Lecture Notes in Artificial Intelligence 3157

Edited by J. G. Carbonell and J. Siekmann

Subseries of Lecture Notes in Computer Science

Chengqi Zhang   Hans W. Guesgen
Wai K. Yeap (Eds.)

PRICAI 2004:
Trends in
Artificial Intelligence

8th Pacific Rim International Conference
on Artificial Intelligence
Auckland, New Zealand, August 9-13, 2004
Proceedings

Springer

Series Editors

Jaime G. Carbonell, Carnegie Mellon University, Pittsburgh, PA, USA
Jörg Siekmann, University of Saarland, Saarbrücken, Germany

Volume Editors

Chengqi Zhang
University of Technology Sydney, Faculty of Information Technology
Broadway, NSW 2007, Sydney, Australia
E-mail: chengqi@it.uts.edu.au

Hans W. Guesgen
The University of Auckland, Department of Computer Science
Auckland 1020, New Zealand
E-mail: hans@cs.auckland.ac.nz

Wai K. Yeap
Auckland University of Technology, Institute for IT Research
Private Bag 92006, Auckland 1020, New Zealand
E-mail: wai.yeap@aut.ac.nz

Library of Congress Control Number: 2004109779

CR Subject Classification (1998): I.2, F.1

ISSN 0302-9743
ISBN 3-540-22817-9 Springer Berlin Heidelberg New York

This work is subject to copyright. All rights are reserved, whether the whole or part of the material is concerned, specifically the rights of translation, reprinting, re-use of illustrations, recitation, broadcasting, reproduction on microfilms or in any other way, and storage in data banks. Duplication of this publication or parts thereof is permitted only under the provisions of the German Copyright Law of September 9, 1965, in its current version, and permission for use must always be obtained from Springer. Violations are liable to prosecution under the German Copyright Law.

Springer is a part of Springer Science+Business Media

springeronline.com

© Springer-Verlag Berlin Heidelberg 2004
Printed in Germany

Typesetting: Camera-ready by author, data conversion by Olgun Computergrafik
Printed on acid-free paper   SPIN: 11308799   06/3142   5 4 3 2 1 0

Preface

The Pacific Rim International Conference on Artificial Intelligence (PRICAI) is a biennial international event which focuses on Artificial Intelligence (AI) theories and technologies, and their applications which are of social and economic importance for countries in the Pacific Rim region. Seven earlier conferences were held in: Nagoya, Japan (1990); Seoul, Korea (1992); Beijing, China (1994); Cairns, Australia (1996); Singapore (1998); Melbourne, Australia (2000); and Tokyo, Japan (2002). PRICAI 2004 was the eigth in the series and was held in Auckland, New Zealand in August 2004.

PRICAI 2004 had attracted a historical record number of submissions, a total of 356 papers. After careful reviews by at least two international Program Committee members or referees, 94 papers were accepted as full papers (27%) and 54 papers (15%) were accepted as posters. Authors of accepted papers came from 27 countries. This volume of the proceedings contains all the 94 full papers but only a 2-page extended abstract of each of the accepted posters. The full papers were categorized into four sections, namely: AI foundations, computational intelligence, AI technologies and systems, and AI specific application areas. Among the papers submitted, we found "Agent Technology" to be the area having the most papers submitted. This was followed by "Evolutionary Computing", "Computational Learning", and "Image Processing".

Many people contributed towards the production of this proceedings. First, we would like to thank the Program Committee members and referees for their extremely hard work and timely return of their comprehensive reports. Without them, it would have been impossible to make decisions and to produce such a high-quality proceedings on time. Second, we would like to acknowledge the contributions of all the authors of the 356 papers submitted. Without their willingness to submit their work to us, there would be no PRICAI.

The technical programs comprised two days of workshops and tutorials, and three days of technical sessions, invited talks and keynote speeches. Proceedings for each workshop and tutorial will be published separately. The three renowned keynote speakers were Prof. Richard Lethrop (University of California, Irvine), Dr. Mehran Sahami (Google, Inc. and Stanford University), and Prof. Carles Sierra (AI Research Institute, Spain). No doubt, their talks will inspire many of our researchers in the Pacific Rim region. We thanked them sincerely for their willingness to come and share their work among us.

Finally, we would like to thank our financial sponsors: AUT, Air Force Office of Scientific Research, Asian Office of Aerospace Research and Development, the University of Auckland, and Franz Inc. for their generosity and willingness to be a part of this wonderful conference. We would also like to thank Saidé Lo, Dr. Vladimir Obolonkin and Kitty Ko at AUT for their endless efforts in organizing the conference.

August 2004
Auckland

Chengqi Zhang
Hans W. Guesgen
Wai K. Yeap

Organization

PRICAI 2004 was organized by the Institute for Information Technology Research, Auckland University of Technology, New Zealand. The conference was held at the Sheraton Hotel, Auckland from 9th August to 13th August, 2004.

Conference Committee

General Co-chairs	Prof. Wai Yeap (Auckland University of Technology)
	Prof. Philip Sallis (Auckland University of Technology)
Program Co-chairs	Prof. Chengqi Zhang (University of Technology, Sydney)
	Assoc. Prof. Hans Guesgen (University of Auckland)
Finance Chair	Prof. Meng Er (Auckland University of Technology)
Workshop Chair	Dr. Bernhard Pfahringer (University of Waikato)
Tutorial Chair	Dr. Alistair Knott (University of Otago)
Doctoral Forum Chair	Prof. Ramakot Sadananda (Asian Institute of Technology)
Conference Chair	Saidé Lo (Auckland University of Technology)

Program Committee

Konagaya Akihiko	Boonserm Kijsirikul	Anthony Robins
Mike Barley	Alfred Kobsa	Akito Sakuria
Gerhard Brewka	Kazuhiro Kuwabara	M. Sasikumar
Longbing Cao	Willem Labuschagne	Abdul Sattar
Jirapun Daengdej	Gerard Ligozat	Zhong Zhi Shi
HongHua Dai	Ji Ming Liu	Arul Siromoney
John Debenham	John Lloyd	Von Wun Soo
Jim Delgrande	Ute Loerch	Venkatesh Svetha
Meng Er	Chee Kit Looi	Hidaeki Takeda
George Ferguson	Dickson Lukose	Lipo Wang
Norman Foo	XuDong Luo	Ian Watson
Christian Freksa	Numao Masayuki	Wayne Wobcke
Sharon X.Y. Gao	Yuji Matsumoto	Hyun Seung Yang
Scott Goodwin	Chris Messon	Roland H.C. Yap
Hans W. Guesgen	Kyong Ho Min	WaiKiang Yeap
Joachim Hertzberg	Antonija Mitrovic	Jeffrey Xu Yu
Jieh Hsiang	Hideyuki Nakashima	XingHuo Yu
ShunChin Hsu	Abhaya Nayak	Minjie Zhang
Mitsuru Ishizuka	Bernhard Nebel	ShiChao Zhang
Margaret Jefferies	Jeng-Shyang Pan	YueJie Zhang
Shyam Kapur	Fred Popowich	Zili Zhang
Ray Kemp	Pat Riddle	Ning Zhong

Referees

Peter Andreae
Quan Bai
Stuart Bain
Matthew Beaumont
Sven Behnke
Pavel Berkhin
Michael Blumenstein
Richard Booth
Michael Brenner
Cliff Brunk
Steve Cassidy
Ratthachat Chatpatanasiri
ShiPei Chen
LieuHen Chen
Yong Cheng
Prabhas Chongstitvatana
Gary Cleveland
Christophe Collet
Michael Cree
Katia Dilkina
Tiansi Dong
Mark Dras
Frank Dylla
Tomio Echigo
Dominik Engel
Vlad Estivill-Castro
Valnir Ferreira
Lutz Frommberger
Gabriel P.C. Fung
Isaac P.W. Fung
ChungHye Han
XiaoShu Hang
Jayprasad J. Hegde
Malte Helmert
Rene Hexel
Shoji Hirano
Joerg Hoffmann
YouPing Huang
He Huang
HsiangCheh Huang
Tudor Hulubei
Ryutaro Ichise
Deepa Joshi

Manolya Kavakli
Jojumon Kavalan
Elizabeth Kemp
Alexander Kleiner
Kitty Ko
Christian Koehler
Mihai Lazarescu
ChangShing Lee
Gang Li
Ling Li
Yuefeng Li
Chunsheng Li
Li Li
QingYong Li
Li Lin
ShunShii Lin
FengTse Lin
WanQuan Liu
WenJun Liu
Alan Loh
JianHua Lu
Stephen Marsland
Jean Claude Martin
Yutaka Matsuo
Michael Mayo
Brendan McCane
Eric McCreath
Thomas Meyer
Kavitha Mohanraj
Diego Molla
YooJin Moon
Reinhard Moratz
Milan Mosny
Vivek Nallur
Gulisong Nasierding
Cholwich Nattee
KeeSiong Ng
Vladimir Obolonkin
Hayato Ohwada
KokLeong Ong
Mehmet Orgun
Maurice Pagnucco
Jignashu Parikh

Patrick Paroubek
Dmitry Pavlov
Tuan Pham
Nghia Pham
Thimaporn Phetkaew
Yusuf Pisan
Arun Pujari
ZhenXing Qin
LiangXi Qin
Jochen Renz
Debbie Richards
Kai-Florian Richter
DongHyun Roh
Ryusuke Sagawa
Chiaki Sakama
YongHo Seo
Qiujian Sheng
YuhPyng Shieh
Toramatsu Shintani
Sukree Sinthupinyo
Cameron Skinner
John Slaney
Nuanwan Soonthornphisaj
Philippe Tarroux
Justin Terry
Jonathan Teutenberg
Nuttakorn Thubthong
YiQing Tu
Rahul D. Vakil
Hans van Ditmarsch
Kimberly Voll
TingTing Wang
JunHu Wang
Keith White
William H. Wilson
Stefan Woelfl
Diedrich Wolter
CheeKit Wong
Min Xu
Yukihiko Yamashita
Hui Yang
YangDong Ye
ShiJim Yen

Manuel Zahariev   HaiJun Zhang   Zheng Zheng
DongMo Zhang   FangWei Zhao   LingZhong Zhou
Yan Zhang   YanChang Zhao   Ling Zhuang

Sponsors

Air Force Office of Scientific Research,
Asian Office of Aerospace Research & Development, Japan
Auckland University of Technology, New Zealand
Franz Inc., USA
University of Auckland, New Zealand

Table of Contents

Invited Talks

Biomedical Artificial Intelligence 1
   Richard Lathrop

Electronics Institutions: Methodology of Multi-agent Systems Development 2
   Carles Sierra

The Happy Searcher: Challenges in Web Information Retrieval 3
   Mehran Sahami, Vibhu Mittal, Shumeet Baluja, and Henry Rowley

PART 1: AI Foundations

Logic and Reasoning

On the Intended Interpretations of Actions 13
   Victor Jauregui, Maurice Pagnucco, and Norman Foo

Temporal Linear Logic for Symbolic Agent Negotiation 23
   Peep Küngas

Dealing with Inconsistent Secure Messages 33
   Qingfeng Chen and Shichao Zhang

Answer Set Computation
Based on a Minimal Model Generation Theorem Prover 43
   Yasuyuki Shirai and Ryuzo Hasegawa

Knowledge Representation and Search

What Is a Qualitative Calculus? A General Framework 53
   Gérard Ligozat and Jochen Renz

Qualitative Direction Calculi with Arbitrary Granularity 65
   Jochen Renz and Debasis Mitra

Power of Brute-Force Search
in Strongly-Typed Inductive Functional Programming Automation 75
   Susumu Katayama

Ontology

Ontology Services-Based Information Integration
in Mining Telecom Business Intelligence 85
   Longbing Cao, Chao Luo, Dan Luo, and Li Liu

Planning

Indexing Approach for Delivery Demands with Time Constraints 95
   Naoto Mukai, Jun Feng, and Toyohide Watanabe

An Hierarchical Terrain Representation for Approximately Shortest Paths 104
   David Mould and Michael C. Horsch

MSIP: Agents Embodying a Category-Based Learning Process
for the ITS Tutor to Self-improve Its Instructional Plans 114
   Roberto Legaspi, Raymund Sison, and Masayuki Numao

Constraint Satisfaction

Circuit Consistencies 124
   Abdellah Idrissi and Ahlem Ben Hassine

Solving Over-Constrained Temporal Reasoning Problems
Using Local Search 134
   Matthew Beaumont, John Thornton, Abdul Sattar, and Michael Maher

Methods of Automatic Algorithm Generation 144
   Stuart Bain, John Thornton, and Abdul Sattar

A Novel Heuristic to Solve IA Network by Convex Approximation and Weights .. 154
   Arun K. Pujari and T. Adilakshmi

Applying An Improved Heuristic Based Optimiser to Solve a Set of Challenging
University Timetabling Problems: An Experience Report 164
   Vincent Tam, Jack Ho, and Alvin Kwan

Extending Unit Propagation Look-Ahead of DPLL Procedure 173
   Anbulagan

Machine Learning

Extended Nearest Feature Line Classifier 183
   Yonglei Zhou, Changshui Zhang, and Jingchun Wang

Sifting the Margin – An Iterative Empirical Classification Scheme 191
   Dan Vance and Anca Ralescu

Accelerating Linear Causal Model Discovery Using Hoeffding Bounds 201
  Gang Li, Honghua Dai, Yiqing Tu, and Tarkan Kurt

Polynomial Time Inductive Inference of Ordered Tree Languages
with Height-Constrained Variables from Positive Data 211
  *Yusuke Suzuki, Takayoshi Shoudai, Satoshi Matsumoto,
  and Tetsuhiro Miyahara*

Fast Incremental Learning of Linear Model Trees 221
  Duncan Potts

A Modified Incremental Principal Component Analysis
for On-Line Learning of Feature Space and Classifier 231
  Seiichi Ozawa, Shaoning Pang, and Nikola Kasabov

PART 2: Computational Intelligence

Computational Learning

An Evolutionary Approach to the Design of Cellular Automata Architecture
for Multiplication in Elliptic Curve Cryptography over Finite Fields 241
  Jun-Cheol Jeon and Kee-Young Yoo

Probability Based Genetic Programming for Multiclass Object Classification 251
  Will Smart and Mengjie Zhang

Design of Nearest Neighbor Classifiers
Using an Intelligent Multi-objective Evolutionary Algorithm 262
  Jian-Hung Chen, Hung-Ming Chen, and Shinn-Ying Ho

Elastic Learning Rate on Error Backpropagation of Online Update 272
  Tae-Seung Lee and Ho-Jin Choi

Learning Dynamics of Neural Networks with Singularity
– Standard Gradient vs. Natural Gradient 282
  Hyeyoung Park, Masato Inoue, and Masato Okada

Feature Selection for Multi-class Problems Using Support Vector Machines 292
  Guo-Zheng Li, Jie Yang, Guo-Ping Liu, and Li Xue

Beyond Learners' Interest: Personalized Paper Recommendation
Based on Their Pedagogical Features for an e-Learning System 301
  Tiffany Tang and Gordon McCalla

Bayesian Network

An Anytime Algorithm for Interpreting Arguments 311
  Sarah George, Ingrid Zukerman, and Michael Niemann

Varieties of Causal Intervention 322
   Kevin B. Korb, Lucas R. Hope, Ann E. Nicholson, and Karl Axnick

Evolutionary Computing

Species Merging and Splitting for Efficient Search
in Coevolutionary Algorithm 332
   Myung Won Kim and Joung Woo Ryu

Exploiting Unexpressed Genes
for Solving Large-Scaled Maximal Covering Problems 342
   Taejin Park and Kwang Ryel Ryu

Combining Extension Matrix and Integer Programming
for Optimal Concept Learning 352
   Xiaoshu Hang and Honghua Dai

HeurEAKA – A New Approach for Adapting GAs to the Problem Domain 361
   J.P. Bekmann and Achim Hoffmann

A Modified Integer-Coding Genetic Algorithm
for Job Shop Scheduling Problem 373
   *Chunguo Wu, Wei Xiang, Yanchun Liang, Heow Pueh Lee,
   and Chunguang Zhou*

Using Evolutionary Learning of Behavior
to Find Weaknesses in Operating Systems 381
   Jörg Denzinger and Tim Williams

Creative 3D Designs Using Interactive Genetic Algorithm
with Structured Directed Graph 391
   Hyeun-Jeong Min and Sung-Bae Cho

Spatiotemporal Parameter Adaptation
in Genetic Algorithm-Based Video Segmentation 401
   Sin Kuk Kang, Eun Yi Kim, and Hang Joon Kim

Object Detection and Removal Using Genetic Algorithms 411
   Eun Yi Kim and Keechul Jung

Neural Networks

Elman's Recurrent Neural Networks Using Resilient Back Propagation
for Harmonic Detection 422
   *Fevzullah Temurtas, Nejat Yumusak, Rustu Gunturkun,
   Hasan Temurtas, and Osman Cerezci*

Neural Based Steganography 429
  V. Kavitha and K.S. Easwarakumar

Neural Network Combines with a Rotational Invariant Feature Set
in Texture Classification 436
  Yongping Zhang and Ruili Wang

Fuzzy Logic

What Concrete Things Does Fuzzy Propositional Logic Describe? 445
  Paul Snow

A Framework for Fuzzy Rule-Based Cognitive Maps 454
  M. Shamim Khan and Sebastian W. Khor

Discontinuity Enhancement Using Fuzziness in DCT Blocks 464
  TaeYong Kim and Jong Soo Choi

PART 3: AI Methodologies and Systems

Data Mining

Is Minimum-Support Appropriate to Identifying Large Itemsets? 474
  Shichao Zhang, Li Liu, Jingli Lu, and Yuming Ou

An Efficient Approach for Mining Periodic Sequential Access Patterns 485
  Baoyao Zhou, Siu Cheung Hui, and Alvis Cheuk Ming Fong

A New Collaborative Recommender System Addressing Three Problems 495
  Byeong Man Kim, Qing Li, Jong-Wan Kim, and Jinsoo Kim

A GA-Based Fuzzy Decision Tree Approach for Corporate Bond Rating 505
  Kyung-shik Shin, Hyun-jung Kim, and Suhn-beom Kwon

Classification and Cluster

Text Classification Using Belief Augmented Frames 515
  Colin Keng-Yan Tan

A Feature Selection for Text Categorization
on Research Support System Papits 524
  *Tadachika Ozono, Toramatsu Shintani, Takayuki Ito,
  and Tomoharu Hasegawa*

Constrained Ant Colony Optimization for Data Clustering 534
  Shu-Chuan Chu, John F. Roddick, Che-Jen Su, and Jeng-Shyang Pan

Case-Based Reasoning

A Kernel-Based Case Retrieval Algorithm with Application to Bioinformatics ... 544
    Yan Fu, Qiang Yang, Charles X. Ling, Haipeng Wang, Dequan Li,
    Ruixiang Sun, Hu Zhou, Rong Zeng, Yiqiang Chen, Simin He,
    and Wen Gao

Building a Case-Based Reasoner for Clinical Decision Support 554
    Anna Wills and Ian Watson

Information Retrieval

Association-Rule Based Information Source Selection 563
    Hui Yang, Minjie Zhang, and Zhongzhi Shi

Distributional Character Clustering for Chinese Text Categorization 575
    Xuezhong Zhou and Zhaohui Wu

Approximately Repetitive Structure Detection for Wrapper Induction 585
    Xiaoying Gao, Peter Andreae, and Richard Collins

Agent Technology

Model Theory for PRS-Like Agents:
Modelling Belief Update and Action Attempts 595
    Wayne Wobcke

Towards Belief Revision Logic Based Adaptive
and Persuasive Negotiation Agents....................................... 605
    Raymond Y.K. Lau and Siu Y. Chan

Agents and Web Services Supported Business Exception Management 615
    Minhong Wang and Huaiqing Wang

Multi-agent Interaction Technology
for Peer-to-Peer Computing in Electronic Trading Environments 625
    Martin Purvis, Mariusz Nowostawski, Stephen Cranefield,
    and Marcos Oliveira

$\mathcal{K}_2$: Animated Agents that Understand Speech Commands
and Perform Actions 635
    Takenobu Tokugana, Kotaro Funakoshi, and Hozumi Tanaka

InCA: A Mobile Conversational Agent 644
    Mohammed Waleed Kadous and Claude Sammut

Determination of Usenet News Groups
by Fuzzy Inference and Kohonen Network 654
   Jong-Wan Kim, Hee-Jae Kim, Sin-Jae Kang, and Byeong Man Kim

Using Context to Solve the Correspondence Problem
in Simultaneous Localisation and Mapping 664
   Margaret E. Jefferies, Wenrong Weng, Jesse T. Baker, and Michael Mayo

Knowledge-Based Interactive Robot:
System Architecture and Dialogue Manager 673
   Pattara Kiatisevi, Vuthichai Ampornaramveth, and Haruki Ueno

Robotics

Complete Coverage by Mobile Robots
Using Slice Decomposition Based on Natural Landmarks 683
   Sylvia C. Wong and Bruce A. MacDonald

Shape Matching for Robot Mapping 693
   Diedrich Wolter and Longin J. Latecki

Covisibility-Based Map Learning Method for Mobile Robots 703
   Takehisa Yairi

PART 4: AI Specific Application Areas

Bioinformatics

Optimal Gene Selection for Cancer Classification
with Partial Correlation and *k*-Nearest Neighbor Classifier 713
   Si-Ho Yoo and Sung-Bae Cho

Prediction of the Risk Types of Human Papillomaviruses
by Support Vector Machines 723
   Je-Gun Joung, Sok June O, and Byoung-Tak Zhang

Computational Methods for Identification of Human microRNA Precursors 732
   Jin-Wu Nam, Wha-Jin Lee, and Byoung-Tak Zhang

Multi-objective Evolutionary Probe Design
Based on Thermodynamic Criteria for HPV Detection 742
   In-Hee Lee, Sun Kim, and Byoung-Tak Zhang

Image Processing and Computer Vision

Synergism in Color Image Segmentation 751
   Yuzhong Wang, Jie Yang, and Peng Ningsong

Face Recognition Using Direct-Weighted LDA 760
  Dake Zhou and Xin Yang

Face Recognition Using Enhanced Fisher Linear Discriminant Model
with Facial Combined Feature 769
  Dake Zhou and Xin Yang

Gradient Vector Flow Snake with Embedded Edge Confidence 778
  Yuzhong Wang and Jie Yang

Object Boundary Edge Selection for Human Body Tracking
Using Level-of-Detail Canny Edges 787
  Tae-Yong Kim, Jihun Park, and Seong-Whan Lee

Unsupervised Multiscale Image Segmentation
Using Wavelet Domain Hidden Markov Tree 797
  Xu Qing, Yang Jie, and Ding Siyi

Adaptive Model for Foreground Extraction in Adverse Lighting Conditions 805
  Stewart Greenhill, Svetha Venkatesh, and Geoff West

Improvement of Binarization Method Using a Water Flow Model
for Document Images with Complex Backgrounds 812
  Hyun-Hwa Oh and Sung-Il Chien

Learning and Integrating Semantics for Image Indexing 823
  Joo-Hwee Lim and Jesse S. Jin

PDA-Based Text Localization System Using Client/Server Architecture 833
  Anjin Park and Keechul Jung

Vision Technique for the Recognition of Billet Characters
in the Steel Plant 843
  Jong-hak Lee, Sang-gug Park, and Soo-joong Kim

Natural Language Processing

Tagging Medical Documents with High Accuracy 852
  Udo Hahn and Joachim Wermter

Pronominal Anaphora Resolution
Using a Shallow Meaning Representation of Sentences 862
  Hilda Ho, Kyongho Min, and Wai Kiang Yeap

Multi-agent Human-Machine Dialogue:
Issues in Dialogue Management and Referring Expression Semantics 872
  Alistair Knott, Ian Bayard, and Peter Vlugter

Coherent Arrangement of Sentences Extracted
from Multiple Newspaper Articles 882
    Naoaki Okazaki, Yutaka Matsuo, and Mitsuru Ishizuka

Improvement of Language Models Using Dual-Source Backoff 892
    Sehyeong Cho

Speech Understanding and Interaction

Speaker Identification Based on Log Area Ratio
and Gaussian Mixture Models in Narrow-Band Speech 901
    David Chow and Waleed H. Abdulla

Automatic Sound-Imitation Word Recognition from Environmental Sounds
Focusing on Ambiguity Problem in Determining Phonemes 909
    Kazushi Ishihara, Tomohiro Nakatani, Tetsuya Ogata,
    and Hiroshi G. Okuno

Statistical Pitch Conversion Approaches Based on Korean Accentual Phrases 919
    Ki Young Lee, Jong Kuk Kim, and Myung Jin Bae

Poster Papers

On the Stability of a Dynamic Stochastic Capacity Pricing Scheme
for Resource Allocation in a Multi-agent Environment 928
    Alain Gaetan Njimolu Anyouzoa and Theo D'Hondt

Part-of-Speech Tagging and PP Attachment Disambiguation
Using a Boosted Maximum Entropy Model 930
    Seong-Bae Park, Jangmin O, and Sang-Jo Lee

Solving Pickup and Delivery Problems
with Refined Construction and Repair Heuristics 932
    Vincent Tam and M.C. Kwan

Mining Multi-dimensional Data with Visualization Techniques 934
    Danyu Liu and Alan P. Sprague

Believability Based Iterated Belief Revision 936
    Pei Yang, Yang Gao, Zhaoqian Chen, and Shifu Chen

On Designing a Reduced-Order Fuzzy Observer 938
    Behzad Moshiri, Farhad Besharati, Abdrreza Dehghani Tafti,
    and Ali Akhavan Bitaghsir

Using Factorization Algorithm for 3D Reconstruction
over Long Un-calibrated Sequences 940
    Yoon-Yong Jeong, Yong-Ho Hwang, and Hyun-Ki Hong

A Hybrid Algorithm for Combining Forecasting Based on AFTER-PSO 942
    Xiaoyue Feng, Yanchun Liang, Yanfeng Sun, Heow Pueh Lee,
    Chunguang Zhou, and Yan Wang

A Multi-strategy Approach for Catalog Integration 944
    Ryutaro Ichise, Masahiro Hamasaki, and Hideaki Takeda

Some Game Theory of Pit... 946
    Hans P. van Ditmarsch

Dynamically Determining Affect During Scripted Dialogue 948
    Tony Meyer

Knowledge and Argument Transformation for Arguing Mobile Agents 950
    Hajime Sawamura and Wataru Kawakami

Improving Newsgroup Clustering by Filtering Author-Specific Words 953
    Yuval Marom and Ingrid Zukerman

Evolving Artificial Ant Systems
to Improve Layouts of Graphical Objects................................ 955
    Vincent Tam, Simon Koo, and Kozo Sugiyama

MASCONTROL: A MAS for System Identification and Process Control 957
    Evelio J. González, Alberto Hamilton, Lorenzo Moreno,
    Roberto L. Marichal, and Vanessa Muñoz

Vision Based Acquisition of Mouth Actions for Human-Computer Interaction ... 959
    Gamhewage C. de Silva, Michael J. Lyons, and Nobuji Tetsutani

Unsupervised Image Segmentation with Fuzzy Connectedness................ 961
    Yuanjie Zheng, Jie Yang, and Yue Zhou

Personalized Image Recommendation in the Mobile Internet 963
    Yoon Ho Cho, Chan Young Kim, and Deok Hwan Kim

Clustering IP Addresses Using Longest Prefix Matching
and Nearest Neighbor Algorithms 965
    Asim Karim, Syed Imran Jami, Irfan Ahmad, Mansoor Sarwar,
    and Zartash Uzmi

A Fuzzy Clustering Algorithm for Analysis of Gene Expression Profiles 967
    Han-Saem Park, Si-Ho Yoo, and Sung-Bae Cho

Evaluation of a Boosted Cascade of Haar-Like Features in the Presence
of Partial Occlusions and Shadows for Real Time Face Detection.............. 969
    Andre L.C. Barczak

Classifying Human Actions
Using an Incomplete Real-Time Pose Skeleton 971
  Patrick Peursum, Hung H. Bui, Svetha Venkatesh,
  and Geoff A.W. West

Multiclass Support Vector Machines Using Balanced Dichotomization 973
  Boonserm Kijsirikul, Narong Boonsirisumpun,
  and Yachai Limpiyakorn

Time Series Pattern Discovery by Segmental Gaussian Models 975
  Imahara Shuichiro, Sato Makoto, and Nakase Akihiko

A Model for Identifying the Underlying Logical Structure
of Natural Language 977
  Vasile Rus and Alex Fit-Florea

A Reputation-Based Trust Model for Agent Societies 979
  Yuk-Hei Lam, Zili Zhang, and Kok-Leong Ong

A Model of Rhetorical Structure Analysis of Japanese Texts and Its Application
to Intelligent Text Processing: A Case for a Smart Help System 981
  Noriko Ito, Toru Sugimoto, Shino Iwashita, Ichiro Kobayashi,
  and Michio Sugeno

Explicit State Duration HMM for Abnormality Detection
In Sequences of Human Activity 983
  Sebastian Lühr, Svetha Venkatesh, Geoff West, and Hung H. Bui

An Augmentation Hybrid System for Document Classification and Rating 985
  Richard Dazeley and Byeong-Ho Kang

Study and Comparison of 3D Face Generation 987
  Mark Chan, Patrice Delmas, Georgy Gimel'farb, Chia-Yen Chen,
  and Philippe Leclercq

Stable Solutions Dealing with Dynamics in Scheduling
Based on Dynamic Constraint Satisfaction Problems 989
  Hiromitsu Hattori, Toramatsu Shintani, Atsushi Isomura,
  Takayuki Ito, and Tadachika Ozono

Analyzing Emotional Space in Sensitivity Communication Robot "Ifbot" 991
  Masayoshi Kanoh, Shohei Kato, and Hidenori Itoh

Human-Centric Approach for Human-Robot Interaction 993
  Mariko Narumi and Michita Imai

Complexity of Coordinating Autonomous Planning Agents 995
  Adriaan ter Mors, Jeroen Valk, and Cees Witteveen

An Approach for Multirelational Ontology Modelling 997
    Pedro J. Vivancos-Vicente, Rafael Valencia-García,
    Jesualdo T. Fernández-Breis, Rodrigo Martínez-Béjar,
    and Fernando Martín-Rubio

SNR-Invariant Normalization of the Covariance Measure
for Template Matching 999
    Jong Dae Kim

Brain Emotional Learning Based Intelligent Controller
Applied to Gas Metal Arc Welding System 1001
    Mahdi Jalili-Kharaajoo

Qualitative Spatial Arrangements and Natural Object Categories
as a Link Between 3D-Perception and Speech 1003
    Reinhard Moratz, Michael Wünstel, and Robert Ross

Integrating Feature Information
for Improving Accuracy of Collaborative Filtering 1005
    Hyungil Kim, Juntae Kim, and Jonathan L. Herlocker

An Ordered Preprocessing Scheme for Data Mining 1007
    Laura Cruz R., Joaquín Pérez, Vanesa Landero N.,
    Elizabeth S. del Angel, Victor M. Álvarez, and Verónica Peréz

Spatial Function Representation and Retrieval 1009
    Yutaka Matsuo, Akira Takagi, Shigeyoshi Hiratsuka, Koiti Hasida,
    and Hideyuki Nakashima

Fuzzy Project Scheduling with Multiple Objectives 1011
    Hongqi Pan and Chung-Hsing Yeh

A New Approach for Applying Support Vector Machines
in Multiclass Problems Using Class Groupings and Truth Tables 1013
    Mauricio Kugler, Hiroshi Matsuo, and Akira Iwata

Imitation of Bee Reproduction as a Crossover Operator
in Genetic Algorithms 1015
    Ali Karcı

An Intelligent Robot Navigation System
Based on Neuro-Fuzzy Control 1017
    Osama Fathy Hegazy, Aly Aly Fahmy, and Osama Mosaad El Refaie

Author Index 1019

Biomedical Artificial Intelligence

Richard Lathrop

Information and Computer Science
University of California
Irvine, CA 92697-3425 USA
rickl@uci.edu

Abstract. This talk will survey the intriguing connections between artificial intelligence and its biomedical application domain. Biology has recently become a data-rich, information hungry science because of recent massive data generation technologies, but we cannot fully analyse this data due to the wealth and complexity of the information available. The result is a great need for intelligent systems in biology. We will visit examples such as machine learning for pharmaceutical drug discovery, optimal heuristic search for protein structure prediction, rule-based systems for drug-resistant HIV treatment, constraint-based design of large self-assembling synthetic genes, and a multiple-representation approach to curing some forms of cancer. The talk will conclude with suggestions for how AI practitioners can begin the explore this rich and fascinating domain.

Electronics Institutions: Methodology of Multi-agent Systems Development

Carles Sierra

AI Research Institute, Spain
sierra@iiia.csic.es

Abstract. Human interactions very often follow conventions; that is, general agreements on language, meaning, & behaviour. By following conventions, humans decrease uncertainties in the behaviour of others, remove conflicts on meaning, give expectations on the outcome of the interaction and simplify the decision process by restricting the potential actions that may be undertaken to a limited set. These benefits explain why conventions have been so widely used in aspects of human interaction such as trading, laws, games, and the like. In some situations, conventions become foundational &, more importantly, some of them become norms. Norms establish how interactions of a certain sort will & must be structured within an organisation &, therefore, they become the essence of what is understood as human institutions. This is so, for instance, in the case of auction houses, courts, parliaments or the stock exchange. Human institutions not only structure human interactions, but they also enforce individual & social behaviour by obliging everybody to act according to the norms.

The notion of electronic institution thus becomes a natural extension of human institutions by permitting not only humans, but also autonomous agents, to interact with one another. I will show in this talk how this concept becomes a very powerful tool to specify, verify and develop Multi-Agent applications. An example of a deployed application to model concurrent auction houses will be explained in detail.

The Happy Searcher: Challenges in Web Information Retrieval

Mehran Sahami, Vibhu Mittal, Shumeet Baluja, and Henry Rowley

Google Inc.
1600 Amphitheatre Parkway
Mountain View, CA 94043
{sahami,vibhu,shumeet,har}@google.com

Abstract. Search has arguably become the dominant paradigm for finding information on the World Wide Web. In order to build a successful search engine, there are a number of challenges that arise where techniques from artificial intelligence can be used to have a significant impact. In this paper, we explore a number of problems related to finding information on the web and discuss approaches that have been employed in various research programs, including some of those at Google. Specifically, we examine issues of such as web graph analysis, statistical methods for inferring meaning in text, and the retrieval and analysis of newsgroup postings, images, and sounds. We show that leveraging the vast amounts of data on web, it is possible to successfully address problems in innovative ways that vastly improve on standard, but often data impoverished, methods. We also present a number of open research problems to help spur further research in these areas.

1 Introduction

Search engines are critically important to help users find relevant information on the World Wide Web. In order to best serve the needs of users, a search engine must find and filter the most relevant information matching a user's query, and then present that information in a manner that makes the information most readily palatable to the user. Moreover, the task of information retrieval and presentation must be done in a scalable fashion to serve the hundreds of millions of user queries that are issued every day to a popular web search engines such as Google.

In addressing the problem of information retrieval on the web, there are a number of challenges in which Artificial Intelligence (AI) techniques can be successfully brought to bear. We outline some of these challenges in this paper and identify additional problems that may motivate future work in the AI research community. We also describe some work in these areas that has been conducted at Google.

We begin by briefly outlining some of the issues that arise in web information retrieval that showcase its differences with research traditionally done in Information Retrieval (IR), and then focus on more specific problems. Section 2 describes the unique properties of information retrieval on the web. Section 3 presents a statistical method for determining similarity in text motivated by both AI and IR methodologies. Section 4 deals with the retrieval of UseNet (newsgroups) postings, while Section 5 addresses the retrieval of non-textual objects such as images and sounds. Section 6 gives a brief overview of innovative applications that harness the vast amount of text available on the Web. Finally, Section 7 provides some concluding thoughts.

2 Information Retrieval on the Web

A critical goal of successful information retrieval on the web is to identify which pages are of high quality and relevance to a user's query. There are many aspects of *web* IR that differentiate it and make it somewhat more challenging than traditional problems exemplified by the TREC competition. Foremost, pages on the web contain links to other pages and by analyzing this web graph structure it is possible to determine a more global notion of page quality. Notable early successes in this area include the PageRank algorithm [1], which globally analyzes the entire web graph and provided the original basis for ranking in the Google search engine, and Kleinberg's HITS algorithm [2], which analyzes a local neighborhood of the web graph containing an initial set of web pages matching the user's query. Since that time, several other linked-based methods for ranking web pages have been proposed including variants of both PageRank and HITS [3][4], and this remains an active research area in which there is still much fertile research ground to be explored.

Besides just looking at the link structure in web pages, it is also possible to exploit the anchor text contained in links as an indication of the content of the web page being pointed to. Especially since anchor text tends to be short, it often gives a concise human generated description of the content of a web page. By harnessing anchor text, it is possible to have index terms for a web page even if the page contains only images (which is seen, for example, on visually impressive home pages that contain no actual text). Determining which terms from anchors and surrounding text should be used in indexing a page presents other interesting research venues.

2.1 Adversarial Classification: Dealing with Spam on the Web

One particularly intriguing problem in web IR arises from the attempt by some commercial interests to unduly heighten the ranking of their web pages by engaging in various forms of *spamming* [5]. One common method of spamming involves placing additional keywords (or even entire dictionaries) in invisible text on a web page so that the page potentially matches many more user queries, even if the page is really irrelevant to these queries. Such methods can be effective against traditional IR ranking schemes that do not make use of link structure, but have more limited utility in the context of global link analysis. Realizing this, spammers now also utilize *link spam* where they will create large numbers of web pages that contain links to other pages whose rankings they wish to raise.

Identifying such spam in both text-based and linked-based analyses of the web are open problems where AI techniques such as Natural Language Processing (NLP) and Machine Learning (ML) can have a direct impact. For example, statistical NLP methods can be used to determine the likelihood that text on a web page represents "natural" writing. Similarly, classification methods can be applied to the problem of identifying "spam" versus "non-spam" pages, where both textual and non-textual (e.g., link) information can be used by the classifier.

Especially interesting is that such classification schemes must work in an *adversarial* context as spammers will continually seek ways of thwarting automatic filters. Adversarial classification is an area in which precious little work has been done, but effective methods can provide large gains both for web search as well as other adversarial text classification tasks such as spam filtering in email [6].

2.2 Evaluating Search Results

Even when advances are made in the ranking of search results, proper evaluation of these improvements is a non-trivial task. In contrast to traditional IR evaluation methods using manually classified corpora such as the TREC collections, evaluating the efficacy of web search engines remains an open problem and has been the subject of various workshops [7][8]. Recent efforts in this area have examined interleaving the results of two different ranking schemes and using statistical tests based on the results users clicked on to determine which ranking scheme is "better" [9]. There has also been work along the lines of using decision theoretic analysis (i.e., maximizing users' utility when searching, considering the relevance of the results found as well as the time taken to find those results) as a means for determining the "goodness" of a ranking scheme. Commercial search engines often make use of various manual and statistical evaluation criteria in evaluating their ranking functions. Still, principled automated means for large-scale evaluation of ranking results are wanting, and their development would help improve commercial search engines and create better methodologies to evaluate IR research in broader contexts.

3 Using the Web to Create "Kernels" of Meaning

Another challenge in web search is determining the relatedness of fragments of text, even when the fragments may contain few or no terms in common. In our experience, English web queries are on average two to three terms long. Thus, a simple measure of similarity, such as computing the cosine of the terms in both queries, is very coarse and likely to lead to many zero values. For example, consider the fragments "Captain Kirk" and "Star Trek". Clearly, these two fragments are more semantically similar than "Captain Kirk" and "Fried Chicken", but a simple term-based cosine score would give the same (zero) value in both cases.

Generalizing this problem, we can define a real-valued kernel function K(x, y), where x and y are arbitrary text fragments. Importantly, we note that K can utilize external resources, such as a search engine in order, to determine a similarity score[1]. To this end, we can perform query expansion [10] on both x and y using the results of a search engine and then compute the cosine between these expanded queries. More formally, let QE(t) denote the query expansion of text t, where (for example) we could define QE(t) as the centroid of the TFIDF vector representations of the top 30 documents returned by a search engine in response to query t. We can now define K(x, y) as the cosine between QE(x) and QE(y). Illustratively, we obtain the following results with such a kernel function, anecdotally showing its efficacy:

---

[1] We could define K(x, y, S) where S represents the search engine used. However, since S generally remains constant, we can define K with respect to just the parameters x and y.

K("Captain Kirk", "Mister Spock") = 0.49
K("Captain Kirk", "Star Trek") = 0.38
K("Captain Kirk", "Fried Chicken") = 0.02

While such a *web contextual kernel* function has obvious utility in determining the semantic relatedness of two text fragments by harnessing the vast quantities of text on the web, open research issues remain. For example, future research could help identify more effective text expansion algorithms that are particularly well suited to certain tasks. Also, various methods such as statistical dispersion measures or clustering could be used to identify poor expansions and cases where a text fragment may have an expansion that encompasses multiple meanings (e.g., an expansion of "Michael Jordan" including terms both about the researcher and the basketball star).

4 Retrieval of UseNet Articles

One of the less visible document collections in the context of general purpose search engines is the UseNet archive, which is conservatively estimated to be at least 800 million documents. The UseNet archive, mostly ignored in traditional academic IR work – with the one exception of the 20 newsgroups data set used in text classification tasks – is extremely interesting. UseNet started as a loosely structured collection of groups that people could post to. Over the years, it evolved into a large hierarchy of over 50,000 groups with topics ranging from sex to theological musings.

IR in the context of UseNet articles raises some very interesting issues. As in the case of the Web, spam is a constant problem. However, unlike the web, there is no clear concept of a home page in UseNet. For example, what should the canonical page for queries such as "IBM" or "Digital Cameras" be? One previously explored possibility is to address retrieval in UseNet as a two stage IR problem: (1) find the most relevant newsgroup, and (2) find the most relevant document within that newsgroup. While this may appear to be a simple scheme, consider the fact that there are at least 20 newsgroups that contain the token "IBM". This leads us to the problem of determining whether the canonical newsgroup should be based on having "IBM" at the highest level (i.e., `comp.ibm.pc`), the group with the most subgroups underneath it (i.e., `comp.sys.ibm.*`), or simply the most trafficked group. Still, other questions arise, such as whether moderated newsgroups should given more weight that unmoderated newsgroups or if the *Big-8* portion of the UseNet hierarchy should be considered more credible than other portions.

At the article or posting level, one can similarly rank not just by content relevance, but also take into account aspects of articles that not normally associated with web pages, such as temporal information (when a posting was made), thread information, the author of the article, whether the article quotes another post, whether the proportion of quoted content is much more than the proportion of original content, etc. Moreover, recognizing that certain postings may be FAQs or "flames" would also aid in determining the appropriate ranking for an article. Along these lines, previous research has examined building models of newsgroups, communication patterns within message threads, and language models that are indicative of content [11][12][13]. Still, questions remain of how to go about using such factors to build an effective ranking function and how to display these results effectively to users.

Furthermore, one can also attempt to compute the inherent quality or credibility level of an author independent of the query, much as PageRank [1] does for the Web. Such a computation would operate on a graph of relatively modest size since, for example, if we were to filter authors to only those that had posted at least twice in a year to the same newsgroup, we would be left with only on the order of 100,000 authors. This is a much more manageable size than the web graph which has several billion nodes. Computing community structures – rather than pure linear structures as in posting threads – can also generate interesting insights as to how various authors and groups participate in and influence discussions.

One of the most comprehensive studies on bulletin board postings (similar to UseNet) is the Netscan project [11]. This work examined characteristics of authors and posting patterns, such as identifying characteristics of people who start discussions, people who "flame", people who cross-post to multiple newsgroups, people who spam, people who seem to terminate threads, etc. More recently, work on filtering technologies in the context of information retrieval [14] has also focused attention on building better models of the likely content in messages and routing them to appropriate people, bringing together work on user modeling, IR, and text analysis.

An advantage of working with the UseNet archive is the fact that it alleviates many of the infrastructural problems that might otherwise slow research in the web domain, such as building HTML parsers, properly handling different languages and character sets, and managing the exceptional volume of available data (even small potions of the Web would require several hundred gigabytes to store). Contrastingly, much of the older UseNet posting archive was previously available on a few CD-ROMs, making the archive relatively easy to store, index and process on a single machine. More recently, researchers have started looking at an even smaller scale problem: culling information from bulletin board postings and trying to ascribe a quality level to the information contained therein. For example, Arnt and Zilberstein [13] analyzed postings on the Slashdot bulletin board (a discussion forum predominated by technology savvy readers), attempting to learn the moderation system used. Slashdot moderators assign both a genre label – such as "informative", "funny", etc. – and a score between -1 and +5 indicating their view on how relevant a posting is. Given these score and label pairs, it is a challenging task to use the rich structure of the domain (i.e., author information, posting content, thread history, etc.) to predict both the label and score for new postings. More generally, improving ranking methods for UseNet or bulletin board postings is an open area of research with many interesting similarities to the web, but also with very many significant differences that make it a fascinating subject of further study.

5 Retrieval of Images and Sounds

With the proliferation of digital still and video cameras, camera phones, audio recording devices, and mp3 music, there is a rapidly increasing number of non-textual "documents" available to users. One of the challenges faced in the quest to organize and make useful all of the world's information, is the process by which the contents of these non-textual objects should indexed. An equally important line of study (although not a focus of this paper) is how to present the user with intuitive methods by which to query and access this information.

Fig. 1. 12 Results obtained by searching Google-Images for "Cars"

The difficulties in addressing the problem of non-textual object retrieval are best illustrated through an example. Figure 1 shows 12 results obtained by searching Google's image repository for "cars". Note the diverse set of content related to cars that is present. In the first 12 results, we see everything from different car poses, pictures of cars on billboards, cars barely visible through the snow, cars for parades, and even hand drawn illustrations. In addressing this sort of diversity, we presently give three basic approaches to the task of retrieving images and music.

1. *Content Detection:* For images, this method means that the individual objects in the image are detected, possibly segmented, and recognized. The image is then labeled with detected objects. For music, this method may include recognizing the instruments that are played as well as the words that are said/sung, and even determining the artists. Of the three approaches, this is the one that is the furthest from being adequately realized, and involves the most signal processing.
2. *Content Similarity Assessment:* In this approach, we do not attempt to recognize the content of the images (or audio clips). Instead, we attempt to find images (audio tracks) that are similar to the query items. For example, the user may provide an image (audio snippet) of what the types of results that they are interested in

finding, and based on low-level similarity measures, such as (spatial) color histograms, audio frequency histograms, etc, similar objects are returned. Systems such as these have often been used to find images of sunsets, blue skies, etc. [15] and have also been applied to the task of finding similar music genres [16].

3. *Using Surrounding Textual Information:* A common method of assigning labels to non-textual objects is to use information that surrounds these objects in the documents that they are found. For example, when images are found in web documents, there is a wealth of information that can be used as evidence of the image contents. For example, the site on which the image appears (for example an adult site or a site about music groups, TV shows, etc.), how the image is referred to, the image's filename, and even the surrounding text all provide potentially relevant information about the image.

All of these approaches can, of course, be used in conjunction with each other, and each provides a fairly diverse set of benefits and drawbacks. For example, surrounding textual information is the easiest method to use; however it is the most susceptible to misclassification of the image content, due to both errors and malicious web site designers. Content Similarity Assessment can provide some indication of the image content, but is rarely able in practice to find particular objects or particular people. Content Detection is the only method that attempts to recognize the objects in the scene; however, building detectors for arbitrary objects is a time consuming task that usually involves quite a bit of custom research for each object. For example, the most studied object detection domain to date is finding faces in images, and work has continued on improving the quality for almost a decade [17][18][19][20]. Work in using these systems to detect people (beyond just finding faces) and cars is progressing [21][22]; extending to arbitrary objects is also the focus of a significant amount of research.

Beyond assigning labels to images, there are a variety of other topics that must be addressed in deciding which images to present to the user. For example, should multiple copies of the same image be presented? What about near-duplicates? Eliminating near-duplicates involves not only comparing the images to find identical copies, but also developing automatic methods to ignore insignificant variations – such as those due to compression formats, scanner calibration error, and small corruptions in files. Another topic that must be addressed is what order to present the images. Is there one ordering that is better than another? Perhaps the relevance of the page on which the images are found should play a factor in the order assessment. Finally, looking into the future, how many of these ideas can be extended to video retrieval? Combining the audio track from videos with the images that are being displayed may not only provide additional sources of information on how to index the video, but also provide a tremendous amount of (noisy) training data for training object recognition algorithms en masse.

6 Harnessing Vast Quantities of Data

Even with the variety of research topics discussed previously, we are only still scratching the surface of the myriad of issues that AI technologies can address with respect to web search. One of the most interesting aspects of working with web data is the insight and appreciation that one can get for large data sets. This has been exemplified by Banko and Brill in the case of word sense disambiguation [23], but as a practical example, we also briefly discuss our own experiences in two different contexts at Google: Spelling Correction and Query Classification.

Spelling Correction. In contrast to traditional approaches which solely make use of standard term lexicons to make spelling corrections, the Google spelling corrector takes a Machine Learning approach that leverages an enormous volume of text to build a very fine grained probabilistic context sensitive model for spelling correction. This allows the system to recognize far more terms than a standard spelling correction system, especially proper names which commonly appear in web queries but not in standard lexicons. For example, many standard spelling systems would suggest the text "Mehran Sahami" be corrected to "Tehran Salami", being completely ignorant of the proper name and simply suggesting common terms with small edit distance to the original text. Contrastingly, the Google spelling corrector does not attempt to correct the text "Mehran Sahami" since this term combination is recognized by its highly granular model. More interesting, however, is the fact that by employing a *context sensitive* model, the system will correct the text "Mehran *Salhami*" to "Mehran *Sahami*" even though "Salami" is a common English word and is the same edit distance from "Salhami" as "Sahami." Such fine grained context sensitivity can only be achieved through analyzing very large quantities of text.

Query Classification into the Open Directory Project. The Open Directory Project (ODP) (http://dmoz.org/) is a large open source topic hierarchy into which web pages have been manually classified. The hierarchy contains roughly 500,000 classes/topics. Since this is a useful source of hand-classified information, we sought to build a query classifier that would identify and suggest categories in the ODP that would be relevant to a user query. At first blush, this would appear to be a standard text classification task. It becomes more challenging when we consider that the "documents" to be classified are user queries, which have an average length of just over two words. Moreover, the set of classes from the ODP is much larger than any previously studied classification task, and the classes are non-mutually exclusive which can create additional confusion between topics. Despite these challenges, we have available roughly four million pre-classified documents, giving us quite a substantial training set.

We tried a variety of different approaches that explored many different aspects of the classifier model space: independence assumptions between words, modeling word order and dependencies for two and three word queries, generative and discriminative models, boosting, and others. The complete list of methods compared is not included since some portions of the study were conducted in an iterative piecemeal fashion, so a direct comparison of all methods applied to all the data is not possible to provide. Nevertheless, we found that the various algorithms performed as expected relative to previously published results in text classification when training data set sizes were small. Interestingly, as we steadily grew the amount of data available for training, however, we reached a critical point at which most of the algorithms were generally indistinguishable in performance. Even more interesting was the fact that as we moved substantially beyond this critical point by adding even more training data, Naïve Bayes (with a few very minor modifications to take into account the confidence associated with the classification and the use of a separate model for single word queries), outperformed – by several percentage points in accuracy – every other algorithm employed, even after substantial effort was placed into making them better. Furthermore, most probability smoothing techniques, which generally seem to help in limited data situations, either showed no appreciably improvements or actually decreased performance in the data rich case for Naïve Bayes.

While the set of alternative algorithms used was by no means exhaustive, and the results here are still somewhat anecdotal, we hypothesize that, as in the case of the Banko and Brill study, an abundance of data often can, and usually does, make up for weaker modeling techniques. This perspective can be unusually liberating – it implies that given enough training data, the simpler, more obvious solutions can work, perhaps even better than more complex models that attempt to compensate for lack of sufficient data points.

7 Conclusions

Web information retrieval presents a wonderfully rich and varied set of problems where AI techniques can make critical advances. In this paper, we have presented a number of challenges, giving an (admittedly brief) overview of some approaches taken toward these problems and outlining many directions for future work. As a result, we hope to stimulate still more research in this area that will make use of the vast amount of information on the web in order to better achieve the goal of organizing the world's information and making it universally accessible and useful.

References

1. Brin, S., Page, L.: The Anatomy of a Large-Scale Hypertextual Web Search Engine. In: Proc. of the 7th International World Wide Web Conference (1998) 107-117
2. Kleinberg, J.M.: Authoritative Sources in a Hyperlinked Environment. Journal of the ACM **46**(5) (1999) 604-632
3. Bharat, K., Henzinger, M.R.: Improved Algorithms for Topic Distillation in a Hyperlinked Environment. In: Proc. of the 21st International ACM-SIGIR Conference on Research and Development in Information Retrieval (1998) 104-111
4. Tomlin, J.A.: A New Paradigm for Ranking Pages on the World Wide Web. In: Proc. of the 12th International World Wide Web Conference (2003) 350-355
5. Henzinger, M.R., Motwani, R., Silverstein, C.: Challenges in Web Search Engines. In: Proc. of the 18th International Joint Conference on Artificial Intelligence (2003) 1573-1579
6. Sahami, M., Dumais, S., Heckerman, D., and Horvitz, E.: A Bayesian Approach to Filtering Junk E-Mail. In: Learning for Text Categorization: Papers from the 1998 Workshop. AAAI Technical Report WS-98-05 (1998)
7. Dumais, S., Bharat, K., Joachims, T., Weigend, A. (eds.): Workshop on Implicit Measures of User Interests and Preferences at SIGIR-2003 (2003).
8. Agosti, M., and Melucci, M. (eds.): Workshop on Evaluation of Web Document Retrieval at SIGIR-1999 (1999)
9. Joachims, T.: Evaluating Retrieval Performance Using Clickthrough Data. In Proc. of the SIGIR-2002 Workshop on Mathematical/Formal Methods in Information Retrieval (2002)

10. Mitra. M., Singhal, A., and Buckley, C.: Improving Automatic Query Expansion. In: Proc. of the 21st Annual International ACM-SIGIR Conference on Research and Development in Information Retrieval (1998) 206-214
11. Smith, M., Kollock, P.: Communities in Cyberspace: Perspectives on New Forms of Social Organization. Routledge Press, London (1999)
12. Fiore, A., Tiernan, S.L., Smith, M.: Observed Behavior and Perceived Value of Authors in Usenet Newsgroups: Bridging the Gap, In: Proc. of the ACM SIGCHI Conference on Human Factors in Computing Systems (2002) 323-330
13. Arnt, A., and Zilberstein, S.: Learning to Perform Moderation in Online Forums. In: Proc. of the IEEE/WIC International Conference on Web Intelligence (2003)
14. Zhang, Y., Callan, J., Minka, T.P.: Novelty and Redundancy Detection in Adaptive Filtering. In: Proc. of the 25th International ACM-SIGIR Conference on Research and Development in Information Retrieval (2002)
15. Smith, J.R., Chang, S.F.: Tools and Techniques for Color Image Retrieval. In: Proc. of SPIE Storage and Retrieval for Image and Video Databases, Vol. 2670. (1996) 426-437
16. Berenzweig, A., Logan, B., Ellis, D., Whitman, B.: A Large-Scale Evaluation of Acoustic and Subjective Music Similarity Measures. In: Proc. of the 4th International Symposium on Music Information Retrieval (2003)
17. Wu, J., Rehg, J.M., Mullin, M.D.: Learning a Rare Event Detection Cascade by Direct Feature Selection. In: Advances in Neural Information Processing Systems 16 (2004)
18. Sung, K., Poggio, T.: Learning Human Face Detection in Cluttered Scenes. In Proc. of Intl. Conf. on Computer Analysis of Image and Patterns (1995)
19. Rowley, H.A., Baluja, S., Kanade, T.: Neural Network-based Face Detection. IEEE Trans. On Pattern Analysis and Machine Intelligence **20**(1) (1998) 23-38
20. Viola, P., Jones, M.: Rapid Object Detection Using a Boosted Cascade of Simple Features. In: Proc. of the IEEE Conf. on Computer Vision and Pattern Recognition (2001) 511-518
21. Schneiderman, H., Kanade, T.: A Statistical Model for 3D Object Detection Applied to Faces and Cars. In: Proc. of IEEE Conf. on Computer Vision and Pattern Recognition (2000)
22. Viola, P., Jones, M., Snow, D.: Detecting Pedestrians Using Patterns of Motion and Appearance. Mitsubishi Electric Research Lab Technical Report. TR-2003-90 (2003)
23. Banko, M., Brill, E.: Mitigating the Paucity of Data Problem: Exploring the Effect of Training Corpus Size on Classifier Performance for NLP. In: Proc. of the Conference on Human Language Technology (2001)

On the Intended Interpretations of Actions

Victor Jauregui, Maurice Pagnucco, and Norman Foo

School of Computer Science & Engineering
The University of New South Wales
Sydney, NSW, 2052, Australia
{vicj,morri,norman}@cse.unsw.edu.au

Abstract. In this paper we address the problem of commonsense reasoning about action by appealing to Occam's razor – we should accept the simplest hypothesis explaining the observed phenomena – to generalise the commonsense law of inertia. In particular, we identify the intended interpretation of an action as the *simplest* transformation induced by an action on a world to produce a possible successor. We formalise the notion of *simplicity* of a transformation as its conditional Kolmogorov complexity. Finally we show that the framework can solve simple commonsense reasoning problems and indicate its role as a first step towards capturing commonsense notions of causation.

1 Introduction

The problem of *commonsense reasoning about action* can be characterised as follows: given a (possibly incomplete) description of a world w, and a generally incomplete specification of an action a, what are the possible *successor worlds*, denoted $Res(a, w)$, which ensue after the action is performed?

Quite generally, an action specifies a mapping, or transformation, between worlds. In the presence of incomplete descriptions, or non-deterministic actions, this mapping may not be unique, but may correspond to a number of possible transformations. When an initial world w is supplied, identifying the successor worlds resulting from an action is tantamount to identifying the intended transformations for the given action description.

The difficulty faced is that, typically, we only characterise an action (incompletely) by its *direct effects* – those effects for which the action is immediately responsible. Consider the following example.

> We have $n > 0$ homogeneous switches, labelled 1 through n. Suppose, initially, all our switches are open (off). Assume, further, that we specify an action which makes the k-th switch (for some k) closed (on).

In particular, note that our action specification has not described the intended transformation completely. We have not, for example, specified what should happen to the j-th switch, for any $j \neq k$.

The *commonsense* intuition, however, is clear; given our incomplete action specification, the most plausible interpretation for the action yields that only the k-th switch closes, while the others remain unaffected. The argument is that because our action specification provides no support for any other switch closing, other than the k-th, had we intended any other effects, these would have been specified in the action description.

We can characterise these notions more formally as follows. Since our action describes only its direct effects, we admit as our potential *candidate* successors all worlds which satisfy the action's direct effects. We denote this set of candidates, $E(a)$. As action a provides an incomplete description, $E(a)$ is likely to be too permissive – our intended worlds will be a selection among these worlds. This amounts to identifying a function S which considers an initial world w and a set of candidate successors and picks out the intended successors. That is, we can express this as $Res(a, w) = S(w, E(a))$, depicting it graphically in Figure 1.

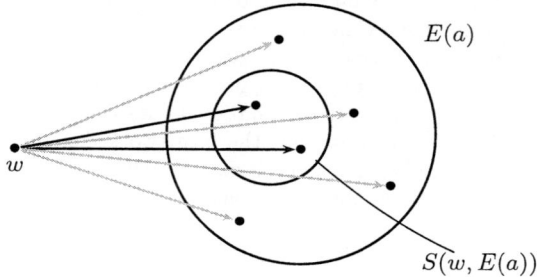

Fig. 1. Candidate mappings associated with an action. Intended mappings are represented by solid lines.

This kind of characterisation has been adopted in the approaches of McCain and Turner [1] and Pagnucco and Peppas [2]. We follow a similar direction but place our emphasis on finding the intended interpretation of an action. In particular, our selection function S selects the intended mappings from w into $E(a)$.

In Figure 1 the candidate mappings into $E(a)$ are depicted in grey with the solid arrows indicating the intended mappings among these. Once we have identified the intended mappings we can readily identify the intended successors.

This paper aims to rationalise our appeals to commonsense in reasoning about action by looking to identify the most plausible transformations which corresponds to an incomplete action specification. Traditionally this has been achieved by appealing to some notion of *minimal change* – any change that is not dictated by the action specification should not take place. We attempt to generalise this commonsense notion by appealing to the more general principle of *Occam's razor*; identifying the simplest transformations consistent with the action description as the intended mappings.

In Section 2 we motivate our work by showing how our intuitions manifest themselves in the situation calculus – the most common framework used to describe reasoning about action problems. In Section 3 we characterise the simplicity of a mapping between worlds by its conditional Kolmogorov complexity, allowing us, in Section 4, to formulate the problem of commonsense reasoning about action in terms of the complexity of a transformation. More specifically, the intended interpretation of an action is identified with the simplest transformations. Section 5 shows that we can capture some of our commonsense intuitions in this framework, providing an elegant solution to Hanks & McDermott's Yale Shooting Problem [3]. We also highlight some limitations in the current formalism indicating there is still substantial work to be done to get the formalisation 'right'. Finally, we conclude in Section 6, with a summary and some motivation for the present framework as an initial step towards the formal characterisation of commonsense notions of causation.

2 Background

The *situation calculus* (see, [4]) is a logical formalism for reasoning about action. It consists of *situations*, which indicate the state of the system we are modelling at a given instant in time; *fluents*, which identify the properties of that system we are interested in modelling; and *actions* which dictate the transitions between states that can take place. To say that the property described by a fluent f holds in situation s we write $Holds(f, s)$. So, for example, if we use the fluent $sw(k)$ to denote that switch k is closed in situation s, we would write $Holds(sw(k), s)$.

The system described in our example above would consist of the fluents: $sw(1), sw(2), \ldots, sw(k), \ldots, sw(n)$ describing whether switch k, for $k = 1, \ldots n$, is open or not. The initial situation, in which all the switches are open, would correspond to the situation term S_0, and would be described by the sentences:

$$\neg Holds(sw(1), S_0), \neg Holds(sw(2), S_0), \ldots, \neg Holds(sw(n), S_0) \qquad (S_0)$$

Actions invoke state transitions which are captured by adding a function term *Result*, which maps an action and a situation to a successor situation.

Describing the direct effects of the action $close(k)$, which, as mentioned earlier, specifies that the k-th switch becomes closed, would be done by the *effect axiom*: $Holds(sw(k), Result(close(k), s))$.

Once supplied an action a and a world w, it remains to characterise the intended successors $Res(a, w)$, via the intended interpretation of the action. In our example, the intuition that the desired mapping is the one that leaves all switches, other than the k-th, unaffected is captured by the *Commonsense Law of Inertia* which according to Shanahan [5] states, among other things, that:

> Normally, given any action (or event type) and any fluent, the action doesn't affect the fluent. [p18]

Moreover, Shanahan argues:

> As a scientific claim, the commonsense law of inertia wouldn't stand up to much scrutiny. But it's much better thought of, not as a statement about the world, but either as a useful representational device or as a strategy for dealing with incomplete information. [p18]

From our perspective the commonsense law of inertia gives a particular rule for capturing our selection criteria S.

In a logical framework, we eliminate unwanted models by adding extra axioms. We characterise the role of S similarly here. In general, for selection criteria S we can identify a set of formulae Γ_S which admits only the intended models. We can think of Γ_S as supplying a description of the intended transformations.

In particular, when S corresponds to the commonsense law of inertia, we can capture the intended mapping by adding *frame axioms*, which describe inertial transformations. Consider the switches example we described earlier with n fluents and possibly m actions ($close(k)$ for $1 \leq k \leq m \leq n$). The following, approximately $\approx 2 \times n \times m$ frame axioms, capture the inertial mapping – with one such set of $\approx 2 \times n$ axioms for each action $close(k)$:

$$\begin{array}{c} Holds(sw(1), s) \rightarrow Holds(sw(1), Result(close(k), s)) \\ \neg Holds(sw(1), s) \rightarrow \neg Holds(sw(1), Result(close(k), s)) \\ \vdots \\ Holds(sw(n), s) \rightarrow Holds(sw(n), Result(close(k), s)) \\ \neg Holds(sw(n), s) \rightarrow \neg Holds(sw(n), Result(close(k), s)) \end{array} \qquad (\Gamma_S)$$

We can observe a significant degree of regularity in these axioms, however. Taking advantage of this we can simplify our description, by treating each fluent uniformly, to $\approx 2 \times m$ axioms of the form (one of these for each action)[1]:

$$\begin{array}{c} \forall f \neq sw(k) \; Holds(f, s) \rightarrow Holds(f, Result(close(k), s)) \\ \forall f \neq sw(k) \; \neg Holds(f, s) \rightarrow \neg Holds(f, Result(close(k), s)) \end{array} \qquad (\Gamma'_S)$$

The important point we wish to make here is that the commonsense law of inertia constitutes a simple rule for completing the description of a transformation given an incomplete action description. The development above showed that this notion of simplicity can be captured by observing regularities to produce a short description of the intended transformation. On this basis, we make more precise Shanahan's claim that the commonsense law of inertia is a useful representational device for dealing with incomplete information. It is 'useful' in the following senses:

- it has a physical justification in Newton's mechanical law of inertia;
- it furnishes a simple rule to describe the intended transformations when provided an incomplete action description.

What remains is to give a more precise notion of simplicity with which to identify 'simple' transformations.

---

[1] Moreover, if we take advantage of the regularity in the actions (which is a feature of this example but would not generalise readily), we can simplify things even further to just two axioms:

$$\begin{array}{c} \forall k \; \forall j \neq k \; Holds(sw(j), s) \rightarrow Holds(sw(j), Result(close(k), s)). \\ \forall k \; \forall j \neq k \; \neg Holds(sw(j), s) \rightarrow \neg Holds(sw(j), Result(close(k), s)). \end{array}$$

3 Measuring Simplicity

Essentially, the main idea of this paper is *to equate commonsense, in reasoning about action, with the simplicity of a transformation*. In the sense that we showed that the commonsense law of inertia appeals to a simple rule, we argue that, in the absence of further information, commonsense inferences are the simplest inferences we can make from the given evidence.

Unfortunately, the simplest inferences we can make are often outside the scope of the language we use for our representations. This is the case, for example, when we use circumscription (see [6]) to characterise the commonsense law of inertia. So the simple analysis provided above, of adding a brief collection of formulae Γ_S to capture the intended transformations, may not be feasible.

Instead, our approach is to look at a well established measure of simplicity – or, its dual, complexity – called *Kolmogorov complexity* (see Li & Vitanyi [7]), which gives the complexity of a string x, and proceed to encode our logical theories into strings to make use of this measure. Let us first define Kolmogorov complexity (the following is an adaptation taken from Li & Vitanyi [7]):

Definition 1. *The **Kolmogorov complexity** of a string x (over some alphabet), denoted $K(x)$, is the length of the shortest program p (usually encoded over the binary alphabet) which when supplied to a universal Turing machine, U, produces x. That is:*

$$K(x) = \min\{|p| : U(p) = x\}. \tag{1}$$

For our purposes we want a measure of the simplicity of a transformation. There is a variant of Kolmogorov complexity we can use for this (see Li & Vitanyi [7]):

Definition 2. *The **conditional Kolmogorov complexity** of a string x given a string y, denoted $K(x|y)$, is the length of the shortest program p which, when given y as input, computes x. That is:*

$$K(x|y) = \min\{|p| : U(p, y) = x\}. \tag{2}$$

The intuition we want to capture is that, if we encode worlds w and v as strings, then the simplicity of the mapping from w to v, imposed by performing action a in world w, is determined by the conditional Kolmogorov complexity $K(v|w)$.

4 Formalising Commonsense Reasoning About Action

Our formalism involves mapping situations to strings, on which the intended mappings correspond to the simplest transformations.

Consider the switches example used earlier. We can map the initial situation S_0, in which all the n switches are initially open (off), to the binary string: $w = 0^n$. Our mapping is straight forward: the truth value of a fluent (i.e., whether the fluent holds or not) is determined by the value of the corresponding bit in the string. In our example, the k-th bit determines whether the k-th switch is open or closed. As such, a world under this encoding is just an n-bit string.

Corresponding to the action description $Holds(sw(k), Result(close(k), s))$, which admits as possible candidate successors those worlds v consistent with the k-th switch being closed, we define our effect function E, such that $E(close(k))$ consists of the set of n-bit strings with the k-th bit set to one, i.e., $E(close(k)) = \{x1y : |x1y| = n, |x| = k-1\}$. Once we have w and have determined $E(a)$ for action a, we need to select the intended mappings from among those candidate mappings of w into $E(a)$. As we outlined above, the intended mappings are the ones with the simplest transformations, which correspond to the shortest programs that transform w into some $v \in E(a)$. Formally:

Definition 3. *Given a world w and an action a, the set of possible successor worlds is the subset of candidate worlds $v \in E(a)$ with minimal conditional Kolmogorov complexity given w. That is:*

$$Res(a, w) = S(w, E(a)) = \min_{v}\{K(v|w) : v \in E(a)\}. \qquad (3)$$

The intuition being that our selection function identifies the simplest transformations; taking the worlds these map to as the desired successors.

The intention is that, because an action will generally be incompletely specified through its direct effects, the various underlying mechanisms that bring about these effects are non-monotonically implied. Moreover, in the absence of further information, we cannot rationally justify any more mechanisms than are necessary to bring about said effects. Li & Vitanyi [7] express this as follows:

> We are to admit no more causes of natural things (as we are told by Newton) than such as are both true and sufficient to explain their appearances.

Significantly, we note that inertial transformations will generally feature prominently among the simplest transformations. This is perhaps indicative of why the commonsense law of inertia is a good heuristic for commonsense reasoning about action. In particular, if we choose our universal Turing machine U in the definition of $K(x|y)$ (2), so that the empty program does altogether nothing, then the inertial transformation, which simply corresponds to the identity map, yields the simplest possible transformation.

Proposition 1. *Let U in (2) be such that $U(\varepsilon, y) = y$, then $K(x|y)$ receives its least value 0, when $x = y$.*

Proof. Since the empty string ε is the unique string with $|\varepsilon| = 0$, and all programs p are encoded by strings, then ε supplies the unique program of length 0 which yields $K(x|x) = 0$. □

5 Results and Discussion

In general, we expect that in a world in which few things change when an action is performed, any changes not specified by the direct effects of an action would require some form of elaboration corresponding to the conjecture of a cause, or explanation, for these changes. In this sense, deviations from inertia would require longer descriptions, excluding them from among the simplest mappings.

Earlier we conjectured that the inertial map would feature prominently among the simplest transformations when few things tend to change. It may be, though, that an action changes many things in a regular (though not inertial) manner, or that the world itself evolves regularly. In such cases the assumptions that justify the commonsense law of inertia break down.

In these instances the most rational choice of succession is that which most closely exhibits the pattern of change indicated by the action description. Our concerns here largely coincide with Solomonoff's in his theory of inductive inference [8]. Indeed, prediction problems, such as the one we are interested in, typically appeal to some form of inductive inference based on past experience. Our framework accommodates such inductive inferences naturally.

We now show that this framework can capture our intuitions with the simple switches example. The simplest transformation (i.e., the intended mapping) which maps a string of n 0's to a string with the k-th bit set to one (that is, into the set $E(close(k))$), intuitively, is the following:

$$\underbrace{0\ldots 000\ldots 0}_{n} \xrightarrow{close(k)} \underbrace{0\ldots 0\overbrace{\vphantom{0}1}^{k-1}0\ldots 0}_{n}$$

This transformation corresponds to the program which moves to the k-th position on the Turing machine tape and writes a '1'. We are faced with the problem that encoding the value of k in our program would incur an overhead which would suggest a preference for changing the earliest bits in the string; as these incur smaller overheads to specify. As no such preference should be implied, we overcome this by factoring out the particular value of k from our program. The way we do this is to define our universal machine U in (2), to have three tapes. The first is the *world-tape*, on which is encoded the initial world w. The world tape will also contain the output after it has undergone the specified transformation. The second tape, called the *program-tape*, contains the program we identify with the transformation to take place on the world tape. The third tape is a *data-tape* containing particular information about the action.

In our example, for the action $close(k)$, on the data tape would appear $k-1$ '1's, constituting the $k-1$ shifts needed to identify the k-th bit. The program tape would then refer to the data tape for this particular information rather than having it coded within the program. By discounting the data tape from consideration of the complexity (size) of the program we remove the bias introduced by the particular, arbitrary ordering of bits (fluents) imposed by the tape.

The key motivation behind this is to keep the program/data distinction. Li & Vitanyi [7] make a similar distinction when they consider *two-part codes*. The program encodes what is referred to as the *model*, which in our case we wish to identify with the *nature* of the transformation (in this case the setting of a bit). The data tape simply encodes particular information regarding the action (in this case the particular value which identifies the bit to alter). With these considerations, below (on the right) we encode the shortest program which transforms n zeros to a string with a '1' at the k-th bit, coinciding with the intended/simplest mapping (on the left):

$$\underbrace{0\ldots000\ldots0}_{n} \xrightarrow{close(k)} \underbrace{0\ldots\overbrace{0\,1\,0}^{k-1}\ldots0}_{n} \quad : \quad \begin{array}{c}(q_0, \overset{\times}{1}, \overset{R}{R}, q_0)\\ (q_0, \overset{\times}{\_}, \overset{1}{\times}, q_H)\end{array}$$

The only alternative simplest program which would map w into $E(close(k))$, is the program which writes k '1's on the tape. This would correspond to:

$$\underbrace{\overbrace{0\cdots00}^{k}\ldots0}_{n} \xrightarrow{close(k)} \underbrace{\overbrace{1\cdots10}^{k}\ldots0}_{n} \quad : \quad \begin{array}{c}(q_0, \overset{\times}{1}, \overset{1}{0}, q_0)\\ (q_0, \overset{\times}{0}, \overset{R}{R}, q_0)\\ (q_0, \overset{\times}{\_}, \overset{1}{\times}, q_H)\end{array}$$

We see that this unintended map is more complex (has a longer program). In fact, this is only the case because we have omitted in the intended program the Turing machine tuples when we don't care about reading a '0' on the data tape. This is no severe restriction as we can always choose a reference machine U, in (2), which adheres to the common convention that if a state-input pair is not found then the machine simply halts.

This example shows that the formalism captures the same intuitions that the commonsense law of inertia does when an action changes few things. The next example shows that it allows us to capture our intuitions when appeals to the principle of minimal change fail.

Consider the Yale Shooting Problem as proposed initially by Hanks & McDermott [3] and cited in Shanahan [5]. The scenario consists of a turkey and a gun; which is used to shoot the turkey. We identify two fluents: *Alive* and *Loaded* to indicate that the turkey is alive and the gun is loaded, respectively. There are also three actions *Load*, *Wait* and *Shoot*, with the obvious meanings. Suppose our initial situation S_0 has the turkey alive and the gun unloaded. These actions are specified according to the following effect axioms:

$$Holds(Loaded, Result(Load, s))$$
$$Holds(Loaded, s) \rightarrow \neg Holds(Alive, Result(Shoot, s))$$

Note that, as the wait action is intended to do nothing, its effect axiom is omitted.

Consider performing the sequence of actions, *Load* then *Wait* followed by *Shoot*. Intuitively we expect the following model, which we have depicted pictorially:

$$\overset{A,\overline{L}}{\bullet} \xrightarrow[\Delta L]{Lo} \overset{A,L}{\bullet} \xrightarrow{Wa} \overset{A,L}{\bullet} \xrightarrow[\Delta \overline{A}]{Sh} \overset{\overline{A},L}{\bullet}$$

where the Δ's below the arrows indicate the occurrence of an abnormality with the respective fluent. Unfortunately, the following anomalous model is also admitted when we minimise change (to see this observe that there are as many Δ's in the anomalous model as in the intended one, however, they occur at different times with different fluents):

$$\overset{A,\overline{L}}{\bullet} \xrightarrow[\Delta L]{Lo} \overset{A,L}{\bullet} \xrightarrow[\Delta \overline{L}]{Wa} \overset{A,\overline{L}}{\bullet} \xrightarrow{Sh} \overset{A,\overline{L}}{\bullet}$$

This second, anomalous model is clearly counter-intuitive. There is no justification for the gun becoming unloaded during the wait action. In our framework we can show that the anomalous model is rejected. This result confirms that, in our approach, the inertial mapping will generally feature among the simplest transformations. In particular, the $Wait$ action, having been specified as not doing anything (thus corresponding to $E(Wait)$ admitting all possible worlds), receives as its intended interpretation the simplest program which does nothing – the empty program. More generally we have:

Proposition 2. *Let w be a world and 'a' an action such that $w \in E(a)$, then the intended mapping is always the inertial mapping. That is, $Res(a,w) = \{w\}$.*

Proof. From Proposition 1, $K(v|w)$ gets its least value for $v = w$. Since $w \in E(a)$, $\{K(v|w) : v \in E(a)\}$ is minimised when $v = w$, yielding $Res(a,w) = \{w\}$. □

Carrying over the arguments from the switches example, the load action receives the program that sets the only bit associated with the *Loaded* fluent and the *Shoot* action gets the program which checks if the *Alive* bit is set and resets it.

The program that performs the composite sequence of actions, consisting of *Load*, *Wait* and *Shoot* actions, we take to be the composition of these programs. This composite program, associated with the composite action, clearly yields only the intended model above and not the anomalous model. In particular, we cannot trade a change during the *Wait* action with a change during the *Shoot* action, as takes place in the anomalous model under minimisation of change.

Unfortunately, though it appears the formalism presented has a number of desirable properties, and generally adheres to our commonsense intuitions, it also suffers a number of obvious deficiencies which suggest the framework, in its present incarnation, is not satisfactory. One such deficiency regards the program/data distinction. Our solution of having separate program and data tapes appears too simplistic. In particular, we have the following.

Proposition 3. *The complexity of a world transformation is bounded by a fixed constant that depends on the universal machine U used in (2).*

Proof. Let u be a program which runs on U that ignores the world tape and interprets the data tape as a program (u encodes a universal program). We can proceed as follows: we encode u on our program tape, supplying, on the data tape, a program p such that $u(p) = v$, for any $v \in E(a)$. Now $U(u,w) = v$, so, by (2), $K(v|w) \leq |u|$. □

This is clearly a severe limitation. What it shows, in particular, is that we have been too simplistic in determining the roles that program and data can play in our formalism. More specifically, what might be required is to place a stronger restriction on what constitutes valid data.

6 Conclusion

The aim of this paper was to provide a formalism for commonsense reasoning about action which appeals to Occam's razor as its guiding principle, generalising the commonsense law of inertia.

We argued that we can identify commonsense with simplicity which we went on to formalise using Kolmogorov complexity. Subsequently, a formalism that identifies the intended interpretations of an action as the simplest transformations that satisfy the direct effects of an action is provided. We showed that it is possible to characterise commonsense intuitions regarding minimal change in this framework, and showed that we can solve the Yale Shooting Problem when minimal change breaks down.

Ultimately, we argued, the present framework still faces significant limitations which render it preliminary. A number of such issues (for example, the problems with the program/data distinction) are currently under investigation.

One of the main motivations behind our work has been to furnish a framework with which we can analyse such aspects of commonsense reasoning as causal reasoning, as identified by McCain & Turner [1], Lin [9], Thielscher [10], Sandewall [11], among others. In this respect, this paper is an attempt to lay the groundwork for such an analysis. In particular, just as the 2nd Law of Thermodynamics identifies a direction of time and hence causation, so we hope that analogous information theoretic arguments may allow us to give a formal characterisation of commonsense notions of causation. The hope is that the framework proposed will supply a natural platform through which to address these concerns.

References

1. McCain, N., Turner, H.: A causal theory of ramifications and qualifications. In Mellish, C., ed.: Proceedings of the 14th International Joint Conference on Artificial Intelligence, Morgan Kaufmann, San Francisco (1995) pp. 1978–1984
2. Pagnucco, M., Peppas, P.: Causality and minimal change demystified. In Nebel, B., ed.: Proceedings of the 17th International Joint Conference on Artificial Intelligence. Volume 1., Seattle, Washington, Morgan Kaufmann (2001) pp. 125–130
3. Hanks, S., McDermott, D.: Nonmonotonic logic and temporal projection. Artificial Intelligence **33** (1987) pp. 379–412
4. McCarthy, J., Hayes, P.: Some philosophical problems from the standpoint of artificial intelligence. In Meltzer, B., Michie, D., eds.: Machine Intelligence 4. Edinburgh University Press (1969) pp. 463–502
5. Shanahan, M.: Solving the frame problem. MIT Press, Cambridge, Mass. (1997)
6. McCarthy, J.: Circumscription – a form of nonmonotonic reasoning. Artificial Intelligence **13** (1980) pp. 27–39
7. Li, M., Vitnyi, P.: An introduction to Kolmogorov complexity and its applications. 2nd edn. Springer-Verlag, New York (1997)
8. Solomonoff, R.: A formal theory of inductive inference. Part I. Information and Control **7** (1964) pp. 1–22
9. Lin, F.: Embracing causality in specifying the indirect effects of actions. In Mellish, C., ed.: Proceedings of the Fourteenth International Joint Conference on Artificial Intelligence, Morgan Kaufmann, San Francisco (1995) pp. 1985–1991
10. Thielscher, M.: Ramification and causality. Artificial Intelligence **89** (1997) pp. 317–364
11. Sandewall, E.: Transition cascade semantics and first assessments results for ramification, preliminary report. Technical Report R-96-19, Department of CIS, Linköping University, Sweden (1996)

Temporal Linear Logic for Symbolic Agent Negotiation

Peep Küngas

Norwegian University of Science and Technology
Department of Computer and Information Science
peep@idi.ntnu.no

Abstract. In this paper we present an application of temporal linear logic (TLL) to symbolic agent negotiation and reasoning. While linear logic gives us control over resources and agent capabilities during negotiation, TLL allows considering time issues as well. That allows us to construct more expressive offers, which would not be possible in linear logic only.

1 Introduction

In heterogeneous multi-agent systems interoperability between agents cannot be taken for granted. Indeed, since agents may enter and leave a system at their will, there should exist a mechanism for automatically adjusting agents' behaviours and goals in order to keep the system in balance. Automatic negotiation is regarded as a mechanism for granting that sort of on-the-fly system integration and management.

So far, in multi-agent systems, mainly game-theoretical negotiation has been applied. The latter is based on a numerical utility function, which is used to choose a strategy for negotiation. However, game-theoretical negotiation suffers at least in three issues. Firstly, a negotiation strategy is chosen before negotiation starts and cannot be changed during negotiation. Secondly, the participating agents cannot hide their internal states from each-other, since the states are used to define the utility function. And thirdly, the negotiation process is based on numerical information, which is hardly interpretable by humans. Thus human participants may not be able to follow the negotiation process by their own and thus cannot evaluate the results.

Symbolic negotiation in contrast is based on logical formalisms and thus overcomes the previously mentioned disadvantages. It means that encapsulation of agent preferences, resources and goals is supported. Additionally, the negotiation process and the result of the process is declarative and thus more easily interpretable than numerical information. And finally, agents are allowed to dynamically adjust their negotiation strategies during negotiation as well.

Several solutions to symbolic negotiation have been described. Küngas and Matskin [7] elaborated the ideas of Harland and Winikoff [3] and demonstrated applicability of linear logic (LL) to agent negotiation. They proposed that distributed LL theorem proving could capture a formalism for agent negotiation.

They also described a formal mechanism for generating new offers. The corresponding framework allows agents to negotiate over resources and exploit capabilities of their partners. Since all participating agents have to achieve their personal goals, each agent has to be sure about resources that can be given away and capabilities that could be executed by other agents. Agent reasoning in [7] is an interactive process involving Partial Deduction (PD) and LL theorem proving. PD is applied there as a method of deducing subproblems, which from negotiation point of view are interpreted as offers.

The main advantages of using LL as a negotiation formalism, over other formalisms, include its resource-consciousness and nonmonotonicity. Additionally, LL could be viewed as a computation-centric logic in contrast to truth-centric logics, which have been prevalent so far. That allows inherently reasoning about changes in a dynamically changing environment.

Although LL provides a rich formalism for representing resources and agent capabilities, it still lacks a construction for specifying another important aspect of dynamic systems, namely time. In this paper we extend the previous work on LL with the notion of time through usage of temporal LL (TLL). Since TLL is an extension of LL, we can implicitly transfer the previous agent negotiation framework in LL to TLL. We present a way to use modalities of TLL to model time issues in negotiation as well. That approach gives us an opportunity to go beyond barely resource-oriented negotiation and construct a more expressive negotiation formalism, which allows solving larger class of problems than LL alone.

Although several articles discuss language and representation issues of symbolic negotiation, we are more concerned with the computational side of negotiation process. This paper presents a formalism for generating new offers using PD during negotiation. We define PD steps as inference figures in TLL. While using those inference figures instead of basic TLL rules, we can achieve more efficient proof search.

The paper is organized as follows. In Section 2 we introduce underlying formalisms. Section 3 describes a motivating example and explicitly emphasises the role of time in symbolic negotiation. Section 4 presents completeness and soundness results of our framework whilst Section 5 reviews related work. The last section concludes the paper and discusses future work.

2 Formal Aspects of Symbolic Negotiation

2.1 Linear Logic and Temporal Linear Logic

LL is a refinement of classical logic introduced by J.-Y. Girard to provide means for keeping track of "resources". In LL a conjunction of two instances of a propositional constant A is not logically equivalent to A. This does not apply in classical logic, since there the truth value of a fact does not depend on the number of copies of the fact. Indeed, LL is not about truth, it is about computation.

In the following we are considering intuitionistic fragment of LL (ILL) consisting of multiplicative conjunction ($\otimes$), additive disjunction ($\oplus$), additive conjunction (&), linear implication (⊸) and "of course" operator (!). In terms of resource acquisition the logical expression $A \otimes B \vdash C \otimes D$ means that resources C and D are obtainable only if both A and B are obtainable. After the sequent has been applied, A and B are consumed and C and D are produced.

The expression $A \vdash B \oplus C$ in contrary means that, if we have resource A, we can obtain either B or C, but we do not know which one of those. The expression $A \& B \vdash C$ on the other hand means that while having resources A and B we can choose, which one of those to trade for C. Therefore it is said that $\oplus$ and $\&$ represent respectively *external* and *internal* choice. The formula !A means that we can use or generate the resource A as much as we want – the amount of the resource is unbounded.

There are several proposals for considering time in LL and they are reviewed in Section 5. We adopt the formalisation of Hirai [4]. His intuitionistic fragment of TLL includes in addition to LL part also modalities $\Box$ and $\bigcirc$. Whilst the first is for reasoning about persistence of resources, the second modality is for reasoning about time. Formula $\bigcirc A$ for instance means that A holds in the next time point. Thus sequent $A \vdash \bigcirc B$ expresses that after consuming A at time point t, B becomes available at time point $t+1$.

To increase the expressiveness of formulae, we use the following abbreviations $a^n = \underbrace{a \otimes \ldots \otimes a}_{n}$ and $\bigcirc^n a = \underbrace{\bigcirc \ldots \bigcirc}_{n} a$, for $n > 0$.

2.2 Agents in TLL

Definition 1. *An agent specification (AS) is presented with the following TLL sequent:*

$$\Gamma; S \vdash \bigcirc^n G,$$

where Γ is a set of extralogical TLL axioms representing agent's capabilities, S is the initial state and G is the goal state of an agent. Index n determines the upper bound for the discrete time steps, in a resulting solution. Both S and G are multiplicative conjunctions of literals.

Definition 2. *Agent capabilities in Γ are in form:*

$$\vdash I \multimap O,$$

where I and O are formulae in conjunctive normal form which are, respectively, consumed and generated when a particular capability is applied.

While in I only modality ! might be used, in O additionally $\bigcirc$ is allowed. Thus we are able to express explicitly that it takes time before effects of application of a capability become evident. This kind of expressivity is extremely relevant if agents have to coordinate their actions. It has to be mentioned that a capability can be applied only, if conjuncts in I form a subset of conjuncts in S.

Definition 3. *Agent specification implementation (ASI) is a (composite) capability*

$$\vdash S \multimap_{\lambda a_1, \ldots, a_n . f} S, n \geq 0,$$

where f is a term representing the function, which generates O from I by applying potentially composite functions over $a_1, \ldots, a_n$.

2.3 Encoding Offers in LL

Harland and Winikoff [3] presented the first ideas about applying LL theorem proving for agent negotiation. Both internal and external nondeterminism in negotiation can be represented with LL. In the case of internal nondeterminism a choice is made by resource provider, whereas in the case of external nondeterminism a choice is made by resource consumer. For instance, formula $Dollar^5 \multimap Beer \oplus Soda$ (at the offer receiver side) means that an agent can provide either some $Beer$ or $Soda$ in return for 5 dollars, but the choice is made by the provider agent. The consumer agent has to be ready to obtain either a beer or a soda. The formula $Dollar \multimap Tobacco \& Lighter$ (again at the offer receiver side) in contrary means that the consumer may select which resource, $Tobacco$ or $Lighter$, s/he gets for a $Dollar$.

There is another kind of nondeterministic construction in LL, namely the ! operator. Since !A means that an agent can generate as many copies of A as required, the number of literals A is unbounded and represents additional kind of nondeterminism. From negotiation point of view, !A represents unbounded access to the resource.

While using TLL we can in addition to the preceding describe also offers like $\bigcirc A \vdash B$. The intuitive meaning of the offer is that resource A could be provided at time point $t+1$, if B is given at t (now). Such offers provide agents with a way to solve certain dependencies between their resources and capabilities. For instance, it may happen that an agent needs resource A for generating C. However, if A is after that no longer needed by the agent, then A could be given away after C has been produced and A still remains.

Definition 4. *Offer is a sequent $A \vdash B$, where A represents resources which are asked, and B represents resources which could be provided by an agent. While A is a LL formula, B is a TLL formula.*

2.4 Partial Deduction and (T)LL

Partial deduction (PD) (or partial evaluation of logic programs first formalised in [8]) is known as one of optimisation techniques in logic programming. Given a logic program, partial deduction derives a more specific program while preserving the meaning of the original program. Since the program is more specialised, it is usually more efficient than the original program, if executed. For instance, let A, B, C and D be propositional variables and $A \multimap B$, $B \multimap C$ and $C \multimap D$ computability statements in LL. Then possible partial deductions are $A \multimap C$, $B \multimap D$ and $A \multimap D$. It is easy to notice that the first corresponds to forward chaining (from initial states to goals), the second to backward chaining (from goals to initial states) and the third could be either forward or backward chaining.

We are applying PD for determining subtasks, which cannot be performed by a single agent, but still are possibly closer to a solution than an initial task. This means that given a state S and a goal G of an agent we compute a new state S' and a new goal G'. This information is forwarded to another agent for further inference.

In order to manage access to unbounded resources, PD steps $\mathcal{R}_{C_l}$, $\mathcal{R}_{L_l}$, $\mathcal{R}_{W_l}$ were defined in [7]. They are formalised as the following LL inference figures (A, B and C are LL formulae):

$$\frac{!A \otimes !A \otimes B \vdash C}{!A \otimes B \vdash C} \mathcal{R}_{C_l} \qquad \frac{A \otimes B \vdash C}{!A \otimes B \vdash C} \mathcal{R}_{L_l} \qquad \frac{B \vdash C}{!A \otimes B \vdash C} \mathcal{R}_{W_l}$$

We define in addition forward and backward chaining PD steps for reasoning under time constraints.

Definition 5. *Forward chaining PD step $\mathcal{R}_f^{\bigcirc}(L_i)$ is a rule*

$$\frac{A \otimes B \vdash \bigcirc^{n-1} C}{A \otimes D \vdash \bigcirc^n C} \mathcal{R}_f^{\bigcirc}(L_i)$$

Definition 6. *Backward chaining PD step $\mathcal{R}_b^{\bigcirc}(L_i)$ is a rule*

$$\frac{A \vdash \bigcirc^{n-1} D \otimes \bigcirc^{n-1} C}{A \vdash \bigcirc^n B \otimes \bigcirc^n C} \mathcal{R}_b^{\bigcirc}(L_i)$$

In both case L_i is defined as an agent capability $\vdash D \multimap \bigcirc B$.

3 A Motivating Example

Let us consider the following scenario with 2 agents in an office environment, where agents have to reserve access to a printer before they can print their documents. Only one agent can access the printer in time. Agent *Mary* has initially reserved access to a printer and would like to print out a document. That is formally described with the following:

$$S_{Mary} = \{Printer\}, \qquad G_{Mary} = \{\bigcirc^n Document\}.$$

Mary's capabilities are limited to document printing, thus Γ_{Mary} consists of one action only:

$$\Gamma_{Mary} = \{\vdash Printer \otimes Paper \multimap_{print} \bigcirc Document \otimes \bigcirc Printer\}.$$

The capability *print* denotes that for printing a document we need access to a printer and some paper, while as a result we get a printout of the document and we still have access to the printer.

Agent *John* has a scanner and some paper. He wants to make a copy of an article and thus is looking for a photocopier. However, there does not seem to be any photocopier available in the office. Fortunately, it turns out that John is skilled in solving technical issues in an office environment and thus can combine a printer and a scanner to produce a system with the same functionality as a photocopier. *John*'s capabilities include also photocopying. The current state S_{John} and the goal G_{John} of *John* are encoded as the following:

$$S_{John} = \{Scanner \otimes !Paper\}, \qquad G_{John} = \{\bigcirc^n Copier \otimes \bigcirc^n Copy\}.$$

John's capabilities to combine machines and to copy are formalised with the following:

$$\Gamma_{John} = \begin{array}{l} \vdash Printer \otimes Scanner \multimap_{combine} \bigcirc Copier, \\ \vdash Copier \otimes Paper \multimap_{copy} \bigcirc Copier \otimes \bigcirc Copy, \end{array}$$

Since *John* is unable to achieve his goal alone, he generates the following offer:

$$!Paper \vdash Printer.$$

The offer is generated in the following way:

$$\cfrac{\cfrac{\cfrac{\cfrac{\cfrac{\cfrac{Pa \otimes S \vdash Pa \otimes S}{Pa \otimes S \vdash \bigcirc^{n-2} Pa \otimes \bigcirc^{n-2} S} Id}{!Pa \otimes Pa \otimes S \vdash \bigcirc^{n-2} S \otimes \bigcirc^{n-2} Pr \otimes \bigcirc^{n-2} Pa} \bigcirc^{n-2} \quad \cfrac{!Pa \vdash Pr}{!Pa \vdash \bigcirc^{n-2} Pr} \bigcirc^{n-2}}{!Pa \otimes S \vdash \bigcirc^{n-2} S \otimes \bigcirc^{n-2} Pr \otimes \bigcirc^{n-2} Pa} L\otimes, R\otimes}{!Pa \otimes S \vdash \bigcirc^{n-1} Co \otimes \bigcirc^{n-1} Pa} \mathcal{R}_{C_l}, \mathcal{R}_{L_l}}{!Pa \otimes S \vdash \bigcirc^n Co \otimes \bigcirc^n C} \mathcal{R}_b^{\bigcirc}(combine)}{\mathcal{R}_b^{\bigcirc}(copy)}$$

We write S, C, Co, Pr and Pa to denote *Scanner*, *Copy*, *Copier*, *Printer* and *Paper*, respectively. Inference figure $\mathcal{R}_b^{\bigcirc}(L_i)$ is described in Section 4.

However, since the offer does not satify her needs, *Mary* derives the following counteroffer:

$$Paper \vdash \bigcirc Printer.$$

Since *Mary*'s offer is subsumed by *John*'s offer, *John* accepts it. Now, when agents start executing their capabilities to achieve their goals, resources are changed according to the negotiation results.

It should be noted that *Mary* cannot give away resource *Printer* immediately, since it is needed for her own purposes as well. However, she can release the resource after she has performed certain operations with it. That arises complicated issues in symbolic negotiation, which could be modelled only through usage of the time notion.

However, in order to construct offers, which include time-dependent information, we need an additional mechanism. In particular, we exchange the roles of agent specification $S \vdash G$ and a particular capability $\vdash I \multimap O$. Thus we apply $\vdash S \multimap G$ to $I \vdash O$. Doing this allows to reason, which resources are missing for applying a particular capability. *Mary* constructed her offer by using capability *print*:

$$\cfrac{\cfrac{Pr \otimes Pa \vdash Pr \otimes Pa}{Pr \otimes Pa \vdash Pr \otimes Pa \otimes (Pr \multimap Doc)} Id \quad \cfrac{\vdash Pr \multimap Doc}{} Axiom}{Pr \otimes Pa \vdash \bigcirc Doc \otimes \bigcirc Pr} R\otimes \quad \cfrac{\cfrac{\cfrac{\cfrac{\cfrac{Pr \vdash Pr}{Pr, Pr \multimap Doc \vdash \bigcirc Doc} Id \quad \cfrac{Doc \vdash Doc}{Doc \vdash \bigcirc Doc} Id}{Pa \vdash \bigcirc Pr \quad Pr \otimes (Pr \multimap Doc) \vdash \bigcirc Doc} L\multimap}{Pa, Pr \otimes (Pr \multimap Doc) \vdash \bigcirc Doc \otimes \bigcirc Pr} R\otimes}{Pr \otimes Pa \otimes (Pr \multimap Doc) \vdash \bigcirc Doc \otimes \bigcirc Pr} L\otimes}{} Cut$$

4 Formalisation of Reasoning About Temporal Constraints

In this section we prove completeness and soundness of PD for TLL.

Definition 7. *Resultant is an* $ASI \vdash I \multimap_{\lambda a_1,...,a_n.f} O, n \geq 0$.

ASI determines which agent capabilities could be applied through PD steps to derive resultant $\vdash S \multimap_{\lambda a_1,...,a_n.f} G, n \geq 0$. It should be noted that resultants are derived by applying PD steps to agent specifications (AS), which are represented in form $A \vdash B$.

Definition 8 (Derivation of a resultant). *Let $\mathcal{R}$ be any predefined PD step. A derivation of a resultant R_0 is a finite sequence of resultants: $R_0 \Rightarrow_\mathcal{R} R_1 \Rightarrow_\mathcal{R} R_2 \Rightarrow_\mathcal{R} \ldots \Rightarrow_\mathcal{R} R_n$, where $\Rightarrow_\mathcal{R}$ denotes to an application of a PD step $\mathcal{R}$.*

Definition 9 (Partial deduction). *Partial deduction of an AS $\Gamma; S \vdash G$ is a set of all possible derivations of $ASI \vdash S \multimap G$ from any resultant R_i. The result of PD is a multiset of resultants R_i.*

One can easily denote that this definition of PD generates a whole proof tree for agent specification $\Gamma; S \vdash G$.

Definition 10. *AS $\Gamma; S \vdash G$ is executable, iff given Γ as a set of agent capabilities, resultant $\vdash S \multimap_{\lambda a_1,...,a_n.f} G, n \geq 0$ can be derived such that derivation ends with resultant R_n, which equals to $\vdash A \multimap A$.*

Soundness and completeness are defined through executability of agent specifications.

Definition 11 (Soundness of PD of an AS). *An $AS \vdash S' \multimap G'$ is executable, if an $ASI \vdash S \multimap G$ is executable in an AS $\Gamma; S \vdash G$ and there is a derivation $\vdash S \multimap G \Rightarrow_\mathcal{R} \ldots \Rightarrow_\mathcal{R} \vdash S' \multimap G'$.*

Completeness is the converse:

Definition 12 (Completeness of PD of an AS). *An $AS \vdash S \multimap G$ is executable, if an $ASI \vdash S' \multimap G'$ is executable in an AS $\Gamma; S' \vdash G'$ and there is a derivation $\vdash S \multimap G \Rightarrow_\mathcal{R} \ldots \Rightarrow_\mathcal{R} \vdash S' \multimap G'$.*

Our proofs of soundness and completeness are based on proving that derivation of a resultant is a derivation in a AS using PD steps, which are defined as inference figures in TLL.

Proposition 1. *Given that L_i is defined as $\vdash D \multimap \bigcirc B$, resource- and time-sensitive backward PD step $\mathcal{R}_b^\bigcirc(L_i)$ is sound with respect to TLL rules.*

Proof.

$$\cfrac{A \vdash \bigcirc^{n-1}D \otimes \bigcirc^{n-1}C \quad \cfrac{\cfrac{\cfrac{\cfrac{\overline{D \vdash D}\; Id \quad \overline{\bigcirc B \vdash \bigcirc B}\; Id}{D \multimap \bigcirc B, D \vdash \bigcirc B}\; L\multimap}{\vdots\; \bigcirc, n-1\times}}{\bigcirc^{n-1}D \vdash \bigcirc^{n}B} \quad \cfrac{\cfrac{\overline{C \vdash C}\; Id}{\vdots\; \bigcirc, n\times}}{\bigcirc^{n-1}C \vdash \bigcirc^{n}C}}{\cfrac{\bigcirc^{n-1}D, \bigcirc^{n-1}C \vdash \bigcirc^{n}B \otimes \bigcirc^{n}C}{\bigcirc^{n-1}D \otimes \bigcirc^{n-1}C \vdash \bigcirc^{n}B \otimes \bigcirc^{n}C}\; L\otimes}\; R\otimes}{A \vdash \bigcirc^{n}B \otimes \bigcirc^{n}C}\; Cut$$

Proposition 2. *Given that L_i is defined as $\vdash D \multimap \bigcirc B$, forward PD step $\mathcal{R}_f^{\bigcirc}(L_i)$ is sound with respect to TLL rules.*

Proof.

$$\cfrac{\cfrac{\cfrac{\overline{A \vdash A}\; Id}{A \vdash \bigcirc A}\; \bigcirc \quad \overline{\bigcirc B \vdash \bigcirc B}\; Id}{\cfrac{A, \bigcirc B \vdash \bigcirc A \otimes \bigcirc B}{A \otimes \bigcirc B \vdash \bigcirc A \otimes \bigcirc B}\; L\otimes}\; R\otimes \quad \cfrac{\cfrac{\cfrac{\overline{A \vdash A}\; Id \quad \overline{B \vdash B}\; Id}{A, B \vdash A \otimes B}\; R\otimes \quad A \otimes B \vdash \bigcirc^{n-1}C}{\cfrac{A, B \vdash \bigcirc^{n-1}C}{\cfrac{\bigcirc A, \bigcirc B \vdash \bigcirc^{n}C}{\bigcirc A \otimes \bigcirc B \vdash \bigcirc^{n}C}\; L\otimes}\; \bigcirc}}{A \otimes \bigcirc B \vdash \bigcirc^{n}C}\; Cut}{\cfrac{A \otimes \bigcirc B \vdash \bigcirc^{n}C}{A \otimes D \vdash \bigcirc^{n}C}\; \mathcal{R}_f(L_i)}$$

A, B, C and D in previous inference figures are formulae of TLL. Since $\bigcirc(A \otimes B)$ in the left hand side of a sequent could be transformed to $\bigcirc A \otimes \bigcirc B$, we do not show the transformation explicitly in previous inference figures.

Theorem 1 (Soundness of PD for TLL). *PD for TLL is sound.*

Proof. Since both PD steps, $\mathcal{R}_f^{\bigcirc}(L_i)$ and $\mathcal{R}_b^{\bigcirc}(L_i)$, are sound, PD for TLL is sound as well. The latter derives from the fact that, if there exists a derivation $\vdash S \multimap G \Rightarrow_{\mathcal{R}} \ldots \Rightarrow_{\mathcal{R}} \vdash S' \multimap G'$, then the derivation is constructed by PD in a formally correct manner.

Theorem 2 (Completeness of PD for TLL). *PD for TLL is complete.*

Proof. When applying PD we first generate all possible derivations until no derivations could be found, or all proofs have been found. According to Hirai [4] theorem proving in propositional TLL is equivalent to reachability checking of timed Petri nets, which is decidable. Therefore it is easy to see that in this way the whole proof tree is generated.

Since the number of derivations is finite, derivation $\vdash S \multimap G \Rightarrow_{\mathcal{R}} \ldots \Rightarrow_{\mathcal{R}} \vdash S' \multimap G'$ would be either discovered or it will be detected that there is no such derivation. Therefore PD for TLL is complete.

5 Related Work

Kanovich et al [6] introduced time to LL on the first order level. However, the encoding is not flexible enough to handle several problems in agent systems. Hirai [4] proposes a framework, which is based on timed Petri nets and embodies both LL and modal logic S4 for time modalities. Thus both, formulae in S4 and

LL are provable in this logic. Its main contribution compared to the work of Kanovich and Ito [5] is that full intuitionistic LL is considered, instead of the fragment of LL without modality !. The latter has the important feature from negotiation point of view – with ! also unbounded access to resource could be offered. Another approach for describing temporal LL through timed Petri nets is given in [11]. However, it lacks completeness theorem for timed Petri nets as stated in [4].

Fisher [2] introduced the idea of agent negotiation as distributed theorem proving in classical logic. In his approach all agents share the common view to the world and if a new clause is inferred, all agents would sense it. Inferred clauses are distributed among agents via broadcasting.

Parsons et al [9] defined negotiation as interleaved formal reasoning and arguing. Arguments and contra arguments are derived using theorem proving taking into consideration agents' own goals. While Parsons et al [9] perform reasoning in classical logic, it is possible to infer missing clauses needed for achieving a goal. The situation gets more complicated, when several instances of formulae are available and, moreover, the actions performed by agents or resources they spend can be interdependent.

Sadri et al [10] propose another logical approach to automated negotiation, which is built on Amgoud et al [1] work on argumentation. The work of Sadri et al is more specialised and detailed than the work by Amgoud et al. That allows deeper analysis of the reasoning mechanism and the knowledge required to build negotiation dialogues.

6   Conclusions

In this paper we extended our previous work on symbolic negotiation. While preserving non-monotonicity and resource-consciousness from earlier work, through the usage of PD in temporal linear logic we introduced time to symbolic negotiation. Thereby we bound together two important aspects of dynamic systems, time and resources, for symbolic negotiation. As a result, the proposed framework allows reasoning about temporal and resource dependencies during symbolic negotiation.

We did not consider here PD strategies, which determine how to choose particular PD steps and agent capabilities in order to achieve desired results. Though, we have recognised the strategies as an extremely important issue, since it relates to the efficiency of the whole PD process. Therefore our future work has a special focus on PD strategies.

Acknowledgements

This work was partially supported by the Norwegian Research Foundation in the framework of Information and Communication Technology (IKT-2010) program – the ADIS project. Additionally I would like to thank the anonymous referees for their comments.

References

1. L. Amgoud, S. Parsons, N. Maudet. Arguments, Dialogue and Negotiation. In Proceedings of 14th European Conference on Artificial Intelligence, Berlin, Germany, August 20–25, 2000, pp. 338–342, IOS Press, 2000.
2. M. Fisher. Characterising Simple Negotiation as Distributed Agent-Based Theorem-Proving – A Preliminary Report. In Proceedings of the Fourth International Conference on Multi-Agent Systems, Boston, July 2000, IEEE Press, 2000.
3. J. Harland, M. Winikoff. Agent Negotiation as Proof Search in Linear Logic. In Proceedings of the First International Joint Conference on Autonomous Agents and Multi-Agent Systems (AAMAS 2002), July 15–19, 2002, Bologna, Italy.
4. T. Hirai. Propositional Temporal Linear Logic and its Application to Concurrent Systems. IEICE Transactions, Vol E83-A, No. 11, pp. 2228–2235, November 2000.
5. M. I. Kanovich, T. Ito. Temporal Linear Logic Specifications for Concurrent Processes (Extended Abstract). In Proceedings of 12th Annual IEEE Symposium on Logic in Computer Science (LICS'97), Warsaw, Poland, June 29–July 2, 1997, pp. 48–57, 1998.
6. M. I. Kanovich, M. Okada, A. Scedrov. Specifying Real-Time Finite-State Systems in Linear Logic. In Proceedings of the 2nd International Workshop on Constraint Programming for Time-Critical Applications and Multi-Agent Systems (COTIC'98), Nice, France, September 7, 1998.
7. P. Küngas, M. Matskin. Linear Logic, Partial Deduction and Cooperative Problem Solving. To appear in Proceedings of DALT 2003, Melbourne, Australia, July 15, 2003, Lecture Notes in Artificial Intelligence, Vol. 2990, Springer-Verlag, 2004.
8. J. W. Lloyd, J. C. Shepherdson. Partial Evaluation in Logic Programming. Journal of Logic Programming, Vol. 11, pp. 217–242, 1991.
9. S. Parsons, C. Sierra, N. Jennings. Agents that Reason and Negotiate by Arguing. Journal of Logic and Computation, Vol. 8, No. 3, pp. 261–292, 1998.
10. F. Sadri, F. Toni, P. Torroni. Logic Agents, Dialogues and Negotiation: An Abductive Approach. In Proceedings of the Symposium on Information Agents for E-Commerce, Artificial Intelligence and the Simulation of Behaviour Convention (AISB-2001), York, UK, March 21–24, 2001.
11. M. Tanabe. Timed Petri Nets and Temporal Linear Logic. In Proceedings of 18th International Conference on Application and Theory of Petri Nets (ICATPN'97), Toulouse, France, June 23–27, 1997, Lecture Notes in Computer Science, Vol. 1248, pp. 156–174, 1997, Springer-Verlag.

Dealing with Inconsistent Secure Messages

Qingfeng Chen and Shichao Zhang

Faculty of IT, University of Technology, Sydney, Australia

Abstract. In this paper we propose a formal framework for dealing with the inconsistency in secure messages with weights, which takes into account both the freshness and dynamic properties of secure messages. This enables us to better measure the inconsistency and generates reliable verification result.

1 Introduction

In e-commerce, the secure messages from different sources or at different moments are often inconsistent. Although the conflicting messages are greatly avoided by using the modern cryptographic algorithms such as the block cipher [5], it signifies the potential risks that we may run into. However, current techniques stress on the handling of incoherence in knowledge base but have not touch on the topic of measuring the inconsistency in secure messages. Fortunately, there are many approaches for dealing with the inconsistency in knowledge bases, such as, arbitration based information merging [3] and majority based information merging [4]. All these methods seem to be helpful for tackling the inconsistency in secure messages.

Unlike the general knowledge, secure message contains some special requirements, such as freshness and dynamic. Before evaluating the inconsistency in secure messages, we must not only ensure they are not reply attacks but also confirm the messages are really derived from the sender and received by whom he claims to be. In addition, the sources of secure messages may be associated with a weight presenting the degree of importance, such as the hierarchy of trust in *Public Key Infrastructure* (PKI) in Figure 1. Moreover, the belief relationship for disjunction connectives in knowledge base cannot be applied in the secure messages for the reason that the principal should not allow to have ambiguous opinion with respect to the supporting of a secure message. For example, let α and β be two secure messages. It is unallowable for the principal P to support $\alpha \vee \beta$ but he must support either α or β.

This paper proposes a formal framework to measure the incoherence in secure messages with weights that represent the degree of importance of message sources. It analyzes the inconsistent secure messages by evaluating the reliability on each of them. In Section 2, it gives the semantics definition. In Section 3, it presents how to measure the inconsistency of secure messages. Some examples are presented in Section 4. Section 5 presents an experiment of the cash withdraw transaction from ATM. Finally, we conclude this paper in Section 6.

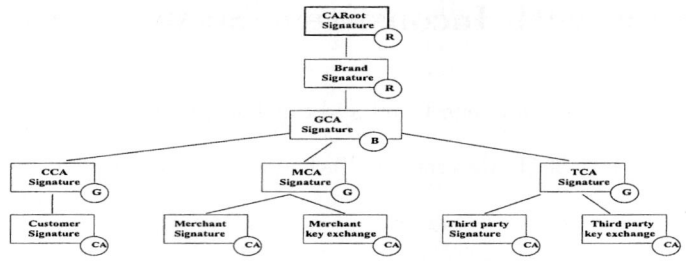

Fig. 1. PKI tree of Trust.

2 Semantics Definition

Suppose $\mathcal{L}$ denotes a set of proposition formulae formed in the usual way from a set of atom symbols $\mathcal{A}$. In particular, $\mathcal{A}$ can contain α and $\neg\alpha$ for some atom α. The logical operators $\wedge$, $\vee$, $\nrightarrow$ and $\rightarrow$ denotes the connectives. We use variables X, Y, P and CA for principals, Greek letters φ, ϕ and ψ for formulae, $T_{expiration}$ for expiration date of message and m, α, γ, θ, μ and $\beta \in \mathcal{A}$ for messages in general. Let $\equiv$ be logical equivalence. A model of a formula ϕ is a possible set of atoms where ϕ is true in the usual sense; Let k be a key.

On the other hand, $e(m, k)$ presents the message m is encrypted by using symmetric key k; $S(m, k)$ presents the signed message m by using the private signature key k; $E(m, k)$ presents the encrypted message by using the public key-exchange key k; and $H(m)$ denotes the hashing of message m. Moreover, we have the following operators:

- <- , -> :: $Message_1 \times Message_2 \longrightarrow Message$, which denotes a set of messages. Moreover, each of them can be the conjunction of several messages.
- - sends - , - :: $Principal_1 \times Principal_2 \times Message \longrightarrow Formula$, which denotes the messages was transmitted from $Principal_1$ to $Principal_2$.
- knows :: $Principal \times Message \longrightarrow Formula$, which denotes the messages have been generated.
- sees :: $Principal \times Message \longrightarrow Formula$, which denotes the messages have been received.
- fresh :: $Message \longrightarrow Formula$
- - believes - , - :: $Principal_1 \times Principal_2 \times Message \longrightarrow Formula$, which denotes $Principal_1$ believes the messages are fresh and sent from $Principal_2$.

Example 1. Suppose m, m_1 and m_2 are messages and P_1 and P_2 are principals. $<m_1, m_2>$ denotes the conjunction messages; "P_1 sends P_2, m" denotes the message m was sent from P_1 to P_2; "P_1 knows m" denotes m has been generated by P_1; "P_2 sees m" presents principal P_2 has received message m; "fresh m" presents m is fresh and not a replay of previous message; "P_2 believes P_1, m" denotes the message m is fresh and really from P_1.

The entailment relationship among the above operators is listed below.

(1) ⊢ P knows m → P sends Q, m
(2) ⊢ P sends Q, m → Q sees m

where we can conclude (⊢ P knows m → P sends Q, m) ∧ (⊢ P sends Q, m → Q sees m) ⟶ Q sees m.

In ENDL logic, *sends*, *knows*, *sees* and *fresh* are primitive operators. We can turn these operators into the following axiom.

⊢ P knows m × P sends Q, m × fresh m × Q sees m ⟶ Q believes P, m

Where the principal P generates the message m and then sends it to the principal Q. If Q receives this message and confirms it is fresh, it is reasonable for principal Q to believe the message m sent from P. However, it does not imply principal Q believes the integrity and confidentiality of m, which needs to be validated further by other methods such as [1]. The *knows*, *sends* and *sees* operators actually presents the dynamic properties of the generating, sending and receiving of secure messages. In addition, the message m can be a conjunction message, such as $m = \alpha \wedge \beta$. Moreover, the implication $\alpha \to \beta$ is used to denote a special message called *rule*, in which the entailment relationship between α and β is defined.

Definition 1. *Let $M = \{m_1, m_2, ..., m_n\}$ be a secure message source. The set of messages derived from sender, receiver and third party are denoted by M_S, M_R and $M_T = \{M_{T_1}, ..., M_{T_m}\}$ respectively.*

where the messages sources can be viewed as databases. They are responsible for recording the messages that have been generated, sent or received by the principals. Ideally, it assumes that these messages should be consistent with each other in the aforementioned verification of secure protocols.

Definition 2. *Let $\alpha \in \mathcal{A}$ be an atom. For brevity, $-\alpha$ is defined to be equivalent to $\neg\alpha$ so $-(-\alpha)$ is α.*

Definition 3. *Let T be a timestamp attached to message m. If $|Clock-T| < \Delta t_1 + \Delta t_2$ regarding received messages or $T < T_{expiration}$ regarding generated messages then m is fresh; otherwise m is viewed as a replay.*

Where *Clock* is the local time, Δt_1 is an interval representing the normal discrepancy between the server's clock and the local clock, and Δt_2 is an interval representing the expected network delay time [2]. In addition, $T_{expiration}$ denotes the expiration date, which was designated to messages when they are generated. The timestamp plays an important role in preventing the replays of previously transmitted secure messages.

Definition 4. *Let $\models_{support}$ be a supporting relationship. For a secure message source M, $M \models_{support}$ is defined as follows, where α is an atom in $\mathcal{A}$, and each of them virtually denotes a message.*

$$\begin{cases} M_S \models_{support} \alpha \text{ iff "} M_S \text{ knows } \alpha \text{" and "} \alpha \text{ is fresh"} \\ M_R \models_{support} \alpha \text{ iff "} M_R \text{ believes } M_S, \alpha \text{" and "} \alpha \text{ is fresh"} \\ M_T \models_{support} \alpha \text{ iff "} M_T \text{ believes } M_S, \alpha \text{" and "} \alpha \text{ is fresh"} \end{cases}$$

where M_S, M_R and M_T present the message sources of sender, receiver and the third party respectively. Among them, the receiver and the third party can receive messages from different senders. In particular, "α is fresh" in these formulae is decided by using $T < T_{expiration}$. On the other hand, the M_R and M_T must check the freshness of α by using $|Clock-T| < \triangle t_1 + \triangle t_2$ when they receive messages from the senders. These will assist them in determining whether they believe the message α or not.

The supporting relation considers the dynamic property of secure message by using the *knows* and *sees* operators that provide user a useful way to describe the dynamic transmission of secure messages. Furthermore, the freshness of secure message is protected by relying on the discriminant of timestamp defined in Definition 3.

As mentioned above, the rule presents a entailment relationship among messages. In particular, the conditions of a rule can be the conclusion of other rule, which is called relevant rule.

Definition 5. *Suppose α_1, ..., α_n (n $\geq$ 1) are secure messages. Let $\alpha_1 \rightarrow \alpha_2$, $\alpha_2 \rightarrow \alpha_3$, ..., $\alpha_{n-1} \rightarrow \alpha_n$ be entailment relationships among them. Then we can deduce a new rule below if they are true.*

$$\alpha_1 \rightarrow \alpha_2 \wedge \alpha_2 \rightarrow \alpha_3 \wedge \ldots \wedge \alpha_{n-1} \rightarrow \alpha_n \longrightarrow \alpha_1 \rightarrow \alpha_n$$

These entailment relationships virtually denotes the operations of encryption, decryption, signature and authentication in cryptography.

Example 2. 1) If *Alice* knows a symmetric key k and message m then she knows $e(m, k)$ that presents the message m was encrypted by k; and 2) if *Alice* knows message m encrypted by k, then she can send encrypted m to *Tom*. A new rule can then be derived from them, If *Alice* knows k and m, then she can send the encrypted m to *Tom* for the reason that the result of the first message is actually the condition of the second message. As a result, *Alice* is able to send the $e(m, k)$ to *Tom*.

Let δ be a conjunction of atoms, and α and β be atoms in the usual sense. They have the following properties.

- *Conjunction*: $M \models_{support} \alpha \wedge \beta$ iff $M \models_{support} \alpha$ and $M \models_{support} \beta$
- *Implication constraint*: If $M \models_{support} \delta \rightarrow \alpha$ and $M \models_{support} \delta$, then $M \models_{support} \alpha$.
- *Transitivity constraint*: If $M \models_{support} \delta \rightarrow \alpha_i$ and $M \models_{support} \alpha_1 \wedge \ldots \wedge \alpha_n \rightarrow \beta$, then $M \models_{support} \alpha_1 \wedge \ldots \wedge \alpha_{i-1} \wedge \delta \wedge \alpha_{i+1} \wedge \ldots \wedge \alpha_n \rightarrow \beta$.

Consider the sensitivity of secure messages, it is hence impractical for a secure message source to support the disjunction messages with 'or' relation, such as $M \models_{support} \alpha \vee \beta$.

A logic with three values is adopted in this paper. In addition to the truth values t and f, an intermediate truth value $u(uncertain)$ is adopted. The truth value u virtually indicates an intermediate level of belief between $true$ (i.e., believable) and $false$ (i.e., unbelievable).

This three-valued logic is chosen for it provides useful ways for depicting the belief in transmitted messages for separating them into three clustering as follows.

1) information in one cluster is definitely insecure to the transaction online;
2) whereas information in the second is surely reliable;
3) the third cluster is the most important, in which information is uncertain to be secure or not.

3 Measuring Incoherence in Secure Messages

This section gives a formal definition of measuring operator having a majority behavior.

Definition 6. *For $\Delta \in \wp(\mathcal{L})$, $M \in \wp(\mathcal{A})$, and M_P derived from principal $P \in \{S, R, T\}$, in which S, R and T denotes the sender, receiver and the third party respectively. Let $M_P \models_{support} \Delta$ denote that $M_P \models_{support} \alpha$ holds for every α in Δ.*

From the last definition, the model of Δ is then defined as follows.

$$model(\Delta) = \{M \in \wp(\mathcal{A}) \mid M \models_{support} \Delta\},$$

where M denotes a message source. The model of Δ presents a set of atoms in M to support Δ.

Example 3. Consider the following set of formulae.

(1) $model(\{\alpha, \beta, \alpha \rightarrow \gamma\}) \equiv \{\alpha, \beta, \gamma\}$
(2) $model(\{\alpha \wedge \beta, -\gamma\}) \equiv \{\alpha, \beta, -\gamma\}$
(3) $model(\{\alpha, \alpha \rightarrow \beta, -\gamma, \beta \wedge -\gamma \rightarrow \theta\}) \equiv \{\alpha, \beta, -\gamma, \theta\}$

In (1), $M \models_{support} \alpha$, $M \models_{support} \beta$ and $M \models_{support} \alpha \rightarrow \gamma \longrightarrow M \models_{support} \gamma$, so we can conclude $\{\alpha, \beta, \gamma\}$ in terms of the *implication constraint*; in (2), $M \models_{support} \alpha \wedge \beta \longrightarrow M \models_{support} \alpha$ and $M \models_{support} \beta$, and $M \models_{support} -\gamma$, so we can conclude $\{\alpha, \beta, -\gamma\}$ in light of the *conjunction* property; in (3), $M \models_{support} \alpha$, $M \models_{support} \alpha \rightarrow \beta \longrightarrow M \models_{support} \beta$, $M \models_{support} -\gamma$ and $M \models_{support} \beta \wedge -\gamma \rightarrow \theta \longrightarrow M \models_{support} \alpha \wedge -\gamma \longrightarrow M \models_{support} \theta$, so we can conclude $\{\alpha, \beta, -\gamma, \theta\}$ in terms of the *implication constraint* and *transitivity constraint* mentioned above.

The above description gives the definition with respect to the supporting relationship between secure messages and message sources. To evaluate the degree of supporting of the secure messages, it is quantified by defining the cardinality of a supporting set of the secure messages.

Definition 7. Let $\alpha \in \mathcal{A}$ be an atom. $|M \models_{support} \alpha|$ is the total number of α supported by the model of M.

Example 4. Let α and β be atoms. If $model(M)$ $\{\alpha, \alpha, \beta, -\beta\}$, then, we can conclude that $|M \models_{support} \alpha| = 2$, $|M \models_{support} \beta| = 1$, and $|M \models_{support} -\beta| = 1$.

Definition 8. *The support function from $\mathcal{A}$ to $[0, 1]$ is defined below when α is not empty, and $|M \models_{support} \emptyset| = 0$.*

$$|M \models_{support} \alpha| = \frac{|\alpha|}{|\alpha \cup -\alpha|} \times 100$$

where $|\alpha|$ is the number of occurrence of the set of α in the model of M. If $|M \models_{support} \alpha| = 0$, then we can say M has no opinion upon α and vice versa; if $|M \models_{support} \alpha| = 1$, it indicates that there is not conflicting message $-\alpha$ in the message source M; if $|M \models_{support} \alpha| = c$, $0 < c < 1$, it presents α is partially supported by M.

In the last definition, we give a function to calculate the degree that a message source M supports α. Then the *reliability* between α and a set of message sources is defined below.

Definition 9. *The set of secure messages $\{M_S, M_R, M_T\}$ is defined as the sum of supports between α and each M_i, $i \in \{S, R, T\}$, and $|M_S \sqcup M_R \sqcup M_T \models_{support} \emptyset| = 0$.*

$$reliability(\alpha) = |M_S \sqcup M_R \sqcup M_T \models_{support} \alpha|$$

where the $\sqcup$ denotes a union operation but the repeated items are reserved, such as $\{\alpha, -\beta\} \sqcup \{\alpha\} = \{\alpha, \alpha, -\beta\}$. Moreover α and β have to be fresh in each source of secure messages in terms of the above definitions. In particular, if $|M_S \sqcup M_R \sqcup M_T \models_{support} \alpha| = 0$ then $reliability(\alpha) = 0$, which presents the set of sources of secure messages does not support α.

The above description assumes that the sources of secure message have equivalent degree of importance. However, they are usually associated with different weights in practical circumstances. For example, *CARoot*, *GCA*, and *CCA* in Figure 1. present a trust tree of certificate authorities, which have different level of authorities.

In this paper, a special supporting relationship called weighted supporting is hence proposed where ϖ is a function that assigns each message source M a nonnegative number representing the weight of M, $0 \leq \varpi \leq 1$. It is possible that M_S and M_R are occasionally treated with equivalent weight under the consideration of fairness. The weight function ϖ in fact presents the degree of importance of the sources of secure messages. If $\varpi_{M_i} > \varpi_{M_j}$, $i \neq j$, it presents M_i is more important than M_j, and more of its opinion will be reflected in the result of measuring of the inconsistency in secure messages. In particular, if the weight of a source of secure messages is assigned zero then it is deemed to be unreliable and its views will not be taken into account when evaluating the reliability.

Definition 10. Let ϖ_S, ϖ_R and ϖ_T be the weights of M_S, M_R and M_T respectively, and let $|\alpha^i|$ be the sum of occurrence of the set of α in message sources $i \in \{S, R, T\}$. The weighted reliability between α and the set of message sources $\{M_S, M_R, M_T\}$ is then defined as follows. In particular, if α is empty then reliability$(\emptyset, \varpi)$ 0.

$$reliability(\alpha, \varpi) = \frac{\sum_{i \in \{S,R,T\}} |\alpha^i| * \varpi_i}{\sum_{i \in \{S,R,T\}} (|\alpha^i| + |-\alpha^i|) * \varpi_i}$$

The above method is adopted to quantify the support between an atom α (a message) and the set of message sources $\{M_S, M_R, M_T\}$. In this paper, we define 50% as the minimum support threshold for reliability of any atoms, written as *minsupport*. In this scenario, the number of occurrence of α and $-\alpha$ are equivalent, so the sources of secure messages are definitely conflicting. We are just able to say the security of message α is uncertain even the reliability of α is over 0.5 but below 1.

In general, if the reliability on message α is higher, it implies that the secure message sources have lower inconsistency with respect to the message α and vice versa.

Based on the above definitions, the belief regarding the secure messages is defined as follows.

Definition 11. Let $\alpha \in \wp(\mathcal{A})$, and ϖ be weights of message sources. The belief of M_S, M_R and M_T in α is defined as follows.

$$belief(\alpha) = \begin{cases} secure & \text{if } reliability(\alpha, \varpi) = 1 \\ insecure & \text{if } reliability(\alpha, \varpi) \leq minsupport \\ uncertain & \text{if } reliability(\alpha, \varpi) > minsupport \end{cases}$$

where the '*secure*' indicates it has no negative object of α within M_S, M_R and M_T, so α is consistent during transmission; the '*insecure*' indicates the belief in α is completely inconsistent; and the '*uncertain*' indicates the message α is partially reliable only but people have to make further verification to confirm its reliability.

4 Examples of Measuring Inconsistency

For simplicity, in the following examples, it assumes that all the messages held by the secure message sources are fresh. Also, the messages are assumed to be generated and sent by the sender and received and seen by whom it claims to be. Let α, β, γ, μ and θ be messages, which can be plain text, encrypted messages, symmetric key, signature key and such like.

Example 5. Suppose $M_S = \{\alpha, \beta, \alpha \wedge \beta \to \gamma\}$, $M_R = \{-\alpha, \beta, -\alpha \wedge \beta \to -\gamma\}$, and $M_T = \{\alpha, \beta, \gamma\}$. Let their weights be $\varpi(M_S) = \varpi(M_R) = 0.3$ but $\varpi(M_T) = 0.4$.

Then $model(M_S) \equiv model(M_T) \equiv \{\alpha, \beta, \gamma\}$ and $model(M_R) \equiv \{-\alpha, \beta, -\gamma\}$, and $reliability(\alpha, \varpi)$ 0.7, $reliability(\beta, \varpi) = 1$ and $reliability(\gamma, \varpi) = 0.7$. So $belief(\alpha) = $ 'uncertain', $belief(\beta) = $ 'secure' and $belief(\gamma) = $ 'uncertain'.

In the message set of M_S, $\alpha \wedge \beta$ is supported by M_S for M_S supports both α and β. The result indicates that β is secure since the belief in β is 1. The reliability of α and γ needs to be validated further for the belief in them is below the minimal support. To better understand this instance, the α, β and γ can be viewed as message m, symmetric key k and encrypted message $e(m, k)$ respectively.

Example 6. Suppose M_S, M_R and M_T are the same as the last example, and $\varpi(M_S) = \varpi(M_R)$ 0.2 but $\varpi(M_T) = 0.6$.

Then $reliability(\alpha, \varpi) = 0.8$, $reliability(\beta, \varpi) = 1$ and $reliability(\gamma, \varpi) = 0.8$. So $belief(\alpha) = $ 'insecure', $belief(\beta) = $ 'secure' and $belief(\gamma) = $ 'uncertain'.

In this case, the third party is allocated a higher weight than last example. Actually, it is usually reasonable to put more trust on the third party like trust center. There is not change to the belief in β for the secure message sources do not contain its negative object. On the other hand, the belief in α and γ increases for more supports are put on them.

Example 7. Let $M_S = \{\alpha, \alpha \rightarrow \gamma, \beta, \theta, \beta \wedge \gamma \wedge \theta \rightarrow \mu\}$, $M_R = \{-\alpha, -\beta \wedge -\gamma, \theta, -\mu\}$, and M_T $\{-\alpha, \beta \wedge \theta, \mu\}$. Suppose the weights of M_S, M_R and M_T are as in the last example.

So $model(M_S) \equiv \{\alpha, \beta, \gamma, \theta, \mu\}$, $model(M_R) \equiv \{-\alpha, -\beta, -\gamma, \theta, -\mu\}$ and $model(M_T) \equiv \{-\alpha, \beta, \theta, \mu\}$, and $reliability(\alpha, \varpi)$ 0.4, $reliability(\beta, \varpi) = 0.8$ and $reliability(\gamma, \varpi) = 0.66$, $reliability(\theta, \varpi) = 1$ and $reliability(\mu, \varpi) = 0.8$. So $belief(\alpha) = $ 'insecure', $belief(\beta) = $ 'uncertain', $belief(\gamma) = $ 'uncertain', $belief(\theta) = $ 'secure' and $belief(\mu) = $ 'uncertain'.

In this scenario, although the message μ is a implicit message in M_S, it can be uncovered by using the transitivity constraint mentioned above. Although the belief in β and μ is uncertain they both have high reliability 0.8, which means their inconsistency is low.

5 Experiments

We use some simulated data to evaluate the inconsistency in secure messages. The used data corresponds to the cash withdrawal transaction from an Automated Teller Machine (ATM). When people make cash withdrawal from an ATM, they need to have knowledge of the related PIN. The customer places their card in the ATM slot and enters their PIN. The customer then inputs the amount requested for withdrawal. The host computer needs to verify that the PIN is the proper one for that card. To ensure the amount dispensed at the machine is identical to the amount debited from the account, a sequence number is included on the response messages from host computer. Moreover, the encryption by using DES algorithm protects the PIN being exposed to eavesdroppers who intercept the communications. It also protects PIN being read by the personnel who have access to the bank's database.

Therefore, the transmitted messages in ATM transaction include PIN (encrypted PIN), Key(symmetric key), $Acct$(account number), $Amount$ and SN (Sequence number). There are three message sources including host computer, ATM, and the third party in this transaction, which are depicted as M_{host}, M_{ATM} and M_T respectively.

- $M_{host} = \{PIN_{host}, Key_{host}, Acct_{host}, Amount_{host}, SN_{host}, Weight_{host}\}$
- $M_{ATM} = \{PIN_{ATM}, Key_{ATM}, Acct_{ATM}, Amount_{ATM}, SN_{ATM}, Weight_{ATM}\}$
- $M_T = \{PIN_T, Key_T, Acct_T, Amount_T, SN_T, Weight_T\}$

Where each item are assigned with values of *1*, *0* or *null* respectively. In particular, *null* value means this item is empty in the message sources. *1* and *0* presents two conflicting situations. The obtained messages are organized as the forms in Table 1.

Table 1. Cash Withdraw from ATM.

	PIN	Key	Acct	Amount	SN	Weight
M_{host}	1	1	1	1	1	0.4
M_{ATM}	1	0	0	0	null	0.3
M_T	1	null	0	1	1	0.3

Then, we can measure the *reliability* for each item, which is depicted in Table 2. in terms of the function given in Definition 10.

Table 2. Reliability on ATM Transaction Data.

	PIN	Key	Acct	Amount	SN
$reliability_{host}$	1	0.57	0.4	0.7	0.7
$reliability_{ATM}$	1	0.43	0.6	0.3	0
$reliability_T$	1	0	0.6	0.7	0.7

In Table 2, the reliability of encrypted PIN is 1, which indicates this item is reliable. As was described in Definition 10, the reliability of null value (empty) is zero. On the other hand, if the value of reliability on a message is big, then we can say the inconsistency of this message is low and vice versa, which provides us an intuitive way to measure the inconsistency in secure messages.

Finally, the beliefs of secure messages are presented in Table 3 according to the given *reliability* in the last Table and the Definition 11.

Table 3. Belief in ATM Transaction Data.

	PIN	Key	Acct	Amount	SN
$belief_{host}$	secure	uncertain	insecure	uncertain	uncertain
$belief_{ATM}$	secure	insecure	uncertain	insecure	insecure
$belief_T$	secure	insecure	uncertain	uncertain	uncertain

From the belief table, we can identify the uncertain messages from the secure and insecure messages. As was mentioned above, they are unreliable and need to be further validated. Therefore, we can guarantee the reliability of verification result to some extent.

6 Conclusions

This paper has developed an intuitive way to measure the incoherence in secure messages by evaluating their reliability. It enables us to identify the uncertain messages from the secure and insecure messages. Our examples and experiments have demonstrated that the designed framework is effective for dealing with the inconsistency in secure messages.

References

1. Chen Q., Zhang C., and Zhang S., An extension of NDL for verifying secure transaction protocols, *Knowledge and Information Systems*, an Internation Journal by Springer, forthcoming in 2004.
2. Denning D., Sacco G., Timestamp in Key Distribution Protocols, *Communications of ACM* 24(8):533-536, August 1981.
3. Liberatore P. and Schaerf M., Arbitration (or How to Merge Knowledge Bases), *IEEE Transaction on Knowledge and Data Engineering*, 10(1), pages: 76–90, 1998.
4. Lin J., and Mendelzon A.O., Knowledge base merging by majority, *In Dynamic Worlds: From the Frame Problem to Knowledge Management*, Kluwer, 1999.
5. Piper F., and Murphy S., Cryptography: A Very Short Introduction, *Oxford University Press*, 2002.

Answer Set Computation Based on a Minimal Model Generation Theorem Prover

Yasuyuki Shirai[1] and Ryuzo Hasegawa[2]

[1] Mitsubishi Research Institute, Inc., Tokyo, 100-8141, Japan
shirai@mri.co.jp
[2] Graduate School of Information Science and Electrical Engineering
Kyushu University, Kasuga City, 816-8580, Japan
hasegawa@ar.is.kyushu-u.ac.jp

Abstract. Answer set programming (ASP) has been a focus as a new declarative programming paradigm. The basic algorithm to compute answer sets based on a model generation theorem proving scheme has been proposed by Inoue [7]. The implementation of the basic algorithm, however, generates enormous redundant combinations of hypotheses. In this paper, we propose a new implementation method based on a minimal model generator MM-MGTP [5], including a new data structure called modal disjunction buffer and some extended operations to avoid redundancy. Some experimental results are shown for comparison with the naive implementation and other systems.

1 Introduction

Answer set programming (ASP) that computes answer sets from extended logic programs including "negation as failure" and classical negation has been a focus as a new declarative programming paradigm. Some efficient systems such as dlv [2], smodels [10] have been proposed. In 1992, Inoue [7] proposed the method to transform extended logic programs with negation as failure (NAF) into NAF-free disjunctive logic programs with modal operator K.

Regarding the modal operator K as a predicate symbol, bottom up theorem proving systems for disjunctive logic programs such as MGTP (Model Generation Theorem Prover) [6] can be applied to compute answer sets from given extended logic programs. The naive implementation of [7], however, causes some problems in terms of efficiency, that is, generating redundant combinations of hypotheses or generating lots of models that are not answer sets.

In this paper, we propose a new implementation method based on a minimal model generator MM-MGTP [5] instead of MGTP, including a new data structure called *modal disjunction buffer* and some extended operations to avoid redundant branches. The outline of the rest of the paper is as follows: in Section 2, we first review the definition, the language and the procedure of MGTP and its extension MM-MGTP. Section 3 defines the embedding method of NAF into MGTP input clauses and the procedure to compute answer sets. Some redundant cases involved in the naive implementation are shown here. Section 4 is the main section in this paper. We show a new method using MM-MGTP and introduce some techniques for efficiency. Section 5 shows some experimental results on Quasigroup existence problems in finite algebra and the 3-coloring problems to compare the naive approach using MGTP and other systems. Section 6 concludes this paper with summary and future works.

2 Minimal Model Generation on MGTP

2.1 MGTP

MGTP is a class of deduction procedures for first-order logic in conjunctive normal form (CNF) that has been successfully used to solve hard combinatorial problems [11]. The procedural semantics of first-order CNF formulas as defined by MGTP is based on bottom-up evaluation. MGTP is closely related to hyper-tableaux [4]. An MGTP program is a set of clauses defined as follows:

$$A_1, \ldots, A_n \to C_1 \vee \cdots \vee C_m. \ (n \geq 0, m \geq 0) \tag{1}$$

where each $A_1, \ldots, A_n, C_1, \ldots, C_m$ is a positive or negative literal. Terms are defined normally. The left-hand side of the implication is called an *antecedent* (that is a conjunction of $A_1, \ldots, A_n$), and the right-hand side is called a *consequent*. A clause is said to be *positive* if its antecedent is *true* ($n = 0$), and *negative* if its consequent is *false* ($m = 0$). A clause for $m \leq 1$ is called a *Horn* clause, otherwise called a *ıon-Horn* clause. A clause is said to be *range-restricted* if every variable in the consequent of the clause appears in the antecedent. MGTP programs must satisfy the range-restrictedness condition.

2.2 The Procedure of MGTP

Each proof step of MGTP is a process of generating a *model candidate* (denoted by M) in bottom up manner, starting with positive clauses.

The following two rules act on the model generation method.

- Model extension rule: If there is a clause, $\mathcal{A} \to \mathcal{C}$, and a substitution σ such that $\mathcal{A}\sigma$ is satisfied in a model candidate M and $\mathcal{C}\sigma$ is not satisfied in M, extend M by adding $\mathcal{C}\sigma$ to M. If $\mathcal{C}$ is disjunctive (that is $m > 1$), generate $M_1, \ldots, M_m$ by adding each disjunct to M (case splitting).
- Model rejection rule: If there is a negative clause whose antecedent $\mathcal{A}\sigma$ is satisfied in a model candidate M, or there are complementary literals L and $\neg L$ in M, reject M.

We call the process to obtain $\mathcal{A}\sigma$, a *conjunctive matching* of the antecedent literals against the elements in a model candidate.

The task of model generation is to try to construct a model for a given set of clauses. If this method finds a model, the given clause set is satisfiable, and if not, unsatisfiable. See some previous papers such as [6, 11] for the detail of the MGTP procedure and some improvements for efficiency.

2.3 MM-MGTP

Although the MGTP procedure ensures that the set of generated models contains all minimal models for a given non-Horn program, it also contains non-minimal models as is the case with conventional tableaux and Davis-Putnam procedures. Hasegawa [5] proposed a minimal model generator MM-MGTP as an extension of MGTP, in which *branching assumptions* and *branching lemmata* are introduced. In [5], non-Horn extension with a disjunction $C_1 \vee C_2 \vee \cdots \vee C_n$ is transformed to a logically equivalent form, that is :

$$(C_1, [\neg C_2], \ldots, [\neg C_n]) \vee (C_2, [\neg C_3], \ldots, [\neg C_n]) \vee \ldots, C_n$$

where negative literals denoted by '[ ]' are called branching assumptions (which are also known under the name of *complementary splitting*). Branching assumptions help to avoid non-minimal models occurring in the left side of a proof tree. Especially, the leftmost model in an proof tree is assured to be minimal. Hasegawa [5] also proposed an additional process called *branching lemma*.

Example 1. Consider the program $\mathcal{P} = \{\rightarrow a \vee b \vee c. \, , \, b \rightarrow a. \, \, c \rightarrow b.\}$. Figure 1 shows a proof tree for $\mathcal{P}$ using branching assumptions (denoted by [ ]). Since on the leftmost branch, a model $\{a\}$ is generated without using branching assumption $[\neg b]$ and $[\neg c]$ to close branches, $\neg a$ can be added as a branching lemma on the right branches to avoid non-minimal models including a ([[ ]] denotes a branching lemma). Similarly, since the branch of b is closed without using a branching assumption $[\neg c]$, a branching lemma $[\![\neg b]\!]$ can also be added to the rightmost branch.

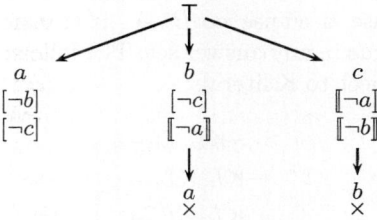

Fig. 1. MM-MGTP Proof Tree.

In the above example, branching assumptions and lemmata avoid the generation of non-minimal models without any other checking. In general, however, branching assumptions and lemmata do not provide the complete procedure to avoid generation of non-minimal models. In order to overcome this, Hasegawa [5] also proposed the other efficient methods to check the minimality based on the relevancy checking. As a result, every model generated by MM-MGTP is minimal.

3 Answer Set Computation on MGTP

3.1 Extended Logic Program and Answer Set Semantics

In this paper, we define extended logic program as a set of rules of the form :

$$A_1, \ldots, A_n, \text{not } B_1, \ldots, \text{not } B_l \to C_1 \vee \cdots \vee C_m \ (n \geq 0, m \geq 0, l \geq 0) \quad (2)$$

where each $A_1, \ldots, A_n, B_1, \ldots, B_l, C_1, \ldots, C_m$ is a positive or negative literal.

Answer set semantics [3] for extended logic programs is defined as follows. For a program $\mathcal{P}$, let $\mathcal{P}_G$ be a ground instances of $\mathcal{P}$. $red(\mathcal{P}_G^S)$ with respect to the set of literals S is obtained by the following operations on $\mathcal{P}_G$.

- For each $B \in S$, delete rules that have $not\ B$ in their antecedent,
- delete all $not\ B$ literals from the remaining rules.

S is an answer set of $\mathcal{P}$ if and only if S is a deductive closure of $red(\mathcal{P}_G^S)$.

3.2 Embedding Negation as Failure into MGTP Clauses

Inoue [7] proposed the method to transform extended logic programs into NAF-free MGTP input clauses. A clause represented in (2) can be transformed to the following MGTP clause[1] using the modal operator K.

$$\begin{aligned}A_1, \ldots, A_n \to \neg KB_1, \ldots, \neg KB_l, C_1 \vee \cdots \vee \\ \neg KB_1, \ldots, \neg KB_l, C_m \vee KB_1 \vee \ldots \vee KB_l.\end{aligned} \quad (3)$$

The literals with K are called *hypothetical literals* (or K *literals*), while literals without it are called *objective literals*. Intuitively, KL means a hypothesis that L holds. As a special case, a clause $not B \to .$ is transformed to $\to KB$. which means that B must be true in any answer set. The following integrity constraints are introduced with respect to K literals:

$$\neg KL, L \to . \quad (4)$$
$$\neg KL, KL \to . \quad (5)$$
$$KL, \neg L \to . \quad (6)$$
$$KL, K\neg L \to \quad (7)$$
$$\neg KL, \neg K\neg L \to . \quad (8)$$

3.3 Answer Set Computation on MGTP

The model generation procedure of MGTP can be applied to the transformed program shown in Section 3.2, regarding K as a predicate symbol and using the

---

[1] Precisely, it is not in the form of MGTP clause defined in (1). The form of the consequent is an abbreviation in the MGTP system.

integrity constraints (4) – (8). All models generated by MGTP for the transformed program include non-answer sets as well as answer sets. Let $obj(M)$ be the set of objective literals in M, that is, $obj(M)$ is obtained by removing K literals from M. Inoue [7] showed that $obj(M)$ is an answer set if and only if $M \in \mathcal{M}$ satisfies the following two conditions:

1. M is a minimal model, that is, there is no $M' \in \mathcal{M}$ such that $M' \subset M$. [2]
2. For every literal L, if $\mathsf{K}L \in M$ then $L \in M$ (called T-*condition*).

Let min be an operation that selects minimal models from a set of models $\mathcal{M}$, and $tcond$ an operation that selects models that satisfy T-condition from a set of models. The result of $obj(tcond(min(\mathcal{M})))$ is equal to the set of all answer sets from the given extended logic program.

In general, a set of models $\mathcal{M}$ generated by the naive implementation of Section 3.2 and Section 3.3 contains lots of non-answer sets and redundant models. The former consists of non-minimal models and models that do not satisfy T-condition such as $\{\mathsf{K}a, \mathsf{K}b, \mathsf{K}c\}$. The latter consists of the duplication of answer sets such as $\{\mathsf{K}a, a, b\}$ and $\{\mathsf{K}b, a, b\}$ that are caused by the different hypotheses.

4 Answer Set Computation Using MM-MGTP

The minimality checking for generated models is the hard part in model checking on answer set computation. If we commit minimal model generation to the MM-MGTP procedure, minimality checking after model generation would be no longer required. In the following subsections, we describe a method using MM-MGTP and some modification for efficiency.

4.1 Transformation into the MM-MGTP Program

In order to avoid non-minimal models, MM-MGTP implements branching assumption scheme, in which each extension of a disjunct contains the negation of each literal that appears on the right side of the disjunct (Section 2). Hence, transformation into the MGTP program shown in (3) can be simplified in MM-MGTP as follows:

$$A_1, \ldots, A_n \rightarrow C_1 \vee \cdots \vee C_m \vee \mathsf{K}B_1 \vee \cdots \vee \mathsf{K}B_l. \tag{9}$$

In the MM-MGTP representation, for negation as failure in the antecedents, it is sufficient to add their K literals on the right side of the consequent. For example, a clause $not\ a, not\ b \rightarrow c$. is transformed to $\rightarrow c \vee \mathsf{K}a \vee \mathsf{K}b$.

---

[2] If the program does not contain non-Horn clauses, the minimality condition is not required [8].

4.2 Modal Disjunction Buffer

Here we introduce a new data structure for disjunctions that consists of K literals. Consider the program $\mathcal{P} = \{\to Ka \vee Kb \vee Kc., \to a \vee Kd \vee Ke.\}$. Although $\mathcal{P}$ has one answer set $\{a\}$ trivially, the combinations of hypotheses literals cause non-answer set models (e.g., $\{Kb, Kd\}, \{Kb, Ke\}, \{Kc, Ke\}$). These models are minimal but dot not satisfy T-condition.

Since K literals never appear in antecedents and are not used in conjunctive matching, disjuncts that consist of only K literals should not be extended in case splitting. We prepare another data structure called *modal disjunction buffer* (*MDB* in short) in which disjuncts consisting of K literals are stored and processed in another way.

For the program $\mathcal{P}$, instead of splitting on Ka, Kb and Kc separately, $Ka \vee Kb \vee Kc$ is put together into the MDB on a new branch that inherits all other information from the upper node. Figure 2 shows the proof tree of the program $\mathcal{P}$ using MDB represented as ☐ in the figure.

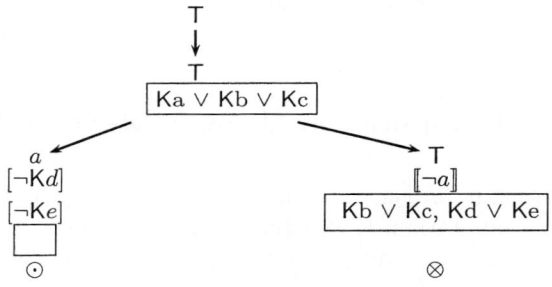

Fig. 2. Case Splitting with Modal Disjunction Buffer.

Although clauses in MDB have no effects on conjunctive matching, subsumption testing, refutation and simplification functions can be extended on MDB as well as objective literals. In the left branch of Figure 2, the MDB becomes empty because of the subsumption testing for the buffer. In the buffer of the right branch, Ka is removed because of refutation testing by the branching lemma $[\![\neg a]\!]$. In the figure, ⊙ means an answer set, and ⊗ means a non-answer set (that does not satisfy T-condition). In Figure 2, the redundant combination of hypothetical literals can be suppressed. The next two subsections describe the extension of these operations.

4.3 Extended Unit Refutation and Simplification

In the MGTP procedure, unit refutation and unit simplification are the substantial operations for pruning redundant branches [11]. These are operated on the complementary pair of literals, that is, L and $\neg L$, to simplify disjunctions or derive refutation.

These two operations can be applied to a set of disjunctions in MDB. In these operations, the notion of complementary literals can be extended to literals that satisfy the integrity constraints shown in (4) – (8).

Example 2. If we have K$a \vee$ Kb in MDB and $\neg a$ and $\neg b$ as results of conjunctive matching, case splitting or branching assumption/lemma, the branch should be closed.

4.4 Extended Subsumption Testing

For a disjunction $\mathcal{C} = L_1 \vee \ldots \vee L_i \vee \ldots \vee L_n$ as a result of conjunctive matching, if $L_i \in M$, then L_i *subsumes* $\mathcal{C}$ and $\mathcal{C}$ cannot be used for model extension. These operations are called *subsumption testing*. The concept of subsumption testing should also be extended to be applied for disjunctions which contain K literals.

We can simply perform subsumption testing for K literals in MDB by considering K as a predicate symbol. Additionally, we can extend this scheme according to the definition of answer set semantics :

1. if $L_i \in M$ and $\mathcal{C} = C_1 \vee \ldots \vee C_m \vee$ K$L_1 \vee \ldots \vee$ K$L_i \vee \ldots \vee$ KL_n is a model extending candidate (i.e., a result of conjunctive matching), $\mathcal{C}$ can be subsumed by L_i and can be removed from the model extending candidates.
2. if $L_i \in M$ and $\mathcal{C} =$ K$L_1 \vee \ldots \vee$ K$L_i \vee \ldots \vee$ KL_n is in MDB, $\mathcal{C}$ can be subsumed by L_i and can be removed from the model disjunction buffer.

It is clear that the extended subsumption testing is sound. In fact, according to the definition of answer set semantics, in the deductive closure of the set of literals including L, rules that contain *not* L in their antecedents (in MGTP representation, rules that contain KL in their consequents) are removed.

Although the extended subsumption testing for MDB has no effect on proof structures, T-condition checks are no longer required owing to this extension. If a model candidate set M include L, the disjunctions including KL in the MDB should have been removed by the subsumption testing. Hence, if the MDB is not empty when a branch is terminated with a model M, M does not satisfy T-condition. From these observations, T-condition checking can be replaced by empty checking for the MDB on the terminated node.

4.5 Extended Conjunctive Matching

If we have a MDB that contains a unit disjunction (e.g., Ka), and a rule $a \rightarrow b$, we can add Kb into a model candidate M to be used for unit refutation and simplification. For example, if we have a branching lemma $[\neg b]$, Kb immediately falsifies that branch.

More formally, *extended conjunctive matching* can be defined as follows : for a model candidate M, a modal disjunction buffer K and a Horn clause $A_1, \ldots, A_n \rightarrow C$, if there exists a substitution σ such that for all $i(1 \leq i \leq n)$, K$A_i\sigma \in K$ or $A_i\sigma \in M$, M can be extended to $M + \{$K$C\sigma\}$.

5 Experiments

We have developed an answer set computation system called NMGTP based on MM-MGTP using Java. The following experiments were executed on Celeron 1.30GHz using Vine Linux 2.5.

Table 1 shows the results for the 3-coloring problems on ladder graphs (10 nodes) by NMGTP, naive implementation on MGTP, dlv[3] and smodels. The 3-coloring problems are well known as benchmark tests for answer set programming (e.g., [10]). As seen in Table 1, NMGTP can avoid redundant branches generated by the naive implementation. The reason that dlv and smodels achieved the excellent results is that the lookahead procedures adopted could be effective for the 3-coloring problems in contrast to QG problems described later, while NMGTP has no lookahead procedures. Moreover, the implementations of dlv and smodels are well tuned in C++, while NMGTP is a prototype system for experiments written in Java.

Table 1. Results for The 3-coloring Problems.

	#Failed Branches	#Answer Sets	#Models	RunTime(msec)
NMGTP	0	486	486	141
naive	118,496	486	190,524	69,548
dlv	–	486	–	< 20
smodels	–	486	–	< 20

Table 2. Results for QG problems.

	Order	#Failed Branches	#Answer Sets	#Models	RunTime(msec)
NMGTP	8	9	1	1	230
naive	8	23	1	1	302
dlv	8	–	1	–	2,640
smodels	8	–	1	–	930
NMGTP	11	112	5	5	3,823
naive	11	> 18,000	–	–	> 1000,000
dlv	11	–	5	–	660,950
smodels	11	–	5	–	231,070

Table 2 shows the results for the Quasigroup existence problems [1] (QG problems in short) in finite algebra (order 8 and 11). QG problems are defined as constraint satisfaction problems on order n Latin squares. QG problems have some variations. We have experimented the problems called QG5. QG5 constraints are defined as $\forall a, b \in G, a \circ a = a, a \circ b \circ a \circ a = b$ where G is a Latin square whose order is n ($|G| = n$) and $\circ$ is a binary operation defined on G.

---

[3] Runtime for dlv is measured by UNIX time command.

```
→ range(1).  → range(2).  → range(3).  → range(4).  → range(5).
→ p(1,1,1).  → p(2,2,2).  → p(3,3,3).  → p(4,4,4).  → p(5,5,5).
range(M), range(N), M ≠ N,
  not p(M,N,2), not p(M,N,3), not p(M,N,4), not p(M,N,5) → p(M,N,1).
.........
p(M,N,X), range(M1), M1 ≠ M → ¬p(M1,N,X).    % distinctness property
p(Y,X,A), p(A,Y,B) → p(B,Y,X).
p(Y,X,A), ¬p(A,Y,B) → ¬p(B,Y,X).
¬p(Y,X,A), p(A,Y,B) → ¬p(B,Y,X).    % QG5 constraints
.........
```

Fig. 3. Problem description for QG5 order 5 (in brief).

The problem description for QG problems in extended logic programming form is shown briefly in Figure 3 where $p(A,B,C)$ means $A \circ B = C$ in G. As shown in the table, NMGTP could solve order 11 in several seconds, while dlv and smodels took more than hundreds seconds. In solving QG problems by dlv or smodels, since a huge number of ground clauses are generated[4], the process of lookahead and constraint propagation on those huge clauses could be overheads, while in NMGTP, instance clauses are only generated as results of conjunctive matching.

6 Summary and Future Work

In this paper, we proposed a new framework called NMGTP for computing answer sets for extended logic programs including negation as failure and classical negation. When using NMGTP, all answer sets can be found without any backtracking. We also proposed some techniques to improve efficiency, and showed the effectiveness of our approaches through some experiments.

There are lots of systems for answer set computation such as dlv [2], smodels [10]. Although the method to handle hypotheses in MDB is similar to those in dlv or smodels, NMGTP works on model generation manner, that is, grounded hypotheses are only generated as results of conjunctive matching as well as objective literals. Some experiments reveals that our approach is effective for the problems such as Quasigroup problems where a huge number of complicated constraint propagations intertwine with each other. Recently, ASSAT[9] achieved some major improvements over dlv or smodels. Unfortunately, ASSAT targets at normal logic programs and does not permit classical negation. We have compared with ASSAT in the limited representation, but it cannot be fair comparison.

As another approach based on MGTP, Shimajiri [12] proposed relevancy testing method that prune redundant branches with respect to T-condition. This approach, however, is not sound for extended logic programs with disjunctions because the minimality condition can not be guaranteed after pruning

---

[4] In dlv case, 141551 ground clauses are generated (order 11).

non-relevant branches. Our approach proposes a sound procedure for extended logic programs including disjunctions.

As a future research, we will investigate implementing some lookahead procedures or backward propagation on MDB. Some experiments such as for block world problems reveal that the lookahead procedures on the set of hypotheses are quite effective to prune redundant branches. We will also introduce some heuristics to select a clause for case splitting. These heuristics gives crucial effects on the size of the proof tree in many cases on answer set programming.

References

1. F. Bennett. Quasigroup Identities and Mendelsohn Designs. *Canadian Journal of Mathematics*, 41:341–368, 1989.
2. T. Eiter, W. Faber, C. Koch, N. Leone, and G. Pfeifer. Dlv - a system for declarative problem solving. In *Proc. of the 8th Int. Workshop on Non-Monotonic Reasoning (NMR'2000)*, 2000.
3. M. Gelfond and V. Lifschitz. The stable model semantics for logic programming. In *Proc. Fifth Int. Conf. and Symp. of Logic Programming*, pages 1070–1080, Seattle, WA, 1988.
4. R. Hähnle. Tableaux and related methods. In A.Robinson and A.Voronkov, editors, *Handbook of Automated Reasoning*. The MIT Press, 2002.
5. R. Hasegawa, H. Fujita, and M. Koshimura. Efficient Minimal Model Generation Using Branching Lemmas. In *Proc. of 17th International Conference on Automated Deduction, Lecture Notes in Artificial Intelligence 1831*, pages 184–199. Springer-Verlag, 2000.
6. R. Hasegawa, H. Fujita, M. Koshimura, and Y. Shirai. A Model Generation Theorem Prover MGTP for First-Order Logic. In *Computational Logic: Logic Programming and Beyond*, pages 178–213, 2002. LNAI 2208.
7. K. Inoue, M. Koshimura, and R. Hasegawa. Embedding Negation as Failure into a Model Generation Theorem Prover. In *Proc. 11th Int. Conf. on Automated Deduction*, pages 400–415. Springer-Verlag, 1992. LNAI 607.
8. K. Inoue and C. Sakama. A Fixpoint Characterization of Abductive Logic Programs. *Journal of Logic Programming*, 27(2):107–136, 1996.
9. F. Lin and Y. Zhao. ASSAT: Computing Answer Sets of A Logic Program By SAT Solvers. In *Proc. of 18th AAAI*, pages 112–118. AAAI Press, 2002.
10. I. Niemelä and P. Simons. Efficient Implementation of the Well-founded and Stable Model Semantics. Research report 7-96, University of Koblenz-Landau, 1996.
11. Y. Shirai and R. Hasegawa. Two Approaches for Finite-Domain Constraint Satisfaction Problem - CP and MGTP -. In L. Sterling, editor, *Proc. 12th Int. Conf. on Logic Programming*, pages 249–263. MIT Press, 1995.
12. Y.Shimajiri, H.Seki, and H.Itoh. Incorporating a Pruning Strategy into the Computation of Stable Models. *Journal of the Japanese Society for Artificial Intelligence*, 12(5), 1997. (in Japanese).

What Is a Qualitative Calculus? A General Framework

Gérard Ligozat[1] and Jochen Renz[2]

[1] LIMSI-CNRS, Université Paris-Sud, 91403 Orsay, France
[2] National ICT Australia*, Knowledge Representation and Reasoning Group
UNSW Sydney, NSW 2052, Australia

Abstract. What is a qualitative calculus? Many qualitative spatial and temporal calculi arise from a set of JEPD (jointly exhaustive and pairwise disjoint) relations: a stock example is Allen's calculus, which is based on thirteen basic relations between intervals on the time line. This paper examines the construction of such a formalism from a general point of view, in order to make apparent the formal algebraic properties of all formalisms of that type. We show that the natural algebraic object governing this kind of calculus is a non-associative algebra (in the sense of Maddux), and that the notion of weak representation is the right notion for describing most basic properties. We discuss the ubiquity of weak representations in various guises, and argue that the fundamental notion of consistency itself can best be understood in terms of consistency of one weak representation with respect to another.

1 Introduction

What is a qualitative temporal or spatial calculus? And: why should we care? An obvious, if not quite satisfactory way of answering the first question would consist in listing some examples of fairly well-known examples: on the temporal side, Allen's interval calculus [1] is the most famous candidate; others are the point calculus [24], the point-and-interval calculus [7], generalized interval calculi [14], or the INDU calculus [20]; on the spatial side, there are Allen-like calculi, such as the directed interval calculus [22], the cardinal direction calculus [16], which is a particular case of the n-point calculi [4], the rectangle calculus [3], and more generally the n-block calculi [5], as well as calculi stemming from the RCC-like axiomatics, such as the RCC-5 and RCC-8 calculi [21], and various kinds of calculi, such as the cyclic interval calculus [2], the star calculi [19], or the preference calculi [8].

Why should we care? A first reason is that, as becomes soon apparent after considering some of the examples, many calculi share common properties, and are used in analogous ways: Take for instance Allen's calculus. It makes use of a set of basic relations, and reasoning uses disjunctions of the basic relations (representing incomplete knowledge), also called (disjunctive) relations. A relation has a converse relation, and relations can be composed, giving rise to an algebraic structure called Allen's algebra (which is a relation algebra, in Tarski's sense [23]). In applications, the knowledge is represented by temporal networks, which are oriented graphs whose nodes stand for

---

* National ICT Australia is funded through the Australian Government's *Backing Australia's Ability* initiative, in part through the Australian Research Council.

intervals, and labels on the arcs which are relations. In this context, a basic problem is determining whether a given network is consistent (the problem is known to be NP-complete, [24]). Finally, when a network is consistent, finding a qualitative instantiation of it amounts to refining the network to an atomic sub-network which is still consistent: and this can be checked at the algebraic level.

Thus, it makes sense to ask the question: to what extent do those properties extend to the other calculi we mentioned above? As first discussed in [17], it soon appears that some properties of Allen's calculus do not extend in general. Some disturbing facts:

- As remarked by [9, 17], the algebras of some calculi are not relation algebras in the sense of Tarski, but more general algebras called non-associative algebras by Maddux (relation algebras being the particular case of associative non-associative algebras). In fact, the INDU algebra is only a semi-associative algebra.
- The natural or intended models of the calculus may not be models in the strong sense or, in algebraic terms, representations of the algebra. This is no new realization: Allen's composition, for instance, expresses necessary and sufficient conditions only if the intervals are in a dense and unbounded linear ordering. But what is less known, apart from the fact that it may be interesting to reason in weaker structures, e.g., about intervals in a discrete linear ordering, is the fact that all such models correspond to weak representations of the algebra, in the sense of [13].
- For some calculi, such as the containment algebra [12] or the cyclic interval calculus [2], it has been observed that some finite atomic constraint networks which are algebraically closed[1] are not consistent. Again, this phenomenon is best expressed, if not explained, in terms of weak relations.
- For Allen's calculus, any consistent atomic network is in fact k-consistent, for all $k < n$, if it has n nodes. Again, the analogous result is false for many calculi, and considering the various weak representations helps to explain why it may be so.

So we cannot hope to have general methods and have to look closer at what the calculi have to offer. Defining a family of calculi by giving examples amounts to a partial extensional definition. But what would an intensional definition be? If we can answer this last question, we have some hope of developing general methods which could be used for whole classes of calculi, instead of specific ones which have to be reinvented for each particular calculus.

Although we do not consider this particular aspect in this paper, an example of a general concept which is valid for a whole class of calculi is the notion of pre-convexity [15] which has been shown as providing a successful way of searching for tractable classes, at least for formalisms based on linear orderings such as Allen's calculus.

The purpose of this paper is to give a precise technical answer to the first question: what is a qualitative calculus? The answer involves a modest amount of – actually, two – algebraic notions, which both extend standard definitions in universal algebra: the notion of a *non-associative algebra* (which generalizes that of a relation algebra), and the notion of a *weak representation*, (which generalizes that of a representation).

---

[1] We use the term *algebraically closed*, or *a-closed*, to refer to the notion which is often (in some cases incorrectly) referred to as path-consistency: for any 3-tuple (i, j, k) of nodes, composing the labels on (i, k) and (k, j) yields a result which contains the label on (i, j).

This paper provides a context for discussing these various points. In section 2, the general construction of JEPD relations is presented in terms of partition schemes. The main operation in that context is weak composition, whose basic properties are discussed. Section 3 describes some typical examples of the construction. It is shown in Section 4 that all partition schemes give rise to non-associative algebras, and in Section 5 that the original partition schemes are in fact weak representations of the corresponding algebra. A proposal for a very general definition of a qualitative calculus is presented in Section 6 as well as a description of the various guises into which weak representations appear: both as particular kind of network and as natural universes of interpretation. Section 7 is concerned with the basic notion of consistency, which appears as a particular case of a more general notion of consistency of one weak representation with respect to another.

2 Developing a New Calculus

Although there seems to be almost no end to defining qualitative spatial or temporal calculi, most constructions are ultimately based on the use of a set of JEPD (jointly exhaustive and pairwise disjoint[2]) relations. This will be our starting point for defining a generic qualitative calculus, in a very general setting.

2.1 Partition Schemes

We start with a non-empty universe U, and consider a partition of $U \times U$ into a family of non-empty binary relations $(R_i)_{i \in I}$:

$$U \times U = \bigcup_{i \in I} R_i \qquad (1)$$

The relations R_i are called *basic relations*. Usually, calculi defined in this way use a partition into a finite number of relations. In order to keep things simple, we assume I to be a finite set. In concrete situations, U is a set of temporal, spatial, or spatio-temporal entities (time points, intervals, regions, etc.). Among all possible binary relations, the partition selects a finite subset of "qualitative" relations which will be a basis for talking about particular situations. For instance, in Allen's calculus, U is the set of all intervals in the rational line, and any configuration is described in terms of the 13 basic relations.

We make some rather weak assumptions about this setup. First, we assume that the diagonal (the identity relation) is one of the R_is, say R_0:

$$R_0 = \Delta = \{(u, v) \in U \times U \mid u = v\} \qquad (2)$$

Finally, we choose the partition in such a way that it is globally invariant under conversion. Recall that, for any binary relation R, $R^\smile$ is defined by:

$$R^\smile = \{(u, v) \in U \times U \mid (v, u) \in R\} \qquad (3)$$

---

[2] Contrary to one of the authors' initial assumption, the JEPD acronym does not seem to be related in any way to the JEPD hypothesis in biblical exegesis, where J, E, P, D stand for the Jehovist, Elohist, Priestly and Deuteronomist sources, respectively!

We assume that the following holds:

$$(\forall i \in I)(\exists j \in I) \quad R_i^\smile = R_j \tag{4}$$

Definition 1. *A partition scheme is a pair $(U, (R_i)_{i \in I})$, where U is a non-empty set and $(R_i)_{i \in I}$ a partition of $U \times U$ satisfying conditions (2) and (4).*

2.2 Describing Configurations

Once we have decided on a partition scheme, we have a way of describing configurations in the universe U. Intuitively, a configuration is a (usually finite) subset $V \subseteq U$ of objects of U. By definition, given such a subset, each pair $(u, v) \in V \times V$ belongs to exactly one R_i for a well-defined i. Later, we will think of V as a set of nodes of a graph, and of the map $\nu : V \times V \to I$ as a labeling of the set of arcs of the graph. Clearly, $\nu(u, u)$ is the identity relation R_0, and $\nu(v, u)$ is the transpose of $\nu(u, v)$. The resulting graphs are called *constraint networks* in the literature. More generally, we can express constraints using Boolean expressions using the R_is. In particular, constraint networks using disjunctive labels are interpreted as conjunctions of disjunctive constraints represented by unions of basic relations on the labels.

2.3 Weak Composition

Up to now, we did not consider how constraints can be propagated. This is what we do now by defining the *weak composition* of two relations. Recall first the definition of the composition $R \circ S$ of two binary relations R and S:

$$(R \circ S) = \{(u, v) \in U \times U \mid (\exists w \in U) \quad (u, w) \in R \enspace \& \enspace (w, v) \in S\} \tag{5}$$

Weak composition, denoted by $R_i \diamond R_j$, of two relations R_i and R_j is defined as follows:

$$(R_i \diamond R_j) = \bigcup_{k \in J} R_k \text{ where } k \in J \text{ if and only if } (R_i \circ R_j) \cap R_k \neq \emptyset \tag{6}$$

Intuitively, weak composition is the best approximation we can get to the actual composition if we have to restrict ourselves to the language provided by the partition scheme. Notice that weak composition is only defined with respect to the partition, and not in an absolute sense, as is the case for the "real" composition.

At this level of generality, some unpleasant facts might be true. For instance, although all relations R_i are non-empty by assumption, we have no guarantee that $R_i \diamond R_j$, or $R_i \circ R_j$ for that matter, are non-empty. A first remark is that weak composition is in a natural sense an upper approximation to composition:

Lemma 1. *For any $i, j \in I$:* $R_i \diamond R_j \supseteq R_i \circ R_j$

Proof. Any $(u, v) \in R_i \circ R_j$ is in some (unique) R_k for a well-defined k. Since this R_k has an element in common with $R_i \circ R_j$, R_k must belong to $R_i \diamond R_j$. □

Lemma 2. *For any $i, j, k \in I$:* $(R_i \diamond R_j) \cap R_k = \emptyset$ *if and only if* $(R_i \circ R_j) \cap R_k = \emptyset$

Proof. Because of Lemma 1, one direction is obvious. Conversely, if $(R_i \diamond R_j) \cap R_k$ is not empty, then, since $(R_i \diamond R_j)$ is a union of R_ls, R_k is contained in it. Now, by definition of weak composition, this means that R_k intersects $R_i \circ Rj$. □

The interaction of weak composition with conversion is an easy consequence of the corresponding result for composition:

Lemma 3. *For all $i, j \in I$:* $(R_i \diamond R_j)^\smile = R_j^\smile \diamond R_i^\smile$

2.4 Weak Composition and Seriality

In many cases, the relations in the partition are *serial* relations. Recall that a relation R is serial if the following condition holds:

$$(\forall u \in U)(\exists v \in U) \text{ such that } (u,v) \in R \tag{7}$$

Lemma 4. *If the relations R and S are serial, then $R \circ S$ is serial, (hence it is non-empty).*

Proof. If R and S are serial, then, for an arbitrary u, choose first w such that $(u,w) \in R$, then v such that $(w,v) \in S$. Then $(u,v) \in (R \circ S)$. □

As a consequence, since all basic relations are non-empty, the weak composition of two basic relations is itself non-empty.

Lemma 5. *If the basic relations are serial, then $\forall i \in I$:* $\bigcup_{j \in I}(R_i \diamond R_j) = U \times U$

Proof. We have to show that, for any given i, and any pair (u,v), there is a j such that (u,v) is in $R_i \diamond R_j$. We know that $(u,v) \in R_k$, for some well-defined k. Because R_i and R_k are serial, for all t there are x and y such that $(t,x) \in R_i$ and $(t,y) \in R_k$. Therefore $(x,y) \in R_i^\smile \circ R_k$, so $R_i^\smile \circ R_k$ is non-empty. Moreover, there is one well-defined j such that $(x,y) \in R_j$. Hence (t,y) is both in R_k and in $R_i \circ R_j$. Therefore, $R_k \subseteq (R_i \diamond R_j)$, hence $(u,v) \in (R_i \diamond R_j)$. □

3 Examples of Partition Schemes

Example 1 (The linear ordering with two elements). Let $U = \{a,b\}$ a set with two elements. Let $R_0 = \{(a,a),(b,b)\}$, $R_1 = \{(a,b)\}$, $R_2 = \{(b,a)\}$. The two-element set U, in other words, is linearly ordered by R_1 (or by R_2). Then $R_1 \circ R_1 = R_2 \circ R_2 = \emptyset$, $R_1 \circ R_2 = \{(a,a)\}$, and $R_2 \circ R_1 = \{(b,b)\}$. Hence $R_1 \diamond R_1 = \emptyset$, $R_2 \diamond R_2 = \emptyset$, $R_1 \diamond R_2 = R_0$, and $R_2 \diamond R_1 = R_0$.

Example 2 (The linear ordering with three elements). Let $U = \{a,b,c\}$ a set with three elements. Let $R_0 = \{(a,a),(b,b),(c,c)\}$, $R_1 = \{(a,b),(b,c),(a,c)\}$, $R_2 = \{(b,a),(c,b),(c,a)\}$. Here, the three-element set U is linearly ordered by R_1 (or by R_2). Then $R_1 \circ R_1 = \{(a,c)\}$, $R_2 \circ R_2 = \{(c,a)\}$, $R_1 \circ R_2 = R_2 \circ R_1 = \{(a,a),(b,b),(a,b),(b,a)\}$. Consequently, $R_1 \diamond R_1 = R_1$, $R_2 \diamond R_2 = R_2$, $R_1 \diamond R_2 = R_2 \diamond R_1 = U \times U$.

Example 3 (The point algebra). The standard example is the point algebra, where U is the set Q of rational numbers, and R_1 is the usual ordering on Q, denoted by $<$. R_2 is the converse of R_1. Because this ordering is dense and unbounded both on the left and on the right, we have $R_1 \circ R_1 = R_1$, $R_2 \circ R_2 = R_2$, $R_2 \circ R_1 = R_1 \circ R_2 = U \times U$.

Example 4 (Allen's algebra). Here U is the set of "intervals" in $\mathbb{Q}$, i.e., of ordered pairs $(q_1, q_2) \in \mathbb{Q} \times \mathbb{Q}$ such that $q_1 < q_2$. Basic relations are defined in the usual way [1]. Since $\mathbb{Q}$ is dense and unbounded, weak composition coincides with composition [13].

Example 5 (Allen's calculus on integers). U is the set of intervals in $\mathbb{Z}$, that is, of pairs $(n_1, n_2) \in \mathbb{Z} \times \mathbb{Z}$ such that $n_1 < n_2$. Weak composition differs from composition in this case: e.g., we still have $\mathsf{p} \diamond \mathsf{p} = \mathsf{p}$, but the pair $([0, 1], [2, 3])$ is in p, but not in $\mathsf{p} \circ \mathsf{p}$.

4 The Algebras of Qualitative Calculi

4.1 Algebras Derived from Partition Schemes

Now we take an abstract algebraic point of view. For each $i \in I$, we introduce a symbol r_i (which refers to R_i) and consider the set $B = \{r_i \mid i \in I\}$. Let A be the Boolean algebra of all subsets of B. The top element of this algebra is denoted by **1**, and the bottom element (the empty set) by **0**. Union, intersection and complementation are denoted by $+$, $\cdot$ and $-$, respectively. Let $\mathbf{1}'$ denote $\{r_0\}$. We still denote by $r_i^{\smile}$ the operation of conversion. On this Boolean algebra, the weak composition function defines an operation which is usually denoted by ;. When tabulated, the corresponding table is called the *weak composition table* of the calculus. The operation of composition on basic symbols is extended to all subsets as follows:

$$\text{For } a, b \in A, (a\,;\,b) = \bigcup_{i,j}(r_i\,;\,r_j), \text{ where } r_i \in a \text{ and } r_j \in b. \tag{8}$$

Since the algebraic setup reflects facts about actual binary relations, the algebra we get in this way would be a relation algebra in Tarski's sense, if we considered composition. In the general case, however, what we are considering is only weak composition, an approximation to actual composition. What happens is that we get a weaker kind of algebra, namely, a *non-associative algebra* [18, 10]:

Definition 2. *A non-associative algebra A is a tuple* $\mathcal{A} = (A, +, -, \mathbf{0}, \mathbf{1}, ;, \smile, \mathbf{1}')$ *such that:*

1. $(A, +, -, \mathbf{0}, \mathbf{1})$ *is a Boolean algebra.*
2. $\mathbf{1}'$ *is a constant,* $\smile$ *a unary and* ; *a binary operation s. t., for any* $a, b, c \in A$:

   (a) $(a^{\smile})^{\smile} = a$ (b) $\mathbf{1}'\,;\,a = a;\ \mathbf{1}' = a$ (c) $a\,;\,(b+c) = a\,;\,b + a\,;\,c$
   (d) $(a+b)^{\smile} = a^{\smile} + b^{\smile}$ (e) $(a-b)^{\smile} = a^{\smile} - b^{\smile}$ (f) $(a\,;\,b)^{\smile} = b^{\smile}\,;\,a^{\smile}$
   (g) $(a\,;\,b) \cdot c^{\smile} = \mathbf{0}$ *if and only if* $(b\,;\,c) \cdot a^{\smile} = \mathbf{0}$

A non-associative algebra is a relation algebra if it is associative.

Maddux [18] also introduced intermediate classes of non-associative algebras between relation algebras (**RA**) and general non-associative algebras (**NA**), namely weakly associative (**WA**) and semi-associative (**SA**) algebras. These classes form a hierarchy:

$$\mathbf{NA} \supseteq \mathbf{WA} \supseteq \mathbf{SA} \supseteq \mathbf{RA} \tag{9}$$

In particular, semi-associative algebras are those non-associative algebras which satisfy the following condition:

$$\text{For all } a, (a\,;\,\mathbf{1})\,;\,\mathbf{1} = a\,;\,\mathbf{1}. \tag{10}$$

Proposition 1. *The algebraic structure associated to a partition scheme is a non-associative algebra. If the basic relations are serial, it is a semi-associative algebra.*

Proof. We have to check points (2(a–g)) of Def.2 (checking the validity on basic relations is enough). The first six points are easily checked. The last axiom, the triangle axiom, holds because of lemma 2. If all basic relations are serial, the condition for semi-associativity holds, because, by lemma 5, $(a\,;\,\mathbf{1}) = \mathbf{1}$ for all basic relations a. □

4.2 What About Associativity?

The non associative algebras we get are not in general associative. E.g., the algebra of Example 1 is not associative: $((r_1\,;\,r_2)\,;\,r_2) = (\mathbf{1}'\,;\,r_2) = r_2$, whereas $(r_1\,;\,(r_2\,;\,r_2)) = (r_1\,;\,\mathbf{0}) = \mathbf{0}$. Although it satisfies the axiom of weak associativity [18], it is not semi-associative, since for instance $(r_1\,;\,\mathbf{1})\,;\,\mathbf{1} = \mathbf{1}$ whereas $r_1\,;\,(\mathbf{1}\,;\,\mathbf{1}) = r_1 + \mathbf{1}'$.

If weak composition coincides with composition, then the family $(R_i)_{i \in I}$ is a proper relation algebra, hence in particular it is associative. However, this sufficient condition is not necessary, as Example 2 shows: although the structure on the linear ordering on three elements has a weak composition which is not composition, it defines the point algebra, which is a relation algebra, hence associative. An example of an algebra which is semi-associative but not associative is the INDU calculus [6]. The semi-associativity of INDU is a consequence of the fact that all basic relations are serial.

5 Weak Representations

In the previous section, we showed how a qualitative calculus can be defined, starting from a partition scheme. The algebraic structure we get in this way is a non-associative algebra, *i.e.*, an algebra that satisfies all axioms of a relation algebra, except possibly associativity.

Conversely, what is the nature of a partition scheme with respect to the algebra? The answer is that it is a weak representation of that algebra. The notion of a weak representation we use here[3] was first introduced in [13] for relational algebras. It extends in a natural way to non-associative algebras.

Definition 3. *Let $\mathcal{A}$ be a non-associative algebra. A* weak representation *of $\mathcal{A}$ is a pair (U, φ) where U is a non empty set, and φ is a map of $\mathcal{A}$ into $\mathcal{P}(U \times U)$, such that:*

1. φ is an homomorphism of Boolean algebras.
2. $\varphi(\mathbf{1}') = \Delta = \{(x,y) \in U \times U \mid x = y\}$.
3. $\varphi(a^{\smile})$ is the transpose of $\varphi(a)$.
4. $\varphi(a\,;\,b) \supseteq \varphi(a) \circ \varphi(b)$.

A weak representation *is a* representation *if moreover:*

5. φ is injective.
6. $\varphi(a\,;\,b) = \varphi(a) \circ \varphi(b)$.

Example 6. Take a set $U = \{u_1, u_2, u_3\}$ with three elements. Let φ be defined by: $\varphi(\mathsf{o}) = \{(u_1, u_2)\}$, $\varphi(\mathsf{o}^{\smile}) = \{(u_2, u_1)\}$, $\varphi(\mathsf{m}) = \{(u_1, u_3)\}$, $\varphi(\mathsf{m}^{\smile}) = \{(u_3, u_1)\}$, $\varphi(\mathsf{d}) = \{(u_3, u_2)\}$, $\varphi(\mathsf{d}^{\smile}) = \{(u_2, u_3)\}$, $\varphi(\mathsf{eq}) = \{(u_1, u_1), (u_2, u_2), (u_3, u_3)\}$, and $\varphi(a) = \emptyset$ for any other basic relation a in Allen's algebra. Then (U, φ) is a weak representation of Allen's algebra which can be visualized as shown in Fig. 1(a).

---

[3] This notion is not to be confused with weak representability as used by Jónsson, see [11, 10].

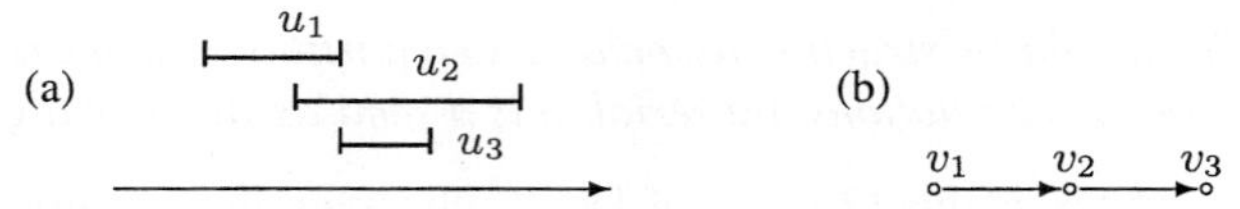

Fig. 1. A weak representation of Allen's algebra (a) and of the point algebra (b).

Example 7 (The point algebra). A weak representation of this algebra is a pair $(U, \prec)$, where U is a set and $\prec$ is a linear ordering on U. It is a representation iff $\prec$ is dense and unbounded. Fig. 1(b) shows a weak representation with three points v_1, v_2, v_3.

5.1 Partition Schemes and Weak Representations

Now we come back to the original situation where we have a universe U and a partition of $U \times U$ constituting a partition scheme. Consider the pair (U, φ), where $\varphi : \mathcal{A} \to \mathcal{P}(U \times U)$ is defined on the basic symbols by:

$$\varphi(r_i) = R_i \tag{11}$$

and is extended to the Boolean algebra in the natural way:

$$\text{For } a \in \mathcal{A} \text{ let } \varphi(a) = \bigcup_{r_i \in a} \varphi(r_i) \tag{12}$$

Proposition 2. *Given a partition scheme on U, define φ as above. Then the pair (U, φ) is a weak representation of $\mathcal{A}$.*

Proof. The only point needing a proof is concerned with axiom 4. For basic symbols, $\varphi(r_i \,;\, r_j) = R_i \diamond R_j$, by definition, while $\varphi(r_i) \circ \varphi(r_j) = R_i \circ R_j$. By lemma 1, the former relation contains the latter. The results extends to unions of relations. □

From this proposition we can assert the (obvious) corollary:

Corollary 1. *The weak representation associated to a partition scheme is a representation if and only if weak composition coincides with composition.*

6 What Is a Qualitative Calculus?

We now have a general answer to our initial question: what is a qualitative calculus?

Definition 4. *A qualitative calculus is a triple $(\mathcal{A}, U, \varphi)$ where:*

1. *$\mathcal{A}$ is a non-associative algebra.*
2. *(U, φ) is a weak representation of $\mathcal{A}$.*

6.1 The Ubiquity of Weak Representations

Summing up, we started with a partition scheme and derived an algebra from it. This algebra, in all cases, is a non-associative algebra. It may or may not be a relation algebra. If the partition scheme is serial, it is a semi-associative algebra. In all cases, anyway, the original partition scheme defines a weak representation of the algebra.

In the next sections, we show that weak representations appear both as constraints (a-closed, normalized atomic networks) and as universes of interpretation. Consequently, many notions of consistency are related to morphisms between weak representations.

6.2 Weak Representations as Constraint Networks

Recall that a (finite) *constraint network on* $\mathcal{A}$ is a pair $\mathcal{N} = (N, \nu)$, where N is a (finite) set of nodes (or variables) and ν a map $\nu : N \times N \to \mathcal{A}$. For each pair (i, j) of nodes, $\nu(i, j)$ is the constraint on the arc (i, j). A network is *atomic* if ν is in fact a map into the set of basic relations (or *atoms*) of $\mathcal{A}$. It is *normalized* if $\forall i, j \in N$ $\nu(i, j) = \mathbf{1}'$ if $i = j$, and $\forall i, j \in N$ $\nu(j, i) = \nu(i, j)^\smile$. A network $\mathcal{N}' = (N, \nu')$ is a *refinement* of $\mathcal{N}$ if $\forall i, j \in N$ we have $\nu'(i, j) \subseteq \nu(i, j)$. Finally, a network is *algebraically closed*, or *a-closed*, if $\forall i, j, k \in N$ $\nu(i, j) \subseteq \nu(i, k) \, ; \, \nu(k, j)$.

Let (N, ν) be a network, and consider for each atom $a \in \mathcal{A}$ the set $\rho(a) = \{(i, j) \in N \times N \mid \nu(i, j) = a\}$. This defines a map from the set of atoms of $\mathcal{A}$ to the set of subsets of $N \times N$, which is interpreted as providing the set of arcs in the network which are labeled by a given atom. If the network is atomic, any arc is labeled by exactly one atom, i.e., the set of non-empty $\rho(a)$ is a partition of $N \times N$ labeled by atoms of $\mathcal{A}$. If it is normalized, this partition satisfies the conditions (2) and (3) characterizing a partition scheme. If the network is a-closed, then (N, ρ), where ρ is extended to $\mathcal{A}$ in the natural way, i.e., as $\rho(b) = \sum_{a \in b} \rho(a)$, is together with N a weak representation of $\mathcal{A}$.

Conversely, for any weak representation (U, φ), we can interpret U as a set of nodes, and $\varphi(r_i)$ as the set of arcs labeled by r_i. Hence each arc is labeled by a basic relation, in such a way that (v, u) is labeled by $r_i^\smile$ if (u, v) is labeled by r_i, and that for all u, v, w the composition of the label on (u, w) with that on (w, v) contains the label on (u, v). Hence a weak representation is an a-closed, normalized atomic network.

Considering a weak representation in terms of a constraint network amounts to seeing it as an intensional entity: it expresses constraints on some instantiation of the variables of the network. Now, weak representations are at the same time extensional entities: as already apparent in the discussion of partition schemes, they also appear as universes of interpretation.

6.3 Weak Representations as Interpretations

Many standard interpretations of qualitative calculi are particular kinds of weak representations of the algebra, namely, representations. Allen's calculus, e.g., is usually interpreted in terms of the representation provided by "intervals", in the sense of strictly increasing pairs in the rational or real line. It has less been pointed out in the literature that in many cases weak representations, rather than representations, are what the calculi are actually about.

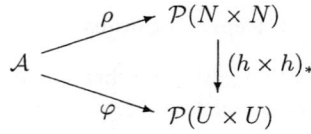

Fig. 2. A general notion of consistency.

As already discussed in [13], a finite weak representation of Allen's algebra can be visualized in terms of finite sets of intervals on a finite linear ordering. More generally, restricting the calculus to some sub-universe amounts to considering weak representations of Allen's algebra: for instance, considering intervals on the integers (Example 5) yields a weak representation. It also makes sense to consider the problem of determining whether constraint networks are consistent with respect to this restrictive interpretation.

Encountering the notion of seriality is not surprising. Recall that a constraint network is k-consistent if any instantiation of $k - 1$ variables extends to k-variables. In particular, a network is 2-consistent if any instantiation of one variable extends to two variables. Hence a partition scheme is serial if and only if the (possibly infinite) "network" U (or weak representation) is 2-consistent. Many natural calculi have consistent networks which are not 2-consistent, e.g., Allen's calculus on integers. Although the 2-element network with constraint d is consistent, it is not 2-consistent: if an interval x has length one, there is no interval y such that ydx.

7 What Is Consistency?

The preceding discussion shows that a weak representation can be considered alternatively as a particular kind of constraint network (an atomic, normalized and a-closed one), or as a universe of interpretation. Now, a fundamental question about a network is whether it is consistent with respect to a given domain of interpretation.

Intuitively, a network $\mathcal{N} = (N, \nu)$ is consistent (with respect to a calculus $(\mathcal{A}, U, \varphi)$) if it has an atomic refinement $\mathcal{N}' = (N, \nu')$ which is itself consistent, that is, the variables N of $\mathcal{N}$ can be interpreted in terms of elements of U in such a way that the relations prescribed by ν' hold in U. More specifically, if (N, ν') is a-closed, normalized, and atomic, consider the associated weak representation (N, ρ). Then the consistency of the network with respect to the weak representation (U, φ) means that there exists an instantiation $h : N \to U$ such that, for each atom $a \in \mathcal{A}$, $(i, j) \in \rho(a)$ implies $(h(i), h(j)) \in \varphi(a)$. Hence consistency of such a network appears as a particular case of compatibility between two weak representations. This means that in fact consistency is a property involving two weak representations:

Definition 5. *Let $\mathcal{N} = (N, \rho)$ and $\mathcal{U} = (U, \varphi)$ be two weak representations of $\mathcal{A}$. Then $\mathcal{N}$ is consistent with respect to $\mathcal{U}$ if there exists a map $h : N \to U$ such that the diagram in Fig. 2 commutes, that is, for each $a \in \mathcal{A}$, $(i, j) \in \rho(a)$ implies $(h(i), h(j)) \in \varphi(a)$.*

This generalization of the notion of consistency emphasizes the fact that it is a notion between two weak representations, where one is interpreted in intentional terms, while the other is used in an extensional way, as a universe of interpretation.

Example 8 (The point algebra). A weak representation in that case is a linearly ordered set. Consider two such weak representations $(N, \prec_N)$ and $(U, \prec_U)$. Then $(N, \prec_N)$ is consistent with respect to $(U, \prec_U)$ iff there is a strictly increasing map $h : N \to U$.

7.1 Inconsistent Weak Representations

In that light, what is the meaning of the existence of inconsistent weak representations? Examples of finite atomic a-closed networks which are not consistent exist e.g. for the cyclic interval calculus or the INDU calculus [17]. In such cases, the universe of interpretation of the calculus (such as intervals on a rational circle, or intervals with duration) has too much additional structure and constraints on its relations for the network to take them into account. Characterizing the cases where this can happen seems to be an open problem in general.

8 Conclusions

This paper proposes to introduce a shift of perspective in the way qualitative calculi are considered. Since Allen's calculus has been considered as a paradigmatic instance of a qualitative calculus for more than two decades, it has been assumed that the algebraic structures governing them are relation algebras, and that the domains of interpretation of the calculi should in general be extensional or, in algebraic terms, representations of these algebras. These assumptions, however, have been challenged by a series of facts: some calculi, as first shown in [9], then by [17], involve non-associative algebras. Also, for many calculi, the domains of interpretation may vary, and do not necessarily constitute representations.

We argued in this paper that a qualitative calculus should be defined abstractly as a triple consisting of a non-associative algebra and a weak representation of that algebra. This abstract definition makes apparent the fact that particular kinds of networks on the one side, and representations of the algebras on the other side, are ultimately of a common nature, namely, both are particular kinds of weak representations. This last fact has of course been known before: for instance, the work described in [10] is about trying to construct representations of a given relation algebra by incrementally enriching a-closed networks using games *à la* Ehrenfeucht-Fraissé. However, we think that putting qualitative calculi in this setting provides a clear way of considering new calculi, as well as an agenda for questions to be asked first: what are the properties of the algebra involved? What are weak representations? Are the intended interpretations representations of the algebra? When are weak representations consistent with respect to which weak representations?

A further benefit of the framework is that it makes clearly apparent what consistency really means: consistency of a network (a network is a purely algebraic notion) with respect to the calculus is a particular case of consistency between two weak representations: it can be defined as the possibility of refining the network into a weak representation which is consistent wrt. the one which is part of the calculus considered.

Obviously, defining a general framework is only an initial step for studying the new problems which arise for calculi which are less well-behaved than Allen's calculus.

A first direction of investigation we are currently exploring consists in trying to get a better understanding of the relationship between consistency and the expressiveness of constraint networks.

References

1. J. F. Allen. Maintaining knowledge about temporal intervals. *CACM*, 26(11):832–843, 1983.
2. P. Balbiani and A. Osmani. A model for reasoning about topologic relations between cyclic intervals. In *Proc. of KR-2000*, Breckenridge, Colorado, 2000.
3. P. Balbiani, J.-F. Condotta, and L. Fariñas del Cerro. A model for reasoning about bidimensional temporal relations. In *Proc. of KR-98*, p. 124–130, 1998.
4. P. Balbiani, J.-F. Condotta, and L. Fariñas del Cerro. Spatial reasoning about points in a multidimensional setting. In *Proc. IJCAI'99 Spat.&Temp. Reasoning WS*, p.105-113, 1999.
5. P. Balbiani, J.-F. Condotta, and L. Fariñas del Cerro. A tractable subclass of the block algebra: constraint propagation and preconvex relations. In *Proc. EPIA'99*, p. 75–89, 1999.
6. P. Balbiani, J.-F. Condotta, and G. Ligozat. On the Consistency Problem for the INDU Calculus. In *Proc. TIME-ICTL-2003*, Cairns, Australia, 2003.
7. R. Dechter, I. Meiri, and J. Pearl. Temporal Constraint Networks. *AIJ*, 49(1-3):61–95, 1991.
8. I. Duentsch and M. Roubens. Tangent circle algebras. In H. de Zwart, editor, *Relational Methods in Computer Science*, p. 300–314. LNCS, Vol.2561. Springer, 2002.
9. M. Egenhofer and A. Rodriguez. Relation Algebras over Containers and Surfaces: An Ontological Study of a Room Space. *Spatial Cognition and Computation*, 1(2):155–180, 1999.
10. R. Hirsch and I. Hodkinson. *Relation Algebras by Games*. North Holland, 2002.
11. B. Jónsson. Representation of modular lattices and relation algebras. *Tr. AMS*, 92:449–464, 1959.
12. P. Ladkin and R. Maddux. On Binary Constraint Problems. *JACM*, 41(3):435-469, 1994.
13. G. Ligozat. Weak Representations of Interval Algebras. In *Proc. AAAI'90*, p. 715–720, 1990.
14. G. Ligozat. On generalized interval calculi. In *Proc. AAAI'91*, p. 234–240, 1991.
15. G. Ligozat. Tractable relations in temporal reasoning: pre-convex relations. In *Proc. of the ECAI-94 Workshop on Spatial and Temporal Reasoning*, p. 99–108, Amsterdam, 1994.
16. G. Ligozat. Reasoning about cardinal directions. *J. of Vis. Lang. & Comp.*, 1(9):23–44, 1998.
17. G. Ligozat, D. Mitra, and J.-F. Condotta. Spatial and Temporal Reasoning: Beyond Allen's Calculus. In *Proc. AAAI Symp. on Found. and Appl. of Spatio-Temporal Reasoning*, 2003.
18. R. Maddux. Some varieties containing relation algebras. *Trans. AMS*, 272(2):501–526, 1982.
19. D. Mitra. Qualitative Reasoning with Arbitrary Angular Directions. In *Proc. of the AAAI-02 W20 Workshop on Spatial and Temporal Reasoning*, Edmonton, Canada, 2002.
20. A. K. Pujari and A. Sattar. A new framework for reasoning about points, intervals and durations. In *Proc. IJCAI'99)*, p. 1259–1267, 1999.
21. D. A. Randell, Z. Cui and A. G. Cohn. A spatial logic based on regions and connection. In *Proc. KR'92*, p. 165–176, 1992.
22. J. Renz. A spatial Odyssey of the interval algebra: 1. Directed intervals. In *Proc. IJCAI'01*, p.51–56, 2001.
23. A. Tarski. On the calculus of relations. *Journal of Symbolic Logic*, 6:73–89, 1941.
24. M. B. Vilain and H. Kautz. Constraint propagation algorithms for temporal reasoning. In *Proc. of AAAI-86*, p. 377–382, 1986.

Qualitative Direction Calculi with Arbitrary Granularity

Jochen Renz[1] and Debasis Mitra[2]

[1] National ICT Australia*
Knowledge Representation and Reasoning Group
UNSW Sydney, 2052, NSW, Australia
[2] Department of Computer Sciences
Florida Institute of Technology
Melbourne, FL 32901, USA

Abstract. Binary direction relations between points in two-dimensional space are the basis to any qualitative direction calculus. Previous calculi are only on a very low level of granularity. In this paper we propose a generalization of previous approaches which enables qualitative calculi with an arbitrary level of granularity. The resulting calculi are so powerful that they can even emulate a quantitative representation based on a coordinate system. We also propose a less powerful, purely qualitative version of the generalized calculus. We identify tractable subsets of the generalized calculus and describe some applications for which these calculi are useful.

1 Introduction

Spatial information is an important part of intelligent systems. There are mainly two different approaches to representing and reasoning about spatial information. One approach tries to represent spatial information in a quantitative, metric way, usually by some kind of coordinate system. Another approach, qualitative spatial representation and reasoning, tries to represent spatial information by specifying qualitative relationships between spatial entities. One of the main motivations of qualitative spatial representation is that it is considered to be similar to the way humans conceptualize spatial information and to the way it is expressed in natural language. An obvious advantage of qualitative spatial representation is the handling of imprecise information. Using qualitative relationships it is possible to express only as much information as is necessary or known. The level of precision which can be represented depends on the granularity of the qualitative relations.

Several aspects of space can be represented in a qualitative way, the most important being topology, direction, and distance [2]. In this paper we focus on qualitative direction, i.e., relationships such as left, right, north, or south. Three kinds of spatial entities are usually distinguished, points, lines or line segments, and extended two- or higher dimensional regions. While regions are certainly the most important spatial entities (real-world objects are three-dimensional extended regions) points are the most basic spatial entities and particularly important for representing directions. All qualitative direction calculi for one or higher dimensional spatial entities are essentially based on qualitative directions over points: line segments can be represented by the two end-points, lines by any two of their points, and direction relations between extended regions depend on certain points of the regions such as the leftmost point or the center of a region. Sometimes regions can even be approximated as points, in particular if the size of the regions is small compared to their distance. Therefore, developing a sophisticated qualitative direction calculus over points and exploring its limits is an essential part of qualitative spatial representation and reasoning.

---

* National ICT Australia is funded through the Australian Government's Backing Australia's Ability initiative, in part through the Australian Research Council

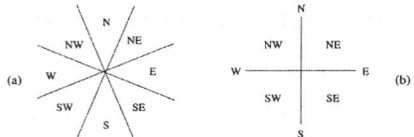

Fig. 1. Cone-based and projection-based qualitative direction calculi [4]

2 Representing Qualitative Direction

The direction between two spatial entities requires to specify either a reference point or a reference direction with respect to which the direction is measured, i.e., direction is essentially a ternary relation. In this paper we consider directions with respect to a given reference direction, i.e., we consider absolute and global directions. Under certain conditions relative directions can be transformed into absolute directions and *vice versa*, so this restriction is not as strong as it seems.

The direction of a point q with respect to another point p can be specified by using the exact angle between the vector pq and the vector which points from p to the given reference direction, where the angle is between $0°$ and $360°$. If the exact angle is not known or not important, which is the case whenever humans without a tool for the exact measurement of directions are involved, then it is better to have a qualitative representation of direction. The goal of a qualitative representation of the direction between points in two-dimensional space is to specify a limited number of relations such that each relation covers a part of the $360°$ range and all relations taken together cover the $360°$ range completely. If in addition the relations do not overlap, they form a jointly exhaustive and pairwise disjoint (JEPD) set of relations, called *basic relations*. The number of basic relations and the way in which they partition the $360°$ range depends on the application and on the required level of granularity. Since the range which has to be covered by the qualitative relations is fixed and well-defined, direction is perfectly suited for calculi with a varying level of granularity. If the given direction information is less precise than that of the basic relations, then the union of different possible basic relations can be used. Complete lack of information can be expressed as the union of all basic relations. Thus, a full set of qualitative relations contains all basic relations B and all possible unions of the basic relations 2^B. An essential requirement for applying standard qualitative reasoning algorithms is that the set of relations is closed under union, intersection, converse, and composition.

Frank [4] distinguished two kinds of calculi for representing absolute directions (see Fig. 1). The *projection-based approach* is based on two orthogonal axes where the four main directions north, east, south, and west are located on, and on the four sectors bounded by the axes which correspond to the directions northeast, southeast, southwest, and northwest. The *cone-based approach* is based on four axes which bound eight equally sized sectors corresponding to the eight above mentioned directions. The computational properties of the projection-based approach, also known as the *cardinal algebra*, has been analyzed by Ligozat [6]. Reasoning over the full cardinal algebra is NP-complete, while there exists a maximal tractable subset which contains all basic relations. For both approaches the granularity of the relations is fixed, which strongly limits their applicability.

3 The Star Calculus

In this section we introduce the *Star calculus* for representing and reasoning about qualitative directions between points in a two-dimensional space with respect to a given reference di-

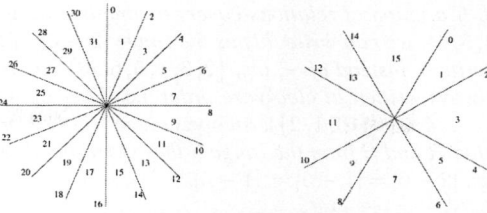

Fig. 2. Two Star calculi: (a) $\mathcal{STAR}_8(0)$, (b) $\mathcal{STAR}_4[30, 60, 120, 150](30)$

rection.[1] The Star calculus is a generalization of several existing calculi such as the different kinds of calculi which Frank distinguished. We give a general specification of a qualitative direction calculus which allows us to define basic relations on an arbitrary fixed level of granularity. We define converse and composition in a general way and prove general computational properties. Using the Star calculus, it is possible to specify qualitative direction relations between two points with respect to a given reference direction. For each point, the Star calculus divides the plane into several zones which form the different relations.

Definition 1 (Star calculus). *Given a two dimensional plane $\mathcal{P}$ and a global reference direction in $\mathcal{P}$. For each point $p \in \mathcal{P}$ the Star calculus $\mathcal{STAR}_m[\delta_1, \ldots, \delta_m](\delta_1)$ where $0 \leq \delta_1 < \ldots < \delta_m < 360$ and $\delta_m - \delta_1 < 180$ specifies m lines which intersect at p while forming the angles δ_j with the reference direction for each $1 \leq j \leq m$. For each point $p \in \mathcal{P}$ these m lines partition $\mathcal{P}$ into $4m + 1$ disjoint zones with respect to the reference direction (see Fig. 2): $2m$ half lines resulting from the m lines, $2m$ two-dimensional sectors each bound by two half lines, and the point p. A unique identifier is assigned to each zone as follows:*

- *The m lines are split into $2m$ half-lines which point from p to the directions δ_j and $(\delta_j+180) \bmod 360$ for $1 \leq j \leq m$. We assign the unique identifiers $0_p, 2_p, \ldots, (4m-2)_p$ in clockwise order starting with the angle δ_1.*
- *The $2m$ half lines and the point p bound $2m$ sectors. We assign these sectors the unique identifiers $1_p, 3_p, \ldots, (4m-1)_p$ in clockwise order starting with the sector bound by p and the half lines 0_p and 2_p.*

Using these zones, $4m + 1$ basic Star relations can be defined as follows:

1. *the identity relation $id \equiv \{(p, p) | p \in \mathcal{P}\}$, and*
2. *the relations $I \equiv \{(p, q) | p, q \in \mathcal{P} \text{ and } q \in I_p\}, \forall I \in \{0, 1, 2, \ldots, 4m - 1\}$*
3. *we denote the relations $\{1, 3, 5, \ldots\}$ as odd relations, and $\{0, 2, 4, \ldots\}$ as even relations*

A Star calculus is the power set of all basic Star relations, i.e., it contains 2^{4m+1} different relations. The set of $4m + 1$ basic relations of a Star calculus $\mathcal{A}$ is denoted $bas(\mathcal{A})$. A Star calculus is called regular, *if all $2m$ zones have equal size, i.e., if the angle between consecutive lines is $180/m$ degrees, and can be written as $\mathcal{STAR}_m(\delta_i)$. The class of all Star calculi based on m lines is denoted $\mathcal{STAR}_m$.*

The union of different basic relations can be written as a set of basic relations, e.g., the union of the basic relations 2, 5, and 6 is written as $\{2, 5, 6\}$. The union of all basic relations, the *universal relation*, is written as $\{*\}$.

---

[1] The Star calculus was introduced in a slightly different form by Mitra [8], but in this paper we provide a rigorous formal definition and analysis of the calculus which results in surprisingly new insights.

Definition 2 (range). *If a union of relations covers a complete range of consecutive basic relations, e.g.* $\{2, 3, 4, 5, 6\}$, *we can write this as the range* $[2 - 6]$. *If the union contains the identity relation, we write $+$ instead of $-$, i.e.,* $\{2, 3, 4, 5, 6, id\}$ *can be written as the range* $[2 + 6]$. *A range is always written in clockwise order, i.e.,* $[2 - 6]$ *is different from* $[6 - 2]$ *(which represents* $\{6, \ldots, 4m - 1, 0, 1, 2\}$*). An open range* $]R - S[$ *or* $]R + S[$ *excludes the first and the last relation R and S from the range if they correspond to half-lines, i.e., if they are even numbers. E.g.,* $]2 - 6[=]1 - 5[= [1 - 5]$.

Let us specify the usual operators for the Star relations. Union and intersection of Star relations are the normal set-theoretic operators. Converse and composition depend on the semantics of the relations. Although a Star calculus can have sectors of different sizes, each relation has a definite converse relation because of the point symmetry of the lines intersecting at p.

Proposition 1 (converse). *Given a Star calculus* $\mathcal{A} \in \mathcal{STAR}_m$. *The converse of the relation id is id. The converse $R^{\smile}$ of a basic relation $R \in bas(\mathcal{A})$ with $0 \leq R \leq 4m - 1$ is given by $(R + 2m) \bmod 4m$. The converse of a union of basic relations is equal to the union of all converse basic relations. The converse of a range $[R \pm S]$ results in $[R^{\smile} \pm S^{\smile}]$. Analogous for open ranges.*

The notion of ranges is particularly helpful for specifying compositions of basic relations since these mostly cover consecutive relations. The composition operator is usually defined as $x(R \circ S)y =_{def} \exists z : xRz \wedge zSy$.

Proposition 2 (composition). *Given a Star calculus* $\mathcal{A} \in \mathcal{STAR}_m$. *Composition $R \circ S$ of two basic relations $R, S \in bas(\mathcal{A})$ can be computed as follows:*

1. *If $R = id$, then $R \circ S = S$,*   2. *If $S = id$, then $R \circ S = R$,*
3. *If $R = S$, then $R \circ S = R$,*   4. *If $R = S^{\smile}$ and R odd, then $R \circ S = \{*\}$,*
5. *If $R = S^{\smile}$ and R even, then $R \circ S = \{R, S, id\}$,*
6. *Let X be the shortest distance between R and S, i.e., $(R + X) \bmod 4m = S$.*
   If $X < 2m$, then $R \circ S =]R - S[$. If $X > 2m$, then $R \circ S =]S - R[$.

It follows from the above rules that $R \circ S = S \circ R$. Please note that the relations resulting from the last composition rule never contain boundary relations corresponding to half lines. This is because id is not contained in these relations, so either with R or with S one is always forced to leave the bounding lines. As usual, the composition of unions of basic relations is the union of the composition of each involved basic relation. It is surprising that the angles of the lines do not seem to be important, but we will see later that this is not always the case.

4 Reasoning over the Star Calculus

Qualitative spatial reasoning consists of several different reasoning problems such as deriving unknown relations from a given set of spatial constraints or eliminating all impossible labels from given spatial constraints in order to obtain the minimal representation. Most of these problems can be reduced to the *consistency problem* $\mathsf{CSPSAT}(\mathcal{S})$ where $\mathcal{S} \subseteq 2^{\mathcal{B}}$ and $2^{\mathcal{B}}$ is closed under the usual operators [10]:

Instance: Given a set $\mathcal{V}$ of n variables over a domain $\mathcal{D}$ and a finite set Θ of binary constraints xRy where $R \in \mathcal{S}$ and $x, y \in \mathcal{V}$.
Question: Is there an instantiation of all n variables in Θ with values from $\mathcal{D}$ which satisfies all constraints?

For Star calculi, the domain $\mathcal{D}$ of variables is the set of all points $p \in \mathcal{P}$.

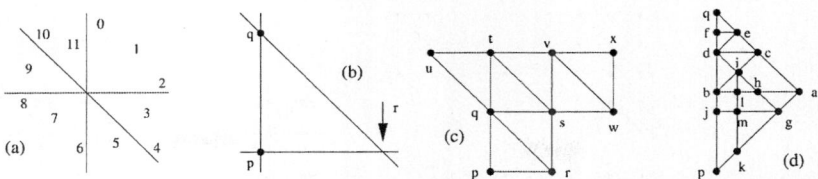

Fig. 3. Constructing the exact position of points with respect to p and q using lines with fixed angles

Theorem 1. *Given a Star calculus $\mathcal{A} \in \mathcal{STAR}_m$. If $m = 1$, then* CSPSAT($\mathcal{A}$) *is tractable. If $m \geq 2$, then* CSPSAT($\mathcal{A}$) *is NP-complete.*

Proof Sketch. Let $m = 1$. We define a x-y-coordinate system in $\mathcal{P}$ where axis x is parallel to the line given by $\mathcal{A}$ and axis y is orthogonal to x. If we consider $p \in \mathcal{P}$ the center of the coordinate system, then the five zones defined by $\mathcal{A}$ with respect to p can be projected onto the two axes and be described as pairs of point algebra relations in the following way $\{\{>\}, \{=\}\}, \{\{<=>\}, \{<\}\}, \{\{<\}, \{=\}\}, \{\{<=>\}, \{>\}\}$, and $\{\{=\}, \{=\}\}$, where the first point relation specifies the projection onto the x axis and the second point relation the projection onto the y axis. This carries over to the Star relations which can be described in the same way. Any set of constraints Θ over $\mathcal{A}$ can be divided into two sets Θ_x and Θ_y of point algebra constraints as described above. First Θ_y is solved while eliminating all unforced equalities. Then all constraints of Θ_x referring to variables which are not equal in the solution of Θ_y are eliminated, resulting in Θ'_x. Θ is consistent iff Θ_y and Θ'_x are both consistent. For $m = 2$, NP-completeness follows from the NP-completeness result by Ligozat [6]. This carries over to all $m > 2$. ∎

The next step is usually to study the computational properties of the basic relations, and, if reasoning over them is tractable, identify maximal tractable subsets. Before doing so, we first have a closer look at the expressiveness of the Star relations. As we will see, they are amazingly powerful as they actually allow us to express geometrical statements. Assume we have a Star calculus with three lines as show in Figure 3(a) and the three constraints $p\{0\}q, q\{4\}r, p\{2\}r$. If the constraints are consistent, then for all consistent instantiations of p and q, the instantiation of r is exactly determined as the intersection of the two lines 2_p and 4_q (see Figure 3(b)). This is an immediate consequence of Euclid's AAS and ASA theorems as the even Star relations have fixed angles. If we have two more constraints $q\{2\}s, r\{0\}s$, then the position of s is also exactly determined with respect to the instantiations of p and q, although the direct relation between p and s can only be expressed as $p\{1\}s$ which is a two-dimensional sector. In the same way we can continue and form an infinite grid of points which are all exactly determined with respect to the instantiations of two points p and q (see Figure 3(c)). If more than three lines are available, it is possible to exactly determine an infinite number of points between two other points of the grid (see Figure 3(d)), i.e., we can get coordinate system with rational values. This demonstrates that Star calculi with three or more lines are so expressive that it is even possible to define coordinate systems, an essentially quantitative entity. This fact is summarized in the following proposition.

Proposition 3 (coordinate systems based on Star relations). *Given a Star calculus $\mathcal{A} \in \mathcal{STAR}_m$ and two points $p, q \in \mathcal{P}$. If $m = 3$, it is possible to define a coordinate system with integer values with respect to two points p and q and the three given angles of $\mathcal{A}$ (see Figure 3(c)). If $m > 3$, it is possible to define a coordinate system with rational values with respect to two points p and q and the given angles of $\mathcal{A}$. (see Figure 3(d)).*

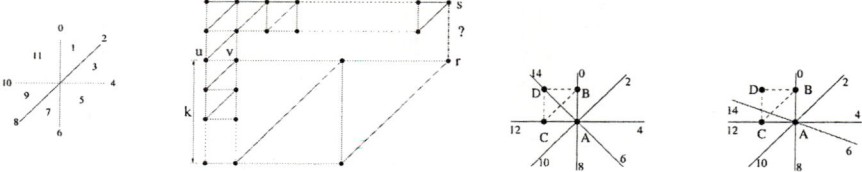

Fig. 4. (a) Construction for the proof of Theorem 2   (b) The Star calculi $\mathcal{A}$ and $\mathcal{B}$ of example 1

Thus, by using a Star calculus with more than two lines, the boundary between qualitative and quantitative representation has disappeared. The quantitative aspect of a coordinate system can be emulated by the Star calculus.

Since the exact positions of points which are enforced by the coordinate system cannot be determined by computing composition and intersection of other Star relations, it is quite obvious that this expressive power cannot be captured by qualitative reasoning methods based only on relational operations. A commonly used method of this kind is that of enforcing k-consistency [7]. A set of constraints Θ is called k-consistent, iff for *each* consistent instantiation of $k - 1$ variables of Θ there is also a consistent instantiation of *any* k-th variable of Θ. The method of enforcing k-consistency consists in eliminating all basic relations of all tuples of k variables that contradict the results of applying all possible compositions within the tuple. Enforcing 3-consistency (also known as the *path-consistency method*), for instance, is done by computing for all triples of variables x, y, z of a set of constraints all entailments $R_{xz} := R_{xz} \cap (R_{xy} \circ R_{yz})$ until a fixed point is reached. If the empty relation occurs, the set is inconsistent. For $k \geq 3$ composition of relations of arity $k - 1$ must be defined and used.

Theorem 2. *Given a Star calculus $\mathcal{A} \in \mathcal{STAR}_m$ with $m \geq 3$ and a constant $k \geq 2$. It is not possible to decide* CSPSAT$(bas(\mathcal{A}))$ *by enforcing k-consistency.*

Proof Sketch. Let $m = 3$. We use a Star calculus such as that in Fig. 4(a) (note that the lines could have arbitrary angles) and emulate a coordinate system with respect to two points u and v, i.e., we assume u has coordinate $(0,0)$ and v has coordinate $(1,0)$. We construct a point s with coordinate $(2k, 2)$ by using a sequence of triangles with length 1. We further define a point r with coordinate $(2k+1, 0)$ by using a sequence of triangles of length 1 followed by a sequence of triangles of length k (see Fig. 4(a)). Let Θ be the set of all constraints between all points involved in the construction where each constraint gives the exact basic relation between the points except for the relation between r and s which we set to $r\{0\}s$. In order to determine that Θ is inconsistent, it is necessary to map the points to a coordinate system or to count the relations which is impossible by trying to enforce k-consistency. Note that more than k variables are necessary in order to construct larger triangles of length k. For $m > 3$ an inconsistent set can be constructed in a similar way by making use of intermediate points on rational coordinates as shown in Figure 3(c). ∎

Note that the qualitative Star relations also depend on other geometrical laws such as the theorems of intersecting lines. The following example gives further indication that qualitative reasoning methods cannot be complete for Star calculi with $m \geq 3$.

Example 1. $\mathcal{A} = \mathcal{STAR}_4[0, 45, 90, 135](0)$ and $\mathcal{B} = \mathcal{STAR}_4[0, 45, 90, 110](0)$. Both calculi define 17 basic relations. Their composition and converse tables are identical. Let Θ be the set of constraints $A\{0\}B, A\{12\}C, C\{2\}B, C\{0\}D, B\{12\}D$ and let φ be the constraint $A\{14\}D$ (see Figure 4(b)). For both calculi Θ is consistent. $\Theta \cup \varphi$ is consistent for $\mathcal{A}$, but inconsistent for $\mathcal{B}$.

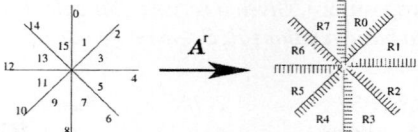

Fig. 5. The revised Star calculus $\mathcal{STAR}_4^r(0)$ obtained from $\mathcal{STAR}_4(0)$.

Despite the negative result of Theorem 2, CSPSAT($bas(\mathcal{A})$) is nevertheless tractable. It is just not possible to decide it with qualitative reasoning methods only, they only give approximate solutions to the consistency problem. It could be solved using quantitative methods such as expressing the constraints as a system of inequalities resulting from the algebraic semantics of the relations, or by combining qualitative reasoning methods with a coordinate system where intermediate results are entered, but this is outside the focus of this paper.

Since we are dealing with qualitative spatial representation and reasoning in this paper, we will in the following try to revise the Star calculus in a way which enables purely qualitative reasoning methods. In doing so, we will try to meet two important requirements for efficient qualitative reasoning over a particular calculus, namely, that tractable qualitative reasoning methods are sufficient for the set of basic relations of the calculus [9] and that all basic relations are contained in the tractable subsets of the calculus [11]. Since both requirements are not supported by the Star calculus, we have to define a revised version of the Star calculus which enables purely qualitative direction relations on arbitrary levels of granularity.

5 A Purely Qualitative Direction Calculus

Responsible for the high expressiveness of the Star calculus and for its ability to emulate a metric representation are the basic relations corresponding to the lines, i.e., the "*one-dimensional relations*". If these were eliminated or subsumed by new relations, it could be possible to obtain a sub-calculus of the Star calculus which allows for efficient qualitative reasoning. Removing the one-dimensional relations or adding them to both neighboring relations leads to relations which are not JEPD anymore. So we have to combine them with only one neighboring relation in order to obtain new basic relations. Since the resulting basic relations should be closed under converse, we have to combine them with either the preceding or the succeeding relations in clockwise order. We choose the first.

Definition 3 (revised Star calculus). *Given a Star calculus $\mathcal{A} \in \mathcal{STAR}_m$ for some $m \geq 2$ and its set of basic relations $bas(\mathcal{A}) = \{0, 1, \ldots, 4m-1, id\}$. The revised Star calculus $\mathcal{A}^r$ is the power set of the jointly exhaustive and pairwise disjoint set of relations $\mathcal{R} = \{R_0, R_1, \ldots, R_{2m-1}, id\}$ which is obtained from $bas(\mathcal{A})$ in the following way (see Figure 5): $R_i := \{2i+1, 2i+2\}$ for $0 \leq i \leq 2m-2$ and $R_{2m-1} := \{4m-1, 0\}$.*

The revised Star calculus consists of $2m + 1$ basic relations. The converse of a basic relation R_i can be computed by $R_i^{\smile} = R_j$ where $j = i + m \mod 2m$. While it is quite easy to guarantee that a system of relations is closed under the converse operator, it is much more difficult to show this for the composition operator. For the revised Star calculus the last composition rule of Prop. 2 is problematic, according to which the result of the composition of two basic relations is an open range. Therefore, the one-dimensional relations which are added to form basic relations of the revised Star calculus are removed again when computing composition, i.e., the revised Star calculus is not closed under composition. In order to fix this problem, we use *weak composition* [3], which is defined as the minimal relation which contains the actual composition, i.e., $R \circ_w S = \{T \mid T \cap (R \circ S) \neq \emptyset \text{ and } T \in bas(\mathcal{A})\}$. It is clear that the revised Star calculus is closed under converse, intersection and weak composition.

Proposition 4 (weak composition). *Given a revised Star calculus $\mathcal{A} \in \mathcal{STAR}_m^r$. The weak composition $R \circ_w S$ of two basic relations $R, S \in bas(\mathcal{A})$ can be computed as follows (again we have $R \circ_w S = S \circ_w R$):*

1. *If $R = id$, then $R \circ_w S = S$,*
2. *If $S = id$, then $R \circ_w S = R$,*
3. *If $R = S$, then $R \circ_w S = R$,*
4. *If $R = S^\smile$, then $R \circ_w S = \{*\}$,*
5. *Let X be the shortest distance between R and S, i.e., $(R + X) \bmod 2m = S$. If $X < m$, then $R \circ_w S = [R - S]$. If $X > m$, then $R \circ_w S = [S - R]$.*

For revised Star calculi weak composition differs from actual composition only for points located on the boundary of sectors of other points. If we can prove that for any consistent set of constraints, there exists a solution where no point lies on a sector boundary of other points, then weak composition can be used instead of composition for determining consistency.

Theorem 3. *Let Θ be a consistent set of constraints over a revised Star calculus $\mathcal{A}$. Then there is an instantiation of all variables in Θ with points of $\mathcal{P}$ such that no point is located on the boundary of a sector defined by another point.*

Proof Sketch. Let θ be a consistent instantiation of Θ. We can transform θ to an instantiation θ' such that no two points in θ' are located on each others sector bounding lines. We first compute the set of constraints Θ_θ over $bas(\mathcal{A})$ which hold between each pair of points in θ. Since Θ_θ is consistent, each point of θ lies in the intersection of the corresponding sectors of all other points. If the intersection forms an extended region and a point p is located at the boundary of it, then p is moved by $\epsilon > 0$ into the interior of the intersection. If the intersection is a line (segment), then there must be at least two points which are located on each others sector bounding line. If only two points are on the line, one can be moved by $\epsilon > 0$ into the interior of the others sector. If more than two points are on the line, the point which does not lie between two other points is moved first. In all cases, no two resulting points of θ' are located on each others bounding lines while all constraints are still satisfied. ∎

In order to determine tractable subsets of the revised Star calculus (the NP-completeness results of the Star calculus also hold for the revised calculus), we can make use of Helly's theorem [1]: "Let F be a finite family of at least $n+1$ convex sets in R^n such that every $n+1$ sets in F have a point in common. Then all the sets in F have a point in common." Applied to our case of two-dimensional space, it is necessary that any three convex sets have a point in common. Since any basic relation of the revised Star calculus (note: also any basic relation of the Star calculus!) is a convex set, any 4-consistent set of constraints Θ over the basic relations is consistent.[4] This is because of the definition of 4-consistency which states that for any consistent triple of variables of Θ a consistent instantiation of any fourth variable can be found. In this case the fourth point must be located in the intersection of the three sectors determined by the relations between each of the three points of the triple and the fourth point, which is the requirement for applying Helly's theorem. This holds for all "convex relations".

Definition 4 (convex relations). *Let $\mathcal{A}$ be a (revised) Star calculus. The set of convex relations $\mathcal{C}_\mathcal{A}$ consists of $\{*\}$ and of all relations of $\mathcal{A}$ which correspond to a range of consecutive basic relations which does not contain a basic relation and its converse: $\mathcal{C}_\mathcal{A} = \{[R \pm S] \mid R, S \in bas(\mathcal{A}), R^\smile, S^\smile \notin [R \pm S]\} \cup \{*\}$*

Theorem 4. *Any 4-consistent set of constraints Θ over the set of convex relations $\mathcal{C}_\mathcal{A}$ of a (revised) Star calculus $\mathcal{A}$ is consistent.*

---

[4] This is true for the Star calculus and for the revised Star calculus. In the following we write "(revised) Star calculus" if something applies to the Star calculus and to the revised Star calculus.

Since this theorem results from Helly's theorem, it is possible to compute an instantiation of Θ without backtracking by starting with three points and sequentially adding the other points in arbitrary order. For the Star calculus, this also applies to pre-convex relations (relations whose topological closure are convex relations) [5], while this concept is not applicable to the revised Star calculus. Unfortunately, this nice theorem is hardly useful for (revised) Star calculi $\mathcal{A} \in \mathcal{STAR}_m^{(r)}$ with $m \geq 3$. Not because it appears to contradict Theorem 2 (which it doesn't), but because 4-consistent sets are very rare and because it is not possible to enforce 4-consistency on every set of constraints over the (revised) Star relations, i.e., there are consistent sets of constraints for which there exists no corresponding 4-consistent set. Even for a revised Star calculus with $m = 3$, there are always consistent sets of constraints where not *all* consistent instantiations of three variables can be extended to a fourth variable: Consider the set of constraints involving the variables p, q, r, s in Figure 3(c). The set is clearly consistent, but when assigning $p = (0,0)$, $q = (0,1)$, and $s = (2,1)$ it is not possible to find a consistent instantiation for r, hence the set is not 4-consistent and cannot be made 4-consistent. In any case, we are mainly interested in consistency, i.e., whether *at least one* consistent instantiation exists. 4-consistency is too restrictive for that purpose. It turns out that the path-consistency method (also known as enforcing 3-consistency, see Section 4) is sufficient in some cases.

Theorem 5. *Given a revised Star calculus $\mathcal{A} \in \mathcal{STAR}_m^r$ with $m \leq 3$. Consistency of a set of constraints Θ over $bas(\mathcal{A})$ can be decided by the path-consistency method.*

Proof Sketch. Proof by induction over the number of variables n of Θ. It clearly holds for $n = 3$. Assume (a) that it holds for $n = k$. Given a path-consistent set Θ with $n = k+1$ variables $\mathcal{V} = \{v_1, \ldots, v_{k+1}\}$. The set $\Theta' \subset \Theta$ contains all constraints over the variables $\mathcal{V} \setminus \{v_{k+1}\}$, it is path-consistent and by assumption consistent. Θ is consistent if there is an instantiation θ' of Θ' such that all sectors of the points in θ' which are supposed to contain $\theta'(v_{k+1})$ have a non-empty intersection. Assume (b) that there is no such θ'. Because of Helly's theorem there must then be three variables v_i, v_j, v_l such that the corresponding sectors of $\theta'(v_i), \theta'(v_j), \theta'(v_l)$ do not have a common intersection. By a case analysis and a proof that the cases are the same for all possible angles of the given lines, we can show that for a Star calculus with $m \leq 3$ every path-consistent set of atomic constraints over four variables is always consistent, and, furthermore, that there is a subset of three variables such that for each consistant instantiation of the subset, there is always a consistent instantiation of the fourth variable. This fact (it is not because of assumption (a)) contradicts assumption (b). Therefore, there is a θ' which can be extended to a consistent instantiation θ of Θ. ∎

6 Applications

All real-world objects are three-dimensional extended entities rather than points, so many applications of qualitative spatial direction relations require calculi developed for more complex spatial entities than points. For these calculi, the Star calculus will definitely be an important basis. Nevertheless, there are also quite some applications where direction relations between points are necessary. Whenever the distance between two extended spatial entities is large relative to their extension, it is more convenient to treat them as point-like entities. Navigation tasks consider almost always point-like entities which have to be navigated from one location to another. For vehicles with automatic navigation devices it is possible to follow an exactly specified direction. When using "normal" vehicles like a car or when hiking, then it is not possible to follow an exact direction. Depending on the navigation tool which is available (if any), a direction can only be specified within a certain angular range. This is where the Star calculus turns out to be useful. It allows to use the finest granulation which can be distinguished by the user. Navigation assistance such as a route description can then be given in terms of Star relations, e.g., "go towards direction R_1 until landmark A can be seen in direction R_2, then turn to direction R_3 and go until..." As briefly described in this example, Star calculi can also be used to locate positions relative to the directions of landmarks, which is one possible qualitative spatial reasoning task. This kind of navigation and reasoning is particularly useful in the open field. A similar task is to reason about positions and routes relative to (cell phone) transmitters. The cells formed by a transmitter cover zones with different angles which can be exactly represented by a Star calculus. Another application is the automatic recognition and interpretation of route sketches. Depending on the precision with which this recognition should be obtained, the granularity of the Star calculus can be chosen. For all these applications revised Star calculi can be used instead of full Star calculi.

7 Discussion

Qualitative directions between points are at the heart of qualitative spatial representation and reasoning. Directions are one of the most important spatial aspect and directions between points are the basis for any calculus over more complex entities. Moreover, there is also a number of applications where directions are required between points. In this paper we proposed a class of direction calculi, the Star calculi, which are a generalization of several existing calculi for representing and reasoning about the qualitative direction between points in a plane. Although it is an important property of qualitative representations that the qualitative relations can be chosen on a level of granularity which is useful for a certain application, previous approaches did not offer the possibility of selecting basic relations on the desired level of granularity. Star calculi offer this possibility and they do so in an unrestricted way. Basic direction relations can be chosen on an arbitrary level of granularity. Star calculi can therefore be adopted to applications in an optimal way. We give general rules for computing composition and converse for the whole class of calculi. This enables us to apply the well-known qualitative reasoning methods. It turns out that Star calculi are so powerful that it is even possible to emulate coordinate systems. The disadvantage of this expressiveness is that qualitative reasoning methods cannot be complete for most Star calculi, but only provide approximate solutions to the reasoning problems. Developing complete reasoning algorithms is a matter of future research. We proposed a less expressive version, the revised Star calculi which do not contain relations corresponding to lines but only to two-dimensional sectors. We analyzed the computational properties and identified tractable subsets for certain classes of the revised calculus. Future work on revised Star calculi should analyze other classes, identify maximal tractable subsets and develop algorithms for finding consistent instantiations.

References

1. V. Chvatal. *Linear Programming*. W.H. Freeman and Company, 1983.
2. A. G. Cohn and S. M. Hazarika. Qualitative Spatial Representation and Reasoning: An Overview. *Fundamenta Informaticae*, 46(1-2):1–29, 2001.
3. I. Düntsch, H. Wang and S. McCloskey. A relation algebraic approach to the Region Connection Calculus. *Theoretical Computer Science*, 255:63–83, 2001.
4. A. Frank. Qualitative spatial reasoning about cardinal directions. In *Proc. ACAI'91*, p.157-167, 1991.
5. G. Ligozat. A new proof of tractability for Ord-Horn relations. In *Proc. AAAI'96*, p.715–720,1996.
6. G. Ligozat. Reasoning about cardinal directions. *J. of Vis. Languages & Computing*, 9:23–44, 1998.
7. A. K. Mackworth. Consistency in networks of relations. *Artificial Intelligence*, 8:99–118, 1977.
8. D. Mitra. Qualitative reasoning with arbitrary angular directions. In: *Proc. of AAAI'02 Workshop on Spatial and Temporal Reasoning*, 2002.
9. J. Renz. Maximal tractable fragments of the Region Connection Calculus: A complete analysis. In *Proc. IJCAI'99*, p.448–454, 1999.
10. J. Renz and B. Nebel. On the complexity of qualitative spatial reasoning: A maximal tractable fragment of the Region Connection Calculus. *Artificial Intelligence*, 108(1-2):69–123, 1999.
11. J. Renz and B. Nebel. Efficient methods for qualitative spatial reasoning. *JAIR*, 15:289–318, 2001.

Power of Brute-Force Search in Strongly-Typed Inductive Functional Programming Automation

Susumu Katayama

University of Miyazaki, Miyazaki 889-2155, Japan
skata@cs.miyazaki-u.ac.jp

Abstract. A successful case of applying brute-force search to functional programming automation is presented and compared with a conventional genetic programming method. From the information of the type and the property that should be satisfied, this algorithm is able to find automatically the shortest Haskell program using the set of function components (or library) configured beforehand, and there is no need to design the library every time one requests a new functional program.
According to the presented experiments, programs consisted of several function applications can be found within some seconds even if we always use the library designed for general use. In addition, the proposed algorithm can efficiently tell the number of possible functions of given size that are consistent with the given type, and thus can be a tool to evaluate other methods like genetic programming by providing the information of thebaseline performance.

1 Introduction

Strong typing is useful for sound programming because it provides constraints for identifying errors in programs at the compilation time. On the other hand, when using a strongly typed functional language like Haskell[3] one can exploit strong typing to enable random programming, that is, when we forget what function to put to some place in our program, we can just combine functions to obtain a type-consistent program that matches, put it there, and then it is often the case the program works correctly. The main topic of this paper is automation of this trial and error process.

Roughly speaking, the approach to construct a set of functions matching the requested type used in this research is doing the following in the breadth-first manner.

1. construct a set of functions whose return type matches the requested type, and
2. for the type of each argument of each function in the set, if ever, do the same thing recursively.

Without the type constraint, repeating that process until small number of depth causes the number of programs explode. However, as we shall see in Section 5, with type constraints the number of matching functions consisted of several functions is sometimes surprisingly small. Its analogy with the cases where doing search for future moves in playing deterministic board games like chess is interesting: because the number of interesting moves is limited by each situation, brute force search without highly heuristic approach like genetic programming can work well.

Strangely enough, while variations of exhaustive search seem successful in playing deterministic board games, in the recent literature I could not find attempts to apply exhaustive search to synthesis of general functions. As for heuristic methods there are some genetic programming approaches. The ADATE System[6] successfully invents some algorithms by using monomorphic, first-order type system and improving synthesized programs that are correct for some examples and incorrect for others. PolyGP[9] uses polymorphic, higher-order type system like the proposed method, and is discussed in Subsection 5.3 in more detail.

2 Foundations of Functional Programming

This section reviews some important ideas of the foundations of functional programming (e.g. [2]) in short, for readers who are not accustomed with them.

2.1 Lambda Calculus

Lambda calculus is a term rewriting system that is Turing-complete. It is itself a very simple functional language. In other words, functional languages are extensions of lambda calculus with syntactic sugars.

In lambda calculus, each variable is a function and can be passed as an argument. Function applications are expressed by just putting the function left-adjacent to its argument like $x\ y$, where y is applied to function x. They are left associative, i.e., $x\ y\ z$ means $(x\ y)\ z$.

$x\ y\ z$ can also be seen as applying two arguments to binary function x. In fact, the set of functions taking a pair of A and B and returning C is isomorphic to the set of functions taking A and returning a function taking B and returning C. This is how lambda calculus usually deals with n-ary functions, when the theory of lambda calculus itself only deals with unary functions.

Let E is a lambda expression (i.e. an expression in lambda calculus). Then the function taking argument variable x and returning E is written as $\lambda\ x.\ E$. Obtaining a function this way is called *lambda abstraction*. Lambda abstraction is a kind of quantification like $\forall$ and $\exists$. Here E may or may not include x. If x is not included in E, x is called *absent* parameter of $\lambda\ x.\ E$.

$\lambda\ x_1\ x_2\ \ldots\ x_n.\ E$ where E is an expression is a shorthand of $\lambda\ x_1.\ \lambda\ x_2.\ \ldots\ \lambda\ x_n.\ E$. This can be viewed as a function taking $x_1, x_2, \ldots, x_n$ as arguments and returning E.

2.2 Combinators

A closed lambda expression, or lambda expression where all the variables appearing is bounded by lambda abstraction is called a *combinator*. All the exported functions in modules in functional languages are combinators.

Some primitive combinators have their names: e.g. $\mathbf{S} = \lambda\ f\ g\ x.\ f\ x\ (g\ x)$ is called distributer and represents term sharing; $\mathbf{K} = \lambda\ x\ y.\ x$ is called cancellator and represents skipping an argument, and sometimes used in $\mathbf{K}\ E$ form to represent a constant function returning E; $\mathbf{I} = \mathbf{SKK} = \lambda\ x.\ x$ represents an identity function.

The set of functions constructed with function applications of **S**'s and **K**'s is Turing-complete. In other words, any computable recursive function can be constructed only with combinations of function applications. This is why we synthesize programs with only function applications in inductive functional programming automation algorithms including the proposed one and genetic programming.

2.3 Typed Lambda Calculus

So far I wrote about type-free lambda calculus and combinatory logic, but most modern functional languages are typed, and are based on typed lambda calculus.

In typed lambda calculus each expression is assigned a type. For example, since **K** takes an argument with a type, say, a and returns a function that takes an argument with another type b and returns a, the type of **K** is $\forall\, a\, b.\, a \rightarrow (b \rightarrow a)$. In this type a and b here are generic type variables that correspond to template type variables in C++, and $x \rightarrow y$ means the function type taking x as the argument and returns y. Because $\rightarrow$ is right-associative, $\forall\, a\, b.\, a \rightarrow (b \rightarrow a)$ can also be written as $\forall\, a\, b.\, a \rightarrow b \rightarrow a$, which intuitively reflects the fact that this function can be interpreted as a binary function taking type a and type b as arguments and returns a.

$E :: t$ means that the type of expression E is t. For example, $\mathbf{K} :: \forall ab.\, a \rightarrow b \rightarrow a$. Also, $\mathbf{S} :: \forall\, a\, b\, c.\, (b \rightarrow c \rightarrow a) \rightarrow (b \rightarrow c) \rightarrow b \rightarrow a$, and $\mathbf{I} :: \forall\, a.\, a \rightarrow a$.

One important fact in assigning types to lambda expressions and combinators is that some lambda expressions have infinite types which are usually prohibited in most typed functional languages. Especially, fixed point combinators which are used to implement recursions are defined with such prohibited subexpressions, and thus general recursions cannot be implemented only with **S** and **K** combinators. A common solution to this limitation is to regard a fixed point combinator $\mathit{fix} :: \forall\, a.\, (a \rightarrow a) \rightarrow a$ as yet another primitive combinator. This issue is discussed further in Subsection 4.2.

3 Implemented System

This section describes the specification and the implementation of the system, but as for the implementation here I provide only a sketch. The full detail of the implementation is written in [5].

3.1 Specification

The system reads a Haskell source file describing the available function set, which I call the *component library*. This algorithm constructs the shortest program with the given type satisfying the given property by combining functions in the component library. If the type is not provided, it is inferred from the property by using the conventional Hindley-Milner style type inference algorithm (e.g. [4]).

The current version of the algorithm can deal only with Hindley-Milner style type system, although Haskell extends it with ad hoc polymorphism or type classes. Also, in the experiments shown later I decided to prohibit functions in containers (such as list of functions, tuple of a function and something, etc.), because it is quite rare that such containers are required, and because by prohibiting them the efficiency improved in a great deal. I did that by introducing two kinds of type variables: one that can match functions and the other that cannot, and made the system identify each type variable.

3.2 System Structure

Figure 1 shows the structure of the implemented system.

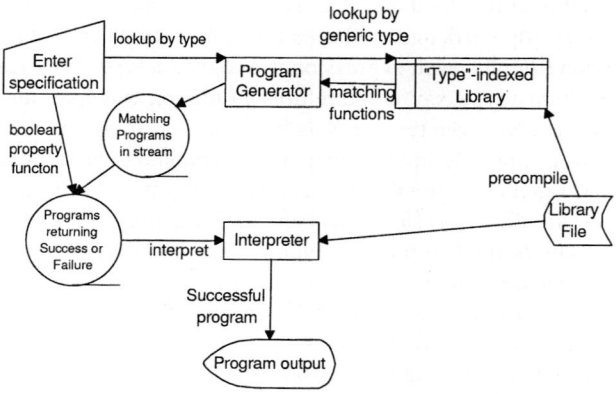

Fig. 1. System structure.

The system runs in the following way:

- when the program is invoked, the library is read to the interpreter and the library trie;
- the user-requested type and property are read; if the type is not provided, it is inferred by a conventional algorithm;
- the program generator returns the infinite set of programs that matches the requested type in the form of lazy infinite list (or stream) that is ordered by the program size;
- each generated program is applied to the property function as the argument, and the interpreter runs the resulting term, which is repeated until the return value is true (or success).

3.3 Program Construction

As written in the Introduction, the approach to construct a set of functions matching the requested type used in this research is essentially,

1. to construct a set of functions whose return type matches the requested type, and
2. to do the same thing recursively for the type of each argument of each function in the set, if ever,

in the breadth-first way instead of the depth-first way because the depth is infinite.

This can be achieved in the following way: let X be the infinite set of matching functions defined above, and

1. as a lazy list produce a subset of X that includes programs with size 1, and try each;
2. as a lazy list produce a subset of X that includes programs with size 2, and try each;
3. as a lazy list produce a subset of X that includes programs with size 3, and try each;
   ... and so forth.

Although this may look complicated, it can concisely be written in modern functional languages by using the monad for breadth-first search defined by Spivey[7][1].

Here I mention an optimization employed to reduce redundancy in the search space. If there is an expression that includes a subexpression $\mathbf{K}\ E_1\ E_2$, the subexpression can always be reduced to the shorter form E_1, and thus such an expression should always be tried beforehand, when trying shorter programs. The same thing applies to $\mathbf{I}\ E_1$. However, if there is a term sharing things are different, i.e., $\mathbf{S}\ E_1\ E_2\ E_3$ reduces to $E_1\ E_3\ (E_2\ E_3)$, and if E_3 is a long expression this reduction may yield a longer expression. Thus, we obtain the following general optimization rule: *always avoid reducible terms unless the head function duplicates a parameter*.

In the later presentation I write $(\rightarrow)\ a\ b$ instead of $a\ \rightarrow\ b$ if the parameter should not be given to this function when producing programs, or in other words, if supplying the parameter makes the term reducible and the parameter is not shared. The prefixed $(\rightarrow)$ has stronger fixity than the infixed $\rightarrow$.

4 Component Library Design

One easy way of designing the component library is to use **SK** plus fix plus constructors and case expressions (or destructors) for each data type. However, this naive way has some tasks that unnecessarily enlarge the search space. This section discusses the policy to design it to avoid unnecessary redundancy in the search space and at the same time to cover large class of functions, based on the results of preliminary experiments.

4.1 Avoiding Absent Parameters

$\mathbf{K} :: \forall\ a\ b.\ a\ \rightarrow\ b\ \rightarrow\ a$ enables absent parameters. On the other hand, if it is used in the component library of the proposed algorithm without any specialization, it causes the search space explode, because its return type a matches any requested type and its argument requests type b, which can match any expression, and thus the algorithm is forced to produce all the expressions without any type constraint as the second argument of $\mathbf{K} :: \forall\ a\ b.\ a\ \rightarrow\ b\ \rightarrow\ a$. Moreover, all the expressions produced in this way are ignored without being used because they are passed as absent parameters, totally wasting the complexity.

One approach to this problem is just to suppress the $\mathbf{K}\ E_1\ E_2$ pattern by defining the type of $\mathbf{K}$ as $\forall\ a\ b.\ a\ \rightarrow\ (\rightarrow)\ b\ a$ and use the optimization written in Section 3.3.

---

[1] Applying Spivey's monad (stream of finite lists) to my algorithm in a straightforward way causes extreme heap use, because some results of computation remains in the memory for later reuse. In order to avoid that by recomputation, in my implementation I used a function taking an integer and returning a finite list as the monad instead.

What follows shows another approach that avoids using **K**. This approach prevents simple programs from being filled up with many meaningless combinators, but requires many destructors for each data type.

If a function without any absent parameter is definable from **S** and **K**, it is provably definable without **K** by introducing the compositor
$\mathbf{B} = \lambda f\, g\, x.\, f\, (g\, x) :: \forall a\, b\, c.\, (c \to a) \to (b \to c) \to b \to a$ and the permutator $\mathbf{C} = \lambda f\, x\, y.\, f\, y\, x :: \forall a\, b\, c.\, (b \to c \to a) \to c \to b \to a$ as primitive combinators and using **S**, **B**, **C**, and **I**.

Note that without **K** more destructors have to be defined. For example, when the type of natural numbers Nat is defined with 0 and successor function s, if one may use **K**, only one destructor for Nat is enough, that is, $caseNat$ defined as follows:

$caseNat \qquad\qquad :: \forall a.\, a \to (Nat \to a) \to Nat \to a$
$caseNat\ x\ f\ 0 \quad\ = x$
$caseNat\ x\ f\ (s\ n) = f\ n$

By using $caseNat$ the function that doubles the argument is defined as $caseNat\ 0$ ($\mathbf{B}\ s\ s$), and the function that returns 0 if the argument is 0 and returns 1 ($=s\ 0$) otherwise can be defined as $caseNat\ 0\ (\mathbf{K}\ (s\ 0))$. However, the latter cannot be defined without **K**.

If **K** may not be used, adding $ifZero$ defined as

$ifZero \qquad\qquad :: \forall a.\, a \to a \to Nat \to a$
$ifZero\ x\ y\ 0 \quad\ = x$
$ifZero\ x\ y\ (s\ n) = y$

is enough. In general, defining for each argument (Nat, in the above case) of each function argument ($f :: Nat \to a$ in the above case) the version using the argument and that not using it should be enough. However, if there are n parameters this policy requires 2^n destructors, which may be a large amount for some data types. In the experiment in Section 5 I reduced the number by permitting **K** with less polymorphic type for some arguments. This issue requires more future discussion, though.

4.2 Fixed Point Combinator and Termination

The fixed point combinator fix is defined as $fix\ f = \mathbf{letrec}\ \{\, x = f\, x\,\}\,\mathbf{in}\, x$, and has type $\forall a.\, (a \to a) \to a$. It is used to implement general recursions. By applying the identity combinator $\mathbf{I} = \lambda x.\, x :: \forall a.\, a \to a$ to fix, we obtain an infinite loop $fix\ \mathbf{I} :: \forall a.\, a$ which matches any type, increasing the search space tremendously.

Again, one can use ($\to$) optimization to fix to solve the above problem. However, it is worth discussing whether we should use fix or not. Although a fixed point combinator makes typed lambda calculus Turing-complete, this means the program may not terminate. Thus, if you want to use fix in a search-based programming automation, you have to define timeout in the interpreter. On the other hand, there is a computer language called **Charity** which is designed always to terminate. Although it cannot implement interpreters for usual programming languages, it is still interesting because it has enough ability to implement total functions such as Ackermann's function that are not primitive recursions.

In the experiments in the next section I used paramorphism (e.g. [1]) for each data type instead of *fix* to obtain terminating programs.

4.3 Resulting Component Library

Based on the discussion so far, I coordinated the component library for the experiments as follows:

      — **Primitive combinators:**
S	$:: \forall a\, b\, c.\, (b \to c \to a) \to (b \to c) \to b \to a$
S	$= \lambda f\, g\, x.\, f\, x\, (g\, x)$
B	$:: \forall a\, b\, c.\, (c \to a) \to (b \to c) \to (\to)\, b\, a$
B	$= \lambda f\, g\, x.\, f\, (g\, x)$
C	$:: \forall a\, b\, c.\, (b \to c \to a) \to c \to (\to)\, b\, a$
C	$= \lambda f\, x\, y.\, f\, y\, x$
I	$:: \forall a.\, (\to)\, a\, a$
I	$= \lambda x.\, x$

      — **K***List* is a version of **K** specialized to ignore list parameters.

K*List*	$:: \forall a\, b.\, a \to (\to)\, [b]\, a$	— $[b]$ means list of b's.
K*List*	$= \lambda x\, y.\, x$	

      — **Natural number constructors:**
zero	$:: Int$
zero	$= 0$
successor	$:: Int \to Int$
successor	$= \lambda x.\, x + 1$

      — **Natural number destructors:**
paraNat	$:: \forall a.\, a \to (Int \to a \to a) \to Int \to a$
paraNat x f 0	$= x$
paraNat x f $(n+1)$	$= f\, n\, (paraNat\, x\, f\, n)$
cataNat	$:: \forall a.\, a \to (a \to a) \to (\to)\, Int\, a$
cataNat x f 0	$= x$
cataNat x f $(n+1)$	$= f\, (cataNat\, x\, f\, n)$
caseNat	$:: \forall a.\, a \to (Int \to a) \to (\to)\, Int\, a$
caseNat x f 0	$= x$
caseNat x f $(n+1)$	$= f\, n$
ifZero	$:: \forall a.\, a \to a \to (\to)\, Int\, a$
ifZero x y 0	$= x$
ifZero x y $(n+1)$	$= y$
predecessor	$:: (\to)\, Int\, Int$
predecessor 0	$= 0$
predecessor $(n+1)$	$= n$

      — **List constructors:**
nil	$:: [a]$	
nil	$= []$	— empty list
cons	$:: a \to [a] \to [a]$	
cons	$= \lambda x\, y.\, (x : y)$	— appends an element to a list.

— **List destructors:**

$$
\begin{aligned}
&paraList &&:: \forall\, a\, b.\ a \to (b \to [b] \to a \to a) \to [b] \to a \\
&paraList\ x\ f\ [] &&= x \\
&paraList\ x\ f\ (a:m) &&= f\ a\ m\ (paraList\ x\ f\ m) \\
&paraList' &&:: \forall\, a\, b.\ a \to ([b] \to a \to a) \to [b] \to a \\
&paraList'\ x\ f\ [] &&= x \\
&paraList'\ x\ f\ (a:m) &&= f\ m\ (paraList'\ x\ f\ m) \\
&caseList &&:: \forall\, a\, b.\ a \to (b \to [b] \to a) \to (\to)\,[b]\,a \\
&caseList\ x\ f\ [] &&= x \\
&caseList\ x\ f\ (a:m) &&= f\ a\ m \\
&caseList' &&:: \forall\, a\, b.\ a \to ([b] \to a) \to (\to)\,[b]\,a \\
&caseList'\ x\ f\ [] &&= x \\
&caseList'\ x\ f\ (a:m) &&= f\ m \\
&head &&:: \forall\, a.\ (\to)\,[a]\,a \qquad\text{— CAR in lisp} \\
&head\ (a:m) &&= a \\
&tail &&:: \forall\, a.\ (\to)\,[a]\,[a] \qquad\text{— CDR in lisp} \\
&tail\ (a:m) &&= m
\end{aligned}
$$

Note that the same component library is used for all the experiments.

5 Experiments

5.1 Task Description

This section presents results from experiments of composing the following functions:

- $nth :: Int \to [a] \to a$ satisfying
  $nth\ 5$ "$widjfgwi$" $==$ 'f' and $nth\ 1$ "$wddidjfgwi$" $==$ 'w',
- $map :: (b \to a) \to [b] \to [a]$ satisfying
  $f\ (\lambda\, c.\ c ==\ 'c')$ "$stock$" $==$ [False, False, False, True, False] and
  $f\ (\lambda\, c.\ c ==\ 'e')$ "$peeped$" $==$ [False, True, True, False, True, False]
- $length :: [a] \to Int$ satisfying f "$hageho$" $== 6$ and f "$hoge$" $== 4$

Correct answers for those tasks are:

$$
\begin{aligned}
nth &= \mathbf{B}\ (cataNat\ head\ (\mathbf{C}\ \mathbf{B}\ tail))\ predecessor \\
map &= \mathbf{B}\ (paraList\ nil)\ (\mathbf{B}\ (\mathbf{C}\ (\mathbf{K}list\ cons))) \\
length &= paraList'\ 0\ (\mathbf{K}list\ successor)
\end{aligned}
$$

In all the tasks the proposed method successfully produced the correct program.

5.2 Results

All the experiments were run on a Pentium4 2.00GHz machine. I used the Glasgow Haskell Compiler ver. 6.2 on Linux 2.4.22, with the -O optimization flag.

Table 1 shows the computation time of the proposed method in seconds. Here I provide the minimum and the maximum of three runs. Note that they do not and should not differ in a great deal between runs, because the algorithm is deterministic.

Table 1. Computation time (sec.) of the proposed method, and the number of type consistent unsuccessful programs tried.

	nth	map	length
min/max of three runs (real)	4.43/4.52	1.59/1.62	0.026/0.044
(user)	4.29/4.37	1.57/1.58	0.010/0.030
# of programs tried until success	619	0	17

Note that all the experiments finished within seconds. This fact suggests some utility in everyday programming.

It is interesting that the number of type-consistent programs until the correct one is found is within hundreds. Table 2 shows the number of possible programs matching each requested type, ordered by the program size.

Table 2. Number of type-consistent programs for each size.

size	1	2	3	4	5	6	7	8
nth	0	0	2	2	40	113	1027	4626
map	0	0	0	0	0	0	2	7
length	0	1	1	18	29	415	1632	14126

5.3 Comparison with Genetic Programming Approach

PolyGP [9] is a genetic programming algorithm that generates type-consistent Haskell programs in the Hindley-Milner type system. It is a pioneering work that for the first time focused on the Hindley-Milner system to moderately limit the search space in inductive programming automation.

Success rate. Unlike my approach presented here, PolyGP is a genetic programming algorithm, and thus it may be unable to find a correct program forever, depending on the initial population. According to [8], 4 of 10 runs for nth and 3 of 10 runs for map are successful. Also, all the successful cases of nth found a correct program within 12000 programs, and those of map found one within 35000. On the other hand, my program always succeeds.

Computation time. Because the original code is not efficient, I applied some optimization and ran it in the environment described at the beginning of Subsection 5.2.

The computation time of PolyGP for map task trying 35000 programs spanned from 31.5 sec to 33.7 sec when I tried 10 runs.

Requirements. PolyGP requires the user to design the fitness function to reflect how good the program behaves. For nth task this is designed by the difference between the integer argument and the actual position of the returned character, and for map task this is the difference in length and contents between the expected output list and the actual list. Programming those fitness functions can sometimes require more labor than programming the target functions such as nth and map.

Also, experiments of PolyGP in [8] use different library for each task, which my algorithm does not require.

One point we should remember is that using different component libraries between different algorithms can make comparisons unfair, because, to consider an extreme case, if the function that is searched for is included in the library it is easy to find it. On the other hand, we should evaluate algorithms under useful conditions in order to obtain informative results. In Section 4 I tried to show that the library is reasonably selected. In addition, I used a common library throughout the experiments to show that it is general, which condition is more pragmatic.

6 Conclusions

A system that generates a shortest type-consistent functional program that satisfies the given property by breadth-first exhaustive search is presented and evaluated. Although the tasks might be too easy for evaluation, I guess the system is still useful when, for example, programming overnight and our mind does not work well, provided the computer answers within seconds.

Also, this paper shows that with an appropriate component library the number of type-consistent programs can be surprisingly small. It is interesting that under strongly-typed environment there seems not to have existed brute-force approaches to inductive programming automation in recent literature (and thus with recent CPU power), although there exist heuristic approaches like genetic programming which may be overkill. I do not think exhaustive search methods can universally be applied to synthesis of large programs, but trying the simplest method before inventing heuristic ones and comparing them might be one good research policy.

References

1. Augusteijn, L.: Sorting Morphisms. Advanced Functional Programming, LNCS 1608 (1999) 1–27
2. Field, A. J., Harrison, P. G.: Functional Programming. Addison Wesley (1988)
3. Hudak, P., Fasel, J. H.: A gentle introduction to Haskell. SIGPLAN Notices **27**(5) (1992) T1–T53
4. Jones, M. P.: Typing Haskell in Haskell. Proc. of the 1999 Haskell Workshop (1999)
5. Katayama, S.: Implementing a breadth-first search algorithm for strongly typed inductive functional programming. submitted to The 2004 International Conference on Functional Programming
6. Olsson, R.: Inductive Functional Programming Using Incremental Program Transformation. Research report 189, Doctor scientiarum thesis, University of Oslo, (1994)
7. Spivey, M.: Combinators for breadth-first search. J. Functional Programming **10**(4) (2000) 397–408
8. Yu, T.: Polymorphism and genetic programming. Proc. of Fourth European Conference on Genetic Programming (2001)
9. Yu, T., Clack, C.: PolyGP: A polymorphic genetic programming system in Haskell. Genetic Programming 1998: Proc. of the Third Annual Conference (1998) 416–421

Ontology Services-Based Information Integration in Mining Telecom Business Intelligence

Longbing Cao[1], Chao Luo[2], Dan Luo[2], and Li Liu[1]

[1] Faculty of Information Technology, University of Technology, Sydney, Australia
[2] Department of Electronics and Information, Liaoning Technical University, China
{lbcao,liliu}@it.uts.edu.au, {chao.luo,dan.luo}@mail.ia.ac.cn

Abstract. Ordinary implementation of mining telecom business intelligence (BI) is to simply pack data warehouse (DW), OLAP and data mining engines together. In practice, this type of system cannot adapt to changing or new requirements emergent in the problem domain. As a result of survey, 85% of DW projects failed to meet their intended objectives. In this paper, an internal linkage and communication channel, namely an ontology service-based match and translation among user interface, DW, and enterprise information systems, is developed, which implements unified naming and directory of ontology services, metadata management and rule generation for ontology mapping and query parsing among conceptual view, analytical view and physical view from top down. A system prototype on top of realistic telecom environment shows that our intelligence integration solution presents much stronger power to deal with operational decision making user-friendly and adaptively compared with those simply combining BI products available from vendors.

1 Introduction

Mining telecom business intelligence is a complicated process [1]. In this activity, the following procedures must be done: (i) building a DW system on top of Enterprise Information Systems (EIS) running in telecom industry, (ii) supporting four-level data analyses in realistic enterprise environment, and finally (iii) providing and delivering customers of BI system with a flexible and adaptive knowledge portal seamlessly and dynamically, which integrates EIS, DW, OLAP and Data Mining (DM).

As a matter of fact, business requirements of operational analysis and internal structures of underlying EIS are always dynamically realistic. However, almost all ordinary solutions, which have been or are transferred from system integrators of BI to users, are prone to provide users with subjects, data models, analytical dimensions and measures predefined in design time. As a result, most established BI systems cannot adapt to changing or new requirements emergent in the problem domain daily. 85% of DW projects failed to meet their intended objectives, and 40% didn't even get off the ground [2]. A fundamental reason for the above failure is the poor integration of information distributed among DW, OLAP and DM engines. Simple packing cannot support dynamically analytical requirements and run-time intelligence mining flexibly and adaptively in the real world.

In this paper, we mainly report some of our explorations in constructing an internal linkage and communication channel for information integration from underlying operational systems. We build an ontology services-based integration infrastructure, which implements unified naming, directory and transport of ontology services, and ontology mapping and query parsing among conceptual view, global view and physical view from business interfaces through DW to EIS. This work is from our activities in building telecom BI system by integrating DW, OLAP, DM and reporting systems commercially available. Our experiments in the real world of telecom industry have shown that it can support online and interactive integration of the above mentioned four modules, rather than simply packing together. It can provide users with development supports for adapting to new and dynamic requirements and changes user-friendly and flexibly.

2 Ontology Service Representation

Before going ahead with describing the ontology service-based integration of DW, OLAP and DM, we need to clarify some basic concepts and representations which are essential in defining integration mechanisms based on ontology services[3,4].

Definition 1 Ontology Relationship ($\mathcal{P}$, r): An ontology relationship defines relations existing between two ontologies. An ontology relationship r could be an instance of set of relations $\mathcal{P}$. In our project[5], we define the following elements in $\mathcal{P}$: Identical, Aggregate, Generalize, Substitute, Disjoin, Overlap, and Associate. We further distinguish and relate two or more ontologies with the following predicates: *same_as*, *part_of*, *is_a*, *equal_to*, *disjoin_to*, *overlap_to*, and *relate_to*. Table 1 shows details about ontology relationships.

Table 1. Ontology relationships

Relations	Description	Predicates
Identical	When the two ontologies O1 and O2 are identical	*same_as*
Aggregate	When ontology O2 is part of ontology O1	*part_of*
Generalize	When ontology O2 is a kind of O1	*is_a*
Substitute	When ontology O2 is equal to O1	*equal_to*
Disjoin	When O2 and O1 have no share in common	*disjoin_to*
Overlap	When O2 and O1 have partial share	*overlap_to*
Associate	When O2 is related to O1 in a relation except of the above six	*relate_to* or user-defined associating predicates

Example 1 The following expression shows that ontology Billing consists of LocalBilling and RemoteBilling, while Localbilling and Remotebilling is in Disjoin.
part_of(Billing, *disjoin_to*(LocalBilling, RemoteBilling))

Definition 2 Ontology Organizational Structure Type ($\mathcal{T}$, τ): An ontology organizational structure type τ consists of many ontology elements linked in some relationships. It is a value element of set of types $\mathcal{T}$ which covers all possible ontology organizational structure types. Some main ontology hierarchy, for instance, Hierarchical,

Egalitarian, and Hybrid [6,7], can be found in telecom EIS like billing system, operational and maintenance system and so forth.

Definition 3 Ontology Service Item Atom: An ontology service is defined by set of items of attributes and their relationships, which are represented in Key Value Tuples (KVT); all attribute items are embodied and extended from item atoms. An item atom is a basic unit which defines a type of attribute the ontology service must hold, and can be expressed in form as $<\mathcal{A}>k : v<\backslash\mathcal{A}>$.

All keys defined in the infrastructure are drawn from a universal namespace, which is extracted and defined by us according to the reality and requirements of analyses in telecom, and encloses complexities in DW, DM and EIS. The pair-element denotes a name in a hierarchical namespace following some type of relationship, where a first token in the tuple is at the highest level in the hierarchy and the rightmost is the leaf.

Definition 4 Ontology Service Description: Following basic item atoms are constituent attributes of an ontology service: <ST>k : v <\ST> is a service type item atom, <SL>k : v<\SL> is a locator item atom, <I>k : v<\I> is an input item atom, <IC>k : v<\IC> is a precondition atom which defines constraints on service, <O>k : v<\O> is an output item atom, the item <IO>k : v<\IO> define constraints across inputs and outputs, <OC>k : v<\OC> is postcondition item of service. Furthermore, each item atom may have a list of items, which is called Item List[8]. For instance, an item list of j inputs is a list of j (j ≥ 1) items as <I>k1:v1, k2:v2, ..., kj:vj<\I>.

For each item atom in a service, there may be some mandatory items and other optional ones. Multiplicity of constraint properties of items can be found in our case, like *MO*: Mandatory One, *MM*: Mandatory Many, *OO*: Optional One, *OM*: Optional Many.

Example 2 The following is service description for the DMAlgorithmRegistration ontology, which registers a globally unique decision tree algorithm with three mandatory inputs and one optional algorithm creating date. All inputs and outputs of the algorithm are separated by semicolons and stored into array in Java, and generates one new decision tree class if registration is successful. A token $/\mathcal{O}$ is marked at the end of all optional items.

    <OS> register: algoid(datamining)
        <ST>Type: DecisionTree<\ST>
        <SL>LocationID: ioas. algorithm.datamining.algoid<\SL>
        <I>Name:String,InputString:StringArray,OutputString:StringArray,Date: Calender/O<\I>
        <IC>InputString: semicolon, OutputString: semicolon<\IC>
        <O>Algo_class: DecisionTreeClass<\O>
        <OC>Status: successful<\OC>
        <IO>Relation: one-one<\IO>
    <\OS>

Accordingly, we can define some basic ontology services (as partially shown in Table 2) needed in the integration of DW, OLAP, DM and reporting system in telecom industry.

Table 2. Partial ontology services

Ontology Service	Verb	Noun-term
SubjectAddition	create	subjectid(serviceroot_subject)
DimensionUpdate	update	dimid(serviceroot_dimension)
MeasureDeletion	delete	measureid(serviceroot_measure)
DMAlgorithmRegistration	register	algoid(algorithmtype)
DMAlgorithmUpdate	update	algoid(algorithmtype)
DMAlgorithmExecution	execute	algoid(algorithmtype)
OntologySearch	search	ontologyid(serviceroot_ontology)

3 Ontology Integration of Business, Data Warehouse and EIS

Our major objective of heterogeneous information translation and integration includes: (i) providing transparent and seamless integration of the underlying heterogeneous resources among telecom operational systems, (ii) supporting smooth transformation from business concepts in user interface to low-level entities in specific resource systems, and (iii) furnishing online interactive techniques for transparent interoperability and smooth translation among levels.

3.1 Ontology Match and Translation Structure

As an approach for overcoming heterogeneity, ontology has been widely investigated and used for explicit description of information in heterogeneous resources. In summary, there are three ways of deploying ontologies: single ontology approach, multiple ontology approach and hybrid ontology approach[6]. It is believed that hybrid ontology approach can overcome drawbacks of single and multiple ontology approaches [6, 7]. However, there is still lot of research work on how to build a hybrid ontology infrastructure for integrating domain specific heterogeneous resources, from business to DW to underlying EIS.

In the process of integrating heterogeneous and distributed information from data sources, we proposed an ontology structure as shown in Figure 1. There are three views coexisted in this ontology system from top down: a top-level conceptual view,

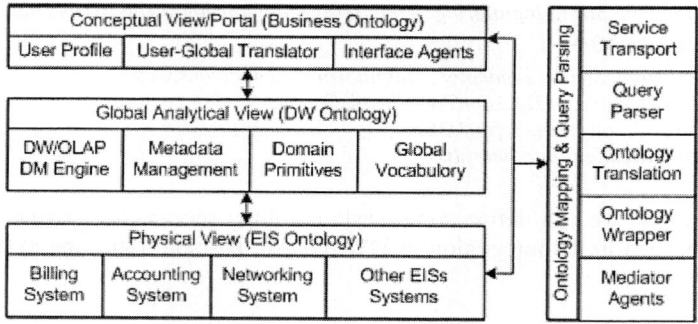

Fig. 1. Ontology match and translation

an analytical view, and a low-level EIS view. A mediator level is built for ontology mapping and query parsing among three levels. A universal namespace, a representation of ontology services, and ontology mapping and query parsing are introduced for uniquely naming, resolving, identifying and transporting ontologies and their relations among levels. In addition, KVT/ Key Value Pairs (KVP) and Key Property Pairs (KPP, here Property is used to define cardinality of an entity) are utilized for describing ontology naming, directory, location and transport services.

3.2 Top-Level Conceptual View

The objective of Conceptual View is to present users with domain specific concepts, objects, business rules, and user interfaces in a conceptual profile user-friendly. The ontologies capture general knowledge about concepts, terminology and relationships from viewpoint of business in the world.

The output of this view is a conceptual ontology base, which includes a Concept Category Directory (CCD). The CCD, which is a hierarchical concept tree implementing telecom business namespace, lists and defines all terms and relationships abstracted in daily business, and generates a list of candidate concepts and expressions based on the business process and activities happened in the user views. Here, a concept rather than an attribute or entity is used to describe the world. For instance, *Conditions...* rather than *Where...* is used in generating a query.

Definition 5 Concept Category Directory Entry: A CCD entry consists of a unique Leading Item (LI, an identifier), and optionally multiple Substitute Items (SI, recommended candidate concepts) as follows:

{{{*Leading Item, MO*}:{*LI_Value*}},{{*Substitute Items, OM*}:{*SI_Value1, SI_Value2,...*}}},

for instance:

{{{*LI_Service_Provider*}:{*Service_Provider_Label*}},{{*SI_Service_Provider*}:{*Service_Provider_Name,Service_Provider_Nickname,Service_Provider_Description*}}}.

3.3 Global Analytical View

The Global Analytical View is a logical aggregated representation of underlying logical elements and relationships locating in DWs, OLAP server and DM engines. So, in terms of domain specific primitives in telecom information systems, this global side ontology wraps technical and business metadata items. These metadata items are defined in set of elements (attributes, dimensions and measures) in data model, source data, ETL, and also actions and rules of interaction between DW and data sources.

Definition 6 Analytical Ontology Directory Entry: It consists of some domain-specific metadata items, which focuses on business and technical metadata required in the problem domain, rather than on business rules and concepts. The following elements are enclosed in it: globally unique identifier(gui), recommended global name(rgn), candidate substitute names(csn), parent object(po, top-level coupled concept name), child objects (co, low-level EIS instances), analytical locator(al, where to find this entry from the bottom EIS resources, including related connection string, schema, metadata of resources, and so forth), close associators (ca, including actions and relationships with other neighboring entries). Furthermore, the cardinality property of an entry is shown in the following:

$$\{\{gui, MO\}, \{rgn, MO\}, \{csn, OM\}, \{po, MO\}, \{co, MM\}, \{al, MO\}, \{ca, OM\}\}$$

All item atom entries are stored into knowledge base and registered into ontology name database. The usage of KVT, KPP, the Pair-Element encoding system, and the introduction of elements *parent* and *child, locator* and *associators,* can solve conflicts of data type, scaling, generalization, naming and location.

Furthermore, in order to build this orderly aggregated analytical level, a metadata management mechanism is necessary and built-in for organizing data model of DW, OLAP and DM engines. It also encloses information about bottom resource primitives, data connections, resource locations, and services and queries distributions.

3.4 Low-Level Physical View Ontology

The Low-level Physical View is a representation of physical entities and relationships related to transactions among underlying information systems. The most common form of Physical View is as tables and attributes located in EIS. EIS enclose multiple enterprise information resources in which store huge amount of operational data and information. On this level, telecom operational systems like BOSS, MIS, ERP, OA are all resource providers of the DW and DM system.

In terms of technical implementation, the multiplicity of this level also brings us a colorful world of physical instances/attributes/relations and so forth. For instance, the counterpoints of *Customer_Name* on user conceptual view, may take names as *Customer_Name, Customer_Label, User_Name, User_Label* etc. in physical systems(Figure 2). These names may be distributed into the following business operational systems like billing system, accounting system, switch system, operation and maintenance system, etc.

4 Ontology Mapping and Query Parsing

The objective of this level is to construct a set of mediation services which implement online ontology mapping and management among top-level concepts, global metadata items and low-level resource attributes. It also implements query parsing from concept-oriented query requests in user interfaces to DW elements, EIS attributes and relations-based query statement in the bottom.

4.1 Ontology Mapping Among User View, Global View and Physical View

Ontology mapping first implements match between user view in concepts and global view in elements and relationships, then transports user requests from global to low-level physical view in concrete attributes existing in information resources.

Figure 2 shows principle we cope with the above three-level match. As described above, three-level views are separated for specific requirements of different levels. The above ontology representation is used to organize elements on each level.

As mentioned before, for each record of conceptual ontology, the unique Leading Item (actor) may have 0 to many Substitute Items (stand-ins). For instance, a leading item of *Customer_Name* may have many stand-ins, for instance, *User_Name, User_Label, Customer_Label*, and so forth. After fixing the mapping from concepts to DW elements and EIS attributes, owners of BI system can define or update itemsets as they have or like by interfaces.

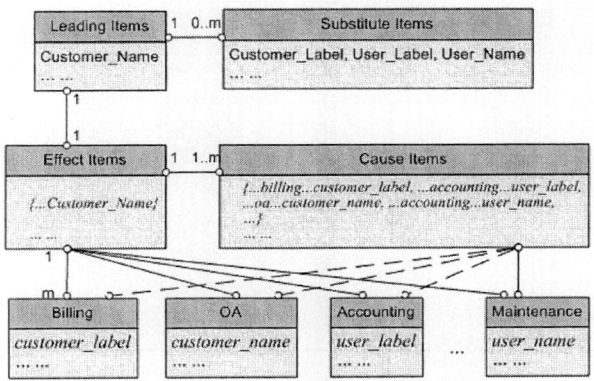

Fig. 2. Ontology mapping

In the global analytical view, there are many Cause-Effect pairs there. For each element of global ontology, there is only one Effect Item, which uniquely identifies a metadata item of global view on the basis of DW models. This Effect Item wraps related element in data model of DW and data marts. On the other side, one to many concrete instances/attributes/relations compose the corresponding Cause Items (as shown in the following pair elements), which are exactly some specific instances, attributes, what we would see in respective EIS and data sources on the low level.

{{Effect Item, MO}, {Cause Items, OM}}

It is noteworthy that here all naming of ontology elements on the high level and the physical level are in the same namespace, level-oriented ontology directories, and based on the same serviceroot. Moreover, an ontology name database is built to manage the naming and labeling, resolving and match of logical name and physical name of ontologies on different levels. A user interface module is developed to deal with activities of Insert, Delete, Modify and Query the logical and physical names of the ontologies in the name database.

4.2 Query Parsing Process

Query processing is defined by parsing rules. A query parsing rule can be generated automatically by selecting metadata items, defining relations (by predefined predicates) among ontology and metadata items, setting limit conditions (constraints) for relevant items and attributes, and grouping and sorting where appropriate.

An interactive module (as shown in Figure 3) is developed to support online definition and generation of query rules on the basis of metadata management. This module not only arranges the translation and integration among conceptual level, DW level and physical level, but also covers metadata items of underlying source data, for instance, ETL rules, and mapping from EIS to concepts directly.

Here, the Relations toolbar is in charge of ontology and metadata relationship management. Limit Condition is used to set constraint property among items. Grouping and Sorting are for arranging items in group or sorting in ascending or descending directions.

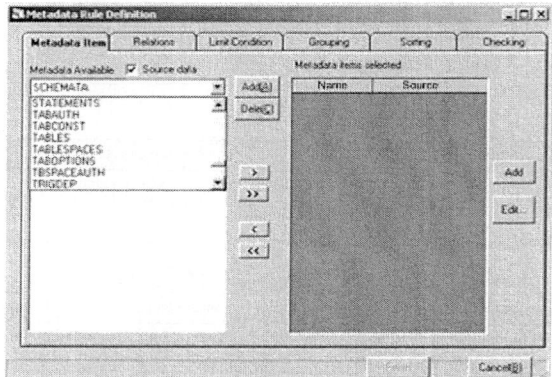

Fig. 3. Interactive query rule generation

As a prerequisite, some modules are developed for construction, registration and maintenance of ontologies and metadata items. Predicates of ontology relationships can be invoked from user interface of ontology construction to define relations among ontologies. Ontology naming and index are managed from ontology registration module and further stored into ontology name database and knowledge base.

5 Case Study: A Prototype for Intelligence Integration in Telecom

According to what we have discussed in the above sections, we have constructed a business intelligence prototype system called IOAS[5]. It has integrated DW server, OLAP server, DM engine on top of realistic business and data in mobile telecom, and formed a unified knowledge portal for enterprise decision making. Figure 5 presents some screen shots of this system.

In the IOAS, IBM DB2 Universal database is used as database server, DB2 Data Warehouse and Oracle OLAP server stores six subjects and six special subjects, Cognos is used for OLAP, ad hoc and predefined reporting presentation, IBM Intelligent Miner mines business intelligence from huge amount of telecom data. Under the IOAS, Informix, Oracle, Sybase, DB2 are used in telecom business operational systems for storage of respective operational transactions.

To users, complexities from multiple heterogeneous information resources, ETL tools, Operational Data Store system, DW system, presentation reports and tools, are shielded and hidden under the one-stop interface. They can easily launch analysis and observations without worries of underlying heterogeneity, symbolization, authorization and information management from DW to bottom data sources.

Fig. 4. Case study: IOAS integrating business intelligence in telecom

6 Performance Evaluation

Compared with solutions simply combining BI products presently available from vendors, our ontology services-based approach presents much stronger power for information integration user-friendly and flexibly from the following aspects:

(1) The integration of analyses, DW, OLAP and DM is not by simple addition on the basis of a reporting system, rather through an internal ontology service-based linkage and communication channel. This three-level hybrid ontology schema sets up some internal mechanisms for supporting ontology mapping, query parsing among business concepts, analysis models and physical entities.
(2) Some user-friendly development supports help users to modify, update, create or re-arrange ontologies and functionalities on different levels in terms of problem domain and requirements. Thus, users can arrange their own three-level ontology base and ontology namespace as required adaptively without modifying the match relations. Again, the metadata management tool helps users to maintain and match ontology mapping and query parsing in terms of their interests.
(3) Representation and directory of ontology services, combined with others like metadata rule definition, support structural and semantic transparency in dealing with the heterogeneity and interoperability among domain specific levels.

Technically, our solution by providing internal location, directory, mediation and transport supports can help BI system users enhance their own capabilities in dealing with changing or new environment flexibly and adaptively in a user-friendly manner.

7 Conclusions and Future Works

In this paper, we studied how to integrate information among reporting, DW, OLAP and DM engines beyond realistic telecom business operational systems. We introduced a three-tier ontology infrastructure implementing transparency from business concepts to underlying EIS. Uniform namespace, ontology representation, and metadata management are used to define, locate and transport ontology elements among three views. An ontology mapping is designed to transparently associate relevant ontologies with Conceptual, Global and Physical Views. Interactive rule generation supports dynamic information translation and query parsing among low-level attributes, metadata items, and concepts-based business profiles.

We further built a BI system prototype on the basis of realistic mobile telecom operational systems and historical data. It has shown that it is more user-friendly, flexible and adaptive for telecom customers to online mine business intelligence from huge amount of business transactions, than simple packing those BI components.

Our future works include but are not limited to the follows:

(1) Representation and deployment of FIPA-compatible ontology services;
(2) Increasing adaptability and run-time working power to deal with dynamically evolutionary business environment and decision-making requirements.

References

[1] Mark Whitehorn, *Business intelligence: the IBM solution*, New Springer, 1999.
[2] Usama M. Fayyad. Tutorial report of Summer school of data mining. Monash Uni, 2003.
[3] FIPA. FIPA0006 and FIPA0086.
[4] Hiroki Suguri et al. Implementation of FIPA Ontology Service.
[5] Longbing Cao, Dan Luo, Chao Luo, Chengqi Zhang. Systematic engineering in designing architecture of telecommunications business intelligence system. *Proceedings of HIS'03*, 1084-1093, IOS press, 2003.
[6] H. Wache, et al. Ontology-based integration of information – a survey of existing approaches. 2001. From webster.cs.uga.edu/~budak/ courses/s02/nis/Survey-2.ppt.
[7] Zhang cui, Dean Jones and Paul O/Brien. Issues in ontology-based information integration. www.csd.abdn.ac.uk/ebiweb/papers/cui.pdf.
[8] Cheng Hian Goh. *Representing and Reasoning about Semantic Conflicts in Heterogeneous Information Sources*. Phd, MIT, 1997.

Indexing Approach for Delivery Demands with Time Constraints

Naoto Mukai[1], Jun Feng[2], and Toyohide Watanabe[1]

[1] Department of Systems and Social Informatics,
Graduate School of Information Science, Nagoya University
Furo-cho, Chikusa-ku, Nagoya, 464-8603, Japan
naoto@watanabe.nuie.nagoya-u.ac.jp
watanabe@nuie.nagoya-u.ac.jp
[2] Department of Information Engineering,
Graduate School of Engineering, Nagoya University
Furo-cho, Chikusa-ku, Nagoya, 464-8603, Japan
feng@watanabe.nuie.nagoya-u.ac.jp

Abstract. Demand-bus system is focused as a new transportation system. Dynamic Vehicle Routing Problem with Time Windows (DVRPTW) we address is a simple environment model for demand-bus system. In the problem, delivery demands with time constraints occur enduringly. Share-ride vehicles transport customers to their destination. In order to solve this problem, we propose CRTPR-Tree which indexes moving vehicles on a road network. A node of the tree consists of a pointer to vehicle (in leaf nodes) or pointers to child nodes (in intermediate nodes), a bounding rectangle, and a time constraint. Moreover, we propose two scheduling algorithms based on time traveling measure (TTM) or time constraint measure (TCM) for delivery orders of customers. We performed experiments with the profitability and the usability on an ideal environment. The experimental results show that our approach produces good effects.

1 Introduction

Traffic congestion is a serious problem in urban area. Traditional traffic system such as fixed bus system is one of the causes of the traffic congestion. Recently, a new transportation system called Demand-bus system, in which customers can choose their ride-on and drop-off positions freely, is focused by traffic companies. The profitability and usability of the system should be analyzed for adapting a wide community in the viewpoint of business.

Demand-bus system is modeled at differently simulated levels as follows. The problem of minimizing the total traveling cost of vehicles, which is called the Vehicle Routing Problem (VRP), has already been addressed in [1, 2]. In VRP, all delivery demands of customers are given as initial conditions before the vehicles start out from their depot. Each vehicle visits the customers and transports to their destinations. The VRP with time-windows constraints of customers (i.e., a customer must be serviced within a time limit), which is called the vehicle routing problem with time-windows (VRPTW), was studied in [3–6]. Central issues to be solved for the problem are "which vehicles are assigned to customers" and "how delivery orders for customers are scheduled". Most of approaches for VRPTW are based on heuristic algorithms such as simulated annealing or genetic algorithm for solving assigning and scheduling.

In our problem, which is called Dynamic Vehicle Routing Problem with Time Windows (DVRPTW), delivery demands with a time constraint occur while vehicles travel enduringly in contrast to VRP or VRPTW. It is difficult to solve the problem in such time-varying environment by the existing approaches based on heuristic algorithms because of their time complexities In order to solve our DVRPTW, we propose CRTPR-Tree for assigning and two scheduling methods based on time traveling measure (TTM) or time constraint measure (TCM) for scheduling. CRTPR-Tree based on TPR-Tree which is a fundamental indexing structure for moving objects. A node of CRTPR-Tree consists of three components: a pointer to a vehicle (in leaf nodes) or pointers to child nodes (in intermediate nodes), a bounding rectangle, and a time constraint. The form of the bounding rectangle depends on the position of the vehicle, road network constraints (i.e., reachable regions of vehicles), and riding and dropping positions of assigned customers. The time constraint is based on the time limit of customers (i.e., whether the customer could arrive his destination within his expectation time or not).

The remainder of this paper is as follows: the formulation of DVRPTW is described in Section 2. Section 3 defines the structure of CRTPR-Tree and bounding rectangles and time constraints. The assigning vehicles and scheduling orders are defined in Section 4. Section 5 reports on our experimental results in the viewpoints of profitability and usability of our approach. Section 6 concludes and offers future works.

2 Formalization of DVRPTW

We formulate DVRPTW as follows. A traffic topology is based on the concept of an undirected graph G. Nodes which represent intersections are given by $P = \{p_1, p_2, \cdots\}$. A node p is a pair of coordinates on x-y dimensions as (px, py). Edges which represent road segments are given by $L = \{[p - p'] : p, p' \in P\}$.

Let $C = \{c_1, c_2, \cdots, c_N\}$ be N customers. The demand of customer c_j is given by $D_j = (r_j, d_j, TL_j)$, where r_j is the ride-on node, d_j is the drop-off node, and TL_j is the time limit of riding time (i.e., the customer wants to arrive at his drop-off node within the time limit). The customer satisfaction CS_j of customer c_j, where σ is control parameter of satisfaction, is defined as Equation (1). PC_j is the proportion of delay time to the time limit where tr_j is ride-on time instant, td_j is drop-off time instant. In particular, if a customer can arrive at his drop-off node within his time limit, his customer satisfaction value is 1; otherwise, the value decreases gradually. For simplicity, we regard the usability of DVRPTW as the total customer satisfaction of customers.

$$PC_j = \frac{(td_j - tr_j) - TL_j}{TL_j}$$

$$CS_j = \begin{cases} 1 & (PC_j \leq 0) \\ exp(\frac{-PC_j}{\sigma}) & (PC_j > 0) \end{cases} \quad (1)$$

Let $V = \{v_1, v_2, \cdots, v_K\}$ be K vehicles. The position of vehicle v_i at the time t is given by $\bar{v}_i(t) = (x_i(t), y_i(t))$. The velocity vector of vehicle v_i at time t is given by $\boldsymbol{v}_i(t) = (vx_i(t), vy_i(t))$. The delivery order of vehicle v_i at time t is given by a queue $q_i(t)$. The ride-on nodes and drop-off nodes of customers are inserted into the queue according to a measure, and satisfied in the order of the queue. Let $d(p_1, p_2)$ be route distance between nodes p_1 and p_2, and L be the length of the queue. The traveling cost $|q_i(t)|$ of vehicle v_i, which shows the total distance of the delivery route, is defined as Equation (2). For simplicity, we regard the profitability of DVRPTW as the traveling cost of vehicles.

$$|q_i(t)| = \sum_{l}^{L-1} d(q_i(t)[l], q_i(t)[l+1]) \quad (2)$$

Our objective is to maximize the customer satisfaction (usability) and to minimize the traveling cost (profitability). Our objective function is defined as Equation (3).

$$max \left(\frac{\sum_{j=1}^{N} CS_j}{\sum_{i=1}^{K} |q_i(t)|} \right) \quad (3)$$

3 CRTPR-Tree

Several indexing structures for moving objects have been proposed. Most fundamental structure is called TPR-Tree[7] which adopts time-parameterized bounding rectangles. Self adjusting structure, which is called Star-Tree, was proposed in [8]. R^{EXP}-Tree extended from TPR-Tree for expiration times of moving objects was proposed in [9]. TPR*-Tree[10] employed a new set of insertion and deletion algorithms.

We propose CRTPR-Tree extended from TPR-Tree for moving objects with a time constraint on a road network. Although it has been applicable to moving objects in any dimension, we focus on moving objects in x-y dimensions in this paper. CRTPR-Tree is a height balanced tree associated with the feature of R-Tree[11].

3.1 Leaf Nodes

In a leaf node, an entry E is a pointer to a vehicle v_i, a bounding rectangle $BR(t)$ which bounds the vehicle v_i, and time constraint $TC(t)$ of the vehicle v_i as Equation (4).

$$E = (v_i, BR(t), TC(t)) \quad (4)$$

Bounding Rectangle. A bounding rectangle $BR(t)$ in a leaf node is defined as intervals on x coordinate and y coordinate as Equation (5).

$$BR(t) = ((BRx^{\perp}(t), BRx^{\top}(t)), (BRy^{\perp}(t), BRy^{\top}(t))) \tag{5}$$

Here, we recall a bounding rectangle of TPR-Tree called Conservative Bounding Rectangle (CBR). CBR spreads with maximum and minimum speeds of bounded vehicles in order to bound vehicles all the time. However, vehicle may deviates from bounding rectangle when it changes direction. And, area of rectangle increases beyond reachable regions of vehicles. These weakness causes deterioration of efficiency and reliability in tree search.

Therefore, we propose a new bounding rectangle which is called RCBR for CRTPR-Tree. For simplicity, we consider only x-coordinate. At first, the interval of RCBR at update time t_{upd} is equal to the position of bounding vehicles v_i as Equation (6).

$$RCBRx^{\perp}(t_{upd}) = RCBRx^{\top}(t_{upd}) = x_i(t_{upd}) \tag{6}$$

Next, we consider a reachable rectangle $RR(t)$ of vehicle v_i. Let I be update interval time, moving distance of vehicle v_i within the interval I is calculated by $dmax_i = v_i \times I$. And, the passed node $p \in P$ is a node which satisfies the condition $d(\bar{v}_i(t), p) \leq dmax_i$. We define the reachable rectangle $RR(t)$ as a rectangle which bounds all passed nodes as Figure 1(a).

Moreover, we define the spread speed $RCBRv$ of RCBR as Equation (7).

$$\begin{aligned} RCBRvx^{\perp} &= min\left(vx_i(t_{upd}), -\frac{|RRx^{\perp}(t_{upd}) - x_i(t_{upd})|}{I}\right) \\ RCBRvx^{\top} &= max\left(vx_i(t_{upd}), \frac{|RRx^{\top}(t_{upd}) - x_i(t_{upd})|}{I}\right) \end{aligned} \tag{7}$$

Thus, the interval of RCBR at time t is defined as Equation (8). As in Figure 1(b), the RCBR spreads with same speed as the vehicle and stops when it reaches at the reachable rectangle in the same direction of the vehicle; on the other hand, RCBR spreads until the reachable rectangle smoothly in the opposite direction of the vehicle. In fact, RCBR never spreads beyond the reachable rectangle and could bound vehicle even though the vehicle turns in a different direction.

$$\begin{aligned} &RCBRx^{\perp}(t) = \\ &max\left(RRx^{\perp}(t_{upd}), RCBRx^{\perp}(t_{upd}) + RCBRvx^{\perp}(t - t_{upd})\right) \\ &RCBRx^{\top}(t) = \\ &min\left(RRx^{\top}(t_{upd}), RCBRx^{\top}(t_{upd}) + RCBRvx^{\top}(t - t_{upd})\right) \end{aligned} \tag{8}$$

Here, we define a demand rectangle DR_j of customer c_j as Equation (9).

$$\begin{aligned} DRx_j^{\perp} &= min(rx_j, dx_j) \\ DRx_j^{\top} &= max(rx_j, dx_j) \end{aligned} \tag{9}$$

Consequently, a bounding rectangle $BR(t)$ of the vehicles v_i assigned to customers $c_j (j = 0, \cdots, k)$ is defined by using $RCBR(t)$ and DRj as Equation (10).

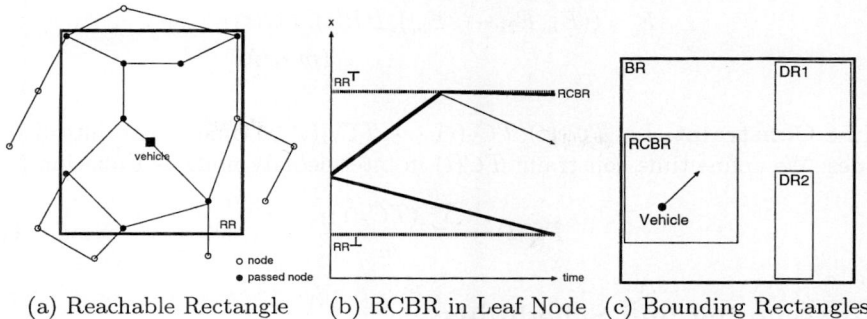

(a) Reachable Rectangle (b) RCBR in Leaf Node (c) Bounding Rectangles

Fig. 1. Shapes of Rectangles.

The bounding rectangle in leaf node implies responsible area of the vehicle for delivery in Figure 1(c).

$$BRx^{\perp}(t) = \min_j(RCBRx^{\perp}(t), DRx_j^{\perp})$$
$$BRx^{\top}(t) = \max_j(RCBRx^{\top}(t), DRx_j^{\top}) \quad (10)$$

Time Constraint. Let $c_j (j = 0, \cdots, k)$ be customers assigned to vehicle v_i. Time constraint $TCC_j(t)$ of customer c_j, where σ is control parameter of constraint and η is minimum value, is defined as Equation (11). $PT_j(t)$ is the proportion of the time limit at time t to expected traveling time of customer c_j. In particular, the time constraint value increases gradually since a customer ride: if a vehicle could not transport the customer within his time limit, the value is 1.

$$PT_j(t) = \begin{cases} \frac{-T_j}{d(b_i, r_j) + d(r_j, d_j)/b_i} & (before\ ride) \\ \frac{(t - tr)_j - T_j}{d(b_i, d_j)/b_i} & (after\ ride) \end{cases}$$

$$TCC_j(t) = \begin{cases} exp\left(\frac{PT_j(t)+1}{\sigma}\right) + \eta & PT_j(t) \leq -1 \\ 1 + \eta & PT_j(t) > -1 \end{cases} \quad (11)$$

Realistically, if there is one customer in a hurry, vehicle must hurry for him. Thus, time constraint $TC(t)$ in leaf node is maximal value of time constraints $TCC(t)_j$ of customers as Equation (12).

$$TC(t) = \max_j(TCC_j(t)) \quad (12)$$

3.2 Intermediate Nodes

In intermediate node, an entry E is pointers to child nodes $E_1, E_2, \cdots, E_m$, a bounding rectangle $BR(t)$ which bounds the time-parameterized bounding rectangles of the child nodes, and time constraint $TC(t)$ as Equation (13). A bounding rectangle $BR(t)$ in an intermediate node is formed as same as a bounding rectangle in a leaf node. Let M be the maximum number of entries in intermediate nodes to be fit in one node.

$$E = ((E_1, E_2, \cdots, E_m), BR(t), TC(t)) \qquad (13)$$
$$(m < M)$$

Time Constraint. Let $TC_1(t), TC_2(t), \cdots, TC_m(t)$ be time constraints of child nodes. We define time constraint $TC(t)$ in intermediate node as Equation (14).

$$TC(t) = \frac{\sum_c (TC_c(t))}{m} \qquad (14)$$

4 Assigning and Scheduling

4.1 Assigning

Assigning is based on indexes of vehicles and two evaluation functions. Let DR_{new} be demand rectangle of new demand and $A(R)$ be area of rectangle R. Nodes of CRTPR-Tree are evaluated by Equation (15) or Equation (16), and a node with lowest value is selected from root to leaf. Equation (15), we denote AA (assigning by area), evaluates responsible delivery areas of vehicles. Equation (16), we denote AAC (assigning by area and constraint), evaluates time constraints of vehicles in addition to responsible delivery area. The parameter η was the minimum value of time constraint as mentioned. Hence, smaller value of the η prioritizes time constraint over area: conversely, larger value prioritizes area over time constraint. The least calculation order of the assigning is $M \cdot \log_M(K)$, where M is the maximum number of entries in an intermediate node, K is the number of vehicles, and $\log_M(K)$ is the ideal height of the tree.

$$A(BR(t) \cup DR_{new}) \qquad (15)$$
$$A(BR(t) \cup DR_{new}) \times TC(t) \qquad (16)$$

4.2 Scheduling

After assigning vehicles, the delivery demands of customers (i.e., ride-on nodes and drop-off nodes) are scheduled by two measures: time traveling measure (TTM) or time constraint measure (TCM).

TTM. The delivery demands are inserted into the queue $q(t)$ to minimize traveling cost $|q(t)|$. For example, pairs of a ride-on node or a drop-off node and a time constraint as $(r, TC(t))$ are illustrated in Figure 2(a). TTM order is shown in Figure 2(b). TTM tries to minimize traveling costs of vehicles. Hence, it appears that traveling cost keeps low value.

TCM. The delivery demands are inserted into the queue $q(t)$ in time constraint $TTC(t)$ order. For example, TCM order is shown in Figure 2(c). TCM tries to transport customers one by one in the order of descending time constraints of customers. Hence, it appears that customer satisfaction keeps high value.

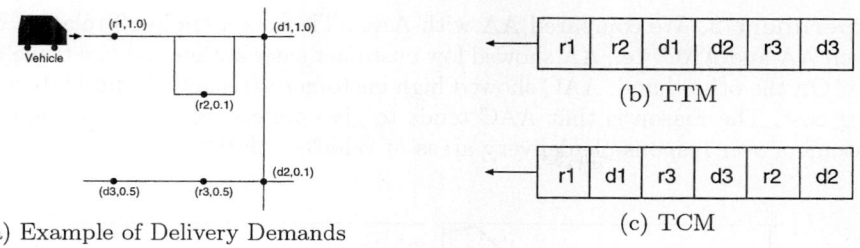

Fig. 2. Delivery Queue.

5 Experiments

5.1 Environment

A CRTPR-Tree which indexes moving vehicles is managed by a server. The server receives positions, velocity vectors, and reachable regions from vehicles periodically and re-creates the CRTPR-Tree at the update time. Parameter setting is as follows: road network is 21 × 21 grid (1000 × 1000 pixels): i.e., all intersections are orthogonal 4-crossed points except for four borders. Iteration is repeated until $t = 10000$, and new demand arises by 10% at each time. Time limit TL of customers is selected from between 1 and 5 times minimum riding time randomly. The another parameters are shown in Table 1(a).

Table 1. Experimental Patterns.

parameter	value
$|v|$	5
M	5
I	30
σ	0.5
η	0.1

(a)Settings

Exp	Patterns	Fig 3
1	P1, P2	a,b
2	P1, P3	c,d
3	P1, P4	e,f

(b)Experiments

Pattern	Rectangle	Assigning	Scheduling
P1	RCBR	AAC	TTM
P2	CBR	AAC	TTM
P3	RCBR	AA	TTM
P4	RCBR	AAC	TCM

(b)Patterns

5.2 Experimental Results

We performed three experiments with varying the number of vehicles from 20 to 30, regarding average of customer satisfaction and total traveling cost in Table 1(b). And, we compared with four patterns $(P1, \cdots, P4)$ in Table 1(c).

Experiment 1. We compared RCBR with CBR. RCBR produces better results than CBR regarding customer satisfaction. Because, RCBR could cut the area of bounding rectangle and curb the number of deviations of vehicles compared to CBR. However, it seems that there is not much difference if update interval is too short, because short interval leads small area of bounding rectangle.

Experiment 2. We compared AA with AAC. There is a trade-off relation between AA and AAC: i.e., AA showed low customer satisfaction and low traveling cost. On the other hand, AAC showed high customer satisfaction and high traveling cost. The reason is that AAC tends to give preference time constrains of customers over responsible delivery areas of vehicles.

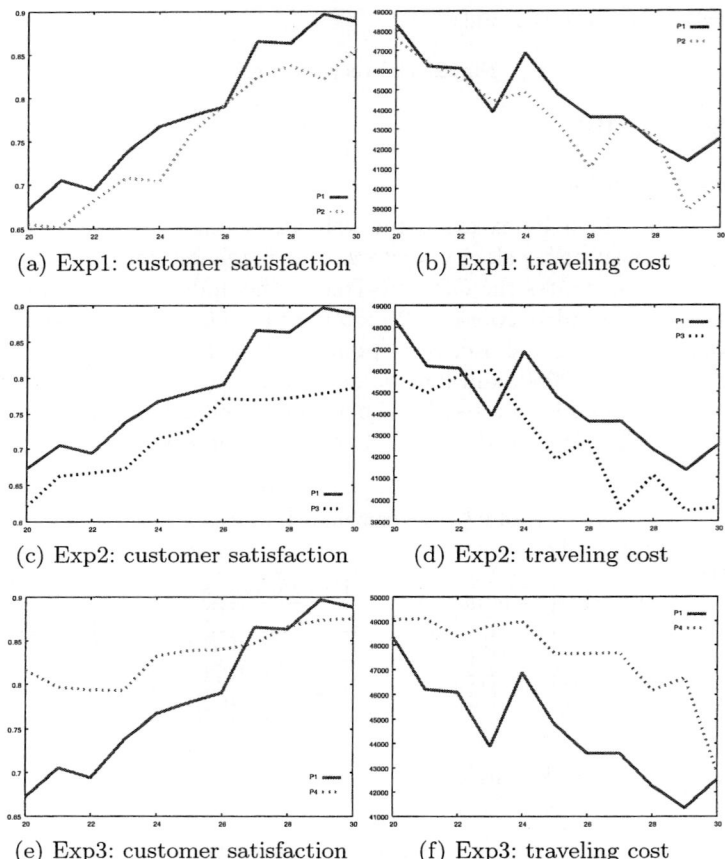

(a) Exp1: customer satisfaction (b) Exp1: traveling cost

(c) Exp2: customer satisfaction (d) Exp2: traveling cost

(e) Exp3: customer satisfaction (f) Exp3: traveling cost

Fig. 3. Experimental Results.

Experiment 3. We compared TTM with TCM. As well as Experiment 2, there is a trade-off relation between TTM and TCM: i.e., TTM showed low customer satisfaction and low traveling cost. On the other hand, TCM showed high customer satisfaction and high traveling cost. The reason is that TCM tries to transport customers one by one. In this paper, we don't consider waiting time of customers, so that customer satisfaction may be down if the waiting time is included in the formula of customer satisfaction.

6 Conclusions

In this paper, we proposed an approach using CRTPR-Tree for DVRPTW. The objective of DVRPTW is to maximize customer satisfaction and to minimize traveling cost. In order to solve the problem, we proposed indexing tree called CRTPR-Tree for moving vehicles. Moreover, we proposed methods for assigning vehicles and scheduling orders. At the last, we performed experiments regarding customer satisfaction and traveling cost. Our experimental results showed distinctive trends case by case. In our future works, heuristic algorithms such as simulated annealing and genetic algorithm will be incorporated into our system. Moreover, we will try to adopt our system to realistic environment.

Acknowledgment

We would like to thank the 21st Century COE Program for 2002. And, we acknowledge to Prof. Naohiro Ishii of Aichi Institute of Technology.

References

1. Desrochers, M., Lenstra, J., Savelsbergh, M., F.Soumis: Vehicle routing with time windows: Optimizatin and approximation. Vehicle Routing: Methods and Studies (1988) 65–84
2. Solomon, M., Desrosiers, J.: Time window constrained routing and scheduling problems. Transportations Science **22** (1988) 1–13
3. Thangiah, S.: Vehicle routing with time windows using genetic algorithms. Application Handbook of Genetic Algorithms: New Frontiers, Volume II. Lance Chambers (Ed.), CRC Press (1995) 253–277
4. Potvin, J.Y., Bengio, S.: The vehicle routing problem with time windows — part II: Genetic search. INFORMS Journal on Computing **8** (1996) 165–172
5. Louis, S.J., Yin, X., Yuan, Z.Y.: Multiple vehicle routing with time windows using genetic algorithms. In Angeline, P.J., Michalewicz, Z., Schoenauer, M., Yao, X., Zalzala, A., eds.: Proceedings of the Congress on Evolutionary Computation. Volume 3., Mayflower Hotel, Washington D.C., USA, IEEE Press (1999) 1804–1808
6. Ibaraki, T., Kubo, M., Masuda, T., Uno, T., Yagiura, M.: Effective local search algorithms for the vehicle routing problem with general time window constraints. In: Proc. of MIC'2001. (2001) 293–297
7. Saltenis, S., Jensen, C.S., Leutenegger, S.T., Lopez, M.A.: Indexing the positions of continuously moving objects. In: Proc. of ACM SIGMOD 2000. (2000) 331–342
8. Procopiuc, C., Agarwal, P., Har-Peled, S.: Star-tree: An efficient self-adjusting index for moving objects. In: Proc. of ALENEX. (2002) 178–193
9. Saltenis, S., Jensen, C.S.: Indexing of moving objects for location-based services. In: Proc. of ICDE 2002. (2002) 463–473
10. Tao, Y., Papadias, D., Sun, J.: The TPR*-tree: An optimized spatio-temporal access method for predictive queries. In: Proc. of Very large data bases. (2003) 9–12
11. Guttman, A.: R-trees: a dynamic index structure for spatial searching. In: Proc. of ACM SIGMOD 1984. (1984) 47–57

An Hierarchical Terrain Representation for Approximately Shortest Paths

David Mould and Michael C. Horsch

Department of Computer Science,
University of Saskatchewan,
Saskatoon, SK, Canada S7N 5A9
{mould,horsch}@cs.usask.ca

Abstract. We propose a fast algorithm for on-line path search in grid-like undirected planar graphs with real edge costs (aka terrains). Our algorithm depends on an off-line analysis of the graph, requiring poly-logarithmic time and space. The off-line preprocessing constructs a hierarchical representation which allows detection of features specific to the terrain. While our algorithm is not guaranteed to find an optimal path, we demonstrate empirically that it is very fast, and that the difference from optimal is almost always small.

1 Introduction

Path planning through terrains is a problem often seen in areas including robotics and computer games. By *terrain*, we mean a planar graph whose nodes are evenly distributed across a portion of the plane, and in which each node is connected to its nearby neighbours and only those. In terrains, edges have non-negative weights representing the cost of traversing the edge (not necessarily distance). The cost of a path is the sum of the weights on all edges along the path. We are specifically interested in applications that require frequent path planning.

Applications requiring computation of shortest paths in graphs (not necessarily terrains) are common; algorithms for this task are well-known. However, general graph search algorithms do not consider the terrain's properties, such as regular connectivity and a tendency to contain regions of similar edge costs, both of which can be exploited to improve search performance.

Our technique, called HTAP, uses a multiscale representation: a "pyramid" of graphs, with the original graph at the bottom and each higher level being a decimated version of the one immediately beneath. The construction of the pyramid extracts features from the terrain so that important decisions about path planning can be made at a higher level of abstraction. When a pathing query is made, we iteratively perform queries at each level of the pyramid beginning at the top; the results from higher levels restrict the region of the graph in which we search at the current level. When we reach the lowest level, i.e., the original graph, the search space is a narrow corridor of constant width. In Fig. 1 (right) we show an example terrain, and the corridor constructed using HTAP;

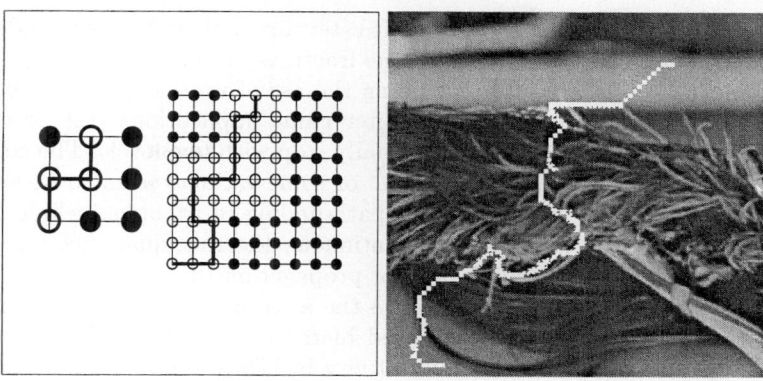

Fig. 1. (left) Two levels of a pyramid: the path, marked in bold, and the corridor derived from the path above, denoted with unfilled circles. (right) A sample terrain with edge costs visualized in greyscale, with the corridor (marked in white) superimposed. Darker regions are cheaper.

the terrain has $243^2 = 59049$ nodes, but the corridor has only 1284 nodes. The HTAP technique is not guaranteed to find an optimal path. It is well-suited to applications in which real-time path-planning is required, and in which the penalty for slight deviations from optimality is not high. Our empirical results (obtained from a prototype implementation which was not highly optimized) indicate that HTAP can be used in real time for a wide range of terrain sizes. The empirical results suggest linear-time on-line complexity for path planning, although a proof of that claim has not yet been obtained. Empirically, the paths returned by HTAP are rarely worse than 1.3 times the cost of the optimal path, and usually much better than 1.1 times optimal.

2 Previous Work

Single source shortest path algorithms such as Dijkstra's algorithm [4] can be too expensive to use repeatedly for on-line or real-time queries. All-pairs algorithms such as Johnson's algorithm [7] have suitable on-line time complexity for repeated path queries, but require quadratic space to store all the paths.

When heuristic information is available, the A* algorithm [5] is often used to solve path planning problems. Its variants include: ϵ-admissible heuristics [11] which attempt to speed up search by relaxing the optimality requirement; iterative deepening A* [8], which improves the memory requirement of A* search; and real-time A* [9]. For terrains, the performance of heuristic search methods can be very slow, because good heuristics are difficult to find. The usual "airdistance" heuristic does not always give a reasonable estimate of the cost-to-goal in terrains with weighted edges, especially when edge costs and distances are measured in different scales. The phenomenon of "flooding," i.e., exploring all vertices in an area near an obstacle to find a way around it, can increase the computational costs dramatically. If a terrain is maze-like, A* guided by a distance heuristic often has to flood large fractions of the terrain to find a path.

Variants of heuristic search, including the use of way-points and multi-level representations, are common in computer game applications [12]. Multi-level representations in these applications usually stop with two levels. The computational costs of heuristic search (using A* or some variant) seem to be accepted as unavoidable. Similar techniques for path-finding in robotics include the use of potential fields, Voronoi regions in continuous domains, quad-tree representations of continuous space and wave-front propagation (flood-fill) [10].

Repeated path planning is central to the area of Intelligent Transportation Systems, and researchers have proposed hierarchical representations to speed up on-line processing [6, 3]. The connectivity in ITS graphs can be quite different from terrains, so these methods for building hierarchies cannot be applied directly and usefully to terrains.

Shortest path problems are also important in graph theory and computational geometry. Chiang and Mitchell [2] give algorithms for the problem of computing shortest paths in a continuous plane containing a set of polygonal obstacles. These require more than quadratic time and space for precomputation, while allowing sublinear time on-line processing. Arikati *et al.* [1] describe a quadratic time preprocessing algorithm and a quadratic space hierarchical representation of a planar graph for linear time on-line shortest path computation.

3 Algorithm

Our pyramid is a multiresolution representation of the graph: the base of the pyramid is the original graph, and each level above the base is a graph with constant-factor fewer nodes. The nodes at a given level which are also present at the level above, we call *survivors*; the process of selecting survivors we call *decimation*. Each node at the base level has a pointer up to its *representative* at each higher level. We use *immediate representative* to refer to the nearest survivor to an arbitrary-level node.

We have the notion of *blocs*, which are purely geometrically determined entities, and *regions*, which are the Voronoi regions for a given subset of survivors. (The Voronoi region for a survivor is the set of nodes closer to that survivor than to any other survivor, where "closer" is with respect to optimal path length in the original graph. Ties are broken arbitrarily.) In our implementation, a bloc is a 3 × 3 grouping of nodes, but any constant grouping could have been used instead. Each node at a level above the bottom has a collection of *children* – nodes at the level below which are nearer to it than to any other node of its level. See Fig. 2 (right) for a picture of the survivor-representative relationships, and Fig. 2 (left) for the difference between blocs and regions.

3.1 Pyramid Representation

The base of the pyramid is the original graph and each upper level is a decimated version of the level beneath. With each original node, we store pointers up to all of its representatives, one per level. With each upper node, we store two pointers: one down to the node in the lower graph which occupies the same position in the terrain, and one up to the node's representative in the level above. A sketch of the up pointers is in Fig. 2 (right); the marked node demonstrates the necessity of maintaining a list of all representatives at the pyramid base, since the sequence of representatives may differ from the sequence of immediate representatives.

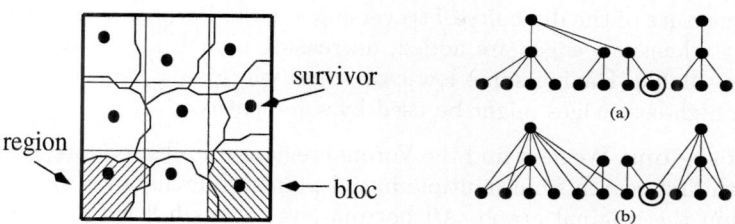

Fig. 2. (left) A sketch of a pyramid level: blocs, regions, and a single survivor per bloc. Two levels of a pyramid. (right) In (a), links between nodes and their immediate representatives; (b), links between bottom nodes and their representatives at all levels. All links are directed upward.

In addition to the information in the pyramid structure, each level of the pyramid is a proper graph, that is, it contains weighted edges between nodes. Details on computing the graph connectivity and edge weights appear below.

3.2 Pyramid Construction

We repeatedly perform the following process, stopping when the newly created level is the largest graph we are willing to risk searching exhaustively.

Suppose we are constructing a new level i, $i > 0$, where $i = 0$ is the bottom of the pyramid. We perform the following steps, explained in greater detail below:
1. Divide the level into blocs.
2. Choose one node from each bloc to survive to the level above (decimation).
3. Find the Voronoi regions for the survivors, in the original graph.
4. Determine which pairs of survivors should be linked by edges.
5. Determine costs for the new edges from the previous step.

Division into blocs. For each node in the current level, we assign a bloc identifier based on its location in the terrain. In our implementation, 3×3 groups of nodes were assigned to a single bloc.

Decimation. From each bloc there will be a single survivor. The challenge is to decimate the graph so as to best preserve its structure, from the point of view of finding short paths. The nodes most worth preserving are those which lie on the greatest number of optimal paths among the entire ensemble of paths; unfortunately, computing all paths is an extremely expensive task. We choose instead to compute a proxy, inspired by the notion of parallel resistance in electrical circuits. The resistance of a node R is given by

$$1/R = 1/c_1 + 1/c_2 + ... + 1/c_n \qquad (1)$$

where c_j is the cost of the jth edge to the node. Within a given bloc, the node with the lowest resistance is the one used by the most paths, and hence the one which survives to the level above. We use resistance because it is a natural measure of the difficulty of traversing a node. Parallel resistance behaves gracefully when new edges are added, decreasing monotonically as more paths become available. Having some low-cost edges will give a node low resistance, but even high-cost edges might be used by some paths.

Voronoi regions. We next find the Voronoi regions for all survivors, making use of breadth-first search from multiple initial points. Our distance metric is path cost within the original graph. All bottom-level nodes fall within the Voronoi region of some survivor; for each bottom-level node, we record which survivor is closest. Also, if the new level $i > 1$, then for every node at level $i - 1$ we record which survivor at level i is closest (the immediate representatives) using the already-determined Voronoi regions.

Placing edges. Initially level i has no edges. We place a new edge between every pair of nodes at level i whose Voronoi regions at the pyramid base are linked by at least one edge.

Finding new edge costs. The cost of the new edge is the path cost of travelling between the two nodes in a subset of the original graph, where the path is restricted to lie within the Voronoi regions of the two nodes in question.

3.3 Query Processing

Each shortest-path query consists of a start and end node. The overall pathfinding exercise is a cascade of searches; at each level below the top, we find a path by searching in a tightly restricted subset of the original graph.

We begin by finding the representatives of both nodes at the top level and finding the optimal path through the entire top-level graph using A* (with the air distance heuristic). Having found a path at a given level, we then mark all children of the nodes on the path as eligible, and find the shortest path one level down, searching only in the eligible corridor. The algorithm ends when a path is found at the pyramid base. Fig. 1 suggests how the corridor is derived from the path one level up and used to constrain the search space.

A subtask of the path query resolution process involves marking the children of a given node, so that we can add the marked nodes to the corridor. However, the nodes do not explicitly store their children. To mark a node's children, we perform the following: we first find a single child, then we flood to find all nodes at the child's level who share its representative. The nodes form a contiguous region (recall that they are the Voronoi region for their representative) and therefore flood-fill can efficiently mark the region. The initial child is found by going to the node's location in the original graph (where pointers to all levels are stored) then taking the pointer up to the proper level. Fig. 2 shows sketches of the pyramid structure.

3.4 Complexity

Construction of the pyramid requires $O(N \log N)$ time, where N is the number of nodes in the original graph. There are $O(\log N)$ levels in the pyramid, and constructing each requires an investigation of every node at the pyramid base. The memory footprint of the pyramid is $O(N \log N)$ because at the base level, every node has a pointer up to every level above, and there are $O(\log N)$ levels. There are $O(N)$ nodes in total in the pyramid, from equation 2 below.

If our survival policy does a good job of making regions of approximately equal size, then the run-time complexity of the algorithm is $O(n)$, shown as follows. At level i, we are seeking a path of length $p^i n$, where n is the length of the bottom-level path, and the linear dimension of the graph was reduced by a factor $p < 1$ at each level of the pyramid. The total computational cost is

$$n + pn + p^2 n + p^3 n + ... + p^k n \leq n(\sum_{i=0}^{\infty} p^i) = n/(1-p). \qquad (2)$$

In general, our algorithm is not guaranteed to find the shortest path. Our empirical results are presented below. Here, following Pearl [11], we consider an abbreviated analysis of the algorithm on a regular 4-connected lattice with each edge having unit cost. In this kind of grid, an optimal path has the property that each edge traversed on the path reduces the Manhattan distance to the goal. By construction (assuming ties are broken in a deterministic manner), each level in the pyramid is a regular lattice with uniform edge costs. An optimal path at level $k+1$ in the pyramid defines a corridor in the kth level of the pyramid which contains an optimal path at level k.

4 Results

Next we report results from our experiments. Each experiment consisted of a single path planning exercise. Endpoints were chosen at random within the map; the optimal path was determined using A* with the air distance heuristic, and compared to the path reported by HTAP. We compare the computational costs of finding paths, in terms of the opened node count, and the path costs themselves, expressed as the ratio of the optimal path to the HTAP path. In reporting the computational costs of using the pyramid to answer path queries, we sum all nodes in all corridors in the pyramid. Even though we might not open a given node when searching the corridor, we had to visit the node to mark it eligible.

We tested HTAP on a number of different maps. Specific maps employed were the *noise map*, where every edge had a cost chosen at random with uniform distribution over $\{1..255\}$; two *maze maps*, hand-drawn mazes whose edge

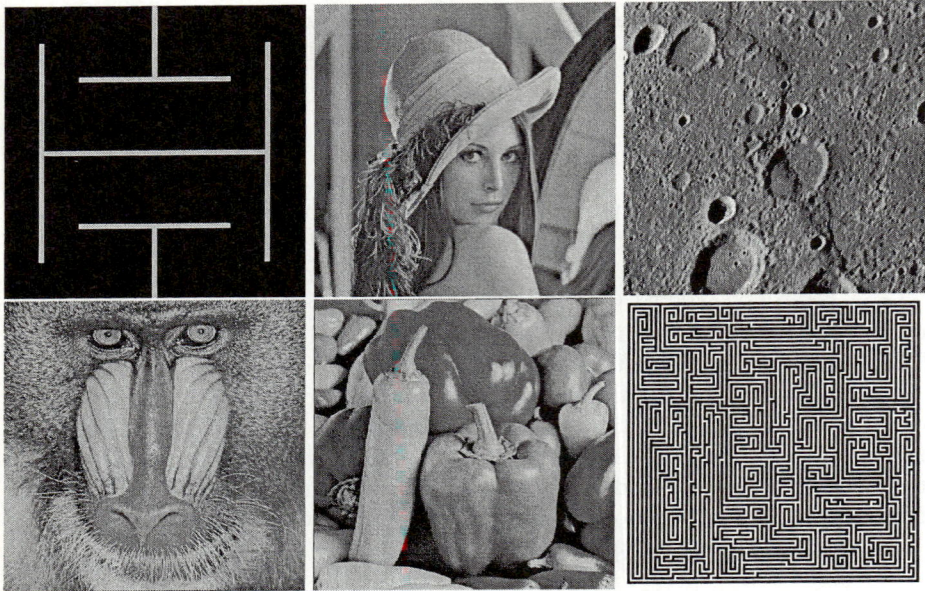

Fig. 3. Visualizations of some of the graphs we used. Above, a simple maze, the Lena image, and a terrain image; below, the mandrill image, the peppers image, and a complex maze.

costs were either 1 (hallway) or 255 (wall); and various image maps, where standard test images were converted to greyscale and edge costs were derived from pixel intensities. Image maps produced edge costs as follows: for two nodes (pixels) having intensities p_1 and p_2 respectively, the cost was $\max(1, (p_1 + p_2)/2)$. Pictures of our maps are shown in Fig. 3.

We chose to use images because they share some characteristics with real terrains. They have a wide range of edge costs, but pixel intensities (and the derived edge costs) tend to be correlated, and in some cases it is possible to divide the terrain into subregions within which costs are roughly uniform. The presence of such subregions is a feature of real terrains. The images we used are standard test images in the computer vision community.

The multiresolution representation allows us to find even long paths very quickly; see Fig. 4 (left) for a time comparison between A* and HTAP. Strikingly, the data points for HTAP are scarcely visible: on the scale of the graph, our computational cost is near zero. The difference illustrated by the graph is the difference between $O(n^2)$ and $O(n)$. Our path costs are also shown by themselves, where the $O(n)$ behaviour is more apparent. There is some variation owing to the slight differences among different region sizes. Each of these graphs shows 5000 random paths on the 729×729 noise map. Also of interest is the comparison between our paths' costs and the optimal paths' costs, shown in Fig. 5; we show an example to give the flavor, with detailed data in the table. From the graph

An Hierarchical Terrain Representation for Approximately Shortest Paths

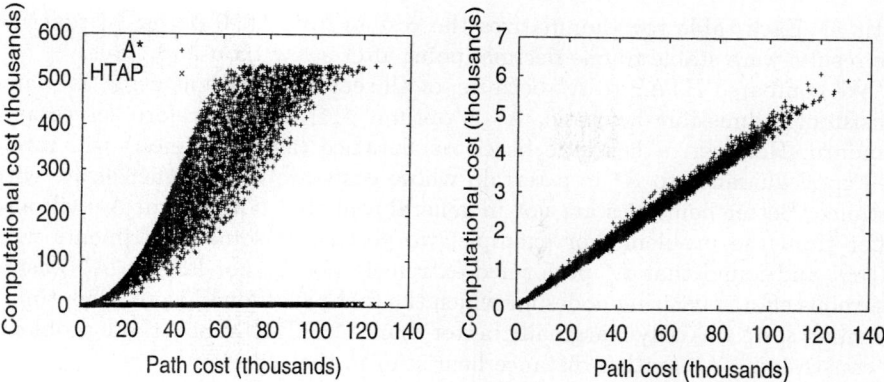

Fig. 4. (left) Comparison of computational costs for HTAP and for A*. The HTAP data points lie along the x-axis and are difficult to see. (right) The HTAP computational costs alone. Note the change in range on the y-axis between the two figures.

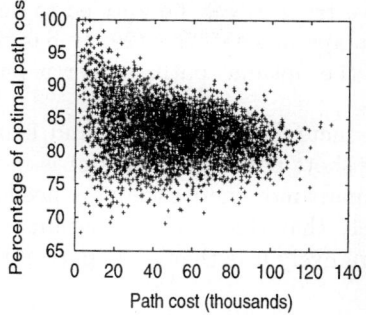

Map	size	1%	5%	10%	25%
noise	243 × 243	0.8	3.4	16.2	95.2
noise	729 × 729	0.1	0.6	3.8	98.4
simple maze	243 × 243	57.1	92.1	96.3	99.2
complex maze	340 × 340	57.1	68.6	77.5	92.6
Lena	512 × 512	25.3	78.4	89.4	97.3
mandrill	512 × 512	15.3	67.0	84.7	96.9
peppers	512 × 512	17.4	71.4	87.1	97.6
terrain	512 × 512	1.3	30.3	72.4	98.5

Fig. 5. (left) Scatter plot of path costs. The horizontal axis is raw path cost and the vertical axis is the ratio of the costs of the optimal path and the reported path. (right) Cumulative distribution of path costs.

we see that the cost of short paths is very likely to be near the optimal path cost, and that while the ratio drops off somewhat as paths become very long, it never drops off too far. Again, the results in the graph are for 5000 random paths on the 729 × 729 noise map. The results for the noise map are representative of results on other maps.

In the table, we report cost differences in terms of the cumulative distribution: what proportion of paths were within 1% of optimal, etc. Percentage values represent the ratio of the optimal path to the reported path. We had virtually no cases where the reported path was worse than 50%. Our results are better for more structured images, which would be more susceptible to compression; even for the largest noise map, however, 95% of our paths were within 25% of optimal. Each table row summarizes the results from 5000 paths; in practice, the results were stable to one decimal point after a few thousand trials.

We compared HTAP to A* because, of all search algorithms using the same consistent, admissible heuristic, A* is optimal [11], and therefore serves as a standard. However, a heuristic based on distance (as is common) will rarely give good guidance to A* in a terrain whose costs are not commensurate with distance. Better heuristics are not in general available. Variants of A* will also suffer from the problem. For example, we performed some experiments with A^*_ϵ[11], and found that A^*_ϵ performed extremely poorly. For large ϵ, A^*_ϵ wasted enormous effort revisiting nodes for which the first paths found were suboptimal. For small ϵ, A^*_ϵ was only marginally better than A*. HTAP avoids these problems by constraining A* (with a distance heuristic) to the corridor.

5 Discussion

Empirical results for HTAP suggest that it is $O(n)$ in the path length, rather than the typical $O(n^2)$ for A* in terrains. It is extremely fast, two orders of magnitude faster than A* on the maps that we tried. It can be applied to very large maps; we have successfully used it on maps of size 729×729. It has the disadvantage that it does not always return the optimal path, rather a path whose cost is not much worse than optimal.

Although fast for long paths, our method incurs some overhead and hence is not very fast for short paths. For extremely short paths, the corridor is more egg-shaped than ribbon-shaped, and contains many more nodes than are needed. However, for short paths it is also highly likely that the corridor contains the optimal path. The longer the corridor, the more likely it is that some part of the optimal path lies outside it.

Our algorithm is best able to find the optimal path when the original graph is well represented by the pyramid: hence, large regions with near-uniform edge costs lose little information when most of the edges are removed. Highly non-uniform regions suffer more, which is why our results on the noise map come so much further short of optimal. The maze maps were difficult because even small lossiness in compression can translate into serious errors in the paths. Note, however, that even in the difficult cases HTAP usually found a very good path.

6 Conclusions and Future Work

We have presented a fast method for finding short paths in the graph. Though the method is not guaranteed to find the shortest path, with high probability it finds a path not much more expensive than the optimal path – and moreover, it finds a path of length n by searching only $O(n)$ nodes. Our method depends on precomputing a multiresolution structure of size $O(N \log N)$ in the number of nodes in the graph; the precomputation is expensive, but runtime queries are processed very quickly. On a 1.8 GHz AMD processor, it requires about 7.5 minutes to compute the pyramid for a 729×729 graph.

We have presented algorithms for building the pyramid and for exploiting it for fast path planning. Future work involves optimizing the pyramid construction and investigating the tradeoffs between performing more computation at runtime and having a higher likelihood of finding the optimal path.

We are interested in investigating the tradeoffs between a wider corridor and a better chance of finding the optimal path. We have considered only static terrains so far, while some application areas involve dynamic terrains; we are therefore interested in looking at incremental modification to the pyramid. Our memory footprint right now is $O(N \log N)$ in the size of the original graph, and we believe that we can reduce it to $O(N)$. We are interested in looking at the effects of different policies for node preservation. We want to investigate a hybrid algorithm, in which a traditional method is first used, and HTAP is used only when the traditional method does not quickly find the solution. Finally, we want to perform more detailed analysis of HTAP's complexity.

References

1. Srinivasa Rao Arikati, Danny Z. Chen, L. Paul Chew, Gautam Das, Michiel H. M. Smid, and Christos D. Zaroliagis. Planar spanners and approximate shortest path queries among obstacles in the plane. In *European Symposium on Algorithms*, pages 514–528, 1996.
2. Yi-Jen Chiang and Joseph S. B. Mitchell. Two-point euclidean shortest path queries in the plane. In *Symposium on Discrete Algorithms*, pages 215–224, 1999.
3. Y. Chou, H.E. Romeijn, and R.L. Smith. Approximating shortest paths in large-scale networks with an application to intelligent transportation systems. *INFORMS Journal on Computing*, 10:163–179, 1998.
4. E. Dijkstra. A note on two problems in connexion with graphs. *Numerische Mathematik*, 1:269–271, 1959.
5. P.E. Hart, N. J. Nilsson, and B. Raphael. A formal basis for the heuristic determiniation of minimum cost paths. *IEEE Trans. Systems Science and Cybernetics*, 4(2):100–107, 1968.
6. Yun-Wu Huang, Ning Jing, and Elke A. Rundensteiner. Hierarchical path views: A model based on fragmentation and transportation road types. In *ACM-GIS*, pages 93–100, 1995.
7. D.B. Johnson. Efficient algorithms for shortest paths in sparse networks. *J. Assoc. Comput. Mach.*, 24(1):1–13, 1977.
8. R.E. Korf. Iterative-deepening A*: An optimal admissible tree search. In *IJCAI-85*, pages 1034–1036, 1985.
9. R.E. Korf. Real-time heuristic search. *Airtificial Intelligence*, 42(3):189–211, 1990.
10. Robin R. Murphy. *Introduction to A.I. Robotics*. MIT Press, 2000.
11. Judea Pearl. *Heuristics: Intelligent Search Strategies for Intelligent Problem Solving*. Addison-Wesley, 1984.
12. Steve Rabin, editor. *AI Game Programming Gems*. Charles River Media, Inc, 2002.

MSIP:
Agents Embodying a Category-Based Learning Process for the ITS Tutor to Self-improve Its Instructional Plans

Roberto Legaspi[1], Raymund Sison[2], and Masayuki Numao[1]

[1] Institute of Scientific and Industrial Research, Osaka University
8-1 Mihogaoka, Ibaraki, Osaka, 567-0047, Japan
{roberto,numao}@ai.sanken.osaka-u.ac.jp
[2] College of Computer Studies, De La Salle University – Manila
2401 Taft Avenue, Manila 1004, Philippines
sisonr@ccs.dlsu.edu.ph

Abstract. We have conceived of a Multi-agent Self-improving Planner (MSIP) within the tutor module of an intelligent tutoring system (ITS). It embodies a learning process that utilizes knowledge about different student categories to adapt and improve its instructional plans on the level of these categories. In this sense, the categories become recipients and effectors of effective plans. The fundamental reason for introducing agents as learning elements is their intrinsic capability to learn and perform autonomously during on-line interaction. This paper discusses each agent's learning task and the representation of the knowledge each acquires. Empirical results drawn from performing the agents' tasks using recorded teaching scenarios validate the MSIP's learning process.

1 Introduction

Tutoring is a specialized kind of instruction far different from the traditional form of teaching because it is structured according to the individual needs of students. An intelligent tutoring system (ITS) is a computer program that can diagnose problems of individual learners. This diagnostic capability enables it to adapt instruction or remediation to the needs of individuals [15]. An adaptive tutor allows its *instructional plans*, i.e., the sequence of teaching activities, to differ from one student to another.

However, more than being adaptive, several authors have noted that computerized tutors should be capable of *self-improvement* (citations in [6]). Self-improvement may involve revising existing plans and/or learning new ones. Though ITSs are generally adaptive, and a few are self-improving [13, 11, 6, 9], it does not follow that the manner by which they learn their plans is *efficient*, i.e., the effective plan is learned at a reasonably short time. A plan is *effective* if at the end of it, the set goal is achieved.

We hypothesize that utilizing the knowledge learned by automatically *categorizing* learners based on some common characteristics can effect an efficient self-improvement process for the ITS tutor. We have conceived of a *Multi-agent Self-improving Planner* (MSIP) which embodies a learning process that implements our hypothesis. Every vital aspect of the learning process, as part of the over-all pedagogic reasoning, is delegated to an agent. The MSIP employs unsupervised machine learning techniques for learning from experience for the provision of intelligent behavior that underlie the learning process.

This paper expounds the MSIP as an agent-based planning module that implements a category-based learning process. Section 2 discusses the MSIP architecture. More importantly, it elucidates the reasons for adopting agents as learning elements. Section 3 explains the experimentation methodology and the real-world data used to conduct the experiments. Sections 4 and 5 elaborate on the dynamics of each agent. Finally, we conclude and state our future direction in Section 6.

2 The MSIP: An Agent-Based Planning Module

Fig. 1 shows the MSIP architecture as well as its external relationships to configurate a complete tutoring system cast in a multi-user environment. The ITS tutor can be viewed as a distributed problem solving [7] architecture with separate agent components for teaching and pedagogic decision making.

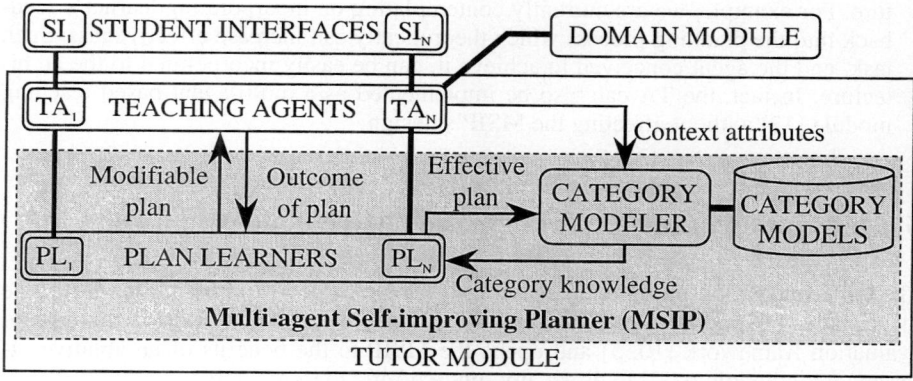

Fig. 1. The MSIP Architecture

The *Teaching Agent* (TA) is the one that directly interacts with the student. It creates a tutorial context profile in terms of student- and session-related attributes. Learner attributes include: cognitive ability (low, moderate, high), which is measured in terms of the student's performance in pre-tests, and prior tests and problem-solving exercises; learning style (visual, audio, kinesthetic) that is determined through an instrument (e.g., the Index of Learning Styles [8]) administered before the session is conducted; knowledge scope, and list of errors committed by the student. The topics in the instructional domain, which is teaching the basic C language constructs, are organized in a taxonomy that describes their relationships (e.g., pre-requisite and co-requisite) in terms of the language constructs' syntax, semantics, and purpose. The knowledge scope points in the taxonomy the last topic taken by the student, which implies that all topics previous to it had been taken as well. At the same time, the TA collaborates with the student to set the session-related attributes: session goal and topic to be tackled. All these context attributes are vital to the operations of the MSIP.

As an agent-based planning module, the MSIP categorizes every student who interacts with the tutor according to the context attributes provided by the TA and learns the best plan to apply to the student based on the category knowledge it possesses. Based on the TA's assessment on how effective a plan is the MSIP self-improves accordingly. Over time, the MSIP eventually learns the effective plan.

The fundamental reason for introducing agents as learning elements is that an agent possesses significant capability to learn and perform autonomously as it interacts online with other agents (whether human or software). Consequently:

1. Their concurrent actions pave the way for efficient learning in an on-line time restricted scenario.
2. Each agent's learning capability can be assessed separately. The efficacy of each agent can be validated and the one that restrains performance can be pinpointed.
3. Simultaneously acquired results can be immediately distributed to be utilized by other agents. The availability of category knowledge, and the increase in the rate by which it can be made available, leads to the desired effectiveness and efficiency in performance at an early stage.
4. By encapsulating the learning tasks within agents, it offers flexibility in architecture design. A new task can be easily implemented as another agent in the architecture. For example, we are currently contemplating on incorporating learner's feedback into the planning process which theoretically can increase effectiveness. Such task, and the agent conceived to achieve it, can be easily incorporated to the architecture. In fact, the TA can also be implemented as a multi-agent-based teaching module [12] without affecting the MSIP's design.

3 Description of the Experimentation Methodology and Data

The experimentation prototype consists only of the MSIP. Minimizing the influence of the other ITS modules in evaluating the efficacy of the MSIP follows the layered evaluation framework [10, 5] and opens the MSIP to the benefits of an ablative assessment methodology [2] to direct any future efforts to improve it.

Moreover, in order to perform significant experiments under the same initial conditions, the MSIP is evaluated using a corpus of recorded teaching scenarios. A *teaching scenario* defines a previously used instructional plan and contains the context (as described by the student and session attributes outlined by the TA) by which it was successfully applied. Reyes [14] provides a case library of recorded verbal protocols of expert-student interactions, which was later on processed by a case-based reasoning tutor in order to derive the instructional plan for each case. The learned plans were later on validated by domain experts as effective. The participants of the recorded interactions include two seasoned instructors and 24 qualified peer tutors, while the students were 120 Computer Science majors who were then taking their initial programming course. For each student an average of three instructional sessions were conducted. One session covers one set of lesson (i.e., a lesson, for example, on all conditional constructs or on just one type of conditional construct). We adapted the case library's 105 unique cases to form our set of teaching scenarios.

4 The Category Modeler

A fundamental question is whether attempting to learn on-line student categories would significantly improve the selection of instructional plans. Evidence show that categorizing learners according to certain features correlates to effective pedagogical reasoning of both human (e.g., [4, 8]) and computerized (citations in [1]) tutors. We entrench on this premise the relevance of automatically learning student categories.

The *Category Modeler* (CM) incrementally builds and updates models of different student categories. Fig. 2 shows the functional view of the CM, its external relationships, and the kinds of knowledge it processes. The *Service Request Handler* (SRH) regulates and services the requests made by the TAs and PLs as it organizes these requests for the *Category Knowledge Manager* (CKM) to know the kind of information that needs to be learned, or retrieved from or stored into the category models. We slowly explicate the different learning aspects within the CM.

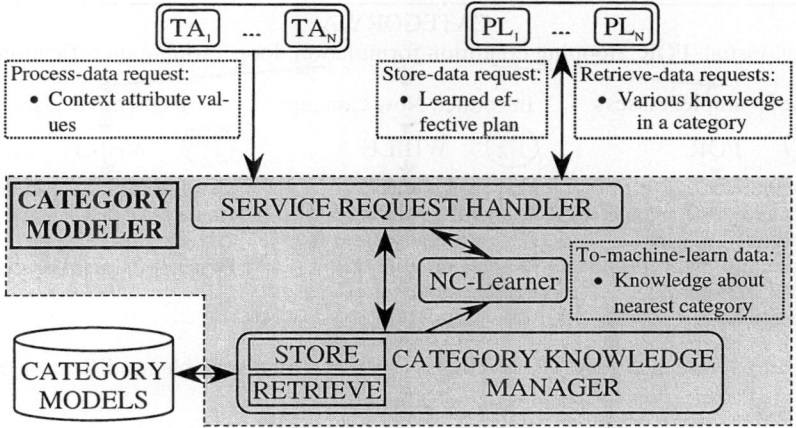

Fig. 2. The functional view of the Category Modeler

A *category model* is an incremental interpretation of the members' behavior whose function is to reproduce the current state of the members' knowledge, their learning patterns and abilities, and the instructional plans that are supposed to work for the category. The model is structured as a tree of depth four wherein the root node contains the vector of student attribute values, and the session attribute values at the intermediary levels distinguish plans in terms of the goal (2nd level) and the domain content, or topic, (3rd level) they address. The leaf nodes contain the instructional plans implemented as ordered lists of teaching activity representations. Hence, a path from the root to one of the leaf nodes specifies the plan for the context specified by the path. Given this representation, category membership is therefore a conjunction of student attribute values (i.e., in terms of common features). This is rather straightforward since we primarily want to acquire a comprehensible explanation of why a category possesses certain plans in relation to its members' features.

When the CM automatically categorized the 105 teaching scenarios, 78 initial category models were learned. The categories in Fig. 3 depict the comprehensible distinction among category models in terms of features-plans correlation. With different cognitive abilities, difference in treatment may lie in the amount and difficulty level of the *activity object* (e.g., the next easy example to show, the next difficult problem or exercise to work on, etc.), and/or the pace by which knowledge should be delivered. With the low level learners of A, support comes through simple and easy to understand activity objects and with the tutor providing sufficient guidance through feedback, advice, and motivation. With B's moderate level learners, the tutor can minimize supervision while increasing the difficulty level of the activity objects. The visual learners of A benefit from graphical presentation (in P1) while the auditory learners in B benefit from more oral explanations (in P4). Transition to a new topic (in the topic taxonomy, the discussion on the FOR construct precedes that of the WHILE) is characterized by plans that preteach vocabulary, integrate new knowledge, contextualize instruction, and test current knowledge (in P2 and P3); while reference to a previous topic may call for summarization and further internalization (in P4).

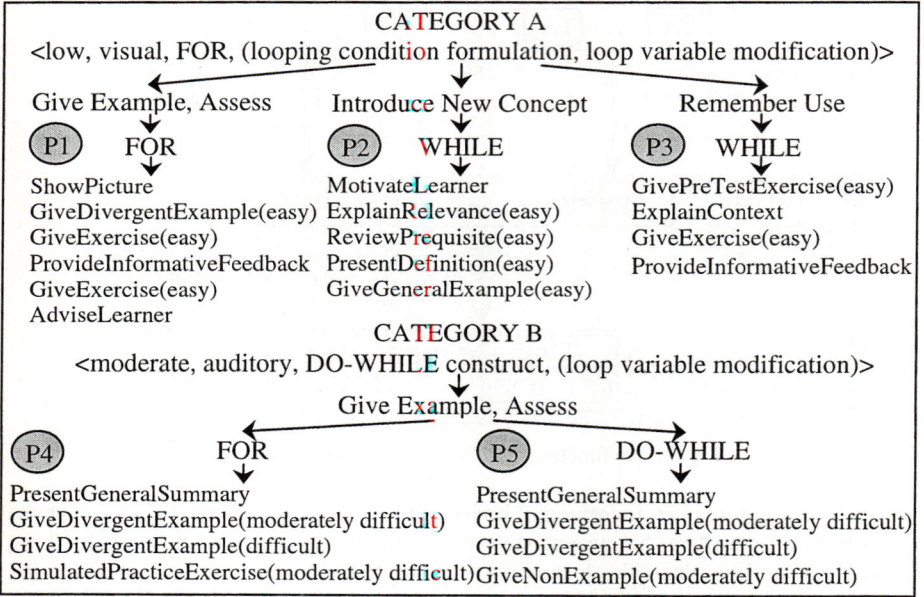

Fig. 3. Two [of the 78 initial] category models that exemplify relations in features and plans

One of the knowledge the PL acquires from the CM is the appropriate initial *local plan*, i.e., the existing plan in the category model, to apply to the student. But what if the student is classified to a new category, which implies the absence of a local plan, where will this initial workable plan come from? A *new category* is formed when the attribute values for the current student are not found in any of the existing models.

It is plausible to find the solution in the *nearest category*, i.e., the category least distant to the new one in terms of their student attribute values. Once the CKM informs the SRH that no local plan exists, the SRH immediately invokes the assistance of the *NC-Learner* (NCL), an agent that machine-learns the nearest category and acquires its local plan. The NCL applies an information-theoretic measure called *cohesion* over the student attribute values in all categories. This is not a Euclidean distance metric in which all features are summed independently, but a measure of distance in terms of relations between attributes as represented by contingency tables. [We refer the reader to [17] for an elaborate discussion on this measure]. Briefly, *cohesion* (C_c) is defined as $C_c = W_c/O_c$ where W_c represents the average distance between members of category C and O_c represents the average distance between C and all other categories. The category that is most cohesive is the one that best maximizes the similarity among its members while concurrently minimizing its similarity with other categories. The NCL pairs the new category to one of the existing categories and treats this pair as one category, say P. The cohesion score can now be computed for P and the rest of the existing categories ($C_p = W_p/O_p$). The computation is repeated, pairing each time the new category with another existing category, until the cohesion score has been computed for all possible pairs. The existing category in the pair that yields the highest cohesion is the nearest category.

Once the NCL learns the nearest category, it requests from the CKM all the knowledge in that category. Once knowledge is provided, it immediately seeks the branches whose goal and topic are identical to, or resemble or relate most to, those of the new category. The NCL finally adopts the plan of the selected branch. Fig. 4 shows a sample outcome of this process. The new category model here was derived from a test case scenario which is not among the 105 initial ones.

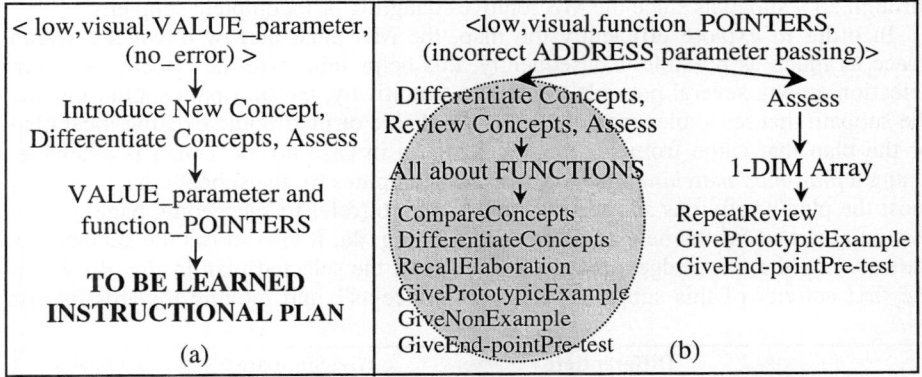

Fig. 4. The figure in (b) describes the nearest category learned by the NCL for the new model in (a). The NCL adopts as workable plan the one at the leaf node of the selected (shaded) path

5 Plan Learner

Even if a local plan is available, there is still no guarantee that it will immediately work for the student. A more accurate behavior is to acquire that plan but then slowly adapt and improve it to fit the student. This intelligent behavior is supported by the MSIP's *Plan Learner* (PL). Fig. 5 shows the PL's learning aspects and components.

Using the category knowledge provided by the CM, the *Map Builder* (MB) learns a map of alternative plans. Initially, the map is formed as a union of plans that worked for categories whose goals are similar to, or form the subgoals of, the current ses-

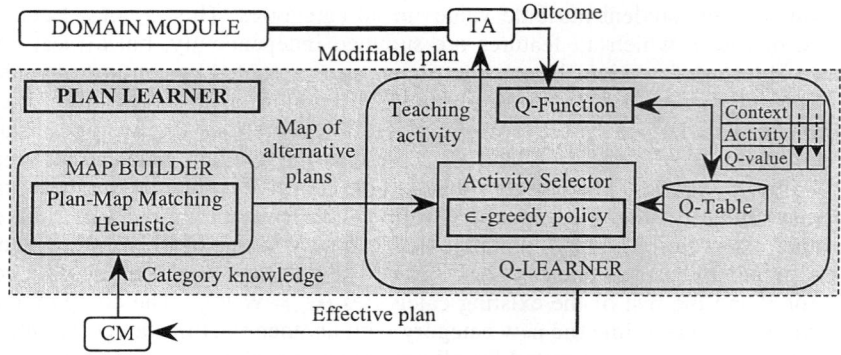

Fig. 5. The functional view of the Plan Learner

sion's goal. This is intuitive since the manner by which activities should be sequenced is explicitly seen in the goal. However, the MB needs to prune this map so as to fit the current context attributes. A teaching activity is retained in the map if: (1) it has been found in the past to be effective for the given context attribute values, (2) it follows tutorial session constraints (e.g., the activity "Compare concepts" apply only if there are two or more topics to be discussed), and (3) it belongs to a path that passes through all n subgoals since the MB removes dangling or incomplete subpaths.

In order to explore efficiently the map, the MB must narrow down the search space as much as possible. Consequently, this helps minimize the effect of random selection among several possible transitions. Intuitively, the best path should include the subpath that resembles most the initial workable or modifiable existing local plan or the plan that came from the nearest category in case no local plan is available. Using a *plan-map matching heuristic*, the MB computes for the subpath that preserves most the plan's activities and their sequence. Fig. 6 (refer to succeeding page) shows the map learned for the new category model in Fig. 4a. It also shows the subpath (as indicated by the thick edges) that resembles most the selected plan in Fig. 4b. From the first activity of this subpath, "Compare concepts", and moving towards its last

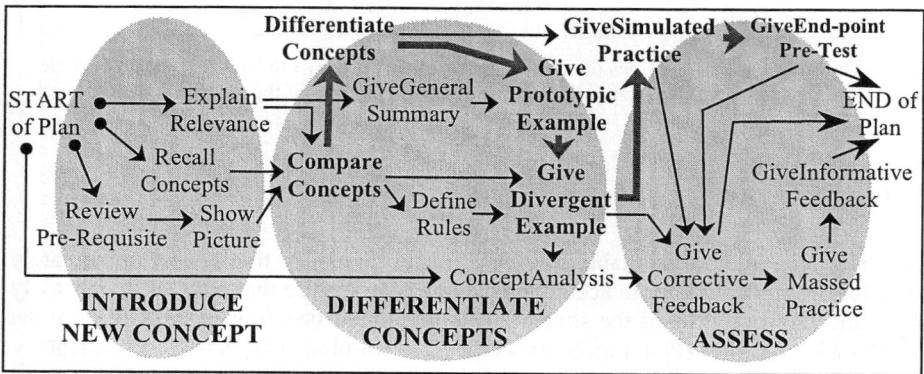

Fig. 6. The map is a directed graph of related teaching activities that need to be carried out in succession. The thick-edged transitions indicate the category-effected subpath that helps reduce the exploration space

activity, "Give end-point pre-test", all transitions that branch away from this subpath are disregarded during exploration. In this way, unnecessary subpaths can be ignored. The MB submits the final map to the Q-learner.

The most essential aspect of the learning process is for the PL to improve the modifiable plan towards the effective version, and it must do so efficiently. To account for this intelligent behavior, the PL utilizes its Q-learning agent, or *Q-learner*. Reinforcement learning (RL) is much more focused on goal-directed learning from interaction as compared to other machine learning approaches [16]. As an RL method, *Q-learning* [18] can process on-line experience with little computation while remaining interactive. More importantly, evidence shows that Q-learning is more efficient when provided with background knowledge [3].

The Q-learner derives a modifiable version of the plan by exploring the map provided by the MB. The Q-learner's activity selection module selects a teaching activity in the map and relays it to the TA. The procedural and content knowledge necessary to carry out each type of activity are encapsulated in the ITS Domain Module. The TA executes the activity and issues to the Q-learner a reinforcement value indicating whether the activity was effective (positive outcome), not effective (negative outcome), or neutral (no outcome) based on its assessment of the student's resulting knowledge state. The Q-function updates its table of Q-values depending on the feedback of the TA. A *Q-value* represents the predicted future (discounted) reward that will be achieved if the teaching activity is applied by the TA in the given tutorial context. Given a perfect version of the Q-function, the effective plan is derived by simply selecting in each context that is reached the activity that yields the largest Q-value. The best plan is the sequence of teaching activities that maximizes the accumulated Q-values. The Q-learner uses an internal ϵ-greedy policy. This means that with probability ϵ, it selects another activity rather than the one it thought was best. This prevents it from getting stuck to a sub-optimal plan. Over time, ϵ is gradually reduced and the Q-learner begins to exploit the activities it finds as optimal.

Using new recorded teaching scenarios as test cases, we experimented on the PL's capabilities in two set-ups: (1) category knowledge is utilized, and (2) the effect of category knowledge is removed, in constructing the map. Each set-up simulates the development of the same test scenario for 50 successive stages; each stage is characterized by a version (or modification) of the PL's plan. Each version is evaluated vis-à-vis the effective (again, as has been validated by experts) plan in the test scenario. The learning performance of the PL is the mean effectiveness in every stage across all scenarios. Fig. 7 shows the PL's learning performance.

It is evident that the PL can find the effective plan with the effectiveness level in each stage increasing asymptotically over time. The absence of category background knowledge restrains the PL's efficiency as well as the effectiveness of the learned instructional plans. When category knowledge is infused, however, the PL achieves its goal at an early stage. Since the PL learns from experience and does not need to start from scratch, the effectiveness of its plans starts at mid-level. It can be expected that as more category models are discovered, the effectiveness value will start at a higher level. Lastly, we have evidence that the PL discovered new plans, which attests to its incremental learning capabilities. Although, it did not discover new successions since it learned the new plans using the existing ones.

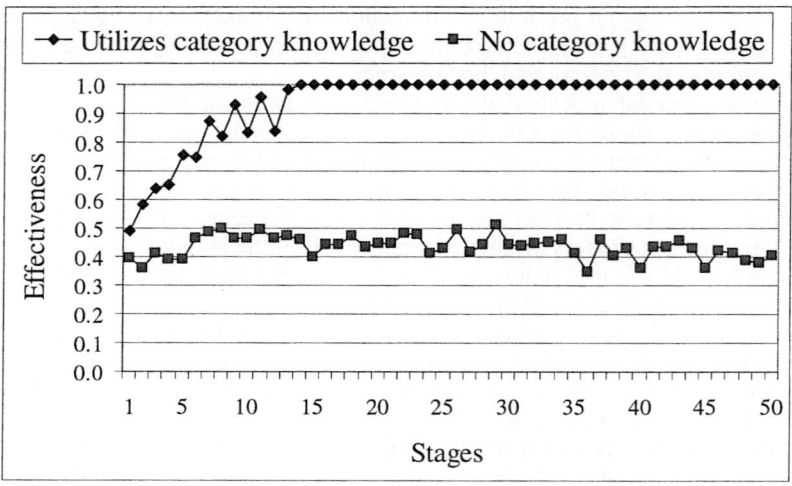

Fig. 7. The PL's learning performance

6 Conclusion and Future Work

A lot of work needs to be done in understanding how ITSs can improve their tutoring capabilities. Hitherto, no ITS self-improved its instructional plans for incrementally learned student categories. We demonstrated empirically that when differences in students' learning behavior are utilized by unsupervised machine learning techniques, it powerfully cued our agent-based planner to efficiently self-improve.

This is a research in progress that can be completed and improved in various ways. Communication protocols need to be set up for the MSIP agents. A comparative study of the MSIP with the few self-improving planners will provide a global view of its performance. Another is to include learner feedback in the planning process (e.g., "It could have helped me more if you conducted <activity> and skipped <another activity>"). Theoretically, such feedback can augment the existing plans with new activity successions. Most importantly, the MSIP's learning capabilities need to be validated in real-time interactions with actual students.

References

1. Arroyo, I., Beck, J., Beal, C., Woolf, B., Schultz, K.: Macroadapting AnimalWatch to gender and cognitive differences with respect to hint interactivity and symbolism. Proceedings of the Fifth International Conference on Intelligent Tutoring Systems (2000)
2. Beck, J.: Directing Development Effort with Simulated Students, In: Cerri, S.A., Gouardes, G., Paraguacu, F. (eds.). Lecture Notes in Computer Science, vol. 2363 (2002) 851-860
3. Bhanu, B., Leang, P., Cowden, C., Lin, Y., Patterson, M.: Real-Time Robot learning. Proceedings of the 2001 IEEE International Conference on Robotics and Automation (2001)

4. Bloom, B.S., et. al.: Taxonomy of Educational Objectives: Handbook I: Cognitive Domain, Longmans, Green and Company (1956)
5. Brusilovsky, P., Karagiannidis, C., Sampson, D.: The Benefits of Layered Evaluation of Adaptive Applications and Services. 8th International Conference on User Modelling, Workshop on Empirical Evaluations of Adaptive Systems (2001)
6. Dillenbourg, P.: The design of a self-improving tutor: PROTO-TEG. Instructional Science, 18(3), (1989) 193-216
7. Durfee, E.H.: Distributed problem solving and planning. Multi-agent systems and applications. Springer-Verlag, New York, Inc. (2001) 118-149
8. Felder, R.M., Silverman, L.K.: Learning and Teaching Styles in Engineering Education. Engr. Education, 78(7), (1988) 674-681 [The paper is preceded by a 2002 preface that states and explains changes in the model]
9. Gutstein, E.: SIFT: A Self-Improving Fractions Tutor. PhD thesis, Department of Computer Sciences, University of Wisconsin-Madison (1993)
10. Karagiannidis, C., Sampson, D.: Layered Evaluation of Adaptive Applications and Services. In: Brusilovsky, P., Stock, O., Strapparava, C. (eds.): Adaptive Hypermedia and Adaptive Web-based Systems. Lecture Notes in Computer Science, vol. 1892. Springer-Verlag, Berlin Heidelberg New York (2000) 343-346
11. Kimball, R.: A self-improving tutor for symbolic integration. In: Sleeman, D.H., and Brown, J.S. (eds): Intelligent Tutoring Systems, London Academic Press (1982)
12. Morin, J.F., Lelouche, R.: Agent-oriented tutoring knowledge modeling in a problem-solving ITS. Proc. of the ACM-SIGART Workshop on Interaction Agents (1998) 26-32
13. O'Shea, T.: A self-improving quadratic tutor. In: Sleeman, D.H., and Brown, J.S. (eds): Intelligent Tutoring Systems, London Academic Press (1982)
14. Reyes, R.: A Case-Based Reasoning Approach in Designing Explicit Representation of Pedagogical Situations in an Intelligent Tutoring System. PhD thesis, College of Computer Studies, De La Salle University, Manila (2002)
15. Sison, R., Numao, M., Shimura, M.: Multistrategy discovery and detection of novice programmer erros. Machine Learning, 38, (2000) 157-180
16. Sutton, R., Barto, A.: Reinforcement Learning: An Introduction. Cambridge, MA: MIT Press (1998)
17. Talmon, J.L., Fonteijn, H., & Braspenning, P.J.: An Analysis of the WITT Algorithm. Machine Learning, 11, (1993) 91-104
18. Watkins, C.J.C.H., Dayan, P.: Q-learning. Machine Learning, 8, (1992) 279-292

Circuit Consistencies

Abdellah Idrissi and Ahlem Ben Hassine

[1] 79, Rue du Port Boyer
44300, Nantes, France
abdelidri@yahoo.fr
[2] JAIST, 1-1, Tatsunokuchi
Ishikawa, 923-1292, Japan
hassine@jaist.ac.jp

Abstract. Partial Consistency is a preeminent property for improving the solving process of a constraint satisfaction problem. This property is depicted by the omnipresence of several levels of consistency among which circuit consistency. Two non-equivalent definitions have been proposed for this level. In this paper we present, first, some concepts of the most local consistencies techniques used in practice. Second, we upraise the ambiguity of the two proposed definitions of circuit consistency property. Then, we rename and redefine them. Finally, we study their capacities of filtering by comparing them with other local consistencies.

Keywords: Constraint Satisfaction, Circuit Consistency.

1 Introduction

Local consistency is a preeminent property in improving the solving process of the constraint satisfaction problems (CSP). Reinforcing local consistency is defined by the process of pruning some inconsistent values from the original problem. Filtering techniques are essential to reduce the search space effectively, they can be used as phase of pre-treatment or throughout the search for a solution. Their aim is to make explicit the implicit constraints appearing in the constraint network. These techniques allow us to avoid discovering many times certain local inconsistencies and consequently prune the search tree. Several local consistencies levels were proposed in the literature. However, choosing which level of consistency we have to apply, we need to compute the compromise between its capacity to prune the search tree and the required time.

In this paper, we focus on the circuit consistency property proposed in [2] and [3]. Two non-equivalent definitions have been proposed for this level. The main contribution of this paper is first to upraise the divergence between the two definitions given for circuit consistency property. Second, to propose new interpretations for this property. Finally, we suggest a classification of the proposed new definitions using to the relation "stronger than". A local consistency LC is *stronger than* another local consistency LC' if for any network of constraints checking LC also checks LC' and a local consistency LC is *strictly stronger* than another local consistency LC' if LC is stronger than LC' and if there is at least a network of constraints checking LC' which do not check LC.

The rest of the paper is organized as follows. Section 2 introduces the local consistencies. Section 3 presents the circuit consistency definitions followed by some discussions. In section 4, we propose the new circuit consistency definitions and study in section 5 their capacities of filtering by comparing them with other local consistencies allowing to identify inconsistent values. Section 6 concludes the paper.

2 Local Consistencies

A constraints satisfaction problems is defined simply by a set of variables provided with a finite domains and a set of constraints relating these variables. The constraints restrict the values the variables can simultaneously take.

More formally a CSP P is a triplet (X, D, C) where: $X=\{X_1,...,X_n\}$ is the set of n variables of the problem. $D=\{D_1,...,D_n\}$ is the set of domains where $D_i=\{v_{i_1}...v_{i_d}\}$ is the set of possible values for the variable X_i and finally $C=\{C_{ij},...\}$ is the set of e constraints of the problem. Each constraint carries on a set of distinct variables. We should note that, in this paper we focus only on binary constraints, where each constraint implies two variables.

Solving a CSP consists in finding a set of assignments of values for the variables such all the constraints are simultaneously respected. This is an NP-complete problem. Therefore it is useful to reduce as much as possible the size of the search space and this by reinforcing, before or during research, some level of local consistency.

Local consistency techniques lie close to the heart of constraint programming's success. They can prune values from the domain of variables, saving much fruitless exploration of the search tree. There are several levels of local consistencies in the literature. In the next section, we will focus our work on the circuit consistency [2]. We will setup it in the hierarchy of local consistencies allowing to remove non-viable values according to the relation "stronger than". But, it is noteworthy that [2] and [3], proposed two different definitions of the circuit consistency. Therefore, we will first point out these two definitions, then we will show that they do not indicate the same local consistency.

3 Circuit Consistency Definitions

3.1 Definitions

Definition 1. *We call* Compatible Value Graph *CVG [2] of a CSP, the n-partite graph defined as follows: for each variable X_i of the CSP, we associate the set of vertices $V_i = \{(X_i, v_{i_1}), ..., (X_i, v_{i_d})\}$ where $D_i = \{v_{i_1}, ..., v_{i_d}\}$; two vertices (X_i, v_{i_k}) and (X_j, v_{j_l}) of the graph are linked if $X_i \neq X_j$ and $R_{ij}(v_{i_k}, v_{j_l})$ (the vertices of each set V_i are not linked).*

We assume that the constraint network is a complete graph, therefore, for each two free variables (not related by a constraint), we can assign for them the universal constraint to complete the graph without changing the set of solutions.

Definition 2. *The* Directed Compatible Value Graph *(DCVG) [2] is defined by choosing an arbitrary order on the variables of the CSP. Let $X_1, ..., X_n$ be this order and $V_1, ..., V_n$ their corresponding sets of vertices in the CVG. The edges between sets of vertices V_i and V_{i+1} for $i = 1, ..., n-1$ are directed from V_i to V_{i+1}, while the edges between V_i and V_j with $i+2 \leq j$ for $i = 1, ..., n-2$ and $j = 3, ..., n$ are directed from V_j to V_i.*

Several DCVG can be defined for the same CVG according to the used variables' order.

Definition 3. *A set V_i of vertices of DCVG graph is* **Circuit Consistent (CC)** *[2], [3] if and only if $\forall (X_i, v_{i_k}) \in V_i$, there exists at least one elementary circuit of length p, for each $p \in \{3, ..., n\}$ passing through (X_i, v_{i_k}) such that the set of vertices of the circuit of length p-1 is a subset of the set of vertices of the circuit of length p. A domain $D_i \in D$ is circuit consistent if the set of the associated vertices V_i is circuit consistent. A CSP P is circuit consistent if and only if $\forall\ D_i \in D$, D_i is circuit consistent and D_i is not empty.*

We notice that the definition of the circuit consistency of a CSP is based only on one DCVG independently of the chosen order among the variables of the problems. However, as we indicated above, for the same CVG many DCVG can be assigned.

Definition 4. *A relaxed compatible value graph RCVG is a partial graph of DCVG obtained by taking only the arcs between V_i and V_{i+1} and those between V_n and V_1.*

Definition 5. *A set V_i of vertices of V is circuit consistent [2], [3] if and only if $\forall (X_i, v_{i_k}) \in V_i$ there exists n-1 vertices (X_j, v_{j_l}), j=1, ..., n $j \neq i$ such that for all j, $R_{ij}(v_{i_k}, v_{j_l})$ there is at least one path of length $p =| j - i\ | mod[n]$ from (X_i, v_{i_k}) to (X_j, v_{j_l}) passing through the set of vertices of the path of length p-1 in the RCVG graph. A domain D_i of D is circuit consistent if the set of the associated vertices V_i is circuit consistent. A CSP P is circuit consistent if and only if $\forall\ D_i \in D$, D_i is circuit consistent and D_i is not empty.*

3.2 Discussions

We notice that the check of the circuit consistency of (X_i, v_{i_k}) using definition 5, requires the handle of a range implying all the variables. Whilst for the definition 3, it imposes an overlap of the circuits of lower size into those of higher size. Figure 2 presents a network of constraints circuit consistent by the definition 3, but which is not circuit consistent by definition 5. The value (X_3, v_2)

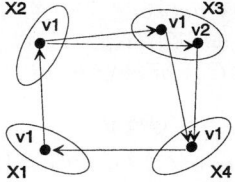 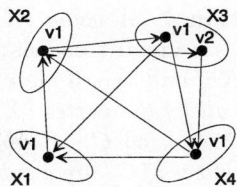

Fig. 1. On the left, Example of relaxed compatible value graph.

Fig. 2. On the right, CN checking CC by def. 3 but not check it by def. 5.

can be extended to the circuit $\{(X_3, v_2), (X_4, v_1), (X_2, v_1)\}$ of length 3 in the DCVG corresponding to the order X_2, X_3, X_4, X_1. The vertices of this circuit are included in the circuit $\{(X_3, v_2), (X_4, v_1), (X_1, v_1), (X_2, v_1)\}$ of the DCVG. The value (X_3, v_2) is circuit consistent by definition 3, but it is not by definition 5, i.e. there exists no value compatible with (X_3, v_2) in the domain of X_1. Therefore, to ensure the equivalence between the two definitions 3 and 5, it would be necessary that the orientation of the DCVG is modified according to the variable to check while ensuring a circular order on the variables, i.e. to check the circuit consistency of the values of D_i one must take X_i as first variable in the order. For the previous example, the order of the variables to consider for the DCVG should be X_1, X_2, X_3, X_4 to check the CC of the values of X_1, and X_2, X_3, X_4, X_1 to check the values of X_2, and soon. Using such dynamic order on the variables of the DCVG, the two definitions 3 and 5 define the same local consistency. Thus for the previous example, it is unnecessary to check the CC for (X_3, v_2) by applying definition 3 since in the DCVG to consider figure 2 there is no circuit of length 3 passing by (X_3, v_2).

Thus, to prove the circuit consistency by definition 3 depends on the used order among the problem variables, i.e. some value can be circuit consistency by an order and not by another one. In the following we will first rename and redefine these two local consistency properties. Second we will discuss their capacities of theoretical filtering by comparing them with other local consistencies allowing to identify inconsistent values.

4 New Circuit Consistency Definitions

Definition 6. *Given a constraints network $\mathcal{R}=(X, D, C)$ with $n = |X|$ and an order $d = (X_{d_1}, X_{d_2}..., X_{d_n})$ on X, one calls* directed graph of the compatible values *of $\mathcal{R}$ and d, noted $DCVG(\mathcal{R}, d)$ the n-partite graph defined as follows:*
- At each variable X_i is associated the set of vertices $V_i = \{ (X_i, v_{i_1}), (X_i, v_{i_2}), ..., (X_i, v_{i_p}) \}$ where $D_i = \{v_{i_1}, v_{i_2}, ..., v_{i_p}\}$.
- There exists an arc from $(X_{d_i}, v_{d_{i_k}})$ to $(X_{d_{i+1}}, v_{d_{i_m}})$ ($i < n$) if and only if $((X_{d_i}, v_{d_{i_k}}), (X_{d_{(i+1)}}), v_{d_{(i+1)_m}}))$ is an authorized pair of values.
- There exists an arc from $(X_{d_i}, v_{d_{i_k}})$ to $(X_{d_j}, v_{d_{j_l}})$ if and only if $((X_{d_i}, v_{d_{i_k}}), (X_{d_j}, v_{d_{j_l}}))$ is an authorized pair of values and $i > j + 1$ with $i \in \{3, 4, ..., n\}$ and $j \in \{1, 2, ..., n-2\}$.

Definition 7. *A value (X_i, v_{i_k}) of a constraints network $\mathcal{R}=(X, D, C)$ with $n = |X|$ is d-circuit consistent (d-CC) where $d = (X_{d_1}, X_{d_2}, ..., X_{d_n})$ is an order on X if and only if there is a series $(C_3, C_4, ..., C_n)$ of circuits of $DCVG(\mathcal{R},d)$ passing all by the vertex (X_i, v_{i_k}) such as:*
- *$\forall j \in \{3, 4, ..., n\}$ C_j is length j.*
- *The vertices of C_j are a subset of the set of vertices of C_k for all $j \in \{3, 4, ..., n-1\}$ and $k \in \{4, 5, ..., n\}$ such as $j < k$.*

Definition 8. *A constraints network $\mathcal{R}=(X, D, C)$ is d-circuit consistent where d is an order on X if and only if $\forall$ $D_i \in D$, $D_i \neq \emptyset$ and all the values of D_i are d-circuit consistent.*

Definition 9. *Given a constraints network $\mathcal{R}=(X, D, C)$ with $n = |X|$ and an order $d = (X_{d_1}, X_{d_2}, ..., X_{d_n})$ on X, one calls Restricted Graph of the Compatible Values of $\mathcal{R}$ and d, noted $RCVG(\mathcal{R}, d)$ the n-partite graph defined by:*
- *At each variable X_i is associated the set of vertices $V_i = \{(X_i, v_{i_1}), (X_i, v_{i_2}), ..., (X_i, v_{i_d})\}$ where $D_i = \{v_{i_1}, v_{i_2}, ..., v_{i_d}\}$.*
- *There exists an arc from $(X_{d_i}, v_{d_{i_k}})$ to $(X_{d_{(i+1)}}, v_{d_{(i+1)_m}})$ $(i < n)$ if and only if $((X_{d_i}, v_{d_{i_k}}), (X_{d_{(i+1)}}, v_{d_{(i+1)_m}}))$ is an authorized pair of values.*
- *There exists an arc from $(X_{d_n}, v_{d_{n_p}})$ to $(X_{d_1}, v_{d_{1_p}})$ if and only if $((X_{d_n}, v_{d_{n_p}}), (X_{d_1}, v_{d_{1_p}}))$ is an authorized pair of values.*

Definition 10. *A value (X_i, v_{i_k}) of a constraints network $\mathcal{R}=(X, D, C)$ is d-dynamic circuit consistent (d-DCC) where $d = (X_{d_1}, X_{d_2}, ..., X_{d_n})$ is an order on X if and only if there exists for any variable $X_h \in X$ different of X_i a value $Val[X_h]$ such as $((X_i, v_{i_k}), (X_h, Val[X_{h_m}]))$ is authorized and $((X_i, v_{i_k}), (X_{d_{j+1}}, Val[X_{d_{j+1}}]), ..., (X_{d_n}, Val[X_{d_n}]), (X_{d_1}, Val[X_{d_1}]), ..., (X_{d_{j-1}}, Val[X_{d_{j-1}}]))$ is a circuit of $RCVG(\mathcal{R}, d)$ where j is defined by $d_j = i$.*

The concept of the d-dynamic circuit consistency can be approached independently of that of RCVG like illustrates it below the equivalent definition.

Definition 11. *A value (X_i, v_{i_k}) of a constraints network $\mathcal{R}=(X, D, C)$ is d-dynamic circuit consistent (d-DCC) where $d = (X_{d_1}, X_{d_2}, ..., X_{d_n})$ is an order on X if and only if there is an instantiation I of X such as:*
- *$I[X_i] = v_{i_k}$.*
- *$\forall j \in \{1, 2, ..., n-1\}$ with $n = |X|$, $((X_{d_j}, I[X_{d_j}]), (X_{d_{j+1}}, I[X_{d_{j+1}}]))$ is an authorized pair of values.*
- *$((X_{d_n}, I[X_{d_n}]), (X_{d_1}, I[X_{d_1}]))$ is an authorized pair of values.*
- *$\forall j \in \{1, ..., n\}$ $(j \neq i)$, $((X_i, v_{i_k}), (X_j, I[X_j]))$ is an authorized pair of values.*

Theorem 1. *Definitions 10 and 11 are equivalent.*

Proof. Let be $\mathcal{R} = (X, D, C)$ a constraints network and $d = (X_{d_1}, ..., X_{d_n})$ an order on X.

- A d-DCC value according to the definition 10 is also d-DCC according to the definition 11. Assume that (X_i, v_{i_k}) a d-DCC consistent value according to the definition 10. Let I the instantiation of X defined by $I[X_i] = v_{i_k}$ and $\forall X_j \in X$ such as $X_j \neq X_i$ $I[X_j] = Val[X_j]$. $\forall j \in \{1, 2, ..., n-1\}$ with $n = |X|$, $((X_{d_j}, I[X_{d_j}]), (X_{d_{j+1}}, I[X_{d_{j+1}}]))$ is an authorized pair of values since by definition of RCVG$(\mathcal{R}, d)$ there is an arc from the vertex $(X_{d_j}, Val[X_{d_j}])$ to the vertex $(X_{d_{j+1}}, Val[X_{d_{j+1}}])$ only if this pair, of values, is authorized and $((X_i, v_{i_k}), (X_{d_{i+1}}, Val[X_{d_{i+1}}]), ..., (X_{d_n}, Val[X_{d_n}]), (X_{d_1}, Val[X_{d_1}]), ..., (X_{d_{i-1}}, Val[X_{d_{i-1}}]))$ is a circuit of RCVG$(\mathcal{R}, d)$. $((X_{d_n}, Val[X_{d_n}]), (X_{d_1}, Val[X_{d_1}]))$ correspond to an arc of a circuit of RCVG$(\mathcal{R}, d)$ and the pair of values $((X_{d_n}, I[X_{d_n}]), (X_{d_1}, I[X_{d_1}]))$ are thus by definition of RCVG$(\mathcal{R}, d)$ a pair of values authorized. Lastly, $\forall j \in \{1, ..., n\}$ such as $j \neq i$, $((X_i, v_{i_k}), (X_j, Val[X_j]))$ are an authorized pair and $((X_i, v_{i_k}), (X_j, I[X_j]))$ is thus also since $I[X_j] = Val[X_j]$. Consequently, (X_i, v_{i_k}) are a d-DCC value according to the definition 11.
- A d-DCC consistent value according to the definition 11 is also according to the definition 10: Assume that (X_i, v_{i_k}) a d-DCC consistent value according to the definition 11. There is an instantiation I checking the four properties of definition 11. For every $X_j \in \mathcal{X}$ such as $X_j \neq X_i$, let us define $Val[X_j]$ by $Val[X_j] = I[X_j]$. According to the definition 11, the pair of values $((X_{d_j}, Val[X_{d_j}]), (X_{d_{j+1}}, Val[X_{d_{j+1}}]))$ is authorized $\forall j \in \{1, 2, ..., n-1\}$ and there is thus an arc from the vertex $(X_{d_j}, Val[X_{d_j}])$ to the vertex $(X_{d_{j+1}}, Val[X_{d_{j+1}}])$ in RCVG$(\mathcal{R}, d)$. Moreover, $((X_{d_n}, Val[X_{d_n}]), (X_{d_1}, Val[X_{d_1}]))$ is authorized and there is thus an arc from the vertex $(X_{d_n}, Val[X_{d_n}])$ to the vertex $(X_{d_1}, Val[X_{d_1}])$ in RCVG$(\mathcal{R}, d)$. $((X_i, v_{i_k}), (X_{d_{h+1}}, Val[X_{d_{h+1}}]), ..., (X_{d_n}, Val[X_{d_n}]), (X_{d_1}, Val[X_{d_1}]), ..., (X_{d_{h-1}}, Val[X_{d_{h-1}}]))$ where h is defined by $d_h = i$ is thus a circuit of RCVG$(\mathcal{R}, d)$ and (X_i, v_{i_k}) is d-DCC according to the definition 10.

Definition 12. *A constraints network $\mathcal{R}=(X, D, C)$ is d-**dynamic circuit consistent (d-DCC)** where d is an order on X if and only if $\forall$ $X_i \in X$, $D_i \neq \emptyset$ and $\forall (X_i, v_{i_k}) \in D$, (X_i, v_{i_k}) is d-dynamic circuit consistent.*

5 Classification of the Consistencies (d-CC and d-DCC)

Theorem 2. *For any order d on the set of variables, the d-dynamic circuit consistency (d-DCC) is strictly stronger than the d-circuit consistency (d-CC).*

Proof. Let be $\mathcal{R}=(X, D, C)$ a constraints network and $d = (X_{d_1}, X_{d_2}, ..., X_{d_n})$ an order on $\mathcal{X}$. Let be $(X_{d_i}, v_{d_{i_k}})$ a d-dynamic circuit consistent value and I an instantiation checking the (X_{d_i}, v_{d_i}) for the conditions of definition 11. There is a series $(C_3, C_4, ..., C_n)$ of circuits of DCVG$(\mathcal{R}, d)$ passing all by $(X_{d_i}, v_{d_{i_k}})$ such as $\forall i \in \{3, 4, ..., n\}$ C_i is length i and $\forall i \in \{3, 4, ..., n-1\}$ and $\forall j \in \{4, 5, ..., n\}$ such as $i < j$, the set of vertices of C_i are a subset of the set of vertices of C_j. Indeed, $\forall p \in \{3, 4, ..., n\}$ it is enough to define C_p by:

- If $p \leq i$, $C_p=((X_{d_i}, v_{d_i}), (X_{d_{i-p+1}}, I[X_{d_{i-p+1}}]), (X_{d_{i-p+2}}, I[X_{d_{i-p+2}}]), ..., (X_{d_{i-1}}, I[X_{d_{i-1}}]))$.
- If not, $C_p=((X_{d_i}, v_{d_i}), (X_{d_{i+1}}, I[X_{d_{i+1}}]), ..., (X_{d_p}, I[X_{d_p}]), (X_1, I[X_1]), ..., (X_{i-1}, I[X_{i-1}]))$.

The value (X_{d_i}, v_{d_i}) are thus d-circuit consistent and the d-dynamic circuit consistency is stronger than d-circuit consistency. Moreover, figure 3(a) presents the graph of inconsistency of a constraints network which is d-circuit consistent but not d-dynamic circuit consistent with $d = (X_1, X_2..., X_n)$. Consequently the d-dynamic circuit consistency is strictly stronger than d-circuit consistency.

Theorem 3. *The arc consistency (AC) and the d-circuit consistency (d-CC) are incomparable according to the relation "stronger than".*

Proof. Figure 3(a) presents the graph of inconsistency of a consistent network of constraints d-circuit consistent (with $d = (X_1, X_2, ..., X_n)$) which is not arc consistent and figure 3(b) presents the graph of inconsistency of a network of constraints arc consistent which is not d-circuit consistent.

Theorem 4. *The d-dynamic circuit consistency (d-DCC) is strictly stronger than the arc consistency (AC).*

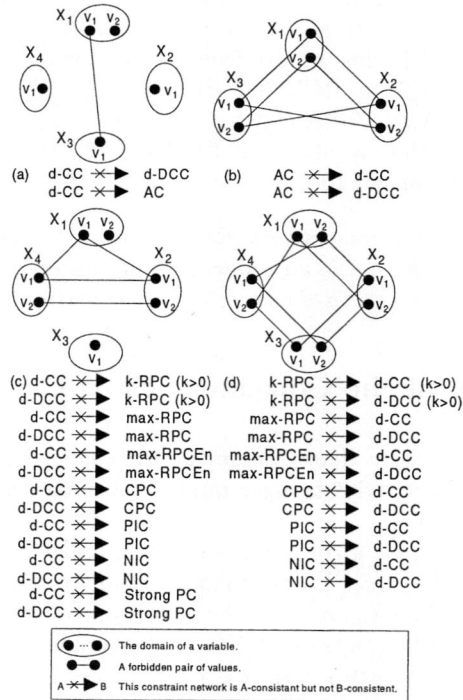

Fig. 3. Comparison between d-CC, d-DCC and other local consistencies.

Proof. That is to say $\mathcal{R}=(X, D, C)$ a network of constraints and (with $d = (X_1, X_2, ..., X_n)$) an order on $\mathcal{X}$. $\forall (X_i, v_{i_k})$ there exists an instantiation I such as $\forall k \in \{1, ..., n\}$ with $k \neq i$, $((X_i, v_i), (X_k, I[X_k]))$ is an authorized pair of values. Consequently, each value of the network $\mathcal{R}$ has at least ONE support on each constraint and $\mathcal{R}$ thus checks the arc consistency. Moreover, figure 3(b) presents the graph of a constraints network arc consistent which does not check the d-dynamic circuit consistency.

Theorem 5. *With respect to the relation "stronger than", the d-circuit consistency (d-CC) and the d-dynamic circuit consistency (d-DCC) are incomparable with the k-restricted path consistency (k-RPC) ($\forall k \geq 1$), the max-restricted path consistency (max-RPC), the max-restricted path consistency enhanced (max-RPCEn), the conservative path consistency (CPC) [5], the path inverse consistency (PIC) [6] and the neighborhood inverse consistency (NIC) [6].*

Proof. Figure 3(c) has the graph of inconsistency of a constraints network d-CC consistency and d-DCC consistency with $d = (X_1, X_2, ..., X_n)$ which does not check the k-RPC ($\forall k \geq 1$), the max-RPC, the max-RPCEn, the CPC, the PIC and the NIC consistency. Moreover, figure 3(d) presents the graph of a constraints network which checks neither the d-CC consistency, nor the d-dynamic CC consistency (with $d = (X_1, X_2, ..., X_n)$) and which checks the k-RPC ($\forall k \geq 1$), the max-RPC, the max-RPCEn, the CPC, the PIC and the NIC.

Theorem 6. *The singleton arc consistency (SAC) is strictly stronger than the d-dynamic circuit consistency (d-DCC).*

Proof. First of all let us prove by recurrence on k that given a constraints network $\mathcal{R}=(X, D, C)$ and $d = (X_1, X_2, ..., X_n)$ an order on X, if a value $(X_{d_i}, v_{d_{i_k}})$ is singleton arc consistent then it exists for all $k \in \{1, 2, ..., n-1\}$ an instantiation I of $\{ X_{d_i}, X_{d_{(i+1) mod(n)}}, ..., X_{d_{(i+k) mod(n)}} \}$ made up only of arc consistent values of $\mathcal{R} \mid_{D_{d_i} = \{v_{d_i}\}}$ and such as:

1. $I[X_{d_i}] = v_{d_{i_k}}$.
2. $\forall j \in \{I, (i+1) mod(n), ..., (i+k-1) mod(n)\}$, $((X_{d_j}, I[X_{d_j}]), (X_{d_{(j+1) mod(n)}}, I[X_{d_{(j+1) mod(n)}}]))$ is an authorized pair of values.
3. $\forall j \in \{1, ..., k\}$, $((X_{d_i}, v_{d_i}), (X_{d_{(i+j) mod(n)}}, I[X_{d_{(i+j) mod(n)}}]))$ is an authorized pair of values.

For $k = 1$ this property is checked. Indeed, if $(X_{d_i}, v_{d_{i_k}})$ is singleton arc-consistent, then $\mathcal{R} \mid_{D_{d_i} = \{v_{d_{i_k}}\}}$ is not arc inconsistent. Let be b a support of $(X_{d_i}, v_{d_{i_k}})$ in the field of $X_{d_{(i+1) mod(n)}}$ in $\mathcal{R} \mid_{D_{d_i} = \{v_{d_{i_k}}\}}$. The instantiation which associates $v_{d_{i_k}}$ to X_{d_i} and b to $X_{d_{(i+1) mod(n)}}$ checks conditions 1 to 3. Let us suppose now the property checked for k ($k < n - 1$) and let us show that it is it also for $k + 1$. That is to say I an instantiation answering the conditions for k. $(X_{d_{(i+k) mod(n)}}, I[X_{d_{(i+k) mod(n)}}])$ is an arc consistent value of $\mathcal{R} \mid_{D_{d_i} = \{v_{d_{i_k}}\}}$ and thus has in $\mathcal{R} \mid_{D_{d_i} = \{v_{d_{i_k}}\}}$ at least a support c in $D_{d_{(i+k+1) mod(n)}}$. $(X_{d_{(i+k+1) mod(n)}}, c)$

Solving Over-Constrained Temporal Reasoning Problems Using Local Search*

Matthew Beaumont[1], John Thornton[1], Abdul Sattar[1], and Michael Maher[2]

[1] School of Information Technology,
Griffith University Gold Coast, Southport, Qld, Australia 4215
{m.beaumont,j.thornton,a.sattar}@griffith.edu.au
[2] Department of Computer Science,
Loyola University, Chicago, IL 60626, USA
mjm@cs.luc.edu

Abstract. Temporal reasoning is an important task in many areas of computer science including planning, scheduling, temporal databases and instruction optimisation for compilers. Given a knowledge-base consisting of temporal relations, the main reasoning problem is to determine whether the knowledge-base is satisfiable, i.e., is there a scenario which is consistent with the information provided. However, many real world problems are over-constrained (i.e. unsatisfiable). To date, there has been little research aimed at solving over-constrained temporal reasoning problems. Recently, we developed standard backtracking algorithms to compute *partial scenarios*, in the spirit of Freuder and Wallace's notion of *partial satisfaction*. While these algorithms were capable of obtaining optimal partial solutions, they were viable only for small problem sizes. In this paper, we apply local search methods to overcome the deficiencies of the standard approach to solving over-constrained temporal reasoning problems. Inspired by our recent success in efficiently handling reasonably large satisfiable temporal reasoning problems using local search, we have developed two new local search algorithms using a random restart strategy and a TABU search. Further, we extend our previous constraint weighting algorithm to handle over-constrained problems. An empirical study of these new algorithms was performed using randomly generated under- and over-constrained temporal reasoning problems. We conclude that 1) local search significantly outperforms standard backtracking approaches on over-constrained temporal reasoning problems; and 2) the random restart strategy and TABU search have a superior performance to constraint weighting for the over-constrained problems. We also conjecture that the poorer performance of constraint weighting is due to distortions of non-zero global minima caused by the weighting process.

1 Introduction

Temporal reasoning plays an important role in many areas of computer science including planning [2], scheduling [7], natural language processing [10], tempo-

---

* The authors gratefully acknowledge the financial support of the Australian Research Council, grant A00000118, in the conduct of this research.

ral databases and instruction optimisation for compilers. Temporal information can generally be broken up into two categories, quantitative information and qualitative information. Quantitative information is specific numerical information about an event, whereas qualitative information is information about the relationship between events. This study is primarily concerned with qualitative temporal information.

Allen's interval algebra [1] models qualitative information about temporal problems by representing the relation between two events as a disjunction of up to thirteen possible atomic relations. The reasoning problem is then the task of finding a consistent labelling of every relation in the problem with one atomic relation from the disjunctive set of relations available. Traditionally interval algebra (IA) problems have been represented as binary temporal constraint satisfaction problems (TCSP), expressed as constraint networks. where the arcs between nodes represent relations and the nodes represent events.

An over-constrained TCSP is a TCSP that has no solution satisfying all the constraints; to "solve" such problems we look for a labelling that is consistent with a maximal number of constraints [4]. In [3], we developed a traditional backtracking approach to solve over-constrained IA problems. While our algorithm was capable of obtaining optimal solutions, it was only viable on small problem sizes. Even with the use of path consistency, the search space is not reduced sufficiently to find a solution in a practical time frame. To overcome this problem we turned to the local search paradigm.

Local search techniques, while not complete, have been shown to be effective on problems that are often too large for traditional backtracking to solve [8, 9, 11, 13]. Unfortunately, the standard approach of representing an IA problem as a TCSP proved impractical for a local search approach, as to find an accurate cost of a potential solution involves a significant search in its own right [3]. By remodelling the problem as a standard CSP using the *end point ordering* model [13] we were able to obtain the cost of potential solutions accurately without the need of a separate search, thus allowing us to apply a local search algorithm in a straight forward and efficient manner.

In this paper, we apply local search methods to overcome the deficiencies of the standard approach to solving over-constrained temporal reasoning problems. Inspired by our recent success [13] in efficiently handling a reasonably large (under-constrained) temporal reasoning problems using constraint weighting local search, we develop two new algorithms using a random restart strategy and a TABU search. Further, we extend our previous constraint weighting algorithm to handle over-constrained problems and present an empirical evaluation of all three algorithms.

The rest of the paper is organised as follows: Section 2 introduces Interval Algebra (IA). Section 3 describes how local search can be applied to temporal reasoning problems by reformulating them using end-point ordering. Section 4 describes local search algorithms for handling over-constrained temporal reasoning problems. Section 5 presents results and analysis of the empirical study. Finally, we conclude the paper with a few remarks on future work.

2 Interval Algebra

Allen's Interval Algebra (IA) provides a rich formalism for expressing qualitative relations between interval events [1]. In IA, a time interval X is an ordered pair of real-valued time points or *end-points* (X^-, X^+) such that $X^- < X^+$. Allen defined a set **B** of 13 basic interval relations such that any pair of time intervals satisfy exactly one basic relation. These relations capture the *qualitative* aspect of event pairs being before, meeting, overlapping, starting, during, equal or finishing each other. Indefinite information is expressed in IA as a disjunction of basic relations, represented as an *interval formula* of the form: $X\{B_1..B_n\}Y$ where $\{B_1..B_n\} \subseteq \mathbf{B}$. For example, the interval formula $X\{m,o\}Y$ represents the disjunction (X meets Y) or (X overlaps Y).

An IA problem has a solution if there is an assignment of an interval to each interval variable such that all interval relations are satisfied. An I-interpretation [6] maps each interval variable to an interval. It *satisfies* a basic relation $X\{B\}Y$ iff the end-points of the intervals assigned to X and Y satisfy the corresponding end-point constraints. We say that an IA problem Θ is I-satisfiable iff there exists an I-interpretation such that at least one basic relation in each interval formula is satisfied. ISAT is the problem of deciding whether Θ is I-satisfiable and is one of the basic tasks of temporal reasoning [6]. This problem is known to be NP-complete [14] in general.

3 End Point Ordering

End-point ordering [13] translates the ISAT problem into a standard CSP, taking the end-point relations of interval formulas to be constraints and the time interval end-points to be variables. The main innovation of our approach is that we define the domain value of each time interval end-point to be the integer valued position or rank of that end-point within the *total ordering of all end-points*. For example, consider the following solution S to a hypothetical IA problem:

$$S = X\{b\}Y \wedge Y\{m\}Z \wedge Z\{bi\}X$$

Given the solution is consistent, a set of possible I-interpretations must exist that satisfy S. One member of this set is given by $I_a = (X^- = 12, X^+ = 15, Y^- = 27, Y^+ = 30, Z^- = 30, Z^+ = 45)$. For each I-interpretation, I_n, there must also exist a *unique* ordering of the time-interval end-points that corresponds to I_n. For example, the ordering of I_a is given by $(X^- < X^+ < Y^- < Y^+ = Z^- < Z^+)$ and is shown in the following diagram:

$$\begin{array}{ccc} \overleftrightarrow{X} & \overleftrightarrow{Y} & \overleftrightarrow{Z} \end{array}$$

As any I-interpretation can be translated into a unique end-point ordering, it follows that the search space of all possible end-point orderings will necessarily contain all possible solutions for a particular problem. In addition, since it is the end-point ordering that is key – and not the values assigned to each endpoint, we

```
function FindBestMoves(Constraints, Cost, e_i^-, e_i^+)
  Moves ← ∅, OuterCost ← 0
  OuterConstraints ← all c_i ∈ Constraints involving (e_i^-, e_i^+)
  d_min^- ← min domain value of e_i^-
  while d_min^- ≤ max domain value of e_i^- do
    (TestCost, OuterCost, d_max^-) ← FindCost(e_i^-, d_min^-, OuterConstraints, OuterCost)
    if OuterCost > Cost then d_max^- ← max domain value of e_i^-
    else if TestCost <= Cost then
      InnerCost ← OuterCost, InnerConstraints ← OuterConstraints
      d_min^+ ← d_min^- + 1
      while d_min^+ ≤ max domain value of e_i^+ do
        (TestCost, InnerCost, d_max^+, RealCost)
                  ← FindCost(e_i^+, d_min^+, InnerConstraints, InnerCost)
        if RealCost < BestRealCost then
          BestRealCost ← RealCost
        if TestCost < Cost then
          Cost ← TestCost
          Moves ← ∅
        else if TestCost = Cost then Moves ← Moves ⊕ ((d_min^- ... d_max^-), (d_min^+ ... d_max^+))
        if InnerCost > Cost then d_max^+ ← max domain value of e_i^+ + 1
        d_min^+ ← d_max^+ + 1
      end while
    end if
    d_min^- ← d_max^- + 1
  end while
  return (Moves, Cost)
end
```

Fig. 1. The modified *FindBestMoves* TSAT Move Selection Function.

can choose convenient values for the end-points. Hence, we can assign an integer to each of the end-points in a way that respects the ordering (e.g. $X^- = 1$, $X^+ = 2$, $Y^- = 3$, $Y^+ = 4$, $Z^- = 4$, $Z^+ = 5$ for the above ordering).

4 Local Search for Over-Constrained Problems

4.1 Constraint Weighting

The original constraint weighting algorithm [13] works with the certainty that a solution to a problem exists and therefore only tracks the weighted cost (since when this cost is zero the unweighted cost will also be zero). As there are no zero cost solutions in an over-constrained problem, the algorithm will fail to recognise that a new optimum cost solution has been found, and at timeout will simply report failure. To solve over-constrained problems we extend the algorithm by tracking the unweighted cost at every move point in the cost function, shown by the FindBestMoves function in Figure 1, where the global variable *BestRealCost* holds the current optimum cost. The algorithm will still navigate the search space with the weighting heuristic and, in addition, the best solution found so far in the search will be recorded and replaced based on the unweighted cost.

4.2 TABU Search

The TABU search is a local search technique that relies on keeping a memory of the recent moves [5]. When a new move is selected, it is compared to the

```
function FindMoves(Constraints, Cost, e_i^-, e_i^+)
  Moves ← ∅, OuterCost ← 0
  OuterConstraints ← all c_i ∈ Constraints involving (e_i^-, e_i^+)
  d_min^- ← min domain value of e_i^-
  while d_min^- ≤ max domain value of e_i^- do
    (TestCost, OuterCost, d_max^-) ← FindCost(e_i^-, d_min^-, OuterConstraints, OuterCost)
    InnerCost ← OuterCost, InnerConstraints ← OuterConstraints
    d_min^+ ← d_min^- + 1
    while d_min^+ ≤ max domain value of e_i^+ do
      (TestCost, InnerCost, d_max^+) ← FindCost(e_i^+, d_min^+, InnerConstraints, InnerCost)
      Moves ← Moves ⊕ ((d_min^- ... d_max^-), (d_min^+ ... d_max^+), TestCost)
      d_min^+ ← d_max^+ + 1
    d_min^- ← d_max^- + 1
  end while
  Sort the Moves into ascending order of TestCost
  return (Moves)
end
```

Fig. 2. The Move Function for TABU.

moves currently kept in memory and, if a match is found, this move is rejected as tabu. This prevents the algorithm from cycling back and forth between a few common moves and effectively getting stuck. If the move selected is not tabu and is different from the current value it is replacing, then the current value is made tabu and is replaced by the new move. The number of moves for which a value remains tabu plays a vital role; if it is to large, then it becomes possible that all available moves are tabu and, if it is too small, it is possible for the algorithm to fall into a cycle and get stuck.

To improve the performance of our TABU search algorithm we allow it to make aspiration moves [5]. An aspiration occurs when there exists one or more tabu moves that could produce a better cost than the current best cost. In this case the algorithm selects the first such move and instantiates it, ignoring that it is currently tabu. However, if non-tabu best cost improving moves exist, these will be preferred and an aspiration will not occur.

4.3 Random-Restart Search

The Random-Restart technique is a simplistic strategy for escaping a local minima. In the event the algorithm detects a local minimum, all the variables in the problem are randomly re-instantiated, and the search is restarted (the algorithm is deemed to be in a minimum when for a pre-defined number of loops the value for Cost has not changed). The Random-Restart algorithm is presented in Figure 4, using the same FindBestMoves presented in [13].

5 Empirical Study

In our earlier work [3], we developed two backtracking based algorithms for handling over-constrained temporal reasoning problems. These algorithms are guaranteed to find the optimal partial solution of the problem. However, our

procedure TABU(*Events, Constraints*)
  Randomly instantiate every event $(e_i^-, e_i^+) \in Events$
  $Cost \leftarrow$ number of unsatisfied constraints $\in Constraints$
  $TABULIST \leftarrow \emptyset$
  while $Cost > 0$ **do**
    for each $(e_i^-, e_i^+) \in Events$ **do**
      Add the range for (e_i^-, e_i^+) to $TABULIST$
      $(Moves) \leftarrow FindMoves(Constraints, Cost, e_i^-, e_i^+)$
      if the cost of the first $Move \in Moves < Cost$ **then** remove every $Move \in Moves \geq Cost$
      $Aspiration \leftarrow$ first $Move \in Moves$
      while $Moves \neq \emptyset$ **do**
        Remove the first $Move \in Moves$
        if (randomly selected $(d_i^-, d_i^+) \in Move) \notin TABULIST$ **then**
          Instantiate (e_i^-, e_i^+) with (d_i^-, d_i^+)
          $Moves \leftarrow \emptyset$
      if no $Move \in Moves$ was instantiated **then**
        Instantiate (e^-, e^+) with randomly selected $(d_i^-, d_i^+) \in Aspiration$
      if cost of selected $Move < Cost$ **then** $Cost =$ cost of $Move$
  end while
end

Fig. 3. The TABU Local Search Procedure for Interval Algebra.

procedure Random-Restart(*Events, Constraints*)
  Randomly instantiate every event $(e_i^-, e_i^+) \in Events$
  $Cost \leftarrow$ number of unsatisfied constraints $\in Constraints$
  $RESTART \leftarrow 0$
  while $Cost > 0$ **do**
    $StartCost \leftarrow Cost$
    for each $(e_i^-, e_i^+) \in Events$ **do**
      $(Moves, Cost) \leftarrow FindBestMoves(Constraints, Cost, e_i^-, e_i^+)$
      Instantiate (e_i^-, e_i^+) with randomly selected $(d_i^-, d_i^+) \in Moves$
    if $Cost < StartCost$ **then** $RESTART \leftarrow 0$
    else if $(++RESTART) >$ MAX_RESTART **then**
      Randomly instantiate every event $(e_i^-, e_i^+) \in Events$
      $TCost \leftarrow$ number of unsatisfied constraints $\in Constraints$
      if $TCost < Cost$ **then** $Cost \leftarrow TCost$
      $RESTART \leftarrow 0$
  end while
end

Fig. 4. The Random-Restart Local Search Procedure for Interval Algebra.

empirical study was based on relatively small sized problems (we used problems with 8-10 nodes in the network with varying degrees).

In [13], we studied the application of local search to under-constrained (solvable) temporal reasoning problems. The main purpose of this study was to investigate practical value of local search techniques in this domain, which was largely unexplored. Our results indicated that a portfolio algorithm using TSAT (local search) and heuristic backtracking would be the best solution on the range of the 80 node problems we considered.

5.1 Problem Generation

For this study, we used Nebel's problem generator [6] to randomly generate problems using the $A(n, d, s)$ model, where n is the number of nodes or events,

d is the degree size (defining the percentage of all possible arcs that are actually constrained) and s is the label size (defining the number of the thirteen possible atomic relations that are actually assigned to a constrained arc). As the results show, by varying the values of d and s it is possible to generate random problems that are either nearly all over-constrained or nearly all under-constrained.

5.2 Results

The purpose of our empirical study is to evaluate comparative performance of the extended weighting, TABU search and Random-Restart algorithms. We used a randomly generated test set using $n = 40$, $d = 25\%, 50\%, 75\%, 100\%$ and $s = 2.5, 9.5$, giving a total of 8 problem sets. To further evaluate the three algorithms, we re-tested the hard solvable problem set for 80 nodes used in our initial study [13]. Each problem set, except the hard set, contains 100 problems, and each problem was solved 10 times with a timeout of 15 seconds. The hard solvable problem set contains 318 problems which were also solved 10 times each with a timeout of 30 seconds. In the results of Table 1, Cost refers to the least number of violated constraints found during a search, and Time and Number of Moves refer to the elapsed time and the number of changes of variable instantiation that had occurred at the point when the least cost solution was found. All experiments were performed on a Intel Celeron 450MHz machine with 160Mb of RAM running FreeBSD 4.2. For TABU search we set the list length of the $TABULIST$ to be 50, for Random-Restart $RESTART$ was set at 250 and for Weighting MAX_FLATS was set to 4 and $MAX\_WEIGHTS$ was set to 10 (refer to [13] for a complete explanation of these parameters).

5.3 Analysis

The experimental results indicate that the problem sets fall into two groups: one where nearly all problems had solutions ($n = 40$ $d = 25$ $s = 9.5$), ($n = 40$ $d = 50$ $s = 9.5$) and the original hard set ($n = 80$ $d = 75$ $s = 9.5$), and the remaining sets where nearly all problems were over-constrained[1]. Looking at the results in Table 1, we can see that random re-start TABU search performs better than Weighting in terms of cost on all over-constrained problem sets. For instance, comparing the mean and min cost columns, Weighting is between 2% to 3% worse for the mean cost and 4% to 20% worse for the min cost (min cost being the minimum cost value found in all runs). In order to more clearly compare the relative performance of the algorithms, we plotted cost descent graphs for each algorithm against time. These graphs record the average best cost achieved at each time point for each problem set. Figure 5 shows a typical over-constrained descent curve (similar shapes were found for all other over-constrained problem sets). Here we see all three algorithms starting in a similar descent, but with Weighting starting to descend at a slower rate well before both TABU and

---

[1] We only assume over-constrainedness as no known complete algorithm can solve these problems

Table 1. Experimental Results.

Problem	Method	Solved %	Cost Mean	Std Dev	Max	Min	Number of Moves Mean	Median	Std Dev	Time Mean
$n = 40$	TABU	0.00	61	8.69	91	37	16203	15838	4304	3.37
$d = 25$	Random-Restart	0.00	61	8.39	86	38	4166	4182	605	1.14
$s = 2.5$	Weighting	0.00	63	8.75	89	40	3234	3175	432	5.22
$n = 40$	TABU	72.00	0	0.59	2	0	1712	38	4111	0.06
$d = 25$	Random-Restart	91.00	0	0.31	2	0	83	39	128	0.03
$s = 9.5$	Weighting	100.00	0	0.00	0	0	30	30	4	0.03
$n = 40$	TABU	0.00	179	9.69	211	151	3598	3548	798	5.58
$d = 50$	Random-Restart	0.00	179	9.53	210	153	3339	3341	554	4.81
$s = 2.5$	Weighting	0.00	185	9.44	219	160	1756	1750	107	6.23
$n = 40$	TABU	0.60	3	1.59	13	0	3894	3977	2543	1.17
$d = 50$	Random-Restart	2.70	3	1.77	10	0	1264	1228	525	0.85
$s = 9.5$	Weighting	96.10	0	0.31	3	0	478	188	870	1.45
$n = 40$	TABU	0.00	310	10.65	341	282	1510	1469	297	7.16
$d = 75$	Random-Restart	0.00	310	10.53	338	280	1705	1663	346	7.32
$s = 2.5$	Weighting	0.00	318	10.49	351	290	1426	1415	96	6.99
$n = 40$	TABU	0.00	16	3.30	28	5	3328	3272	714	6.33
$d = 75$	Random-Restart	0.00	16	3.20	26	7	3218	3207	512	5.52
$s = 9.5$	Weighting	0.00	18	3.70	31	6	2952	2913	402	7.17
$n = 40$	TABU	0.00	433	7.72	454	410	905	892	172	8.38
$d = 100$	Random-Restart	0.00	433	7.51	454	405	1004	988	185	7.90
$s = 2.5$	Weighting	0.00	443	6.36	460	424	1252	1243	89	6.68
$n = 40$	TABU	0.00	37	4.70	50	24	1945	1905	391	8.18
$d = 100$	Random-Restart	0.00	36	4.70	55	25	2158	2109	413	8.31
$s = 9.5$	Weighting	0.00	45	4.65	58	29	2107	2075	287	6.61
$n = 80$	TABU	0.60	4	2.54	19	0	2092	2125	1081	8.33
$d = 75$	Random-Restart	3.18	4	2.60	19	0	1717	1666	710	7.41
$s = 9.5$	Weighting	99.97	0	0.02	1	0	215	200	69	4.80

Random-Restart. A probable cause for the poorer performance of Weighting on the over-constrained problems is that by adding weight to unsatisfied constraints, a weighting algorithm distorts the original cost surface (i.e. by changing the relative cost of the constraints). In an under-constrained problem this will not change the relative cost of a solution, as this is always zero. However, in an over-constrained problem, the weighting process can *disguise* an optimal minimum cost solution by adding weights to the constraints that are violated in that solution. In that case, the search may be guided away from potentially optimal regions of the search space. As both TABU and Random-Restart are guided by the true unweighted cost, they are not subject to such misguidance.

Conversely, on all the under-constrained problem sets, Weighting has a distinct advantage, as shown in the results table and in the graph of Figure 6. This performance is paralleled in other studies that have shown weighting to outperform standard local search heuristics on a range of difficult constraint satisfaction and satisfiability problems [12]. The results and graphs also show there is little difference between the long-term performance of TABU and Random-Restart. This is somewhat surprising, as we would expect TABU to have an advantage over a simple restart(i.e. if TABU provides good guidance in escaping a local minimum this should lead us more efficiently to a more promising solution than restarting the algorithm). Random-restart is generally effective on cost surfaces where local minima occur discontinuously, i.e. where they occur singly and are

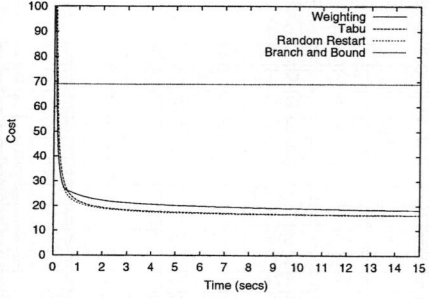 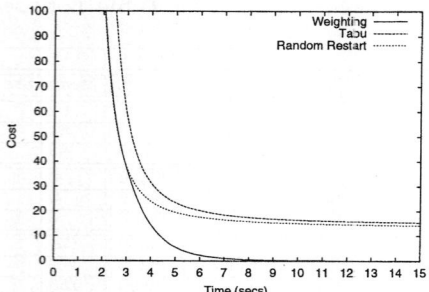

Fig. 5. Over-constrained descent graph for $n = 40$, $d = 75$, $s = 9.5$.

Fig. 6. Under-constrained descent graph for $n = 80$, $d = 75$, $s = 9.5$.

fairly distant from each other. Our results may imply such a cost surface, or alternatively there may be more work needed in optimising TABU's performance.

To obtain a clearer picture of the advantages of local search in the over-constrained domain, we ran an existing branch and bound algorithm (known as Method 1 in [3]) on a range of the over-constrained problems. The graph in Figure 5 shows the descent curve of this algorithm on the ($n = 40$ $d = 75$ $s = 9.5$) problems in comparison to our three local search techniques (similar curves were obtained across the range of our over-constrained problem sets). These results showed branch and bound was unable to make any significant cost descent within a 100 second cut-off period.

6 Conclusion

We have demonstrated that a local search approach to solving over-constrained temporal reasoning problems is both practical and efficient. While we do not have an absolute measure of optimum cost for our problem sets (as no known complete algorithm is able to solve them), our 40 node graphs show that a local search is able to reach a flat area on a descent curve within a few seconds. This should be compared to the performance of existing backtracking techniques, which have trouble finding solutions for over-constrained random problems of greater than ten nodes [3]. We have also introduced and compared three new local search algorithms for over-constrained temporal reasoning. Our results indicate that the existing Weighting algorithm does not compare well to the relatively simple TABU and Random-Restart local search heuristics on over-constrained problems, but is still superior in the under-constrained domain.

Our work opens up several possibilities for further research. Firstly, existing work on constraint weighting has shown that hybrid constraint weighting and TABU search algorithms perform well on over-constrained problems with hard and soft constraints [12]. Hence, it would be interesting to explore such hybrid algorithms in the temporal reasoning domain. Additionally, as many real world problems resolve into hard (mandatory) and soft (desirable) constraints, it would be useful to extend our work to look at such realistic problems.

References

1. J. Allen. Maintaining knowledge about temporal intervals. *Communications of the ACM*, 26(11):832–843, 1983.
2. J. Allen and J. Koomen. Planning using a temporal world model. In *Proceedings of the 8th International Joint Conference on Artificial Intelligence (IJCAI)*, pages 741–747, Karlsruhe, W.Germany, 1983.
3. M. Beaumont, A. Sattar, M. Maher, and J. Thornton. Solving over-constrained temporal reasoning problems. In *Proceedings of the 14th Australian Joint Conference on Artificial Intelligence (AI 01)*, pages 37–49, 2001.
4. E. Freuder and R. Wallace. Partial constraint satisfaction. *Artificial Intelligence*, 58(1):21–70, 1992.
5. F. Glover. Tabu search: Part 1. *ORSA Journal on Computing*, 1(3):190–206, 1989.
6. B. Nebel. Solving hard qualitative temporal reasoning problems: Evaluating the efficiency of using the ORD-Horn class. *Constraints*, 1:175–190, 1997.
7. M. Poesio and R. Brachman. Metric constraints for maintaining appointments: Dates and repeated activities. In *Proceedings of the 9th National Conference of the American Association for Artificial Intelligence (AAAI-91)*, pages 253–259, 1991.
8. B. Selman, H. Levesque, and D. Mitchell. A new method for solving hard satisfiability problems. In *Proceedings of the Tenth National Conference on Artificial Intelligence (AAAI-92)*, pages 440–446, 1992.
9. Y. Shang and B. Wah. A discrete Lagrangian-based global search method for solving satisfiability problems. *J. Global Optimization*, 12:61–99, 1998.
10. F. Song and R. Cohen. The interpretation of temporal relations in narrative. In *Proceedings of the 7th National Conference of the American Association for Artificial Intelligence (AAAI-88)*, pages 745–750, Saint Paul, MI, 1988.
11. J. Thornton. *Constraint Weighting Local Search for Constraint Satisfaction*. PhD thesis, School of Information Technology, Griffith University Gold Coast, Australia, January 2000.
12. J. Thornton, S. Bain, A. Sattar, and D. Pham. A two level local search for MAX-SAT problems with hard and soft constraints. In *Proceedings of the Fifteenth Australian Joint Conference on Artificial Intelligence (AI 2002)*, pages 603–614, 2002.
13. J. Thornton, M. Beaumont, A. Sattar, and M. Maher. Applying local search to temporal reasoning. In *Proceedings of the Ninth International Symposium on Temporal Representation and Reasoning (TIME-02)*, pages 94–99, 2002.
14. M. Vilain and H. Kautz. Constraint propagation algorithms for temporal reasoning. In *Proceedings of the Fifth National Conference on Artificial Intelligence (AAAI-86)*, pages 377–382, 1986.

Methods of Automatic Algorithm Generation

Stuart Bain, John Thornton, and Abdul Sattar

Institute for Integrated and Intelligent Systems
Griffith University
PMB 50, Gold Coast Mail Centre, 9726, Australia
{s.bain,j.thornton,a.sattar}@griffith.edu.au

Abstract. Many methods have been proposed to automatically generate algorithms for solving constraint satisfaction problems. The aim of these methods has been to overcome the difficulties associated with matching algorithms to specific constraint satisfaction problems. This paper examines three methods of generating algorithms: a randomised search, a beam search and an evolutionary method. The evolutionary method is shown to have considerably more flexibility than existing alternatives, being able to discover entirely new heuristics and to exploit synergies between heuristics.

1 Introduction

Many methods of adapting algorithms to particular constraint problems have been proposed in the light of a growing body of work reporting on the narrow applicability of individual heuristics. A heuristic's success on one particular problem is not an *a priori* guarantee of its effectiveness on another, structurally dissimilar problem. In fact, the "no free lunch" theorems [1] hold that quite the opposite is true, asserting that a heuristic algorithm's performance, averaged over the set of all possible problems, is identical to that of any other algorithm. Hence, superior performance on a particular class of problem is necessarily balanced by inferior performance on the set of all remaining problems.

Adaptive problem solving aims to overcome the difficulties of matching heuristics to problems by employing more than one individual heuristic, or by providing the facility to modify heuristics to suit the current problem. However, much of the research into adaptive algorithms is concerned with the identification of which heuristics, from a set of completely specified heuristics, are best suited for solving particular problems. Heuristics in these methods are declared *a priori*, based on the developer's knowledge of appropriate heuristics for the problem domain. This is disingenuous, in that it assumes knowledge of the most appropriate heuristics for a given problem, when the very motivation for using adaptive algorithms is the difficulty associated with matching heuristics to problems.

Our previous work [2] introduced a new representation for constraint satisfaction algorithms that is conducive to automatic adaptation by genetic programming. Additionally, it was demonstrated that from an initial random and poor-performing population, significantly improved algorithms could be evolved. In this paper we examine other methods to automatically search the space of algorithms possible within this representation. These methods are a beam search, a random search as well as the previously considered evolutionary method.

Existing work on adaptive algorithms will be reviewed in section 2, before the representation to be used in the current experiments is discussed in section 3. The three methods of exploration will be described in section 4, with details of the experiments conducted to evaluate their performance in searching the space of algorithms.

2 Background

A popular paradigm for representing finite domain problems is that of the *constraint satisfaction problem* (CSP). All CSPs are characterised by the inclusion of a finite set of variables; a set of domain values for each variable; and a set of constraints that are only satisfied by assigning particular domain values to the problem's variables. Whilst a multitude of algorithms have been proposed to locate solutions to such problems, this paper focuses on methods that can adapt to the particular problem they are solving. A number of previously proposed adaptive methods will first be discussed.

The MULTI-TAC system developed by Minton [3, 4] is designed to synthesise heuristics for solving CSPs. Such heuristics are extrapolated from "meta-level theories" i.e. basic theories that describe properties of a partial solution to a CSP. The theories explicated for use with MULTI-TAC lead primarily to variable and value ordering heuristics for complete (backtracking) search. Exploration is by way of a beam search, designed to control the number of candidate heuristics that will be examined. Unlike some of the other adaptive methods, MULTI-TAC is able to learn new heuristics from base theories.

The use of chains of low-level heuristics to adapt to individual problems has also been proposed. Two such systems are the Adaptive Constraint Satisfaction (ACS) system suggested by Borrett et al. [5] and the hyper-heuristic GA (HHGA) system proposed by Han and Kendall [6]. ACS relies on a pre-specified chain of algorithms and a supervising "monitor" function that recognises when the current heuristic is not performing well and directs the search to advance to the next heuristic in the chain. In contrast to a pre-specified chain, the hyper-heuristic system evolves a chain of heuristics appropriate for a particular problem using a genetic algorithm. Although Borrett exclusively considers complete search methods, their work would allow the use of chains of local search algorithms instead. The same can be said *vice versa* for Han and Kendall's work which considered chains of local search heuristics.

Gratch and Chien [7] propose an adaptive search system specifically for scheduling satellite communications, although the underlying architecture could address a range of similar problems. An algorithm is divided into four seperate levels, each in need of a heuristic assignment. All possibilities for a given level are considered before committing to a particular one, at which point the search proceeds to the next level. In this way, the space of possible methods is pruned and remains computationally feasible. However, such a method is unable to recognise synergies that may occur between the various levels.

The premise of Nayerek's work [8] is that a heuristic's past performance is indicative of its future performance within the scope of the same sub-problem. Each constraint is considered a sub-problem, with its own cost function and a set of associated heuristics. A utility value for each heuristic records its past success in improving its constraint's cost function, and provides an expectation of its future usefulness. Heuristics are in no way modified by the system, and their association to a problem's constraints must be determined *a priori* by the developer.

Epstein et al. proposed the Adaptive Constraint Engine (ACE) [9] as a system for learning search order heuristics. ACE is able to learn the appropriate importance of individual heuristics (termed "advisors") for particular problems. The weighted sum of advisor output determines the evaluation order of variables and values. ACE is only applicable for use with complete search, as a trace of the expanded search tree is necessary to update the advisor weights.

With the exception of MULTI-TAC, the primary limitation of these methods is their inability to discover new heuristics. Although ACE is able to multiplicatively combine two advisors to create a new one, it is primarily, like Nayerek's work, only learning which heuristics are best suited to particular problems. Neither [7], which learns a problem-specific conjunctive combination of heuristics, nor [6], which learns a problem-specific ordering of heuristics, actually learn *new* heuristics.

A secondary limitation of these methods (specifically observed in MULTI-TAC and Gratch and Chien's work) is their inability to exploit synergies, i.e. heuristics that perform well in conjunction with other methods but poorly individually. A discussion of synergies is not applicable to the remaining methods, except for the hyper-heuristic GA, where the use of a genetic algorithm permits their identification. Other factors that should be mentioned include the ability of the methods to handle both complete and local search; the maximum complexity of the heuristics they permit to be learned; and whether the methods are able to learn from failure. These properties are summarised for each method in the taxonomy of Table 1 below.

Table 1. Taxonomy of Algorithm Adaptation Methods.

Name	Learns Local or Complete	Learns New Heuristics	Exploits Synergies	Learns From Failure	Unlimited Complexity	Method of Search
MULTI-TAC	Both	Yes	No	Yes	No	Beam
ACS	Both	No	Yes	No	No	N/A
HHGA	Both	No	Yes	No	No	Evolutionary
Gratch	Both	No	No	Yes	No	Beam
Nayarek	Local	No	Yes	Yes	No	Feedback
ACE	Complete	No	Yes	No	No	Feedback

3 A New Representation for CSP Algorithms

A constraint satisfaction algorithm can be viewed as an iterative procedure that repeatedly assigns domain values to variables, terminating when all constraints are satisfied, the problem is proven unsolvable, or the available computational resources have been exhausted. Both backtracking and local search algorithms can be viewed in this way. The traditional difference between the two methods is that backtracking search instantiates variables only up to the point where constraints are violated, whereas all variables are instantiated in local search regardless of constraint violations. Despite these differences, at every iteration both types of search make two decisions: "What variable will be instantiated next?" and "Which value will be assigned to it?".

Bain et al. [2] proposed a representation capable of handling both complete and local search algorithms, together with a method of genetic programming to explore the space of algorithms possible within the representation. In combination, the representation and genetic programming meet all five criteria discussed in the preceeding section. Although the representation is capable of handling complete search methods, the rest of this paper will concentrate on its use with local search.

Algorithms in this representation are decomposed into three seperate heuristics: the *move contention function*; the *move preference function*; and the *move selection function*. At every iteration, each move (an assignment of a value to a variable) is passed to the *move contention function* to determine which moves will be considered further. For example, we may only consider moves that involve unsatisfied constraints as only these moves offer the possibility of improving the current solution. Each move that has remained in contention is assigned a numeric preference value by the *move preference function*. An example preference function is the number of constraints that would remain unsatisfied for a particular move. Once preference values have been assigned, the *move selection function* uses the preference values to choose one move from the contention list to enact. A number of well-known local search algorithms cast in this representation are shown in Table 2. Extensions for representing a range of more complicated algorithms are discussed in [2].

Table 2. Table of Well-Known Local Search Heuristics.

GSAT	{ CONTEND all-moves-for-unsatisfied-constraints; PREFER moves-on-total-constraint-violations; SELECT randomly-from-minimal-cost-moves }
HSAT	{ CONTEND all-moves-for-unsatisfied-constraints; PREFER on-left-shifted-constraint-violations-+-recency; SELECT minimal-cost-move }
TABU	{ CONTEND all-moves-not-taken-recently; PREFER moves-on-total-constraint-violations; SELECT randomly-from-minimal-cost-moves }
WEIGHTING	{ CONTEND all-moves-for-unsatisfied-constraints; PREFER moves-on-weighted-constraint-violations; SELECT randomly-from-minimal-cost-moves }

Table 3. Function and Terminal Sets for Contention.

Functions for use in Contention Heuristics	
InUnsatisfied :: Move → Bool	True iff Move is in an unsatisfied constraint.
WontUnsatisfy :: Move → Bool	True iff Move won't unsatisfy any constraints.
MoveNotTaken :: Move → Bool	True iff Move hasn't been previously taken.
InRandom :: Move → Bool	True iff Move is in a persistent random constraint. The constraint is persistent this turn only.
AgeOverInt :: Move → Integer → Bool	True iff this Move hasn't been taken for Integer turns.
RandomlyTrue :: Integer → Bool	Randomly True Integer percent of the time.
And, Or :: Bool → Bool → Bool	The Boolean AND and OR functions. Definitions as expected.
Not :: Bool	The Boolean NOT function. Definition as expected.
Terminals for use in Contention Heuristics	
Move :: Move	The Move currently being considered.
NumVariables :: Integer	The number of variables in the current problem.
True, False :: Bool	The Boolean values True and False.
10, 25, 50, 75 :: Integer	The integers 0 and 1.

Table 4. Function and Terminal Sets for Preference.

Functions for use in Preference Heuristics	
AgeOfMove :: Move → Integer	Returns the number of turns since Move was last taken.
NumWillSatisfy, NumWillUnsatisfy :: Move → Integer	Returns the number of constraints that will be satisfied or unsatisfied by Move, respectively.
Degree :: Move → Integer	Degree returns the number of constraints this Move (variable) affects.
PosDegree, NegDegree :: Move → Integer	Return the number of constraints satisfied by respective variable settings.
DependentDegree, OppositeDegree :: Move → Integer	DependentDegree returns PosDegree if Move involves a currently True variable or NegDegree for a False variable. The reverse occurs for OppDegree.
TimesTaken :: Move → Integer	Returns the number of times Move has been taken.
SumTimesSat, SumTimesUnsat :: Move → Integer	Returns the sum of the number of times all constraints affected by Move have been satisfied or unsatisfied respectively.
SumConstraintAges :: Move → Integer	For all constraints Move participates in, returns the sum of the length of time each constraint has been unsatisfied.
NumNewSatisfied, NumNeverSatisfied :: Move → Integer	Returns the number of constraints that will be satisfied by Move that are not currently satisfied, or have never been satisfied, respectively.
RandomValue :: Integer → Integer	Returns random value between 0 and Integer-1.
Plus, Minus, Times :: Integer → Integer → Integer	Returns the arithmetic result of its two integer arguments.
LeftShift :: Integer → Integer	Returns its input shifted 16 bits higher.
Terminals for use in Contention Heuristics	
Move :: Move	The Move currently being considered.
NumVariables, NumConstraints :: Integer	The number of variables and constraints in the current problem.
NumFlips :: Integer	The number of Moves that have already been made.
0, 1 :: Integer	The integers 0 and 1.

Table 5. Function and Terminal Sets for Selection.

Functions for use in Selection Heuristics	
RandomFromMax, RandomFromMin, RandomFromPositive, RandomFromAll :: Integer → MoveList → CostList → Move	The first two functions make a random selection from the maximum or minimum cost moves, respectively. The third makes a random selection from all moves with a positive preference value. The final function makes a random selection from all moves in the preference list.
Terminals for use in Selection Heuristics	
NumContenders :: Integer	The number of moves in contention.
ListOfMoves :: MoveList	The list of moves determined by the contention stage.
ListOfCosts :: CostList	The list of costs determined by the preference stage.

4 Adapting Algorithms

To study the performance of the three methods considered in this paper, namely beam search, evolutionary search and a random search, experiments were conducted to evolve algorithms for solving Boolean satisfiability problems. Such problems have been widely studied and have a known hardness distribution. The problem selected (uf100-01.cnf) is taken from the phase-transition region, which is the area where the problems are (on average) the most difficult for traditional backtracking search routines.

4.1 Beam Search

Beam search is an effective method of controlling the combinatorial explosion that can occur during a breadth first search. It is similar to a breadth first search, but only the most promising nodes at each level of search are expanded. The primary limitation of beam search is its inability to recognise and exploit synergies that may exist in the problem domain. With respect to evaluating algorithms, this may be two heuristics that perform poorly individually but excellently together.

To determine whether such synergies occur, a study of possible contention heuristics was conducted using a beam search. The set of possible contention heuristics for the first level of beam search were enumerated from the function and terminal sets shown in Table 3. These heuristics contain at most 1 functional node and are shown in Table 6. As contention heuristics are Boolean functions that determine whether particular moves warrant further consideration, each subsequent level of the beam search will consider more complicated heuristics, by combining additional functional nodes using the Boolean functions: AND, OR and NOT.

As contention heuristics cannot be considered in isolation from preference and selection heuristics, the preference and selection heuristics of the GSAT algorithm were adopted for this experiment. This provides an initial 16 algorithms for evaluation, the results for which are shown in Table 6. Accompanying these are the results for the beam search, which extends the heuristics to all Boolean combinations of up to 2 functional nodes[1]. For a beam width of p, only

---

[1] With the exception of redundant combinations like "a AND a" and "False OR b".

Table 6. Beam Search Results.

Problem: uf100-01, Tries: 500, Cutoff: 40000								
Heuristics with up to one functional node				Beam search up to two functional nodes				
Rank	Algorithm	Percent Solved	Best Avg. Flips	Beam Width	Domain Size	Best Avg. Flips	Percent Improv.	Best % Solved
1	AgeOverInt(Move, 10)	76	21924					
2	RandomlyTrue(50)	71	20378	2	4	20105	1.34	69%
3	RandomlyTrue(25)	67	23914	3	9	11262	44.73	98%
4	RandomlyTrue(75)	50	24444	4	16	11262	44.73	98%
5	True	36	28111					
6	RandomlyTrue(NumVariables)	35	28846	6	25	11262	44.73	98%
7	InUnsatisfied(Move)	1	39455	7	36	1988	90.24	100%
8	AgeOverInt(Move, 25)	1	39893			:		
9	RandomlyTrue(10)	0	39936			:		
10	False	0	40000			:		
11	AgeOverInt(Move, 75)	0	40000			:		
12	AgeOverInt(Move, 50)	0	40000		No further improvement			
13	AgeOverInt(Move, NumVariables)	0	40000			:		
14	InRandom(Move)	0	40000			:		
15	MoveNotTake(Move)	0	40000			:		
16	WontUnsatisfy(Move)	0	40000	16	196	1988	90.24	100%

the heuristics composed entirely from the p best performers are considered, i.e. when the beam width is 2, only heuristics composed of "AgeOverInt(Move, 10)" and "RandomlyTrue(50)" are considered.

The heuristics examined in the first level of beam search have been delineated into two groups based on the percentage of problems that each was able to solve. Although significant performance improvements can be observed when the better-performing heuristics are combined, the most drastic improvement occurs after the inclusion of one of the poorly-performing heuristics. The "InUnsatisfied(Move)" heuristic, although obvious to human programmers, is not at all obvious to beam search, where its poor individual performance denotes it as a heuristic to be considered later, if at all. Whilst it may be possible to locate good heuristics using beam search, the width of the beam necessary eliminates much of the computational advantage of the method.

4.2 Evolutionary Exploration of the Search Space

Genetic programming [10] has been proposed for discovering solutions to problems when the form of the solution is not known. Instead of the linear (and often fixed length) data structures employed in genetic algorithms, genetic programming uses dynamic, tree-based data structures to represent solutions. The two methods are otherwise quite similar, using equivalent genetic operators to evolve new populations of solutions. When genetic programming is used to evolve algorithms, the data structures are expression trees modelling combinations of heuristics. The fitness function used by the genetic operators relies on solution rates and other performance metrics of the algorithms under test.

Two of the limitations identified from existing work, the inability to exploit synergies and the inability to learn from failure, are overcome with genetic programming. Synergies can be exploited as individuals are selected probabilistically to participate in cross-over. Poorly performing individuals still have a possibility of forming part of a subsequent generation. Genetic programming is also able to learn from failure, as the fitness function can comprise much more information than just whether or not a solution was found. Specifically in local search, information about a candidate algorithm's mobility and coverage [11] can prove useful for comparing algorithms.

As well as combining different contention, preference and selection heuristics in novel ways, the inclusion of functions like "AND", "OR", "PLUS" and "MINUS" permit a range of new heuristics to be learned. No limit is placed on the complexity (size) of the algorithms that may be learned, which will vary depending on the fitness offered by such levels of complexity. Fixed levels of complexity were an additional limiting factor of some existing work.

Details and results of the experiment can be found in Table 7. These results show that the genetic programming method rapidly evolves good performing algorithms from an initially poor performing population. Although the experiment was continued for 100 generations, there was little improvement after generation 30.

Table 7. Conditions and Results for the Genetic Programming Experiment.

Experiment Conditions		Experimental Results				
Population Composition		Gen.	Mean Success	Mean Unsat.	Best Avg. Moves	Best So Far
Population Size	100					
Elitist copy from previous gen.	25	0	0.04%	34.89	38435	38435
Randomly selected and crossed	70	10	9.52%	13.45	9423	9423
New elements generated	5	20	65.68%	3.16	1247	1247
Evaluation of Algorithm Fitness		30	83.23%	2.35	981	981
$F_i = Standardised(UnsatConstraints_i) +$		40	85.12%	3.04	1120	981
$100 * SuccessRate_i$		50	89.88%	3.14	1131	981
Test Problem	uf100-01	60	91.96%	2.15	898	898
Number of runs for each algorithm	25	70	88.96%	1.90	958	898
Maximum moves per run	40000	80	89.04%	2.64	1062	898
Mean number of moves required		90	90.56%	1.35	876	876
by the state-of-the-art [12]	594	99	92.88%	1.73	1070	876

4.3 Random Exploration of the Search Space

In order to demonstrate that the observed performance improvements in the evolutionary experiment over time are not purely the result of fortuitously generated algorithms, the experiment was repeated without the genetic operators. That is, each generation of the population was composed entirely of randomly generated elements. As genetic programming must begin with a similar randomly generated population, any observed differences in overall performance between the random experiment and the evolutionary experiment, can be attributed to the genetic operators of selection, cross-over and cloning.

With the exception of the differences in population composition, parameters for this experiment were the same as for the previous experiment. Results are shown in Table 8, when three different (practical) limits are placed on the size of

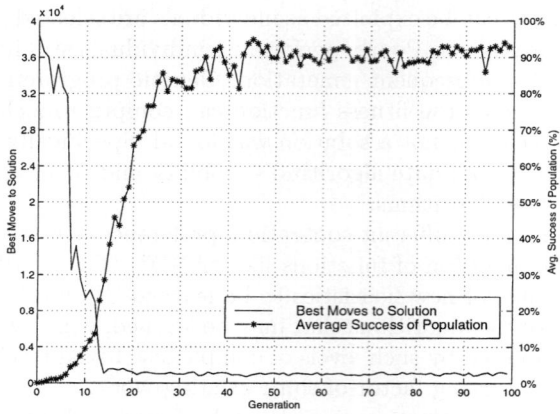

Fig. 1. Results for the genetic programming experiment.

the generated contention and preference trees[2]. Only the best average moves to solution (so far) and the best success rate (so far) are reported, as generational averages have no meaning within the context of this experiment. The results clearly show that a random exploration of the search space does not approach the performance of an evolutionary method.

Table 8. Results for the Random Exploration Experiment.

Gen.	Node Limit = 6		Node Limit = 20		Node Limit = 80	
	Best Average Moves	Best Success %	Best Average Moves	Best Success %	Best Average Moves	Best Success %
0	33981	32	38424	4	40000	0
10	33543	32	33531	20	23671	64
20	33543	32	6301	100	23671	64
30	6959	92	6301	100	23671	64
40	6959	92	6301	100	23671	64
50	6959	92	6301	100	23671	64
60	6959	92	6301	100	20814	88
70	6959	92	6301	100	6726	100

5 Conclusions and Future Work

This paper has demonstrated that within the space of algorithms, synergies do exist between heuristics, so a heuristic that performs poorly individually may perform well in conjunction with other heuristics. For this reason, beam search is not the most appropriate method for searching the space of algorithms.

Furthermore, the usefulness of genetic programming was demonstrated by comparing it with an entirely random method of search. As genetic programming

---

[2] Selection heuristics are restricted by the function and terminal sets to have exactly 4 nodes.

begins with a similar, entirely random set of solutions, the observed performance improvements are attributable to the genetic operators. Even with a fixed set of functions and terminals, albeit one large enough to be combined in many novel ways, an initial random and poorly-performing population of algorithms was significantly improved by the application of genetic programming operating within our recently proposed representation.

Acknowledgments

The authors would like to acknowledge the support of the Australian Research Council Large Grant A00000118 in conducting this research.

References

1. Wolpert, D.H., Macready, W.G.: No free lunch theorems for optimization. IEEE Transactions on Evolutionary Computation **1** (1997) 67–82
2. Bain, S., Thornton, J., Sattar, A.: Evolving algorithms for constraint satisfaction. In: 2004 Congress on Evolutionary Computation, Portland, Oregon (2004) To Appear.
3. Minton, S.: An analytic learning system for specializing heuristics. In: IJCAI '93: Proceedings of the 13th International Joint Conference on Artificial Intelligence, Chambéry, France (1993) 922–929
4. Minton, S.: Automatically configuring constraint satisfaction programs: A case study. Constraints **1** (1996) 7–43
5. Borrett, J.E., Tsang, E.P.K., Walsh, N.R.: Adaptive constraint satisfaction: The quickest first principle. In: European Conference on Artificial Intelligence. (1996) 160–164
6. Han, L., Kendall, G.: An investigation of a Tabu assisted hyper-heuristic genetic algorithm. In: 2003 Congress on Evolutionary Computation. Volume 3., IEEE Press (2003) 2230–2237
7. Gratch, J., Chien, S.: Adaptive problem-solving for large-scale scheduling problems: A case study. Journal of Artificial Intelligence Research **1** (1996) 365–396
8. Nareyek, A.: Choosing search heuristics by non-stationary reinforcement learning. In: M.G.C. Resende and J.P. de Sousa (Eds), Metaheuristics: Computer Decision Making, Kluwer Academic Publishers (2001) 523–544
9. Epstein, S.L., Freuder, E.C., Wallace, R., Morozov, A., Samuels, B.: The adaptive constraint engine. In Hentenryck, P.V., ed.: CP '02: Principles and Practice of Constraint Programming. (2002) 525–540
10. Koza, J.: Genetic Programming: On the programming of computers by means of natural selection. MIT Press, Cambridge, Massachusetts (1992)
11. Schuurmans, D., Southey, F.: Local search characteristics of incomplete SAT procedures. Artificial Intelligence **132** (2001) 121–150
12. Hutter, F., Tompkins, D., Hoos, H.: Scaling and probabilistic smoothing: Efficient dynamic local search for SAT. In: CP '02: Principles and Practice of Constraint Programming, Springer Verlag (2002) 233–248

A Novel Heuristic to Solve IA Network by Convex Approximation and Weights

Arun K. Pujari and T. Adilakshmi

Artificial Intelligence Lab
University of Hyderabad
Hyderabad, 50046, India
akpcs@uohyd.ernet.in

Abstract. In this paper we propose a new heuristic to determine a solution of a general interval algebra(IA) network. We make use of a tractable upper approximation by replacing each disjunction of the IA network by its interval closure. The resulting network becomes a convex network and it is well known that the consistency of the convex network can be decided in polynomial time. We start with a singleton labeling of the approximation and gradually work towards a consistent singleton labeling of the original network. We propose a scheme of ranking the basic relations in a disjunction and our search process moves in the decreasing order of this rank to find a solution. We exploit the properties of convex relations and weighted relations to design our heuristic for the general class of problems. The experiment reveals that the convex approximation finds consistency for more number of problems than the algorithm without approximation.

1 Introduction

Temporal reasoning arises while dealing with problems involving time. It has been a central research topic in AI since several years. Representing and reasoning about incomplete and imprecise temporal information is essential in many AI applications, such as knowledge representation, natural language understanding, commonsense reasoning, planning, scheduling and multimedia presentation. Numerous frameworks have been proposed till date addressing various aspects- Point Algebra [11] for time events, Interval Algebra(IA) [1] for time intervals and INDU [7] for interval durations. All these formalisms fall into one general framework. Each of these provides a set of jointly exhaustive and pairwise disjoint (JEPD) binary relations and represents the temporal knowledge as a network of binary constraints. In such a temporal constraint network, variables are represented as time points and/or intervals and constraints between them represent temporal information as collection (disjunction) of qualitative and/or metric relations. A major reasoning problem in this framework is to decide satisfiability of given information.

Interval Algebra [1] consists of thirteen basic JEPD interval relations namely, eq, b, bi, d, di, o, oi, s, si, m, mi, f, and fi. The constraints in an IA network are disjunctions of these thirteen relations. The problem of determining satisfiability (and hence, that of obtaining a solution) of an IA network is known to be NP-hard. There are certain subclasses of relations that admit polynomial time algorithms. For instance, if the IA network has all convex relations then path-consistency suffices to determine consistency of the network and path-consistency can be accomplished in polynomial time [4, 5, 9]. For the general IA network, it is necessary to resort to some sort of heuristic and backtracking for deciding consistency and obtaining a solution.

In the present work we propose a new heuristic for determining a solution of the IA network. The basic idea of our approach is as follows. We start with a tractable upward approximation of any IA network. By upward approximation, we mean that a constraint along any edge of the approximated network is a superset of the corresponding constraint of the given network. The solution of the tractable approximation can be obtained in polynomial time. If the approximated network is inconsistent then so is the original network. Let us assume that we get a solution of the approximation as a consistent singleton labeling. If this consistent singleton labeling is also a singleton labeling of the original network, then it is a solution of the original network. Otherwise, we propose a method of gradually working towards a consistent labeling of the original network from the consistent labeling of the approximation. There are two critical decisions necessary for such a scheme. First of all, it is to decide the singleton labeling of the approximation that becomes the starting point of the search process. The second is the scheme of moving iteratively towards the solution of the original network. We adopt a technique of ranking the individual atomic relations of an edge such that the rank of a relation intuitively corresponds to its likelihood to be part of a solution. We start with the highest ranked relation along every edge and then iteratively select relations in the decreasing order of the rank till we obtain a consistent labeling of the original network. We propose a ranking scheme based on numerical values so that higher the value of a relation more likely is the relation being part of consistent instantiation. We show experimentally that the proposed methods work well for very large number of randomly generated problems. Since we use numerical weights for ranking of the relation the convergence of the network is hard to analyze. As a result it is hard to determine in advance the number of steps required to get a solution. Our experiments reveal that the number of steps is a linear function of the size of the network for most of the randomly generated networks. Our algorithm takes a pre-specified number of steps and in case no solution is obtained by then, it assumes the network to be inconsistent. Thus the proposed heuristic is sound but not complete.

In Section 2, we discuss the method of tractable approximation of an IA network. Section 3 introduces the process of ranking the individual relations with respect to numerical weights of a constraint. In Section 4, we propose our new heuristic and in Section 5 experimental results are reported.

2 Upper Approximation

2.1 Definitions and Notations

Interval Algebra (IA) consists of thirteen JEPD relations: eq, b, bi, d, di, o, oi, s, si, m, mi, f, and fi. IA_i is denoted the ith basic relation for $1 \le i \le 13$. Any subset of relations is denoted as α. An IA network is a binary constraint network with n interval variables and a set of binary constraints C^{ij} between an ordered pair of variables (i,j).

Each C^{ij} is a disjunction of basic relations (individual basic relation is denoted by C^{ij}_m) and is represented as a subset. A singleton labeling of a network, denoted as $\tau(N)$, is obtained by replacing each C^{ij} by one of its basic relations C^{ij}_m, for some m. There may be many singleton labelings of a network. A consistent singleton labeling is a solution of the network.

2.2 Interval Closure

The atomic relation IA_i can be encoded as pairs of integers (x, y), $0 \le x \le 4, 0 \le y \le 4$ in a distributed lattice[4]. For two atomic relations $IA_r = (x_1, y_1)$ and $IA_s = (x_2, y_2)$, $IA_r < IA_s$ if and only if $x_1 < x_2$ and $y_1 < y_2$. For any two atomic relations IA_r and IA_s such that $IA_r \le IA_s$, an interval in the lattice $[IA_r, IA_s]$ is the set of all relations between IA_r and IA_s. Convex relations [4] are the relations corresponding to intervals in the lattice. For instance, {o, s, d, fi, eq, f} is a convex relation as it contains all elements of the lattice between o and f. For any IA relation α, the interval closure $I(\alpha)$ is defined as the smallest convex relation containing α [4]. For notational convenience, we represent IA_r by r.

It is easy to compute $I(\alpha)$ for a given IA relation $\alpha = \{r_1, r_2, ..., r_k\}$. We can view each atomic relation r_i as a pair of integers to be represented as an element in the lattice. Thus $\alpha = \{(x_1, y_1), (x_2, y_2), ..., (x_k, y_k)\}$. Define $x_{min} = Min(x_i)$ and define in the similar manner y_{min}, x_{max} and y_{max}. $I(\alpha)$ is the lattice interval defined by [r, s] such that $r = (x_{min}, y_{min})$ and $s = (x_{max}, y_{max})$. For example, if $\alpha = \{d, eq, si\}$ then $I(\alpha)$ is the set of all the relations between (1,2) and (2,4), that is $I(\alpha) = \{s, eq, si, d, f, oi\}$.

For an IA network N, I(N) is the network obtained from N by replacing the relation α along every edge by $I(\alpha)$. I(N) is a tractable upper approximation of N. We call this as *convex approximation* of N. We know that consistency of I(N) can be decided in polynomial time and we can also find a solution of I(N) in polynomial time. If I(N) is inconsistent (not satisfiable) then so is N. If any solution of I(N) is a singleton labeling $\tau(N)$ of N then it is also the solution of N. Thus, in some instances it is possible to get a solution of N in polynomial time even when we do not know whether N is convex.

3 Ranking of Relations

Several formalisms are proposed that assign weights to relations in IA network [2], [8], [10]. In [2], Bhavani and Pujari propose EvIA network where a numerical weights of atomic relations are handled in the line of evidence operations of evidential reasoning. We use the similar formalism so that the importance of each atomic relation can be quantified and weights can be used as a heuristic to find a solution of the given network.

As a deviation from the traditional manner of representing a constraint as the disjunction of atomic relations, we represent a constraint as a vector $W \in R^{13}$ such that

$0 \leq W_m \leq 1$, $1 \leq m \leq 13$ and $\Sigma W_m = 1$. The value 0 for W_m implies that the corresponding atomic relation IA_m is absent in the disjunction. We represent the composition table [3] as a 3-dimensional binary matrix **M**, such that $M_{ijm} = 1$ if and only if the atomic relation IA_m belongs to the composition of the atomic relations IA_i and IA_j. The composition of two weighted relations W^{ik} and W^{kj} resulting in a relation W^{ij} is denoted as $W^{ik} \otimes W^{kj}$. Its each component is defined as follows.

$$W_m^{ij} = \sum_u \sum_v M_{uvm} W_u^{ij} W_v^{jk}, \quad 1 \leq m \leq 13$$

The inverse is defined in the usual manner. The intersection of two weighted relations W^{ij} and V^{ij} is denoted as $U^{ij} = W^{ij} \cap V^{ij}$ such that

$$U_m^{ij} = \frac{W_m^{ij} V_m^{ij}}{\sum_m W_m^{ij} V_m^{ij}}, \quad 1 \leq m \leq 13$$

The conventional path consistency algorithm [3] attempts to eliminate iteratively the relations that are contradictory to the relations obtained through different paths and retains only those relations that are common. On the same line, we propose *weighted_pc* algorithm for weighted IA network. This algorithm modifies the weights of the atomic relations such that the common relation has stronger weight and the relation that is not supported by many paths has weight close to zero. Intuitively, the relation with high weight has high likelihood of consistency. The algorithm also detects inconsistency when the result of intersection of weighted vectors is a 0-vector. We give below the formal description of *weighted_pc* algorithm. It is easy to see that if the weight vectors are restricted to be binary then the algorithm is equivalent to the conventional path consistency algorithm.

Table 1. Weighted_pc algorithm: The algorithm takes a weighted network as input and returns the network with modified weight or exits when it detects inconsistency.

```
weighted_pc(W(N))
Input : A weighted network W(N)
Output: Modified network W(N)
initialize: status = unknown
  do for each pair (i,j)
    do for k = 1 to n, k ≠ i and k ≠ j
      compute  Wik ⊗ Wkj
        if Wij ∩(Wik ⊗ Wkj)= 0
          then exit with status = inconsistent
          else compute Wij(k) ← Wij ∩ (Wik ⊗ Wkj)
        if Wij(k)∩ Wij(h) = 0 for any h < k
          then exit with status = inconsistent
    enddo
    compute average over k of Wij(k)
    replace Wij by the average value
  enddo
```

4 New Heuristic

In this section we propose the new heuristic for finding a solution of a general IA network. As mentioned earlier, we start with a singleton labeling of I(N). The upper approximation I(N) of N is first converted to a weighted network WI(N) by the algorithm *convert(N, W(N))* (table 2).

Table 2. Algorithm to convert an IA network to an weighted network by assigning equal weights to disjuncts.

```
Convert (N,W(N))
Input: IA network N
Output: Weighted network W(N)
do for each pair i, j
     if the constraint Cij has k atomic relations i.e.,
     Cij ={r1, r2, ..., rk}
     then compute the weight vector Wij as
```
$$W_m^{ij} = \begin{cases} \dfrac{1}{k}, & r_m \in C^{ij} \\ 0, & otherwise \end{cases}$$
```
enddo
```

We start with equal weights for the basic relations in a disjunction. The *weighted_pc* algorithm is used to modify the weights so that more frequently generated relations acquire higher weights. We then generate a singleton labeling for I(N) by selecting for every edge the atomic relation with highest weight. We check whether this singleton labeling is a solution of N and this is done by the conventional path consistency method. If it is not a solution then we identify the atomic relations that are not in N but appear in the singleton labeling. We modify WI(N) by assigning zero weights to these relations and normalizing the weight vectors. The process is repeated with another round of *weighted_pc* till we get a consistent singleton labeling of N. Since it is difficult to estimate the number of iterations necessary to get a solution, we recommend 9n iterations.

The intuition behind the proposed heuristic is as follows. When we use composition and intersection operations in a path consistency method, we generate atomic relations with varying frequency. For instance, when two relations α and β are used in a composition, an atomic relation IA_m is generated $\Sigma_{i \in \alpha, j \in \beta} \mathbf{M}_{ijm}$ times. The same relations may also be generated along many combinations along the paths between i and j through different k. On the other hand, if a particular atomic relation is not generated at least in one instance, then it is ignored throughout. As we start with equal weights, the more frequently generated relations accumulate higher values and some relations get zero value. Thus the relation with highest value is supported by many paths and this relation is likely to be consistent with other edges. In case it is not so, we should look for another relation that gathers higher weight in the absence of the highest weight relation. However, we only delete the relations that are added due to upper approximation. The advantage of taking Interval Closure as the upper approximation is due to the minimality property of the convex IA network. The justification of the selecting the relations with highest weights is clear. However, in order to justify that by taking interval closure of the network makes the heuristic more robust, we carry out the experiments of the same heuristic with the interval closure and without it. The experimental results are described in the following section.

Table 3. The proposed heuristic.

```
Algorithm highest_weight heuristic
Input: IA network N, max_iteration
Output: A solution of N
compute the interval closure I(N) of N
path_consistency(I(N))
convert (I(N), WI(N))
do while iteration < max_iteration
iteration = 1
weighted_pc (WI(N))
    get singleton labeling τ(I(N))of I(N) by selecting
    the atomic relation corresponding to highest weight
    along every edge of WI(N).
path-consistency(τ(I(N)))
    if success
        if the τ(I(N)) is also a singleton labeling of N
            This is done by checking that the atomic re-
            lations of τ(I(N)) are members of the corre-
            sponding constraints of N.
        then exit with τ(I(N))as the solution of N
        else identify the atomic relations in τ(I(N)) that
        are not in N and change their weights to 0 in
        WI(N).
iteration = iteration +1
end while
```

5 Experimental Results

We carried out elaborate experiments with very large number of problem instances. The objective of the experimental analysis is essentially to determine the robustness of the proposed algorithms. Realizing that the algorithm is not complete, we attempt to determine the instances when our algorithm finds a solution for the networks that are known to be consistent. The experimental analyses are also to evaluate the benefit of starting with convex approximation of the given network.

Random instances of the IA network are generated in a similar method as described in [6]. A model A(**n, d, t**) is generated with n number of nodes, **d** percentage of edges of the network representing the density of the graph, and **t**, the constraint tightness, as the average number of relations per edge. For instance **n** = 30, **d** = 40, and **t** = 6, IA network is of 30 nodes, average number of atomic relations of 40% of the edges are 6 and remaining 60% edges of the network are labeled with universal constraint. Different networks (100 problem instances) are randomly generated for each combinations of **n, d** and **t** by varying **n** from 10 to 60 and **d** in the range of 10 to 70, and **t** = 8. Each problem instance is made consistent by adding a known solution to the network. We compare the performance of the algorithm with the similar algorithm that does not make use of convex approximation I(N).

We observe that for networks known to be consistent, convex approximation finds consistency for more number of problems. Experimental analysis demonstrates that these heuristic strategies can be very practical to determine a solution for the general IA network. Figures 1, 2 and 3 are x-y plots for density **d** vs. the percentage of solved instances for 20, 30 and 40 nodes, respectively. Figures 4, 5 and 6 are x-y plots for nodes **n** vs. the percentages of solved instances. Figure 4 depicts the average number of problems solved for different values of **d** between 10 to 70. Following [6], we identify the hard region of the problem instances in terms of $\mathbf{d} = (100 * d') / (n-1)$, where $d' = 9.5$. Figure 5 gives the graph corresponding to the hard region and figure 6, for the problems, which are outside hard region.

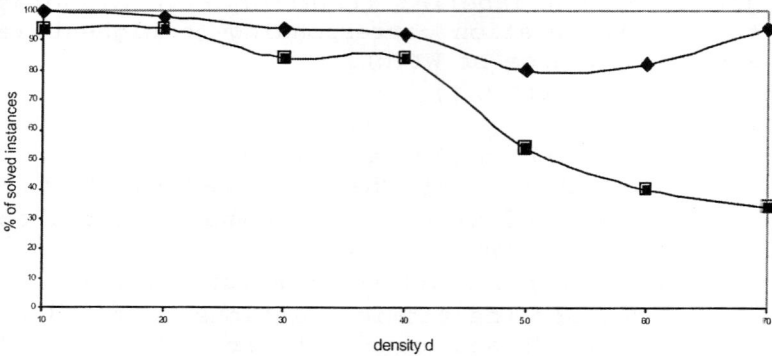

Fig. 1. The performance analysis for the IA network with n= 20, t=8 and for different d. The graph depicts the percentages of problem instances for which solution can be found in 5n iterations. It also gives a comparative analysis of the performance with ♦ and without ■ convex approximation.

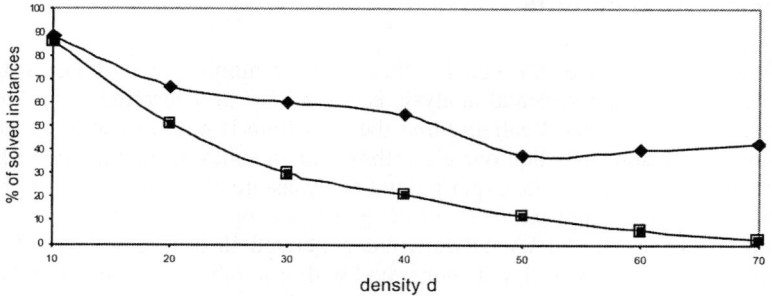

Fig. 2. Similar study as that of Figure 1 for n= 30.

A Novel Heuristic to Solve IA Network by Convex Approximation and Weights 161

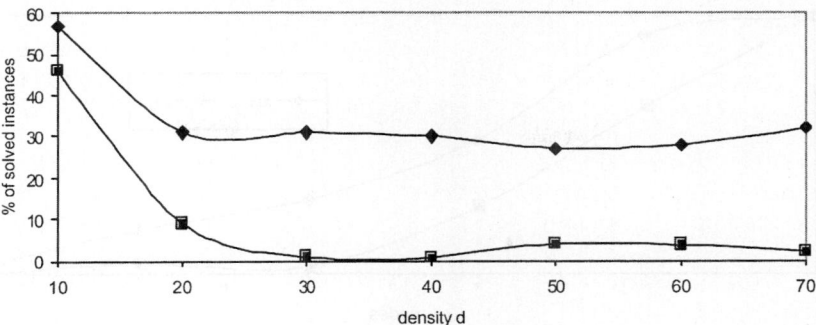

Fig. 3. Similar study as that of Figure 1 for n= 40.

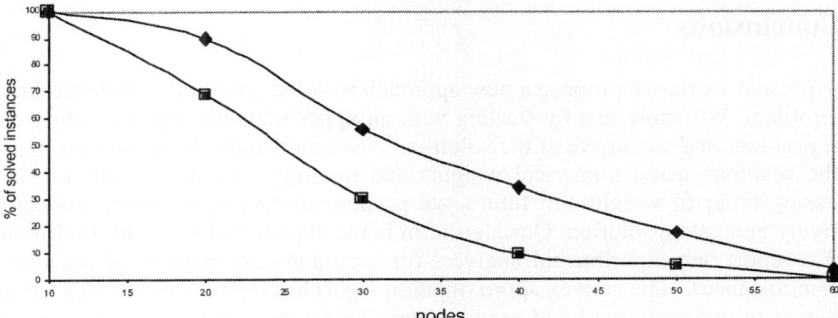

Fig. 4. The performance analysis for the IA network for different values of n. The graph depicts the percentages of problem instances for which solution can be found in 5n iterations. It also gives a comparative analysis of the performance with ♦ and without ■ convex approximation.

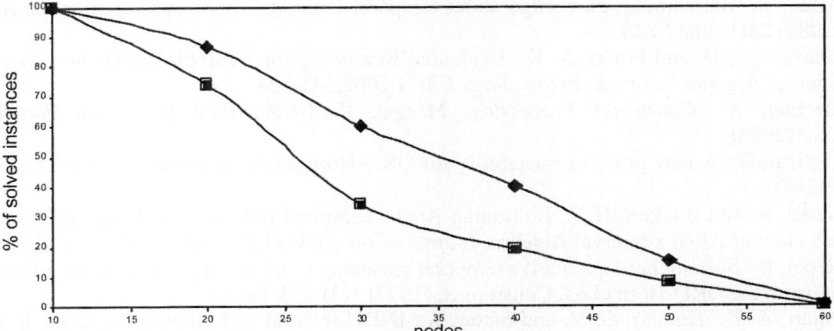

Fig. 5. The performance analysis for the IA network for different values of n and for hard problem instances. The graph depicts the percentages of problem instances for which solution can be found in 5n iterations. It also gives a comparative analysis of the performance with ♦ and without ■ convex approximation.

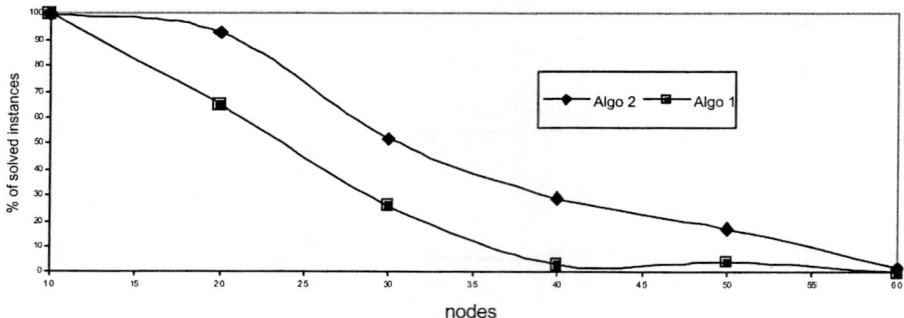

Fig. 6. The performance analysis for the IA network for different values of n and for easy problem instances.

6 Conclusions

In the present work, we propose a new approach to solve temporal constraint satisfaction problem. We show that by starting with an upper tractable approximation of the given problem one can arrive at the solution. We demonstrate this paradigm by ranking the relations using numerical weights and moving towards the solution in the decreasing order of weights. In future, we propose to investigate other strategies to iteratively generate a solution. Our algorithm is incomplete but efficient. In this work, we also report our experimental analyses for hard and easy regions of the space of problem instances. The convex approximation algorithm reports consistency for more number of problems in hard and easy regions. This demonstrates that one can check the consistency of the network by working with convex approximation.

References

1. Allen, J.: Maintaining knowledge about temporal intervals. *Communication of the ACM*, (1983) 26(11):832-843.
2. Bhavani, S. D. and Pujari, A. K.: Evidential Reasoning for Heuristic Algorithms to Solve Interval Algebra Network. *Proceedings KBCS-2002*,525-534.
3. Dechter, R.: *Constraint Processing*. Morgan Kaufmann Publishers, San Francisco, USA(2003).
4. Ligozat, G.: A new proof of tractability for ORD-Horn relations. *Proceedings of AAAI-96*, 395-401.
5. Nebel, B. and Buckert, H. J.: Reasoning About Temporal Relations: A Maximal Tractable sub class of Allen's Interval Algebra, *Journal of the ACM* (1995) 42 : 43-66.
6. Nebel, B.: Solving hard qualitative temporal reasoning problems: Evaluatting the efficiency of using the ORD-Horn class. Constraints, (1997) 1(3):175-190.
7. Pujari, A. K., Kumari, G. V. and Sattar, A.: INDU-interval and duration network. In *Proceedings of Sixteenth Australian joint conference on AI*, (1999) pages 291-303. Springer-Verlag.
8. Rossi, F., Venable K. B., Khatib, L., Morris, P. and Morris, R.: Two solvers for tractable temporal constraints with preferences. *Proc. AAAI 2002 workshop on preferences in AI and CP Edmonton, Canada*.

9. VanBeek, P.: Reasoning about qualitative temporal information. *Artificial Intelligence* (1992) 58:297-324.
10. VanBeek, P. and Manchak, D. W.: The design and experimental analysis of algorithms for temporal reasoning. *JAIR 4* (1996) 1-18.
11. Vilain, M. and Kautz, H.: Constraint propagation algorithm for temporal reasoning, *Proc. of AAAI-86*, Morgan Kaufman.

Applying An Improved Heuristic Based Optimiser to Solve a Set of Challenging University Timetabling Problems: An Experience Report

Vincent Tam[1], Jack Ho[1], and Alvin Kwan[2]

[1] Department of E.E.E., The University of Hong Kong
Pokfulam, Hong Kong
phone: +852-2859-2697
vtam@eee.hku.hk

[2] C.I.T.E., School of Professional And Continuing Education
The University of Hong Kong, Pokfulam, Hong Kong
cmkwan@hkucc.hku.hk

Abstract. University timetabling problems (UTPs) represent a class of challenging and practical constrained optimization problems with its unique requirements when compared to school timetabling. In the past, researchers had proposed different intelligent search methods, that can be generally classified as the constructive or local search methods, to automate school and/or university timetabling. In this paper, we considered a flexible local search scheme combining both min-conflicts and look-forward heuristics to effectively solve general university timetabling problems. Our search proposal augmented with a k-reset repair operator achieved impressive results when compared to that of a general finite-domain constraint solving system, namely the *ZDC*, on a set of challenging UTPs obtained from an international timetabling competition. A preliminary analysis of their search results was conducted.More importantly, our search proposal of combined heuristics sheds light on various directions to effectively handle other complex or large-scale scheduling problems.

1 Introduction

Timetabling problems generally represents a class of *NP*-complete [2] and complex combinatorial optimization problems, frequently involving a large number of variables in real-world applications. Owing to the NP-complete nature, even solving a timetabling problem involving a small number of variables and a relatively simple set of constraints may require a huge amount of time and efforts to produce a feasible solution if any. Solving large-scale school timetabling problems [4, 6] by hands is often impractical or even infeasible due to the limited time. Researchers in the area of Algorithm Design and Analysis [2], Artificial Intelligence [1, 3] and Operations Research [5] have tried various search approaches including the genetic algorithms (GA) [10], simulated annealing (SA) [5] and tabu search (TS) [12] to hopefully provide an automated decision support system to solve most of these diffcult scheduling problems. Yet no "**effective and generic**"[1] timetabling technique has been achieved so far.

---

[1] Clearly, timetabling is an application-specific problem. Here, we are not considering a generic solution that can solve all timetabling problems. We only aim to ultimately obtain an automated timetabling technique without much effort in parameter tunning to produce *satisfactory* performance in solving most, say over 80%, of the real-life cases.

Basically, there are two major approaches to tackle the school or university timetabling problems as specific instances of the discrete constrained optimization problems (COPs) [9, 12]. The first is the traditional constructive search approach often involving some form of backtracking search. An example is the branch-and-bound (BnB) method [12]. The second approach involves some kinds of local search methods such as the GA or SA working on an initial and complete solution with a number of iterative repairs until a predetermined resource like the maximum number of iterations is exhausted. Besides, there are search hybrids [10, 12] proposed to combine the possible advantages of both approaches. A previous work by Yoshikawa et. al [13, 14] focused on only using the min-conflict heuristic (MCH) to generate an initial solution by assigning a value with the minimum number of constraint violations to each variable. After a fairly good-quality initial solution is generated, their search proposal relies on a heuristic billiard-move operator to iteratively repair on the current and complete assignment of lessons for school/university timetabling. Besides initialization heuristics, Kwan et. al [6] have attempted various lesson or timeslot selection heuristics to try to improve the performance of the billiard-move based heuristic search methods in handling real-life instances of school timetabling problems (STPs) in Hong Kong.

After all, none of the previous work on school/university timetabling has ever considered to *actively* apply the MCH as a repair heuristic during the search process for solving the timetabling problem at hand. In pursuit of this interesting idea, we quickly adapted a previous MCH-based search proposal by Stuckey et. al [10] to combine the MCH and look-forward heuristics to effectively solve any general timetabling problem, and then applied our adapted heuristic search framework to successfully solve a set of 20 challenging UTPs obtained from the PATAT International Timetabling Competition [8] organised by the famous Meta-Heuristic Network [8]. Undoubtedly, our proposal of combined heuristics not only gained remarkable success to effectively solve *all* 20 instances of challenging UTPs when compared fairly with a general constraint solving system, namely the *ZDC* as newly built by the Constraint Group [15] in the University of Essex, but also shed light on solving other complex or large-scale scheduling problems.

This paper is organized as follows. Section 2 discusses some previous works on school/university timetabling, the challenging UTPs that we are interested in and some related consideration. In Section 3, we describe our search proposal to combine both MCH and look-forward heuristics so as to tackle the challenging UTPs or possibly other school timetabling problems. Section 4 gives the empirical evaluation of our search proposal against that of the *ZDC* constraint solving system on a set of challenging UTPs. Lastly, we conclude our work in Section 5.

2 Preliminaries

This section describes the basic concepts or definitions required for our subsequent discussion. First, we review some previous works in solving school or university timetabling problems (UTPs). Then, a set of challenging UTPs that we will later use for benchmarking will be clearly explained before examining our search proposal in Section 3.

2.1 Previous Works

To solve high-school timetabling problems in Japan, Yoshikawa et. al [13, 14] proposed a combined search method using a novel initialization algorithm, namely the *Really-Full-Lookahead-Greedy* (RFLG) algorithm, to generate a high-quality initial lesson assignments, and the strongly biased Min-Conflicts Hill-Climbing (MCHC) [9] to iteratively refine the current assignments until a satisfactory solution was produced. The RFLG algorithm firstly made use of full arc-consistency technique to check and ensure initial assignments only occurred among the arcconsistent variables (lessons). For those arc-inconsistent variables excluded in the first step, RFLG would later assign a value (timeslot) with the least penalty value to each of them. The RFLG algorithm was designed to generate a relatively high-quality initial solution which would then be further refined by the MCHC strongly biased toward any local minimum. In each iteration, the MCHC repetitively selected any inconsistent variable for reassignment to achieve the least penalty values, with ties broken randomly. As a whole, their proposed combination of the RFLG and MCHC could successfully produce high-quality solutions in solving 2 real-life instances of high-school timetabling and 1 practical university timetabling application in Japan. Besides, Kwan et. al [6] carefully considered the possible impacts of various complex constraint types on the lesson selection, and proposed a new constrainedness measure, the K_{app} value, to effectively guide the most-constrained-variable-first (MCVF) ordering when solving 3 real-life instances of high school timetabling problems in Hong Kong. Later, they suggested another new contention measure [6] to guide the timeslot selection process. The basic idea is: the less contended a timeslot is, the more likely it should be assigned to the currently selected lesson. Obviously, allocating the more "free" timeslots may help to avoid any unnecessary "backtracks" due to resource conflicts early in the search stage.

2.2 The University Timetabling Problems

The 20 challenging university timetabling problems (UTPs) were obtained from the International Timetabling Competition 2002 [8]. The competition was organized by the Metaheuristics Network and sponsored by the International Series of Conferences on the Practice and Theory of Automated Timetabling (PATAT) from October 2002 to March 2003.

A major reason that we were interested in the 20 challenging UTPs was simply because ALL 20 instances in the competition were reductions of various typical university timetabling problems. All challenging instances of UTPs adopted a 5-day cycle with 9 periods per day. In each problem instance, the total number of lessons, each with its corresponding list of students, a list of required features for each lesson, the total number of available rooms, the corresponding room capacities, and finally the corresponding lists of room features were clearly specified. Besides, there were two basic categories of constraints: *hard* or *soft*.

The hard constraints included:
- Any student should not attend more than one lesson at any time.
- There should be at most one lesson scheduled at each room at any time.
- The room assigned to a lesson should contain all the features required by the lesson.
- The room should be large enough for the lesson assigned.

The soft constraints were:
- Any student should not have a lesson at the last period of a day.
- Any student should not have lessons at more than two consecutive periods in a day.
- Any student should not attend only one lesson in a day.

There is at least one perfect solution for each of the 20 challenging UTPs. Therefore, the designated algorithm should be able to find solutons for all 20 instances without violating any hard constraints within a predetermined time limit depending on a specific combination of the hardware and operating systems used.

3 Combining the Min-conflicts and Look-Forward Heuristics

Since most existing work can be too specific in design or inappropriate for scheduling based on individual student's preference, we devise a new combination of the min-conflict [9] and look-forward [10] heuristics as a general-purpose search scheme for tackling the challenging UTPs. In fact, our preliminary evaluation of Yoshikawa's proposal readily confirms that Yoshikawa's proposed RLFG algorithm can be computationally expensive in solving the challenging set of UTPs. Thus, unlike Yoshikawa's proposal [13] that relied on the full look-ahead (arc-consistency) technique to produce a good-quality initial solution to be iteratively improved by the min-conflicts hill-climbing (MCHC) heuristic only, our search proposal starts with a randomized initial solution and aggressively uses both MCHC and the more intelligent look-forward heuristics. The MCHC is used to bias toward any local minimum of constraint violations while the look-forward, as originally proposed by Stuckey and Tam [10], aims to guide any strongly biased heuristic search more intelligently by trying different plausible neighboring states to sensibly break ties during the search. Together, the MCHC and look-forward heuristics complement each other with impressive results achieved on a set of hard graph-coloring problems [11]. In this work, we quickly adapt the original look-forward heuristic operator through an integration with the interesting billiard-move operator as suggested in Yoshikawa's work for handling UTPs. Besides, we try out several heuristic variable ordering techniques to guide our proposed search scheme more intelligently.

Our proposed search framework can be divided into 3 major parts. The first part is mainly used for initializing the relevant data structures, domains and variables; preparing of the heuristic minimal width ordering (MWO) [12] of all variables; and properly setting up a queue of variables with constraint violations and a tabu-list to avoid cycling before the search starts. The second part represents the main body of the search algorithm in which we firstly apply the MCHC followed by the adapted *look_forward_billiard_movement* operator when no "recent" improvement on the previous solution is made. The last part denotes the constraint relaxation codes which provides flexibility to relax the more diffcult soft constraints in order to focus the search effort on the more important constraints and finally return the best satisfactory solution ever found. Clearly, on certain easy UTPs, the last part of our search algorithm can be flexibly removed.

The major operators of our search proposal to combine both the min-conflicts and look-forward heuristics are explained below. For more detail, refer to [11]. The empirical evaluation of our above search proposal will be given in Section 4.

- The apply_MCH operator: a relatively expensive operator in terms of both time and space complexities. It performs the steepest-descent step by examining all the all the values in the domain of a variable. The value that causes the minimum number of constraint violations will be selected. Ties are broken randomly.
- The MWO_sorting operator: The minimal width ordering (MWO) heuristic strategy gives all variables a total ordering with the minimal width and then labels the variables accordingly. Basically, MWO aims at reducing the needs for backtracking through labeling the less constrained variables, as determined in its constraint graph, first. For detail, refer to [12].
- The look_forward_billiard_movement operator: The basic idea of the original look_forward operator is to carefully investigate the ties resulting from the apply_MCH operator. The look_forward operator aims at finding a value from the ties to intelligently guide the search towards a more promising solution. When ties are formed, the concerned variable will be assigned to every single value in the ties with the remaining variables being modified by a low-cost heuristic operator that we have quickly adapted from the billiard_movement operator [14] proposed by Yoshikawa et. al [13, 14] for timetabling. The original billiard_movement operator selects an unassigned lesson L_1 for assignment to another timeslot T_1 originally occupied by L_2 only if the originally assigned lesson L2 can successfully shifted to another available timeslot T_2, thus acting like the bombardment of billiard balls in a pool. Our newly adapted billiard_movement operator will thoroughly examine all the possible billiard movements for each lesson L_t in ties with the current assignment ($T_x = L_y$). And the new assignment resulting from such thorough examination and causing the smallest number of constraint violations will ultimately be selected. For detail, refer to [11].

4 Experimental Results

To demonstrate the feasibility of our search proposal combining both minconflicts and look-forward heuristics, a prototype, namely the *MCH+LF_Bill* optimiser, was tested on a challenging set of 20 university timetabling problems (UTPs) [8] obtained from the International Timetabling Competition 2002 available from October 2002 to March 2003. Our prototype was implemented in Java and executed on an Intel Pentium 1.9*GHz* machine under the Microsoft Windows XP platform. For benchmarking, we installed a stable version of the general finite-domain constraint solving system, namely *ZDC* Version 1.81 available from the Constraint Group [15] in the University of Essex, on our only notebook computer installed with a Pentium 800*MHz* processor and Microsoft Windows 98 operating system due to their unique support for the reliable performance of the *ZDC* system. Both computers were equipped with 256 Mbytes of RAM. For a fairer comparison, both our heuristic-based optimiser and the *ZDC* system are allowed with 30 CPU minutes only, though on different environments, to solve each instance of the challenging UTPs. In addition, we only focus on the penalty value of their final solution returned, with a penalty value of 1 accumulated for each "soft" constraint violated in the returned solution, for the following comparison. All the figures reported below for our heuristics based search proposals are averages over 10 runs for reliable performance in each test case.

Table 1. The Performance of Our Search Proposal Against That of the *ZDC* System on A Set of 20 Challenging UTPs.

	Case 1				Case 2			
	ZDC		MCH+LF_Bill		ZDC		MCH+LF_Bill	
Prob.	APV	HPV	APV	HPV	APV	HPV	APV	HPV
01	72	597	0	566	?	?	167	167
02	19	514	0	496	?	?	202	203
03	107	613	0	543	?	?	235	243
04	240	924	18	844	?	?	445	457
05	146	947	0	743	?	?	532	546
06	59	809	0	764	?	?	374	383
07	215	928	0	886	?	?	543	571
08	247	829	0	690	?	?	198	198
09	!	!	0	534	?	?	184	184
10	!	!	0	525	?	?	190	190
11	190	680	0	543	?	?	209	210
12	!	!	0	509	?	?	357	369
13	232	796	0	581	?	?	392	402
14	452	1248	0	885	?	?	662	677
15	333	1011	0	704	?	?	479	489
16	141	720	0	578	?	?	121	121
17	102	861	0	787	?	?	509	532
18	119	653	0	501	?	?	184	185
19	!	!	0	808	?	?	376	383
20	34	731	0	753	?	?	164	166

Table 1 summarizes the penalty results of our search proposal, the *MCH+LF_Bill* optimiser, against that of the *ZDC* system on all instances of the challenging UTPs for 2 different cases. The results for the Case 1 in which we considered all hard constraints and only the first soft constraint, namely the *no_last_period_constraint*, as stated in Section 2.2 are shown in the left portion of Table 1, whereas the results for the Case 2 where we considered all hard constraints together with the first and second soft constraints, namely the *no_last_period* and *no_3_consecutive_periods* constraints, are given in right half of the table. For all the case tested, both our proposed *MCH+LF_Bill* optimiser and the relevant *ZDC* optimiser, particularly the Guided Local Search (GLS) optimiser being used, could successfully solve **all hard constraints** in the final solution returned. Therefore, we focus our comparison solely on the penalty values reflecting the number of soft constraints violated in the final solutions. For each optimiser examined, the leftmost column focuses on the actual penalty values (APV) solely due to the soft constraint(s) considered whereas the second column denotes the the hypothetical penalty values (HPV) taking into account of all 3 soft constraints stated in Section 2.2 to reflect its overall solution quality for reference. Of course, we considered only 1 or 2 such soft constraints in the actual search process. Besides, an "!" symbol is used to denote the case where the *ZDC* system failed to return a solution after exceeding the time limit of 30 CPU minutes while a "?" symbol is used to represent the case where the *ZDC* system was run out of memory during program execution. Obviously, the smaller the actual or hypothetical penalty value (APV or HPV), the smaller the number of soft constraints violated by the ultimate solution returned by the concerned optimiser, therefore the more favorable the optimiser is. For both Case 1 and 2, our proposed *MCH+LF_Bill* optimiser combining both effective MCH and *look_forward* heuristics **consistently outperformed** the finite-domain constraint solving system *ZDC* in terms of both smallest actual and hypothetical penalty values (APV and HPV) returned to tackle all these 20 challenging UTPs except the last problem of Case 1 in which the HPV of our proposed *MCH+LF_Bill* optimiser is only slightly larger than that of the *ZDC* optimiser probably due to the probabilistic search behavior of our proposed *look_forward_billiard_ movement* operator in this specific case. The detailed explanation for this special case prompts for further investigation. Specifically for Case 1, our proposed *MCH+LF_Bill* optimiser could successfully solve *all* hard and soft constraints considered with its APVs returned as 0 for all 20 challenging problems except problem 04 with its APV as 18 showing the exceptional diffculty of this particular UTP as confirmed by our preliminary analysis [11] provided later. On the other hand, the *ZDC* optimiser always return a relatively larger APVs, and even failed to return a solution for 4 UTPs, including the problem 09, 10, 12 and 19, after 30 CPU minutes. In this particular aspect, the soft constraint *no_last_period* is still relatively easy for our effective search proposal to tackle. However, for the Case 2 involving both soft constraints as *no_last_period* and no *3_consecutive_periods*, the *ZDC* optimiser ran out of memory for 20 UTPs likely due to the intensive computation required to check for the newly included soft constraint: *no_3_consecutive_periods*. Besides, the APVs and HPVs returned for our proposed *MCH+LF_Bill* optimiser are fairly close to each other or sometimes even the same, implying that the newly introduced soft constraint *no_3_consecutive_periods* is also presented as a great challenge to our heuristic search framework. After all, these results clearly demonstrate the effectiveness and reliable performance of our heuristics based search framework over the general constraint solving sytems such as the *ZDC* system[2] [15] to handle challenging UTPs.

Clearly, the *apply MCH* operator performed well in the challenging UTPs. The major weakness of our search proposal was the lack of an appropriate search restart scheme when the whole search landscape was trapped into local minima. The *look_forward_billiard_movement* operator, though succeeded to improve the solution quality to a large extent, may sometimes fail to further improve the search landscape when the corresponding penalty values dropped below a certain value as observed in our preliminary analysis. Table 2 showing the variations of total penalty values against the number of iterations for our search proposal "without any time bound on the CPU time" but simply halted after no improvement on penalty value over 30 consecutive iterations clearly illustrate this interesting phenomenon. For problem 04, our proposed *MCH+LF_Bill* optimiser goes through a very rugged landscape to drastically decrease the penalty value from the initial 120 to around 20 in the first 2, 000 iterations, and successfully finds a feasible solution to all hard and relevant soft constraints after another 5, 000+ iterations. Conversely for problem 10, our search proposal exhibits a very sharp drop in penalties in the first 3000 iterations, later followed by another slow drop around 14, 000 to 18, 000 iterations, and lastly remains almost level off from 25, 000 iterations onwards. The specific reason(s) behind this opposite phenomenon prompt us for further investigation.

---

[2] It is worthwhile to note that like many other constraint solving systems, the *ZDC* system is still under development with constant revisions. So, it is always possible that the *ZDC* system may effectively handle all these challenging UTPs in its future version(s).

Table 2. The Preliminary Analysis of Our Search Proposal on 2 Selected UTPs.

(a) Penalty changes for prob. 04

(b) Penalty changes for prob. 10

5 Conclusion

Most previous works for school or university timetabling tends to be too specific and often based on the rigid model of class-based scheduling. Among these works, Yoshikawa et. al [13] proposed a combined searchmethod using the *ReallyFull-Lookahead-Greedy* (RFLG) algorithm [14], to generate a good-quality initial solution, and the strongly biased Min-Conflicts Hill-Climbing (MCHC) [9] to iteratively repair the current solution until a satisfactory solution was produced. A direct result of their proposal was the constraint handling system COAS-TOOL [13] that had been successfully applied to tackle 3 real-life instances of school or university timetabling problems (UTPs) in Japan. In this paper, instead of relying on the RFLG or other initialization method to produce a good-quality initial solution, we proposed a *MCH+LF_Bill* optimiser combining both MCH and the intelligent look-forward to *aggressively* guide the search for *better* improvements from the current search position until a feasible and nearoptimal solution is obtained, or a resource limit as specified in CPU minutes or the maximum number of iterations is reached. We implemented a prototype of our proposed *MCH+LF_Bill* optimiser in Java for running on a Pentium $1.9GHz$ machine installed with theWindows XP operating system, and compared against a general finite-domain constraint solving system, namely the ZDC system, on a set of 20 challenging UTPs obtained from the International Timetabling Competition 2002 [8] organized by the Metaheuristics Network. Our search prototype successfully solved/optimised for all 20 instances of the hard UTPs for two different cases considered within a reasonable period of time, and compared favorably to the results obtained by the ZDC system. More importantly, we conducted a preliminary analysis on the performance of our search proposal in solving these challenging UTPs. The preliminary analysis clearly indicates that there is still much room for improve our search proposal to tackle hard UTPs or other related scheduling problems.

There are many interesting directions for future investigation. First, a more detailed and thorough analysis to look for any opportunity for improving our proposed search framework should be interesting. Second, improving our heuristic search proposal with a max-search [12] strategy that will opportunistically restart the current search with the best solution found to avoid our heuristic operators being trapped in local minima should be able to improve the overall search effectiveness. Lastly, it should be interesting to examine the effects of various heuristic ordering strategies on our search proposal in solving general UTPs.

References

1. E. Aarts and J. Korst. Boltzmann machines for traveling salesman problems. *European Journal of Operational Research*, 39:79–95, 1989.
2. Thomas H.Cormen, Charles E.Leiserson, Ronald L.Rivest, "Introduction to Algorithms", The MIT Press, McGraw-Hill Book Company, 1990.
3. A. Davenport, E. Tsang, C. Wang, and K. Zhu. GENET: A connectionist architecture for solving constraint satisfaction problems by iterative improvement. In *Proceedings of AAAI'94*, 1994.
4. Gotlieb, "The Construction of Class-Teacher Timetables", Proceedings of IFIP Congress 62, 1963, Pages 73-77.
5. D. Johnson, C. Aragon, L. McGeoch, and C. Schevon. Optimization by simulated annealing: an experimental evaluation; Part II, graph coloring and number partitioning. *Operations Research*, 39(3):378 – 406, 1991.
6. Alvin C.M. Kwan, H.L. Chan, "Efficient Lesson Selection Heuristic for High-School Timetabling", Proceedings of the IASTED International Conference Artificial Intelligence and Soft Computing, August 9-12, 1999.
7. Alvin C.M. Kwan, Ken C.K. Chung, Kammy Yip, Vincent Tam, "An Automated School Timetabling System Using Hybrid Intelligent Techniques", (ISMIS'2003), Japan, October, 2003.
8. The Meta-Heuristics Network. The International Timetabling Competition 2002 (October 2002 to March 2003) at http://www.idsia.ch/Files/ttcomp2002/ - sponsored by the International Series of Conferences on the Practice and Theory of Automated Timetabling (PATAT).
9. Steven Minton, Andy Philips, Mark D.Johnston, Philip Laird, "Minimizing Conflicts: A Heuristic Repair Method for Constraint-Satisfaction and Scheduling Problems", Artificial Intelligence, 58, 1992, Pages 161-205.
10. Peter J. Stuckey, Vincent Tam, "Improving Evolutionary Algorithms for Efficient Constraint Satisfaction", The International Journal on Artificial Intelligence Tools, the World Scientific Publishers, Vol. 8, No. 4, pages 363 - 383, December, 1999.
11. V. Tam and D. Ting. "Combining the Min-Conflicts and Look-Forward Heuristics to Effectively Solve A Set of Hard University Timetabling Problems" Proceedings of the IEEE ICTAI'03, pp. 492 - 496, Sacramento, USA, November 3-5, 2003.
12. E. Tsang. *Foundations of Constraint Satisfaction*. Academic Press, 1993.
13. Masazumi Yoshikawa, Kazuya Kaneko, Yuriko Nomura, Masanobu Wantanabe, "A Constraint-Based Approach to High-School Timetabling Problems: A Case Study", AAAI-94, Pages 1111-1116.
14. Masazumi Yoshikawa, Kazuya Kaneko, Yoichiro Nakakuki, "Improving a Heuristic Repair Method for Large-Scale School Timetabling Problems", CP99, 1999, Pages 275-288.
15. The *ZDC* Constraint Solving System (Version *1.81*). Available at http://cswww.essex.ac.uk/Research/CSP/cacp/cacpdemo.html.

Extending Unit Propagation Look-Ahead of DPLL Procedure

Anbulagan

Logic and Computation Program, Canberra Research Laboratory
National ICT Australia Limited
Locked Bag 8001, Canberra, ACT 2601, Australia
anbulagan@nicta.com.au

Abstract. The DPLL (Davis-Putnam-Logemann-Loveland) procedure is one of the most effective methods for solving SAT problems. It is well known that its efficiency depends on the choice of the branching rule. Different branching rules are proposed in the literature. Unit propagation look-ahead (UPLA) branching rule was one of the main improvements in the DPLL procedure (e.g.,[10]). The UPLA branching rule integrated in *satz* SAT solver [10] performs a series of variable filtering process at each node as a static variable filtering agency. In this paper we introduce and experiment with dynamic variable filtering (DVF) based branching rule which extends the UPLA heuristic process for doing more filtering and choosing a best branching variable from an irreducible sub-formula. To enhance the performance of DVF branching rule, we integrate neighborhood variable ordering heuristic (NVO) for exploring only the neighborhood variables of the current assigned variable. Experimental results of DVF+NVO branching rule on a number of real-world benchmark instances and quasigroup problems prove our approaches to be useful in many circumstances.

1 Introduction

The satisfiability (SAT) problem is central in mathematical logic, artificial intelligence and other fields of computer science and engineering. In conjunctive normal form (CNF), a SAT problem can be represented as a propositional formula $\mathcal{F}$ on a set of Boolean variables $\{x_1, x_2, ..., x_n\}$. A literal l is then a variable x_i or its negated form $\bar{x}_i$, and a clause c_i is a logical *or* of some literals such as $x_1 \vee x_2 \vee \bar{x}_3$. A propositional formula $\mathcal{F}$ consists of a logical *and* of several clauses, such as $c_1 \wedge c_2 \wedge ... \wedge c_m$, and is often simply written as a set $\{c_1, c_2, ..., c_m\}$ of clauses.

Given $\mathcal{F}$, the SAT problem involves testing whether all the clauses in $\mathcal{F}$ can be satisfied by some consistent assignment of truth values $\{true, false\}$ to the variables. If this is the case, $\mathcal{F}$ is satisfiable; otherwise it is unsatisfiable.

One of the best known and most widely used algorithms to solve SAT problems is the DPLL (Davis-Putnam-Logemann-Loveland) procedure [3]. Many SAT solvers such as Posit [5], Tableau [2], *satz* [10], and *cnfs* [4] are based on this procedure. DPLL essentially enumerates all possible solutions to a given SAT problem by setting up a binary search tree and proceeding until it either finds a satisfying truth assignment or concludes that no such assignment exists. It is well known that the search tree size of a SAT problem is generally an exponential function of the problem size, and that the branching variable selected by a branching rule at a node is crucial for determining the size of the sub-tree rooted at that node. A wrong choice may cause an exponential increase of the sub-tree size. Hence, the actual performance of a DPLL procedure depends significantly on the effectiveness of the branching rule used.

In general, the branching rules compute $w(x_i)$ and $w(\bar{x}_i)$, where the function w measures the quality of branching to literals (x_i) or $(\bar{x}_i)$. The DPLL procedure should select the branching variable (x_i) such that $w(x_i)$ and $w(\bar{x}_i)$ are the highest. Whether to branch on (x_i) or $(\bar{x}_i)$ is only important for the satisfiable problems because the literals chain created, when the truth value is appropriately assigned to the branching variables, will reduce the search tree size. We can reduce the search tree size that a DPLL procedure explores if we extend the branching rule with an appropriate heuristic.

Much of the research on DPLL has focussed on finding clever branching rules to select the branching variable that most effectively reduces the search space. Among them, Li and Anbulagan have performed a systematic empirical study of unit propagation look-ahead (UPLA) heuristics in [10] and integrated the optimal UPLA in *satz* SAT solver. The effectiveness of UPLA in *satz* has made this solver one of the best solvers for solving hard random and a number of real-world SAT problems.

The UPLA branching rule of *satz* performs a series of variable filtering process at each node as a *static* variable filtering agency. The UPLA heuristic itself carries out one of the following actions during two propagations of a free variable at each search tree node: detecting a contradiction earlier, simplifying the formula, or weighing the branching variable candidates. Intuitively, at a node, the formula simplification process by UPLA can cause the previously selected branching variable candidates become ineffective. To handle the problem, in this paper we introduce and experiment with dynamic variable filtering (DVF) based branching rule.

The key idea underlying this new branching rule is to further detect failed literals that would remain undiscovered using a UPLA branching rule, before choosing a branching variable. In other words, we perform more reasoning in the open space between the UPLA heuristic and the MOMS (Maximum Occurrences in clause of Minimum Size) heuristic in the actual DPLL branching rule. To test this idea, we use *satz*215 (the best version of the *satz* DPLL procedure) where we simply replace its branching rule by a new branching rule. The new rule allows filtering of free variables, and at the same time reduces the sub-formula size at each node until the filtering process is saturated. Then, it chooses a best branching variable from an irreducible sub-formula.

Since the DVF based branching rule examines all free variables many times at each node, we attempt to limit the number of free variables examined by only exploring the neighborhood variables of the current assigned variable. For this purpose, we additionally integrate the neighborhood variable ordering (NVO) heuristic for enhancing the performance of DVF.

The experimental results of DVF+NVO branching rule on a number of real-world benchmark instances and quasigroup problems prove our approaches to be useful in many circumstances. This study also raises a number of other possibilities for enhancing the performance of DVF+NVO branching rule to solve more SAT problems, e.g., by avoiding redundant unit propagation searches for variables remain unchanged between iteration of UPLA heuristic.

In the next section we describe the background of this work in more detail. In section 3 we present the DVF based branching rule and its extension, which integrates the NVO heuristic. In section 4, we present some experimental results to give a picture of the performance of our new branching rules on a number of structured SAT problems. Finally, we conclude the paper with some remarks on current and future research.

2 Unit Propagation Look-Ahead Based Branching Rule

The UPLA heuristic plays a crucial role in a DPLL procedure and is used to reach dead-ends earlier with the aim of minimising the length of the current path in the search tree. The earlier SAT solvers which used the power of UPLA partially were *POSIT* [5] and *Tableau* [2]. Then Li and Anbulagan conducted a systematic empirical study to explore the real power of the UPLA heuristic and integrated the optimal UPLA heuristic in a SAT solver called *satz* [10]. The success of *POSIT*, *Tableau*, and *satz* in solving hard random 3-SAT and a number of real-world problems shows the effectiveness of this heuristic.

We distinguish the UPLA heuristic from the conventional unit propagation procedure (UP) that is usually used in DPLL as follows: UP is executed to reduce the size of a sub-formula possessing unit clauses *after* a branching variable is selected, while UPLA is integrated in the branching rule itself and is executed at each search tree node. In figure 1, we present a branching rule which integrates the UPLA heuristic on top of the MOMS heuristic.

Given a variable x_i, the UPLA heuristic examines x_i by adding the two unit clauses possessing x_i and $\bar{x}_i$ to $\mathcal{F}$ and independently making two unit propagations. These propagations result in a number of newly produced binary clauses, which are then used to weigh the variable x_i. This is calculated in figure 1, using the function $diff(\mathcal{F}_1, \mathcal{F}_2)$ which returns the number of new binary clauses in $\mathcal{F}_1$ that were not in $\mathcal{F}_2$. Let $w(x_i)$ be the number of new binary clauses produced by setting the variable to *true*, and $w(\bar{x}_i)$ be the number of new binary clauses produced by setting the variable to *false*. When there is no contradiction found during the two unit propagations, then variable x_i will be piled up to the branching variable candidates stack $\mathcal{B}$. The DPLL procedure then uses a MOMS heuristic to branch on the variable x_i such that $w(\bar{x}_i)*w(x_i)*1024+w(\bar{x}_i)+w(x_i)$ is the highest. The branching variable selected follows the two-sided Jeroslow-Wang (J-W) rule [7] designed to balance the search tree.

```
B := ∅;
For each free variable xᵢ, do
Begin
    let 𝓕'ᵢ and 𝓕''ᵢ be two copies of 𝓕
    𝓕'ᵢ := UP(𝓕'ᵢ ∪ {xᵢ});  𝓕''ᵢ := UP(𝓕''ᵢ ∪ {x̄ᵢ});
    If both 𝓕'ᵢ and 𝓕''ᵢ contain an empty clause then backtrack();
    else if 𝓕'ᵢ contains an empty clause then xᵢ := false; 𝓕 := 𝓕''ᵢ;
    else if 𝓕''ᵢ contains an empty clause then xᵢ := true; 𝓕 := 𝓕'ᵢ;
    else
        B := B ∪ {xᵢ}; w(xᵢ) := diff(𝓕'ᵢ, 𝓕) and w(x̄ᵢ) := diff(𝓕''ᵢ, 𝓕);
End;

For each variable xᵢ ∈ B, do 𝓜(xᵢ) := w(x̄ᵢ) * w(xᵢ) * 1024 + w(x̄ᵢ) + w(xᵢ);
Branch on the free variable xᵢ such that 𝓜(xᵢ) is the highest.
```

Fig. 1. The UPLA based branching rule.

The UPLA heuristic also allows the earlier detection of the so-called failed literals in $\mathcal{F}$. These are literals l where $w(l)$ counts an empty clause. For such variables, DPLL immediately tries to satisfy $\bar{l}$. If there is a contradiction during the second unit propagation, DPLL will directly perform backtracking, else the size of the sub-formula is reduced which allows the selection of a set of best branching variable candidates at each node in search tree.

So, during two propagations of a free variable through the UPLA heuristic, the following three circumstances can occur:

- The free variable selected becomes a candidate for the branching variable.
- Only one contradiction is found during two unit propagations, meaning the size of formula $\mathcal{F}$ will be reduced during the other successful unit propagation process.
- Two contradictions are found during two unit propagations causing the search to backtrack to an earlier instantiation.

Daniel Le Berre suggested the further detection of implied literals within UPLA heuristic [9], resulting in the latest and best version of *satz*, *satz*215. The *satz*215 DPLL procedure generally uses a reasoning based on unit propagation to deduce implied literals in order to simplify $\mathcal{F}$ before choosing a best branching variable. For example, if $\mathcal{F}$ contains no unit clause but two binary clauses $(x \vee y)$ and $(x \vee \bar{y})$, unit propagation in $\mathcal{F} \cup \{\bar{x}\}$ leads to a contradiction. Therefore, x is an implied literal and could be used to simplify the formula $\mathcal{F}$ directly.

Intuitively, at a node, the formula simplification process of UPLA in *satz*215 can cause the previously selected branching variable candidates become ineffective. To handle the problem, in the next section we propose a new branching rule which does more reasoning to choose a best branching variable from an irreducible sub-formula. We term this reasoning technique the *dynamic variable filtering* (DVF) heuristic.

3 Dynamic Variable Filtering Based Branching Rule

The main objective of using UPLA in *satz*215 DPLL procedure is to detect contradictions earlier or to find a set of best branching variable candidates. In reality, UPLA heuristic in *satz*215 performs a series of variable filtering processes at each node as a static variable filtering agency, because it will only perform between one to three filtering processes at each node (depending on the search tree height). During the filtering process, some variables are assigned the value *true* or *false* through a forced unit propagation when a contradiction occurs during another unit propagation. Note that the UPLA examines a free variable by performing two unit propagations. This process will automatically reduce the size of sub-formula and collect the (almost) best branching variable candidates at each node of the search tree.

```
Do
    ℱ_init := ℱ;  ℬ := ∅;
    For each free variable x_i, do
    Begin
        let ℱ'_i and ℱ''_i be two copies of ℱ
        ℱ'_i := UP(ℱ'_i ∪ {x_i}); ℱ''_i := UP(ℱ''_i ∪ {x̄_i});
        If both ℱ'_i and ℱ''_i contain an empty clause then backtrack();
        else if ℱ'_i contains an empty clause then x_i := false; ℱ := ℱ''_i;
        else if ℱ''_i contains an empty clause then x_i := true; ℱ := ℱ'_i;
        else
            ℬ := ℬ ∪ {x_i}; w(x_i) := diff(ℱ'_i, ℱ) and w(x̄_i) := diff(ℱ''_i, ℱ);
    End;
Until (ℱ = ℱ_init);

For each variable x_i ∈ ℬ, do ℳ(x_i) := w(x̄_i) * w(x_i) * 1024 + w(x̄_i) + w(x_i);
Branch on the free variable x_i such that ℳ(x_i) is the highest.
```

Fig. 2. The DVF based branching rule.

Our work is based on the insight that the size of a sub-formula during the variable filtering process can be further reduced in the UPLA based DPLL procedures. Here, we propose a new heuristic called the *dynamic variables filtering* (DVF) heuristic that further filters the free variables and at the same time reduces the sub-formula size at each node until the filtering process is saturated. We illustrate the new branching rule powered by DVF heuristic in figure 2.

We expect this new heuristic to perform better than the UPLA heuristic in terms of reducing the search tree size. To verify this, we carried out an empirical study and modified the branching rule of the DPLL procedure *satz*215[1] for our purpose. The *satz*215 DPLL procedure is the best version of *satz* in our experiments. A new DPLL procedure based on the DVF heuristic, *ssc*34, are proposed.

---
[1] Available from www.laria.u-picardie.fr/~cli/EnglishPage.html

The $ssc34$ solver is the same as the $satz215$ solver, except we replace the branching rule used in $satz215$ with the DVF heuristic based branching rule. It performs the variable filtering process until the sub-formula cannot be further reduced at each node before a branching variable selected. In fact, $ssc34$ examines the free variables many times using the UPLA heuristic at each search tree node. One might think that this saturation process is very costly, but it is not the case.

3.1 Neighborhood Variable Ordering Heuristic

Since DVF based branching rule of $ssc34$ examines all free variables many times using the UPLA heuristic at each node, we attempt to limit the number of free variables examined by only exploring the neighborhood variables of the current assigned variable. For this purpose, we create the $ssc355$ DPLL procedure by integrating a simple *neighborhood variable ordering* (NVO) heuristic in $ssc34$. Bessière et. al. [1] proposed a formulation of the dynamic variable ordering heuristic in the CSP domain that takes into account the properties of the neighborhood of the variable. The main objective of our simple NVO heuristic in $ssc355$ is to restrict the number of variables examined by UPLA in the DVF heuristic.

4 Experimental Evaluation

To evaluate the effectiveness of our proposed filtering techniques, we compare $ssc34$ and $ssc355$ DPLL procedures with $satz215$ on a number of structured SAT benchmark instances. These instances are well known in the literature and taken from different domain problems, such as bounded model checking, circuit verification, planning, scheduling, security and quasigroup problems. All instances have been downloaded from SATLIB (www.satlib.org) except the $lg*$ problems which have been downloaded from SIMLIB (www.mrg.dist.unige.it/star/sim/). The test consists of 125 instances where 57 of them are satisfiable and the other 68 are unsatisfiable. The number of variables of those instances varies from 317 to 939,040 and the number of clauses varies from 27 to 228,329. This experiment was conducted on a Intel Pentium 4 PC with a 3 GHz CPU under Linux. The run time is expressed in seconds. The time limit, to solve a problem, is set to 3600 seconds.

4.1 Performance on Real-World Instances

In table 1, we present the comparative results of $satz215$ (uses UPLA heuristic), $ssc34$ (uses DVF heuristic) and $ssc355$ (uses DVF+NVO heuristics) on the well known real-world instances. The table shows the search tree size (number of branching nodes) and the run time (in seconds) required to solve a given problem. The bracketed numbers in the problem column indicate the number of instances solved for that class of problems. For those problems, the $\#Vars$, $\#Cls$, *Search Tree Size*, and *Time* indicate the sum from all instances solved.

Table 1. Run time (in seconds) and search tree size of real-world SAT problems. The best performances are in bold.

Domain	Problem	#Vars	#Cls	Search Tree Size			Run Time		
				satz215	ssc34	ssc355	satz215	ssc34	ssc355
BMC	barrel5	1407	5383	1072	1200	**472**	33.28	**20.13**	38.41
	barrel6	2306	8931	4304	2600	**2560**	270.53	**102.70**	407.41
	barrel7	3523	13765	12704	**2643**	8656	1895.57	**594.00**	3344.53
	longmult8	3810	11877	11931	10881	**7449**	234.91	1012.22	**485.56**
	longmult9	4321	13479	18453	14447	**10917**	**459.39**	1825.39	1131.52
	longmult10	4852	15141	23854	n/a	**13207**	**735.78**	> 3600	1311.43
	longmult11	5403	16863	28951	n/a	**14558**	**997.61**	> 3600	1617.30
	longmult12	5974	18645	29574	n/a	**15268**	**1098.05**	> 3600	1819.64
	longmult13	6565	20487	28686	n/a	**15278**	**1246.26**	> 3600	2126.64
	longmult14	7176	22389	29721	n/a	**15598**	**1419.23**	> 3600	2419.84
	longmult15	7807	24351	32719	n/a	**17375**	**1651.43**	> 3600	3002.06
	queueinvar12	1112	7335	276	195	**94**	**0.81**	4.05	3.24
	queueinvar14	1370	9313	1019	399	**169**	**1.96**	12.68	6.45
	queueinvar16	1168	6496	293	287	**110**	**1.05**	6.23	4.06
	queueinvar18	2081	17368	5695	**1566**	1797	**11.51**	72.85	35.61
	queueinvar20	2435	20671	8865	2607	**2238**	**18.85**	144.60	70.35
CIRCU	eq_checking (34)	18055	31162	11677	2961	**2834**	5.68	5.90	**5.41**
	par16 (10)	6740	23350	5813	5894	**4717**	**11.75**	23.85	24.77
PLAN	bw_large.c	3016	50457	**4**	**4**	15	20.75	**21.99**	
	bw_large.d	6325	131973	705	n/a	**466**	**220.26**	> 3600	1081.17
	hanoi4	718	4934	8055	8197	**4462**	**4.91**	18.00	13.77
	lg28	7022	212453	n/a	n/a	**37**	> 3600	> 3600	**14.60**
	lg283	7268	227148	n/a	n/a	**93**	> 3600	> 3600	**30.29**
	lg284	7268	227293	n/a	n/a	**33**	> 3600	> 3600	**15.15**
	lg285	7295	228325	n/a	n/a	**37**	> 3600	> 3600	**15.16**
	lg286	7295	228329	n/a	n/a	**39**	> 3600	> 3600	**17.12**
	lg291	6668	166247	n/a	n/a	**3072**	> 3600	> 3600	**885.44**
	log.a	828	6718	12640	0	0	2.64	0.13	**0.12**
	log.b	843	7301	6	293	0	**0.08**	0.54	0.10
	log.c	1141	10719	507	1632	1	**0.35**	3.47	0.23
	log.d	4713	21991	0	520	1	**0.67**	51.31	5.53
SCHED	e0ddr2-10-by-5-1	19500	103887	1	1	29	**14.97**	40.75	153.03
	e0ddr2-10-by-5-4	19500	104527	n/a	1	n/a	> 3600	**57.34**	> 3600
	enddr2-10-by-5-1	20700	111567	0	0	1	**35.66**	74.11	127.55
	enddr2-10-by-5-8	21000	113729	0	2	222	**48.10**	58.02	108.64
	ewddr2-10-by-5-1	21800	118607	0	0	2	**24.58**	57.04	125.81
	ewddr2-10-by-5-8	22500	123329	0	3	0	**23.25**	46.43	60.68
SECUR	cnf-r1 (8)	2920867	35391	225	0	0	**1.40**	2.64	1.05
	cnf-r2 (8)	2986215	63698	17	0	0	**2.42**	4.05	2.20
	cnf-r3-b1-k1.1	21536	8966	2008485	**1265**	3551	2965.68	**70.65**	124.32
	cnf-r3-b1-k1.2	152608	8891	n/a	3002	**1500**	> 3600	174.00	**52.62**
	cnf-r3-b2-k1.1	152608	17857	128061	0	0	792.00	1.05	**0.88**
	cnf-r3-b2-k1.2	414752	17960	181576	0	0	1253.54	**1.19**	1.09
	cnf-r3-b3-k1.1	283680	26778	31647	0	0	447.66	**1.89**	1.51
	cnf-r3-b3-k1.2	676896	27503	38279	0	0	600.35	**2.25**	1.64
	cnf-r3-b4-k1.1	414752	35817	11790	0	0	347.51	**3.00**	2.41
	cnf-r3-b4-k1.2	939040	35963	20954	0	0	623.98	**3.37**	2.71

Bounded model checking (BMC) is the problem of checking if a model satisfies a temporal property in paths with bounded length k. We experiment with SAT-encoded BMC domain problems. We select the most representative barrel*, longmult* and queueinvar* instances from this domain. All instances are unsatisfiable. The results on BMC problems indicate that $ssc355$ has its best performance, in term of search tree size, even though it still suffers from run time point of view. This means that on BMC domain problems, the DVF+NVO branching rule performs well to choose a best branching variable from an irreducible sub-formula.

We solve the equivalence verification and parity instances from circuit domain (CIRCU) problems. All equivalence verification instances are unsatisfiable and all parity instances are satisfiable. The $ssc355$ has its best performance from search tree size point of view.

We solve also the blocks world, hanoi and logistics instances from planning domain (PLAN) problems. The lg^* problems are unsatisfiable, while the other problems of this domain are satisfiable. The results on those problems indicate that $ssc355$ has its best performance in general. The DVF+NVO based DPLL procedure can solve the lg^* problems, while the $satz215$ and $ssc34$ unable to solve those problems in the given time limit.

The $ssc34$ DPLL procedure can solve all job shop scheduling instances from scheduling domain (SCHED) problems. All instances are satisfiable. The $satz215$ and $ssc355$ fail to solve the problem $e0ddr2$-10-by-5-4 in one hour.

We solve the data encryption standard (DES) instances of security domain (SECUR) problems. These are SAT-encoding of cryptographic key search problem. All instances are satisfiable. The $ssc355$ DPLL procedure has its best performance on those problems. While the UPLA branching rule has the difficulty to solve those problems.

The simplistic version of NVO heuristic performed well on longmult* instances of BMC domain and the instances of planning domain. These results encourage us to explore further the power of NVO heuristic. Moreover, the DVF+NVO branching rule can solve all the problems in our experiment, except the $e0ddr2$-10-by-5-4 job shop scheduling problem. While UPLA branching rule fails to solve 8 problems and the DVF one fails to solve 13 problems in given time limit.

4.2 Performance on Quasigroup Problems

The quasigroup problems were given by Fujita, Slaney, and Bennett in their award-winning IJCAI paper [6]. The best way to view a quasigroup problem is in terms of the completion of a Latin square. Given N colors, a Latin square is defined by an N by N table, where each entry has a color and where there are no repeated colors in any row or column. N is called the *order* of the quasigroup.

In table 2, we present the comparative results of $satz215$, $ssc34$ and $ssc355$ on the well known quasigroup problems. The column SAT, in the table, denotes the status of solution which indicates satisfiable ("Y") or unsatisfiable ("N"). The $ssc355$ DPLL procedure has a best performance for most of the problems, in terms of search tree size, while the $satz215$ has a best performance from the run time point of view. These results explain that the NVO heuristic of $ssc355$ performs well in solving the quasigroup problems with larger neighborhoods, while its inefficiency comes from the redundant unit propagation searches.

5 Conclusion

UPLA branching rule fails to choose the best branching variable because it limits the variable filtering process. Its ineffectiveness makes many real-world problems

Table 2. Run time (in seconds) and search tree size of quasigroup problems. The best performances are in bold.

Problem	SAT	#Vars	#Cls	Search Tree Size			Run Time		
				satz215	ssc34	ssc355	satz215	ssc34	ssc355
qg1-07	Y	343	68083	2	4	2	5.31	5.25	**4.61**
qg1-08	Y	512	148957	2644	8	1	36.48	23.17	**21.71**
qg2-07	Y	343	68083	1	1	2	6.26	6.11	**5.41**
qg2-08	Y	512	148957	2788	6067	2380	**33.17**	65.34	53.27
qg3-08	Y	512	10469	18	0	0	**0.10**	0.21	0.18
qg3-09	N	729	16732	1034	736	695	**2.51**	4.24	6.64
qg4-08	N	512	9685	30	30	30	**0.09**	0.21	0.17
qg4-09	Y	729	15580	82	0	9	**0.25**	0.40	0.34
qg5-09	N	729	28540	1	1	1	0.40	0.58	**0.36**
qg5-10	N	1000	43636	2	1	2	**0.71**	0.89	0.81
qg5-11	Y	1331	64054	3	0	1	**1.39**	3.60	7.90
qg5-12	N	1728	90919	3	1	2	**2.55**	4.45	4.23
qg5-13	N	2197	125464	669	3150	245	**75.55**	2192.63	154.75
qg6-09	Y	729	21844	1	0	0	**0.25**	0.51	0.87
qg6-10	N	1000	33466	3	1	1	0.45	0.57	**0.44**
qg6-11	N	1331	49204	63	19	41	**1.86**	4.67	4.14
qg6-12	N	1728	69931	1024	925	720	**29.10**	276.70	70.41
qg7-09	Y	729	22060	0	0	0	**0.35**	0.69	0.87
qg7-10	N	1000	33736	1	1	2	0.50	0.66	**0.57**
qg7-11	N	1331	49534	7	1	4	**1.12**	1.41	1.51
qg7-12	N	1728	70327	154	42	88	**5.89**	23.42	10.26
qg7-13	Y	2197	97072	24	1405	492	**3.33**	1316.80	98.37

difficult for the DPLL procedure. In order to improve the power of UPLA, we have proposed the DVF and DVF+NVO branching rules which perform more variable filtering at each node.

The experimental results of DVF+NVO branching rules on a number of real-world benchmark instances and quasigroup problems prove our approaches to be useful in many circumstances. The DPLL procedure based on DVF+NVO branching rule performed well particularly on planning and security problems.

The work presented in this paper is a first attempt at building an efficient SAT solver. In our future work, we envisage at least three further improvements of our current approach. Firstly, it is clear that savings can be made by avoiding redundant unit propagation searches for variables that remain unchanged between iterations of UPLA. Secondly, further improvements of the NVO heuristic appear promising, as our first implementation is fairly simplistic. Finally, we are also looking at integrating a backjumping technique into DVF.

Acknowledgments

We would like to thank Andrew Slater for helping us to run the experiments. We would also like to thank the anonymous reviewers for their valuable comments and suggestions on a previous version of this paper. National ICT Australia is funded through the Australian Government's *Backing Australia's Ability* initiative, in part through the Australian Research Council.

References

1. Bessière, C., Chmeiss, A., and Sais, L. *Neighborhood-based Variable Ordering Heuristics for the Constraint Satisfaction Problem*. In Proceedings of Seventh International Conference on Principles and Practice of Constraint Programming, 2001, Paphos, Cyprus, pp. 565-569.
2. Crawford, J. M., and Auton, L. D. Experimental Results on the Crossover Point in Random 3SAT. *Artificial Intelligence Journal*, 1996, Vol. 81, no. 1-2.
3. Davis, M., Logemann, G. and Loveland, D. *A Machine Program for Theorem Proving*. Communication of ACM 5 (1962), pp. 394-397.
4. Dubois, O., and Dequen, G. *A Backbone-search Heuristic for Efficient Solving of Hard 3-SAT Formulae*. In Proceedings of 17th International Joint Conference on Artificial Intelligence, 2001, Seattle, Washington, USA.
5. Freeman, J. W. *Improvements to Propositional Satisfiability Search Algorithms*. Ph.D. Dissertation, Department of Computer and Information Science, University of Pennsylvania, Philadelphia, PA, (1995).
6. Fujita, M., Slaney, J., and Bennett, F. *Automatic Generation of Some Results in Finite Algebra*. In Proceedings of 13th International Joint Conference on Artificial Intelligence, 1993, Chambery, France, pp.
7. Hooker, J. N., Vinay, V. *Branching Rules for Satisfiability*. Journal of Automated Reasoning, 15:359-383, 1995.
8. Jeroslow, R., Wang, J. *Solving Propositional Satisfiability Problems*. Annals of Mathematics and AI, 1, 1990, pp. 167-187.
9. Le Berre, D. *Exploiting the Real Power of Unit Propagation Lookahead*. In Proceedings of Workshop on the Theory and Applications of Satisfiability Testing, 2001, Boston University, MA, USA.
10. Li, C. M., and Anbulagan. *Heuristics Based on Unit Propagation for Satisfiability Problems*. In Proceedings of 15th International Joint Conference on Artificial Intelligence, 1997, Nagoya, Aichi, Japan, pp. 366-371.

Extended Nearest Feature Line Classifier

Yonglei Zhou, Changshui Zhang, and Jingchun Wang

Department of Automation, Tsinghua University,
Beijing 100084, P.R. China
zhouyonglei98@mails.tsinghua.edu.cn

Abstract. An extended nearest feature line (ENFL) classifier is proposed to handle the discrimination problems. The ENFL borrows the concept of feature line spaces from the nearest feature line (NFL) method, to make use of the information implied by the interaction between each pair of points in the same class. Instead of the NFL distance, a better distance metric is designed in the ENFL. The ENFL is very effective in the cases with a small training set. The experimental evaluation shows that in the given feature space, the ENFL consistently achieves better performance than NFL and conventional nearest neighbor methods.

1 Introduction

We address a discrimination problem with C classes and N training samples. The training samples consist of measurement vectors and known class labels. Given a training set as $X = \left\{ \{x_i^c\}_{i=1}^{N_c} \right\}_{c=1}^{C}$, where $\{x_i^c\}_{i=1}^{N_c}$ denotes the sample subset for the c-th class and N_c is the subset's size which satisfy $N = \sum_{c=1}^{C} N_c$, the task is to predict the class membership of an unlabeled sample x.

The k-nearest-neighbor method (k-NN)[4] is a simple and efficient approach to this task. We find the k nearest neighbors of x in the training set and classify x as the majority class among the k nearest neighbors. In a given feature space, it's very important to select an appropriate distance metric for k-NN.

There have been various distance metrics used in k-NN, which can be divided into two categories. The distance metrics in the first category are defined between an unlabeled point and a labeled point in the feature space, e.g. Euclidean distance, Hamming distance, Cosine distance, Kullback-Liebler (KL) distance[8] etc. Using these distance metrics, the training points are regarded as some isolated ones in the feature space. Hence, some useful information implied by the interaction of samples is ignored. Different from the first category, those in the second category make use of some prior knowledge for the whole training set, such as Mahalanobis distance, Quadratic distance. Especially, a discriminant adaptive nearest neighbor (DANN) classification method is proposed in [5], where a local linear discriminant analysis (LDA) is adopted to estimate an effective local Quadratic distance metric for computing neighborhoods. However, these distance metrics are only effective when the training set is large enough.

In this paper, we concern the discrimination problems with multiple but finite samples for each class, e.g. face recognition task. In these problems, 1-NN (also called as NN for simplicity) is frequently adopted because of the small training set. And the mentioned distance metrics in the second category are inappropriate. In [1][2], a nearest feature line (NFL) method is proposed to make use of the information implied in each pair of points of the same class by constituting some feature line (FL) spaces. The feature line (FL) is a straight line passing through two points of the same class in the feature space. The NFL distance is defined as the Euclidean distance between a unlabeled point and its projection to the FL. The experimental results have shown the NFL can produces consistently superior results over the NN methods based on many conventional distances[1][2]. However, the NFL distance will cause some problems, which weakens the NFL's performance in some cases such as the example in Fig. 1. Hence, an extended nearest feature line method (ENFL) is proposed to strengthen the original NFL by using a new distance metric. The generalization of the ENFL is better than that of the NFL and other conventional NNs. The experimental results substantiate the strength of the ENFL, especially in the cases when only a small training set is available and the data distribution in the feature space is nonlinear.

The remainder of this paper is organized as follows. In section 2, some related work are referred to briefly. In Section 3, the ENFL method is proposed. In Section 4, an extensive experimental evaluation is carried out using some UCI datasets and the AR face database. Some conclusions are drawn in section 5.

2 Related Work

A discriminant adaptive nearest neighbor (DANN) method is proposed in [5], where a local LDA metric Σ_0 for the test point x_0 is learned using its nearest neighbor points through an iterative process. At completion, use the Quadratic distance $d(x, x_0) = (x - x_0)^T \Sigma_0 (x - x_0)$ to obtain x_0's k-nearest neighbors for classification. Obviously, some prior knowledge has been introduced to the DANN. For example, the local data distribution is assumed to be Gaussian and linear separable. The DANN classifier can be expected to achieve better performance than the conventional NN classifiers. However, a large sample set is needed for good estimation of the local Quadratic metric. Hence, in the small training set case, the DANN will be weakened.

The nearest feature line (NFL) method[1][2] constructs some feature line spaces to make use of the information implied by the interaction between each pair of training points in the same class. A feature line (FL) is defined as a straight line $\overline{x_i^c x_j^c}$ passing through two points x_i^c and x_j^c which belong to the same class(see Fig. 2). All FLs in the same class constitute an FL Space of that class, $S_c = \{\overline{x_i^c x_j^c} | 1 \leq i, j \leq N_c, i \neq j\}$, and there are C FL spaces.

In the NFL classifier, the distance between a point and its projection onto the FL is calculated and used as the metric. The projection of the test point x on the FL $\overline{x_i^c x_j^c}$ can be obtained as $x_p^{c,ij} = x_i^c + \mu(x_j^c - x_i^c)$, where $\mu = (x - x_i^c) \cdot (x_j^c - x_i^c)/(x_j^c - x_i^c) \cdot (x_j^c - x_i^c)$. Then the NFL distance is described as

$$d_{NFL}(x, \overline{x_i^c x_j^c}) = ||x - x_p^{c,ij}||.$$

According to the NN rule, x is classified into the class c^o, which satisfies

$$d_{NFL}(x, \overline{x_{i^o}^{c^o} x_{j^o}^{c^o}}) = \min_{1 \leq c \leq C} \min_{1 \leq i,j \leq N_c, i \neq j} d_{NFL}(x, \overline{x_i^c x_j^c}).$$

The experimental results in [1][2] have shown that in the given feature space, the NFL consistently achieves better performance than the NN.

Using the NFL distance d_{NFL} in the FL spaces is equivalent to extending each pair of training points in the same class to an infinite number of points lying on the corresponding FL. And this infinite extension of the training set will cause problems, which has been referred to in [3]. That is, the extension part of one class has possibility to cross those of other classes, especially in the nonlinear cases such as the example illustrated in Fig. 1. If it occurrs, the recognition rate will be lowered. Hence, a new distance metric is needed to make better use of the information implied by each pair of feature points in the same class.

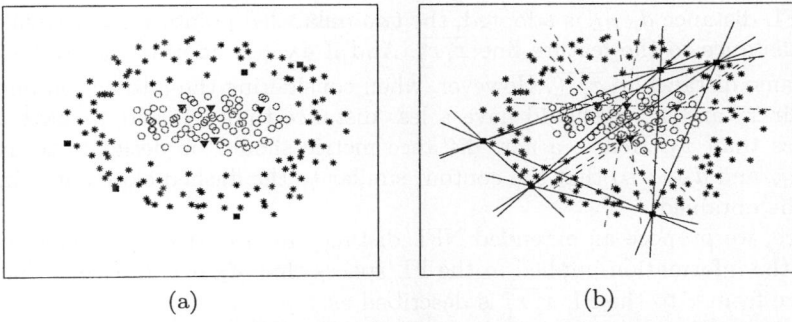

(a)   (b)

Fig. 1. The points come from two categories: class 1 denoted by circles and class 2 denoted by asterisks. (a) Five training points are randomly selected from each class, denoted by solid triangles and squares respectively. (b) The feature line spaces. As can seen, the extension parts of class 1 and class 2 are interwoven.

3 Extended Nearest Feature Line Classifier (ENFL)

Similar to the NFL, the NN based on Euclidean distance can also be reformulated in the FL space by setting the distance metric as

$$d_{NN}(x, \overline{x_i^c x_j^c}) = \min\{d(x, x_i^c), d(x, x_j^c)\}.$$

However, it does not make use of the virtue of the FL spaces. The reason is that while calculating the distance $d_{NN}(x, \overline{x_i^c x_j^c})$, the pair of points, x_i^c and x_j^c, are treated as isolated ones.

Let us discuss the effects of various distance metrics in the FL spaces using a concept of equal-distance surface (also called a contour in 2-dimensional cases). An equal-distance surface of an FL is defined as a surface in the feature space on which the points have some same distance to the FL. For a 2-dimensional

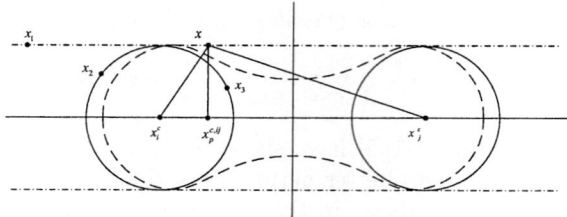

Fig. 2. The contours for an FL with different distance metrics. Two real-line circles are for Euclidean distance. Two parallel dashdotted lines are for the NFL distance. And the dashed close curve is the contour expected to be obtained.

case illustrated in Fig. 2, the contour for an FL with Euclidean distance consists of two circles or a close curve formed by the intersection of two circles, and the contour for an FL with the NFL distance is two parallel lines. As seen in Fig. 2, if the NFL distance d_{NFL} is adopted, the two unlabeled points x and x_1 will have same distance to the feature line $\overline{x_i^c x_j^c}$. And if d_{NN} is adopted, x_2 and x_3 will have same distance to $\overline{x_i^c x_j^c}$. However, when considering the interaction between the pair x_i^c and x_j^c, x should have a less distance than x_1, and x_3 have a less distance than x_2. Hence, a new distance metric should be designed to extend the d_{NN} and d_{NFL} so that the contour similar to the dashed close curve in Fig. 2 can be obtained.

Here, we propose an extended NFL distance metric d_{ENFL} to make better use of the information implied in the FL spaces than d_{NN} and d_{NFL}. The new distance from x to the FL $\overline{x_i^c x_j^c}$ is described as

$$d_{ENFL}(x, \overline{x_i^c x_j^c}) = \frac{||x - x_i^c|| \cdot ||x - x_j^c||}{||x_i^c - x_j^c||}.$$

The denominator in d_{ENFL} is introduced to adjust each FL's influence area according to the distance between the pair of points. That is, it can strengthen the effect of those FLs whose corresponding pairs of points have large distances.

The contours for an FL with the ENFL distance d_{ENFL} are illustrated in Fig. 3. Obviously, these contours reflect the interaction between the pair of points in the same class and meet our need.

According to the NN rule, x is classified into the class c^o, which satisfies

$$d_{ENFL}(x, \overline{x_{i^o}^{c^o} x_{j^o}^{c^o}}) = \min_{1 \leq c \leq C} \min_{1 \leq i,j \leq N_c, i \neq j} d_{ENFL}(x, \overline{x_i^c x_j^c}).$$

We call the NN classifier based on d_{ENFL} as the extended NFL classifier (ENFL).

The classification results for the example in Fig. 1 with 3 distance metrics are shown in Fig. 4, which indicate that the ENFL has better generalization than the NFL and the NN based on Euclidean distance.

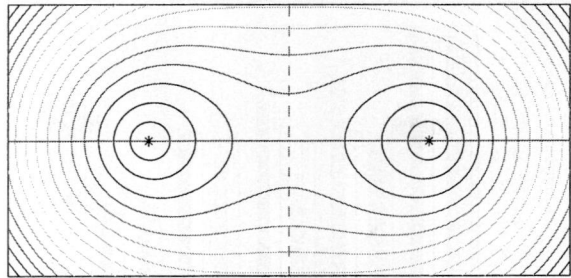

Fig. 3. The contours for an FL with d_{ENFL}. Two points denoted by asterisks are the pair of points used to construct the FL.

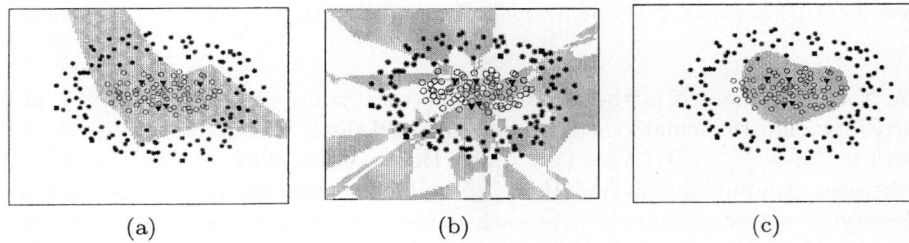

Fig. 4. The classification results for the example illustrated in Fig. 1 with five training samples per class, using NN classifiers based on (a)Euclidean distance, (b)the NFL distance, and (c) the ENFL distance.

4 Experimental Evaluation

To substantiate the strength of the ENFL, we apply it to real data classification tasks. Here, we evaluate the ENFL's performance over some UCI datasets and the AR face database, versus the NFL and the NN based on Euclidean distance.

4.1 UCI Datasets

We select five typical datasets from the UCI data repository: 'Wine', 'Ionosphere', 'Spectf', 'Sonar' and 'Diabetes'.

To do the experiment, each dataset is randomly divided into 5 disjoint subsets of equal size. For each time, we select three subsets to constitute the training set and treat the remainder as the testing set. Thus, there are totally 10 different trials over each dataset. Using the results of these trials, we can calculate the mean and standard deviation of the recognition rates for each method.

The ENFL, the NFL, the NN and the k-NN ($k = 3, 7$) based on Euclidean distance are performed in this task. As shown in Fig. 5, nearly over all five datasets, the ENFL achieves better performance than other methods.

Let us focus our attention on the computational loads of NN, NFL and ENFL for classifying a testing sample. In NN, we need calculate the Euclidean distance

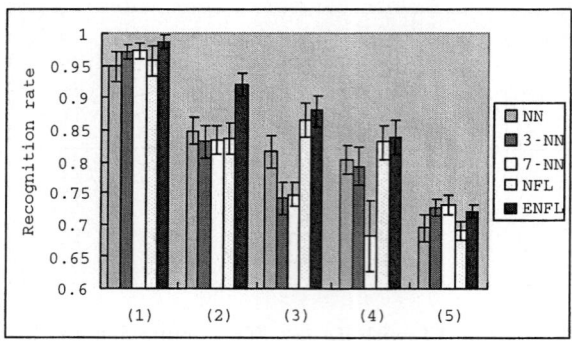

Fig. 5. Recognition rates of the ENFL versus the NFL, the NN and the k-NN ($k = 3, 7$) over five UCI datasets: (1)Wine, (2)Ionosphere, (3)Spectf, (4)Sonar and (5)Diabetes.

for N times, where N is the number of the total training samples. In NFL and ENFL, we must calculate the NFL distance and the ENFL distance respectively both for $M = \sum_{c=1}^{C} N_c(N_c - 1)/2$ times. Hence, either NFL or ENFL will have a heavier computational load than NN will. The average time consumed for classifying a testing sample over each dataset is reported in Table 1. All the tests are done on a 1.5GHz PC processor. From Table 1, we can find that the computational load of NFL is heavier than that of ENFL. The reason is that in the NFL distance, the testing point's projection on the FL must be recalculated for each time, while in the ENFL distance, the distances between the testing point and all training points can be precalculated and stored.

Table 1. The average time consumed for classifying a testing sample over each dataset, with the millisecond (ms) as the unit.

	Wine	Ionosphere	Spectf	Sonar	Diabetes
NN	0.0140	0.0499	0.0788	0.0601	0.0326
NFL	0.619	8.57	13.1	5.24	13.0
ENFL	0.169	2.62	3.38	1.44	3.29

4.2 Face Recognition

Face recognition task is carried out using AR face database, which contains over 4,000 color images corresponding to 126 people's faces. Each person in these database participated in two sessions, separated by two weeks.

In this experiment, 50 persons are randomly selected from the total 126 persons and 7 frontal view faces with no occlusions are selected for each person from the first session. We have manually carried out the localization step, followed by a morphing step so that each face occupies a fixed 27×16 array of pixels. And they are converted to gray-level images by adding all three color channels, i.e., $I = (R + G + B)/3$. The selected images of two subjects from the AR face

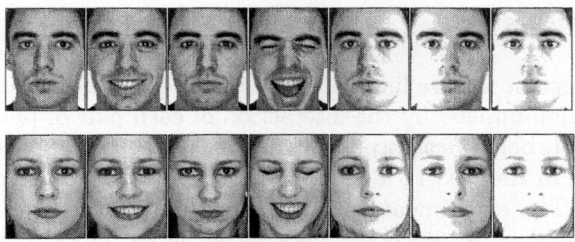

Fig. 6. Selected images of two subjects from the AR face database after preprocessing.

database are shown in Fig. 6, which have been preprocessed. The gray-level images are finally normalized to zero mean and unit variance, and reshaped to 432 sized vectors, which constitute our own data set $X = \{x_i\}_{i=1}^{350}$. In practice, the data space is too large to allow fast and robust recognition. Principle Component Analysis (PCA)[7] is adopted here for dimensionality reduction. Hence, the data set X is transformed into d-dimensional PCA space, $Y = \{y_i\}_{i=1}^{350}$. N samples per subject are used as the training samples and the rest as the testing ones. We randomly select them to do the test and repeat the procedure for 10 times. Note that the training sample number per subject is not necessary to be same.

In the first test, the training sample number per subject is fixed as 3 and we evaluate the performance of the ENFL, the NFL and the NN based on Euclidean distance with various principle component (PC) numbers. In the second test, the PC number is fixed as 20 and we change the training sample number per subject from 2 to 6 to evaluate the same three methods. As shown in Fig. 7, in this experiment, the ENFL method is comparable to the NFL method, and both of them are superior to the NN method, nearly with an 8 percent increase in recognition rate. If the training sample number per subject and the PC number are fixed as 3 and 40, the average time consumed for recognizing a face image is: 0.0455ms for NN, 0.125ms for NFL and 0.06ms for ENFL.

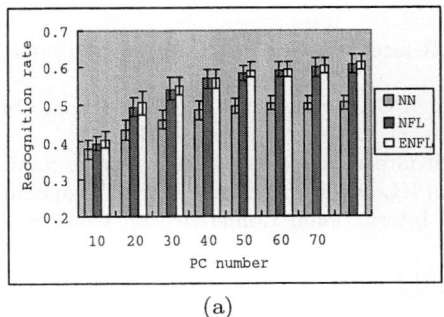
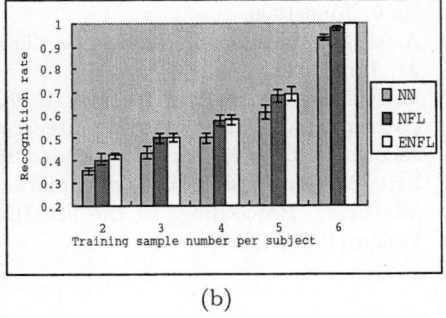

(a)   (b)

Fig. 7. Recognition rates of the ENFL over AR face data set, versus the NFL and the NN based on Euclidean distance. (a)The training sample number per subject is fixed as 3 while changing the PC number. (b) The PC number is fixed as 20 while changing the training sample number per subject.

5 Conclusions

An extended nearest feature line (ENFL) method is proposed to make good use of the information implied by the interaction of each pair of points in the same class. The ENFL borrows the concept of feature line (FL) spaces from the the NFL. However, in the ENFL, a new distance metric is presented instead of the NFL distance. The experimental results show that in the given feature space, the ENFL classifier consistently achieves better performance than both the NFL classifier and the NN classifier based on Euclidean distance.

Acknowledgements

This work was supported by National High Technology Research and Development Program of China(863 Program) under contract No.2001AA114190.

The authors would like to thank anonymous reviewers for their helpful comments, also thank Jianguo Lee for helpful conversations about this work.

References

1. S.Z. Li and J. Lu. Face Recognition Using the Nearest Feature Line Method, IEEE Trans. Neural Networks, vol. 10, no.2, pp. 439-443, Mar. 1999.
2. S.Z. Li, Kap Luk Chan and Changliang Wang. "Performance Evaluation of the Nearest Feature Line Method in Image Classification and Retrieval". IEEE Trans. On Pattern Analysis and Machine Intelligence, vol. 22, No.11, November 2000.
3. Li.Zhao, Wei.Qi, S.Z.Li, S.Q.Yang, H.J.Zhang, A New Content-based Shot Retrieval Approach: Key-frame Extraction based Nearest Feature Line (NFL) Classification, ACM Multimedia Information Retrieval 2000, Oct 2000, Los Angeles, USA.
4. T. M. Cover and P. Hart, "Nearest Neighbor Pattern Classification," Annals of Statistics, 1967.
5. Trevor Hastie and Robert Tibshirani, "Discriminant Adaptive Nearest Neighbor Classfication," IEEE Trans. on Pattern Analysis and Machine Intelligence, vol. 18, No.6, June 1996.
6. A. M. Martinez and R. Benavente, "The AR-face database," CVC Technical Report 24, June 1998.
7. Aleix M. Martinez and Avinash C. Kak, "PCA versus LDA," IEEE Trans. On Pattern Analysis and Machine Intelligence, vol. 23, No.2, February 2001.
8. Jacob Goldberger, Shiri Gordon and Hayit Greenspan, "An Efficient Image Similarity Measure Based on Approximations of KL-Divergence Between Two Gaussian Mixtures," Proceedings of the 9th IEEE International Conference on Computer Vision (ICCV 2003).

Sifting the Margin
– An Iterative Empirical Classification Scheme

Dan Vance[1] and Anca Ralescu[2]

[1] University of Cincinnati, ECECS Department,
Cincinnati, Ohio, USA
Dvance@ECECS.UC.edu

[2] University of Cincinnati, ECECS Department,
Cincinnati, Ohio USA
Aralescu@ECECS.UC.edu

Abstract. Attribute or feature selection is an important step in designing a classifier. It often reduces to choosing between computationally simple schemes (based on a small subset of attributes) that do not search the space and more complex schemes (large subset or entire set of available attributes) that are computationally intractable. Usually a compromise is reached: A computationally tractable scheme that relies on a subset of attributes that optimize a certain criterion is chosen. The result is usually a 'good' sub-optimal solution that may still require a fair amount of computation. This paper presents an approach that does not commit itself to any particular subset of the available attributes. Instead, the classifier uses each attribute successively as needed to classify a given data point. If the data set is separable in the given attribute space the algorithm will classify a given point with no errors. The resulting classifier is transparent, and the approach compares favorably with previous approaches both in accuracy and efficiency.

1 Introduction

A typical 2-class classification problem can be stated as follows, given a vector $X = [x_1, x_2, ..., x_n]$ classify it into one of two classes, based on the values of all or a subset of its components, $(x_i)_{i=1,...,n}$. In general, the components are called *attributes* and their values are called *features*. However, often these terms are used interchangeably.

A brute force algorithm that searches through all the subsets of $\{x_i; i=1,..., n\}$ in order to identify the best subset (a 'good' predictor for which the number of errors is minimized), has exponential complexity and therefore alternate approaches have been developed. A review [13], even concise of these approaches, exceeds the scope of this paper. It suffices to say that often such approaches either identify a *best* subset of attributes, or construct new attributes from the given ones. The main idea underlying these methods is to find those attributes that can account for the classification for *all* (or nearly all) of the training set.

2 The Margin Algorithm

The work presented here departs from the previously described approach by allowing the use of different attributes in different areas of the feature space. Example 1 illustrates this approach on a small data set.

Example 1: Consider a simple artificial dataset. Class A consists of 34 points, Class B consists of 232 points. Each has a normal distribution. Class A has $mean_A = (50.21, 52.73)$ and standard deviation $s_A = (20.42, 23.12)$. Class B has $mean_B = (115.82, 111.73)$ and standard deviation $s_B = (28.94, 27.79)$. In Figure 1, all the data points are plotted. An intuitive approach to separating the classes would be to find the mean of each cluster, create an axis connecting the two means, and find a line that crosses this axis that *best* separates the clusters.

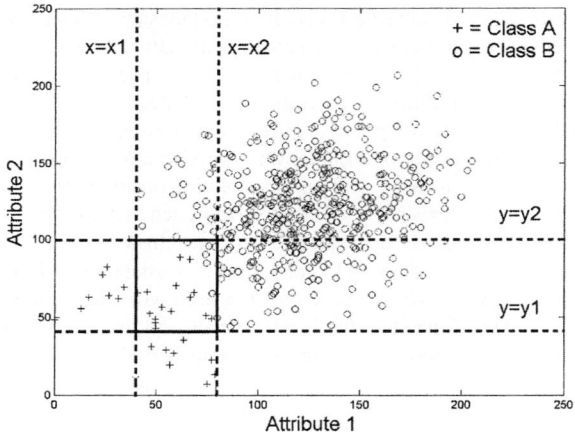

Fig. 1. The data set for Example 1 is shown with margins. The rectangle is the area where points cannot be classified.

In Figure 1 a dashed vertical line, $x = x_1$, is drawn where x_1 is the maximum coordinate for points in A and another dashed vertical line, $x = x_2$, is drawn where x_2 is the minimum x coordinate for points in B. The interval determined by these can be used to classify some of the points: those whose x coordinates fall to the left and right of the interval. However, the points with the x coordinate within the interval are not classified using their x coordinates. Classification is without error at this stage. Margin is willing to accept a few errors in order to classify many more points, so the interval can be further narrowed. One *marches* its endpoints towards the opposite means until the final positions are reached. The final position forms the *margin*, m_x, for this attribute. Points whose x coordinates fall in this margin cannot be classified by this attribute without too great a penalty (a tradeoff has been reached). Since this example is just to illustrate the idea, the final position reached by the algorithm is not shown.

For these points a similar construction of a margin is done in the y attribute. In Figure 1, a dashed horizontal line, $y = y_1$, is drawn where y_1 is the maximum y coordinate for the points from m_x that that are in A and another dashed horizontal line, $y = y_2$, is draw, where y_2 is the minimum y coordinate for the points from m_x which are in B. The values y_1 and y_2 determine the margin, m_y, for the attribute y. The lines start at the means and are *marched* toward the opposite mean until the final positions are reached. The points with the x coordinates in m_x whose y coordinates fall outside m_y are classified either as A or B, while those whose y coordinates fall inside m_y cannot be classified (by this procedure). Again, for this example, the final position reached by the algorithm is not shown.

Figure 1 shows the combination of the results from the margins for the x-axis and the y-axis. The points inside the rectangle are not classified. All other points can be classified correctly. In this simplistic version of the algorithm, accuracy is 93%. The 'errors' are the 18 of 266 points remaining unclassified. Even without the final positions that the algorithm attains for the margins, most points have been classified.

Real datasets give a more interesting problem. Suppose one adds the points A_1, B_1, A_2, and B_2 to Example 1.

B_1-------------meanA---- B_2---------------------- A_2-----meanB------------------A_1

A_1 and B_1 are outliers (or noise) at the extremes of their distributions and are not in the overlap region. The decision is made *a priori* to accept these points as misclassified by the algorithm. Points A_2 and B_2 are added in the overlap region. The 2 margin edges start at $mean_A$ and at $mean_B$. Each edge is *marched* toward the opposite mean. As we *march* toward the opposite means, if one stops these edges at the first incorrect classification (A_2 or B_2), one could miss large numbers of points that would be classified correctly. The following remarks are useful at this point:
1. The lines are *marched* as before within 2 standard deviations from the means. This ensures that 98% or more of all data points are considered.
2. A fixed number of iterations is used. This is based on the value of increments of the standard deviation. For example, when this increment is 0.1 the number of iterations is 441.
3. After each iteration, the algorithm counts the number of correctly classified points.
4. The 2 standard deviations (1 from each class) from the iteration giving the highest classification accuracy are selected as the final result.

In essence, the procedure truncates the extremes of each distribution in the area of overlap. Also some misclassification of the training data are allowed in the hope that more of the points are classified correctly.

As it can be seen from Example 1, when projected on a particular attribute, say x_1, the data points from the two classes may overlap. The region of overlap is called here *margin*. If the margin is known, then the data points that fall outside it can be classified based on the values for the attribute x_1. For the data points inside the margin, attribute x_1 is not useful. For these points the values of the attribute x_2 may be considered to further classification. Their margin (along x_2) is used to classify the remaining points. It is easily seen that the classification surface induced by such an algorithm is parallel to the coordinate axes (or, in higher dimensions, coordinate planes). It can also be seen that if the points are not separable by such surfaces (even though they may be separable, linearly or otherwise), the procedure outlined will not succeed in completely separating the training points and indeed may fail to separate *any* subset of these. Therefore, in the remaining part of this paper it is assumed that the two classes are separable (to some extent) along at least some of the attributes and the algorithm attempts to find these attributes and the separating surfaces corresponding to them.

Intuitively, the concept of margin along attribute x_i is defined as the largest region in the domain for x_i that contains examples from the two classes. To express formally this concept the following notation is introduced.

Let x_i, $i = 1, ..., n$ denote the attributes for a two class classification problem. Let *TRAIN* denote the training set for this problem, that is $TRAIN = \{(x_1, ..., x_n, y)\}$ $y \in \{A, B\}$ where the values for y indicate the class (A or B) that the vector ($x_1, ..., x_n$) belongs to. Let X_i denote the domain of the attribute x_i as represented in *TRAIN*. Let X^y_i the domain of the attribute x_i represented in class y. Obviously, $X_i = X^A_i \cup X^B_i$.

Definition 1: The margin m_i along attribute x_i is defined as follows:
$m_i \subseteq X^A_i \cap X^B_i$ and $\forall S \subseteq X^A_i \cap X^B_i$, it follows that $S \subseteq m_i$ (1)

Definition (1) states a property of maximality for the margin among all those subsets of the feature space that contain points from both classes. However, for practical purposes (in order to increase the number of correctly classified data points, at the expense of a fewer misclassified), this property is not always required.

2.1 Margin Along a Single Attribute

It can be seen that X_i can now be written as $X_i = (X^A_i \setminus X^B_i) \cup m_i \cup (X^B_i \setminus X^A_i)$, where \ denotes set difference. Assuming that m_i the margin for the attribute x_i has been found, the classification of data points is done as follows.

Simple class complexity: In scanning the training data set in a given direction, all of the examples of class A appear to one side of the margin, followed by the margin, followed by all of the examples for class B (without loss of generality, assume that class A is to the left of class B). If $m_i = [a_i, b_i]$ and the class for the data point x is given by the rule:

Class(x) = A   if $x < a_i$
B   if $x > b_i$ (2)
none   otherwise

The values x for which $Class(x) =$ none are those which belong to the margin.

Increased class complexity: In this case $m_i = \cup^m_{j=1}[a_{ij}, b_{ij}]$ such that for each $j = 1, ..., m$ classes alternate. The approach can be reduced to the previous, by applying the classification rule iteratively in the space for the attribute x_i with the margin $[a_{ij}, b_{ij}]$, where $a_{ij}, = \min\{a_{ij}; j = 1, ..., m\}$ and $b_{ij}, = \max\{b_{ij}; j = 1, ..., m\}$. The remaining part of this paper assumes simple class complexity.

2.2 Sifting the Margin

The quality of the margin determines the classification accuracy along the corresponding attribute. In practice the classifier has very little knowledge on the actual attribute values corresponding to each class. Therefore, the main part of deriving the classifier is to estimate the margins for each attribute. Informally, the procedure for learning the margin, starts with an estimate at each class mean for training data and iterates by updating these estimates. In these iterations more training data are allocated to their correct class by the 'sift'.

Let m_A^i and m_B^i denote the means of the two classes along attribute i. Again, without loss of generality assume that class A is to the left of class B, i.e., that $m_A^i < m_B^i$. The number of standard deviations for each class determines the margin. The margins are found for each attribute, using η_A and η_B. The underlying class distribution is considered Normal (the Central Limit Theorem justifies this assumption is justified for large classes). This means that with high probability the class values fall within two standard deviations from the class mean. The margin, $m_i = [a_i, b_i]$ for the ith attribute for the jth increment of η_A and kth increment of η_B is updated accordingly. The quantities η_A and η_B are the learning constants. Their values determine the accuracy and the speed of the convergence of the algorithm.

Table 1. Iterative Margin Pseudocode

TRAIN: the training data set
<u>Initialize</u>: *max_correct* = 0, *number_correct* = 0

For $\eta_A = 0, \ldots, 2$ step 0.1 (A = class A)
 For $\eta_B = 0, \ldots, 2$ step 0.1 (B = class B)
  For all x in the dataset,
   For $i = 1$ to k (i = attribute number)
    If x is correctly classified by rule (2), then increment *number_correct*
    Endif
   Endfor
   If *number_correct* > *max_correct*, then *max_correct* = *number_correct*
    and $m_i = [a_i, b_i]$ by rule (3)
   Endif
  Endfor
 Endfor
Endfor

2.3 Using the Margin for Several Attributes

Let $X = \{x_1, \ldots, x_n\}$ denote the collection of attributes of interest (in general, this is the collection of attributes specified for all of the points in the training set *TRAIN*. Further it is assumed that for all attributes the classes have simple complexity (or, alternatively, only that subset is considered for which this is true).

As the margin edges are marched, they approach each other and eventually pass one another. Rule (3) is detailed here.

$Max_A = m^i_A + \eta_A s^i_A$ (m = mean), $Min_B = m^i_B - \eta_B s^i_B$ (s = standard deviation)

If $Max_A <= Min_B$
$\quad a_i = Max_A$
$\quad b_i = Min_B$
Else (3)
$\quad a_i = Min_B$
$\quad b_i = Max_A$
Endif

2.4 Computational Aspects

The complexity of the algorithm is determined by the complexity of the sifting portion of the algorithm and the complexity of the classification portion of the algorithm. The former is linear in the number of attributes and size of the training set, i.e., it is $O(C_1|X||TRAIN|)$ where the constant C_1 is determined by the step in the two 'for loops'.

The latter is linear in the number of currently used attributes, that is, $O(C_2|A|)$ where $|X| \geq |A|$. Note that this is an upper limit. In practice, most of the classification is accomplished by 1 attribute. In analyzing the algorithm using all the attributes two situations must be considered:
1. The two classes are separable along their attributes or a subset of these.
2. The two classes are not separable.

In case 1, a more exact evaluation of complexity can be done by taking into account the size of the training subsets considered for each attribute and the probability of selecting, at each step, that attribute corresponding to a maximum reduction of this subset. Accuracy of the algorithm in this case does not depend on the order in which the attributes are considered, *if* there are no misclassifications (such as in carefully constructed artificial datasets). Since in fact this is not reasonable for real-world data, exploration of order of presentation of the attributes needs to be considered at a future date. It is expected that for a given attribute, the further apart the means of the 2 classes, and the tighter the clustering of each class, the closer one would come to this ideal artificial dataset. In short, we would expect to try a measure such as J_3 to order the presentation of attributes to the algorithm.

In case 2, the margin for any given attribute, i.e., the collection of training points not classified by the classification rule for that attribute, is not empty. In this case the order of attributes becomes more interesting and it is desired that the attributes are considered in order of their classification accuracy or a measure such as J_3. Since, in general it is not known a priori that the classes are separable along attribute axes, attributes should be considered in increasing order of a measure calculated from the size of their domains and corresponding margin (e.g. smallest margin relative to the attribute domain). In experiments thus far, this aspect has not been implemented.

3 Experimental Results

The approach outlined in the preceding sections has been tested on the artificial dataset described in Example 1 and two real datasets as follows:

Real Datasets - Two real datasets from the UC Irvine [1] repository are used to illustrate the performance of the algorithm.

Wisconsin breast cancer dataset: Of the 699 samples, there are 16 with missing attributes, and those are removed (solely for simplicity of programming; the algorithm doesn't require their removal). The dataset is then split into a training set of approximately 1/2 the original number of points and the balance is used as a test dataset. On a trial run the algorithm classifies the training data with 95.6% accuracy and the test data with 94.6% accuracy. On a training run of the entire dataset, 25 of 444 benign cases (5.6%),and 9 of 239 malignant cases were misclassified (4.8%), respectively. Only 3 of the 683 cases were not classified (0.004%). Margin had 94.6% accuracy.

Table 2. Wisconsin Breast Cancer – 10 runs

Run #	η_A	η_B	% Correct of Training Data	% Correct of Test Data
1	2	2	93.0	94.2
2	0	0.1	94.7	95.5
3	0	0	95.6	94.6
4	0	0	96.9	95.6
5	1.9	1.7	94.7	95.1
6	1.8	2	96.9	92.5
7	0	0.3	94.3	94.1
8	0	0.3	96.5	95.5
9	2	1.6	94.3	95.3
10	1.7	1.8	93.4	94.4
Mean:	.94	.98	95.0	94.7

Pima Indians Diabetes dataset: The Pima Indians Diabetes dataset is usually a difficult dataset to classify. It consists of 768 points. In the current approach are divided into a training set with 1/2 of the available data and the balance is used as a test dataset. On a trial run the algorithm classifies the training data with 74.3% accuracy and the test data with 78.4% accuracy. This compares favorably with other results in the literature.

4 Comparison to Other Classifiers

Table 3. Accuracy: Margin vs. Other Algorithms

	Classifier	Diabetes	Breast Cancer
Neural Nets	Extracted Rules from Pruned Neural Nets [8]	-	97%
	Extracted Rules from Feedforward Networks [9]	-	97%
	Continuous Network [9]	-	97%
	Rprop [10]	76%	-
Genetic Programming	Forward Feed Neural Net in Genetic Programming [10]	77%	-
	Linear Genetic Programming [10]	76%	-
Linear Discriminant	Linear Discriminant (1) [11]	67%	-
Gaussian process	Gaussian process (1) [11]	67%	-
SVM	SVM (1) [11]	64%	-
Bayesian Learning with Fuzzy Rules	Fuzzy Rules [12]	-	96%
Misc.	best of Statlog Project – compares 20 classification methods [13]	78%	-
	Bayesian estimator [13]	78%	96%
	LogitBoost [13]	-	97%
Ensemble Methods	best of Ensemble Methods [14]	74%	77%
Decision Trees	C4.5 [15], [6], [7]	68-71.5%	94-95.7%
	CVC4.5 [6]	72-73%	94%
	C4.5* (2) [6]	75%	96%
	CI2-2L [7]	70%	95%
	IB1 [7]	71%	96%
	Margin	*78%*	*95%*

As seen in Table 3, the Margin algorithm compares favorably with other methods. Pre-processing is not needed, as it is for some of these methods. These results are not a strict comparison. For example, authors varied in using 1/3 to 2/3 of the data for training and the balance for testing. We used multiple random sub-sampling. Other researchers used the same method or k-fold cross validation.

While at first glance, this may appear to be a Top-Down Inductive Decision Tree (TDIDT) algorithm that produces trees such as those made by C4.5, it is constructed in a different manner.

1. The criterion by which Margin's decision tree is constructed is not information theoretic as with ID3/C4.5, but more structural.
2. Margin uses the means and standard deviations to proceed through the data in partitioning of data. TDIDT uses statistical information to choose attributes directly.

3. Margin does most of the classification by the 'sift' through the 1st or 2nd margin.
4. Margin is a very transparent approach using 1 attribute to classify a point as in a particular class. TDIDT has a series of rules to make the classification decision.
5. TDIDT does allow a 'pruning', but it is not to be expected necessarily. Classification is assumed to be after a series of decisions, thus later in general than by Margin.

These differences make the implementation of Margin very easy and straightforward compared to C4.5. Both C4.5 and Margin perform well on the Wisconsin Breast Cancer data, but Margin out-performs C4.5 for the Pima Indians Diabetes data.

Margin is a decision tree, as shown here:

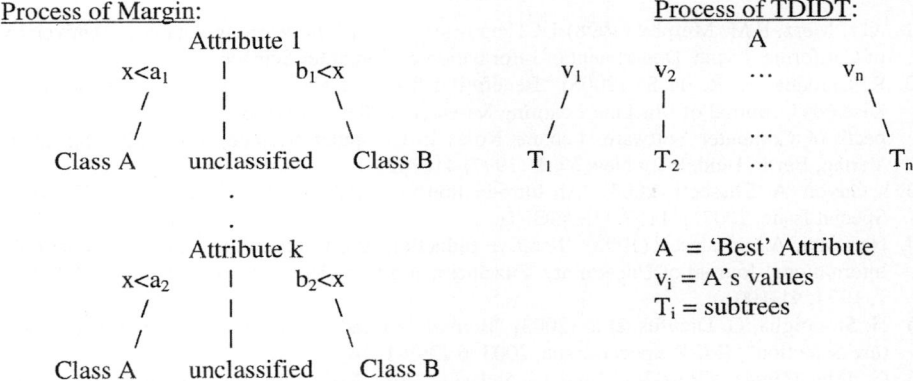

5 Conclusions

An algorithm for finding classification surface parallel to the attribute axes has been proposed. This algorithm departs from the usual approach in which feature identification by allowing classification to be made according to different attributes in different regions of the feature space. The correctness of classification and the efficiency each depends on the order in which the attributes are processed to some extent. While the complexity is linear in n, it can possibly be further improved (but still linear in n) by using attributes in decreasing order of their classification ability. This would mean that successive iterations would not need to consider as many points as with other choices. There is no guarantee that there is a best order of attributes with this filter.

A hypothesis that is currently being tested is that using local $\eta_A(i)$ and $\eta_B(i)$ for attribute $i = 1, ..., k$ would allow more precise measurement of the overlap and therefore better classification performance. This can be accomplished without additional complexity. The current algorithm keeps a global 'best' η_A and η_B (the values for all attributes). By saving the local best and (for each attribute) as the algorithm goes through the same exact steps no complexity is added.

While the current algorithm has been shown to work with these databases, a broader spectrum of databases needs to be tested. In particular, testing with databases of more than two classes needs to be done.

Acknowledgements

Both authors were partially supported by the grant N000140310706 from the Department of the Navy and by the Ohio Board of Regents.

References

1. C.J. Merz, P.M. Murphy (1998) UCI repository of machine learning databases. University of California, Irvine, Department of Information & Computer Sciences
2. R. Caruana, V. R. de Sa (2003) "Benefitting from the Variables that Variable Selection Discards", Journal of Machine Learning Research, 2003, 1245-1264. (eds.): Theoretical Aspects of Computer Software. Lecture Notes in Computer Science, Vol. 1281. Springer-Verlag, Berlin Heidelberg New York (1997) 415–438
3. I. Guyon, A. Elisseeff (2003) "An Introduction to Variable and Feature Selection", JMLR Special Issue, 2003, p 1157-1182GGGH.
4. Narazaki, A.L. Ralescu (1992) "Iterative Induction of a Category Membership Function", International Journal of Uncertainty, Fuzziness, and Knowledge-Based Systems, Vol. 2, No. 1, 1994, 91-100.
5. H. Stoppiglia, G. Dreyfus, et al (2003) "Ranking a Random Variable for Variable and Feature Selection", JMLR Special Issue, 2003, p 1399-1414
6. G. John (1994) "Cross-Validated C4.5: Using Error Estimation for Automatic Parameter Selection", Technical Report STAN-CS-TN-94-12, CS Department, Stanford University, October 1994
7. Z. Zheng (1993) "A Benchmark for Classifier Learning", Technical Report 474, Proceedings of the 6th Australian Joint Conference on AI, p 281-286, World Scientific, 1993
8. R. Setiono (1996) "Extracting Rules from Pruned Neural Networks for Breast Cancer Diagnosis", Artificial Intelligence in Medicine, Vol. 8, No. 1, February 1996, p 37-51
9. J. Taha, J. Ghosh (1997) "Evaluation and Ordering of Rules Extracted from Forwardfeed Networks", Proceedings of the IEEE International Conference on Neural Networks, p 221-226, 1997
10. A. Tsakonas, G. Dounias (2002) "A Scheme for the Evolution of Feedforward Networks using BNF-Grammar Driven Genetic Programming", Proceedings EUNITE-02. Algarve, Portugal, 2002
11. W. Ju et al (2003) "On Bayesian Learning of Sparse Classifiers", September 2003
12. C. Pina-Reyes, M. Sipper (1998) "Evolving Fuzzy Rules for Breast Cancer Diagnosis", Proceedings of 1998 International Symposium on Nonlinear Theory and Applications (NOLTA'98), Vol. 2, p 369-372, Lausanne, 1998
13. P. Yau et al (2002) "Bayesian Variable Selection and Model Averaging in High Dimensional Multinomial Nonparametric Regression", Journal of Computational and Graphical Statistics, Vol. 12, No. 1, p23-32, March 2003
14. D. Bahler, L. Navarro (2000) "Combining Heterogeneous Sets of Classifiers: Theoretical and Experimental Comparison of Methods", 17th National Conference on Artificial Intelligence (AAAI 2000), Workshop on New Research Problems for Machine Learning, 2000
15. J. Aguilar, J Riquelme, M. Toro (2000) "Data Set Editing by Ordered Projection", 14th European Conference on Artificial Intelligence, August 2000

Accelerating Linear Causal Model Discovery Using Hoeffding Bounds

Gang Li, Honghua Dai, Yiqing Tu, and Tarkan Kurt

School of Information Technology, Deakin University,
221 Burwood Highway, Vic 3125, Australia
{gangli,hdai,ytu,tkurt}@deakin.edu.au

Abstract. Efficiently inducing precise causal models accurately reflecting given data sets is the ultimate goal of causal discovery. The algorithms proposed by Dai et al. has demonstrated the ability of the Minimum Message Length (MML) principle in discovering *Linear Causal Models* from training data. In order to further explore ways to improve efficiency, this paper incorporates the *Hoeffding Bounds* into the learning process. At each step of causal discovery, if a small number of data items is enough to distinguish the better model from the rest, the computation cost will be reduced by ignoring the other data items. Experiments with data set from related benchmark models indicate that the new algorithm achieves speedup over previous work in terms of learning efficiency while preserving the discovery accuracy.

1 Introduction

The problem of automatically selecting a good model has been variously described as training a neural network, constructing a classifier, or discovering a causal model. This kind of model selection is usually a search through model space with some criterion of 'fitness' such as regression/classification accuracy, or minimum message length etc. As a method of model selection, the Greedy search, calculates the 'fitness' of models it meets and picks the best one. The time cost concerned is proportional to the size of the data set $|D|$ used for validation. Suppose that T greedy search steps will be used, then the amount of time cost is $\mathcal{O}(T \times |D|)$, which might be expensive for large data sets.

In this paper, we focus on the task of linear causal model discovery [1]. Actually, linear causal model discovery is a NP-hard problem, except a special case in which each node has no more than one parent. The obvious method of reducing computation cost is to increase the amount of pruning and reduce the model space [2].

The algorithm we propose in this paper, *MMLCI-HB*, aims to improve the efficiency of linear causal model discovery by minimizing the size of data set $|D|$ used at each step of the greedy search, while producing approximate the same results as would be got from the full data set.

The paper is organized into 5 sections. After a recap of *Linear Causal Model* and its MML-based discovery algorithms in Section 2, we propose the *MMLCI-HB* algorithm using the concept of *Hoeffding Bounds* in Section 3. Then in

Section 4 we give the experimental results, and finally in Section 5 we conclude with several challenges for future research.

2 Linear Causal Model and MMLCI Algorithms

2.1 Linear Causal Model

In social sciences, there is a class of limited *Graphical Model*, usually referred as *Linear Causal Models*, including *Path Diagram*, and *Structural Equations Model* [3]. In *Linear Causal Models*, effect variables are strictly linear functions of exogenous variables. Although this is a significant limitation, its adoption allows for a comparatively easy environment in which to develop causal discovery algorithms. Informally speaking, a *Linear Causal Model* is a limited *Directed Graphical Model* in which every variable concerned is a continuous variable, and the model consists two parts: *Structure*, which qualitatively describes the relation among different variables; and *Parameters*, which quantitatively describe the relation between variable and its parents.

2.2 MMLCI Algorithms

In 1996, Wallace et al. successfully introduced the *Minimum Message Length* (MML) principle [4] to the discovery of *Linear Causal Models*. In 1997, Dai et al. further studied the reliability and robustness issues in causal discovery [5], and closely examined the relationships among the complexity of the causal model to be discovered, the strength of the causal links, the sample size of given data set and the discovery ability of individual causal discovery algorithms. Their algorithm is usually referred to as *MMLCI-I* [6]. In 2002, Dai and Li proposed the *MMLCI-II*, which adopts a refined MML-based encoding scheme for linear causal model [7] and solves the negative message length problem existing in *MMLCI-I*. In 2004, the *MMLCI-III* is introduced, and it incorporates ensemble methods to improve the accuracy of the discovery result [8]. In general, two key issues exist in these MML-based causal discovery algorithms:

Evaluating the MML cost of models, which requires an efficient encoding schema for the model itself and the training data set. The evaluation actually reflects the 'fitness' (minimum message length) of each candidate model with the data set;

Searching through the space of all possible models. Different search strategies can be used, such as the greedy search as in *MMLCI-I* and *MMLCI-II*, the ensemble search as in *MMLCI-III*, or MCMC and Genetic search as in [6].

According to the MML principle [4], the shorter the encoding message length is, the better is the corresponding model. Given a data set D, the total message length for a linear causal model $LCM = \langle S, \Theta_S \rangle$ can be approximated by [7]:

$$\begin{aligned}
msgLen(D, LCM) &= msgLen(S) + msgLen(\Theta_S) + msgLen(D|S, \Theta_S) \\
&= msgLen(S) + msgLen(\Theta_S) + \sum_{t=1}^{|D|} msgLen(D_t|S, \Theta_S)
\end{aligned} \quad (1)$$

Where $|D|$ is the size of data set D, and D_t is the t-th instance of the data set D, $msgLen(S)$ is the encoding length of model structure, while $msgLen(\Theta_S)$ is the encoding length for the local parameters, and $msgLen(D_t|S,\Theta_S)$ is the encoding length for the data item D_t assuming the model. The detailed encoding scheme can be found in [7].

As for searching, greedy search is the basic strategy used in *MMLCI-I* and *MMLCI-II*, and it is also used in the base learner of *MMLCI-III*. In each greedy search step, the whole data set D will be used to decide whether the candidate model is better than the current model, and in this process, we have to calculate the encoded message length for each data item D_t. This paper is based on the idea that: if in each greedy search step, only necessary part of the data set will be used to compare two models, the computational cost could be saved by calculating only the message length for those necessary data items.

3 MMLCI-HB Algorithm

3.1 Hoeffding Bounds

Hoeffding Bounds are one of the most fundamental tools used to determine the sample size needed to bound the error in the probability estimate. They are frequently used in the analysis of many problems arising in both statistics and machine learning [9]. Given a sequence of independent and bounded data items, Hoeffding Bounds help upper-bound the probability that the estimated mean of these data items deviates much from the true mean [10].

Theorem 1. *Suppose $x_1, \ldots, x_n$ are n independently sampled data items from the range $[l, u]$, then for any $\epsilon > 0$ we have*

$$p(|E - \tilde{E}| > \epsilon) < e^{-2n\epsilon^2/R^2} \quad (2)$$

Where $\tilde{E} = \frac{\sum x_i}{n}$ is the estimated mean after n independently sampled data item, E is the unknown true mean. and $R = u - l$.

For a proof of this theorem, please see [10].

The Hoeffding Bounds can also be interpreted as: with confidence $1 - \delta$, the estimate of the mean $\tilde{E}$ is within ϵ of the true mean E, i.e., $p(|E - \tilde{E}| > \epsilon) < \delta$. Combined this with equation 2 and solving for ϵ gives us a bound on how close the $\tilde{E}$ is to E after n data items were sampled, with confidence $1-\delta$: $\epsilon = \sqrt{\frac{R^2 \ln(1/\delta)}{2n}}$. From Hoeffding Bounds, it is easy to get the following corollary:

Corollary 1. *Suppose $x_1, \ldots, x_n$ are n independently sampled data items from the range $[l, u]$, $\tilde{E} = \frac{\sum x_i}{n}$ is the estimated mean of these sampled data items. With confidence $1 - \delta$, the unknown true mean of these data items will fall into this range:*

$$[\tilde{E} - \sqrt{\frac{R^2 \ln(1/\delta)}{2n}}, \tilde{E} + \sqrt{\frac{R^2 \ln(1/\delta)}{2n}}] \quad (3)$$

Where $R = u - l$.

As indicated above, Hoeffding Bounds has found broad applicability in many different areas. For example, Maron and Moore proposed a technique for finding a good model for the data by quickly discarding bad models [9, 11]. Devroye et al. illustrate the application of this Bounds in pattern recognition. This bounds have the very attractive property that it is independent of the distribution of data items, and this property makes it especially attractive in the search of linear causal model.

3.2 Accelerating the MMLCI Algorithm

As for the discovery of linear causal model, from eq. 1 it is clear that all sampled data item D_t will be used at each step of model searching, and this is potentially computational extensive. This searching could be accelerated if the same result might be returned using a small fraction of the data. In order to apply Hoeffding Bounds to the linear causal model discovery, we need to provide a bound on partial sums of the encoded message length for data items $D_1, D_2, \ldots$.

From Corollary 1, it is easy to estimate the bounds on the partial sums of data items:

Corollary 2. *Suppose $x_1, \ldots, x_n$ are n independently sampled data items from the range $[l, u]$, $\tilde{S} = \sum x_i$ is the partial sums of these sampled data items. With confidence $1 - \delta$, the true sums Sum will fall into this range:*

$$[\tilde{S} - \sqrt{\frac{nR^2 \ln(1/\delta)}{2}}, \tilde{S} + \sqrt{\frac{nR^2 \ln(1/\delta)}{2}}] \tag{4}$$

Where $R = u - l$.

Given a data set D with n data items, and a linear causal model $LCM = \langle S, \Theta_S \rangle$, the encoding length of D using model LCM is $\sum_{t=1}^{|D|} msgLen(D_t|S, \Theta_S)$.

Suppose the message length $msgLen(D_t|S, \Theta_S)$ to be n independently sampled variables, given a desired probability $1-\delta$, the Hoeffding Bounds guarantees that the partial sum of message lengths will fall in this range:

$$[\sum_{t=1}^{|D|} msgLen(D_t|S, \Theta_S) - \sqrt{\frac{nR^2 \ln(1/\delta)}{2}}, \sum_{t=1}^{|D|} msgLen(D_t|S, \Theta_S) + \sqrt{\frac{nR^2 \ln(1/\delta)}{2}}] \tag{5}$$

Where R is the length of the range of possible message length.

In each greedy searching step in the linear causal model discovery, using eq. 1 and eq.5, the lower and the upper bounds of $msgLen(D, LCM)$ can be estimated as:

$$[msgLen(S, \Theta_S) + \sum_{t=1}^{|D|} msgLen(D_t|S, \Theta_S) - \sqrt{\frac{nR^2 \ln(1/\delta)}{2}},$$
$$msgLen(S, \Theta_S) + \sum_{t=1}^{|D|} msgLen(D_t|S, \Theta_S) + \sqrt{\frac{nR^2 \ln(1/\delta)}{2}}] \tag{6}$$

When comparing two candidate models, in order to choose one over the other with high confidence, we need to use enough data items to make the upper bound of one model is still less than the lower bound of the other model. This leads to our *MMLCI-HB* algorithm, as described in Algorithm 1.

Algorithm 1 MMLCI-HB Algorithm.

Input: a training data D, search step limit $StepLimit$, number of sub data sets C, the confidence $1 - \delta$, optional seeding model M_{seed}
Output: a linear causal model M

$\quad M \Leftarrow M_{seed}$; $Steps \Leftarrow 0$;
$\quad$ Slice D into C parts: $D^{(1)}, \ldots, D^{(C)}$;
$\quad$ **repeat**
$\quad\quad M' \Leftarrow$ Generate a candidate model from M;
$\quad\quad M.MML[0] \Leftarrow msgLen(M_S, M_{\Theta_S})$;
$\quad\quad M'.MML[0] \Leftarrow msgLen(M'_S, M'_{\Theta_S})$;
$\quad\quad t \Leftarrow 0$;
$\quad\quad$ **repeat**
$\quad\quad\quad t \Leftarrow t + 1$;
$\quad\quad\quad n_t \Leftarrow$ the size of $\bigcup_{k=1}^{t} D^{(k)}$
$\quad\quad\quad$ **if** $M.MML[t]$ is not available **then**
$\quad\quad\quad\quad M.MML[t] \Leftarrow M.MML[t-1] + msgLen(D^{(t)}|M_S, M_{\Theta_S})$;
$\quad\quad\quad$ **end if**
$\quad\quad\quad \epsilon_M \Leftarrow \sqrt{\frac{n_t R_M^2 \ln(1/\delta)}{2}}$;
$\quad\quad\quad$ Update the $LB(M.MML[t])$ and $UB(M.MML[t])$;
$\quad\quad\quad M'.MML[t] \Leftarrow M'.MML[t-1] + msgLen(D^{(t)}|M'_S, M'_{\Theta_S})$;
$\quad\quad\quad \epsilon_{M'} \Leftarrow \sqrt{\frac{n_t R_{M'}^2 \ln(1/\delta)}{2}}$;
$\quad\quad\quad$ Update the $LB(M'.MML[t])$ and $UB(M'.MML[t])$;
$\quad\quad\quad$ **if** $UB(M'.MML[t]) < LB(M.MML[t])$ **then**
$\quad\quad\quad\quad M \Leftarrow M'$;
$\quad\quad\quad\quad$ break;
$\quad\quad\quad$ **else if** $UB(M.MML[t]) < LB(M'.MML[t])$ **then**
$\quad\quad\quad\quad$ discard M';
$\quad\quad\quad\quad$ break;
$\quad\quad\quad$ **end if**
$\quad\quad$ **until** $(t == C)$
$\quad\quad$ **if** $(t == C)$ **then**
$\quad\quad\quad M \Leftarrow$ the model with minumum message length;
$\quad\quad$ **end if**
$\quad$ **until** $Steps > StepLimit$
$\quad$ return model M;

Starting with a seed model, a directed acyclic graph provided by user or a null graph without any edge, the *MMLCI-HB* algorithm still adopts the framework of greedy search: generate some candidate models, select the best one, and then repeat until a predefined limit is reached. First, the training data set D is divided into C sub data sets $D^{(1)}, \ldots, D^{(C)}$; Then, at each greedy search step, sub data sets are fed into the algorithm, and the lower and the upper bounds of message lengths of the candidate models are then calculated, until one model's upper bound is less than the other models' lower bounds, or all sub data sets have been used (In this case, the model with the minimum message length will be selected). If only part of the original data set D is used at this search step, the computational cost is saved from avoiding the calculation for the other data items.

In the implementation of the *MMLCI-HB* algorithm, the following issues need to be considered:

The length of the range. For a linear causal model M, the length R_M of the range of possible message length for data items, is an important factor for the accuracy of the lower and the upper bounds. In our implementation, it is estimated as twice of the difference between the maximum and the minimum message length for data items assume M is true.

The number of sub data sets. The original data set is divided into C sub data sets, and in each search step, these C sub data sets are fed into the algorithm one by one until the best model can be distinguished from the other candidate models. A larger value of C will tend to get a more accurate approximation to the minimal number of required data items, and make it possible to save more computation from estimating the message length of other data items, while at the same time, more time will be spent on comparison.

MML Array. For each candidate model M, an array of MML estimation will be maintained. Each array consists of $(C+1)$ elements, and the first element contains the message length of $msgLen(M_S, M_{\Theta_S})$, and the i-th element contains the message length of $msgLen(\bigcup_{j=1}^{i} D^{(j)}, M)$. When the t-th sub data set is fed into the algorithm, there is no need to recalculate the length of previous sub data sets, and the encoded message length $M.MML[t]$ can be from $M.MML[t-1]$ and estimation of $msgLen(D^{(t)}|M)$.

4 Experimental Results

In this section, we evaluate the performance of the *MMLCI-HB* algorithm proposed in this paper, and the following four algorithms are compared:

- the *MMLCI-HB* algorithm as proposed in this paper;
- the *MMLCI-II* algorithm as in [7]. According to [12], this is a fast algorithm with a reasonable accuracy;
- the *MMLCI-III* algorithm as in [8]. This algorithm incorporates ensemble learning into causal discovery, and it can discover very accurate result though it is time extensive;
- the *MMLCI-III-HB* algorithm: we replace the base learner in *MMLCI-III* by the *MMLCI-HB* algorithm.

The performance of these algorithms will be compared by their time cost and the accuracy: if a causal discovery algorithm works perfectly, it should reproduce exactly the model used to generate the data. In practice, sampling errors will result in deviations from the original model, but algorithm which can reproduce a model structure similar to the original, and secondarily coefficient values similar to the original, must be considered to be more accurate than those which do not.

4.1 Examination of the Induced Models

Eight data sets reported in related literature [1, 6] are re-examined: *Fiji, Evans, Blau, Rodgers, case9, case10, case12 and case15*. The details of these data sets are described in Table 1, and all the original models are shown in Figure 1.

Table 1. Information of Data Set.

Data Set	Number of Nodes	Sample Size
Fiji	4	1000
Evans	5	1000
Blau	6	1000
Rodgers	7	1000
Case9	9	1000
Case10	10	1000
Case12	12	1000
Case15	15	1000

All those four compared algorithms are implemented in Matlab. In the *MMLCI-HB* algorithm, and the *MMLCI-III-HB* algorithm, the parameters are set like this: C is set to be 10, so that each sub data set consists of 100 data items; and the δ is set to be 0.0001%, so that each step will select the model with 99.9999% confidence. For the algorithm *MMLCI-III* and *MMLCI-III-HB*, the ensemble size is set to be 10.

Table 2 gives the comparison of *the Minimum Number of Needed Manipulations*, which is the number of *adding, deleting, and reversing* needed to transform the recovered structure to the original model. From Table 2, we can see that the *MMLCI-HB* algorithm performs similar to the *MMLCI-II* algorithm, while the *MMLCI-III* algorithm performs similar to the *MMLCI-III-HB* algorithm. This indicates that the introduction of Hoeffding Bounds into causal discovery won't lose the accuracy of discovered results.

4.2 Time Comparison

Table 3 compares the time cost of these four algorithms in discovering causal models. From the Table, we can see that the *MMLCI-HB* algorithm is faster than the *MMLCI-II* algorithm, and the *MMLCI-II-HB* algorithm is faster than the *MMLCI-III* algorithm.

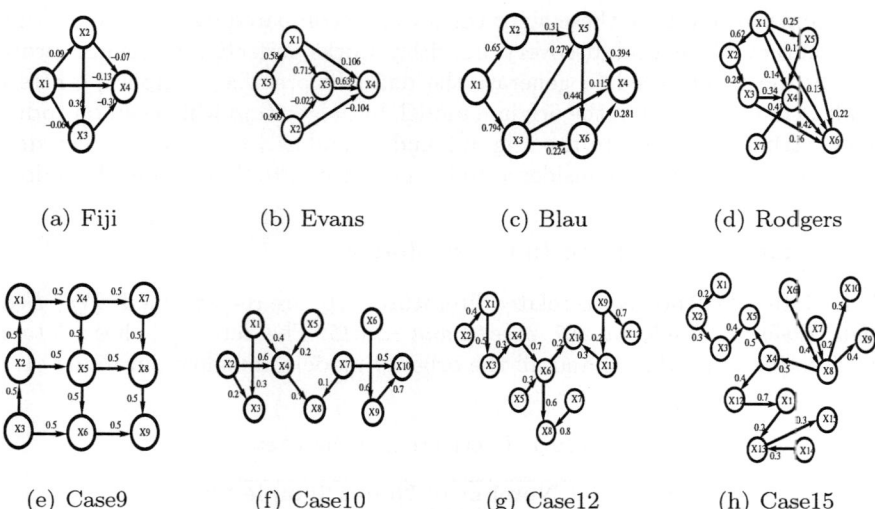

Fig. 1. Original Models used in this experiment.

Table 2. Number of Needed Manipulations.

Data Set	MMLCI-HB	MMLCI-II	MMLCI-III	MMLCI-III-HB
Fiji	3	3	3	3
Evans	6	6	3	3
Blau	3	3	1	1
Rodgers	5	5	0	0
Case9	0	0	0	0
Case10	0	0	0	0
Case12	0	0	0	0
Case15	0	0	0	0

This acceleration comes from time saving at greedy search steps in which only part of the training data set is needed to distinguish models. For smaller models such as *Fiji* and *Evans*, the acceleration is very manifest, and this is because for these models, normally only several hundreds data items are enough to be used to induce the model. However, for larger models, usually most of the data items will be needed, and the kind of time saving is less. Therefore, for models *Case10*, *Case12* and *Case15*, the time saving is negligible.

Finally, it should be noted that the *MMLCI-HB* algorithm could be slower than the *MMLCI-II* algorithm, especially when all data items are needed to distinguish models at each search step. In this case, there is no time saved from the estimation of message length, while some extra calculation has to be spent on estimation and comparison of message length bounds, although it is only a little bit extra time.

Table 3. Comparison of Time Complexity (in *seconds*).

Data Set	MMLCI-HB	MMLCI-II	MMLCI-III	MMLCI-III-HB
Fiji	0.37	0.96	11.37	5.48
Evans	1.03	2.25	25.01	11.92
Blau	2.31	3.42	36.29	25.14
Rodgers	6.18	8.94	101.75	87.18
Case 9	12.51	16.32	172.06	138.77
Case 10	18.94	20.10	217.50	205.16
Case 12	35.77	36.20	391.44	367.43
Case 15	263.92	265.50	3012.76	2985.84

5 Conclusion

For the task of linear causal model discovery, computational cost is related to both the size of model space and the size of training data set. The discovery process can be sped up by two different strategies: *pruning the model space* or *using a small data set*.

This paper takes the second strategy to do the acceleration, and the Hoeffding Bounds are incorporated to decide the suitable number of data items to distinguish the best model from all candidate models. The proposed *MMLCI-HB* algorithm adopts the same framework of the greedy searching as in *MMLCI-I*, *MMLCI-II*. At each search step, the *MMLCI-HB* algorithm will try to use a small number of data items to estimate the lower and the upper bounds of the message length, if with a high probability, the best model can be distinguished from the other models, the calculation of the message length for other data items will be avoided.

Experiments show that the proposed *MMLCI-HB* algorithm can achieve acceleration of both the greedy search algorithm as in [6, 7] and the ensemble discovery algorithm [8], while keeping the accuracy of the final discovery results.

Future work can be carried out on the following aspects:

1. A refined method to estimate the length R of the range of possible message length for data item;
2. The largest data set size used in greedy search step can be used as an estimation to the size of needed data set required to discover linear causal model from.

References

1. Wallace, C., Korb, K., Dai, H.: Causal discovery via MML. In: Proceedings of the 13th International Conference on Machine Learning **(ICML'96)**. (1996) 516–524
2. Li, G., Dai, H., Tu, Y.: Identifying markov blankets using lasso estimation. In: Proceedings of The 8th Pacific-Asia Conference on Knowledge Discovery and Data Mining (PAKDD-2004), Sydney, Australia (2004)
3. Bollen, K.: Structural Equations with Latent Variables. Wiley, New York (1989)

4. Wallace, C., Boulton, D.: An information measure for classification. Computer Journal **11** (1968) 185–194
5. Dai, H., Korb, K., Wallace, C., Wu, X.: A study of causal discovery with small samples and weak links. In: Proceedings of the 15th International Joint Conference On Artificial Intelligence **IJCAI'97**, Morgan Kaufmann Publishers, Inc. (1997) 1304–1309
6. Dai, H., Li, G.: An improved approach for the discovery of causal models via MML. In: Proceedings of The 6th Pacific-Asia Conference on Knowledge Discovery and Data Mining (PAKDD-2002), Taiwan (2002) 304–315
7. Li, G., Dai, H., Tu, Y.: Linear causal model discovery using MML criterion. In: Proceedings of 2002 IEEE International Conference on Data Mining, Maebashi City, Japan, IEEE Computer Society (2002) 274–281
8. Dai, H., Li, G., Zhou, Z.H.: Ensembling causal discovery. In: Proceedings of The 8th Pacific-Asia Conference on Knowledge Discovery and Data Mining (PAKDD-2004), (Sydney, Australia)
9. Maron, O., Moore, A.W.: Hoeffding races: Accelerating model selection search for classification and function approximation. In: Advances in Neural Information Processing Systems. Volume 6., Providence, RI, Morgan Kaufmann (1994) 59–66
10. Hoeffding, W.: Probability inequalities for sums of bounded random variables. Journal of the American Statistical Association 58 (1963) 13–30
11. Maron, O., Moore, A.W.: The racing algorithm: Model selection for lazy learners. Artificial Intelligence Review 11 (1997) 193–225
12. Dai, H., Li, G., Tu, Y.: An empirical study of encoding schemes and search strategies in discovering causal networks. In: Proceedings of 13th European Conference on Machine Learning (Machine Learning: ECML 2002), Helsinki, Finland, Springer (2002) 48–59

Polynomial Time Inductive Inference of Ordered Tree Languages with Height-Constrained Variables from Positive Data

Yusuke Suzuki[1], Takayoshi Shoudai[1],
Satoshi Matsumoto[2], and Tetsuhiro Miyahara[3]

[1] Department of Informatics, Kyushu University, Kasuga 816-8580, Japan
{y-suzuki,shoudai}@i.kyushu-u.ac.jp
[2] Department of Mathematical Sciences, Tokai University, Hiratsuka 259-1292, Japan
matumoto@ss.u-tokai.ac.jp
[3] Faculty of Information Sciences,
Hiroshima City University, Hiroshima 731-3194, Japan
miyahara@its.hiroshima-cu.ac.jp

Abstract. Due to the rapid growth of tree structured data or semistructured data such as Web documents, efficient learning of structural features from tree structured data becomes more and more important. In order to represent tree structured patterns with rich structural features, we introduce a new type of structural variables, called height-constrained variables. An (i,j)-height-constrained variable can be replaced with any tree such that the trunk length of the tree is at least i and the height of the tree is at most j. Then, we define a term tree as a rooted tree pattern with ordered children and height-constrained variables. The minimal language (MINL) problem for term trees is to find a term tree t such that the language generated by t is minimal among languages, generated by term trees, which contains all given tree structured data. Let $\mathcal{OTT}^h$ be the set of all term trees with (i,j)-height-constrained variables for any i and j ($1 \leq i \leq j$) and no variable-chain. We assume that there are at least two edge labels. In this paper, we give a polynomial time algorithm for the MINL problem for $\mathcal{OTT}^h$. Thus we show that the class $\mathcal{OTT}^h$ is polynomial time inductively inferable from positive data.

1 Introduction

Due to the rapid growth of Internet usage, tree structured data or semistructured data such as Web documents have been rapidly increasing. Such tree structured data are represented by rooted trees with ordered children and edge labels, according to Object Exchange Model [1]. So efficient learning from tree structured data becomes more and more important. In order to represent tree structured patterns common to tree structured data, we have proposed *ordered term trees* which are rooted trees with ordered children and structured variables [9–11]. In this paper we call ordered term trees *term trees* simply. Conventional term trees have one type of variables, which can be replaced with arbitrary trees of arbitrary height. In this paper we introduce a new kind of variables, called *height-constrained variables*, in order to represent tree structured patterns with rich structural features. An (i,j)-*height-constrained variable* can be replaced with any tree g such that the trunk length of g, which is defined as the length between the root and a leaf of g which is identified with the lower vertex of the variable, is at least i and the height of g is at most j.

In Fig.1, the variables with label "x", "y" and "z" of the term tree t_1 can be replaced with the trees g_1, g_2 and g_3, respectively. We gave a data mining method from semistructured data using term trees as common tree structured patterns or tree wrappers [7]. Also we have implemented an information extraction system from HTML documents of search sites by using term trees. Such tree structured data in the same search site have repeated structures of subtrees and have large varieties in width of subtrees. But the height of such subtrees are constrained. So term trees with height-constrained variables which are replaced with trees of constrained height are useful tree structured patterns. A term tree t is said to be *linear*, or *regular*, if all variable labels in t are mutually distinct. The minimal language (MINL) problem for term trees is to find a term tree t, called a *minimally generalized term tree*, such that the language generated by t is minimal among languages generated by term trees, which contains all given tree structured data. Consider the examples in Fig. 1. t_1 is a minimally generalized term tree explaining the trees T_1, T_2 and T_3. The term tree t_2 also explains the three trees. But t_2 is overgeneralized and meaningless.

Let Λ be a set of edge labels which has at least two edge labels. Let $\mathcal{OTT}_\Lambda^h$ be the set of all linear term trees with (i,j)-height-constrained variables for any i and j $(1 \leq i \leq j)$ and no variable-chain. In Sec. 3, we give a polynomial time algorithm for the MINL problem for $\mathcal{OTT}_\Lambda^h$. Thus we show that the class $\mathcal{OTT}_\Lambda^h$ is polynomial time inductively inferable from positive data. In Sec. 4, we show that a problem for optimizing the size of a minimally generalized term tree with variable-chains is NP-complete. A term tree is different from other representations of tree structured patterns such as in [3, 5] in that a term tree has structured variables which can be substituted by trees and a term tree represents not a substructure but a whole tree structure. As related works, in [6, 9, 10], we showed that some fundamental classes of linear ordered or unordered term tree languages *without* height-constrained variables are efficiently learnable.

2 Preliminaries

In this paper, we deal with ordered term trees consisting of two-port variables only. The general definition of ordered term trees with multiple-port variables are given in [10]. For a set S, the number of elements in S is denoted by $|S|$.

Definition 1 (Term trees). Let $T = (V_T, E_T)$ be a rooted tree with ordered children, called an *ordered tree*, or a *tree* where V_T is a set of vertices and E_T is a set of edges. Let E_g and H_g be a partition of E_T, i.e., $E_g \cup H_g = E_T$ and $E_g \cap H_g = \emptyset$. And let $V_g = V_T$. A triplet $g = (V_g, E_g, H_g)$ is called an *ordered*

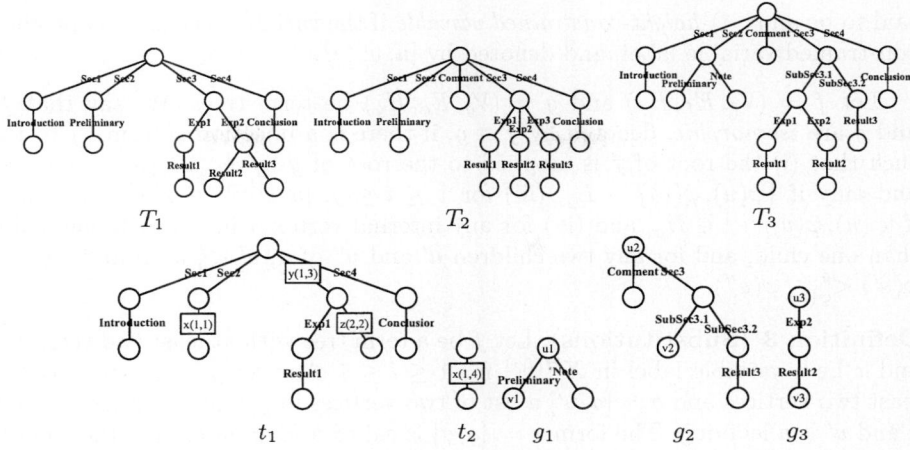

Fig. 1. Term trees t_1, t_2 and trees T_1, T_2, T_3. Vertices are denoted by circles in a standard way. Variables are denoted by squares each of which connects to two vertices which are called the parent port and the child port of the variable. A notation $x(i,j)$ in a square shows that the square is an (i,j)-height-constrained variable with a variable label x.

term tree, or a *term tree* simply. And elements in V_g, E_g and H_g are called a *vertex*, an *edge* and a *variable*, respectively. The root of g is the root of T.

Here we use the same terminologies as in graph theory. For a term tree g and its vertices v_1 and v_i, a *path* from v_1 to v_i is a sequence $v_1, v_2, \ldots, v_i$ of distinct vertices of g such that for any j with $1 \leq j < i$, there is an edge or a variable which consists of v_j and v_{j+1}. If v is adjacent to v' with an edge or a variable and v lies on the path from the root to v', v is said to be the *parent* of v' and v' is a *child* of v. The *height* of g is the length of the longest path from the root to a leaf. We use a notation $[v, v']$ to represent a variable in H_g such that v is the parent of v'. Then we call v the *parent port* of $[v, v']$ and v' the *child port* of $[v, v']$. For a term tree g, all children of every internal vertex u in g have a total ordering. The ordering on the children of u is denoted by $<_u^g$. We assume that every edge and variable of a term tree is labeled with some words from specified languages. A label of a variable is called *variable label*. Λ and X denote a set of edge labels and a set of variable labels, respectively, where $\Lambda \cap X = \phi$. A term tree $g = (V_g, E_g, H_g)$ is called *linear* (or *regular*) if all variables in H_g have mutually distinct variable labels in X. In this paper, we discuss with linear term trees only. Thus we assume that all term trees in this paper are linear.

Definition 2 (Height-constrained variables). Let $X^{\mathcal{H}}$ be an infinite subset of a variable label set X. For two integers $1 \leq i \leq j$, let $X^{\mathcal{H}(i,j)}$ be an infinite subset of $X^{\mathcal{H}}$. We assume that $X^{\mathcal{H}} = \bigcup_{1 \leq i \leq j} X^{\mathcal{H}(i,j)}$ and $X^{\mathcal{H}(i,j)} \cap X^{\mathcal{H}(i',j')} = \emptyset$ for $(i,j) \neq (i',j')$. A variable label in $X^{\mathcal{H}(i,j)}$ is called an (i,j)-*height-constrained variable label* for any $1 \leq i \leq j$. Especially a $(1,j)$-height-constrained variable label is called a j-*height-bounded variable label*. A variable $[u,v]$ of a term tree is said to be an (i,j)-*height-constrained variable* if the variable has an (i,j)-height-constrained variable label, and denoted by $[u,v]^{(i,j)}$.

Let $f = (V_f, E_f, H_f)$ and $g = (V_g, E_g, H_g)$ be term trees. We say that f and g are *isomorphic*, denoted by $f \equiv g$, if there is a bijection φ from V_f to V_g such that (i) the root of f is mapped to the root of g by φ, (ii) $\{u,v\} \in E_f$ if and only if $\{\varphi(u), \varphi(v)\} \in E_g$, (iii) for $1 \leq i \leq j$, $[u,v]^{(i,j)} \in H_f$ if and only if $[\varphi(u), \varphi(v)]^{(i,j)} \in H_g$, and (iv) for any internal vertex u in f which has more than one child, and for any two children u' and u'' of u, $u' <_u^f u''$ if and only if $\varphi(u') <_{\varphi(u)}^g \varphi(u'')$.

Definition 3 (Substitutions). Let f be a term tree with at least two vertices, and x be a variable label in $X^{\mathcal{H}(i,j)}$ for $1 \leq i \leq j$. And let g be a tree with at least two vertices and $\sigma = [u, u']$ a list of two vertices in g where u is the root of g and u' is a leaf of g. The form $x := [g, \sigma]$ is called a *binding* for x if the length of the path between u and u', called the *trunk length* of the binding, is at least i and the height of g is at most j. A new term tree $f\{x := [g, \sigma]\}$ is obtained by applying the binding $x := [g, \sigma]$ to f in the following way. Let $e = [v, v']^{(i,j)}$ be an (i,j)-height-constrained variable in f with the variable label x. Let g' be one copy of g and w, w' the vertices of g' corresponding to u, u' of g, respectively. For the variable $e = [v, v']^{(i,j)}$, we attach g' to f by removing the variable e from H_f and by identifying the vertices v, v' with the vertices w, w' of g', respectively. A *substitution* θ is a finite collection of bindings $\{x_1 := [g_1, \sigma_1], \cdots, x_n := [g_n, \sigma_n]\}$, where x_i's are mutually distinct variable labels in $X^{\mathcal{H}}$ and g_i's are term trees. The term tree $f\theta$, called the *instance* of f by θ, is obtained by applying the all bindings $x_i := [g_i, \sigma_i]$ on f simultaneously. The root of the resulting term tree $f\theta$ is the root of f. Next we define the ordering of children. Let f be a term tree and θ a substitution. Suppose that v has more than one child and let u' and u'' be two children of v of $f\theta$. If v is the parent port of variables $[v, v_1]^{(i_1, j_1)}, \ldots, [v, v_k]^{(i_k, j_k)}$ of f with $v_1 <_v^f \cdots <_v^f v_k$ ($1 \leq i_\ell \leq j_\ell, 1 \leq \ell \leq k$), we have the following four cases. Let g_i be a term tree which is substituted for $[v, v_\ell]^{(i_\ell, j_\ell)}$ for $\ell = 1, \ldots, k$. Case 1: If $u', u'' \in V_f$ and $u' <_v^f u''$, then $u' <_v^{f\theta} u''$. Case 2: If $u', u'' \in V_{g_\ell}$ and $u' <_v^{g_\ell} u''$ for some ℓ, then $u' <_v^{f\theta} u''$. Case 3: If $u' \in V_{g_\ell}$, $u'' \in V_f$, and $v_\ell <_v^f u''$ (resp. $u'' <_v^f v_\ell$), then $u' <_v^{f\theta} u''$ (resp. $u'' <_v^{f\theta} u'$). Case 4: If $u' \in V_{g_\ell}$, $u'' \in V_{g_{\ell'}}$ ($\ell \neq \ell'$), and $v_\ell <_v^f v_{\ell'}$, then $u' <_v^{f\theta} u''$. If v is not a parent port of any variable, then $u', u'' \in V_f$, therefore we have $u' <_v^{f\theta} u''$ if $u' <_v^f u''$.

For example, let t_1 be a term tree in Fig. 1 and $\theta = \{x := [g_1, [u_1, v_1]], y := [g_2, [u_2, v_2]], z := [g_3, [u_3, v_3]]\}$ be a substitution, where g_1, g_2 and g_3 are trees in Fig. 1. Then the instance $t_1\theta$ of the term tree t_1 by θ is the tree T_3.

A term tree with no variable is called a *ground term tree*, which is a standard tree. We denote by $\mathcal{OT}_\Lambda$ the set of all ground term trees whose edge labels are in Λ. For a term tree t, the *term tree language* $L_\Lambda(t)$ of t is defined as $\{s \in \mathcal{OT}_\Lambda \mid s \equiv t\theta$ for a substitution $\theta\}$. $\mathcal{OTT}_\Lambda^{\mathcal{H}}$ denotes the set of all term trees such that all the variables have labels in $X^{\mathcal{H}}$ and all the edges have labels in Λ. Let g be a term tree in $\mathcal{OTT}_\Lambda^{\mathcal{H}}$. A sequence of variables $[u_0, u_1]^{(i_1, j_1)}, [u_1, u_2]^{(i_2, j_2)}, \ldots, [u_{k-1}, u_k]^{(i_k, j_k)}$ ($2 \leq k$) of g is said to be a *variable-chain* if (i) u_0 is the root of g, has at least two children, or connects to the parent with an edge, and (ii) u_i has exactly one child for any i with $1 \leq i \leq k-1$, and (iii) u_k is a leaf, has at least two children, or connects to a child with an edge. In this paper, we show the following class $\mathcal{OTT}_\Lambda^h$ is polynomial time inductively inferable from positive data when $|\Lambda| \geq 2$.

$$\mathcal{OTT}_\Lambda^h = \{g \in \mathcal{OTT}_\Lambda^\mathcal{H} \mid g \text{ has no variable-chain}\} \quad (|\Lambda| \geq 2).$$

It is an open problem whether or not the class $\mathcal{OTT}_\Lambda^\mathcal{H}$ is polynomial time inductively inferable from positive data.

Let Λ be a set of edge labels and $\mathcal{TT}_\Lambda$ a set of term trees with edge labels in Λ. A *minimally generalized term tree* in $\mathcal{TT}_\Lambda$ explaining a given set of trees $S \subseteq \mathcal{OT}_\Lambda$ is a term tree t such that $S \subseteq L_\Lambda(t)$ and there is no term tree $t' \in \mathcal{TT}_\Lambda$ satisfying that $S \subseteq L_\Lambda(t') \subsetneq L_\Lambda(t)$. Angluin [4] gave a useful sufficient condition for inferability called finite thickness. $\mathcal{TT}_\Lambda$ is said to have *finite thickness*, if for any nonempty finite set $S \subseteq \mathcal{OT}_\Lambda$, the cardinality of $\{t \in \mathcal{TT}_\Lambda \mid S \subseteq L_\Lambda(t)\}$ is finite. Moriyama and Sato [8] introduced a notion of M-finite thickness by generalizing finite thickness. $\mathcal{TT}_\Lambda$ is said to have *M-finite thickness* if for any nonempty finite set $S \subseteq \mathcal{OT}_\Lambda$, (1) the number of minimally generalized term trees $t \in \mathcal{TT}_\Lambda$ explaining S such that $L_\Lambda(t)$ contains S is finite, and (2) for any $t \in \mathcal{TT}_\Lambda$, $S \subseteq L_\Lambda(t)$ implies that there exists a minimally generalized term tree t' explaining S such that $S \subseteq L_\Lambda(t') \subseteq L_\Lambda(t)$. For $t \in \mathcal{TT}_\Lambda$, a *finite telltale* of t is a finite set $S \subseteq \mathcal{OT}_\Lambda$ such that for any $t' \in \mathcal{TT}_\Lambda$, $S \subseteq L_\Lambda(t')$ implies $L_\Lambda(t') \not\subseteq L_\Lambda(t)$. Moreover we consider the following two computational problems.

Membership Problem for $\mathcal{TT}_\Lambda$.
Instance: A term tree $t \in \mathcal{TT}_\Lambda$ and a tree $T \in \mathcal{OT}_\Lambda$.
Question: Is there a substitution θ such that $T \equiv t\theta$?

Minimal Language Problem (MINL) for $\mathcal{TT}_\Lambda$.
Instance: A nonempty set of trees $S \subseteq \mathcal{OT}_\Lambda$.
Question: Find a minimally generalized term tree $t \in \mathcal{TT}_\Lambda$ explaining S.

Lemma 1. $\mathcal{OTT}_\Lambda^h$ *has M-finite thickness.*

We note that $\mathcal{OTT}_\Lambda^h$ does not have finite thickness. But it is easy to see the above lemma since for any $S \subseteq \mathcal{OT}_\Lambda$ and (i,j)-height-constrained variables of any minimally generalized term tree t explaining S, i and j are not greater than the maximum height of trees in S. Below we assume that a set Λ of edge labels has at least two labels, i.e., $|\Lambda| \geq 2$.

Lemma 2. *For any $t = (V_t, E_t, H_t) \in \mathcal{OTT}_\Lambda^h$, there exists a finite tell-tale of t.*

Proof. (Sketch) First we construct a finite set S which should be a finite telltale. Let $u_0, u_1, ..., u_k$ be new vertices. Let a and b be two distinct edge labels in Λ. We denote by $\{u, u'\}^\lambda$ an edge labeled with λ. Let $g^{\lambda_1 \lambda_2 \cdots \lambda_k}$ be a tree $(\{u_0, u_1, ..., u_k\}, \{\{u_0, u_1\}^{\lambda_1}, \{u_1, u_2\}^{\lambda_2}, ..., \{u_{k-1}, u_k\}^{\lambda_k}\})$ where $\lambda_\ell \in \{a, b\}$ $(1 \leq \ell \leq k)$. For a variable $e = [v, v']^{(i,j)}$ of t, let $x(e)$ be the variable label of e and we define a binding $x(e) := [g^{\lambda_1 \lambda_2 \cdots \lambda_k}, [u_0, u_k]]$ for all $i \leq k \leq j$. Totally we make $\sum_{k=i}^{j} 2^k$ bindings for a variable $e = [v, v']^{(i,j)}$. Let $B(e)$ be the set of all the bindings for a variable $e = [v, v']^{(i,j)}$. We define a finite subset $S \subseteq \mathcal{OT}_\Lambda$ as $S = \{t\theta \mid \theta = \bigcup_{e \in H_t} \{b(e)\}$ where $b(e) \in B(e)$ for $e \in H_t\}$. Next we show that for any $t' = (V_{t'}, E_{t'}, H_{t'}) \in \mathcal{OTT}_\Lambda^h$, $S \subseteq L_\Lambda(t') \subseteq L_\Lambda(t)$ implies $t' \equiv t$. Let $V'_t := \{v \in V_t \mid v$ is one of the followings: the root of t, a leaf of t, or a vertex which is not the root and has at least two children$\}$. We define $V'_{t'} \subseteq V_{t'}$ in the same way. Since $S \subseteq L_\Lambda(t') \subseteq L_\Lambda(t)$, there exists a bijection $\xi : V'_{t'} \to V'_t$ which keeps the ancestor-descendant relation, i.e., for $v, v' \in V'_{t'}$, v' is an ancestor of v if and only if $\xi(v')$ is an ancestor of $\xi(v)$. For any $v \in V'_{t'}$, let $na(v)$ be the nearest ancestor of v. Let $t'[na(v), v]$ be the chain consisting of variables and edges from $na(v)$ to v of t' and $t[na(\xi(v)), \xi(v)]$ the chain consisting of variables and edges from $na(\xi(v))$ to $\xi(v)$ of t. Then we can show that $t'[na(v), v] \equiv t[na(\xi(v)), \xi(v)]$ since $S \subseteq L_\Lambda(t')$ and $L_\Lambda(t') \subseteq L_\Lambda(t)$. This implies $t' \equiv t$. □

In [2], we gave a polynomial time matching algorithm for **Membership Problem for** $\mathcal{OTT}_\Lambda^\mathcal{H}$ by extending the matching algorithm in [9]. The algorithm also works on $\mathcal{OTT}_\Lambda^h$ because $\mathcal{OTT}_\Lambda^h$ is a subclass of $\mathcal{OTT}_\Lambda^\mathcal{H}$.

Lemma 3. Membership Problem for $\mathcal{OTT}_\Lambda^h$ *is solvable in polynomial time.*

In Sec. 3, we give a polynomial time algorithm for **Minimal Language Problem for** $\mathcal{OTT}_\Lambda^h$. Moriyama and Sato [8] showed sufficient conditions for polynomial time inductive inferability. In our case, it can be stated as follows.

Theorem 1 (Moriyama and Sato [8]). *If TT_Λ has M-finite thickness, then TT_Λ is polynomial time inductively inferable from positive data if and only if for each term tree $t \in TT_\Lambda$, there exists a finite tell-tale of $L_\Lambda(t)$ and both* **Membership Problem for** TT_Λ *and* **Minimal Language Problem for** TT_Λ *are computable in polynomial time.*

Finally we have the following main theorem from Lemmas 1, 2, 3, and 4 and Theorem 1.

Theorem 2. *The class $\mathcal{OTT}_\Lambda^h$ ($|\Lambda| \geq 2$) is polynomial time inductively inferable from positive data.*

3 An Efficient MINL Algorithm for Term Trees with Height-Constrained Variables

We give an algorithm MINL^h (Fig. 2) which computes **Minimal Language Problem for** $\mathcal{OTT}_\Lambda^h$ ($|\Lambda| \geq 2$). Let t be a term tree in $\mathcal{OTT}_\Lambda^h$, u a vertex of a term tree t, and v a child of u. Let λ be an element of Λ. We suppose that $e = [u, v]^{(i,j)}$ is an (i, j)-height-constrained variable ($1 \leq i \leq j$) of t and $x(e)$ is the variable label of e. Then we define the following 10 substitutions, called *refinement operators*, for t.

Algorithm $\text{MINL}^h(S)$;
input: a set of trees $S \subseteq \mathcal{OT}_\Lambda$;
begin
  Let Λ_S be the set of all edge labels which appear on edges of trees in S;
  Let h_S be the maximum height of trees in S and $t := (\{u,v\}, \emptyset, \{[u,v]^{(1,h_s)}\})$;
  // VARIABLE-EXTENSION
  while there are $e \in H_t$ and $1 \leq \ell \leq 5$ s.t. $S \subseteq L_\Lambda(t\mathcal{R}_\ell(e))$ **do** $t := t\mathcal{R}_\ell(e)$;
  // EDGE-REPLACEMENT
  while there are $e \in H_t$, $\lambda \in \Lambda_S$, and $6 \leq \ell \leq 9$ s.t. $S \subseteq L_\Lambda(t\mathcal{R}_\ell(e)_\lambda)$ **do** $t := t\mathcal{R}_\ell(e)_\lambda$;
  // HEIGHT-CONSTRAINT
  while there is $e \in H_t$ s.t. $S \subseteq L_\Lambda(t\mathcal{R}_{10}(e)_\lambda)$ **do** $t := t\mathcal{R}_{10}(e)$;
  output t
end.

Fig. 2. Algorithm MINL^h.

$\mathcal{R}_\ell(e) = \{x(e) := [t_\ell, [u,v]]\}$ ($\ell = 1,2,3,4,5$) (Fig. 3)
$\mathcal{R}_6(e)_\lambda = \{x(e) := [t_6, [u,v]]\}$ if $i = 1$ (Fig. 4)
$\mathcal{R}_\ell(e)_\lambda = \{x(e) := [t_\ell, [u,v]]\}$ ($\ell = 7,8,9$) (Fig. 4)
$\mathcal{R}_{10}(e) = \{x(e) := [t_{10}, [u,v]]\}$ (Fig. 5)

We denote by $s(t)$ a ground term tree obtained by replacing all (i,j)-height-constrained variables in t with an edge-chain of length i. For term trees t and t', we write $t \approx t'$ if we ignore edge labels of t and t' and $s(t) \equiv s(t')$.

Lemma 4. *Let Λ be a set of edge labels where $|\Lambda| \geq 2$. The algorithm MINL^h finds a minimally generalized term tree in $\mathcal{OTT}_\Lambda^h$ explaining a given set S of trees in $\mathcal{OT}_\Lambda$ in polynomial time. Then* **Minimal Language Problem for** $\mathcal{OTT}_\Lambda^h$ *is computable in polynomial time.*

Proof. (Sketch) We prove the following three claims to show the correctness of the algorithm MINL^h. *Claim 1.* Let t be the term tree just after VARIABLE-EXTENSION for an input S. Let t' be a minimally generalized term tree explaining S. If $S \subseteq L_\Lambda(t') \subseteq L_\Lambda(t)$ then $t' \approx t$. *Claim 2.* Let t be the term tree just after EDGE-REPLACEMENT. Let t' be a term tree with $S \subseteq L_\Lambda(t') \subseteq L_\Lambda(t)$. Then there exists a bijection ξ from $V_{t'}$ to V_t such that $\{v,v'\}$ is an edge in t' if and only if $\{\xi(u), \xi(v')\}$ is an edge in t, moreover both the edges have the same edge labels. *Claim 3.* Let t be the term tree just after HEIGHT-CONSTRAINT and t' a term tree with $S \subseteq L_\lambda(t') \subseteq L_\Lambda(t)$. From Claim 2, there exists a bijection ξ from $V_{t'}$ to V_t. Then, $[v,v']$ is an (i,j)-height-constrained variable in t' if and only if $[\xi(v), \xi(v')]$ is an (i,j)-height-constrained variable in t. □

4 Hardness Result

In this section, we consider the following problem for the class $\mathcal{OTT}_\Lambda^\mathcal{H}$.

Minimal Language Problem of Maximum Variable Size for $\mathcal{OTT}_\Lambda^\mathcal{H}$.
Instance: A nonempty set of trees $S \subseteq \mathcal{OT}_\Lambda$, a positive integer K.
Question: Find a minimally generalized term tree $t = (V, E, H) \in \mathcal{OTT}_\Lambda^\mathcal{H}$ explaining S such that $|H| \geq K$

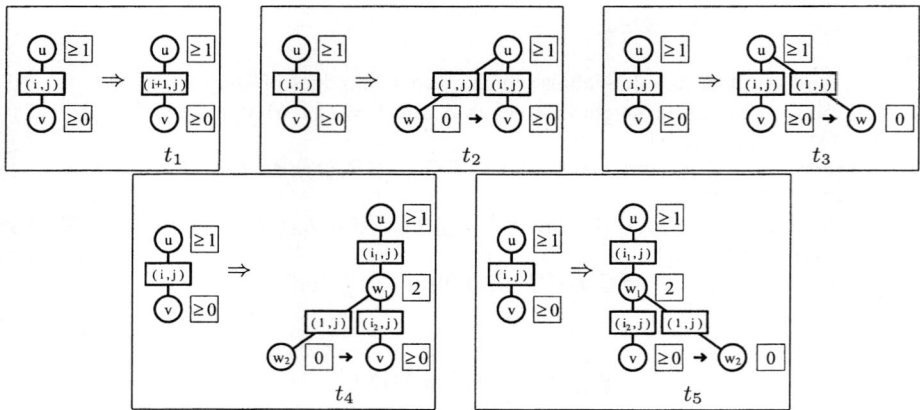

Fig. 3. Refinement operators $\mathcal{R}_\ell(e)$ ($\ell = 1, 2, 3, 4, 5$). For term trees t_4 and t_5, we assume $i = i_1 + i_2$. The digit in a box $\boxed{k}$ (resp. $\boxed{\geq k}$) near u shows that the number of children of u is equal to k (resp. is more than or equal to k). A single right arrow shows that the right vertex of it is the immediately right sibling of the left vertex.

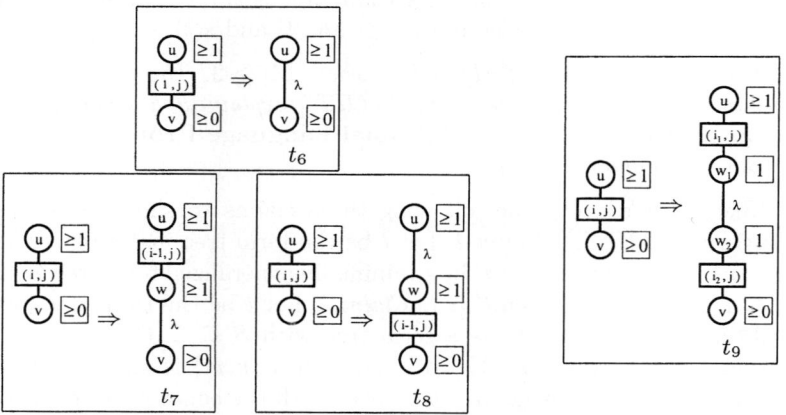

Fig. 4. Refinement operators $\mathcal{R}_\ell(e)_\lambda$ ($\ell = 6, 7, 8, 9$). For a term tree t_9, we assume $i = i_1 + i_2 + 1$.

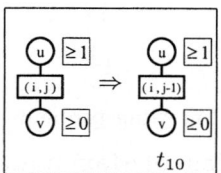

Fig. 5. Refinement operator $\mathcal{R}_{10}(e)$.

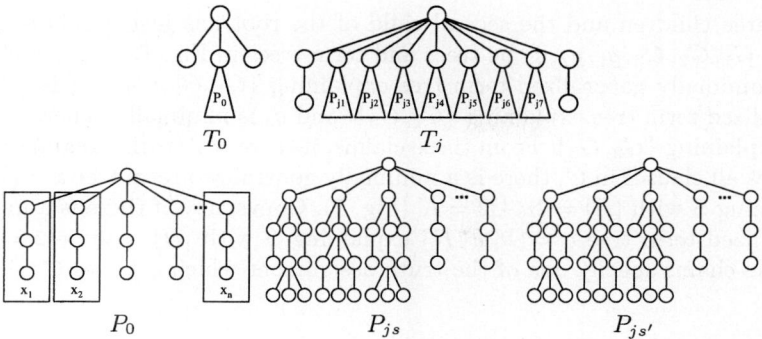

Fig. 6. $S = \{T_1 \ldots, T_m, T_0\}$ is a sample set used in the reduction in Theorem 3. For example, P_{js} and $P_{js'}$ ($1 \le s, s' \le 7$) correspond to truth assignments for $(x_1, x_2, x_3) = (true, false, true)$ and $(true, false, false)$, respectively.

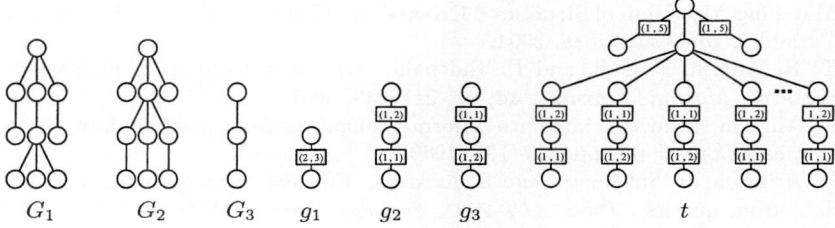

Fig. 7. Trees G_1, G_2, G_3, term trees g_1, g_2, g_3, and a minimally generalized term tree $t = (V, E, H)$ explaining S.

Theorem 3. Minimal Language Problem of Maximum Variable Size for $\mathcal{OTT}_\Lambda^\mathcal{H}$ is NP-complete.

Proof. Membership in NP is obvious. We transform 3-SAT to this problem. Let $U = \{x_1, \ldots, x_n\}$ be a set of variables and $C = \{c_1, \ldots, c_m\}$ a collection of clauses over U with $|c_j| = 3$ for any j ($1 \le j \le m$). For a tree T and a vertex u of T, we denote the subtree consisting of u and the descendants of u by $T[u]$. Let P_0 be the tree which is described in Fig. 6. The root of P_0 has n children $v_1, v_2, \ldots, v_n$. For each i ($1 \le i \le n$), $P_0[v_i]$ corresponds to the truth assignment to x_i. We construct trees $T_1, \ldots, T_m$ and C in the following way. T_j ($1 \le j \le n$) is described in Fig. 6. The root of T_j has 9 children $v_{j0}, v_{j1}, \ldots, v_{j8}$. The 7 subtrees $T_j[v_{j1}], \ldots, T_j[v_{j7}]$ correspond to the truth assignments that satisfy c_j. Each $T_j[v_{ji}]$ ($1 \le i \le 7$) is constructed as follows. Let $c_j = \{\ell_{j1}, \ell_{j2}, \ell_{j3}\}$ where $\ell_{jk} = x_{n_{jk}}$ or $\neg x_{n_{jk}}$ ($1 \le k \le 3, 1 \le n_{jk} \le n$). The 7 truth assignments to $(x_{n_{j1}}, x_{n_{j2}}, x_{n_{j3}})$ make c_j true. For the ith truth assignment ($1 \le i \le 7$) and all $1 \le n_{j1}, n_{j2}, n_{j3} \le n$, P_{ji} is obtained from P_0. This resulting tree P_{ji} becomes $T_j[v_{ji}]$. Let T_0 be the tree in Fig. 6 which contains P_0 as a subtree. Then we have the following two claims for $S = \{T_1, \ldots, T_m, T_0\}$ and $K = 2n + 2$. *Claim 1.* Let t be a minimally generalized term tree explaining S. Then the root of t has just three children and the second child of the root has just n children. *Claim 2.* Let $G_1, G_2, G_3, g_1, g_2, g_3$ be trees and term trees in Fig. 7, respectively. Then g_1 is minimally generalized term tree explaining $\{G_1, G_2, G_3\}$, g_2 is minimally generalized term tree explaining $\{G_1, G_3\}$, and g_3 is minimally generalized term tree explaining $\{G_2, G_3\}$. From these claims, if there is a truth assignment which satisfies all clauses in C, there is a minimally generalized term tree $t = (V, E, H)$ explaining S with $|H| = 2n + 2 = K$ (Fig. 7). Conversely, if there is a minimally generalized term tree $t = (V, E, H)$ explaining S with $|H| = 2n + 2 = K$, the variable-chains specify one of the truth assignment which satisfies C. □

References

1. S. Abiteboul, P. Buneman, and D. Suciu, Data on the web: From relations to semistructured data and XML, Morgan Kaufmann, 2000.
2. K. Aikou, Y. Suzuki, T. Shoudai, T. Uchida, and T. Miyahara, A Polynomial Time Matching Algorithm of Structured Ordered Tree Patterns with Height-Constrained Variables, *to be submitted*, 2004.
3. T. R. Amoth, P. Cull, and P. Tadepalli, On exact learning of unordered tree patterns, *Machine Learning*, **44**, pp. 211–243, 2001.
4. D. Angluin, Inductive inference of formal languages from positive data, *Information and Control*, **45**, pp. 117–135, 1980.
5. H. Arimura, H. Sakamoto, and S. Arikawa, Efficient learning of semi-structured data from queries, *Proc. ALT-2001, Springer-Verlag, LNAI 2225*, pp. 315–331, 2001.
6. S. Matsumoto, Y. Suzuki, T. Shoudai, T. Miyahara, and T Uchida, Learning of Finite Unions of Tree Patterns with Repeated Internal Structured Variables from Queries, *Proc. ALT 2003, Springer-Verlag, LANI 2842*, pp. 144–158, 2003.
7. T. Miyahara, Y. Suzuki, T. Shoudai, T. Uchida, S. Hirokawa, K. Takahashi, and H. Ueda, Extraction of tag tree patterns with contractible variables from irregular semistructured data, *Proc. PAKDD 2003, Springer-Verlag, LNAI 2637*, pp. 430–436, 2003.
8. T. Moriyama and M. Sato, Properties of language classes with finite elasticity, *IEICE Transactions on Information and Systems*, **E-78-D(5)**, pp. 532–538, 1995.
9. Y. Suzuki, R. Akanuma, T. Shoudai, T. Miyahara, and T. Uchida, Polynomial time inductive inference of ordered tree patterns with internal structured variables from positive data, *Proc. COLT-2002, Springer-Verlag, LNAI 2375*, pp. 169–184, 2002.
10. Y. Suzuki, T. Shoudai, T. Uchida, and T. Miyahara, Ordered term tree languages which are polynomial time inductively inferable from positive data, *Proc. ALT-2002, Springer-Verlag, LNAI 2533*, pp. 188–202, 2002.
11. Y. Suzuki, T. Shoudai, S. Matsumoto and T. Uchida, Efficient Learning of Unlabeled Term Trees with Contractible Variables from Positive Data, *Proc. ILP-2003, Springer-Verlag, LNAI 2835*, pp.347–364, 2003.

Fast Incremental Learning of Linear Model Trees

Duncan Potts

University of New South Wales, Australia
duncanp@cse.unsw.edu.au

Abstract. A linear model tree is a decision tree with a linear functional model in each leaf. In previous work we demonstrated that such trees can be learnt incrementally, and can form good models of non-linear dynamic environments. In this paper we introduce a new incremental node splitting criteria that is significantly faster than both our previous algorithm and other non-parametric incremental learning techniques, and in addition scales better with dimensionality. Empirical results in three domains ranging from a simple benchmark test function to a complex ten dimensional flight simulator show that in all cases the algorithm converges to a good final approximation, although the improved performance comes at the cost of slower initial learning.

1 Introduction

In many real-time applications a fast response is required from the system. Often processing power is restricted by the hardware available and the performance of the software is a prime concern. For example an autonomous agent operating in an outdoor environment may need to constantly process the latest sensor information to determine the next action, and a large processing delay may be unacceptable. In such situations there may be the need for fast incremental learning upon which we can confidently place an upper bound on the processing time for a training example.

In this paper we shall focus on the problem of inducing models of continuous non-linear dynamic environments, although the methods developed have a potentially much wider applicability. It is envisioned that in the future the model will be used to control the agent, however in this work we only address the system identification task of constructing such a model. A non-linear model can be formulated in continuous time as

$$\dot{\mathbf{z}} = f(\mathbf{z}, \mathbf{u}) \tag{1}$$

where $\mathbf{z}$ is an n dimensional state vector and $\mathbf{u}$ is an m dimensional input ($\dot{\mathbf{z}}$ is the rate of change of $\mathbf{z}$ with respect to time) [1]. The problem then becomes one of incrementally learning an approximation to the function f using the states experienced by the agent.

When there is little prior knowledge it is beneficial to consider non-parametric techniques where the number of learning parameters is adjusted by the algorithm. Schaal and Atkeson [2] developed an algorithm based on locally weighted learning that not only dynamically allocates models as required, but also adjusts the shape of each local weighting function. The algorithm performs well for data with a low intrinsic dimensionality, even if the input data itself has a high number of dimensions. However there are several parameters that are hard to specify without trial and error, and the range of inputs and a metric over the input space must be defined in advance.

A decision tree with a linear model in each leaf (a linear model tree) can also approximate a non-linear function. The induction of such trees in a batch manner has received significant attention in the literature, however our previous work has only recently addressed the incremental induction of model trees [3].

The contribution of this paper is to present a new incremental node splitting rule based on a previously published batch technique. Empirical testing in three domains compares the new rule with existing incremental and batch methods.

2 Linear Model Trees

Learning each component of $\dot{\mathbf{z}}$ in (1) can be formulated as a typical regression problem

$$y = f(\mathbf{x}) + \epsilon$$

where $f(\mathbf{x})$ is the component of $\dot{\mathbf{z}}$ and $\mathbf{x} = [\mathbf{z}^T \ \mathbf{u}^T \ 1]^T$ is a $d = n+m+1$ dimensional column vector of regressors (the constant regressor is added to simplify the notation). The observed values y are corrupted by independent zero-mean Gaussian noise ϵ with unknown variance σ^2. The aim of a regression analysis is to find an approximation $\hat{f}(\mathbf{x})$ to $f(\mathbf{x})$ that minimises some cost function (e.g. sum of squared errors) over a set of training examples.

For a linear model tree, $\hat{f}(\mathbf{x})$ is a decision tree with a linear model in each leaf. The decision tree partitions the input space and within each leaf

$$\hat{f}(\mathbf{x}) = \mathbf{x}^T \hat{\theta}$$

where $\hat{\theta}$ is a column vector of d parameters. The linear least squares estimate of the function $f(\mathbf{x})$ is the value of $\hat{\theta}$ that minimises

$$J = \sum_{i=1}^{N}(y_i - \mathbf{x}_i^T \hat{\theta})^2$$

over the N training examples $\langle \mathbf{x}_i, y_i \rangle$ in the leaf. Defining the $N \times 1$ vector $\mathbf{y}$ and the $N \times d$ matrix $\mathbf{X}$

$$\mathbf{y} = \begin{bmatrix} y_1 \\ \vdots \\ y_N \end{bmatrix} \quad \text{and} \quad \mathbf{X} = \begin{bmatrix} \mathbf{x}_1^T \\ \vdots \\ \mathbf{x}_N^T \end{bmatrix}$$

the linear least squares estimate is

$$\hat{\theta}_{LS} = [\mathbf{X}^T \mathbf{X}]^{-1} \mathbf{X}^T \mathbf{y} \qquad (2)$$

The residual for each example is the difference between the value y_i and the prediction $\hat{f}(\mathbf{x}_i)$, and the residual sum of squares (RSS) is the minimum value of J (occurring when $\hat{\theta} = \hat{\theta}_{LS}$). Both $\hat{\theta}_{LS}$ and RSS can be calculated for each node incrementally using the recursive least squares (RLS) algorithm. The difficulty lies in defining the tree structure itself.

3 Related Work

The general approach to building trees from a training set is to start at the root and perform top down induction. At each node the training set is recursively partitioned using a splitting rule until the tree is sufficiently large. Several splitting rules measure error to the average y value [4, 5] and are therefore only applicable when the leaves contain constant values. However when linear models are fitted to each leaf distance to the linear regression plane should be used instead.

RETIS [6] minimises the total residual sum of squares over the two linear models on each side of every candidate split. The number of potential split values increases with the number of examples (assuming the regressors are drawn from a continuous set), and $\hat{\theta}_{LS}$ must be calculated using (2) for the two subsets of examples on each side of every split. It therefore quickly becomes intractable to test all potential split values with this technique.

Several methods have been proposed to simplify the problem [7–9] and have proven effective in a batch setting where typically an overly large tree is grown initially, and a pruning process is later applied to try and optimise the prediction capability on unseen examples. For an incremental algorithm, however, it is desirable to limit the growth of the tree in the first place and avoid any complex pruning procedure. The algorithm must therefore determine not only *where* to make a split but also *when*, and the splitting rules considered so far do not help. There is clearly no need to make any split if the examples in a leaf can all be explained by a single linear model, however the leaf should be split if the examples suggest that two separate linear models would give significantly better predictions.

Fortunately this problem has also received attention in the statistics community, enabling us to determine the likelihood of the examples in the leaf occurring under the hypothesis that they were generated from a single linear model. The best split is the one least likely to occur under this hypothesis. However if this probability is not significant, then no splitting should occur until further evidence is accumulated. Our previous work [3] uses a similar principle, but the splitting rule is slow because a linear model is built on each side of every candidate split. The splitting rule in the next section only requires a single linear model in each leaf.

Several researchers have considered the incremental induction of classification trees (where each leaf determines an element from a finite set of classifications) [10] and regression trees (where each leaf contains a constant) [11]. However these techniques cannot be extended to linear model trees because the splitting decision is significantly more complex.

4 Incremental Induction Algorithm

4.1 Fast Splitting Rule

The question of whether the examples were generated by a single linear model can be tested as a hypothesis. The null hypothesis is that the underlying function is linear over the entire node ($H_0 : f(\mathbf{x}) = \mathbf{x}^T \theta$) while the alternative hypothesis is that it is not. Both SUPPORT [12] and GUIDE [13] are batch algorithms that compute the residuals from a single linear model and compare the distributions of the regressor values from the two sub-samples associated with the positive and negative residuals. Under the null hypothesis it would be expected that the means and variances of the regressors in these two sub-samples are not significantly different. However under the alternative hypothesis a difference in the regressor means or variances may arise from any curvature in the function being approximated. The fast incremental splitting rule is based on the SUPPORT technique which is analysed below to show how the degree of confidence in the split is obtained and what approximations are required in an incremental setting.

Assume that $\hat{f}(\mathbf{x})$ is the linear model constructed from all N examples at the node. The N_1 examples with non-negative residuals are put into subset 1, and the N_2 with negative residuals are put into subset 2. Label the regressor j for each example i in subset k as x_{ijk}. Let $\bar{x}_{jk}$ denote the mean of regressor j over the examples in subset k, and let s_j^2 denote the pooled variance estimate of x_j over both subsets. The statistic

$$T_j^{(1)} = \frac{\bar{x}_{j1} - \bar{x}_{j2}}{s_j \sqrt{\frac{1}{N_1} + \frac{1}{N_2}}} \qquad (3)$$

tests for the difference in means. Define $z_{ijk} = |x_{ijk} - \bar{x}_{jk}|$, let $\bar{z}_{jk}$ denote the mean of the z values for each subset, and let w_j^2 denote the pooled variance of the z values over both subsets. The statistic

$$T_j^{(2)} = \frac{\bar{z}_{j1} - \bar{z}_{j2}}{w_j \sqrt{\frac{1}{N_1} + \frac{1}{N_2}}} \qquad (4)$$

tests for the difference in variances. Under the null hypothesis both statistics are distributed according to the Student's t distribution with $N-2$ degrees of freedom. The largest in absolute size $T = \max_{j,n} |T_j^{(n)}|$ is used to select the best split attribute j, and the corresponding split value is the average of the class means $\bar{x}_{j1}$ and $\bar{x}_{j2}$. Denote the probability under the Student's t distribution where $|t| > T$ as α.

The key advantage of such a statistical test in an incremental implementation is that if the probability α is not small enough to discount H_0 with the desired degree of confidence, no split should be made at all. Moreover only a single linear model is maintained within each leaf and therefore the training function (see Table 1) is fast.

Table 1. Leaf training function.

---
function Train(leaf t, example $\langle \mathbf{x}, y \rangle$, stopping parameter δ)
1   update leaf model m with $\langle \mathbf{x}, y \rangle$ (using RLS)
2   calculate $T = \max_{j,n} |T_j^{(n)}|$ using (3) and (4), and the associated p-value (α)
3   **if** $\alpha < \alpha_{split}$ and $\delta > \delta_0$
4   split the leaf
5   **end if**
   end Train

Unfortunately neither t statistic can be calculated exactly in an incremental algorithm because the classification of a residual as positive or negative requires the exact regression plane, which at any intermediate stage in a sequence of incremental calculations is an approximation to its final value. In the same manner an exact calculation of z requires an exact regressor mean $\bar{x}_{jk}$ which is also unavailable at intermediate stages. Our implementation uses the latest regression plane and regressor means to classify a residual as positive or negative and calculate z.

4.2 Stopping, Pruning and Smoothing

Stopping, pruning and smoothing are implemented in the same manner as our previous work [3]. The only difference is that the stopping parameter δ is calculated in the parent of each leaf (using the linear models in its children) and the value is passed down to the leaf (see Table 1).

4.3 Training Complexity

Assuming that the stopping rule has limited the growth of the tree, the time taken to pass each training example down to a single leaf in the tree according to the tests in the intermediate nodes is bounded by the depth of the tree. The RLS update of a single linear model takes $O(d^2)$, and therefore the overall training complexity is $O(Nd^2)$ where N is the total number of training examples.

The algorithm therefore fulfills our goal of scaling linearly with the number of examples. Also pleasing is the $O(d^2)$ increase with dimensionality, and the fact that a strict bound can be placed on the worst case processing time for a training example (if the tree has stopped growing).

5 Experimental Results

The new incremental model tree induction algorithm (Fast-IMTI) is empirically tested in three domains, and results are compared with the following algorithms:

1. The incremental adaptive locally weighted learning algorithm RFWR [2].
2. Our previous incremental model tree induction algorithm (Slow-IMTI) [3].
3. The batch model tree induction algorithm SUPPORT [12] with linear models.

RFWR has since been adapted to improve its dimensionality reduction capability [14], however the test domains do not contain redundant dimensions and the original algorithm, without any ridge regression parameters, is more competitive. RFWR requires a metric to be defined over the input space, therefore each regressor is scaled to the range $(-1,+1)$ and the metric is the standard Euclidean distance. RFWR is also sensitive to the magnitude of the outputs which are therefore also scaled to the range $(-1,+1)$ prior to training (with the exception of the 2D test function).

To ensure the IMTI algorithms are invariant to the output scale, the stopping parameter δ_0 (which controls the trade-off between the asymptotic model size and prediction error) is multiplied by the output variance for each output component. The IMTI split error $\alpha_{split} = 0.01\%$, hence a split is only made when there is less than a 0.01% chance that the data in the node came from a single linear model. This low level reduces the number of incorrect splits when testing many times. In addition a node is only split if each new leaf contains at least $3d$ examples. The IMTI pruning error $\alpha_{prune} = 0.1\%$. The number of candidates $\kappa = 10$ for Slow-IMTI. SUPPORT uses $v=10$ and MINDAT=30 unless otherwise stated. Both IMTI and SUPPORT are implemented with Gaussian smoothing [3] and a smoothing parameter $\rho = 4$. Further parameters in RFWR and SUPPORT limit the number of linear models, resulting in a certain degree of asymptotic error. These parameters are optimised in each domain to give the best predictions while keeping the model complexities within a comparable range.

Training is performed using a single stream of non-repeating examples, such as would be obtained by an agent in the real world. The batch SUPPORT algorithm is re-run for each point on the following graphs. Results show the mean of 20 trials, and error bars and numerical errors reported in tables indicate one unbiased estimate of the standard deviation.

5.1 2D Test Function

Initial tests are performed using the same function as Schaal and Atkeson [2],

$$y = \max\left\{e^{-10x_1^2}, e^{-50x_2^2}, 1.25e^{-5(x_1^2+x_2^2)}\right\} + \epsilon$$

where ϵ is independent zero-mean Gaussian noise with variance σ^2 and $\sigma = 0.1$. Training examples are drawn uniformly from the square $-1 \leq x_1 \leq +1, -1 \leq x_2 \leq +1$. The algorithms are tested using 2000 examples drawn in a similar manner, but without noise.

The stopping parameter $\delta_0 = 0.01$ for Fast-IMTI and $\delta_0 = 0.005$ for Slow-IMTI. RFWR uses the parameters published in Schaal and Atkeson [2] and learning rates set to 250. SUPPORT uses $f = 0.1$ and $\eta = 0.4$.

Figure 1a compares the normalised root mean square errors (nRMSE) showing that all algorithms converge to a similar accuracy. Figure 1b compares the training performances, demonstrating the linear scaling of the IMTI algorithms with the number of examples and the clear computational advantage of Fast-IMTI.

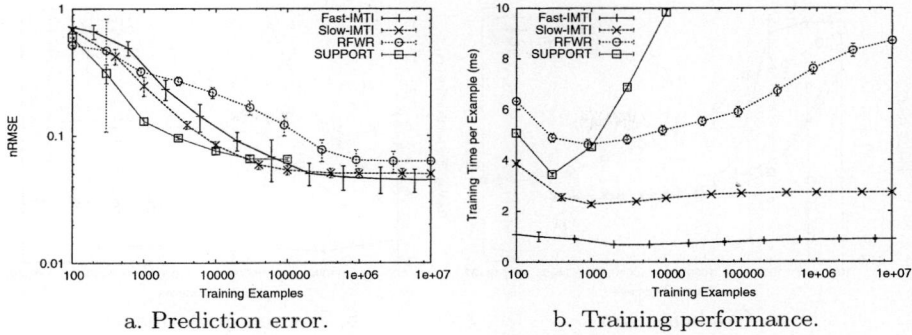

a. Prediction error.   b. Training performance.

Fig. 1. Comparison of algorithms on the 2D test function.

5.2 Pendulum in Continuous Time

A pendulum rotating 360° around a pivot P is a simple non-linear dynamic environment with a closed form for the gradient, allowing gradient errors to be examined. The dynamic model of the pendulum can be written

$$\dot{\mathbf{z}} = \begin{bmatrix} 0 & 1 \\ -\frac{g\sin\theta}{l\theta} & -\frac{\mu}{ml^2} \end{bmatrix} \mathbf{z} + \begin{bmatrix} 0 \\ \frac{1}{ml^2} \end{bmatrix} u \qquad (5)$$

where $\mathbf{z} = [\theta \; \dot{\theta}]^T$, θ is the pendulum angle, g is gravity, $m = l = 1$ are the mass and length of the pendulum, $\mu = 0.1$ is a drag coefficient and u is the torque applied to the pendulum. Define $\mathbf{x} = [\mathbf{z}^T \; u]^T$ and $\mathbf{y} = \dot{\mathbf{z}} + \epsilon$ where ϵ is a vector of independent zero-mean Gaussian noise with variance σ^2 and $\sigma = 0.1$. Training examples of $\langle \mathbf{y}, \mathbf{x} \rangle$ are drawn uniformly from the input domain $-\pi \leq \theta \leq +\pi, -5 \leq \dot{\theta} \leq +5$ and $-5 \leq u \leq +5$. The algorithms are tested using 5000 examples drawn in a similar manner, but without noise.

The stopping parameter $\delta_0 = 2 \times 10^{-4}$ for Fast-IMTI and $\delta_0 = 2 \times 10^{-5}$ for Slow-IMTI. The RFWR initial distance metric $\mathbf{D}_0 = 5\mathbf{I}$, the penalty $\gamma = 10^{-9}$ and the learning rates are 100. SUPPORT uses the parameters $f=0.1$ and $\eta=0.5$.

Figure 2 compares the gradient errors nRMSE(Grad) (defined in [3]) and training times. Again Fast-IMTI has a clear computational advantage although it suffers from a period of slow initial learning.

5.3 Flight Simulator

Learning to fly an aeroplane is a complex high-dimensional task. These experiments use the same simulator as previously published work [15]. The system is sampled 4 times per second, and 6 state measurements (altitude, roll, pitch, yaw rate, climb rate and air speed) combine with 4 actions (2 stick directions, thrust and flaps) to make a 10 dimensional regressor vector $\mathbf{x}$. The learning task is to predict the 6 values of the next state.

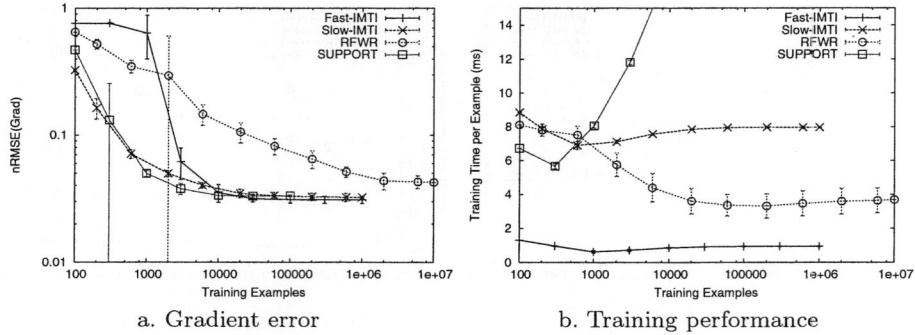

a. Gradient error　　　　　　　b. Training performance

Fig. 2. Comparison of algorithms on the continuous pendulum.

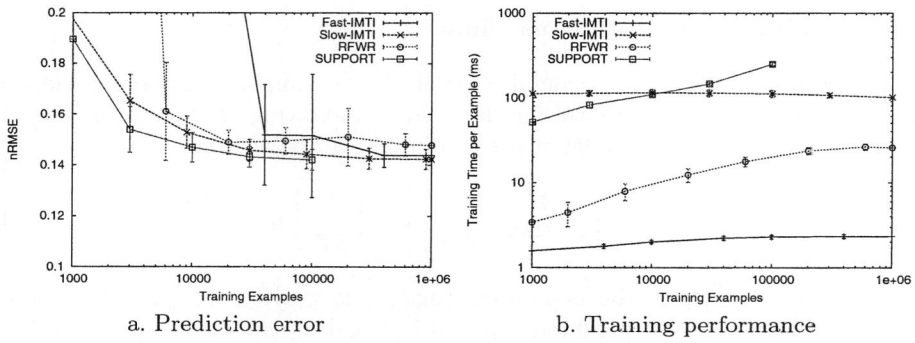

a. Prediction error　　　　　　　b. Training performance

Fig. 3. Comparison of algorithms on the flight simulator.

Training examples are taken directly from a trace of the aircraft flying so that successive regressors are highly correlated. Simulated turbulence is set to the highest level resulting in complex noise characteristics that deviate substantially from the independent Gaussian assumption. The algorithms are tested using 10,000 examples randomly drawn from a similar trace.

The stopping parameter $\delta_0 = 0.005$ for both Fast-IMTI and Slow-IMTI. The RFWR initial distance metric $\mathbf{D}_0 = 2.5\mathbf{I}$, the penalty $\gamma = 10^{-6}$ and the learning rates are 1000. SUPPORT uses the parameters MINDAT=50, $f=0.2$ and $\eta=0.5$.

Figure 3a compares the prediction errors and shows that although Fast-IMTI eventually converges to an accurate approximation, it takes significantly longer to do so. All three model tree algorithms appear to converge to a more accurate model than RFWR. Figure 3b compares the training times[1], showing the large computational advantage of Fast-IMTI in this higher dimensional problem.

---

[1] Note the log-log scale, and that the flight experiments were performed on a different platform and performance cannot be compared directly with Figs. 1b and 2b.

Table 2. Model complexities.

	TOTAL NUMBER OF LOCAL LINEAR MODELS		
	2D TEST FUNCTION	PENDULUM	FLIGHT SIMULATOR
Fast-IMTI	89±11	27±2	24±6
Slow-IMTI	58±4	27±1	58±17
RFWR	92±3	28±4	42±6
SUPPORT	61±3	25±1	45±7

5.4 Model Complexities

Table 2 compares the complexities of the models built by each algorithm in each domain. The local models in the leaves of the model trees are simple linear models that predict only a single output component and contain d parameters, however the local RFWR models are multivariate linear models predicting all output components which each contain $d \times n$ parameters. Therefore the model tree representation is significantly more compact for the pendulum and flight simulator. Slow-IMTI learns a simpler model than Fast-IMTI for the lower dimensional problems, although Fast-IMTI appears to construct a more efficient representation for the complex flight simulator.

6 Conclusions and Future Work

This paper introduces a fast new splitting rule (Fast-IMTI) for the incremental induction of linear model trees. The splitting rule requires that only a single linear model is built in each leaf of the tree, and is therefore significantly faster than our previous algorithm (Slow-IMTI) in which a linear model is constructed on each side of every candidate split in each leaf. The training time for the new splitting rule scales $O(d^2)$ with dimensionality compared with $O(d^3)$ for Slow-IMTI [3]. This explains the pronounced difference between the Fast-IMTI and Slow-IMTI training times for the flight simulator where $d = 10$. The Fast-IMTI algorithm is also significantly faster than the alternative non-parametric incremental learner RFWR in all domains tested.

All three model tree learners form a more efficient representation than RFWR, giving more accurate predictions from a smaller model. In addition they do not require a metric over the input space and there are no learning rates to be tuned, thus avoiding a major cause of instability in many gradient descent systems. However the Fast-IMTI algorithm does appear to suffer from slow initial learning, especially in the more complex domains. It is therefore most effective when processing resources are limited but training data is abundant. One possible area for investigation is a combination of the two IMTI algorithms that exhibits the best features of each.

Future work will also concentrate on integrating system identification and control. Nakanishi et al. [16] have developed a provably stable adaptive controller based on the representation learnt by RFWR, and perhaps a similar approach can be applied to incrementally induced linear model trees.

References

1. Slotine, J., Li, W.: Applied nonlinear control. Prentice-Hall (1991)
2. Schaal, S., Atkeson, C.: Constructive incremental learning from only local information. Neural Computation **10** (1998) 2047–2084
3. Potts, D.: Incremental learning of linear model trees. In: Proceedings of the 21st International Conference on Machine Learning. (2004)
4. Frank, E., Wang, Y., Inglis, S., Holmes, G., Witten, I.: Using model trees for classification. Machine Learning **32** (1998) 63–76
5. Quinlan, J.: Combining instance-based and model-based learning. In: Proceedings of the 10th International Conference on Machine Learning. (1993) 236–243
6. Karalic, A.: Employing linear regression in regression tree leaves. In: Proceedings of the 10th European Conference on Artificial Intelligence. (1992) 440–441
7. Malerba, D., Appice, A., Bellino, A., Ceci, M., Pallotta, D.: Stepwise induction of model trees. In: AI*IA 2001: Advances in Artificial Intelligence, Lecture Notes in Artificial Intelligence **2175**. Springer (2001)
8. Dobra, A., Gehrke, J.: SECRET: A scalable linear regression tree algorithm. In: Proceedings of the 8th ACM SIGKDD International Conference on Knowledge Discovery and Data Mining. (2002)
9. Li, K., Lue, H., Chen, C.: Interactive tree-structured regression via principal Hessian directions. Journal of the American Statistical Association **95** (2000) 547–560
10. Utgoff, P., Berkman, N., Clouse, J.: Decision tree induction based on efficient tree restructuring. Machine Learning **29** (1997) 5–44
11. Munos, R., Moore, A.: Variable resolution discretization in optimal control. Machine Learning **49** (2002) 291–323
12. Chaudhuri, P., Huang, M., Loh, W., Yao, R.: Piecewise-polynomial regression trees. Statistica Sinica **4** (1994) 143–167
13. Loh, W.: Regression trees with unbiased variable selection and interaction detection. Statistica Sinica **12** (2002) 361–386
14. Vijayakumar, S., Schaal, S.: Locally weighted projection regression: Incremental real time learning in high dimensional space. In: Proceedings of the 17th International Conference on Machine Learning. (2000) 1079–1086
15. Isaac, A., Sammut, C.: Goal-directed learning to fly. In: Proceedings of the 20th International Conference of Machine Learning. (2003) 258–265
16. Nakanishi, J., Farrell, J., Schaal, S.: A locally weighted learning composite adaptive controller with structure adaptation. In: IEEE International Conference on Intelligent Robots and Systems. (2002)

A Modified Incremental Principal Component Analysis for On-Line Learning of Feature Space and Classifier

Seiichi Ozawa[1], Shaoning Pang[2], and Nikola Kasabov[2]

[1] Graduate School of Science and Technology, Kobe University
1-1 Rokko-dai, Nada-ku, Kobe 657-8501, Japan
ozawasei@kobe-u.ac.jp
[2] Knowledge Engineering & Discover Research Institute
Auckland University of Technology, Private Bag 92006,
Auckland 1020, New Zealand
{shaoning.pang,nik.kasabov}@aut.ac.nz

Abstract. We have proposed a new concept for pattern classification systems in which feature selection and classifier learning are simultaneously carried out on-line. To realize this concept, Incremental Principal Component Analysis (IPCA) and Evolving Clustering Method (ECM) was effectively combined in the previous work. However, in order to construct a desirable feature space, a threshold value to determine the increase of a new feature shoule be properly given in the original IPCA. To alleviate this problem, we can adopt the accumulation ratio as its criterion. However, in incremental situations, the accumulation ratio must be modified every time a new sample is given. Therefore, to use this ratio as a criterion, we also need to develop a one-pass update algorithm for the ratio. In this paper, we propose an improved algorithm of IPCA in which the accumulation ratio as well as the feature space can be updated on-line without all the past samples. To see if correct feature construction is carried out by this new IPCA algorithm, the recognition performance is evaluated for some standard datasets when ECM is adopted as a prototype learning method in Nearest Neighbor classifier.

1 Introduction

In real-world applications such as pattern recognition, we often confront difficult situations where a complete set of training samples is not given in advance. In face recognition tasks, for example, human faces have large variations depending on expressions, lighting conditions, make-up, hairstyles, and so forth. When a human is registered in a person identification system, it is difficult to consider all variations in face images in the first place [1]. Another difficulty in the realistic recognition problems lies in the uncertainty of data distribution; that is, we cannot know what training samples will appear in the future. Hence, it is quite difficult to extract essential features only from initially given training samples.

To solve these problems, we should select appropriate features on-line based on the property of an input data stream. This means that not only classifier but also feature space must be incrementally trained. For this purpose, a new concept of incremental learning have been proposed in which the feature selection and classifier learning are simultaneously carried out on-line [2, 3]. One of the great advantages in this concept is that classification systems can improve their performance constantly even if an insufficient number of training samples are given at the early stage, often resulting in inappropriate selection of features and poor classifier performance.

To realize the above two desirable characteristics in recognition systems, we have proposed a one-pass incremental learning scheme which consists of Incremental Principal Component Analysis (IPCA) [4] and Evolving Clustering Method (ECM) [5]. In order to construct a proper feature space, however, a suitable threshold value to determine the dimensional augmentation should be given in IPCA; this optimization often leads to annoying parameter search. This paper presents a remedy for this problem by introducing the accumulation ratio into IPCA as its criterion. Since the accumulation ratio is usually calculated from all the given samples, in order to develop one-pass incremental learning algorithm for feature space and classifier, we have to devise an incremental update algorithm for this ratio without keeping any past training samples.

2 Incremental Principal Component Analysis (IPCA)

2.1 Original IPCA Algorithm

Principal Component Analysis (PCA) is one of the most popular and powerful feature extraction techniques in pattern classification problems. Although PCA is not suited for incremental learning purposes, Hall and Martin have devised a method to update eigenvectors and eigenvalues in an incremental way [4].

Assume that N training samples $\boldsymbol{x}_i \in \mathcal{R}^n$ ($i = 1, \cdots, N$) have been presented so far, and an eigenspace model $\Omega = (\bar{\boldsymbol{x}}, \boldsymbol{U}, \boldsymbol{\Lambda}, N)$ is constructed by calculating the eigenvectors and eigenvalues from the covariance matrix of $\boldsymbol{x}_i$, where $\bar{\boldsymbol{x}}$ is a mean input vector, $\boldsymbol{U}$ is a $n \times k$ matrix whose column vectors correspond to the eigenvectors, and $\boldsymbol{\Lambda}$ is a $k \times k$ matrix whose diagonal elements correspond to the eigenvalues. Here, k is the number of dimensions of the current eigenspace.

Let us consider the case that the $(N+1)$th training sample $\boldsymbol{y}$ is presented. The addition of this new sample will lead to the changes in both of the mean vector and covariance matrix; therefore, the eigenvectors and eigenvalues should also be recalculated. The mean input vector $\bar{\boldsymbol{x}}$ is easily updated as follows:

$$\bar{\boldsymbol{x}}' = \frac{1}{N+1}(N\bar{\boldsymbol{x}} + \boldsymbol{y}). \quad (1)$$

The problem is how to update the eigenvectors and eigenvalues.

When the eigenspace model Ω is reconstructed to adapt to a new sample, we must check if the dimensions of the eigenspace should be changed or not. If the new sample has almost all energy in the current eigenspace, the dimensional augmentation is not needed in reconstructing the eigenspace. However, if it has some energy in the complementary space to the current eigenspace, the dimensional augmentation cannot be avoided. This can be judged from the norm of the following residue vector $\boldsymbol{h}$:

$$\boldsymbol{h} = (\boldsymbol{y} - \bar{\boldsymbol{x}}) - \boldsymbol{U}\boldsymbol{g} \tag{2}$$

where

$$\boldsymbol{g} = \boldsymbol{U}^T(\boldsymbol{y} - \bar{\boldsymbol{x}}). \tag{3}$$

Here, T means the transposition of vectors and matrices. When the norm of $\boldsymbol{h}$ is larger than a threshold value η, it must allow the number of dimensions to increase from k to $k+1$, and the current eigenspace must be expanded in the direction of $\boldsymbol{h}$. Otherwise, the number of dimensions remains the same.

It has been shown that the eigenvectors and eigenvalues should be updated based on the solution of the following intermediate eigenproblem [4]:

$$\left(\frac{N}{N+1} \begin{bmatrix} \boldsymbol{\Lambda} & \boldsymbol{0} \\ \boldsymbol{0}^T & 0 \end{bmatrix} + \frac{N}{(N+1)^2} \begin{bmatrix} \boldsymbol{g}\boldsymbol{g}^T & \gamma\boldsymbol{g} \\ \gamma\boldsymbol{g}^T & \gamma^2 \end{bmatrix} \right) \boldsymbol{R} = \boldsymbol{R}\boldsymbol{\Lambda}' \tag{4}$$

where $\gamma = \tilde{\boldsymbol{h}}^T(\boldsymbol{y} - \bar{\boldsymbol{x}})$, $\boldsymbol{R}$ is a $(k+1) \times (k+1)$ matrix whose column vectors correspond to the eigenvectors obtained from the above intermediate eigenproblem, $\boldsymbol{\Lambda}'$ is the new eigenvalue matrix, and $\boldsymbol{0}$ is a k-dimensional zero vector. Using $\boldsymbol{R}$, we can calculate the new $n \times (k+1)$ eigenvector matrix $\boldsymbol{U}'$ as follows:

$$\boldsymbol{U}' = [\boldsymbol{U}, \hat{\boldsymbol{h}}]\boldsymbol{R} \tag{5}$$

where

$$\hat{\boldsymbol{h}} = \begin{cases} \boldsymbol{h}/\|\boldsymbol{h}\| & \text{if } \|\boldsymbol{h}\| > \eta \\ \boldsymbol{0} & \text{otherwise.} \end{cases} \tag{6}$$

Here, η is a small threshold value which is set to zero in the original IPCA [4]. As you can see from Eq. (5), $\boldsymbol{R}$ operates to rotate the eigenvectors; hence, let us call $\boldsymbol{R}$ a rotation matrix in the following. Note that if $\hat{\boldsymbol{h}} = \boldsymbol{0}$, $\boldsymbol{R}$ degenerates into a $n \times k$ matrix; that is, the dimensions of the updated eigenspace remains the same as those of the previous eigenspace.

2.2 A New Criterion for Increasing Eigenspace Dimensionality

As seen in Eq. (6), the dimensional augmentation is carried out whenever the norm of a residue vector is larger than a threshold value η. However, this is not a good criterion in practice because a suitable threshold can be varied depending on the magnitude of input values. If the threshold is too small, we cannot get an efficient feature space with small dimensions; this may result in deteriorating generalization performance and computational efficiency.

To reduce this dependency in determining appropriate feature space dimensions, the following accumulation ratio is often used as its criterion:

$$A(k) = \frac{\sum_{i=1}^{k} \lambda_i}{\sum_{j=1}^{n} \lambda_j} \tag{7}$$

where λ_i is the ith largest eigenvalue, k and n are the numbers of dimensions of the current feature space and input space, respectively. By specifying an appropriate threshold value θ, we can determine the feature space dimensions by searching for a minimum k such that $A(k) > \theta$ holds. In general, the update of Eq. (7) cannot be done without the training samples given previously. This is a serious problem when we device a one-pass incremental learning algorithm. To solve this problem, we propose an incremental update algorithm of $A(k)$ without keeping all the past training samples.

First let us consider the numerator of Eq. (7). Using the fact that the total amount of eigenvalues is equivalent to the summation of variances σ_i^2, the numerator is given by

$$\sum_{i=1}^{k} \lambda_i = \sum_{i=1}^{k} \sigma_i^2 = \frac{1}{N} \sum_{i=1}^{k} \sum_{j=1}^{N} \{u_i^T (x^{(j)} - \bar{x})\}^2 \tag{8}$$

where u_i is the ith column vector of U.

Assume that a new sample y is given, the new mean $u_i^T \bar{x}'$ of feature values on u_i is calculated as follows:

$$u_i^T \bar{x}' = \frac{1}{N+1} u_i^T (N\bar{x} + y) \tag{9}$$

From Eqs. (8) and (9), the total amount of new eigenvalues is given by

$$\sum_{i=1}^{k} \lambda_i' = \sum_{i=1}^{k} \sigma_i'^2 = \sum_{i=1}^{k} \frac{1}{N+1} \left[\sum_{j=1}^{N} \{u_i^T (x^{(j)} - \bar{x}')\}^2 + \{u_i^T (y - \bar{x}')\}^2 \right]$$

$$= \frac{N}{N+1} \sum_{i=1}^{k} \lambda_i + \frac{N}{(N+1)^2} \|U_k^T (y - \bar{x})\|^2 \tag{10}$$

where $U_k = \{u_1, \cdots, u_k\}$. In the similar manner, the denominator in Eq. (7) is also obtained as follows:

$$\sum_{i=1}^{k} \lambda_i' = \frac{N}{N+1} \sum_{i=1}^{n} \lambda_i + \frac{N}{(N+1)^2} \|y - \bar{x}\|^2. \tag{11}$$

Then, the following new ratio $A'(k)$ is calculated from Eqs. (10) and (11):

$$A'(k) = \frac{N(N+1) \sum_{i=1}^{k} \lambda_i + N\|U_k^T (y - \bar{x})\|^2}{N(N+1) \sum_{i=1}^{n} \lambda_i + N\|y - \bar{x}\|^2} \tag{12}$$

Note that no past samples are needed for the incremental update of $A'(k)$ here.

In the proposed method, the dimensional augmentation is judged from the accumulation ratio $A(k)$. Hence, the new eigenvector matrix U' in Eq. (5) is modified as follows:

$$U' = [U, \hat{h}]R \tag{13}$$

where

$$\hat{h} = \begin{cases} h/\|h\| & \text{if } A(k) < \theta \\ 0 & \text{otherwise.} \end{cases} \qquad (14)$$

Here, θ is a threshold value.

3 Proposed Learning Scheme

3.1 Incremental Prototype Update for k-NN Classifier

As stated in Section 2, IPCA is utilized for reducing the dimensions of input data and constructing an appropriate feature space based on an incoming data stream. In IPCA, depending on input data, the following two operations are carried out: eigen-axes rotation and dimensional augmentation of a feature space. On the other hand, ECM can evolve the prototypes which correspond to the representative points in the feature space constructed by IPCA. Hence, when the rotation and dimensional augmentation are carried out, all prototypes must be modified so as to keep the consistency between the old and new eigenspaces.

Let the jth prototype in the current eigenspace $\Omega = (\bar{x}, U, \Lambda, N)$ be $\tilde{p}_j$ ($j = 1, \cdots, L$) and let the corresponding prototype in the original input space be p_j. Here, L is the number of prototypes. For these two prototypes, the following relation holds:

$$\tilde{p}_j = U^T(p_j - \bar{x}). \qquad (15)$$

Assume that the $(N+1)$th sample y is added and the eigenspace Ω is updated by $\Omega' = (\bar{x}', U', \Lambda', N+1)$. Substituting Eqs. (1) and (5) into Eq. (15), the updated prototypes $\tilde{p}'_j$ are given as follows [3]:

$$\tilde{p}'_j = U'^T(p_j - \bar{x}') = R^T \begin{bmatrix} \tilde{p}_j \\ \hat{h}^T(p_j - \bar{x}) \end{bmatrix} + \frac{1}{N+1} U'^T(\bar{x} - y). \qquad (16)$$

When no dimensional augmentation is needed, $\hat{h} = 0$ holds from Eq. (6). Then, Eq. (16) reduces to

$$\tilde{p}'_j = R^T \tilde{p}_j + \frac{1}{N+1} U'^T(\bar{x} - y) \qquad (17)$$

where no information on p_j is needed in the prototype update. However, when the dimensional augmentation as well as the rotation occurs, the original prototypes p_j are necessary for the exact calculation of the new prototype $\tilde{p}'_j$. That is to say, unless we keep the original prototypes in memory, it is impossible to carry out this prototype update.

To do that, we have proposed the approximation for the first term in the right hand side of Eq. (16):

$$\tilde{p}'_j \simeq R^T [\tilde{p}_j^T, 0]^T + \frac{1}{N+1} U'^T(\bar{x} - y) \qquad (18)$$

where $[\tilde{\boldsymbol{p}}_j^T, 0]^T$ is a $(k+1)$-dimensional column vector which is given by adding a zero element to the current prototype $\tilde{\boldsymbol{p}}_j$. This approach is efficient in memory use, but we have to mind the approximation error when the accumulation ratio for the feature space is not so large.

3.2 Learning Algorithm

Let us assume that a small number of training samples are given in advance to form an initial eigenspace. Then, the proposed one-pass incremental learning algorithm is shown below:

Step 0: Calculate the eigenvector matrix $\boldsymbol{U}$ and eigenvalue matrix $\boldsymbol{\Lambda}$ from the covariance matrix of initial training samples. Calculate the projection of all the initial training samples $\boldsymbol{x}_i$ into the eigenspace to obtain the feature vectors $\tilde{\boldsymbol{x}}_i$. Apply ECM (see the details in [6]) to these feature vectors, and obtain the prototypes $\tilde{\boldsymbol{p}}_j$.

Step 1: Apply IPCA to the $(N+1)$th training sample $\boldsymbol{y}$ and update the current eigenspace model $\Omega = (\bar{\boldsymbol{x}}, \boldsymbol{U}, \boldsymbol{\Lambda}, N)$ as follows:
  1. Solve an intermediate eigenproblem in Eq. (4) to obtain a rotation matrix $\boldsymbol{R}$ and an eigenvalue matrix $\boldsymbol{\Lambda}'$.
  2. Update the accumulation ratio $A'(k)$ based on Eq. (12).
  3. Update the mean input vector $\bar{\boldsymbol{x}}'$ and eigenvector matrix $\boldsymbol{U}'$ based on Eqs. (1) and (13), respectively.
  4. Increase the total number of training samples N by one.

Step 2: If the dimensional augmentation is not needed in IPCA, update all the current prototypes $\tilde{\boldsymbol{p}}_j$ based on Eq. (17). Otherwise, update them based on Eq. (18).

Step 3: For the training sample $\boldsymbol{y}$, obtain the feature vectors $\tilde{\boldsymbol{y}}$ using the updated eigenvector matrix $\boldsymbol{U}'$ and mean vector $\bar{\boldsymbol{x}}'$ as follows: $\tilde{\boldsymbol{y}} = \boldsymbol{U}'^T(\boldsymbol{y} - \bar{\boldsymbol{x}}')$

Step 4: Apply ECM to $\tilde{\boldsymbol{y}}$, and obtain the updated prototypes $\tilde{\boldsymbol{p}}_{j'}$.

Step 5: Go back to Step 1.

When a query input is presented for classification purpose, the distances to all the prototypes are calculated, and then the k nearest neighbor (k-NN) method can be applied to determine the class. Note that the classification process is carried out on-line during the training of the feature space and prototypes. However, we do not need any modification on the k-NN classifier even if the rotation and augmentation are carried out, because this classifier uses only the distance between a query input and a prototype.

4 Experiments

To investigate the effectiveness of the proposed incremental learning scheme, the performance is evaluated for the three standard datasets in UCI Machine Learning Repository [7]: Segmentation data, Vowel data, and Sonar data. The dataset information is summarized in Table 1. In the Sonar dataset, the training

Table 1. Evaluated UCI datasets. The item 'accuracy' means the highest accuracy shown on the UCI web site [7].

name	input dim.	class	train. data	test data	accuracy [%]
Segmentation	19	7	210	2100	-
Vowel	10	11	528	462	56
Sonar	60	2	208	-	83

and test samples are not divided. Hence, we split this dataset into two halves, and the evaluations are conducted through two-fold cross-validation.

Before the learning starts, first we construct an initial feature space using a small portion of training samples; that is, these training samples are used for calculating eigenvectors and their eigenvalues through conventional PCA. While the incremental learning is carried out, training samples are randomly drawn from the rest of the training dataset one by one, then the eigenspace is updated by IPCA shown in Section 2. Since the events of incremental learning may not happen at regular time intervals, we use the term *incremental learning stages* instead of the usual time scale. Here, the number of learning stages is equivalent to the number of all training samples that are not used as the initial dataset.

4.1 Study on Threshold Value η

In the original IPCA, the threshold value η in Eq. (6) is set to zero. However, since the norms of residue vectors are rarely zero in practice, a small value is usually set to η to avoid generating a redundant feature space. As easily expected, if the value is too large, a compact feature space is acquired but the performance may get worse due to the lost of useful information. Generally, it is not easy to find a suitable η and it may be varied depending on the scale of input data.

As a preliminary experiment, let us see the influence of η to the recognition performance. Here, Nearest Neighbor (NN) classifier is used for evaluating the recognition performance. The prototypes for NN classifier are trained by ECM in which the same training dataset as in IPCA is used. The training of the feature space and prototypes are conducted based on the procedure shown in 3.2.

Figure 1 shows typical time courses of recognition accuracy, accumulation ratio, and feature space dimensions. In these experiments, η are varied from 0.1 to 1.2, and 10% of the entire training samples are used for obtaining initial eigen spaces; that is, the remaining 90% samples are trained one by one. As you can see from Fig. 1, the influences of η to the recognition accuracy and the generated feature space are quite different depending on the datasets. In Sonar data, it seems that η greatly influence to the construction of feature spaces. If $\eta = 1.2$, the small dimensional feature space is generated but the recognition accuracy is deteriorated due to the low accumulation ratio. If $\eta = 0.1$, the best accuracy is acquired but the dimensions of the feature space become very large. On the other hand, for Vowel data and Segmentation data, there are less influence of η to both accuracy and dimensions. These results indicate that the threshold value η should be optimized for each dataset.

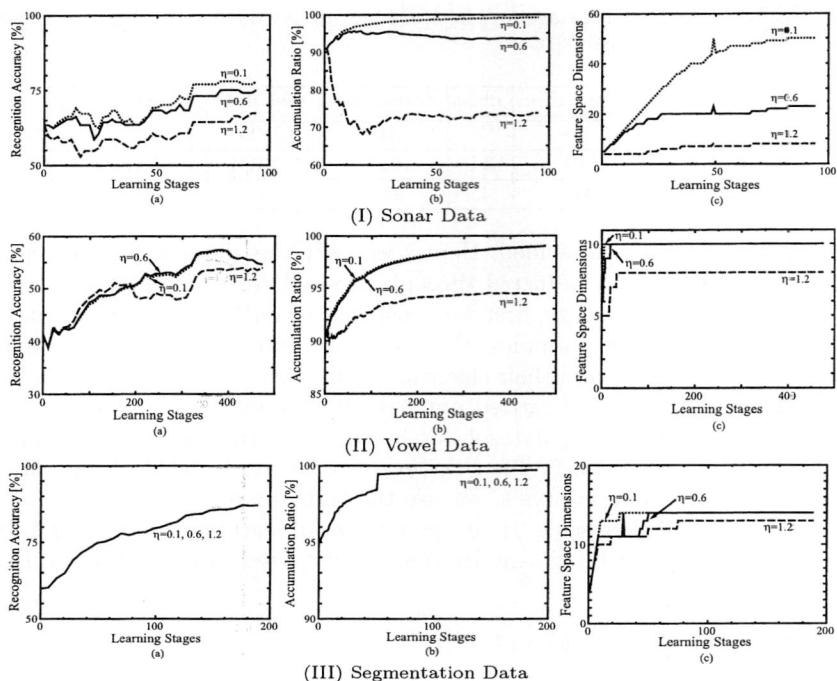

Fig. 1. Typical time courses of (a) recognition accuracy [%], (b) accumulation ratio [%], and (c) feature space dimensions when the original IPCA is applied.

The proposed method mentioned in 3.2 can be adopted to avoid such a nuisance optimization. In the next experiment, the recognition performance and appropriateness of acquired feature spaces are evaluated for the modified IPCA using the above three UCI datasets.

4.2 Evaluation of Proposed IPCA

Even in the proposed IPCA, a threshold value θ in Eq. (14) for the accumulation ratio must be properly given in order to specify how much signal energy should be retained to construct effective feature spaces. To find appropriate threshold values, θ is varied from 0.85 to 0.999 here. In general, the performance of incremental learning depends on the order of giving training samples. Hence, we shall evaluate the performance averaged over ten different learning conditions (i.e., ten different streams of training samples). To see the effectiveness of incremental feature construction, the evaluation for initial feature spaces is also carried out for comparative purposes. More concretely, the eigenvectors are selected only from an initial training set such that the accumulation ration is over 0.999, and the feature space spanned by these eigenvectors is fixed over the entire learning stages but the prototype learning is carried out by ECM.

Tables 2(a)-(c) show the recognition accuracy, accumulation ratio $A(k)$, and dimensions of feature space k at the final incremental learning stage for the

Table 2. Recognition accuracy [%], accumulation ratio $A(k)$, and dimensions of feature space k at the final incremental learning stage for the three UCI datasets: (a) Sonar data, (b) Vowel, and (c) Segmentation. In PCA, the feature space is calculated only from an initial training set, and then it is fixed over the entire learning stages.

(a) Sonar

	$\theta=0.85$	$\theta=0.9$	$\theta=0.95$	$\theta=0.999$	PCA
Accuracy [%]	77.8	79.4	80.0	79.4	76.2
$A(k)$ [%]	85.6	90.4	95.2	99.9	70.9
k	15.3	19.5	26.5	53.5	9

(b) Vowel

	$\theta=0.85$	$\theta=0.9$	$\theta=0.95$	$\theta=0.999$	PCA
Accuracy (%)	55.4	56.3	57.8	56.0	56.5
$A(k)$ (%)	87.2	92.3	96.6	100	100
k	6.1	7.2	8.2	10	10

(c) Segmentation

	$\theta=0.85$	$\theta=0.9$	$\theta=0.95$	$\theta=0.999$	PCA
Accuracy (%)	79.4	80.9	81.4	87.3	79.5
$A(k)$ (%)	94.3	96.8	97.8	100	86.4
k	4.4	4.6	4.8	8.6	6

three UCI datasets. In any case, the percentage of initial training samples is set to 10%.

As seen from the results, we can find some threshold values that gives better final recognition accuracy as compared with the results of PCA. Moreover, this final accuracy increases when a large threshold value θ is given. For Sonar data and Vowel data, it seems that there is an optimal value for θ around 0.95. Comparing the feature space dimensions k in these two cases with the previous results in Fig. 1 (see the cases of $\eta = 0.1$ or 0.6), we can see that high-performance compact feature spaces are constructed by the proposed IPCA. It is considered that this result comes from the property of the proposed IPCA; that is, keeping the accumulation ratio at a specified value throughout the learning stages seems to be effective to construct efficient (i.e., low-dimensional) feature spaces.

For Segmentation data, on the other hand, the optimal θ is 0.999 and the accumulation ration $A(k)$ becomes 100%. This result shows that the optimal θ can be different depending on the datasets. However, since we know by experience that there is an optimal value around 0.95 in many cases, we can easily search for the optimal value using the cross-validation. This optimization process is much easier than the search for the optimal value of η in the original IPCA.

5 Conclusions and Future Works

In our previous works [2, 3], we have proposed an adaptive evolving connectionist model in which Incremental Principal Component Analysis (IPCA) and Evolving

Clustering Method (ECM) are effectively combined. This learning scheme gives a new concept for pattern recognition systems: feature selection and classifier learning are simultaneously carried out on-line.

In order to construct a proper feature space based on this approach, a suitable threshold value to determine the dimensional augmentation should be given in the IPCA algorithm. This optimization often needs a little annoying process; therefore, the accumulation ratio is introduced into IPCA as its criterion. To implement this approach, first we devised the incremental update algorithm for the accumulation ratio without the past training samples. Next, we presented a new incremental learning scheme for feature space and classifier. From several experiments using the three standard datasets in UCI machine learning repository, we verified that the proposed IPCA worked well without elaborating sensitive parameter optimization and its recognition accuracy outperforms that of the previously proposed learning scheme [3].

There are still several open problems. One is that the computation costs for feature space update could be expensive especially for large dimensional data because the current IPCA algorithm must be applied to each given training sample. To alleviate this problem, we should introduce a batch-mode learning strategy into IPCA. Another problem is that the eigen-features are not always effective for classification purposes. Recently kernel PCA is widely noticed as high-performance features; hence, the extension of incremental learning approach to kernel PCA should be our next research target.

References

1. S. L. Toh and S. Ozawa, "A Face Recognition System Using Neural Networks with Incremental Learning Ability," *Proc. 8th Australian and New Zealand Conf. on Intelligent Information Systems*, pp. 389-394 (2003)
2. S. Pang, S. Ozawa, and N. Kasabov, "One-pass Incremental Membership Authentication by Face Classification," *Proc Int. Conf. on Biometric Authentication 2004* (in press)
3. S. Ozawa, S. Pang, and N. Kasabov, "On-line Feature Selection for Adaptive Evolving Connectionist Systems," *Proc Int. Conf. on Fuzzy Systems & Innovational Computing 2004* (in press)
4. P. Hall and R. Martin, "Incremental Eigenanalysis for Classification," *Proc. British Machine Vision Conference*, vol. 1, pp. 286-295 (1998)
5. N. Kasabov, *Evolving Connectionist Systems: Methods and Applications in Bioinformatics, Brain Study and Intelligent Machines*. Springer-Verlag (2002)
6. N. Kasabov and Q. Song, "DENFIS: Dynamic Evolving Neuro-fuzzy Inference System and Its Application for Time-series Prediction," *IEEE Trans. on Fuzzy systems*, vol. 10, no. 2, pp. 144-154 (2002)
7. http://www.ics.uci.edu/mlearn/MLRepository.html

An Evolutionary Approach to the Design of Cellular Automata Architecture for Multiplication in Elliptic Curve Cryptography over Finite Fields[*]

Jun-Cheol Jeon and Kee-Young Yoo

Department of Computer Engineering, Kyungpook National University,
Daegu, 702-701 Korea
jcjeon33@infosec.knu.ac.kr, yook@bh.knu.ac.kr

Abstract. Cellular Automata (CA) has been used in evolutionary computation for over a decade and Elliptic Curve Cryptography (ECC) has recently received a lot of attention due to their important and practical applications in public key cryptographys. The two elliptic curve operations are the Add and Double, which are computed by field arithmetic operations, such as additions, modular multiplications, modular squarings and divisions. The addition operation for field elements is trivial and squaring is so much faster than regular multiplication. Divisions which are the important contributors for the run time also can be implemented by repeating multiplications. Thus we propose an special and efficient multiplication architecture based on CA in ECC over $GF(2^n)$. The proposed evolutionary computation architectures can be used in the effectual hardware design of coprocessor for ECC since they have high regularity and a reduced latency.

Keywords: Elliptic Curve Cryptography, Finite Fields, Cellular Automata, Evolutionary Computation, Multiplication, Irreducible Polynomial.

1 Introduction

In cryptography, to achieve a high level of security, many of public-key algorithms, that rely on computations in $GF(2^n)$, require large field size, some as large as $GF(2^{2000})$. Hence, there is a need to develop an efficient algorithm for the multiplication in $GF(2^n)$. However, significantly smaller parameters can be used in ECC than in other competitive graphys such RSA and ElGamal, but with equivalent levels of security. Some benefits of having smaller key sizes include faster computations, and reductions in processing power, storage space and bandwidth. This makes ECC ideal for constrained environments such as pagers, PDAs, cellular phones and smart cards [6].

Elliptic Curve Cryptography was introduced by Victor Miller and Neal Koblitz in 1985. ECC proposed as an alternative to established public-key cryptosystem such as RSA and ElGamal, have recently gained a lot attention in industry and academia [1,2].

---

[*] Corresponding Author: Kee-Young Yoo
This work was supported by the Brain Korea 21 Project in 2004.

The main reason for attractiveness of ECC is the fact that there is no sub-exponential algorithm known to solve the discrete logarithm problem on a properly chosen elliptic curve.

The two elliptic curve operations that are most relevant to the complexity of multiplying a group element by a constant are the Add and Double operations, which are composed of field arithmetic operations such as additions, modular multiplications, modular squarings and divisions. The mostly cost field arithmetic operation is division [3]. Moreover the division can be computed by applying AB multiplication repeatedly. Fast computation of an arithmetic operation can generally be classified into two approaches: a faster or smaller architecture design or noble algorithm generation, and this paper focused on the former approach.

Finite field $GF(2^n)$ arithmetic operations have recently been applied in a variety of fields, including cryptography and error-correcting codes [4]. A number of modern public key cryptography systems and schemes, for example, Diffie-Hellman key pre-distribution, the Elgamal cryptosystem, and ECC, require the operations of division, exponentiation, and inversion, which are normally implemented using AB or AB^2 multiplier [5].

Cellular automata, which is introduced by Von Neumann in [7] has been accepted as a good computational model for the simulation of complex physical systems. It has been used for various applications, such as evolutionary computations, parallel processing computations and number theory etc. Zhang in [8] proposed architecture with programmable cellular automata and a cell complexity of 3-SWITCH+2-XOR, while Choudhury in [9] designed an LSB multiplier based on a CA with a cell complexity of 2-AND+2-XOR.

This paper proposes architectures for modular AB multiplication based on CA architecture. We focused on the architectures in ECC, which uses restricted irreducible polynomials, specially, trinomials. The multiplication structure which is firstly attempted using trinomials based on CA architecture has a time complexity of $n(T_{AND}+T_{XOR})$ and hardware complexity of $n(AND+XOR+REGISTER)+XOR$. Our architecture offers a fair area/time performance trade-off.

The remainder of this paper is organized as follows. The conceptional background, including finite fields, ECC, and CA are described in section 2. Section 3 presents the proposed multiplication architecture based on CA using irreducible trinomials. In section 4, we presents discussion and performance analysis. Finally, section 5 gives concluding remarks.

2 Preliminaries

In this section, we present mathematical background in the finite field and ECC, and the characteristics and properties of CA.

2.1 Finite Fields

A finite field or Galois Field(GF), which is a set of finite elements, can be defined by commutative law, associative law, and distributive law and facilitates addition, subtraction, multiplication, and division. Numbers of architectures have already been developed to construct low complexity bit-serial and bit-parallel multiplications using various irreducible polynomials to reduce the complexity of the modular multiplication. Since a polynomial basis operation does not require a basis conversion, it can be readily matched to any input or output system. Also, due to its regularity and simplicity, the ability to design and expand into high-order finite fields with polynomial basis is easier to realize than with other basis operations [10].

The finite field $GF(2^n)$ can be viewed as a vector space of dimension n over $GF(2^n)$. That is, there exists a set of n elements $\{1, \alpha, \ldots, \alpha^{n-2}, \alpha^{n-1}\}$ in $GF(2^n)$ such that each $A \in GF(2^n)$ can be written uniquely in the form $A = \sum A_i \alpha^i$, where $A_i \in \{0,1\}$. This section provides one of the most common based of $GF(2^n)$ over $GF(2)$ [10], polynomial bases. Let $f(x) = x^n + \sum_{i=0}^{n-1} f_i x^i$, where $f_i \in \{0,1\}$, for $i = 0, 1, \ldots, n-1$, be an irreducible polynomial of degree m over $GF(2)$. For each irreducible polynomial, there exists a polynomial basis representation. In such a representation, each element of $GF(2^n)$ corresponds to a binary polynomial of degree less than n. This is, for $A \in GF(2^n)$ there exist n numbers $A_i \in \{0,1\}$ such that $A = A_{n-1}\alpha^{n-1} + A_{n-2}\alpha^{n-2} \ldots + A_1\alpha + A_0$.

The field element $A \in GF(2^n)$ is usually denoted by the bit string $(A_{n-1} \ldots A_1 A_0)$ of length n. The following operations are defined on the elements of $GF(2^n)$ when using a polynomial representation with irreducible polynomial $f(x)$. Assume that $A = (A_{n-1} \ldots A_1 A_0)$ and $B = (B_{n-1} \ldots B_1 B_0)$.

1) Addition: $A + B = C = (C_{n-1} \ldots C_1 C_0)$, where $C_i = (A_i + B_i) \bmod 2$. That is, addition corresponds to bitwise exclusive-or.

2) Multiplication: $A \cdot B = C = (C_{n-1} \ldots C_1 C_0)$, where $C(x) = \sum_{i=0}^{n-1} C_i x^i$ is the remainder of the division of the polynomial $(\sum_{i=0}^{n-1} A_i x^i)(\sum_{i=0}^{n-1} B_i x^i)$ by $f(x)$.

In many applications, such as cryptography and digital communication applications, the polynomial basis is still the most popularly employed basis [10]. In the following, we confine our attention to the computations that use the polynomial basis.

2.2 Elliptic Curve Cryptography

In ECC, computing kP is the most important operation, where k is an integer and P is a point on the elliptic curve. This operation can be computed using the addition of two points k times. ECC can be don with at least two types of arithmetic, each of which gives different definitions of multiplication [11]. The types of arithmetic are

1) Z_p arithmetic(modular arithmetic with a large prime p as the modulus)
2) $GF(2^n)$ arithmetic, which can be done with shifts and exclusive-ors. This can be thought of as modular arithmetic of polynomials with coefficients mod 2.

We focused on $GF(2^n)$ arithmetic operation. Let $GF(2^n)$ be a finite field of characteristic. Then the set of all solution to the equation

$$E: y^2 + xy = x^3 + a_2x^2 + a_6, \text{ where } a_2, a_6 \in GF(2^n), a_6 \neq 0,$$

together with special point called the point at infinity O is a non-supersingular curve over $GF(2^n)$. Let $P_1 = (x_1, y_1)$ and $P_2 = (x_2, y_2)$ be points in $E(GF(2^n))$ given in affine coordinates [12]. Assume $P_1, P_2 \neq O$, and $P_1 \neq -P_2$. The sum $P_3 = (x_3, y_3) = P_1 + P_2$ is computed as follows:

If $P_1 \neq P_2$ (called point addition)

Then $\lambda = (y_1 + y_2)/(x_1 + x_2)$, $x^3 = \lambda^2 + \lambda + x_1 + x_2 + a_2$, $y^3 = (x_1 + x_3)\lambda + x_3 + y_1$

If $P_1 = P_2$ (called point doubling)

Then $\lambda = y_1 / x_1 + x_1$, $x^3 = \lambda^2 + \lambda + a_2$, $y^3 = (x_1 + x_3)\lambda + x_3 + y_1$

From these formulas, we can determine the number of field operations required for each kind of elliptic curve operation. The addition algorithm for field elements is trivial: the two blocks of bits are simply combined with the bit-wise XOR operation. Because our field has characteristic 2, subtraction is the same as addition. The squaring can be substituted by multiplication. Division also can be computed by repeating multiplications. Thus the most considerable contributors are multiplications.

Addition and multiplication in $GF(2^n)$ should be performed using one of the irreducible binary polynomials of degree n such as $n \in \{113, 131, 163, 193, 233, 239, 283, 409, 571\}$ [12]. As before this restriction is designed to facilitate interoperability while enabling implementers to deploy efficient implementations capable of meeting common security requirements. The rule used to pick acceptable reduction polynomials was: if a degree n binary irreducible trinomial:

$$f(x) = x^n + x^k + 1, \text{ for } n > k \geq 1$$

exists, use the irreducible trinomial with k as small as possible; otherwise use the degree n binary irreducible pentanomial:

$$f(x) = x^n + x^{k_3} + x^{k_2} + x^{k_1} + 1, \text{ for } n > k_3 > k_2 > k_1 \geq 1.$$

These polynomials enable efficient calculation of field operations. The second reduction polynomial at $n=239$ is an anomaly chosen since it has been widely deployed [12]. Our scheme is focused on trinomials as reduction polynomials.

2.3 Cellular Automata

A CA is an array of cells where each cell is in any one of its permissible states. At each discrete time step (clock cycle), the evolution of a cell depends on its transition rule. CAs can be characterized based on four properties: the cellular geometry, neighborhood specification, number of states per cell, and rule to compute to successor state. The next state of a CA depends on the current state and rules [7]. CA can also be classified as linear or non-linear. If the neighborhood is only dependent on an XOR operation, the CA is linear, whereas if it is dependent on another operation, the CA is non-linear. If the neighborhood is only dependent on an EXOR or EXNOR operation, then the CA can also be referred to as an additive CA.

Among additive CAs, CA of which dependency on neighbors is shown only in terms of XOR is called a non-complemented CA, and the corresponding rule is called the non-complemented rule. If the dependency on neighbors is shown only in terms of XNOR, the CA is called a complemented CA, and the corresponding rule is called the complemented rule. A hybrid CA can be subject to either the complemented or non-complemented rule. Also, there are the 1-dimensional, 2-dimensional, and 3-dimensional CAs according to the structure of arrangement of cells [7].

Furthermore, if the same rule applies to all the cells in a CA, the CA is called a uniform or regular CA, whereas if different rules apply to different cells, it is called a hybrid CA. And in the structure of CAs, the boundary conditions should be taken into consideration, where the boundary conditions incur since there exist no left neighbor of the leftmost cell and right neighbor of the rightmost cell among the cells composing CA. According to the conditions, they are divided into three types.

1) Null Boundary CA (NBCA): CA of which left neighbor of the leftmost cell and right neighbor of the rightmost cell are regarded to be '0'.
2) Periodic Boundary CA (PBCA): CA of which leftmost cell and rightmost cell are regarded to be adjacent to each other, i.e., the left neighbor of the leftmost cell becomes the rightmost cell, and the right neighbor of the rightmost cell becomes the leftmost cell.
3) Intermediate Boundary CA (IBCA): The left neighbor of the leftmost cell is regarded to be the second right neighbor, and right neighbor of the rightmost cell is regarded to be the second left neighbor.

The evolution of the ith cell in a 1-dimensional 3-neiborhood CA can be represented as a function of the present states of the $(i-1)$th, ith, and $(i+1)$th cells as: $Q_i(t+1) = f_i(Q_{i-1}(t), Q_i(t), Q_{i+1}(t))$, where f_i represents the transition rule for the ith cell. If next state determine by 1 bit shifting to the left, then it can be expressed as $Q_i(t+1) = Q_{i-1}(t)$, $(0 \leq i \leq n-1)$, where $Q(t+1)$ denotes the next state for cell $Q(t)$. It means that the next state of ith cell only depends on the right neighborhood of current ith cell. The proposed structure carries out efficient modular reduction based on PBCA.

3 Proposed Architecture for Multiplication Based on PBCA

In this section, we propose efficient multiplication architecture based on cellular automata using irreducible trinomials.

3.1 Proposed Multiplication Architecture

This subsection presents efficient multiplication algorithm using irreducible trinomials based on PBCA by the MSB-first method on the finite field $GF(2^n)$. Let us suppose that $A(x)$ and $B(x)$ are the elements on $GF(2^n)$. Then the two polynomials $A(x)$, $B(x)$ are as follows:

$$A(x) = A_{n-1}x^{n-1} + \ldots + A_1 x^1 + A_0 \tag{1}$$

$$B(x) = B_{n-1}x^{n-1} + \ldots + B_1 x^1 + B_0 \tag{2}$$

$A(x)B(x) \bmod P(x)$ can be expressed as $A(x)(B_{n-1}x^{n-1} + B_{m-2}x^{n-1} + \cdots + B_1 x^1 + B_0) \bmod P(x)$ by replacing equation (2). Then the equation satisfies

$$[A(x)B_{n-1}x^{n-1} + A(x)B_{n-2}x^{n-2} + \cdots + A(x)B_1 x^1 + A(x)B_0] \bmod P(x).$$

It is also represented as

$$[A(x)B_{n-1}x^{n-2} + A(x)B_{n-2}x^{n-3} + \cdots + A(x)B_1]x \bmod P(x) + A(x)B_0,$$

so that we induce the following equation (3).

$$\{[A(x)B_{n-1}x \bmod P(x) + A(x)B_{n-2}]x \bmod P(x) + \ldots + A(x)B_1\} x \bmod P(x) + A(x)B_0 \tag{3}$$

A definite algorithm for implementing equation (3) in the above is as follows:

[Algorithm 1] Multiplication Algorithm using general irreducible polynomials

    Input : $A(x)$, $B(x)$, $P(x)$
    Output : $A(x)B(x) \bmod P(x)$

    Step 1 : $R(x) = 0$
    Step 2 : for $i = n-1$ to 0
    Step 3 : $\quad R(x) = R(x) \cdot x \bmod P(x) + A(x)B_i$

The $R(x) \cdot x \bmod P(x)$ operation and $A(x)B_i$ ($0 \leq i \leq n-1$) operation can be performed simultaneously in Step 3 on Algorithm 1, where the basic computations for implementing the above are as follows:

    C1 : 1-bit left shift: $R(x) \cdot x$
    C2 : Modular reduction: $R(x) \cdot x \bmod P(x)$
    C3 : $A(x)B_i$ ($0 \leq i \leq n-1$)

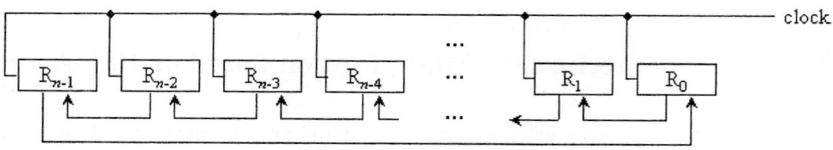

Fig. 1. Periodic boundary cellular automata structure reflecting **C1**, $Q_i(t+1) = Q_{i-1}(t)$

First, in order to perform **C1**, which requires a 1bit left-shift to implement $R(x) \cdot x$, Cellular automata using n-bit register is used. The next state of each register is defined as the state of the right neighbor in cellular automata expressed as $Q_i(t+1) = Q_{i-1}(t)$. Here, the leftmost register and rightmost register of the cellular automata are adjacent.

In order to perform **C2**, which is the modular reduction, modular reduction operations are required due to the 1bit left-shift resulting from **C1**. The following equation yields $R(x) \cdot x \bmod P(x)$.

$$((R_{n-1} \wedge P_{n-1}) \oplus R_{n-2})x^{n-1} + ((R_{n-1} \wedge P_{n-2}) \oplus R_{n-3})x^{n-2} + \ldots + ((R_{n-1} \wedge P_k) \oplus R_{k-1})x^k + \\ \ldots + ((R_{n-1} \wedge P_2) \oplus R_1)x^2 + ((R_{n-1} \wedge P_1) \oplus R_0)x^1 + ((R_{n-1} \wedge P_0) \oplus 0) \quad (4)$$

In equation (4), P_i ($0 \leq i \leq n-1$) has zero values but P_k and P_0 have always '1' since we only consider trinomial as irreducible polynomial introduced in section 2.2. The resultant equation by operating **C1** and **C2** is shown as follows.

$$R_{n-2} \cdot x^{n-1} + R_{n-3} \cdot x^{n-2} + \ldots + (R_{n-1} \oplus R_{k-1})x^k + \ldots + R_1 \cdot x^2 + R_0 \cdot x^1 + R_{n-1}, \quad (5)$$

where $P(x) = x^n + x^k + 1$. Fig. 2 shows periodic boundary cellular automata structure considering modular reduction.

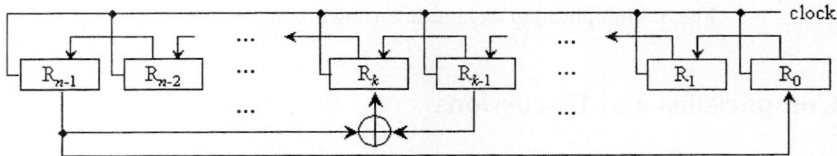

Fig. 2. Periodic Boundary Cellular automata structure reflecting *C*1 and *C*2

C3 can be easily obtained using n AND gates since each element of $A(x)$ should be multiplied by the element B_i, $i(0 \leq i \leq n-1)$ in order to perform **C3**. The method is presented for obtaining AB based on Algorithm 1 using described **C1**, **C2**, and **C3**. The proposed multiplication architecture is shown in Fig.3 as **C1** and **C2** are performed simultaneously. The proposed algorithm based on irreducible trinomials, $T(x)$, is shown as follows.

[Algorithm 2] Proposed Multiplication Algorithm using trinomial for ECC

> Input : $A(x)$, $B(x)$, $T(x)$
> Output : $A(x)B(x) \bmod T(x)$
>
> Step 1 : $R(x)=0$
> Step 2 : for $i = n-1$ to 0
> Step 3 : $R(x) = R_{n-2} \cdot x^{n-1} + R_{n-3} \cdot x^{n-2} + \ldots + (R_{n-1} \oplus R_{k-1})x^k + \ldots + R_1 \cdot x^2$
> $\qquad\qquad + R_0 \cdot x^1 + R_{n-1} + A(x)B_i$

To perform our structure based on Algorithm 2, cellular automata shown in Fig.2 is initialized as zero values.

The proposed architecture can be divided into two parts. The upper part performs $A(x)B_i$ ($0 \leq i \leq n-1$) and the lower part executes 1bit-circularly-left-shift and modular reductions. It is possible to perform multiplication in n clock cycles using n AND gates, $n+1$ XOR gates and only n-bit register.

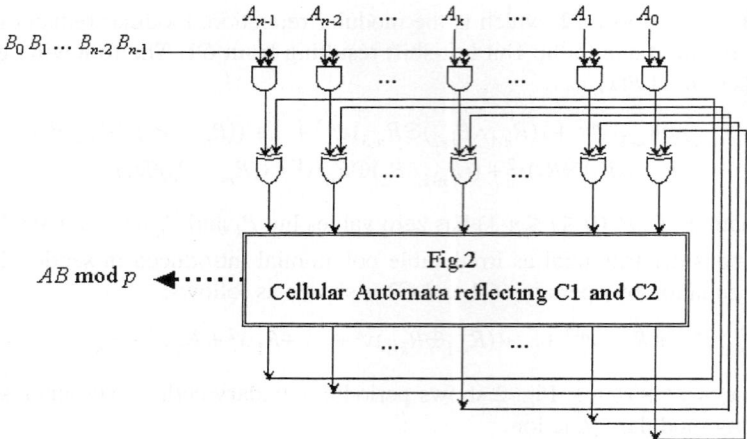

Fig. 3. Multiplication architecture using irreducible trinomials

4 Comparisons and Discussions

As usually, parallel fashion architectures need much more hardware equipments than serial fashion architectures, and latency is reverse. However the proposed architecture has better complexities than serial or parallel fashion architectures on the fields of the both sides, area and time. Our I/O format, the multiplicand input parallel while the multiplier input serial fashion, differs from typical ways. Thus there are advantages compared to typical architectures.

1) Faster implementation: Bit-serial architectures, for small silicon area, usually take much more time to perform the operations, and it hardly reduces time complexity since they compute the operation in sequence. But our architecture has taken special I/O format so we could achieve a better implementation as fast as parallel architecture.
2) Smaller silicon area: Bit-parallel architectures, such as systolic architectures, usually demand wide silicon area though they are faster. Our architecture is not only much smaller but also faster as much as parallel-in parallel-out fashion architectures.
3) Expansion for other cryptosystems: Another advantage is that our architecture can be expanded for other public cryptosystems using general irreducible polynomials, but existing systolic architectures including Wang's in [13] and Wei's in [14] can be hardly reduced their complexities though they use the restricted irreducible polynomials for ECC, because the binary value of irreducible polynomial in systolic array should be computed with other inputted values whenever it passes through every register. Thus though some of the binary values in irreducible polynomial have zero values, the architecture should input zeros while our architecture does not need to input the values.

Moreover, our architecture is the first attempt for ECC only, our concept is easily expanded for division and inversion architectures which are the important contributors for the run time in ECC. The following comparison table includes the case when our architecture uses general irreducible polynomials.

Table 1. Performance comparison

Circuit / Item	Fenn [15]	Zhang [8]	Choudhury [9]	Proposed architectures based on CA	
Function	AB	AB	AB+C	AB	AB
Number of Cell	$n+1$	n^2	n	n	n
Cell complexity	1-AND +1-XOR	3-AND +2-XOR	2-AND +2-XOR	1-AND +1-XOR	1-AND +1-XOR
Registers	$2n+2$	n	$2n$	n	n
AND gate	$2n-1$	$3n$	n	n	n
XOR gate	$2n-2$	$2n$	$2n$	$n+1$	$2n$
Critical path	$T_{AND}+\log_2 n T_{XOR}$	$T_{AND}+2T_{XOR}$	$T_{AND}+T_{XOR}$	$T_{AND}+T_{XOR}$	$T_{AND}+T_{XOR}$
Latency	$2n+1$	n	n	n	n
Irreducible Polynomial	General	General	General	Trinomial	General
I/O format	Serial-in serial-out	Parallel-in parallel-out	Parallel-in parallel-out	Serial and Parallel-in parallel-out	

Fenn designed two types of bit-serial *AB* multipliers based on LFSR architecture with a critical path of $(T_{AND}+\log_2 n T_{XOR})$. over GF($2^n$) [15]. Zhang in [7] proposed an architecture with programmable cellular automata and a cell complexity of 3-AND+2-XOR, while Choudhury in [8] designed an LSB multiplier based on a CA with a latency of $n(T_{AND}+T_{XOR})$. In contrast, the proposed structure based on an CA, had a latency of $n(T_{AND}+T_{XOR})$ and hardware complexity of n(AND+XOR+REGISTER) +XOR. Though general irreducible polynomial polynomials are applied to our architecture, only $(n-1)$ more XOR gates are required. Consequently the proposed structure exhibited considerable advantages over the other conventional systems.

5 Conclusions

This paper has presented multiplication architecture based on CA architecture using irreducible trinomials, which are restricted in ECC. Our architecture has been designed by characteristics of irreducible trinomials and periodic boundary CA. The proposed architecture has been minimized the both time complexity and hardware complexity such that it has only time complexity of $n(T_{AND}+T_{XOR})$ and area complexity of n(AND+XOR+REGISTER)+XOR. Moreover our architecture can be expanded for other public cryptosystems using general irreducible polynomials, it just requires only (n-1) more XOR gates. Therefore they show outstanding advantages in both area and time compared to typical structures. Our architecture has a regularity and modularity. Accordingly, it can be used as a basic arithmetic architecture in ECC.

References

1. N.Koblitz, Elliptic curve cryptosystems, Mathematics of Computation, Vol. 48, pp.203-209 (1987).
2. V.Miller, Use of Elliptic Curves in Cryptography, Advances in Cryptology-CRYPTO'85, Springer-Verlog Lecture Notes in Computer Science, Vol. 218, Berlin, (1986).
3. A.J.Menezes, Elliptic Curve Public Key Cryptosystems, Boston, MA: Kluwer Academic Publishers (1993).
4. T. R. N. Rao and E. Fujiwara, *Error-Control Coding for Computer Systems*, Englewood Cliffs, NJ: Prentice-Hall (1989).
5. W. Drescher, K. Bachmann, and G. Fettweis, "VLSI Architecture for Non Sequential Inversion over GF(2^m) using the Euclidean Algorithm," *The International Conference on Signal Processing Applications and Technology*, Vol.2, pp.1815-1819 (1997).
6. I. Lopez, R.Dahab, An overview of Elliptic Curve Cryptography, University of Campinas Press, Brazil (2000).
7. J. Von Neumann, *The theory of self-reproducing automata*, University of Illinois Press, Urbana and London (1966).
8. C. N. Zhang and M. Y. Deng, and R. Mason, "A VLSI Programmable Cellular Automata Array for Multiplication in GF(2^n)," *PDPTA '99 International Conference*, (1999).
9. P. Pal. Choudhury and R. Barua, "Cellular Automata Based VLSI Architecture for Computing Multiplication And Inverses In GF(2^m)," *IEEE 7th International Conference on VLSI Design*, pp. 279-282 (1994).
10. A. J. Menezs, Applications of Finite Fields, Boston, MA: Kluwer Academic Publishers (1993).
11. C. Kaufman, R. Perlman, M. Speciner, Network Security private communication in a public world, New Jersey: Prentice Hall (2002).
12. SEC 1: Elliptic Curve Cryptography version 1.0, Certicom Reserch (2000).
13. S. W. Wei, "VLSI architecture of divider for finite field GF(2^m)", *IEEE International Symposium on Circuit and Systems*, Vol.2, pp. 482-485 (1998).
14. C. L. Wang, J. H. Guo, "New Systolic Arrays for $C+AB^2$, inversion, and division in GF(2^m)", *IEEE Trans. on Computer*, Vol.49, No.10, pp.1120-1125 (2000).
15. S. T. J. Fenn, M.G. Parker, M. Benaissa, and D. Tayler, "Bit-serial multiplication in GF(2^m) using irreducible all-one polynomial," *IEE Proc. Comput. Digit. Tech.*, Vol.144, No.6, pp. 391-393 (1997).

Probability Based Genetic Programming for Multiclass Object Classification

Will Smart and Mengjie Zhang

School of Mathematical and Computing Sciences
Victoria University of Wellington, P.O. Box 600, Wellington, New Zealand
{smartwill,mengjie}@mcs.vuw.ac.nz

Abstract. This paper describes a probability based genetic programming (GP) approach to multiclass object classification problems. Instead of using predefined multiple thresholds to form different regions in the program output space for different classes, this approach uses probabilities of different classes, derived from Gaussian distributions, to construct the fitness function for classification. Two fitness measures, overlap area and weighted distribution distance, have been developed. The approach is examined on three multiclass object classification problems of increasing difficulty and compared with a basic GP approach. The results suggest that the new approach is more effective and more efficient than the basic GP approach. While the area measure was a bit more effective than the distance measure in most cases, the distance measure was more efficient to learn good program classifiers.

1 Introduction

Classification tasks arise in a very wide range of applications, such as detecting faces from video images, recognising words in streams of speech, diagnosing medical conditions from the output of medical tests, and detecting fraudulent credit card transactions [1,2]. In many cases, people (possibly highly trained experts) are able to perform the classification task well, but there is either a shortage of such experts, or the cost of people is too high. Given the amount of data that needs to be classified, automated classification systems are highly desirable. However, creating automated classification systems that have sufficient accuracy and reliability turns out to be very difficult.

Genetic programming (GP) is a relatively recent and fast developing approach to automatic programming [3,4]. In GP, solutions to a problem are represented as computer programs. Darwinian principles of natural selection and recombination are used to evolve a population of programs towards an effective solution to specific problems. The flexibility and expressiveness of computer program representation, combined with the powerful capabilities of evolutionary search, make GP an exciting new method to solve a great variety of problems.

GP research has considered a variety of kinds of classifier programs, using different program representations, including decision tree classifiers and classification rule sets [5]. Recently, a new form of classifier representation – numeric expression classifiers – has been developed using GP [6–9]. This form has been successfully applied to real world classification problems such as detecting and recognising particular classes of objects in images [7, 8, 10, 11], demonstrating the potential of GP as a general method for classification problems.

The output of a numeric expression GP classifier is a numeric value that is typically translated into a class label. For the simple binary classification case, this translation can be based on the sign of the numeric value [7, 6, 8, 12–15]; for multiclass problems, finding the appropriate boundary values to separate the different classes is more difficult. The emphasis of previous approaches was often on separating the program output space into regions (referred to as the *basic GP approach*), with each region indicating a different class. This includes a primary static method such as object classification map or static range selection [9, 6, 11], dynamic range selection [6], centred and slotted dynamic class boundary determination methods [14, 15]. Past work has demonstrated the effectiveness of these approaches, particularly the dynamic methods, on a number of object classification problems.

In the static methods, the region boundaries of program output space were fixed and predefined. In the dynamic methods, class boundaries were automatically found during the evolutionary process. While the static methods often need a hand crafting of good boundaries, the dynamic methods usually involve a long time search to automatically find good boundaries. Both approaches usually take very long training times and often result in unnecessarily complex programs, and sometimes poor performances[11, 15].

1.1 Goals

To avoid the above disadvantages, the goal of this paper is to investigate a new approach to the use of Gaussian distribution and probability in genetic programming for multiclass classification problems. Rather than setting up class region boundaries for classification, this approach uses Gaussian distribution to model the behaviour of each program based on the training examples for each class. This approach is examined on three multiclass object classification problems of increasing difficulty and compared with the basic GP approach [11] on the same problems. Specifically, we are interested in:

- How can the fitness function be constructed using the Gaussian distribution?
- How can the classification accuracy be calculated?
- Can this approach do a good enough job on the given problems?
- Will the new approach outperform the basic GP approach for the same problems?

1.2 Structure

This paper is organised as follows. Section 2 describes genetic programming applied to classification. Section 3 describes the new fitness function for classification. Section 4 describes the object classification problems to be applied. Section 5 presents the results and section 6 gives the conclusions.

2 GP Applied to Multiclass Classification

2.1 Terminals and Functions

Terminals. In this approach, we used two kinds of terminals: *feature terminals* and *numeric parameter terminals*.

Feature terminals form the inputs from the environment. The feature terminals considered in this approach are the means and variances of certain regions in object cutout images. Two such regions were used, the entire object cutout image and the central square region. This makes four feature terminals. The values of the feature terminals would remain unchanged in the evolutionary process, but different objects usually have different feature values.

Notice that these features might not be sufficient for some difficult object classification problems. However, they have been found reasonable in many problems and the selection of good features is not the goal of this paper.

Numeric parameter terminals are floating point numbers randomly generated using a uniform distribution at the beginning of evolution. Unlike feature terminal, the values of this kind of terminals are the same for all object images.

Functions. In the function set, the four standard arithmetic and a conditional operation were used to form the function set:

$$FuncSet = \{+, -, *, /, if\} \quad (1)$$

The $+$, $-$, $/$ and $*$ operators are addition, subtraction, multiplication and "protected" division with two arguments. The *if* function takes three arguments. If the first argument is negative, the *if* function returns its second argument; otherwise, it returns its third argument.

2.2 Fitness Function

In the basic GP approach, We used classification accuracy on the training set as the fitness function. To calculate the accuracy, we used a variant version of the *program classification map* [11] to perform object classification. This variation situates class regions sequentially on the floating point number line. The object image will be classified to the class of the region that the program output with the object image input falls into. Class region boundaries start at some negative number, and end at the same positive number. Boundaries between the starting point and the end point are allocated with an identical interval of 1.0. For example, a five class problem would have the following classification map.

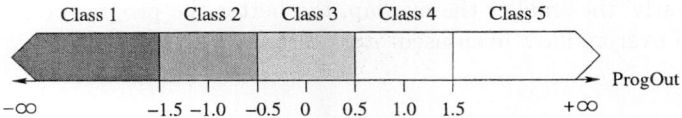

In the new approach, we applied the Gaussian distribution and used probability to construct the fitness function and to calculate the final classification accuracy. The details are presented in section 3.

2.3 Parameters and Termination Criteria

The parameter values used in this approach are shown in table 1. The evolutionary process is run for a fixed number (*max-generations*) of generations, unless it finds a program that solves the classification perfectly (100% accuracy), at which point the evolution is terminated early.

Table 1. Parameters used for GP training for the three datasets.

Parameter Names	Shapes	coins	faces	Parameter Names	Shapes	coins	faces
population-size	300	500	500	reproduction-rate	10%	10%	10%
initial-max-depth	3	3	3	cross-rate	60%	60%	60%
max-depth	5	8	8	mutation-rate	30%	30%	30%
max-generations	51	51	51	cross-term	15%	15%	15%
object-size	16×16	70×70	92×112	cross-func	85%	85%	85%

3 Constructing Fitness Function Using Gaussian Models

In our new approach, we used Gaussian distribution and probability models to construct the fitness function of each program and used multiple programs to calculate the accuracy of a genetic program classifier.

For a set of training data, we assume that the behaviour of a program classifier is modelled using multiple Gaussian distributions, each of which corresponds to a particular class. The distribution of a class is determined by evaluating the program on the examples of the class in the training set. This was done by taking the mean and standard deviation of the program outputs for those training examples for that class.

For presentation convenience, we first use a two-class problem to describe the fitness measures, then describe the fitness function for multiclass classification problems and the calculation of classification accuracy.

3.1 Fitness Measures

Figure 1 shows three example sets of normal curves for a two class problem. If a program can successfully classify all the training examples (the ideal case), the two curves will be fairly separated (figure 1 c); if the two curves are clearly overlapped, some examples will be incorrectly classified by the program (figure 1 a, b). Clearly, the smaller the overlap, the better the program classifier. Two measures of overlap have been used: *area* and *distance*.

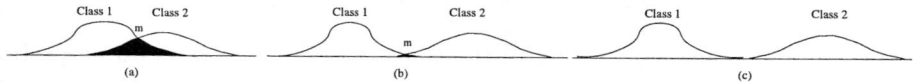

Fig. 1. Example normal distributions for a two-class problem.

Area Measure. In figure 1, the overlap area is shown in solid black. Assuming the intersection point of the two normal curves is m (m was found by a binary search), the area under the left distribution in the region $[m, \infty)$ plus the area under the rightmost distribution in the region $(-\infty, m)$ form the overlap area. Note that to calculate the areas directly is an NP-complete problem and an approximation must be made, which should be close enough to use.

At the beginning of evolution, the standard normal distribution $P(x)$ (Eq. 2) is sampled from its centre (0) to some large number (i.e. 20) at regular intervals α (i.e. 0.04). The area under the distribution at each point x is calculated using Eq. 3 and the value is stored for later use to simplify the computation.

$$P(x) = \frac{\exp(\frac{-x^2}{2})}{\sqrt{2\pi}} \tag{2}$$

$$A(x) = \sum_{i=0}^{\frac{x}{\alpha}} \alpha P(\alpha i) \tag{3}$$

When the area under a normal distribution with mean μ and standard deviation σ is to be calculated (during evolution), Eq. 4 is used.

$$A(\mu, \sigma, x) = A(\frac{x - \mu}{\sigma}) \tag{4}$$

Accordingly, the approximation of the overlap area in figure 1 (a) will be A_o:

$$A_o = 1 - A(\mu_1, \sigma_1, m) - A(\mu_2, \sigma_2, m) \tag{5}$$

The overlap area has a possible maximal approximation of 1.0 (where the distributions have the same mean), and a possible minimum of zero (where the distributions have different means, but both standard deviations are zero).

Distance Measure. We also used a second measure, "weighted distribution distance" of the two distributions to evaluate the overlap, as shown in Eq. 6.

$$d = 2 \times \frac{|\mu_1 - \mu_2|}{\sigma_1 + \sigma_2} \tag{6}$$

Under this measure, the worse case is 0, when μ_1 and μ_2 are the same. In the ideal case, this distance will be very large (go to ∞).

In order to make the range of the distance measure the same as for the area measure (0 best, 1 worst), we used the following standardised distribution distance measure d_s in this approach.

$$d_s = \frac{1}{1 + d} \tag{7}$$

3.2 Fitness Function

For multiclass classification, there are three or more classes. The fitness function is determined by considering all the overlaps between every two classes. Assuming the number of classes is n, then there will be $C_n^2 = \frac{n \times (n-1) \times ... \times 2 \times 1}{2}$ overlaps of distributions. The fitness of a program is calculated based on Eq. 8.

$$fitness = \sum_{i=1}^{C_n^2} M_i \qquad (8)$$

where M_i is a fitness measure of the ith overlap of distributions of two classes, which can be either the area measure (Eq. 5) or the distance measure (Eq. 7).

3.3 Classification Accuracy

Classification accuracy is calculated by the number of objects correctly classified by a GP system as a percentage of the total number of objects in a data set. To measure which class a given pattern (object example) belongs to, we used *multiple best programs* rather than the single best program in the population. Assuming l best programs in the population are used, the probability $Prob_c$ of a given pattern being of class c can be calculated by Eq. 9.

$$Prob_c = \prod_{i=1}^{l} P(\mu_{i,c}, \sigma_{i,c}, r_i) \qquad (9)$$

where P is the normal probability function (Eq. 10), r_i is the output result of program i with the pattern to be classified, $\mu_{i,c}$ and $\sigma_{i,c}$ are the mean and standard deviation of the outputs of program i for class c.

$$P(\mu, \sigma, x) = \frac{\exp(\frac{-(x-\mu)^2}{2\sigma^2})}{\sigma\sqrt{2\pi}} \qquad (10)$$

Based on Eq. 9, the probability of the pattern being of each class can be calculated. The class with the largest probability is used as the class of the pattern.

4 Data Sets

We used three data sets providing object classification problems of increasing difficulty in the experiments. Example images are shown in figure 2.

The first set of images (figure 2a) was generated to give well defined objects against a relatively clean background. The pixels of the objects were produced using a Gaussian generator with different means and variances for each class. Three classes of 960 small objects were cut out from those images to form the classification data set. The three classes are: black circles, grey squares, and light circles. For presentation convenience, this dataset is referred to as *shapes*.

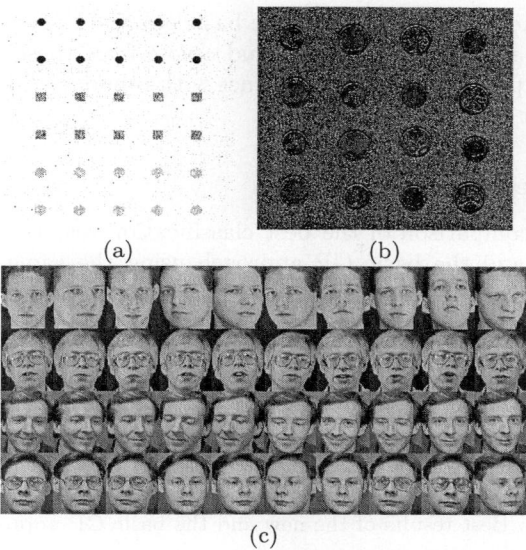

Fig. 2. Dataset examples: (a) Shapes, (b) Coins, and (c)Faces.

The second set of images (figure 2b) contains scanned 5 cent and 10 cent New Zealand coins. The coins were located in different places with different orientations and appeared in different sides (head and tail). In addition, the background was quite cluttered. We need to distinguish different coins with different sides from the background. Five classes of 576 object cutouts were created: 5 cent heads, 5 cent tails, 10 cent heads, 10 cent tails, and the cluttered background. Compared with the *shapes* data set, the classification problem in this data set is much harder. Although these are still regular, man-made objects, the problem is very hard due to the cluttered background and a low resolution.

The third data set consists of 40 human faces (figure 2c) taken at different times, varying lighting slightly, with different expressions (open/closed eyes, smiling/non-smiling) and facial details (glasses/no-glasses). These images were collected from the first four directories of the ORL face database [16]. All the images were taken against a dark homogeneous background with limited orientations. The task here is to distinguish those faces into the four different people.

For the shapes and the coins data sets, the objects were equally split into three separate data sets: one third for the training set used directly for learning the genetic program classifiers, one third for the validation set for controlling overfitting, and one third for the test set for measuring the performance of the learned program classifiers. For the faces data set, due to the small number of images, ten-fold cross validation was applied.

5 Results and Discussion

This section presents a series of results of the new method on the three object classification data sets. These results are compared with those for the basic GP approach. To make a fair comparison, the basic approach uses the same number of best programs as the new approach, and a vote from these programs is then applied. For all experiments, we run 50 times with random seeds and the average results on the test set were presented.

5.1 Overall Results

Table 2 shows a comparison of the best classification results obtained by both the new method and the basic GP approach using the same sets of features, functions and parameters. On all the three data sets, the new approach achieved very good results and always outperformed the basic approach, in terms of both classification accuracy and training time. This trend is particularly clear for relatively difficult problems such as in the coins and faces data sets. This indicates that the new approach is more effective than the basic GP approach and is more efficient to learn good classifiers for these problems.

Table 2. Best results of the new and the basic GP approaches.

Dataset	Strategy	Generations	Time (s)	Test Accuracy (%)
Shapes	Basic approach	11.70	3.29	98.64
	New approach	0.86	0.29	99.96
Coins	Basic approach	41.02	6.07	90.46
	New approach	19.42	2.93	98.41
Faces	Basic approach	8.60	0.38	86.75
	New approach	4.66	0.24	97.75

5.2 Different Programs and Fitness Measures in the New Approach

We used two fitness measures to evaluate the programs and used multiple programs to obtain the classification results. This section is to compare the two fitness measures and to investigate how many programs should be used.

Table 3 shows a comparison of the results on the three data sets using different numbers of programs and the two fitness measures in the new approach.

As can be seen from table 3, different numbers of programs for classification resulted in different performances. This is particularly true for difficult object classification problems. It seems that at certain numbers, the method achieved a high accuracy and spent a short training time, but the numbers leading to good results for various data sets appeared to be different. It generally needs an empirical search to obtain such good numbers for different data. However, if this can improve the performance, such a search is a small price to pay.

In terms of two fitness measures, the results suggest that the area measure resulted in better performance in accuracy in most cases, but it also took a bit longer time to learn the good program classifiers. This is mainly because the computational complexity of the area measure is greater than the distance measure. Nevertheless, both measures achieved quite good results, which were better than the basic approach for the same problems.

Table 3. Results for different programs and the two fitness measures.

Dataset	Programs Used	Generations Fitness Measure		Time (s) Fitness Measure		Test Accuracy (%) Fitness Measure	
		Distance	Area	Distance	Area	Distance	Area
Shapes	1	0.88	0.86	0.26	0.29	97.48	99.96
	3	0.38	0.34	0.19	0.20	99.84	99.83
	5	0.14	0.12	0.15	0.16	99.81	99.80
	10	0.04	0.04	0.14	0.15	99.79	99.78
	20	0.06	0.06	0.16	0.18	99.68	99.68
	50	0.30	0.16	0.30	0.27	99.46	99.46
Coins	1	32.98	33.78	4.55	5.37	94.23	97.49
	3	18.70	19.42	2.47	2.93	97.81	98.41
	5	14.96	15.76	1.96	2.39	98.12	98.38
	10	14.62	14.26	2.06	2.27	98.46	98.60
	20	10.82	9.06	1.60	1.57	98.40	98.25
	50	14.54	13.32	2.84	2.90	98.06	98.29
Faces	1	5.13	4.66	0.20	0.24	96.35	97.75
	3	2.09	1.73	0.08	0.10	96.95	95.90
	5	1.56	1.49	0.07	0.09	96.10	96.10
	10	1.03	0.88	0.05	0.06	95.45	94.70
	20	0.64	0.68	0.04	0.06	93.25	93.25
	50	0.25	0.18	0.03	0.04	91.20	90.30

6 Conclusions

The main goal of this paper was to construct the fitness function using Gaussian distributions in genetic programming for multiclass object classification problems. This goal was achieved by introducing two measures for the overlaps of distributions between every two classes on the training examples. A second goal was to investigate whether this new approach was better than a basic GP approach using the same set of features (terminals) and functions. Both approaches were examined on three object classification problems of increasing difficulty. The results suggest that the new approach is better than the basic approach in terms of both classification accuracy and training time.

Two fitness measures, *overlap area* and *distribution distance*, were applied to constructing the fitness function. Both measures achieved much better results than the basic approach on the three classification problems of increasing difficulty. Although the overlap area measure resulted in better performance in most cases, it also took longer time to evolve good program classifiers due to its greater complexity of computation than the distance measure.

Unlike most existing GP approaches for classification problems, where only the best learned/evolved program classifier was applied to the object examples to measure the accuracy, this approach used multiple top programs for classification and the class with the largest probability is used as the class of the object pattern.

While this approach does not need to manually define the fixed class boundaries, it does need to find a good number of programs used for object classification. The results suggest that there does not appear to be a reliable way to find a good number of programs, which is most likely problem dependent and needs an empirical search. However, if this can greatly improve the performance, such a search is a small price to pay.

Although developed for multiclass object classification problems, this approach is expected to be able to be applied to general classification problems.

For the future work, we will further investigate the number of programs for object classification, investigate the effectiveness of the new approach on other data sets, and compare this approach with other learning methods such as decision trees and neural networks.

References

1. J. Eggermont, A. E. Eiben, and J. I. van Hemert. A comparison of genetic programming variants for data classification. In *Proceedings of the Third Symposium on Intelligent Data Analysis (IDA-99), LNCS 1642*. Dpringer-Verlag, 1999.
2. Helen Gray. Genetic programming for classification of medical data. In John R. Koza, editor, *Late Breaking Papers at the 1997 Genetic Programming Conference*, pages 291–297. Standford University, 1997.
3. Wolfgang Banzhaf, Peter Nordin, Robert E. Keller, and Frank D. Francone. *Genetic Programming: An Introduction on the Automatic Evolution of computer programs and its Applications*. Morgan Kaufmann Publishers, 1998.
4. John R. Koza. *Genetic programming : on the programming of computers by means of natural selection*. Cambridge, Mass. : MIT Press, London, England, 1992.
5. John R. Koza. *Genetic Programming II: Automatic Discovery of Reusable Programs*. Cambridge, Mass. : MIT Press, London, England, 1994.
6. Thomas Loveard and Victor Ciesielski. Representing classification problems in genetic programming. In *Proceedings of the Congress on Evolutionary Computation*, volume 2, pages 1070–1077. 2001. IEEE Press.
7. Andy Song, Vic Ciesielski, and Hugh Williams. Texture classifiers generated by genetic programming. In David B. Fogel, et al. editors, *Proceedings of the 2002 Congress on Evolutionary Computation*, pages 243–248. IEEE Press, 2002.
8. Walter Alden Tackett. Genetic programming for feature discovery and image discrimination. In Stephanie Forrest, editor, *Proceedings of the 5th International Conference on Genetic Algorithms*, pages 303–309. 1993. Morgan Kaufmann.
9. Mengjie Zhang and Victor Ciesielski. Genetic programming for multiple class object detection. In Norman Foo, editor, *Proceedings of the 12th Australian Joint Conference on Artificial Intelligence*, pages 180–192, Sydney, Australia, December 1999. Springer-Verlag. LNAI 1747.
10. Mengjie Zhang, Peter Andreae, and Mark Pritchard. Pixel statistics and false alarm area in genetic programming for object detection. In Stefano Cagnoni, editor, *Applications of Evolutionary Computing, Lecture Notes in Computer Science, LNCS Vol. 2611*, pages 455–466. Springer-Verlag, 2003.
11. Mengjie Zhang, Victor Ciesielski, and Peter Andreae. A domain independent window-approach to multiclass object detection using genetic programming. *EURASIP Journal on Signal Processing, Special Issue on Genetic and Evolutionary Computation for Signal Processing and Image Analysis*, 2003(8):841–859, 2003.
12. Daniel Howard, S. C. Roberts, and R. Brankin. Target detection in SAR imagery by genetic programming. *Advances in Engineering Software*, 30:303–311, 1999.

13. Jamie R. Sherrah, Robert E. Bogner, and Abdesselam Bouzerdoum. The evolutionary pre-processor: Automatic feature extraction for supervised classification using genetic programming. In John R. Koza, et al. editors, *Genetic Programming 1997: Proceedings of the Second Annual Conference*, pages 304–312, 1997.
14. Will Smart and Mengjie Zhang. Classification strategies for image classification in genetic programming. In Donald Bailey, editor, *Proceeding of Image and Vision Computing Conference*, pages 402–407, New Zealand, 2003.
15. Mengjie Zhang and Will Smart. Multiclass object classification using genetic programming. In Guenther R. Raidl, et al. editors, *Applications of Evolutionary Computing*, Volume 3005, *LNCS*, pages 367–376, 2004. Springer Verlag.
16. F. Samaria and A. Harter. Parameterisation of a stochastic model for human face identification. In *2nd IEEE Workshop on Applications of Computer Vision*, Sarasota (Florida), July 1994. ORL database is available at: www.cam-orl.co.uk/facedatabase.html.

Design of Nearest Neighbor Classifiers Using an Intelligent Multi-objective Evolutionary Algorithm

Jian-Hung Chen, Hung-Ming Chen, and Shinn-Ying Ho

Department of Information Engineering and Computer Science,
Feng Chia University, Taichung 407, Taiwan
Tel:886-4-24517250 ext. 3723, Fax: 886-4-24516101
jh.chen@ieee.org, hmchen@ms25.url.com.tw, syho@fcu.edu.tw

Abstract. The goal of designing optimal nearest neighbor classifiers is to maximize classification accuracy while minimizing the sizes of both reference and feature sets. A usual way is to adaptively weight the three objectives as an objective function and then use a single-objective optimization method for achieving this goal. This paper proposes a multi-objective approach to cope with the weight tuning problem for practitioners. A novel intelligent multi-objective evolutionary algorithm IMOEA is utilized to simultaneously edit compact reference and feature sets for nearest neighbor classification. Two comparison studies are designed to evaluate performance of the proposed approach. It is shown empirically that the IMOEA-designed classifiers have high classification accuracy and small sizes of reference and feature sets. Moreover, IMOEA can provide a set of good solutions for practitioners to choose from in a single run. The simulation results indicate that the IMOEA-based approach is an expedient method to design nearest neighbor classifiers, compared with an existing single-objective approach.

1 Introduction

The nearest neighbor (1-nn) classifier is commonly used due to its simplicity and effectiveness [1]-[5]. According to 1-nn rule, an input pattern is assigned to the class of its nearest neighbor from a labeled reference set. The goal of designing optimal 1-nn classifiers is to maximize classification accuracy while minimizing the sizes of both reference and feature sets. Ho et al. [4] proposed an intelligent genetic algorithm IGA for simultaneous reference set editing and feature selection to design 1-nn classifiers, using a weighted-sum approach by combining multiple objectives into a single-objective function. However, in order to obtain good solutions using the weighted-sum approach, domain knowledge and large computational cost are required for determining a set of good weight values.

In this paper, a multi-objective approach utilizing a novel intelligent multi-objective evolutionary algorithm IMOEA [6], [7] is proposed to solve the problem of designing optimal 1-nn classifiers. The proposed approach can cope with the weight tuning problem for practitioners. Furthermore, IMOEA can efficiently obtain a set of non-dominated solutions in a single run, compared with a single-objective EA using multiple runs in terms of solution quality and computation cost. Two comparison studies are designed to evaluate performance of the proposed approach. It is shown empirically that the IMOEA-designed classifiers have high classification accuracy and small sizes of reference and feature sets. The experimental results indicate that the IMOEA-based approach is an expedient method to design nearest neighbor classifiers, compared with an existing single-objective approach.

The organization of this paper is as follows. The investigated problem is described in Section 2. Section 3 presents the design of optimal 1-nn classifiers using IMOEA. Section 4 reports the experimental results and Section 5 concludes this paper.

2 The Investigated Problem

2.1 Designing 1-nn Classifier

The investigated problem of designing optimal 1-nn classifiers is described as follows [4], [5]:

Let $X = \{X_1, ..., X_n\}$ be a set of features describing objects as n-dimensional vectors $x = [x_1, ..., x_n]^T$ in R^n and let $Z = \{z_1, ..., z_N\}$, $z_j \in R^n$, be a data set. Associated with each z_j, $j=1, ..., N$, is a class label from a set $C = \{1, ..., c\}$. The criteria of *data editing* and *feature selection* are to find subsets $S_1 \subseteq Z$ and $S_2 \subseteq X$ such that the classification accuracy is maximal and the sizes of the reduced sets, card(S_1) and card(S_2), are minimal, where card($\cdot$) denotes cardinality. Define a real-valued function $P_{1\text{-nn}}(V, S_1, S_2)$ as the classification accuracy of a 1-nn classifier with S_1 and S_2:

$$P_{1\text{-}nn} : P(Z) \times P(X) :\rightarrow [0,1], \tag{1}$$

where $P(Z)$ is the power set of Z and $P(X)$ is the power set of X. The classification accuracy $P_{1\text{-nn}}$ uses a counting estimator $h^{CE}(v_j)$ [11] measured on a given validation set $V = \{v_1, ..., v_m\}$, as shown in Equation (2). If v_j is correctly classified using S_1 and S_2 by the 1-nn rule, $h^{CE}(v_j) = 1$, and 0 otherwise.

$$P_{1-nn}(V, S_1, S_2) = \sum_{j=1}^{m} h^{CE}(v_j)/m \tag{2}$$

The problem is how to search for S_1 and S_2 in the combined space such that $P_{1\text{-nn}}$ is maximal, and card(S_1) and card(S_2) are minimal.

Essentially, the investigated problem has a search space of C($N+n$, card(S_1)+card(S_2)) instances, i.e., the number of ways of choosing card(S_1)+card(S_2) out of $N+n$ binary decision variables with three incommensurable and competing objectives. The investigated problem can be formulated as the following multi-objective optimization problem:

$$\begin{cases} \text{Maximum } f_1 = P_{1-nn} \\ \text{Minimum } f_2 = card(S_1) \\ \text{Minimum } f_3 = card(S_2) \end{cases} \tag{3}$$

2.2 Review of Weighted-Sum Approaches

For editing a reference set, Kuncheva et al. [1] and Cano et al. [3] found that EAs using a weighted-sum objective function can offer high classification accuracy and a good data reduction ratio for designing 1-nn classifiers. To edit a reference set and select useful features simultaneously, Kuncheva et al. proposed a GA with a weighted-sum approach, using a fitness function F as follows [4], [5]:

$$F = P_{1-nn}(V, S_1, S_2) - \alpha \left(\frac{card(S_1) + card(S_2)}{N+n} \right). \qquad (4)$$

The sum of card(S_1) and card(S_2) is used as a penalty term. The weight value α is used to tune the degree of penalty.

Generally, the number $N+n$ of binary decision variables is large. Large parameter optimization problems often pose a great challenge to engineers due to the large parametric space, the possibility of large infeasible and non-uniform areas, and the presence of multiple peaks. Despite having been successfully used to solve many optimization problems, conventional GAs cannot efficiently solve large parameter optimization problems. Therefore, Ho et al. [4] proposed IGA using the fitness function F in Equation (4) to solve the investigated problem with a large number of decision variables. It have been shown empirically that the IGA-designed classifiers outperform some existing methods, including Kuncheva's GA-based method [5] in terms of both classification accuracy and the number card(S_1)×card(S_2). However, different data sets represent different classification problems with different degrees of difficulties [3]. Without using domain knowledge, it is difficult for practitioners to determine appropriate weight values in the weighted-sum approach and the results may be sensitive to weight values. In order to obtain high performance, multiple experiments with different weight values for different data sets are necessary in the weighted-sum approach.

3 IMOEA-Designed 1-nn Classifier

3.1 Chromosome Representation

The feasible solution S corresponding to the reduced reference and feature sets is encoded using a binary string consisting of $N+n$ bits. The first N bits are used for $S_1 \subseteq Z$ and the last n bits for $S_2 \subseteq X$. The i-th bit has a value 1 when the respective element of $Z(X)$ is included in $S_1(S_2)$, and 0 otherwise. The search space consists of 2^{N+n} points. For example, considering the reduced reference set $\{z_3, z_5, z_6, z_8\}$ and feature set $\{X_2, X_3, X_5, X_6\}$, the corresponding chromosome is S = [0 0 1 0 1 1 0 1 0 0 1 1 0 1 1] with N=9 and n=6.

3.2 Fitness Assignment

The fitness assignment strategy of IMOEA uses a generalized Pareto-based scale-independent fitness function GPSIFF considering the quantitative fitness values in the Pareto space for both dominated and non-dominated individuals [6], [7]. GPSIFF makes the use of Pareto dominance relationship to evaluate individuals using a single measure of performance. Let the fitness value of an individual Y be a tournament-like score obtained from all participant individuals by the following function:

$$GPSIFF(Y) = p - q + c, \tag{5}$$

where p is the number of individuals which can be dominated by Y, and q is the number of individuals which can dominate Y in the objective space. Generally, a constant c can be optionally added in the fitness function to make fitness values positive. In this study, c is the number of all participant individuals. Note that GPSIFF is to be maximized in IMOEA.

3.3 Intelligent Crossover (IC)

In the conventional crossover operations of GAs, two parents generate two children with a combination of their chromosomes using *randomly* selected cut points. The merit of IC is that, the systematic reasoning ability of orthogonal experimental design (OED) [4], [6]-[8] is incorporated in the crossover operator to economically estimate the contribution of individual genes to a fitness function, and then the better genes are intelligently picked up to form the chromosomes of children. The procedure of IC, theoretically analysis and experimental studies for illustrating the superiority of IC with the use of OED can be found in [4], [6]-[8].

3.3.1 Orthogonal Array and Factor Analysis

Orthogonal array (OA) is a factional factorial matrix, which assures a balanced comparison of levels of any factor or interaction of factors. It is a matrix of numbers arranged in rows and columns where each row represents the levels of factors in each experiment, and each column represents a specific factor that can be changed from each experiment. The array is called orthogonal because all columns can be evaluated independently of one another, and the *main effect* of one factor does not bother the estimation of the main effect of another factor. A two-level OA used in IC is described as follows. Let there be γ factors with two levels for each factor. The total number of experiments is 2^γ for the popular "one-factor-at-a-time" study. The columns of two factors are orthogonal when the four pairs, (1,1), (1,2), (2,1), and (2,2), occur equally frequently over all experiments. Generally, levels 1 and 2 of a factor represent selected genes from parents 1 and 2, respectively. To establish an OA of γ factors with two levels, first we obtain an integer $\omega = 2^{\lceil \log_2(\gamma+1) \rceil}$, where the bracket represents a ceiling operator. Then, build an orthogonal array $L_\omega(2^{\omega-1})$ with ω rows and $(\omega-1)$ columns and use the first γ columns; the other $(\omega-\gamma-1)$ columns are ignored. The algorithm of constructing OAs can be found in [13]. OED can reduce the number of experiments for factor analysis.

After proper tabulation of experimental results, we can further proceed *factor analysis* to determine the relative effects of various factors. Let y_t denote a function value of the combination t, where $t = 1, \ldots, \omega$. Define the main effect of factor j with level k as S_{jk} where $j = 1, \ldots, \gamma$ and $k = 1, 2$:

$$S_{jk} = \sum_{t=1}^{\omega} y_t \cdot F_t, \tag{6}$$

where $F_t = 1$ if the level of factor j of combination t is k; otherwise, $F_t = 0$. Since GPSIFF is to be maximized, the level 1 of factor j makes a better contribution to the function than level 2 of factor j does when $S_{j1} > S_{j2}$. If $S_{j1} < S_{j2}$, level 2 is better. If $S_{j1} = S_{j2}$, levels 1 and 2 have the same contribution. The main effect reveals the individual effect of a factor. The most effective factor j has the largest main effect difference $MED = |S_{j1} - S_{j2}|$. After the better one of two levels of each factor is determined, a reasoned combination consisting of γ factors with better levels can be easily derived. The reasoned combination is a potentially good approximation to the best one of the 2^γ combinations.

3.3.2 Procedures of Intelligent Crossover

Two parents breed two children using IC at a time. How to use OA and factor analysis to perform the IC operation with γ factors is described as the following steps:

Step 1: Randomly divide the parent chromosomes into γ pairs of gene segments where each gene segment is treated as a factor.

Step 2: Use the first γ columns of OA $L_\omega(2^{\omega-1})$ where $\omega = 2^{\lceil \log_2(\gamma+1) \rceil}$.

Step 3: Let levels 1 and 2 of factor j represent the jth gene segment of a chromosome coming from parents, respectively.

Step 4: Simultaneously evaluate the fitness values y_t of the ω combinations corresponding to the experiments t, where $t = 1, ..., \omega$.

Step 5: Compute the main effect S_{jk} where $j = 1, ..., \gamma$ and $k = 1, 2$.

Step 6: Determine the better one of two levels for each gene segment. Select level 1 for the jth factor if $S_{j1} > S_{j2}$. Otherwise, select level 2.

Step 7: The chromosome of the first child is formed using the combination of the better gene segments from the derived corresponding parents.

Step 8: Rank the most effective factors from rank 1 to rank γ. The factor with a large MED has a high rank.

Step 9: The chromosome of the second child is formed similarly as the first child except that the factor with the lowest rank adopts the other level.

For one IC operation, the two children are more promising to be new non-dominated individuals. The individuals corresponding to OA combinations are called *by-products* of IGC. The by-products are well planned and systematically sampled within the hypercube formed by parents, so some of them are promising to be non-dominated individuals. Therefore, the non-dominated by-products will be added to the elite set in IMOEA.

3.4 Intelligent Multi-objective Evolutionary Algorithm

IMOEA uses an elite set E with capacity N_{Emax} to maintain the non-dominated individuals generated so far. The used IMOEA in the investigated problem is as follows:

Step 1: (Initialization) Randomly generate an initial population of N_{pop} individuals and create an empty elite set E and an empty temporary elite set E'.

Step 2: (Evaluation) Compute all objective function values of each individual in the population. Assign each individual a fitness value by using GPSIFF.
Step 3: (Update elite sets) Add the non-dominated individuals in both the population and E' to E, and empty E'. Considering all individuals in E, remove the dominated ones. If the number N_E of non-dominated individuals in E is larger than N_{Emax}, randomly discard excess individuals.
Step 4: (Selection) Select N_{pop}-N_{ps} individuals from the population using binary tournament selection and randomly select N_{ps} individuals from E to form a new population, where $N_{\text{ps}}=N_{\text{pop}} \cdot p_s$. If $N_{\text{ps}} > N_E$, let $N_{\text{ps}}= N_E$.
Step 5: (Recombination) Perform the IC operations for $N_{\text{pop}} \cdot p_c$ selected parents. For each IC operation, add non-dominated individuals derived from by-products and two children to E'.
Step 6: (Mutation) Apply bit mutation with p_m to the population.
Step 7: (Termination test) If a stopping condition is satisfied, stop the algorithm. Otherwise, go to Step 2.

4 Experimental Results

The 11 well-known data sets with numerical attribute values are used to evaluate performance of the proposed approach. All the data sets are available from [12]. To assure fair performance comparisons by avoiding the dependence on the training and test data, the following data partition is used. First, the patterns with the same class label are put together without changing their order in the original data file. Subsequently, the patterns with odd index values are assigned to the set V_1 and the other patterns are assigned to the set V_2. When $V_1(V_2)$ is used as a training set, $V_2(V_1)$ is a test set. In the training phase, the training set is used to select the reduced sets S_1 and S_2, and calculate the classification accuracy $P_{1\text{-nn}}$. The test classification accuracy is measured using the test set.

The coverage metric C(A, B) of two solution sets A and B [9] is used to compare the performance of two corresponding algorithms considering the three objectives:

$$C(A,B) = \frac{|\{a \in A; b \in B; a \succeq b\}|}{|B|}. \tag{7}$$

C(A, B) = 1 means that all individuals in B are weakly dominated by A. On the contrary, C(A, B) = 0 means that none of individuals in B are weakly dominated by A. The comparison results of two solution sets using the coverage metric are depicted using box plots. For easy understanding, the data reduction ratio Drd is used to measure the efficiency of editing reference sets:

$$Drd = \frac{card(S_1)}{N}. \tag{8}$$

The feature reduction ratio Frd is used to measure the efficiency of editing feature sets:

$$Frd = \frac{card(S_2)}{n}. \qquad (9)$$

The parameter settings of IGA are as follows: $N_{pop}=30$, $p_s=0.4$, $p_c=0.6$ and $p_m=0.05$. The fitness function of IGA is F in Equation (4). Nine different weight values of α, α=0.1, 0.2, 0.3, 0.4, 0.5, 0.6, 0.7, 0.8 and 0.9 are used. In order to make comparisons with multi-objective solutions, the nine experiments using nine different weight values ranged from 0.1 to 0.9 are regarded as an IGA run. The parameter settings of IMOEA are as follows: $N_{pop}=30$, $N_{Emax}=30$, $p_s=0.4$, $p_c=0.6$ and $p_m=0.05$. The factor value of OA is 7 in both IGA and IMOEA. The stopping condition is the number of function evaluations $N_{eval}=10000$. Thirty independent runs were performed. Each of IGA, and IMOEA performed 30 independent runs. The solution sets of 30 runs are compared using the coverage metric.

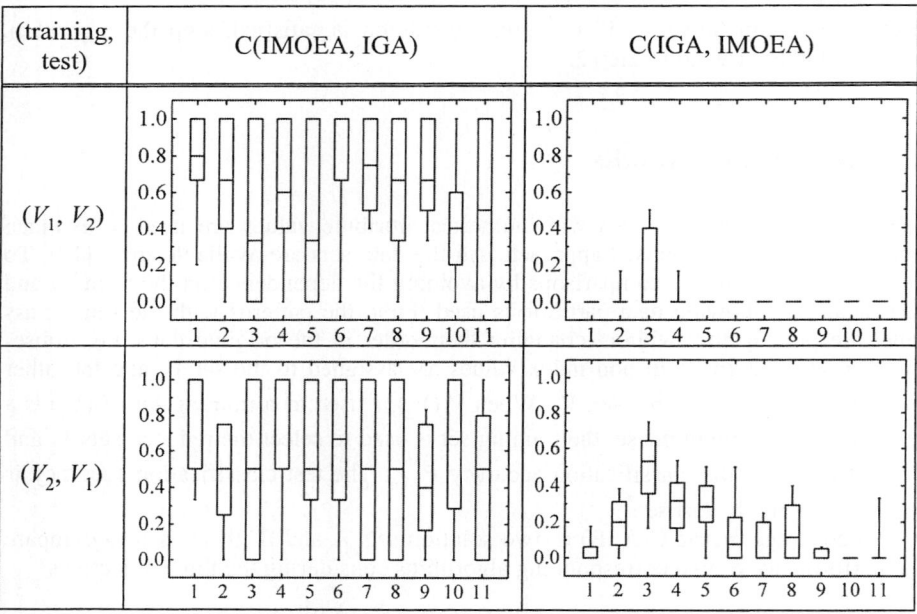

Fig. 1. Box plots based on the coverage metric C. The vertical axis is the value of C and the horizontal axis is the index of data sets.

Fig. 1 shows the coverage metric of C(IGA, IMOEA) and C(IMOEA, IGA) from 30 runs, for the (training, test) data sets (V_1, V_2) and (V_2, V_1). Observing the median in the box plots, the results shows that the solutions of IMOEA weakly dominate 40%-80% solutions of IGA, and the solutions of IGA weakly dominate 5%-40% solutions of IMOEA. The results reveal that IMOEA can evolve a set of non-dominated solutions that cover the solutions of IGA.

Due to its nature, IMOEA tries to optimize the three objectives and tends to obtain widespread solutions on all the three objectives. Considering only $P_{1\text{-nn}}$, it is not fair to perform t-test on all the classification accuracy of the IMOEA-designed classifiers

Table 1. Results of average classification accuracy, data reduction ratio and feature reduction ratio on DROP5 and C4.5.

Data set	DROP5		C4.5	
	$P_{1\text{-nn}}$	Drd	$P_{1\text{-nn}}$	Frd
(1) cmc	0.4888	28.31%	0.5050	100.00%
(2) glass	0.6692	30.29%	0.6730	77.78%
(3) haberman	0.7256	13.72%	0.7160	66.67%
(4) heartc[†]	0.5418	19.86%	0.5420	96.15%
(5) iris	0.9200	20.67%	0.9265	37.50%
(6) liver-disorder	0.5883	30.14%	0.6580	100.00%
(7) new-thyroid	0.9210	12.56%	0.9255	80.00%
(8) pima	0.7227	20.18%	0.7055	87.50%
(9) sonar	0.7694	27.36%	0.7405	16.67%
(10) wdbc	0.9367	8.97%	0.9170	21.67%
(11) wine	0.9439	12.35%	0.9320	26.92%
Average	0.7480	20.40%	0.7492	64.62%

[†]Six patterns with missing attribute values are excluded.

Table 2. Results of t-test on the classification accuracy of the selected IMOEA-designed classifiers, the C4.5 classifiers and DROP5, with 29 degrees of freedom at the 0.05 the significance level. The solutions of IMOEA are selected using Equation (4) with $\alpha=0.5$.

Data set	IMOEA($\alpha=0.5$)		t-test	
	$P_{1\text{-nn}}$	Deviation	DROP5	C4.5
(1) cmc	0.4461	0.0103	Lose	Lose
(2) glass	0.6698	0.0183	Equal	Equal
(3) haberman	0.6891	0.0176	Lose	Lose
(4) heartc[†]	0.5340	0.0159	Lose	Lose
(5) iris	0.9400	0.0174	Win	Win
(6) liver-disorder	0.5872	0.0237	Equal	Lose
(7) new-thyroid	0.9464	0.0153	Win	Win
(8) pima	0.6711	0.0155	Lose	Lose
(9) sonar	0.8001	0.0199	Win	Win
(10) wdbc	0.9426	0.0073	Win	Win
(11) wine	0.9306	0.0158	Lose	Equal

to the baseline classification accuracy. Therefore, Equation (4) is adopted as a simple decision making model to select a solution from a set of non-dominated solutions. Table 1 reports the results of C4.5[10] and DROP5[11]. Table 2 reports the results of the t-test on the classification accuracy of the selected IMOEA-designed classifiers using $\alpha=0.5$ with the C4.5 and the DROP5 classifiers. Table 3 reports the data and the feature reduction ratios of the selected IMOEA-designed classifiers. It shows that the selected IMOEA-designed classifiers offer smaller data and feature reduction ratios than those of the IGA-designed classifiers. From Tables 1-3, the simulation results indicate that the proposed approach can achieve better data and feature reduction ratios without losses in generalization accuracy.

Table 3. Results of average data and feature reduction ratio on the IGA-designed classifiers, the selected IMOEA-designed classifiers and the C4.5 classifiers. The solutions of IMOEA are selected using Equation (4) with $\alpha=0.5$.

Data set	IGA		IMOEA($\alpha=0.5$)	
	Drd	*Frd*	*Drd*	*Frd*
(1) cmc	47.15%	32.67%	41.48%	14.67%
(2) glass	37.88%	16.67%	27.95%	11.11%
(3) haberman	25.54%	39.67%	22.50%	35.67%
(4) heartc†	38.30%	15.77%	33.52%	8.69%
(5) iris	4.52%	33.00%	6.47%	25.00%
(6) liver-disorder	36.56%	25.83%	26.25%	17.83%
(7) new-thyroid	13.88%	24.00%	9.52%	20.00%
(8) pima	36.60%	27.25%	30.75%	15.63%
(9) sonar	33.00%	13.68%	23.69%	2.45%
(10) wdbc	24.96%	20.27%	18.58%	5.27%
(11) wine	12.99%	11.15%	7.19%	7.69%
Average	28.31%	23.63%	22.54%	14.91%

5 Conclusions

In this paper, we have proposed an approach to designing optimal 1-nn classifiers using a novel intelligent multi-objective evolutionary algorithm IMOEA with intelligent crossover based on orthogonal experimental design. The proposed approach copes with the weight tuning problem for practitioners. It has been shown empirically that the IMOEA-designed classifiers have high performance, compared with the IGA-based in terms of classification accuracy, the size of reference set and the size of feature set. Moreover, IMOEA provides a set of solutions for practitioners to choose from. IMOEA can be easily applied without using domain knowledge to efficiently design 1-nn classifiers with high-dimensional patterns with overlapping. The simulation results indicate that the IMOEA-based approach is a good alternative method to design nearest neighbor classifiers, compared with the existing single-objective approach.

References

1. L.I. Kuncheva, J.C. Bezdek, Nearest prototype classification clustering, genetic algorithms, or random search?, IEEE Trans. on Systems, Man and Cybernetics-Part C, 28 (1) (1998) 160-164.

2. M.L. Raymer, W.F. Punch, E.D. Goodman, L.A. Kuhn, A.K. Jain, Dimensionality reduction using genetic algorithms, IEEE Trans. on Evolutionary Computation, 4 (2) 2000 164-171.
3. J.R. Cano, F. Herrera and M. Lozano, Using evolutionary algorithms as instance selection for data reduction in KDD: an experimental study, IEEE Trans. on Evolutionary Computation, 7 (6) 2003 561-575.
4. S.-Y. Ho, C.-C. Liu, S. Liu, Design of an optimal nearest neighbor classifier using an intelligent genetic algorithm, Pattern Recognition Letters, 23 (13) (2002) 1495-1503
5. L.I. Kuncheva, L.C. Jain, Nearest neighbor classifier: Simultaneous editing and feature selection, Pattern Recognition Letters, 20 (1999) 1149-1156.
6. S.-Y. Ho, X.-I Chang, An efficient generalized multiobjective evolutionary algorithm, in: Proc. of the Genetic and Evolutionary Computation Conference GECCO-99, Orlando, July 1999, pp. 871-878.
7. J.-H. Chen, S.-Y. Ho, Evolutionary multi-objective optimization of flexible manufacturing systems, in: Proc. of the Genetic and Evolutionary Computation Conference GECCO-2001, San Francisco, July 2001, pp. 1260-1267.
8. S.-Y. Ho, Y.-C. Chen, An efficient evolutionary algorithm for accurate polygonal approximation, Pattern Recognition, 34 (2001), 2305-2317.
9. E. Zitzler, L. Thiele, Multiobjective evolutionary algorithms: A comparative case study and the strengthen Pareto approach, IEEE Trans. on Evolutionary Computation, 3 (4) (1999), 257-271.
10. J.R. Quinlan, C4.5: Programs for Machine Learning, San Mateo, Morgan Kauffman, Los Altos, CA, 1993.
11. R.D. Wilson and T.R. Martinez, Reduction Techniques for Instance-based Learning Algorithms, Machine Learning 38 (2000), 257–286.
12. C.L. Blake, C.J. Merz, UCI Repository of machine learning databases, 1998. Available from <http://www.ics.uci.edu/~mlearn/MLRepository.html>.

Elastic Learning Rate on Error Backpropagation of Online Update[*]

Tae-Seung Lee[1] and Ho-Jin Choi[2]

[1] School of Electronics, Telecommunication and Computer Engineering,
Hankuk Aviation University,
200-1, Hwajeon-dong, Deokyang-gu, Koyang-city, Kyonggi-do, 412-791, Korea
thestaff@hitel.net
[2] Software Technology Institute, Information and Communications University,
517-10, Dogok-dong, Kangnam-gu, Seoul, 135-854, Korea
hjchoi@icu.ac.kr

Abstract. The error-backpropagation (EBP) algorithm for learning multilayer perceptrons (MLPs) is known to have good features of robustness and economical efficiency. However, the algorithm has difficulty in selecting an optimal constant learning rate and thus results in non-optimal learning speed and inflexible operation for working data. This paper introduces an elastic learning rate that guarantees convergence of learning and its local realization by online update of MLP parameters into the original EBP algorithm in order to complement the non-optimality. The results of experiments on a speaker verification system with Korean speech database are presented and discussed to demonstrate the performance improvement of the proposed method in terms of learning speed and flexibility for working data of the original EBP algorithm.

Keywords: machine learning, neural networks, speech interaction

1 Introduction

The error-backpropagation (EBP) algorithm is prevailing in multilayer-perceptron (MLP) learning. For training MLPs, the EBP algorithm is widely used due to its robustness in overfitting and its economical efficiency in terms of the number of learning parameters and the size of required memory [1], [2]. In the EBP algorithm, selection of an appropriate constant learning rate is important for the learning speed and recognition rate of an MLP. In general, an "optimal" learning rate lies within a range of "effective" learning rates which provide near-best performance [3]. This range is obtained from training data and then applied to working data, assuming that the properties of the training data are the same as those of the working data.

We notice that the original EBP algorithm has a drawback in selecting an optimal learning rate because it uses learning rates which are constant. In reality, the optimal learning rate does change according to the global and local progress of a given learning experiment. The learning rate in the initial stage of learning may be different from that of the final stage. Learning rates for various learning models may not be the same

---

[*] This research was supported by University IT Research Center Project.

even in the same stage of learning. Moreover, for the range of effective learning rates, the properties of working data are likely to be different from those of training data, contrary to the assumption mentioned above. In this case, the optimal learning rate selected for the training data may be different from that for the working data. Thus, it would be more reliable to keep the effective range as broad as possible. The original EBP algorithm keeps its learning rate constant for the whole process of learning, neglecting that proper learning rate may change with the progress of learning. This behavior of EBP results in lazy learning. Moreover, sticking to a constant learning rate tends to narrow down the effective range where the optimal learning rate can be located. This defect would reduce the flexibility of the EBP algorithm when applied to the working data.

In this paper, we propose a modified EBP algorithm which adopts "elastic" learning rates in the online update mode so that faster learning speed and broader effective range can be obtained. The algorithm senses all the aspects of dynamicity in MLP learning and applies appropriate learning rates according to the progress of learning. The dynamic range of elastic learning rates is searched beforehand by applying various constant learning rates of the original EBP, in order to assure the convergence of the given learning. The elastic learning rate catches the detailed progress of learning, and the online update of the MLP parameters realizes the learning pattern by pattern. This paper discusses the performance of the proposed method through experiments using a speaker verification system based on MLPs and a Korean speech database for connected four-digit speech.

2 MLP Learning with EBP and Its Non-optimality

MLPs learn models of learning by establishing decision boundaries that discriminate the model areas. If patterns of models are fully presented in an iterative manner and internal parameters of an MLP are adjusted so that all patterns of each model are classified into their corresponding model, the decision boundaries will finally be settled within the optimal positions.

The commonly used EBP algorithm updates the weights of an MLP using the information related to a given pattern and current weights status as the following formulae:

$$w_{ij}(n+1) = w_{ij}(n) + \Delta w_{ij}(n)$$
$$= w_{ij}(n) - \eta \frac{\partial e_p(n)}{\partial w_{ij}(n)} \cdot \quad (1)$$

$$e_p(n) = \frac{1}{2} \sum_{k=1}^{M} e_k^2(n) \cdot \quad (2)$$

$$e_k(n) = d_k(n) - y_k(n) \cdot \quad (3)$$

here, w_{ij} stands for weighted link from computational node j to node i, n for update count of weighted link, e_p for summation of error energies from all output nodes for given pattern p, and e_k, d_k and y_k stand for error, learning objective output, and network output, respectively, of output node k. M designates the number of output nodes and η the learning rate determining how much portion of the change of weighted link Δw_{ij} is applied to the update.

The objective of learning is in general designated to 1 if the output node corresponds to the model of the current pattern, or to 0 or -1 otherwise, according to whether the type of activation function is binary or bipolar, respectively. Updates of weighted links continue until some criteria are satisfied. For a typical case, the summation of e_p's for all learning patterns goes down below a certain value. After learning is complete, the network outputs (each converging to its own objective) are derived from the learned weighted links and the decision boundaries are formed along the valleys between the output peaks of all models.

To obtain the best discrimination of an MLP and learning duration of the all models with the EBP algorithm, distinct learning rates η's must be searched. Too large or too small η tends to lead poor discrimination and long duration. In general, various η's need to be tested by decreasing from large to small values (or vice versa) within a suitable range, and the optimal η need to be selected to obtain the best discrimination and shortest duration of learning.

However, the optimal η for the best learning changes according to global and local progress of learning. One epoch is the duration in which all patterns to be learned are presented once. As learning epochs proceed, the temporal value of η should decrease by large to prevent the learning from oscillating around the desired objective. Even within a single epoch, proper η may differ from pattern to pattern because individual learning of a pattern progresses differently from those of other patterns. The original EBP algorithm adopts a constant η and does not consider such variation of learning progress, hence cannot achieve the optimal learning. That is, it cannot obtain both the best discrimination and the shortest duration at once.

The optimal η is located within a range of effective η's, which provide near-best performance. This range is obtained from training data and applied to working data, assuming that the properties of training data are the same as those of working data. In reality, however, the properties of working data are not necessarily the same as those of training data, simply because the amount of the latter is generally larger than that of the former and thus the latter has more variation. Accordingly, the optimal η selected for training data may not guarantee the best performance for working data. To obtain as high performance for working data as possible, it is therefore important for the range of effective η's to be as broad as possible so that more variation of working data is prepared for.

3 Proposed Method

To enable the EBP algorithm to prepare for the variation of learning progress and the difference between training and working data of an MLP, we present a modified EBP algorithm. The modification aims to achieve three goals: (1) to guarantee the convergence of learning, (2) to catch the progress of individual pattern, and (3) to realize the individual progress of each pattern to the MLP.

First, to guarantee the convergence of learning. To achieve this goal we adopt a kind of "elastic" learning rate. By this means, dynamic excitation by learning patterns should not cause a given learning to become distant from the desired objective. To acquire the final convergence in learning, empirical information can be utilized that has been obtained by previous searches for training data. In the proposed method, we adopt the upper and lower limits of the constant learning rates each of which has led to convergence in preceding evaluations using the original EBP algorithm. Any of elastic learning rates within this range will guarantee convergence.

Second, to catch the individual progress of each learning pattern. Establishing decision boundaries can be analyzed by local error gradient of model-specific output node. When the local error gradient of output node k is designated as δ_k, the corresponding model generates δ_k during learning and it repulses the decision boundaries which are shaped arbitrarily at the first stage of learning, establishing them gradually as borders of model areas. δ_k is calculated by error e_k and the first differential function of output activation function φ. The value of the first differential function is obtained from the weighted and summed input v_k to output node k. The calculus form of δ_k is expressed as follows:

$$\delta_k = e_k \cdot \varphi'(v_k). \qquad (4)$$

e_k and $\varphi'(v_k)$ yield significant values to the patterns located nearby decision boundaries contact to the model area of node k and the patterns within the areas of other models over the decision boundaries. Learning continues until δ_k is minimized for the given pattern and the value of δ_k shows how much the pattern must be learned hereafter at a point of learning time. Among the ingredients of δ_k, e_k can more effectively present the progress of learning of a pattern due to its linearity as seen in Eqn 3, so it is adopted to catch the individual progress of each learning pattern.

Third, to apply the individual progress of the given pattern to an MLP. The offline update mode of the EBP algorithm calculates the changes of weighted link vector for all learning patterns, averages them, and updates the weighted link vector once per an epoch as follows:

$$w_{ij}(t+1) = w_{ij}(t) - \frac{\eta}{N} \sum_{p=1}^{N} \frac{\partial e_p(t)}{\partial w_{ij}(t)}. \qquad (5)$$

where, t stands for epoch count and N for the number of patterns given during an epoch. Compared with the offline mode, the online mode shown as Eqn. 1 updates the weighted link vector whenever the change of weighted link vector is calculated for each pattern. In the offline mode, all the patterns have to be learned with the same learning rate. In the online mode, however, each pattern can have opportunity to be learned with the proper learning rate as to its local learning progress because of its property of pattern by pattern update.

The three means presented above construct the following formulae for the update of weighted link vector in the proposed method:

$$f(n) = \frac{e_C^{\,2}(n) - e_{OBJ}}{R_{ACT} - e_{OBJ}}. \qquad (6)$$

$$\eta(n) = \begin{cases} f(n) \cdot L_{HIGH} & \text{if } f(n) \cdot L_{HIGH} > L_{LOW} \\ L_{LOW} & \text{otherwise} \end{cases}. \qquad (7)$$

$$w_{ij}(n+1) = w_{ij}(n) - \eta(n)\frac{\partial e_p(n)}{\partial w_{ij}(n)}. \tag{8}$$

where, $e_C^2(n)$ stands for error energy form of the error yielded by the output node to where the given pattern belongs, R_{ACT} for the possible range of the error energy for the same output node, e_{OBJ} for the objective error energy of given learning, and L_{HIGH} and L_{LOW} for the upper and lower limit, respectively, such that the range established by them guarantees the learning to converge. $f(n)$ stands for error energy normalization function to gauge the learning progress of the pattern and normalize it into the range from 0 to 1. $f(n)$ presents high values for deficiently learned patterns and low values for sufficiently learned patterns. $\eta(n)$ stands for elastic learning rate scaled from the normalized error energy of the pattern into the range limited by L_{HIGH} and L_{LOW}. Eqn. 8 is the finally obtained expression which the elastic learning rate is adopted into the original EBP algorithm in the online mode.

4 Performance Evaluation

To evaluate the proposed method, we use the speaker verification system implemented in [4] as a test bed. This section describes briefly the system, the speech database used, and the conditions of experiment, then analyzes and discusses the results of the experiment.

The speaker verification system isolates words from input utterance, classifies the isolated words into nine streams of Korean continuants (/a/, /e/, /ə/, /o/, /u/, /ɨ/, /i/, /l/, nasals), and learns an enrolling speaker for each continuant using MLPs. The system then calculates identity scores for customer speakers. Since the system uses the continuants as speech recognition units, the underlying densities exhibit mono-modal distribution [5]. Thus, it is good enough for each MLP to have a two-layered structure that includes one hidden layer [6], [7]. Since the MLPs need to learn only two models, i.e., one for the enrolling speaker and the other for the background speakers, they can learn the models using one output node and two hidden nodes. In total, nine MLPs are provided for the nine continuants.

The speech data used in this experiment are the recorded voice of connected four digits, spoken by 40 Korean male and female speakers. The digits are ten Arabic numerals pronounced in Korean as /goN/, /il/, /i/, /sam/, /sa/, /o/, /yug/, /cil/, /pal/, /gu/, each corresponding to a digit from 0 to 9. Each speaker utters 35 words of different 4-digit strings four times, when the utterance is recorded in 16-bit resolution and 16-kHz sampling. Three of the four utterance samples are used to enroll the speaker, and the last utterance is used for verification. In order to learn the enrolling speakers discriminatively, additional 29 male and female speakers are participated as background speakers for MLPs other than the above 40 speakers.

In our experiment, the conditions for MLP learning are set up as follows [8]:

- Input patterns are normalized such that the elements of each pattern vector are placed into the range from -1.0 to +1.0.
- The learning targets of output node are +0.9 for the enrolling speaker and -0.9 for the background speakers to obtain faster speed in EBP learning.
- Speech patterns are presented in an alternating fashion for the two models during learning. In most cases, however, the numbers of patterns for the two models are not the same. Accordingly, the patterns are presented repetitively (more than once)

for the model with fewer patterns until all the patterns have been presented once for the model with more patterns. This completes one epoch of learning.
- Since learning may stop at a local minimum, the epochs of learning are limited to 1000 maximum.

In our experiment, each of the 40 speakers can be treated as both the enrolling speaker and the test speaker. When one of them is picked as the test speaker, then the other 39 speakers are used as imposters. As a result, 35 tests using the 35 words are performed for a true speaker and 1,365 (35 * 39) tests for the imposters. In total, we performed 1,400 (35 * 40) trials of test for true speaker and 54,600 (35 * 40 * 39) trials for imposters.

The experiment aims to demonstrate the performance of the proposed method as compared to the original EBP algorithm, using the speaker verification system as the test bed. Here we first obtain the best performance of the system using the original online EBP algorithm and the optimized performance using the proposed method. Then, the two methods are compared for learning duration and operational flexibility to conclude that the proposed method exhibits superior performance.

In the results of our experiment, error rate stands for equal error rate, and the number of learning epochs for average number of epochs used to enroll a speaker for an isolated word. These values are calculated by taking the average of values obtained from three trials of learning, each trial being set to the same MLP conditions.

Fig. 1 depicts the changes in the performance of the system implemented using the original online EBP algorithm, measured with respect to various values of learning rate and objective error energy. The values in the figure chase the trajectories of the numbers of learning epochs and verification errors, with a fixed value of 0.01 for learning objective error energy in the case of figure (a) and a fixed value of 0.5 for learning rate in the case of figure (b). In figure (a), the best learning rate, 0.5, is obtained when the number of learning epochs is 172.3 and the error rate is 1.65 %. In figure (b), the best learning objective error energy, 0.005, is obtained when the number of learning epochs is 301.5 and the error rate is 1.59 %.

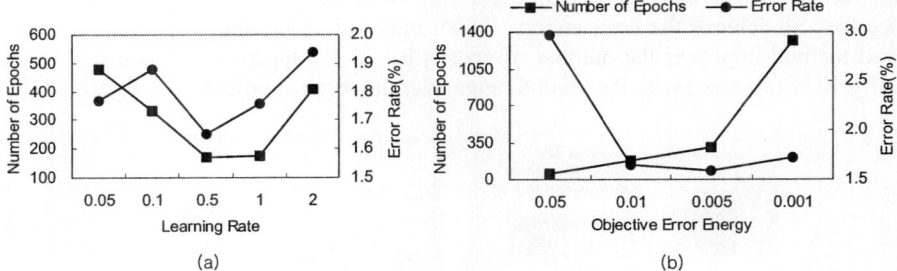

Fig. 1. Performance of the original online EBP algorithm for the ranges of (a) learning rate and (b) objective error energy

Fig. 2 depicts the changes in the performance of the system implemented using the proposed method, measured with respect to various values of upper and lower limits. Note that all the performance points in the figure assume a fixed value of 0.005 for (learning) objective error energy. The values in the figure chase the trajectories of the numbers of learning epochs (figure (a)) and verification errors (figure(b)), when the upper and lower limits are set to the combination as depicted. These limits, especially the lower limits, have guaranteed the convergence in the search of learning parameter with the original online EBP. In figure (a), for every upper limit specified, the smallest number of epochs is obtained when the lower limit is 0.5, and the best such number is 214.5 when the upper limit is 2. In figure (b), any particular relationships of the error rates to the upper and lower limits are not found, but the error rates lie in a narrow range between 1.58 % and 1.69 % for all combinations of the upper and lower limits. The best performance, number of epochs 255.2 and error rate 1.58 %, is determined at the upper limit 2 and the lower limit 0.5 in the search.

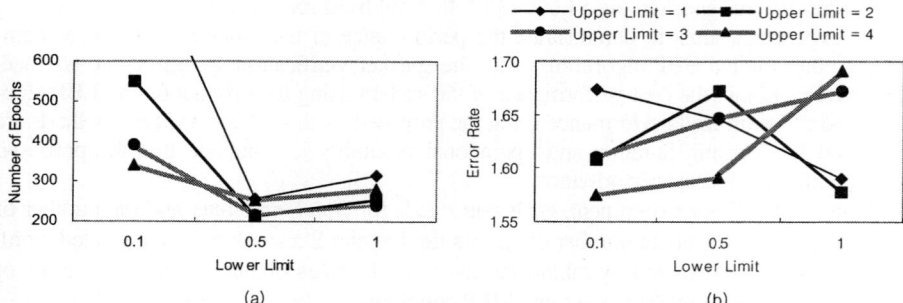

Fig. 2. Performance of the proposed method for various ranges of upper and lower limits: (a) number of epochs and (b) error rate

Fig. 3 compares the best performance of the proposed method with the original online EBP algorithm. Figure (a) compares them with respect to number of epochs and error rate, and figure (b) shows the rates of improvement in the number of epochs. Note that the performance of the proposed method is shown for two different ranges of upper and lower limits: [1..2] and [0.5..2]. In our experiment, the first range achieves no increase in the error rate but the second range increases the error rate by 0.08 % over the best error rate of the original online EBP algorithm. Both ranges are meaningful, however, since they all achieve the error energy, 0.005, imposed as learning objective. The proposed method improves the number of epochs by 20 % (approx.) with the first range and by 40 % (approx.) with the second range over the original online EBP algorithm.

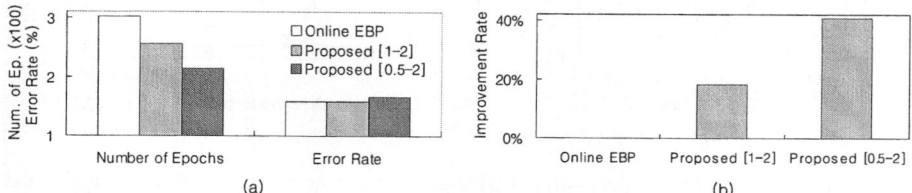

Fig. 3. (a) Performance comparison of the proposed method with the original online EBP algorithm and (b) the rates of improvement in the number of epochs

Fig. 4 shows the enhanced flexibility of the proposed method over the original online EBP algorithm. For the range [0.1..2] of constant learning rates, the original algorithm shows the best performance of 301.5 for the number of epochs and 1.59 % for error rate, and the worst performance of 1315.3 and 1.88 % respectively. For the range [0.1..2] of lower limits with an upper limit added by 2 to a lower limit (i.e., keeping the width of the range as 2), the proposed method presents the best performance of 209.4 and 1.63 %, respectively, and the worst performance of 566.8 and 1.76 %, respectively, for the number of epochs and error rate. The differential rates between the best and the worst for the number of epochs and error rate are 336 % and 18 %, respectively, with the original online EBP algorithm, and 166 % and 8 %, respectively, with the proposed method. From these numbers, we can say that the flexibility of the proposed method is more than two times of that of the original online EBP algorithm.

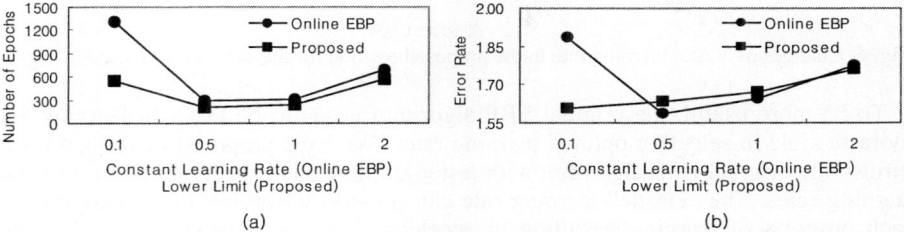

Fig. 4. Enhanced flexibility of the proposed method over the original online EBP algorithm for (a) number of epochs and (b) error rate

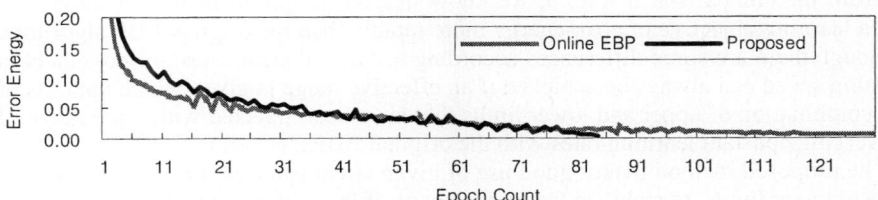

Fig. 5. Decreasing curves of error energy for the original online EBP algorithm and the proposed method in a typical learning sample

To observe the internal behavior of the proposed method, we depict in Fig. 5 the decreasing curves of error energy for the original online EBP algorithm and the proposed method, both using a typical learning sample. In addition, we depict in Fig. 6 the changes of elastic learning rate in the proposed method. The learning experiment is conducted using the constant learning rate 0.5 in the original online EBP algorithm and using the range [0.5..3] in the proposed method. As in Fig. 5, the decreasing curve of the proposed method exhibits slower movement in the initial stage of learning than the original online EBP algorithm, but goes steeper and more linear in the middle and final stages. These characteristics after the middle stage may be interpreted from the changes of elastic learning rate as shown in Fig. 6, where one unit in the horizontal scale represents one epoch consisting of 580 learning patterns (and the epochs are depicted till 55). After the point about 8 of epoch count, elastic learning rates over 0.5 are rarely detected and the magnitudes of the learning rates become lowered. This implies that many learning patterns are sufficiently learned earlier to that point except a few of patterns and these patterns raise high learning rates, but that even the learning rates get down rapidly in frequency and magnitude. The high learning rates partly generated for the poorly-learned drop more error energy for an epoch of the entire patterns, and this effect makes the curve of error energy linearly decreasing and the duration of learning short.

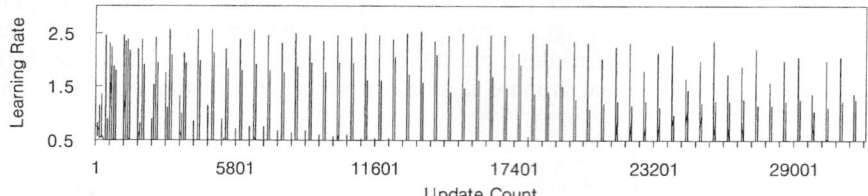

Fig. 6. Changes of elastic learning rate in the proposed method for the same sample used in Fig. 5

To be more useful, the original EBP algorithm needs to be faster in learning and more flexible in selecting optimal learning rates. We have proposed modifications to furnish the original EBP algorithm with faster learning and broader range of effective learning rates. The "elastic" learning rate can provide a learning rate appropriate to each progress of learning, resulting in accelerated learning speed. In addition, the selection of the optimal learning rate for working data can be flexible by the elastic learning rate because the range of effective learning rates becomes broader than that of the original EBP algorithm.

From the comparison in Fig. 3, we know that the proposed method achieves the given learning objective of error energy more rapidly than the original EBP algorithm. Although there are some differences according to marked error rates, improvement in learning speed can always be achieved if an effective range is given which consists of any combination of upper and lower limits that have been selected within the range of converging constant learning rates with the original EBP algorithm.

The proposed method makes good use of given circumstances, i.e. the range of upper and lower limits, to stabilize the performance of learning and to result in a broader range of effective performance as shown in Fig. 4. The proposed method exhibits near-invariant performance for the range of lower limits (with fixed interval to upper limits). For the same range, the original EBP algorithm with constant learning rates shows even worse performance in the lower end of the range and the range which provides effective performance must be more narrowed. The reason for the invariant performance of proposed method is that the method finds most proper learning rate within the range and applies it to update of weighted link vector for each pattern. Therefore, even if the properties of working data would be considerably different from that of learning data, the performance in learning speed and error rate for the working data would not be injured significantly.

The heart of the proposed method is the steady and active reduction of errors by the elastic learning rate as shown in Figs. 5 and 6. The elastic learning rate of the proposed method attacks the errors by the most power within limits to guarantee convergence of learning. This property enables the original EBP algorithm to keep the errors of an MLP steadily decreasing and acquire faster learning and more flexibility by the simple means.

5 Conclusion

The results we have presented in this paper are good evidence to verify the more fleet learning and the higher pliability of the proposed method over the original EBP algorithm. In spite of its high capability, the original EBP algorithm suffers from slow learning for learning data and difficulty in selecting an optimal learning rate for working data. To reform these inferiorities, we have suggested the revised version of the EBP algorithm and demonstrated the performance improvement through the experiments of learning on the MLP-based speaker verification system with the Korean speech database. The proposed method would be useful for other MLP-applied signal processing system when the EBP algorithm is adopted for learning MLPs, as well as pattern recognition applications demonstrated in this paper.

References

1. Lawrence, S. and Giles, C. L.: Overfitting and Neural Networks: conjugate gradient and backpropagation. IEEE-INNS-ENNS International Joint Conference on Neural Networks **1** (2000) 114-119
2. Towsey, M., Alpsan, D., Sztriha, L.: Training a Neural Network with Conjugate Gradient Methods. IEEE International Conference on Neural Networks **1** (1995) 373-378
3. Wilson, D. R. and Martinez, T. R.: The Need for Small Learning Rates on Large Problems. International Joint Conference on Neural Networks **1** (2001) 115-119
4. Lee, T., Hwang, B.: Continuants Based Neural Speaker Verification System. Lecture Notes in Artificial Intelligence **2972** (2004) 89-98
5. Savic, M., Sorensen, J.: Phoneme Based Speaker Verification. IEEE International Conference on Acoustics, Speech, and Signal Processing **2** (1992) 165-168
6. Delacretaz, D. P., Hennebert, J.: Text-Prompted Speaker Verification Experiments with Phoneme Specific MLPs. IEEE International Conference on Acoustics, Speech, and Signal Processing **2** (1998) 777-780
7. Lippmann, R. P.: An Introduction to Computing with Neural Nets. IEEE Acoustics, Speech, and Signal Processing Magazine **4** (1987) 4-22
8. Bengio, Y.: Neural Networks for Speech and Sequence Recognition. International Thomson Computer Press, London Boston (1995)

Learning Dynamics
of Neural Networks with Singularity
– Standard Gradient vs. Natural Gradient

Hyeyoung Park[1], Masato Inoue[2,3], and Masato Okada[3,4]

[1] Computer Science Dept., Kyungpook National University,
Sankyuk-dong, Buk-gu, Daegu, 702-701, Korea
hypark@knu.ac.kr
[2] Department of Computational Intelligence and Systems Science,
Interdisciplinary Graduate School of Science and Engineering,
Tokyo Institute of Technology, Yokohama 226-8502, Japan
inoue@sp.dis.titech.ac.jp
[3] RIKEN BSI, Hirosawa 2-1, Wako, Saitama 351-0198, Japan
[4] "Intelligent Cooperation and Control", PRESTO, JST,
c/o RIKEN BSI, Saitama 351-0198, Japan
okada@brain.riken.jp

Abstract. In hierarchical models, such as neural networks, there exist complex singular structures. The singularity is known to affect estimation performances and learning dynamics of the models. Recently, there have been a number of studies on properties of obtained estimators for the models, but there are few studies on the dynamical properties of learning used for obtaining the estimators. Using two-layer neural networks, we investigate influences of singularities on dynamics of standard gradient learning and natural gradient learning under various learning conditions. In the standard gradient learning, we found a quasi-plateau phenomenon, which is severer than the well known plateau in some cases. The slow convergence due to the quasi-plateau and plateau becomes extremely serious when an optimal point is in a neighborhood of a singularity. In the natural gradient learning, however, the quasi-plateau and plateau are not observed and convergence speed is hardly affected by singularity.

1 Introduction

A learning model has a set of modifiable parameters, which plays a role of coordinates in the parameter space. Learning is a process of searching an optimal point step by step in the parameter space. In a hierarchical set of models, a low order model is included in the parameter space of a larger order model as a union of subspaces. On the points within the subspaces corresponding to a lower order model, the Fisher information matrix degenerates and the subspaces make singularities. Therefore, a parameter space has a complex singular structure, which is responsible for various nontrivial properties of hierarchical models. All problems related to this singularity are generally called singularity problems.

There are two important issues on singularity problems. One is estimation performances of the models in the singular case that the optimum is on a singular point in the parameter space. Since the Fisher-Cramér-Rao paradigm does not hold at singularities, the classical theoretical results on properties of statistical estimators cannot be applied in the singular case. This is a fatal problem in model selection of hierarchical models, and we need a new statistical theory for the singular case. Recently, some asymptotic properties of maximum likelihood estimator and Bayesian predictive distribution have been studied[2–4, 11], and the results showed that the properties of the estimators in singular case are strictly different from those in regular case.

The other important issues in singularity problems is dynamical properties of learning in the models, which is affected by the singular structure. Since we need to use learning process to obtain an estimator, it is very important to see what occurs around the singularities during learning. The importance should be especially emphasized when the optimum is on a singular point or in a neighborhood of a singular point. Therefore, we need to investigate three types of learning task classified by the position of optimal point in parameter space; regular case, singular case, and near-singular case. Furthermore, the dynamics of different learning algorithms are strictly different, and thus we also need to see the different properties of different learning algorithms.

The conventional works on learning dynamics have been done only for restricted cases. Saad and Solla[10] and Inoue et al[5] investigated dynamics of soft-committee machines, and discussed about plateau caused by permutation symmetry which is one of singularity. However, the soft-committee machine is not a hierarchical model, and thus it is not sufficient to investigate various phenomena might be caused by singularities. Riegler and Biehl [8] investigated the dynamics of general multilayer perceptrons (MLP), but they mainly investigated regular cases, which is far from singularities. Amari et al[2], Rattray et al[9], and Inoue et al[5] discussed the difference between standard gradient and natural gradient, and showed that natural gradient can efficiently avoid the bad influence of singularity. However, these works were also restricted because they used simple cone models and soft-committee machines.

In this paper, we investigate dynamics of MLP in three types of learning task to see influences of singularity in various situations. We also compare dynamics of natural gradient and standard gradient for MLP. This work could be a preliminary step to one of important topics that should be discussed in studies on singularity problems.

2 Model with Singularity

A multilayer perceptron (MLP) is a representative learning model with hierarchical singularity. A simple MLP is defined as

$$\zeta' = f_{J,w}(\boldsymbol{\xi}) = \sum_{i=1}^{K} w_i g(\boldsymbol{J}_i \cdot \boldsymbol{\xi}). \qquad (1)$$

Here, $\boldsymbol{\xi} \in \Re^N$ denotes the input vector; $\boldsymbol{J}_i \in \Re^N$ and $w_i \in \Re$ denote the weight parameters connected to the i-th hidden unit; N denotes the number of input nodes; and $g(\cdot)$ denotes an activation function. We also assumed that there exist a teacher network of same architecture with M hidden units and parameter $\boldsymbol{B}_n \in \Re^N$ and $v_n \in \Re$ $(n = 1, \ldots, M)$. For a given input $\boldsymbol{\xi}$, the teacher network generates an output $\zeta = f_{\boldsymbol{B},v}(\boldsymbol{\xi})$.

The MLP has a hierarchical structure, which means that an MLP with K-hidden units are included in the parameter space of an MLP with $K + 1$ or more hidden units. As an example, let us consider an MLP with 2 hidden units. Parameters of the MLP are given by $\boldsymbol{J}_1, \boldsymbol{J}_2, w_1,$ and w_2. When the parameters satisfy a condition defined by

$$w_1 w_2 \|\boldsymbol{J}_1\| \|\boldsymbol{J}_2\| \|\boldsymbol{J}_1 - \boldsymbol{J}_2\| = 0, \qquad (2)$$

a hidden unit is redundant, and the MLP has exactly same behavior to an MLP with 1 hidden unit.

An important thing is that all the points satisfying the condition (2) are singular. When we use an MLP for learning, we usually do not know the optimal network size, and use sufficiently large network. Therefore it is often the case that we use K-hidden units even though the optimal network has $K - 1$ or less hidden units. In this case, the optimum is located in the singular subspaces. We call this case a singular case. In the singular case, the optimum is not represented by only one points, but some subspaces, which means that the goal of learning is not unique. These unusual situations make some influence on learning dynamics. More important and frequent case is not exact singular, but near-singular case. This could be the most common case that we meet in real applications. In the near-singular case, we can guess the nontrivial singular structure can affect the dynamics. Therefore, in order to investigate the influence of singularity, we need to investigate the three types of learning; singular, near-singular, and regular case, but conventional studies focused only on the regular case or soft committee machine in which the optimum is always uniquely determined. The MLP used in this paper can represent the three essential types of learning task. By using it, we can investigate essential properties of dynamics related to singularities.

3 Analysis of Learning Dynamics

3.1 Gradient Descent Learning

We investigate two on-line gradient descent learning algorithm; the steepest gradient learning and the natural gradient learning. At each learning step, new training data $(\boldsymbol{\xi}, \zeta)$ is generated from the teacher network. The student network is trained to decrease the squared error defined as

$$E^{\text{trn}}(\boldsymbol{\xi}, \zeta) = \frac{1}{2}[f_{\boldsymbol{B},v}(\boldsymbol{\xi}) - f_{\boldsymbol{J},w}(\boldsymbol{\xi})]^2 = \frac{1}{2}\left[\sum_{i=1}^{K} w_i g(x_i) - \sum_{n=1}^{M} v_n g(y_n)\right]^2, \qquad (3)$$

where $x_i = \boldsymbol{J}_i \cdot \boldsymbol{\xi}$, $y_n = \boldsymbol{B}_n \cdot \boldsymbol{\xi}$. When we use standard gradient learning, the update term is given by

$$\Delta \boldsymbol{J}_i = -\frac{\eta}{N}\delta_i \boldsymbol{\xi}, \quad \Delta w_i = -\frac{\eta}{N}g(x_i)e_{\boldsymbol{\xi}} \quad (4)$$

where $e_{\boldsymbol{\xi}} = \left[\sum_{j=1}^{K} w_j g(x_j) - \sum_{n=1}^{M} v_n g(y_n)\right]$, $\delta_i = w_i g'(x_i)e_{\boldsymbol{\xi}}$, and η is a learning rate.

For the natural gradient learning, we need to assume a stochastic model of the student network, which is defined by a conditional probability distribution of output ζ' for a given input $\boldsymbol{\xi}$, $p(\zeta'|\boldsymbol{\xi};\boldsymbol{\Upsilon})$, where $\boldsymbol{\Upsilon} = [w_1,..,w_K,\boldsymbol{J}_1^T,..,\boldsymbol{J}_K^T]$. The most typical one is the standard normal distribution which is written by

$$p(\zeta'|\boldsymbol{\xi}; J, w) = \frac{1}{\sqrt{2\pi}}\exp\left\{-\frac{1}{2}(\zeta' - f_{J,w}(\boldsymbol{\xi}))^2\right\}. \quad (5)$$

Then the Fisher information matrix for the (stochastic) student network is given by $\langle \nabla \log p(\zeta'|\boldsymbol{\xi};\boldsymbol{\Upsilon})\nabla \log p(\zeta'|\boldsymbol{\xi};\boldsymbol{\Upsilon})^T\rangle_{\boldsymbol{\xi}}$, where ∇ denotes partial derivation with respect to the parameter $\boldsymbol{\Upsilon}$; $\langle \cdot \rangle_{\boldsymbol{\xi}}$ denotes an expectation with respect to random input $\boldsymbol{\xi}$; and T denotes the transposition.

For the multilayer perceptrons defined in Section 2, the Fisher information matrix $\boldsymbol{G}$ can be written by using four blocks of matrix such as

$$\boldsymbol{G} = \begin{bmatrix} \boldsymbol{G}_{ww} & \boldsymbol{G}_{wJ} \\ \boldsymbol{G}_{wJ}^T & \boldsymbol{G}_{JJ} \end{bmatrix} = \begin{bmatrix} [G_{w_i w_j}]_{i,j=1..K} & [G_{w_i J_j}]_{i,j=1..K} \\ [G_{w_i J_j}]_{i,j=1..K}^T & [G_{J_i J_j}]_{i,j=1..K} \end{bmatrix}, \quad (6)$$

where

$G_{w_i w_j} = \langle g(x_i)g(x_j)\rangle_{\boldsymbol{\xi}}$, $G_{w_i J_j} = \langle w_j g(x_i)g'(x_j)\boldsymbol{\xi}\rangle_{\boldsymbol{\xi}}$, $G_{J_i J_j} = \langle w_i w_j g'(x_i)g'(x_j)\boldsymbol{\xi}\boldsymbol{\xi}^T\rangle_{\boldsymbol{\xi}}$.

By assuming the random input $\boldsymbol{\xi}$ is subject to the standard multivariate normal distribution and using $g(u) = \text{erf}(u/\sqrt{2})$, we can obtain the explicit form of $\boldsymbol{G}$[12]. We can also write $\boldsymbol{G}^{-1}$ in similar form such as

$$\boldsymbol{G}^{-1} = \begin{bmatrix} \boldsymbol{G}^{ww} & \boldsymbol{G}^{wJ} \\ (\boldsymbol{G}^{wJ})^T & \boldsymbol{G}^{JJ} \end{bmatrix} = \begin{bmatrix} [G^{w_i w_j}]_{i,j=1..K} & [G^{w_i J_j}]_{i,j=1..K} \\ [G^{w_i J_j}]_{i,j=1..K}^T & [G^{J_i J_j}]_{i,j=1..K} \end{bmatrix}, \quad (7)$$

and each block can be written by

$$G^{w_i J_j} = \phi_{ij}\boldsymbol{U}^T, \quad G^{J_i J_j} = \theta_{ij}\boldsymbol{I} + \boldsymbol{U}\boldsymbol{\Theta}_{ij}\boldsymbol{U}^T, \quad \boldsymbol{U} = [\boldsymbol{J}_1,\ldots,\boldsymbol{J}_K], \quad (8)$$

where the scalars $G^{w_i w_j}$ and θ_{ij}, a $1 \times K$ vector $\boldsymbol{\phi}_{ij}$, and a $K \times K$ matrix $\boldsymbol{\Theta}_{ij}$ can be deterministically calculated for given parameter $\boldsymbol{J}$ and w (See [12] for details). Using the obtained $\boldsymbol{G}^{-1}$, the update term of natural gradient learning is given by

$$\tilde{\Delta}\boldsymbol{J}_i = \sum_{k}^{K}\left((G^{w_k J_i})^T \Delta w_k + G^{J_i J_k}\Delta \boldsymbol{J}_k\right), \tilde{\Delta} w_i = \sum_{k}^{K}\left(G^{w_i w_k}\Delta w_k + G^{w_i J_k}\Delta \boldsymbol{J}_k\right). \quad (9)$$

3.2 Statistical Mechanical Approach

Using statistical mechanical approach[8, 10], we investigate average dynamics at thermodynamic limit, i.e., the limit of $N \to \infty$. The estimation accuracy of the learning is evaluated using the generalization error, which is defined as

$$E^{\text{gen}} = \left\langle \frac{1}{2} \{ f_{\boldsymbol{B},w}(\boldsymbol{\xi}) - f_{\boldsymbol{J},w}(\boldsymbol{\xi}) \}^2 \right\rangle_{\boldsymbol{\xi}}. \tag{10}$$

Under the assumption that each element of the input vector is iid with zero mean and unit variance, the generalization error at the thermodynamic limit can be deterministically described by using new order parameters defined as $R_{in} \equiv \boldsymbol{J}_i^T \boldsymbol{B}_n$, $Q_{ij} \equiv \boldsymbol{J}_i^T \boldsymbol{J}_j$, and $T_{nm} \equiv \boldsymbol{B}_n^T \boldsymbol{B}_m$. Especially when $g(u) = \text{erf}(u/\sqrt{2})$, the explicit form of E^{gen} is given by

$$E^{\text{gen}} = \frac{1}{\pi} \left[\sum_{i,j}^{K} w_i w_j \arcsin \left(\frac{Q_{ij}}{\sqrt{1+Q_{ii}}\sqrt{1+Q_{jj}}} \right) \right.$$
$$+ \sum_{m,n}^{M} v_m v_n \arcsin \left(\frac{T_{mn}}{\sqrt{1+T_{mm}}\sqrt{1+T_{nn}}} \right) \tag{11}$$
$$\left. -2 \sum_{i}^{K} \sum_{n}^{M} w_i v_n \arcsin \left(\frac{R_{in}}{\sqrt{1+Q_{ii}}\sqrt{1+T_{nn}}} \right) \right]$$

Therefore, in order to investigate learning dynamics, it is sufficient to obtain motion equations of the order parameters R_{in} and Q_{ij}, and the parameter w_i. From the definition of the order parameters, their update terms of standard gradient learning can be easily obtained as

$$\Delta R_{in} = \Delta \boldsymbol{J}_i \cdot \boldsymbol{B}_n, \quad \Delta Q_{ij} = \Delta \boldsymbol{J}_i \cdot \boldsymbol{J}_j + \Delta \boldsymbol{J}_j \cdot \boldsymbol{J}_i + \Delta \boldsymbol{J}_i \cdot \Delta \boldsymbol{J}_j. \tag{12}$$

In the thermodynamic limit $N \to \infty$, we introduce a new time variable α ($\Delta \alpha = 1/N$), which can be interpreted as a continuous time variable. Then the motion equations are obtained as

$$\frac{dR_{in}}{d\alpha} = -\eta \left\langle \delta_i y_n \right\rangle_{\boldsymbol{\xi}}, \quad \frac{dQ_{ij}}{d\alpha} = -\eta \left\langle \delta_i x_j + \delta_j x_i \right\rangle_{\boldsymbol{\xi}} + \eta^2 \left\langle \delta_i \delta_j \right\rangle_{\boldsymbol{\xi}}, \quad \frac{dw_i}{d\alpha} = -\eta \left\langle g(x_i) e_{\boldsymbol{\xi}} \right\rangle_{\boldsymbol{\xi}}. \tag{13}$$

In the case of $g(u) = \text{erf}(u/\sqrt{2})$, the motion equations can be given by compact forms with Q_{ij}, R_{in}, T_{nm}, w_i, and v_n [6].

For the natural gradient learning, we can also apply the same method to obtain the motion equations of the order parameters, R_{in} and Q_{ij}, and parameter w_i, which are given by

$$\frac{dR_{in}}{d\alpha} = -\eta \left[\sum_k^K \theta_{ik} \langle \delta_k y_n \rangle_\xi + \boldsymbol{R}_{\bullet n} \sum_k^K \left(\phi_{ki}^T \langle g_k e_\xi \rangle_\xi + \boldsymbol{\Theta}_{ik} \langle \delta_k \boldsymbol{x} \rangle_\xi \right) \right], \tag{14}$$

$$\frac{dQ_{ij}}{d\alpha} = -\eta \left[\boldsymbol{Q}_{\bullet i} \sum_k^K \left(\phi_{kj}^T \langle g_k e_\xi \rangle_\xi + \boldsymbol{\Theta}_{jk} \langle \delta_k \boldsymbol{x} \rangle_\xi \right) + \boldsymbol{Q}_{\bullet j} \sum_k^K \left(\phi_{ki}^T \langle g_k e_\xi \rangle_\xi + \boldsymbol{\Theta}_{ik} \langle \delta_k \boldsymbol{x} \rangle_\xi \right) \right.$$
$$\left. + \sum_k^K \left(\theta_{ik} \langle \delta_k x_j \rangle_\xi + \theta_{jk} \langle \delta_k x_i \rangle_\xi \right) \right] + \eta^2 \left[\sum_{k,l}^K \theta_{ik} \theta_{jl} \langle \delta_k \delta_l \rangle_\xi \right], \tag{15}$$

$$\frac{dw_i}{d\alpha} = -\eta \left[\sum_k^K \left(G^{w_i w_k} \langle g_k e_\xi \rangle_\xi + \phi_{ik} \langle \delta_k \boldsymbol{x} \rangle_\xi \right) \right], \tag{16}$$

where $\boldsymbol{R}_{\bullet n} = [R_{1n}, .., R_{Kn}]$, $\boldsymbol{Q}_{\bullet i} = [Q_{1i}, .., Q_{Ki}]$, $\boldsymbol{x} = [x_1, .., x_K]^T$, and $g_k = g(x_k)$. The motion equations of natural gradient given in [5,9] is for a soft committee machines, and we generalized it for MLP. Detail descriptions for the equations will be given in [7].

4 Results

4.1 Definition of Learning Tasks

Using the motion equations given in Section 3, we analyzed the dynamics of the standard gradient and natural gradient learning. To see how singularity affects learning dynamics, we first classified learning tasks into three types according to the condition of optimal point as mentioned in section 2; regular, singular, and near-singular types. We focused on the case $K = M = 2$, so that the optimal parameters can be directly represented by the parameter of teacher network, $\boldsymbol{B}_1$, $\boldsymbol{B}_2$, v_1, and v_2. In investigations, we used three conditions of teacher parameter to represent three types of learning task: $\boldsymbol{B}_1 \perp \boldsymbol{B}_2$ for regular case, $\boldsymbol{B}_1 = \boldsymbol{B}_2$ for singular case, and $\boldsymbol{B}_1 \cong \boldsymbol{B}_2$ for near-singular case. The condition were defined more concretely using order parameter $\boldsymbol{T} = [T_{nm}]_{n,m=1,2}$ and $\boldsymbol{v} = (v_1, v_2)$ (See Table 1). Note that the teacher network defined for singular can be realized with other parameter conditions, such as $\boldsymbol{J}_1 = 1$, $w_1 = 1$, and $w_2 = 0$. That is, the goal of learning is not uniquely determined.

Table 1. Conditions for teacher network parameters

Task	Regular	Singular	Near-singular
$\boldsymbol{T}, \boldsymbol{v}$	$\begin{bmatrix} 1 & 0 \\ 0 & 1 \end{bmatrix}, \begin{bmatrix} 0.5 \\ 0.5 \end{bmatrix}$	$\begin{bmatrix} 1 & 1 \\ 1 & 1 \end{bmatrix}, \begin{bmatrix} 0.5 \\ 0.5 \end{bmatrix}$	$\begin{bmatrix} 1 & 0.9 \\ 0.9 & 1 \end{bmatrix}, \begin{bmatrix} 0.5 \\ 0.5 \end{bmatrix}$

For tracing motions of learning parameters, we defined their initial conditions as

$$\boldsymbol{Q} = [Q_{ij}]_{i,j=1,2} = \begin{bmatrix} 1 & 0 \\ 0 & 1 \end{bmatrix}, \quad \boldsymbol{R} = [R_{in}]_{i,n=1,2} = \begin{bmatrix} 10^{-2} & 0 \\ 0 & 10^{-2} \end{bmatrix} \tag{17}$$

For the parameter (w_1, w_2), we tried various initial states: $\boldsymbol{w} = (w_1, w_2) = (0.1, 0.1 - \varepsilon)$, $\varepsilon = 0.02, 0.04, 0.09$.

4.2 Dynamics of Standard Gradient

We first analyzed dynamics of standard gradient learning. Time evolutions of the generalization error for three types of learning task are shown in Fig. 1(a). The value of ε was set to 0.02. Note that the learning curves for the three cases are strictly different. In the regular case, we can see a well known plateau discussed in [10]. In the singular case, we can see a new type of slow dynamics, which we call a quasi-plateau[6]. In this situation, the convergence of singular case without plateau takes more time than regular case with plateau. For the near-singular case, we can see that both of plateau and quasi-plateau appear. Conventional studies insisted that the plateau was the main cause of slow convergence of MLP learning, but we here show the exitance of another interesting phenomenon, the quasi-plateau. Considering that the near-singular case are often in real applications, we can say that the quasi-plateau should be regarded as one of main causes of slow learning observed in real applications. The results of on-line learning simulations with finite input dimension ($N = 100$) is also well fitted to the theoretical result.

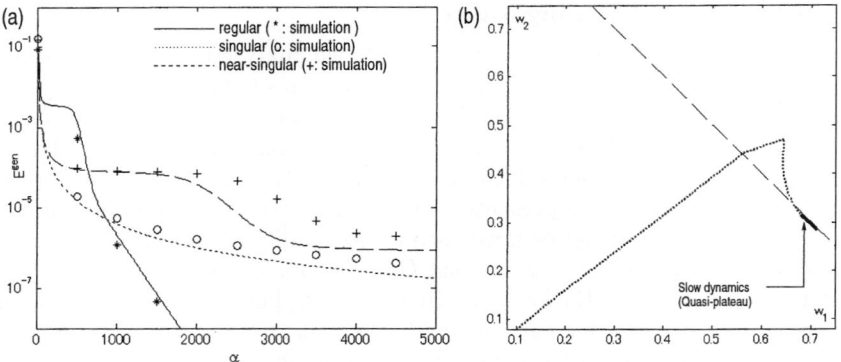

Fig. 1. (a) Evolution of generalization error for three types of learning task (b) Learning trajectory of (w_1, w_2) in singular case

Next, we should discuss when the slow dynamics occur. It has been shown that the plateau is due to the permutation symmetry ($\bm{J}_1 = \bm{J}_2$)[5, 10]. When permutation symmetry occurs, the learning becomes very slow, and it takes long time to break the symmetry. However, in the singular case, the optimal network can be realized at $\bm{J}_1 = \bm{J}_2$, and the permutation symmetry does not have to be broken. This is the reason why the plateau disappears in singular case. An interesting thing is the existence of another slow dynamics in singular case. To explain it, we shows the trajectory in the parameter space of w_1 and w_2 in Fig. 1(b). The dashed straight line shows $w_1 + w_2 = v_1 + v_2 = 1$. All the points on this line can be optima of learning when $\bm{J}_1 = \bm{J}_2$, and they are also singular points at the same time. Therefore, in the singular case, the learning becomes very slow around the optimal subspace. In Fig. 1(b), the thick line-segment is the trajectory at time $\alpha = 300, .., 10000$. One can see the parameters slowly move along the close neighborhood of the optimal subspace, making quasi-plateau. Detail discussions on quasi-plateau will be given in [6].

Even though the plateau and quasi-plateau occurs at permutation symmetry, the quasi-plateau differs from the plateau in the point that it occurs only when the parameters are near by the singular subspace satisfying both condition of $w_1 + w_2 = 1$ and $J_1 = J_2$. In the regular case, the permutation symmetry is broken before the condition $w_1 + w_2 = 1$ is satisfied, and thus the quasi-plateau is not observed. In near-singular case, the optimal point is close to the singular subspace, and the condition $J_1 \cong J_2$ is preserved in some extent when the condition $w_1 + w_2 = 1$ is satisfied. This tells the reason why both of plateau and quasi-plateau are observed in near-singular case.

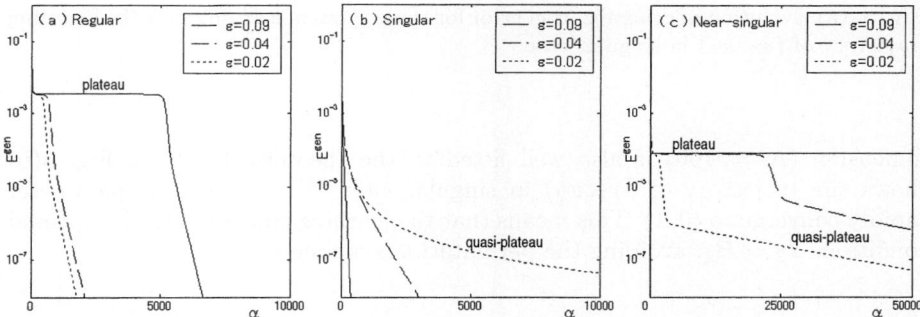

Fig. 2. Evolution of generalization error for three types of learning task with different initial condition ε

We also investigated the dependency of convergence speed on initial conditions by changing value of ε. For all the cases, the convergence speed strongly depends on ε, and interesting thing is that the plateau is extended at large ε, and the quasi-plateau is apparent at small ε. By the existence of both of plateau and quasi-plateau, most strong dependency is shown in near-singular case. This implies that it is difficult to avoid slow convergence by changing ε. As value of ε increases the length of plateau is extremely extended. In addition, even in the case of small ε with relevantly short plateau, the convergence speed in near-singular case was still slower than either regular case or singular case because of the quasi-plateau. From the results of this work, we can say that the quasi-plateau is very important phenomenon making convergence extremely slow.

4.3 Dynamics of Natural Gradient

We did the same analysis for dynamics of the natural gradient learning. Fig. 3(a) shows the evolutions of generalization error for three types of learning task. We can see that the convergence speed of natural gradient learning does not depend on the type of learning task. The on-line learning simulation with finite input

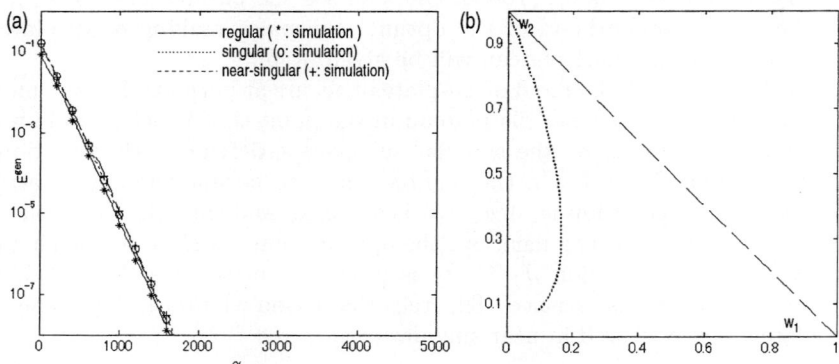

Fig. 3. (a) Evolution of generalization error for three types of learning task (b) Learning trajectory of (w_1, w_2) in singular case

dimension ($N = 100$) is also well fitted to the theoretical results. Fig. 3(b) shows the trajectory of (w_1, w_2) in singular case. We can see the parameter rapidly converge to $(0, 1)$. This means that the learning converges to the optimal condition, $\boldsymbol{J}_2 = \boldsymbol{B}_2$, avoiding the permutation symmetry.

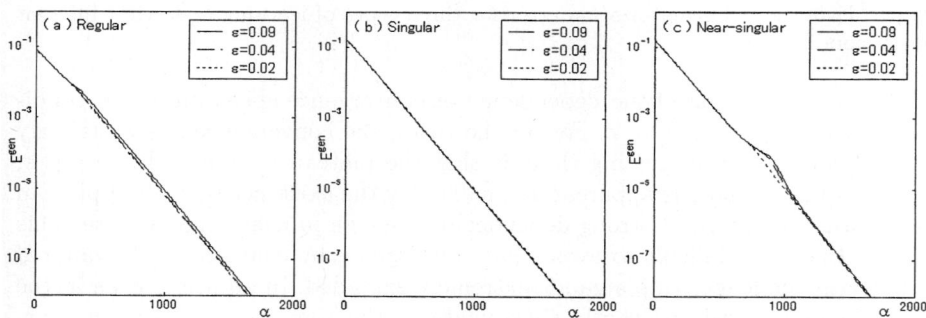

Fig. 4. Evolution of generalization error in natural gradient learning for three types of learning task with different initial condition ε

We also investigated the learning curves for different initial conditions. In Fig. 4, the learning curves of natural gradient show little difference for various initial values of ε as well as various types of learning task. Especially, we can confirm that the natural gradient remarkably improves the strong dependency on value of ε shown in the standard gradient learning for near-singular case.

5 Conclusions

We investigated the influence of singularity on learning dynamics, which is one of main issues on singularity problems but have not been elaborately studied. From the investigation using statistical mechanics, we found a new type of slow dynamics in standard gradient learning, which we call a quasi-plateau. The mechanism of the quasi-plateau differs from the well known plateau, and it is one of main causes of slow convergence. The influence of plateau and quasi-plateau is maximized in near-singular case, which we can often meet in real applications. We also derived motion equations of natural gradient for MLP, and investigated its dynamics. We confirmed that all the unpleasant phenomena shown in standard gradient learning almost disappeared in natural gradient learning. This work is a preliminary step toward understanding the dynamical properties of learning model with complex singularities. Further studies on asymptotic dynamics and noise fluctuation should be done.

References

1. Amari S.,Ozeki, T., "Differential and algebraic geometry of multilayer perceptrons." *IEICE Trans. Fundamentals*, E84-A, 31–38, 2001.
2. Amari S.,Ozeki, T., Park, H., "Learning and Inference in Hierarchical Models with Singularities," *Sys. and Comm. in Japan*, 34, 34–42, 2003.
3. Fukumizu, K., "Likelihood ratio of unidentifiable models and multilayer neural networks", *The Annals of Statistics*, 3, 833-851,(2003).
4. Hagiwara, K., "On the problem in model selection of neural network regression in overrealizable scenario", *Neural Computation*, 14, 1979–2002, 2002.
5. Inoue, M., Park, H. and Okada, M., "On-line learning theory of soft committee machines with correlated hidden units - Steepest gradient descent and natural gradient descent -", *J. Phys. Soc. Jpn*, 72, 4, 805-810, 2003.
6. Park. H., Inoue, M., Okada, M. "Learning dynamics of multilayer perceptrons with Singular structures", submitted to *J. Phys. A*, 2003.
7. Park. H., Inoue, M., Okada, M., Amari, S., "Learning dynamics of multilayer perceptrons with Singular structures", in Preparation.
8. Riegler, P. and Biehl, M., "On-line backpropagation in two-layered neural networks", *J. Phys. A; Mathe. Gen.*, 28, L507-L513, 1995.
9. Rattray M., Saad D. and Amari S., "Natural gradient descent for on-line learning", *Physical Review Letters*,81, 5461–5464, 1998.
10. Saad, D. and Solla, A. "On-line learning in soft committee machines", *Physical Review E,* 52, 4225–4243, 1995.
11. Watanabe, S., "Algebraic analysis for non-identifiable learning machines", *Neural Computation*, 13, 899–933, 2001.
12. Yang, H. and Amari, S., Complexity Issues in Natural Gradient Desent Method for Training Multilayer Perceptrons, *Neural Computaion*, 10, 2137-2157, 1998.

Feature Selection for Multi-class Problems Using Support Vector Machines

Guo-Zheng Li, Jie Yang, Guo-Ping Liu, and Li Xue

Institute of Image Processing & Pattern Recognition, Shanghai Jiao Tong University,
Shanghai, China, 200030

Abstract. Since feature selection can remove the irrelevant features and improve the performance of learning systems, it is an crucial step in machine learning. The feature selection methods using support vector machines have obtained satisfactory results, but the previous works are usually for binary classification, and needs auxiliary techniques to be extended to multiple classification. In this paper, we propose a prediction risk based feature selection method using multiple classification support vector machines. The performance of the proposed method is compared with the previous methods of optimal brain damage based feature selection methods using binary support vector machines. The results of experiments on UCI data sets show that prediction risk based feature selection method obtains better results than the previous methods using support vector machines for multiple classification problems.

1 Introduction

Feature selection is one of the key topics in machine learning and other related fields [1–3], it can remove the irrelevant even noisy features and hence improve the quality of the data set and the performance of learning systems. In the recent years, many feature selection algorithms have been developed, but no optimal algorithms can actually be suitable for all problems. Since neural computing does not make assumption of the possible distribution of the data, only when the training data sets are available, can feature selection using neural computing perform well and really improve the performances of the neural learning machines [4, 5].

Support vector machines(SVMs) proposed in 1990s have exhibited excellent performance in many applications and become the standard tools in neural computing [6, 7]. Compared with other neural computing methods like multiple layer perceptron neural network trained by back propagation algorithms, SVMs realize the data dependent principle of structure risk minimization, have better generalization ability and can obtain the optimal solution[8].

Although SVMs are powerful algorithms, too many irrelevant features can reduce their performances, so feature selection for SVMs are proposed[5, 3]. Weston et al. proposed to use the leave-one-out error bound as the selection criteria[9]; Guyon et al. used the second derivative of the object function as the criteria [5]. Rakotomamonjy used the zero oder and first order of the above criteria and proved that the optimal damage brain measure used by Guyon et al. is better than others[10]. It is worth noting that all the above algorithms are based on binary classification SVMs.

Since SVMs classification algorithms are designed for binary classification problems, the techniques like one against one or one against all are needed to build multiple classification SVMs. At the same time, the capability of the feature selection methods using binary SVMs is limited. Weston et al. computed the sum of measures of the corresponding features in each binary SVMs of the multiple classification SVMs to evaluate the features in multiple classification problems [11].

In order to use the multiple classification SVMs as the learning machine to help to select the features effectively, we propose to use the prediction risk based feature selection method [12]. The rest of this paper is arranged as follows: Prediction risk based feature selection method using multiple classification SVMs is described in Section 2; Section 3 focuses on experiments on multi-class UCI data sets; and in Section 4, we will give some discussions.

2 Prediction Risk Based Feature Selection Method

We use feature selection to improve the accuracy of multiple classification support vector machines, which will firstly be introduced in brief.

Support vector machines(SVMs) proposed in the 1990s have become state-of-the-arts methods in machine learning fields [8,7] and exhibited excellent performance in many applications such as digit recognition[13], text categorization[14], computer vision[15], biological data mining [5], and medical diagnosis [16], etc.

In this paper, the version of 2-norm soft margin SVMs [7] is used for the binary classification machines, which minimize the training error as well as the 2-norm of slack variables according to the statistical learning theory [8]. The object function is defined as:

$$\mathcal{L} = \sum_{i=1}^{\ell} \alpha_i - \frac{1}{2} \sum_{i,j=1}^{\ell} y_i y_j \alpha_i \alpha_j K(\boldsymbol{x}_i, \boldsymbol{x}_j) - \frac{1}{2C} \langle \boldsymbol{\alpha} \cdot \boldsymbol{\alpha} \rangle$$

where C is the parameter to control the trade off of training error and the norm of slack variables, $\boldsymbol{\alpha}$ is the Lagrange multiplier vector, and $K(\boldsymbol{x}_i, \boldsymbol{x}_j)$ is the kernel function[17] introduced into SVMs to solve the nonlinear problems. Radial basis function(RBF) kernel is considered as a superior choice [18]:

$$K(\boldsymbol{x}, \boldsymbol{z}) = \exp(-\|\boldsymbol{x} - \boldsymbol{z}\|^2/\sigma^2).$$

where $\boldsymbol{x}, \boldsymbol{z}$ are input examples, σ is the radius.

There are several methods to construct multiple classification machines based on binary classification SVMs, among them one against one method is recommended[19]. If there are k classes in the data set, $k(k-1)/2$ binary SVMs are trained on each pair of class labels. In this work, one against one method is used to build the multiple classification, and voting method of *maximum win* strategy is used to predict the labels of test examples.

For more details of SVMs, please refer to http://www.kernel-machines.org.

2.1 The Previous Work

Some embedded feature selection methods using binary classification SVMs have been proposed. Guyon et al. proposed to use optimal brain damage as the selection criteria [5]. Furthermore, optimal brain damage has been studied by Rakotomamonjy and proved to be better than the other measures proposed before[10].

Optimal brain damage(OBD) proposed by LeCun et al.[20] uses the change of the object function as the selection criteria, which is defined as the second order term in Taylor series of the object function:

$$S_i = \frac{1}{2}\frac{\partial^2 \mathcal{L}}{\partial (w^i)^2}(Dw^i)^2.$$

in which $\mathcal{L}$ is the object function of learning machines, and w is the weight of features.

OBD has been used in the feature selection for artificial neural networks and obtained satisfactory results[21]. In binary classification SVMs, OBD has performed well in the gene analysis problems[5].

For binary classification SVMs, the measure of OBD is defined[5] as

$$S_i = \frac{1}{2}\boldsymbol{\alpha}^T K(\boldsymbol{x}_k, \boldsymbol{x}_h)\boldsymbol{\alpha} - \frac{1}{2}\boldsymbol{\alpha}^T K(\boldsymbol{x}_k^{-i}, \boldsymbol{x}_h^{-i})\boldsymbol{\alpha}$$

where $\boldsymbol{\alpha}$ is the Lagrange multipliers in SVMs, and $-i$ in $K(x_k^{-i}, x_h^{-i})$ means the component i has been removed. The feature corresponding to the least S_i will be removed.

The methods proposed in the previous works are based on binary classification SVMs. If we want to extend them to multiple classification SVMs, we have to compute the measures of each individual binary classification SVMs. One way is that we compute the sum of the measures of each individual SVMs for the corresponding features, and remove the features with the least sum of measures. However, all these methods are based on individual SVMs not on the multiple classification SVMs, so we propose the prediction risk based feature selection method for the multi-class problems which uses the multiple classification SVMs directly.

2.2 Prediction Risk Based Feature Selection Method

Prediction risk based feature selection method proposed by Moody et al. [12], evaluates the features by computing the change of training error when the features are replaced by their mean values,

$$S_i = \text{ERR}(\bar{x}^i) - \text{ERR}$$

where ERR is the training error. ERR($\bar{x}^i$) is the test error on the training set and defined as:

$$\text{ERR}(\bar{x}^i) = \frac{1}{N} \sum_{j=1}^{N} \left(\tilde{y}(x_j^1, ..., \bar{x}^i, ..., x_j^M) \neq y_j \right),$$

in which, M, N are the number of features and instances respectively, $\bar{x}^i$ is the mean value of the ith feature and $\tilde{y}()$ is the prediction value of the jth example with the ith feature replaced by its mean value.

The feature corresponding to the least S_i will be removed, because its change causes the least error which indicates it is the least important one.

This measure was used to perform feature selection for the regularized forward neural networks and obtained better results than other measures like fuzzy gain, output sensitivity[22].

In order to remove the features effectively, we use the sequential backward search algorithms [23], which removes one feature in one step according to the measures. The algorithms used in this paper is named as SVM-SBS in the following. The best feature subset is the one with the least test error on the test sample.

Algorithm SVM-SBS

Surviving feature subset $u = [1, 2, ..., M]$, the discarded feature list $r = [\ ]$ and the test error list $e = [\ ]$ are initialized firstly. Then, training sample $x_{r0} = [x_r^1, ..., x_r^i, ..., x_r^M]^T$ with the target values y_r and the test sample x_{s0} with the target values y_s are input into SVM-SBS.

Step 1: Restrict training sample to good feature indices $x_r = x_r(:, u)$, and in the first iteration, $x_r = x_{r0}$.

Step 2: Train the multiple classification machines to get M-SVM(x_r, y_r).

Step 3: Test the model on the test sample, classification error rate is computed $e_t = \text{M-SVM}(x_s(:, u), y_s)$, and update the error list $e = [e_t, e]$.

Step 4: Compute the selection criteria S_i for all i on the training sample using the evaluation method in the above two subsections.

Step 5 Find the feature with smallest selection criterion $h = \arg \min(S)$.

Step 6: Update the discarded feature list $r = [u(h), r]$ and eliminate the feature with smallest selection criterion $u = u(1 : h - 1, h + 1 : \text{length}(u))$.

If length(u) > 1 goto step 1.

Step 7: Output the test error list e on the test sample and the discarded feature list r.

3 Experiments on the UCI Data Sets

3.1 The Used UCI Data Sets

In order to compare the different feature selection methods for multiple classification problems using support vector machines, we use twelve of multi-class data sets from UCI data repository [24]. Data sets selected for comparison are listed in Table 1.

Table 1. The properties of the UCI data sets for comparison.

Data set	Number of instances	Number of attributes	Number of Classes
all-bp	3772	29	3
all-hyper	3772	29	5
all-hypo	3772	29	4
backup	683	35	19
fisher	47	35	4
glass	214	9	6
lung	32	56	3
processed-cl.	303	13	5
processed-va	200	13	5
soybean-l	305	34	19
soybean-s	47	35	4
stepp-order	47	35	4

For all the data sets, we first replace the symbols with numerical values in the data sets, then, all the attributes are transformed into the interval of [-1,1] using an affine transformation. At last, we split the data set equally into two parts according to the number of instances of each class, one part is used as training sample, the other is used as test sample, such operation is performed 100 times.

3.2 Experimental Methods and Results

In order to compare the two feature selection methods, we choose the same parameters $C = 100$ and $\sigma = 0.5$ for the SVMs on all data sets. Although they are not the optimal parameters, we consider them reasonable. OBD based feature selection methods and prediction risk based methods using SVMs are performed on the data sets using the SVM-SBS algorithm. Both evaluation methods are applied in SVM-SBS to selected features on the training data sets and compute the test error of the selected feature subset of the corresponding test data set. The test error is defined as the classification error rate:

$$\text{ERR}(\boldsymbol{x}_s) = \frac{1}{N} \sum_{j=1}^{N} (\tilde{y}_j(\boldsymbol{x}_{sj}) \neq y_j),$$

where N is the number of test instances, $\tilde{y}_j$ is the prediction value of $\boldsymbol{x}_j$.

This calculation is performed 100 times. Finally, the statistical results of the average error and its corresponding standard deviation for each number of feature subset are computed. Results of the least average error of each data set and its corresponding standard deviation are listed in Table 2.

Since prediction risk feature selection is an embedded method, the computation is efficiency and mainly focused on the training of SVMs. The CPU time of each time of selection using the SVM-SBS algorithm is varied on different data sets and no more than one second on a computer with one PIV 1.2G CPU of intel and 512M memory.

Table 2. Statistical results of the test error on UCI data sets by different feature selection methods.

Data set	Prediction risk based method	OBD based method	All features
all-bp	0.0418±0.0076	**0.0408±0.0087**	0.0646±0.0432
all-hyper	0.0305±0.0366	**0.0262±0.0040**	0.0355±0.0206
all-hypo	**0.0249±0.0111**	0.0394±0.0165	0.0504±0.0168
backup	**0.1032±0.0329**	0.1457±0.1600	0.2354±0.0841
fisher	**0.0013±0.0077**	0.0072±0.0216	0.3344±0.0753
glass	**0.4019±0.0924**	0.4362±0.0967	0.4362±0.0967
lung	0.4580±0.1169	**0.4415±0.1468**	0.5987±0.1217
processed-cl.	0.2334±0.0375	0.2334±0.0375	0.2334±0.0375
processed-va	**0.3537±0.0556**	0.3574±0.0532	0.3574±0.0532
soybean-l	**0.1841±0.0460**	0.3384±0.2639	0.4752±0.1961
soybean-s	0.0257±0.0219	**0.0253±0.0443**	0.3597±0.0728
stepp-order	**0.0128±0.0257**	0.0195±0.0456	0.3446±0.0765
Average	**0.1559±0.0410**	0.1759±0.0749	0.2938±0.0745

From Table 2, we can see that: 1) Compared with the total feature set, both methods significantly reduce the classification error rate, except on one data set; 2) On seven out of twelve data sets prediction risk based method obtains better results than OBD based method does, and on four data sets prediction risk based method performs worse than OBD based method does; 3) For the average values, prediction risk based feature selection method obtains 2 percent better results than OBD does on the average error and 3 percent better results on the standard deviation error.

One typical selection process is on the data set of backup, whose results of the average error and the corresponding standard deviation are plotted on Figure 1. From Figure 1, we can see the results of the test error become small first and then high when more features are eliminated.

4 Discussions

Prediction risk based feature selection method for multi-class problems using support vector machines is proposed and obtains better results than optimal brain damage based feature selection method on twelve of multi-class data sets from UCI data repository.

We think two factors may account for the better performance of the proposed method. One is that the two feature selection method are based on two different measures, prediction risk and optimal brain damage, the former is something like the wrapper method [2] which can obtain the least error for specific learning machines. The second reason is that prediction risk based method uses the whole multiple classification support vector machines to evaluate the features, while optimal brain damage method is based on binary support vector machines, and

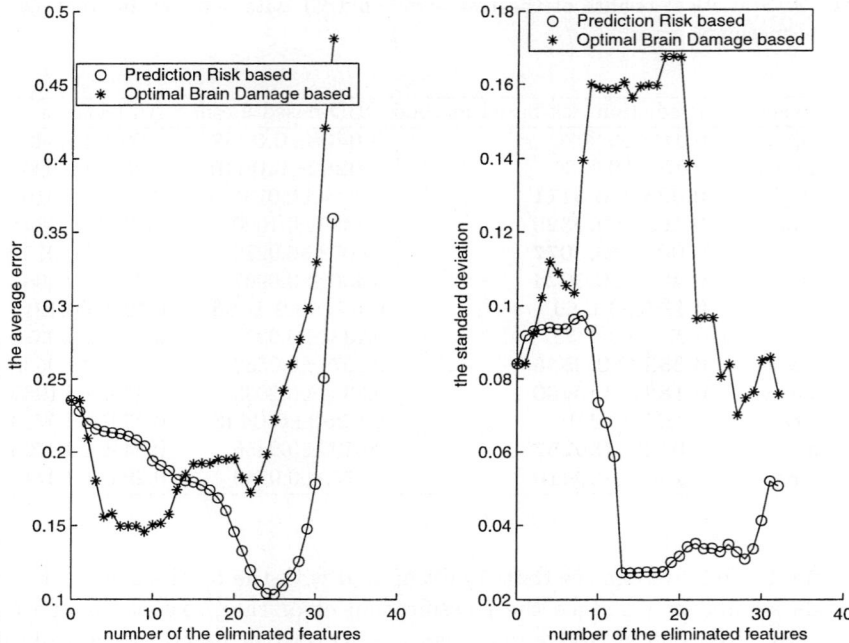

Fig. 1. The feature selection process of the embedded algorithms on the data set of backup.

needs auxiliary techniques to evaluate the features, perhaps another auxiliary method can help to obtain better results.

We can also find both feature selection methods can greatly reduce the test error of the used data sets, the reduction magnitude is about 13 percent of the test error on the total feature set. This indicates that almost all the data sets have some redundant features or even noisy features, and these features hurt the performance of the used learning machine. Thus, feature selection is needed to perform on all the data sets for learning machines.

Feature selection using support vector machines is a general method which does not make any assumption of the data distribution. However, one or several outlier examples may cause unexpected results, outlier detection should be considered before the feature selection is performed in the real world applications. In addition, how about the performance of the proposed method compared with other ad hoc feature selection methods like spectral clustering and mutual information methods is still an open issue, which needs a thorough investigation.

Acknowledgments

This work is financially supported by the Natural Science Foundation of China under the grant number of 50174038. Thanks also go to the anonymous reviewers for their valuable advices.

References

1. Dash, M., Liu, H.: Feature selection for classification. Intelligent Data Analysis **1** (1997) 131–156
2. Kohavi, R., George, J.H.: Wrappers for feature subset selection. Artificial Intelligence **97** (1997) 273–324
3. Guyon, I., Elisseeff, A.: An introduction to variable and feature selection. Journal of machine learning research **3** (2003) 1157–1182
4. Reed, R.: Pruning algorithms — a survey. IEEE Transactions on Neural Networks **4** (1993) 740–747
5. Guyon, I., Weston, J., Barnhill, S., Vapnik, V.: Gene selection for cancer classification using support vector machines. Machine Learning **46** (2002) 389–422
6. Haykin, S.: Neural Networks: A Comprehensive Foundation. 2 edn. Printice Hall, New Jersey (1999)
7. Cristianini, N., Shawe-Taylor, J.: An Introduction to Support Vector Machines. Cambridge University Press, Cambridge (2000)
8. Vapnik, V.: Statistical Learning Theory. Wiley, New York (1998)
9. Weston, J., Mukherjee, S., Chapelle, O., Pontil, M., Poggio, T., Vapnik, V.: Feature selection for SVMs. In: Advances in Neural Information Processing Systems. Volume 13. (2001)
10. Rakotomamonjy, A.: Variable selection using SVM-based criteria. Journal of machine learning research **3** (2003) 1357–1370
11. Weston, J., Elisseeff, A., Bakir, G., Sinz, F.: The spider. http://www.kyb.tuebingen.mpg.de/bs/people/spider/index.html (2004)
12. Moody, J., Utans, J.: Principled architecture selection for neural networks: Application to corporate bond rating prediction. In Moody, J.E., Hanson, S.J., Lippmann, R.P., eds.: Advances in Neural Information Processing Systems. Volume 4., Morgan Kaufmann Publishers, Inc. (1992) 683–690
13. LeCun, Y., Jackel, L.D., Bottou, L., Brunot, A., Cortes, C., Denker, J.S., Drucker, H., Guyon, I., Müller, U.A., Säckinger, E., Simard, P., Vapnik, V.: Comparison of learning algorithms for handwritten digit recognition. In Fogelman-Soulié, F., Gallinari, P., eds.: Proceedings ICANN'95 – International Conference on Artificial Neural Networks, Volume II. (1995) 53–60
14. Joachims, T.: Text categorization with support vector machines. In: Proceedings of European Conference on Machine Learning(ECML). (1998)
15. Pontil, M., Verri, A.: Object recognition with support vector machines. IEEE Trans. on PAMI **20** (1998) 637–646
16. El-Naqa, I., Yang, Y., Wernick, M.N., Galatsanos, N.P., R, N.: Support vector machine learning for detection of microcalcifications in mammograms. In: Proceedings of IEEE International Symposium on Biomedical Imaging. (2002) 201–204
17. Mercer, J.: Functions of positive and negative type and their connection with the theory of integral equations. Philos. Trans. Roy. Soc. London **A 209** (1909) 415–446
18. Keerthi, S.S., Lin, C.J.: Asymptotic behaviors of support vector machines with gaussian kernel. Neural Computation **15** (2003) 1667–1689
19. Hsu, C.W., Lin, C.J.: A comparison of methods for multi-class support vector machines. IEEE Transactions on Neural Networks **13** (2002) 415–425
20. LeCun, Y., Denker, J.S., Solla, S.A.: Optimal brain damage. In Touretzky, D., ed.: Advances in Neural Information Processing Systems, Morgan Kaufmann, Inc. (1990) 598–605

21. Cibas, T., Soulie, F., Gallinari, P.: Variable selection with neural networks. Neurocomputing **12** (1996) 223–248
22. Verikas, A., Bacauskiene, M.: Feature selection with neural networks. Pattern Recognition Letters **23** (2002) 1323–1335
23. Marill, T., Green, D.M.: On the effectiveness of receptors in recognition system. IEEE Transaction on Information Theory **9** (1963) 11–17
24. Blake, C., Keogh, E., Merz, C.J.: UCI repository of machine learning databases. Technical report, Department of Information and Computer Science, University of California, Irvine, CA (1998) http://www.ics.uci.edu/ mlearn/MLRepository.htm.

Beyond Learners' Interest:
Personalized Paper Recommendation Based on Their Pedagogical Features for an e-Learning System

Tiffany Tang[1,2] and Gordon McCalla[2]

[1] Department of Computing, Hong Kong Polytechnic University
Hung Hom, Kowloon, Hong Kong
cstiffany@comp.polyu.edu.hk
[2] Department of Computer Science, University of Saskatchewan
Saskatoon, Saskatchewan, Canada
mccalla@cs.usask.ca

Abstract. Delivering personalized recommendations for e-learning is different from that in many other domains (i.e. e-commerce, news, etc.) in that we should not only consider users' interest, but also their pedagogical features such as their learning goals, and background knowledge etc. To attack this problem, in this paper in the context of recommending research papers for learners, we introduce the notion of pedagogy-oriented similarity measurement and propose two pedagogy-oriented recommendation techniques: model-based and hybrid recommendations. To compare these two techniques, we carried out an experiment using artificial learners. Experiment results are encouraging, showing that hybrid collaborative filtering, which can lower the computational costs will not compromise the overall performance of the recommender system. In addition, as more and more learners participate in the learning process, both learner and paper models can better be enhanced and updated, which is especially desirable for web-based learning systems.

1 Introduction

Recommender systems (**RS**) have been explored mostly in applications other than e-learning, such as e-commerce or news recommendation. In e-commerce, it is imperative to provide personalized experiences for consumers involved, which has proved to be effective for cross-selling, up-selling, and mass marketing [7]. In e-learning, however, we want to recommend items such as papers, web pages, and other papers where learners' (consumers') pedagogical characteristics should be considered. To maximize the utility of learning, the recommending mechanism should consider not only learners' interest towards the items like most other RSs do, but also their knowledge of domain concepts, for instance, not to recommend highly technical papers to a first-year-undergraduate student or popular-magazine articles to a senior-graduate student. In addition, items contained in recommendation list might not be entirely interesting to learners. If the system continues to recommend something that cannot stimulate learners' interest in one way or another, it is also undesirable. Therefore, making recommendations in a pedagogically ordered list is very important, which is quite different from recommendation in e-commerce, where site managers prefer to leave the list unordered to avoid leaving the impression that a specific recommendation is the best choice [7]. For example, some instructors will recommend their students to read an interesting magazine article, such as a related article in *Communications of ACM*, before a technical paper, because they believe it will help their student understand the technical paper or make them less intimidated. Finally, for e-learning, customization should also be made not only towards learning items, but also towards their pedagogical presentations [5, 10].

To address these issues, in this paper we will discuss our work on recommending research papers for learners engaged in an evolving e-learning system [9]. Our system is designed to recommend research literatures for students in the area of data mining and its applications. This study extends our work in [10] and mainly focuses on proposing model-based and collaborative filtering based recommendation techniques in this domain, and show through an artificial-learner-based simulation to study the effect and benefits of introducing pedagogical similarity for e-learning.

1.1 Motivation

In our study, we will consider a special kind of user data, i.e. pedagogy-oriented data, which is unique to the e-learning domain. The pedagogy-oriented data is different in the sense that it can directly *affect* as well as *inform* recommendation process; thus, enhancing the quality of recommendations in the context of the web-based learning environments. This pedagogical feature can be determined two factors: 1). User's knowledge state; 2). User's knowledge goals. Although other factors such as user's learning preferences might also be one of the learning factors, we will instead give higher weights on the above two factors; thus, making them two of the biggest contributing factors for pedagogy-oriented personalized recommendation. Before we proceed, let us first look at a motivational example of how different recommendations can be in e-learning and other domains.

An Example. Suppose we have already had the following three types of users, A, B and C as shown in Table 1.

Table 1. A comparison of user model A, B and C

	User A	User B	User C
Knowledge in Statistics	strong	strong	weak
Knowledge in Computer Sci.	strong	strong	weak
Interest	Application of data clustering in bioinformatics	data mining & web mining applications on E-commerce	Data mining & web mining application in e-commerce
Paper Preferences	Technical/ theoretical	Application and magazine survey, technical/theoretical	Application and magazine survey

From table 1, we can conclude that user B and C have some overlapping interests, but since their knowledge background especially with respect to their technical background is different, the paper recommended to them would be different. But for User

A and B, although they have different application interest, their technical background is similar; therefore, they might receive similar technical papers. It can also be implied that user models A and C have no overlapping areas. But it is still possible for them to receive the same paper(s): for example, seminal paper(s) on data mining, state-of-the-art discussion papers on data mining etc. Therefore, it is obvious that making recommendations for our system is different from that in other domains where users' interests were the most important in order to retain them by way of delivery personalized recommendations.

1.2 Related Work

There are several related works concerning tracking and recommending technical papers. [1] define the paper recommendation problem as: *"Given a representation of my interests, find me relevant papers."* Bollacker *et al.* [2] refine CiteSeer, NEC's digital library for scientific literature, through an automatic personalized paper-tracking module which retrieves each user's interests from well-maintained heterogeneous user profiles. [12] discuss an enhanced digital book with a spreading-activation-geared mechanism to make customized recommendations for readers with different type of background and knowledge. [6] investigate the adoption of collaborative filtering techniques to recommend papers for researchers; however, the paper did not address the issue of how to recommend a research paper, rather, how to recommend *additional* references for a target research paper. In the context of an e-learning system, additional readings cannot be recommended purely through an analysis of the citation matrix of a target paper. These works are different from ours in that we not only recommend papers according to learners' interests, but also pick up those *not-so-interesting-yet-pedagogically-suitable* papers for them. In some cases pedagogically valuable papers might not be interesting and papers with significant influence on the research community might not be pedagogically suitable for learners. We argue that the main goal of recommending papers is to provide learners with necessary knowledge of a given topic and personalize the learning environment which motivates them to explore more. As part of our previous study, in order to understand what average learners actually want from the system we carried out a survey that is described in more details in [10].

The rest of this paper is organized as follows. In the next section, we will present our problem statement and introduce model-based and collaborative filtering based recommendation techniques. In Section 3, we will discuss in details the simulations we conducted as a way of assessing and comparing our proposed recommendation techniques. Experiment results and discussions will be provided in Section 4, and we conclude this paper by pointing out our future research plans.

2   Our Approach: Pedagogy-Oriented Paper Recommendation

Our goal can be stated as follows:

Given a collection of papers and a learner's profile, recommend and deliver a set of materials in a pedagogically appropriate sequence, so as to meet both the learner's pedagogical needs and interest.

To be precise, *papers* include online reading materials which can help learners understand the topic being taught, such as conference papers, journal papers, magazine articles etc. Ideally, the system will maximize a learner's utility such that the learner gains a maximum amount of knowledge and is well motivated in the end. However, the model-based recommendation, which is achieved through a careful assessment of learner characteristics and then matches these models against papers, is very costly due to the following reasons:

- when a new paper is added into the system, a detailed identification is required (e.g. tagging it with a detail information of the background knowledge needed for understanding it), which cannot be done automatically;
- when a learner gains some new knowledge after reading a paper, a new matching process is required in order to find the next suitable paper for him/her, resulting in the updating of his/her learner model.

Alternatively, we can use a collaborative filtering technique (CF) to reduce the complexity of the recommendation process. The idea of CF is to let peer learners to filter out those not suitable materials, while the system does not need to know the detailed characteristics of them. Hence, the matching process is not performed from learner models to learning materials, but from one learner model to other learner models. Since the system also utilizes some characteristics of papers discussed in [10], then it is not a pure CF but a hybrid-CF. The remaining question is whether or not the hybrid-CF is as effective as the model-based recommendation. To answer this question, we carried out an experiment using artificial learners for two types of pedagogical-oriented recommendation techniques: pure model-based which makes recommendations based on the matching of learner models to papers, and hybrid CF which is based on peer learner recommendation. Details will be given out in the next section.

3 Evaluating Pedagogy-Oriented Hybrid Recommendation Technique

3.1 Simulation Setup

For the purpose of testing, we first generate 500 artificial learners and use 50 papers related to data mining as the main learning materials. The RS then delivers recommendations of 15 papers to each learner according to each individual learner model (pure model-based). Each learner rates these papers according to their properties. After that, we generate 100 additional artificial learners, who become the target learners. Then, two recommendation techniques are applied for these target learners in order to evaluate their differences as well as performances. The first technique is the same as the technique used in the first 500 learners, i.e. model-based recommendation. The second technique uses a hybrid-recommendation technique (model based with collaborative filtering).

Learner Properties. In the simulation, we use minimal learner properties to generate artificial learners, as shown below:
- *Learner ID #.*
- *Background knowledge* as vector $[(k_1, k_2) (k_3, k_4) (k_5, k_6) k_7, k_8, k_9, k_{10}]$, where k_i represents its strength on knowledge i-th, and $k_i \in [0, 1]$. We assume that k_1 and k_2 are

two basic mathematics topics, k_3 and k_4 are two discrete mathematics topics taught in computer science or mathematics, k_5 and k_6 are two statistics topics, k_7 is algorithm analysis, and k_8, k_9 and k_{10} are topics in database, bioinformatics, and AI in education. k_1 is derived from truncated inverse standard lognormal distribution with $\sigma = 1$ and reduced by factor 1/5. And k_2 is lower than k_1 by the factor which also follows truncated standard lognormal distribution with $\sigma = 1$ and reduced by factor 1/10. k_3, k_4 and k_5 are derived from truncated inverse lognormal distribution with $\sigma = 1$ and reduced by factor 1/5. k_6 is derived from truncated standard lognormal distribution with $\sigma = 1$ and reduced by factor 1/5. k_7 is derived from uniform distribution U[0, 1]. k_8, k_9 and k_{10} are derived from truncated standard lognormal distribution with $\sigma = 1$ and reduced by factor 1/5.

- *Interest toward specific topics* as vector $[I_1, I_2, I_3, ..., I_{12}]$, where I_i represents its interest on topic i-th, and $I_i \in [0, 1]$. We assume that all interests except I_1 (general topical knowledge) are generated randomly following uniform distribution. And I_1 is generated using truncated inverse standard lognormal distribution with $\sigma = 1$ and reduced by factor 1/5.
- *Motivation* as value $M \in [0, 1]$. Where 1 represents that the learner's willingness to spend more time to learn something not covered/understood before, and 0 represents the learner's unwillingness to explore any piece of knowledge not covered in the paper. M is generated using truncated standard lognormal distribution with $\sigma = 1$ and reduced by factor 1/5.

Paper Properties. We use the following properties for the papers.
- *Paper ID #.*
- *Technical knowledge* as vector $[(k_1, k_2) (k_3, k_4) (k_5, k_6) k_7, k_8, k_9, k_{10}]$, where k_i denotes the extensiveness of the knowledge i-th used inside the paper. The extensiveness of a knowledge means that a learner needs a good background of the corresponding knowledge in order to be able to understand the paper thoroughly. If the learner lacks that knowledge, then it can gain the corresponding knowledge by reading the paper carefully and spending more time to look at the references. We assume $k_i \in [0, 1]$, and each of them represents the same topic as that described in learner properties. This feature indirectly affects the technical level of the paper.
- *Paper topics* as vector $[I_1, I_2, I_3, ..., I_{10}]$, where I_i denotes the corresponding topic in learner's interest.
- *Authority level* which is used to determine whether the paper is an important paper or not, for example, a classical paper or highly cited paper, etc.

Learning Constraints.
Five core papers, i.e. papers that are pedagogically required for all learners (for example, the seminal paper by Agrawal in 1994 introduced, for the first time, the notion of association rule mining and its technique), will be recommended by the system regardless of learners' interests or knowledge. Those papers are core papers in the simulated course. And they are specifically chosen as follow: either paper ID #1 or #2, either paper #5 or #6, paper #8, one of paper #26 or #27 or #35, and either paper #33 or #48. Moreover, at least two papers with high technical level should be recommended to the learner. And totally 15 papers must be read and rated by each learner.

The above requirements define the constraints of recommendation, which differentiates the recommendation in e-learning system from that in other application areas.

3.2 Model-Based Recommendations

Rule Generations. The model-based recommendation is based on the following rules (learner-centric):
- System starts with recommending acceptable papers in terms of learners' knowledge level (understandable) and the similarity of learners' interest towards the topic in the paper (the understandable level and the interest similarity will be described later). Up to eight authoritative papers will be selected first; if no more authoritative papers can be selected, then the system will recommend non-authoritative papers.
- Two interested papers, but with very high technical level will be recommended, in order to improve learner's knowledge.
- Some not-interested-yet-pedagogical-useful (authoritative) papers will be provided as the part of the learning requirement in the end.

After learners finish a paper, some additional knowledge may be acquired, which depends on the learner motivation. In our simulation, we assume that the increment is based on:

IF $paper.k_j > learner.k_j$ **AND** $paper.authority = $ TRUE **THEN**
$learner.k_j = (paper.k_j - learner.k_j) \times learner.M \times Interest \times w_1 + learner.k_j$

IF $paper.k_j > learner.k_j$ **AND** $paper.authority = $ FALSE **THEN**
$learner.k_j = (paper.k_j - learner.k_j) \times learner.M \times Interest \times w_2 + learner.k_j$

Where w_1 and w_2 represent factors that might affect learning speed after reading an authoritative/non-authoritative paper. They are two of the control variables in our experiment. And *Interest* represents the similarity of learner interest to the paper's topic which will be described later. Moreover, the total gain made by the learner is defined as the value added from reading the paper, or

Value added $= \Sigma_i ((new)\ learner.k_i - (old)\ learner.k_i)$

The rule to measure a learner's understanding (*Understand*) will be based on the knowledge gap between the learner's knowledge and those required to fully understand the paper. In addition, the similarity of learners' interest to the paper's topic (*Interest*) is generated according to the following rules:

$y = 1$ if $\exists j$ such that $learner.I_j$ and $paper.I_j \geq 0.9$
$y = 0.9$ if $\exists j$ such that $learner.I_j$ and $paper.I_j \geq 0.8$
...
$y = 0.1$ if $\exists j$ such that $learner.I_j$ and $paper.I_j \geq 0.0$
Interest = **Max**(y)

Rating Generation Rules. After a learner reads a paper, we need rating-generation rules to generate learner rating toward the paper. We use the following rules in our simulation: 1). If learners are interested in the topic AND understand the paper, a higher rating is generated. Or, matching based on both interests and background knowledge; generate higher ratings 4 or 5 under the following formula.

Rate = Round (*Interest* × *Understand* × 2) + 3   if *Interest* ≥ 0.7 and *Understand* ≥ 0.7

2). Learners give ratings to a paper based on the amount of knowledge that could be acquired (*value added*) AND the understanding of the paper (easy to follow, or *pedagogical-readiness*), OR the importance of the paper to their interest.

Rating Implications. If the rating is high (e.g. 4 or 5), learner motivation will increase randomly following uniform distribution to upper bound value 1, with increasing rate x. If the rating is low (e.g. 1 or 2), learner motivation will decrease randomly also following uniform distribution to lower bound 0, also with decreasing rate x. If the rating falls into the medium of the scale (e.g. 3), learner motivation unchanged. x is another control variable which represents how much motivation a learner gain/loss after reading a paper.

3.3 Hybrid Recommendations

The following rules are used for the hybrid recommendation.
- *Neighborhood finding*: for each target learner (*tlearner*) find five neighbors (*nlearner*) based on the similarity of their interest and background knowledge. The similarity measurement is calculated based on the following:
  Positive Similarity = Σ (*nlearner.I$_i$*)   if *tlearner.I$_i$* $\geq$ *nlearner.I$_i$*
  Negative Similarity = Σ (*nlearner.I$_i$* – *tlearner.I$_i$*)   if *tlearner.I$_i$* < *nlearner.I$_i$*
  Similarity = *Positive Similarity* - *Negative Similarity*

The *similarity* formula is used to find similarity in learner background knowledge. The rationale to adopt this measurement is when a learner has a lower interest than a target learner, then the magnitude of learner's interest is credible for recommending a paper to the target learner, therefore, the positive similarity measures the total of learners' interest in such condition. However, if the learner's interest is higher than the target learner's interest, then an error may appear regarding the learner's recommendation, and the gap between those two interests may be the cause of the error. Therefore, the negative similarity denotes the sum of the gaps. The same is used for the similarity measure of two learners' background knowledge.

- From these five nearest neighbors, we can get a set of candidate papers based on their ratings. In our simulation, each learner has rated 15 papers; therefore, at least 15 papers will be in the candidate set. Then, we order those papers in candidate set from the highest ratings from the closest neighbor to the lowest rating from the furthest neighbor.

- The system will recommend up to eight authoritative papers starting from those receiving the highest rating followed by recommending non-authoritative papers. Then, the system will choose and recommend two very interesting and highly technical papers, and recommend five pedagogically required papers, if the learner has not read them. Finally, the system recommends the rest of the papers according to the rating order, until up to 15 papers in total.

3.4 Evaluation Metrics and Control Variables

Those commonly adopted metrics [4], (e.g. ROC) in the research community cannot be applied here due to the inherent features of recommendation for e-learning. These metrics, for example, ROC, are mainly adopted to test the "satisfaction' of users in terms of item interest-ness. However, we argue that since the most critical feature of recommending learning items is to facilitate learning (not just to provide 'interesting'

items), it is not applicable in our domain. Therefore, we propose two new metrics as follows:
- *Average learner motivation* after recommendation
- *Average learner knowledge* after recommendation

And for the purpose of comparison, we compare the percentage differences between model-based recommendation and hybrid recommendation.

In our simulation, control variables w_1, w_2 and x are adjusted to differentiate artificial learners as follows. $x = 1$ for fast motivation change (FMC), $x = 0.3$ for moderate (MMC), $x = 0.1$ for slow (SMC), and $x = 0$ (NMC). Moreover, we use eight pairs of (w_1, w_2), which are (1, 0), (U[0, 1], 0), (U[0, 0.3], 0), (1, U[0, 0.3]), (U[0, 1], U[0, 0.3]), (U[0, 0.3], U[0, 0.3]), (1, U[0, 1]), (U[0, 1], U[0, 1]), (1, 1), where U[0, y] means a random value generated from a uniform distribution function. The pair value represents the effect of authoritative and non-authoritative papers in the increment of the learner's knowledge. For example, (1, 0) indicates that only authoritative papers can fully increase a learner's knowledge. And (1, 1) indicates that both authoritative and non-authoritative papers are equally weighted and can fully increase a learner's knowledge. Each group of experiment is repeated thirty times for statistical analysis.

4 Experiment Results and Discussions

4.1 Experiment Results

Table 2 shows the result of the experimentation. The value shown in each cell is the pair value of the percentage difference between model-based recommendation and the hybrid-CF technique in terms of average learner knowledge and motivation. A negative value indicates that the model-based recommendation technique is better than hybrid-CF. And a positive value represents the reverse situation. For example, the pair value (**0.65; 2.93**) represents that using hybrid-CF is 0.65% and 2.93% better than using model-based in terms of the average learner knowledge and motivation respectively. All results are checked by t-test for equal mean hypothesis (assuming different variance). The value in italics inside the table shows that the null hypothesis is not rejected (for $\alpha = 0.05$), or the difference between model-based and hybrid-CF is not statistically significant. If we exclude zero and italic values in Table 2, then there are 14 and 6 negative values for the difference of learner knowledge and motivation respectively, with the lowest value equals to -1.05% and -5.68% respectively. And there are 8 and 12 positive values for the difference of leaner knowledge and motivation, with the highest value equals to 1.20% and 19.38%, respectively. Thus, we conclude that using hybrid-CF results in a lower performance in terms of learner average knowledge. However, since hybrid-CF usually needs lower computational cost than model-based recommendation (which is not measured here) and the performance loss is not big, hence hybrid-CF is very promising in e-learning system.

So far, it is unclear why the individual result of our simulations, especially some values which show high differences, especially when motivation change quickly (FMC). However, we can conclude that using hybrid-CF may not always result in a lower performance. And if it happens, the difference may not higher than 5%. This conclusion is useful, since hybrid-CF needs lower cost than model-based recommendation. Thus, if the performance lost is not big, then hybrid-CF should be used instead of the traditional model-based recommendation.

Table 2. The differences between model-based and hybrid recommendation (in percentage %). The first value in each cell represents the difference of final knowledge and the second value represents the difference of final motivation.

(w_l, w_s)	FMC	MMC	SMC	NMC
(1, 0)	**0.59; 2.77**	**-0.70**; *-0.06*	**-0.77**; *-0.42*	*-0.43; 0.00*
(U[0, 1], 0)	**0.98; 7.97**	**-0.28; 3.85**	*0.21; -0.32*	**0.54**; *0.00*
(U[0, .3], 0)	*-0.47;* **15.15**	**-0.52**; *0.75*	*0.33; -5.42*	**1.09**; *0.00*
(1, U[0, .3])	**-0.57; 1.61**	**-1.05; -1.05**	**-0.76**; *-0.90*	*-0.29; 0.00*
(U[0, 1], U[0, .3])	*0.30;* **8.09**	**-0.44; 3.41**	*0.22; -0.01*	**0.69**; *0.00*
(U[0, .3], U[0, .3])	**-0.85; 19.38**	**-0.69**; *-0.19*	*0.06; -5.68*	**1.20**; *0.00*
(1, U[0, 1])	**-0.52; 1.13**	**-0.96; -0.8**	**-0.82; -0.84**	*-0.27; 0.00*
(U[0, 1], U[0, 1])	**0.96; 7.36**	*-0.15;* **4.68**	*0.16; -0.06*	**0.88**; *0.00*
(1, 1)	*-0.34;* **1.47**	**-0.69; -1.31**	**-0.47**; *-0.81*	*-0.43; 0.00*

4.2 Discussions

Effectiveness of Artificial Learner

Computer simulation has long served as a tool of applying artificial intelligence on intelligent tutoring systems [3, 8]. Although a simulation program can only model part of the real environment where real learners involve, it can afford a powerful tool for gaining insights for paper recommendations in complex settings. Therefore, the simulation discussed in this paper can serve as a guide in our future study. In fact, we have designed a follow-up human subject study, which extends the resulting recommendations made by the artificial learners on the real human learners.

Personalization for Adaptive Learning Environments

It is noted that in our study, we attempt to personalize additional learning pieces to students based not only on their interests, but also on their pedagogical characteristics. Although personalizing learning contents have been studied mainly in the adaptive hypermedia community for years [11], their main implementations of personalization have largely focused on personalized link generation, content sequencing etc. To the best of our knowledge, automated paper recommender has rarely been studied.

5 Concluding Remarks

In this paper, we pointed out the differences of making recommendations in e-learning and other domains. We propose two pedagogy-oriented recommendation techniques: model-based and hybrid recommendations. We argue that while it is feasible to apply both of these techniques in our domain, a hybrid collaborative filtering technique is more efficient to make "just-in-time" recommendations. In order to assess and compare these two techniques, we carried out an experiment using artificial learners. Experiment results are encouraging, showing that hybrid collaborative filtering, which can lower the computational costs, will not compromise the overall performance of the RS. In addition, as more and more learners participate in the learning process, both learner and paper models can better be enhanced and updated, which is especially desirable for web-based learning systems. Currently, we have tested the recommendation mechanisms with real learners, and the results are very encouraging, which will be reported in another paper. We plan to run a larger scale of human learner study in the near future.

References

1. Basu, C., Hirsh, H., Cohen, W. and Nevill-Manning, C. Technical paper recommendations: a study in combining multiple information sources. *JAIR*, 1, 231-252. 2001.
2. Bollacker, K., Lawrence, S. and C. Lee Giles, C. L. A system for automatic personalized tracking of scientific literature on the web. *ACM DL*, 105-113. 1999.
3. Chan, T. and Baskin, A.B. Learning companion systems. *ITS 1990*, 6-33. 1990.
4. Herlocker, J., Konstan, J., Borchers, A. and Riedl, J. An algorithmic framework for performing collaborative filtering. *SIGIR'99*, 230-237. 1999.
5. Kobsa, A., Koenemann, J. and Pohl, W. Personalized hypermedia presentation techniques for improving online customer relationships.*The Knowledge Engineering Review* 16(2): 111-155. 2001.
6. McNee, S, Albert, I., Cosley, D., Gopalkrishnan, P., Lam, S., Rashid, A., Konstan, J. and Riedl, J. On the Recommending of Citations for Research Papers. *ACM CSCW'02*, 116-125. 2002.
7. Schafer, J., Konstan, J. and Riedl, J. Electronic Commerce Recommender Applications. *Data Mining and Knowledge Discovery*, 5, (1/2): 115-152. 2001.
8. Tang, T.Y. and Chan, K. C. C. Feature construction for student group forming based on their browsing behaviors in an e-learning system. *PRICAI 2002*, 512-521. 2002.
9. Tang, T.Y and McCalla, G. Smart recommendations for an evolving e-learning system. In *Workshop on Technologies for Electronic Documents for Supporting Learning, AIED'2003*.
10. Tang, T.Y. and McCalla, G. On the pedagogically guided paper recommendation for an evolving web-based learning system. *Proc. of FLAIRS Conference*, 2004. AAAI Press.
11. Weber, G.,and Brusilovsky, P. ELM-ART: an adaptive versatile system for web-based instruction. *International Journal of AI in Education*, 12: 1-35. 2001.
12. Woodruff, A., Gossweiler, R., Pitkow, J., Chi, E. and Card, S. Enhancing a digital book with a reading recommender. In *ACM CHI 2000*, 153-160. 2000.

An Anytime Algorithm for Interpreting Arguments

Sarah George, Ingrid Zukerman, and Michael Niemann

School of Computer Science and Software Engineering
Monash University, Clayton, VICTORIA 3800, Australia
{sarahg,ingrid,niemann}@csse.monash.edu.au

Abstract. The problem of interpreting Natural Language (NL) discourse is generally of exponential complexity. However, since interactions with users must be conducted in real time, an exhaustive search is not a practical option. In this paper, we present an anytime algorithm that generates "good enough" interpretations of probabilistic NL arguments in the context of a Bayesian network (BN). These interpretations consist of: BN nodes that match the sentences in a given argument, assumptions that justify the beliefs in the argument, and a reasoning structure that adds detail to the argument. We evaluated our algorithm using automatically generated arguments and hand-generated arguments. In both cases, our algorithm generated good interpretations (and often the best interpretation) in real time.

1 Introduction

Discourse interpretation is a complex task that is essential for human-computer interaction. This complexity arises from the large number of choices to be made at different stages of the interpretation process, e.g., there are several possible referents for each noun, each sentence could have more than one meaning, and sentences may relate to each other in a variety of ways. As a result, the problem of finding an interpretation of Natural Language (NL) discourse is exponential. However, interactions with users must be conducted in real time. This precludes an exhaustive search for the best interpretation of a user's discourse, and leads us to the idea of a "good enough" interpretation.

Anytime algorithms were introduced by Dean [1] and Horvitz *et al.* [2] in the late 1980's to produce approximate solutions to complex problems in limited time. In this paper, we present an anytime algorithm for discourse interpretation. Our algorithm receives as input probabilistic arguments presented by users to an argumentation system called BIAS (*Bayesian Interactive Argumentation System*). These arguments are composed of NL sentences linked by means of argumentation connectives (a small sample argument is shown in Fig. 1).

Our system uses Bayesian networks (BNs) [3] as its knowledge representation and reasoning formalism. Our domain of implementation is a murder mystery, which is represented by a 32-node BN. An interpretation of an argument consists of nodes in the domain BN that match the sentences in the argument, assumptions (values for BN nodes) that account for the beliefs stated in the argument, and a reasoning structure (a subnet of the domain BN) that connects the identified nodes. For instance, the subnet in Fig. 1 illustrates an interpretation generated for the argument on the left-hand-side. The italicized nodes are those mentioned in the argument, and the grey, boxed node is an assumption (inferred by the system) that accounts for the beliefs in the argument.

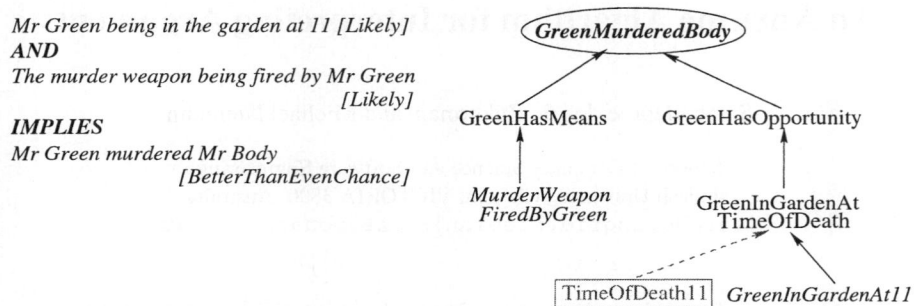

Fig. 1. Sample argument and interpretation.

In the next section, we discuss related research. We then define interpretations in the context of BNs, and describe our anytime algorithm for argument interpretation. In Section 5, we evaluate our algorithm's performance, followed by concluding remarks.

2 Related Research

Discourse interpretation systems typically employ different resources to fill in information omitted by a user, e.g., [4, 5]. However, most interpretation systems developed to date have focused on the procedures and knowledge sources required for generating interpretations, ignoring issues of efficiency and real-time performance.

These issues have been addressed by anytime algorithms in the context of planning, diagnosis and decision-making under uncertainty, e.g., [1, 6]. In areas more related to our work, anytime algorithms have been used in a system that generates proofs for hypotheses [7], and in spoken dialogue systems [8, 9].

Haenni [7] applied an anytime algorithm based on the Dempster-Schaefer formalism for generating proofs for hypotheses. Like BIAS, his system aims for a concise proof. However, he used heuristics to select propositions to be included in the proof, while we use a complex function that combines different attributes of an interpretation. The anytime algorithm described in [8] improves the quality of the surface realization of spoken responses to users' queries, while the algorithm presented in [9] interprets users' spoken queries. Both systems are implemented in the travel timetable domain. Our work resembles most that of Fischer *et al.* [9] in the sense that their system also maps users' queries to points in a network (although they use a semantic network), and they also use a cost function to assess the quality of an interpretation. However, their domain of discourse is significantly more restricted than ours.

3 What Is an Interpretation?

An interpretation of an argument in the context of a BN is a tuple $\{NC, AC, IG\}$, where NC is a *node configuration*, AC is an *assumption configuration*, and IG is an *interpretation graph*.

A **Node Configuration** is a set of nodes in the domain BN that match the sentences in an argument. Each node in the BN is associated with one or more *canonical sentences* that express its content. For instance, the canonical sentence for GreenHasOpportunity in Fig. 1 is "Mr Green had the opportunity to murder Mr Body". BIAS uses a cosine similarity measure [10] complemented with an automatically-derived word-similarity score [11] to estimate the similarity between an input sentence and a canonical sentence associated with a node. For example, an input sentence such as "Mr Green had the chance to kill Mr Body" is considered similar to "Mr Green had the opportunity to murder Mr Body" and (a little less similar) to "Mr Green murdered Mr Body". Hence, arguments that contain this sentence yield node configurations that include GreenHasOpportunity and GreenMurderedBody. The process for proposing candidate node configurations is described in Section 4.1.

An **Assumption Configuration** is a set of assumptions made by BIAS to account for the beliefs in an argument. For example, for the argument in Fig. 1 to make sense, the system has to assume that the time of death was 11. At present, our BN nodes are binary. Hence, the possible assumptions are: SET TRUE – assume that a node is True; SET FALSE – assume that a node is False; and UNSET – assume no direct evidence for this node.

An **Interpretation Graph** is a subnet of the domain BN which links the nodes that correspond to the antecedents in an argument (according to a particular node configuration) to the nodes that correspond to the consequents. Note that a good interpretation graph is not necessarily the minimum spanning tree that connects the nodes in question, as this spanning tree may have blocked paths (through which evidence cannot propagate in a BN [3]), which render an interpretation invalid.

4 Anytime Algorithm

Algorithm *GenerateInterpretations* (Fig. 2) receives as input an argument *Arg*, and returns the best N (=4) interpretations among those considered in the available time. To this effect, it matches the sentences in the argument to nodes in the domain BN (Step 1), makes assumptions that are warranted by the beliefs in the argument (Step 2), and proposes subnets of the BN that connect the nodes in the argument (Step 3). Each of these steps selects the "best" component of an interpretation based on local knowledge. However, this component is not necessarily the best overall when considered in conjunction with the other components. Fig. 3(a) depicts the search tree generated by our algorithm, where each level of the tree corresponds to a different component. Fig. 3(b) instantiates this search tree with respect to a small example.

4.1 Getting a Node Configuration

Algorithm *GetNodeConfig* (Fig. 2) receives as input the sentences in an argument, and returns a set of matching nodes – one node per sentence. The algorithm selects a node configuration from a list called *NodeConfigList*. This list comprises two main parts: {*PrevNodeConfigList, MakeNewConfig*}, where *PrevNodeConfigList* is a list of previously generated node configurations, and *MakeNewConfig* is a call to a function that

Algorithm *GenerateInterpretations(Arg)*
while {there is time}
{
   1. // Get a node configuration in the domain BN that matches the argument
      $NC \leftarrow GetNodeConfig(Arg)$
   2. // Get an assumption configuration that accounts for the beliefs stated for the nodes in NC
      $AC \leftarrow GetAssumptionConfig(Arg,NC)$
   3. // Get an interpretation graph that connects the nodes in NC
      $IG \leftarrow GetInterpretationGraph(NC,AC)$
   4. Evaluate interpretation $\{NC, AC, IG\}$.
   5. Retain top N (=4) interpretations.
}

Algorithm *GetNodeConfig(Arg)*   (Section 4.1)

1. Select an element from *NodeConfigList* at random (all previously generated configurations are equiprobable, and the probability of generating a new configuration is $Pr_{new}\%$ (=5%) of the probability of any of the previous configurations).
2. If *MakeNewConfig(Node)* was called,   (Section 4.4)
Then insert the node configuration returned by this function in *PrevNodeConfigList*.
3. Return the chosen configuration.

Algorithm *GetAssumptionConfig(Arg,NC)*   (Section 4.2)

1. If *AssumptionConfigList* is empty
   (a) Call *MakeNewConfig(Assumption)* K times (= 200), where each time *MakeNewConfig* returns the best assumption configuration. (Section 4.4)
   (b) Assign the top k (=3) assumption configurations to *AssumptionConfigList*.
2. Select an element from *AssumptionConfigList* at random.
3. Return the chosen configuration.

Algorithm *GetInterpretationGraph(NC,AC)*   (Section 4.3)
Call *MakeNewConfig(InterpretationGraph)*, and return the configuration it produced.

Algorithm *MakeNewConfig(ConfigType)*   (Section 4.4)

1. If the priority queue is empty, propose an initial configuration, calculate its probability, and add the configuration and its probability to the priority queue.
2. Remove the first configuration from the queue.
3. Generate the children of this configuration, calculate their probability, and insert them in the queue so that the queue remains sorted in descending order of probabilities.
4. Return the chosen (removed) configuration.

Fig. 2. Anytime algorithm for argument interpretation.

returns the next best configuration of a given type, e.g., a node or assumption configuration, or an interpretation graph (Section 4.4).

For the example in Figure 3(b), *PrevNodeConfigList* is initially empty, hence *MakeNewConfig(Node)* must be called, returning node configuration NC_1. This configuration is added to *PrevNodeConfigList*, and returned by *GetNodeConfig*. Now, *NodeConfigList* contains two elements: $\{NC_1, MakeNewConfig\}$, where NC_1 is selected with probability 0.952, and *MakeNewConfig* with probability 0.048 (=5% of 0.952). If *MakeNewConfig* is selected next time *GetNodeConfig* is called, then *NodeConfigList* will contain three elements: $\{NC_1, NC_2, MakeNewConfig\}$.

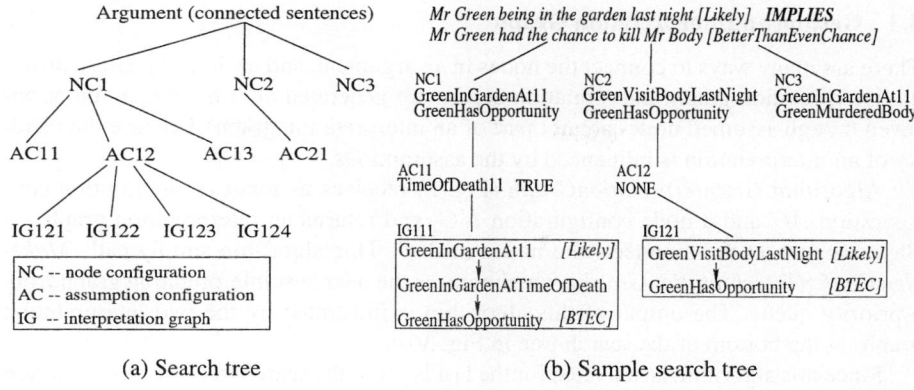

Fig. 3. Process for generating interpretations.

Algorithm *GetNodeConfig* reduces the fan-out factor of node configurations by having an initial low probability of generating a new node, and further reducing this probability as the list of configurations grows. This low fan-out is due to the fact that the intended node configuration is usually among the top three returned by our parser.

Note that when a node configuration is generated, a belief mentioned regarding a particular statement becomes associated with the node that matches that statement. For example, in Fig. 3(b), the belief of BetterThanEvenChance given for the sentence "Mr Green had the chance to kill Mr Body" is associated with node GreenHasOpportunity for node configuration NC_1, and with GreenMurderedBody for NC_3.

4.2 Getting an Assumption Configuration

For each node configuration, the system determines whether it needs to make assumptions so that the beliefs in the BN resulting from Bayesian propagation match the beliefs stated in an argument. For instance, if "Mr Green being in the garden last night" is interpreted as GreenInGardenAt11 (Fig. 3(b)), then BIAS must assume that the time of death was 11 (TimeOfDeath11 TRUE) for the beliefs in the BN to match those in the argument (AC_{11}). In contrast, if this sentence is interpreted as GreenVisitBodyLastNight, no assumptions are required (AC_{12}).

Algorithm *GetAssumptionConfig* (Fig. 2) receives as input an argument *Arg* and a node configuration NC, and returns an assumption configuration, i.e., a set of nodes in the BN accompanied by their assumed beliefs. This algorithm randomly selects an assumption configuration from a list of configurations denoted *AssumptionConfigList*, which is composed of the top k (=3) assumption configurations among those returned by *MakeNewConfig* (Section 4.4).

For the example in Figure 3(b), assume that we are under node configuration NC_1, and that *AssumptionConfigList* is empty. Hence, *MakeNewConfig(Assumption)* is called K times, returning each time the best assumption configuration. After these K calls, the top k configurations are retained: $\{AC_{11}, AC_{12}, AC_{13}\}$. From now on, every time *GetAssumptionConfig* is called, it selects one of these configurations at random.

4.3 Getting an Interpretation Graph

There are many ways to connect the nodes in an argument, and each way yields a different interpretation graph. Interpretation graphs are generated after making assumptions (even though assumed nodes are not part of an interpretation graph), because the validity of an interpretation is influenced by the assumptions.

Algorithm *GetInterpretationGraph* (Fig. 2) receives as input an assumption configuration AC and a node configuration NC, and returns an interpretation graph – a Bayesian subnet that connects the nodes in NC. This algorithm simply calls *MakeNewConfig(InterpretationGraph)*, which returns the next best interpretation graph from a priority queue. The output of this algorithm is illustrated by the two interpretation graphs at the bottom of the search tree in Fig. 3(b).

Since this algorithm is activated for the last layer of the search tree, the interpretation graphs it returns do not need to be cached for further processing, as opposed to node configurations and assumption configurations.

4.4 Making a New Configuration

MakeNewConfig is at the core of our anytime algorithm. It returns a new configuration every time it is called (Fig. 2). This may be a node configuration, an assumption configuration or an interpretation graph. The algorithm maintains a priority queue of configurations and their probabilities. Each time it is called, it removes the configuration at the top of the queue, generates its "child configurations" (configurations derived from the selected one), inserts them in the queue, and returns the selected configuration.

Algorithm *MakeNewConfig* performs three activities that require calls to specialized functions: *propose an initial configuration*, *generate children of a configuration*, and *calculate the probability of a configuration*. A *static* approach is applied to perform the first two activities for node and assumption configurations, and a *dynamic* approach for interpretation graphs.

Static Approach. In order to generate the next node or assumption configuration, the algorithm maintains a structure called *Score Table*, which maps an input element to a decision (e.g., a sentence to a matching node, or a node to an assumption about it). This structure is obtained from our sentence parser or our assumption generator.

The Sentence Score Table is a list where each element corresponds to a sentence in the argument. Each sentence in turn is associated with a list of <node: probability> pairs – one pair for each node in the domain BN – ordered in descending order of probability (Fig. 4(a)). Each pair represents the probability that this node is intended by the sentence in question, which is calculated based on the similarity between this sentence and the canonical sentences for the node [11].

Each element in the Assumption Score Table corresponds to a node in the BN. Each node is associated with a list of <assumption: probability> pairs – one pair for each type of assumption (Fig. 4(b)). Each pair represents the probability of making this assumption about the node in question, which is obtained using heuristics such as the following: not changing the belief in a node has the highest probability, and asserting the belief in a node has a higher probability than contradicting it (e.g., a belief of 0.8 has a higher probability of being assumed true than false).

sentence$_1$ sentence$_2$ ... sentence$_m$ n_1: 0.2 n_{15}: 0.4 ... n_3: 0.3 n_{24}: 0.15 n_{10}: 0.3 ... n_{20}: 0.1 ... ... n_{32}: 0.0 n_2: 0.01 ... n_{13}: 0.02 (a) Sentence Score Table	node$_1$ node$_2$ ... node$_{32}$ UNSET: 0.8 SET TRUE: 0.95 ... UNSET: 0.5 SET TRUE: 0.1 UNSET: 0.04 ... SET TRUE: 0.3 SET FALSE: 0.1 SET FALSE: 0.01 ... SET FALSE: 0.2 (b) Assumption Score Table

Fig. 4. Sample Score Tables for node configurations and assumption configurations.

The three activities mentioned above are performed as follows.

Propose an initial configuration – Select the first row from the Score Table.

Generate children of a configuration – The ith child is generated by moving down one place in list i in the Score Table, while staying in the same place in the other lists.

Calculate the probability of a configuration – For node configurations, this probability is the product of the probabilities of the entries in a configuration. For assumption configurations, this probability is a function of the "cost" of making a set of assumptions (the higher the product of the probabilities of the entries in an assumption configuration, the lower the cost) and the "savings" due to a closer match between the beliefs stated in an argument and those in the BN as a result of making the assumptions (the calculation of this component is described in [12]). For instance, for the example in Fig. 1, the time of death assumption reduces the discrepancy between the user's stated belief in GreenMurderedBody and that in the BN in the absence of this assumption.

To illustrate the operation of this algorithm, consider the Sentence Score Table in Fig. 4(a). Initially, the first row is selected, yielding nodes $\{n_1, n_{15}, \ldots, n_3\}$ which have probability $0.2 \times 0.4 \times \ldots \times 0.3$. Prior to returning this configuration to *GetNodeConfig*, its children are generated: $\{\underline{n_{24}}, n_{15}, \ldots, n_3\}, \{n_1, \underline{n_{10}}, \ldots, n_3\}, \ldots$, their probabilities are calculated, and they are inserted in the queue in descending order of their probability. Next time *MakeNewConfig* is called for node configurations, the first configuration in the queue will be removed, its children will be generated, and so on.

Dynamic Approach. This procedure is described in detail in [12]. Here we provide a brief outline.

Propose an initial configuration – Generate the minimum spanning tree that connects the nodes corresponding to the argument.

Generate children of a configuration – The children of an interpretation graph are generated by iteratively "growing" the graph, i.e., adding nodes and arcs.

Calculate the probability of a configuration – The probability of an interpretation graph is a function of its size (the larger the graph the lower its probability), its structural similarity with the argument, and the probability that its nodes were implied by the argument (nodes that were previously seen by the user are more likely than nodes with which the user is unfamiliar).

4.5 Algorithm Analysis

Our anytime algorithm may be classified as *interruptible* [6], as it can be interrupted at any time to produce results whose quality is described by its *Conditional Performance Profile (CPP)*. Notice, however, that our algorithm has a small fixed-time component due to the K calls to *MakeNewConfig* from *GetAssumptionConfig*.

The operation of *GetAssumptionConfig* differs from that of *GetNodeConfig* and *GetInterpretationGraph* as follows. *GetAssumptionConfig* makes a random selection from a static list of the k best assumption configurations (selected from K assumption configurations generated by *MakeNewConfig* for a particular node configuration), while the other two procedures iteratively call *MakeNewConfig* to obtain a new node configuration or interpretation graph. This difference is due to the fact that the process which generates the children of a node configuration or an interpretation graph reliably proposes items of decreasing goodness, while this is not necessarily the case for the process which generates the next assumption configuration. This is because the assumptions are generated from the top of the Assumption Score Table, but their goodness can be determined only after Bayesian propagation is performed.

5 Evaluation

Our evaluation focuses on the anytime algorithm, i.e., the time BIAS takes to produce a good interpretation, rather than on BIAS' ability to produce plausible interpretations (which was evaluated in [12]).

Our evaluation consists of two experiments: one where the system interprets automatically generated arguments, and one where it interprets hand-generated arguments. The arguments in both experiments were designed to test the effect of three factors on BIAS' performance: *argument size*, *interpretation complexity*, and *belief distortion*.

Argument size measures the number of nodes in an argument. We considered three argument sizes: Small (2-3 nodes), Medium (4-5 nodes) and Large (6-7 nodes).

Interpretation complexity measures how much of an "inferential leap" is performed in order to connect between the nodes in an argument. The complexity of an interpretation is approximated by means of the number of nodes in the minimum spanning tree that connects the nodes in an argument. We considered three levels of complexity for our automatic evaluation: 0 (the minimum spanning tree includes only the nodes in the argument), +2 (the minimum spanning tree includes 2 additional nodes), and +4 (4 additional nodes). Our hand-generated evaluation had interpretations with a complexity of up to +7.

Belief distortion measures how far the beliefs in an argument are from those inferred by BIAS. For instance, if the argument states that a node is Likely while BIAS believes it is VeryLikely, there is a distortion of 1. Belief distortions are related to assumptions, since BIAS may be forced to make assumptions in order to reconcile the beliefs in an argument with BIAS' propagated beliefs. We considered 5 levels of *total distortion* between an argument and its interpretation (from 0 to 4) for both experiments. 0 distortion means that the beliefs in the argument match those in the interpretation, and a distortion of 4 means that the total discrepancy between the beliefs in the nodes in the argument and BIAS' beliefs is 4 – this may be due to a large discrepancy in one node, or small discrepancies in several nodes.

An Anytime Algorithm for Interpreting Arguments

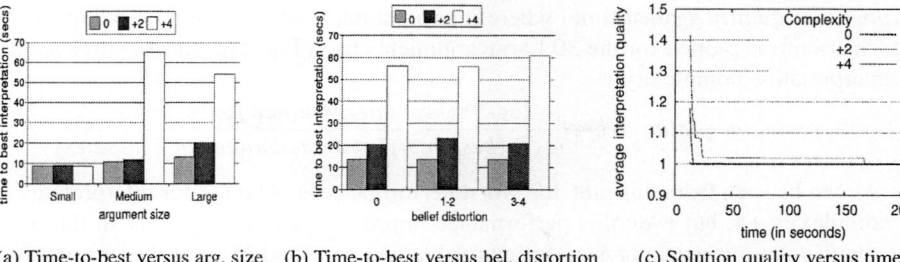

(a) Time-to-best versus arg. size (90 arguments)   (b) Time-to-best versus bel. distortion (138 Large arguments)   (c) Solution quality versus time (30 Large arguments)

Fig. 5. Performance of our anytime algorithm for automatically generated arguments.

Our automatically generated arguments were produced by randomly selecting a certain number of nodes from our domain BN, and positioning them in the BN so that there are enough intervening nodes – this achieves a desired level of complexity. The propagated beliefs in the nodes in these arguments were then altered to achieve different levels of belief distortion. Our hand-generated arguments were based on arguments entered by people (obtained in previous system trials [12]). These arguments were manually modified in order to obtain enough sample arguments to test the above three factors.

Our experiments focused on two aspects of an interpretation: assumptions and interpretation graphs. Hence, our test arguments consist of implications that connect between nodes in the BN (rather than between NL sentences). Our interpretation algorithm was run for 5 minutes to obtain a performance profile over time. Its performance for our experiments is described below.

Automatically Generated Arguments. We ran our interpretation algorithm on a total of 228 automatically generated arguments, which varied in argument size, interpretation complexity and belief distortion. Fig. 5 depicts different aspects of the performance of our anytime algorithm for these experiments.

Fig. 5(a) shows the effect of argument size and interpretation complexity on the average time taken to find the best interpretation for 90 arguments, while keeping the belief distortion to 0. This chart indicates that argument size has a small influence on system performance (the best interpretation was found in less than 20 seconds), except when the complexity of the interpretation is +4 (4 nodes in addition to those in the argument) and the argument is Medium or Large. In these cases, the average time required to find the best interpretation exceeds 50 seconds. Although the performance for Medium arguments appears worse than that for Large arguments, this difference is not statistically significant, as the standard deviation is quite large.

Fig. 5(b) shows the effect of belief distortion and interpretation complexity on the average solution time for 138 Large arguments (the performance for Medium arguments is consistent with that for Large arguments). Belief distortion seems to have little effect on algorithm performance (with the best interpretation found in around 20 seconds), while once more, the main influencing factor is interpretation complexity.

These results prompted us to examine the CPP (conditional performance profile) of our algorithm in relation to interpretation complexity. Fig. 5(c) plots average *in-*

terpretation quality against time, where interpretation quality is defined below. This information was plotted for the 30 Large arguments from Fig. 5(a) for the three levels of interpretation complexity.

$$interpretation\ quality = \frac{-\log_2 \Pr(best\ interpretation\ found\ so\ far)}{-\log_2 \Pr(best\ interpretation\ obtained\ in\ 5\ minutes)}$$

As can be seen from this plot, the worst performance is obtained for interpretations of complexity +4, but even this performance improves significantly early in the process, with solutions reaching near-optimum obtained at around 25 seconds. The plot for complexity +2 reaches the best interpretation at about 16 seconds, and the plot for complexity 0 is nearly invisible, as it reaches the best interpretation quality immediately.

User-Based Arguments. Our results for user-based arguments are significantly better than those obtained for the automatically generated arguments. In fact, the best solution was obtained in under 3 seconds for all our hand-generated arguments, which had levels of complexity of up to +7. This indicates that the automatically generated arguments produce very harsh evaluation conditions, which constitute an upper bound for the performance expected under actual working conditions.

6 Conclusion

We have offered an anytime algorithm that generates "good enough" interpretations of probabilistic arguments in the context of a BN. These interpretations consist of BN nodes that match the sentences in an argument, assumptions that justify the beliefs in the argument, and a reasoning structure that adds detail to the argument. Our evaluation focused on interpreting arguments that required making additional assumptions and postulating interpretation graphs (rather than proposing different node configurations). Our anytime algorithm generated a good interpretation for automatically generated arguments in under 25 seconds, and the best interpretation for hand-generated arguments in under 3 seconds. In both cases creditable performance was achieved in real time. However, this discrepancy in run times suggests that our algorithm's performance for automatically generated arguments constitutes an upper bound for its performance under actual conditions, which is very encouraging.

Acknowledgments

This research is supported in part by the ARC Centre for Perceptive and Intelligent Machines in Complex Environments. The NL parser was implemented by Tony Ng.

References

1. Dean, T., Boddy, M.S.: An analysis of time-dependent planning. In: AAAI-88 – Proceedings of the 7th National Conference on Artificial Intelligence, St. Paul, Minnesota (1988) 49–54
2. Horvitz, E., Suermondt, H., Cooper, G.: Bounded conditioning: flexible inference for decision under scarce resources. In: UAI89 – Proceedings of the 1989 Workshop on Uncertainty in Artificial Intelligence, Windsor, Canada (1989) 182–193

3. Pearl, J.: Probabilistic Reasoning in Intelligent Systems. Morgan Kaufmann Pub., San Mateo, California (1988)
4. Raskutti, B., Zukerman, I.: Generation and selection of likely interpretations during plan recognition. User Modeling and User Adapted Interaction **1** (1991) 323–353
5. Carberry, S., Lambert, L.: A process model for recognizing communicative acts and modeling negotiation subdialogues. Computational Linguistics **25** (1999) 1–53
6. Zilberstein, S., Russell, S.: Approximate reasoning using anytime algorithms. In Natarajan, S., ed.: Imprecise and Approximate Computation. Kluwer Academic Pub. (1995) 43–62
7. Haenni, R.: Anytime argumentative and abductive reasoning. Soft Computing Journal **8** (2003)
8. Jokinen, K., Wilcock, G.: Confidence-based adaptivity in response generation for a spoken dialogue system. In: Proceedings of the Second SIGdial Workshop on Discourse and Dialogue, Aalborg, Denmark (2001)
9. Fischer, J., Haas, J., Nöth, E., Niemann, H., Deinzer, F.: Empowering knowledge based speech understanding through statistics. In: ICSLP'98 – Proceedings of International Conference on Spoken Language Processing. Volume 5., Sydney, Australia (1998) 2231–2235
10. Salton, G., McGill, M.: An Introduction to Modern Information Retrieval. McGraw Hill (1983)
11. Zukerman, I., George, S., Wen, Y.: Lexical paraphrasing for document retrieval and node identification. In: IWP2003 – Proceedings of the Second International Workshop on Paraphrasing: Paraphrase Acquisition and Applications, Sapporo, Japan (2003) 94–101
12. Zukerman, I., George, S.: A probabilistic approach for argument interpretation. To appear in User Modeling and User-Adapted Interaction, Special Issue on Language-Based Interaction: User Modeling and Adaptation (2004)

Varieties of Causal Intervention

Kevin B. Korb, Lucas R. Hope,
Ann E. Nicholson, and Karl Axnick

School of Computer Science and Software Engineering
Monash University
Clayton, Victoria 3800, Australia
{korb,lhope,annn}@csse.monash.edu.au

Abstract. The use of Bayesian networks for modeling causal systems has achieved widespread recognition with Judea Pearl's *Causality* (2000). There, Pearl developed a "do-calculus" for reasoning about the effects of deterministic causal interventions on a system. Here we discuss some of the different kinds of intervention that arise when indeterminstic interventions are allowed, generalizing Pearl's account. We also point out the danger of the naive use of Bayesian networks for causal reasoning, which can lead to the mis-estimation of causal effects. We illustrate these ideas with a graphical user interface we have developed for causal modeling.

1 Introduction

Little progress has been made in understanding the nature of causality in the last 2500 years, after Aristotle made the first serious foray. David Hume made some negative observations about what causality is not – pointing out, for example, that causal relations are not directly observable. What causality may actually be remains a perplexing problem, but progress has been made in relating it to other concepts whose understanding appears to be more accessible. The influential, and first, text on learning Bayesian networks from data, *Causation, Prediction and Search* (1993) [12], notably eschewed any attempt to define the central concept, focusing instead on the relation between (undefined) causal structure and probabilistic structure. More recently, Judea Pearl has used Bayesian networks to make progress in understanding philosophical problems about causal concepts, giving accounts of counterfactual reasoning [10], experimental methods [9] and token causality [6, 7]. James Woodward, among others, is using Pearl's account of causal intervention to improve upon an old philosophical tradition, attempting to make sense of causality in terms of manipulation [14]. This convergence of artificial intelligence (automated Bayesian networks) and philosophy is, we think, wholly to the good and promises to be fruitful for both sides of the collaboration.

The philosophical use of Bayesian networks largely depends upon a causal interpretation of the arc structure and the probabilistic interpretation of causality, stemming from the work of Patrick Suppes [13] and Wesley Salmon [11]. Although there is some dispute within the AI community about the merits of the causal interpretation, most of this seems to be fueled by the observation that any Bayesian network can be reordered back-to-front and still represent the very same probability distribution, using Chickering's arc reversal rule [3]. What that observation ignores is that any such reordering can only lead from simple to complex networks when they begin from a perfect map – that is, one whose arcs are both necessary and sufficient for identifying a probabilistic dependency in the system being modeled[1]. A causal interpretation of the Bayesian network implies that we can use the network for causal reasoning and not just probabilistic reasoning. And this further implies the ability to use such models to reason hypothetically about the consequences of interventions. Thus, the difference between the "statistically equivalent" models $Cancer \leftarrow Gene \rightarrow Smoking$ and $Smoking \rightarrow Gene \rightarrow Cancer$ may be determininable by experimentally setting the value of $Smoking$, though not by any observation of the three variables.

Judea Pearl has notably discussed causal interventions and their modeling with Bayesian networks in *Causality* [10]. There, he favors representing an intervention on a variable C by arc-cutting: by setting C to a desired value and cutting all arcs from its parents. He formalizes this approach in his "do-calculus." An alternative method is to introduce a new node I_c as an additional parent of C, where setting (or observing) I_c to be TRUE models an intervention. Once the alterations to the network are applied for either method of modeling intervention, ordinary Bayesian network propagation rules can be used. The arc-cutting method is in many ways simpler, but we suggest the simplicity comes at a price: foregoing the possibility of modeling many situations realistically.

In this paper we describe extensions to these techniques for modeling interventions with Bayesian networks and especially (re)introducing indeterminism into that modeling. We hope this will contribute to the collaboration of AI and philosophy of science, as well as open up the wider practical application of Bayesian networks. After a brief defence of indeterminism, we proceed by defining the concept of intervention and presenting a classification system for different kinds of intervention. We then discuss the concept of the effectiveness of an intervention, and finally we describe our programmatic representation of interventions and a GUI for managing them in a Bayesian network tool.

2 Indeterministic Causal Models

One curiosity of the collaboration between AI and philosophy of science thus far is a widespread agreement that, at bottom, these networks are deterministic, despite that fact that they are explicitly probabilistic models. Pearl, for one, is adamant that a deterministic conception of causality is required and for three reasons [10, pp. 26-7][2]:

1. Determinism is intuitive.
2. Counterfactuals and causal explanation can only be made sense of given a deterministic interpretation.
3. The deterministic interpretation is more general, since any indeterministic model can be transformed into a deterministic model.

---

[1] Granted, this claim has not yet exactly been proved in the literature. Indeed, it is demonstrably false in cases of measure zero, that is, cases where parameters in the network must be given an *exact* value for the network to be a perfect map. However, outside of measure zero cases, the relation between network minimality and causality is very clear empirically and, we believe, susceptible to compelling arguments. Presenting these, however, would take us beyond the scope of this paper.

[2] For a philosopher voicing the same opinion see, for example, [2].

Whether determinism is intuitive or not, we shall leave to the reader. However, we note in passing that there is a growing consensus amongst philosophers of science that such intuitions are insufficient reason for dismissing the probabilistic analysis of causality, which is explicitly indeterministic. Pearl has been collaborating with Joseph Halpern in developing an important account of causal explanation [6, 7]; we hope, however, that an indeterministic account of causal explanation is not actually impossible, since we are developing one.

As for Pearl's last point, it is undeniable that any Bayesian network can be converted into a deterministic model. The point, however, is empty, since equally every deterministic system can be represented as an indeterministic system. Even were things otherwise, it would remain deniable that the deterministic version is the proper vehicle for interpreting the original. We illustrate with a simple three-variable model which is linear (the simplest kind of Bayesian network). Structurally we have: $X \to Z \leftarrow Y$. The more common way to write linear models is with equations of this type:

$$Z = a_1 X + a_2 Y + U$$

Here, a_1 is a coefficient representing the degree of dependency of Z upon X and a_2 the dependency of Z upon Y. But, Z is not a strict function of any of X or Y or the combination of the two: there is a residual degree of variation, described by U. U is variously called the residual, the error term, the disturbance factor, etc. Whatever it's called, once we add it into the model, the model is deterministic, for Z certainly is a function – a linear function, of course – of the combination of X, Y and U. Does this make the physical system we are trying to model with the equation (or, Bayesian network) deterministic? Well, only if as a matter of fact U describes a variable of that system. Since as a matter of actual *practice* U is typically identified only in negative terms, as what is "left over" once the influences of the other parents of Z have been accounted for, and since in that typical practice U is only ever measured by measuring Z and computing what's left over after our best prediction using X and Y, it is simply not plausible to identify this as a variable of the system. What is represented by U is everything that either is unknown about this system or else is *unknowable* about this system, the ineradicable indeterminism in its fundamental relationships. Any justification for bundling all such unknowns and unknowables into a "known" variable can only lie in an a priori argument for determinism. But since indeterministic worlds are describable and, for all we can see, consistent, such an a priori argument would be ruling out a posteriori possibilities, which is something any reasonable a priori theory should not aspire to do. In short, the identification of causal models with their deterministic counterparts has been achieved only by presumption[3].

3 Observation Versus Intervention

Unfortunately, while the causal interpretation of Bayesian networks is becoming more widely accepted, the distinction between causal reasoning and observa-

---

[3] To convert any deterministic system into an indeterministic system, simply remove the error terms. If there are none, the system is surely correctly described as deterministic, but that is no bar to *representing* it with an indeterministic system having only extreme probability parameters.

tional reasoning remains for many obscure. This is particularly true in application areas where the use of regression models, rather than Bayesian networks, is the norm, since regression models (in ordinary usage) simply lack the capability of modeling interventions.

We illustrate the difference between intervention and observation with a simple example. Figure 1 presents a three-variable causal model of coronary heart disease (CHD) risk, which is loosely based upon models of the Framingham heart disease data (e.g., [1, 4]). As is normal, each arrow represents a direct and unerasable causal connection between variables[4]. Two contributing factors for CHD are shown: hypertension (HT; elevated blood pressure) at age 40 and HT at age 50. The higher the blood pressure, the greater the chance of CHD, both directly and indirectly. That is, hypertension at 40 directly causes heart disease (in the terms available in this simplified network of three variables!), but also indirectly through HT at 50. In this simplified model, the direct connection between HT at 40 and CHD between 50 and 60 represents all those implicit causal processes leading to heart disease which are *not* reflected in the later HT.

Figure 2(a) shows the results of observing no HT at age 50. The probability of CHD has decreased from a baseline of 0.052 to 0.026, as expected. But what if we intervene (say, with a medication) to lower blood pressure as in Figure 2(b)? The probability is reduced by a lesser amount to 0.033. By intervening on HT at 50 we have cut the indirect causal path between HT at 40 and CHD, but we have not cut the direct causal path. That is, there are still implicit causal processes leading from HT at 40 to CHD which the proposed intervention leaves intact. Observations of low HT at 50 will in general reflect a lower activation of those implicit processes, whereas an intervention will not. In short, it is better to have low blood pressure at 50 *naturally* than to achieve that by artificial means – and this causal model reflects these facts.

A real-world example of people getting this wrong is in the widespread use of regression models in public health. To assess the expected value of intervention on blood pressure at age 40, for example, regression models of the Framingham data have been used [1, 4]. If those models had exactly the same structure as ours, then (aside from being overly simplistic) there would be no actual problem, since HT at 40 being a root node there is no arc-cutting needed. However, the models actually used incorporate a reasonable number of additional variables, including parents of HT at 40, such as history of smoking, cholesterol levels, etc. By simply *observing* a hypothetical low blood pressure level and computing expected values, these models are being used for something they are incapable of representing[5]. The mis-estimation of effects may well be causing bad public policy decisions.

---

[4] Unerasable means that, no matter what other variables within the network may be observed, there is some joint observational state in which the parent variable can alter the conditional probability of the child variable. In case this condition does not hold we have an unfaithful model, in the terminology of [12]. We will not be considering such models here.

[5] In order to be *capable* of representing interventions we require a graphical representation in which the parental effects upon an intervened-upon variable can be cut (or altered). This minimally requires moving from ordinary regression models to path models or structural equation models, and treating these in the ways suggested in this paper.

326   Kevin B. Korb et al.

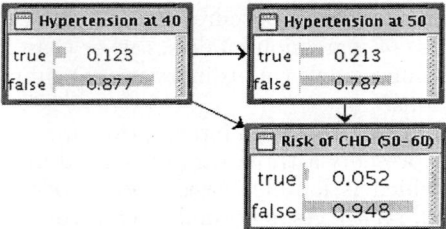

Fig. 1. A causal model linking hypertension at age 40 and 50 with risk of coronary heart disease.

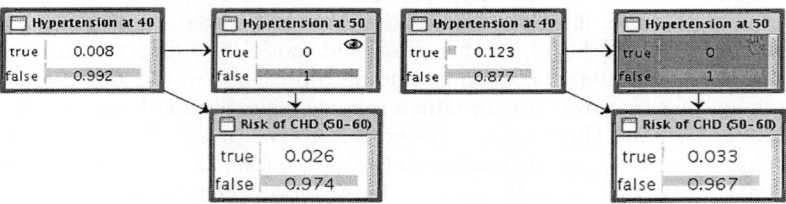

Fig. 2. The hypertension causal model where HT at age 50 is (a) observed as low (b) set to low.

4 Defining an Intervention

In ordinary usage, an intervention represents an influence on some causal system which is extraneous to that system. What kind of influence we consider is not constrained. It may interact with the existing complex of causal processes in the system in arbitrary ways. For example, a poison may induce death in some animal, but it may also interact with an anti-toxin so that it does not. Or again, the action of the poison may be probabilistic, either depending on unknown factors or by being genuinely indeterministic. Also, an intervention may impact on multiple factors (variables) in the system simultaneously or be targeted to exactly one such variable. In the extant literature of both philosophy and computer science there seems to have been an implicit agreement only to consider the very simplest of cases. In that literature, interventions are deterministic, always achieving their intended effect; and their intended effect is always to put exactly one variable into exactly one state. As a consequence, interventions never interact with any other causes of the targeted variable, rather their operation renders the effect of those other parents null. While such a simple model of interaction may be useful in untangling some of the mysteries of causation (e.g., it may have been useful in guiding intuitions in Halpern and Pearl's study of token causation, [6, 7]), it clearly will not do for a general analysis. Nor will it do for most practical cases. Medical interventions, for example, often fail (patients refuse to stop smoking), often interact with other causal factors (which explains why pharmacists require substantial training before licensing), often impact on multiple variables (organs) and often, even when successful, fail to put any variable into exactly one state (indeterminism!). Hence, we now provide a more general definition of intervention (retaining, however, reference to a single target variable in the system; this is a simplifying assumption which can easily be discharged).

Definition 1 *An intervention on a variable C in a causal model M transforms M into the augmented model M' which adds $I_c \to C$ to M where:*

1. I_c *is introduced with the intention of changing C.*
2. I_c *is exogenous in M'.*
3. I_c *directly causes (is a parent of) C.*

We take it that interventions are *actions* and, therefore, intentional. In particular, there will be some intended *target distribution* for the variable C, which we write $P^*(C)$. I_c itself will just be a binary variable, reflecting whether an intervention on C is attempted or not. However, this definition does not restrict I_c's interaction with C's other parents, leaving open whether the target distribution is actually achieved by the intervention. Also, the definition does allow variables other than C to be directly caused by I_c; hence, anticipated or unanticipated side-effects are allowed.

5 Categories of Intervention

We now develop this broader concept of intervention by providing a classification of the different kinds of intervention we have alluded to above. We do this using two "dimensions" along which interventions may vary. The result of the intervention is the adoption by the targeted variable of a new probability distribution over its states (even when a single such state is forced by the intervention, when the new probability distribution is degenerate), whether or not this achieved distribution is also the target distribution. To be sure, the new distribution will be identical to the original distribution when the intervention is not attempted or is entirely ineffectual. This special case can be represented

$$P_{M'}(C|\pi_c, \neg I_c) = P_M(C|\pi_c) \tag{1}$$

where π_c is the set of the original parents of C.

Dimensions of Intervention

1. The degree of *dependency* of the effect upon the existing parents.
   (a) An entirely independent intervention leads to an achieved distribution which is a function only of the new distribution aimed for by the intervention. Thus, for an independent intervention, we have

$$P_{M'}(C|\pi_c, I_c) = P^*(C) \tag{2}$$

   (b) A dependent intervention leads to an achieved distribution which is a function of both the target distribution and the state of the variable's other parents.

   An independent intervention on C simply cuts it off from its parents. Dependent interventions depend for their effect, in part, on the pre-existing parents of the target variable. The dependency across the parents, including the new

I_c, may be of any variety: linear, noisy-or, or any kind of complex, non-linear interaction. These are precisely the kinds of dependency that Bayesian networks model already, so it is no extension of the semantics of Bayesian networks to incorporate them. Rather, it is something of a mystery that prior work on intervention has ignored them.

2. Deterministic versus stochastic interventions.
   (a) A deterministic intervention aims to leave the target variable in one particular state – i.e., the target distribution is extreme.
   (b) A stochastic intervention aims to leave the target variable with a new distribution with positive probability over two or more states.

A deterministic intervention is by intention simple. Say, get Fred to stop smoking. By factoring in the other dimension, allowing for other variables still to influence the target variable, however, we can end up with quite complex models. Thus, it might take considerable complexity to reflect the interaction of a doctor's warning with peer-group pressure.

The stochastic case is yet more complex. For example, in a social science study we may wish to employ stratified sampling in order to force a target variable, say age, to take a uniform distribution. That is an independent, stochastic intervention. If, unhappily, our selection into experimental and control groups is not truly random, it may be that this selection is related to age. And this relation may induce any kind of actual distribution over the targeted age variable.

Any non-extreme actual distribution will be subject to changes under Bayesian updating, of course, whether it is for a targeted variable or not. For example, a crooked Blackjack dealer who can manipulate the next card dealt with some high probability, may intervene to set the next deal to be an Ace with probability 0.95. If the card is later revealed to be an Ace, then obviously that probability will revised to 1.0.

Most interventions discussed in the literature are independent, deterministic interventions, setting C to some one specific state, regardless of the state of C's other parents. We can call this sort of intervention Pearlian, since it is the kind of intervention described by Pearl's "do-calculus" [10]. This simplest kind of intervention can be represented in a causal model simply by cutting all parent arcs into C and setting C to the desired value.

6 Modeling Effectiveness

There is another "dimension" along which interventions can be measured or ranked: their effectiveness. Many attempted interventions have only some probability, say r, of taking effect – for example, the already mentioned fact that doctors do not command universal obedience in their lifestyle recommendations. Now, even if such an intervention is of the type that when successful will put its target variable into a unique state, the attempt to intervene will not thereby cut-off the target variable from its parents; it is not Pearlian. The achieved distribution will, in fact, be a mixture of the target distribution and the original distribution, with the mixing factor being the probability r of the intervention succeeding.

Classifying or ranking interventions in terms of their effectiveness is often important. However, we have not put this scale on an equal footing with the other two dimensions of intervention, simply because it is conceptually derivative. That is, any degree of effectiveness r can be represented by mixing together the original with the target distribution with the factor r. In case the intended intervention is otherwise independent of the original parents, we can use the equation:

$$P_{M'}(C|\pi_c, I_c) = r \times P^*(C) + (1-r) \times P_M(C|\pi_c) \qquad (3)$$

This being a function of all the parents of C, it is a subspecies of dependent interventions.

In practical modeling terms, to represent such interventions we maintain two Bayesian networks: one with a fully effective intervention and one with no intervention. (Note that the first may still be representing a dependent intervention, e.g., one which interacts with the other parents.) There are then two distinct ways to use this mixture model: we can do ordinary Bayesian net propagation, combining the two at the end with the weighting factor to produce new posterior distributions or expected-value computations; or, if we are doing stochastic sampling, we can flip a coin with bias r to determine which of the two models to sample from.

7 Representing Interventions

Any Bayesian network tool can be used to implement interventions just by generating the augmented model manually, as in Section 4[6]. However, manual edits are awkward and time consuming, and they fail to highlight the intended causal semantics. Hence, we have developed a program, the *Causal Reckoner*, which runs as a front-end to the BN tool Netica [8] [7].

The *Causal Reckoner* makes Pearlian interventions as easy as observing a node and implements more sophisticated interventions via a pop-up, and easy to use, GUI. The mixture modeling representation of effectiveness (§6) is implemented via a slider bar, and the target distribution is set by gauges. The full scope of possible interventions is not yet implemented (e.g., causally interactive interventions), as this requires arbitrary replacement of a node's CPT.

Our program provides better visualization and intervention features than any other we have seen. Indeed, *Genie* [5] is the only program with similar capabilities that we know of; it has the feature of 'controlling' nodes to perform Pearlian interventions. Our visualization for basic interventions is shown in Figure 2(b) in Section 3. The node is shaded and a hand icon (for "manipulation") is displayed. We don't show the intervention node, simplifying and saving screen space.

When visualizing less than fully effective interventions, it is useful to report extra information. Figure 3(a) shows a 90% effective intervention intended to set low blood pressure at age 50. The target distribution is shown to the right of the node's actual distribution, which is a mixture of the original and target distributions. In the hypertension example, the intervention can be interpreted as a drug which fails in its effect 10% of the time. A drug with a weaker effect is shown in Figure 3(b).

---

[6] Alternatively, decision nodes can be used to model Pearlian interventions, since their use implies the arc-cutting of such interventions. However, that is an abuse of the semantics of decision nodes which we don't encourage.

[7] The software can be downloaded from: http://www.datamining.monash.edu.au/cgi-bin/cgiwrap/mdmc/run-cvstrac.cgi/causal/wiki.

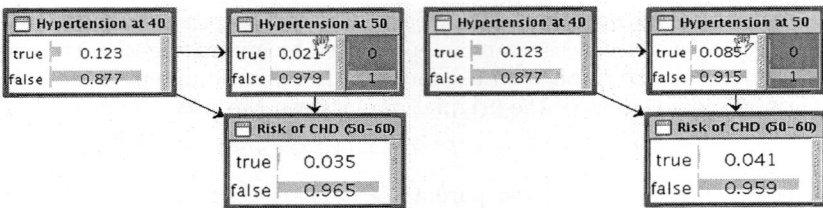

Fig. 3. The hypertension causal model: (a) with 90% effective interventions and (b) 60% effective interventions.

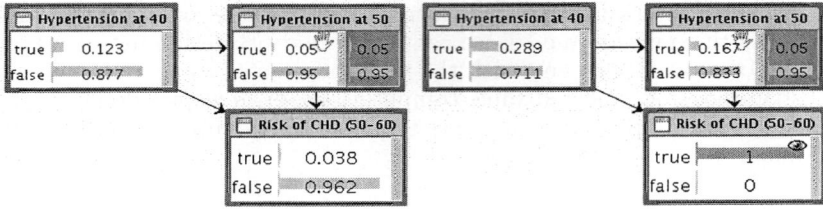

Fig. 4. (a) The hypertension causal model where a stochastic medical intervention has been made. In (b) an observation has also been entered.

Even a fully effective intervention can result in an actual distribution that deviates from the target distribution. This can happen when the intervention is stochastic, since other observational evidence also must be incorporated. Figure 4(a) shows the hypertension example given a fully effective stochastic intervention. Take a drug that sets the chance of low blood pressure to 95%, irrespective of other causal influences. This particular drug reduces the chances of CHD from 0.052 to 0.038. But what if the patient gets CHD anyway? Figure 4(b) shows that under this scenario, it is less likely that the drug *actually* helped with hypertension, since people with hypertension are more susceptible to CHD than others.

In short, the *Causal Reckoner* provides a GUI for mixing observations and interventions seamlessly. We can take existing networks in any domain and investigate various intervention policies quickly, without the trouble of creating new nodes and manually rewriting arbitrarily large CPTs.

8 Conclusion

Recent research exploring the causal interpretation of Bayesian networks has been very fruitful. However, the theory needs to find its way into practical application. For that purpose, tools such as the *Causal Reckoner* are needed to make it easy to model causal interventions and reason about their consequences and more difficult to make blunders, such as substituting an observational value for an intervention value.

In addition to these virtues of our work, we believe the nearly universal tendency to focus on deterministic models and deterministic interventions, while in part motivated by a healthy preference for the simple, either dismisses whole regions of potentially important applications or else invites new blunders in oversimplifying them. By taking seriously the indeterminism of the probabilistic relations in Bayesian networks, we have readily found a variety of intervention models that Pearlian interveners have yet to consider, including partially effective interventions, stochastic interventions and causally interactive interventions. Furthermore, it is clear that a great many real systems exhibit just these features.

Acknowledgements

We thank Charles Twardy for helpful discussions.

References

[1] Keaven M. Anderson, Patricia M. Odell, Peter W.F. Wilson, and William B. Kannel. Cardiovascular disease risk profiles. *American Heart Journal*, 121:293–298, 1991.

[2] Nancy Cartwright. What is wrong with Bayes nets? *The Monist*, 84:242–264, 2001.

[3] D. Chickering. A transformational characterization of equivalent Bayesian network structures. In D. Poole P. Besnard and S. Hanks, editors, *Proc of the 11th Conference on Uncertainty in AI*, pages 87–98, San Fransisco, CA, 1995. Morgan Kaufmann.

[4] R.B. D'Agostino, M.W. Russell, and D.M. Huse. Primary and subsequent coronary risk appraisal: new results from the framingham study. *American Heart Journal*, 139:272–81, 2000.

[5] Marek J. Druzdzel. SMILE: Structural modeling, inference, and learning engine and GeNIe: A development environment for graphical decision-theoretic models. In *Proceedings of the Sixteenth National Conference on Artificial Intelligence (AAAI-99)*, pages 902–903, Orlando, FL, July 18–22 1999.

[6] Joseph Y. Halpern and Judea Pearl. Causes and explanations: A structural-model approach – Part I: Causes. In J. Breese and D. Koller, editors, *Uncertainty in AI*, pages 194–202, 2001.

[7] Joseph Y. Halpern and Judea Pearl. Causes and explanations: A structural-model approach – Part II: Explanation. In *IJCAI '01*, 2001.

[8] Norsys. Netica. http://www.norsys.com, 2000.

[9] J. Pearl. Statistics, causality, and graphs. In A. Gammerman, editor, *Causal Models and Intelligent Data Management*, pages 3–16. Springer, Berlin, 1999.

[10] J. Pearl. *Causality: models, reasoning and inference*. Cambridge University Press, Cambridge, UK, 2000.

[11] Wesley Salmon. Probabilistic causality. *Pacific Phil Qtly*, 61:50–74, 1980.

[12] P. Spirtes, C. Glymour, and R. Scheines. *Causation, prediction and search*. Springer-Verlag, New York, 1993.

[13] Patrick Suppes. *A Probabilistic Theory of Causality*. Amsterdam, 1970.

[14] James Woodward. Causation and manipulability. In Edward N. Zalta, editor, *The Stanford Encyclopedia of Philosophy*. Fall 2001.

Species Merging and Splitting
for Efficient Search in Coevolutionary Algorithm

Myung Won Kim and Joung Woo Ryu

School of Computing, Soongsil University 1-1, Sangdo 5-Dong, Dongjag-Gu, Seoul, Korea
mkim@comp.ssu.ac.kr, ryu0914@orgio.net

Abstract. Coevolutionary algorithm takes advantage of the reduced search space by evolving species associated with subsets of variables independently but cooperatively. In this paper we propose an efficient coevolutionary algorithm combining species splitting and merging together. Our algorithm conducts efficient local search in the reduced search space by splitting species for independent variables while it conducts global search by merging species for interdependent variables. We have experimented the proposed algorithm with several benchmarking function optimization problems and the inventory control problem, and have shown that the algorithm outperforms existing coevolutionary algorithms.

1 Introduction

Evolutionary algorithm is a general and efficient optimization method and it is successfully applied to various problems including resource management, scheduling, and pattern recognition. However, one of the common problems of the algorithm is that search time grows exponentially as the dimension of search space expands.

Recently, attempts have been made to improve the search speed of the evolutionary algorithm. Potter and DeJong have proposed the cooperative coevolutionary algorithm which improves the search speed significantly [1]. In the algorithm a complete solution is divided into a set of subcomponents corresponding to a single variable called species each of which evolves independently but cooperatively. Each species evolves independently using its own evolution strategy and it corresponds to the search of the 1-dimensional space of a single variable and consequently it allows efficient search. In the algorithm, however, each species cooperates with other species in such a way that an individual of the species is evaluated by evaluating a complete chromosome that is assembled from itself and the best individuals of other species. In this way species evolves independently but cooperatively. And it shows especially good results when it is applied to the problems of concept learning and the task assignment problem between agents [2,3,4]. But the method can be even less efficient than ordinary algorithms in particular cases that there are lots of Nash equilibrium points and that variables are strongly interdependent. In order to overcome this problem, K. Weicker and N. Weicker proposed adaptive cooperative coevolution algorithm with which they solved the problem by combining species representing variables if there is variable interdependency [5]. But when most variables are interdependent with one another and after combining all species representing the variables, evolutionary speed sharply decreases as it does in ordinary algorithms due to the rapid expansion of search space.

In this paper we propose a new coevolutionary algorithm as an improvement of Weickers' algorithm. In our algorithm species are not only merged but also split into subcomponent species if necessary. Merging species allows more global but slow evolutionary search while splitting species allows local but fast evolutionary search. Efficiency can be achieved by combining species merging and splitting appropriately. In our algorithm species are split when they are independent while species are merged when they are interdependent. We use species interdependency as a decision criterion for dynamically controlling species merging and splitting.

The paper is organized as follows. In Section 2 we describe existing evolution algorithms and compare them with our algorithm. In Section 3 we describe our algorithm based on merging and splitting of species in detail. Section 4 describes the experimental results of our algorithm on the benchmarking function optimization problems, and the inventory control problem. Finally, we conclude our paper.

2 Existing Coevolutionary Algorithms

2.1 Cooperative Coevolution

Conventional genetic algorithm, proposed by John Holland is a general and global search method based on the natural selection and evolution mechanism. Genetic algorithm initializes and maintains a population of chromosomes that encode potential solutions to a given problem. Each chromosome is generally a fixed length sequence of bits put in order. The algorithm is briefly described in the following. First, the initial population of chromosomes are generated usually at random. Then each chromosome of the population is evaluated resulting in the fitness score. Genetic operators such as crossover and mutation are applied to generate a new population of chromosomes. Crossover generates two offspring chromosomes from their parent chromosomes by exchanging parts of the parent chromosomes. In crossover, parent chromosomes are selected in a way that more fit chromosomes are more likely selected. Mutation randomly changes small segments of a chromosome in order to introduce a diversity of chromosomes. This process of generating a new population and evaluation is repeated until the termination criteria are met. When the algorithm terminates, the best fit chromosome will be taken as a solution to the given problem.

Potter and DeJong proposed the cooperative coevolutionary genetic algorithm (CCGA) improving the conventional genetic algorithm, which suffers from slow evolution when search space is large. In CCGA each chromosome is divided into its subcomponents each of which corresponds to partial solutions associated with one or more variables involved in the objective function to be optimized. We call a collection of such a specified subcomponent a species. In the algorithm each species evolves independently but cooperatively in such a way that each chromosome of a species is evaluated by assembling it together with representative chromosomes of the other species. In this way each species evolves independently while it collaborates with the other species in evaluation. In CCGA each species is associated with a single variable and by allowing each species evolve independently the algorithm reduces the search space significantly.

If we let p be the number of species, the fitness of $c_i^{S_k}$ the i-th chromosome of species S_k, is determined as in Eq. 1.

$$F^{CCGA}(c_i^{S_k}) = F(\langle c_{elite}^{S_1}, c_{elite}^{S_2}, ..., c_i^{S_k}, ..., c_{elite}^{S_p} \rangle) \tag{1}$$

$c_{elite}^{S_k}$ in the equation represents the elite (the best fit) chromosome of species S_k, $\langle \rangle$ represents reconstruction of a complete chromosome by assembling chromosomes of its species, and F represents the fitness function of complete chromosomes. Each species evolves one generation at a time in a round robin fashion. The conventional evolutionary algorithm searches the whole search space, however, CCGA searches the 1-dimensional space for a single variable at a time, as shown in Fig. 1, consequently the search space is significantly reduced and it causes fast evolution.

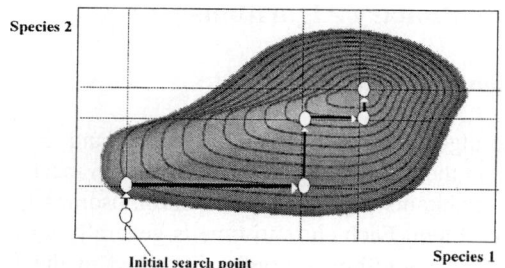

Fig. 1. Evolution Search in CCGA

Although its evolution speed is fast, CCGA can be less efficient than the ordinary algorithm for problems in which there are strong variable interdependency such that there are many Nash equilibrium points [6]. Potter and DeJong also proposed a variant (CCGA2) of the original CCGA (CCGA1) to alleviate the local optimum problem of the original CCGA, particularly when variables are strongly interdependent. The evolution method of CCGA2 is similar to that of CCGA1 but it differs from CCGA1 in the evaluation method. In order to evaluate a species chromosome two complete chromosomes are assembled by selecting the best fit species chromosomes and selecting them randomly. Each of them is evaluated and the maximum is chosen to be the fitness score of the species chromosome. This allows to escape Nash equilibrium points in CCGA2.

2.2 ACC(Adaptive Cooperative Coevolution)

The Adaptive Cooperative Coevolution Algorithm (ACC) was proposed by K. Weicker and N. Weicker to improve CCGA by allowing global search for those strongly interacting variables [5]. It is similar to CCGA except that species can be merged. During evolution in ACC, species interdependency is computed and maintained by a dependency matrix, and it is used to control species merging. Two species are merged if their interdependency exceeds a given threshold. In the following we describe how species interdependency is computed. Let Γ be the set of all variables to be considered to optimize the given objective function and the number of species at generation t be $s(t)$. And let $S_{V_k}(t)$ represent the species associated with a set of variables V_k ($\bigcup_{k=1}^{s(t)} V_k = \Gamma, V_k \cap V_j = \phi (k \neq j)$) at generation t. Then, the fitness of the i-th chromosome $c_i^{S_{V_k}(t)}$ of species $S_{V_k}(t)$ is determined as

$$F^{ACC}\left(c_i^{S_{V_k}(t)}\right) = max \begin{pmatrix} F\left(\langle c_{elite}^{S_{V_1}(t)}, c_{elite}^{S_{V_2}(t)}, ..., c_i^{S_{V_k}(t)}, ..., c_{elite}^{S_{V_{s(t)}}(t)} \rangle\right) \\ F\left(\langle c_{elite}^{S_{V_1}(t)}, ..., c_{rand}^{S_{V_j}(t)}, ..., c_i^{S_{V_k}(t)}, ..., c_{elite}^{S_{V_{s(t)}}(t)} \rangle\right) \end{pmatrix} \quad (2)$$

where $c_{elite}^{S_{V_k}(t)}$ represents the elite chromosome of species $S_{V_k}(t)$ and $c_{rand}^{S_{V_j}(t)}$ represents a randomly chosen chromosome of $S_{V_j}(t)$. The first term of the right hand side of Eq. 2 evaluates the chromosome $c_i^{S_{V_k}(t)}$ collaborating with the elite chromosomes of the other species as CCGA1 does while the second term evaluates the chromosome collaborating with the elite chromosomes of the other species except the j-th species for which a randomly chosen chromosome is used. In this evaluation, when the second term of *max* of Eq. 2 is greater than the first term (so, chosen to be the fitness score), we increase the value of dependency between species $S_{V_j}(t)$ and $S_{V_k}(t)$ in the dependency matrix. During evolution we merge two species when the value of dependency between them exceeds a given threshold. If there is no interdependency among species, the first term of *max* will always be chosen as the fitness score and the evolution will progress as in CCGA1. Variables corresponding to the merged species will evolve at the same time and it allows more global search to possibly escape a local optimum. The process of merging species in ACC is done as follows. Suppose we merge two species $S_{V_j}(t)$ and $S_{V_k}(t)$ associated with variable sets V_j and V_k, respectively. The merged species $S_V(t)$ is determined as follows.

$$merge(S_{V_j}(t), S_{V_k}(t)) = S_V(t) \quad (3)$$

where $V = V_j \cup V_k$. $c_i^{S_V(t)}$, the i-th chromosome of the merged species $S_V(t)$, is given as

$$c_i^{S_V(t)} = \begin{cases} c_{elite}^{S_{V_j}(t)} \circ c_{elite}^{S_{V_k}(t)} : if\ i=1, \\ c_{elite}^{S_{V_j}(t)} \circ c_{rand}^{S_{V_k}(t)} : if\ 2 \le i \le \left\lceil \frac{n}{2} \right\rceil, \\ c_{rand}^{S_{V_j}(t)} \circ c_{elite}^{S_{V_k}(t)} : otherwise \end{cases} \quad (4)$$

where ∘ represents a concatenation of two species chromosomes.

3 SMCA: Splitting and Merging Coevolutionary Algorithm

When it is applied to problems in which variables are strongly interdependent, ACC is no longer efficient because species are merged into a large species as evolution progresses and the evolution speed gets slow down since the search space expands rapidly. To solve this problem of ACC, we propose a new coevolution algorithm called SMCA in which species are not only merged but also split if necessary.

In SMCA, species are merged in a similar way in ACC. SMCA starts with the set of base species each of which is associated with a single variable. During evolution process, interdependencies between species are maintained by a dependency matrix. Two species are merged when their associated interdependency value exceeds a given threshold. A merged species is split into a set of base species if it fails to improve its elite chromosome within a certain period of time. Split species can be merged again based on interdependency between species. Merged species allow more global search, however, they slow down the search speed while split species speed up the search but it may suffer from local search. SMCA combines local but fast search and global but slow search by combining merging and splitting of species appropriately.

3.1 Species Merging

In SMCA its merging method is similar to that of ACC. Let $S_V(t)$ represent a merged species of species $S_{V_j}(t)$ and $S_{V_k}(t)$ where $V = V_j \cup V_k$, $c_i^{S_V(t)}$ the i-th chromosome of $S_V(t)$ is determined as follows.

$$c_i^{S_V(t)} = \begin{cases} c_{elite}^{S_{V_j}}(t) \circ c_{elite}^{S_{V_k}}(t) : if\ i=1, \\ c_{elite}^{S_{V_j}}(t) \circ c_{rand}^{S_{V_k}}(t) : if\ 2 \le i \le \left\lceil \frac{n}{3} \right\rceil, \\ c_{rand}^{S_{V_j}}(t) \circ c_{elite}^{S_{V_k}}(t) : if\ \left\lceil \frac{n}{3} \right\rceil < i \le \left\lceil \frac{2n}{3} \right\rceil, \\ c_{rand}^{S_{V_j}}(t) \circ c_{rand}^{S_{V_k}}(t) : otherwise \end{cases} \quad (5)$$

As the result, the merged species $S_V(t)$ consists of four different kinds of chromosomes created by merging species chromosomes in four different ways; (1) the elite chromosomes of both species, (2) the elite chromosome of species $S_{V_j}(t)$ and randomly chosen chromosomes of species $S_{V_k}(t)$, (3) randomly chosen chromosomes of species $S_{V_j}(t)$ and the elite chromosome of species $S_{V_k}(t)$, and (4) randomly chosen chromosomes of both species. Here, we set the size of population of each kind of chromosomes except (1) to be one third of the population of the merged species. As in ACC, a species is merged when the value of species interdependency in the dependency matrix exceeds a given threshold.

3.2 Species Splitting

Species splitting is to speed up evolution by reducing the search space. If a merged species does not improve the fitness of its elite chromosome within a certain period of time, we consider that the search point places where search is slow and we try to split species for speeding up evolution by chance.

For $V \subseteq V_k$, let $\text{proj}(c_i^{S_{V_k}(t)}, V)$ represent a function of extracting genes that encode variables in set V from the i-th chromosome $c_i^{S_{V_k}(t)}$ of species $S_{V_k}(t)$. In this case, if $P = \{U_1, U_2, ..., U_m\} \left(\bigcup_{i=1}^{m} U_i = V_k, U_i \cap U_j = \phi \; (i \neq j) \right)$ is a partition of variable set V_k, $S_{U_i}(t)$, the i-th species split from species $S_{V_k}(t)$, and $c_j^{U_i(t)}$, the j-th chromosome of species $S_{U_i}(t)$, are determined as follows.

$$\text{split}(S_{V_k}(t), P) = \{S_{U_1}(t), S_{U_2}(t), ..., S_{U_m}(t)\}$$
$$S_{U_i}(t) = (c_1^{S_{U_i}(t)}, c_2^{S_{U_i}(t)}, ..., c_n^{S_{U_i}(t)}) \quad (6)$$

$$c_j^{S_{U_i}(t)} = \text{proj}(c_j^{S_{V_k}(t)}, U_i) : 1 \leq i \leq n, 1 \leq j \leq m \quad (7)$$

In other words, the original species is split into a set of different species each of which corresponds to a set of variables. Apparently many different ways of splitting are possible depending on how the set of variables associated with the species to split is partitioned. In this paper, to make our algorithm simple, we split a species into a set of single variable species.

4 Experiments

4.1 Function Optimization

We experimented with our algorithm on some of the benchmark function optimization problems including the Ackley function, the Rosenbrock function, and the Schwefel function. For comparison purposes, we used each function in its original form and in its coordinate rotated form to introduce variable interdependency [7]. Parameters and methods used in our function optimization experiments are shown in Table 1.

Table 1. Experiment Parameter Values

parameters	value
population size	100
bits/variable	16
crossover rate	0.6
mutation rate	1/(chromosome length)
selection method	fitness proportionate
crossover method	2 point crossover

We compare the average performance over 10 runs of our algorithm and others as shown in Figs. 2, 3, and 4.

The original form of the Ackley function is defined as

$$F(\vec{x}) = -20\exp(-0.2\sqrt{\frac{1}{n}\sum_{i=1}^{n}x_i^2}) - \exp(\frac{1}{n}\sum_{i=1}^{n}\cos(2\pi x_i)) + 20 + e, -20 \leq x_i \leq 20 \quad (8)$$

The global optimum of the function is $F(\vec{x}) = 0$ at $\vec{x} = (0, 0, \ldots, 0)$. The Ackley function does not have variable interdependency in its original form but its rotated form has variable interdependency. In our experiment n (dimension) is fixed to 30.

The Rosenbrock function is given as in Eq. 9 and it has a weak variable interdependency in its original form.

$$F(\vec{x}) = \sum_{i=1}^{n/2}[100(x_{2i} - x_{2i-1}^2)^2 + (1 - x_{2i-1}^2)^2], -2.048 \leq x_i \leq 2.048 \quad (9)$$

The Rosenbrock function has its global minimum at the point $\vec{x} = (1, 1, \ldots, 1)$. An interesting characteristic of this function is that variable interdependency exists only between variables x_{2i} and x_{2i-1} when $0 < i \leq n/2$.

The Schwefel function has a term that contains the sine function and oscillation is getting larger as it moves outward from the center $\vec{x} = (0, 0, \ldots, 0)$. The original form of the function is defined as

$$F(\vec{x}) = \sum_{i=1}^{n}[-x_i \cdot \sin(\sqrt{|x_i|})], -500 \leq x_i \leq 500 \quad (10)$$

The global optimum of this function is $F(\vec{x}) = -n \cdot 418.9829$ at the point $\vec{x} = (420.9687, 420.9687, \ldots, 420.9687)$.

In summary, CCGAs are efficient when no variable interdependency exist, however, otherwise they are not efficient. ACC is efficient even when variable interdependency exists, however, it quickly saturates when strong variable interdependency exists. The experiment results clearly show that SMCA is consistently efficient no matter how much variable interdependency exists.

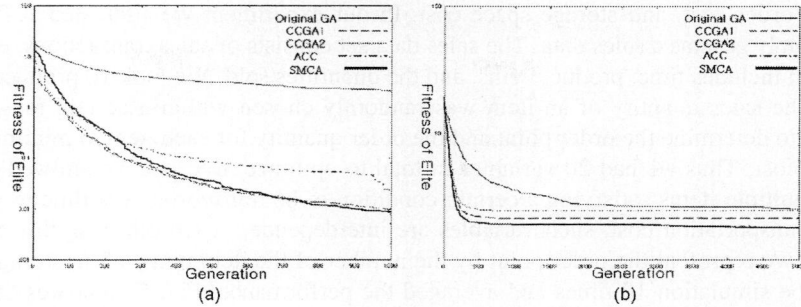

Fig. 2. (a): Ackley and (b): Rotated Ackley

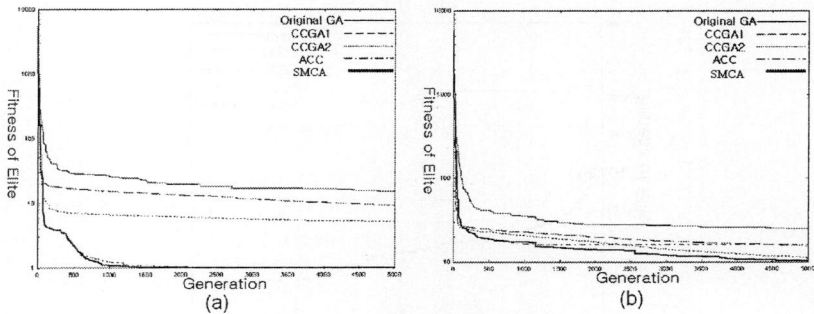

Fig. 3. Rosenbrock and (b): Rotated Rosenbrock

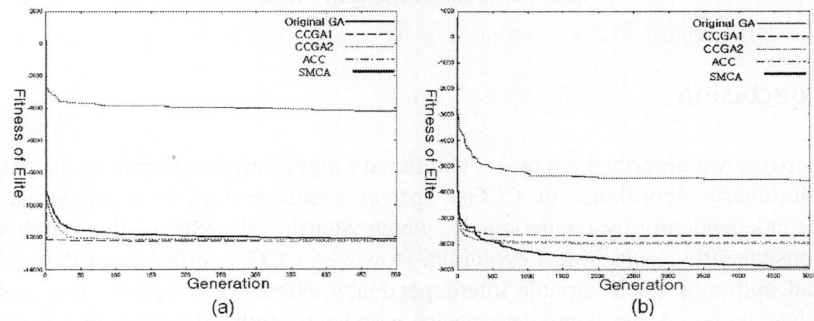

Fig. 4. (a): Schwefel and (b): Rotated Schwefel

4.2 ICP (Inventory Control Problem)

ICP is one of common practical optimization problems [8]. Traditionally, ICP is reduced to the problem of deciding when (order point) to place replenishment order and how many units of individual items (order quantity) to order to minimize the total cost, which is composed of various types of costs such as lost sales cost, transportation cost, order cost, and storage space cost. In our experiment we simulated ICP using randomly generated sales data. The sales data set consists of sales transactions, each of which includes time, product items, and the quantities sold. We took 10 product items and the sales quantity of an item was randomly chosen within a certain range. We need to determine the order point and the order quantity for each item to minimize the total cost. Thus we had 20 variables in total to optimize. Because we allowed orders for multiple items satisfying a certain condition to be transported at a time to reduce the transportation cost, such variables are interdependent each other. In this experiment we represent the order point by the number of the item units left in storage. We ran the simulation 10 times and averaged the performance. Fig. 5 compares the performances of different algorithms and it is clear that SMCA outperforms other existing algorithms.

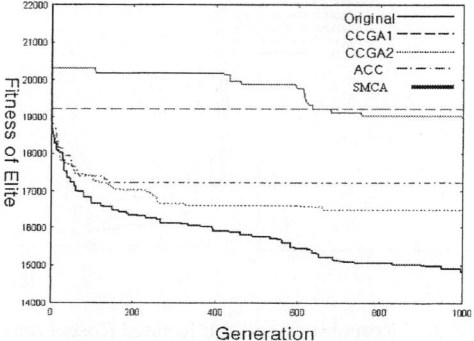

Fig. 5. Performance Comparison for ICP

5 Conclusion

In this paper we described a new coevolutionary algorithm that improves the existing coevolutionary algorithms. In CCGA species corresponding to a single variable evolve independently by cooperatively, which significantly reduces the search space and consequently results in fast evolution. However, CCGA suffers from the problem of local optimum when variable interdependency exists. To overcome this problem ACC was proposed and it merges species associated with interdependent variables. Merging species allows more global search than splitting species. However, ACC also suffers from slow evolution when variables are strongly interdependent. In this case species are quickly merged into a larger species, causing the expanded search space. SMCA, however, combines species merging and splitting appropriately in order to take advantage both of fast evolution of CCGA and of global search of ACC. Our experiment results have shown that SMCA outperforms existing evolutionary algorithms.

Acknowledgement

This research was supported by the Soongsil University Research Fund.

References

[1] M. A. Potter and K. A. DeJong, "A cooperative coevolutionary approach to function optimization," Proc. of the Third Conference on Parallel Problem Solving from Nature, Springer-Verlag, pp.249-257, 1994.
[2] M.A. Potter and K.A DeJong, "Cooperative Coevolution: An Architecture for Evolving Coadapted Subcomponents," Evolutionary Computation 8(1), MIT press, pp.1-29, 2000.
[3] M. Mundhe and S. Sen, "Evolving agent societies that avoid social dilemmas," Proc. Of GECCO-2000, Las Vegas, Nevada, pp.809-816, July 2000.
[4] L. Pagie and M. Mitchell, " A Comparison of Evolutionry and Coevolutionary Search," Journal of Computational Intelligence and Applications, Vol. 2, No. 1, pp. 53-69, 2002.
[5] K. Weicker and N. Weicker, "On the improvement of coevolutionary optimizers by learning variable interdependencies," Congress on Evolutionary Computation (CEC99), pp.1627-1632, 1999.
[6] J. Nash, *Non-cooperative games*, Annals of Mathematics 5(2), pp. 286-295, 1951.
[7] R. Salomon, "Reevaluating genetic algorithm performance under coordinate rotation of benchmark functions," BioSystems 39, pp.210-229, 1996
[8] R. Eriksson and B. Olsson, "Cooperative Coevolution in Inventory Control Optimisation," Proc. of 3rd International Conference on Artificial Neural Networks and Genetic Algorithms (ICANNGA97), Norwich, UK, April 1997.

Exploiting Unexpressed Genes for Solving Large-Scaled Maximal Covering Problems

Taejin Park and Kwang Ryel Ryu

Department of Computer Engineering, Pusan National University
Jangjeon-Dong San 30, Kumjeong-Ku, Busan 609-735, Korea
{parktj,krryu}@pusan.ac.kr

Abstract. We introduce a genetic algorithm incorporating unexpressed genes to solve large-scaled maximal covering problems (MCPs) efficiently. Our genetic algorithm employs new crossover and mutation operators specially designed to work for the chromosomes of set-oriented representation. The unexpressed genes are the genes which are not reflected in the evaluation of the individuals. These genes play the role of preserving information susceptible to be lost by the application of genetic operators but potentially useful in later generations. By incorporating unexpressed genes, the algorithm enjoys the advantage of being able to maintain diversity of the population preventing premature convergence. Experiments with large-scaled real MCP data have shown that our genetic algorithm outperforms simulated annealing and tabu search which are popularly used local neighborhood search algorithms for optimization.

1 Introduction

A *maximal covering problem* (MCP) is the problem of selecting q columns from a given binary $m \times n$ matrix to maximize the number of rows each of which is covered by at least one 1 in the corresponding row of any selected q columns. In the example of Figure 1 where $m = 5$, $n = 6$, and $q = 3$, the set of columns $\{c_1, c_2, c_5\}$ is a solution which covers the most number of rows. The rows covered in this example are r_1, r_3, r_4, and r_5, where r_1 is covered by c_1 and c_5, r_3 by c_1, r_4 by c_2, and r_5 by c_5. MCP is the frequently used model for the optimization problems of providing maximum service with limited resources, examples of which include the facility location problem and the crew scheduling problem for airlines, railways, or subways.

	c_1	c_2	c_3	c_4	c_5	c_6
r_1	**1**		1		**1**	
r_2			1			1
r_3	**1**			1		
r_4		**1**				
r_5					**1**	

Fig. 1. An example maximal covering problem.

C. Zhang, H.W. Guesgen, W.K. Yeap (Eds.): PRICAI 2004, LNAI 3157, pp. 342–351, 2004.

This paper presents a novel approach to solving large-scaled MCPs by applying a genetic algorithm. There have been many successful applications employing hybrid of genetic algorithm and local search to exploit the global perspective of genetic algorithm and the fast convergence of local search [6, 7]. Our genetic algorithm also employs greedy heuristic in the crossover and mutation operators to improve the efficiency of search. More importantly, we propose a new chromosome structure incorporating *unexpressed genes* as a means of maintaining diversity of the population. The unexpressed genes refer to the genes that are not expressed in the phenotype and thus are not reflected in the evaluation of an individual. The role of the unexpressed genes is to preserve some of the potentially useful information which is doomed to be lost by the application of genetic operators. The incorporation of the unexpressed genes contributes a lot to the diversification of search by preventing premature convergence of the population. Experiments with large-scaled MCPs have shown that the proposed genetic algorithm incorporating the unexpressed genes outperforms the neighborhood search algorithms in terms of both solution time and quality.

The next section describes the chromosome structure and crossover operator devised for solving MCPs. Section 3 introduces the unexpressed genes that we propose in this paper. Section 4 explains our mutation operator specially designed for solving MCPs. Section 5 reports experimental results comparing the performance of our genetic algorithm with those of other neighborhood search methods. Finally, section 6 gives some conclusion and the direction of future works.

2 Chromosome Representation and Greedy Crossover

A solution of an MCP with an $m \times n$ matrix is a set of q columns selected from the n columns of the matrix, where q is a predetermined number given by the problem. A solution is evaluated by an objective function which basically counts the number of rows covered by the selected q columns. Depending on the application domain of the problem, the objective function sometimes also considers the quality of the columns constituting the solution and other problem-specific constraints. Figure 2 shows a chromosome representation one may easily think of when he or she wants to solve an MCP. It is just a string or set of indexes of q selected columns where the order of the columns is meaningless.

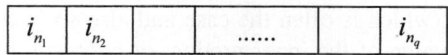

Fig. 2. Set-oriented chromosome representation for MCP.

Under this representation, we cannot use single or multiple-point crossover because it might produce illegal strings having repeated column indexes. What we need is an operator which chooses a subset of the columns of selected parents. Given two parent chromosomes P_1 and P_2, our crossover operator thus produces one child P_c by selecting q columns from $P_1 \cup P_2$. A random selection of columns, however, is not likely to produce a good child covering more rows than any of its parents. Therefore, our crossover operator selects columns by using a *greedy-adding heuristic* with the hope that the resulting subset covers maximum number of rows. Figure 3 shows the algorithm of our greedy crossover operation.

```
Algorithm GreedyCrossover
   input: parent chromosomes P₁, P₂ (|P₁|=|P₂|=q)
   output: child chromosome P_c
P = P₁∪P₂;
P_c = ∅ ;
while |P_c| ≠ q
   find j with maximum  δ(j) where j∈P;
   (tie-breaking is done by comparing S_p(j))
   P_c := P_c∪{j};
   P  := P - {j};
return P_c;
```

Fig. 3. Algorithm of greedy crossover.

$\delta(j)$ in the above algorithm heuristically measures the goodness of a column j in the following way:

$$\delta(j) = Eval(P_c \cup \{j\}) - Eval(P_c) \qquad (1)$$

where $Eval(P)$ is the number of rows covered by the set of columns in P. The best column according to this heuristic is the one that, when added to the current subset, contributes the most to the increase in the number of rows covered. Although not shown formally in the above algorithm, there is an important tie-breaking strategy which plays a significant role in enhancing the performance of our genetic algorithm: When there are more than one columns with maximum $\delta(j)$, we select the column whose similarity to all the columns in P (= $P_1 \cup P_2$) is the lowest. The similarity $S_P(j)$ of column j to all the columns in P (including j itself) is measured by calculating the inner product of the column vectors as follows:

$$S_P(j) = \sum_{v \in P} j \cdot v = j \cdot \sum_{v \in P} v \qquad (2)$$

Note that the columns of any MCP are binary vectors. If the columns have almost the same number of 1s (which is often the case and also so in the MCPs used in our experiments), then the value of the inner product of two such binary vectors j and v becomes bigger as the Hamming distance of the two gets smaller. $S_P(j)$ is calculated ahead of time for each of the columns before entering the **while** loop of the algorithm of Figure 3.

Given a set of columns P, a column with low $S_P(j)$ is the one that covers many rows which are different from those covered by the other columns in P. The reason for preferring the column with the lowest $S_P(j)$ for tie-breaking is that by selecting such a column it is expected that the columns to be selected in succession in the next iteration will be likely to cover more rows which are not covered by the columns selected so far. Suppose on the contrary that we select the column with the highest $S_P(j)$ among the columns with the same maximum $\delta(j)$. Then the column to be added in the next iteration would be so similar to the one just selected that it is not likely to cover more new rows.

3 Incorporation of Unexpressed Genes

While the greedy crossover described in the previous section is very good at producing individuals having good column combination of high coverage, the population as a whole rapidly loses those columns which are not selected by the crossover over the generations. This loss of diversity leads to premature convergence. The purpose of incorporating unexpressed genes is to preserve the columns which are not selected by the crossover but suspected to be potentially useful in later generations. Figure 4 shows the chromosome structure having unexpressed genes, where the chromosome C consists of the expressed part $E(C)$ with q columns and the unexpressed part $U(C)$ with r columns. Although only $E(C)$ is looked at when C is evaluated, both parts are involved when crossover is applied. Given the parents P_1 and P_2, the expressed part $E(P_c)$ of the child P_c is produced by the same greedy crossover operator described in Figure 3 except that this time q columns are selected from the pool of almost $2(q+r)$ different columns[1] of both the expressed and unexpressed parts of the two parents.

expressed part: $E(C)$				unexpressed part: $U(C)$			
i_{e_1}	i_{e_2}	......	i_{e_q}	i_{u_1}	i_{u_2}	......	i_{u_r}

Fig. 4. Chromosome with unexpressed genes.

After the columns for $E(P_c)$ is selected, the unexpressed part $U(P_c)$ is produced again from both the expressed and unexpressed parts of P_1 and P_2 by selecting the columns which are the most dissimilar to those already selected for $E(P_c)$, as described in the algorithm of Figure 5. The similarity $S_{E(Pc)}(j)$ of column j to the columns in $E(P_c)$ is calculated similarly as in equation (2):

$$S_{E(P_c)}(j) = \sum_{v \in E(P_c)} j \cdot v = j \cdot \sum_{v \in E(P_c)} v \qquad (3)$$

By forcing the unexpressed part to become as different from the expressed part as possible, the resultant chromosome, when it becomes a parent, is expected to serve as a pool of more diverse columns from which better new children may be produced for the next generation. The unexpressed genes formed this way contribute a lot to prevention of premature convergence by maintaining the diversity of the population.

---

[1] The number of different columns can be smaller than $2(q+r)$ if the same column appears in both parents.

```
Algorithm GreedyCrossover-UnexpressedGenes
    input: parent chromosomes P₁, P₂ (|P₁|=|P₂|=q)
    output: unexpressed part U(P_c) of child P_c
P = P₁ ∪ P₂;
U(P_c) = ∅ ;
while |U(P_c)| ≠ q
    find j which has minimum S_{E(Pc)}(j) where j ∈ P;
    U(P_c) = U(P_c) ∪ {j};
    P = P - {j};
return U(P_c);
```

Fig. 5. Crossover algorithm for generating the unexpressed part.

4 K-Exchange Mutation

For the chromosome representation of Figure 2 or 4 devised for MCP, we propose a mutation operation which is similar to the k-exchange neighbor generation method used by previous research for solving MCPs by applying local search algorithms [5]. As shown in the algorithm of Figure 6, our k-exchange mutation first performs a mutation test by applying a predetermined mutation probability not at the level of individual genes (columns) but at the level of chromosome. Once the chromosome is determined to be mutated, k columns are removed and then k new columns are inserted. This k-exchange mutation is applied only to the expressed part.

```
Algorithm K-ExchangeMutation
    input: chromosome C, inteter k
    output: mutated chromosome C
if MutationTest(C) = pass then
    RemoveColumns(C, k);
    InsertColumns(C, k);
return C;
```

Fig. 6. Algorithm of k-exchange mutation.

The procedure for removing k columns is described in Figure 7. To remove a column, a column j is first randomly selected and then removed according to the probability inversely proportional to the following $\gamma(j)$ value

$$\gamma(j) = Eval(C) - Eval(C - \{j\}) \qquad (4)$$

where $Eval(C)$ is the number of rows covered by the columns of C as in equation (1). The value $\gamma(j)$ is the decrease in the number of rows covered by removing the column j. Since bigger $\gamma(j)$ value indicates that column j is having a more important role in covering the rows, its removal probability $P_r(j)$ should be lower.

```
Algorithm RemoveColumns
  input: chromosome C, integer k
  output: chromosome C with k columns removed
  while |C| > q - k
    randomly select a column j;
    calculate γ(j);
    derive removal probability $P_r(j)$ from γ(j);
    remove j from C with probability $P_r(j)$;
  return C;
```

Fig. 7. Algorithm for removing k columns.

After k columns are removed, k new columns to be inserted are selected one by one from the pool of n columns of the $m \times n$ matrix of the given MCP by using the greedy-adding heuristic as used by the greedy crossover operator described in section 2, except that tie-breaking is done randomly without calculating the column similarity. The process of selecting k columns from the set of n columns, although greedy, can be computationally expensive especially when n is very large. However, it is not such a big burden at all for running the genetic algorithm because the mutation rate is so low. The role of the k-exchange mutation is to supply new columns into the population without sacrificing much of the quality of the individual chromosomes mutated.

As mentioned above, the k-exchange mutation is not applied to the unexpressed part. Instead, mutation for the unexpressed part is simply done by replacing each column by another which is randomly selected from the set of n columns, just to promote the diversity. Empirical study has shown that the mutation rate for the unexpressed part should be much higher than that of the k-exchange mutation for the expressed part.

5 Experimental Results and Discussions

We used a real subway crew scheduling data for the experiments, where $m = 814$, $n = 179,514$, $q = 83$, and each column covers exactly 10 rows. Since 18 columns are already fixed to satisfy the constraints related to some labor regulations, what is left is the selection of 65 additional columns out of 179,514 columns to cover the remaining 634 rows still not covered. All the experiments were done on a Pentium IV 2G Hz server with 1G RAM.

We implemented two versions of genetic algorithm: one with the unexpressed genes (GAUG) and the other without (GA). For GAUG, the population size was 1,500 and 3-exchange mutation with mutation rate of 0.01 was used. The mutation rate for the unexpressed part was 0.1 and the length of the unexpressed part was set to 80. For GA, the only difference was its population size of 3,346 considering the fact that the length of the individual chromosome is only 65 compared to 145 of GAUG (3,346 ≈ 1,500×145/65). The evaluation of each individual is made by counting the number of rows covered by the columns of only the expressed part, and fitness scaling was not used. The initial population was generated not randomly but by using the greedy-adding heuristic. However, the columns for the unexpressed part were still selected randomly. For the selection stochastic universal sampling method was used.

We also implemented two popular neighborhood search algorithms, i.e., tabu search (TS) and simulated annealing (SA), for performance comparison. To be fair, the initial solution for both algorithms was generated by using the greedy-adding heuristic, and neighborhood solutions were generated by using the k-exchange method which is similar to the k-exchange mutation. However, it turned out to be better to have the value of k range from 1 to 5 instead of the fixed value of 3.

Each of the above algorithms was run for 10 times given 60 minutes of CPU time and the number of rows still left uncovered[2] was counted. Table 1 shows the best, the worst, and the average results of these experiments. We can see that GAUG is a clear winner. In additional experiments with artificially generated MCP data of various sizes which were still large-scaled, we obtained similar results as can be seen in Table 2. In this table, q is the number of columns to be selected.

Table 1. Experimental results with the subway crew scheduling MCP data.

Algorithm	Best	Average	Worst
GAUG	5	6.5	8
GA	15	15.9	17
SA	7	8.0	10
TS	9	10.0	12

Table 2. Experimental results with artificially generated MCP data of various sizes.

MCP data			GAUG			SA		
# Rows	# Columns	q	Best	Avg.	Worst	Best	Avg.	Worst
312	55,807	39	1	2.4	3	2	3.0	4
384	54,738	42	6	6.9	8	7	7.6	8
453	72,094	45	6	6.7	7	6	7.3	9
520	92,139	53	4	4.8	6	4	4.9	6
634	142,265	65	5	5.5	6	5	6.0	9

Figure 8 compares the curves obtained by averaging at every minute the ten runs of the four algorithms for the given 60 minutes of CPU time. Although the quality of solution improves rather slowly during early iterations, GAUG eventually outperforms all the other methods. As can be seen by the curve of GA, however, genetic

---

[2] For our crew scheduling problem, a heuristic iterative repair algorithm is run as a postprocessing to take care of the rows uncovered. The failure to cover all the rows is usually due to the columns that cover the rows already covered by others. Therefore, given a maximal covering solution, the iterative repair algorithm first identifies those rows covered by multiple columns and then heuristically modifies such columns and other related columns until all the rows are covered. As there are more rows left uncovered in the given maximal covering solution, we observe a significant (more than linear) increase in time needed for the repair.

algorithm without the unexpressed genes performs the worst due to severely premature convergence. The reason for little improvement by both genetic algorithms at the beginning is that they were given relatively good initial populations by using the greedy-adding heuristic.

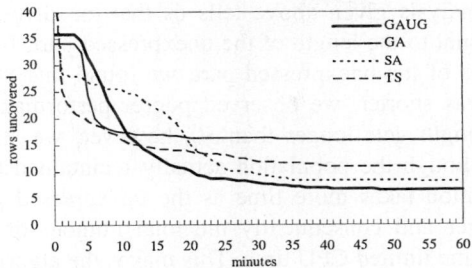

Fig. 8. Average search behaviors for the crew scheduling MCP data.

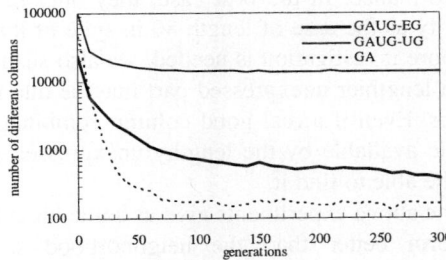

Fig. 9. Change in the number of different columns in the population over generations.

To see how much the unexpressed genes contribute to promoting the diversity of the population and thus preventing premature convergence, the number of different columns residing in the population was counted over generations. Figure 9 shows the changes in the number of different columns over generations. The genetic algorithm that does not have the unexpressed part (GA) started with more than 46,000 different columns in its initial population. This number decreased very rapidly to about only 160 in 300 generations. For the genetic algorithm having the unexpressed genes, the numbers of different columns were counted separately for the expressed part (GAUG-EG) and the unexpressed part (GAUG-UG). The initial number of different columns in the expressed part was about 24,000 which is a little more than half of the number of GA because the population size of GAUG was set to about half of that of GA. GAUG-EG also decreases rapidly but not so much as GA. The reason is that the crossover, although greedy, selects columns from a more diverse and bigger pool of columns consisting of both the expressed and unexpressed parts of the parents. The major source of diversity, as expected, is the unexpressed part. GAUG-UG started from about 100,000 and did not go down below 13,000. Remember that the columns for the unexpressed part are selected by giving high priority to the columns that are different from those selected for the expressed part, to keep the population as diverse as possible. Note also that the mutation rate for the unexpressed part is 0.1 which is ten times higher than that for the expressed part. After 300 generations, while the population of GA contains only about 160 different columns, the population of GAUG still maintains about 13,400 different columns in total.

The empirical analysis given above tells us that the diversity of the population should be proportional to the length of the unexpressed part. In separate experiments with various lengths of the unexpressed part, we found that 80 was the best length. When the length was shorter, we observed poorer performance due to the lack of diversity. As the length gets longer than 80, however, we still observed no better performance even though the population actually maintained better diversity. Since the crossover operation takes more time as the unexpressed part gets longer, each iteration takes longer and consequently the total number of generations becomes smaller given the same limited CPU time. This makes the algorithm hard to find good solutions. In additional experiments with extended CPU time of up to two hours, various versions of the algorithm with lengthy unexpressed parts were still unable to show any better performance. In the best case, they only reached almost the same level of solution quality as the case of length 80 in spite of the much longer processing time. Although more investigation is needed, we also suspect that the disappointing performance with lengthier unexpressed part may be due to the greedy nature of our crossover operator. Even if a real good column combination exists in the larger pool of columns made available by the lengthy unexpressed part, the greedy crossover simply may not be able to find it.

The results of all the above experiments give us some hints to the question of what makes GAUG perform better than the neighborhood search algorithms. The neighborhood generation scheme of the neighborhood search algorithms and the greedy crossover of our genetic algorithm both use the similar greedy-adding heuristic. However, the neighborhood generation scheme has to scan through the pool of almost 180,000 columns to find k columns for replacement every time it generates a neighbor from a current solution. This means that the algorithm cannot search for enough number of iterations given a limited CPU time because the neighbor generation process in each iteration takes nontrivial time. In an effort to increase the total number of iterations, we modified the neighbor generation scheme in such a way that it selects columns from a random sub-pool of the 180,000 column pool with the sub-pool sampled anew every iteration. As a matter of fact we have also tried various sizes of sub-pools, but the results were all disappointing. Although the total number of iterations increased, the final quality of solution found was not very satisfactory perhaps because of failure to generate real good neighbors from the reduced column sub-pools.

In contrast, the crossover operator of GAUG generates child chromosomes by selecting q (= 65) columns from a small pool of only $2(q+r)$ (= 290) columns of parent chromosomes, which is computationally much less demanding. While the neighborhood search algorithms solve a single large-sized problem in each iteration, our genetic algorithm solves a lot of tiny problems in parallel[3] at each generation to find a good subset of columns. One of the keys to the success of genetic algorithm, therefore, is that the chromosomes that are the small column pools constituting the tiny problems must be diverse and good in their quality. Our genetic algorithm not only improves quality of the chromosomes through evolution by application of genetic operations but also maintains diversity by incorporating the unexpressed genes.

6 Conclusion and Future Works

In this paper we presented a genetic algorithm which can solve large-scaled MCPs efficiently. The proposed algorithm uses new crossover and mutation operators specially designed for solving MCPs. Perhaps the most important contribution of this paper is the incorporation of the unexpressed genes as a means of maintaining diversity to prevent premature convergence. Experiments with large-scaled MCP data have shown that our proposed algorithm outperforms neighborhood search algorithms such as the tabu search and simulated annealing. In future work, we would like to see if the proposed chromosome structure with unexpressed genes could be used to solve other optimization problems requiring set-oriented representation.

References

1. B.T. Downs, J.D. Camm, An Exact Algorithm for the Maximal Covering Problem, Naval Research Logistics, 43, 435-461, 1996.
2. R.D. Galvao, C. ReVelle, A Lagrangean Heuristic for the Maximal Covering Location Problem, European Journal of Operational Research, 88, 114-123, 1996.
3. J.E. Beasley and P.C. Chu, A Genetic Algorithm for the Set Covering Problem, European Journal of Operational Research, 94, 392-404, 1996
4. L.A.N. Lorena, L.S. Lopes, Computational Experiments with Genetic Algorithms Applied to Set Covering Problems, Pesquisa Operacional, 41-53, 1996
5. J. Hwang, C. S. Kang, Kwang Ryel Ryu, Yongho Han, Hyung Rim Choi, A Hybrid of Tabu Search and Integer Programming for Subway Crew Scheduling Optimization, IASTED-ASC, 72-77, 2002.
6. T. Kido, H. Kitano, M. Nakanishi, A Hybrid Search for Genetic Algorithms: Combining Genetic Algorithms, TABU Search, and Simulated Annealing, Proceedings of the Fifth International Conference on Genetic Algorithms, pp 641, 1993.
7. D. Levine. Application of a hybrid genetic algorithm to airline crew scheduling. Computers & Operations Research, 23(6):547-558, 1996.

---

[3] We can logically view that the crossover is done in parallel.

Combining Extension Matrix and Integer Programming for Optimal Concept Learning

Xiaoshu Hang and Honghua Dai

School of information technology, Deakin University, Australia
{xhan,hdai}@deakin.edu.au

Abstract. This paper proposes two integer programming models and their GA-based solutions for optimal concept learning. The models are built to obtain the optimal concept description in the form of propositional logic formulas from examples based on completeness, consistency and simplicity. The simplicity of the propositional rules is selected as the objective function of the integer programming models, and the completeness and consistency of the concept are used as the constraints. Considering the real-world problems that certain level of noise is contained in data set, the constraints in model 11 are slacked by adding slack-variables. To solve the integer programming models, genetic algorithm is employed to search the global solution space. We call our approach IP-AE. Its effectiveness is verified by comparing the experimental results with other well-known concept learning algorithms: AQ15 and C4.5.

1 Introduction

Inductive learning is a very well known machine learning method used to derive general rules or patterns from given examples and has been widely used in many areas including data mining and cognitive science. There are quite a number of approaches introduced in the last twenty years for inductive learning. They are mainly classified into two groups. One is covering algorithms such as AQ11,AQ15[1] with the learning results in rules; the other is divide-and-conquer algorithms such as ID3,C4.5[2] with the learning results in a decision tree. The extension matrix algorithm was also a covering algorithm. This approach has been implemented and the algorithm is called AE with the advantage of simplicity and strong knowledge representation capability[3,4].

Concept learning has being faced with some NP-hard problems which impede obtaining the best rules of the target concept. These problems include the shortest rules, the optimal coverage and the optimal feature subset[5]. The problem of optimal concept learning is essentially a problem of optimization, especially an optimization with constraints. Therefore, we are inspired to represent the problem of optimal concept learning as an integer programming model, and then solve the model to obtain the optimal concept description. We find that the joint-point between a sample dataset and an integer programming model is an extension matrix. Therefore, given a dataset, we first create an extension matrix of positive examples against negative examples based on which an integer programming model is built. And then we use genetic algorithm to solve the model to obtain the optimal description of the target concept.

The rest of the paper is arranged as follows: Section 2 introduces the representation of extension matrix. In section 3, two integer programming models are introduced. In section 4, the genetic algorithm is used to solve the integer programming model in order to obtain the best concept description. Section 5 gives the experimental results of our approach and section 6 comes the conclusions.

2   Concept Learning Based on Extension Matrix

Suppose $E = D_1 \times D_2 \times \cdots \times D_n$ represents a finite n-dimensional vector space, where D_j represents a finite set of characters whose cardinality is denoted by $|D_j|$. The attribute set of objects in E is $X = \{x_1, x_2, \cdots, x_n\}$, where the range of the jth attribute x_j is D_j. $e_1^*, e_2^*, \cdots, e_t^*$ are the examples(objects) of E where $* \in \{+,-\}$. A positive example of E is denoted by $e_i^+ = <v_{i1}, v_{i2}, \cdots, v_{in}>$ where $v_{ij} \in D_j$. PE and NE are the positive example set and negative example set, respectively.

$$PE = \{e_1^+, e_2^+, \cdots, e_{K_p}^+\}, \; K_p \leq t, \; 1 \leq i \leq K_p$$
$$NE = \{e_1^-, e_2^-, \cdots, e_{K_n}^-\}, \; K_n \leq t, \; 1 \leq j \leq K_n,$$

PE and NE are said to be consistent with respect to X if $PE \cup NE = E$ and $PE \cap NE = \emptyset$. We introduce a concept *extension matrix* on which our integer programming models are built.

Given a positive example $e_i^+ = <v_{i1}^+, v_{i2}^+, \cdots, v_{in}^+>$ and a negative example set $NE = \{e_1^-, e_2^-, \cdots, e_m^-\}$ in which $e_i^- = <v_{i1}^-, v_{i2}^-, \cdots, v_{in}^->$. Using dead element "*" replaces element v_{ij}^- of NE if $v_{ij}^+ = v_{ij}^-$, so that we get a matrix $EM(e_i^+|NE)$ called extension matrix of positive example e_i^+ against NE.

$$EM(e_i^+ | NE) = \begin{bmatrix} r_{11} & r_{12} & \cdots & r_{1n} \\ r_{21} & r_{22} & \cdots & r_{2n} \\ \cdots & \cdots & \cdots & \cdots \\ r_{m1} & r_{m2} & \cdots & r_{mn} \end{bmatrix}, \; r_{ij} = \begin{cases} v_{ij}^-, & if \; v_{ij}^+ \neq v_{ij}^- \\ *, & if \; v_{ij}^+ = v_{ij}^- \end{cases}$$

In an extension matrix $EM(e_i^+|NE)$, a set of m non-dead elements r_{ij_i} ($i=1,\cdots,m$, $j_i \in \{1,\cdots,n\}$) from the m different rows respectively form a path $\{r_{1j_1}, \cdots, r_{mj_n}\}$ in the matrix that corresponds to a conjunctive formula covering e_i^+ against NE.

$$L = \bigwedge_{i=1}^{n} \left[x_{j_i} \neq r_{ij_i} \right]$$

where $\left[x_{j_i} \neq r_{ij_i} \right]$ is an atom in variable-value logic.

For a given example set E, in which PE and NE are consistent, $EM(PE|NE)$ is called the extension matrix of positive example set PE against negative example set NE and is defined as fellows:

$$EM(PE|NE) = EM(e_1^+|NE) \wedge EM(e_2^+|NE) \ldots \wedge EM(e_{K_n}^+|NE)$$

with

$$r_{ij} = \begin{cases} *, & if \; \exists k \in \{1,2,\ldots,Kn\} : r_{i,j} \; in \; EM(e_k^+|NE) \; is \; * \\ v_{ij}, & if \; v_{ij} \; in \; each \; EM(e_k^+|NE), k = 1,2,\ldots,Kn \end{cases}$$

3 Two Integer Programming Models for Concept Learning

Integer programming is a mathematical technique that is concerned with optimization. It tries to find the best possible answer to a problem in a wider field of operations research. Many optimization-based problems, such as the *fixed-charge network flow* problem and the famous *travelling salesman problem*(TSP), are often modelled by integer programming techniques[6].

Linear integer programming problems have the general form of

$$\min\{c^T x : Ax = b, x \geq 0, x \in Z^n\} \quad (1)$$

where Z^n is the space of n-dimensional integer vectors.

Model 1: In this model, the data sample is supposed to meet the completeness and consistency. Let E be the example set, and PE and NE be the positive example set and negative example set, respectively. The extension matrix EM(PE|NE) of PE against NE is generated as follows:

$$EM(PE|NE) = \begin{bmatrix} r_{11} & r_{12} & \cdots & r_{1m} \\ r_{21} & r_{22} & \cdots & r_{2m} \\ \cdots & \cdots & \cdots & \cdots \\ r_{m1} & r_{m2} & \cdots & r_{mn} \end{bmatrix}$$

Suppose that each example consists of n attributes so the extension matrix EM(PE|NE) consists of m rows and n columns. First, we define the given coefficients in the objective function as follows:

$$c_{i,j} = \begin{cases} 1, & \text{if } r_{i,j} \text{ is a non}-\text{dead element} \\ 0, & \text{if } r_{i,j} \text{ is a dead element} \end{cases}$$

Then the integer programming model is represented as follows:

Objective function: $\quad Z = \text{Min} \sum_{i=1}^{n} \sum_{j=1}^{|D_i|} c_{i,j} x_{i,j}$

$$\text{Subject to} \quad \forall k(k=1,\ldots,m) : \sum c_{i,j,k} x_{i,j,k} \geq 1 \quad (2)$$

The decision variable $x_{i,j}$ is binary and specifies whether or not the corresponding element will be included in the final formula. If $x_{i,j}=1$ then the atom $[x_j \neq r_{i,j}]$ is included in the final formula. The objective function aims at seeking for the shortest formula, the complementary rule of which will cover all the positive examples in PE. The constraints in the model are used to ensure that for each row of the extension matrix there is at least one non-dead element to be selected as an atom in the final formula. Therefore we have m constraints for the extension matrix.

Example 1. Table1 is an example set of pneumonia and tuberculosis from [4]. The positive example set PE has 5 instances of pneumonia and the negative example set NE has also 5 instances of tuberculosis. Suppose pneumonia is the target concept to be learnt.

Table 1. Samples of Pneumonia and Tuberculosis

No	FEVER	COUGH	X-RAY	ESR	AUSCULTATION	DISEASE
1	high	heavy	flack	normal	bubble-like	
2	medium	heavy	flack	normal	bubble-like	
3	low	slight	spot	normal	dry-deep	Pneumonia
4	high	medium	flack	normal	bubble-like	
5	medium	Slight	flack	normal	bubble-like	
1	absent	slight	strip	normal	normal	
2	high	heavy	hole	fast	dry-peep	
3	low	slight	strip	normal	normal	Tuberculosis
4	absent	slight	spot	fast	dry-peep	
5	low	medium	flack	fast	Normal	

To acquire the concept description for pneumonia, the extension matrix EM(PE|NE) of PE against NE is generated as follows:

$$E(PE \mid NE) = \begin{bmatrix} absent & * & strip & * & normal \\ * & * & hole & fast & * \\ * & * & strip & * & normal \\ absent & * & * & fast & * \\ * & * & * & fast & normal \end{bmatrix}$$

Table 2. Decision variables and their corresponding values

FEVER={high, medium, low, absent}	x_{11} x_{12} x_{13} x_{14}
COUGH={slight, medium, heavy}	x_{21} x_{22} x_{23}
X-RAY={flack, spot, strip, hole}	x_{31} x_{32} x_{33} x_{34}
ESR={normal, fast}	x_{41} x_{42}
AUSCULTATION={bubble-like, dry-peep, normal}	x_{51} x_{52} x_{53}

The integer programming model for concept learning is built on EM(PE|NE) as follow:

Objective function Min $Z = x_{14} + x_{33} + x_{34} + x_{42} + x_{53}$

$$s.t. \begin{cases} x_{14} + x_{33} + x_{53} \geq 1 \\ x_{34} + x_{42} \geq 1 \\ x_{33} + x_{53} \geq 1 \\ x_{14} + x_{42} \geq 1 \\ x_{42} + x_{53} \geq 1 \end{cases}$$

Model 2: In this model, considering some real world problems that are characterized by certain levels of noise in the sample data, the integer programming model should be modified to account for this incomplete or inconsistent data. The final set of rules is so found as to cover as more positive examples but as few negative examples as possible.

In this case, the extension matrix may not contain non-dead element in each row, which means some rows are dominated by dead element "*". Therefore, the constraint of the modified IP-model contains two parts. One is the slacked restriction for each row by adding a slack-variable s_i; the other is the specified minimum consistency α that the final formula must satisfy. The integer programming model is formulated as follows:

$$\text{Objective function:} \quad Z = Min \sum_{i=1}^{n} \sum_{j=1}^{m} c_{i,j} x_{i,j}$$

$$\text{Subject to} \quad \begin{array}{l} \forall k(k=1,...,m): \sum_{i=1}^{n} c_{i,j_k} x_{i,j_k} + s_k \geq 1 \\ \sum_{k=1}^{m} s_k \leq m(100-\alpha)/100 \end{array} \quad (3)$$

Where s_i is a slack-variable that enable us to control the coverage of positive examples and negative examples by the final formula and α is the specified minimum consistency. If α is high then fewer negative examples are covered by the final formula, so a rational setting for α is obtained by the empirical methods.

In some cases, EM(PE|NE) may not exist. Our algorithm deals with this case by repeating the same process until PE is empty. It creates an extension matrix by randomly selecting an example from PE and then builds the IP model as the fitness function of the GA module and then evolves the initialized population till the best possible formula is found. The formula covers all negative examples in NE and its complementary rule covers some of positive examples which need to be deleted. The process repeats until the PE is empty. The algorithm is described as follows:

Algorithm: IP-AE for optimal concept learning
Input: a sample dataset and a group of parameters
Output: a group of propositional logic formula describing the target concept

1. Create extension matrix EM(PE| NE) of the problem of concept learning;
2. If E(PE(PE| NE) does not exist then
3.   While PE is not empty
4.   Randomly select an example e_i in PE;
5.   Create E(e_i| NE) ;
6.   Build the corresponding IP-model based on which the fitness function is designed;
7.   Using GA to find the best formula F in $E(e_i/NE)$ and its complementary version;
8.   Delete all the positive examples covered by the complementary rule of F in PE;
9.   Endwhile
10. else
11.   Build the corresponding IP-model based on which the fitness function is designed;
12.   Using GA to find the best formula F in E(PE | NE) ;
13. endif
14. Output the complementary rule of formula F;

4 GA-Based Solution to IP-Models

4.1 Coding

We employ binary encoding scheme in this paper. The length of a chromosome is $\sum D_j$ (j=1,...,n). When the extension matrix is generated, the objective function Z(X) of the integer programming model is determined by simply adding up all the decision variables corresponding to the non-dead elements in the extension matrix. Each decision variable corresponds a bit in the chromosome.

4.2 Fitness Function

For a constraint optimization problem, we need to consider that some individuals may not satisfy the constraints. Generally, a penalty function is added into the fitness function to deal with this situation. An individual incurs a penalty if it does satisfy the constraint. Therefore, the fitness function includes two parts: Z(X) and Φ(X). Z(**X**) refers to the total number of terms in the objective function of the integer programming model. The constraint is rewritten as follows:

$$\Phi(X) = P\sum_{k=1}^{m}\omega_k \quad \omega_k = \begin{cases} 1, & if \sum_{i=1}^{n} c_{ki}x_{ij_k} = 0 \\ 0, & if \sum_{i=1}^{n} c_{ki}x_{ij_k} \neq 0 \end{cases},$$

It represents the total number of positive examples which are not covered by the formula multiple a big penalty factor P. Φ=0 if all positive examples are covered by the formula.

$$f = Max\ (W - Q * Z(X) - \Phi(X)) \qquad (4)$$

where W is a big enough constant and Q is a positive coefficient.

5 Experimental Results

To compare with other methods, we choose the congressional voting records data set for our experiment. The data set includes votes for each of the U.S. House of Representatives Congressmen on the 16 key votes identified by nine different types of votes. The problem is to classify a Congressman as a Democrat or a Republican based on the sixteen votes. It consists of 267 Democrat and 168 Republic voting records. Each attribute has a domain of three different values(yea, nay and abstain), so the total length of a chromosome is 48 bits. We learn the target concept Democrat by employing the 267 examples as positive ones and the 167 example as negative ones. The extension matrix EM(PE| NE) in this case does not exist, so the program repeats the process of constructing an EM(e^+| NE) and IP model and solving it until PE is empty. The parameters are set up as: the probability of crossover Pc=0.8, mutating probability Pm=0.08, the population size N=100, W=1000, Q=10, P=50 and the maximal iterative number M=500.

Table 3. Rules produced by IP-AE for recognizing Democrats

No	Rules
1	If [vote4=nay]and [vote3=yea or abstain] then democrat
2	If [vote4=nay]and [vote12=yea or nay] and [vote6=yea] then democrat
3	If [vote7=nay]and [vote11=yea] and [vote3=yea] then democrat
4	If [vote4=nay]and [vote2=yea] then democrat
5	If [vote4=abstain]and [vote9= yea or nay] and [vote11=yea or abstain]then democrat
6	If [vote10=nay] and [vote11=yea]and [vote9=yea] then democrat
7	If [vote7=nay] and [vote10=nay] and [vote12=nay] and [vote15=yea] then democrat
8	If [vote4=nay] and [vote5=nay] and [vote15=yea] then democrat
9	If [vote16=nay] and [vote11=yea] and [vote13=nay] then democrat
10	If [vote16=nay] and [vote11=yea] and [vote1=nay] and [vote2=nay] then democrat
11	If [vote16=abstain] and [vote11=yea] and [vote1=yea] then democrat
12	If [vote16=abstain] and [vote13=yea] and [vote3=yea] then democrat

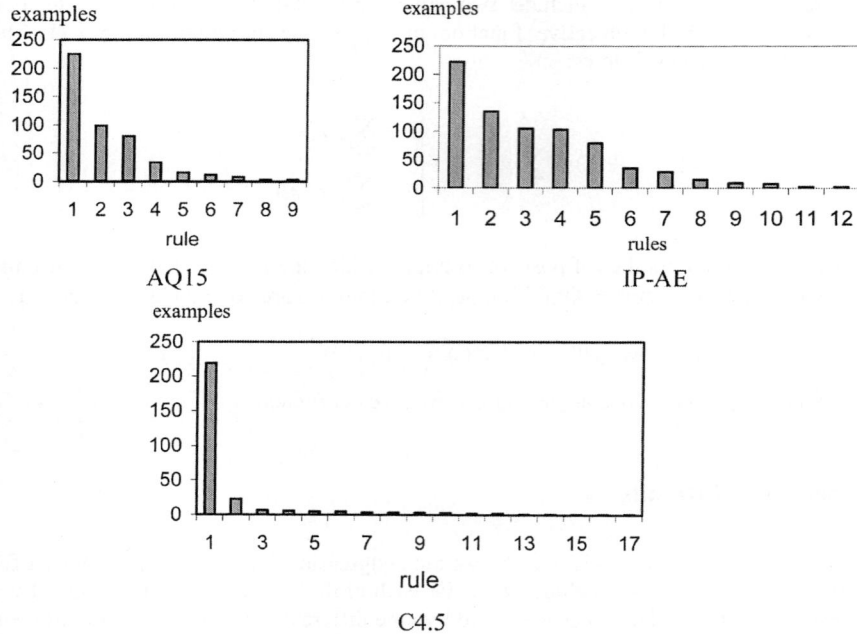

Fig 1. Coverage of rules in each algorithm

12 rules represented in the conjunction of disjunction of atoms for describing Democrats are produced by IP-AE (see Table 3). We compare our experimental results with the two well-known algorithms: AQ15 and C4.5. AQ15 generates 9 rules in the conjunction of disjunction of atoms[10], while C4.5 produces 17 classification rules in conjunctive normal form. To fairly compare IP-AE with the two methods, we convert all the rules in each method into CNF(conjunctive normal form). The total number of rules in CNF and their average rule length in each method are shown in Table 4, from which we can see that IP-AE has 17 rules and the shortest average rule length which means a higher

readability. Figure2 exhibits the visual representation of the coverage of each rule. In contrast to AQ15 and C4.5, IP-AE has a fewer number of rules and shorter average rule length. The reason is that we select simplicity as the objective function of the IP model, which means we prefer seeking for the shortest formula in the extension matrix, correspondingly its complementary rule is also the shortest and covers all the positive examples in PE when $EM(PE|NE)$ exists or covers the most positive examples in PE when $EM(e^+|NE)$ exists.

We are more concerned with the comparison of the classification performance of IP-AE with that of other algorithms. The most commonly used measure for classification performance is predictive accuracy and cross-validation, especially 10-fold cross-validation, which aims at estimating the error of a hypothesis generated by a concept learning algorithm. That is, randomly divide the complete data set into 10 equally sized disjoint subsets, and then in turn select 9 of the 10 subsets as the training set leaving the last one as the test set. A predictive accuracy is calculated after each run and a *t-statistic* test based on the 10 runs is performed with 95% confidence interval on the mean of predictive accuracy. The error rate in Table 5 refers to the misclassification rate. The difference in both the predictive accuracy and misclassification rate suggest that IP-AE outperforms all of these approaches.

Table 4. Comparison of simplicity of concept description

Approach	Conjunctive Normal Form	
	Number of Rules	Average length
AQ15[10]	32	3.34
C4.5	17	4.47
IP–AE	**17**	**3.17**

Table 5. Comparison of classification performance

Approach	Predictive Accuracy	95% confidence interval	Error rate
AQ15[10]	0.956	0.023	0.044
C4.5	0.944	0.041	0.048
IP–AE	**0.958**	**0.035**	**0.041**

6 Conclusions

This paper proposes two integer programming models for optimal concept learning from examples. The two models are designed by seeking for the shortest formula as the objective functions and by using completeness and consistency as constraints. Considering certain level of noise in real data set, the constraints in model II are slacked by adding some slack-variables. To solve the integer programming models, genetic algorithms are used to search the best possible solution in the global solution space. Our experimental results show that the integration of integer programming model with the assistance of one or more intelligent computational approaches such as genetic algorithm could be very helpful to optimal knowledge acquisition.

References

1. R.S. Michalski, I. Mozetic, J. Hong, and N. Lavrac, "*The MultiPurpose Incremental Learning System aq15 and Its Testing Application to Three Medical Domains,*" Proc. Fifth Nat'l Conf. Artificial Intelligence, pp. 1041-1045, 1986.
2. Quinlan, J.R. Simplifying decision trees, International Journal of Man-Machine Studies, 27, 221-234,1987.
3. R.S.Michalski, J.G.Carbonell & T.M.Mitchell, Machine learning: An artificial intelligent approach. Springer-Verlag,1983.
4. J.Hong, R.S.Michalski & C.Uhrik. An Extension matrix approach to the general covering problem, In SPIE Application of artificial intelligence vol. 635,1996.
5. X.Wu, Rule induction with extension matrices, Journal of the American society for information science, Vol.49,Number 5,pp 435-454,1998.
6. A.Gonzalez and R. Perez, SLAVE: A genetic learning system based on an iterative approach, IEEE Transaction on Fuzzy Systems, vol. 7(2) pp. 176-191, 1999.
7. S. Vinterbo. A genetic algorithm for a family of set cover problems. Technical report, Dept. of Computer and Information Science, Norwegian University of Science and Technology, 1999.
8. T.Briji, K.Vanhoof & G.Wets, Reducing redundancy in characteristic rule discovery by using IP-techniques, Intelligent Data Analysis Journal, 4(3), 2000.
9. Jamie Twycross, Steve Cayzaer, An immune-based approach to document classification, http://citeseer.nj.nec.com/558965.html
10. Mitchell A. Potter and Kenneth A. De Jong, The Coevolution of antibodies for concept learning. In the fifth international conference on parallel problem solving form nature, Sep.1998,Amterdam.
11. K.D. Jong, W.Spears, & D.Gordon, Using genetic algorithms for concept learning. In *Machine Learning, 13*, 161-188, 1993.
12. Tjen-Sien Lim, Wei-Yin Loh, Yu-Shan Shih, A Comparison of Prediction Accuracy, Complexity, Training Time of Thirty-three Old New Classification Algorithms , Machine Learning, vol. 40, pp. 203--228, 2000.
13. Cios K.J., Wedding D.K. and Liu N. 1997. CLIP3: cover learning using integer programming, http://isl.cudenver.edu/Projects/Clip3/default.htm.
14. Günter Rudolph: An Evolutionary Algorithm for Integer Programming. PPSN 1994: 139-148.

HeurEAKA – A New Approach for Adapting GAs to the Problem Domain

J.P. Bekmann[1,2] and Achim Hoffmann[1]

[1] School of Computer Science and Engineering,
University of New South Wales, NSW 2052, Australia
[2] National ICT Australia (NICTA), A.T.P, NSW 1430, Australia

Abstract. We propose a new approach for the efficient development of effective heuristic problem solvers for combinatorial problems. Our approach is based on Genetic Algorithms (GA) and addresses the known problem of allowing the efficient adaptation of a general purpose GA to a given problem domain. The adaptation is done by building a knowledge base that controls part of the GA, i.e. the fitness function and the mutation operators. The knowledge bases are built by a human who has at least a reasonable intuition of the search problem and how to find a solution. The human monitors the GA and intervenes when he/she feels that the GA produces individuals which have only a small chance of leading to an acceptable solution or the human helps by providing rules describing how to generate an individual with high chances of success.
We use an incremental knowledge acquisition approach based on Nested Ripple Down Rules. We provide initial experiments on an industrially relevant domain of channel routing in VLSI design. Industrial algorithms have been developed over decades in this domain. Our results so far are extremely encouraging, as we managed to solve some benchmark problems with a relatively small knowledge base in conjunction with a general purpose GA.

1 Introduction

Finding solutions to difficult search problems still represents a major problem, despite considerable progress in some areas, such as Constraint Satisfaction Problems (CSPs). While Genetic Algorithms (GA) have for a long time been considered to be generic general purpose search techniques which can be applied to all sorts of search problems, in practice it usually proves to be rather difficult to adapt a general purpose GA design to a particular problem type at hand [1, 2]. Suitable mutation operators and selection criteria need to be developed along with designing appropriate parameters for the GA, including population size, number of generations, mutation rate, the use of cross-over etc. In this paper we present a new approach to address this difficulty: our approach aims at making the process of developing a problem specific version of a GA as easy as possible. In order to achieve this objective, we propose a new framework that allows one to incrementally develop a knowledge base that controls the generation of new individuals, in order to steer the GA through the overall search space. The basic idea being that often GAs create individuals of which a human could judge that the chances of leading to an acceptable solution are very low. The generation of such individuals can be suppressed by providing suitable knowledge that explains why those indivuals are so unlikely to lead to a solution. Also, the same idea applies to those individuals a human could state with some confidence as having a good chance of leading to a solution. Similarly, our framework allows one to provide rules that tell how to generate such individuals. The incremental aspect of our framework ensures that previously provided knowledge about the quality of individuals is maintained while additional knowledge is integrated into the knowledge base by only being applicable to those cases where the existing knowledge base did not judge in accordance with the human. In other words, the adverse interaction of multiple rules in a knowledge base is effectively avoided.

Our framework HeurEAKA (Heuristic Evolutionary Algorithms using Knowledge Acquisition) allows the GA to run in conjunction with the current - initially empty - knowledge base on problem instances. The evolutionary process can be monitored by the human and individuals can be evaluated. If a particular individual is generated that appears undesirable or suboptimal, the human could enter a new rule that prevents such behavoir in future or provide an improved alternative action. The user might also also add a rule which imposes a fitness penalty on such individuals. More generally, the user formulates rules based on characteristics of selected individuals, and these are applied in the general case by the GA.

This paper is organised as follows: in the next sections we briefly review the basics of GAs. In section 3 we present our overall framework along with the knowledge acquisition approach. Section 4 presents a case study where our framework was applied to the problem of channel routing, an industrially relevant problem from the realm of VLSI design. The following section 5 discusses our results and the lessons learnt so far. This is followed by the conclusions in section 6.

2 Genetic Algorithms

Evolutionary algorithms are loosely based on processes observed in nature, most notably made famous by Charles Darwin. In the evolutionary computation, there are various approaches in applying these principles to search and optimisation. These include genetic algorithms, evolution strategy, evolutionary programming and genetic programming.

Basic evolutionary algorithms are relatively easy to implement. A solution candidate of the problem to be solved is encoded into a genome. A collection of genomes makes up a population of potential solutions. The GA performs a search through the solution space by modifying the population, guided by an evolutionary heuristic. When a suitable solution has been identified, the search terminates.

A genetic algorithm usually starts with a randomly initialized population of individuals, and searches through the solution space guided by a *fitness* value assigned to individuals in the population. Based on probabilistic operators for selection, mutation and crossover, the GA directs the search to promising areas. GAs have been applied to a wide variety of domains, and were found to be quite effective at solving otherwise intractible problems [3] .

GAs do suffer from a variety of problems, most notably the "black art" of tuning GA parameters such as population size, selection strategies, operator weightings, as well as being very sensitive to problem encoding and operator formulation [1]. Holland [4] formulated this as the manipulation of building blocks relevant to the problem encoding. We aim to address some of these issues with an explicit formulation of domain knowledge using well suited KA techniques.

3 Architecure of HeurEAKA

The system architecture has four main modules - a GA module, a KB module, a user interface (UI) and a *primitives* module. The latter being tailored to the particular problem domain.

A *primitives interface* is defined through which the GA and KB access problem specific functionalities.

Overall, the system operation consists of the GA search strategy calling on problem specific elements defined in the KB by a user or in the primitives module by the system engineer/user.

3.1 Characteristics of the Genetic Algorithm Module

Genome encoding and manipulation is treated by the GA as opaque. All manipulations take place indrectly via the *primitives interface* (see Section 4.1).

In order to generate new indivduals, the GA has to select parents from the current population and then generate offspring either by mutation or by crossover. Further, some individuals of the current generation should be selected for removal and replaced by newly generated individuals.

Offspring of selected parents are either created via a crossover copy operation or as a mutated copy. A coin-flip determines which operator will be applied. The crossover operator mimics natural evolutionary genetics and allows for recombination and distribution of successful solution sub-components in the population.

In order to select individuals either as a parent for a new individual or as a candidate to be removed from the population, the knowledge base is invoked to determine the fitness of an individual as explained below. In order to generate suitable offspring, another knowledge base is invoked which probabilistically selects mutation operators.

3.2 Knowledge Acquisition Implementation

Our knowledge acquisition approach for building the knowledge base for fitness determination and the knowledge base for selecting operators for offspring generation is based on the ideas of ripple down rules (RDR) [5]. RDR builds a rule base incrementally based on specific problem instances for which the user explains their choices. An extension of RDR allows hierarchical structuring of RDRs - "nested RDR" (NRDR) [6]. NRDR allows re-use of definitions in a KB, and the abstraction of concepts which make it easier to describe complex problems on the knowledge level and also allow for more compact knowledge bases for complex domains.

Ripple Down Rules Knowledge Base: We use single classification RDRs (SCRDRs) for both types of knowledge bases. A single classification RDR is a binary tree where the root node is also called the default node. To each node in the tree a rule is associated, with a condition part and a conclusion which is usually a class - in our case it is an operator application. A node can have up to two children, one is attached to an *except* link and the other one is attached to the so-called if-not link. The condition of the default rule in the default node is always true and the conclusion is the default conclusion. When evaluating a tree on a case (the object to be classified), a *current conclusion* variable is maintained and initialised with the default conclusion. If a node's rule condition is satisfied, then its conclusion overwrites the *current conclusion* and the except-link, if it exists, is followed and the corresponding child node is evaluated. Otherwise, the if-not link is followed, if it exists, and the corresponding child node is evaluated. Once a node is reached such that there is no link to follow the *current conclusion* is returned as a result. Figure 1 shows a simple RDR tree structure. In other RDR implementations, any KB modification would be done by adding exception rules, using conditions which only apply to the current case. By doing this, it is ensured that proper performance of the KB on previous cases is maintained.

Nesting RDRs allows the user to define multiple RDRs in a knowledge base, where one RDR rule may use another, nested RDR tree in its condition, and in HeurEAKA as an action. I.e. the nested RDR tree is evaluated in order to determine whether the condition is satisfied. A strict hierarchy of rules is required to avoid circular definitions etc.

For the purpose of controlling the Genetic Algorithm, in our approach all conclusions are actually actions that can be applied to the case, which is an individual genome. The rules are formulated using the Rule Specification Language as detailed below.

Fitness Knowledge Base. The user specifies a list of RDRs which are to be executed when the fitness of a genome is determined. The evaluation task can thus be broken into components as needed, each corresponding to a RDR. The evaluator executes each RDR in sequence.

Mutation Knowledge Base. For determining a specific mutation operator a list of RDRs provided by the user is consulted. Each RDR determines which specific operator would be applied for modifying an individual. Unlike for the evaluation, for mutation only one of the RDRs for execution will be picked probabilistically using weights supplied by the user.

Rule Specification Language (RSL): Conditions and actions for a rule are specified in a simple language based loosely on "C" syntax. It allows logical expressions in the condition of a rule, and a list of statements in the action section. The use of variables scoped to the rule is also supported. Types include integers, floats, enumerations, booleans and types defined via the *primitives interface*. (Variables can also be defined with a KB wide scope).

RSL supports simple control structures such as *while*, *do..while* and *if* (the use of which is discouraged since conditionals should ideally be handled in a rule's condition).

An example of a rule would be:
variables: *int iCount = 5; bool lIsGood;*
condition: *iCount > 0||someRdr(iCount)*
actions: *lIsGood = checkSomeOtherRdr(iCount); .print(lIsGood);*

This rule uses two variables. The condition contains a reference to a separately defined RDR *someRdr* which takes an integer parameter. The action contains two statements, the first relying on the boolean condition returned from the evaluation of *checkSomeOtherRdr(iCount)*, the other is a built-in command (in this language these are identified by a leading period) supported for debugging purposes.

User Interaction and Knowledge Acquisition for the GA takes place as a process of iteration: on each individual the fitness KB is applied and a set of rules executed. The user can review these rules and make modifications if necessary. Fig. 1 shows in bold a rule a user might have added for the case where conditions $ad\bar{g}hij$ hold. This would cause action Z to be executed, instead of W.

Fig. 2 illustrates the KA refinement cycle. The same applies for mutation, where one mutation RDR is selected randomly and then evaluated to obtain a specific mutation operator that modifies the genome.

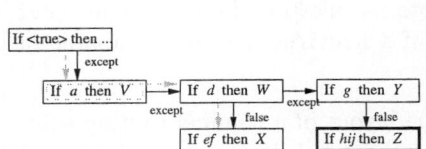

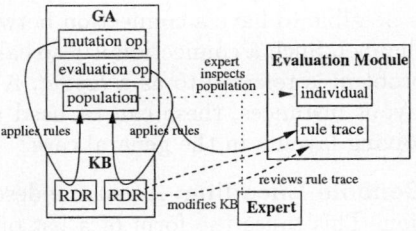

Fig. 1. A simple RDR structure. The dashed line indicates the path taken & rule executed (V) for $a\overline{de}$, the bold box indicates how action Z would be added for $ad\bar{g}hij$.

Fig. 2. The GA consults the KB when evaluating and mutating a genome. Picking an individual, the expert can iteratively review the corresponding rule trace and modify the KB.

In order to build knowledge bases that guide the GA search, the user can monitor the individuals generated and the fitness values assigned to individuals. A user can step back, forward and review the application of RDR rules to the genome, and make modifications to the respective KB by adding exception rules.

Since the evaluation of a set of RDRs can cause a number of actions to be executed, it is necessary to allow the user to step through an execution history to help improving it. For this, records of genomes and variable instantiations are maintained. A suitable user interface is necessary here and an example for the channel routing problem is shown in the following section.

4 Experiments

Due to space limitations the following description is only indicative and not a complete description of all features available in our system.

4.1 VLSI Demonstrator

In order to demonstrate that genetic algorithms enhanced with knowledge acquisition can be used to develop algorithms for solving complex combinatorial problems, detailed channel routing, which is an industrially relevant problem within the realm of VLSI design, was chosen to demonstrate our approach. A channel routing problem is given by a channel of a certain width, see Fig 3. On both sides of the channel are connection points. Each connection point belongs to a certain electrical net and all connection points of the same net need to be physically connected with each other by routing a wire through the channel and, of course, without two nets crossing. The width of the channel determines how many wires can run in parallel through the channel. The length of the channel determines how many connection points on both sides of the channel there may be. Furthermore, the layout is done on a small number of different layers (e.g. 2 to 4 layers), to make a connection of all nets without crossing possible at all. It is possible to have a connection between two adjacent layers at any point in the channel. Such a connection is also called a *via*. A solution to the channel routing problem is referred to as a *layout*. A KB contains rules for the manipulation of layout instances, these can be used as part of a heuristic algorithm capable of solving layouts in the general case.

Genome Encoding: A genome describes the layout of a channel routing solution. This takes the form of a list of wires, each containing a sequential list of nodes. Each node has three coordinates corresponding to the row, column and layer number. A wire begins with a node corresponding to a pin on the bottom of the channel and ends with one corresponding to the pin at the top of the channel.

A layout is characterized by the number of columns and rows (tracks), how many pins are to be found on either side of the channel and what the pin configuration is. A problem instance used for the system would be given by the VLSI layout problem to be solved. A genome will usually not represent a valid solution as some wires are usually crossing. Only when all those crossings have been eliminated and not more than the prescribed number of layers are used would the fitness value of a genome reach a satisfactory level.

HeurEAKA – A New Approach for Adapting GAs to the Problem Domain

Genome Random Initialization: A layout is defined with a fixed number of wires, columns and (generally) a fixed pin configuration. When the GA starts, a population of random layouts complying with these constraints is generated. For this pin pairs are connected, with the minimum number of random nodes (2) to bridge any horizontal distance.

Genome Crossover: It is important to choose crossover operators such that they maintain usable sub-components within the genome (in GA parlance these are referred to as building blocks). This is attempted by leaving whole wires intact, and swapping sequential groups of wires. In this case the wires between two parents are exchanged using a two point crossover. An example might be the crossover of parent A $\{1_A, 2_A, 3_A, 4_A, 5_A\}$ and parent B $\{1_B, 2_B, 3_B, 4_B, 5_B\}$ at wires 2 and 4, giving children $\{1_A, 2_B, 3_B, 4_A, 5_A\}$ and $\{1_B, 2_A, 3_A, 4_B, 5_B\}$.

Genome Mutation: The KB contains rules designed to manipulate the layout, typically they would describe the resolution of a conflict identified using the *.findconflict* command (a primitive function returning a conflict found in the layout).

Genome Evaluation: Rules added by the user determine the fitness of a genome. Typically the user would add rules based on the number of layers used in the layout, as well as the number of conflicts. This exerts evolutionary pressure on the search towards finding conflict less layouts with the minimum number of layers. The length of wires, number of *vias* (layer transitions) are also useful fitness critera.

Primitives Interface / Rule Specification Language Extensions: Primitives relating to the channel layout problem are supplied. These include the types *wire* and *node*, as well as other layout-specific commands. Figure 4 shows an example of a rule for raising a segment based on a conflict. High level operators are NRDRs which form a useful vocabulary for intuitive descriptions on the knowledge level. For example $RaiseHorizSegment(N)$ is defined as $Ne = N.next; Ne.insert(N.x, N.y, N.z + 1); Ne.insert(Ne.x, Ne.y, Ne.z + 1);$. Most of the KB resembles rules as seen in Fig. 4.

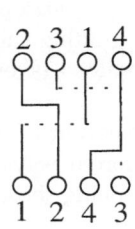
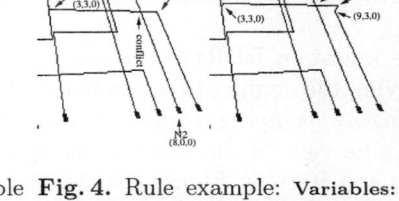

Fig. 3. A simple channel routing problem.

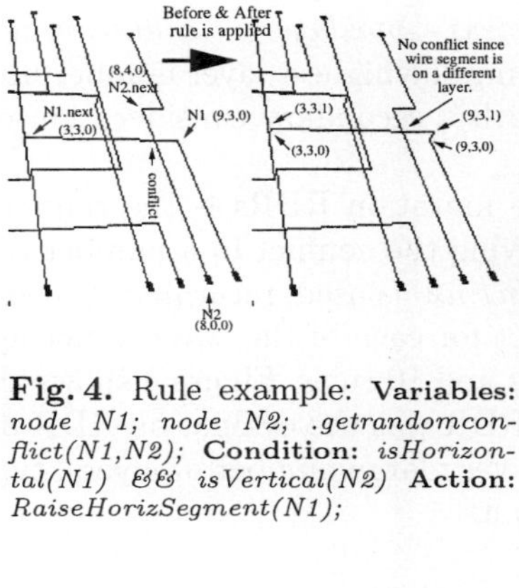

Fig. 4. Rule example: **Variables:** *node N1; node N2; .getrandomconflict(N1,N2);* **Condition:** *isHorizontal(N1) && isVertical(N2)* **Action:** *RaiseHorizSegment(N1);*

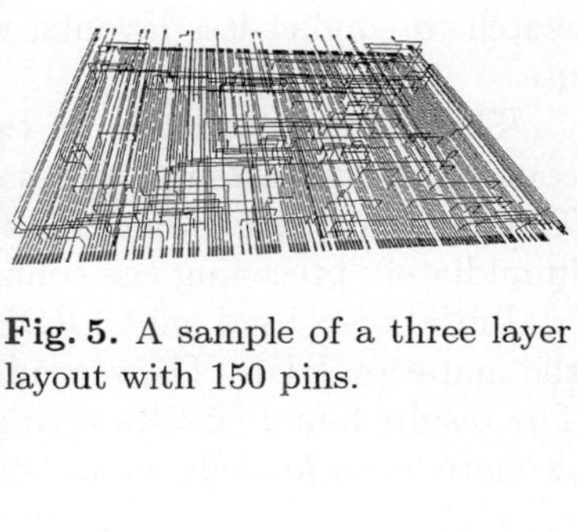

Fig. 5. A sample of a three layer layout with 150 pins.

User Interface: Our tool based on the HeurEAKA framework is shown in the following figures. Figure 6 shows a screenshot of how the user can interact with the KB and sample layouts, adding and refining rules as needed. It was found necessary to have a good visualization and debugging interface to be able to productively create and test rules. The GA is controlled via the interface displayed in Fig. 7. The user may start, stop, restart and step through a GA's execution. If desired, an individual genome can be selected and further analyzed as shown in Fig. 6.

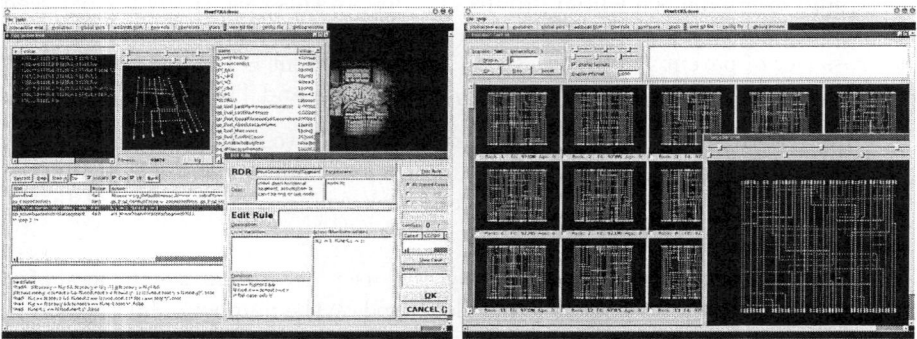

Fig. 6. The interactive screen allows the user to step through rule application, changing the KB as needed.

Fig. 7. The GA window displays snapshots of the population at given intervals. The user can start, stop and step through evolution.

4.2 Channel Routing Experiments

In order to test the approach and the implemented tool, a KB was created. Initial tests were done with a KB containing 2 RDRs and 10 rules, later tests were run with 50 RDRs and 167 rules. On average the KA process took approximately 10 minutes per rule.

The main evaluation operator contained essentially one RDR, with the main rule being: *.fitness = pg_defaultfitness - .maxlayers - .countconflicts * 5;* (*.maxlayers* is a primitive function returning the highest layer number used), guiding the search to conflict-less layouts, with a secondary consideration of reduced layer use.

The primary structure of the mutation RDRs is the random selection of a conflict, and an attempt at resolving the conflict in a number of different ways. The function *.getrandomconflict(n1,n2)* is used, returning two nodes, being those immidiately preceding the conflict for each of the two conflicting wires.

Initial tests used only 2 RDRs and 10 rules. Figure 4 shows the main rule for the mutation RDR. The second RDR was the evaluation RDR described above. The results found layouts with a very large number of layers, typically 20 layers or more, even for only small layouts.

Subsequent tests were done with a more sophisticated KB. The mutation operator typically contained 15 high level RDRs to choose from, including, high-level operators such as, *LowerSingleSegment*, *MoveDownHorizontalSegment*, *MoveSegmentLeftorRightN*, *RaiseWholeWire*, *SplitHorizontalSegment*. In total 49 RDRs and 167 rules were used.

GA Configuration: Based on empirical tests, a population size of 500 for small, and 2000 for large layouts was used.

Layer Restriction: Initial tests using the 167 rule KB were run for 3 layer layouts, with some found for up to 150 pins a side, an example is shown in Fig. 5. We decided to concentrate on 2 layer solutions as they are more comparable to other attempts at solving the CRP, and the theoretical limits are better understood for 2 layer layouts.

Two strategies were selected for finding 2 layer layouts: incremental layering and static layer restriction. The former forcing the search to optimize for a single layer first, when convergence appears to have taken place, an additional layer was added. The latter simply allowed the search to use two layers from the start. Solutions using the static strategy were found slightly faster. Figure 9 shows the distinctive "step" in the incremental strategy, where a second layer is added after convergence of single layer search.

Channel Width / Number of Tracks: In order to control layout *density* the number of long distance crossing connections was limited in the problem specifications. The *density* for a 2-layer problem is defined as the maximum over all positions p along the length of the channel as follows: the number of nets which have at least one connection point on the left as well as one connection point o the right of p. This determines the theoretical lower limit on tracks needed to solve the problem.

Table 1. Results for 2 layer layouts with different number of pins and tracks. Note that $\frac{mutations}{popsize}$ for different layer strategies are not comparable. Less tracks or higher density make the problem harder.

pins on side (channel len.)	density	tracks	layer stategy	$\frac{mutations}{popsize}$	successful seeds	avg. conflicts for failed seeds
30	10	25	inc	220	100%	-
30	10	25	static	128	100%	-
30	20	35	inc	616	85%	2
30	20	25	inc	333	29%	4
50	24	40	inc	581	16%	3.5
50	24	40	static	766	16%	3.6
50	24	35	inc	1372	10%	4.9
70	39	60	static	1028	16%	5.2
70	39	55	inc	776	10%	8.9
70	39	50	static	1496	20%	7.3
80	44	70	static	1392	40%	6

5 Discussion

The experiments show that it is feasible to attempt solutions to complex problems using the HeurEAKA framework - in this case we applied it to the domain

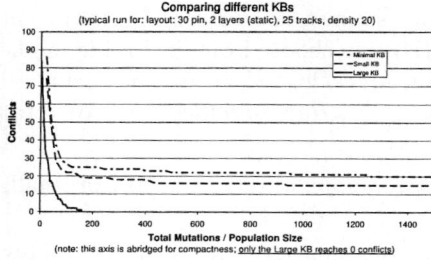 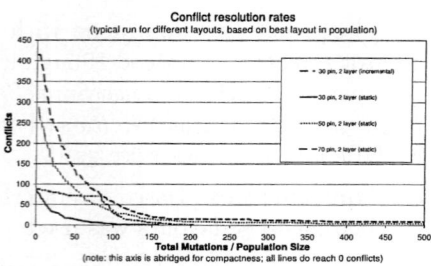

Fig. 8. Quasi random mutations "minimal" and a primitive KB "small" are unable to solve the 30 pin layout problem. The more mature KB can solve it effectively.

Fig. 9. Comparison of different conflict resolution rates, given different layout sizes and layer allocation strategies (static vs incremental).

of detailed Channel Routing Problem (CRP). We were able to effectively perform KA using ripple-down rules based knowledge acquisition, which formed an effective KB for the GA.

The development of the problem specific components of HeurEAKA did require some effort in addition to KB construction, it would be commensuate with any other attempt at solving a CRP problem, since basic encoding and access of a layout is necessary. We argue that the additional effort usually spent on adapting and tuning GAs towards a problem domain is in excess of ours.

A number of studies have been made in the application of GAs to CRP. They fall mainly into 3 categories: regular GAs, GA with case based reasoning (CBR) and hybrid solutions. For regular genetic algorithms as well as hybrid solutions, the development of the mutation algorithms require specific domain knowledge - in some cases, existing CR techniques [7, 8]. As seen in figure 8, a GA with no use of domain knowledge ("minimal KB") is inefficient, or even unable to solve complex problems. Goeckel et al. [7] show that the use of informed operators results in finding of better solutions for the CRP.

It is known that the development of representation and mutation techniques for genetic algorithms is often quite difficult [1]. Instead of relying on the definition of operators through expert introspection and trial and error, we allow the user to formulate them by exploring example cases. There is an approach somewhat related in the use of case based reasoning for GA in VLSI design [9]. Here, however, previous cases are selected by an expert and only used for injection into a GA search, rather than formulation of operators. It does not build on generalizations and expert insight learnt from these cases, thus being far less powerful.

On average rules took approximately 10 minutes each to formulate, taking about 30 hours for the formulation of a viable algorithm. The formulation of effective CRP algorithms has been the subject of much study and industry-standard algorithms took many years to perfect [10]. In our case KA was done by a novice in CRP, using mainly intuition and being able to incrementally specify rules in a natural way on the knowledge level. Thus the effort and expertise required was significantly less than commercial routing solutions.

Our experiments show that reasonable solutions can be found using our approach. The size of layouts and track sizes look comparable to those benchmarks used with other CRP algorithms [11] and [7] - many are in the 12-23 column range, some up to 129. However, direct comparison needs extension to supporting same-side pin connections in the HeurEAKA tool. The results outlined in the previous section look promising, and with the continued development of the KB, should produce even better layouts in the future.

By demonstrating our framework to the well understood domain of CRP, we hope to be able to benchmark our results against existing algorithms. Having proved our techniques, we hope to apply it in other domains where little prior expert knowledge or known algorithms exist. Here, the value of interactive exploration and intuitive explanation as a sufficient and efficient basis for problem solving would be particularly highlighted.

6 Conclusion

In this paper we have presented a framework for solving complex combinatorial problems based on interaction of a human expert and an evolutionary algorithm. We outline how our approach makes it easier to tackle such problems than the conventional design of algorithms.

Given that the development of standard genetic algorithms still requires considerable effort in the formulation and tuning of operators, we introduce a method that is better suited to integrate domain knowledge. We used NRDR, an unconventional KA technique, by integrating it into the design process to provide an intuitive method of supporting an expert's development effort. By demonstrating the approach in the domain of detailed channel routing, we have shown that the approach looks promising in achieving results comparable to conventional algorithms developed with vastly more effort.

We also hope to extend the RDR techniques used to provide some automated support for rule formulation such as the automatic evaluation of proposed new rules on databases of genomes that were generated through previous genetic searches. The current framework provides some support for statistical evaluation of rule effectiveness in the search for solutions, but they need to be improved. Currently rule usage is tracked in relation to frequency of application to successful candidates as well as fitness contribution. Extensions could include the ability to review them against a case history and statistical measures relating their use in successful and unsuccessful evolutionary paths.

The KB used in the presented experiments for CRP is sufficient to solve some benchmark problems. However, in future work we plan to extend it to be able to tackle more challenging problems. If we can show the competetiveness of these solutions, we hope to apply the framework to problems in other domains.

References

1. Rothlauf, F.: Representations for Genetic and Evolutionary Algorithms. Springer Verlag (2002)
2. Goldberg, D.E.: The Design of Innovation: Lessons from and for Competent Genetic Algorithms. Volume 7, Kluwer Series on Genetic Algorithms and Evolutionary Computation. Kluwer Academic Publishers (2002)
3. De Jong, K., Spears, W.: Using genetic algorithm to solve NP-complete problems. In Schaffer, J.D., ed.: Proc. of the Third Int. Conf. on Genetic Algorithms, San Mateo, CA, Morgan Kaufmann (1989) 124–132
4. Holland, J.: Adaptation in Natural and Artificial Systems. University of Michigan Press. (1975)
5. Compton, P., Jansen, R.: Knowledge in context: A strategy for expert system maintenance. In: 2nd Australian Joint Artificial Intelligence Conference. Volume 1. (1989) 292–306
6. Beydoun, G., Hoffmann, A.: Theoretical basis for hierarchical incremental knowledge acquisition. In: International Journal in Human-Computer Studies. (2001) 407–452
7. Gockel, N., Pudelko, G., Drechsler, R., Becker, B.: A hybrid genetic algorithm for the channel routing problem. In: International Symposium on Circuits and Systems, volume IV. (1996) 675–678
8. Lin, Y., Hsu, Y., Tsai, F.: Silk: A simulated evolution router. In: IEEE Transactions on CAD. Volume 8.10. (1989) 1108–1114
9. Liu, X.: Combining genetic algorithm and casebased reasoning for structure design (1996)
10. Lengauer, T.: Combinational Algorithms for Integrated Circuit Layout. B.G. Teubner/John Wiley & Sons (1990)
11. Lienig, J., Thulasiraman, K.: A new genetic algorithm for the channel routing problem. In: 7th International Conference on VLSI Design, Calcutta (1994) 133–136

A Modified Integer-Coding Genetic Algorithm for Job Shop Scheduling Problem

Chunguo Wu[1], Wei Xiang[2], Yanchun Liang[1,2]
Heow Pueh Lee[2], and Chunguang Zhou[1]

[1] College of Computer Science and Technology, Jilin University, Key Laboratory of Symbol Computation and Knowledge Engineering of the Ministry of Education, Changchun 130012, China
liangyc@ihpc.a-star.edu.sg
[2] Institute of High Performance Computing, Singapore 117528, Singapore

Abstract. An operation template is proposed in this paper for describing the mapping between operations and a subset of natural numbers. With such operation template, a job shop scheduling problem (JSSP) can be transformed into a traveling salesman problem (TSP), hence the integer-coding genetic algorithm for TSP can be easily applied and modified. A decoding strategy, called virtual job shop, is proposed to evaluate the fitness of the individual in GA population. The integration of the operation template and virtual job shop makes the existing integer-coding GA possible for solving an extension of a classical job shop scheduling problem.

1 Introduction

The job shop scheduling problem (JSSP) is widely acknowledged as one of the most difficult NP-hard problems. A classical $n \times m$ JSSP can be described as follows: Given a finite set of n jobs $J = \{J_i \mid i \in N(n)\}$ to be machined on a finite set of m machines $M = \{M_j \mid j \in N(m)\}$, where $N(\cdot)$ is a subset of natural number set. Each job must be processed on every machine and has pre-determined operations which are assigned in some sequence. The problem is to determine the operation sequences on each machine in order to satisfy one or more objectives concurrently. Typically, the most common objective is the completion of all jobs in the shortest makespan.

There are many reported studies on JSSP for the past 40 years. The solution techniques available for solving JSSP can be classified into two groups: exact methods and approximation methods. The survey on both exact methods and approximation methods for JSP can be found in Ref. [1]. Most of the reported studies on JSSP deal with a classical JSSP, which is a simplified $n \times m$ job shop scheduling problem that has the following basic assumptions: (1) Each job must pass through every machine once and once only, (2) The operation cannot be interrupted, (3) Every machine can process at most one job at a time.

The real-world scheduling problem is however, more complex. For example, not all jobs have to pass through every machine, and sometimes some un-successive operations of a job may need to pass through one machine many times. This work is proposed to deal with such an extension of the classical JSSP.

The remainder of the paper is organized as follows. Section 2 describes the extension of classical JSSP problem examined in this work. Section 3 presents the modified integer-coding GA, including an innovated operation template, chromosome coding, virtual job-shop decoding, and fitness evaluation. Section 4 gives a validation of the proposed algorithm by three benchmark JSSP problems. Section 5 is the conclusion and discussion.

2 Job Shop Scheduling Problem Description

In a classical $n \times m$ JSSP, each job can only pass through every machine once, that is, there are at most m operations in a job. In real-world scheduling, it is quite common that a job need to be processed repeatedly in numbers of machines. Hence, an extension of a classical $n \times m$ JSSP is studied in this work. We flexible the following assumption of JSSP: (1) Each job may not need to pass through every machine; (2) Un-successive operations of a job may pass through one machine many times.

To build the model of such job shop scheduling problem, job set and machine set are defined as follows:

$$\mathbf{J} = \{J_i \mid i \in \mathbf{N}(n)\}, \tag{1}$$

$$\mathbf{M} = \{M_j \mid j \in \mathbf{N}(m)\}, \tag{2}$$

The number of operations in job i is represented as n_i ($i \in \mathbf{N}(n)$), thereby, the total number of operations is

$$p = \sum_{i=1}^{n} n_i . \tag{3}$$

Each operation can be represented as a four tuple: $p(i,k,j,t)$, where i represents job number, k represents operation number of job i, j is the required machine number, t is the processing time on this machine.

3 Integer Coding Based Genetic Algorithm

There exist many mature techniques for solving different TSP. Genetic algorithm (GA) for TSP is one of them. In solving an n-city TSP, the gene coding of GA is actually a number coding of these n cities, that is, each chromosome is an order set of natural numbers ranged from 1 to n. Some researches studied the same coding method to solve JSSP [3, 4]. Yamada et al. represented a JSSP to a set of permutations of operations number on every machine [4]. Such coding method requires to solve m sub-sequencing problems and makes the algorithm inefficient. Furthermore, it had additional requirement that each job must have m operations, which reduced the flexibility of JSSP. In this work, all operations are mapped to numbers coding ranged from 1 to p. Then a JSSP can be translated to a TSP, hence the integer-coding genetic algorithm for TSP can be easily applied. In this section, some modifications on integer-coding GA for TSP to solve JSSP are presented, those general issues on GA like selection and genetic operators (crossover, mutation, and reversion) can be referred to Liang et al.'s work [5].

3.1 Operation Template

Definition 1: Operation template is defined as the mapping between a set of natural numbers and operations, if

1) For an arbitrary operation $p(i,k,j,t)$, there has one and only one natural number $l \ (l \in \mathbf{N}(p))$ according to the mapping,

2) For an arbitrary natural number $l \ (l \in \mathbf{N}(p))$, there has one and only one operation $p(i,k,j,t)$ according to the mapping.

An operation template is noted as $\mathbf{T}$, then the mapping relationship between $l \ (l \in \mathbf{N}(p))$ and operation $p(i,k,j,t)$ can be noted as:

$$p(i,k,j,t) = \mathbf{T}(l), \qquad (4)$$

$$l = \mathbf{T}^{-1}(p(i,k,j,t)). \qquad (5)$$

To construct an operation template, each operation can either be assigned a un-repeated natural number in $\mathbf{N}(p)$, or be assigned sequenced number according to the operation sequence number. An operation template $\mathbf{T}$ is the mapping between the defined numbers and operations. Once the operation template is constructed, it should not be changed anymore. For example, for a given 3×3 JSSP shown in Table 1, the total number of operations for this problem is nine. Each row in this table represents a job. Each operation consists of a machine number and the processing time for that operation.

Table 1. 3×3 JSSP

Job no.	Oper. 1	Oper. 2	Oper. 3
1	2, 3	3, 7	1, 5
2	1, 6	3, 9	2, 8
3	3, 4	1, 3	2, 9

Continuous numbers are assigned to operations for all jobs, that is, natural numbers 1 to 9 are assigned to nine operations. Each operation is represented as four tuple as stated in section 2. For example, operation 1 is represented as (1, 1, 2, 3) which means job1's operation 1 is processed on machine2 by 3 processing time. Number one is mapped to Operation 1, number two is mapped to Operation 2, and so on. Hence an operation template for this JSSP problem is generated as a mapping between each number and each four-tuple represented operation. Figure 1 is the constructed operation template.

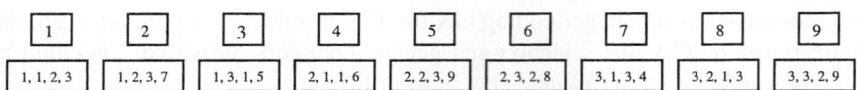

Fig. 1. Operation Template T

3.2 Chromosome Representation

Each individual chromosome in the population represents a schedule, a permutation of the operations for all jobs. An individual chromosome is a chain of each nature number which represents a respective operation. An example of a chromosome is shown in Figure 2. Each chromosome can be mapped to a sequence of operations (a schedule) based on the operation template. Figure 3 shows the respective sequence of operations to the chromosome in Figure 2.

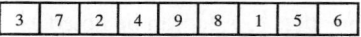

Fig. 2. A chromosome representation

| 1, 3, 1, 5 | 3, 1, 3, 4 | 1, 2, 3, 7 | 2, 1, 2, 6 | 3, 3, 2, 9 | 3, 2, 1, 3 | 1, 1, 2, 3 | 2, 2, 3, 9 | 2, 3, 2, 8 |

Fig. 3. A sequenced operations corresponding to the chromosome in Fig. 2 based on the operation template

3.3 Decoding Strategy

Any individual chromosome in a population can be mapped to a sequence of operations according to the operation template. Such a sequence of operations represents a schedule. Recall that the operations in each job have precedence constraints, therefore not all the permutations represent feasible schedules directly. To ensure the feasibility of each schedule, in this work, a specific decoding is developed to decode each chromosome to a feasible schedule.

The procedure of decoding is actually to simulate the virtual processing according to the sequenced operations presented in individual chromosome. In this work, a decoding procedure called Virtual Job Shop is proposed.

3.3.1 Virtual Job Shop

Virtual job shop can be regarded as the general decoding procedure to decode the chromosome from first gene to the last one. The detail procedure can be stated as follows:

1. Scan the genes contained in the chromosome.
2. The first available operation is added to the task queue of its corresponding machine.
3. Repeat the step 1 and 2 till all of the operations are arranged into their machine task queues.
4. According to the task queues, calculate the operating time for each operation by the Gantt chart.

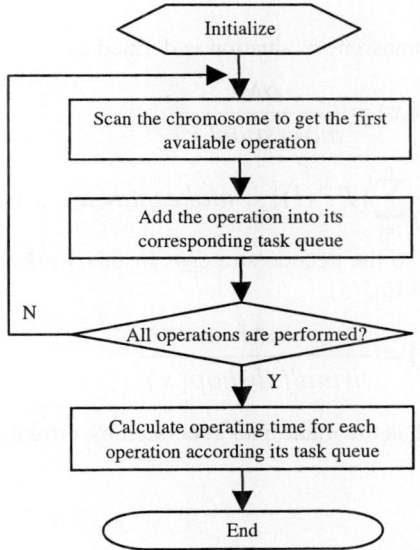

Fig. 4. Flowchart of virtual job shop

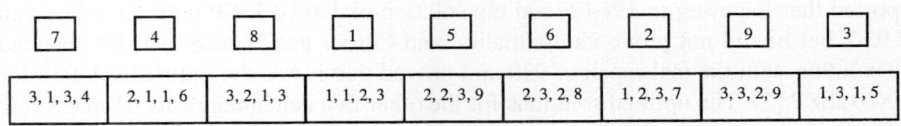

Fig. 5. The feasible schedule after virtual job shop decoding

Fig. 4 shows the flowchart of virtual job shop's decoding procedure. For example, by virtual job shop's decoding, an individual chromosome shown in Fig. 2 is finally decoded to a real schedule shown in Fig. 5. The Gantt chart of this schedule is shown in Fig. 6.

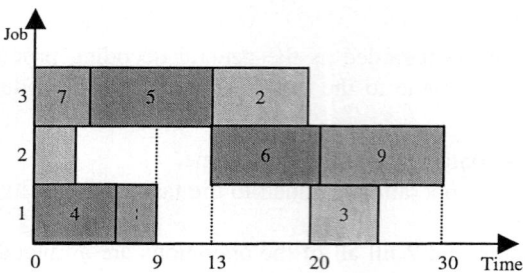

Fig. 6. Gantt chart for the schedule

3.4 Fitness Evaluation

The fitness function for chromosome evaluation is defined as

$$f(x) = \frac{\alpha M}{makespan(x)}, \tag{6}$$

where $\alpha \in (0, 1]$, $M = \dfrac{1}{m}\sum_{l=1}^{p}(T^{-1}(l))_4$, $makespan(x)$ is the completion time for all operations according to the decode strategy. In this work the fitness function has the form as that shown in Eq. (5).

$$f(x) = \frac{\alpha M}{virtualjobshop(x)}, \tag{7}$$

where $VirtualJobShop(x)$ is the makespan generated by virtual job shop decoding strategy.

4 Validation

The JSSP benchmarks constructed in Ref. [6] are the three popular ones, among which the second one (10×10 JSSP) is investigated by many researchers. Jacek et al. reported that Lageweg in 1984 found the solution of 10×10 JSSP with the makespan of 930, but he did not prove its optimality, and Carlier and Pinson in 1989 obtained the solution with the makespan of 930 and proved that it was the optimal solution for 10×10 JSSP [2]. The optimal solutions for the other two benchmarks are 55 and 1165, respectively.

Table 2 gives the GA running parameters in this work and table 3 presents results of five runs for the benchmarks attached in Ref. [6]. Table 3 shows that the benchmark of 6×6 JSSP is relatively easy to be solved and its optimal solution could be found for each run. The benchmark of 10×10 JSSP is most difficult to be solved, whose average relative error is 9.35%. The benchmark of 20×5 JSSP ranks medially between them according to the extent of difficult solution, whose average relative error is 7.30%.

There are n jobs and m machines in an $n \times m$ JSSP. Generally, if the number of operations is not specified explicitly, the jobs need to pass through each machine exact onece in an $n \times m$ JSSP. Hence, the number of operations for an $n \times m$ JSSP is $n \times m \times m$. Thus, the 10×10 benchmark has 1000 operations and 20×5 benchmark has 500 operations. As far as the operation number, it is reasonable that the 10×10 benchmark is more difficult to be solved than 20×5 benchmark. We also test the proposed algorithm with some other parameter sets, such as $P_c = 0.8$, $P_m = 0.003$, $popsize = 150$, $maxgen = 600$ and $P_c = 0.65$, $P_m = 0.005$, $popsize = 200$, $maxgen = 600$. But the results are very similar to those shown in Table 3.

Table 2. GA Running Parameters

p_c	p_m	$popsize$	$maxgen$
0.95	0.015	100	600

Table 3. Computation Results

Time number	Instances 6×6 (55)		
	makespan	Time (s)	Error (%)
1	55	2.13	0
2	55	2.35	0
3	55	2.34	0
4	55	2.47	0
5	55	2.72	0
average	55	2.40	0

Time number	Instances 10×10 (930)		
	makespan	Time (s)	Error (%)
1	1028	102.98	10.54
2	998	92.30	7.31
3	1043	86.53	12.15
4	1017	101.88	9.35
5	998	95	7.31
average	1017	95.74	9.35

Time number	Instances 20×5 (1165)		
	makespan	Time (s)	Error (%)
1	1236	57.54	6.09
2	1265	60.75	8.58
3	1247	49.88	7.04
4	1241	72.59	6.52
5	1263	42.62	8.41
average	1250	56.68	7.30

5 Conclusion and Discussion

To enable the ample existing integer-coding GA for TSP to be applied to solve JSSP, this paper proposes the concepts of operation template and virtual job shop. The operation template is used to decide operation sequences given by the chromosomes and the virtual job shop to calculate the makespans of the operation sequences. The utilization of the operation template and virtual job shop makes the JSSP could be solved easily using the existing integer-coding GA for TSP.

Acknowledgments

The first and third authors are grateful to the support of the science-technology development project of Jilin Province of China under Grant No. 20030520, the doctoral funds of the National Education Ministry of China under Grant No. 20030183060, and the key science-technology project of the National Education Ministry of China under Grant No. 02090.

References

1. Anant Singh Jain, Sheik Meeran. A state-of-the-art review of job-shop scheduling techniques. Department of Applied Physics, Electronic and Mechanical Engineering, University of Dundee, Dundee, Scotland, UK.
2. B. Jacek, D. Wolfgang, P. Erwin. The job shop scheduling problem: conventional and new solution techniques. European journal of operational research 93, 1-33 (1996).
3. R. Cheng, M. Gen, Y. Tsujimura. A Tutorial Survey of Job-Shop Scheduling Problems using Genetic Algorithms-I. Representation, Computers & Industrial Engineering, 30(4), 983-997 (1996).
4. T. Yamada and R. Nakano. Job-shop Scheduling. In: Genetic Algorithm in Engineering Systems, IEE control engineering series 55, 1997.
5. Y.C. Liang, H.W. Ge, C.G. Zhou, H.P. Lee, W.Z. Lin, S.P. Lim, K.H. Lee. Solving traveling salesman problems by genetic algorithms, Progress in Natural Science 13(2), 1-7 (2003).
6. H. Fisher and L. Thompson. "Probabilistic learning combination of local job-shop scheduling rules," Industrial Scheduling, Prentice Hall, Englewood Cliffs, New Jersey, 1963.

Using Evolutionary Learning of Behavior to Find Weaknesses in Operating Systems

Jörg Denzinger and Tim Williams

Department of Computer Science, University of Calgary,
2500 University Drive NW, Calgary, Alberta, T2N 1N4 Canada
{denzinge,timw}@cpsc.ucalgary.ca

Abstract. System security is an ongoing struggle between system designers and the hacking community. Human creativity within this community pushes software into areas never anticipated by the designers, thus revealing weaknesses. Evolutionary algorithms offer designers a new way to examine the viability of their code. Because of the use of randomness as well as direction based on evaluation, these algorithms help to simulate some aspects of the human creative process. In this work we show that already rather simple evolutionary searches allow us to find weaknesses in an operating system, a Linux version, resulting in a crash of the system and the necessity to reboot – a serious system flaw and security risk.

1 Introduction

In a world where more and more things are controlled by computers using more and more complex program systems, unanticipated behavior of these complex systems becomes more and more a problem (see [1]). The need to interact with human beings or other computer systems brings with it the danger of having to react to unforeseen situations, where the system behavior then becomes unpredictable, unreliable and potentially harmful (see [9]). System crashes due to "hostile" user behavior and viruses are examples of harmful interactions, where human beings use observations of a system, intuitive thinking and some basic knowledge about the system and its environment to wreak havoc around the world (see [2], [3], [10], [12] and for a more defensive approach [5]).

Naturally, testing and verification are intended to prevent coming into harmful situations within a system. But, in addition to never having enough resources, state-of-the-art testing methods do not really address the issue of unforeseen behavior of users or other systems, simply because they are unforeseen. The standard tests trying to cover the possible paths through program structures (see [11]) do not help a lot for programs that allow for input at every time and they do nothing about other systems, like the operating system or compilers, that the tested system relies on. Formal verification methods suffer from the same problems and additionally cannot cope with larger systems. Scenario based testing focuses on testing system behavior in its full context, but it requires someone envisioning the scenarios and then tests if the system reactions are adequate. It is not able to *find* scenarios that lead to unwanted behavior. In fact, in todays testing often there is nearly no focus on unwanted things, i.e. on trying to test for negative conditions.

If we look at how human users abuse systems by bringing them into unforeseen situations and taking advantage of the then "confused" system, then we can observe that a lot of human abilities come into play that are at the core of AI research: appropriate use of knowledge, learning from observations, dealing with not always predictable environments, and the use of intuition to suggest behavior. Consequently, AI techniques should play a key role in testing complex systems, but, so far, this is not the case.

In this paper, we present an on-line learning system, based on evolutionary techniques, that is used to test the Linux operating system (version 2.2.10) for user behavior that can crash the system. The basic idea of our EvoAttack system is to evolve sequences of operating system calls that are evaluated with regard to a given fitness function and that "breed" new sequences that hopefully achieve higher fitness levels. The best sequences are retained and re-evaluated in every generation of sequences. The computer system on which the sequences are evaluated is put under more and more "pressure" (relative to the fitness measure) until a sequence is produced that gets the target system to show a certain effect as the result of the cumulative efforts of all sequences it was exposed to.

The effect that our EvoAttack system wants to produce is a crash of the targeted system. Despite the fact that operating systems are very susceptible to timing issues and have a lot of safeguards to prevent user-level processes from harming the system kernel, EvoAttack was able to generate sequences of system call sequences that brought the target system into a state requiring a reboot in 70 percent of the "attack" attempts. And one of the fitness functions that were able to achieve this just measured the execution time of the system call sequences, a measure that can be easily obtained by outside observation.

2 Some Linux Essentials

The current three leading commercial operating systems all follow very different design philosophies which affect not only how they are written but how they function and how they are tested. The operating systems in question are:

- Linux: a monolithic kernel with loadable modules
- Microsoft Windows 2000: an object oriented kernel
- Apples OS-X which is a micro-kernel based on the Mach kernel

Each of these designs have large followings and different strengths and weaknesses. The kernel used for testing was a version of Linux (2.2.10), a reliable and well documented operating systems kernel. It is monolithic in nature, which means that the majority of the operating system resides as a single large block of code. This code is comprised of several major subsections, such as memory management, scheduling and resource management, which are eventually linked together to form the core or kernel of the operating system. Kernel developers

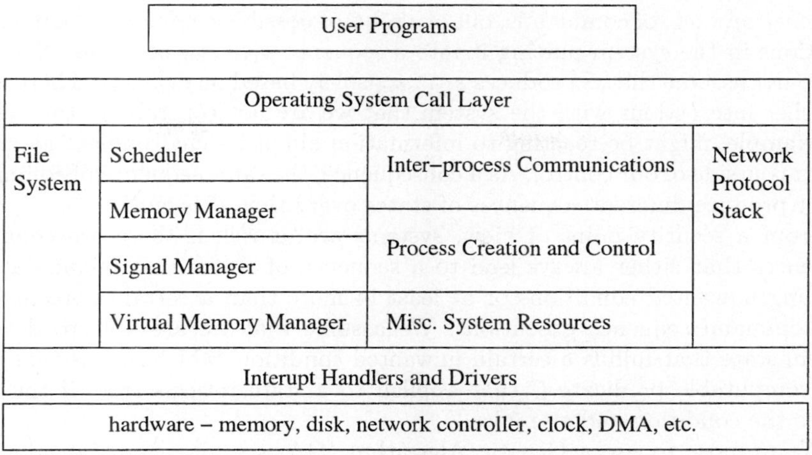

Using Evolutionary Learning of Behavior   383

```
                      ┌─────────────────────────────┐
                      │        User Programs        │
                      └─────────────────────────────┘
┌──────────────────────────────────────────────────────────────────┐
│                    Operating System Call Layer                   │
├────────────┬──────────────────────┬──────────────────┬───────────┤
│  File      │  Scheduler           │  Inter-process   │  Network  │
│  System    ├──────────────────────┤  Communications  │  Protocol │
│            │  Memory Manager      ├──────────────────┤  Stack    │
│            ├──────────────────────┤  Process Creation│           │
│            │  Signal Manager      │  and Control     │           │
│            ├──────────────────────┼──────────────────┤           │
│            │ Virtual Memory Mgr.  │ Misc. System     │           │
│            │                      │ Resources        │           │
├────────────┴──────────────────────┴──────────────────┴───────────┤
│                  Interupt Handlers and Drivers                   │
├──────────────────────────────────────────────────────────────────┤
│     hardware – memory, disk, network controller, clock, DMA, etc.│
└──────────────────────────────────────────────────────────────────┘
```

Fig. 1. Basic Block Diagram of Linux Kernel.

Leffler, McKusick, Karels and Quarterman ([8]) in their work on the design of a version of UNIX called 4.3BSD, describe the functions supplied by their UNIX kernel. "The UNIX kernel provides four basic facilities: processes, a filesystem, communications, and system startup." The Linux kernel provides the same basic functionality. Figure 1 shows a very basic block diagram of this kernel.

There are really only two ways of accessing the kernel. The first method uses software interrupts and is known as the system call layer, this is the method accessible to common user programs. The second method uses hardware interrupts and allows access via the kernels driver level code. By only allowing access to the kernel through these two tightly controlled mechanisms a large number of potential security flaws are avoided. It is the software interrupt mechanism, typically called the operating systems call interface, that provides the starting point for many system attacks. Our research makes use of standard, legal system calls and therefore accesses the kernel, from user space, via software interrupts. Our method is equally applicable to other kernel access vectors such as the packets delivered via the Ethernet controller, thus opening the way to the testing of both protocol stack and web applications.

3 Evolutionary On-Line Learning for Threat Testing

The goal of threat based testing of a system is not to verify correct functionality, the assumption is that current "positive" test methods are sufficient for this level of testing. The threat testing methodology we propose here focuses on the idea of generating an interaction sequence with the system under test that puts this system into a state that fulfills some conditions(s) that are unwanted and/or intended to be normally unattainable, thus constituting a *threat* to the system.

To explain the general method, we assume that the system $\mathcal{S}$ to be tested accepts some interactions with the outside world that can be described as a sequence $c_1,...,c_m$ of commands, out of a set $\mathcal{C}$ of possible commands, that achieve reactions in the system putting it into a sequence $s_1,...,s_m$ of states. Note that we do not assume that $\mathcal{S}$ produces $s_1,...,s_m$ solely based on $c_1,...,c_m$. There might be other interactions with the system that we are not controlling; the system, for example, might be reacting to information about its environment gained by sensors outside of our control. As a consequence, the same sequence of commands might produce different sequences of states every time it is run.

From a security point of view, systems are at risk if there are command sequences that either always lead to a sequence of states that include a state fulfilling unwanted conditions or at least in more than a certain percentage of the command sequence executions. We assume that we are able to detect a system state that fulfills a certain unwanted condition, which means that there is a computable predicate $\mathcal{G}$ that applied to a state returns true, if the state fulfills the condition and else false.

We propose to use a Genetic Algorithm (GA, see [6] for an introduction) to produce command sequences that lead to states fulfilling $\mathcal{G}$. A GA works on a set of so-called individuals. Each individual is evaluated according to a so-called fitness function f_{fit} and new individuals are created by combining old individuals, selected based on their fitness but also including some random component, using so-called Genetic Operators. After a certain number of new individuals are generated, the same number of old indidviduals, usually the ones with the lowest fitness, are deleted to make room for the new individuals. The remaining old individuals together with the new ones constitute the new starting point for the next generation cycle.

This basic algorithm is well known and has many variants dealing with how the mixture of fitness value and randomness in the selection is achieved and what Genetic Operators are defined, for example. The key components to connect the general algorithm to the application for which it is used are how an individual is defined and how its f_{fit}-value is computed. Naturally, the structure of an individual also influences what can be used as a Genetic Operator.

From the point of view of threat testing of a system $\mathcal{S}$, the obvious candidate for individuals are command sequences. The fitness value of an individual should indicate first, whether the sequence led to a state fulfilling $\mathcal{G}$ and if not, it should at least indicate how near the sequence came to such a state. Since we assume that $\mathcal{S}$ is not only dependent on the command sequence constituting an individual, the fitness should not be based on one evaluation by feeding the sequence to $\mathcal{S}$, but it should combine several such evaluation runs.

But for complex systems that, due to other influences on them, are rather unpredictable or even indeterministic, this approach to testing it with regard to $\mathcal{G}$ is too simple, resp. the search spaces the GA faces are too big and too volatile to be conquered by the testing GA. While the basic approach described above can also be seen as an off-line learning approach, we suggest to modify it to achieve an on-line learning threat testing system.

We still want to use sequences of commands as individuals, but we use sequences of a fixed length k and k is not very large. We also still propose to evaluate the individuals by sending them as command sequence to $\mathcal{S}$ and the fitness measure is still how near executing the sequence came to achieve $\mathcal{G}$. But this fitness measure is not solely based on the sequence that was just executed, it is based on all sequences that were evaluated before as well as on all other outside influences that occured since the system $\mathcal{S}$ was in use. So, the whole unpredicatability of the system $\mathcal{S}$ is not seen as a liability anymore, we use it to our advantage. This means that the fitness of an individual depends on when we do the evaluation and therefore we repeat the evaluation of all individuals in a generation every time we start the repetition of the basic loop of the GA. Thus individuals that seem to bring the system nearer to a state fulfilling $\mathcal{G}$ at one point in time either add to the pressure towards $\mathcal{G}$ or they will be discarded later. Hence we have an *on-line learning* system.

The fitness function depends a lot on the tested system $\mathcal{S}$ and the condition $\mathcal{G}$. But the possible Genetic Operators can be easily defined in general. If we have two command sequences $c_1,...,c_k$ and $c'_1,...,c'_k$, then Crossover randomly selects an i with $1 \leq i \leq k$ and the resulting sequence is $c_1,...,c_i,c'_{i+1},...,c'_k$. To perform a Mutation on $c_1,...,c_k$, we again select a random i and a command $c \in \mathcal{C}$ with $c \neq c_i$ and the new individual is $c_1,...,c_{i-1},c,c_{i+1},...c_k$.

While this concept of threat testing was inspired by works on learning behavior for agents, like [4], this kind of usage of these methods is new. [11] suggested the usage of evolutionary methods to develop tests covering the branches in programs controlling embedded systems. But these systems do not exhibit at all the level of undeterministic behavior we are dealing with and they are far away from the complexity of the systems we are targeting. Also, knowledge about the program structure is necessary for Wegener's approach to work, whereas our method does not depend on the program structure at all. [7] also uses evolutionary methods to evolve new tests for a controller, but out of a set of known faults of this controller. Obviously, this is mainly a recombination effort, not the construction of a new threat, as in our approach.

4   Crashing Linux

Our testing methodology focuses on the idea of generating, within the operating system, a variety of states that are unwanted and intended to be normally unattainable. In this case the goal was to drive the operating system into an unusable state. A typical experimental run ranged in duration from 2 to 3.5 days which limited the actual number of runs included in our evaluation. From a security point of view, the results are, however, significant (over 70 percent success rate), since essentially already one successful run could cause a lot of damage.

We used a fully instrumented Linux (version 2.2.10) kernel for these experiments. This version of the kernel, although older, is stable, familar and well documented. There are a few documented flaws of this kernel version, which was one of our reasons for choosing it, since initially we wanted to target these flaws with our EvoAttack system. Naturally, after the initial experiments that found

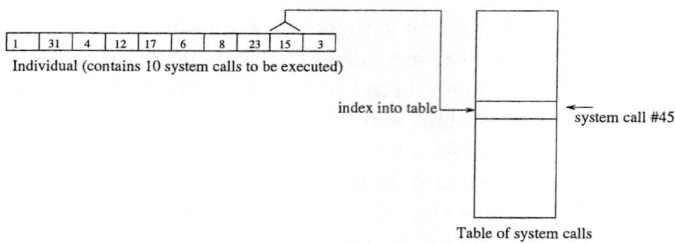

Fig. 2. Example of gene to actual call mapping.

different, unknown problems, we concentrated on evaluating these new problems. A second reason was that revealing new flaws would not compromise the currently deployed systems. Most routines were compiled with the gcc instrumenting option and a trace routine was provided to log when a kernel routine was entered or exited. A custom driver was written to allow access to the kernel trace buffer created via the instrumentation routines. The behaviour which can be monitored easily consists of kernel execution times and internal kernel execution paths. The entrance and exit times of each kernel routine are monitored and the execution of each system call is traced. System memory usage was not monitored due to the already large size of the test data structures. The data captured allows for the analysis of many values such as:

- total call time
- time spent in certain kernel areas or routines
- internal execution path, entry into error processing routines
- variations in time or path execution from a statistical normal

An individual, within the EvoAttack system, is comprised of a sequence of valid operating system calls. Not all of the kernels system calls were part of the acceptable list since some calls, such as kill, would cause an early termination of the individual. Therefore each element of the call sequence is an index into an array of possible system calls and not the actual call number as pushed onto the stack and seen by the kernel (see Figure 2). Most of the operating system calls require parameter values. While we think that these can also be evolved, for our experiments we used fixed values for each call. The selected values are legitimate values for the particular call and do not cause any known harm.

The implementation of our test system involved the use of two separate computers. The target system, which ran the actual individuals and performed the kernel tracing, communicated with a host system via the parallel link. The host system implemented the GA and calculated the fitness functions. The isolation of the target was required to minimize the execution of system calls that were not directly related to the tested individuals. The communications link was controlled by direct access to the parallel port and not by the execution of any related system calls. The kernel trace buffer was accessed from user space via a custom driver written for this purpose. It should be noted that the target system's performance is significantly less than that of the host. This was done for two reasons: cost and timing. The first reason is self explanatory but the rational for timing needs to be examined. Some of the interrupts generated by a system are not directly influenced by the speed of the processor. For example, the system clock generates ticks at the same rate regardless of the processor clock rate. This means that the ratio of interrupts serviced vs kernel code executed will be much higher on lower speed systems. This allows less chance for the kernel to recover from interrupt related problems.

The host randomly creates the initial generation of individuals. An individual is sent to the target via the parallel link. Execution of each individual is done by creating a user level task, starting the trace, executing the individual's call sequence, terminating the trace and then allowing the task to terminate. The trace is then transmitted to the host for analysis.

In order to implement threat testing, we needed a fitness function. Since the actual target state or error is not known before testing, the initial search space is large. To help with the exploitation of the search space, certain kernel stress conditions, such as increased activity and/or execution time within the kernel are used as fitness functions. EvoAttack was quite successful using only these two, rather primitive, fitness functions. The first, $f_{fit,time}$, was a measure of the time spent in execution for each individual (a function which does not require kernel tracing to measure). The second fitness function, $f_{fit,call}$, was a measure of the number of kernel routines used by an individual during execution. This function made heavy use of the kernel trace facilities that we had provided. In keeping with our need to isolate the target system both functions were calculated by the host based on the trace information provided by the target.

The initial population were 100 random individuals (produced using 32 different system calls). Each individual contains a sequence of 10 system calls. Our GA then used a simple elitist selection method for the selection of parents and the creation of the next generation. All of the individuals of the generation are ranked, based on their fitness value. The lowest 12 percent of the population are removed and the top 24 percent of the population is allowed to breed. New individuals are created via the usual random point crossover. All of the resulting population is then considered for exposure (based on a programmable mutation rate) to a single point mutation operator. This is realized by either incrementing or decrementing the value representing the call. The choice of increment of decrement is random.

Each individual in the new generation is executed and a new fitness value calculated. Note that this value is dependent on previously evaluated individuals! It is useful to think of a kernel as a state machine whose operation is affected, not only by inputs and previous states, but also by time. Events, both random and periodic (typically hardware interrupts), cause the system to jump into specific interrupt service routines. These routines access and modify kernel data structures. When a data structure is modified by the interrupt handler, it could occur at a time when another section of the kernel had partly completed a modification to the same data structure. This sort of race condition is commonly faced by most shared memory systems. The kernel uses flags and interrupt masks to min-

Table 1. Evaluation results with different fitness functions.

Fitness function	Runs	Mut. Rate	Success Rate	Observed Error Types
$f_{fit,time}$	8	75%	57.1%	1,2,3
$f_{fit,time}$	5	65%	60.0%	1,2,3
$f_{fit,time}$	7	40%	71.4%	1,2,3
$f_{fit,call}$	10	65%	70.0%	2,3

imize the possiblity of data corruption. The main problem with this situation, as it pertains to testing, is that an interrupt can change the operating systems internal state and therefore the execution path taken by the kernel's code. For example, if an interrupt affects a flag, which is then tested and acted on by the kernel, the outcome will be different if the flag is tested before or after the interrupt changes it. A microsecond's difference in interrupt arrival time between two test runs can cause significantly different operating systems states.

5 Experimental Evaluation

For our experiments, we tested a machine that was only running the individuals for evaluation; no other user processes were active on the target. So, problems due to the interaction of several user processes are outside of the scope of our experiments. As mentioned earlier, it was anticipated that the final fitness functions would be very complex, however the two most primitive functions proved to be more than enough to provide our proof-of-concept.

Using the total execution time of the individual as the first fitness function $f_{fit,time}$ proved to be successful (see Table 1). The crash rate was dependent on the mutation rate ranging from 40 to 75 percent. As was expected, the runs with somewhat lower mutation rates yielded better results, due to a greater exploitation of the results of individuals and less exploration of new sequences. The error conditions experienced by the test system consisted of three types:

1. the inability for root (or any user) to log into the system. Although the login prompt accepted input, the password prompt would never appear.
2. the inability to execute most programs. The system would generate a segmentation fault (usually indicative of a memory/pointer problem) upon the attempted execution of most commands. The system memory utilization did not appear to rise and fall substantially and no swap memory was in use.
3. the target program would stop communications, this error was always observed in conjunction with one of the other error conditions.

All of these faults could be related to issues within the memory management subsystem of the kernel.

The second fitness function $f_{fit,call}$ was simply the total number of calls to kernel routines during the execution of the individual. As a fitness function, this yielded even better results than the use of execution times (see Table 1), perhaps due to the increased error recovery and cleanup which can be complex,

Table 2. Subsequences for $f_{fit,call}$ shortly before a crash.

Subsequence	In top 24 Individuals	In all Individuals
29,13,13,25,31,29,1	57.9%	19.8%
29,13,13,25,31,29	57.9%	20.9%
29,13,13,25,31	57.9%	21.5%
29,13,13,25	68.4%	26.9%
29,13,13	68.4%	27.2%
29,13	78.9%	32.3%

but potentially fast, activities. All errors were of the second and third type described above (segmentation fault and communications error).

Using the second fitness function, distinct subsequences were observed by the end of the test. The top 24 individuals (after ranking) are the ones used in the creation of new individuals so it is their sequences which will be reinforced in the new generation. Table 2 presents an analysis of the subsequences of system calls observed in the last generation of a successful test where the target system crashed during the execution of the 20th individual in generation 590. We observed rather long subsequences – which would be called building blocks in evolutionary computation. For example, more than 50 percent of the top 24 percent individuals included the subsequence 29,13,13,25,31,29,1 that was also in nearly 20 percent of all individuals generated in this run. Among the longest sequences occuring in more than one individual was 29,13,13,25,31,29,1,27,16, which maps to the following C system calls:

```
29: pipe(Tpfd);                              29: pipe(Tpfd);
13: stat (Tname,(struct stat *)Tbuf);         1: read(Tfd, Tbuf, Tcnt);
13: stat (Tname,(struct stat *)Tbuf);        27: rmdir ("testdir");
25: rename (Tnewname,"testname3");           16: setuid (Myuid);
31: setgid(Mygid);
```

This represents a sequence of system calls which is very unusual and not likely to occur in normal user programs.

All in all, our experiments show that our method of threat testing can reveal weaknesses in operating systems. Since operating systems are among the very complex systems and very difficult to test with regard to unwanted behavior, we see our EvoAttack system as proof that using AI can improve testing, and as a consequence system security and reliability, a lot. Threat based testing can be a very valuable addition to the testers' arsenal of tools, since it covers areas not examined well by other mechanisms. Threat testing should not be used alone since there is naturally no guarantee that 10 runs without a crash mean that a system has no problems.

6 Conclusion and Future Work

We presented an AI-based method for testing complex systems with regard to the possibility that interactions with the system can threaten it, resulting in unwanted or even dangerous behavior. In our proof of concept, our threat testing of a stable version of the Linux operating system revealed the possibility to crash the system from a normal user account. This was achieved with either of two rather primitive fitness functions that guided the evolutionary on-line learning that is the core of our method. One of these functions only measured the execution time of the interaction commands, a measure that can be easily taken without any additional specialized access to the system. The reveiled problem has to be considered a serious flaw of the tested system that was only revealed by our threat testing method.

As stated above, so far we consider our research into this topic only as a proof of concept. There are many possible improvement and additional goals that have to be addressed in the future. In addition to applying the general method of threat testing to additional applications (starting with more current versions of Linux, different operating systems, and other kinds of complex program systems, like web servers or data base systems), we expect the development of fitness functions measuring different kinds of threats an important area. We did not expect that the simple fitness functions we tried first, to get a feeling of what happens, would already be successful. With the use of threat testing by system developers, many systems should not be susceptible to such rather simple threats in the future. But there will be more intelligent threats and consequently the fitness functions will have to incorporate more knowledge to test for such threats.

References

1. J. Branke. Evolutionary Optimization in Dynamic Environments, Kluwer, 2002.
2. D. Boneh and D. Brumley. Remote timing attacks are practical, Proceedings of the 12th Usenix Security Symposium, 2003, pp. 1-14.
3. D.E. Denning. Information Warfare and Security, Addison-Wesley, 1999.
4. J. Denzinger and M. Kordt. Evolutionary On-line Learning of Cooperative Behavior with Situation-Action-Pairs, Proc. ICMAS-2000, IEEE, 2000, pp. 103–110.
5. S. Hofmeyr and S. Forrest. Architecture for an artificial immune system, Evolutionary Computation Journal, 8(4), 2000, pp. 443–473.
6. D.E. Goldberg. The Design of Innovation: Lessons from and for Competent Genetic Algorithms, Kluwer, 2002.
7. A.C. Schultz, J.J. Grefenstette and K.A. De Jong. Adaptive Testing of Controllers for Autonomous Vehicles, Proc. Symposium on Autonomous Underwater Vehicle Technology, IEEE, 1992, pp. 158–164.
8. S.J. Leffler, M.K. McKusick, M.J. Karels, and J.S. Quarterman. The Design and Implementation of the 4.3BSD UNIX Operating System, Addison-Wesley, 1989.
9. G. Thaller. Software Engineering for Real-time and Embedded Systems, BHV-Verlag, 1997.
10. United States Army. Army Field Manual- F100-6: Information Operations, 1996.
11. J. Wegener. Evolutionary testing of embedded systems, In *Evolutionary Algorithms for Embedded Systems Design*, Kluwer, 2003, pp. 1–34.
12. The WildList Organization International. PC viruses in-the-wild - real-time, http://www.wildlist.org/WildList/Real-Time.htm, as seen Oct 2003.

Creative 3D Designs Using Interactive Genetic Algorithm with Structured Directed Graph*

Hyeun-Jeong Min and Sung-Bae Cho

Dept. of Computer Science, Yonsei University
134 Shinchon-dong, Sudaemoon-ku, Seoul 120-749, Korea
{solusea,sbcho}@cs.yonsei.ac.kr

Abstract. We propose a methodology for representing artificial creatures like 3D flowers. Directed graph and Lindenmayer system (L-system) are commonly involved in AI-based creativity research for encoding creatures. It is difficult for L-systems to directly feed back real morphologies structurally from their genotypes, since they are a grammatical rewriting system and also use parameters such as loops, procedure calls, variables, and primitive parameters for representing their genotypes. In this paper flower genotypes are manifested by a knowledge-based structured directed graph (SDG) and phenotypes are represented a flower morphology resulting from the derivation and graphical representation of the genotypes. Evolution is simulated using an interactive genetic algorithm (IGA), where a SDG is useful for genotypic representation of creatures and IGA uses human evaluation for the fitness function. We have applied the creation of 3D flowers using the knowledge-based SDG and IGA. Experimental results show that realistic flower morphologies can be created by the proposed method.

1 Introduction

Art, music, and designs have been emerging from computers for many years in artificial life (A-life), which is the study of life and life-like processes having autonomy, adaptation, self-replication and self-repairing [1, 2]. It can automatically create satisfactory artificial characters having actions or morphologies and also generate new population. Besides a binary encoding, directed graph (DG) or Lindenmayer system (L-system) is used to represent genotypes for creating individuals using evolutionary algorithm. This paper provides a glimpse of the creativity in specific domains when DG is used in combination with interactive genetic algorithm (IGA) techniques. We specifically focus on artificial flowers, demonstrating how realistic-looking creatures reflecting human's preference can be modeled with genetically generated DG.

In DG proposed by K. Sims for creating 3D creatures [3], each of creatures is represented by composition of nodes and edges. It is convenient to define a morphological structure of individuals more quickly and easily and users can intuitively figure

---

* This work was supported by Korea Science and Engineering Foundation (KOSEF) through the Biometrics Engineering Research Center (BERC) at Yonsei University.

out the real morphology of a genotype represented by DG. K. Sims generated various creatures and locomotion in his previous researches such as swimming, walking, jumping, and following actions of creatures having various morphologies. It takes however a long time for generating these creatures in his method because there are many cases for their genotypes.

The approach is based on the use of an IGA and a knowledge-based SDG that generates a simplification of flower morphology similar to real flowers in nature. The fitness functions must provide an evaluation score for every solution. For creative products in computers especially like design and art, a common problem in applying evolutionary computation techniques to artistic domains is the difficulty of deriving formal fitness functions to evaluate the individuals [4]. IGA is a technique which involves developing the automatic design methods for the systems that are based on user's preference and subjective evaluation. We apply the knowledge-based genotypic representation and the evaluation of phenotypes by IGA that is useful in generating natural morphology rapidly since it has no evaluation function and is evaluated by human beings, and we have to deal with few individuals in limited generations.

Here we consider a kind of SDG as genotypic representations and evolve translated phenotypes by interactive genetic algorithm (IGA) for automatically creating natural artificial flowers. The next section explains the related works of automatically generating creatures using evolutionary algorithm and genotypic representation by SDG, and section 3 describes how structured directed graph and IGA proposed in this paper can be used. Finally sections 4 and 5 provide results, discussion, and suggestions for the future work

2 Related Works

L-systems were originally introduced to model the development of simple multicellular organisms in terms of division, growth, and death of individual cells [5, 6]. Ochoa generated artificial 2D plant morphologies by mathematical formalism known as L-systems [7]. The applications of L-systems have subsequently been extended to plants and complex branching structures. The parametric L-systems, which are a particularly convenient programming tool for expressing growing models of plants having symmetric structure and have rewriting processes for reuse of rules and parameters for various morphologies. G. Hornby used L-systems for encoding in evolutionary algorithm to create virtual creatures having hundreds of parts, and presented co-evolving morphology and controller by using oscillator circuits controlling each actuated joint of creature [8]. Moreover, he defined generative representations which identified by their ability to reuse elements of the genotype and compared it against direct representation [9].

DG representation to specify the construction of creatures by K. Sims used nodes for body segments, which are composed of another nested graph for the body segment's neural controller for behaviors such as walking, swimming, jumping and following [10]. DGs were presented as an appropriate basis for a grammar that could be used to describe both the morphology and nervous systems of virtual creatures like L-system. New features and functions that are appropriate for the environment can be generated or existing ones can be removed so that the levels of complexity can also evolve. Moreover he generated virtual creatures that competed in a physically simulated three-dimensional world and had various morphologies by these DGs and nested graphs for their genotype [11]. B. Lintermann and O. Deussen presented a modeling method that allowed easy generation of many branching plants including flowers, bushes, and trees [12]. They defined a set of components describing structural and geometrical elements of plants and users could get immediate feedback on what they had created. K. Sims generated various creatures and their locomotion using DG. On the other hand, we could generate creatures fast by a simplification of representations and structures of real objects.

The GOLEM created by H. Lipson consisted of bars and actuators for structures and artificial neurons for behavior control [13]. J. Ventrella presented an animation system developed for the exploration of emergent morphology and behaviors using genetic algorithm for evolving populations composed of improved and realistic behaviors [14]. His creatures were encoded as fixed-length vectors of parameters for constructing a creature. Various morphologies were described in Framsticks simulator for modeling, simulating and optimizing virtual agents, with three-dimensional bodies and embedded control system [15]. J. Bongard and R. Pfeifer generated growing creatures under a simulated genetic process by defining gene expression rules that determine the division of body segments [16]. H. Kawamura and H. Ohmori proposed stable frame structures using genetic algorithm [17].

We can represent the genotype of creatures using L-system and DG respectively. It is difficult to grasp an entire structure of morphology and users also get no direct feedback from the generated rules because L-system uses parameters and rewriting rules [12]. The L-system is suitable for generating growing models, that is, the growth processes of plants can be captured as well, and it can also generate artificial creatures of symmetric structure. On the other hand, in the knowledge-based SDG, users can directly remind phenotypes because of structurally defined genotypes in DG. In this paper, we utilize SDG for easily representing global aspects of creatures. For this purpose we can generate natural morphology within the real world even though evolution is iterated. Additionally, we have applied IGA using user's emotional evaluation for automatically generating a simplification of real flowers in nature. In this paper, we take a chrysanthemum as an example.

3 Creating 3D Artificial Flowers

From the modeling point of view, the global characteristics of plants have to be directly dealt with. We use an evolutionary algorithm for automatically creating populations. We have to distinctly define the criteria of fitness evaluation for using an evolutionary algorithm, but it is difficult to apply the conventional evolutionary algorithm since humans' emotional evaluation is required for creating a more natural morphology of flowers. Therefore, in this paper we present the domain-specific SDG as the genotypic representation of real morphology and IGA for an automatic creation of natural flower morphology.

3.1 Structured Directed Graph

In DG, individuals are encoded with nodes and edges. Each node in the DG contains information describing rigid objects such as dimension and color of each part, and each edge also contains the information of positions and orientations for connecting edges to each part. Figure 1 shows that the structure of a real flower [18] and the corresponding genotypic representation with DG.

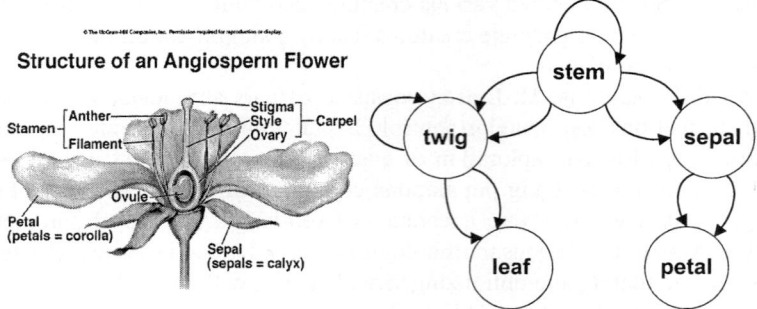

Fig. 1. Real flower morphology and the corresponding representation of genotype.

Directed graph $DG=(V, E)$ has a set of vertices and a set of edges between the vertices. Vertex and edge in directed graph described in Figure 1 are defined as follows.

$V(DG) = \{v_{stem}, v_{twig}, v_{sepal}, v_{petal}, v_{leaf}\}$
$E(DG) = \{<v_{stem}, v_{stem}>, <v_{stem}, v_{twig}>, <v_{stem}, v_{sepal}>, <v_{twig}, v_{twig}>, <v_{twig}, v_{leaf}>,$
$<v_{sepal}, v_{petal}>\}$

We can represent adjacency matrix of DG with 5×5 matrix because $DG=(V, E)$ and $|V| = 5$, and each element of this matrix is defined as follows.

$$a_{ij} = \begin{cases} n, & \text{if } (v_i, v_j) \in E(DG) \text{ and } i \neq j \\ n/r, & \text{if } (v_i, v_j) \in E(DG) \text{ and } i = j \\ 0, & \text{otherwise} \end{cases}$$

where n and r represent the number of edges and recursion count, respectively.

We have to define parameters in nodes and edges of DG for the detailed morphology. In an evolutionary process, parameter values of each node and edge are initially chosen randomly, but they can be automatically generated through operations. Defining this SDG with genotypic representation of an individual, we can easily define the whole structure of an individual and get direct feedback to a representation of real morphology. Figure 2 shows the two-dimensional matrix representing the relation of each node and edge in the DG and an example of a flower morphology created. In the table n is the number of edges and r is the recursion count of rigid parts. In this matrix (v_i, v_j) denotes the ith column and jth row and each node has n edges and r parts for recursive connection of the same node. Also (v_i, v_j) has n connections with different edges and nodes. For instance, if a stem node has 5 edges with twig node, a stem part can connect 5 twig parts.

Node	stem	twig	sepal	petal	leaf
stem	n/r	n	n	0	n
twig	0	n/r	n	0	n
sepal	0	0	0	n	0
petal	0	0	0	0	0
leaf	0	0	0	0	0

Fig. 2. The relation of edges and nodes in a genotype and the phenotype.

For representing the genotype with DG, each node is defined from the components of a real flower, and has parameters such as color, shape, and dimension of each component. Moreover, each edge has connection parameters such as position, orientation, and joint type for connection of nodes. Table 1 shows the parameters and values of a genotype within this DG. The range of colors represents the kind of colors in each part such as green, dark green, yellow, etc, and the shape represents the shape of rigid objects for its phenotype.

Table 1. Genotypic representation using directed graph.

DG	Component	stem	twig	petal	sepal	leaf
Node	Color	0~3	0~2	0~12	0~5	0~5
	Dimension	0~8	0~8	0~12	0~3	0~12
	Shape	Cylinder	Cylinder	Ellipsoid	Ellipsoid	Ellipsoid
Edge	Position	(x, y, z)	(x, y, z)	(x, y, z)	(x, y, z)	(x, y, z)
	Orientation	angle	angle	angle	angle	angle
	Joint type	fixed	fixed	fixed	fixed	fixed

3.2 Interactive Genetic Algorithm

GA proposed by John Holland in early 1970s applies some of natural evolution mechanisms such as crossover, mutation, and selection of the fittest to optimization and machine learning. GA is a very efficient search method, and has been applied to many problems concerning optimization and classification [19]. In IGA that is the similar method with GA except fitness evaluation part, a user evaluates the fitness to each individual in a population. IGA can interact with user and can stir up user's emotions or preferences in the course of evolution [20]. Therefore, the IGA is suitable for solving problems that cannot be easily solved by GA, like the generation of natural flower morphology in this paper.

The knowledge-based SDG is encoded by the information of their parts and nodes. The parts consist of dimensions, colors, shapes, and counts about each part of a flower, and the nodes consist of positions and orientations for connection and counts. The criterion used for the selection of individuals, who pass their genetic information from one generation to the next, is rank-based selection which is used to avoid undesirable convergence effects. Selection is not determined by the actual fitness value but by an individual's position within a fitness rank scale.

node	stem	twig	sepal	petal	leaf		node	stem	twig	sepal	petal	leaf
stem	3	2	1	0	2		stem	2	2	1	0	0
twig	0	2	1	0	4	×	twig	0	2	1	0	2
sepal	0	0	0	10	0		sepal	0	0	0	12	0
petal	0	0	0	0	0		petal	0	0	0	0	0
leaf	0	0	0	0	0		leaf	0	0	0	0	0

⇩

node	stem	twig	sepal	petal	leaf		node	stem	twig	sepal	petal	leaf
stem	2	2	1	0	2		stem	3	2	1	0	0
twig	0	2	1	0	2		twig	0	2	1	0	2
sepal	0	0	0	10	0		sepal	0	0	0	12	0
petal	0	0	0	0	0		petal	0	0	0	0	0
leaf	0	0	0	0	0		leaf	0	0	0	0	0

Fig. 3. An example of crossover operation in IGA.

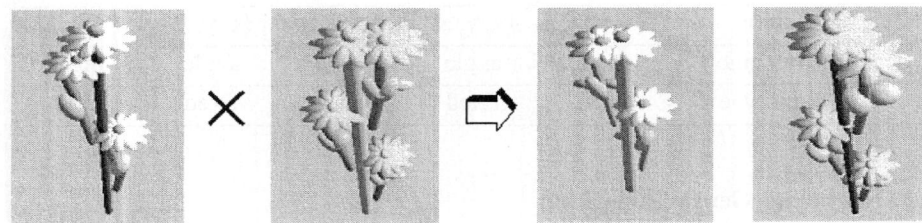

Fig. 4. An example of phenotypic representations with crossover in Figure 3.

Each individual in a population evolves to get higher fitness as it goes from generation to generation. A crossover operation exchanges edges and parameters in randomly selected parts between two individuals, and a mutation operation modifies the parameters in edges and nodes for the selected individual. We define the nodes in genotypic representation for IGA operations as the structures of a real flower such as stem, twig, sepal, petal, and leaf. We can create various phenotypes from the primitive structure of a flower by changing the values of the parameters in edges and nodes. For example, if the (stem, twig) and (sepal, petal, leaf) of nodes cross each other, the parameters in nodes and edges of 2 individuals selected to cross over each other. The relations of nodes and edges in DG are represented by 5×5 matrix, and an example of IGA is shown in Figure 3 and Figure 4 using this matrix.

4 Experimental Results

In this section we describe the experimental set-up to generate flower morphologies by the proposed method. First of all, we define the genotype of the flower structure by DG. Secondly, we represent each individual acquired by changing parameters in edges and nodes of each part, and evaluate each individual from IGA up to the last generation. We use an API program named 3D MathEngine that is now used in commercial to represent morphology and locomotion of individuals [21]. Using this program, we can represent and define a position and orientation of 3D rigid parts for generating individuals. We simplify the components of phenotypes and use rigid objects given by MathEngine such as a cube, cylinder, ellipsoid, and corn for shapes of each part.

We have developed the interface of the prototype system, and in IGA we have defined 6 individuals, 10 generations, and 5 levels of fitness evaluation. Nodes in DG are divided into 5 parts which are the stem, twig, leaf, sepal, and petal, and each node is connected to the edges of corresponding node by randomly generated parameters.

In this experiment, the conditions of IGA are given as follows.

- The number of individuals in a population is 6,
- The maximum number of generations is 10,
- The selection rate is 0.8,
- The crossover rate is 0.8,
- The mutation rate is 0.05,
- The fitness value is between 1 and 5 (the worst is 1), and
- IGA evaluation by 13 subjects.

Since IGA differs from the conventional GA due to humans' subjective evaluation, it is difficult to show the usefulness of IGA. We have carried out a convergence test and a schema analysis to evaluate the performance of this method.

4.1 Convergence Test

Convergence test uses the variation of mean values of fitness evaluations by subjects. To show the convergence of the method as an experimental result, we have requested 13 subjects to find natural flower morphology using the proposed method. Figure 5 shows the variations of fitness on average and the best, while subjects search for a more natural morphology. In this figure, the x-axis is the number of generations and the y-axis relates to the fitness values from 1 to 5. By the iteration of generations in IGA, we can observe that a more natural flower is generated.

4.2 Analysis of Schemas

This method analyzes the frequency of genes of individuals in populations at each generation of IGA process. It shows how the good characteristic schema is inherited through IGA. We define schemas such as the components like shape, color, and count of nodes for representing actual morphology. Each node consists of stem, twig, sepal, petal, and leaf, and the morphology of flower changes to various shapes by the defined schemas. Figure 6 shows how many schemas appear in populations in each generation and the phenotype having the best schema of fitness 5. The schemas selected in Figure 6 are shown in Table 2.

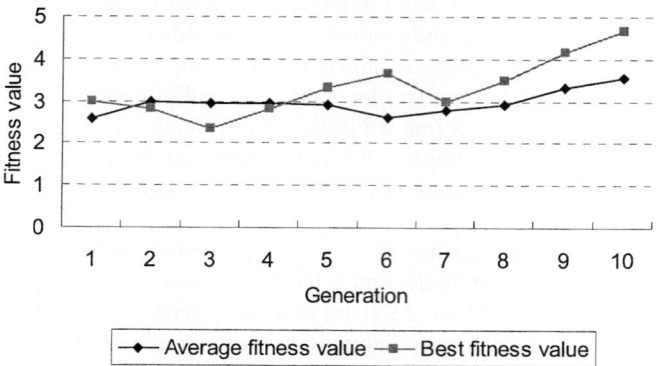

Fig. 5. Fitness changes on searching for natural flower.

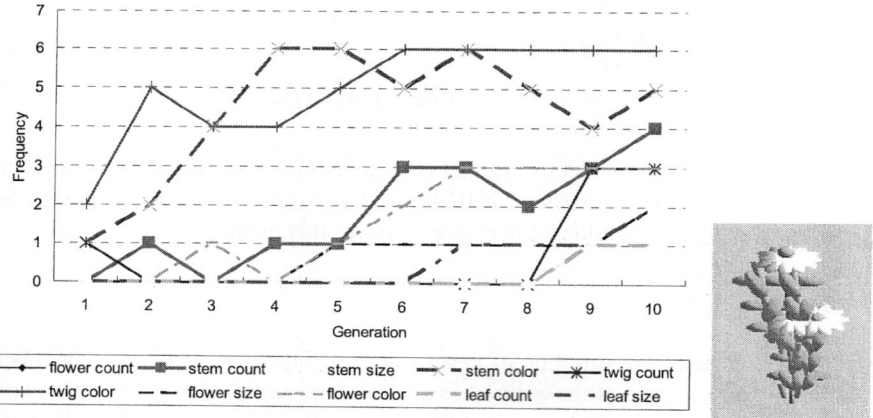

Fig. 6. The variation in generations of frequency of schemas and the fitness of populations.

Table 2. The schemas in the best solution of Figure 6.

Schema	Value	Schema	Value
Flower count	3	Stem count	4
Flower color	2 (Floral white)	Stem color	3 (Green)
Flower size	8 {0.12, 0.5, 0.1}	Stem size	0 {0.05, 1.2}
Twig count	12	Twig color	1 (Green yellow)
Leaf count	18	Leaf size	0 {0.3, 0.15, 0.1}

We have randomly selected an individual from the last population through the evaluation of a convergence test. In Figure 6, we realize that the characteristic schemas which do not appear in a population of the first generation increase. To analyze these schemas, we select the individual having the best fitness value in the last population. We analyze schemas of each population through the IGA process. Since we define ellipsoid shape for leaf, petal, and sepal and the cylinder shape for stem and twig, we define schemas for the shapes of each part as its size like {radius, height} or {x, y, z}.

To analyze the schemas included in the best solution, we define more effective ones which consist of natural flower morphology as the number of flowers, flower size, flower color, the number of stems, stem color, the number of twigs, twig color, the number of leaves, and leaf size. The size, color, and count of each part affect the evaluation to a more natural morphology similar to real flowers. Figure 6 shows the frequency of these schemas, and we can observe that they appear more and more as iterations even though they do not appear in individuals at the first population.

5 Conclusions

We have presented an automatic creation method of morphologies by using IGA which is suitable for sensitive problems due to humans' evaluation, and a creation of natural morphology to real character with the knowledge-based SDG which can create structures similar to real shapes. We have created flowers in three-dimensional world with evolutionary process.

We can reproduce the best characteristic parts by iteration of nodes in genotypic representation using SDG. Moreover, in contrast to previous approaches, our system lets users get direct feedback because it is represented structurally by SDG. In the future work we will focus on a representation of natural locomotion and the creation of other morphologies using SDG.

References

1. Langton, C. G.: Artificial life. *Santa Fe Institute Studies in the Sciences of Complexity*, vol. 6 (1989) 1-44
2. Bentley, P. J. and Corne, D. W.: *Creative Evolutionary Systems*. Morgan Kaufmann (2002)
3. Sims, K.: Artificial evolution for computer graphics. *Published in Computer Graphics*, vol. 25, no. 4 (1991) 319-328
4. Biles, J. A.: Life with GenJam: Interacting with a musical IGA. *Proc. of 1999 IEEE Int. Conf. on Systems, Man, and Cybernetics*, vol. 5, (1999) 652-656
5. Lindenmayer, B.: Mathematical models for cellular interaction in development I+II. *Journal of Theoretical Biology* (1968) 280-315
6. Hammel, M. and Prusinkiewicz, P.: Simulating the development of Fraxinus pennsylvanica shoots using L-systems. *Proceedings of the Sixth Western Computer Graphics Symposium* (1995) 49-58

7. Ochoa, G.: On genetic algorithms and Lindenmayer systems. *Parallel Problem Solving from Nature V* (1998) 335-344
8. Hornby, G. S. and Pollack, J. B.: Evolving L-systems to generate virtual creatures. *Computers & Graphics*, vol. 25 (2001) 1041-1048
9. Hornby, G. S. and Pollack, J. B.: Creating high-level components with a generative representation for body-brain evolution. *Artificial Life*, vol. 8, no. 3 (2002) 223-246
10. Sims, K.: Evolving virtual creatures. Computer Graphics, Annual Conference Series, *SIGGRAPH'94 Proceedings* (1994) 15-22
11. Sims, K.: Evolving 3D morphology and behavior by competition. *The Fourth International Workshop on the Synthesis and Simulation of Living Systems* (1994) 28-39
12. Lintermann, B. and Deussen, O.: Interactive modeling of plants. *IEEE Computer Graphics*, vol. 19, no. 1 (1999) 56-65
13. Lipson, H. and Pollack, J. B.: Automatic design and manufacture of robotic lifeforms. *Nature* 406 (2000) 974-978
14. Ventrella, J.: Explorations in the emergence of morphology and locomotion behavior in animated characters. *Proceedings of the Forth Workshop on Artificial Life* (1994) 463-441
15. Komosinski, M.: The framsticks system: Versatile simulator of 3D agents and their evolution. *The International Journal of Systems & Cybernetics*, vol. 32, no. 1/2 (2003) 156-173
16. Bongard, J. C. and Pfeifer, R.: Repeated structure and dissociation of genotypic and phenotypic complexity in artificial ontogeny. *Genetic and Evolutionary Computation Conference* (2001) 829-836
17. Kawamura, H. and Ohmori, H.: Computational morphogenesis of discrete structures with concideration of connection variables. *Memoris of the School of Engineering*, Nagoya Univ. vol. 53 (2002) 28-55
18. University of Oklahoma's botany 1114, "Flowers and flower morphology," http://bomi.ou.edu/bot1114/botany10/lab/flowers/flower10.html
19. Goldberg, D. E.: Genetic Algorithms in Search, *Optimization & Machine Learning*, Addison-Wesley Publishing Co. Inc. (1989)
20. Taylor, T. and Massey, C.: Recent developments in the evolution of morphologies and controllers for physically simulated creatures. *Artificial Life*, vol. 7, no. 1 (2001) 77-87
21. Kim, H.-S. and Cho, S.-B.: Application of interactive genetic algorithm to fashion design. *Engineering Applications of Artificial Intelligence*, vol. 13, no. 6 (2000) 635-644

Spatiotemporal Parameter Adaptation in Genetic Algorithm-Based Video Segmentation

Sin Kuk Kang[1], Eun Yi Kim[2,*], and Hang Joon Kim[1]

[1] Department of Computer Engineering, Kyungpook National Univ.,
1370 Sangyuk-dong, Puk-gu, Daegu, 702-701 Republic of Korea
{skkang,kimhj}@ailab.knu.ac.kr
[2] Department of Internet and Multimedia Engineering, Konkuk Univ.,
Mojin-dong, Gwangjin-gu, Seoul, 143-701, Republic of Korea
Tel. +82-2-450-4135, Fax. +82-2-450-4072
eykim@konkuk.ac.kr

Abstract. This paper presents a novel technique for the automatic adaptation of GA parameters within GAs, for video sequence segmentation. In our approach, the mating rates are not constant, but spatio-temporally varying. The variation of mating rates depends on the time and the degree of activity of each chromosome in between the successive frames. Experimental results show that the proposed approach can enhance the computational efficiency and the quality of the segmentation results than standard methods.

1 Introduction

In recent years, genetic algorithms (GA) have received considerable attention regarding their potential as a good solution in the field of segmentation problems [1-6]. Their main attractive is their ability to efficiently deal with hard complex combinatorial problem. They are also attractive because they can achieve an efficient parallel exploration of search space without getting stuck in local optima. Therefore, over the last few years, GAs have attracted increasing attention for use in segmenting variety of images [2-5]. These studies show that GAs are successfully used for image or video segmentation problems, yet relatively low search efficiency is still prevalent problem in GAs. The efficiency is determined through controlling a balance between exploitation and exploration in the search space, and then the balance is strongly affected by strategy parameters such as population size, crossover rate and mutation rate [1,6]. Crossover controls the size of the solution space that can be explored, while mutation creates new chromosomes that may be useful. A high mutation rate allows the fast exploration of the whole solution space and reduces the chance of entrapment in local minima. However, it can cause significant disruption to the exploitation of local regions. Meanwhile, a high crossover allows for further exploration of the solution space and reduces the chance of settling for a false optimum; yet, if it

---

* The corresponding author.

is too high, it can waste a lot of computation time in exploring unpromising regions. Consequently, search efficiency has been a problem with traditional genetic algorithms because it is difficult to choose a value for each parameter and to find the values efficiently. In most applications of GAs, fixed parameters are used; the parameter values are determined using a set-and-test approach. However, the use of constant parameters is in contrast to the general evolutionary spirit, as a GA is an intrinsically dynamic and adaptive process. Therefore it is natural to try to modify the value of strategy parameters during the run of the algorithms.

This paper presents a novel technique for the automatic adaptation of GA parameters within GAs, for video sequence segmentation. In our approach, the mating rates are not constant, but spatio-temporally varying. The variation of mating rates depends on the time and the degree of activity of each chromosome in between the successive frames. In the proposed method, the segmentation of the current frame in the video is successively obtained by chromosomes that evolve using DGAs. Unlike the standard DGA, chromosomes are initiated using the segmentation results of the previous frame instead of the random values and then the unstable chromosomes corresponding to the moving objects parts have the larger mating rates than stable chromosomes, to adapt the changes in between the successive frames. The proposed method with automatic adaptation of GA parameter can provide effective exploitation and exploration of the solution space, thus improving the performance relative to speed and segmentation quality.

The organization of the remainder of the paper is as follows. Section 2 describes the segmentation algorithm and the proposed method for automatic parameter adaptation is proposed in Section 3. Experimental results using natural video sequences are then reported in Section 4, followed by the conclusion.

2 Segmentation Algorithm

Video segmentation is carried out by chromosomes that evolve using DGAs. A chromosome consists of a label and feature vector allocated to one site at a specific time. The population of chromosomes is given initial values then evolved by iteratively performing GA operators, such as selection, crossover, and mutation, until the stopping criterion is satisfied. These operators eventually lead to a stable label configuration, which is taken as the resulting segmentation.

The main feature of the proposed method is to dynamically adapt the mating rates as the segmentation processes with time. This automatic adaptation of mating rates will introduce in the next section.

2.1 Chromosome

A chromosome $C_{st}=(l_{st}, f_{st})$ is allocated at site s at time t of the input video sequence, wherein l_{st} is the label and f_{st} is the estimated RGB-color vector. A chromosome is real-coded. As such, the chromosome is composed of four integer fields, each of which represents a label and each color in the feature vector.

Each chromosome has a fitness value, and then its fitness is defined as the Euclidean distance between the estimated color vector and the observed color vector at the location of the chromosome on the current frame. Therefore, to minimize its fitness value, each chromosome is evolved by iteratively performing selection, crossover, and mutation. In a DGA, these operators function on the neighbors of a chromosome rather than the whole population. Here, the neighbors of a chromosome are composed of the chromosomes located within a $w \times w$ window centered on the pixel (s,t).

In the proposed method, each chromosome has an *evolution probability* that represents its likelihood of being evolved by crossover and mutation. The probability of a chromosome C_{st} is denoted as PE_{st}, and defined as follows:

$$PE_{st} = \frac{\Delta g(s,t)}{\max\{\ \Delta g(0,t),\ \ldots\ ,\ \Delta g(s,t),\ \ldots\ ,\ \Delta g(M_1 \times M_2 - 1, t)\ \}}, \quad (1)$$

where $\Delta g(s,t) = |\ g(s,t) - g(s,t-1)\ |$ is the local fitness variance of chromosome C_{st} at time t. Accordingly, the evolution probability of a chromosomes is directly proportional to the variance of its local fitness.

Based on their evolution probabilities, the chromosomes are classified as either stable or unstable chromosomes. A chromosome is categorized as unstable if the following condition is satisfied:

$$PE_{st} \geq \frac{1}{2}(\ 1 - C_r (\text{or } M_r)\ ), \quad (2)$$

where C_r and M_r are crossover rate and mutation rate, respectively. Given the rates of mating operators, certain chromosomes with evolution probabilities above the threshold are selected as unstable.

2.2 Evolution Strategy

The chromosomes mapped to the first frame are evolved using conventional DGAs [5]. That is, the chromosomes are initialized with totally random values, and all of them have the same evolution probabilities. On the other hand, the chromosomes of the subsequent frames are initiated from the segmentation results of the previous frame, and then classified into stable and unstable ones according to their evolution probabilities. The difference between stable and unstable chromosomes is that the operators applied to stable chromosomes differ from those applied to unstable chromosomes. Stable chromosomes undergo neither crossover nor mutation, whereas unstable chromosomes are evolved using all GA operators for each generation. This prevents the stable chromosomes converged to the stable solution during segmentation of the previous frame from being disrupted by sudden fitness changes, and allows the unstable chromosomes corresponding to the moving objects parts for adapting the changes in between the successive frames.

GA operators and stopping criterion used in the respective evolution mechanisms are as follows:

- **Selection.** The selection scheme is elitist, whereby the chromosome with the highest fitness in the neighborhood is selected.
- **Crossover.** Crossover is a variant of uniform crossover [1]. First, a neighboring chromosome is randomly picked in the window. Then, one component in the feature vector is chosen and replaced by the corresponding value of the feature vector in the current chromosome, thereby yielding two new chromosomes, one of which is then selected.
- **Mutation.** For mutation, a random position is chosen along the gene of the chromosome, then the corresponding value is added to the value sampled from the normal distribution. That is,

$$C_{st}(i)' = C_{st}(i) + \sigma_i \times N(0,1), \qquad (3)$$

where $C_{st}(i)$ is the ith component of the real-coded chromosome C_{st}, and $C_{st}(i)'$ is the new component produced by mutation. Finally, σ_i is the step-size for the ith component, and N represents the normal distribution.
- **Stopping Criterion.** For the stopping criterion, stability is defined as the fraction of pixels that have the same label in both the current and previous generations. Then, a stability criterion and a stopping criterion are defined, respectively. The stability criterion is reached if the stability is above a stability threshold. The stopping criterion is reached when the stability is above the maximal stability, or when the frequency reaching to the stability criterion is above a predefined number (stability number). The stopping criterion is also reached when the number of generations is higher than the maximal number.

3 Parameter Adaptation

The main feature of the proposed method is to dynamically adapt the mating rates as the segmentation processes with time. *At the current generation number k, the rates are defined as the fraction of the unstable chromosomes out of all the chromosomes*, whose equation is

$$M(k)(\text{or } C(k)) = \frac{num(\ \{\ C_{st}\ |\ PE_{st} \geq 0.5(1 - M_r(\text{or } C_r))\ \}\ )}{num(\ \{\ C_{st}\ |\ 0 \leq s \leq (H-1)\times(W-1)\ \}\ )}, \qquad (4)$$

where $num(\cdot)$ is the function to count the member in a set. As can be seen in Eq. (4), the rates are mainly dependent on the evolutional probabilities of chromosomes at a specific step. Starting with the initial parameters, M_r and C_r, the mating rates are dynamically changed according to Eq. (4).

The main features of the proposed adaptation procedure are

- The mating rates are temporally varying. Within a frame, the mating rates will be decreased gradually along with the elapse of generation.
- The mating rates are spatially varying. Between frames, the larger mating rates will be applied to the regions (or parts) including the highly active objects.

3.1 Temporal Adaptation of Parameters

The chromosomes at the early generation step have large fitness variance in between the generation as they start with the random values, so that they will have the larger evolution probabilities. On contrast, the chromosomes have the fitness variance close to zero, since they reach to a stable configuration, thus they have the smaller evolution probabilities. Hence, the mating rates will be decreased gradually along with the elapse of generation.

Figs. 1 and 2 show the variation of mating rates according to the generation step, when segmenting the video sequence *Claire* and *Table Tennis*. In experiments, the initial crossover rate and mutation rate were set to 0.1 and 0.01. Once given the initial parameters, the mating rates were gradually decreased as the segmentation processes with time, which is shown in Figs. 1 and 2.

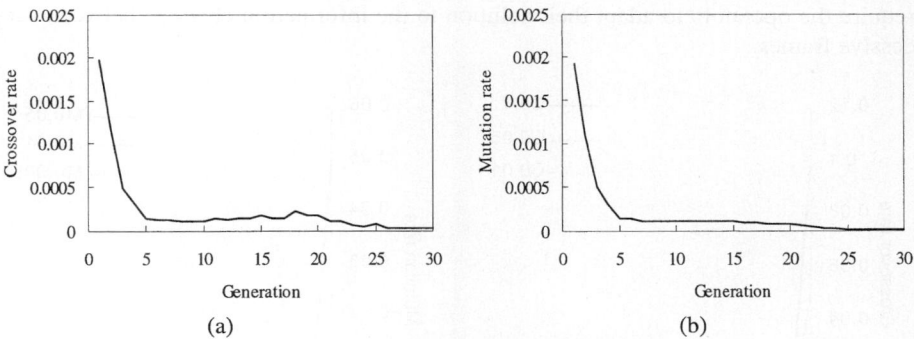

Fig. 1. Temporal variation of mating rates, when segmenting *Claire*: (a) crossover rates; (b) mutation rates

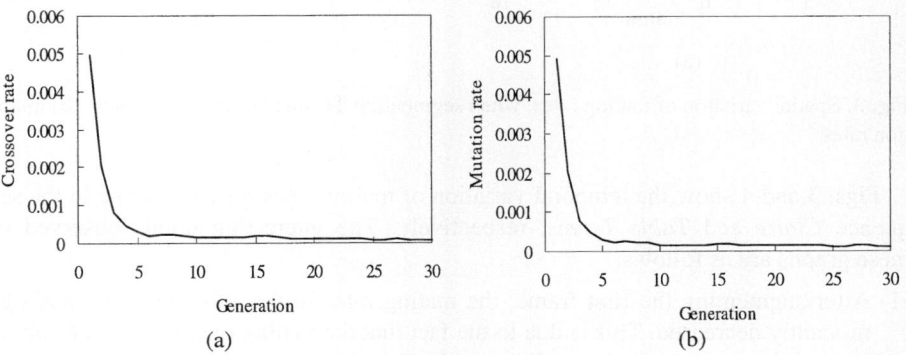

Fig. 2. Temporal variation of mating rates, when segmenting Tennis: (a) crossover rates; (b) mutation rates

3.2 Spatial Adaptation of Parameters

In the proposed method, the segmentation of current frame is successively obtained using the segmentation result of the previous frame. That is, chromosomes of the current frame are initialized with the segmentation result of the previous frame. Then, the chromosomes corresponding to the moving objects have larger fitness variance than the chromosomes corresponding to background, due to the significant difference between their estimated color vectors and the observed vector. On the other hand, the chromosomes corresponding to background or non-moving parts have local energy variances close to zero. Therefore, chromosomes corresponding to moving object parts have higher evolution probabilities to be evolved by crossover and mutation. This is extremely desirable when considering an actual video, as those chromosomes allocated to background are converged to a stable solution during the segmentation of the previous frame, therefore, their solutions do not need to be improved by crossover and mutation. In the mean time, those chromosomes allocated to moving object parts require the operators to adapt their solution to the information changed between successive frames.

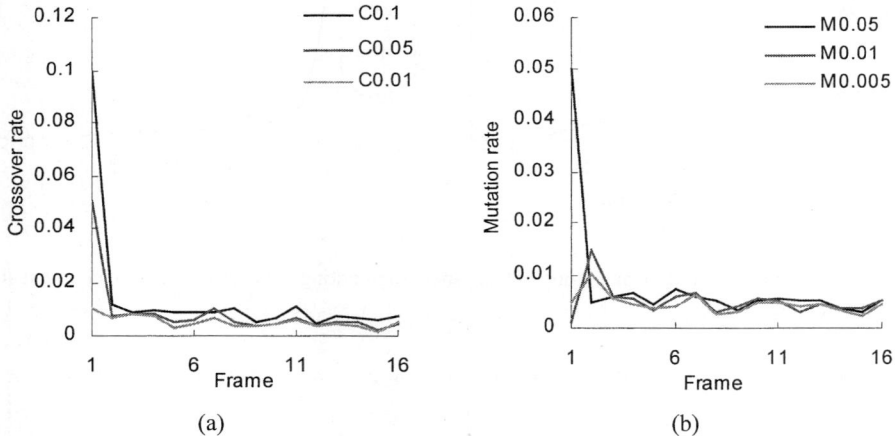

Fig. 3. Spatial variation of mating rates, when segmenting Tennis: (a) crossover rates; (b) mutation rates

Figs. 3 and 4 show the temporal variation of mating rates for each frame in the sequence *Claire* and *Table Tennis*, respectively. The interesting points observed in these graphs are as follows:

(1) After segmenting the first frame, the mating rates in the subsequent frames significantly decreased. This is due to the fact that the mating operators in the subsequent frames are applied to only unstable chromosomes after starting the segmentation result of the previous frame.
(2) There is not significant difference among average mating rates for the several initial rates. This experimentation shows that the proposed method is not affected by the initial values.

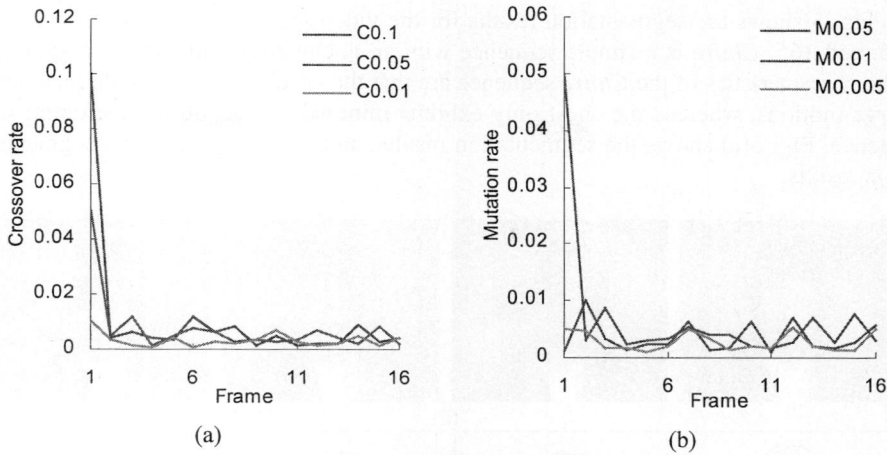

Fig. 4. Spatial variation of mating rates, when segmenting Tennis: (a) crossover rates; (b) mutation rates

(3) When comparing the graphs at Figs. 1-4, average mating-rates in the *Table Tennis* are larger than those in *Claire*. These differences are due to the characteristics of the segmented sequences. The *Claire* sequence has the small motion, whereas the *Table Tennis* sequence has relatively large motions during the entire sequence. Accordingly, the more representative solutions are required to enable the chromosomes initialized with the segmentation results of the previous frame to track the changes between successive frames. As a result, the larger mating rates are needed.

From these features, we obtain the fact that the mating rates in the proposed adaptation method are affected by the characteristics of the videos not by the initial mating rates.

Consequently, the proposed spatiotemporally adjustable parameter adaptation facilitates an effective exploration for solution space and eventually creates a faster convergence speed and better segmentation results.

4 Experimental Results

To assess the validity of the proposed method, it was tested on several well-known video sequences, and the results were compared with those of conventional GA-based methods. It should be noted that since the DGA parameter, such as window size and mating rates, all have an influence on the performance of the algorithms, these parameters were determined empirically. The parameters used for the experiments were as follows: the stability threshold was set at 99.9%, the stability number at 100, the maximal stability at 100%, the maximum number of generations at 1000, and the label size at 64. The DGA parameters were fixed according to the type of tested video sequence. The window size was 5×5 and the initial crossover and mutation rate 0.1 and 0.01, respectively.

Fig. 5 shows the segmentation results for the video sequence *Claire* at time 1, 65, 96, and 165. *Claire* is a simple sequence with an uncluttered stationary background. The characteristics of the *Claire* sequence are that the head and face include relatively large motions, whereas the chest only exhibits minimal motion during the entire sequence. Fig. 5(a) shows the segmentation results, and Fig. 5(b) shows the segmentation results.

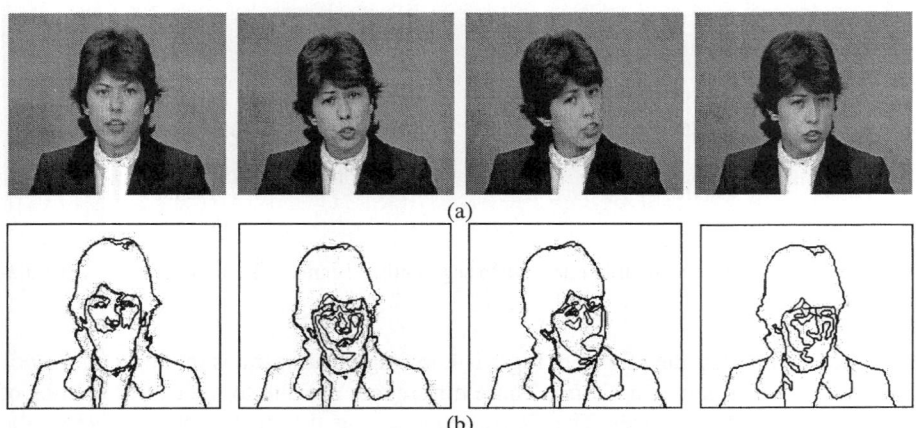

Fig. 5. Segmentation results of sequence *Claire*: (a) Original frames at time 1, 65, 96, and 165, (b) Segmentation results

Fig. 6 shows the results of the video sequence *Table Tennis* at time 1, 4, and 10. The scene was decomposed into five objects: the background, ball, left hand, right arm with a racquet, and background. In this sequence, the objects are not absolutely rigid, and different areas have different kinds of motion. In particular, the left hand was not explicitly shown in the simulation results as indeed it disappears as the se-

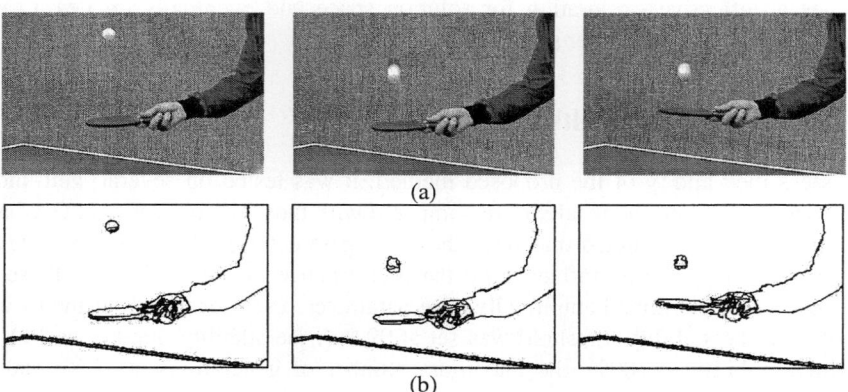

Fig. 6. Segmentation results of sequence *Table Tennis*: (a) Original frames at time 1, 4, 10, and 14. (b) Segmentation results

quence unravels. Figs. 6(a) and (b) show the segmentation results in terms of the object boundaries and regions, respectively. With the proposed method, to improve the computational efficiency, only unstable chromosomes are evolved by crossover and mutation. Nonetheless, the objects boundaries were correctly tracked. In addition, those regions corresponding to the same video object part between two frames were colored with the same color, which can be used as an important cue for object tracking.

To prove its effectiveness, the proposed method was compared with Andrey et al.'s method as regards the speed and quality of the segmentation results. Andrey et al. proposed a DGA based segmentation method for gray-level images [5]. In their work, the segmentation is performed by a population of units that iteratively evolves according to simple and local evolutionary rules. The work adapts the set-and-test approach for mating rates. Their work showed how DGAs could be generalized to an unsupervised segmentation problem, and the effectiveness of DGAs for an unsupervised image segmentation.

Then, to quantitatively measure the quality of the segmentation results, the standard uniform function F was applied, as proposed by Liu et al and used in [3,7]. The function is defined as

$$F(\omega_t) = \frac{1}{1000 \times image\_size} \sqrt{R} \times \sum_{i=1}^{R} \frac{e_i^2}{\sqrt{A_i}},$$

where ω_t is the image to be segmented, R the number of regions in the segmented image ω_t, A_i, the area or number of pixels in the ith region, and e_i, the color error in region i. e_i is defined as the sum of the Euclidean distance of the color vectors between the estimated original image and the observed input image of each pixel in the image. The smaller the value of F, the better the segmentation results. The smaller the value of F, the better the segmentation results.

Table 1 shows the performance comparison of the two methods when segmenting the sequences *Claire* and *Table Tennis*. These comparisons show that the proposed method could improve both the quality of the segmentation results and the convergence speed. Consequently, the proposed method demonstrated a superior performance when compared with standard DGA-based algorithms.

Table 1. Summary of Performance

Methods	Video sequences	Average number of generations to segment a frame	Average value of $F(\omega)$
Conventional method	Claire	152.79	15.52
	Tennis	130.13	31.96
Proposed method	Claire	38.69	15.19
	Tennis	45.83	29.42

5 Conclusion

This paper presented a new unsupervised method for segmenting a video sequence. Each frame in a sequence was modeled using an MRF, which is robust to degradation. Since this is computationally intensive, a new segmentation algorithm based on GA that can improve computationally efficiency was developed. Experimental results demonstrated the effectiveness of the proposed method.

Acknowledgement

This work was supported by grant No. R04-2003-000-10187 from the Basic Research Program of the Korea Science & Engineering Foundation. This research was supported in part by University IT Research Center Project.

References

1. Gen, M., and Cheng, R.: Genetic algorithms and engineering optimization, John Wiley and sons, Inc. (2000)
2. Gene K. Wu and T. R. Reed: Image sequence processing using spatiotemporal segmentation. IEEE Trans. Circuits Syst. Video Technol., 9-5 (1999) 798-807.
3. Kim, E. Y., S. W. Hwang, S. H. Park and H. J. Kim: Spatiotemporal Segmentation using Genetic Algorithms. Pattern Recognition. 34-10 (2001) 2063-2066.
4. S. M. Bhandarkar and H. Zhang: Image segmentation using evolutionary computation. IEEE Trans. Evolutionary Computation. 3-1 (1999) 1-21.
5. Andrey, P. and P. Tarroux: Unsupervised segmentation of Markov random field modeled textured images using selectionist relaxation. IEEE Trans. Pattern Anal. Machine Intell. 20-3(1998) 659-673.
6. D. E. Goldberg: Genetic Algorithms in Search, Optimization and Machine Learning. Addison Wesley. (1989)
7. J. Liu and Y. H. Yang: Multiresoultion color image segmentation. IEEE Trans. PAMI. 16-7 (1994) 689-700.

Object Detection and Removal Using Genetic Algorithms

Eun Yi Kim[1] and Keechul Jung[2]

[1] Dept. of Internet and Multimedia Engineering, Konkuk Univ., Seoul, Korea
eykim@konkuk.ac.kr
[2] School of Media, College of Information Science, Soongsil Univ., Seoul, Korea
kcjung@computing.ssu.ac.kr

Abstract. This paper proposes an approach for automatic object detection and removal in video sequences based on genetic algorithms (GAs) and spatiotemporal restoration. Given two consecutive frames, first, objects in the current frame are detected and tracked by a GA-based segmentation method. Second, two stages are performed for the restoration of the regions occluded by the detected text regions: temporal and spatial restorations. The performance of object detection is enhanced by the new proposed evolution method based on GAs. The combination of temporal and spatial restoration shows great potential for automatic removal of extracted objects of interest in various kinds of video sequences, and is applicable to many video re-using applications.

1 Introduction

Recently, digital videos and images have been widely used in many applications. Accordingly, how to structure, index, and retrieve video data becomes an important issue in multimedia applications. Moreover, automatic video editing including object removal and replacement gives us more possibility in re-using video data. For example, indirect advertisements are prevalent and easily found in TV programs and movie scenes. Examples include logos or banners on clothes, electrical home appliances, furniture, etc. In cases in which indirect advertisement is not permitted, these are conventionally manually erased after taking a picture, or taped by sticky bands before taking a picture. Unlike such methods, we hope to develop a system that can detect these objects and remove them. Objects of interest in these fields can be blotches, scratches, flaws, noises, or text characters in images or videos.

There are some related research areas in image processing and computer graphics. Detection and removal of blotches and line scratches in an image sequence is closely related to text detection and removal in video sequences [1]. However, the text included in images is usually bigger than blotches and scratches, and therefore it is inappropriate to use the blotch/scratch-oriented techniques for text removal. Bertalmio et al. presented a method that used a partial differential equation for the inpainting problem, and applied it to remove pre-specified regions and artificially inserted text in images [2]. Chan and Shen proposed a similar approach based on curvature driven diffusions [3]. As the application part of the flaw removal in photographs, films, and images, Wei and Levoy used tree-structured vector quantization for texture synthesis [4]. These approaches may hardly produce good results in cases in which the surrounding areas of the region to be restored are poorly textured. Irani and Peleg used image motion information extracted from an image sequence for image enhancement and reconstruction of occlusion [5]. Yoon and Bae presented the motion-compensated recovery of an occluded region for caption replacement [6]. These investigations showed interesting results for the occluded background recovery. However, these techniques used multiple frames for occlusion recovery, and therefore took a long time to estimate motion information. Additionally, when caption and background regions span many frames together without moving, these methods are inapplicable to the restoration of background regions occluded by captions.

In this paper, we describe automatic object segmentation and removal technique in video sequences. We need two techniques for this purpose; one for detecting, segmenting, and tracking region-of-interests (ROIs) in an image, and the other for removing the ROIs in the video sequence. For detecting, segmenting, and tracking the ROIs in an image we use an GA(Genetic Algorithm)-based method. For restoring the background regions, we perform temporal restoration between consecutive frames and then spatial restoration in the rest. 2D motion information extracted from object tracking information is used for temporal restoration, and then residual pixels remaining after temporal restoration are restored by using an inpainting algorithm [2]. We call it *spatiotemporal restoration*.

The reasons for using a combined approach of temporal restoration and spatial restoration can be stated as follows: (1) The ROIs in the compressed domain such as MPEG are usually extremely degraded, and therefore it is difficult to get reasonable results using only spatial information in a frame for the occluded region's restoration; (2) although it may give better results to use several consecutive frames for the restoration, the computational burden of extracting motion information continuously through several frames is relatively high; (3) for some ROIs (for example, stationary objects on a stationary background) temporal information is not available. For these reasons, we use a combined method of temporal restoration and spatial restoration.

2 Object Detection Using Genetic Algorithms

The object detection is performed by spatial segmentation, temporal segmentation, and object extraction and tracking. The spatial segmentation divides each frame in the sequence into regions, and the temporal segmentation produces a change detection mask (CDM). Objects are then extracted for each frame by combining the spatial segmentation result and the CDMs, and tracked.

2.1 Spatial Segmentation

The spatial segmentation of each frame in the sequence is formulated in MRF-MAP framework, and then the energy function of each MRF is optimized using a new GA-based evolutionary method.

2.1.1 Image Modeling Using MRFs

The input image G was considered as degraded by i.i.d zero-mean Gaussian white noise $N=\{n_{ij}\}$. Let $S=\{(i,j):1 \le i \le M_1, 1 \le j \le M_2\}$ denote the $M_1 \times M_2$ lattice, such that an element in S indexes an image pixel. Let $\Lambda=\{\lambda_1, \ldots, \lambda_R\}$ denote the label set and $X=\{X_{ij}|\ X_{ij} \in \Lambda\}$ be the family of random variables defined on S. The neighborhood of S can be defined as $\Gamma=\{\eta_{ij}\}$, where η_{ij} is a set of sites neighboring (i,j). Then, X is an MRF on S with respect to Γ because the two conditions of [7] are satisfied. Let ω be a realization of X. The goal is to identify ω which maximizes the posterior distribution for a fixed input image g. That is, to determine

$$\arg\max_{\omega} P(X=\omega|G=g) \propto \arg\max_{\omega} P(g|\omega)P(\omega) \qquad (1)$$

Eq. (1) is divided into likelihood function and prior probability, which are defined in [7]. Using these components, Eq. (1) can be represented by the following equation, which is defined as a *posterior energy function*.

$$\arg\min_{\omega}\{\sum_{c \in C}[S_c(\omega)+T_c(\omega)]+\frac{[g-F(\omega)]^2}{2\sigma^2}+\frac{1}{2}\log(2\pi\sigma^2)\} \qquad (2)$$

In Eq. (2), σ is the noise variance and $F(\bullet)$ is the mapping function that the label of a pixel corresponds to the estimated color vector. And C is a possible set of cliques. Then spatial potentials $S_c(\omega)$ and imposes the spatial continuity of the labels and temporal potentials $T_c(\omega)$ is to achieve the temporal continuity of the labels. These potentials are defined in detail in [3]. Let ρ_{ij} denote a set of cliques containg pixel (i,j). Since C is equal to the sum of ρ_{ij} for all pixels, the function in Eq. (2) can be rewritten as the sum of the local energy U_{ij} for all pixels.

$$\arg\min_{\omega} \sum_{(i,j) \in S} \{\sum_{c \in \rho_{ij}}[S_c(\omega_{ij})+T_c(\omega_{ij})]+\frac{[g_{ij}-F(\omega_{ij})]^2}{2\sigma^2}+\frac{1}{2}\log(2\pi\sigma^2)\} \qquad (3)$$

As a result, instead of maximizing the posterior distribution, the posterior energy function is minimized to identify the optimal label.

2.1.2 Segmentation Algorithm

In this paper, minimization of energy function is distributed into chromosomes that evolve by DGAs. A chromosome consists of a label and a feature vector, which are described in [7]. Its fitness is defined as the local energy U_{ij}. A set of chromosomes is called a population and represents a segmentation result. According to their fitnesses, the chromosomes are classified into two groups: stable and unstable chromosomes. When the chromosomes are mapped to an actual video sequence, the stable and unstable chromosomes correspond to the background and moving object parts, respectively.

In the proposed method, the segmentation of the frames in a sequence is successively obtained. For the first frame, the chromosomes are initiated with random values, whereas, for later frames they are started from the segmentation of the previous frame. The segmentation for the starting frame is determined using Kim et al.'s segmentation algorithm [7]. Thereafter, the remaining frames are segmented using the algorithm outlined as in Fig. 1. At intervals of T, the system receives the input $I(t)$ and $C(t-1)$, that is, the current frame and segmentation result of the previous frame, respectively. Starting with the segmentation results of the previous frame, the chromosmes are evolved through iteratively performed selection and genetic operations. In the selection process, the chromosomes are updated to new chromosomes, $C(t)$, by an elitist selection scheme. Thereafter, in the Decision Module, the chromosomes are classified into two groups according to their fitness: stable chromosomes, $S\_C(t)$, and unstable ones, $U\_C(t)$. In the current frame, the chromosomes are sorted in an increasing order based on their fitnesses. Given the probabilities of genetic operations, certain chromosomes with lower fitnesses are selected as being unstable: prior to crossover and mutation, the unstable chromosomes are determined in accordance with their probabilities. Only the unstable chromosomes are evolved by crossover and mutation, which are described in detail in [7]. It should be noted that the probabilities of genetic operations have an influence on the performance of the algorithms. Accordingly, these parameters were determined empirically. In Fig. 1, $U\_C'(t)$ and $U\_C''(t)$ are chromosomes evolved by crossover and mutation, respectively. $S\_C(t)$ is then delayed for τ_k, the time taken for the genetic operations within a generation. These operations are iteratively performed until the stopping criterion is satisfied. For the stopping criterion, the equilibirum is defined in [7]. The stopping criterion is reached when the euqilibrium is above the equilibrium threshold or the number of generations is more than the maximal number.

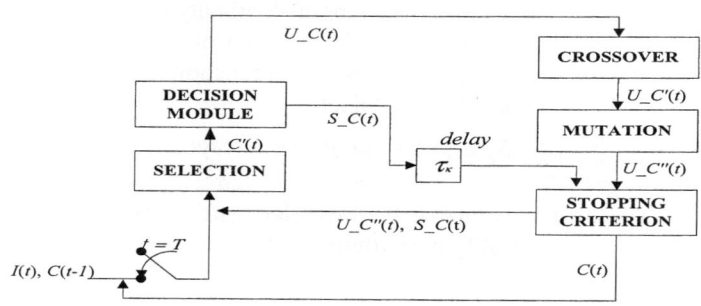

Fig. 1. Spatial segmentation algorithm.

2.2 Temporal Segmentation and VOP Extraction

To overcome the missing problem and enhance the coherent segmentation results of moving objects, temporal segmentation is performed by two steps: detection by adaptive thresholding and use of historical information. After producing initial CDM is produced by adaptive thresholding [8], the result is modified by history information.

Here, the ***history information*** of a pixel means whether or not the pixel belongs to the moving object parts in the previous frame. This history information is represented as a matrix of a frame size $H = \{h_{ij} \mid 0 \leq i \leq M_1, 0 \leq j \leq M_2\}$, then each element in the matrix has a '0' or '1' value. A pixel has h_{ij} of one if it belonged to part of a video object in the previous frame, otherwise it has h_{ij} of zero. The CDM is then modified with this history information using the simple rule: If it belongs to part of a video object plane in the previous frame and its label is the same as the corresponding pixel in the previous frame, the pixel is marked as the foreground area in the current frame.

After spatial segmentation and temporal segmentation are performed, both results are combined to yield video object planes. This combination is very simple. Let $R_t = \{R_{kt} \mid k = 1,2,...,r\}$ denote the segments for the current frame F_t. Then region R_{kt} is marked as a foreground region, only if the majority part of the region belongs to the foreground part of the CDM_t.

2.3 Object Tracking

The core of the proposed object-tracking method is the natural correspondence to be established by our spatial segmentation. Those regions corresponding to the same objects in successive frames can retain the same label throughout a whole video sequence, referred to as ***natural correspondence***.

Let $Q = \{Q_i \mid i \in \Lambda\}$ denote a VOP present in F_t, which Q_i denote a region forming the Q. Plus the region Q_i has the label i. Similarly, let $P = \{P_i \mid i \in \Lambda\}$ denote a VOP present in F_{t-1}. Then Q has the natural correspondence with a parent satisfying the following condition:

$$\frac{Sim(Q,Q^*)}{\sum_{i \in \Lambda} \mid num(Q_i) \mid} \geq \theta_{N\_C}, \tag{4}$$

where θ_{N_C} is the threshold. And the Q^* is the parent that has the most similar label distribution and similar size to Q, and $Sim(\cdot,\cdot)$ is the function computing the similarity of P and Q, whose equation are

$$Q^* = \arg \max_{P \in VOP(t-1)} Sim(Q,P) \quad (5) \qquad Sim(Q,P) = -\sum_{i \in \Lambda} \mid num(Q_i) - num(P_i) \mid^2, \tag{6}$$

where $num(\bullet)$ is the function counting the pixels. In Eq. (6), the similarity between two VOPs is measured relative to the label distribution and size of the regions forming them. If there is a big difference between the numbers of pixels assigned to a label i in Q and P, or if most regions in the current VOP have different labels from the regions in a previously detected VOP, the similarity is decreased. Here, θ_{N_C} is fixed to -200.

Fig. 2 shows some examples of natural correspondence. Figs. 2(a) and (d) show the spatial segmentation results at time 3 and 4 in *Table Tennis*. The corresponding spatiotemporal segmentation results are shown in Figs. 2(b) and (e), then Figs. 2(c) and (f) show the regions corresponding to moving objects, where each region is colored in accordance with its label. In Figs 2(c) and (f), those regions corresponding to the same object parts in the successive are colored with the same color, thereby establishing a natural correspondence between the objects.

3 Object Removals Using Spatiotemporal Restoration

We perform the removal of ROIs using a combined method of temporal restoration in consecutive frames and spatial restoration for the residual regions. The spatiotemporal restoration is completed as a weighted sum of the spatial restoration and temporal restoration as following Eq. (7).

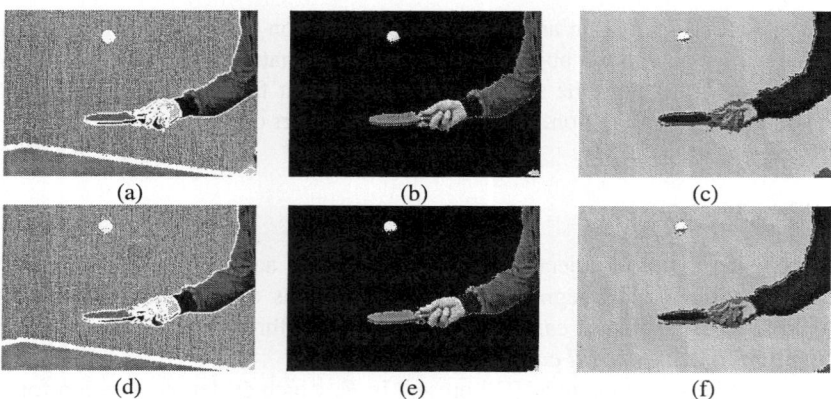

Fig. 2. Example of natural correspondence in *Table Tennis*. (a) Spatial segmentation result at time 3. (b) VOPs at time 3. (c) Colored regions representing VOPs at time 3. (d) Spatial segmentation result at time 4. (e) VOPs at time 4. (f) Colored regions representing VOPs at time.

$$\hat{I}(i,j,t) = \alpha \hat{I}_T(i,j,t) + (1-\alpha)\hat{I}_S(i,j,t) \tag{7}$$

where α is a weighting coefficient, $\hat{I}_T(i,j,t)$ and $\hat{I}_S(i,j,t)$ are the results of temporal restoration and spatial restoration at time t for a site (i, j) respectively.

3.1 Sequence Classification

Most of the moving objects in a video sequence have several characteristics. Therefore, if we make use of these characteristics for spatiotemporal restoration, the computational time can be reduced and more accurate motion estimation can be achieved. For example, if it is known in advance that the background is stationary, the time for estimating background motion vectors can be precluded. Furthermore, when a sequence has the frame differences in background regions resulting from noises not from real movements of a camera or objects, incorrect temporal restoration produced by misestimating of motions can be prevented. Thus the occluded regions are restored using accurate motion information in the temporal restoration step. After estimating global motions and object tracking, input video images are classified using simple classification rules in which text motion and background frame difference are utilized. Table 1 shows the simple classification rules. Symbols T1 and T2 are threshold values for motion estimation.

Table 1. Four-type classification rules of a sequence for spatiotemporal restoration.

ROI's motion	Frame Difference in Background	Types
< T1	< T2	Stationary Object on Stationary Background
	≥ T2	Stationary Object on Varying Background
≥ T1	< T2	Moving Object on Stationary Background
	≥ T2	Moving Object on Varying Background

3.2 Spatiotemporal Restoration

To restore the occluded regions in a video sequence, we use both spatial and temporal information. For the temporal restoration, we use the object motions estimated in the sequence classification, and the background motions selectively estimated using minimum absolute difference (MAD). The temporal restoration at time t using motion estimation results is performed as follows.

$$\hat{I}_T(i,j,t) = I(i+d_1^b, j+d_2^b, t-1), \tag{8}$$

where $(i+d_1^b, j+d_2^b) \notin ObjectArea(i,j,t-1)$. *ObjectArea* stands for the occluded regions by the extracted VOPs in each frame and $ObjectArea(i,j,t-1) = ObjectArea(i+d_1^t, j+d_2^t, t)$. $I(i,j,t-1)$ is the pixel value of the position (i,j) at time t-1. d^t and d^b are the motion vector and the background motion vector of the block including (i,j), which is extracted from the tracking information, respectively. After forward mapping from the previous frame to the current frame using estimated motion vectors, the object pixels in the occluded regions in a current frame are restored temporally by copying the corresponding background pixels in the previous frame. If the pixels to be copied in a previous frame are the object pixels, we do not copy them.

To remove the occluded pixels remaining after temporal restoration, we use the 'image inpainting' algorithm as the spatial restoration algorithm. The image inpainting algorithm devised by Bertalmio et al. [2], is a method for restoring damaged parts of an image and filling in automatically the selected regions with surrounding information. As detailed by Bertalmio et al, the basic idea of the inpainting algorithm is that the information surrounding the region to be inpainted is propagated inside along the isophote lines arriving at the region boundaries [2]. In the n'th inpainting time, the improved version of the image pixel $I^n(i,j)$ is as follows.

$$I^{n+1}(i,j) = I^n(i,j) + \Delta t\, I_t^n(i,j), \tag{9}$$

where $I^n(i,j)$ is each of the image pixels inside the region to be inpainted and $\Delta t I^n(i,j)$ stands for the update of the image pixel $I^n(i,j)$ with the rate of improvement, Δt. This update term contains not only the information to propagate, but also the isophote direction using a 2-D Laplacian operator.

Inpainting Algorithm

1. Preprocessing (anisotropic diffusion)
2. For each pixel in the region to be inpainted
2.1. Compute the vertical/horizontal smoothness variations using 2-D Laplacian
2.2. Compute the isophote direction
2.3. Propagate 2D-smoothness variations along to the isophote line
2.4. Compute the magnitude of the pixel to be inpainted
2.5. Update the value of the pixel through the combination of 2.1, 2.2, 2.3 and 2.4
3. Iterate steps 2.1 to 2.5

During the spatial restoration, anisotropic diffusion [2,9] was interleaved with one per tenth inpainting loop to ensure noise insensitivity and preserve the sharpness of edges.

$$\frac{\partial}{\partial t}I(x,y,t) = g(\nabla I)\kappa(x,y,t)|\nabla I(x,y,t)|, \forall(x,y)\in\Omega, \tag{10}$$

where $g(\nabla I) = e^{(-(\|\nabla I\|/K)^2)}$, $\kappa(x,y,t)$ is the Euclidean curvature of the isophote line and ∇I, Ω, K is the image gradient, the regions to be inpainted, and a normalizing constant, respectively. We performed the spatial restoration algorithm until the pixel values in the regions to be restored did not change.

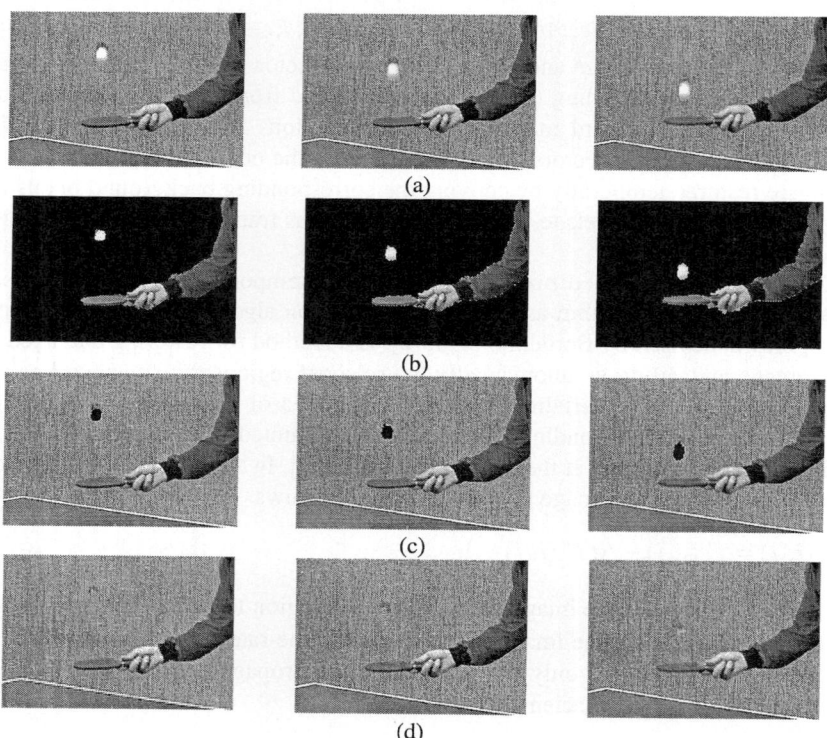

Fig. 3. Results of object detection, removal and restoration for Tennis: (a) Three frames from the sequence, (b) VOPs for each frame, (c) Removal of a ball from the original frames, (e) Restoration of removed region.

4 Experimental Results

To assess the validity of the proposed method, we have tested the proposed method using the natural video sequence collected from movies and animations.

Fig. 3 shows the object extraction, tracking and restoration results of *Table Tennis*. Fig. 3(a) shows the original frames, and Figs. 3(b) shows moving VOPs extracted from each frame. And Fig. 3(c) shows the results that VOPs of balls are removed from the original frames, then Fig. 3(d) shows the spatiotemporal restoration results. The proposed segmentation method produced a meaningful partition with accurately object boundaries and were perfectly tracking of the multiple moving objects through a whole video sequence. As shown in the Fig. 3(d), the extracted ball is completely recovered, however, the shadow-like region, which is due to the MPEG compression, is not extracted, therefore, it does not restored at all.

To fully assess the effectiveness of the proposed object segmentation method and restoration method, they were applied to the outdoor scenes including very fast moving objects on the complex background. Fig. 4 shows the results for the road scenes. Fig. 4(a) shows a succession of certain frames from a traffic monitoring sequence. Then, the succession of extracted VOPs from the sequence is shown in Figs. 4(b). The tracking of the vehicles was also correct, in spite of the fast motion of the vehicles and their relatively small sizes. However, it is not easy to extract the vehicles, which have fast motion and it makes also difficult to make a restoration stage. The crude boundaries of the extracted vehicles make lots of noise in an inpainting job and vehicle's shadow affects the spatiotemporal restoration stages too.

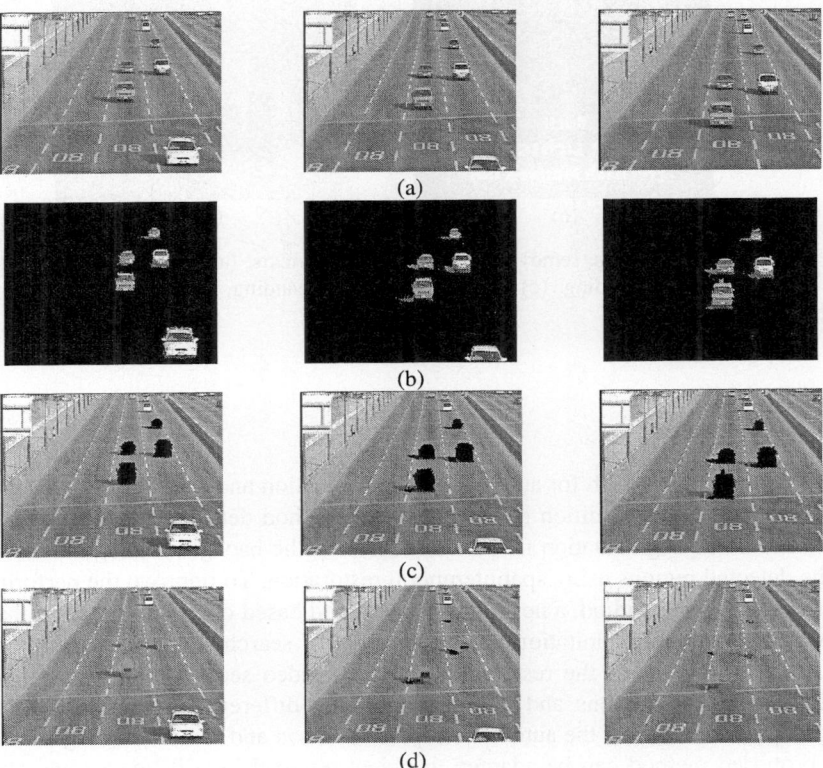

Fig. 4. Results of object detection, removal and restoration for road scenes: (a) Three frames from the sequence, (b) VOPs for the extracted vehicles, (c) Removal of specific cars from the original frames, (d) Restoration of removed region.

Fig. 5 shows the intermediate results of text removal: Fig. 5(a) shows an input image obtained from digital TV, then Fig. 5(b) shows an original extracted text pixels using double thresholding denoted with white pixels. Figs. 5(c) and (d) show an example of expanded image and a final result image, respectively.

As shown in Figs. 3 and 4, the proposed object detection method can produce meaningful partitions from video sequences where no priori information is not known. Although there are still some noise and un-recovered regions, we can have positive results for automatic object extraction and restoration.

Fig. 5. Results of detection, removal, and restoration for texts: (a) Input image, (b) Extracted text regions before expanding, (c) Text region after expanding, (d) Restoration of removed region.

5 Conclusion

In this paper, an approach for automatic object detection and removal technique using for object-based video edition is proposed. Our method detected ROIs automatically using GA-based segmentation method and restored the background regions occluded by the detected regions using spatiotemporal restoration. To improve the performance of object detection method, a new evolution method based on GAs were used that can allows for effective exploitation and exploration of search space. In addition to increase the efficiency of the restoration, an input video sequence was classified according to object motions and background frame difference. Experimental results suggest potential uses of the automatic object detection and removal in digital videos. The proposed method can be adapted to object removal in still images and stationary/moving objects on the stationary background as well.

Acknowledgement

This work was supported by grant No. R04-2003-000-10187-0 from the Basic Research Program of the Korea Science & Engineering Foundation.

References

1. Kokaram, A. C., R. D. Morris, W. J. Fitzgerald and P. J. W. Rayner: Interpolation of Missing Data in Image Sequences. IEEE Transaction on Image Processing, 4-11 (1995) 1509-1519.
2. Bertalmio M., G. Sapiro, Vicent Caselles and Coloma Ballester: Image Inpainting. Siggraph 2000 Conference Proceedings. (2000) 417-424.
3. Chan T. and J. Shen: Inpainting, zooming, and edge coding, Special Session on Inverse Problems and Image Analysis at the AMS Annual Conference. (2001) January.
4. Wei L. Y. and M. Levoy: Fast Texture Systhesis using Tree-structured Vector Quantization. Siggraph 2000 Conference Proceedings. (2001) 479-488.
5. Irani M., S. Peleg: Motion Analysis for Image Enhancement: Resolution, Occlusion, and Transparency. Journal on Visual Communications and Image Representation, 4-4 (1993) 324-335.
6. Yoon H. S. and Y. L. Bae: A Method for Recovering Original Image for Video caption Area and Replacing Caption Text. International Workshop of Content-based Multimedia Indexing. (2001) Sep.
7. Kim, E. Y., S. W. Hwang, S. H. Park and H. J. Kim: Spatiotemporal Segmentation using Genetic Algorithms. Pattern Recognition. 34-10 (2001) 2063-2066.
8. Habili, N., A. Moini, and N. Burgess: Automatic thresholding for change detection in digital video. Proc. SPIE. 4067(2000) 133-142.
9. Perona P. and J. Malik: Scale-space and edge detection using anisotropic diffusion. IEEE Trans. on Pattern Analysis and Machine Intelligence. 12-7 (1990) 629-639.

Elman's Recurrent Neural Networks Using Resilient Back Propagation for Harmonic Detection

Fevzullah Temurtas[1], Nejat Yumusak[1], Rustu Gunturkun[2], Hasan Temurtas[2], and Osman Cerezci[3]

[1] Sakarya University, Department of Computer Engineering, Adapazari, Turkey
[2] Dumlupinar University, Technical Education Faculty, Kutahya, Turkey
[3] Sakarya University, Department of Electric - Electronic Engineering, Adapazari, Turkey

Abstract. In this study, the method to apply the Elman's recurrent neural networks using resilient back propagation for harmonic detection is described. The feed forward neural networks are also used for comparison. The distorted wave including 5th, 7th, 11th, 13th harmonics were simulated and used for training of the neural networks. The distorted wave including up to 25th harmonics were prepared for testing of the neural networks. Elman's recurrent and feed forward neural networks were used to recognize each harmonic. The results obtained using Elman's recurrent neural networks are better than the results values obtained using the feed forward neural networks for resilient back propagation.

1 Introduction

Power quality has received increased attention in recent years with the widespread application of nonlinear loads employing advanced solid-state power switching devices in a multitude of industrial and commercial applications. The operation of solid-state power switching devices in power electronic converters deteriorates the power quality by injecting harmonics into the power system causing increased distortions, equipment and load malfunctions and losses [1-3].

AC power systems have a substantial number of large harmonic generating devices, e.g. adjustable speed drives for motor control and switch-mode power supplies used in a variety of electronic devices such as computers, copiers, fax machines, etc. These devices draw non-sinusoidal load currents consisting primarily of lower-order 5th, 7th, 11th, and 13th harmonics that distort the system power quality. [3]. With the widespread use of harmonic-generating devices, the control of harmonic currents to maintain a high level of power quality is becoming increasingly important. Harmonic standards (e.g. IEEE 519 and IEC 555) have been developed to address limits in allowable harmonics [4].

An effective way for harmonic elimination is the harmonic compensation by using active power filter. Active power filter detect harmonic current from distorted wave in power line, then generates negative phase current as same as detected harmonic to cancel out the harmonic in power system. Using of the artificial neural networks is one of the methods for harmonic detection. [6-9].

The back propagation (BP) algorithm is widely recognized as a powerful tool for training feed forward neural networks (FNNs). But since it applies the steepest descent method to update the weights, it suffers from a slow convergence rate and often yields suboptimal solutions [10,11]. A variety of related algorithms have been introduced to address that problem. A number of researchers have carried out comparative studies of MLP training algorithms [10-12]. The BP with momentum and adaptive learning rate algorithm [12], Resilient BP [10] used in this study are these type algorithms.

In this study, the method to apply the Elman's recurrent neural networks [8,9] for harmonic detection process in active filter is described. The feed forward neural networks were also used for comparison. The distorted wave including 5th, 7th, 11th, and 13th harmonics are used to be input signals for these neural networks at the training state. The output layer of network is consisted of 4 units in according to each order of harmonic. By effect of learning representative data, each component of harmonic is detected to each according unit. That means neural network structures can decompose each order of harmonic and detect only harmonic without fundamental wave in the same time.

2 Elman's Recurrent Neural Network for Harmonic Detection

Because of non-sinusoidal load currents consisting primarily of lower-order 5th, 7th, 11th, and 13th harmonics that distort the system power quality, we consider about 5th, 7th, 11th, and 13th harmonics detection. At the first step we used the feed forward neural network [8,9]. This network was a multilayer network (input layer, hidden layer, and output layer). The hidden layer neurons and the output layer neurons use nonlinear sigmoid activation functions.

At the second step, because of the time series nature of the distorted wave, we used Elman's recurrent neural network (RNN) [8,9] for harmonic detection as seen in Figure 1. This network is also a multilayer network (input layer, recurrent hidden layer, and output layer). The hidden layer neurons and the output layer neurons use nonlinear sigmoid activation functions.

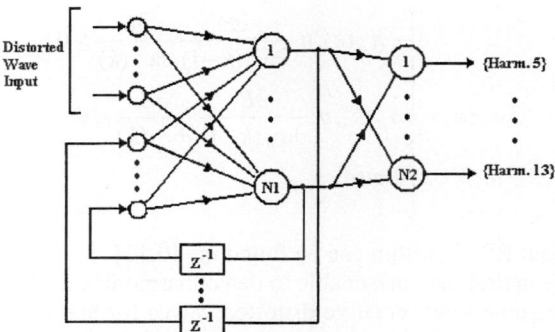

Fig. 1. Elman's recurrent neural network structures for harmonics detection

In this study, 20 hidden layer neurons and 4 output layer neurons were used for both FNN and Elman's RNN and the number of the inputs were 4 for both network structures.

3 Training of the Networks

The back propagation (BP) method is widely used as a teaching method for an ANN. The main advantage of the BP method is that the teaching performance is highly improved by the introduction of a hidden layer [12].

The BP algorithm with momentum gives the change $\Delta w_{ji}(k)$ in the weight of the connection between neurons i and j at iteration k as,

$$\Delta w_{ji}(k) = -\alpha \frac{\partial E}{\partial w_{ji}(k)} + \mu \Delta w_{ji}(k-1) \quad (1)$$

where, α is called the learning coefficient, μ is the momentum coefficient, E is the sum of squared differences error function, and $\Delta w_{ji}(k-1)$ is the weight change in the immediately preceding iteration.

The performance of the BP algorithm is improved if the learning rate is allowed to change during the training process in response to the complexity of the local surface error. Training time can also be decreased by the use of an adaptive learning rate, which attempts to keep the learning rate step size as large as possible while keeping learning stable. This algorithm is commonly known as the gradient descent with momentum and adaptive learning rate (GDX) [12]. GDX is one of the high performance BP training algorithms which used in this paper. Other high performance BP training algorithm used in this study is Resilient BP (RP) [10,12]. Standard BP algorithm is also used for comparison.

RP was developed by Riedmiller and Braun [10]. In contrast to other gradient algorithms, this algorithm does not use the magnitude of the gradient. It is a direct adaptation of the weight step based local gradient sign. The RP algorithm generally provides faster convergence than most other algorithms [10,12]. Local information for each weight's individual update value, $A_{ji}(k)$, on the error function E is obtained according to [10,12].

When the update value for each weight is adapted, the delta weights are changed as follows:

$$\Delta w_{ji}(k) = \begin{cases} -A_{ji}(k), & if \; \frac{\partial E}{\partial w_{ji}(k-1)} \frac{\partial E}{\partial w_{ji}(k)} > 0 \\ A_{ji}(k), & if \; \frac{\partial E}{\partial w_{ji}(k-1)} \frac{\partial E}{\partial w_{ji}(k)} < 0 \\ 0, & else \end{cases} \quad (2)$$

More details about RP algorithm can be found in [10,12].

In order to make neural network enable to detect harmonics from distorted wave, it is necessary to use some representative distorted waves for learning. These distorted waves are made by mixing the component of the 5th, 7th, 11th, and 13th harmonics in fundamental wave. For this purpose, 5th harmonic up to 70%, 7th harmonic up to 40%, 11th harmonic up to 10% and 13th harmonic up to 5% were used and approximately 2500 representative distorted waves were generated for training process.

During the training process, the distorted waves were used for recognition. As the result of recognition, output signal from each output unit gives the coefficient of each harmonic included in the input distorted wave and these harmonics are eliminated from the distorted wave (see Figure 2). Equations [8,9] used in the elimination process are shown in (3), and (4).

$$I_f(t) = I_d(t) - \sum_h I_h(t) \qquad (3)$$

$$I_h(t) = A_h Sin(2\pi ft + \theta) \qquad (4)$$

where, $I_f(t)$ is the active filtered wave, $I_d(t)$ is the distorted wave, h = 5,7,11,13, A_h are coefficients of lower-order 5th, 7th, 11th, and 13th harmonics, f = 50 Hz, θ is phase angle and equal to zero in this study.

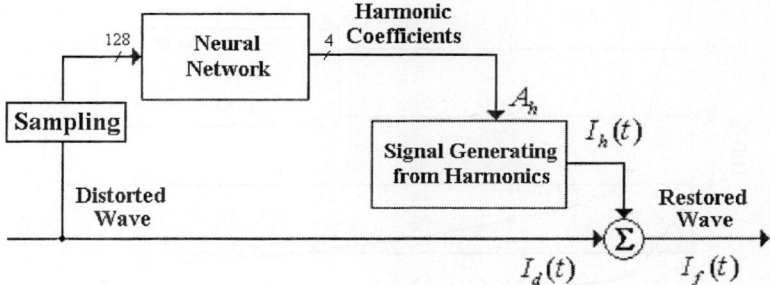

Fig. 2. Process for restoring wave

4 The Quality of Power System Waves

The common index used to determine the quality of power system currents and voltages are total harmonic distortion (THD) [4,9], which is defined as

$$THD = \sqrt{\frac{\sum_2^\infty I_h^2}{I_1^2}} \qquad (5)$$

where I_h represents the individual harmonics and I_1 is the fundamental component of the load wave.

5 Results and Conclusions

The non sinusoidal load currents consist also that the higher order harmonics such as 17th, 19th, etc., but they do not carry any significant current [1]. So, for the performance evaluation of the neural network structures, 5th harmonic up to 70%, 7th harmonic up to 40%, 11th harmonic up to 10% and 13th harmonic up to 5%, 17th harmonic up to 5%, 19th harmonic up to 2.5%, 23rd harmonic up to 2.5%, 25th harmonic up to 2% were used [13] and approximately 250 representative distorted waves were generated as a test set.

For the training and test processes, input signals of the neural networks are the amplitudes of one period of distorted wave. The amplitudes are taken 128 point at regular interval of time axis. The amplitudes are used to be input signals of the neural networks without any pre processing. At the training phase, the higher order harmonics such as 17th, 19th, etc., are ignored for *THD* calculations.

Figure 3 shows the training results of the feed forward neural networks. As seen in this figure, the results of the adaptive back propagation algorithm are better then that of the standard back propagation algorithm. From the same figure, it can be seen easily that the RP training algorithm provides faster convergence than other algorithms in the harmonics detection.

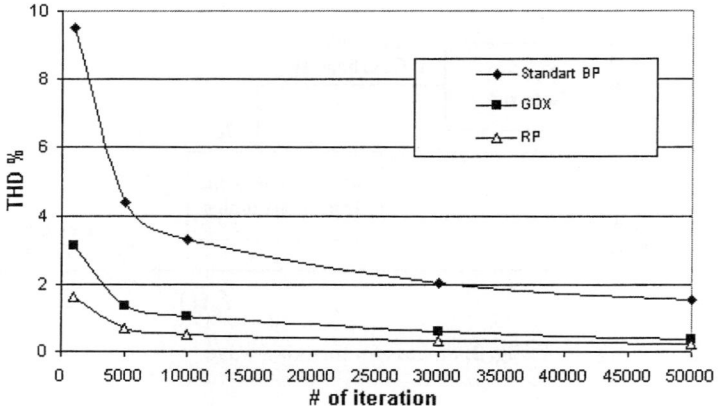

Fig. 3. Training results of feed forward neural networks

Figure 4 shows the training results of Elman's recurrent neural networks. As seen in this figure, the results of the adaptive back propagation algorithm is better then that of the standard back propagation algorithm and the RP training algorithm provides faster convergence than others.

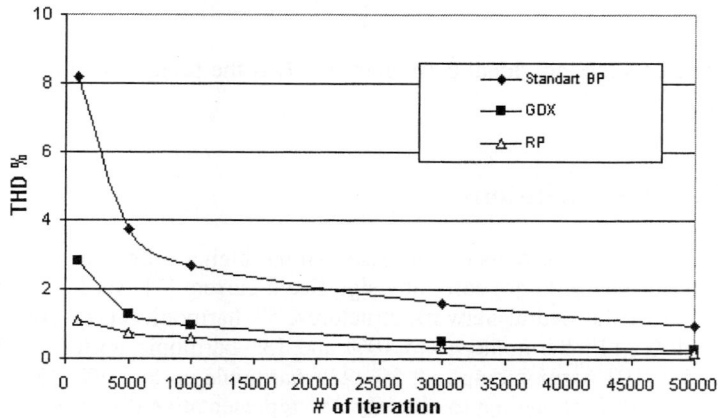

Fig. 4. Training results of Elman's recurrent neural networks

After the training process is completed, the general distorted waves (test set) were used for recognition. As the result of recognition, output signal from each output unit means the coefficient of each harmonic which is including in the input distorted wave and these harmonics are eliminated from the distorted wave.

Table 1 shows the average *THD* values of restored waves obtained by using the feed forward and Elman's recurrent neural networks for training and the test set. The sample source wave and the restored waves are shown in Figure 5.

Table 1. Average *THD* values

Neural Network	Training Algorithm	Training Average THD (%){5^{th}, ..., 13th harmonics}	Test Average THD (%){5^{th}, ..., 25th harmonics}
Before compensation		46.22	46.36
Feed forward NN	Standard BP	1.96	4.14
	GDX	0.35	3.66
	RP	0.22	3.65
Elman's RNN	Standard BP	0.97	3.77
	GDX	0.28	3.66
	RP	0.18	3.65

The recommendation IEEE 519 allows a total harmonic distortion (*THD*) of 5% in low-voltage grids [14]. As seen in the table 1, average *THD* value is 46.36% before compensation and obtained average *THD* values are less then 5% after compensation for all networks. These *THD* values are suitable to the recommendation IEEE 519. 3.65% of these *THD* values come from the higher order harmonics such as 17th, 19th, etc which are not used in the training. This means that there is an improvement potential. The *THD* values obtained by using Elman's recurrent neural networks are better than the *THD* values obtained by using the feed forward neural networks. This can be because of that the feedback structures of the Elman's RNN are more appropriate for the time series nature of the waves.

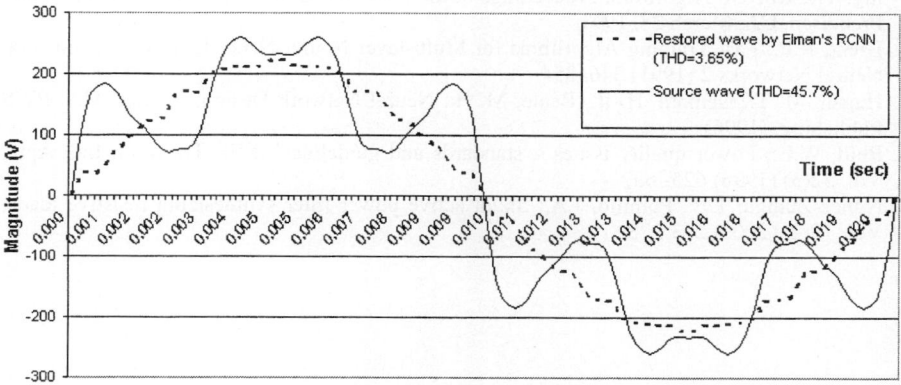

Fig. 5. Sample source and restored waves (by Elman's RCNN)

As the result, the possibility of the feed forward and Elman's recurrent neural networks to detect harmonics is confirmed by compensating the distorted waves and it can be said that the Elman's recurrent neural networks are more effective than the feed forward to use for active filter. And it is also confirmed that the RP training algorithm provides faster convergence than standard and adaptive back propagation algorithms in the harmonics detection.

References

1. Ryckaert, W.R.A., Ghijselen, J.A.L., Melkebeek, J.A.A.: Harmonic mitigation potential of shunt harmonic impedances, Electric Power Systems Research, Vol. 65 (2003) 63-69
2. Rastegar, S.M.R., Jewell, W.T.: A new approach for suppressing harmonic disturbances in distribution system based on regression analysis, Electric Power Systems Research Vol. 59 (2001) 165-184
3. Unsal, A., Von Jouanne, A.R., Stonic, V.L.: A DSP controlled resonant active filter for power conditioning in three phase industrial power system, Signal Processing, Vol. 82 (2001) 1743-1752
4. IEEE Standarts 519-1992, IEEE Recommended Practice and Requirements for Harmonics Control in Electric Power Systems, Piscataway, NJ, (1992)
5. IEEE Recommended Practices for Power System Analysis, IEEE Inc., New York, NY (1992)
6. Pecharanin, N., Sone, M., Mitsui, H.: An application of neural network for harmonic detection in active filter, ICNN (1994) 3756-3760
7. Rukonuzzaman, M., Nakaoka, M.: Adaptive neural network based harmonic detection for active power filter, IEICE Transactions On Communications, E86B (5) (2003) 1721-1725
8. Temurtas, F., Gunturkun, R., Yumusak, N., Temurtas, H., Unsal, A.: An application of Elman's Recurrent Neural Networks to Harmonic Detection, IEA-AIE 04, Lecture Notes in Artificial Intelligence, 3029 (2004) 1043-1052
9. Temurtas, F., Gunturkun, R., Yumusak, N., Temurtas, H.: Harmonic Detection using Feed Forward and Recurrent Neural Networks for Active Filters, Electric Power Systems Research, accepted (2004)
10. Riedmiller, M, and Braun, H.: A Direct Adaptive Method for Faster backpropagation learning: The RPROP Algorithm, Proceedings of the IEEE Int. Conf. On Neural Networks, San Francisco, CA, March 28, 1993.
11. Brent, R.P.: Fast Training Algorithms for Multi-layer Neural Nets, IEEE Transactions on Neural Networks 2 (1991) 346–354
12. Hagan, M. T., Demuth, H. B., Beale, M. H.: Neural Network Design, Boston, MA: PWS Publishing, (1996)
13. Reid, W.E.: Power quality issues – standards and guidelines, IEEE Trans. on Ind. App., Vol. 32(3) (1996) 625- 632
14. Nunez-Zuniga, T.E., Pomilio, J.A.: Shunt active power filter synthesizing resistive loads, Vol. 17(2) (2002) 273-278

Neural Based Steganography

V. Kavitha[1] and K.S. Easwarakumar[2]

[1] Department of Information Technology, Noorul Islam College of Engineering
Kumaracoil, Kanyakumari District, India
kavinaya@india.com

[2] Department of Computer Science & Engineering, Anna University,
Guindy, Chennai 600 025, India
easwarakumar@yahoo.co.in, easwara@cs.annauniv.edu

Abstract. Steganography is the art of hiding messages inside a multimedia block. Data hiding can be done in different medias like text, images, and audio signals. It is very difficult for the hackers to find whether the media has any valid data or not. The goal of this research is to indirectly hide the data into a graphical image using a neural algorithm, as it adds additional complexity for the hackers. Our approach hides indirectly the secured binary bits along with some selected graphical image bits, based on the neural network algorithm, to get cipher bits. The generated cipher bits are then placed in least significant bit (LSB) position of the transmitted graphical image. In reverse process, this method regenerates the original data bits. The neural model used here is the multi-layer feed forward network.

1 Introduction

Steganography is a method that hides vital information inside any other harmless messages, so that the hacker cannot even identify or detect that there is a second secret message present. Text, digital images, video and audio tracks are ideal for this purpose. Binary files with certain degree of irrelevancy and redundancy can be used to hide data. The advantage of steganography is that it can be used to secretly transmit messages without the fact of the transmission being discovered.

The embedding algorithm is used to hide secret messages inside a cover or a carrier document: the embedding process is protected by a key word so that only who possess the secret keyword can access the hidden message. The detector function is applied to a carrier through and returns the hidden secret message. In steganography, the embedded message has nothing to do with the cover and the issue concerned is the bandwidth of the hidden message. The most well-known steganography techniques are Analog of One-Time Pad and LSB Encoding.

Neural networks are simplified models of the biological nervous system, and therefore have drawn their motivation from the kind of computing performed by a human brain. A neural network is a highly interconnected network of a large number of processing elements called neurons in an architecture inspired by the brain. Neural network learns by examples. Neural network is trained with known examples of a problem to acquire knowledge about it.

This paper concentrates on embedding the cipher text generated out of neural network in the graphical image that has to be transmitted. The secrecy lies in the design of neural algorithm. The neural algorithm that has been chosen to train the secret data bits and selected image bits, which has to be transacted through a secured channel between the source and destination. This makes the steganography process that hides the data in a more efficient manner. The neural algorithm is designed with respect to the input patterns. The main advantage of this proposal is that the secret data is not transmitted as it is. The added advantage is that the cipher text generated depends on the design of neural algorithm.

1.1 Image Steganography

An image is an array of numbers that represents light intensities at various pixels. These pixels make up the image's raster data. An image size of 640 by 480 pixels, utilizing 256 colours (8 bits per pixel) is fairly common. Such an image would contain around 300 kilobits of data. Digital images are typically stored in either 24-bit or 8-bit per pixel files. 24-bit images are sometimes known as true colour images. Obviously, a 24-bit image provides more space for hiding information; however, the 24-bit images are generally large and not that common. 24-bit image of size 1024 by 768 pixels would have the size in excess of 2 megabytes. The generated cipher text is hidden in the least significant bit of the RGB.

1.2 LSB Encoding

The least significant bit insertion method is probably the most well-known image steganography technique. It is a common, simple approach to embed information in a graphical image file. Unfortunately, this LSB insertion method is extremely vulnerable to attacks. When applying LSB techniques to each byte of a 24-bit image, three bits can be encoded into each pixel. (As each pixel is represented by three bytes.) Any changes in the pixel bits will be indiscernible to the human eye [2]. The main advantage of LSB insertion is that data can be hidden and the human eye would be unable to notice it. Steganography process stores directly the encrypted data, to be transmitted, in the LSB of the graphical image. This neural network based steganography indirectly stores the data that has to be transmitted by generating cipher text with the contents of image.

2 Design Architecture

The neural based steganography trains the patterns that is formed from the original data and the selected bits from the graphical image, and produces the cipher text. The cipher text is then embedded in the LSB of the graphical image, and then transmitted to the receiver. The secrecy lies in the design of neural algorithm that is used to train the pattern. The chosen neural algorithm has to be exchanged between the sender and receiver through a secured channel. The design architecture of neural based steganography data hiding and retrieval are depicted in figures 1 and 2.

In general, neural algorithm accepts n input pattern that has to be trained, where n equals to 2^{k+1}, for an input pattern having k+1 bits. An input pattern having k+l bits: one bit from the secret information and k bits selected from the cover. The number of neurons in the input layer is designed with k+1 neurons. The number of neurons in the hidden layer depends on the problem domain. The output is limited to the maximum of three bits, because a pixel of RGB components provides three LSB for storing the cipher text. An m bit secret massage can be hidden only in m/3 pixels of the image. The encryption process encrypts k+1 bits at a time to three bits cipher text. Back Propagation Networks is used to train input patterns by randomly choosing the weight values and training the patterns till mean squared error. The weight values are adjusted with respect to BPN algorithm [6]. The training of input pattern in BPN is

Each input unit (X_i, i=0,1,...,K) receives input signal X_i and broad casts this signal to all units in the hidden layer.

Each hidden unit (Y_j, j=0,...,M) sums its weighted input signals.

$$Y\_in_j = V_{oj} + \sum_{i=1}^{K} X_i V_{ij} . \quad (1)$$

applies its activation function to compute its output signal as,

$$Y_j = f(Y\_in_j) . \quad (2)$$

and sends this signal to all output units.

Each output unit (Z_k, k=0,...,2) sums its weighted input signals as,

$$Z\_in_k = W_{0k} + \sum_{j=1}^{M} Z_j W_{jk} . \quad (3)$$

applies its activation function to compute its output signal as,

$$Z_k = f(Z\_in_k) . \quad (4)$$

and sends this signal to all output units.

Each output unit (Z_k, k=0,...,2) updates its bias and weights (j=0,...,M)

$$W_{jk} (new) = W_{jk} (old) + \Delta W_{jk} . \quad (5)$$

Each hidden unit (Y_j, j=0,...,M) updates its bias and weights (i=0,...,K)

$$V_{ij} (new) = V_{ij} (old) + \Delta V_{ij} . \quad (6)$$

In data retrieval process, the bits in the input patterns are formed with the combination of the cipher and selected bits from cover. The same neural algorithm is used for decryption process. Thus, neural base steganography satisfies confidentiality.

In this architecture the neural algorithm acts as a keyword, which is used to hide secret messages inside a carrier document. The keyword is protected by how the input patterns, which comprises of secret binary messages along with selected bits from carrier document with neural algorithm, are trained. The recovery process will reconstruct the original message bits.

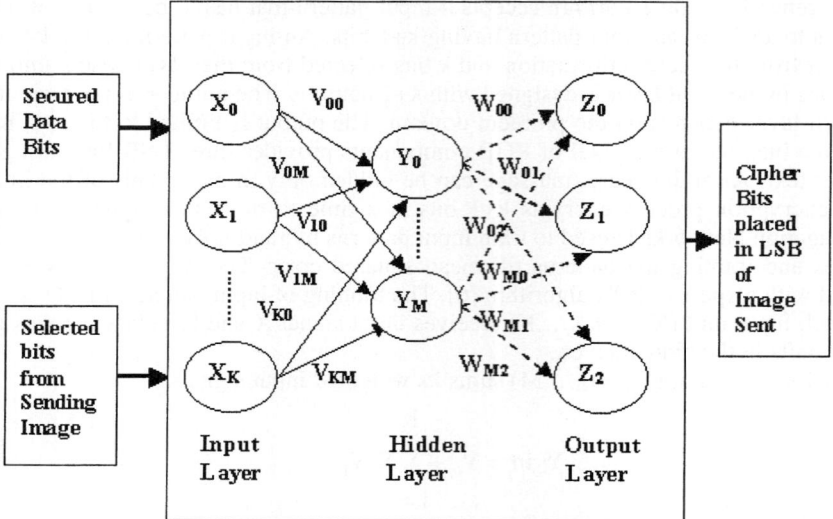

Fig. 1. Neural based steganography – Data hiding

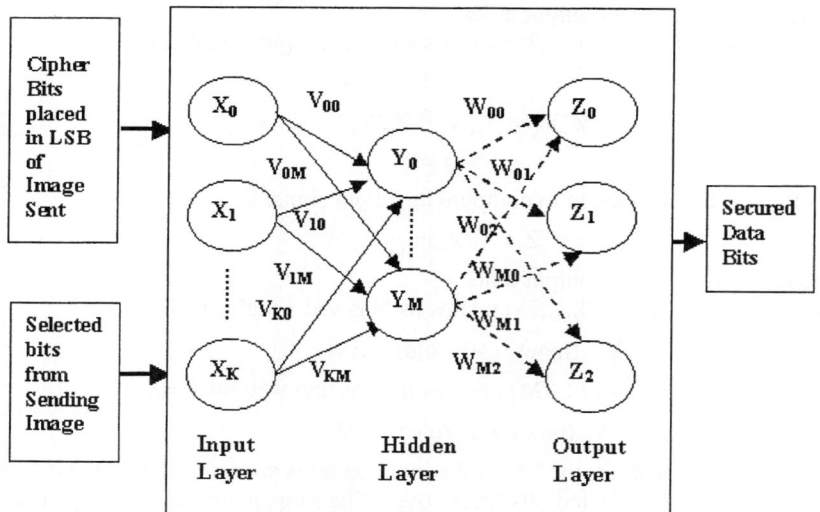

Fig. 2. Neural based steganography – Data retrieving

3 Neural Algorithm for Steganography

The neural based steganography is explained by choosing text as a secret message and the graphical image as the carrier medium. The LSB of the 24-bit Bitmap Picture (BMP) is used to hold the cipher bits. The secret message and the graphical image are converted to binary bits and the input pattern is generated. In the below example a single bit secret message is combined with the single bit binary image to form four possible input pattern as shown in Table 1. The neural algorithm is designed to respond in binary. The output bits generated so called the cipher are embedded in the LSB. Thus, the secret message is indirectly hidden in the cover. The neural network for the above example is shown in fig. 3

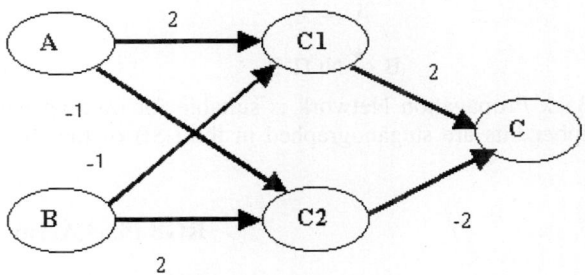

Fig. 3. Neural Network for the above example

The binary value of input secret message "Attack postponed" is 01000001..... (here ASCII value is chosen) is combined with consecutive image bits, from the starting position, of each pixel and is trained with the neural algorithm with the following training pattern shown in the Table 1. The cipher 0001 is embedded in the LSB of RGB. The retrieval process combines the cipher and image bits to reconstructs the original data from the trained network. The selection of image bits can be distributed. The input pattern combination can be a single secret bit with any number of selected image bits. Thus, neural base steganography satisfies confidentiality.

Table 1. Training Pattern

Input Pattern		Target Pattern
Data	Image	Cipher
0	0	1
0	1	0
1	0	0
1	1	1

The message "Attack postponed" is converted to its binary equivalent from through the process of binarization. In this example, MSB (Most Significant Bit) of the RGB components are the selected bits of the graphical image. The secret data bits and selected graphical image bits act as input. The neural network for the above example is designed with two input neurons and output neuron with two neurons in the middle layer. The training pattern is nothing but the Exclusive-NOR. The weight values are set to train the input pattern. The trained neural network fires the output neurons for this input patterns. The output from the output layer is placed in LSB (Least Significant Bit) of the image. The activation function for the given example in hidden layer is given by,

$$C1 = A \text{ OR } (\text{NOT } B). \tag{7}$$

$$C2 = B \text{ OR } (\text{NOT } A). \tag{8}$$

The output layer activation function is,

$$C = C1 \text{ AND } C2. \tag{9}$$

The input given for the neural network is,

$$A \leftarrow A \tag{10}$$

$$B \leftarrow \text{NOT } B \tag{11}$$

In general, Back Propagation Network is suitable for training the complex input patterns. The cipher bits are steganographed in the LSB of the RGB pixel array as shown in Fig 4.

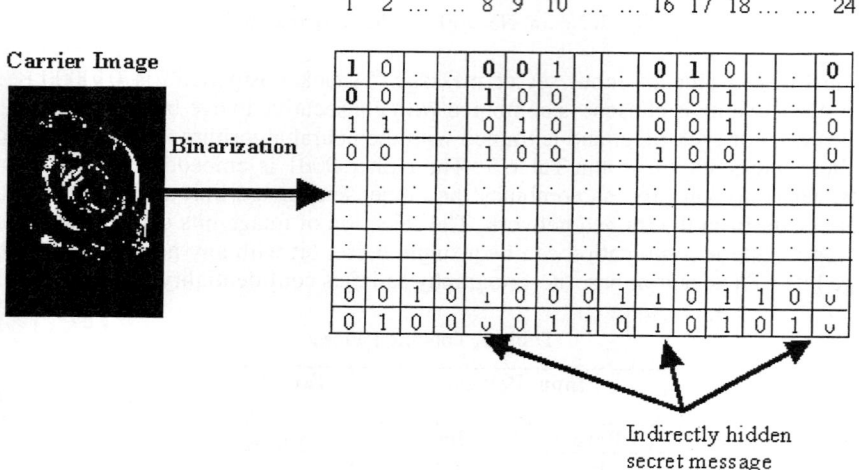

Fig. 4. Embedded neural based steganography pixel array

Here, the output cipher bits are obtained as

Data bits	: 0 1 0 0 ....
Selected image bits	: 1 0 1 0 ....
Equivalent cipher bits:	**0 0 0 1** ....

The overall process is depicted in the following algorithm.

Due to embedding the secret data indirectly, based on neural algorithm, into an image and is transmitted indirectly, it is sure that the confidentiality is more as compared to directly embedding the data into an image. This approach produced more than 90% of confidentiality, in the test trail.

Algorithm 1 (Neural based steganography)

Input: Message bits, selected cover image bits, cover image
Output: Stego image

1. Design principles of training pattern
- Form the input pattern by selecting one bit of secret text and k bits image.
- Choose the number of bits required in the target output pattern.

2. Design of neural network
- Design the neural network with the above training pattern by deciding the number of input neurons, middle layer neurons and output neurons.

3. Train the pattern
- *while* data bits of secret message present *do*
    The input is fed into the trained network and the output generated is stored in the LSB of RGB pattern of the image.
  end while

End (Algorithm 1)

4 Conclusion

The method depicted in this paper has an added advantage of providing confidentiality, as it indirectly embed the data into an image. This makes difficult for the hackers to steal the information. The number of output bits chosen here is limited to three, however it can be tried to extend further. Neural based steganography provides a great potential for defense purposes.

References

1. F.A.P. Peticolas, R.J. Anderson, and M.G.Kuhn, *Information Hiding – A Survey*, Proc, IEEE, vol.87, no.7, 1999,pp.1062 – 1078.
2. N.F. Johnson and S. Jajodia, Exploring Steganography: Seeing the Unseen, *Computer* vol.31, no.2, 1998,pp 26-34.
3. R.J. Anderson and F.A.P. Peticolas, On the Limits of Steganography, *Journal of Selected Areas in Comm.*, vol.16, no.4, 1998, pp.474-481.
4. C. Cachin, *An Information – Theoretic Model for Steganography*, Cryptology ePrint Archive, Report 2000/028, 2002.
5. A. Westfeld, *F5 – A Steganographic Algorithm: High Capacity Despite Better Steganalysis*, Proc. 4th Int'l Work-shop Information Hiding, Springer – Verlag, 2001, pp.289-302.
6. R. Beale and T. Jackson, *Neural Computing: An Introduction*, Adam Hilger, 1990.
7. Y.H. Pao, Adaptive pattern recognition and neural networks, Addision Wesley, 1989.
8. S. Rajasekaran, G.A. Vijayalakshmi Pai, *Neural Networks, Fuzzy Logic, and Genetic Algorithms Synthesis and Applications*, Prentice – Hall of India Private Limited, New Delhi, 2003.

Neural Network Combines with a Rotational Invariant Feature Set in Texture Classification

Yongping Zhang[1] and Ruili Wang[2]

[1] Bioengineering Institute, The University of Auckland
Level 6, 70 Symonds St., Auckland, New Zealand
Zhangyp1963@yahoo.com
[2] Institute of Information Sciences and Technology, Massey University
Private Bag 11222, Palmerston North, New Zealand
R.Wang@Massey.ac.nz

Abstract. In this paper, a new combine method for texture description is introduced, which has successfully applied to pollen surface image discrimination in combination with a multilayer perceptron (MLP) neural network. Through wavelet decomposition and a details reconstruction process, a set of rotation invariant statistic features was formed to characterize textures. In this method, the joint probability of a grey level image and its corresponding details image was calculated. By using MLP as classifier, in experiments with sixteen types of airborne pollen grains, more than 95 percent pollen images were correctly classified.

1 Introduction

Texture feature is one of the most widely used visual features in pattern recognition and computer vision. Texture contains important information about the surface structure of objects and their relationship to the surrounding environment [1]. In the last few decades, many approaches have been used to compute the texture features, including statistic methods, structural methods and transforms based methods, and to which new achievements are constantly being added [1-16].

Many studies have shown that use of wavelet transforms for texture description can achieve good classification performance [2, 6-12]. Smith and Chang used the statistic feature of subbands as the texture representation [6]. Gross et al. characterised texture by using wavelet transform in combination with KL expansion [7].

A combined approach of wavelet transform with co-occurrence matrix was also carried out by Thyagarajan et al. in [8]. In this paper, a novel co-occurrence matrix is introduced for texture description based on wavelet transforms, such matrix is corresponding to the joint distribution of the original greyscale image and the details derived from wavelet transforms.

Distinguishing the pollen species through the analysis of their surface images has become a new application field of computer vision; not only because of the requirement for automatic counting but also because of the need for building reference pollen image collections for teaching and research [18-27]. It is of considerable interest to develop corresponding systems capable to automatically recognise the pollen grains, to count them per types and to retrieve pollen images [22 -26].

In spite of the clear importance of automated pollen analysis, only a few researchers have addressed this area of study. In the method used by Langford [26], grey level histogram is computed for feature extraction. Treloar used the simple geometric features, such as area, perimeter and compactness, in combination with histogram features to form a feature vector [24]. Li and Flenley computed the second order statistic features based on grey level co-occurrence matrix to describe surface texture of pollen grains [25]. Ronneberger used the 3D grey scale invariant with confocal microscopy to discriminate pollen grains [27]. In the present work, we use our combined algorithm to extract texture features of surface images and use a MLP neural network to classify the extracted feature vectors.

2 Wavelet-Based Feature Set

In this section, we introduce the combined features. First we define the details reconstruction and then we introduce a novel method for feature extraction.

2.1 Orthogonal Wavelet Decomposition and Details Reconstruction

As well-known, the orthogonal wavelet decomposition of a given image possesses a pyramidal structure. In Fig.1 the data structure of three levels wavelet decomposition was shown. On the each level, one approximation image and three details images can be got; those details images are horizontal, vertical and diagonal details respectively. The resulting images are also called subband images. Fig.2 shows an example of wavelet decomposition for a pollen texture image, in which the Daubechies wavelet 'db8' are used.

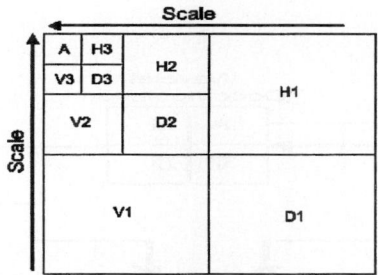

Fig. 1. The data structure of 2D wavelet decomposition.

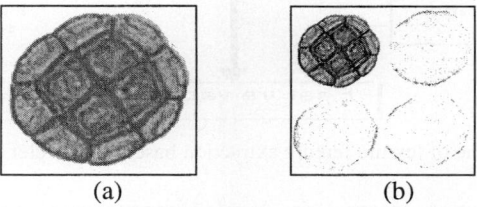

Fig. 2. Wavelet decomposition of image. (a) The original image (surface image of pollen grain *Acacia dealbata*). (b) The result of decomposition.

For image analysis, the four subband images are usually assumed to be independent. So the features are extracted in each subband independently [12]-[14]. However for most cases, across the three details subbands there are certain dependencies, and certain relations exist between the approximation and the details. On the other hand, such a method of separate consideration may lose rotational invariance because the corresponding details subband will change much when the input image is rotated. Therefore, we reconstruct a new details image only using the three details subbands, and compute the corresponding statistic features of the approximation sunband and the new details image, and to compute the joint distribution of the original image and the new details image. In Fig. 3 (a) only the details subbands of Fig. 2(b) are retained by setting the approximation subband as null. By using a wavelet reconstruction algorithm on the new subbands data, a details image is generated as shown in Fig. 3(b).

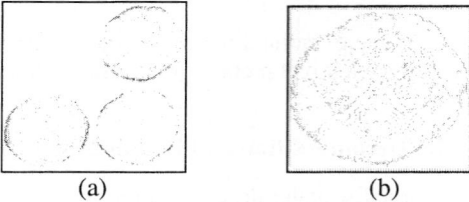

(a) (b)

Fig. 3. Details reconstruction. (a) The remaining details subbands data of Fig. 2 (b). (b) The reconstruction result only using details subbands data.

2.2 Texture Features

After the details reconstruction is performed, we provide a scheme for feature extraction as shown in Fig. 4.

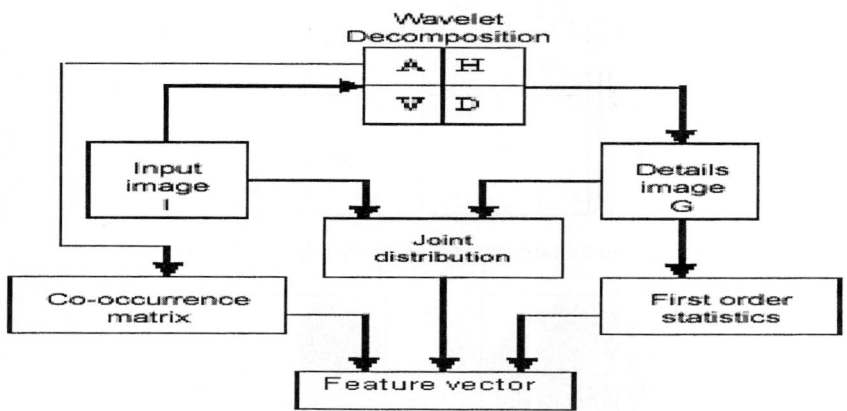

Fig. 4. The scheme of texture feature extraction based on wavelet decomposition.

For the approximation image, grey-level co-occurrence matrices (GLCM) are computed and the common five features are extracted for each co-occurrence matrix. These features include *Angular Second Moment* (ASM), *Contrast* (CON), *Entropy*

(ENT), *Correlation* (COR), and *Inverse Difference Moment* (IDM). For a given displacement vector, the corresponding GLCM is essentially a two-dimensional histogram of the occurrence of pairs of grey-levels. The mathematic definition of co-occurrence matrix as the follows:

$$p_\delta(i,j) = \frac{\#\{p_1, p_2 \in I \mid p_2 = p_1 + \delta, I(p_1) = i, I(p_2) = j\}}{\#I} \quad (2)$$

where I presents the image function, also the image domain and $\delta = (a, b)$ presents the orientation vector (or displacement). In order to obtain rotation invariant features, the GLCM features corresponding to four directions (0°, 45°, 90° and 135°) are firstly calculated, and then average them.

For describing the details image, first-order statistics is used. Energy, mean and standard deviation are computed from the resultant reconstruction image.

In the reports existed, the distributions of grey level and details were computed independently. But for a given image, there is a tight relation between the two distributions. To form effective feature vector, we compute the joint distribution of the original image and its detail image. First of all, like the above, a co-occurrence matrix Q is calculated as:

$$q(i,j) = \frac{\#\{p \in I \mid I(p) = i, G(p) = j\}}{\#I} \quad (3)$$

where G presents the details image reconstructed from the wavelet decomposition of the input image I, which is re-quantized (discretized) to certain grey levels. This matrix indicates the joint probability distribution of grey level and details.

Based on this co-occurrence matrix Q, we compute the following seven features:

Small Detail Emphasis (SDE):

$$SDE = \sum_{i,j} q(i,j)/(1+j^2) \quad (4)$$

This is a measure that emphasizes the details. Small Detail Emphasis will be large when there are lots of pixels with small detail value.

Large Detail Emphasis (LDE):

$$LDE = \sum_{i,j} j^2 q(i,j) \quad (5)$$

This is a measure that also emphasizes the details. Large Detail Emphasis will be large when there are lots of pixels with big detail value.

Gray Distribution Non-uniformity (GDNU):

$$GDNU = \sum_i [\sum_j q(i,j)]^2 \quad (6)$$

The sum $\sum_j q(i,j)$ in the bracket of (Expression 6) gives the total number of pixels with a certain grey level i. The distribution will be large when the details are not evenly distributed over the different intensities.

Details Distribution Non-uniformity (DDNU):

$$DDNU = \sum_j [\sum_i q(i,j)]^2 \quad (7)$$

The sum $\sum_i q(i,j)$ in the bracket of (7) gives the total number of pixels with certain detail value j. The distribution will be large when the grey levels are not evenly distributed over the different detail values.

Energy (ENE):

$$ENE = \sum_{i,j} q(i,j)^2 \quad (8)$$

Energy measures the uniformity of joint distribution.

Entropy (ENT):

$$ENT = -\sum_i \sum_j q(i,j) \log q(i,j) \quad (9)$$

Entropy is highest when all entries in Q are of similar magnitude, and small when the entries in Q are unequal.

Inverse Difference Moment (IDM):

$$IDM = \sum_i \sum_j q(i,j) / (1 + (i-j)^2) \quad (10)$$

The descriptor will have a large value in the cases that the largest elements in Q are along the principal diagonal.

We can call the above seven features as grey-detail co-occurrence matrix (GDCM) features. Up to date, totally fifteen features have been extracted. In the present research we use these features as texture representation.

2.3 Examples

For the feature extraction experiments, six Brodatz texture images D16, D19, D9, D112, D38 and D12 [30] (see Fig. 5) are used. Each Brodatz image of 512×512 is rotated in six directions (0, 30, 60, 90, 120, 150 degree), and each resulting image is cut into 4 subimages of 256×256. A total of 144 (6×4×6) images are produced from the texture album. The texture features of these images are extracted by using our method. Fig. 6 presents the scatter diagram of three features for all the 144 images. There are not any overlapping parts among the six groups. The results demonstrate the effectiveness of our texture description method.

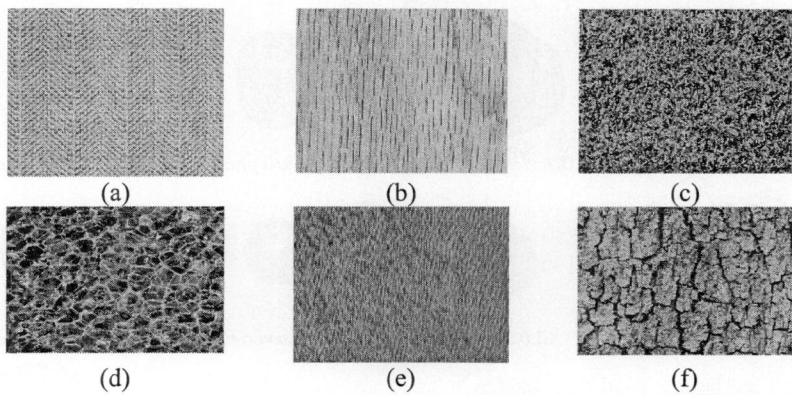

Fig. 5. Brodatz texture images. (a) weave, (b) wood, (c) grass, (d) bubbles, (e) water, (f) bark.

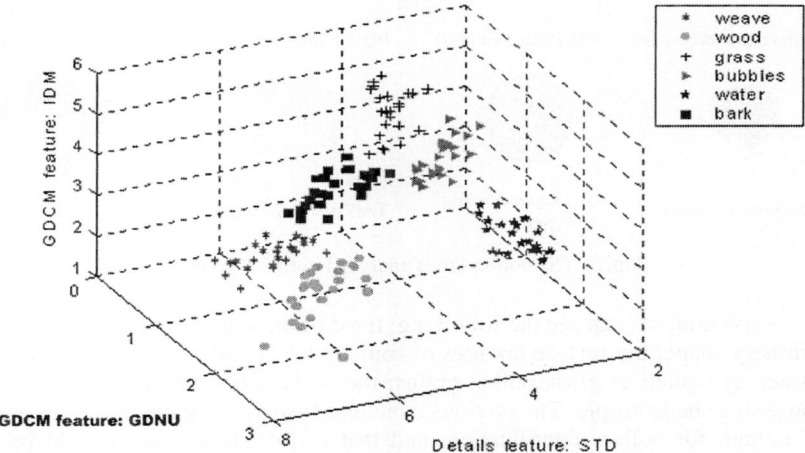

Fig. 6. Scatter diagram of three features: GDCM features **GDNU** and IDM, details feature STD.

3 Pollen Image Classification

We have applied the new texture features to discriminate the airborne pollen grains. The classification results verify the robustness of our combined method by providing high percentage of correct classification for texture images obtained from sixteen types of pollen grains.

3.1 Materials

In this research, sixteen types of airborne pollen grains are considered and their typical surface images shown in Fig. 7. Amongst them, *Agrostis Capillaries* (AC), *Alopecuris Pratensis* (AP), *Festuca Arundibaceae* (FA), *Phalaris Minor* (PM), *Triticum Aestivum* (TA) and *Zea Mays* (ZM) are grasses.

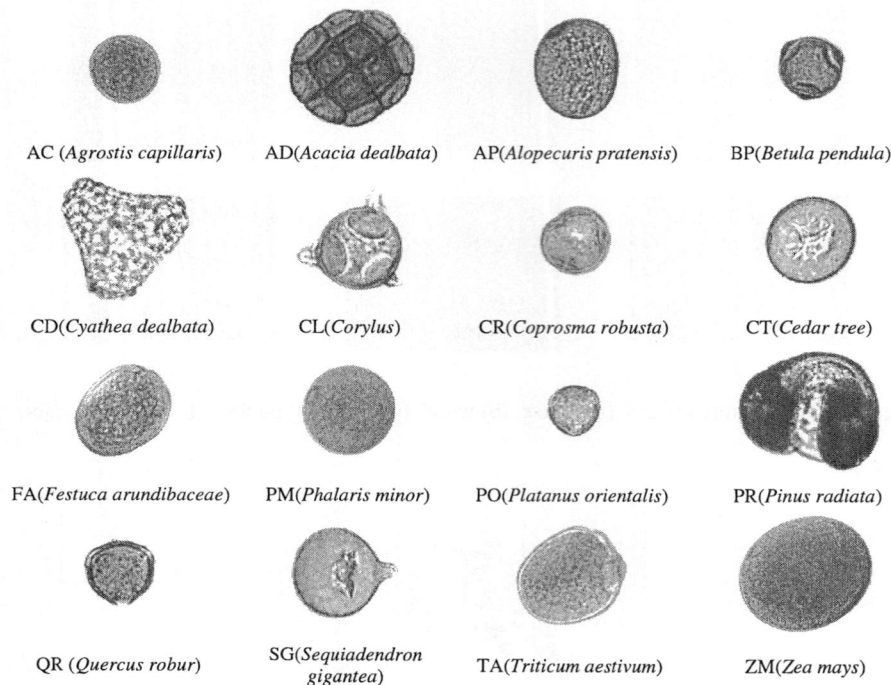

Fig. 7. The pollen types analysed in this research.

By observation, we can see the following: most of these pollen images have a similar periphery shape; the surface textures of some types are difficult to discriminate for the human eye, such as grass pollen grains; the surface texture distribution of most types appear to be isotropic. The obvious conclusions are that shape information alone is not enough for pollen identification, and that texture descriptors should be rotational invariant.

3.2 Classification Experiments

For each type of pollen grains, fifteen images were sampled. By using the ratio of interclass/intraclass distance as a measurement, totally seven features: two GLCM features (ENT and IDM) for approximation image, three GDCM features (DDNU, ENE and IDM) for joint distribution, and two first-order statistic features (mean and standard deviation) for details image were selected from the feature set to represent pollen surface texture.

For classification of pollen images, the MLP neural network of 7×15×16 was employed, and back-propagation algorithm was used for network training. The classification results are summarized in Table 1. In this experiment, 95.4 percent of pollen images are correctly classified.

4 Conclusions

A novel combined feature set has been developed and evaluated for texture classification. The feature set was obtained by using wavelet transformation in combination with co-occurrence probabilities. Through wavelet decomposition and reconstruction, the approximation and new details images was generated for a given image. The GLCM features for the approximation image, the first-order statistic features for the details image, and the joint distribution features for original image and the reconstructed details image were computed for texture description.

Table 1. The confusion matrix for sixteen types of pollen grains.

	AC	AD	AP	BP	CD	CL	CR	CT	FA	PM	PO	PR	QR	SG	TA	ZM
AC	15															
AD		14													1	
AP			14					1								
BP				15												
CD					15											
CL						13							1	1		
CR							14						1			
CT								15								
FA			3						11	1						
PM							1			14						
PO											15					
PR				1								14				
QR													15			
SG														15		
TA															15	
ZM																15

The proposed method also has been successfully applied to identification of pollen grains. By feature selection, seven features are used as texture descriptors to present pollen images, and the MLP neural network is used to discriminate features of sixteen type pollen grains. A classification rate of more than 95 percent was achieved.

References

1. Ojala, T., Pietikainen, M.: A comparative study of texture measures with classification based on feature distributions, Pattern Recognition, Vol. 29(1), (1996) 51-59.
2. Randen, T., HusØy, H.J.: Filtering for texture classification: A comparative study, IEEE Transactions on Pattern Analysis and Machine Intelligence, Vol. 21(4), (1999) 291-310.
3. Reed, T.R., Buf, J.M.H.: A review of recent texture segmentation and feature extraction techniques", Computer Vision, Image Processing and Graphics, Vol. 57(3) (1993) 359-372.
4. Haralick, R.M., Shanmugam, K., Dinstein, I.: Texture features for image classification. IEEE Trans. on Sys, Man, and Cyb, SMC-3 (6) (1973).
5. Kaplan, L.M. et. al.: Fast texture database retrieval using extended fractal features, In Storage and Retrieval for Image and Video Databases VI (Sethi, I K and Jain, R C, eds), Proc. SPIE 3312, (1998) 162-173.

6. Smith, J.R., Chang, S.: Transform features for texture classification and discrimination in large image databases, In Proc. IEEE Int. Conf. on Image Proc. (1994).
7. Gross, M. H., Koch, R., Lippert, L., Dreger. A.: "Multiscale image texture analysis in wavelet spaces, In Proc. IEEE Int. Conf. on Image Proc. (1994).
8. Thyagarajan, K.S., Nguyen, T., Persons, C.: A maximum likelihood approach to texture classification using wavelet transform, In Proc. IEEE Int. Conf. on Image Proc.(1994).
9. Do, M.N., Vetterli, M.: Texture similarity measurement using Kullback-Leibler distance on wavelet subbands, In Proc. of IEEE Int. Conf. on Image Proc. (2000).
10. Ma, W.Y., Manjunath, B.S.: A texture thesaurus for browsing large aerial photographs, Journal of the American Society for Information Science Vol. 49(7), (1998) 633-648.
11. Manjunath, B.S., Ma, W.Y.: Texture features for browsing and retrieval of large image data, IEEE Transactions on Pattern Analysis and Machine Intelligence, Vol. 18, (1996) 837-842.
12. Charalampidis, D., Kasparis, T.: Wavelet-based rotational invariant roughness features for texture classification and segmentation, IEEE Trans. on Image Proc., Vol. 11(8), (2002) 825-837.
13. Jain, A.K., Farrokhnia, F.: Unsupervised Texture Segmentation Using Gabor Filters, Pattern Recognition, 24, (1991) 1167-1186.
14. Laws, K.I.: Textured image segmentation, PhD Thesis, University of Southern California, Electrical Engineering (1980).
15. Siew, L.H., Hodgson, R.M., Wood, E. J.: Texture Measures for Carpet Wear Assess-ment, IEEE Transactions on Pattern Analysis and Machine Intelligence, PAMI-10, (1988) 92-105.
16. Hu, M.K.: Visual Pattern Recognition by Moment Invariants, IRE Transactions on Information Theory, IT-8, (1962) 179-187.
17. Smith, G., Burns, I.: Measuring texture classification algorithms", Pattern Recognition Letters, Vol. 18, (1997) 1495-1501.
18. Benyon, F.H.L, Jones, A.S., Tovey, E.R., Stone, G.:Differentiation of allergenic fungal spores by image analysis, with application to aerobiological counts, Aerobiologia Vol.15, (2000) 211-223.
19. France, I., Duller, A.W.G., Lamb, H.F., Duller G.A.T.: A comparative study of model based and neural network based approaches to automatic pollen identification, British Machine Vision Conference Vol 1, (1997) 340-349.
20. Jones, A.S.: Image analysis applied for aerobiology, 2nd European Symposium on Aerobiology, (2000) pp.2. Vienna, Austria.
21. Taylor, P.E., Flagan, R.C., Valenta, R. Glovsky, M.M.: Release of allergens as respirable aerosols: a link between grass pollen and asthma". Journal of Allergy and Clinical Immunology Vol. 109 (2002) 51-55.
22. Stillman, E.C., Flenley, J.R.: The needs and prospects for automation in palynology, Quaternary Science Reviews Vol. 15 (1996) 15.
23. Fountain, D.W.: Pollen and inhalant allergy, Biologist Vol.49 (1), (2002) 5-9.
24. Trelor, W.J.: Digital image processing techniques and their application to the automation of palynology, Ph. D. Thesis (1992), University of Hull, Hull UK.
25. Li, P., Flenley J.R.: Pollen texture identification using neural networks, Grana Vol. 38 (1999) 59-64
26. Langford, M., Taylor, G.E., Flenley, J.R.: Computerised identification of pollen grains by texture analysis, Review of Palaeobotany and Palynology, Vol. 64, (1990) 197-203
27. Ronneberger, O.: Automated pollen recognition using grey scale invariants on 3D volume image data. 2nd European Symposium on Aerobiology. (2000) p.3. Vienna, Austria.
28. Mallat, S.: A Wavelet Tour of Signal Processing, Academic Press (1998), San Diego
29. Pandya, A.S., Macy, R.B.: Pattern Recognition with Neural Networks in C++. CRC and IEEE Press, (1996) Florida.
30. http://sipi.usc.edu/services/database/database.cgi?volume=textures

What Concrete Things Does Fuzzy Propositional Logic Describe?

Paul Snow

P.O. Box 6134 Concord, NH 03303-6134 USA
paulusnix@cs.com

Abstract. Outside of the fuzzy community, questions persist about the most common fuzzy logic as a guide to propositional truth and so, despite many practical successes, about its fitness for describing real phenomena. The paper assesses the realistic expressiveness of the logic by showing that any ordinary and non-fuzzy linear programming model can be mechanically translated into a fuzzy propositional model, and *vice versa*. Since linear programs are realistic, versatile, and robust, the fuzzy propositional logic cannot be otherwise.

1 Introduction

A long-standing artificial intelligence controversy has been the interpretation of fuzzy propositional logic, its relationship to ordinary Boolean logic, and the sources of its practical successes. For instance, Elkan [1, 2] questioned both the philosophical justification for fuzzy propositional inferences as well as the scalability of fuzzy AI applications. His remarks met with rejoinders from several fuzzy authors [also in 2]. The issues continue to be vigorously discussed in AI circles, and remain unresolved.

As used in this paper, 'fuzzy propositional logic' means the assignment of values chosen from anywhere within the closed unit interval to propositional formulas, with the rules:

$\tau(A)$ and $\tau(B)$ are the values assigned to formulas A and B
$\tau(A \wedge B) = \min[\tau(A), \tau(B)]$
$\tau(A \vee B) = \max[\tau(A), \tau(B)]$
$\tau(\sim A) = 1 - \tau(A)$

It is uncontroversial that this logic originates in a multivalued logic proposed by Jan Lukasiewicz [3] in the 1920's and 30's, whose rules were, for values in the closed unit interval:

$\tau(\sim A) = 1 - \tau(A)$
$\tau(A \Rightarrow B) = 1$ if $\tau(B) \geq \tau(A)$; otherwise $1 - \tau(A) + \tau(B)$
$\tau(A \vee B) = \tau[(A \Rightarrow B) \Rightarrow B]$
$\tau(A \wedge B) = \tau[\sim(\sim A \vee \sim B)]$

Routine algebra confirms that his disjunction and conjunction are, respectively, max and min.

Contemporary fuzzy practice differs from these roots in an emphasis upon graduated membership in sets (*i.e.* a multivalued predicate logic, a topic Lukasiewicz did not much pursue), a variety of definitions of implication, and in some applications, substituting other functions for conjunction, disjunction, and negation. Nevertheless, the core of the interpretive controversies has been the basic propositional logic founded upon max, min, and unit complementation, and it is that core which is discussed here.

The persistence of contention is easily explained. When the logic is interpreted as an account of propositional truth, it conflicts with many people's deeply held ideas about the nature of truth.

The obvious examples of conflict are that classical contradictions (*e.g.* $A \wedge \sim A$) are not necessarily false and that classical tautologies (*e.g.* $A \vee \sim A$) are not necessarily true. More generally, there are unboundedly many Boolean equivalences which are not equivalences in multivalued logic, as was pointed out by Lukasiewicz himself [3].

Elkan was particularly disturbed that formulas like $\sim A \vee B$ and $\sim A \sim B \vee B$ fail to be equivalent, *i.e.* they do not always receive the same truth value. Elkan's intuition compels him to assent that these formulas, which define Boolean implication, should be equivalent.

In his view, their failure to be equivalent was liable to lead to anomalies in chained inferences using fuzzy propositional logic. Concern about chained inferences formed much of the basis for Elkan's broader conjecture that fuzzy applications could not reliably scale to address complex tasks.

Rebuttal from within the fuzzy community to this and similar objections often invokes the notion of 'partial truth.' The idea of fuzzy partial truth is to treat words like *tall* in the statement "John is tall" as predicates which any individual might satisfy to some degree, including, but not confined to, yes or no. Since partial truth differs from categorical truth, it is argued to be harmless and appropriate that classical equivalences are not generally preserved.

Lukasiewicz also thought that his logic addressed aspects of propositional truth which Boolean logic does not, but different aspects than partial truth. The vagueness and imprecision which are often mentioned by later authors play no role in Lukasiewicz's interpretation.

Other formal foundations for the logic's truth values have been proposed, including random sets, likelihood and utility models, distance from a prototype, and abstract measure theory approaches. Bilgic and Turksen survey these interpretations of truth values in [4].

Those authors also document an interpretive dialog within the fuzzy community itself: whether the propositional logic essentially refers to subjective experience, or whether it also describes aspects of objective reality. Like objectivist perspectives in other domains, fuzzy objectivism does not foreclose metaphorical reference to subjective experience, nor other reconciliations with subjectivism.

This paper makes no attempt to resolve the discussions between communities surrounding the logic as an account of truth. Rather, the paper explores a primarily objectivist thesis that regardless of what else it may be, fuzzy propositional logic is an accurate depiction of concrete situations in the real world and of well-defined abstractions of real phenomena.

Starting from an established result about the relationship between fuzzy propositional logic and a class of games, it is shown that computation of a category of true bounds on the value of any linear program restates the evaluation of syntactically and algorithmically related fuzzy propositional formulas. These results do not depend upon 'fuzzy linear programming', a popular hybrid that combines fuzzy predicate methods with linear programming.

Throughout this paper, *linear program* has its usual applied meaning. A linear function of a finite set of variables is to be optimized subject to a finite set of simultaneous linear constraints, including non-negativity, which imply a bound on the function being optimized. The value of a linear program is the optimal constraint-satisfying value of the specified function. As is routine, values are normalized to lie in the closed unit interval. This normalization amounts to a choice of origins and measurement-units for the real-world quantities that appear in the program.

The modeling scope of fuzzy propositional logic visibly coincides with that of conventional linear programming, distinguished by the precision of the solution, and sometimes not even by that. As such, it is readily understandable that the logic is a candidate for a wealth of realistic modeling roles, objective and subjective alike. The logic therefore deserves tolerant consideration even by scholars whose ideas about truth are altogether conventional.

2 The Logic Represents and Evaluates Extensive Games Exactly

The following tree

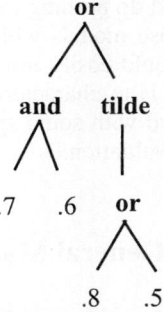

may be immediately interpreted as the parse tree of the fuzzy infix expression

$$(.7 \wedge .6) \vee \sim (.8 \vee .5)$$

The figure can also be interpreted as a representation of a two-person *extensive* game (a constant-sum game with alternating turns where each player knows the history of both players' moves, *e.g.* chess), told initially from the perspective of one of the players. The *tilde* indicates that the subtree descended from it is drawn to describe a portion of the game from the other player's perspective. Further *tilde*s along a path would toggle the perspective back and forth between the two players.

From whichever player's perspective is currently relevant, *or* represents the selection of the best alternative while *and* represents the selection by the other player of what is worst for the current reference player. Typically, evaluation proceeds upwards from the leaves, and a value transmitted through a *tilde* node is complemented to reflect the alternation in whose interest is being discussed.

Gaines [5] attributes the first discussion of the isomorphism between the Lukasiewicz logic and extensive games to Robin Giles [6]. Giles' Lukasiewicz games are strikingly similar to the game interpretation of the ordinary two-valued logic studied by van Benthem [7].

Both Giles and van Benthem emphasize a specific type of extensive game, a hypothetical argument between someone who asserts the truth of a formula and someone else who asserts the contrary. Each author derives a proof theory for their respective logics, identifying 'proof' with the existence of a winning strategy for one or the other hypothetical advocate.

Our concern in this paper, however, is not about any single kind of extensive game, like hypothetical argumentation. Rather, we wish to know what the syntactical isomorphism between any two-person extensive game tree and some fuzzy formula, and *vice versa*, says about the applied modeling scope of the logic.

The availability of the extensive game interpretation affords immediate reassurance about one of Elkan's specific concerns, that long chains of inference in fuzzy propositional logic might be inherently unreliable. There is a large body of AI experience with long-chain reasoning in games. Neither in theory nor in practice does the size and complexity of an extensive game degrade the reliability of conclusions drawn from its game tree.

Extensive games are an important category of social phenomena in their own right. Literal extensive games like chess have been widely studied within AI from its beginnings. As metaphors, extensive games have informed the analysis of realistic subjects ranging from auctions to nuclear warfare.

If fuzzy propositional logic could do nothing except represent and correctly evaluate literal extensive games and those models which have taken the explicit form of extensive games, then the logic would easily amass an impressive roster of applied successes. The remaining question is to characterize the full range of subject matter which could in principle be modeled with some specific fidelity by extensive games, or equivalently, by fuzzy formula evaluation.

3 Extensive Games Bound General Matrix Games

This section recounts some established aspects of constant-sum game theory. It contains the background for the proposition to be presented in the next section.

The extensive game is not the most general type of two-person constant-sum game. Drawing on the conventions codified by von Neumann [8], which are standard in game theory, a general game is represented as a matrix indicating the pay-offs to one player for each combination of the players' strategies in the game represented by the matrix.

A *strategy* is a complete recital of how a player plays the game. In the example game of the last section, one player has only two possible strategies: to choose the left or the right fork at the one decision juncture where this player moves. Let us call this player "Row."

The other player, call him or her "Column," has four possible strategies: if Row moves left, to choose the right or the left fork at the resulting node, and a similar dichotomy if Row moves right. We can denote Column's four strategies as (L, L), (R, L), (L, R), and (R, R).

The pay-off matrix, with values reflecting Row's interests (there is obviously a complementary pay-off matrix from Column's perspective), is:

What Concrete Things Does Fuzzy Propositional Logic Describe?

	L, L	R, L	L, R	R, R
Left	.7	.6	.7	.6
Right	.2	.2	.5	.5

The matrix is interpreted to depict a game which is strategically equivalent to the original, but is played with different rules.

In the new game, each player has a single move, choose one row or one column, and they choose simultaneously, without knowledge of the other's choice. Of course, what they are choosing in the new game is a strategy in the old one, which when executed incorporates all the information available to them in the original version.

This is a theoretical and not a practical modeling device (imagine the matrix for chess). Nevertheless, it is standard that every two-person constant sum game can in principle be represented this way.

Associated with every game matrix are two hypothetical extensive games. One is the game which differs from the actual matrix game conventions in that Column chooses first, and Row responds, knowing Column's move. The other is the game where Row chooses first, and Column responds knowingly. Both hypothetical games for the example are drawn here from Row's perspective:

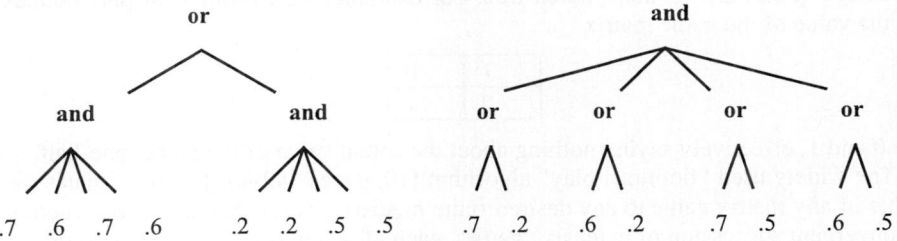

These two extensive games are the identification of Row's pure strategy maximin value and Column's pure strategy minimax value. These quantities are familiar objects of study in game theory.

In general, the two values need not coincide. Whether they do or not, von Neumann showed that there is a maximin mixed strategy (a probability distribution over Row's choices and a corresponding probability distribution over Column's) which yields a single equilibrium expected value for the game.

It is a standard result that this equilibrium value is no greater than the pure strategy maximin value and no less than the pure strategy minimax value. Of course, if the maximin and minimax values are equal, then that is the equilibrium value of the game.

The method of von Neumann's proof was to show that every game matrix corresponds to a pair of linear programs, one for each player. The values of the programs are the value of the matrix game and its complement.

Note that the two hypothetical games and the game matrix to which they pertain are all *dual*. That is, if one of them is given, then the other two can be constructed mechanically from the one that is given. Although their values are generally different, they represent one another in the sense that all the information needed to construct all three is present in each one.

Finally, in the special case where the original game is an extensive game, then it is easy to show that the hypothetical extensive games are strategically equivalent to the original game. Since the original game has a definite value, *i.e.* the pure strategy maximin and minimax values are equal, then this and its complement are also the values of the linear programs associated by von Neumann's Theorem with the game.

4 The Expressiveness of Fuzzy Formulas and Their Evaluation

The converse of von Neumann's Theorem was proven by George Dantzig [9]; see also Appendix 5.3 of [10] for some refinement of Dantzig's demonstration. Any linear program with a definite value can be represented as a constant-sum game. The optimal value of the program and the value of the representing game are the same.

Of course, the game which represents an arbitrary linear program need not be an extensive game. From the discussion of the preceding section, however, the value of the representing game, like games in general, is bounded by a pair of syntactically related extensive games.

That is almost enough to identify the scope of fuzzy formula evaluation with that of linear programming. However, there are cases where the bounds provided by the extensive games are vacuous, albeit true. For example, the hypothetical play bounds on the value of the game matrix

1	0
0	1

are 0 and 1, effectively saying nothing about the actual value of the game, one-half.

The widely used "fictitious play" algorithm [10, pages 442-446], approximates the value of any matrix game to any desired finite precision by mechanically constructing a convergent succession of extensive games, each of which offers a true bound on the value of the matrix. Each element of the sequence is a function of one or the other player's optimal plays in the extensive games which appear earlier in the sequence.

The sequence can begin with the maximin or minimax extensive games. Since they are dual to the matrix, and the algorithm requires no other input, one could construct the sequence of extensive games entirely from its first element.

The algorithm's existence complements the other results already discussed to establish that fuzzy propositional logic provides primitives sufficient for modeling the full range of linear programming applications to whatever precision may be desired. It is interesting that the structure of the fictitious play algorithm abstracts the architecture of hierarchical fuzzy controllers, such as those described in Berenji's contribution to [2, page 9].

Combining all of these results permits the following description of fuzzy evaluation's modeling scope.

> **Proposition.** (1) For every fuzzy propositional formula, a linear program of the same value can be syntactically constructed, (2) for every linear program of definite value, there exists a syntactically constructed fuzzy formula and its dual, whose fuzzy values bound the value of the program above and below, and (3) the bounds of part (2) can be mechanically refined to any finite precision by the successive values of a convergent sequence of fuzzy formulas.

The first part follows directly from the isomorphism between the parse and game trees and von Neumann's Theorem. The second part relies on Dantzig's Theorem for the existence of a suitable matrix game, and the standard results about the pure strategy bounds, whose derivations are isomorphic to a pair of extensive games, and so to fuzzy formulas. The third part characterizes the fictitious play algorithm.

In other words, whatever a fuzzy formula depicts can be depicted by a linear program with the same value. Conversely, whatever can be depicted by a linear program can in principle be depicted by fuzzy formulas, each offering a true bound on the value of the program, and those bounds can be refined indefinitely by evaluating other truly bounding fuzzy formulas. So, to within any finite precision, the expressiveness of fuzzy evaluation exactly coincides with that of linear programming.

The corresponding situation for Boolean propositional logic is weaker. There is, of course, a linear program for every Boolean formula. Programs whose matrices refer to three or more distinct quantities, however, cannot be represented by Boolean formulas in the ways discussed here for fuzzy ones. The two-by-two zero-one matrix presented a few paragraphs ago can be represented and vacuously bounded by Boolean formulas, but to refine those bounds within the formalism requires at least one more value than Boolean propositional logic provides.

That the evaluations referred to in the second and third parts of the Proposition involve bounds is unsurprising. Fuzzy approaches are often used as approximation techniques, as linear programming itself sometimes is. Approximation is a respectable modeling strategy.

The second and third parts of the Proposition also effectively address the overall concerns about fuzzy scalability voiced by Elkan and others. It is uncontroversial that linear programming is impressively scalable. While modeling complicated systems is typically more demanding than modeling simple ones, the use of fuzzy propositional logic would not in itself erect any special impediment to mastering complexity.

Clearly, the logic can be embedded within other modeling schemata, making combinations whose scopes exceed that of linear programs. For example, graduated constraint satisfaction [11] enlists the propositional logic in a program whose explicit constraints are neither necessarily algebraic nor necessarily linear.

Within a formally propositional framework, the core logic is often enhanced by the introduction of an implication operator chosen from among a wide variety of available candidates. Such a maneuver can also result in a combination whose scope would exceed that of single linear programs.

The Proposition concerns only core fuzzy propositional formulas as stand-alone representation tools. That is facially a lower bound on the logic's potential for realistic application.

5 Conclusions

The Elkan affair was a landmark in a perennial series of exchanges among AI communities. Much of what was said during that episode, on both sides, had been said before in earlier debates, and much of it has been repeated since.

Without doubt, Elkan was sincere in his concern about a logic whose ideas regarding implication differ from those of the logic with which he was most familiar. His intuition failed him, however, when it counseled that the unfamiliar logic thereby possessed some inherent flaw which would defeat its use in large and complex applications. It does not, and we know that because linear programming does not.

It is widely remarked that in natural modes of reasoning, *if A then B* has several potential meanings, of which *B or not A* is just one. The chief attraction of *B or not A* may be that it is the best that can be done under the constraint that implication's definition must resolve to expressions in *and*, *or*, and *not*, as every Boolean truth function must.

Multivalued logics do not labor under that constraint, opening the way for truth-valued syntactical expression of other possible and reasonable meanings of *if...then*. With that freedom comes an authentic problem in selecting the 'right' implication operator. It is fair to say that that problem and the opportunities that come with it were and are active research subjects in the fuzzy community. Perhaps Elkan ought to have considered that circumstance more deeply.

Elkan was on firmer ground when he observed that practical success would not compel the conclusion that any particular truth-related interpretation of the logic was correct. There is some inevitability to that since there are at least two incompatible truth-related interpretations, fuzzy partial truth and Lukasiewicz's.

Some of the other interpretations discussed in connection with [4] also explain the logic, without being especially truth-related. Resolution of the broader philosophical issues in the ongoing debates lies beyond practical success.

For many people, philosophical stories like the one about partial truth are satisfying and helpful to them as they organize their thoughts during the handicraft portions of model building. There are also other people who find the same philosophical stories both off-putting and no help at all as they organize their own thoughts for modeling.

It is foreseeable what the reaction of some in the latter group might be to the results discussed in this paper. "If I am ever tempted to use fuzzy methods, then I shall use linear programming instead." That reaction ought to be untroubling to a fuzzy advocate, since it is unlikely that someone who said such a thing would ever be so tempted in the first place.

Where the results might be most useful is after a model has been built, and its fitness is to be assessed by the world at large. It difficult to accept a model, or to judge it reliable, if one utterly rejects its foundations. Foundational doubts can survive even the most extensive empirical testing and validation. Some people outside the community gravely doubt fuzzy propositional logic as a foundation for describing anything real.

The isomorphism between fuzzy propositional logic and a 'neutral' methodology removes one possible ground for prioristic rejection of a fuzzy model. There is no rational basis for dismissing a fuzzy model just because it is a fuzzy model, regardless of one's views about the nature of truth. The evaluator must consider the possibility that the model might work, even if the evaluator would have organized his or her thoughts differently when building it.

Acknowledgment

Portions of this paper were developed during a visit to the Cork Constraint Computation Centre, supported by Science Foundation Ireland Grant 00/PI.1/C075.

References

1. Elkan, C.: The Paradoxical Success of Fuzzy Logic. Proceedings AAAI Conference. MIT Press, Cambridge MA (1993) 698-703
2. Elkan, C.: The Paradoxical Success of Fuzzy Logic. IEEE Expert **9**(4) (1994) 3-49 (with discussion)
3. Lukasiewicz, J.: Philosophical Remarks on Many-valued Systems of Propositional Logic. In Borkowski, L. (ed.): Jan Lukasiewicz. Selected Works. North-Holland, Amsterdam (1970) 153-178
4. Bilgic, T. and Turksen, I.B.: Measurement of Membership Functions: Theoretical and Experimental Work. In Dubois, D. and Prade, H. (eds.): Handbook of Fuzzy Sets and Systems, Volume I. Kluwer, Dodrecht (1999) chapter 3
5. Gaines, B.R.: Fuzzy and Probability Uncertainty Logics. Information and Control **38** (1978) 154-169
6. Giles, R.: Lukaisewicz Logic and Fuzzy Set Theory. International Journal of Man-Machine Studies **8** (1976) 313-327
7. van Benthem, J.: Action and Procedure in Reasoning. Cardozo Law Review **22** (2001) 1575-1593
8. von Neumann, J.: On the Theory of Games of Strategy. In Tucker, A.W. and Luce, R.D. (eds.): Contributions to the Theory of Games. Princeton, Princeton NJ (1959), 13-42
9. Dantzig, G.B.: A Proof of the Equivalence of the Programming Problem and the Game Problem. In Koopmans, T.C. (ed.): Activity Analysis of Production and Allocation. Wiley, New York (1951) 330-335
10. Luce, R. D. and Raiffa, H.: Games and Decisions. Wiley, New York (1957)
11. Snow. P. and Freuder, E.C.: Improved Relaxation and Search Methods for Approximate Constraint Satisfaction with a Maximin Criterion. Proceedings of the Conference of the Canadian Society for Computational Studies of Intelligence (1990) 227-230

A Framework for Fuzzy Rule-Based Cognitive Maps

M. Shamim Khan and Sebastian W. Khor

School of Information Technology
Murdoch University, Perth, WA, Australia
{s.khan,s.khor}@murdoch.edu.au

Abstract. Fuzzy Cognitive Maps (FCM), as defined originally, are limited in their capacity to model real-world scenarios, due to the rather simple representation of causal relationships between interrelated concepts. They can model a world that has only monotonic cause-effect relationships. Unlike this traditional FCM, which uses a linear function to represent the strength of relationship between two concepts, and a non-linear transfer function, to update the value of a concept during simulation, the FCM proposed by us uses fuzzy rules based on membership functions, and an aggregation operator respectively to serve these two purposes. This allows representation of non-monotonic causality, which is typical of many scenarios.

1 Introduction

Fuzzy cognitive maps (FCM) [3, 8] have been used to represent and analyse causal relationships in a number of application areas including policy analysis [12], social systems [14], decision support [5], data warehouse diffusion [6], and scenario planning and monitoring [7].

In this paper, we highlight the limitation of the traditional FCM, and propose a new model, based on fuzzy logic, for the mapping of FCM input state space to the output state space, and an aggregation operator for combining multiple causal inputs to a concept node. Initial experiments to evaluate this model are reported with some results.

Section 2 provides an introduction to the architecture and operation of FCMs. A major limitation of the conventional FCM is described in section 3. The proposed FCM model based on fuzzy logic is discussed in section 4. Section 5 presents some preliminary experimental results based on an implementation of the proposed model, followed by some concluding remarks in section 6.

2 Architecture and Operation of a Fuzzy Cognitive Map

An FCM, represented by a directed graph, is used to model a scenario as a collection of concepts or events (shown as nodes), and the causal relations between them (shown by directed edges). A node that has a causal influence on another node is called a cause node, and a node that is subject to that influence is called the effect node. The direction of the edges indicates the direction of causality. Edges are labelled with signed weights to indicate promoting (positive) or inhibiting (negative) influences and the strengths of these influences. FCM edge strengths are usually expressed by domain experts using fuzzy linguistic expressions such as, *moderate positive, weak negative* and so on. In the example FCM shown in Fig.1, the nodes N_1, N_2, and N_3 have causal influences on the node N_4, represented by the weights $w_{1,4}$, $w_{2,4}$ and $w_{3,4}$ respectively.

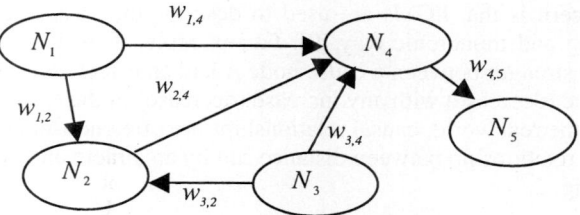

Fig. 1. A simple example of a fuzzy cognitive map.

The combined effect of causal nodes N_i on an effect node N_j is known as the activation of node N_j, and is given by

$$a_j = \sum_{i=1}^{n} c_i \bullet w_{ij} \quad (1)$$

where, c_i is the state of cause node N_i and w_{ij} represents the weights from node N_i to the effect node N_j, and n is the total number of cause nodes. The activation a_j is then transformed using a non-linear transfer function T to produce the new state c_j of the effect node N_j.

$$c_j = T(a_j) \quad (2)$$

A commonly used transformation function is the sigmoid (logistic) function:

$$c_j = 1/(1+e^{-xa_j}) \quad (3)$$

where the parameter x determines how quickly the output approaches the limiting values of 0 and 1.

Given the state vector, $C(k)$, representing all concept node values at any time step k, calculation of the state vector $C(k+1)$ at the next time step is performed by multiplying C by the FCM weight matrix E, and then transforming the result as follows:

$$C(k+1) \quad = \quad T[C(k) \bullet E] \quad (4)$$

FCMs can simulate the dynamic evolution of a scenario with time through repeated computation of the new state vector according to (4). A more detailed account of the operation, use and construction of FCMs is given in [5].

3 Limitations of the Fuzzy Cognitive Map

FCMs are often regarded as a paradigm similar to that of artificial neural networks (ANN). Typically, neural networks contain many links (usually in the 10s and some cases 100s) joining the nodes together. The assumption is that, with a large number of nodes and their interconnections, the network becomes more tolerant of any distortion in the network. Any distortion in one part of the network is compensated for in other parts. However, FCMs do not have this advantage in that the number of links to a node is small, often just one or two. Carvalho [2] observes that feedback loops (which are often present in an FCM, though not mandatory) actually aggravate the errors present in the network as the simulation progresses.

Another concern is that FCMs are used to describe the causal relations in a forward-inferencing and monotonic way [9]. For example, if there is a positive causal link of a certain strength between a cause node A and an effect node B, the state value of B will increase (decrease) with any increase (decrease) in the state value of A.

However, in the real world, causal relationships are often non-monotonic. Consider for example the relationship between distance run by an athlete and her running speed as depicted in Fig. 2.

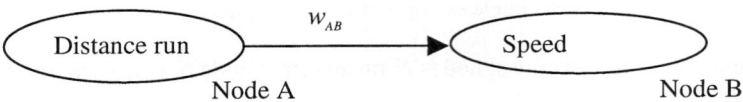

Fig. 2. A non-monotonic causal relationship.

Initially, the speed will increase with increasing distance, but as more distance is covered, the speed will drop with increasing distance. It is not possible for the traditional FCM to simulate such a situation with just the two concepts and their causal link, without introducing one or more other concepts and associated causal links. The fuzzy rule-based FCM model proposed by us can represent such a scenario by expressing domain knowledge using rules.

4 An FCM Based on Fuzzy Logic

We propose using fuzzy logic [16, 17] to map the input (cause node) states to the output (effect node) states. Our proposed model differs from that of Carvalho's rule based FCM [1]. Carvalho views states as additive and cumulative so that the state values can be 'carried over' when they exceed the maxima. This may apparently happen in a multiple-input-single-output situation. We take the view that each state has a maximum and minimum limit. When there are more than one nodes asserting a causal influence on an effect node, their influence is limited to a certain degree. This limit is expressed in the form of a weight vector such that the total of the causality is within the interval [0, 1]. This is explained further in Subsection 4.3.

4.1 The Single Causal Node Case

Consider again the causal relationship between an athlete's speed and the distance covered as represented in Fig. 2. Suppose we have the following fuzzy rules defined:

```
1) If distance_run is nil, then speed is nil
2) If distance_run is vShort, then speed is low
3) If distance_run is short, then speed is fast
4) If distance_run is medium, then speed is vFast
5) If distance_run is long, then speed is medium
6) If distance_run is vLong, then speed is low
```

Let $\mu R (x,y)$ be the degree of the membership of the relation $R (x, y)$, where $x \in A$ and $y \in B$. The degree of membership of each rule is then subject to a defuzzification process, as shown in Fig. 3.

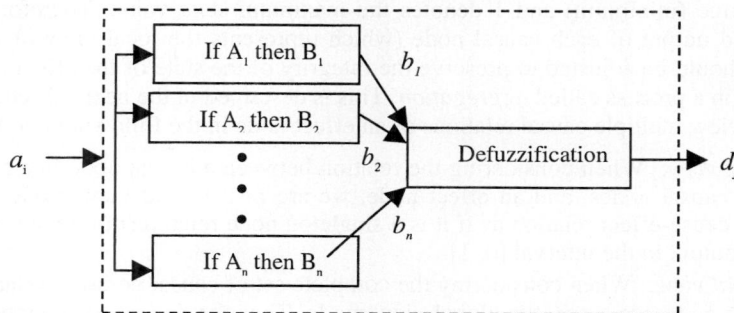

Fig. 3. Fuzzy rules and defuzzification process to derive the new state dj of node Nj. a_i is the state value of causal node N_i and b_j is its value after application of the respective rule. d_j is the output value of N_j after defuzzification.

As shown in figure 3, the output of the fuzzy rules is the entire fuzzy subset $b = \{b_1, ..., b_n\}$. The defuzzification process is to derive a single output value d_j for the effect node C_j. There are many defuzzification processes, the most popular being the Mamdani-type [4] and Sugeno-type [13] inference systems. We have adopted the Mandani-type inference and defuzzification in our experimental simulations. A single output value is derived by computing the centroid of the aggregate output fuzzy subsets. Our model differs from SAM [10] in two important aspects. In SAM, the fired then-parts over a multiple subsets of rules are simply summed and then defuzzified (which is equivalent to our *global view* level described below in subsection 4.2). In our proposed model, the summation and defuzzification is over a single subset of fuzzy rules between a cause node and an effect node, and is performed at the *local view* level. The SAM model thus assumes that the subsets of rules are compatible and can be 'added'. As can be seen from our experiment on corn crop yield, in reality, the rules differ in terms of number as well as shape.

Since there is only a single causal node, the application of an *aggregation operator* (presented in subsection 4.3 below) has no effect on the output d_j. This results in a more accurate modelling of the athlete's performance. Thus, the modified FCM not only embodies the knowledge on whether and how the speed of the athlete increases or decreases with distance, but also outputs the actual speed. Fuzzy sets allow linguistic description of the states of the nodes and their causal relationships. Thus the modified FCM can model human perception and description of the problem domain more closely.

4.2 The Multiple Causal Nodes Case

Consider the factors that affect the yield of a crop. Fig. 4 shows a simple view of the proposed FCM modelling the causal relationship between crop yield and determinant factors of rainfall, sunlight, temperature and fertilizer. Each of the causal nodes can be viewed effectively as having a single relation with the effect node *Yield*. Thus, the initial computation of the aggregate output fuzzy sets for each of the causal node is similar to that of a single causal node. In our example, the result is a set of four defuzzified output values for the effect node *Yield*. It is reasonable to assume that the final state of the effect node should lie within the interval [0, 1], where 0 denotes nil state value (minimum) and 1 denotes the maximum state value. Therefore, the defuzzified output of each causal node (which represents the local view of the causal node) should be adjusted to preserve the integrity of the state of the effect node. This is done in a process called *aggregation*. This is described in the next subsection.

We view multiple causal relations of an effect node in the following two ways:

- *Local view*: When considering the relation between a causal node in a set of multiple causal nodes, and an effect node, we are in the local view mode. We view each cause-effect relation as if it is a singleton node relationship, with the defuzzified output in the interval [0, 1].
- *Global view*: When considering the complete set of causal nodes in relation to the effect node, we are in the global view mode. Thus the degrees of memberships of the defuzzified outputs from the individual causal nodes have to be scaled to match their actual contribution to the influence on the effect node. The scaling is performed by the *aggregation operator*.

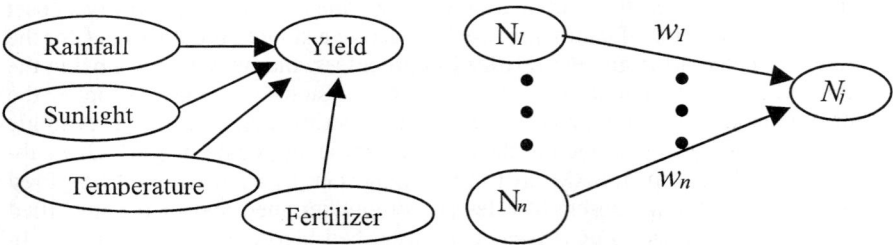

Fig. 4. A simple FCM modelling the relationship between crop yield and multiple contributing factors.

Fig. 5. Multiple cause nodes N_i, $i = \{1, \ldots, n\}$, the effect node N_j, and the weight vector w.

4.3 Aggregation Operator

Consider the causal nodes N_i, $i = 1, \ldots n$, related to an effect node N_j, together with associated weights w_{ij}, as depicted in Fig. 5. The defuzzified outputs c_i, $i = 1, \ldots n$ from the n individual causal nodes are scaled and combined using an n-dimensional aggregation operator A, $A: R^n \rightarrow R$, with an associated n-dimensional weight vector

$$W = (w_1, w_2, \ldots, w_n)^T, \quad \sum_{i=1}^{n} w_i = 1,$$

and is given by:

$$A(c_i, ..., c_n) = \sum_{i=1}^{n} w_i d_i \qquad (5)$$

The *aggregation operator* is ordered not as in the ordered weighted averaging (OWA) operator [15], but pair-wise with respect to the defuzzified output d_i. While it is possible to express weights w_i for the respective cause nodes in accordance with their relative potential influence on the effect node, a simpler approach is to treat the causal influences to be equally important. Thus, the weight for the causal link from node N_i to the effect node N_j is $w_i = 1/n$, where n is the number of cause nodes having an influence on the effect node N_j.

In the global view, the operator A behaves as if the whole set of multiple causal nodes that have an influence on the effect node, is a singleton node with a single weight $w = 1$, thus guaranteeing the integrity of the resultant effect node state to be within the interval [0, 1]. We call the set of multiple causal nodes the compound causal node.

As for the case of a single causal node, the weight $w = 1$ guarantees that the new state of the effect node is within [0, 1] since the output from defuzzification is in [0,1].

The new state value of an effect node as a result of the causal influences is expressed as the degree of its memberships in its participation as the causal node of some other effect node. Thus, the state of a causal node can influence the state of an effect node, which in turn influences another node, and so on.

5 Experiments and Results

The University of Missouri Extension Soil Testing labs has analysed various soil and plant samples, and has drawn some findings regarding the best crop yield factors [11]. We utilised their findings as the basis of our first experiment. We chose corn and the four factors identified as important for optimum corn crop yield: potassium, organic matter, phosphorus, and Ph level of soil. We constructed the fuzzy rules based on the findings. Presented in Fig. 6 are the membership functions of the four factors, showing the degrees of memberships of the factors present in the soil samples. Fig. 7 shows the membership function of corn yield.

The fuzzy rules for the four factors are as shown in Table 1. We conducted the FCM simulations to study the effects of varying the membership grade of one yield factor, while keeping the other three factors constant at 0.1. We varied the membership grades from 0 to 1 at fixed intervals to generate 25 samples for the simulation, the results of which are shown in Fig. 8.

Among the four factors, Ph level of the soil plays the most crucial role in corn crop yield, and it has a narrower effective range. The yield due to phosphorus and potassium plateau off after certain levels of input quantity. On the other hand, excessive organic matter is bad as yield actually drops quite significantly. Thus, the proposed FCM has the capacity to model non-monotonic situations effectively. The traditional FCM is unable to simulate such situations.

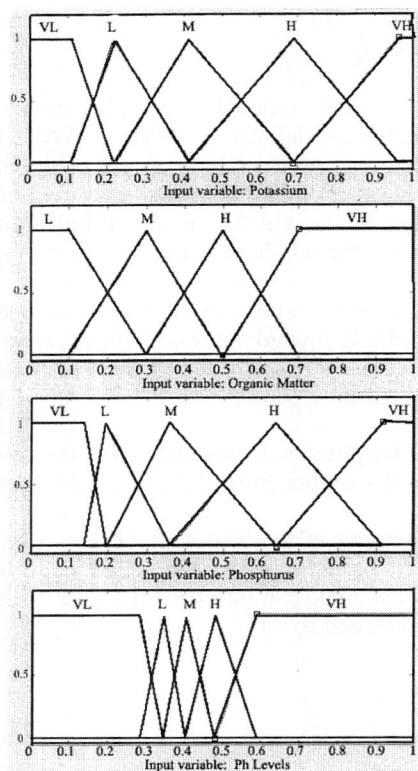

Fig. 6. Membership functions of four factors important for corn crop yield: Potassium, organic matter, phosphorus, and Ph level of soil.

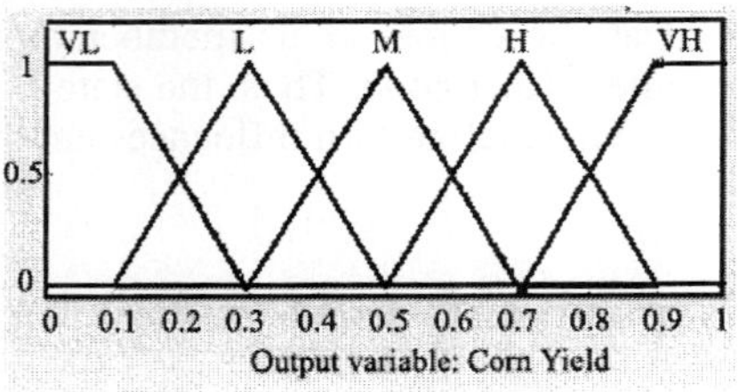

Fig. 7. Membership function of corn crop yield.

Table 1. Fuzzy rules relating the four yield factors: potassium, organic matter, phosphorus and Ph level of soil, to corn crop yield.
VL denotes very low, L: low, M: medium, H: high, VH: very high

Potassium (K)	Organic Matter (OM)	Phosphorus (P)	Ph levels (Ph)
If K is VL, then yield is VL	If OM is L, then yield is VL	If P is VL, then yield is L	If Ph is VL, then yield is VL
If K is L, then yield is VL	If OM is M, then yield is H	If P is L, then yield is L	If Ph is L, then yield is L
If K is M, then yield is H	If OM is H, then yield is VH	If P is M, then yield is VH	If Ph is M, then yield is H
If K is H, then yield is VH	If OM is VH, then yield is M	If P is H, then yield is VH	If Ph is H, then yield is VH
If K is VH, then yield is H		If P is VH, then yield is VH	If Ph is VH, then yield is VL

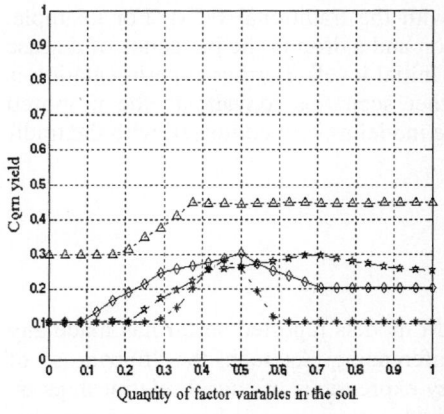 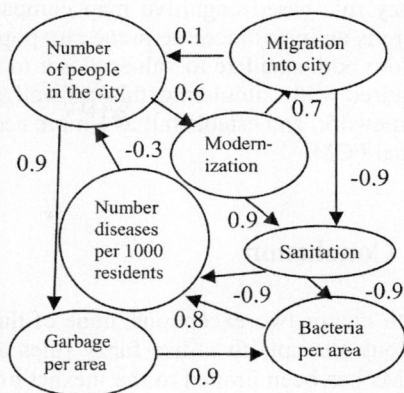

Fig. 8. FCM predicted variations in corn crop yield with each one of four yield factors.

Fig. 9. Example FCM dealing with public health issues in a city (from [3]).

In the second experiment, we used an example FCM from [3] as shown in **Fig. 9**. This example models the causal relationships between a city's population, migration, modernization, and some public health issues. The fuzzy rules for each causal link were created, based on the causal weights as well as any non-monotonic causalities perceived in the original FCM in [3]. Simulation of this scenario using an FCM is meant to serve as a decision support tool by revealing the variation with time of the various parameters of concern to city planners.

Initially, the states of all nodes were set arbitrarily at 0.5. The simulation iterated through a number of cycles, each of which represents a time step, before converging to a stable state as shown in Fig. 10(b). Fig. 10(a) shows the same for a simulation using traditional FCM methodology done for a comparison with the rule-based FCM.

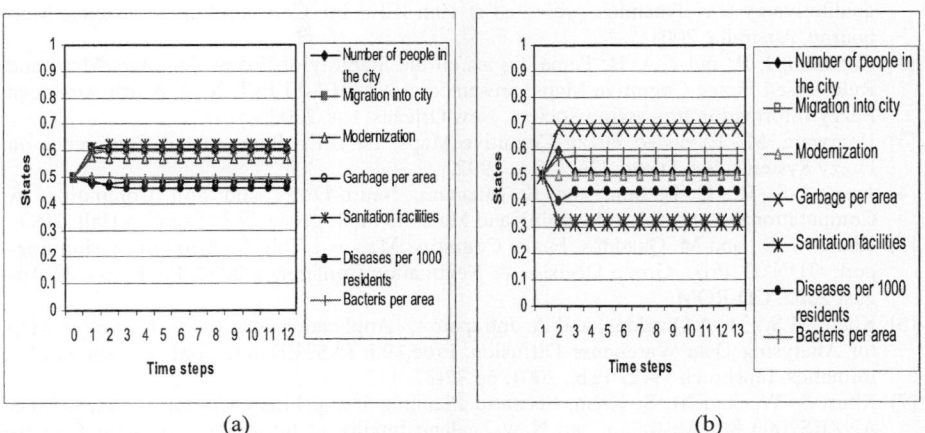

Fig. 10. State values at various time steps during simulation of example model of public health in a city [3], using (a) traditional FCM simulation and (b) Fuzzy rule-based cognitive map simulation

Initial observation shows a greater degree of fluctuation of concept states for the fuzzy rule-based cognitive map compared with the traditional FCM. For example, there is an initial increase in the city population and a drop in the incidence of disease before both stabilize to values closer to their initial levels. Further experimentation is required with simulating this as well as other scenarios to validate the proposed framework, and establish it as a more accurate modeling tool compared with the traditional FCM.

6 Conclusion

With one or two exceptions, none of the FCM models reported so far has made any serious attempts to utilise fuzzy rules and inferencing. As such, the "fuzziness" of FCMs has been limited to the inexact or fuzzy expressions of causal relationships by domain experts. The FCM framework described in this paper is based on fuzzy reasoning. As an improvement over the conventional FCM, it avoids accumulation of errors in the simulation of a scenario involving feedback. It is also capable of representing both monotonic as well as non-monotonic causalities.

We have introduced the use of fuzzy rules to express causality in an FCM. A methodology for combining such rules to implement representation of non-monotonic causality has been presented, along with an aggregation operator for combining multiple causal influences. Some initial experiments to validate this new fuzzy rule-based cognitive map framework have been described. Results of further experiments to validate this will be reported on in future.

References

[1] Carvalho, J. P. and J. A. Tomé, Rule based fuzzy cognitive maps - expressing time in qualitative system dynamics, presented at 10th IEEE Int. Conf. on Fuzzy Systems, Melbourne, Australia, 2001.
[2] Carvalho, J. P. and J. A. B. Tomé, Issues on the Stability of Fuzzy Cognitive Maps and Rule-Based Fuzzy Cognitive Maps, presented at NAFIPS-FLINT 2002, North American Fuzzy Information Processing Society, New Orleans, LA, 2002.
[3] Hagiwara, M., Extended Fuzzy Cognitive Maps, 1st IEEE International Conference on Fuzzy Systems, San Diego, CA, USA, 1992.
[4] Jang, J.-S. R., C.-T. Sun, and E. Mizutani, Neuro-Fuzzy and Soft Computing: A Computational Approach to Learning and Machine Intelligence. N.J.: Prentice Hall, 1997.
[5] Khan, M. S., and M. Quaddus, Fuzzy Cognitive Map as a Tool for Group Decision Support, GDN'02, Proc. Group Decision & Negotiation Conference 2002, Perth 26 - 29 August 2002, CD-ROM.
[6] Khan, M.S., M. A.Quaddus, and A. Intrapairot, Application of a Fuzzy Cognitive Map for Analysing Data Warehouse Diffusion, Proc.19th IASTED Int. Conf. on Applied Informatics, Innsbruck 19-22 Feb., 2001, pp.32-37.
[7] Khor, S. W., and M. S. Khan, Scenario Planning Using Fuzzy Cognitive Maps, Proc. ANZIIS2003 8th Australian and New Zealand Intelligent Information Systems Conference, Sydney 10–12 December 2003, pp.311-316.
[8] Kosko, B., Fuzzy Cognitive Maps, Int. Journal of man-machine studies, vol. 24, 1986, pp. 66-75.

[9] Kosko, B., Neural networks and fuzzy systems: a dynamical systems approach to machine intelligence. New Jersey, USA: Prentice-Hall, Inc., 1992.
[10] Kosko, B., Fuzzy Engineering. New Jersey, USA: Prentice-Hall, Inc., 1997.
[11] Lorenz, T., Soil test and plant analysis summary for year 2000, in AG Connection, vol. 7, 2001, pp. 3-6.
[12] Perusich, K., Fuzzy Cognitive Maps for Policy Analysis, presented at International Symposium on Technology and Society (ISTAS'96), Purdue University, 1996.
[13] Sugeno, M., Industrial Application of Fuzzy Control. N.Y., USA: Elsevlier Science, 1985.
[14] Taber, R., Fuzzy Cognitive Maps Model Social Systems, AI Expert, vol. 9, 1994, pp. 18-23.
[15] Yager, R. R., On ordered weight averaging aggregation operators in multicriteria decision making, IEEE Transactions on Systems, Man, and Cybernetics, vol. 18, pp. 183-190, 1988.
[16] Zadeh, L. A., Fuzzy sets, *Information and Control*, vol. 8, pp. 338-353, 1965.
[17] Zadeh, L. A., Fuzzy Algorithm, *Information and Control*, vol. 12, pp. 94-102, 1968.

Discontinuity Enhancement Using Fuzziness in DCT Blocks

TaeYong Kim and Jong Soo Choi

Graduate School of Advanced Imaging Science, Multimedia and Film, Chung-Ang University, HukSuk-dong 17, DongJak-gu, Seoul, 156-756, Republic of Korea
kimty@cau.ac.kr, jschoi@imagelab.cau.ac.kr

Abstract. Though there have been many methods to detect features in spatial domain, in the case of a compressed image it has to be decoded, processed and encoded again. Alternatively, we can manipulate a compressed image directly in the Discrete Cosine Transform (DCT) domain that has been used for compressing videos or images in the standards like MPEG and JPEG, and we have proposed a model-based discontinuity evaluation technique in the DCT domain that has problems in the rotated or non-ideal discontinuities. In this paper, we propose a fuzzy filtering technique that consists of height fuzzification, direction fuzzification, and fuzzy filtering of discontinuities. The enhancement achieved by the fuzzy filtering includes the linking, thinning, and smoothing of discontinuities in the DCT domain. Although the detected discontinuities are rough in a low-resolution image for the size (8 × 8 pixels) of the DCT block, experimental results show that this technique is fast and stable to enhance the quality of discontinuities.

1 Introduction

For image or video content understanding, the object boundary is one of the most important features. An edge is the boundary between two regions with relatively distinct intensity or color properties, which is one of the basic types of discontinuities in a digital image. This discontinuity has been detected by gradient detection techniques with low-pass filtering [1],[7] in the spatial domain. However, with these methods each compressed input video has to be fully decoded, processed and encoded again.

Alternatively, we can manipulate a compressed video directly without decoding. Due to a much lower data transmission rate and the removal of unnecessary decoding/encoding processes, the compressed domain approach has great potential for reducing the computational complexity of processing. Algorithms in the DCT domain show computational speedups of 50 or more over the corresponding processing of the uncompressed data [8], [9].

Our previous work[4] derived DCT properties related to a standard discontinuity and proposed a model-based discontinuity evaluation technique in the DCT domain. This technique consists of the direction verification and the position alignment method with an evaluation criterion, which enables an evaluation regardless of positions and directions of discontinuities. In the DCT domain discontinuity detection, it is imperative to bring ambiguity and uncertainty in the model definition or in the height evaluation. Since the discontinuity in a DCT block is not an ideal step and the shearing process to rotate a discontinuity needs much time, the technique is used without rotation process and the resultant discontinuities are sparse and isolated.

In this paper, we propose a fuzzy filtering technique to link disconnected discontinuities, to thin bulky discontinuities, and to smooth isolated discontinuities, which is performed only when an ambiguity configuration has been detected, guaranteeing a processed feature highly faithful. To enhance discontinuities in the DCT domain, we first detect a dominant height with the ambiguity by the difference against ideal model, and then we define directional fuzziness using the characteristics of frequencies. With the memberships of heights and directions we filter the discontinuities to enhance the quality of discontinuities, and this technique has proven to be fast and stable as shown in the experiments.

2 Discontinuity Detection in the DCT Domain

In this section, we briefly review our previous work [4] that detects a representative discontinuity height in a DCT block, and suggest modification for real-time applications.

2.1 Discontinuity Position Alignment

The compression process in JPEG or MPEG is done on an 8×8-block basis. The following equations are the mathematical definition of the 8×8 FDCT and IDCT:

$$F(u,v) = \frac{1}{4} C(u)C(v) \sum_{i=0}^{7} \sum_{j=0}^{7} f(i,j) \cos\frac{\pi u(2i+1)}{16} \cos\frac{\pi v(2j+1)}{16}$$

$$f(i,j) = \frac{1}{4} \sum_{u=0}^{7} \sum_{v=0}^{7} C(u)C(v) F(u,v) \cos\frac{\pi u(2i+1)}{16} \cos\frac{\pi v(2j+1)}{16}, \quad (1)$$

where $C(u)$, $C(v) = \frac{1}{\sqrt{2}}$ for u, $v = 0$, or 1 otherwise.

In an ideal step discontinuity model, intensity levels in an 8×8 block are separated by a local discontinuity between $j = 3$ and $j = 4$ in Eq. (1), which is formulated by the intensity function $f(i,j) = a$ at $j = 0, 1, 2, 3$ or $f(i,j) = b$ at $j = 4, 5, 6, 7$, where $-127 \leq a$, $b \leq 127$ and $h = |a - b|$.

Alignment is a process to shift an arbitrary discontinuity position k to "4", where $1 \leq k \leq 7$. To achieve the position alignment, we compensate the values of a given set of DCT coefficients, which is the same operation as the position of a discontinuity is shifted in the spatial position. The compensation frequency values are derived by $c_k(h,v) = F_4(0,v) - F_k(0,v)$, where F_k are DCT coefficients with a discontinuity at position k. In the case of $k = 3$, the derivation is

$$c_3(h, v) = F_4(0, v) - F_3(0, v)$$
$$= -\frac{2}{\sqrt{2}} h \{ cos \frac{7\pi v}{16} \}, \quad (2)$$

and compensation frequencies for the rest of the positions can also be formulated by changing the frequencies. The compensated (shifted) DCT coefficients $\hat{F}_k$ are obtained by $\hat{F}_k(0, v) = F(0, v) + c_k(h, v)$, where $1 \le v \le 7$, h is discontinuity height and k in $\hat{F}_k(0, v)$ represents the position of a discontinuity before alignment.

2.2 Alignment Verification and Height Evaluation

Using the approximated gradient direction described in [4], which is mentioned in Section 3.2, we can estimate the direction of a discontinuity and rotate the slant discontinuities to horizontal or vertical direction by shearing operation in the DCT domain[9].

For the position verification, we use the symmetry, which is defined as flipping an image according to its middle-vertical axis and inverting signs in the spatial domain. For an input block $f(i, j)$ and an output block $g(i, j)$, the symmetry can be expressed as $g(i, j) = -f(i, 7 - j)$, where $0 \le i, j \le 7$. In the compressed domain, the output block can be directly computed from the input block, i.e., $G(u, v) = -cos(\pi v)F(u, v)$. If the block has a step discontinuity at $k = 4$ then $G(u, v) = -cos(\pi v)F(u, v) = F(u, v)$. So, $\hat{F}(0, 2)$, $\hat{F}(0, 4)$ and $\hat{F}(0, 6)$ must be zero in the aligned coefficients. Thus, the verification measure of the discontinuity position is defined as follows:

$$D_k = \hat{F}_k(0, 2)^2 + \hat{F}_k(0, 4)^2 + \hat{F}_k(0, 6)^2, \quad (3)$$

where $k = 1, 2, \ldots, 7$. Each position k is verified by D_k with a fixed value of height h. Because D_k has the smallest value at the aligned position regardless of the height, the position(k) of a dominant discontinuity is detected whose D_k in Eq. (3) has a minimum value.

When the position of a dominant discontinuity is found, D_k can be simplified by substituting the fixed (aligned) position for the variable k. Since cosine frequency is even and periodic, D_k can be further expanded by substituting the known position k and height variable h,

$$D_k(\tilde{h}) = \hat{F}_k(0, 2)^2 + \hat{F}_k(0, 4)^2 + \hat{F}_k(0, 6)^2$$
$$= (\tilde{h} - h)^2 (\alpha_{k_2}^2 + \alpha_{k_4}^2 + \alpha_{k_6}^2), \quad (4)$$

where $\tilde{h}$ is the estimated height, $c_k(h, v)$ is the compensation at k, and α_{k_2}, α_{k_4} and α_{k_6} are constants for frequencies at k.

After rearranging the DCT coefficients by rotation and alignment, since D_k's with various heights follow a hyperbolic curve and have a global minimum value, we use the method of *gradient descent* [3] to enhance the performance and to reduce the noisy discontinuities, and finally we estimate the dominant height ($\tilde{h}$) of a DCT block.

2.3 Inter-block Height

The heights (h_{inter}) and the directions (θ) of inter-block discontinuities are calculated easily by differentiating each DC coefficient ($F_{nDC} = F_n(0,0)/8$), which is the average intensity of an n-th block[2],

$$h_{inter} = ||\nabla \mathbf{F_{nDC}}|| = [F_{nDCx}^2 + F_{nDCy}^2]^{\frac{1}{2}}, \quad (5)$$

where $\nabla \mathbf{F_{nDC}} = [F_{nDCx}\ F_{nDCy}]^T = [\frac{\partial F_{nDC}}{\partial x}\ \frac{\partial F_{nDC}}{\partial y}]^T$, and $\theta_n = \tan^{-1}(\frac{F_{nDCy}}{F_{nDCx}})$.

3 Discontinuity Enhancing with Height and Direction Fuzziness

Since the difference between the formation of DCT coefficients of a detected discontinuity and that of the ideal one reflects the ambiguity of the estimated height, in this section, we analyze the ambiguity in the dominant discontinuity of a DCT block, define fuzzy membership schemes of height and direction, and enhance discontinuities by using a fuzzy filter.

3.1 Height Fuzziness

If the discontinuity in a DCT block is ideal, then the derived height ($\tilde{h}$) has no ambiguity and the $D_k(\tilde{h})$ has to be zero in Eq. (4). Otherwise the $D_k(\tilde{h})$ is not zero and reflects the ambiguity of the detected discontinuity which is common in real images as considered at the previous section. Thus, we define a confidence membership scheme of height using the ambiguity (A_n) in a DCT block.

$$A_n = \sqrt{D_n(\tilde{h})}, \quad \mu_{hn} = 1 - \frac{A_n}{A_{max}}, \quad (6)$$

where A_{max} represents the maximum ambiguity in an image, and μ_{hn} is the height confidence membership of n-th DCT block.

Since the height calculated by the inter-block detection in Eq. (5) is the difference of averaging 64 pixels and is robust against noise, we assign the height confidence membership to one if it is above a given threshold or μ_{hn} if it is below the threshold.

3.2 Direction Fuzziness

The frequencies in a DCT block represent the formation of a discontinuity if the DCT block has a dominant one. If the discontinuity in a DCT block is not isolated, the direction of a discontinuity has the consistency with those of neighbor blocks. We define the direction of a discontinuity as the angle with respect to x axis.

Frequencies in a DCT block can be divided horizontally, vertically, and diagonally according to their positions as shown in Figure 1 (a). This division

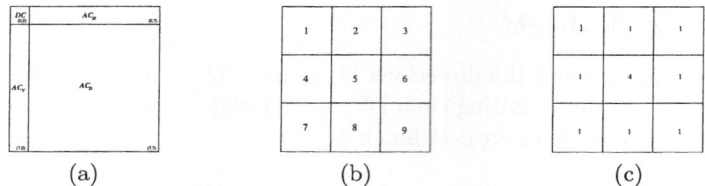

Fig. 1. Frequency division and neighbor blocks of a DCT block: (a) division of a DCT block, (b) numbering convention of neighbor DCT blocks, and (c) weighted crisp mean filter.

represents the characteristics of a discontinuity. If a discontinuity is formed vertically, only the horizontal ACs have values, and if a discontinuity is formed horizontally, only the vertical ACs have values. In the case of a diagonal discontinuity all ACs have values, and all these cases can be characterized by the ratio of absolute summations. We formulate the summations of all ACs, horizontal ACs, vertical ACs, and diagonal ACs as AC_A, AC_H, AC_V, and AC_D, respectively.

$$AC_A = \sum_{u=0}^{7}\sum_{v=0}^{7}|F(u,v)| - F(0,0), \quad AC_H = \sum_{v=1}^{7}|F(0,v)|,$$

$$AC_V = \sum_{u=1}^{7}|F(u,0)|, \quad AC_D = \sum_{u=1}^{7}\sum_{v=1}^{7}|F(u,v)| \quad (7)$$

To find a discontinuity direction, the differentiation in a digital image can be approximated by using the difference. If a gray block has a vertical step discontinuity with h, $\sum_{j=1}^{7}|\frac{\partial f}{\partial x}| = \sum_{j=1}^{7}|f'_j(i,j)| \approx \sum_{j=1}^{7}|f(i,j) - f(i,j-1)| = h$. In the DCT domain, the summation of DCT coefficients obtained from a differentiated vertical step discontinuity is formulated as follows:

$$AC_H = \sum_{v=1}^{7}|F(0,v)| = \sum_{v=1}^{7}|\frac{2}{\sqrt{2}}\sum_{j=0}^{7}f'_j(0,j)\cos\frac{\pi v(2j+1)}{16}| = 6.47h,$$

and $\frac{AC_V}{AC_A} = \frac{AC_D}{AC_A} = 0$, $\frac{AC_H}{AC_A} = 1$. Similarly, if a gray block has a diagonal step discontinuity with h, the summations in the DCT domain are $AC_H = AC_V = 2.60h$ and $AC_D = 9.56h$, and ratios are $\frac{AC_H}{AC_A} = \frac{AC_V}{AC_A} = 0.18$ and $\frac{AC_D}{AC_A} = 0.65$. Using these directional measures and ratios, the fuzzy memberships of four directions are derived.

If AC_A is less than experiential constant ϵ, which includes $AC_V \times AC_H = 0$ case, since the small value of AC_A has little information about the direction and pixels have uniform gray levels in spatial domain, then the height membership that is below the threshold (T_h) becomes 0.5, and the same direction with the inter-block direction θ has the highest membership and the others become zero.

Otherwise, there is enough information to estimate the direction of a representative discontinuity, we use the following directional memberships ($\mu_{direction}$).

If $AC_V \times AC_H > 0$, than

$$\mu_{45} = \frac{1}{0.7}\frac{AC_D}{AC_A}, \quad \mu_0 = \frac{AC_V}{AC_A} - \mu_{45} \times 0.18, \quad \mu_{90} = \frac{AC_H}{AC_A} - \mu_{45} \times 0.18,$$
$$\mu_{135} = \max\{1 - \mu_{45} - \max(\mu_0, \mu_{90}), 0\}. \tag{8}$$

If $AC_V \times AC_H < 0$, than

$$\mu_{135} = \frac{1}{0.7}\frac{AC_D}{AC_A}, \quad \mu_0 = \frac{AC_V}{AC_A} - \mu_{135} \times 0.18, \quad \mu_{90} = \frac{AC_H}{AC_A} - \mu_{135} \times 0.18,$$
$$\mu_{45} = \max\{1 - \mu_{135} - \max(\mu_0, \mu_{90}), 0\}, \tag{9}$$

where constants 0.7 and 0.18 are derived from Eq. (7). The rates of $\frac{AC_D}{AC_A}$, $\frac{AC_V}{AC_A}$, and $\frac{AC_H}{AC_A}$ are invariant regardless of various discontinuity heights when an ideal discontinuity is formed diagonally (45° or 135°) at the block center. However, by the quantization truncation and various discontinuity positions, $\frac{AC_D}{AC_A}$ varies in [0.65, 0.7], and $\frac{AC_V}{AC_A}$ and $\frac{AC_H}{AC_A}$ vary in [0.15, 0.18]. We use the maximum values of rates for normalization in Eqs. (8) and (9).

In the case of an ideal step discontinuity, $\tan^{-1}(\frac{AC_V}{AC_H})$ can be approximated for $\tan^{-1}(\frac{\partial f}{\partial y}/\frac{\partial f}{\partial x})$ to estimate a block direction [4]. However, discontinuities in a real image are not ideal steps and have ambiguities introduced during the imaging process by such factors as diffraction, lens aberration, motion of the object, wrong focus and atmospheric turbulence. The fuzzy memberships in Eqs. (8) and (9) can reflect degrees of ambiguities. As the diagonal direction of a discontinuity approaches the horizontal or vertical direction, the value of $\frac{AC_D}{AC_A}$ decreases and $\frac{AC_H}{AC_A}$ or $\frac{AC_V}{AC_A}$ increases monotonically. Thus, the fuzzy memberships (μ_0, μ_{45}, μ_{90}, and μ_{135}) represent the confidences of four directions of a dominant discontinuity in a DCT block.

3.3 Discontinuity Filtering

With an assumption that a discontinuity is not isolated, if an n-*th* DCT block is lower than a threshold (T_h) – it is not the feature yet – and has one neighbor (8-connected) feature block that has a height above the threshold, then we check that the block will be a feature by using the following filtering scheme.

$$\hat{H}_5 = \frac{1}{\mu_0 + \mu_{45} + \mu_{90} + \mu_{135}}\{\mu_0\frac{\mu_{h4}H_4 + \mu_{h5}H_5 + \mu_{h6}H_6}{\mu_{h4} + \mu_{h5} + \mu_{h6}} + \mu_{45}\frac{\mu_{h3}H_3 + \mu_{h5}H_5 + \mu_{h7}H_7}{\mu_{h3} + \mu_{h5} + \mu_{h7}} + \mu_{90}\frac{\mu_{h2}H_2 + \mu_{h5}H_5 + \mu_{h8}H_8}{\mu_{h2} + \mu_{h5} + \mu_{h8}} + \mu_{135}\frac{\mu_{h1}H_1 + \mu_{h5}H_5 + \mu_{h9}H_9}{\mu_{h1} + \mu_{h5} + \mu_{h9}}\}, \tag{10}$$

where μ_0, μ_{45}, μ_{90}, and μ_{135} are directional confidence memberships for 5*th* DCT block by Eq. (8) or Eq. (9). H_i, which is $\tilde{h}$ in Eq. (4) or h_{inter} in Eq. (5), and μ_{hi}

are height and its confidence membership of i-*th* neighbor block according to the order shown in Figure 1 (b). This filtering weighs the neighbor blocks differently depending on its own direction and neighbor block's height certainties. This fuzzy weighted mean processing makes the height of center block affected much by higher confidence blocks and less by lower confidence blocks by using the height and the direction memberships of neighbor blocks. If all memberships in Eq. (10) equal one then the filter becomes a weighted crisp filter as shown in Figure 1 (c), which is commonly used in conventional filtering methods.

After filtering with Eq. (10), if the filtered height $\hat{H}_5$ is greater than the low threshold ($T_l = T_h - \delta$) like *hysteresis thresholding* in Canny detection [1], the block becomes a discontinuity feature to link the neighbor (8-connected) features. Its purpose is to keep the discontinuities connected as much as possible.

If an n-*th* DCT block is higher than a threshold (T_h) – it is the feature already – and has no 8-connected feature block (it is isolated) or the block is not a bridged block (even if the block is removed, the link is not broken), then $\hat{H}_5$ is compared to T_h. If the $\hat{H}_5$ is lower than T_h then the block is removed for thinning or smoothing.

4 Experimental Results

In the experiments, our discontinuity filtering method applies to images obtained from image database or broadcasting. We used 3×3 window for filtering, $\epsilon = 500$ for checking monochrome block, and $\delta = 0.2 \times T_h$ for low hysteresis threshold T_l. To detect discontinuities in DCT domain we used two angles of shearing ($45°$ and $135°$) and two rotations ($90°$ and $180°$), which cover eight directions of discontinuity. The FDCT and IDCT implementation is based on an algorithm described in [6].

Figure 2 (a) shows a standard image that is popular in image processing. Detected edges by Canny detector (high threshold=0.8, low threshold=0.5 and $\sigma = 2$) in spatial domain and its reformed discontinuities for the ideal blocks are displayed in Figures 2 (b) and (c). We detect discontinuities by inter- and inner-block evaluation method with $T_h = 50$ as shown in Figure 2 (d). Highlighted blocks in Figure 2 (d) are detected by inner-block detection, and others are detected by inter-block detection. We enhance the discontinuities by crisp filtering using the mask in Figure 1 (c), and resultant discontinuities are shown in Figure 2 (e). Because the crisp filter does not consider the ambiguity in neighbor blocks, the enhanced discontinuities are disconnected and isolated. In Figure 2 (f) discontinuities enhanced by the fuzzy filter are depicted. The resultant discontinuities enhanced by fuzzy filtering are well connected and little isolated. Even though inner-block shearing, which takes the majority of processing time, is skipped in this filtering, the fuzzy filtering enhances slant discontinuities and connects them. Especially vertical discontinuities placed in the left part of the picture are well enhanced.

Figure 3 (a) shows an MPEG-2 image (704×480 pixels) that is from broadcasting. Detected edges by Canny detector (high threshold=0.8, low thresh-

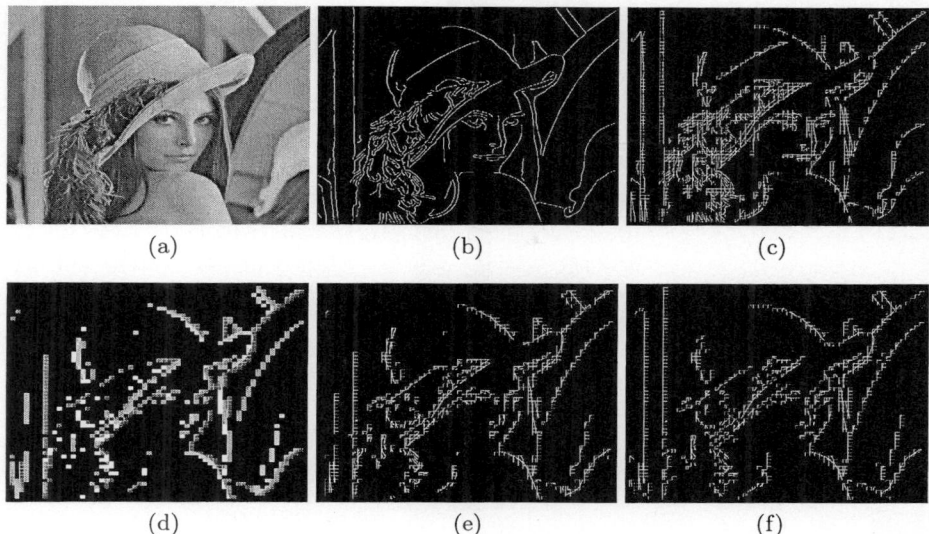

Fig. 2. Standard model image and detected discontinuities: (a) original Lena image (512 × 512 pixels), (b) detected edges by Canny detector (high threshold=0.8, low threshold=0.5 and $\sigma = 2$) in spatial domain, (c) reformed discontinuities from Canny edges for the ideal blocks, (d) detected discontinuities by DCT evaluation ($T_h = 50$), (e) enhanced discontinuities by crisp filtering, and (f) enhanced discontinuities by fuzzy filtering.

Table 1. Comparison of processing times (msec) with image sizes (pixels). T_{d0} and T_{d10} are elapsed detection time without shearing and 10% shearing, respectively. T_s is detection without shearing plus fuzzy filtering time, T_t is IDCT and FDCT transform time, and T_{td} is IDCT and FDCT transform time plus spatial edge detection time.

Image size	T_{d0}	T_s	T_{d10}	T_t	T_{td}
512 × 512	7	11	202	49	258
704 × 480	8	10	195	51	186

old=0.5 and $\sigma = 2$) in spatial domain and its reformed discontinuities are displayed in Figures 3 (b) and (c). We detect discontinuities by inter- and inner-block evaluation method with $T_h = 30$ as shown in Figure 3 (d). The enhanced discontinuities by crisp filtering and fuzzy filtering are shown in Figure 3 (e) and (f), respectively. Highlighted blocks are enhanced blocks by the crisp filter or the fuzzy filter in comparison to Figure 3 (d). As shown in Figure 3 (f) discontinuities enhanced by fuzzy filtering are thin and well connected.

Table 1 represents the processing times for each operation or transform. All times are measured by averaging 100 operations in a LINUX system. In the table, T_{d0} is elapsed detection time without shearing, and T_{d10} is detection time with 10% shearing. T_s is detection without shearing plus filtering time, T_t denotes the elapsed IDCT and FDCT transform time without any operation, and

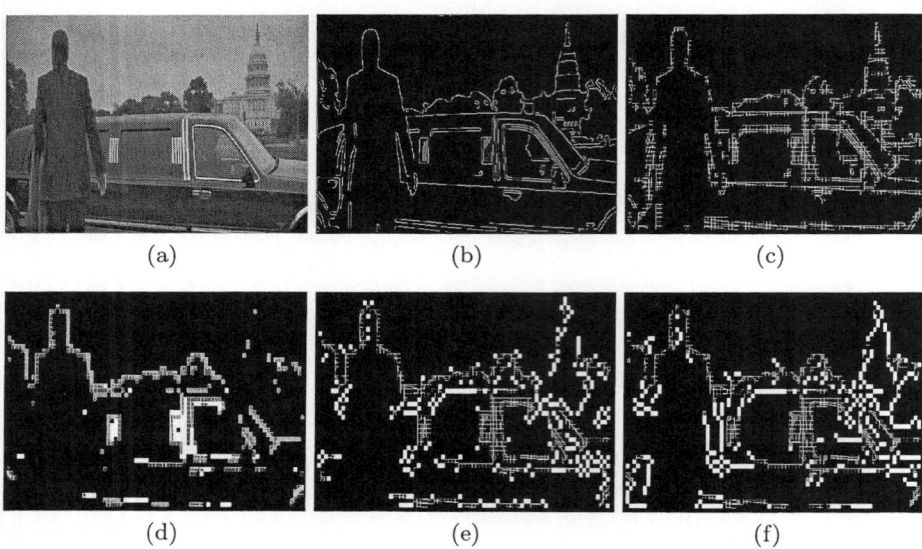

Fig. 3. MPEG-2 image from broadcasting and detected discontinuities: (a) original MPEG-2 movie image (704 × 480 pixels), (b) detected edges by Canny detector (high threshold=0.8, low threshold=0.5 and $\sigma = 2$) in spatial domain, (c) reformed discontinuities from Canny edges, (d) detected discontinuities by DCT evaluation ($T_h = 30$), (e) enhanced discontinuities by crisp filtering, and (f) enhanced discontinuities by fuzzy filtering.

T_{td} represents the elapsed IDCT and FDCT transform time with spatial edge detection time.

As shown in the table, the processing time of discontinuity detection with fuzzy filtering in the DCT domain is much faster than that of the IDCT and FDCT transforms. Since the detection in the DCT domain is performed without shearing and the fuzzy filter enhances the discontinuities, the overall detection and filtering speed of our method is about 20 times faster than that of a conventional edge detection method, without loss of much information.

5 Conclusion

The discontinuity detection method in the DCT domain has a tradeoff between in speed and in accuracy. To enhance the accuracy with preserving the advantage of efficiency, we suggest a fuzzy filtering method. Using the height and the direction memberships in a block and its neighbor blocks, the non-detected blocks are enhanced to connect its neighborhood and detected blocks are smoothed to remove isolated. As shown in the experiments, the technique is efficient in enhancing discontinuities with preserving accuracy.

This detection and filtering technique can be used for the compressed images and videos in the applications like MPEG-2 video indexing and retrieval to improve performance. However, more research is required to complement inaccurate or rough discontinuities in a low-resolution image.

Acknowledgement

We thank the financial support from the Ministry of Education of Korea under the BK21 program.

References

1. John Canny, "A Computational Approach to Edge Detection", *IEEE Trans. on PAMI*, Vol. 8, (1986) 679–698.
2. Rafael C. Gonzalez and Richard E. Woods, *Digital Image Processing*, Addison Wesley, 1993, 197–201.
3. Robert M. Haralick and Linda G. Shapiro, *Computer and Robot Vision*, Addison Wesley, 1992, 605–606.
4. TaeYong Kim and Joon Hee Han, "Model-based Discontinuity Evaluation in the DCT Domain," *Signal Processing*, Vol. 81, No.4, (2001) 871–882.
5. Les Kitchen and Azriel Rosenfeld, "Edge Evaluation Using Local Edge Coherence", *IEEE Trans. on SMC*, Vol. SMC-11, (1981) 597–605.
6. C. Loeffler, A. Ligtenberg and G. Moschytz, "Practical Fast 1-D DCT Algorithms with 11 Multiplications", *Proc. Int'l. Conf. on Acoustics, Speech, and Signal Processing*, (1989) 988–991.
7. D. Marr and E. Hildreth, "Theory of Edge Detection", *Proceeding of Royal Society of London*, Vol. B-207, (1980) 186–217.
8. Bo Shen and Ishwar K. Sethi, "Inner-Block Operations On Compressed Images", *ACM Multimedia '95*, (1995) 489–498.
9. Brian C. Smith and Lawrence A. Rowe, "Algorithms for Manipulating Compressed Images", *IEEE Computer Graphics & Applications*, (1993) 34–42.

Is Minimum-Support Appropriate to Identifying Large Itemsets?

Shichao Zhang[1], Li Liu[1], Jingli Lu[2], and Yuming Ou[2]

[1] Faculty of IT, University of Technology, Sydney, Australia
[2] Computing School, Guangxi Normal University, Guilin, China

Abstract. Apriori-like algorithms have been based on the assumption that users can specify the minimum-support for their databases. In this paper, we propose a fuzzy strategy for identifying interesting itemsets without specifying the true minimum-support. This strategy allows users to specify their mining requirements in commonly sentences. And our algorithm generates potentially useful itemsets in fuzzy sets.

1 Introduction

Since its introduction [1], the Apriori algorithm has been a prevailing approach of identifying large (frequent) itemsets for association analysis. And a great many approaches have been developed for improving and innovating the Apriori algorithm. However, Apriori-like algorithms are based on the assumption that users can specify the minimum-support appropriate to their databases. The minimum-support threshold directly impacts on both the performance and automation of association analysis algorithms. This is because a minimum-support may be too big to find anything, whereas a small one may degrade the system performance dramatically. Thus users must specify a suitable minimum-support for a database to be mined. Unfortunately, because users are often without knowledge concerning their databases, it is impossible to specify the minimum-support appropriate to their databases. Even though a minimum-support is explored under the supervisor of an experienced miner, we cannot examine whether or not the results (mined with the hunted minimum-support) are just what users want. The following story gains an insight into the difficulty of exploring a suitable minimum-support for a mining task.

Consider the tumor dataset D at http://www.stat.cmu.edu/datasets/tumor, which contains 86 records. Let JOHN be the user of D and ZHANG the developer.

ZHANG: John, please specify a minimum-support for your dataset D. JOHN: 0.7. ZHANG: My god! It is too big to find anything. Please try to specify a small one.
JOHN: Mmm..., how about 0.2? ZHANG: It is still too big because only 9 items are identified. You need to specify a very small one.
JOHN: Try 0.06, please. ZHANG: We may identify a few of association rules because only 35 itemsets are identified. You should specify a smaller one.

JOHN: How about 0.006? **ZHANG:** That is great! We have found 5735 itemsets.
JOHN: So what! Is these itemsets what I want? **ZHANG:** !?

From this story, the user-specified minimum-support is appropriate to the database to be mined only if the distribution of items in the database is known. Existing association analysis algorithms are consequently referred to the mining strategies with *database-dependent minimum-support*. This encourages us to develop new mining strategies without *database-dependent minimum-support*.

Current techniques for addressing the minimum-support issue are underdeveloped. Some approaches touch on the topic. In proposals for marketing, Piatetsky-Shapiro and Steingold have proposed to identify only the top 10% or 20% of the prospects with the highest score [3]. In proposals for dealing with temporal data, Roddick and Rice have discussed the independent thresholds and context dependent thresholds for measuring time-varying interestingness of events [4]. In proposals for exploring new strategy, Hipp and Guntzer have presented a new mining approach that postpones constraints from mining to evaluation [2]. In proposals for identifying new patterns, Wang et al. have designed a confidence-driven mining strategy without minimum-support [5]. In proposals for circumventing the minimum-support issue, Yan et al. have advocated an evolutionary mining strategy based on a genetic algorithm [6]. However, the first four approaches attempt to avoid specifying the minimum-support in some extent, whereas the last two approaches solve the minimum-support issue by coding techniques.

In this paper, we propose a fuzzy strategy for identifying interesting itemsets without specifying *the true minimum-support* (that is appropriate to the database to be mined). This strategy allows users to specify their mining requirements in commonly sentences. And our algorithm generates potentially useful itemsets in fuzzy sets.

In fact, if users want to identify large itemsets, the 'large' is already a threshold from fuzzy viewpoint, referred to *the fuzzy threshold*. Certainly, users may want to identify 'more or less large', 'very large' or 'completely large' itemsets. And all the 'more or less large', 'very large' and 'completely large' can be thresholds from fuzzy viewpoint. Therefore, it is reasonable to generates potentially useful itemsets in fuzzy sets. This has indicated that the key problem should be how to efficiently find all the interesting itemsets from databases without specifying the true threshold. This paper provides some basic techniques for attacking this key problem.

In Section 2 we begin with tackling the minimum-support issue in existing association analysis systems. In Section 3 presents an efficient mining algorithm based on our fuzzy mining strategy. In Section 4, we evaluate the proposed approach experimentally. Finally, we summarize our contributions in Section 5.

2 Problem Statement

Let $I = \{i_1, i_2, \cdots, i_N\}$ be a set of N distinct literals called *items*. D is a set of variable length transactions over I. A transaction is a set of items, i.e., a subset of I. A transaction has an associated unique identifier called TID.

In general, a set of items (such as the antecedent or the consequent of a rule) is referred to as an *itemset*. The number of items in an itemset is the *length* (or the *size*) of the itemset. Itemsets of some length k are referred to as k-itemsets.

Each itemset has an associated statistical measure called *support*, denoted as $supp$. For an itemset $A \subseteq I$, $supp(A)$ is defined as the fraction of transactions in D containing A.

An association rule is an implication of the form $A \rightarrow B$, where $A, B \subset I$, and $A \cap B = \emptyset$. The *support* of a rule $A \rightarrow B$ is denoted as $supp(A \cup B)$. The *confidence* of the rule $A \rightarrow B$ is defined as $conf(A \rightarrow B) = supp(A \cup B)/supp(A)$.

Support-confidence framework [1]: The problem of mining association rules from a database D is how to generate all rules $A \rightarrow B$, having both support and confidence greater than, or equal to, a user-specified minimum support (*minsupp*) and a minimum confidence (*minconf*) respectively.

The first step of the support-confidence framework is to generate frequent itemsets using the Apriori algorithm. In other words, for a given database, the Apriori algorithm generates those itemsets which their supports are greater than, or equal to, a user-specified minimum support. As have argued previously, the above definition has shown that the *Apriori* algorithm and *Apriori*-like algorithms rely on the assumption: users can specify the *minsupp*. This paper provides an approach of tackling the minimum-support problem.

2.1 Distribution of Itemsets

Generally, for a database D, let the support of itemsets in D be distributed in an interval $[a, b]$, where $a = Min\{supp(X)|X$ is an itemsemt in $D\}$ and $b = Max\{supp(X)|X$ is an itemsemt in $D\}$. The itemsets in D can be classified into four classes by their supports, which are depicted in Figure 1.

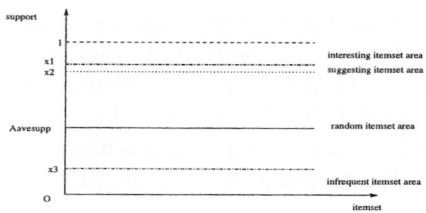

Fig. 1. Interestingness of Itemsets.

In Figure 1, $support = A_{avesupp}$ is a reference line for measuring the interestingness of itemset A, where '$A_{avesupp}$' is the average support of all itemsets in D. That is,

$$A_{avesupp} = \frac{\sum_{A \text{ is an itemset in } D} supp(A)}{\text{Number of itemsets in } D}$$

The support interval $[a,b] \subseteq [0,1]$ is partitioned into four subintervals of $[0,x_3]$, $(x_3,x_2]$, $(x_2,x_1]$, and $(x_1,1]$, where $1 > x_1 \geq x_2 \geq A_{avesupp} \geq x_3 > 0$, referred to as interesting, suggesting, random, and infrequent itemset area, respectively. An itemset with support in one of these four subintervals is respectively called an interesting, suggesting, random, or infrequent itemset. For any itemset A in the interesting itemset area, A is of interest if it satisfies some constraints.

For the database D, the distribution of the supports of itemsets in D, referred to as the *support distribution*, is very important for generating interesting itemsets. If the support distribution in D is symmetrical, $A_{avesupp}$ is a good reference point, written as $GORP$, for generating interesting itemsets. However, the support distribution in a database can be extremely gradient. Therefore, we take into account the lean of the support distribution when generating the $GORP$ appropriate to the database. For example, Assume that most of itemsets in D have low supports and others have extremely high support, and $A_{avesupp}$ may be bigger than $(a+b)/2$ (the median of these supports). If $A_{avesupp}$ is still taken as the $GORP$, we may discover little patterns from D. Similarly, when most of itemsets in D have high supports and others have extremely low support, and the $A_{avesupp}$ can be lesser than $(a+b)/2$. If $A_{avesupp}$ is taken as the $GORP$, we may discover a great many patterns from D.

Based the above analysis, we use the measure, *Lean*, for evaluating the support distribution when generating the $GORP$ for D. The *Lean* will be approximated in next subsection.

2.2 Parameter Estimation

This subsection estimates the parameters: *Lean*, $[a,b]$ and $A_{avesupp}$ for a database.

For the database D, suppose that there are N distinct items, $I = \{i_1, i_2, \cdots, i_N\}$ in D, and there are n records D_i, with each containing m items on an average. Using the *Apriori* algorithm, we assume that $Apriori(D,k)$ generates a set of all k-itemsets in D, where $k \geq 1$. Without any prior knowledge we could estimate a, b and $A_{avesupp}$ as follows.

(1) $a = \frac{1}{n}$
(2) $b = $ the maximum of the supports of k-itemsets in $Apriori(D,k)$ for a certain k.
(3) Approximating average support:

$$A_{avesupp} = \frac{1}{m-k+1} \sum_{i=k}^{m} (\frac{m}{N})^i \qquad (1)$$

It is easy to understand the assignment of a. For b, we can determine k according to a mining task.

For $A_{avesupp}$, we need two assumptions: (1) all items are equally likely to occur and (2) the items occur independent on each other. Then the number of records containing a specific item is $\frac{mn}{N}$, and its support is $support_1 = \frac{mn}{Nn} = \frac{m}{N}$.

In fact, $support_1$ can be taken as the approximate average support of 1-itemsets. According to the assumptions, the approximate average support of 2-itemsets is $support_2 = \frac{m}{N}\frac{m}{N}$ Generally, the average support of j-itemsets is $support_j = (\frac{m}{N})^j$ Consequently, because m is the average number of items in records, we can approximate $A_{avesupp}$ as

$$\frac{1}{m-k+1}((\frac{m}{N})^k + (\frac{m}{N})^{k+1} + \cdots + (\frac{m}{N})^m)$$

We now illustrate the use of the above technique by an example. Consider a dataset from the Synthetic Classification Data Sets (http://www.kdnuggets.com/). The main properties of the dataset are as follows. There are 1000 attributes and 100000 rows. The average number of attributes per row is 5. Let $k = 2$ for computing b and the maximum support of 2-itemsets is 0.0018. Then, we have: $a = 10^{-5}$, $b = 0.0018$, and $A_{avesupp} \approx 6.27 \times 10^{-6}$

Note that, due to the assumption of independency, $A_{avesupp}$ is a constant when n is large enough. This is consistent with the probability theory.

It is often impossible to analyze the *Lean* of the support distribution for all itemsets in the database D due to the fact that there may be billions of itemsets in D when D is large. Therefore, we should find an approximate lean for the support distribution. In our approach, we use the sampling techniques in [7] to approximate the lean of the support distribution in D when D is very large.

For a sample SD of D, we can obtain the support of all itemsets in SD and calculate the average support of itemsets, written as $A_{Savesupp}$. The $Lean_S$ of SD is as follows.

$$Lean_S = \frac{\sum_{j=1}^{m} 1(supp(i_j) < A_{Savesupp}) - \sum_{i=1}^{m} 1(supp(i_j) > A_{Savesupp})}{m} \quad (2)$$

where $supp(i_j)$ is the support of the itemset i_j and m is the number of itemsets in SD.

It is undoubted, $Lean_S$ is certainly larger than *Lean*. However, from the sampling techniques in [7], $Lean_S$ is approximately identical with the gradient degree the distribution of itemsets in D. Therefore, we take the gradient degree of $Lean_S$ as the gradient degree *Lean*.

After *Lean*, a, b, and $A_{avesupp}$ are calculated, an approximate *GORP* for D can be estimated using the fuzzy rules in next subsection.

2.3 Fuzzy Rules

Let *Fsupport* be the mining requirements in commonly sentences (or the fuzzy threshold specified by users). *Fsupport* is a fuzzy set, such as 'large' and 'very large'.

In our fuzzy mining strategy, the sets of the fuzzy sets of parameters $Fsupport$, $Lean$ and $GORP$ are $F\_Fsupport$, F_Lean and F_GORP as follows:

$$F\_Fsupport = \{(VS)\ Very\ small, (S)\ small, (SS)\ More\ or\ less\ small, (M) \quad (3)$$
$$Medium, (SL)\ More\ or\ less\ large, (L)\ large, (VL)\ Very\ large\}$$
$$F\_Lean = \{(L)\ Left\ gradient, (S)\ Symmetry, (R)\ Right\ gradient\} \quad (4)$$
$$F\_GORP = \{(VL)\ Very\ Low, (L)\ Low, (SL)\ more\ or\ less\ Low,$$
$$(M)\ Medium, (SH)\ more\ or\ less\ High,$$
$$(H)\ High, (VH)\ Very\ High\} \quad (5)$$

where, 'Left gradient' means that $Lean < 0$, 'Symmetry' means that $Lean = 0$, and 'Right gradient' means that $Lean > 0$.

Note that we can use more fuzzy sets than the above to describe the states of $Fsupport$, $Lean$ and $GORP$. For simplification, the above $F\_Fsupport$, F_Lean and F_GORP are used in our mining strategy.

For F_GORP, let $F \in F\_GORP$. The right part of F is $\{F, \cdots, VH\}$, written as F_{right}. For example, $VL_{right} = F\_GORP$ and $M_{right} = \{M, SH, H, VH\}$. Based on the above assumptions, the fuzzy rule FR in our fuzzy mining strategy is

IF $Fsupport$ is $A \wedge$ and $Lean$ is B
THEN $GORP$ is C

where A, B and C are fuzzy sets.

The following Table 1 is an example for illustrating the construction of fuzzy rules.

Table 1. Fuzzy rules.

	VS	S	SS	M	SL	L	VL
L	VL	SL	M	SH	H	VH	VH
S	VL	L	SL	M	SH	H	VH
R	VL	VL	L	SL	M	SH	VH

In Table 1, the first column is the fuzzy sets in F_Lean; the first row is the fuzzy sets in $F\_Fsupport$; and others are the outputs generated for $GORP$. Each output is a fuzzy rule.

2.4 Generating Interesting Itemsets

Let the range of the support of itemsets in D be $[a, b]$, the triangular function of $GORP$ is illustrated in Figure 2.

Figure 2 has demonstrated the triangular membership function of $GORP$ with respect to the fuzzy sets in F_GORP. In Figure 2, for the support x of an itemset A in D, the line $support = x$ intersects each fuzzy set in F_GORP at a

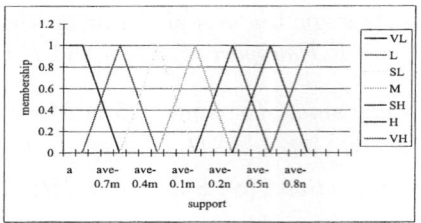

Fig. 2. Fuzzy triangular functions for parameter $GORP$.

certain point pair $(x, \mu_F(x))$. It says that $\mu_F(x)$ is the degree of A belonging to fuzzy set F.

We now define the procedure of identifying potentially interesting itemsets as follows.

Let the range of the support of itemsets in D be $[a, b]$, $Fsupport$ is $A(\in F\_Fsupport)$ and $Lean$ is $B(\in F\_Lean)$, '$GORP$ is $F \in F\_GORP$ obtained by using the above fuzzy rules. Identifying interesting itemsets is to generate the set of the Potentially interesting Itemsets (PI), written as $\pi_{D/F}$. And $\pi_{D/F}$ is defined as

$$\pi_{D/F} = \{A \in Itemset(D) | \exists F' \in F_{right} \wedge \mu_{F'}(supp(A)) > 0\}$$

where, $Itemset(D)$ is the set of all itemsets in D, $supp(A)$ is the support of A.

A potentially interesting itemset A is represented as

$$(A, supp(A), \mu_F(supp(A))) \qquad (6)$$

where, $supp(A)$ is the support of A, $\mu_F(supp(A))$ is the degree of A belonging to fuzzy set F and

$$\mu_F(x) = \begin{cases} 0, & if\ x \leq a_F \\ \frac{x - a_F}{c_F - a_F} & if\ x \in (a_F, c_F) \\ 1, & if\ x \geq c_F \end{cases} \qquad (7)$$

where, a_F is the left endpoint of the triangular membership function of F and c_F is the center point of the triangular membership function of F.

2.5 An Example

Let $TD1$ be a transaction database with 10 transactions: $\{\{A, B, D\}; \{A, B, C, D\}; \{B, D\}; \{B, C, D, E\}; \{A, C, E\}; \{B, D, F\}; \{A, E, F\}; \{C, F\}; \{B, C, F\}; \{A, B, C, D, F\}\}$. Assume $Fsupport = L\ (large)$.

For $TD1$, let $k = 2$. We have: $a = 0.1$, $b = 0.6$, $A_{avesupp} = 0.23721$, and $Lean = 0.5349$.

This means $Lean = R$. According to the fuzzy rules, we obtain $GORP = SH$ and $SH_{right} = \{SH, H, VH\}$. Hence, the set of the Potentially interesting Itemsets is

$$\pi_{TD1/SH} = \{X \in Itemset(TD1) | \exists F' \in SH_{right} \wedge \mu_{F'}(supp(X)) > 0\}$$
$$= \{A, B, C, D, E, F, AB, AC, AD, BC, BD, BF, CD, CF, ABD, BCD\}$$

Assume the membership function of fuzzy set SH for $TD1$ is

$$\mu_{SH}(x) = \begin{cases} 0, & if \ x \leq 0.23721 \\ \frac{50000}{7713}x - \frac{7907}{5142} & if \ x \in (0.23721, 0.39147) \\ 1, & if \ x \geq 0.39147 \end{cases} \quad (8)$$

According to Eq. (6), we can represent the Potentially interesting Itemsets as follows

$(A, 0.5, 1), (B, 0.7, 1), (C, 0.6, 1), (D, 0.6, 1), (E, 0.3, 0.4070386)$
$(F, 0.5, 1), (AB, 0.3, 0.4070386), (AC, 0.3, 0.4070386), (AD, 0.3, 0.4070386)$
$(BC, 0.4, 1), (BD, 0.6, 1), (BF, 0.3, 0.4070386), (CD, 0.3, 0.4070386)$
$(CF, 0.3, 0.4070386), (ABD, 0.3, 0.4070386), (BCD, 0.3, 0.4070386)$

3 An Efficient Algorithm for Identifying Itemsets of Potential Interest

Based on this fuzzy mining strategy and the support-confidence framework, we can define that J is a *potentially interesting itemset* if and only if

$$\begin{aligned} pii(J) = supp(J) &> a_F \wedge \\ \exists X, Y : X \cup Y &= J \wedge \\ X \cap Y &= \emptyset \wedge \\ supp(X \cup Y)/supp(X) &\geq minconf \wedge \\ supp(X \cup Y) &\not\approx supp(X)supp(Y) \end{aligned} \quad (9)$$

where, a_F is the left endpoint of the triangular membership function of F and $F \in F\_GORP$ is a fuzzy set obtained by the above fuzzy rules in Section 2; $minconf$ is the thresholds of the minimum confidence (for the purpose of association-rule analysis). We now construct an efficient algorithm for finding itemsets of potential interest, named as $FuzzyMS$.

Algorithm 1 *FuzzyMS*

Input: *D: data set; Fsupport: a fuzzy threshold (the user-specified mining requirement);*
Output: *Interestset: the set of potentially interesting itemsets with supports and membership values;*
(1) //producing a sample SD of D and estimating the parameter $Lean$
  let set $SD \leftarrow$ a sample of D;
  let set $A_{Savesupp} \leftarrow$ the average support of itemsets in SD;
  calculate $Lean_S \leftarrow \frac{\sum_{j=1}^{m} 1(supp(i_j) < A_{Savesupp}) - \sum_{i=1}^{m} 1(supp(i_j) > A_{Savesupp})}{m}$;
  let set $Lean \leftarrow Lean_S$;

(2) //estimating the parameters a, b and $A_{avesupp}$
   let set $Fsupport \leftarrow$ user's mining requirement;
   let set $Interestset \leftarrow \emptyset$;
   scan D;
   let $a \leftarrow \frac{1}{|D|}$;
   let $b \leftarrow$ the maximum of the supports of 1-itemsets;
   let set $m \leftarrow$ average number of attributes per row;
   let $A_{avesupp} \leftarrow \frac{1}{m-k+1}\sum_{i=k}^{m}(\frac{m}{N})^i$;
   Generate fuzzy concept of $Lean$ according to $Lean_S$;
   Generate '$GORP$ is F' according to fuzzy concepts $Fsupport$ and $Lean$;
   let $a_F \leftarrow$ the left endpoint of the triangular membership function of F;
   let $c_F \leftarrow$ the center point of the triangular membership function of F;
(3) //generating all potentially interesting 1-itemsets
   let $L_1 \leftarrow \{(A, supp(A), \mu_F(supp(A))| A \in Apriori(D, 1, a_F)\ if\ pii(A)\}$;
   let $Interestset \leftarrow Interestset \cup \{(A, supp(A), \mu_F(supp(A)))| A \in L_1\}$;
(4) //generate all candidate i-itemsets of potential interest in D
   for $(i = 2;\ L_{i-1} \neq \emptyset;\ i++)$ **do**
      let $L_i \leftarrow Apriori(D, i, a_F)$;
(5) //Pruning all uninteresting i-itemsets in L_i
      for any itemset A in L_i **do**
         if $\neg pii(A)$ **then**
            let $L_i \leftarrow L_i - \{A\}$;
      end
      let $Interestset \leftarrow Interestset \cup \{(A, supp(A), \mu_F(supp(A)))| A \in L_i\}$;
   end
(6) **output** the potentially interesting itemsets $Interestset$ in D;
(7) **endall**.

The algorithm $FuzzyMS$ generates all itemsets of potential interest in the database D for the given $Fsupport$. It is a $Apriori$-like algorithm without the true minimum-support.

The approximation of the desired factors $Lean$ for the database, D, are carried out by sampling in Step (1). Step (2) firstly estimates the parameters a, b and $A_a vesupp$. Secondly, the fuzzy concept ($\in F\_Lean$) of $Lean$ is generated according to $Lean_S$. Thirdly, the fuzzy concept F ($\in F\_GORP$) of $GORP$ is reasoned according to $Fsupport$ and $Lean$ using the fuzzy rules. Finally, the desired parameters a_F and c_F are obtained.

The rest part of our algorithm (from Step (3) to (7)) is $Apriori$-like. Step (3) generates the set L_1 from $Apriori(D, 1, a_F)$, where $Apriori(D, i, a_F)$ generates a set of all potentially interesting i-itemsets in D for $i \geq 1$ using the Apriori algorithm (with a_F as the minimum-support). And any 1-itemsets A in L_1 is appended to $Interestset$ if $pii(A)$ is true. Step (4) generates all sets L_i for $i \geq 2$ by a loop, where L_i is the set of all potentially interesting i-itemsets in D generated in the ith pass of the algorithm, and the end-condition of the loop is $L_{i-1} = \emptyset$. In Step (5), for $i \geq 2$, all uninteresting i-itemsets are pruned from the set L_i. That is, for any itemset $A \in L_i$, if $pii(A)$ is false, A must be pruned from L_i. And any i-itemsets A in L_i is appended to $Interestset$ if $pii(A)$ is true. Step (5) outputs all potentially interesting itemsets in $Interestset$, where each itemset A in $Interestset$ must satisfy that $pii(A)$ is true and A is represented of the form $(A, supp(A), \mu_F(supp(A)))$.

4 Experiments

Our experiments were conducted on a Dell Workstation PWS650 with 2GB main memory and Win2000 OS. We evaluate our algorithm using both real databases and synthesized databases. Below is two groups of our experiments.

Firstly, the Teaching Assistant Evaluation dataset on ftp://www.pami.sjtus.edu.cn/ is chosen. The Teaching Assistant Evaluation dataset has 151 records, the average number of attributes per row is 6.

For the Teaching Assistant Evaluation dataset, let the users' mining requirement is 'Mining large itemsets'. The running results are shown in Figure 3.

```
The itemsets is right gradient
User's motivation is some or less high or high
The user MinSupport is 0.800000
The real MinSupport is 0.029371
Note
4:Medium;      5:More or Less High
6:High ;       7:Very High
 19       3.3%      [4:0.999][5:1.35e-003]
 67       3.3%      [4:0.999][5:1.35e-003]
 68       4.0%      [4:0.958][5:4.21e-002]
 56       4.0%      [4:0.958][5:4.21e-002]
  7       5.3%      [4:0.917][5:8.29e-002]
 25       6.0%      [4:0.876][5:0.124]
 30       6.6%      [4:0.876][5:0.124]
 32       6.6%      [4:0.876][5:0.124]
  4       6.6%      [4:0.876][5:0.124]
```

Fig. 3. Running results.

Figure 3 was cut from screen. Where we have generated not only the support of itemsets, but also the degree of itemsets belonging to fuzzy set $GORP = SH$. This guides more information than the support does, and thus provides a selective chance for users when the interesting itemsets are applied to real applications.

To assess the efficiency, five synthesized databases are used. The main properties of the five databases are as follow: the average number $|T|$ of attributes per row is 5, the average size $|I|$ of maximal frequent sets is 4, $|D|$ is the number of transactions. These databases are DB1:T5.I4.D1K, DB2:T5.I4.D5K, DB3:T5.I4.D10K, DB4:T5.I4.D50K and DB5:T5.I4.D100K. Let $Fsupport = Medium$. The efficiency is illustrated in Figure 4.

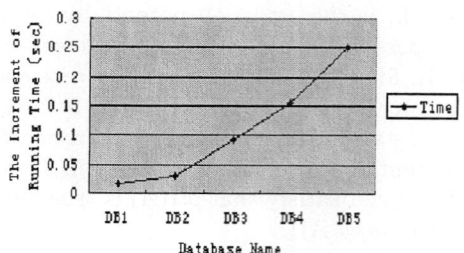

Fig. 4. Running time.

From Figure 4, we have seen that the most increment of running time is 0.1s when enlarging the size of databases from 50K to 100K.

From the above observations, our algorithm is effective, efficient and promising.

5 Summary

In this paper, we have proposed a fuzzy strategy for identifying interesting itemsets without specifying the true minimum-support. Our mining strategy is different from existing Apriori-like algorithms because our mining strategy allows users to specify their mining requirements in commonly sentences and our algorithm generates potentially useful itemsets in fuzzy sets. To evaluate our approach, we have conducted some experiments. The results have demonstrated the effectiveness and efficiency of our mining strategy.

References

1. R. Agrawal, T. Imielinski, and A. Swami, Mining association rules between sets of items in large databases. In: *Proceedings of the ACM SIGMOD 1993*, 1993: 207-216.
2. J. Hipp and U. Guntzer, Is Pushing Constraints Deeply into the Mining Algorithms Really What We Want? *SIGKDD Explorations*, 4 1(2002): 50-55.
3. G. Piatetsky-Shapiro and S. Steingold, Measuring Lift Quality in Database Marketing. *SIGKDD Explorations*, 2 2(2000): 76-80.
4. J. F. Roddick and S. Rice, What's Interesting About Cricket? – On Thresholds and Anticipation in Discovered Rules. *SIGKDD Explorations*, 3 1(2001): 1-5.
5. Ke Wang, Yu He, David Cheung, Francis Chin, Mining Confident Rulees without Support Requirement. In: *Proceedings of the CIKM 2001*, Atlanta, 2001.
6. Xiaowei Yan, Chengqi Zhang and Shichao Zhang, A Database-independent Approach of Mining Association Rules with Genetic Algorithm. In: *Proceedings of the IDEAL03*. Hong Kong, 21-23 March 2003.
7. Chengqi Zhang, Shichao Zhang and Geoffrey Webb, Identifying Approximate Itemsets of Interest in Large databases. *Applied Intelligence*, 18(2003): 91-104.

An Efficient Approach for Mining Periodic Sequential Access Patterns

Baoyao Zhou, Siu Cheung Hui, and Alvis Cheuk Ming Fong

School of Computer Engineering, Nanyang Technological University
Blk N4, #02A-32, Nanyang Avenue, Singapore 639798
zhouby@pmail.ntu.edu.sg, {asschui,ascmfong}@ntu.edu.sg

Abstract. Web usage mining discovers interesting and frequent user access patterns from web logs. Most of the previous works have focused on mining common sequential access patterns of web access events that occurred within the entire duration of all web access transactions. However, many useful sequential access patterns occur frequently only during a particular periodic time interval due to user browsing behaviors and habits. It is therefore important to mine periodic sequential access patterns with periodic time constraints. In this paper, we propose an efficient approach, known as TCS-mine (Temporal Conditional Sequence mining algorithm), for mining periodic sequential access patterns based on calendar-based periodic time constraints. The calendar-based periodic time constraints are used for describing real-life periodic time concepts such as *the morning of every weekend*. The mined periodic sequential access patterns can be used for temporal-based personalized web recommendations. The performance of the proposed TCS-mine algorithm is evaluated and compared with a modified version of WAP-mine for mining periodic sequential access patterns.

1 Introduction

Web usage mining [1], also known as web log mining, aims to discover interesting and frequent user access patterns from web browsing data that are stored in web server logs, proxy logs or browser logs. The discovered knowledge can be used for many practical applications such as web recommendations, adaptive web sites, and personalized web search and surfing. Many approaches [2-5] have been proposed for discovering sequential patterns from transaction databases. However, most of the pervious works only focused on mining common sequential access patterns of web access events, which occurred frequently within the entire duration of all web access transactions. In practice, many useful sequential access patterns occur frequently only in a particular periodic time interval such as *the morning of every weekend*, but not in other time intervals due to user browsing behaviors and habits. Such sequential access patterns are referred to as *periodic sequential access patterns*, where periodic time intervals are real-life time concepts such as *year*, *month*, *week* and *day*. With periodic sequential access patterns, we can recommend or predict the occurrence of a web page during a particular time interval.

Recently, temporal association rule mining algorithms [6-8] have been proposed for mining temporal web access patterns. These works have discussed different ways for defining time constraints. However, such algorithms are mainly based on association rules that ignore the sequential characteristics of web access patterns. In addition, these algorithms also encounter the same problem as most Apriori-based algorithms that require expensive scans of database in order to determine which of the candidates are actually frequent. Different from temporal association rule mining, we propose an efficient approach, known as TCS-mine (Temporal Conditional Sequence mining algorithm), to mine periodic sequential access patterns from web access transaction databases. We also define calendar-based periodic time constraints, which can be used for describing real-life time concepts.

The rest of this paper is organized as follows. In Section 2, we discuss calendar-based periodic time constraints. The proposed TCS-mine algorithm is presented in Section 3. The experimental results are shown in Section 4. Finally, the conclusions are given in Section 5.

2 Calendar-Based Periodic Time Constraints

In this section, we define the calendar-based periodic time constraints that consist of calendar template and calendar instance.

Definition 1: A *calendar template* is defined as $C_T = (U_1 I_1, U_2 I_2, ..., U_n I_n)$. Each U_i is a calendar unit such as *year*, *month*, *week*, *day*, etc. and I_i is a closed interval that contains all valid time values (positive integers) of U_i.

A calendar template represents a hierarchy of calendar units and valid time intervals. For example, a typical calendar template can be in the form of (*year* [1999, 2004], *month* [1, 12], *day* [1, 31]) or (*day-of-week* [1, 7], *hour* [0, 23]).

Definition 2: Given a calendar template $C_T = (U_1 I_1, U_2 I_2, ..., U_n I_n)$, a *calendar instance* is denoted as $(I_1', I_2', ..., I_n')$, where I_i' is an nonempty set of positive integers and $I_i' \subset I_i$, or is a wild-card symbol * that represents all valid time values in I_i.

Calendar instances are formed from calendar template by setting some calendar units to specific values. It can then be used for describing real-life time concepts. For example, given C_T = (*day-of-week* [1, 7], *hour* [0, 23]), we can have C_I = ({6, 7}, {5, 6, 7, 8}) for *the early morning of every weekend* or C_I = (*, {19, 20, 21}) for *the evening of everyday*. In practice, some real-life time concepts such as *morning* or *evening* may have different meanings to different people depending on their personal behaviors and habits. For example, some people consider that *morning* is from sunrise to noon, while others consider that it is from 5 AM to 9 AM. Therefore, calendar instances can be defined according to actual practical requirements. We give some special calendar instances based on C_T = (*day-of-week* [1, 7], *hour* [0, 23]) in Table 1.

Definition 3: A *calendar-based periodic time constraint C*, denoted as $C = [C_T, C_I]$, consists of a calendar template C_T with one calendar instance C_I.

For example, C = [(*day-of-week* [1, 7], *hour* [0, 23]), ({6, 7}, {8, 9})] represents "*8:00 AM to 9:59 AM of every weekend*". Given $C = [C_T, C_I]$, we say time *t is covered by C* if *t* belongs to the time interval defined by *C*. For example, t_1 = "2003-11-08 08:22:45 Saturday" and t_2 = "2003-11-02 09:45:30 Sunday" are covered by *C*.

Table 1. Some special calendar instances.

Time Concept	Calendar Instances
early morning	(*, {5, 6, 7, 8})
morning	(*, {9, 10, 11})
noon	(*, {12})
afternoon	(*, {13, 14, ..., 17})
evening	(*, {18, 19, 20, 21})
night	(*, {22, 23, 0, ..., 4})
weekdays	({1, 2, ..., 5}, *)
weekend	({6, 7}, *)

3 TCS-mine: Mining Periodic Sequential Access Patterns

In this section, we propose an efficient approach, known as TCS-mine (Temporal Conditional Sequence mining algorithm), for mining periodic sequential access patterns from a given web access transaction database.

We first review some concepts on sequential access pattern mining. Web logs can be regarded as a collection of sequences of access events from one user or session in timestamp ascending order. Preprocessing tasks [9] including data cleaning, user identification, session identification and transaction identification can be applied to the original web log files to obtain the web access transactions. Let E be a set of unique access events, which represents web resources accessed by users, i.e. web pages, URLs, or topics. A web access sequence $S = e_1 e_2 \ldots e_n$ ($e_i \in E$ for $1 \leq i \leq n$) is a sequence of access events, and $|S| = n$ is called the *length* of S. Note that it is not necessary that $e_i \neq e_j$ for $i \neq j$ in S, that is repeat of items is allowed. A web access transaction, denoted as $WAT = (t, S)$, consists of a transaction time t and a web access sequence S. All the web access transactions in a database can belong to either a single user (for client-side logs) or multiple users (for server and proxy logs). The proposed algorithm does not depend on the type of web logs that contains the web access transactions. Suppose we have a set of web access transactions with the access event set, $E = \{a, b, c, d, e, f\}$. A sample web access transaction database is given in Table 2.

Table 2. A database of web access transactions.

Transaction Time	Web Access Sequence
2003-11-01 20:21:10 Saturday	abdac
2003-11-02 21:45:22 Sunday	eaebcac
2003-11-05 18:23:24 Wednesday	cacbb
2003-11-08 21:10:10 Saturday	babfae
2003-11-08 21:30:20 Saturday	afbacfc

In $S = e_1 e_2 \ldots e_k e_{k+1} \ldots e_n$, $S_{prefix} = e_1 e_2 \ldots e_k$ is called a *prefix sequence* of S, or a *prefix sequence* of e_{k+1} in S. And $S_{suffix} = e_{k+1} e_{k+2} \ldots e_n$ is called a *suffix sequence* of S or a *suffix sequence* of e_k in S. A web access sequence can be denoted as $S = S_{prefix} + S_{suffix}$. For example, $S = abdac$ can be denoted as $S = a+bdac = ab+dac = \ldots = abda+c$. Let S_1 and S_2 be two suffix sequences of e_i in S, and S_1 is also the suffix sequence of e_i in S_2. Then S_1 is called the *sub-suffix sequence* of S_2 and S_2 is the *super-suffix sequence* of S_1. The suffix sequence of e_i in S without any super-suffix sequence is called the *long suffix sequence* of e_i in S. For example, if $S = abdacb$, then $S_1 = cb$ is the sub-suffix sequence of $S_2 = bdacb$ and S_2 is the super-suffix sequence of S_1. S_2 is also the long suffix sequence of a in S. Given a web access transaction database $WAT_{DB} = \{(t_1, S_1), (t_2, S_2), ..., (t_m, S_m)\}$ in which S_i ($1 \leq i \leq m$) is a web access sequence, and t_i is a transaction time. Given a calendar-based periodic time constraint C, $WAT_{DB}(C) = \{(t_i, S_i) | t_i$ is covered by C, $1 \leq i \leq m\}$ is a subset of WAT_{DB} under C. $|WAT_{DB}(C)|$ is called the *length* of WAT_{DB} under C. The *support* of S in WAT_{DB} under C is defined in equation (1).

$$\sup(S, C) = \frac{|\{S_i | S \in S_i, (t_i, S_i) \in WAT_{DB}(C)\}|}{|WAT_{DB}(C)|} \quad (1)$$

A web access sequence S is called a *periodic sequential access pattern*, if $\sup(S, C) \geq MinSup$, where *MinSup* is a given support threshold. Let's consider the sample database in Table 2. Suppose *MinSup* = 75% and calendar-based periodic time constraint C = [(*day-of-week* [1, 7], *hour* [0, 23]), ({6, 7}, {20, 21})]. It is required to find all web access patterns supported by at least 75% access sequences within the time interval from 8:00 PM to 9:59 PM of every weekend from the sample database.

3.1 Overview of TCS-mine

As shown in Figure 1, the proposed TCS-mine algorithm consists of the following steps: (1) Constraint Preprocessing; (2) Constructing Event Queues for Conditional Sequence Base; (3) Single Sequence Testing for Conditional Sequence Base; (4) Constructing Sub-Conditional Sequence Base; and (5) Recursive Mining for Sub-Conditional Sequence Base.

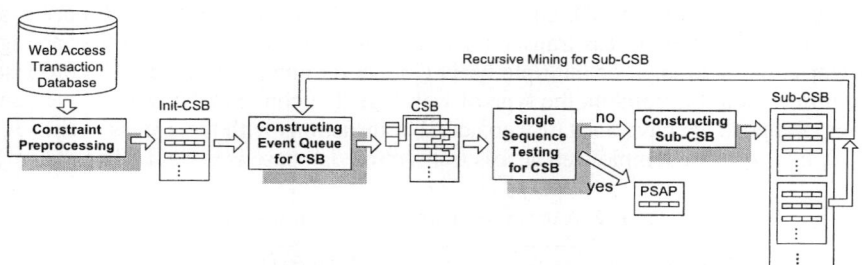

Fig. 1. Overview of the proposed TCS-mine algorithm.

3.2 Constraint Preprocessing

The first step in the TCS-mine algorithm is to filter the web access transaction database by discarding all transactions that do not satisfy the given calendar-based periodic time constraint. The remaining *constraint-satisfied* transactions are then used to construct the initial conditional sequence base. The *initial conditional sequence base* and *conditional sequence base* are defined as follows.

Definition 4: The *initial conditional sequence base*, denoted as *Init-CSB*, is the set of all *constraint-satisfied* transactions in the given web access transaction database, where constraint-satisfied transactions are web access transactions whose transaction times are covered by the given calendar-based periodic time constraint.

Definition 5: The *conditional sequence base* of an event e_i based on prefix sequence S_{prefix}, denoted as $CSB(S_c)$, where $S_c = S_{prefix} + e_i$, is the set of all long suffix sequences of e_i in sequences of a certain dataset. If $S_{prefix} = \varnothing$, the dataset is equal to the initial conditional sequence base of the given web access transaction database. Otherwise, it is the conditional sequence base $CSB(S_{prefix})$.

We also call $CSB(S_c)$ the conditional sequence base of conditional prefix S_c. The initial conditional sequence base can also be denoted as $CSB(\varnothing)$, with $S_c = \varnothing$.

The **ConsPreprocessing** algorithm for constraint preprocessing of transactions from the web access transaction database WAT_{DB} is given in Figure 2.

```
Algorithm: ConsPreprocessing
Input:
1:   C = [C_T, C_I] - calendar-based periodic time constraint
2:   WAT_DB = {WAT_i |WAT_i = (t_i, S_i), 1 ≤ i ≤ n} - web access transaction
     database, and WAT_i is a web access transaction
Output:
Init-CSB - initial conditional sequence base of WAT_DB
Method:
1:   Initialize Init-CSB = ∅.
2:   For each WAT_i ∈ WAT_DB, if t_i is covered by C, insert S_i into Init-
     CSB.
3:   Return Init-CSB.
```

Fig. 2. The algorithm for constraint preprocessing of transactions.

Example: Given a calendar-based periodic time constraint $C = [(day\text{-}of\text{-}week\ [1, 7]$, $hour\ [0, 23])$, $(\{6, 7\}, \{20, 21\})]$, as the time of the third transaction in Table 2 is "2003-11-05 18:23:24 Wednesday", it is not covered by C. So the web access sequence *bbcac* is discarded. After preprocessing, the *Init-CSB* of the sample database contains {*abdac, eaebcac, babfae, afbacfc*}.

3.3 Constructing Event Queues for Conditional Sequence Base

The second step of the TCS-mine algorithm is to construct event queues for $CSB(S_c)$ (for *Init-CSB*, $S_c = \varnothing$). The process performs the following four steps: (1) finding conditional frequent events from $CSB(S_c)$; (2) creating a Header Table; (3) constructing event queues; and (4) deleting non-frequent events.

The *conditional frequent event* is defined as follows.

Definition 6: The *conditional frequent event* is the event whose support in the given conditional sequence base is not less than the support threshold, *MinSup*.

To find *conditional frequent events* in $CSB(S_c)$, we need to identify those events with support of greater than or equal to *MinSup*. This is given in equation (2) below. In equation (2), $|\{S_j|\ e_i \in S_j, S_j \in CSB(S_c)\}|$ is the number of sequences which contains the item labeled e_i in $CSB(S_c)$, and $|Init\text{-}CSB|$ is the length of *Init-CSB*.

$$\sup(e_i) = \frac{|\{S_j \mid e_i \in S_j, S_j \in CSB(S_c)\}|}{|Init - CSB|} \geq MinSup \qquad (2)$$

Then, all the conditional frequent events form the entire Header Table of $CSB(S_c)$. A linked-list structure for each conditional frequent event e_i, called e_i-queue, is created. Each item of e_i-queue is the first item labeled e_i in sequences of $CSB(S_c)$. The head pointer of each event queue is recorded in the Header Table. Finally, as all the items of sequences in $CSB(S_c)$ which are labeled as non-frequent events are not needed anymore, they are discarded. The **ConstructEQ** algorithm for constructing event queues for $CSB(S_c)$ is given in Figure 3.

```
Algorithm: ConstructEQ
Input:
1:   MinSup - support threshold
2:   CSB(S_c) - conditional sequence base of S_c
3:   E = {e_i|1 ≤ i ≤ n} - all access events in CSB(S_c)
Output:
CSB(S_c) with Header Table HT and event queues
Method:
1:   Create an empty Header Table HT for CSB(S_c).
2:   For each e_i ∈ E, if sup(e_i) ≥ MinSup, insertn e_i into HT.
3:   For each conditional sequence ∈ CSB(S_c) do
     a: For each e_i ∈ HT, insert the first item labeled e_i in this se-
        quence into e_i-queue.
     b: Delete all items of events ∉ HT from this sequence.
4:   Return CSB(S_c) with HT and event queues.
```

Fig. 3. The algorithm for constructing event queues for CSB.

Example: For the *Init-CSB* = {*abdac, eaebcac, babfae, afbacfc*}, the result after constructing the Header Table and event queues is given in Figure 4. Each access event is denoted as (*event:count*), where *event* is the event name and *count* is the number of sequences which contains the item labeled as *event* in *Init-CSB*. To be qualified as a conditional frequent event (with *MinSup* = 75% and |*Init-CSB*| = 4), an event must have a count of at least 3. Therefore, the conditional frequent events are (*a*:4), (*b*:4) and (*c*:3). The *a*-queue, *b*-queue and *c*-queue are shown by the dashed lines starting from the Header Table. The items labeled as non-frequent events *d*, *e* and *f* in each sequence are deleted. Similarly, for any subsequent conditional sequence base, the Header Table and event queues can also be constructed using the **ConstructEQ** algorithm.

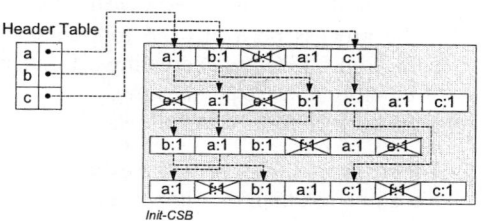

Fig. 4. *Init-CSB* with the Header Table and event queues.

3.4 Constructing Sub-conditional Sequence Base

The *sub-conditional sequence base* is defined as follows.

Definition 7: $CSB(S_{prefix}+e_i)$ is called the *sub-conditional sequence base* of $CSB(S_{prefix})$, if $e_i \neq \emptyset$.

For each access event e_i in the Header Table of $CSB(S_c)$, the **ConstructSubCSB** algorithm for constructing $CSB(S_c+e_i)$ based on $CSB(S_c)$ is given in Figure 5.

```
Algorithm: ConstructSubCSB
Input:
1:  CSB(S_c) - conditional sequence base of S_c
2:  e_i - a given event in Header Table of CSB(S_c)
Output:
CSB(S_c+e_i) - conditional sequence base of e_i based on CSB(S_c)
Method:
1:  Initialize CSB(S_c+e_i) = ∅.
2:  For each item in e_i-queue of CSB(S_c), insert its suffix sequence
    into CSB(S_c+e_i).
3:  Return CSB(S_c+e_i).
```

Fig. 5. The algorithm for constructing Sub-CSB.

Example: For the *Init-CSB* shown in Figure 4, we obtain all suffix seqnences of a by following the a-queue as $CSB(a)$, which is one of the sub-conditional sequence base of *Init-CSB*. The result is shown in Figure 6. $CSB(a)$ contains {bac:1, $bcac$:1, ba:1, $bacc$:1}. Note that bac:1 is the abbreviation of $(b:1)(a:1)(c:1)$.

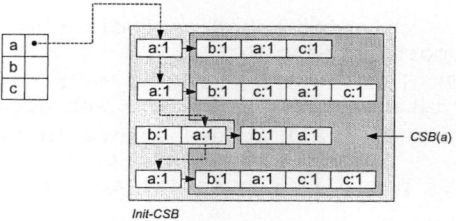

Fig. 6. Construction of $CSB(a)$ based on *Init-CSB*.

3.5 Single Sequence Testing for Conditional Sequence Base

In this step, if all the sequences in $CSB(S_c)$ can be combined into a single sequence, the mining of $CSB(S_c)$ will be stopped. This single sequence will be used to form a part of the final periodic sequential access patterns. Otherwise, we construct Sub-CSBs for $CSB(S_c)$ and perform recursive mining. The **TestCSB** algorithm for testing whether all the sequences in $CSB(S_c)$ can be combined into a single sequence is given in Figure 7.

Example: For $CSB(a)$ = {bac:1, $bcac$:1, ba:1, $bacc$:1}, the first item of each sequence can be combined into one item (b:4), but the second item cannot. The combination is stopped and returns the *failed* flag. For $CSB(aa)$ = {c:2, cc:1}, the sequences can be combined into a single sequence c:3 and the *successful* flag is returned.

```
Algorithm: TestCSB
Input:
1: CSB(S_c) - conditional sequence base of S_c
2: HT - Header Table of CSB(S_c)
Output:
1: test result - successful or failed flag
2: SingleSeq - single sequence of CSB(S_c)
Method:
1: Initialize SingleSeq = ∅.
2: If CSB(S_c) = ∅, return successful and SingleSeq = ∅.
3: For i = 1 to maximum length of sequences ∈ CSB(S_c) do
   a: If all the ith items in each sequence ∈ CSB(S_c) are the
      same event e. And if total count of these items ≥ MinSup
      ×|Init-CSB|, create a new item e with the count and in-
      sert it into SingleSeq.
   b: Otherwise, return failed and SingleSeq = ∅.
4: Return successful and SingleSeq.
```

Fig. 7. The algorithm for testing conditional sequence base.

3.6 The Complete TCS-mine Algorithm

The complete **TCS-mine** algorithm is shown in Figure 8.

```
Algorithm: TCS-mine
Input:
1: C = [C_T, C_I] - calendar-based periodic time constraint
2: MinSup - support threshold
3: WAT_DB = {WAT_i |WAT_i = (t_i, S_i), 1 ≤ i ≤ n} - web access
   transaction database, and WAT_i is a web access transaction
4: E = {e_i|1 ≤ i ≤ n} - all access events in WAT_DB
Output:
PSAP - the set of periodic sequential access patterns
Method:
1: Initialize PSAP = ∅.
2: Use ConsPreprocessing to construct Init-CSB (CSB(S_c), S_c =
   ∅).
3: Use ConstructEQ to construct event queues for CSB(S_c).
4: Use TestCSB to test single sequence for CSB(S_c).
   a: If test is successful, insert all ordered combinations
      of items in frequent sequence FS = S_c+SingleSeq into
      PSAP.
   b: Otherwise, for each e_j in Header Table of CSB(S_c), use
      ConstructSubCSB to construct CSB(S_c+e_j). Set S_c = S_c+e_j
      and recursively mine CSB(S_c) from step 3.
5: Return PSAP.
```

Fig. 8. The algorithm for mining periodic sequential access patterns.

Example: The complete periodic sequential access patterns with $C = [(day\text{-}of\text{-}week [1, 7], hour [0, 23]), (\{6, 7\}, \{20, 21\})]$ and $MinSup = 75\%$ is shown in Table 3.

Table 3. The periodic sequential access patterns of the sample database.

Length of Patterns	Periodic Sequential Access Patterns
1	a:4, b:4, c:3
2	aa:4, ab:4, ac:3, ba:4, bc:3
3	aac:3, aba:4, abc:3, bac:3
4	$abac$:3

4 Experiments

In this section, we present the performance of TCS-mine and compare it with the temporal version of the WAP-mine [4] (or TWAP-mine) algorithm for mining periodic sequential access patterns. WAP-mine is one of the most efficient algorithms that mine common sequential access patterns from a highly compressed data structure known as WAP-tree. As evaluated in [4], the performance of the WAP-mine algorithm is an order of magnitude faster than other Apriori-based algorithms. Therefore, we only compare the TCS-mine algorithm with the TWAP-mine algorithm here.

In order to deal with calendar-based periodic time constraints, the step on *Constraint Preprocessing* discussed in Section 3.2 is applied to TWAP-mine for extracting all the constraint-satisfied transactions from the original web access transaction database. The WAP-tree is then constructed from the constraint-satisfied transactions, and the WAP-mine algorithm is used to mine the periodic sequential access patterns.

The two algorithms, TCS-mine and TWAP-mine, are implemented in C++. All experiments are performed on a 1600 MHz Intel Pentium 4 PC machine with 384 MB memory, running on Microsoft Windows 2000 Professional. The Microsoft Anonymous Web Data (http://kdd.ics.uci.edu/databases/msweb/msweb.html) is used to test the two algorithms. This dataset contains logs on which areas of www.microsoft.com each user has visited and has a total of 32,711 transactions, with each transaction containing from 1 up to 35 page references from a total of 294 pages. We set the calendar-based periodic time constraint C = [(*day-of-week* [1, 7], *hour* [0, 23]), ({1, 2, ..., 5}, *)], which means *every hour of every weekday*. As a result, 22,717 constraint-satisfied transactions are used for the measurement.

To measure the performance, two experiments have been conducted. In the first experiment, we have measured the scalability of the two algorithms with respect to different support thresholds. This experiment uses the 22,717 constraint-satisfied web access sequences with different support thresholds (from 0.2% to 2.4%). The experimental results in Figure 9(a) have shown that the run time of the TWAP-mine increases sharply, when the support threshold decreases, and the TCS-mine always costs less time than the TWAP-mine. In the second experiment, we have measured the scalability of the two algorithms with respect to different sizes of the constraint-satisfied web access sequences. The experiment uses a fixed support threshold (0.2%) with different databases (with sizes vary from 4,000 to 22,717 constraint-satisfied web access sequences). The experimental results in Figure 9(b) have shown that the TCS-mine has better scalability than the TWAP-mine while the size of input database becomes larger.

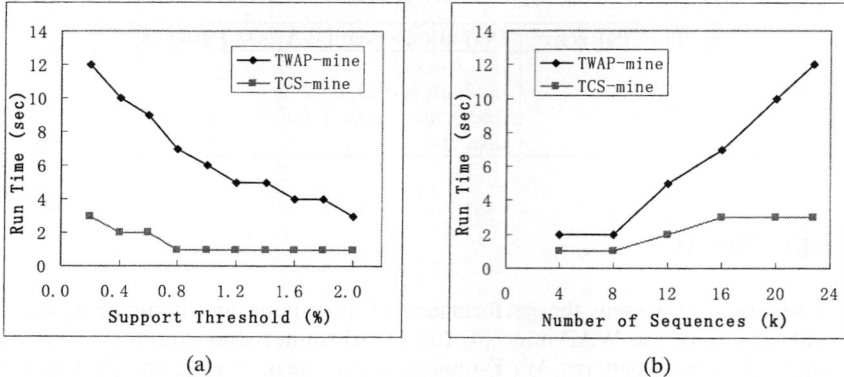

Fig. 9. Scalability with different (a) support thresholds and (b) number of input sequences.

5 Conclusions

In this paper, we have proposed an efficient approach, known as TCS-mine for mining periodic sequential access patterns based on calendar-based periodic time constraints that can be used for describing real-life time concepts. The performance of the TCS-mine algorithm has been evaluated and compared with a temporal version of the WAP-mine algorithm.

References

1. R. Kosala, H. Blockeel: Web Mining Research: A Survey. ACM SIGKDD Explorations, Vol. 2. (2000) 1-15
2. R. Agrawal, and R. Srikant: Mining Sequential Patterns. Proc. of the 11th Intl. Conf. on Data Engineering, Taipei, Taiwan, (1995)
3. R. Srikant, and R. Agrawal: Mining Sequential Patterns: Generalizations and Performance Improvements. Proc. of the 5th Intl. Conf. on EDBT, Avignon, France (1996) 3-17
4. J. Pei, J. Han, B. Mortazavi-asl, and H. Zhu: Mining Access Patterns Efficiently from Web Logs. Proc. of PAKDD2000, Kyoto, Japan, (2000)
5. B. Y. Zhou, S. C. Hui, and A. C. M. Fong: CS-mine: An Efficient WAP-tree Mining for Web Access Patterns. Proc. of the 6th APWeb Conf., Hangzhou, China, (2004).
6. B. Ozden, S. Ramaswamy, and A. Silberschatz: Cyclic Association Rules. Proc. of the 14th Intl. Conf. on Data Engineering, (1998) 412-421
7. S. Ramaswamy, S. Mahajan, and A. Silberschatz: On the Discovery of Interesting Patterns in Association Rules. Proc. of the 24th Intl. Conf. on VLDB, New York, USA, (1998)
8. Y. Li, P. Ning, X. S. Wang, and S. Jajodia: Discovering Calendar-based Temporal Association Rules. Proc. of the 8th Intl. Symp. on Temporal Representation and Reasoning, (2001)
9. R. Cooley, B. Mobasher, and J. Srivastava: Data Preparation for Mining World Wide Web Browsing Patterns. Journal of Knowledge and Information Systems, Vol. 1, No. 1. (1999)

A New Collaborative Recommender System Addressing Three Problems*

Byeong Man Kim[1], Qing Li[1], Jong-Wan Kim[2], and Jinsoo Kim[3],**

[1] Department of Computer Science, Kumoh National Institute of Technology, Korea
[2] School of Computer and Information Technology, Daegu University, Korea
[3] Division of Computer and Applied Science, Konkuk University, Korea
jinsoo@kku.ac.kr

Abstract. With the development of e-commerce and information access, a large amount of information can be found online, which makes a good recommendation service to be urgently necessary. While many collaborative recommender systems (CRS) have succeeded in capturing the similarity among users or items based on ratings, there are still some challenges for them to be a more efficient RS. In this paper, we address three problems in CRS, that is user bias, non-transitive association, and new item problem, and show that the ICHM suggested in our previous work is able to solve the addressed problems. A series of experiments are carried out to show that our approach is feasible.

1 Introduction

Recommender systems (RS) have an obvious appeal in an environment where the amount of on-line information vastly outstrips any individual's capability to survey it. Recommendation systems are now an integral part of some e-commerce sites such as Amazon, Yahoo and CDNow.

Recommender systems are characterized with "individualized" that separate them from search engines which focus on the "matching": the search engines are supposed to return all those items that match the query ranked by degree of match.

At the initial stage, a preliminary recommender system applied the content-based filtering mechanism to provide recommendation service. It selects the right information for users by comparing representations of searching information to user preference which can be indicated implicitly or explicitly. For example, search engines recommend web pages with contents similar to user queries [17]. Content-based information filtering has proven to be effective in locating textual items relevant to a topic.

Later, collaborative filtering (CF) debuted as a prevailing and efficient technique for RS, which was developed by GroupLens [14] and Ringo [16]independently. Collaborative filtering (CF) is the technique of using peer opinions to

---

* This work was supported by grant No. R05-2004-000-10190-0 from the Korea Science and Engineering Foundation.
** Corresponding Author.

predict the interests of others. A target user is matched against the database to discover neighbors which are other users who have historically similar tastes. Items that neighbors like are then recommended to the target user, as he or she will probably also like them. Collaborative RS have been widely applied to various applications from the textual items to audio, multimedia ones. For example, GAB system [17] recommends web pages based on the bookmarks; Jeter system recommends joke [6]; MovieLens system recommends movies; Flycasting system recommends online radio [8]. Most of prevalent CF systems focus on calculating the user-user similarity to make predictions, which is so called user-based CF. However, Sarwar [15] has proved that item-based CF is better than user-based CF on precision and computation complexity.

Although collaborative RS has been very successful in application which shows a better performance than content-based RS. Some researches have pointed out the content information of item helps to provide good recommendation service [1], [2], [5].

In this paper, we use the ICHM method suggested in [11] to solve the three following challenges. The application of ICHM to the three challenges indicates that the ICHM shows a better performance than the pure item-based CF method.

The first challenge is the non-transitive association [18]. In user-based CF, if two users have both read and liked similar items, but not the same ones, the relationship between them is lost. Such a problem is called user-based non-transitive association problem. By using the item similarity instead of user similarity, the item-based framework avoids the user-based non-transitive association problem. However, it brings out the item-based non-transitive association. For example, if two similar items have never been read or rated by the same user. The relationship between them is lost. As for a pure item-based CF, those two items can not be classified into the same similar community. Similar items in different groups will definitely affect the quality of recommendation service negatively.

The second one is user bias from historical ratings. For example, as Table 1 shows, music 3 and 4 has the same historical ratings as music 1 and 2. According to item-based collaborative technique, music 3 and 4 have the same opportunity to be recommended to user 1 by the system. However, if music 1, 2 and 3 belongs to rock music and music 4 belongs to country music, it is obvious that music 3 should have the privilege to be delivered to Jack because he prefers rock music that can be inferred by historical ratings.

The third one is cold start problem. It is hard for pure CF to recommend a new item, since no user made any rating on this new item, which makes it impossible to deliver this new item to its own community where items have the similar ratings from users. The same to the new user, however, it can be partially solved by the gauge set as Jeter RS [6] did.

2 ICHM Overview

ICHM was suggested in [11], and has been successfully applied to a movie RS based on the text information [12] with adaption and a music RS based on audio

Table 1. User bias from historical rating.

Item ID	Jack	Oliver	Peter	Rock	Country
Item 1	5	4	3	Y	N
Item 2	4	4	3	Y	N
Item 3		4	3	Y	N
Item 4		4	3	N	Y

features [13]. Here we just briefly describe this approach and our tiny adjusted part, please refer to the original work for details.

In this approach, it integrates the semantic contents of items and user ratings to calculate the item-item similarity. The procedure of ICHM is described as follows:

1. Apply clustering algorithm to group the items into similar communities, and then use the result, which is the relationship between items and similar item communities, to create a group-rating matrix.
2. Compute the similarity: apply Pearson correlation-based algorithm to calculate the similarity of group-rating matrix and then item-rating matrix. At last, the total similarity is the linear combination of the above two.
3. Make predictions for item by performing a weighted average of deviations from the neighbor's mean [4].

2.1 Construction of Similar Item Communities for Group-Rating Matrix

The goal of construction of similar item communities for group-rating matrix is to group the items into several cliques and provide content-based information for collaborative similarity calculation. Each item has it's own attributes. For example, movie items contain such attributes as actor, actress, director, genre, and synopsis. Thus, we can group the items based on those attributes. Since the result of clustering aims at building the relationship among all items, we build cliques over all items instead of the nearest neighbor between all possible pairs.

K-means Clustering Algorithm is a simple and fast clustering method, which has been popularly used [7]. So we apply it to group the items with some adjustments. The difference is that we apply the fuzzy set theory to represent the affiliation between an object and a cluster. As shown in Figure 1, firstly, items are grouped into a given number of clusters. After completion of grouping, the possibility of one object (here one object means one item) in a certain cluster is calculated as follows:

$$Pro(j,k) = 1 - \frac{CS(j,k)}{MaxCS(i,k)} \qquad (1)$$

where $Pro(j,k)$ means the possibility of object j belonging to the cluster k; The $CS(j,k)$ means the counter-similarity between the object j and the cluster k,

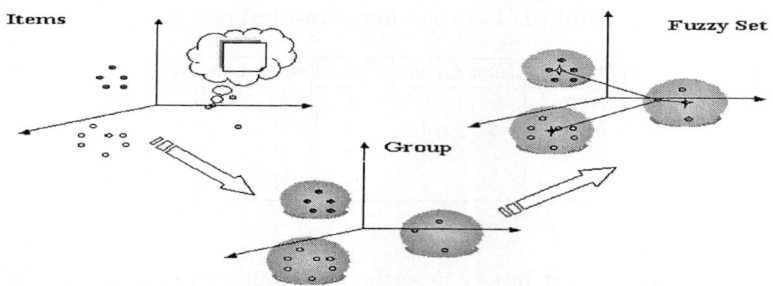

Fig. 1. Adjusted k-means algorithm.

which is calculated based on the Euclidean distance; $MaxCS(i,k)$ means the maximum counter-similarity between an object and the cluster k.

However, as for clustering algorithms, how to choose the initial cluster center is a critical problem. We recommend the refinement algorithm suggested by Bradley [3].

2.2 Similarity

After grouping the items, we can get a new rating matrix and make predictions for users by considering that matrix additionally when calculating the similarity between items. We use the item-based collaborative algorithm to calculate the similarity and make the predictions.

Pearson correlation-based similarity. The most common measure for calculating the similarity is the Pearson correlation algorithm. Pearson correlation measures the degree to which a linear relationship exists between two variables. The Pearson correlation coefficient is derived from a linear regression model, which relies on a set of assumptions regarding the data, namely that the relationship must be linear, and the errors must be independent and have a probability distribution with mean 0 and constant variance for every setting of the independent variable [10].

$$sim(k,l) = \frac{\sum_{u=1}^{m}(R_{u,k} - \overline{R}_k)(R_{u,l} - \overline{R}_l)}{\sqrt{\sum_{u=1}^{m}(R_{u,k} - \overline{R}_k)^2}\sqrt{\sum_{u=1}^{m}(R_{u,l} - \overline{R}_l)^2}} \quad (2)$$

where $sim(k,l)$ means the similarity between the item k and l; m means the total number of users who rate on both the item k and l; $\overline{R}_k, \overline{R}_l$ are the average ratings of the item k and l, respectively; $R_{u,k}, R_{u,l}$ mean the rating of user u on the item k and l respectively.

Firstly, we calculate the similarity of group-rating matrix and then item-rating matrix. At last, the total similarity is the linear combination as follows.

$$sim(k,l) = sim(k,l)_{item} \times (1-c) + sim(k,l)_{group} \times c \quad (3)$$

where $sim(k,l)$ means the similarity between the item k and l; c means the combination coefficient; $sim(k,l)_{item}$ means the similarity between the item k and l, which is calculated from the item-rating matrix; $sim(k,l)_{group}$ means the similarity which is calculated from the group-rating matrix.

2.3 Collaborative Prediction

Prediction for an item is then computed by performing a weighted average of deviations from the neighbor's mean. Here we use top N rule to select the nearest N neighbors based on the similarities of items. The general formula for a prediction on the item k of user u is:

$$P_{u,k} = \overline{R}_k + \frac{\sum_{i=1}^{n}(R_{u,i} - \overline{R}_i) \times sim(k,i)}{\sum_{i=1}^{n}|sim(k,i)|} \quad (4)$$

where $P_{u,k}$ represents the predication for the user u on the item k; n means the total neighbors of item k; $R_{u,i}$ means the rating of user u on the item i; $\overline{R}_k$ is the average ratings on item k; $sim(k,i)$ means the similarity between item k and its' neighbor i; $\overline{R}_i$ means the average ratings on the item i.

In Equation 4, $\overline{R}_k$ is the average rating of all ratings on item k. As for the new item, no user makes any rating on items, $\overline{R}_k$ should be zero. Since this standard baseline of user ratings equals to zero, it is unreasonable for us to apply Equation 4 to new items. Therefore, as for new items, we use $\overline{R}_{neighbors}$, the average rating of all ratings on the new items' nearest neighbors instead of $\overline{R}_k$, which is inferred from the group-rating matrix.

3 Contribution of ICHM

Recall that we have mentioned three challenges for CF in the introduction part. The follows illustrate how ICHM faces those challenges.

Table 2. Item non-transitive problem.

ItemID	Item — rating			Group— rating	
	Jack	Oliver	Peter	cluster1	cluster2
Item 1	5		1	98%	4%
Item 2		4		96%	5%
Item 3				98%	4%

The first case explains how this method can solve the item-based non-transitive association. From Table 2 we can not make predictions for item 1 or 2 by a pure item-based CF. Whereas, ICHM puts up a reasonable solution by considering the group-rating matrix which can provide the relationship among the items based on the item features. For instance, we can't get the similarity between item 1 and 2 in Table 2 if we only consider the item-rating matrix. But, with the help of group-rating matrix, we can easily know that the similarity between item 1 and 2 is around 1. Therefore, we can apply the Equation 4 to make a predictive rating for Oliver's preference of item 1.

$$Prediction_{oliver's\ preference\ on\ item1} = 4 + \frac{(4-3)\times 1}{1} = 5$$

From calculation, we can recommend item 1 to Oliver. Using the same method, we also can make Jack and Peter's predictions for item 2.

Table 3. User bias problem.

ItemID	Item − rating			Group− rating	
	Jack	Oliver	Peter	cluster1	cluster2
Item 1	5	4	3	98%	2%
Item 2	4	4	3	90%	10%
Item 3		4	3	98%	2%
Item 4		4	3	2%	98%
Item 5				98%	2%

The second case illustrates how our suggested approach deals with the user bias from historical ratings. As we know, the predictions for Jack on item 3 and 4 are the same in Table 3 by a pure item-based collaborative filtering. But when considering grouping-rating matrix, from the table, we can get the similarity among items as follows.

$Sim(1,3)_{group-rating} = \frac{(0.98-0.5)(0.98-0.5)+(0.02-0.5)(0.02-0.5)}{\sqrt{(0.98-0.5)^2+(0.02-0.5)^2}\times\sqrt{(0.98-0.5)^2+(0.02-0.5)^2}} = 1$

$Sim(2,3)_{group-rating} = \frac{(0.9-0.5)(0.98-0.5)+(0.1-0.5)(0.02-0.5)}{\sqrt{(0.9-0.5)^2+(0.1-0.5)^2}\times\sqrt{(0.98-0.5)^2+(0.02-0.5)^2}} = 1$

$Sim(1,3)_{item-rating} = 1$
$Sim(2,3)_{item-rating} = 1$
$Sim(1,3)_{total} = Sim(1,3)_{group-rating}\times 0.5 + Sim(1,3)_{item-rating}\times 0.5 = 1.0$
$Sim(2,3)_{total} = Sim(2,3)_{group-rating}\times 0.5 + Sim(2,3)_{item-rating}\times 0.5 = 1.0$
Also, we can get

$$Sim(1,4)_{total} = 0,\ Sim(2,4)_{total} = 0$$

At last, we calculate the predictions for Jack as follows.

$$Prediction_{Jack's\ preference\ on\ item3} = 3.5 + \frac{(5-3.5)\times 1 + (4-3.5)\times 1}{1+1} = 4.5$$
$$Prediction_{Jack's\ preference\ on\ item4} = 3.5 + 0 = 3.5$$

The system will assign a privilege to item 3 when it provides recommendation service for Jack according to the above calculation. The result is reasonable because, from his historical ratings, Jack shows a strong preference on items which belong to the cluster 1, and item 3 has a strong relationship to the cluster1 while item 4 does not. For example, Jack bought many rock music CDs during the past time, if one new rock music CD and one new country music CD have the same chance to be recommended to Jack, usually, new rock music CD has a higher probability to be selected by Jack because Jack is a rock music fan.

In addition, if certain piece of item 5 is added into the database as Table 3 shows, with the help of group-rating matrix, we can find that Jack shows more interest on this new piece of music than others. So to speak, the new item problem is also done.

All those challenges seem to be successfully settled with the help of group-rating matrix. However, it depends on the assumption that the information from group-rating matrix is accurate. The following experimental evaluation section examines whether the contents from items can provide that useful information and how they affect the recommendation.

4 Experimental Evaluation

Currently, we perform experiments on a real movie rating data collected from the MovieLens web-based recommendation system. The data set contained 100,000 ratings from 943 users and 1,682 movies, with each user rating at least 20 items. The ratings in the MovieLens data were explicitly entered by users, and are integers ranging from 1 to 5. We divide data set into a training set and a test data set. 20% of users are randomly selected to be the test users, and 80% of users are randomly selected to be the training set.

In the MovieLens data, there are only genre information of movies. Therefore, we collect the movie semantic information, that is genre, actor, actress, director and Synopsis, from Internet Movie Database (http://www.imdb.com) to construct group-rating matrix from the training data set.

The following two key elements are considered in our study to measure the quality of our recommender system [4].

- **Coverage metrics:** Coverage mainly measures the percentage of items for which a RS is capable of making predictions.
- **Accuracy metrics:** Since most metrics generally support similar conclusions, we only report Mean Absolute Error (MAE) in our study. MAE has widely been used in evaluating the accuracy of a recommender system. The MAE is calculated by summing these absolute errors of the corresponding rating-prediction pairs and then computing the average. Generally, smaller MAE means better performance.

4.1 Uncertain Factors in ICHM

In ICHM, there are two uncertain factors, that is No. of clusters for items to construct the group-rating matrix and the weights of two matrices for calculating total similarity. We treat the weights of two matrices as equal in ICHM. From experiments, we found that the recommendation performance was not very sensitive to the No. of clusters as Figure 2 shows. So we set it to 20 in our following experiments.

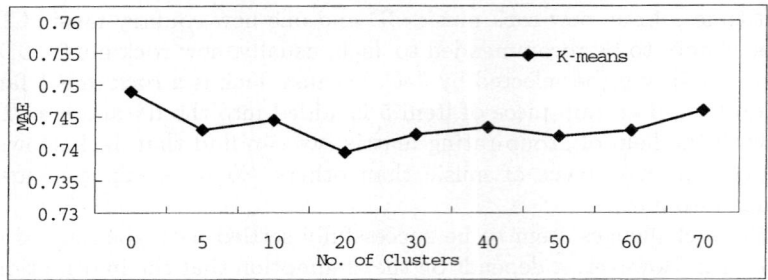

Fig. 2. Number of item cluster.

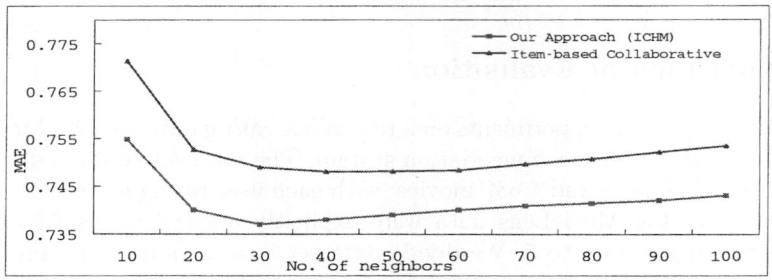

Fig. 3. Comparison.

4.2 Is the Group-Rating Matrix Valuable?

In order to observe the contribution of group-rating matrix, we implement the pure item-based RS and compare with ICHM at the different number of neighbors. From Figure 3 and Table 4, it can be observed that ICHM has a favorable performance, which means we can get useful information from group-rating matrix.

Table 4. Coverage.

No. of neighbors	30	40	50	60	80	100
Coverage (ICHM)	94%	96%	98%	99%	99%	99%
Coverage (Item-based CF)	86%	91%	95%	96%	96%	96%

4.3 How Does the Content Information Affect Performances?

In order to observe the contribution of each content information. We construct group-rating matrix by movie synopsis, genre, character(actor+actress), director, respectively. In our experiments, we found that the semantic information extracted from synopsis contributed greatly to the recommendation performance as Figure 4 shows. What's more, when all of those contents combined together, it achieved a little better performance than individual contribution.

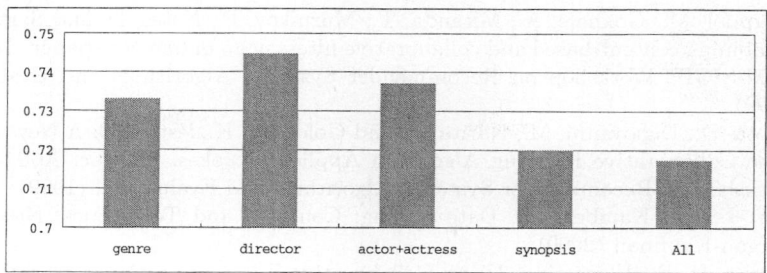

Fig. 4. Comparison.

4.4 New Item Problem

As for new item problem, we randomly selected the number of items from 5 to 25 with the step of 5, and delete all the ratings of those items and treat them as new items. We can observe from Table 5 that ICHM deals reasonably with the new objects.

Table 5. MAE of new items.

MAE	5	10	15	20	25
New items	0.756	0.762	0.78	0.787	0.81
All items excludes new ones	0.745	0.750	0.751	0.755	0.756

5 Conclusion

In this paper, we applies the ICHM method to solve the three challenges in CF framework. Our work indicates that the ICHM shows a better performance than the pure item-based CF method. This also shows that the correct application of content information can provide a good recommendation service.

References

1. Balabanovic, M. and Shoham, Y.. Fab: Content-Based, Collaborative Recommendation, Communications of the ACM, 40(3), pp.66-72. (1997)
2. Basu C., and Cohen.Using Socail and Content-based information in Recommendation. In Proc. of the AAAI-98. (1998).
3. Bradley, P.S. and Fayyad U.M..Refining Initial Points for K-Means Clustering. In Proc. of ICML '98. San Francisco, USA, pages 91–99. (1998).
4. Breese J. S., Heckerman D., and Kardie C.. Em-pirical Analysis of Predictive Algorithms for Col-laborative Filtering. In Proc. Of the 14th Conference on Uncertainty in AI, pp.43-52. (1998).

5. Claypool, M., Gokhale, A., Miranda, T., Murnikov, P., Netes, D. and Sartin, M.. Combining content-based and collaborative filters in an online newspaper , In Proc. ACM-SIGIR Workshop on Recommender Systems: Algorithms and Evaluation. (1999).
6. Gupta, D., Digiovanni, M., Narita, H. and Goldberg, K..Jester 2.0: A New Linear-Time Collaborative Filtering Algorithm Applied to Jokes, In Proc. ACM-SIGIR Workshop on Recommender Systems: Algorithms and Evaluation. (1999).
7. Han, J., and Kamber, M.. Data mining: Concepts and Techniques. New York: Morgan-Kaufman (2000).
8. Hauver, D. B.. Flycasting: Using Collaborative Filtering to Generate a Play list for Online Radio, In Int. Conf. on Web Delivery of Music. (2001).
9. Herlocker, J., Konstan, J., Borchers A., and Riedl, J.. An algorithmic framework for performing collaborative Filtering, In Proc. ACM-SIGIR Conf., 1999, pp. 230-237. (1999).
10. McClave, J. T. and Dietrich, F. H.. Statistics. San Francisco: Ellen Publishing Company (1998).
11. Qing Li, Byeong Man Kim. Clustering Approach for Hybrid Recommender System, In Proc. of the 2003 IEEE/WIC International Conference on Web Intelligence, pp. 33-38. (2003).
12. Qing Li, Byeong Man Kim. Constructing User Profiles for Collaborative Recommender System, In Proc. of Sixth Asia Pacific Web Conf., 2004,pp. 100 - 110. (2004).
13. Q. Li,B.M. Kim,G. D. Hai,D.HOh. A Collaborative Music Recommender based on Audio Features,In Proc. of ACM-SIGIR Conf..(2004).
14. Resnick, P., Iacovou, N., Suchak, M., Bergstorm, P. and Riedl, J.. GroupLens: An open architecture for collaborative filtering of Netnews, In Proc. ACM Conf. on Computer-Supported Cooperative Work, pp.175-186. (1994).
15. Sarwar, B. M., Karypis, G., Konstan, J. A. and Riedl, J.. Item-based Collaborative Filtering Recommendation Algorithms, In Proc. Tenth Int. WWW Conf. 2001, pp. 285-295. (2001).
16. Upendra, S. and Patti, M., Social Information Filtering: Algorithms for Automating "Word of Mouth". In Proc. ACM CHI'95 Conf., pp.210-217. (1995).
17. Wittenburg, K., Das, D., Hill, W. and Stead, L.. Group Asynchronous Browsing on the World Wide Web. Proc. of Fourth International World Wide Web Conference, pp 51-62. (1995).
18. Zan Huang, Hsinchun Chen and Daniel Zeng. Applying associative retrieval techniques to allevi-ate the sparsity problem in collaborative filtering. ACM TOIS archive Volume 22, Issue 1. (2004).

A GA-Based Fuzzy Decision Tree Approach for Corporate Bond Rating

Kyung-shik Shin[1], Hyun-jung Kim[1], and Suhn-beom Kwon[2]

[1] Ewha Womans University, College of Business Administration
11-1 Daehyun-Dong, Seodaemun-Gu, Seoul 120-750, Korea
ksshin@ewha.ac.kr, charitas@empal.com
[2] Kookmin University, School of e-Business
861-1, Jeungreung Dong Sungbuk Gu Seoul 136-702, Korea
sbkwon@mail.kookmin.ac.kr

Abstract. The induction based on a tree structure is an appropriate representation of the complex human reasoning process such as a corporate bond rating application. Furthermore, the fuzzy decision tree (FDT) can handle the information about vague and incomplete classification knowledge represented in human linguistic terms. In addition, FDT is more flexible by relaxing the constraint of mutual exclusivity of cases in decision tree. We propose a hybrid approach using FDT and genetic algorithms (GA) enhances the effectiveness of FDT to the problem of corporate bond rating classification. This study utilizes a hybrid approach using GA in an attempt to find an optimal or near optimal hurdle values of membership function in FDT. The results show that the accuracy of the integrated approach proposed for this study increases overall classification accuracy rate significantly. We also show that the FDT approach increases the flexibility of the classification process.

1 Introduction

The early studies of bond rating applications tend to use statistical techniques such as multiple discriminant analysis (MDA) model [2][3][22], which is most common means for classifying bonds into their rating categories. However, statistical methods have some limitations in applications due to the violation of multivariate normality assumptions for independent variables, which is frequently occurred in financial data. Therefore, a number of studies have demonstrated that artificial intelligence approaches such as inductive learning [25], artificial neural networks [11][20][21][28], and case-based reasoning [5][17][26][27] can be alternative methodology for corporate bond rating classification problems. The basic principle underlying artificial intelligence approaches is to articulate the knowledge framework of domain expertise to solve complex problems and to learn from problem-solving experiences. Since experts have linguistic terms in their knowledge, and linguistic terms in classification problems often refer to sets of numbers with ill-defined boundaries, it is difficult even for experts to capture and represent such knowledge under crisp set concepts.

Constructing decision trees generated by inductive learning methods from existing cases is useful for automated acquisition of expert knowledge. However, the crisp clear cut for attribute segmentation makes the data excessively partitioned, and the instances classified into a single class with attribute values around class boundaries may confuse the conclusion and result in wrong predictions. Instead of excessively generalized decision trees by using numeric attribute segmentation, the fuzzy decision trees (FDT) is regarded as a useful approach, which identifies more than one possible classification for a given instance, to make a proper conclusion for each instance. And it is obvious that the overlapped data between boundaries of a clear-cut point, which is consistent with human information processing, has been misclassified. Compared with MDA and the conventional decision tree algorithm such as ID3, the FDT approach is also important to build a more flexible system by relaxing the constraint of the mutual exclusivity of cases.

This paper investigates the effectiveness of a hybrid approach using genetic algorithms (GA) in an attempt to find an optimal or near optimal hurdle value of each fuzzy term for deciding the confident degrees of membership grade in FDT. Since the FDT based on gradation instead of sharp distinction can make a case to be associated with more than one leaf in a decision tree with different membership degrees, the existing FDT system simply memorizes all cases or selected cases whose membership grade is above a predefined constant value. Considering that filtering based on the confidence of the membership value plays a very important role for building a successful FDT system, a reasonable technique to measure each hurdle value of fuzzy terms is necessary. That is, selectivity based on the degrees of membership grade is preferable rather than using all cases, and so our particular interest lies in finding the efficient and effective criterion that is worth memorizing. Our proposed approach is demonstrated by applications to corporate bond rating.

The remainder of this paper is organized as follows. Next section contains the methodologies used in this study and a hybrid structure of FDT supported by GA. In the experiment and result section, the specific information about data for this study is described and empirical results are summarized and analyzed. The final section includes the conclusion and future research issues.

2   Hybrid Approach of FDT with GA

The process of a hybrid system consists of the following steps: the first process is to construct the FDT to handle vague and incomplete classification knowledge more naturally represented by common linguistic terms using fuzzy set based on a tree structure. The second process is to find each hurdle value of fuzzy terms in FDT using GA. For understanding the integration structure of FDT using GA (GA-FDT), the basic concept of GA is briefly reviewed. Then, the hybrid method is presented in detail.

GA is stochastic search techniques that can search large and complicated spaces on the ideas from natural genetics and evolutionary principle [9][13][15]. They have been demonstrated to be effective and robust in searching very large spaces in a wide range of applications [10][12][14][18][19]. GA performs the search process in four stages: initialization, selection, crossover, and mutation [9][30]. In the initialization stage, a population of genetic structures (called chromosomes) that are randomly distributed in the solution space is selected as the starting point of the search. After the initialization stage, each chromosome is evaluated using a user-defined fitness function. Chromosomes with a good performance may be chosen for replication several times whereas poor-performing structures may not be chosen at all. Such a selective process causes the best-performing chromosomes in the population to occupy an increasingly larger proportion of the population over time. Crossover causes to form a new offspring between two randomly selected "good parents". Crossover operates by swapping corresponding segments of a string representation of the parents and extends the search for a new solution in far-reaching direction. The crossover occurs only with some probability (the crossover rate). There are many different types of crossover that can be performed: the one-point, the two-point, and the uniform type [29]. Mutation is a GA mechanism where we randomly choose a member of the population and change one randomly chosen bit in its bit string representation.

2.1 Fuzzy Decision Tree Induction

In constructing FDT, the first process is fuzzification on the basis of the membership function. After a decision tree has been generated from an inductive learning method using symbols represented by linguistic fuzzy term, a decision tree is converted into a fuzzy decision tree in which classes associated with leaves are multiple predictions with the degree of possibilities for every class.

Fuzzification. The fuzzification process transforms the continuous financial ratios into linguistic terms and assigns the membership value for fuzzy preference on the basis of the membership function to the ratios. Thus, constructing the fuzzy membership functions is considered to have a critical impact on the performance of the proposed hybrid model. Previous studies have proposed numerous methods to determine the number of membership functions and to find optimal parameters of membership functions such as Kohonen's learning vector quantization algorithm, fuzzy c-means clustering algorithm and subtractive clustering method and so on [4][6][8]. Optimal parameters are identified by the class prototype with the shortest distance or the closest similarity that distinguishes the distinctions of given patterns.

In this study, we use an approach suggested by Klimasauskas (1992) for generating the fuzzy membership functions, which finds an effective cluster in a crisp set and converts inputs into the fuzzy membership value associated with each class. We utilize statistical clustering algorithm such as k-means clustering algorithm to formulate the membership functions corresponding to the categorized linguistic terms by determining the centroid, lower and upper boundary value of clusters of the input variable. The formula used to transform an input value X_i in the set [a,b] to the degree of membership in fuzzy sets, $F_i(X_i)$, is shown as follows;

$$F_i(X_i) = \max(0, 1 - K \times |X_i - C|) \qquad (1)$$

where   K: the scale factor = $2 \times (1-M)/(b-a)$
C: the center between the boundaries
M: the value of fuzzy membership function at the boundary

According to the formula of computing the degree of membership in a fuzzy set, the shape of the fuzzy set is controlled by the centroid, upper and lower boundary of each cluster. The value of fuzzy membership function at the boundary (M) is set at 0.5 in this study, which means that we consider fuzzy terms whose membership values are higher than 0.5 relatively reliable.

In this study, in which we experiment the bond rating classification, three fuzzy sets corresponding to the linguistic terms high, middle, and low, respectively assumed for each of the input variables are shown in Figure 1.

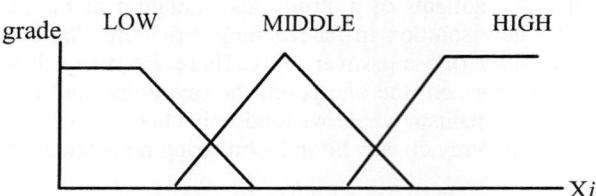

Fig. 1. The membership functions of fuzzy terms

Induction of Decision Trees. Compared with statistical methods such as MDA, one advantage of the decision trees induction is that it is free from parametric assumptions used to generate knowledge structures that underlie statistical methods. The decision trees induction is currently the best-known recursive machine learning technique to partition training cases into tree-type rules and to classify new cases. It generates a reasonably simple tree by progressively selecting attributes to branch the tree. This process discovers categorization patterns, and assembles these patterns into classifiers, and makes predictions using these classifiers without much computation.

Since the induction algorithms such as ID3 was introduced by Quilan (1986) in extracting classification rules from symbolic data based on the information theoretic measure, the induction algorithms have been used for assessing the discriminatory power of each attribute in constructing a decision tree. The tree building process in ID3 is guided by the search heuristics based on the concept of maximizing the value of information gain or reducing the information disorder called entropy. The heuristics is applied recursively at each node, and guides in selecting the attribute and splitting branches. Thereafter, Quinlan (1993) made C4.5 to deal with missing values, continuous variables, and pruning of decision trees and provided C5.0 to analyze substantial databases containing thousands of cases. We use C5.0 as an induction algorithm, which has been adopted by commercial package, *Clementine 5.2*.

Construction of FDT. For the fuzzy decision trees induction, we use the fuzzy inductive learning method (FILM) approach suggested by Jeng, Jeng and Liang (1997) that integrates the fuzzy set theory into the tree induction process [16]. Compared with a typical decision tree, a main advantage of FDT is that it allows the classification process to be more flexible and increases overall classification accuracy rate because of the reduced sensitivity to slight changes of the boundaries of splitting as shown in the following example. Table 1 shows the example of attribute X_i represented by linguistic terms and fuzzy membership values. Figure 2 illustrates the result of a decision tree and a fuzzy decision tree of the sample cases in Table 1.

Since the membership of a decision tree dichotomizes the case into a binary class, that is, a case either belongs or does not belong to a split node, a decision tree using crisp sets concept cannot represent the slight difference of the case feature. For example, if a decision tree defines high as X_i whose value is 3 or low, a case company C may be assessed to belong to leaf high and cannot be categorized to leaf low under crisp set concepts. On the other hand, when the crisp hurdle values of a decision tree are replaced by fuzzy terms and values, the categorization using fuzzy sets assigns a case to more than one class with different degrees of possibility at the same time. For example, a case company C may be assessed to have 0.5 possibility belonging to leaf high, 0.67 possibility belonging to leaf middle, and 0.3 possibility belonging to leaf low.

Table 1. The example of fuzzy representation

Firm	Rating	X_i	Fuzzy X_i / membership value
Company A	A1	0.5	low / 0.7
Company B	A1	2.2	low / 0.56, middle / 0.55
Company C	A2	3.5	low / 0.3, middle / 0.67, high / 0.5
Company D	B	3.8	middle / 0.56, high / 0.54
Company E	B	5.0	high / 0.71
...	...	...	...

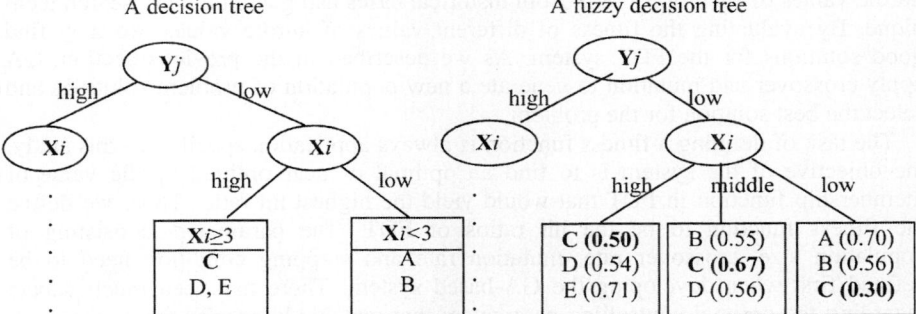

Fig. 2. A decision tree versus a fuzzy decision tree

Since the boundaries of splitting in FDT are not exactly divided in which the gradual transition membership value of fuzzy sets is presented by possibilities rather than binaries, for predicting the class of a new case analyzed using the membership for classification instead of using a single threshold value, a case occasionally comes up with the number of results which conflict one another. Therefore, a hurdle value, which is generally called an α-cut, is indispensable to differentiate membership values considered very close to a member of a set. For example, if we may consider those whose membership grades of "high" are above 0.2, X_i belongs to a set "high" when its membership grade is greater than or equal to the 0.2-cut.

For constructing a solution to a new case, there are many different ways to find which class the case belongs to. In this study, we apply the simplest defuzzification procedure that chooses the majority class among the candidate classes above an optimized α-cut of the membership value. In case that the classification result of the new case obtained from the previous criterion is contradictive, we follow the second criterion that chooses the one that has the highest value, which is calculated by summarizing the membership value of traced nodes, among the candidate ratings reasoned based on a FDT structure.

2.2 Hybrid Structure of a GA-FDT System

Our particular interest lies in improving the effectiveness of calculating the class membership process of tree leaves in a FDT system. Though there are numerous studies to report the usefulness of FDT in classification studies [1][7][16][31], there is a major drawback in building a model in which the existing FDT system simply memorizes all cases or selected cases whose membership grade is above a predefined constant value.

Considering that the degrees of membership grade play a very important role for a successful FDT system, a reasonable technique to measure each hurdle value of fuzzy terms is necessary. One way to assign hurdle values of each fuzzy term is to have a human expert assign for them. However, though the expert is expected to have the knowledge and experience required to decide which set of hurdle values of each fuzzy term would be the most effective to solve a specific problem, even for experts, it is not easily verified a priori in an imprecisely represented domain. As an alternative approach, we introduce the notion of machine learning to learn the optimal set of hurdle values of each fuzzy term from historical cases using evolutionary search technique. By evaluating the fitness of different values of hurdle values, we may find good solutions for the FDT system. As we described in the previous section, GA apply crossover and mutation to generate a new population of problem solutions and select the best solution for the problem.

The task of defining a fitness function is always application specific. In this study, the objective of the system is to find an optimal or near optimal hurdle value of membership function in FDT that would yield the highest hit ratio. Thus, we define the fitness function to be the hit ratios of FDT. The parameters consisting of population size, crossover rate, mutation rate and stopping condition need to be defined first when developing the GA-based system. There has been much debate regarding the optimal controlling parameters that we should specify for experiment. For this experiment, we use 100 organisms in the population, 0.5 in the crossover rate and 0.06 in the mutation rate. As a stopping condition, we use 1,000 trials. These processes are performed by a prototype system implemented in VB supported by Evolver Developer's Kit (EDK) version 4.0.2.

3 Experiments and Results

3.1 Data and Variables Selection

The research data consists of 297 financial ratios and the corresponding bond rating of 1,816 Korean companies whose commercial papers have been rated from 1997 to 2000. The bond ratings are provided by National Information and Credit Evaluation, Inc., one of the most prominent bond rating agencies in Korea. Credit grades are classified as 5 coarser rating categories (A1: 3.2%, A2: 13.3%, A3: 32.3%, B: 43.0%, C: 8.3%) according to credit levels.

The data set is arbitrarily split into three subsets; about 40% of the data is used for a training (A) set, 40% for a training (B) set and 20% for a validation set. The training (A) data is used to construct FDT and the training (B) data is used to find optimal hurdle values of FDT in genetic learning. The validation data is used to test the results with the data that is not utilized to develop the model. The number of the training (A) and (B) cases and the validation cases are 727, 727 and 362, respectively.

We apply two stages of the input variable selection process. At the first stage, we select 106 variables by 1-way ANOVA for the numeric type and Kruskal–Wallis test for the symbolic type between each financial ratio as an input variable and credit grade as an output variable. In the second stage, we select 9 variables using a MDA stepwise method to reduce dimensionality. We select input variables satisfying the univariate test first, and then select significant variables by the stepwise method for refinement. The selected variables for this research are shown in Table 2.

Table 2. Definition of variables

Variable	Definition	Data type
X1	Net income to total asset	Numeric
X2	Net interest coverage ratio	Numeric
X3	Times interest earned	Numeric
X4	Net income to capital stock	Numeric
X5	Equity to total asset	Numeric
X6	Fixed assets to total asset	Numeric
X7	Current liabilities to total asset	Numeric
X8	Transition of ordinary profit	Symbol
X9	Transition of operating activities cash flows	Symbol

In this study, in which we experiment the bond rating classification, two qualitative variables are coded into five types according to the yearly sign transition of ordinary profit (X8) and operating activities cash flows (X9) respectively for three-year period. Each of the quantitative variables (X1-X7) is transformed into three fuzzy sets corresponding to the linguistic terms: high, middle, and low, respectively.

3.2 Results and Analysis

To investigate the effectiveness of the integrated approach for deciding the confident degrees of membership grade in GA-FDT in the context of the corporate bond rating classification problem, we set GA to search each hurdle value of fuzzy terms. The derived results by genetic search are summarized in Table 3. To reduce the impact of random variations in the GA search process, we replicate the experiment several times and suggest the best set of hurdle values.

Table 4 shows the comparison of the results of the classification techniques applied for this study. Each cell contains the accuracy of the classification techniques by classes. Since bond-rating prediction is multiple classification problems, it is difficult to design generally a well-performed model that can obtain the high classification accuracy.

Table 3. The optimized hurdle values of each fuzzy term in FDT using GA

GA-FDT	X1	X2	X3	X4	X5	X6	X7
High	0.20	0.17	0.64	0.87	0.13	0.03	0.64
Middle	0.51	0.00	0.00	0.11	0.96	0.00	0.70
Low	0.33	0.27	0.73	0.60	0.00	0.87	0.28

The results obtained are compared with those of the conventional FDT (pure-FDT) with a predefined -cut and MDA. Overall, the classification accuracy of GA-FDT is higher than that of MDA and pure-FDT. Among the pure-FDT models, the pure-FDT model with 0.1-cut has the highest level of accuracy in the given data sets and the pure-FDT model with 0.0-cut and 0.2-cut is the next best group which has a high accuracy. Based on the empirical results, we conclude that the confident degrees of membership grade in FDT plays an important role in building a successful FDT since the hurdle values of each fuzzy terms derived from the genetic search process can improve the performance of an FDT system as GA finds optimal or near optimal solution for the specified objective function.

Table 4. Classification performance of the validation set

Ratings (total hit)	Accuracy (number of hit)					
	MDA	Pure-FDT				GA-FDT
		0.0-cut	0.1-cut	0.2-cut	0.3-cut	
A1 (10)	40.0 (4)	20.0 (2)	40.0 (4)	40.0 (4)	40.0 (4)	20.0 (2)
A2 (50)	26.0 (13)	20.0 (10)	26.0 (13)	32.0 (16)	34.0 (17)	46.0 (23)
A3 (116)	48.3 (56)	46.6 (54)	46.6 (54)	46.6 (54)	46.6 (54)	76.7 (89)
B (156)	50.6 (79)	78.2 (122)	80.1 (125)	73.1 (114)	66.0 (103)	92.3 (144)
C (30)	36.7 (11)	53.3 (16)	53.3 (16)	53.3 (16)	53.3 (16)	36.7 (11)
Average (362)	45.0 (163)	56.4 (204)	58.6 (212)	56.4 (204)	53.6 (194)	74.3 (269)

McNemar test results for the comparison of the predictive performance between the comparative models and the GA-FDT model for the validation cases are summarized in Table 5.

The results of McNemar tests support that the GA-FDT model has higher classification accuracy than MDA and pure-FDT with significant levels. It also appears that the pure-FDT models perform significantly better than MDA. Furthermore, the pure-FDT models with various -cut do not significantly outperform each other except that the pure-FDT with 0.1-cut outperforms the pure-FDT with 0.3-cut at 5% statistical significance level. The overall result shows that the integrated GA-FDT approach proposed for this study performs better than MDA and pure-FDT.

Table 5. McNemar values for the comparison of performance between models

		Pure-FDT				(Significance level) GA-FDT
		0.0-cut	0.1-cut	0.2-cut	0.3-cut	
MDA		0.001***	0***	0.002***	0.017**	0***
Pure-FDT	0.0-cut		0.215	1	0.314	0***
	0.1-cut			0.215	0.033**	0***
	0.2-cut				0.164	0***
	0.3-cut					0***

** significant at 5%, *** significant at 1%

4 Conclusions

In this study, we propose a hybrid approach using FDT and GA enhances the effectiveness of FDT to the problem of corporate bond rating classification. In this approach, the genetic search technique is used in an attempt to find optimal or near optimal hurdle values of each fuzzy term. The preliminary results demonstrate that this approach increases overall classification accuracy rate significantly. In addition, these results support that GA is an effective method for knowledge extraction, since we can obtain the near optimal hurdle values of membership function in FDT using GA. We also show that the FDT approach increases the flexibility of the classification process.

Our study has the following limitations that need further research. First, in setting up the GA optimization problem, we must select several parameters such as stopping conditions, the population size, crossover rate, mutation rate and so on. The values of these parameters can greatly influence the performance of the algorithm. The varying parameters also generate a lot of groups for our general result. The second limitation is that this study only focuses on optimizing the hurdle value set of each fuzzy term in a FDT system, though the determination of the tree structure, classes and membership functions has a critical impact on the performance of the resulting system. A GA approach could potentially be used to optimize other specific points of the FDT process. We believe that the potential is great for further research with hybrid approaches using GA and also different intelligent techniques as ways to improve the performance of the applications.

References

1. Apolloni, B., Zamponi, G., Zanaboni, A.M.: Learning Fuzzy Decision Trees. Neural Networks. 11 (1998) 885-895
2. Baran, A., Lakonishok, J., Ofer, A.R.: The Value of General Price Level Adjusted Data to Bond Rating. Journal of Business Finance and Accounting. 7 (1980) 135-149
3. Belkaoui, A.: Industrial Bond Ratings: A New Look. Financial Management. 9 (1980) 44-51
4. Bezdek, J.C.: Pattern Recognition with Fuzzy Objective Function Algorithms. Plenum Press, New York (1987)
5. Buta, P.: Mining for Financial Knowledge with CBR. AI EXPERT. 9 (1994) 34-41
6. Chen, M.S., Wang, S.W.: Fuzzy Clustering Analysis for Optimizing Fuzzy Membership Functions. Fuzzy Sets and Systems. 103 (1999) 239-254
7. Chiang, I., Hsu, J.Y.: Fuzzy Classification Trees for Data Analysis. Fuzzy Sets and Systems. 130 (2002) 87-99
8. Chiu, S.: Fuzzy Model Identification Based On Cluster Estimation. J. Intell. Fuzzy Systems. 2 (1994) 267-278
9. Davis, L.: Handbook of Genetic Algorithms. Van Nostrand Reinhold, NY (1991)
10. Colin, A.M.: Genetic Algorithms for Financial Modeling. In: Deboeck, G.J. (Eds.): Trading on the Edge. John Wiley, New York (1994) 148-173
11. Dutta, S., Shekhar, S.: Bond Rating: A Non-conservative Application of Neural Networks. Proceedings of IEEE International Conference on Neural Networks. San Diego, CA (1988)
12. Fogel, D.B.: Applying Evolutionary Programming to Selected Traveling Salesman Problems. Cybernetics and Systems. 24 (1993)
13. Goldberg, D.E.: Genetic Algorithms in Search, Optimization and Machine Learning. Addison-Wesley, MA (1989)

14. Han, I., Jo, H., Shin, K.S.: The Hybrid Systems for Credit Rating. Journal of the Korean Operations Research and Management Science Society. 22 (1997) 163-173
15. Holland, J.H.: Adaptation in Natural and Artificial Systems. The University of Michigan Press, Ann Arbor (1975)
16. Jeng, B., Jeng, Y., Liang, T.: FILM: a Fuzzy Inductive Learning Method for Automated Knowledge Acquisition. Decision Support Systems. 21 (1997) 61-73
17. Kim, K.S., Han, I.: The Clustering-indexing Method for Case-based Reasoning Using Self-organizing Maps and Learning Vector Quantization for Bond Rating Cases. Expert Systems with Applications. 12 (2001) 147-156
18. Klimasauskas, C.C.: Hybrid Fuzzy Encoding for Improved Backpropagation Performance. Advanced Technology for Developers. 1 (1992) 13-16
19. Koza, J.: Genetic Programming, The MIT Press, Cambridge (1993)
20. Maher, J.J., Sen, T.K.; Predicting Bond Ratings Using Neural Networks: A Comparison with Logistic Regression. Intelligent Systems in Accounting, Finance and Management. 6 (1997) 59-72
21. Moody, J., Utans, J.: Architecture Selection Strategies for Neural Networks Application to Corporate Bond Rating. In: A. Refenes: Neural Networks in the Capital Markets. John Wiley (1995).
22. Pinches, G.E., Mingo, K.A.: A Multivariate Analysis of Industrial Bond Ratings. Journal of Finance. 28 (1973) 1-18
23. Quinlan, J.R.: Induction of Decision Trees. Machine learning. 1 (1986) 81-106
24. Quinlan, J.R.: C4.5: Programs for Machine Learning. Morgan Kaufmann Publishers, Los Altos, CA (1993)
25. Shaw, M., Gentry, J.: Inductive Learning for Risk Classification. IEEE Expert. (1990) 47-53
26. Shin, K.S., Han, I. A.: Case-based Approach Using Inductive Indexing for Corporate Bond Rating. Decision Support Systems. 32 (2001) 41-52
27. Shin, K.S., Han, I.: Case-based Reasoning Supported by Genetic Algorithms for Corporate Bond Rating. Expert Systems with Applications. 16 (1999) 85-95
28. Singleton, J.C., Surkan, A.J.: Bond Rating with Neural Networks. In: A. Refenes: Neural Networks in the Capital Markets. John Wiley (1995)
29. Syswerda, G.: Uniform Crossover in Genetic Algorithms. In: Schaffer, J.D. (Eds.): Proc. 3rd Int. Conf. Genetic Algorithms. Morgan Kaufmann, San Maeto, CA (1989)
30. Wong, F., Tan, C.: Hybrid neural, genetic and fuzzy systems. In: Deboeck, G.J. (Eds.): Trading on the Edge. John Wiley, New York (1994) 245-247
31. Yuan,Y., Shaw, M.J.: Induction of Fuzzy Decision Trees. Fuzzy Sets and Systems. 69 (1995) 125-139

Text Classification Using Belief Augmented Frames

Colin Keng-Yan Tan

Department of Computer Science,
School of Computing,
National University of Singapore
ctank@comp.nus.edu.sg

Abstract. In this paper we present our work on applying Belief Augmented Frames to the text classification problem. We formulate the problem in two alternative ways, and we evaluate the performance of both formulations against established text classification algorithms. We also compare the performance against a text classifier based on Probabilistic Argumentation System, an alternative argumentation system similar to Belief Augmented Frames. We show that Belief Augmented Frames are a promising new approach to text classification, and we present suggestions for future work.

1 Introduction

Belief Augmented Frames (BAFs) were introduced by Tan and Lua in [1] and [2]. Briefly, a BAF is a classical artificial intelligence frame enhanced with belief masses. A system of logic called BAF-Logic is also defined to perform reasoning on these frames and propositions about their relationships with each other.

In this paper we apply BAFs to the problem of classifying text data. We propose two alternative ways of formulating text classification in the BAF framework, and we compare the classification accuracy results against established algorithms like Naïve Bayes, k Nearest Neighbors (k-NN), Expectation Maximization, Maximum Entropy, Probabilistic Indexing and tf-idf.

In addition we also model the problem in the Probabilistic Argumentation System (PAS) framework. PAS was proposed by Picard in [3] and [4], and is based on a set of assumptions and propositions, each weighted by probabilities. In this paper we again present two alternative PAS formulations, in direct parallel with the BAF formulations. This allows us to compare the performance of the BAF formulations with PAS.

2 Related Work

The text classification problem is an AI research topic, especially given the burgeoning number of documents available in the form of web pages and other electronic texts like emails, discussion forum postings and other electronic documents.

Briefly text classification is the task of assigning a document d_i to one or more classes c_j. An excellent introduction to this topic may be found in [5], where the following two observations were made:

- Categories are just symbolic labels. No additional knowledge of their "meaning" is available.
- The assignment of a document to a class is made solely on the contents of the document, and not on metadata. This is particularly important for certain types of electronic texts like emails and discussion forum postings, where metadata on the contents of the document are available in the form of Subject fields or Newsgroup names. For such documents it is crucial that this information is removed so that recognition results are not skewed.

Extensive research has been carried out on text classifications, for example in [6] and [7]. Attempts have also been made to incorporate background knowledge to improve classification performance, like in [8] and [9], or the rather novel use of string kernels and support vector machines [10]. In [11] Stricker et. al. use neural networks to solve the related "routing task".

For this paper we have confined our comparisons to established algorithms like Naïve Bayes, as well as the alternative argumentation system PAS. Comparisons with these novel approaches will be left for a later work.

3 Belief Augmented Frames

A Belief Augmented Frame is an extension to the standard AI frames. Each frame consists of slots. Each slot may be empty, or may be linked to other BAFs. BAFs are hierarchical, and groups of BAFs may be linked to a single super-BAF through "parent" propositions. A super-BAF is likewise linked to its children through "child" propositions. BAFs may represent real world objects like cars and people, or may represent abstract ideas like color and numbers, or a concept like "car", as opposed to an actual car object. Both frames and slots are enhanced with belief values to perform uncertain reasoning.

We now look at some formal definitions in the BAF framework, followed by details on how belief measures are combined.

3.1 Definitions

Definition 1. A Belief Augmented Frame Knowledge Base (BAF-KB, or simply KB) is defined to be a set of concepts C. Informally, a concept $c_i \in C$ corresponds to an idea or a concrete object in the world. For example, "train", "orange", "car" and "sneeze" are all valid concepts in the BAF-KB. In this paper we will not differentiate between a tangible object (for example a particular car) versus an abstract idea (for example the color blue, or the idea of a car). The words "object" and "concept" will be used interchangeably.

Definition 2. A Supporting Belief Mass (or just simply "Supporting Mass") φ^T measures how much we believe in the existence of a concept or that a proposition between concepts is true. A Refuting Belief Mass ("Refuting Mass") φ^F measures how much believe that a concept does not exist, or a proposition between two concepts is untrue. In general, $0 \leq \varphi^T, \varphi^F \leq 1$, and φ^T and φ^F may not sum to 1. The last condition is in fact the reason why we have both a supporting and a refuting belief mass; this allows us to eliminate the constraint that $\varphi^F = 1 - \varphi^T$, allowing us to model ignorance. The Supporting and Refuting Belief Masses for the existence of a concept c_i are denoted as φ^T_i and φ^F_i respectively, and for the kth proposition between concept c_i and c_j they are denoted as φ^T_{ijk} and φ^F_{ijk} respectively. Note that by this definition, it is possible that φ^T and φ^F may sum to more than 1.

Definition 3. A concept $c_i \in C$ is defined as a 4-tuple $(cl_i, \varphi^T_i, \varphi^F_i, AV_i)$, where cl_i is the name of the concept, φ^T_i is our supporting belief mass that this concept exists, φ^F_i is our refuting belief mass. AV_i is a set of propositions relating c_i with some $c_j \in C$. Note that there is no restriction that $i \neq j$, so a concept may be related with itself.

Definition 4. A proposition $av_{ijk} \in AV_i$ is the kth proposition between a concept c_i to a concept c_j. A proposition av_{ijk} consists of a 4-tuple $(al_{ijk}, cd_j, \varphi^T_{ijk}, \varphi^F_{ijk})$, where al_{ijk} is the name of the kth ($k \geq 1$) proposition between c_i and c_j, cd_j is the label for c_j, φ^T_{ijk} is our supporting belief mass that the kth proposition between c_i and c_j is true, while φ^F_{ijk} is our refuting belief mass.

Definition 5. The Degree of Inclination DI_i for the existence of a concept c_i and DI_{ijk} for the kth proposition between concepts c_i and c_j is defined as the difference between the supporting and refuting belief masses:

$$DI_i = \varphi^T_i - \varphi^F_i \quad (1)$$

$$DI_{ijk} = \varphi^T_{ijk} - \varphi^F_{ijk} \quad (2)$$

For convenience we use the notation DI when it is immaterial whether we are referring to DI_i or DI_{ijk}. DI measures the truth or falsehood of a statement, and is bounded by $[-1, 1]$. A possible interpretation for DI is shown in figure 2 below:

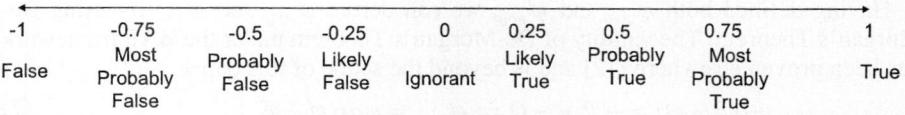

Fig. 1. Possible interpretations for the Degree of Inclination DI, which spans the range $[-1, 1]$.

Definition 6. The Utility Function U_i and U_{ijk} is defined as:

$$U_i = \frac{1 + DI_i}{2} \quad (3)$$

$$U_{ijk} = \frac{1 + DI_{ijk}}{2} \quad (4)$$

For notational convenience we will use U to refer to either U_i or U_{ijk}. U shifts the range of DI from $[-1, 1]$ to $[0, 1]$ to allow φ^T and φ^F to be used as a utility function (hence its name) for decision making. It is also possible to normalize the U values so that they may be used as probability estimates.

3.2 Combining Belief Masses

In the previous section we defined the concepts in the BAF framework. In particular we established a system of representing belief and disbelief in the existence of a concept, or of the propositions relating concepts.

In this section we define how belief measures are to be combined. This forms the basis of BAF-Logic, which we will use to model our text classification problem.

To simplify notation, we will use single-letter propositional symbols like P and Q to represent the fact that a concept c_i exists, or a proposition av_{ijk} exists between concepts c_i and c_j. We write (P, ϕ^T_P, ϕ^F_P) to represent a proposition P with supporting belief mass ϕ^T_P and refuting belief mass ϕ^F_P.

Note that while we use propositional logic style symbols like P and Q to express symbols, BAF-Logic (as defined later) is a first-order logic system. Clauses are defined over entire classes of objects instead of for individual objects.

Definition 7. Given a proposition (P, ϕ^T_P, ϕ^F_P) and given a proposition (Q, ϕ^T_Q, ϕ^F_Q), we define:

$$\phi^T_{P \wedge Q} = min(\phi^T_P, \phi^T_Q) \tag{5}$$

Intuitively, this states that since it is critical that both P and Q must be true for $P \wedge Q$ to be true, our knowledge of $P \wedge Q$ being true will only be as good as our most unreliable piece of evidence supporting $P \wedge Q$.

Definition 8. Continuing with propositions P and Q above, we define:

$$\phi^T_{P \vee Q} = max(\phi^T_P, \phi^T_Q) \tag{6}$$

Again this states that since $P \vee Q$ is true when either P is true or Q is true, we are willing to invest as much confidence in $P \vee Q$ as the strongest piece of evidence supporting $P \vee Q$.

Having defined both $\phi^T_{P \vee Q}$ and $\phi^T_{P \wedge Q}$, we can derive $\phi^F_{P \vee Q}$ and $\phi^F_{P \wedge Q}$ by using De-Morgan's Theorem. The validity of De-Morgan's Theorem under the BAF framework has been proven elsewhere [12] and is beyond the scope of this paper.

$$\neg (P \wedge Q) = \neg P \vee \neg Q \Rightarrow \phi^F_{P \wedge Q} = max(\phi^F_P, \phi^F_Q) \tag{7}$$

$$\neg (P \vee Q) = \neg P \wedge \neg Q \Rightarrow \phi^F_{P \vee Q} = min(\phi^F_P, \phi^F_Q) \tag{8}$$

Definition 9. By definition, the supporting belief mass ϕ^T_P is a measure of how confident we are that a proposition P is true, while the refuting belief mass ϕ^F_P is a measure of how confident we are that the proposition is not true. We can define the logical negation $\neg P$ as:

$$\phi^T_{\neg P} = \phi^F_P \tag{9}$$

$$\phi^F_{\neg P} = \phi^T_P \tag{10}$$

BAFs have several more key features like various operations to declare concepts and propositions, and "daemons", small scripts attached to slots that can respond to slot values. These features, while useful, are not considered in the current work.

Having defined the key ideas of BAFs, we can now examine how we can represent the text classification problem in this framework.

4 Text Classification and the BAF Framework

Given a document d_i represented by terms $(t_{i0}, t_{i1}, t_{i2}, \ldots t_{i,n-1})$, our task is to classify the document into one of a finite set of classes c_j. We can model each class as a BAF, with slots representing their relationship either with the terms found in the documents to be classified, or with the documents themselves. We explore these two possible ways of modeling this task within the BAF framework.

4.1 First Formulation – Classification Based on Individual Word Scores

In the initial formulation, we assumed that a document d_i belongs to class c_k, if, for every term t_{ij}, the following relationship holds:

$$d_i \in c_k \leftarrow (t_{i0} \in c_k \wedge t_{i1} \in c_k \wedge t_{i2} \in c_k \wedge \ldots \wedge t_{i,n-1} \in c_k) \quad (11)$$

Likewise:

$$d_i \notin c_k \leftarrow \vee_{m,\, m \neq k} (t_{i0} \in c_m \wedge t_{i1} \in c_m \wedge t_{i2} \in c_m \wedge \ldots \wedge t_{i,n-1} \in c_m) \quad (12)$$

This can be formulated trivially in BAF-Logic:

$$\varphi^T_{di \in ck} = min(p(c_k \mid t_{i0}), p(c_k \mid t_{i1}), \ldots, p(c_k \mid t_{i,n-1})) \quad (13)$$

$$\varphi^F_{di \in ck} = max(min(p(c_m \mid t_{i0}), p(c_m \mid t_{i1}), \ldots, p(c_m \mid t_{i,n-1})), min(p(c_n \mid t_{i0}), \quad (14)$$

$$p(c_n \mid t_{i1}), \ldots, p(c_n \mid t_{i,n-1})), \ldots)), m, n \text{ etc} \neq k$$

The term probabilities $p(c_k \mid t_{ij})$ are derived using Bayesian probabilities:

$$p(c_k \mid t_{ij}) = \frac{p(t_{ij} \mid c_k) p(c_k)}{p(t_{ij})} \quad (15)$$

Thus in the first formulation we apply BAF-Logic combination rules to individual document terms, to determine our belief that document d_i belongs to class c_k.

The overall class score is given by:

$$U_{d_i \in c_k} = \frac{1.0 + DI_{d_i \in c_k}}{2} \quad (16)$$

Where:

$$DI_{d_i \in c_k} = \varphi^T_{d_i \in c_k} - \varphi^F_{d_i \in c_k} \quad (17)$$

Equations 16 and 17 are the Utility and Degree of Inclination scores respectively, as defined in Definitions 6 and 5 above.

4.2 Second Formulation – Classification Based on Complete Document Score

In the second formulation, we apply the Naïve Bayes approach to first classify an entire document. Thus:

$$p(c_k | d_i) = \prod_j p(c_k | t_{ij}) \quad (18)$$

Here $p(c_k | t_{ij})$ is defined as per Equation 15 above.

It is trivial to formulate the supporting belief for document d_i belonging to class c_k. It is simply the score $p(c_k | d_i)$. Formulating the disputing belief (or disbelief) is also straightforward:

$$d_i \notin c_k \leftarrow d_i \in c_m \vee d_i \in c_n \vee d_i \in c_p \vee \ldots, \; m, n, p, \text{etc} \neq k \quad (19)$$

In BAF-Logic, we can formulate both the supporting and refuting beliefs:

$$\varphi^T_{d_i \in c_k} = p(c_k | d_i) \quad (20)$$

$$\varphi^F_{d_i \in c_k} = \max(p(c_m | d_i), p(c_n | d_i), p(c_p | d_i), \ldots) \quad (21)$$

For scoring, we define our degree of utility and degree of inclination functions as shown in equations 16 and 17 above.

5 Text Classification and Probabilistic Argumentation Systems

The text classification problem was formulated in two ways in the PAS framework, shadowing the two formulations of the BAF framework. The degree of support (dsp) of $d_i \in c_k$ is given by:

$$dsp(d_i \in c_k) = \frac{p(qs(d_i \in c_k)) - p(qs(\bot))}{1 - p(qs(\bot))} \quad (22)$$

In the first PAS formulation we consider the weights of the individual words. The quasi-support $qs(d_i \in c_k)$ is given by:

$$qs(d_i \in c_k) = (t_{i0} \in c_k \wedge t_{i1} \in c_k \wedge t_{i1} \in c_k \ldots \wedge t_{i,n-1} \in c_k) \wedge \neg (t_{i0} \in c_m \wedge t_{i1} \in c_m \wedge \quad (23)$$
$$t_{i1} \in c_m \ldots \wedge t_{i,n-1} \in c_m), \; m \neq k$$

Thus $p(qs(d_i \in c_k))$ is given by:

$$p(qs(d_i \in c_k)) = \Pi_j p(c_k | t_{ij})(\Sigma_{m, m \neq k} \Sigma_j (1.0 - p(c_m | t_{ij})) \quad (24)$$

Each $p(c_k | t_{ij})$ is computed as at Equation 15 above. In the second formulation, we consider the score of the document as a whole. Thus:

$$qs(d_i \in c_k) = (d_i \in c_k) \wedge \neg (d_i \in c_m \vee d_i \in c_n \vee \ldots), \; m, n \text{ etc} \neq k \quad (25)$$

Thus we can find $p(qs(d_i \in c_k))$:

$$p(qs(d_i \in c_k)) = p(c_k | d_i) [\Sigma_{m, m \neq k}(1.0 - p(c_m | d_i))] \quad (26)$$

Note that in either formulation, it is not contradictory to find a term t_{ij} to be in class c_k and any other class at the same time. We propose therefore that:

$$p(qs(\bot)) = 0 \tag{27}$$

Thus $dsp(qs(d_i \in c_k))$ is now:

$$dsp(d_i \in c_k) = p(qs(d_i \in c_k)) \tag{28}$$

Having formulated our problem in both the BAF and PAS frameworks, we now proceed with details of the experiments.

6 Experiment Details and Results

We now present our experiment details and results.

6.1 Experiment Details

The experiments were conducted using Andrew McCallum's Bag of Words Library (Bow) [13]. The Bow library provides facilities for gathering word statistics quickly from very large corpuses, and provides word weighting using Naïve Bayes, tf-idf and several other methods. We extended *rainbow*, the text classification front-end for Bow with the two BAF and two PAS formulations.

We used the *20 Newsgroups* corpus for training and testing. 80% of the corpus amounting to about 16,000 documents was used for gathering word statistics, while 20%, or about 4,000 documents was used for testing. The choice of documents for training and testing was done randomly by the Bow library.

A total of 10 trials were performed for each classification method and the average score was taken. All headers were removed when indexing the documents. This is important because the headers contain the names of the Newsgroups, which will affect our recognition results (as well as contradict the common assumption in text classification that the docments do not contain any information hinting to its correct class).

We now look at the results of the experiments.

6.2 Experiment Results

Figure 2 shows the results of our experiments:

BAF1 is the formulation using individual word scores, while BAF2 is the formulation using overall document scores. Likewise with PAS1 and PAS2. The remaining methods shown are Naïve Bayes, tf-idf, k-Nearest Neighbor (kNN), Expectation Maximization (EM), Maximum Entropy (MAXENT), and Probabilistic Indexing (PRIND), all standard methods provided by *rainbow*.

We see a very large improvement in classification results if we considered overall document scores (BAF2) over individual word scores (BAF1), from 68.98% to 82.36%. PAS shows similar though less dramatic results when shifting from using individual word scores (PAS1) to overall document scores (PAS2), with results improving from 65.87% to 67.46%.

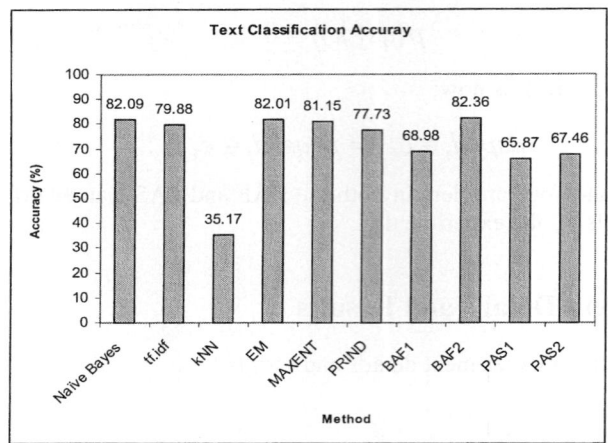

Fig. 2. Classification Accuracy by Method.

These results support the idea that using overall document class scores to do text classification using argumentation systems gives better results than using individual word scores. PAS however appears to perform worse than the remaining methods.

BAF2 shows a small margin of improvement over Naïve Bayes, the closest competitor, with a recognition score of 82.36% against 82.09%. Thus it appears that considering the possibility that a document belongs to another class (Equation 21) appears to have a positive effect on the classification scores, albeit a rather small one (0.27%).

Computation effort, however, is not significantly more than Naïve Bayes, making this improvement worth investigating further, especially since the reasons for the improvement is unclear. Much more study will be made into this.

The next closest classifier in terms of classification accuracy is the Expectation Maximization classifier (82.01%). However this classifier takes significant amounts of computing effort to train. The other methods like Maximum Entropy (81.15%) and Probabilistic Indexing (77.73%) show appreciable difference in classification accuracy over BAF2.

7 Conclusion and Suggestions for Further Research

Our experiment results show that our approach in using BAF-Logic to classify text documents is a promising one.

This is especially so considering that many other useful features of BAFs (for example, hierchical structures allowing for abstraction of document classes, daemons attached to BAF slots allowing for flexible responses to associations with other BAFs) were not employed or covered in this paper.

We have evaluated BAFs only against established text classification methods. Comparisons with more novel methods introduced in Section 2 need to be made. It will also be worthwhile seeing how BAFs can be improved using background knowledge and other supporting information.

Thus it is clear from this initial study that BAFs are potentially an excellent, novel and rich framework for text classification, and will form the basis for a new research direction in this field.

References

1. Tan, C. K. Y., Lua, K. T., "Belief Augmented Frames for Knowledge Representation in Spoken Dialog Systems", First International Indian Conference on Artificial Intelligence, Hyderabad, India, 2003.
2. Tan, C. K. Y., Lua, K. T., "Discourse Understanding with Discourse Representation Structures and Belief Augmented Frames", 2nd International Conference on Computational Intelligence, Robotics and Autonomous Systems, Singapore, 2003.
3. Picard, J., "Probabilistic Argumentation Systems Applied to Information Retrieval", Doctoral Thesis, Universite de Neuchatel, Suisse, 2000.
4. Picard, J., "Using Probabilistic Argumentation Systems to Search and Classify Web Sites", IEEE Data Engineering Bulletin, 2001.
5. Sebastiania, F., "Machine Learning in Automated Text Categorization" Proceedings of THAI-99, European Symposium on Telematics, Hypermedia and Artificial Intelligence, 1999.
6. Cohen, W., Hirsh, H., "Joins that Generalize, Text Categorization using WHIRL", Proceedings of the 4th International Conference on Knowledge Discovery and Data Mining, pp. 169-173, Menlo Park, California, AAAI Press, 1998.
7. Nigam, K., McCallum, A., "Text Classification from Labeled and Unlabeled Documents using EM", Machine Learning, pp. 103-134, 2000.
8. Zelikovitz, S., Hirsh, H., "Improving Text Classification with LSI using Background Knowledge", IJCAI-01 Workshop Notes on Text Learning: Beyond Supervision, 2001.
9. Zelikovitz, S., Hirsh, H., "Integrating Background Knowledge into Nearest Neighbor Text Classification", Proceedings of the 6th Intenational Conference on Case Based Reasoning, 2002.
10. Lodi, H., Saunders, C., Shawes-Taylor, J., Cristianini, N., Watkins, C., "Text Classification using String Kernels", NIPS, 2002.
11. Stricker, M., Vichot, F., Dreyfus, G., Wolinski, F., "Training Context-Sensitive Neural Networks with Few Relevant Examples for the TREC-9 Routing", 2001.
12. Colin Keng-Yan Tan, "Belief Augmented Frames", pp. 50-62, Doctoral Thesis, National University of Singapore, Singapore, 2003.
13. McCallum, A., "Bow: A Toolkit for Statistical Language Modeling", Text Retrieval, Classification and Clustering, http://www-2.cs.cmu.edu/~mccallum/bow/, 1996.

A Feature Selection for Text Categorization on Research Support System Papits

Tadachika Ozono, Toramatsu Shintani, Takayuki Ito, and Tomoharu Hasegawa

Nagoya Institute of Technology, Gokiso, Showa-ku, Nagoya, Aichi, 466-8555, Japan
{ozono,tora,itota,tomoha}@ics.nitech.ac.jp
http://www-toralab.ics.nitech.ac.jp/index.html

Abstract. We have developed a research support system, called Papits, that shares research information, such as PDF files of research papers, in computers on the network and classifies the information into types of research fields. Users of Papits can share various research information and survey the corpora of their particular fields of research. In order to realize Papits, we need to design a mechanism for identifying what words are best suited to classify documents in predefined classes. Further we have to consider classification in cases where we must classify documents into multivalued fields and where there is insufficient data for classification. In this paper, we present an implementation method of automatic classification based on a text classification technique for Papits. We also propose a new method for using feature selection to classify documents that are represented by a bag-of-words into a multivalued category. Our method transforms the multivalued category into a binary category to easily identify the characteristic words to classify category in a few training data. Our experimental result indicates that our method can effectively classify documents in Papits.

1 Introduction

We have developed a research support system, called Papits [Fujimaki 02], [Ozono 02]. Papits has several functions that allow it to manage research information, i.e., a paper sharing function, a paper classifier, a paper recommender, a paper retriever, and a research diary. The paper sharing function facilitates to share research information, such as the PDF files of research papers, and to collect papers from Web sites. The function of automatic classification can classify research information into several research fields. This function enables users to search papers based on category of their interest. Automatic classification in Papits has a structure that gradually improves accuracy through feedback from users. In this paper, we mainly discuss paper classification.

In automatic text classification, one of the main problems is how to identify what words are best suited to classify documents in predefined classes. Feature selection techniques are therefore needed to identify these words, and one such technique uses the information gain (IG) metric [Quinlan 86] assessed over the set of all words encountered in all texts [Lewis 94,Soucy 01]. Soucy [Soucy 01] proposed a feature selection method based on IG and a new algorithm that selects features according to their average cooccurrence. It yielded good results on binary class problems. Automatic classification in Papits needs to classify documents to be classified into the multivalued category, since researches are organized by several fields. Since there are a lot of research fields, it is hard to collect enough training data. When the number of training data in one category is small, feature selection becomes sensitive to noise and irrelevant data. Further, as previously pointed out, there may not necessarily be enough training data. This paper proposes a feature selection method for classifying documents, which is represented by a bag-of-words, into the multivalued category. It transforms the multivalued category into a binary category, and features are selected using IG.

The remainder of this paper is organized as follows: First, we show an outline of our Papits research support system. Second, we describe classification method and propose the feature selection algorithm for managing research papers. Third, we discuss the experimental results we obtained using our algorithm and proves its usefulness. Fourth, we discuss the functions of Papits. Fifth, we compared our work with related works. Finally, we conclude with a brief summary and discuss future research directions.

2 Research Support System Papits

This section presents an outline of Papits, which is a research support system, implemented as a web application (using WebObjects[1]). Users can access via a web browser. Papits has several functions that manage research information, i.e., paper sharing, a paper classifier, a paper recommender, a paper retriever, and a research diary. The knowledge management of Papits supports surveys by through these functions. This paper mainly discusses the paper classifier function, which can provide intense support to surveys on fields of research interest. When users want to look for papers they are interested in, they can easily find these by tracing the category or retrieving or using the recommender.

Figure 1 illustrates the Papits automatic classification process. Papits first collects papers from users, web sites, and the other sources. In this step, the papers have not been yet classified. The unclassified papers are classified by a classifier that uses manually classified papers in the document DB as training data. Here, we have assumed that classification aided by the user is correct, and papers classified by the classifier cannot be guaranteed to be perfectly correct. Papers classified by the classifier are stored in databases as automatic classified papers, and is not used as training data.

While browsing for a paper, if a user corrects or certifies a category for that paper, it is stored as manually classified paper. Training data increases by going through this step, and classification accuracy improves.

Figure 2 has the results obtained for classification in Papits. When a user wants to look for papers of interest, it can be found based on the category of

---

[1] Web Objects is a tool for creating a Web Application, developed by Apple

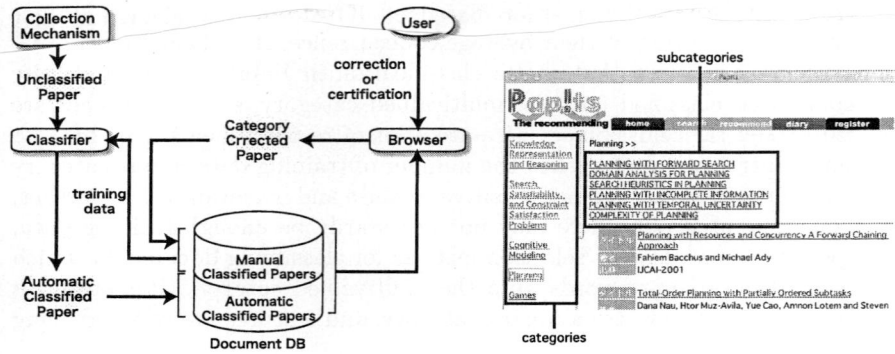

Fig. 1. Work Flow of Classification in Papits.

Fig. 2. Browsing classified papers.

interest. Additionally, users can narrow the range of the field of survey based on subcategories. In this way, users can scrutinize their field of interest through the automatic paper classifier.

3 Automatic Classification

Automatic classification helps users locate papers by following their category of interest. The main problem in automatic text classification is to identify what words are the most suitable to classify documents in predefined classes. This section discusses the text classification method for Papits and our feature selection method.

3.1 Text Classification Algorithm

k-Nearest Neighbor (kNN) and Support Vector Machine (SVM) have frequently been applied to text categorization [Yang 99]. [Yang 99] describes kNN and SVM are an almost equivalent performance. Section 4 discusses the experimental results using these text classification algorithms.

kNN. The kNN algorithm is quite simple: kNN finds the k nearest neighbors of the test document from the training documents. The categories of these nearest neighbors is used to weight the category candidates. The similarity score of each neighbor document to the test document is used as the weight for the categories of the neighbor document. If several k nearest neighbors share a category, then the per-neighbor weights of that category are added, and the weighted sum is used as the likelihood score for that category with respect to the test document. By sorting the scores of the candidate category, a ranked list is obtained for the test document.

Typical similarity is measured with a cosine function:

$$\cos(x_1, x_2) = \frac{\sum_{j=1}^{n} a_j(x_1) \cdot a_j(x_2)}{\sqrt{\sum_{j=1}^{n} a_j(x_1)^2 \cdot \sum_{j=1}^{n} a_j(x_2)^2}}$$

where x_1 and x_2 are documents, and x is a document vector $\langle a_1(x), a_2(x), \cdots, a_n(x)\rangle$. $a_j(x)$ is the weight of the j-th feature (word) on x. We assumed that the weight of each feature would be the same:

- $a_j(x) = 1$: if the j-th word is in document x
- $a_j(x) = 0$: otherwise

SVM. The formulation of SVM is constructed starting from a simple linear maximum margin classifier [Burges 98]. A general linear SVM can be expressed as equation (1)

$$f(\boldsymbol{x}) = \boldsymbol{w} \cdot \boldsymbol{x} - b \qquad (1)$$

where $f(\boldsymbol{x})$ is the output of the SVM, $\boldsymbol{x}$ is the input document, b is a threshold, $\boldsymbol{w} = \sum_i \alpha y_i \boldsymbol{x_i}$, $\boldsymbol{x_i}$ is a stored training document, $y_i \in \{-1, +1\}$ is the desired output of the classifier, and α_i are weights. The margin for this linear classifier is $\frac{1}{||w||}$. Hence the training problem is to minimize $||w||$ with respect to constraint (1).

The linear formulation can not classify nonlinearly separable documents. SVMs get around this problem by mapping the sample points into a higher dimensional space using a kernel function. A general non-linear SVM can be expressed as equation (2)

$$f(\boldsymbol{x}) = \sum_i \alpha_i y_i K(\boldsymbol{x_i}, \boldsymbol{x}) - b \qquad (2)$$

where K is a kernel function which measures the similarity of a stored training documents $\boldsymbol{x_i}$ to the input $\boldsymbol{x}$, $y_i \in \{-1, +1\}$ is the desired output of the classifier, b is a threshold, and α_i are weights which blend the different kernels.

The formulation of SVM was based on a two-class problem, hence SVM is basically a binary classifier. Several different schemes can be applied to the basic SVM algorithm to handle the n-category classification problem. One of schemes to handle the n-category is one-versus-rest approach. The one-versus-rest approach works by constructing a set of n binary classifiers for a n-category problem. The k-th classifier is trained with all of the documents in the k-th category with positive labels, and all other documents with negative labels. The final output is the category that corresponds to the classifier with the highest output value.

$$f(\boldsymbol{x}) = \arg\max_k \sum_{i=1} \alpha_i^k y_i K^k(\boldsymbol{x_i}, \boldsymbol{x}) - b$$

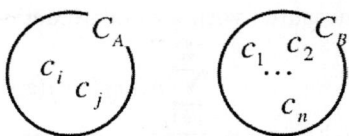

Fig. 3. The multivalued category into the binary category.

V = set of words, sorting by information gain (initial condition = {})
D = set of documents
C = set of categories
k = arbitrary number of features
l = arbitrary number of categories
$IG_{C_A,C_B}(w, D)$: IG of documents D on word w, relative to categories C_A and C_B
add(V, w, IG) : word w is added to V sorted by IG value

1:**Feature_Selection_Algorithm()**
2: **for** each combination C_A of C choose 1 or 2 categories
3:    $C_B = C - C_A$
4:    $IGvalue = IG_{C_A,C_B}(w, D)$
5:    **if** ($max < IGvalue$) **then**
6:       $max = IGvalue$
7:    add(V, w, max)
8: **return** k higher ranks of V.

Fig. 4. Proposing Feature Selection Algorithm.

3.2 An Algorithm for Feature Selection

Feature selection techniques are needed to identify the most suitable words to classify documents, and to reduce the computation costs of classifying new documents. In Papits, automatic classification needs to classify documents into the multivalued category, because research is organized in various fields. However, feature selection becomes sensitive to noise and irrelevant data compared to cases with few categories. There may also not be enough registered papers as training data to identify the most suitable words to classify into the multivalued category in Papits. We propose feature selection to classify documents, which is represented by a bag-of-words, into the multivalued category.

Several existing feature selection techniques use some metric to determine the relevance of a term with regard to the classification criterion. IG is often used in text classification in the bag-of-words approach [Joachims 98, Nigam 99], [Sahami 98].

$$\text{IG}(A, X) = \left(-\sum_{c \in C} \frac{|X_c|}{|X|} \log_2 \frac{|X_c|}{|X|}\right) - \left(-\sum_{v \in Values(A)} \sum_{c \in C} \frac{|X_{c,v}|}{|X|} \log_2 \frac{|X_{c,v}|}{|X_v|}\right)$$

where C is the set of all categories, and each of category is denoted as c. A is an arbitrary feature (word), v is a value of A, and the set of value of feature A

is denoted as $Values(A) = \{0, 1\}$. If feature A is in a document, then value v is 1. Otherwise v is 0. X denotes a set of all documents, and $X_c, X_v, X_{c,v}$ denote sets of documents that are included in category c, taking feature value v, and belonging to category c as well as taking the feature value v. $|X|$ indicate the number of elements of set X.

In this formula, as the number of elements of C increases, documents are divided into more categories. Hence, the IG value becomes sensitive to noise and the irrelevant data. Our method transforms the multivalued category into a binary category, increases the number of data in one category, and does feature selection using IG. Figure 3 presents the idea behind this method with the set of categories $\{c_1, c_2, \cdots, c_i, \cdots, c_j, \cdots, c_n\}$. If suitable words to classify into documents various combinations of categories are found, since a document category is predicted by a combination of words, we thought it would be possible to classify each category by combining these words. For example, let us suppose the following case:

- set C_A consists of categories c_i and c_j
- set C_B consists of categories other than c_i and c_j
- set C_S consists of categories c_i and c_k
- set C_T consists of categories other than c_i and c_k
- word w_a is suitable to classify C_A and C_B
- word w_b is suitable to classify C_S and C_T

If a combination of w_a and w_b can be found, a classifier can classify original categories c_i, c_j, and c_k. Our feature selection method can be used to locate w_a and w_b.

Figure 4 shows the proposed feature selection algorithm. First, new category C_A is a set that consists of two or less categories that are selected from a set of categories C, and C_B is a set of elements of C except for categories that constitute C_A. For all combinations of these, IG is assessed over the set of all words encountered in all texts, let the highest value of IG be the importance of word w. IG for new categories $\{C_A, C_B\}$ is determined by the following:

$$\text{IG}_{C_A, C_B}(A, X) = -\left(\frac{|X_{C_A}|}{|X|} \log_2 \frac{|X_{C_A}|}{|X|} + \frac{|X_{C_B}|}{|X|} \log_2 \frac{|X_{C_B}|}{|X|}\right)$$
$$+ \sum_{v \in Values(A)} \left(\frac{|X_{C_A,v}|}{|X|} \log_2 \frac{|X_{C_A,v}|}{|X_v|} + \frac{|X_{C_B,v}|}{|X|} \log_2 \frac{|X_{C_B,v}|}{|X_v|}\right)$$

X_{C_A} and X_{C_B} denote sets of documents that are included in categories C_A and C_B. $X_{C_A,v}$ and $X_{C_B,v}$ denote taking feature value v and its belonging to categories C_A and C_B respectively. Finally, the best k words according to this metric are chosen as features.

4 Evaluation

4.1 Experimental Setting

This section evaluates the performance of our algorithms by measuring its ability to reproduce manual category assignments on a data set.

We will now describe the data sets and the method of evaluation. The data set is a set of papers from IJCAI'01 proceedings. We used 188 papers that had extracted titles, authors, and abstracts from PDF files as data. These papers had been manually indexed by category (14 categories). Each category corresponded to a section of IJCAI'01 Proceedings and selection was done as follows: *Knowledge Representation and Reasoning, Search, Satisfiability, and Constraint Satisfaction Problems, Cognitive Modeling, Planning, Diagnosis, Logic Programming and Theorem Proving, Uncertainty and Probabilistic Reasoning, Neural Networks and Genetic Algorithms, Machine Learning and Data Mining, Case-based Reasoning, Multi-Agent System, Natural Language Processing and Information Retrieval, Robotics and Perception, Web Applications.*

Our method of feature selection, called "Binary Category", and another using IG were used over this data set. The method of comparison used the IG metric assessed over the set of all words encountered in all texts, and then the best k were chosen words according to that metric. We called this "Multivalued Category". After the best features were chosen with Multivalued Category and Binary Category. We estimated the accuracy of classification by classifier using kNN and SVM in each case of k. SVM training is carried out with the TinySVM [Kudo 01]. To handle the n-category classification problem, we applied one-versus-rest approach to TinySVM classifier tool.

To estimate accuracy for selected features, we used a n-fold cross-validation. The data set is randomly divided into n sets with approximately equal size. For each "fold", the classifier is trained using all but one of the n groups and then tested on the unseen group. This procedure is repeated for each of the n groups. The cross-validation score is the average performance across each of the n training runs. We used a 10-fold cross-validation for our experiments.

4.2 Performance Measures

N-best accuracy was used for evaluation. We considered two kinds of criteria for accuracy, "N=1" and "N=3".

- "N=1" meant that the most suitable category predicted by kNN and SVM corresponded to the original target document category, then a correct prediction was considered.
- "N=3" meant that at least one of three higher suitable categories that were predicted by kNN and SVM corresponded to the original target document category, a correct prediction was considered.

4.3 Experimental Results

Figure 5, Figure 6, Figure 7, and Figure 8 has the results obtained through the different feature selection methods we tested. The results using the kNN classifier are presented in Figure 5 and Figure 6. The other results, Figure 7 and Figure 8, are used the SVM classifier. The horizontal axis is the number of features, and the vertical axis is the accuracy score(%) for "N=1" and "N=3".

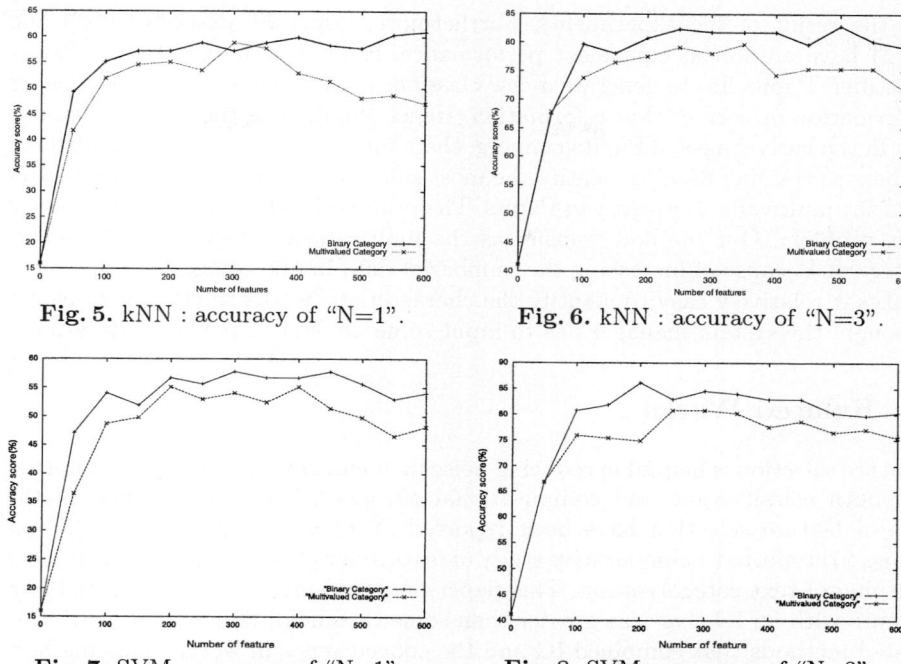

Fig. 5. kNN : accuracy of "N=1".   **Fig. 6.** kNN : accuracy of "N=3".

Fig. 7. SVM : accuracy of "N=1".   **Fig. 8.** SVM : accuracy of "N=3".

Additionally, we experimented the classification of kNN and SVM using an unbounded number of features. The results of the experiments were that Accuracy scores of kNN classification were "N=1" : 36.7% and "N=3" : 61.2%, those of SVM classification were "N=1" : 35.6% and "N=3" : 61.0%. The accuracy of using an unbounded number of features was lower than that of feature selections. For the result given above, feature selection was proven helpful in improving classification. Furthermore, almost every result of accuracy scores was Binary Category method > Multivalued Category method. In almost all cases, "N=1" results of Figure 5 and Figure 7, revealed a higher accuracy for the Binary Category method than for the Multivalued Category method. Moreover, the Binary Category method at "N=3", Figure 6 and Figure 8, was much more accurate than the Multivalued Category method with a fewer number of features. This helped to reduce the impact of noise and irrelevant data, and therefore our feature selection method could reduce the computation costs of classifying new documents without reducing accuracy.

For comparison of kNN (Figure 5, Figure 6) and SVM (Figure 7, Figure 8), their accuracy performance is approximate equivalent. This result was in agreement with [Yang 99].

5 Discussion

The Papits classifier uses kNN instead of SVM. From accuracy performance point of view, there is not so much difference between kNN and SVM, base on the result of the experiments. Furthermore, [Yang 99] describes kNN and SVM have an almost equivalent performance. If SVM is applied to the Papits classifier, Papits has to generate a new classifier whenever users input new paper information or correct that information. Hence Papits uses the kNN algorithm.

In the early stages of Papits running, there may also not be enough registered papers as training data to identify the most suitable words to classify the papers into the multivalued category in Papits. The proposed method in this paper solve this problem. Our method transforms the multivalued category into a binary category. Because of increasing the number of data in one category, our method makes it relatively easy to identify the characteristic words to classify category. Though, the system manager has to input some amount of paper information.

6 Related Works

Feature selection is helpful in reducing noise in document representation, improving both classification and computational efficiency. Therefore, several methods of feature selection have been reported [Yang 97,Soucy 01,John 94].Yang [Yang 97] reported a comparative study of feature selection methods in statistical learning of text categorization. This paper proposed methods that selected any feature with an IG that was greater than some threshold. Soucy [Soucy 01] presented methods that combined IG and the cooccurrence of words. This method selects a set of features according to an IG criterion, and refines them based on the cooccurrence with a predetermined subset of highly ranked features. This method evaluates a task of binary classification. Text classification in Papits needs to classify documents to be classified into the multivalued category. Hence it is hard to collect enough training data. Our method considers the case that Papits stores a few training data, transforms the multivalued category into a binary category to easily identify the characteristic words. John [John 94] proposed feature selection in the wrapper model. This method finds all strongly suitable features and a useful subset of the weakly relevant features that yields good performance. The processing cost to identify weakly relevant features was very expensive, because the wrapper model repeats evaluation with respect to every subset of features. Our method considered subsets of categories. Subsets of categories are much smaller than that of features.

7 Conclusion and Future Work

In this paper, we introduced an approach and a structure to implement automatic classification in Papits. This structure gradually increased the accuracy by using feedback from users. In this system, papers classified by the classifier were not used as training data, since these cannot guarantee a perfectly correct prediction. An unclassified paper is classified by a classifier that only uses manually classified papers in the document DB as training data.

The main problem for the automatic text classification is to identify what words are most suitable to classify documents in predefined classes. Automatic classification in Papits needs to classify documents into the multivalued category, since research is organized by field. To solve this problem, we proposed a feature selection method for text classification in Papits. It transforms the multivalued category into a binary category and was helpful in reducing noise in document representation and improving classification and computational efficiency, because it increased the amount of data in one category, and selected features using IG. We experimentally confirmed its efficacy.

One direction for future study is to develop a means of determining parameters that are suited to the task required, such as the number of features and the number of combinations of categories.

References

[Burges 98] C. J. C. Burges. A tutorial on support vector machines for pattern recognition. *Data Mining and Knowledge Discovery*, 2(2),pp.121-167 1998.

[Fujimaki 02] N. Fujimaki, T. Ozono, and T. Shintani. Flexible Query Modifier for Research Support System Papits. *Proceedings of the IASTED International Conference on Artificial and Computational Intelligence*(ACI2002), pp.142-147, 2002.

[Joachims 98] T. Joachims. Text Categorization with Support Vector Machines: Learning with Many Relevant Features. *Proceedings of the European Conference on Machine Learning*, 1998.

[John 94] G. H. John, R. Kohavi, K. Pfleger. Irrelevant Features and the Subset Selection Problem. *Proceedings of the Eleventh International Conference on Machine Learning*, pp.121-129, 1994.

[Kudo 01] T. Kudo. TinySVM: Support Vector Machines. <http://cl-aist-nara.ac.jp/ taku-ku/software/TinySVM>,2001

[Lewis 94] D. Lewis and M. Ringuette. A comparison of two learning algorithms for text categorization. *Third Annual Symposium on Document Analysis and Information Retrieval*, pp 81-93, 1994.

[Nigam 99] K. Nigam, J. Lafferty and A. McCallum. Using Maximum Entropy for Text Classification. *IJCAI-99 Workshop on Machine Learning for Information Filtering*, 1999.

[Ozono 02] T. Ozono, S. Goto, N. Fujimaki, and T. Shintani. P2P based Knowledge Source Discovery on Research Support System Papits. *The First International Joint Conference on Autonomous Agents & Multiagent Systems*(AAMAS 2002), 2002.

[Quinlan 86] J. R. Quinlan. Induction of decision trees. *Machine Learning*, 1 (1) pp 81-106, 1986.

[Sahami 98] M. Sahami, S. Dumais, D. Heckerman and E. Horvitz. A Bayesian approach to filtering junk e-mail. *AAAI/ICML Workshop on Learning for Text Categorization*, 1998.

[Soucy 01] P. Soucy and G. W. Mineau. A Simple Feature Selection Method for Text Classification. *Proceedings of International joint Conference on Artificial Intelligence*(IJCAI'01), pp. 897-902, 2001.

[Yang 99] Y. Yang and X. Liu. A re-examination of text categorization methods. *22nd Annual International SIGIR*, pp.42-49, 1999.

[Yang 97] Y. Yang and J. O. Perdersen. A Comparative Study on Feature Selection in Text Categorization. *Proceedings of the Fourteenth International Conference on Machine Learning*(ICML'97), 1997.

Constrained Ant Colony Optimization for Data Clustering

Shu-Chuan Chu[1,3], John F. Roddick[1], Che-Jen Su[2], and Jeng-Shyang Pan[2,4]

[1] School of Informatics and Engineering,
Flinders University of South Australia,
GPO Box 2100, Adelaide 5001, South Australia
roddick@infoeng.flinders.edu.au
[2] Department of Electronic Engineering,
Kaohsiung University of Applied Sciences
Kaohsiung, Taiwan
jspan@cc.kuas.edu.tw
[3] National Kaohsiung Marine University
Kaohsiung, Taiwan
[4] Department of Automatic Test and Control,
Harbine Institute of Technology
Harbine, China

Abstract. Processes that simulate natural phenomena have successfully been applied to a number of problems for which no simple mathematical solution is known or is practicable. Such meta-heuristic algorithms include genetic algorithms, particle swarm optimization and ant colony systems and have received increasing attention in recent years.
This paper extends ant colony systems and discusses a novel data clustering process using Constrained Ant Colony Optimization ($CACO$). The $CACO$ algorithm extends the Ant Colony Optimization algorithm by accommodating a quadratic distance metric, the *Sum of K Nearest Neighbor Distances* ($SKNND$) metric, constrained addition of pheromone and a shrinking range strategy to improve data clustering. We show that the $CACO$ algorithm can resolve the problems of clusters with arbitrary shapes, clusters with outliers and bridges between clusters.

1 Introduction

Inspired by the food-seeking behavior of real ants, the ant system [1] and ant colony system [2] algorithms have demonstrated themselves to be efficient and effective tools for combinatorial optimization problems. In simplistic terms, in nature, a real ant wandering in its surrounding environment will leave a biological trace - pheromone - on its route. As more ants take the same route the level of this pheromone increases with the intensity of pheromone at any point biasing the path-taking decisions of subsequent ants. After a while, the shorter paths will tend to possess higher pheromone concentration and therefore encourage subsequent ants to follow them. As a result, an initially irregular path from nest to food will eventually focus to form the shortest path or paths. With appropriate abstractions and modifications, these natural observations have led to a successful computational model for combinatorial optimization. The ant system and ant colony system algorithms [1, 2] have been applied successfully in many difficult applications such as the quadratic assignment problem [3], data mining [4], space-planning [4], job-shop scheduling and graph coloring [5]. A parallelised ant colony system has also been developed by the authors [6, 7].

Clustering is an important technique that has been studied in various fields with applications ranging from similarity search, image compression, texture segmentation, trend analysis, pattern recognition and classification. The goal of clustering is to group sets of objects into classes such that similar objects are placed in the same class while dissimilar objects are placed in separate classes. Substantial work on clustering exists in both the statistics and database communities for different domains of data [8–18].

The Ant Colony Optimization with Different Favor ($ACODF$) algorithm [19] modified the Ant Colony Optimization (ACO) [2] to allow it to be used for data clustering by adding the concept of simulated annealing [20] and the strategy of tournament selection [21]. It is useful in partitioning the data sets for those with clear boundaries between classes, however, it is less suitable when faced with clusters of arbitrary shape, clusters with outliers and bridges between clusters.

An advanced version of the ACO algorithm, termed the Constrained Ant Colony Optimization ($CACO$) algorithm, is proposed here for data clustering by adding constraints on the calculation of pheromone strength. The proposed $CACO$ algorithm has the following properties:

- It applies the quadratic metric combined with the *Sum of K Nearest Neighbor Distances* ($SKNND$) metric to be instead of the Euclidean distance measure.
- It adopts a constrained form of pheromone updating. The pheromone is only updated based on some statistical distance threshold.
- It utilises a reducing search range.

2 Constrained Ant Colony Optimization

Ant Colony Optimization with Different Favor ($ACODF$) applies ACO for use in data clustering. The difference between the $ACODF$ and ACO is that each ant in $ACODF$ only visits a fraction of the total clustering objects and the number of visited objects decreases with each cycle. $ACODF$ also incorporates the strategies of simulated annealing and tournament selection and results in an algorithm which is effective for clusters with clearly defined boundaries. However, $ACODF$ does not handle clusters with arbitrary shapes, clusters with outliers and bridges between clusters well. In order to improve the effectiveness of the clustering the following four strategies are applied:

Strategy 1: While the Euclidean distance measure is used in conventional clustering techniques such as in the $ACODF$ clustering algorithm, it is not suitable for clustering non-spherical clusters, (for example, a cluster with a slender shape). In this work we therefore opt for a quadratic metric [22] as the distance measure. Given an object at position O and objects X_i, $i = 1, 2, \ldots, T$, (T is the total number of objects), the quadratic metric between the current object O and the object X_m can be expressed as

$$D_q(O, X_m) = (O - X_m)^t W^{-1}(O - X_m) \tag{1}$$

where $(O - X_m)$ is an error column vector and W is the covariance matrix given as

$$W = \frac{1}{T} \sum_{i=1}^{T} (X_i - \bar{X})(X_i - \bar{X})^t \tag{2}$$

and $\bar{X}$ is the mean of X_i, $i = 1, 2, \ldots, T$ defined as

$$\bar{X} = \frac{1}{T} \sum_{i=1}^{T} X_i \tag{3}$$

W^{-1} is the inverse of covariance matrix W.

Strategy 2: We use the *Sum of K Nearest Neighbor Distances (SKNND)* metric in order to distinguish dense clusters more easily. The example shown in Figure 1 shows an ant located at A which will tend to move toward C within a dense cluster rather than object B located in the sparser region. By adopting $SKNND$, as the process iterates, the probability for an ant to move towards the denser clusters increases. This strategy can avoid clustering errors due to bridges between clusters.

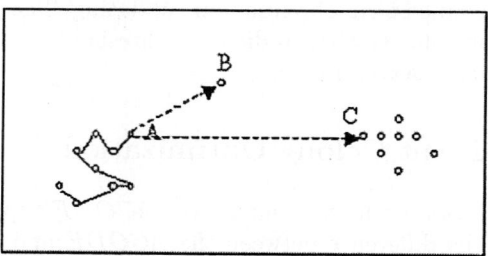

Fig. 1. Using $SKNND$, ants tend to move toward objects located within dense clusters.

Strategy 3: As shown in Figure 1, as a result of strategy 2, ants will tend to move towards denser clusters. However, the pheromone update is inversely proportional to the distance between the visited objects for conventional search formula [2] and the practical distance between objects A and C could be farther than that between objects A and B reducing the pheromone level and causing a clustering error. In order to compensate for this, a statistical threshold for the kth ant is adopted as below.

$$L_{ts}^k = AvgL_{path}^k + StDevL_{path}^k \qquad (4)$$

where $AvgL_{path}^k$ and $StDevL_{path}^k$ are the average of the distance and the standard deviation for the route of the visited objects by the kth ant expressed as

$$AvgL_{path}^k = \frac{\sum L_{ij}^k}{E}, \quad if\ (X_i, X_j)\ path\ visited\ by\ the\ k^{th}\ ant \qquad (5)$$

$$StDevL_{path}^k = \sqrt{\frac{\sum(L_{ij}^k - AvgL_{path}^k)^2}{E}}, \qquad (6)$$

$if\ (X_i, X_j)\ path\ visited\ by\ the\ k^{th}\ ant$

where E is the number of paths visited by the kth ant. We may roughly consider objects X_i and X_j to be located in different clusters if $L_{ij}^k > L_{ts}^k$. The distance between objects X_i and X_j cannot be added into the length of the path and the pheromone cannot be updated between the objects.

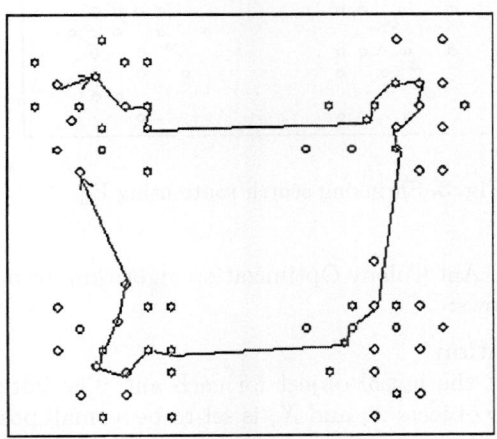

Fig. 2. Conventional search route.

Strategy 4: The conventional search formula [2] between objects r and s is not suitable for robust clustering as object s represents all un-visited objects resulting in excessive computation and a tendency for ants to jump between dense clusters as shown in Figure 2. In order to improve clustering speed and eliminate this jumping phenomenon, the conventional search formula [2] is modified to be

$$P_k(r,s) = \begin{cases} \frac{[\tau(r,s)] \cdot [D_q(r,s)]^{-\beta} \cdot [SKNND(s)]^{-\gamma}}{\sum_{u \in J_k^{N_2}(r)} [\tau(r,u)] \cdot [D_q(r,u)]^{-\beta} \cdot [SKNND(u)]^{-\gamma}}, & if\ s \in J_k^{N_2}(r) \\ 0, & otherwise \end{cases} \qquad (7)$$

where $J_k^{N_2}(r)$ is used to shrink the search range to the N_2 nearest un-visited objects. N_2 is set to be some fraction of the object (in our experiments we used 10%), $D_q(r,s)$ is the quadratic distance between objects r and s. $SKNND(s)$ is the sum of the distances between object s and the N_2 nearest objects. β and γ are two parameters which determine the relative importance of pheromone level versus the quadratic distance and the Sum of N_2 Nearest Neighbor Distance, respectively. We have found that setting β to 2 and γ to between 5 and 15 results in robust performance. As shown in Figure 3, the jumping phenomenon is eliminated after using the shrinking search formula.

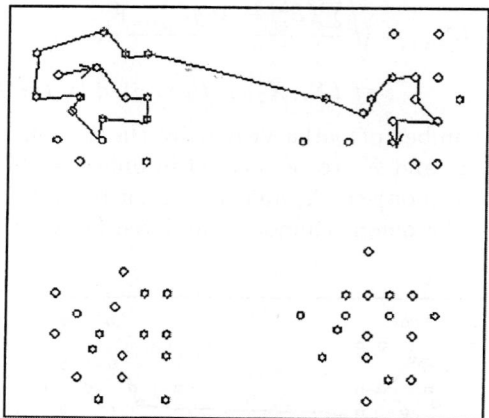

Fig. 3. Shrinking search route using Eq. (7).

The Constrained Ant Colony Optimization algorithm for data clustering can be expressed as follows:

Step 1: Initialization
Randomly select the initial object for each ant. The initial pheromone τ_{ij} between any two objects X_i and X_j is set to be a small positive constant τ_0.

Step 2: Movement
Let each ant moves to N_1 objects only using Eq. (7). In our initial experiments, N_1 was set to be 1/20 of the data objects.

Step 3: Pheromone Update
Update the pheromone level between objects as

$$\tau_{ij}(t+1) = (1-\alpha)\tau_{ij}(t) + \Delta\tau_{ij}(t+1) \tag{8}$$

$$\Delta\tau_{ij}(t+1) = \sum_{k=1}^{T} \Delta\tau_{ij}^k(t+1) \tag{9}$$

$$\Delta\tau_{ij}^k(t+1) = \begin{cases} \frac{Q}{L_k} & , \text{ if } ((i,j) \in \text{ route done by ant } k, \text{ and } L_{ij}^k < L_{ts}^k \\ 0 & , \text{ otherwise} \end{cases} \tag{10}$$

where τ_{ij} is the pheromone level between objects X_i and X_j, T is the total number of clustering objects, α is a pheromone decay parameter and Q is a constant and is set to 1. L_k is the length of the route after deleting the distance between object X_i and object X_j in which $L_{ij}^k > L_{ts}^k$ for the kth ant.

Step 4: Consolidation

Calculate the average pheromone level on the route for all objects as

$$Avg\tau = \frac{\sum_{i,j \in E} \tau_{ij}}{E} \qquad (11)$$

where E is the number of paths visited by the kth ant. Disconnect the path between two objects if the pheromone level between these two objects is smaller than $Avg\tau$. All the objects thus connected together are deemed to be in the same cluster.

3 Experiments and Results

The experiments were carried out to test the performance of the data clustering for Ant Colony Optimization with Different Favor ($ACODF$), $DBSCAN$ [14], $CURE$ [11] and the proposed Constrained Ant Colony Optimization ($CACO$). Four data sets, Four-Cluster, Four-Bridge, Smile-Face and Shape-Outliers were used as the test material, consisting of 892, 981, 877 and 999 objects, respectively.

In order to cluster a data set using $CACO$, N_1 and γ are two important parameters which will influence the clustering results. N_1 is the number of objects to be visited in each cycle for each ant. If N_1 is set too small, the ants cannot finish visiting all the objects belonged to the same cluster resulting in a division of slender shaped cluster into several sub-clusters. Our experiments indicated that good experimental results were obtained by setting N_1 to $\frac{1}{20}$. γ also influences the clustering result for clusters with bridges or high numbers of outliers. We found that γ set between 5 and 15 provided robust results. The number of ants is set to 40.

$DBSCAN$ is a well-known clustering algorithm that works well for clusters with arbitrary shapes. Following the recommendation of *Ester et al.*, $MinPts$ was fixed to 4 and ϵ was changed during the experiments. $CURE$ produces high-quality clusters in the existence of outliers, allowing complex shaped clusters and different size. We performed experiments with shrinking factor is 0.3 and the number of representative points as 10, which are the default values recommended by *Guha et al.* (1998).

All the experiments demonstrate $CACO$ algorithm can correctly identifies the clusters. For the reason of saving the space, we only describe the last experiment to partition the shape-outliers data set. $ACODF$ algorithm cannot correctly partition the Shape-Outliers data set shown in Figure 4. Figure 5 shows the clusters found by $DBSCAN$, but it also makes a mistake in that it has fragmented the clusters in the right-side 'L'-shaped cluster. Figure 6 shows that

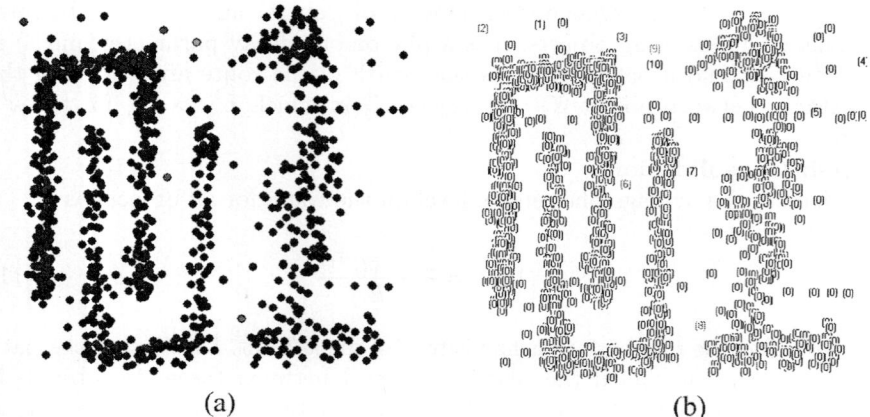

Fig. 4. Clustering results of Shape-Outliers by *ACODF* algorithm. (a) cluster represented by colour, (b) cluster represented by number.

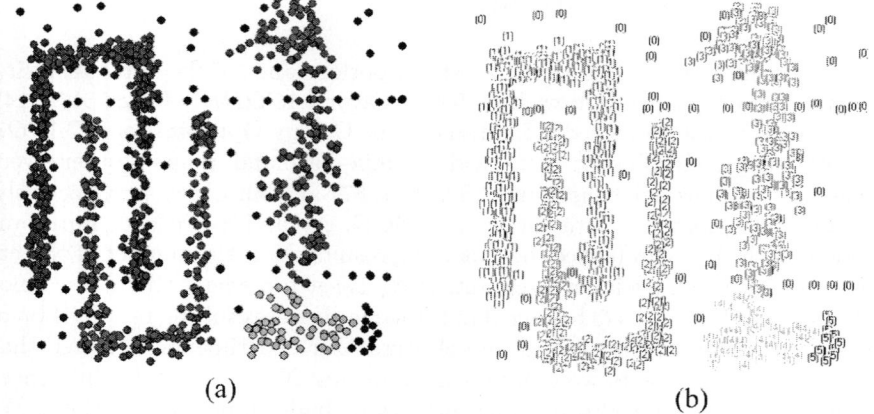

Fig. 5. Clustering results of Shape-Outliers by *DBSCAN* algorithm. (a) cluster represented by colour, (b) cluster represented by number.

CURE fails to perform well on Shape-Outliers data set, with the clusters fragmented into a number of smaller clusters. Looking at Figure 7, we can see that *CACO* algorithm correctly identifies the clusters.

4 Conclusions

In this paper, a new Ant Colony Optimization based algorithm, termed Constrained Ant Colony Optimization (*CACO*), is proposed for data clustering. *CACO* extends Ant Colony Optimization through the use of a quadratic metric, the *Sum of K Nearest Neighbor Distances* metric, together with constrained addition of pheromone and shrinking range strategies to better partition data sets

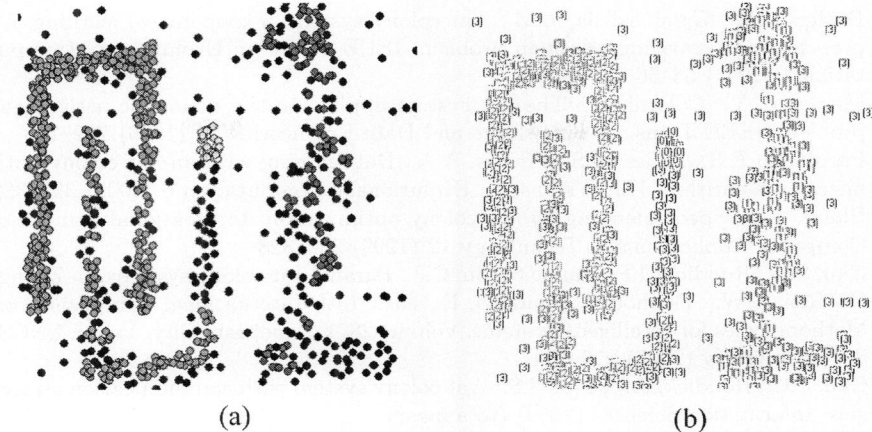

Fig. 6. Clustering results of Shape-Outliers by $CURE$ algorithm. (a) cluster represented by colour, (b) cluster represented by number.

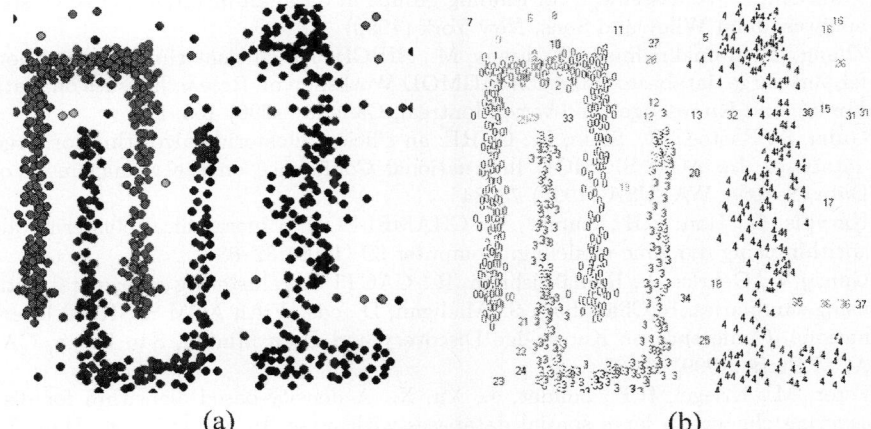

Fig. 7. Clustering results of Shape-Outliers by $CACO$ algorithm. (a) cluster represented by colour, (b) cluster represented by number.

with clusters with arbitrary shape, clusters with outliers and outlier points connecting clusters. Preliminary experimental results compared with the $ACODF$, $DBSCAN$ and $CURE$ algorithms, demonstrate the usefulness of the proposed $CACO$ algorithm.

References

1. Dorigo, M., Maniezzo, V., Colorni, A.: Ant system: optimization by a colony of cooperating agents. IEEE Trans. on Systems, Man, and Cybernetics-Part B: Cybernetics 26 (1996) 29–41

2. Dorigo, J.M., Gambardella, L.M.: Ant colony system: a cooperative learning approach to the traveling salesman problem. IEEE Trans. on Evolutionary Computation 1 (1997) 53–66
3. Maniezzo, V., Colorni, A.: The ant system applied to the quadratic assignment problem. IEEE Trans. on Knowledge and Data Engineering 11 (1999) 769–778
4. Parpinelli, R.S., Lopes, H.S., Freitas, A.A.: Data mining with an ant colony optimization algorithm. IEEE Trans. on Evolutionary Computation 6 (2002) 321–332
5. Bland, J.A.: Space-planning by ant colony optimization. International Journal of Computer Applications in Technology 12 (1999) 320–328
6. Chu, S.C., Roddick, J.F., Pan, J.S., Su, C.J.: Parallel ant colony systems. In Zhong, N., Raś, Z.W., Tsumoto, S., Suzuki, E., eds.: 14th International Symposium on Methodologies for Intelligent Systems. Volume 2871., Maebashi City, Japan, LNCS, Springer-Verlag (2003) 279–284
7. Chu, S.C., Roddick, J.F., Pan, J.S.: Ant colony system with communication strategies. Information Sciences (2004) (to appear)
8. MacQueen, J.: Some methods for classification and analysis of multivariate observations. In: 5th Berkeley symposium on mathematics, statistics and Probability. Volume 1. (1967) 281–296
9. Kaufman, L., Rousseeuw, P.J.: Finding groups in data: an introduction to cluster analysis. John Wiley and Sons, New York (1990)
10. Zhang, T., Ramakrishnan, R., Livny, M.: BIRCH: An efficient clustering method for very large databases. In: ACM SIGMOD Workshop on Research Issues on Data Mining and Knowledge Discovery, Montreal, Canada (1996) 103–114
11. Guha, S., Rastogi, R., Shim, K.: CURE: an efficient clustering algorithm for large databases. In: ACM SIGMOD International Conference on the Management of Data, Seattle, WA, USA (1998) 73–84
12. Karypis, G., Han, E.H., Kumar, V.: CHAMELEON: a hierarchical clustering algorithm using dynamic modeling. Computer 32 (1999) 32–68
13. Ganti, V., Gehrke, J., Ramakrishnan, R.: CACTUS – clustering categorical data using summaries. In Chaudhuri, S., Madigan, D., eds.: Fifth ACM SIGKDD International Conference on Knowledge Discovery and Data Mining, San Diego, CA, ACM Press (1999) 73–83
14. Ester, M., Kriegel, H.P., Sander, J., Xu, X.: A density-based algorithm for discovering clusters in large spatial databases with noise. In Simoudis, E., Han, J., Fayyad, U., eds.: Second International Conference on Knowledge Discovery and Data Mining, Portland, Oregon, AAAI Press (1996) 226–231
15. Sheikholeslami, G., Chatterjee, S., Zhang, A.: WaveCluster: A multiresolution clustering approach for very large spatial databases. In: 1998 International Conference Very Large Data Bases (VLDB'98), New York (1998) 428–439
16. C, A.C., S, Y.P.: Redefining clustering for high-dimensional applications. IEEE Trans. on Knowledge and Data Engineering 14 (2002) 210–225
17. Estivill-Castro, V., Lee, I.: AUTOCLUST+: Automatic clustering of point-data sets in the presence of obstacles. In Roddick, J.F., Hornsby, K., eds.: International Workshop on Temporal, Spatial and Spatio-Temporal Data Mining, TSDM2000. Volume 2007., Lyon, France, LNCS, Springer-Verlag (2000) 133–146
18. Ng, R.T., Han, J.: Clarans: A method for clustering objects for spatical data mining. IEEE Transactions on Knowledge and Data Engineering 14 (2002) 1003–1016
19. Tsai, C.F., Wu, H.C., Tsai, C.W.: A new data clustering approach for data mining in large databases. In: International Symposium on Parallel Architectures, Algorithms and Networks, IEEE Press (2002) 278–283

20. Kirkpatrick, S., Gelatt, J.C.D., Vecchi, M.P.: Optimization by simulated annealing. Science 220 (1983) 671–680
21. 21, A.: Genetic algorithms for function optimization. PhD thesis, University of Alberta, Edmonton, Canada (1981)
22. Pan, J.S., McInnes, F.R., Jack, M.A.: Bound for minkowski metric or quadratic metric applied to VQ codeword search. IEE Proc. Vision Image and Signal Processing 143 (1996) 67–71

A Kernel-Based Case Retrieval Algorithm with Application to Bioinformatics

Yan Fu[1,2], Qiang Yang[3], Charles X. Ling[4], Haipeng Wang[1], Dequan Li[1],
Ruixiang Sun[2], Hu Zhou[5], Rong Zeng[5], Yiqiang Chen[1], Simin He[1], and Wen Gao[1,2]

[1] Institute of Computing Technology, Chinese Academy of Sciences,
Beijing 100080, China
{yfu,hpwang,dqli,yqchen,smhe,wgao}@ict.ac.cn
[2] Graduate School of Chinese Academy of Sciences,
Beijing 100039, China
{rxsun,wgao}@gscas.ac.cn
[3] Department of Computer Science, Hong Kong University of Science and Technology,
Clear Water Bay, Kowloon, Hong Kong
qyang@cs.ust.hk
[4] Department of Computer Science, The University of Western Ontario,
London, Ontario N6A 5B7,Canada
cling@csd.uwo.ca
[5] Research Center for Proteome Analysis, Key Lab of Proteomics, Institute of Biochemistry and Cell Biology, Shanghai Institutes for Biological Sciences, Chinese Academy of Sciences,
Shanghai 200031, China
{hzhou,zr}@sibs.ac.cn

Abstract. Case retrieval in case-based reasoning relies heavily on the design of a good similarity function. This paper provides an approach to utilizing the correlative information among features to compute the similarity of cases for case retrieval. This is achieved by extending the dot product-based linear similarity measures to their nonlinear versions with kernel functions. An application to the peptide retrieval problem in bioinformatics shows the effectiveness of the approach. In this problem, the objective is to retrieve the corresponding peptide to the input tandem mass spectrum from a large database of known peptides. By a kernel function implicitly mapping the tandem mass spectrum to a high dimensional space, the correlative information among fragment ions in a tandem mass spectrum can be modeled to dramatically reduce the stochastic mismatches. The experiment on the real spectra dataset shows a significant reduction of 10% in the error rate as compared to a common linear similarity function.

1 Introduction

Case-based reasoning (CBR) relies on the use of a similarity function to rank previous cases for solving new problems [13, 14]. Over the years, CBR has enjoyed tremendous success as a technique for solving problems related to knowledge reuse, with many important industrial applications [22]. The central component of a CBR system is a similarity function, based on which cases are retrieved and ranked for adaptation and further solution [13, 14]. Because of its importance, various methods have been proposed to compute the similarity between cases, including that of [2, 3, 14, 18, 19].

Although various methods for learning the weights have been designed, no specific similarity function has been designed to take advantage of the correlative information between features using a nonlinear similarity function. An exception is the collaborative filtering framework, in which a linear weighting function is used to represent the correlative information.

This paper presents a general approach to engineering nonlinear similarity functions for scoring cases, and highlights an application [11] of the new method to the peptide retrieval problem in bioinformatics. A central characteristic of this problem is that the correlated features should play a more important role in scoring the cases than other, non-correlated features. In order to emphasize the correlations, we apply the kernel functions to those correlated features. This implicitly translates the cases from the original space to a feature space with new dimensions for combinations of correlated features. Thanks to the kernel trick, nonlinear similarity functions can be constructed in the original space with slight overhead. We show that the resulting similarity function dramatically improves the retrieval accuracy.

Mass spectrometry is currently one of the most important techniques for proteomics research [1]. Protein identification via tandem mass spectrometry (MS/MS) is the central task in MS/MS based proteomics. For example, for the diagnosis and therapy of diseases, investigation on the differently expressed proteomes in normal and abnormal cells is very important. High precision and high-throughput protein identification via MS/MS needs not only elaborate biophysical instruments but also powerful computer algorithms. The basic computational problem is to retrieve the peptide sequence from which the observed MS/MS spectrum was derived through a search for the most similar theoretical MS/MS spectrum in a large database of known peptides. In this paper, we show that the peptide retrieval problem can be expressed as a case-based reasoning problem, in which the peptide sequences correspond to the cases while MS/MS spectra correspond to the features of cases. By using a kernel function to improve a common linear similarity measure for comparing MS/MS spectra, we show that much better retrieval accuracy can be obtained.

Below, we first introduce how to design kernel-based nonlinear similarity functions for the case retrieval. Then we apply the proposed approach to the peptide retrieval problem.

2 Applying the Kernel Trick to Similarity Measurement

For the measurement of the similarity between cases, they are usually presented as feature vectors. One of the simplest similarity measures between two vectors is their dot product, i.e. $\langle \mathbf{x}, \mathbf{y} \rangle$, where $\mathbf{x}, \mathbf{y}$ are n-dimensional feature vectors. For the binary features, the dot product counts the number of features that two cases possess in common. The cosine of the angle between vectors and the Euclidean distance can both be expressed in terms of the dot products, i.e.

$$\cos(\mathbf{x},\mathbf{y}) = \langle \mathbf{x},\mathbf{y}\rangle \big/ \sqrt{\langle \mathbf{x},\mathbf{x}\rangle \cdot \langle \mathbf{y},\mathbf{y}\rangle}, \text{ and}$$

$$d(\mathbf{x},\mathbf{y}) = \sqrt{\|\mathbf{x}-\mathbf{y}\|^2} = \sqrt{\langle \mathbf{x},\mathbf{x}\rangle + \langle \mathbf{y},\mathbf{y}\rangle - 2\langle \mathbf{x},\mathbf{y}\rangle}.$$

In reality, similar cases may not be close to each other geometrically in the original vector space, which we call the input space. In such cases, we may wish to map the original space to a new, usually higher dimensional space with an aim for the similar cases to get closer in the new space. The transformed space is called the feature space. For instance, when the elements of the input vector highly correlate with each other, we may want the feature space to include as new dimensions all the d-order products of the dimensions in the input space. However, the dimensionality of the feature space might be too high to compute efficiently and explicitly.

The kernel trick, popularly used in the machine learning [20], overcomes this difficulty gracefully. A kernel is a function k such that for all $\mathbf{x}, \mathbf{y} \in A$ (usually $A = R^n$),

$$k(\mathbf{x}, \mathbf{y}) = \langle \phi(\mathbf{x}), \phi(\mathbf{y}) \rangle,$$

where ϕ is a mapping from the input space A to a feature space B. Usually, ϕ is a nonlinear mapping and the feature space B is of very high, or even infinite, dimensions. Therefore, any computation that is exclusively based on the dot product in the feature space can be performed with the kernel $k(\mathbf{x}, \mathbf{y})$ from the input space, thus avoiding the explicit mapping ϕ from the input space to the feature space.

For example, the polynomial kernel, $\langle \mathbf{x}, \mathbf{y} \rangle^d$, implicitly maps the n-dimensional input space to a much higher dimensional feature space with all d-order products of the dimensions of the input space as new dimensions. For instance, when $d = 2$ and $\mathbf{x}, \mathbf{y} \in R^2$, we have

$$\langle \mathbf{x}, \mathbf{y} \rangle^d = \langle \phi(\mathbf{x}), \phi(\mathbf{y}) \rangle,$$

$$\phi(\mathbf{x}) = (x_1^2, x_2^2, x_1 x_2, x_2 x_1).$$

Kernels have been widely used recently to extend linear learning algorithms to nonlinear versions, e.g. [5, 17]. However, kernels are not limited to learning algorithms. Being the dot products in the feature space, kernels can be used to construct nonlinear version of any linear algorithm as long as only the dot product is involved. In the case of the case retrieval problem, we obtain the following kernel-based similarity and distance measures for cases $\mathbf{x}$ and $\mathbf{y}$ (where we use a $\cos'(\mathbf{x},\mathbf{y})$ and $d'(\mathbf{x},\mathbf{y})$ for the new cosine and distance functions):

$$k(\mathbf{x}, \mathbf{y}),$$

$$\cos'(\mathbf{x}, \mathbf{y}) = k(\mathbf{x}, \mathbf{y}) / \sqrt{k(\mathbf{x}, \mathbf{x}) \cdot k(\mathbf{y}, \mathbf{y})}, \text{ and}$$

$$d'(\mathbf{x}, \mathbf{y}) = \sqrt{k(\mathbf{x}, \mathbf{x}) - 2k(\mathbf{x}, \mathbf{y}) + k(\mathbf{y}, \mathbf{y})}.$$

The success of these similarity and distance measures depends on the proper definition of the kernel $k(\mathbf{x}, \mathbf{y})$, which should incorporate the available apriori knowledge in the specific domain. In the following, we show how a kernel can incorporate the domain knowledge and is directly used as the similarity measure in a bioinformatic application. We first introduce the peptide retrieval problem in detail.

3 The Peptide Retrieval Problem

Via MS/MS, protein identification problem is divided into peptides identification subproblem. In the mass spectrometer, peptides derived from digested proteins are ionized. Peptide precursor ions of a specific mass-charge ratio (m/z) are fragmented by the collision-induced dissociation (CID). Product ions are detected. The measured m/z and intensity of the product ions form the peaks in the MS/MS spectrum. A peptide is a string of amino acid residues joined together by peptide bonds. For the low-energy CID, the b-y type backbone cleavage is most frequent and usually occurs only once in each peptide, resulting in b and y series of fragment ions, as shown in Fig. 1. The b fragments are the N-terminal sub-strings of amino acid residues dissociated from the cleaved peptide precursors, while the y fragments are the C-terminal sub-strings. The fragments can be singly charged or multiply charged and may possibly lose a neutral water or ammonia molecule. Besides these fragments, the noise and product ions derived from unexpected peptide cleavages also present themselves as peaks in the MS/MS spectrum.

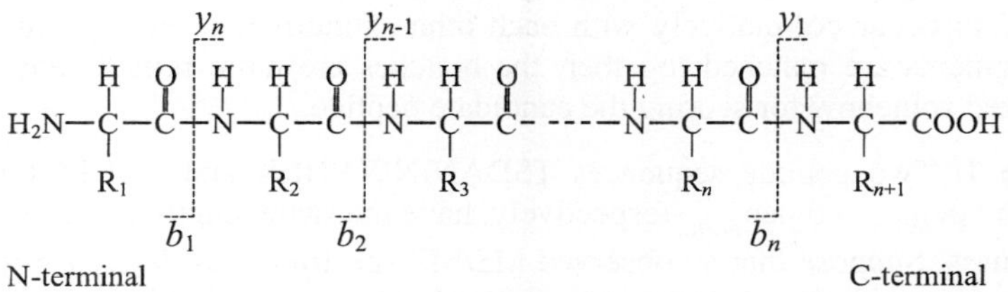

Fig. 1. b and y fragment ions resulting from peptide bonds cleavage by collision-induced dissociation

To identify the peptide sequence of the observed MS/MS spectrum, the database searching approach has been widely used. The peptide retrieval problem can be expressed as follows: given the experimental MS/MS spectrum S, the peptides database D, and background conditions C, find the peptide pep^* in D from which S derived. During a retrieval, peptide sequences in the database are fragmented theoretically to construct the theoretical MS/MS spectra. The experimental and theoretical MS/MS spectra are compared to find the target peptide. Expressed in terms of case retrieval, peptide sequences correspond to the cases while MS/MS spectra correspond to the features of cases. This paper focuses on the use of dot product similarity to compare MS/MS spectra for scoring the peptides in the peptide retrieval problem.

Various strategies have been proposed for scoring peptides in existing peptide retrieval software tools [4, 6, 7, 8, 10, 15, 23]. In existing peptide-scoring algorithms, the *Spectral Dot Product* (*SDP*) is often involved directly or indirectly and plays an important role. In *SDP*, the thereotical and experimental MS/MS spectra are represented as two N-dimensional spectral vectors, denoted by $\mathbf{c} = [c_1, c_2, ..., c_N]$ and $\mathbf{t} = [t_1, t_2, ..., t_N]$, respectively, where N is the number of different m/z values used, c_i and t_i are binary values $\{0, 1\}$ or the intensities of the peaks at the i-th m/z value in MS/MS spectra. The *SDP* is defined as

$$SDP = \langle \mathbf{c}, \mathbf{t} \rangle = \sum_{i=1}^{N} c_i t_i \cdot \quad (1)$$

The *SDP*-based cosine function of the angle between spectral vectors was used as an MS/MS spectrum similarity measure [21]. Sonar MS/MS [9, 10] explicitly adopted the spectral vector representation and the *SDP* for scoring peptides. The notion of cross-correlation in the SEQUEST [7] is in nature equivalent to the *SDP*. The shared peak count in early work is the special case of the *SDP* with c_i and t_i being binary values. An inherent drawback of the *SDP* is that it does not especially leverage correlative information among the dimensions of spectral vectors corresponding to different fragments. This increases the possibility of stochastic mismatches.

4 The Kernel-Based Correlative Similarity Function

Our most important observation about the MS/MS spectrum is that the fragments resulting from peptide bonds cleavage by CID rarely occur independently; most often they tend to occur correlatively with each other. Intuitively, when positively correlated fragments are matched together, the matches are more reliable and should be emphasized somehow for scoring the candidate peptide.

Example 1. Two peptide sequences TSDANINWNNLK and FQDLVDAVRAEK, denoted by pep_{corr} and $\text{pep}_{\text{incorr}}$ respectively, have the same length and nearly the same peptide mass. Suppose that an observed MS/MS spectrum was derived from the peptide precursors with the sequence pep_{corr}. To identify the peptide sequence, a retrieval is performed against the database containing the two peptide sequences pep_{corr} and $\text{pep}_{\text{incorr}}$. For simplicity, the *y* series of fragments is used to construct theoretical MS/MS spectra. Compared with the observed spectrum, the correct peptide pep_{corr} has six matched fragments including y_3, y_4, y_5, y_6, y_7, and y_8 as shown in Fig. 2, while the peptide $\text{pep}_{\text{incorr}}$ has seven matched fragments including y_2, y_4, y_5, y_6, y_9, y_{10}, and y_{11}. Although there are more matched fragments for the peptide $\text{pep}_{\text{incorr}}$, the matches for the pep_{corr} are more consecutive and therefore should be considered as strong indicators of correct answer.

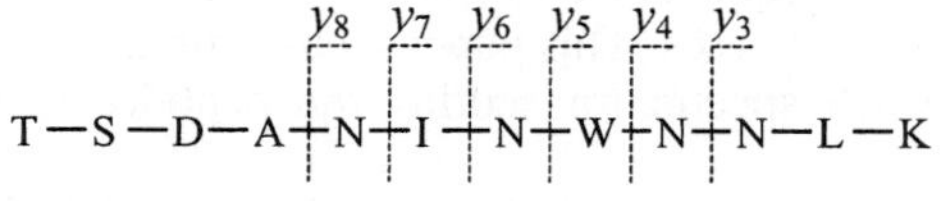

$$\begin{array}{cccccc} y_8 & y_7 & y_6 & y_5 & y_4 & y_3 \end{array}$$
$$\text{T}-\text{S}-\text{D}-\text{A}+\text{N}+\text{I}+\text{N}+\text{W}+\text{N}+\text{N}-\text{L}-\text{K}$$

Fig. 2. Consecutive fragments produced from the fragmentation of the peptide precursors with sequence TSDANINWNNLK

To consider the correlation among fragments, we may exhaustively examine whether each possible combination of correlated fragments is matched as a whole. However, there may be too many such combinations to count one by one. Alternatively, since we are only interested in the overall similarity between two MS/MS spectra rather than the detailed matching results of the individual fragment combinations, we can design the similarity function with kernels as a final sum of all the matching results. To this end, all predicted fragments in the theoretical MS/MS spectrum are arranged in a manner we call the correlative matrix, as shown in Fig. 3, thus making correlated fragments cluster into the local correlative windows. This kind of local correlation can be emphasized with the locally improved polynomial kernel [16].

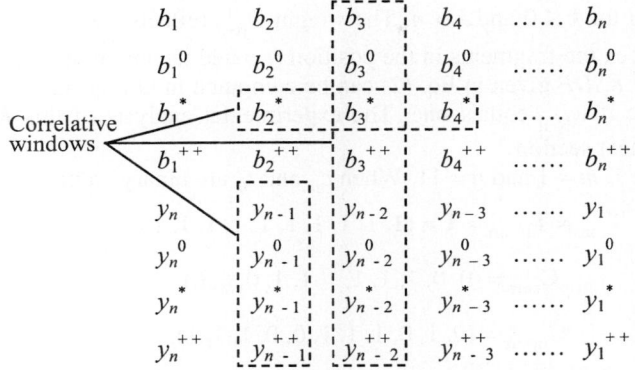

Fig. 3. Correlative matrix and correlative windows. The subscript number indicates the fragmentation position as illustrated in Fig. 1, superscripts 0 and * indicate a neutral loss of H_2O and NH_3, respectively

We assume that all predicted fragments have their corresponding unique m/z values. The only influence of this assumption is that the shared m/z values are emphasized to some extent. We regard such emphasis as reasonable, since the shared m/z values should be of more importance than other, unique m/z values. Under this assumption, all non-zero dimensions in the theoretical spectral vector $\mathbf{t}$ can be arranged into a matrix $\mathbf{T} = (t_{pq})_{m \times n}$ in accordance with their fragment types and fragmentation positions, where m is the number of fragment types and $n+1$ is the residue number of the peptide precursor. For example, $t_{2,3}$ corresponds to the fragment b_3^0 in Fig. 3. For an experimental spectral vector $\mathbf{c}$, the dimensions at the m/z value corresponding to t_{pq} are also arranged into a matrix $\mathbf{C} = (c_{pq})_{m \times n}$. Under the above assumption, we have

$$SDP = \langle \mathbf{c}, \mathbf{t} \rangle = \sum_{p=1}^{m} \sum_{q=1}^{n} c_{pq} t_{pq}.$$

The correlative window may be defined according to the biologists' expert knowledge about how fragments are correlated. With the observation that the continuity of matched fragments is the most important correlation, we define the *Kernel Spectral Dot Product (KSDP)* [11] for consecutive fragments with locally improved kernel as follows,

$$K(\mathbf{c}, \mathbf{t}) = \sum_{i=1}^{m} \sum_{j=1}^{n} win_{ij}(\mathbf{c}, \mathbf{t}), \qquad (2)$$

$$win_{ij}(\mathbf{c}, \mathbf{t}) = \left[\sum_{k=j-l_1}^{j+l_2}\left(w_{|k-j|}(c_{ik}t_{ik})^{1/d}\right)\right]^d,$$

where positive integers l_1 and l_2 are $\lfloor(l-1)/2\rfloor$ and $\lceil(l-1)/2\rceil$ respectively, the window power d is a positive integer and defines the maximum number of consecutive fragments to be considered. Integer l is the size of the correlative window. c_{ik} and t_{ik} are set to zero for $k \leq 0$ and $k > n$. The weight $w_{|k-j|}$ reflects the assumed correlating strength between the fragments in the position (i,j) and its neighbor with $|k-j|$ residues near to it. The *KSDP* given in Eq. (2) can be computed in O(lmn) time in general and in O(mn) time if $w_{|k-j|}$ equals one. The experimental analysis of this *KSDP* is presented in the next section.

In Example 1, $m = 1$ and $n = 11$. When c_{ik} and t_{ik} are binary values, we have

$$\mathbf{T}_{corr} = \mathbf{T}_{incorr} = \mathbf{T} = (1, 1, 1, 1, 1, 1, 1, 1, 1, 1, 1),$$

$$\mathbf{C}_{corr} = (0, 0, 1, 1, 1, 1, 1, 1, 0, 0, 0),$$

$$\mathbf{C}_{incorr} = (0, 1, 0, 1, 1, 1, 0, 0, 1, 1, 1).$$

Therefore,

$$SDP_{corr} = \langle \mathbf{T}_{corr}, \mathbf{C}_{corr}\rangle = 6,$$

$$SDP_{incorr} = \langle \mathbf{T}_{incorr}, \mathbf{C}_{incorr}\rangle = 7,$$

$$KSDP_{corr}\big|_{l=5,d=3,w=1} = \sum_{j=1}^{11}\left[\sum_{k=j-2}^{j+2}(c_{corr1,k}t_{1,k})\right]^3 = 450,$$

$$KSDP_{incorr}\big|_{l=5,d=3,w=1} = \sum_{j=1}^{11}\left[\sum_{k=j-2}^{j+2}(c_{incorr1,k}t_{1,k})\right]^3 = 289.$$

Thus, The correct peptide obtains a lower *SDP* score but a higher *KSDP* score in virtue of the kernel function to correlate consecutive fragments.

5 Experimental Results

The MS/MS spectra used for experiments come from a dataset of ion trap spectra reported in [12]. 18 purified proteins were mixed and digested with trypsin. 22 LC/MS/MS runs were performed on this digested mixture. The generated MS/MS spectra were searched using the SEQUEST software against a database including human protein sequences and the 18 control mixture proteins (denoted by "human plus mixture database"). Search results were manually examined, and 2757 of them were confirmed as true positives.

From the 2757 spectra with their peptide sequences correctly recovered, 2054 spectra with their peptide terminus consistent with the substrate specificity of trypsin are selected for our experiments to make the experiments more manageable. To reduce the noise in the original spectra, only the 200 most intense peaks are retained in each spectrum. In retrieval, trypsin and up to two missed cleavage sites are specified for theoretically digesting the sequences in the database. 3 daltons and 1dalton are set as the matching tolerances for the precursor and the fragment respectively. b, b^{++}, b^0, y, y^{++}, and y^0 are specified as the predicted fragment types.

To tune the two parameters, window size l and window power d, experiments are performed for $l \in \{1, 2, 3, 4, 5, 6, 7, 8\}$ and $d \in \{2, 3, 4\}$ against the human plus mixture database. The *KSDP* given in Eq. (2) is directly used as the similarity function with c_{ik} and t_{ik} being binary values and $w_{|k-j|}$ equal to one. The error rates vs. the parameters are illustrated in Fig. 4, in which erroneous identification indicates the fact that the correct peptide does not rank first in the search result.

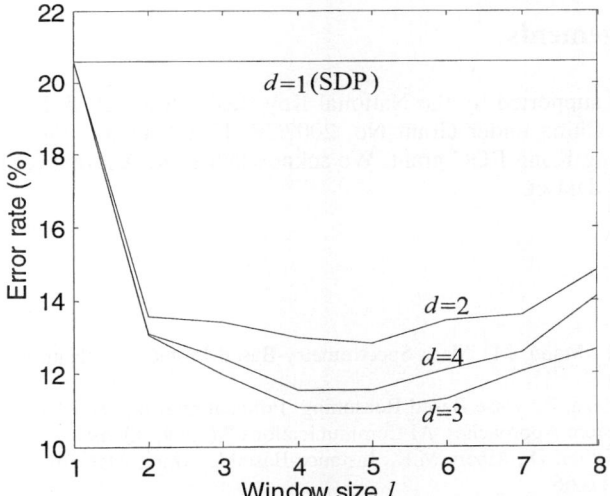

Fig. 4. Error rates vs. the window size l and window power d in *KSDP* given in Eq. (2)

Compared with the *SDP*, the *KSDP* decreases the error rate by 10% at best in this experiment. The lowest error rate is obtained when $d = 3$ and $l = 4$ or 5. It can also be observed that for all tested values of l, the lowest error rate is obtained when $d = 3$; and, for all tested values of d, the lowest error rate is obtained when $l = 4$ or 5. Therefore, we have a good reason to regard window size 4 or 5 and window power 3 as the approximate optimal parameters.

When $l = 1$ or $d = 1$, the *KSDP* given in Eq. (2) reduces to the *SDP* given in Eq. (1). When l and d become larger than one, the kernel function takes effect and the error rate drops rapidly. It is clearly shown in Fig. 4 that nearly all the error rates for $l > 1$ are remarkably lower than that for $l = 1$. The same claim stands for the parameter d. The role of the kernel to reduce stochastic mismatches is significant.

6 Conclusions and Future Work

This paper provides an approach to utilizing the correlative information among features to compute the similarity of cases for case retrieval. This is achieved by extending the dot product-based linear similarity measures to their nonlinear versions with kernel functions. An application to the peptide retrieval problem in bioinformatics shows the effectiveness of the approach. The common linear similarity measure for tandem mass spectra, *Spectral Dot Product* (*SDP*), is extended to the *Kernel SDP* (*KSDP*) to take advantage of the correlative information among fragment ions. The experiments on a previously reported dataset demonstrate the effectiveness of the *KSDP* to reduce stochastic mismatches. In the future, we wish to apply the proposed method to other case retrieval problems.

Acknowledgements

This work was supported by the National Key Basic Research & Development Program (973) of China under Grant No. 2002CB713807. Qiang Yang was also supported by a Hong Kong RGC grant. We acknowledge Dr. Andrew Keller for providing the MS/MS dataset.

References

1. Aebersold, R., Mann, M.: Mass Spectrometry-Based Proteomics. Nature 422(2003) 198–207
2. Agnar, A., Plaza, E.: Case-Based Reasoning: Foundational Issues, Methodological Variations, and System Approaches. AI Communications 7 (1994) 39–59
3. Aha, D.W., Kibler, D., Albert, M.K.: Instance-Based Learning Algorithms. Machine Learning 6 (1991) 37–66
4. Bafna, V., Edwards, N.: SCOPE: a Probabilistic Model for Scoring Tandem Mass Spectra against a Peptide Database. Bioinformatics 17 Suppl. 1 (2001) S13–S21
5. Boser, B.E., Guyon, I.M., Vapnik, V.N.: A Training Algorithm for Optimal Margin Classifiers. In: Haussler, D. (ed.): Proceedings of the Fifth Annual Workshop on Computational Learning Theory. ACM Press, Pittsburgh, PA (1992) 144–152
6. Clauser, K.R., Baker, P., Burlingame, A.L.: Role of Accurate Mass Measurement (± 10 ppm) in Protein Identification Strategies Employing MS or MS/MS and Database Searching. Anal. Chem. 71 (1999) 2871–2882
7. Eng, J.K., McCormack, A.L., Yates, J.R.: An Approach to Correlate Tandem Mass Spectral Data of Peptides with Amino Acid Sequences in a Protein Database. J. Am. Soc. Mass Spectrom. 5 (1994) 976–989
8. Fenyö, D., Qin, J., Chait, B.T.: Protein Identification Using Mass Spectromic Information. Electrophoresis 19 (1998) 998–1005
9. Fenyö, D., Beavis, R.C.: A Method for Assessing the Statistical Significance of Mass Spectrometry-Based Protein Identifications Using General Scoring Schemes. Anal. Chem. 75 (2003) 768–774
10. Field, H.I., Fenyö, D., Beavis, R.C.: RADARS, a Bioinformatics Solution that Automates Proteome Mass Spectral Analysis, Optimises Protein Identification, and Archives Data in a Relational Database. Proteomics 2 (2002) 36–47

11. Fu, Y., Yang, Q., Sun, R., Li, D., Zeng, R., Ling, C.X., Gao, W. Exploiting the kernel trick to correlate fragment ions for peptide identification via tandem mass spectrometry. Bioinformatics (2004) 10.1093/bioinformatics/bth186
12. Keller, A., Purvine, S., Nesvizhskii, A.I., Stolyar, S., Goodlett, D.R., Kolker, E.: Experimental Protein Mixture for Validating Tandem Mass Spectral Analysis. Omics 6 (2002) 207–212
13. Kolodner, J.L.: Case-Based Reasoning. Morgan Kaufmann Publisher, California (1993)
14. Leake, D.B., Kinley, A., Wilson, D.: Case-Based Similarity Assessment: Estimating Adaptability from Experience. In: Proceedings of the 14th National Conference on Artificial Intelligence. AAAI Press, Menlo Park, California (1997)
15. Perkins, D.N., Pappin, D.J., Creasy, D.M., Cottrell, J.S.: Probability-Based Protein Identification by Searching Sequence Databases Using Mass Spectrometry Data. Electrophoresis 20 (1999) 3551–3567
16. Schölkopf, B., Simard, P., Smola, A.J., Vapnik, V.: Prior Knowledge in Support Vector Kernels. In: Jordan, M., Kearns, M., Solla, S. (eds.): Advances in Neural Information. Processing Systems 10. MIT Press, Cambridge, MA (1998) 640–646
17. Schölkopf, B., Smola, A.J., Müller, K.R.: Nonlinear Component Analysis as a Kernel Eigenvalue Problem. Neural Computation 10 (1998) 1299–1319
18. Smyth, B., Keane, M.T.: Remembering to Forget: A Competence Preserving Deletion Policy for Case-Based Reasoning Systems. In: Proceedings of the 14th International Joint Conference on Artificial Intelligence, Morgan-Kaufmann (1995) 377–382
19. Smyth, B., Keane, M.T.: Adaptation-Guided Retrieval: Questioning the Similarity Assumption in Reasoning. Artificial Intelligence 102 (1998) 249–293
20. Vapnik, V.N.: The Nature of Statistical Learning Theory. Springer, New York (1995)
21. Wan, K.X., Vidavsky, I., Gross, M.L.: Comparing Similar Spectra: from Similarity Index to Spectral Contrast Angle. J. Am. Soc. Mass Spectrom. 13 (2002) 85–88
22. Watson, I.: Applying Case-Based Reasoning: Techniques for Enterprise Systems. Morgan Kaufmann Publisher, Inc., California, USA (1997)
23. Zhang, N., Aebersold, R., Schwikowski, B.: ProbID: A Probabilistic Algorithm to Identify Peptides through Sequence Database Searching Using Tandem Mass Spectral Data. Proteomics 2 (2002) 1406–1412

Building a Case-Based Reasoner for Clinical Decision Support

Anna Wills and Ian Watson

Department of Computer Science
University of Auckland, New Zealand
awil176@ec.auckland.ac.nz, ian@cs.auckland.ac.nz
www.cs.auckland.ac.nz/~ian/

Abstract. Orion Systems International Limited has recognised the need in the healthcare industry for an application to provide robust clinical decision support. One possible approach is to develop a case-based reasoner to support decisions made in the disease management process. We have undertaken a project to investigate the validity of using case-based reasoning for this task, specifically focusing on the management of treatment of diabetes patients. An application that uses case-based reasoning has been developed and tested. This paper describes the pre-processing of cases, the development of a case representation and similarity metrics and evaluation. Results show that case-based reasoning could be a valid approach, but more investigation is needed.

1 Introduction

Orion Systems International Limited intend on entering a new market area with a clinical decision support system. A number of Orion's system modules already rely on some form of decision support, however this is minimal. This future system will support decisions made throughout the disease management process - ensuring the deliverance of the right care, in the right quantity, at the right place and at the right time. This project investigates the use of a case-based reasoning (CBR) method for implementation of such a system.

The CBR-Works tool was used to create an application and a diabetes dataset from the UCI Machine Learning Repository was used to test it. Similarity functions were created both through knowledge elicitation and experimentation. CBR-Works is a state-of-the-art commercial CBR application development tool that provides support for a variety of retrieval algorithms and an excellent range of customizable similarity metrics (Schulz 1999). The following sections present some background, describe the application and its evaluation, discuss the results and draw some conclusions from the project's findings.

2 Background

Why Build a System? The cost of diabetes treatment is enormous, with only 3.1% of the U.S. population being affected, but accounting for 11.9% of the U.S. healthcare expenditure. Tighter control over the blood glucose levels of diabetes patients through more intensive management may incur higher up-front costs (labour, medication and supplies) but these would be overshadowed by a significant reduction in the expenditure relating to the development and progression of complications of diabetes and the frequency of these complications. The reduction of diabetes complications will also improve quality of life for many patients. (AACE 2002).

Why Use CBR? The activities of the CBR cycle closely match the process requirements of a knowledge management system, making CBR a good contender for any decision support system (Watson 2002). Looking specifically at implementing a clinical decision support system, the most obvious competition for CBR would be a rule-based approach. However, rules for such a system would undoubtedly become very complex and difficult to understand.

"Cognitive Science research shows that experts use experience when reasoning about a problem, rather than first principles". (Sterling 2001).

Storing experience lends itself well to a case-based approach, whereas encoding experience knowledge in rules is not as intuitive. CBR systems also automatically adapt with experience, while rule-based approaches may need more user-interaction and understanding.

CBR has been used in other medical decision support systems. An integration of CBR and rule-based reasoning was used in systems for the planning of ongoing care of Alzheimer's patients (Marling and Whitehouse 2001) and for the management of Diabetes patients (Bellazi et al. 1999).

Diabetes. Patients with IDDM (Insulin Dependent Diabetes Mellitus) are insulin deficient. Once being administered with insulin they are at risk of hypoglycemia (low blood glucose) and hyperglycemia (high blood glucose). The aim of therapy for IDDM is to keep the average blood glucose level as close to the normal range as possible. The blood glucose measurement of a patient is affected by diet, exercise and exogenous insulin treatments. Three types of insulin formulations are administered for patients in our dataset (Regular, NPH and Ultralente), each formulation having a different duration of action.

3 The Application

3.1 Case Acquisition

Acquiring data proved to be a very difficult task, with obstacles ranging from privacy issues to the lack of a consistent medical record structure. We finally settled on using the "Diabetes Data" dataset from the UCI Machine Learning Repository to allow us to develop a proof of concept.

This dataset consists of 70 files corresponding to 70 different patients, with each file containing a number of record entries for blood glucose readings, insulin doses or other special events. The patient files vary in size, number of entries and timeframe of entries.

Each entry consists of an *entry code*, a *value* and a *timestamp*. The *entry code* specifies what treatment the entry relates to, for example, a pre-breakfast blood glucose measurement, a regular insulin dose, or an above-average exercise session. The *value* is then the corresponding measurement, for example, the blood glucose measurement in mg/dl or the units of regular insulin administered. (The value field is not relevant for the special events, an entry with this event code simply represents the occurrence of that event). The *timestamp* is very fine-grained, detailing the date and time of treatment for the specific record entry.

3.2 Case Representation

The data was pre-processed to delete invalid values that were not consistent with the type checking in CBR-Works; change *entry codes* to their corresponding string references (e.g. 33 to 'Regular Insulin Dose'), for ease of understanding while testing; and add *patientID* numbers.

An important question that needed to be answered at this point was 'what *is* a case?' The progress of diabetes patients is usually monitored by analysing patterns. The HbA1c test is an example of this. The HbA1c test provides an average blood glucose reading over a period of six to twelve weeks by measuring the number of glucose molecules attached to hemoglobin. (CCHS October 2002, Geocities October 2002). Therefore, it makes sense for the final system to also analyse and compare patterns of events, rather than just single events.

However, we started with a simple case representation of a single entry with attributes: *patientID* (integer), *eventType* (taxonomy), *value* (integer) and *timestamp* (timestamp). We then queried the casebase with single events to find similar cases. For this we set up the data in a Microsoft Access database and imported it into CBR-Works. Only a small amount of manual adjustment was needed once cases were imported.

Once this basic retrieval system was working, cases were extended to represent all the events for a specific patient in a single day. Each day has attributes: *DayID* (integer), *Date* (date), *PatientID* (integer) and *EntryRefs* (set of references to entry concepts). This case structure required the cases to be entered manually because the variable length set structure (*EntryRefs*) is not recognised by simple relational databases and therefore could not be imported into CBR-Works in the same way as with the previous case representation.

3.3 Similarity

Similarity measures are comprised of three elements: local similarity functions, attribute weights and an amalgamation function (Stahl 2002). This section describes the measurement methods used for each of these. The similarity measurement methods were constructed using a hybrid bottom-up and top-down approach (Stahl 2002). Measurement methods were defined as far as possible using domain knowledge available (bottom-up) and refined using a top-down approach, by analysing the output and in some cases, adjusting the method to produce a more desirable output.

Local Similarity Functions and Attribute Weights. The attributes involved in the similarity calculation for comparing entries are *eventType* and *value* and these have equal weightings. Only the attribute containing the set of entry references is used for comparing days. Similarity functions for each these *'discriminant'* attributes are described below.

'EventType' Local Similarity Function. This only compares 'like with like' for events, so *EventType*s are 100% similar to an identical *EventType* and 0% similar to any other.

'Value' Local Similarity Function. For the basic case representation that compared a single event with another single event, rules were written to change the similarity function for the value attribute, depending on the *EventType*. For blood glucose measurements a symmetric polynomial function on [case value - query value] with a 'gradient manipulator' of seven was used (see fig. 1). For insulin doses and other events a symmetric step function at zero was used (see fig. 1), because these must be identical to be comparable. However, for the extended case, CBR-Works was too limiting to use the rules, so a more general similarity function was applied to all *EventType* values. A symmetric smooth-step function at one was used (see Fig. 1). When comparing insulin doses and other events with this function, a very low similarity measurement would serve as a warning for values not being identical, while non-identical blood glucose measurement comparisons would still show as being slightly similar.

'EventRefs' Local Similarity Function. A similarity function for *EventRefs* was programmed, which finds the average similarity over the set. Each set member in the

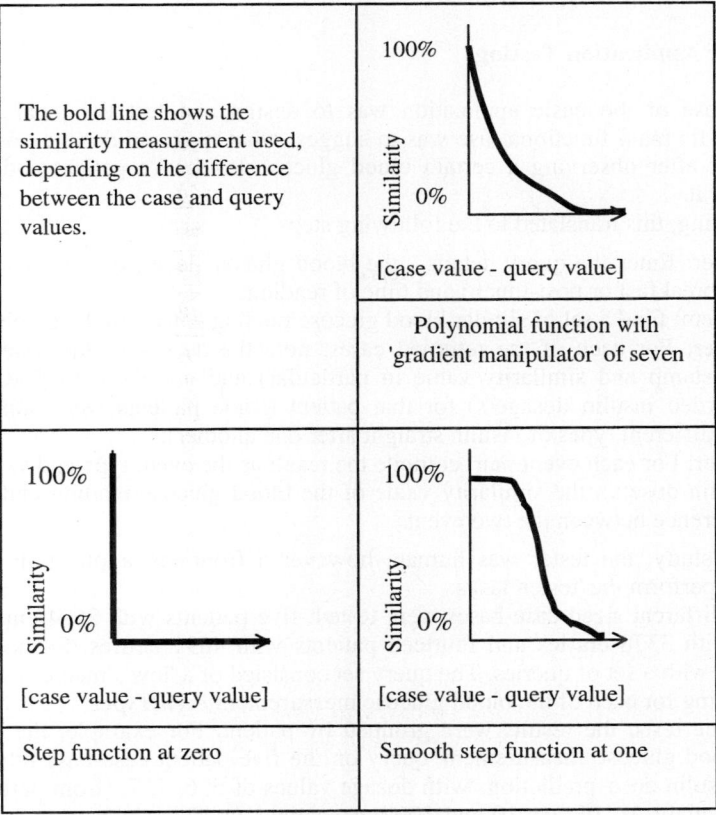

Fig. 1. Similarity functions used for the value attribute

query is compared to each set member in the case and the maximum similarity is found for each query member. These similarity values are then averaged.

Amalgamation Function. To calculate the similarity of days, an average function was used, with all discriminant attributes contributing equally to the similarity. A minimum function was used for entries, so the total similarity is the lowest of all discriminant attribute similarity values. This means that when the *eventType*s are identical, the similarity of the *value* attribute will dictate the total similarity and when they are not the same the total similarity will be zero (i.e. the similarity of the *eventType*s).

4 Evaluation

Extensive informal testing was conducted during construction of the application, to assist with the development of suitable similarity functions.

Two formal testing sessions were performed, the first after completing the basic event comparison application and the second after extending a case to represent the events in a whole day.

4.1 Basic Application Testing

The purpose of the basic application was to design and test the local similarity functions. Its main functional use was to suggest what type and dosage of insulin to administer after observing a certain blood glucose level in a patient and when to administer it.

For testing, this translated to the following steps:

1. Tester: Enter the query details - the blood glucose level, type of reading (e.g. pre-breakfast or post-lunch) and time of reading;
2. System: Find a set of similar blood glucose reading entries in the casebase;
3. Tester: For each of the returned cases, note the details of the case (patient, timestamp and similarity value in particular) and use these to find the next recorded insulin dosage(s) for that patient (some patients were administered two different types of insulin straight after one another);
4. Tester: For each event pair, compile the result as the event type and value of the insulin dose(s), the similarity value of the blood glucose reading and the time difference between the two events.

In our study, the tester was human, however a front-end application could be written to perform the 'tester' tasks.

Three different sized case-bases were tested: five patients with 2604 entries; nine patients with 3378 entries and fourteen patients with 4691 entries. Each case-base was tested with a set of queries. The query set consisted of a 'low', 'medium' and 'high' *value* reading for each of the blood glucose measurement *eventType*s.

In all the tests, the results were grouped by patient. For example, the 'low pre-supper blood glucose measurement' query on the five patient case-base returned ten 'regular insulin dose' predictions with dosage values of 6, 6, 7, 7, (from patient 1), 8, 8, (from patient 2), 10, 10, 10 and 10 (from patient 3). This shows that the type of

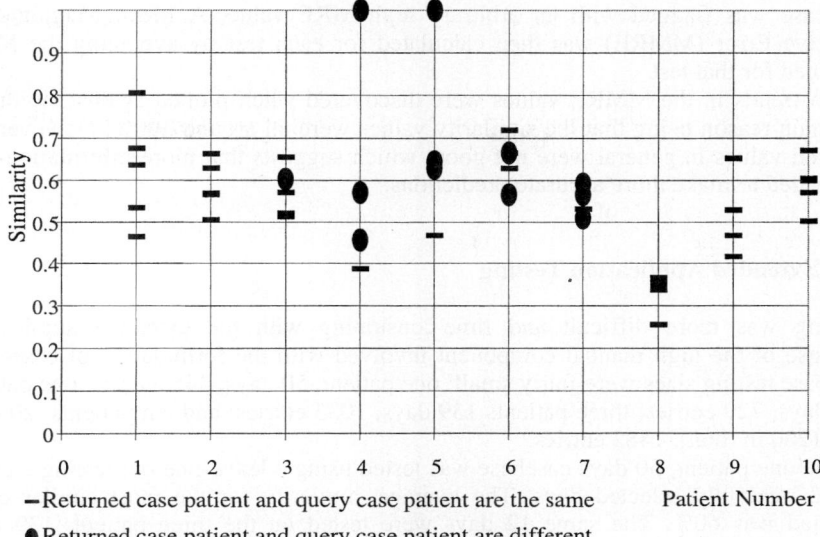

Fig. 2. Similarity values for retrieved cases for 50 cases from the ten patient casebase

insulin and dosage value is dependent on which patient it is to be administered to, as well as the blood glucose level observed.

The smallest case-base with entries from five patients returned good results with an average similarity of 0.973 over all the test cases (for all ten cases retrieved in every test). This increased slightly to 0.981 for nine patients and 0.984 for fourteen patients. However, more interestingly, the diversity in the returned set (both in dosage values and dosage types) increased with the larger case-bases. Again, this highlights the differences in treatment patterns between patients.

Some of the dataset records were taken from paper records with "logical time" slots (breakfast, lunch, dinner, bedtime). These were assigned fictitious timestamps in the dataset of 08:00, 12:00, 16:00 and 22:00 respectively. This did not pose a problem for the testing, (as had been imagined), because all the time differences between blood glucose readings and dosage administrations for 'correct' times were three minutes or less anyway, the majority being zero minutes (i.e. immediately). Consequently, the 'time lapse before administering the dosage' value was not important.

The accuracy of the system was also evaluated. The accuracy measurement used was the Magnitude of Relative Error (MRE) (Mendes et al. 2002), defined as:

$$MRE = \frac{|Actual\ Value - Predicted\ Value|}{Actual\ Value} \qquad (1)$$

MRE was calculated for a randomly chosen set of 20 cases for each casebase size, using the leave-one-out testing method. All the test cases were for blood glucose measurement events and for each test the case(s) with the highest similarity was (were) found, along with the consequential insulin dose(s). These *predicted* insulin doses were compared with the *actual* insulin doses to find the MRE for each test. When the incorrect type of insulin was administered (e.g. NPH instead of Regular), the case was flagged with an arbitrary high MRE value. A Mean Magnitude of Relative Error (MMRE) was then calculated for each test by averaging the MREs obtained for that test.

No trends in the MMRE values were discovered when plotted against similarity, the main reason being that the similarity values were all around 100%. However, the MMRE values in general were not good, which suggests that more information may be needed to make more accurate predictions.

4.2 Extended Application Testing

Testing was more difficult and time-consuming with the extended application. Because of the high manual component involved with the formulation of cases, the casebase testing sizes were fairly small: one patient, 50 days, 345 entries; one patient, 100 days, 729 entries; three patients 139 days, 1035 entries; and ten patients, 20 days each (200 in total), 1482 entries.

The one patient, 50 days casebase was tested using a leave-one-out testing method on 12 randomly selected days. The average similarity for the most similar cases returned was 60%. The same 12 days were tested on the three patient, 139 days casebase and exactly the same most similar cases were returned and therefore the same average similarity was observed. This suggests that it is possible that only information recorded about the current patient (i.e. that patient's history) is useful. Patients have different insulin metabolism rates and insulin tolerance levels, which influence the decision on the type and amount of insulin to be administered. It is quite likely there are other factors not included in the dataset which should also be considered for these decisions.

This observation was investigated further by testing the ten patient case-base. This case-base was made up of 20 days of entries for each of the ten patients. A leave-one-out testing method was used on five randomly chosen cases for each patient (50 in total). Figure 2 shows these results displayed in a scatterplot.15 out of the 50 most similar cases returned were from a patient other than the one in the query, (for patients three to seven only). The average similarity of these 15 cases was 69% (with two 100% values) and the average similarity of the other 35 cases was 54%. These results are more promising for the real-life situation of comparing a newly diagnosed patient with data from previous patients, however in this dataset the results show that there is only a small group of patients for whom this would be effective (patients 3 to 7). In a large dataset there are likely to be many different groups of similar patients. Therefore, a method for finding the correct group for a newly diagnosed patient is another issue for further investigation - more background patient data would probably be needed.

The one patient, 50 days casebase and the one patient 100 days casebases were tested using a leave-one-out testing method on all 50 days from the first case-base. Only four of the 50 cases returned more similar cases with the larger case-base. Three of these four were in the last ten days, suggesting that the similarity of two days may also be related to the time difference between them.

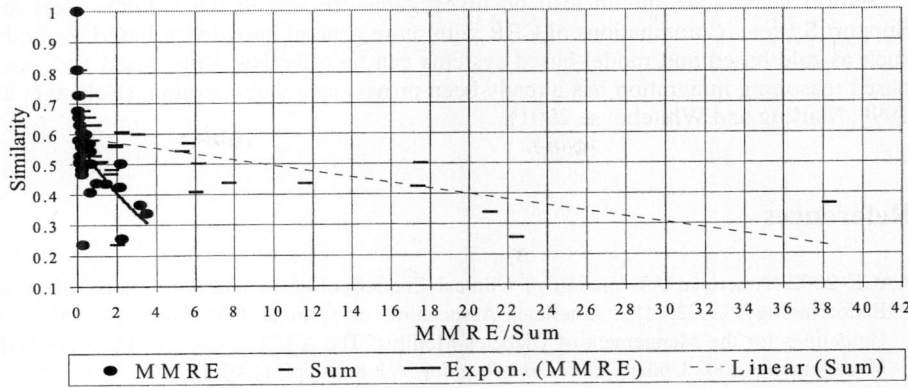

Fig. 3. Accuracy (MMRE and the sum of MREs) versus similarity for 30 leave-one-out tests on the ten patient casebase

The extended application was also tested for accuracy using the MRE and MMRE tests on the ten patient case-base. A leave-one-out test was performed on 30 randomly chosen days. MRE was calculated for each entry in the query case and retrieved case. MMRE and the sum of all MREs for each of the 30 tests was calculated and plotted against the similarity of the two cases. Figure 3 displays the results from these tests. The downwards sloping trendlines represent the relationship between similarity and accuracy - as one decreases, so does the other. This is a desirable outcome for our application.

The testing results for both applications are promising, but would be more reliable if tested on larger datasets. With larger datasets, we would expect more patients with similar treatment patterns, which should produce more convincing results. We would also expect patients with more diverse treatment patterns, to cover more patient types.

The specialized similarity measurements that were implemented in the basic comparison application could be used in the extended application using a different development tool. This may also produce more interesting and conclusive results.

5 Conclusion

We are unable to draw precise conclusions as to the appropriateness of CBR for Orion's Clinical Decision Support System. However, this research produced some promising results that are being investigated further, with a dataset with more patient information; such as: age, weight, medical history, insulin tolerance etc. One of the problems with case acquisition mentioned earlier was the lack of a consistent medical record structure. This is of importance when deciding what information is needed by the system, especially if it is to be used by different healthcare providers with a variety of medical record structures.

The idea of progressively extending the representation of a case should be continued, comparing patterns over longer time periods such as weeks, fortnights and months.

Hybrid techniques should also be investigated for use in the Clinical Decision Support System. Combinations of CBR with more general knowledge based methods, such as rule-based and model-based systems can be effective. Rule-based and case-based reasoning integration has already been proven as a viable option. (Bellazi et al. 1999, Marling and Whitehouse 2001).

References

AACE 2002. American Association of Clinical Endocrinologists, and American College of Endocrinology, 2002. The American Association of Clinical Endocrinologists Medical Guidelines for the Mangement of Diabetes Mellitus: The AACE System of Intensive Self-Management - 2002 Update. *Endocrine Practice* Vol. 8 (Suppl. 1):40-82.

Bellazi, R., Montani, S., Portinale, L. and Riva, A., 1999. Integrating Rule-Based and Case-Based Decision Making in Diabetic Patient Management. In ICCBR-99, LNAI 1650, 386-400. Berlin: Springer.

CCHS (Cleveland Clinic Health System), http://www.cchs.net/hinfo/, Last visited: October 2002.

Geocities, http://www.geocities.com/diabeteschart/ hba1ctest.html. Last visited: October 2002.

Marling, C. and Whitehouse, P., 2001. Case-Based Reasoning in the Care of Alzheimer's Disease Patients. In ICCBR 2001, LNAI 2080, 702-715. Berlin: Springer.

Mendes, E., Watson, I., Triggs, C., Mosley, N., Counsell, S. 2002. A Comparison of Development Effort Estimation Techniques for Web Hypermedia Applications. In Proceedings IEEE Metrics Symposium, June, Ottawa, Canada.

Schulz S., 1999. CBR-Works - A State-of-the-Art Shell for Case-Based Application Building. In Proceedings of the German Workshop on Case-Based Reasoning, GWCBR'99 (1999). Lecture Notes in Artificial Intelligence. Springer-Verlag.

Stahl, A., 2002. Defining Similarity Measures: Top-Down vs. Bottom-Up. In Advances in Case-Based Reasoning. 6th European Conference, ECCBR 2002, Aberdeen, Scotland, UK, September 2002 Proceedings, 406-420. New York: Springer.

Sterling, W., 2001. A Massive Repository for the National Medical Knowledge Bank. Teradata Development Division, NCR Corporation, CA.

Watson, I. 2002. Applying Knowledge Management: Techniques for Building Organisational Memories. In Advances in Case-Based Reasoning. 6th European Conference, ECCBR 2002, Aberdeen, Scotland, UK, September 2002 Proceedings, 6-12. New York: Springer.

Association-Rule Based Information Source Selection*

Hui Yang[1], Minjie Zhang[1], and Zhongzhi Shi[2]

[1] School of IT and Computer Science, University of Wollongong, Wollongong, Australia
{hy92,minjie}@uow.edu.au
[2] Institute of Computing Technology, Chinese Academy of Science, Beijing, P.R.China
shizz@ics.ict.ac.cn

Abstract. The proliferation of information sources available on the Wide World Web has resulted in a need for database selection tools to locate the potential useful information sources with respect to the user's information need. Current database selection tools always treat each database independently, ignoring the implicit, useful associations between distributed databases. To overcome this shortcoming, in this paper, we introduce a data-mining approach to assist the process of database selection by extracting potential interesting association rules between web databases from a collection of previous selection results. With a topic hierarchy, we exploit intraclass and interclass associations between distributed databases, and use the discovered knowledge on distributed databases to refine the original selection results. We present experimental results to demonstrate that this technique is useful in improving the effectiveness of database selection.

1 Introduction

With the explosive growth of information sources available on the Wide World Web, the web has become an enormous, distributed, and heterogeneous information space. To effectively and efficiently find interesting information from the huge amount of resource existing on the web, one of the important steps is to firstly select a subset of distributed collections which are most likely to contain relevant documents regarding the user query before extracting useful information in individual information sources. As a result, **information source selection** (or **resource discovery**) problem is becoming an increasingly important research issue in the distributed information retrieval (DIR) area [4].

Nowadays, several database selection approaches have been introduced to help select the most relevant information sources from the Wide World Web and have received encouraging achievements [2, 3]. Unfortunately, these methods always treat each database independently, ignoring the implicit, useful associations between distributed databases. But the discovery and analysis of the useful information about the relations between the databases will be beneficial to the performance improvement of database selection.

Data mining, an important part of knowledge discovery, is concerned with the process of extracting implicit, previously unknown, and potentially useful information

---

* The research was supported by URC Small Grand-227381019 of Wollongong University.

from given data. Algorithms for data mining focus on the discovery of relevant and interesting patterns within large amounts of data. To the best of our knowledge, very little work has been done on the mining of association rules between distributed databases used for database selection in distributed information retrieval (DIR). The work in this paper could be viewed as a step towards combining data mining techniques with the problem of database selection.

Given a collection of previous database-selection results, a data-mining algorithm is developed to discover knowledge on the databases by extracting potential relations between distributed databases with the use of a topic hierarchy. The discovered knowledge provides assistance in refine the relatively rough original results that are obtained from the database selection tools. Here, what is needed to emphasize is that the aim of this paper is not intended to propose an alternative database selection approach, but provide a subsidiary means to refine the final results on the basis of original selection results with the discovered associations between the databases so as to improve the effectiveness of database selection. Therefore, this association-rule approach can be regarded as a step towards the post-processing of database selection. The contributions of this paper are summarized as follows:

(1) A new methodology for the problem of database selection is proposed from the viewpoint of data mining.
(2) In consideration of the diversity of topic contents of distributed web databases, a topic-based association-rule mining process is accomplished by a twofold approach: first, to generate associations between the databases within the same topic class (i.e., intraclass); and then to deduce the association rules between relevant topics (i.e., interclass) such as parent-child classes and sibling classes in the hierarchical structure.

The remainder of this paper is organized as follows: in the next section, we firstly introduce some background knowledge of our current work. In Section 3, the details of discovering association rules between distributed databases using hierarchical topics are given. In the same section, we also discuss how association rule technique can be applied to the database-selection process. Experimental setup and experimental methodologies are given in Section 4. In Section 5, the performance study of the proposed approach is performed on the Reuters-21578 data set, and the results of the experiments are analyzed. Finally, Section 6 concludes the paper with a brief discussion of future work.

2 Background Knowledge of a Topic-Based Database Selection

This paper is, in fact, the extension of our previous work on database selection. In [6], we proposed a topic-based database selection approach. We firstly partition multiple, distributed web databases based on their subject contents into a structured hierarchy of topics using a Bayesian network learning algorithm. Given a user query, the task of database selection is decomposed into two distinct stages: First, at the category-specific search stage, the system identifies one or more specific topic domains that best match the user's information need. Second, at the term-specific search stage, the selection system computes the likelihood of the databases associated with the relevant topics chosen at the first stage, and selects the potential most appropriate databases based on the ranking scores of the likelihood.

Since our topic-based database-selection approach is based on a topic hierarchy, we consider integrating the topic hierarchy with the discovery of associations between distributed databases. The main reason for using the topic hierarchy has two aspects: one is *the efficiency of data mining*. For a large collection of previous database-selection results, the use of a topic hierarchy can decompose the data mining task into a set of smaller subtasks, each of which only corresponds to the mining of a focused topic domain in the hierarchical tree, therefore making the accomplishment of the data-mining work more effective and efficient; he other is *the search of relevant association rules*. Given a user query, once the database-selection result is returned, the association rules associated with the specific topics that the user is interested in will be directly used for the refinement of the original selection result. As a result, the expense and time of the search for relevant association rules in the association space will be much reduced.

In our work, we utilize a topic hierarchy to assist in the discovery of association rules between databases. Figure 1 shows an example of a simple topic hierarchy. Let C be a classification hierarchy on the topics, which organizes the relationships between the topics in a tree form. Obviously, the relationships between different topics appearing in the structured hierarchy can be classified into three major types of relationships: *parent-child*, *ancestor-descendant*, and *sibling*. For example, in Figure 1, topic "*software*" is the *parent* of topic "*database*", which is semantically more general and broader than topic "*database*". Similarly, topic "*computers*" is the *ancestor* of topic "*database*". Topic "*programming*" is one of the children of topic "*software*", which is defined as a *sibling* to topic "*database*". For each topic in a hierarchical structure, the system stores the knowledge of relationships between this topic and other topics in the hierarchy including parent-child, ancestor-descendent, and sibling relations.

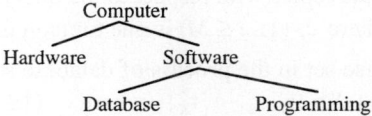

Fig. 1. A simple example of the topic hierarchical structure

3 The Discovery of Association Rules Between Web Databases Using a Topic Hierarchy

3.1 Association Rules

Formally, as defined in [1], let $I = \{i_1, i_2, \cdots, i_m\}$ be a set of binary attributes called items. Let D be a collection of transactions, where each transaction $T \in D$ is a set of items such that $T \subseteq I$ and it is given with a unique identification *TID*. Given an itemset $X \subseteq I$, a transaction T is said to contain X if $X \subseteq T$. An association rule is an implication of the form $X \Rightarrow Y$, where $X, Y \subseteq I$ and $X \cap Y = \varnothing$; and X is called the *antecedent* of the rule and Y is called the *consequence* of the rule. The association rule $X \stackrel{s,c}{\Rightarrow} Y$ holds in the transaction set D with *support s* if $s\%$ of transactions in D contain X and Y, and *confidence c* if $c\%$ of transactions in D that contain X also contain Y:

Given a minimum support threshold called *minsup* and a minimum confidence threshold called *minconf*, the problem of discovering association rules from the transaction set D is to generate all association rules that have support and confidence greater than the specified minimum support *minsup*, and minimum confidence *minconf*, respectively. These rules are called *strong rules*.

In general, the problem of association rule mining can be decomposed into two subproblems: first, find all the itemsets that have support above the specific minimum support, *minsup*. These itemsets are called *large itemsets* or *frequent itemsets*; second, generate the association rules from the above large itemsets that have found. Given a large itemset with size k, a k-itemset ζ, $\zeta = i_1 i_2 \cdots i_k$, $k \geq 2$, the antecedent of the rule will be a subset X of ζ such that X has j ($1 \leq j < k$) items, and the consequence Y will be the itemset $\zeta - X$, if support (ζ) /support (X) >*minconf*, then the rule $X \Rightarrow Y$ is a valid rule.

3.2 A Formal Model of Association Transactions for Database Selection

In the context of distributed information retrieval (DIR), we need to adapt data mining techniques to database selection. The first issue to deal with is to develop a formal model of association transactions for database selection.

Definition 1: A *query* transaction T in a *topic-based* DIR system is a 4-tuple $T=<Q, C, S, D>$ where

- Q is a user query that can be denoted as $Q = \{q_1, q_2, \cdots, q_N\}$, where q_i ($1 \leq i \leq N$) is a query term (word) occurring in the query Q.
- C is a set of appropriate topics with respect to the query, which can be denoted as $C = \{c_1, c_2, \cdots, c_M\}$, where c_i ($1 \leq i \leq M$) is one topic in the topic hierarchy.
- S is a selected database set in the process of database selection. The database set S can be described as $S = \{s_1, s_2, \cdots, s_K\}$, where s_j ($1 \leq j \leq K$) is a web database which is likely to contain relevant information for the user query.
- D is a set of retrieved documents that come from the selected database set S and satisfy the user query. Document set D can be defined as $D = \{d_{11}, \cdots, d_{ij}, \cdots, d_{LK}\}$, where L is the total number of retrieved documents; and K is the number of the databases in the database set S; d_{ij} ($1 \leq i \leq L$, $1 \leq j \leq K$) represents the ith web document which comes from database s_j in the database set S.

With the database set S and the topic categories C in the query transaction, we construct a topic-based database-selection transaction that represents a database-selection result. Unfortunately, this type of database-selection transactions focuses on the binary attribute of the database items, which is only concerned with whether a database appears in a transaction or not, but does not take the relevance degree of a database to the user query into account. For example, given a user query, the DIR system returns a query result of 7 relevant web documents. Among them, 5 documents come from database s_1, and 2 documents comes from database s_2. The database-selection transaction can only reflect the fact that the databases s_1 and s_2 are selected as the relevant databases to the query, which leads to the loss of important information about different relevance degrees of individual databases to the user query. To let the database-selection transactions express the information about the relevance degree of databases to the query, with fuzzy set theory, we extend the traditional association rule by assigning a weight to each database item in the transaction, to indicate the relevance (importance) degree of such a database.

Definition 2: A topic-based *database-selection* transaction τ is a 2-tuple $\tau=<C, S>$ where C is the same as Definition 1; and S is a set of weighted databases searched by the DIR system, which can be described as $S = \{<s_1, w_1>, <s_2, w_2>, \cdots, <s_K, w_K>\}$, where a pair $<s_j, w_j>$ is called a *weighted database item* s_j^w ($1 \leq j \leq K$), and s_j is a *database* item and w_j is a weight associated with *database* item s_j.

Obviously, a topic-based *database-selection* transaction T is the combination of topic items and weighted database items. A simple example of a database selection transaction is show as follows:

$$\text{Transaction } T_1: T_1 = \{<c_1, c_2>, <s_1, w_1>, <s_2, w_2>\}.$$

Here, we use fuzzy set concept to express the relevance (importance) degree of each database in database set S to the user query. A fuzzy set is defined as a collection of elements with the associated membership value between 0 (complete exclusion) and 1 (complete inclusion). The membership value represents the degree of membership of an element in a given set [5]. A fuzzy set A in the database set S is defined as a set of ordered pairs:

$$A = \{(s_j, u_A(s_j)) \mid s_j \in S\} \tag{1}$$

where $u_A(s_j)$ is called the membership function. The membership function maps each database s_j in database set S to a membership grade between 0 and 1. The membership function $u_A(s_j)$ can be described as

$$w_j = u_A(s_j) = \frac{\sum_i d_{ij}}{\sum_i \sum_t d_{it}} \tag{2}$$

where d_{it} ($1 \leq i \leq L$, $1 \leq t \leq K$) represents the ith retrieved document which appears in database s_t in the database set S (recall Definition 1). $\sum_i d_{ij}$ denotes the number of the documents retrieved from database s_j. w_j, the weight associated with database s_j, is assigned by the membership function $u_A(s_j)$, and $\sum_j w_j = 1$ ($1 \leq j \leq K$).

3.3 The Discovery of Fuzzy Association Rule with a Topic Hierarchy

In this subsection, we will first give the definition of fuzzy association rule (FAR). Then we will discuss the issues and problems in the mining of intraclass association rules and interclass association rules, respectively.

3.3.1 Fuzzy Association Rule

We use the term *weighted database itemset* to represent a set of weighted database items with set membership value [0,1] in the database-selection transactions.

Definition 3: A *weighted database k-itemset* δ in a transaction is a set of weighted database items, $\delta = \{s_1^w, s_2^w, \cdots, s_k^w\}$, where s_i^w ($1 \le i \le k$) is a *weighted database item* (recall Definition 2).

Definition 4: *Item()* is a database function which extracts the database set from a *weighted database itemset* δ.

For example, given a *weighted database k-itemset* δ, $Item(\delta) = \{s_1, s_2, \cdots, s_K\}$, where s_i ($1 \le i \le k$) is a *database* item in the itemset δ.

Definition 5: Given a set of transactions T, an interesting *fuzzy association rule* (FAR) is defined as an implication of the form $X \stackrel{s,c,r}{\Rightarrow} Y$, where X and Y are two *weighted database itemsets*, and $item(X) \cap item(Y) = \emptyset$. We said that the fuzzy association rule holds in the transaction set T with *support* s if *s%* of transactions in T contain $item(X)$ and $item(Y)$, *confidence c* if *c%* of transactions in T that contain $item(X)$ also contain $item(Y)$, and *relevance* $r \in [0,1]$ if the weight of each item in the itemsets, $item(X)$ and $item(Y)$, is greater than the relevance threshold r.

Here, the *relevance* concept is introduced to develop effective pruning techniques to identify potentially important database items for the fuzzy association rule mining. To efficiently discover the interesting rules, we push *relevance* constraint in the candidate itemset generating phase of the association rule mining algorithm in order to only retain the suitable candidate itemsets which have the database items with higher weight in the transactions, hence discarding those trivial ones with low weight. This pruning saves both the memory for storing large itemsets and mining efforts. Intuitively, *relevance* parameter can be viewed as an indicator of the required relevance (importance) degree of each item in the *large weighted database itemsets* to a specific topic.

In sum, given a transaction set T, our objective is to discover a set of fuzzy association rules which have *support*, *confidence* and *relevance* satisfying the specific minimums, *minsup*, *minconf* and *minrele*.

3.3.2 The Discovery of Intraclass Association Rules

As previously mentioned, the connections among the databases in the context of a topic hierarchy can be grouped into two major types of association rules: one is *intraclass association rules* within the same topic class, the other is *interclass association rules* between relevant topic classes. Now, we first will discuss how to mine intraclass association rules between the databases on a specific topic. Here, we are only interested in a subset of transactions which are labeled with the specific topic considered.

Definition 6: An interesting *intraclass association rule* is described as $X \stackrel{s,c,r}{\Rightarrow} Y \mid C = c_i$, where c_i is the specific topic considered; and the parameters X, Y, s, c, r are the same as Definition 5.

We present an Aprior-like algorithm to perform the generation of an intraclass association rule. The three major mining steps are described as follows:

(1) Generate all *large database itemsets* which have *support* greater than the specific minimum support *minsup*. For a database itemset ζ, if in the transaction set, the fraction of transactions containing the itemset ζ is greater than *minsup s*, we call ζ a *large database itemset*.

(2) For each of the above large database itemsets, the weight w_i of each database item s_i in a *large database itemset* ζ is calculated by first summing the weights of item s_i in all the transactions containing the itemset δ, and then dividing it by the total number of the transactions containing the itemset ζ, which is defined as

$$w_i = \frac{\text{Sum of the weights of item } s_i \text{ in all the transactions containing the itemset } \delta}{\text{the total number of all the transactions containing the itemset } \delta} \quad (3)$$

If the weights of all the database items in the itemset ζ are all greater than specified minimum relevance *minrele r*, the itemset ζ is called a *large weighted database itemset*.

(3) Once all the *large weight database itemsets* are found, the potentially interesting association rules can be derived from the large itemsets in a straightforward manner. For each *large weight database itemset*, all association rules that have greater than the specified minimum confidence *miniconf* will be derived. For example, for a *large weighted database itemset* ζ, and any X ($X \subset \zeta$), if *support* (*item*(ζ)) / *support* (*item* (ζ) –*item* (X)) > *minconf*, the rule $X \Rightarrow (\zeta - X)$ will be derived.

It is important to note that for each intraclass association rule, it in fact contains two types of information: one is the information on the coourence between the databases, and the other is the information on different relevance degree of individual databases to the specific topic considered. For example, there is an intraclass association rule, that is, *Rule A*: $\{<s_1, 0.4>, <s_2, 0.2>\} \Rightarrow \{<s_3, 0.1>\} | C=$"*software*", which indicates that for topic domain "*software*", if the databases s_1, s_2 are chosen by a database-selection tool, then it is likely that database s_3 will also be selected; on the other hand, it implies that the content of database s_1 is more relevant to topic "*software*" than that of the databases s_2 and s_3, since its potential relevance weight is 0.4, the biggest one among the three databases.

Intraclass association rules can be used to improve the performance of database selection. Consider such a scenario that assumes that a user is searching the information of topic "*software*" on the Internet. The *original* database-selection result by a database-selection tool is the databases s_1 and s_2 which are considered to contain the documents of interest. With *Rule A*, we can add database s_3 into the extended search space, because since the databases s_1 and s_2 have been chosen, and according to *Rule A*, database s_3 will be selected as a potentially useful database with respect to topic "*software*". At the same time, among these three databases, we will rank database s_1 ahead of the databases s_2 and s_3 in the *final* result since database s_1 is more important than other two databases according to *Rule A*.

3.3.3 The Discovery of Interclass Association Rules

As described earlier, a *database-selection* transaction is probably labeled with multiple topics. It is necessary to identify the correlations among the databases in the context of the closely-related topics. In order to simplify the explanation, our work will be introduced based on the assumption that there are a pair of related topics in the topic hierarchy, which will be easily extended to any number of related topics in the hierarchy.

Now we firstly introduce the notion of *overlap* factor. The *overlap* factor is the ratio of the transactions containing both topics c_i, c_j to the transactions that topic c_i or topic c_j appears in, which can be presented as

$$o_{c_i c_j} = \frac{transaction(c_i) \cap transaction(c_j)}{transaction(c_i) \cup transaction(c_j)} \quad (4)$$

It is obvious that the *overlap* factor is an indicator of the correlation degree of topics c_i and c_j. When $o_{c_i c_j}$ is greater than the specified overlap threshold *minover*, we treat the topics c_i and c_j as a "strong" correlated topic pair. Here, we try to discover some potentially interesting associations between "strong" correlated topic pairs.

Definition 7: An interesting *interclass association rule* is described as

$$X \stackrel{s,c,r}{\Rightarrow} Y \mid C = <c_i, c_j>, \text{ and } o_{c_i c_j} > overlap\_threshold$$

where the relationship of the topic pair $<c_i, c_i>$ is either parent-child or siblings, and topic c_i and topic c_j are "strong" correlated. The parameters X, Y, s, c, r are the same as Definition 5.

Once the "strong" correlated topic pairs are determined, the algorithm of mining association rules in each "strong" correlated topic pair will be the same as the one for the mining of intraclass association rules (recall Subsection 3.3.2).

Interclass association rules can be used to improve the performance of database selection. For example, in some cases, the user may be interested in the information of one more topics such as two specific siblings with "strong" correlation. In this case, the interclass association rules about these two siblings can be used either to expand the database search space or to help determine the final database ranking order of the selection result.

4 Experimental Design

As described previously, the goal of our work is considered as a step of the post-processing of database selection, which perfects the relative-rough original database-selection results from the database selection tool by using the potentially useful associations among the databases. Therefore, the objective of our experiments is to compare the selection performance of the refined results obtained by the association-rule approach with that of the original results. We conducted a series of experiments on 20 databases that consist of documents from the Reuters-21578 text dataset (http://www.research.att.com/~lewis/~reuters21578.html) - a well-known text categorization dataset for database selection. Each database contains documents of several topic classes.

In this paper, we use the mean-squared root error metric, which is the variation of the well-known Mean Squared Error (MSE) [2]. The mean-squared root error of the collection ranking for a single query is calculated as:

$$Error = \frac{1}{|C|} \cdot \sqrt{\sum_{i \in C}(O_i - R_i)^2} \quad (5)$$

where: (1) O_i is the position of database s_i in the optimal relevance-based ranking O_Q given a query Q. The optimal ranking O_Q is produced based on the following two criteria: (a) the number of relevant topics in the databases. If database s_i has more classes than database s_j, then s_i is ranked ahead of s_j. That is, $Rank(s_i, s_j) = \{s_i, s_j\}$. (b) the number of relevant documents in the databases. If database s_i has more documents associated with relevant classes than database s_j, then s_i is ranked ahead of s_j. That is, $Rank(s_i, s_j) = \{s_i, s_j\}$. (2) R_i is the position of database s_i in the selection ranking result which is based on the likelihood scores of databases. The database with the largest value of likelihood is ranked 1, the database with second largest value is ranked 2, and so on; (3) C is the set of collections being ranked.

5 Performance Study

5.1 Analysis of Execution Time and the Number of Association Rules

This subsection discusses the effects of the variety of minimum support threshold on the execution time and on the number of association rules generated at different topic levels in the hierarchy. We vary the values of the minimum support threshold in wide range in order to observe all possible differences in the mining. In this manner, we can more clearly determine the effect of the support parameter on the execution time and the size of association rules.

Figure 2-3 show the running time and the number of association rules with respect to the minimum support threshold. It is observed that the smaller the minimum support threshold, the larger the number of the discovered association rules and the more time it takes to generate the rules. The reason for this is that when the minimum support threshold was set to be very small, the size of the candidate itemsets became large. As a result, more association rules would be generated from the candidate itemsets. However, our association-rule mining algorithm requires all the candidate itemsets to be in memory during the mining process, which leads to most of the available memory space is occupied by the candidate itemsets and consequently less memory is used for the generation of association rules.

It is also easily noted that the effects of various minimum support thresholds on the execution time and the number of association rules vary at different topic levels in the hierarchy. The higher the topic level, the fewer the number of association rules generated and the less the execution time should be taken. This is understandable that since the total number of the query transactions at the high level is much more than that of lower levels, the support threshold at the high level should be very smaller. Hence, we had to flexibly define the support thresholds at different topic levels in order to capture the interesting associations as many as possible.

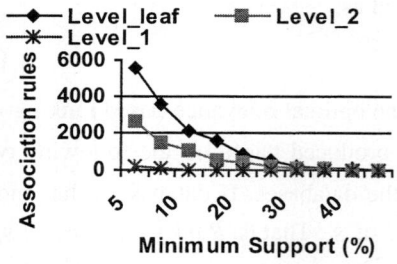 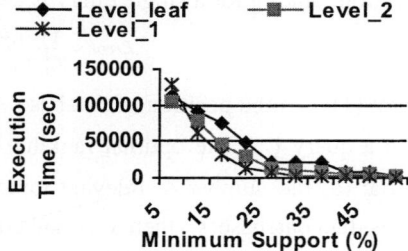

Fig. 2. The effect of different support thresholds on the number of association rules

Fig. 3. The effect of different support thresholds on execution time

5.2 Comparison of Selection Performance

Comparing the original selection results by the database selection tool, we examine the selection performance of the refined results obtained by the association-rule (AR) approach with different minimum support thresholds. In Figure 4, we find that the selection performance of the refined results strongly outperforms that of the original ones in the Reuters_21578 dataset. This should not be surprising, because the AR approach provides a much better opportunity to distinguish the relevant databases with the use of the discovered associations between the databases. From Figure 4, it clearly shows that with the AR approach, the mean-squared root error of the refined results is significantly reduced by 24.9% on average against that of the original results. This suggests that potential interesting association rules between the databases should be one of the key factors that affect the selection accuracy.

It is also interesting to note that the selection-performance differentiation in the variety of support thresholds is related to the number of association rules used for selection. Noted that here we mainly examine the effect of associations between the topics at the leaf level on database-selection performance, since the topics at the leaf level include the majority of the topics in the hierarchy. As shown in Figure 5, the selection accuracy increased as the minimum support threshold decreased. It means that the more association rules were used, the larger the chance became to discovery the useful correlations between the databases. However, we can also see that the AR approach with sup_0.1 slightly outperforms that the AR approach with sup_0.2, but the AR approach with sup_0.1 counts the total of about 4,000 association rules and the AR approach with sup_0.2 only counts about 1,500 association rules. The possible reason for this may be because although the AR approach with sup_0.2 has fewer association rules, it still contains most of the potential useful association rules that are large enough to enable significant improvement on database selection performance. It implies that when the collection of query transactions becomes huge, it is possible to choose the larger minimum support threshold with consideration of the trade-off between the memory space occupied and the number of association rules used.

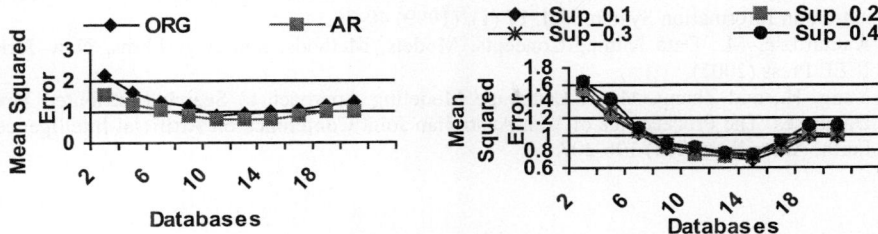

Fig. 4. The comparison of the refined selection results by the association-rule approach (*minsup*=0.2) with the original selection results

Fig. 5. Selection performance of the association rule approach with different support thresholds

6 Conclusion and Future Works

Information retrieval researchers have developed some sophisticated database-selection tools to locate most relevant databases on the web for the users' information needs. However, they always overlook the potentially useful correlations between the databases at the process of database selection. This paper introduces the use of association rules for the problem of database selection. With the assistance of data mining tools, we extract patterns or associations between distributed databases from a collection of previous selection results, and the discovered knowledge on the databases is in turn used to refine the results from the database selection tools so as to further improve the accuracy of database selection. An association-rule mining approach is proposed to generate intraclass and interclass associations between the databases with the use of a topic hierarchy. We tested the effectiveness of our algorithm on the Reuters-21578 dataset and the experimental results are promising and show some potential in future study on database selection.

However, we view this work as a first step, with a number of interesting problems remaining open and subjected to further research. For example, we are investigating ways to develop more effective discovery algorithms. It appears possible to find other mining algorithms that could perform faster or better the discovery of association rules. Second, the interclass associations described in this paper only involve adjacent topics such as parent-child classes and sibling classes in the hierarchy. Therefore, to discover associations between the child classes with different parent classes is another issue worth exploration. Finding such rules needs future work.

References

[1] Agrawal, R., Imielinski, T., and Swami, A.: Mining Association Rles between Sets of Items in Large Databases. Proceedings of the 1993 Acm Sigmod International Conference on Management of Data, (1993) 26-28.

[2] Callan, J. P., Lu, Z., and Croft, W. B.: Searching Distributed Collections with Inference Networks. Proceedings of the 19th Annual International Acm Sigir Conference on Research and Development in Information Retrieval, (1995) 21-29.
[3] Gravano, L., Garcia-Molina, H., and Tomasic, A.: Gloss: Text-Source Discovery over the Internet. ACM Transactions on Database Systems,Vol. 24 (2). (1999) 229-264.
[4] Hawking, D., and Thistlewaite, P.: Methods for Information Server Selection. ACM Transaction on Information System,Vol. 17 (1). (1999) 40-76.
[5] Kantardzic, M.: Data Mining-Concepts, Models, Methods, and Algorithms, New Jork: IEEE Press (2002).
[6] Yang, H., and Zhang, M.: A Language Modeling Approach to Search Distributed Text Databases. The Proceedings of 16th Australian Joint Conference on Artificial Intelligence, Perth, Australia, (2003) 196-207.

Distributional Character Clustering for Chinese Text Categorization

Xuezhong Zhou and Zhaohui Wu

College of Computer Science, Zhejiang University, Hangzhou, 310027, P.R.China
{zxz,wzh}@cs.zju.edu.cn

Abstract. A novel feature generation method-distributional character clustering for Chinese text categorization, which avoids word segmentation, is presented and experimentally evaluated. We propose a hybrid clustering criterion function and bisecting divisive clustering algorithm to improve the quality of clusters. The experimental results show that distributional character clustering is an effective dimensionality reduction method, which reduce the feature space to very low dimensionality (e.g. 500 features) while maintaining high performance. The performance is much better than information gain. Moreover, Naïve Bayes classifier with distributional character clustering has state-of-the-art performance in Chinese text classification.

Keywords: Chinese Text Categorization, Distributional Character Clustering, Hybrid Clustering Criterion

1 Introduction

Content-based document management tasks have gained a prominent status in the information systems fields in the past 25 years [1]. Text Categorization (TC) is the fundamental task, which has been intensively studied for the using of machine learning approaches during 1990s[2]. However, a common and often overwhelming characteristic of text data is extremely high dimensionality and sparse representation of a single document, and very few irrelevant features were found in text because of the complex semantics of natural language [3]. Recently, combined with information theoretic method, distributional word clustering was proposed by several researchers, whose classification performance is striking [4,5,6,7,8].

Because of the unique linguistics and complex ambiguities in Chinese natural language, many term selection and extraction methods may not be applicable to Chinese. The experiment results of previous Chinese TC work are not inspiring [9]. Compared with English TC, Chinese TC has the characteristics such as: (1) Word segmentation is needed. (2) High word dimensionality but limited characters. (3) Character may be the more suitable feature for Chinese TC than word. In this paper we try to combine character with distributional term clustering to provide a novel Chinese TC method without word segmentation. We enhance distributional term clustering to Chinese TC by using character feature, hybrid clustering criterion and bisecting clustering algorithm. It shows that TC accuracy based on Distributional Clustering (DC) is much higher than Information Gain (IG), which is a high performance feature selection method comparatively studied by Yang [10]. Furthermore, it is found that character cluster feature provides very low and more effective representation than Chinese word feature when combined with Naïve Bayes classifier.

2 Distributional Character Clustering and Hybrid Clustering Criterion

In this section, we first quickly review the information theory concept Kullback Leibler divergence used in the previous related works [4,6], then propose the hybrid clustering criterion and the bisecting divisive clustering algorithm.

Let X be a random variable that takes on values from the set χ with probability distribution $p(x)$, then relative entropy between two probability distributions $p(x)$ and $m(x)$ is defined as

$$KL(p(x),m(x)) = H_{P\|M}(X) = \sum_{x \in \chi} p(x) \ln \frac{p(x)}{m(x)} \tag{2.1}$$

Kullback Leibler (KL) divergence (relative entropy) is not a symmetric function and will be unbounded when $m(x)$ is zero. Even more, it is non-negative and does not satisfy the triangle inequalities. A weighted KL divergence, which is symmetric, is used in this paper.

To optimize the character clusters, we provide a hybrid clustering criterion function with KL-divergence, which is minimized to get refined clusters. Let $W = \{w_1, w_2, ..., w_n\}$ be the word set, and $W_s = \{W_1, W_2, ..., W_m\}$ be the word cluster set. The hybrid clustering criterion combining the internal and external clustering criterion is defined as

$$H(W_j, W_s) = \frac{I(\{W_j\})}{E(W_s)} \tag{2.2}$$

where $E(W_s)$ is external similarity of clusters, which is defined as

$$E(W_s) = \sum_{j=1}^{m} p(W_j) KL(p(C|W_j), p(C|W_s)) \tag{2.3}$$

and $I(\{W_j\})$ is the internal similarity of clusters, which is defined as

$$I(\{W_j\}) = \sum_{k=1}^{m} \sum_{w_t \in W_j} p(w_t) KL(p(C|w_t), p(C|W_j)) \tag{2.4}$$

In (2.3) and (2.4), $p(C|Ws)$, $p(C|W_j)$ and $p(C|w_t)$ represent respectively the conditional distribution on class of word clusters set, word cluster and word. $p(C|W_j)$ and $p(C|w_t)$ have the same definitions as[6]. $p(C|Ws)$ is defined as

$$p(C/W_s) = \sum_{j} p(W_j) \frac{p(C|W_j)}{\sum_{i=1}^{m} p(W_i)} \tag{2.6}$$

where $p(W_j) = \sum_{w_t \in W_j} p(w_t)$ if W_s contains all the words of W (no preprocess of feature selection methods are used), then $\sum_{i=1}^{m} p(W_i)=1$.

Algorithm Bisecting Divisive Clustering (P,Π,l,k,W_s)
Input: P is the set of distributions, $\{p(C|w_t):1 \le t \le m\}$, Π is the set of all word priors, $\{\pi_t = p(w_t) : 1 \le t \le m\}$, l is the number of document classes, k is the number of desired clusters.
Output: W_s is the set of word clusters $\{W_1,W_2,...,W_k\}$
Step 1: Initialization: for every word w_t, assign w_t to W_j such that $p(c_j|w_t)=\max_i p(c_i|w_t)$.
This gives l initial word clusters.
Step 2: Bisecting divisivision: Suppose we always let the $k > l$. Using the following function to compute the entropy of initial clusters and pick up a cluster to split.
$$\arg\max_i \sum_{w \in W_i} \pi_t KL(p(C|w_t),p(C|W_i))$$
    Step 2.1: Pick up a cluster whose entropy is the largest.
    Step 2.2: Find 2 sub-clusters using classical K-means algorithm (bisecting).
    Step 2.3: Repeat the above two steps until the number of clusters k is reached.
Step 3: Refinement: adjust the word w_t to new word cluster W_j according to
$$\arg\min_j KL(p(C|w_t),p(C|W_j))$$
Step 4: Stop if the change of objective function (2.2) is much small (such as 10^{-4}), otherwise goto step 3.

Fig. 1. The bisecting divisive clustering algorithm

The object function (2.2) is intuitively reasonable. The goal of hybrid clustering criterion is to refine the clusters to be more internal similar and less external similar when the object function is minimized. That is, we try to minimize the KL divergence of different words in one single cluster and maximize the KL divergence between different word clusters.

The bisecting divisive algorithm is to make a tradeoff between clustering efficiency and effectiveness (The algorithm is described in pseudo code as Fig.1.). Combined with bisecting divisive algorithm, hybrid clustering criterion gets the competitive higher accuracy than the internal clustering criterion of [6] in our experiment.

3 Related Work

Text classification has been intensively studied based on the bag-of-words text representation. Because of the high dimensionality, many feature selection/extraction methods are proposed to address the problem of dimensionality reduction. Furthermore, text classification is highly related to the natural language. Therefore, the linguistic complexity is the essential problem of text classification. In this section, we review some related work of this paper.

3.1 Chinese Text Categorization

Like the traditional TC research, most of the Chinese TC researches are focus on the word based feature extraction and classifiers [9,11,12,13]. But the results is poor comparable for the using of latent different word segmentation methods. Meanwhile, there have been several studies on character-based Chinese TC [14,15,16]. Peng et al.[15] provides a unified n-gram language model for TC, in which the experiment results have showed that 1-gram character maybe is a good feature representation in Chinese TC, but higher order n-gram is not preferred because of the high dimensionality and sparse problem. A comparative study on text representations and classifiers shows that word segmentation do have substantial influence on the performance of word-based TC and character feature is an efficient text representation in Chinese TC [17]. The published results on CNA news corpus indicate two main obstacles in Chinese TC [9]: (1) very high word dimensionality, about 10^5-10^6 number of words drawn from a modest corpus (2) low classification accuracy, the best microaccuracy of k-NN does not exceed 80%.

3.2 Distributional Word Clustering

Lewis has been the first to investigate the impact of term clustering in text classification. But the experiment result is inferior to the single term indexing, probably due to the disappointing performance of reciprocal nearest neighbor clustering and the Reuters corpus used [18]. Distributional Word Clustering (DWC) was first used by Pereira et al.[4] to address the problem of data sparse in statistics language model. They use the soft clustering and KL-divergence (relative entropy) to measure the dissimilarity between two words and aim to classify nouns according to their distribution as direct objects of verbs. It was applied to text classification in [5] as feature extraction method and showed a prominent result on dimensionality reduction while only losing a few percent in text classification accuracy, which is better than some other dimensionality reduction methods such as LSI&PLSI, MI and χ^2 statistics etc.. Slonim[7] and Bekkerman et al.[8] combined DWC with Information Bottleneck method to yield a significant improvement in classification accuracy (up to 18% when the train sample is relative small) over the performance using the words directly. DWC combined with SVM gets the best-known multi-label classification performance on 20Newsgroups, which was proposed in [8]. Moreover, the text representation quality with respect to dataset was discussed because word-cluster feature is inferior to word feature on the Reuters and WebKB datasets. Recently, Dhillon et al. [6] enhanced word clustering for hierarchical text classification and have a state of art performance.

We now list the main contributions of this paper. Character is a particular efficient feature in Chinese TC, which has rarely been studied. We put forward distributional character clustering for Chinese text classification, which is a novel character-based feature generation method without word segmentation. To get the more optimized term clusters, we propose a hybrid clustering criterion with KL-divergence. Furthermore, a systematic comparative experiment is conducted to evaluate the performance of hybrid distributional character clustering method. The experimental results show that distributional character clustering for Chinese TC has several remarkable advantages such as very low, limited feature dimensionality, no need of word segmentation and state-of-the-art performance etc..

4 Text Classifiers

We introduce the classifiers namely Naïve Bayes, Support Vector Machine and Naïve Bayes with cluster features in the experiment in the next several sections.

4.1 Naïve Bayes

Naïve Bayes is a simple yet efficient classifier widely used in the machine learning research. Let $C=\{c_1,c_2,...,c_k\}$ be the set of k classes, and let $W=\{w_1,w_2,...,w_n\}$ be the set of words/features contained in these classes. The Naïve Bayes model assumes that all of the attributes w_i are independent given the category label c_j. Given a new document d, the probability that d belongs to c_i is given by Bayes rule,

$$P(c_i/d) = \frac{p(d/c_i) \cdot p(c_i)}{p(d)} \quad (4.1)$$

According to the class-conditional independence of words, the most possible class for d can be computed as

$$c^*(d) = \mathrm{argmax}_{c_i} \ p(c_i/d) = p(c_i) \prod_{i=1}^{n} p(w_t/c_i)^{n(w_t,d)} \quad (4.2)$$

where $n(w_t,d)$ is the number of occurrences of word w_t in document d, and the quantities $P(w_t/ci)$ are usually maximum likelihood estimates with a Laplace prior:

$$P(w_t/c_i) = \frac{1 + \sum_{d_j \in c_i} n(w_t, d_j)}{n + \sum_{t=1}^{n} \sum_{d_j \in c_i} n(w_t, d_j)} \quad (4.3)$$

The class priors $p(c_i)$ are estimated by the maximum likelihood estimate

$$p(c_i) = \frac{|c_i|}{\sum_j |c_j|} \quad (4.4)$$

4.2 Support Vector Machine

Support Vector Machine (SVM) is a statistical machine learning method, which is based on the principle of Structure Risk Minimization [19]. Considering the linearly separable data space, the training result of SVM is a decision function named optimal separating hyperplane, which separates the positive and negative examples with the largest margin. The examples that are closest to optimal separating hyperplane are termed support vectors. Fig 2 shows the optimal separating hyperplane σ (in blue) and support vectors (the red dot).

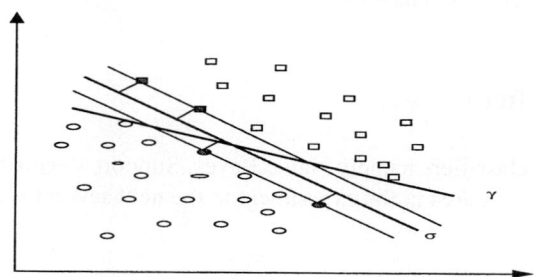

Fig. 2. The optimal separating hyperplane and support vectors

Definitely, let $D=\{y_i, \vec{x}_i\}$ be a train set, where $\vec{x}_i$ is the sample vector and $y_i \in \{+1, -1\}$ is class label, +1 represents the positive sample, while −1 represents the negative sample. Now while in linear separable space, the aim of SVM is to find the $\vec{w}$ and b to assure:

$$\vec{w} \cdot \vec{x}_i - b \geq +1 \quad y_i = +1 \quad (4.5)$$

$$\vec{w} \cdot \vec{x}_i - b \leq -1 \quad y_i = -1 \quad (4.6)$$

In the case of non-linear space, SVM maps the input space to high dimensional space by kernels. [19] has a detailed introduction of SVM.

SVM first introduced by Joachims as a text classifier in [3], and Yang et al. have the comparative study of different classifier in [20]. It showed that SVM is the best text classifier at present, but it is trained very slowly and is a binary classifier. This paper uses a linear SVM text classifier provided by Bow [21].

4.3 Naïve Bayes with Cluster Features

The Naïve Bayes method can be simply translated into using character/word clusters instead of characters/words. The probabilities $p(W_s|c_i)$ are computed similar as $p(w_t|c_i)$ in (4.3) as

$$p(W_s|c_i) = \frac{\sum_{d_j \in c_i} n(W_s, d_j)}{\sum_{s=1}^{m} \sum_{d_j \in c_i} n(W_s, d_j)} \quad (4.7)$$

where $n(W_s, d_j) = \sum_{w_t \in W_s} n(w_t, d_j)$ and m is the number of cluster features.

Now the Naïve Bayes rule(4.1)for classifying a test document d can be rewritten as

$$c^*(d)=\arg\max_{c_i} \log p(c_i)+ \sum_{s=1}^{m} p(W_s|d)\log p(W_s|c_i) \qquad (4.8)$$

where $p(W_s|d)=n(W_s|d)/|d|$. From the definition of formula (4.8), we know that if m is equal to the word vocabulary, then formula (4.8) will decrease to (4.1). Otherwise, if m is equal to 1, then Naïve Bayes classifier will regard the whole word vocabulary as one word cluster. Therefore, we can draw a conclusion that Naïve Bayes with cluster features will get best performance when m has some "mid-values" other than 1 and the number of word capacity.

5 Experimental Results

This section provides empirical evidence of this paper. All the DC related experiment results are based on the simple Naïve Bayes classifier, which is provided by Bow library [21].

5.1 The Data Sets

The corpus used in this paper called CXWAtelenews contains about 2400 Chinese telecommunication articles of China Xinhua Wire Agency, which is mainly drawn from the corpus collected by Fudan University, China. There are 16 topic classes such as economics, politics, military and computer etc. in the corpus. To get the overall recognition of the performance of different methods, we split the corpus into train/test set from 10% to 90% as test set when run different classifiers. The training set and testing set do no overlap and do not contain repeated documents. During word indexing, we use a public word segmentation tool called ICTCLAS (the declared word segmentation precision is 97.58%), and the capacity of result word vocabulary is 50861. We do not use any stoplist and preprocess methods. The capacity of the result character vocabulary is 5163 and also no preprocess is used.

5.2 Evaluation

As a uni-labeled text classification, we used MicroAccuracy [8][9] (equals to precision and recall in uni-labeled case) to measure the performance of classifiers in this article. Let $|C|$ be the number of sample categories, and the number of samples belongs to ith category be C_i. H_{ij} represents the number of samples of ith category, which is classified as jth category, so the accuracy of ith category is defined as

$$Acc(i)=\frac{H_{ii}}{C_i} \qquad (5.1)$$

and the MicroAccuracy is:

$$MA(C)=\frac{\sum_{i=1}^{i=|C|} H_{ii}}{\sum_{i=1}^{i=|C|} C_i} \qquad (5.2)$$

5.3 The Results

The experiment is performed to evaluate the performance of distributional character clustering as a text representation method. Furthermore, we conduct the experiment to show the performance of distributional character clustering as a feature generation method. Additional, we evaluate the hybrid clustering criterion function over internal clustering criterion function proposed in [6].

Table 1. MicroAccuracy of Naïve Bayes with Word, Character and Distributional Character Clustering and SVM. Test Set (0.1-0.9) means that we let the test set be 10%-90% of the whole corpus

Classifers\Test Set	0.1	0.2	0.3	0.4	0.5	0.6	0.7	0.8	0.9
NB(C)	0.842	0.838	0.830	0.825	0.818	0.813	0.802	0.771	0.707
NB(W)	0.771	0.770	0.757	0.745	0.721	0.696	0.665	0.627	0.569
SVM(C)	0.867	0.883	0.875	0.857	0.877	0.842	0.831	0.856	0.799
SVM(W)	0.863	0.881	0.869	0.852	0.855	0.834	0.849	0.807	0.762
NB(C:500)	0.838	0.820	0.805	0.818	0.812	0.790	0.788	0.770	0.714
NB(Hybrid C:500)	0.864	0.837	0.841	0.825	0.823	0.806	0.797	0.772	0.708
NB(IG C:500)	0.815	0.810	0.810	0.796	0.800	0.793	0.784	0.764	0.738

Table 2. MicroAccuracy of IG, internal clustering criterion, hybrid clustering criterion Naïve Bayes Classifier using character feature with 30% test set

The Number of Features	Hybrid Clustering Criterion	Internal Clustering Criterion	IG
5	0.463	0.490	0.225
15	0.744	0.724	0.362
25	0.764	0.771	0.486
50	0.783	0.788	0.564
80	0.799	0.800	0.619
90	0.810	0.799	0.633
100	0.804	0.804	0.627
200	0.811	0.807	0.729
300	0.827	0.827	0.748
400	0.842	0.814	0.772
500	0.841	0.805	0.810
600	0.829	0.822	0.809
700	0.826	0.814	0.823
800	0.829	0.826	0.824
900	0.842	0.831	0.825
1000	0.837	0.816	0.827

5.4 Analysis

From the figures above, we can draw some conclusions as follows:

- **Distributional Character Clustering (DCC) is an effective low dimensionality feature extraction method.** As Table 2 shows, DCC performs much better than IG while in low feature size. With only 15 features, DCC acquires about above 0.70 MA, but the MA of IG is only about 0.36. Hybrid clustering criterion is bet-

ter than IG in all the cases from feature number of 5 to 1000. Furthermore, hybrid distributional character clustering with only 500 features even performs better than character feature with all vocabulary. The experiment results show that DCC is a very robust and efficient dimensionality reduction method, which is also described in [5].
- **Compared with the internal clustering criterion, hybrid clustering criterion has higher performance.** To optimize the clusters set, we use the hybrid clustering criterion, which is better than the internal clustering criterion of [6] from our experiment. Table 1 and Table 2 show that the hybrid clustering criterion has higher performance over internal clustering criterion in most cases.
- **Character is an effective feature representation in Chinese TC without word segmentation, which has low, almost fixed dimensionality and high performance.** Character-based SVM performs higher performance than word-based SVM in most cases, and even it is interesting that character-based NB is much better than word-based NB (Table 1). However, the word segmentation used in this paper is with about 97.58% high precision.

6 Conclusions and Future Work

In this paper, we apply the DC method to Chinese text classification and propose a novel Chinese text representation approach without word segmentation-distributional character clustering to improve the classification performance. Other than the letters in English, characters have more contribution to the topic of documents in Chinese (Most characters have semantic senses). Distributional character clustering does not need the word segmentation and performs state-of-the-art performance in the experiments. It is an efficient dimensionality reduction method to solve VSM sparse problem in Chinese TC, which reduces the feature dimensionality to very low (e.g. 500 features) but with high accuracy. However, the classification is based on the simple Naïve Bayes classifier in our experiments, we will combine the method with Support Vector Machines (SVM) to acquire higher performance. Moreover, we will apply Multiple Cause Mixture Model (MCMM) or use annealing algorithms to acquire the optimized soft cluster features in our future work.

Acknowledgements

We gratefully acknowledge Andrew McCallum for making the Bow software library publicly available. We are also grateful to Chinese Natural Language Processing Platform Group for their Chinese word segmentation tools (ICTCLAS). This research is partly supported by National Basic Research Priorities Programme of China Ministry of Science and Technology under grant number 2002DEA30042.

References

1. Ricardo A. et. al.: Ribeiro-Neto: Modern Information Retrieval. ACM Press / Addison-Wesley, 1999
2. Sebastiani, F.: Machine Learning in Automated Text Categorisation. ACM Computing Surveys, Vol. 34, No. 1, pp. 1-47, March 2002
3. Joachims, T.: Text categorization with support vector machines: learning with many relevant features. ECML-98, pp.137-142
4. Pereira, F. et. al.: Distributional clustering of English words. ACL-93, pp. 183-190
5. Baker, L., McCallum, A.: Distributional Clustering of Words for Text Classification. SIGIR-98, pp. 96-103
6. Dhillon, I. et.al.: Enhance word clustering for hierarchical text classification. SIGKDD-02, pp.23-26
7. Slonim, N. et. al.: Unsupervised Document Classification using Sequential Information Maximization. SIGIR-02, pp. 11-15
8. Bekkerman, R. et.al.: Distributional Word Clusters vs. Words for Text Categorization. JMLR, 1 (2002) 1-48
9. Tsay, J. and Wang, J.: Design and Evaluation of Approaches to Automatic Chinese Text Categorization. JCLCLP, Vol. 5, No. 2, August 2000, pp. 43-58
10. Yiming Yang and Jan O. Pederson: A Comparative Study on Feature Selection in Text Categorization. ICML-97, pp. 412-420
11. He, J. et. al.: On Machine Learning Methods for Chinese Document Categorization. Applied Intelligence, 3,18, 311-322,2003
12. Tan, A.-H. and Yu, P.: A Comparative Study on Chinese Text Categorization Methods, PRICAI-00, pp. 24-35
13. Wong, C. K. P. et. al.: Text Categorization using Hybrid (Mined) Terms, Proceedings of IRAL-00, pp. 217-218
14. Peng, F.C. et.al.: Text Classification in Asian Languages without Word Segmentation. IRAL-03.
15. Peng, F.C., Schuurmans D. and Wang S.J.: Augmenting Naive Bayes Classifiers with Statistical Language Models. JIR, 7, 317–345, 2004.
16. Cao, S, Zeng, F and Cao, H.: The System for Automatic Text Categorization based on Character Vector, Journal of Shanxi University (China), 22(2), 144-149.1999
17. Zhou X.Z., Fang Q., Wu Z.: A Comparative Study on Text Representation and Classifiers in Chinese Text Categorization. ICCPOL-03, pp. 454-461
18. Lewis, D.: An evaluation of phrasal and clustered representations on a text categorization task. SIGIR-92, pp. 37 – 50.
19. Vapnik, V.: The Nature of Statistical Learning Theory, Springer, New York. 1995.
20. Yiming Yang and Xin Liu: A re-examination of text categorization methods. SIGIR-99, pp.: 42-49
21. McCallum A.K.: Bow: A toolkit for statistical language modeling, text retrieval, classification and clustering. http://www-2.cs.cmu.edu/~mccallum/bow, 1996.

Approximately Repetitive Structure Detection for Wrapper Induction

Xiaoying Gao, Peter Andreae, and Richard Collins

School of Mathematical and Computing Sciences
Victoria University of Wellington
Wellington, New Zealand
{Xiaoying.Gao,Peter.Andreae,Richard.Collins}@mcs.vuw.ac.nz

Abstract. In recent years, much work has been invested into automatically learning wrappers for information extraction from HTML tables and lists. Our research has focused on a system that can learn a wrapper from a single unlabelled page. An essential step is to locate the tabular data within the page. This is not trivial when the structures of data tuples are similar but not identical. In this paper we describe an algorithm that can automatically detect approximate repetitive structures within one sequence. The algorithm does not rely on any domain knowledge or HTML heuristics and it can be used in detecting repetitive patterns and hence to learn wrappers from a single unlabeled tabular page.

1 Introduction

The amount of information on the Web is continuing to grow rapidly and there is an urgent need to create information extraction systems that can turn some of the online information from "human-readable only" to "machine readable". Information extraction systems that extract data tuples from particular information sources are often called wrappers. Building wrappers by hand is problematic because the number of wrappers needed is huge and the format of many sources is frequently updated. One solution is to be found in wrapper induction systems that learn wrappers from example Web pages.

A lot of wrapper induction systems have been constructed [1-4], especially for information extraction from HTML tables and lists; this research differs from most other systems in that our system aims to learn from a single unlabeled tabular page, and the page does not have to contain HTML tables or lists nor be generated by a program using predefined templates.

Some researchers have developed systems that learn wrappers from unlabelled Web pages [5-7], but these systems all require at least two training pages. Also, these systems are based on the assumption that the pages are generated by programs using predefined templates. There are many cases in which there is only one page available and the page is manually crafted so that the data formats are not regular and are often updated. Our research focuses on learning a wrapper from one single page, where the page contains a set of tuples of data items presented in a format that a human reader would perceive as a regular structure, even if the underlying HTML is not completely regular.

This paper focuses on the task of automatically detecting a region of approximately repetitive tabular data on a single page and identifying the sequence of "approximate repeat units" (ARUs) in that region that contain the data tuples. Extracting the data tuples from the ARUs is a separate process that is described in another paper [8].

The algorithm we describe is domain independent and does not rely on any HTML heuristics. So it does not require the tabular data to be presented in HTML tables or lists. Even in a page with tables or lists, the ARUs do not necessarily correspond to table rows or list items. For example, a page containing data tuples with five fields might present each tuple as two adjacent table rows with two fields in the first row and three fields in the second row. In this case, each ARU consists of two rows of the HTML table.

In this paper, we first formalise our problem, and then introduce our algorithm that automatically detects approximate repetition within one sequence. We then present our experimental results on using this algorithm in wrapper induction, and finally conclude and discuss future work.

2 Formalisation of the Problem

A web page can be represented by a string of tokens $t_1, t_2, \ldots t_n$, where each token represents a sequence of characters on the page. The tokens must be abstractions of the character strings so that tokens can be matched to determine their similarity. We currently use a different token type for each type of HTML tag, and two tokens types for text — one for numbers and the other for all other text. For a more sophisticated tokeniser, the tokens would not be atomic, and there would be a multivalued scale of similarity of tokens. However, for the sake of clarity of exposition of the algorithm, we will use single letters to represent tokens for most of the paper, and will ignore partial similarities of tokens. We assume that the page contains at least one region of semi-structured data so that a set of data tuples are presented on the page, and that the tokens in the region contain either values of the data tuples or formatting/presentation information.

The problem addressed in this paper is to find a region of the page ($t_k, \ldots t_m$) that can be partitioned into two or more subsequences of tokens $ARU_1, ARU_2, \ldots, ARU_r$ where the ARU_i are all similar to each other. The measure of similarity should be such that ARUs corresponding to the data tuples on a page will be considered similar. Part of the problem is to define a syntactic definition of similarity that accommodates the kinds of errors and irregularities on real pages, but still captures the repetitive structure. For example, if a page is represented in a token string "XYABCDEABDEAPCDEXYET", the system should identify the sequence of three ARUs: "ABCDE", "AB-DE", "APCDE". Note that the second ARU has a missing token ("C" is missing) and the third ARU has a mismatching token ("P" instead of "B"). Alternatively, we could describe the first and third ARU as having an additional token "C".

If a page has nested approximately repetitive structures, our task is to detect the exterior repetitive structure. The interior repetitive structure could then be found by reusing this algorithm on one of the ARUs. If a page has multiple approximately repetitive structures, our algorithm should be able to find all of them.

3 The Approximate Repeat Units Detection Algorithm

The ARUs detection algorithm is based on the observation that if a sequence of tokens contains a region consisting of m repeat units and the sequence is matched against itself, offset by the length of k repeat units, then the first $m-k$ repeat units will match against the last $m-k$ repeat units. Therefore, if we match a token sequence against itself at all possible offsets to find matching subsequences, we should be able to identify any repetitive regions and also the length of the repeat units. If the repeat units are identical, such matching is easy. If the repeat units are only approximately the same, with some mismatched, missing or additional tokens, then a more complicated matching, such as the Smith-Waterman algorithm [9], is required to find a good approximate match.

The limitation of the Smith-Waterman algorithm is that it will only find the best matching subsequence of two sequences, whereas we need to find *all* good matching subsequences within a single sequence. Our algorithm uses a dynamic programming algorithm, similar to Smith-Waterman, to construct a matrix representing all the matching subsequences, and then analyses the matrix to identify the approximately repetitive regions and the approximate repeat units.

3.1 Step1: Building the Matrix

Given a sequence of n tokens, $t_1, t_2, \ldots t_n$, the first step of the algorithm constructs an $n \times n$ matrix H of scores, where H_{ij} is the similarity score of the highest scoring pair of subsequences ending at the tokens t_i and t_j respectively. The score $H_{ij} = 0$ if there are no approximately similar subsequences ending at t_i and t_j. The similarity score of two subsequences is the sum of the token similarities of paired tokens minus any penalties for additional tokens in one subsequence that are not paired with tokens in the other subsequence.

Since the sequence is being matched against itself, $H_{ij} = H_{ji}$, and therefore the algorithm only needs to compute the upper right triangle of the matrix. Also, we are not interested in the trivial match of the whole sequence against itself exactly, so we set $H_{ii} = 0$. The algorithm builds the matrix from the top-left corner: for each cell it finds the best way to extend a pair of subsequences to include the new tokens. We can extend pairs of subsequences to include the tokens t_i and t_j in three different ways:

- We can extend a pair of subsequences ending at t_{i-1} and t_{j-1} by one token each, to include t_i paired with t_j.
- We can extend a pair of subsequences ending at t_{i-k} and t_j by including $t_{i-k+1}, t_{i-k+2}, \ldots, t_i$ as additional tokens in the first subsequence, not paired with any tokens in the second subsequence.

– We can extend a pair of subsequences ending at t_i and t_{j-k} by including $t_{j-k+1}, t_{j-k+2}, \ldots, t_j$ as additional tokens in the second subsequence, not paired with any tokens in the first subsequence.

The algorithm chooses whichever extension results in the best score for the new pair of subsequences.

The algorithm records which extension had the best score by storing a backpointer from (i, j) to the cell that it was extended from. The backpointers are stored in a matrix BP. Figure 1 shows the matrix H constructed for a short sequence of 11 tokens: "XABCDEABDEY". Note that the subsequence $t_2 \ldots t_6$ ("ABCDE") matches the subsequence $t_7 \ldots t_{10}$ ("ABDE"), with just one additional token. Each cell contains a score, which is greater than 0 if the two subsequences have an adequate similarity. The matrix BP is overlaid so that cells calculated by extending the subsequences of a previous cell have backpointers to previous cell. The path of backpointers from a cell shows the matching subsequences ending at that cell. The cells with bold scores represent the locally best matching subsequence. Note that the additional token (t_4) in the first subsequence appears in the path as a vertical backpointer.

		0	1	2	3	4	5	6	7	8	9	10	11
0			X	A	B	C	D	E	A	B	D	E	Y
1	X	0	0	0	0	0	0	0	0	0	0	0	0
2	A			0	0	0	0	0	1	0	0	0	0
3	B				0	0	0	0	0	**2**	0.7	0.3	0
4	C					0	0	0	0	0.7	1.7	0.3	0
5	D						0	0	0	0.3	**1.7**	1.3	0
6	E							0	0	0	0.3	**2.7**	1.3
7	A								0	0	0	1.3	2.3
8	B									0	0	1.0	1.0
9	D										0	0	0
10	E											0	0
11	Y												0

Fig. 1. Similarity Score Matrix H.

The similarity score of tokens t_i and t_j is given by $S_{i,j} = 1$ if t_i and t_j match, and $S_{i,j} = -\frac{1}{3}$ if they do not match. The penalty for a string of k additional tokens is $1 + \frac{k}{3}$. We place a limit, r, on the number of consecutive mismatching and additional tokens, so that $H_{ij} = 0$ if $S_{i-k, j-l} < 0$ for all $1 \leq k, l \leq r$.

The algorithm is given in Figure 2.

Initialise H:
$\quad H_{i0} = H_{0i} = 0$ for $0 \leq i \leq n$
$\quad H_{ij} = 0 \qquad$ for $1 \leq j \leq i \leq n$
For $1 \leq i \leq j \leq n$
$\quad$ If $S_{i-k,j-l} < 0$ for all $1 \leq k, l \leq r$
$\qquad H_{i,j} = 0, BP_{ij} = $ null
$\quad$ Else
$\qquad$ Compute max of
$\qquad\quad S_0 = 0$
$\qquad\quad S_1 = H_{i-1,j-1} + S_{i,j}$
$\qquad\quad S_2 = \max_{1 \leq k < i} \left(H_{i-k,j} - (1 + \frac{k}{3})\right)$
$\qquad\quad S_3 = \max_{1 \leq k < j} \left(H_{i,j-k} - (1 + \frac{k}{3})\right)$
$\qquad$ Set $H_{ij} = $ maximum score.
$\qquad$ If maximum score was S_0: $BP_{ij} = $ null
$\qquad$ Else set BP_{ij} to the cell from which the best score was extended.

Fig. 2. Algorithm to calculate the matrix H.

3.2 Step 2: Finding Best Paths

Our algorithm finds the approximate repeat units by analysing the paths defined by the backpointer matrix, BP, and the corresponding scores in the matrix H. The paths in BP represent pairs of matched subsequences. The set of paths always forms a forest of trees, since nearby paths merge and share a common root. For example, figure 1 contains just a single tree of paths, with all the paths ending at the cell $(2,7)$. matched subsequences.

We are only interested in the "best path" in each tree, representing the best matching pair of subsequences beginning at the root. The best path in a tree is the path from the root to the cell in the tree with the highest score in the matrix H. The best path collection is built by tracing paths back from every non-null cell in BP. The best path for each root is defined to start from the closest cell to the root with a score greater than or equal to 1, and to end at the cell with the best score.

For the token sequence in Figure 1, there is just one root, and the best path starts at $(2,7)$ and ends at $(6,10)$ corresponding to the pair of subsequences "ABCDE" and "ABDE". There is only one root because there is only one repetitive region, and the region contains only two approximate repeat units, so that there is only one offset of the sequence (an offset of 5 tokens) that generates a good match. Figure 3 shows a bigger example using the token string "XYABCED-ABDEAPCDETXYET", which contains a region with three ARU's, and some small regions with minor repetition. All the best paths are shown in Table 1. The region with three ARUs generates two best paths, one with an offset of 5 (matching the first two ARUs against the last two ARUs) and one with an offset of 9, (matching the first ARU against the last ARU).

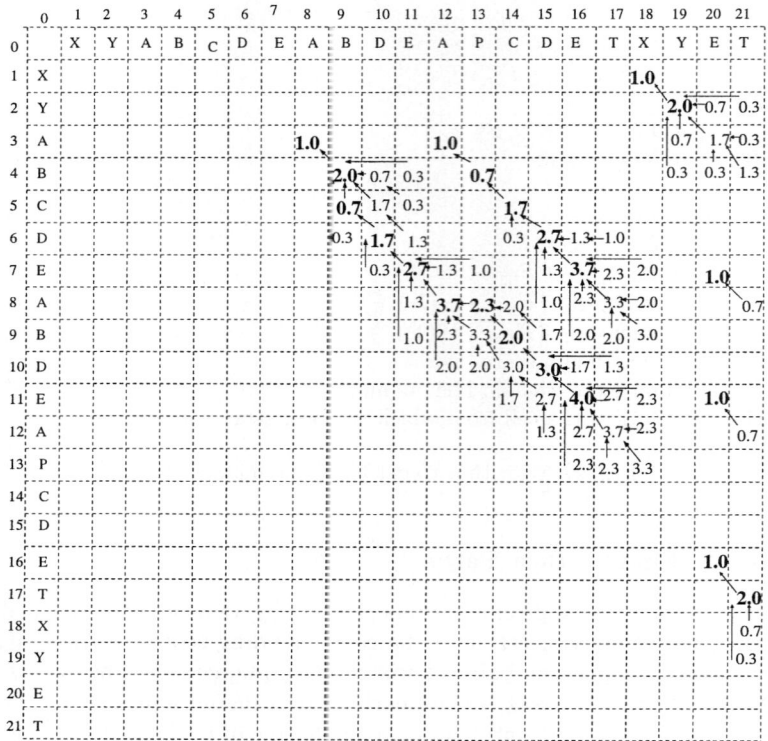

Fig. 3. Example with larger repetitive region.

3.3 Step 3: Identifying Repetitive Regions and ARUs

A repetitive region with k ARUs will typically give rise to $k-1$ best paths, each one representing a match of the first m ARUs with the last m ARUs. The offsets of the paths correspond approximately to multiples of the length of the ARUs. The paths will also typically begin at the beginning of the first ARU and end at the end of the last ARU. Our algorithm exploits this structure to identify repetitive regions and the ARUs.

The algorithm attempts to group the best paths according to the following criteria:

- Paths starting at cells in approximately the same row, and
- Paths ending at cells in approximately the same column, and
- Paths with offsets (the difference between the row and column of the starting cell) that are approximately multiples of the smallest offset in the group.

We consider a number to be approximately equal to another if their difference is at most r - the maximum number of consecutive mismatches or additional tokens. Paths that are not grouped with any other paths are discarded. In the

Table 1. Best paths in the example shown in Figure 3.

No	Best paths	offset	Score	Subsequences
1	(3, 8) to (11, 16)	5	4	ABCDEAB-DE : AB-DEAPCDE
2	(3, 12) to (7, 16)	9	3.7	ABCDE : APCDE
3	(1, 18) to (2, 19)	17	2	XY : XY
4	(7, 20) to (7, 20)	13	1	E : E
5	(11, 20) to (11, 20)	9	1	E : E
6	(16, 20) to (17, 21)	4	2	ET : ET

example in Figure 3, the first two paths are grouped together and the other four are discarded.

From each group of paths, the algorithm constructs the description of a repetitive region and its ARUs:

- If the lowest row of the starting cells of the paths in the group is min, then the repetitive region starts at token t_{min}.
- If the highest column of the ending cells of the paths in the group is max, then the repetitive region ends at token t_{max}.
- Each column of a starting cell of a path in the group is the beginning of an ARU.

In the example in Figure 3, the repetitive region consists of tokens $t_3 \ldots t_{16}$ and the ARUs consist of tokens $t_3 \ldots t_7$ ("ABCDE"), $t_8 \ldots t_{11}$ ("ABDE"), and $t_12 \ldots t_{16}$ ("APCDE").

4 AutoWrapper and Experimental Results

AutoWrapper[8] is a system we built that learns a wrapper from a single, unlabeled, tabular Web page. The earlier version[8] used handcrafted heuristics to identify candidate rows of the table. We have now extended AutoWrapper to use the ARU detection algorithm described above to find the tabular region and the approximate repeat units; Autowrapper then uses these as the candidate rows to build a wrapper.

We tested AutoWrapper on two sets of data and the experimental results are shown in Tables 2 and 3. The first set of data shown in Table 2 was downloaded from RISE (Repository of Online Information Sources Used in Information Extraction Tasks) at http://www.isi.edu/info-agents/RISE. Experimental results for the five Web sites are known in the literature [10, 3, 5] and Table 2 shows a comparison of AutoWrapper with the three other systems — Wien [10], Stalker [3] and RoadRunner [5]. The second set of data used in Table 3 were downloaded from the VUW (Victoria University of Wellington) web site at http://www.mcs.vuw.ac.nz. The pages are semi-structured, but there is only one page of each kind, so that automatic extraction from one single page is essential.

It can be seen from Table 2 that AutoWrapper gets better results than Wien since AutoWrapper works well for data with optional or missing items while

Table 2. Comparative results.

No.	Site	Source and URL	Wien	Stalker	RoadRunner	AutoWrapper
1	OKRA	RISE	√	√	√	√
2	BigBook	RISE, bigbook.com	√	√	√	√
3	La Weekly	RISE, laweekly.com	×	√	√	√ not perfect
4	Address Finder	RISE, iaf.net	×	√	×	×
5	Quote Server	RISE	×	√	– no info	√

Table 3. Results on pages from http://www.mcs.vuw.ac.nz.

No.	Site	Source and URL	Results
6	Graduate course	VUW, /courses/grad-courses.shtml	√
7	People, Staff page	VUW, /people/	×
8	Publications	VUW, /comp/Publications/index-byname.html	√ not perfect
9	Seminars	VUW, /events/seminars/upcoming-seminars.html	√
10	SE research group	VUW, /research/se-vuw/about.shtml	√

Wien cannot; Stalker achieves better results than AutoWrapper, but Stalker requires labeled examples (as does Wien); AutoWrapper achieves results comparable to RoadRunner, but RoadRunner requires at least two pages, whereas AutoWrapper only needs one page.

Our system achieves about 70% success rate in both sets of data, considering Nos.3 and 8 as partial success. The experiments demonstrate that our system works on tabular pages with mismatch and additional tokens (Nos. 3, 5, 6, 10), data tuples presented in multiple rows (No. 1), non-table-list sites (Nos. 3, 10), and manually crafted sites (No. 10). For all web sites, AutoWrapper only requires a single unlabeled Web page. The algorithm is domain independent and does not rely on any HTML heuristics, and it works on semi-structured pages in different domains.

AutoWrapper failed on No. 4 and No. 7 due to the diversity of their data formats. The data tuples in No. 4 can have three to seven fields and the fields can come in a different order. No. 7 has a special format with six tables (as group names) and six lists (staff in each group), where each table is followed by a list and the length of the list varies from 1 to 20. AutoWrapper can detect the repetitive structure in Nos.3 and 8, but can not extract all the information. No. 3 has a list of credit cards presented as plain text at the end of a text paragraph and our tokeniser can not distinguish the list from the rest of the text. No. 8 presents the author as the title and publications as a list, where our system can extract the publications but the author is ignored as optional tokens.

5 Related Work

Most wrapper induction systems require labeled training examples [1,3,11]. There are three systems [5–7] that learn wrappers from unlabeled pages. Road-Runner [5] automatically generates wrappers by comparing HTML pages and analysing their similarities and differences, and it works well on tables and lists generated based on predefined templates. It outperforms other wrapper induction systems in that it can handle nested lists. Another system [6] uses AutoClass for automatic classification of data and uses grammar induction of regular languages for wrapper induction. It induces the structure of lists by exploiting the regularities both in the format of the pages and the data contained in them, while most other systems only consider formats and treat one text string as one single field. This system can therefore extract multiple data fields from one text string and it works on text-rich tables or lists. Another approach that also use grammatical inference for wrapper learning is [7]. All three systems require at least two pages for training the system, while our system requires a single page.

The problem of finding patterns in strings is also studied in the field of molecular biology. A lot of approaches are devoted to the discovery of patterns in biosequences. Our ways of calculating $H_{i,j}$ are similar to the Smith-Waterman algorithm [9], first published in a biology journal in 1970s. It can find the two subsequences of characters with the maximum similarity from two string sequences. Our algorithm finds patterns within one sequence and it needs one input instead of two. We also introduce a limit on the number of consecutive mismatching and additional tokens.

6 Conclusion and Future Work

We sucessfully built a wrapper induction system that can learn wrappers from one single unlabeled tabular training page. Our system is based on an algorithm that automatically detects approximate repeats within one sequence. The algorithm is domain independent and does not rely on any HTML heuristics. Our system AutoWrapper was tested on two data sets and achived about 70% success rate. The experiments show that our system works well on data with mismatching and additional tokens, on manaully crafted pages that are not program generated as well as on tabular pages that are not HTML tables or lists.

One limitation we have noticed is that the tokens in a page are not equally important. We are exploring ways to improve the algorithm by introducing weights to tokens and introducing partial similarity for token comparison. In the future, we will also explore other application areas of this algorithm, particularly how it can improve the performance of our information extraction agents [12].

References

1. N. Kushmerick, D. S. Weld, and R. Doorenbos. Wrapper induction for information extraction. In *IJCAI-97*, pages 729–735, Nagoya, Japan, 1997.
2. D. Freitag. Information extration from html: Application of a general machine learning approach. In *AAAI-98*, 1998.
3. I. Muslea, S. Minton, and C. Knoblock. A hierarchical approach to wrapper induction. In *The 3rd conference on Autonomous Agents(Agent'99)*, 1999.

4. S. Soderland. Learning to extract text-based information from the world wide web. In *Proceedings of Third International Conference on Knowledge Discovery and Data Mining (KDD-97)*, 1997.
5. Valter Crescenzi, Giansalvatore Mecca, and Paolo Merialdo. Roadrunner: Towards automatic data extraction from large web sites. In *Proceedings of 27th International Conference on Very Large Data Bases*, pages 109–118, 2001.
6. Kristina Lerman, Craig Knoblock, and Steven Minton. Automatic data extraction from lists and tables in web sources. In *Automatic Text Extraction and Mining workshop (ATEM-01), IJCAI-01, Seattle, WA*, 2001.
7. Theodore W. Hong and Keith L. Clark. Using grammatical inference to automate information extraction from the Web. *Lecture Notes in Computer Science*, 2168:216–223, 2001.
8. Xiaoying Gao, Mengjie Zhang, and Peter Andreae. Learning information extraction patterns from tabular web pages without manual labelling. In *IEEE/WIC International Conference on Web Intelligence (WI'03) October 13 - 17, 2003 Halifax, Canada*, pages 495–498, 2003.
9. T. F. Smith and M. S. Waterman. Identification of common molecular subsequences. *J. of Mol. Biol.*, 147:195–197, 1981.
10. N. Kushmerick. *Wrapper Induction for Information Extraction*. PhD thesis, Department of Computer Science and Engineering, University of Washington, 1997.
11. William Cohen, Matthew Hurst, and Lee S. Jensen. A flexible learning system for wrapping tables and lists in html documents. In *In The Eleventh International World Wide Web Conference WWW-2002*, 2002.
12. X. Gao and L. Sterling. Knowledge-based information agents. In J. G. Carbonell and J. Siekmann, editors, *Lecture Notes in Artificial Intelligence*, pages 229–238. Springer, 2001.

Model Theory for PRS-Like Agents: Modelling Belief Update and Action Attempts

Wayne Wobcke

School of Computer Science and Engineering
University of New South Wales
Sydney NSW 2052, Australia
wobcke@cse.unsw.edu.au

Abstract. In this paper, we extend our earlier work on modelling the mental states of PRS-like agents by considering the dynamics of belief and modelling of action attempts. The major constraint on our theory is that belief update is modelled within the theory of action as part of the logic ADL, a logic of belief, desire and intention that incorporates propositional dynamic logic. Some logical properties of belief update and attempts are given. The account provides a more complete modelling of both the statics and dynamics of agent programs based on the PRS-like architecture, and thus is a suitable foundation for developing model checking algorithms for this class of agents.

1 Introduction

In previous work, we developed a modelling of the mental states of a class of BDI agents based on a new logic called Agent Dynamic Logic (ADL) that combines elements from Emerson and Clarke's Computation Tree Logic [3], Pratt's Propositional Dynamic Logic [6] and Rao and Georgeff's BDI Logic [7]. The motivation of that work was to develop a logical framework that is closely aligned to the operational behaviour of a range of BDI agent architectures – those based on the PRS system – which we called *PRS-like* architectures. We take the PRS-like family to include PRS itself, Georgeff and Lansky [4], as well as derivative architectures such as UM-PRS, C-PRS, AgentSpeak(L), JACK Intelligent Agents™ and JAM.

The formalism in that paper was explicitly limited to modelling an agent's mental state at single points in time, and did not address the issue of the relationships between an agent's mental states at different time points, i.e. the *dynamics* of mental states. Subtly, even though the formalism is based on temporal logic and thus includes aspects of the past and future, especially in that an intention is characterized as some action the agent believes it will eventually successfully perform, this is not enough to capture the commitment through time to those intentions as the future unfolds, and as it becomes necessary to update beliefs and make choices to commit to particular intentions.

The main objective of this paper is to extend our earlier modelling to incorporate belief update in a purely semantical way. This is done by further restricting the class of PRS interpretations to those in which belief update conforms to the standard operational definition used in the PRS-like architecture. The major technical constraint that we adhere to in this paper is that the belief update of an agent must be modelled as a by-product of action performance within possible worlds models that correspond to execution structures of the agent. This enables belief update to be formalized within Agent Dynamic Logic as part of the semantics of actions; this in turn being possible only because of the restricted belief update functions used by PRS-like systems.

The issues involved in developing a purely semantical account of PRS-like agents turn out to be quite complex, and relate to other fundamental issues such as the notion of "possibility" underlying possible worlds models as used in BDI logic, Bratman's two faces of intention (future and present directed) [1] and his idea of acting with an intention (doing one thing in order to achieve some intended effect), the treatment of action success and failure in BDI models, the modelling of attempted actions (the agent intends an action but can plan only to attempt the action) and the relation between intention and control (the agent should attempt only actions somehow under its direct control). Of course, these issues are themselves interrelated. Accordingly, we begin the paper with a summary of how these issues relate to the semantics of PRS-like architectures, then proceed to the technical definitions of Agent Dynamic Logic.

2 Motivation

One key aspect of the present approach to modelling PRS-like agents is to characterize beliefs, desires and intentions using the dynamic logic of action, where the semantics of an agent program is defined purely in terms of its execution structures. This is in line with work in Computer Science where the semantics of programs is given in terms of state transition relations, enabling model checking algorithms that construct such execution structures to be used for verifying properties of programs. However, the semantics of BDI agent programs is often given in terms of possible worlds models, e.g. Cohen and Levesque [2], Rao and Georgeff [7], Wooldridge [10], where the connection (if any) of the possible worlds models to execution structures is at best indirect.

A core issue to be resolved is what "possible" means in such models – far from being a peripheral question, this turns out to be central to the correct modelling of belief update functions using execution structures. In our framework, basic *execution structures* are analogous to computation trees where the transitions between states are all generated by transition relations defining the semantics of actions; the beliefs of an agent are modelled as a set of "epistemic alternatives". The natural way to model belief update is to derive a set (or sets) of epistemic alternatives for the belief state(s) after the agent executes an action from the initial set of epistemic alternatives and the semantics of the action performed. Putting these ideas together gives a significant restriction: the execution structures of the epistemic alternatives of the agent must all be somehow realizable (generable from transition relations). The agent is not free to imagine (believe possible) execution structures that are not realizable.

A simple example illustrates the nature of this restriction. Suppose the agent has a plan for starting a car that consists of the action of turning the key in the ignition. The semantics of "turning the key" is that when the battery is charged, the car starts, and when the battery is dead, the car does not start. If the agent does not have any belief about the battery, its belief state is characterized by two epistemic alternatives. Suppose the battery is in fact dead and the agent turns the key. In that alternative where the battery is dead (the "actual world"), the car doesn't start and in the resulting state the battery is still dead. However, in the other *epistemic* alternative (where the battery is charged), executing the action does *not* result in a state in which the car starts, because whether the car starts is determined by which world is the actual world (which world the agent is "in"), not by what the agent believes (even more, the agent may observe that the car doesn't start, and may come to believe the battery is dead because of this). This scenario is different from that where there is an alternative actual world in which the battery is actually charged, where the car starts in both epistemic alternatives of the agent, assuming successful key turning, etc.

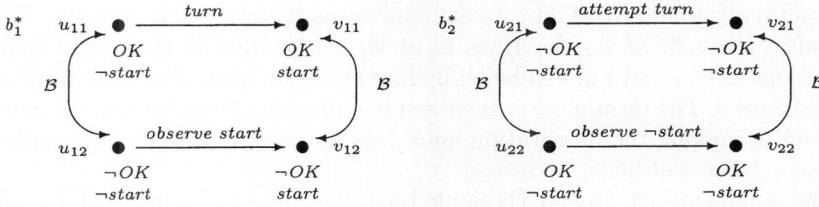

Fig. 1. Execution structures for differing actual worlds b_1^* and b_2^*

The scenarios are as illustrated in Figure 1. There are two execution structures, differing according to which world corresponds to the "actual world", denoted b_1^* and b_2^* in the figure. The transitions corresponding to turning the key in the actual worlds are assumed to be as described above; the transitions in the epistemic alternatives correspond to updates based on observations made of the actual world, e.g. the transition from u_{12} to v_{12} is a transition allowed by the action *observe start*, assuming here successful execution of the action and that the agent observes (only) whether the car starts. The sets of resulting states $\{v_{11}, v_{12}\}$ and $\{v_{21}, v_{22}\}$ characterize the updated belief states of the agent after executing the action in the respective actual worlds (b_1^* and b_2^*). In our semantics, there are thus two grades of "epistemic alternatives" – that arising from the agent's ignorance of which world it is inhabiting (which we call alternative actual worlds), and within some actual world, ignorance of what the state is in that world (which we call epistemic alternatives).

Belief update is modelled as defined in the standard operational definitions of PRS-like agent architectures. However, we make some simplifying assumptions about what the agent observes at any given point in time. First, we assume that the agent's observations are veridical (the agent only observes what is true). This simplifies the way that the set of states modelling the agent's beliefs after performing an action are related to the states resulting from the transition relation modelling the action performed (specifically, when the initial state in the actual world is one of the agent's epistemic alternatives and the agent observes all relevant changes, the resulting state after action execution is also one of the agent's epistemic alternatives). Second, we assume the agent observes whether the postcondition of the intended action holds in the resulting state. Together with the first assumption, it follows that the agent knows (after the event) whether the actions it attempts are successful, and that this is reflected in its beliefs.

3 Agent Dynamic Logic

In this section, we summarize our extended approach to defining the semantics of PRS-like agents' mental state dynamics; the initial theory without reference to dynamics was given in Wobcke [9]. The framework is based on a new logic called Agent Dynamic Logic (ADL) that combines aspects of Computation Tree Logic (CTL), Propositional Dynamic Logic (PDL) and the BDI Logic of Rao and Georgeff (called here BDI-CTL). In combining modal and dynamic logics, ADL is related to the logic of van der Hoek *et al.* [8], and similar to their approach, we use actions *observe p* to model belief update resulting from observations of basic propositions p. The term *observe* is chosen to emphasize that the agent is actively involved in making the observation, and does not simply receive information in a passive process of belief update.

The language ADL (Agent Dynamic Logic) is based on both BDI-CTL, which extends CTL with modal operators for modelling beliefs, desires (goals) and intentions, and PDL, which includes modal operators corresponding to program terms. Our definitions of BDI-CTL are modifications of Rao and Georgeff's in that, though there are three modal operators, B (belief), G (goal) and I (intention) in the language, the operators G and I are defined in terms of other primitives. We assume there is a base propositional language $\mathcal{L}$ for expressing time-independent properties of states. The language of ADL includes the formulae of BDI-CTL (which includes the CTL state formulae) plus formulae built using the PDL constructs, as defined more precisely below. We assume knowledge of the basic CTL definitions.

Definition 1. *A BDI interpretation is a tuple $\langle \mathcal{T}, \prec, \mathcal{S}, \mathcal{W}, \mathcal{A}, \mathcal{B}, \mathcal{I} \rangle$ where $\langle \mathcal{T}, \prec \rangle$ is a time tree, $\mathcal{S}$ is a nonempty set of states, $\mathcal{W}$ is a nonempty set of worlds based on $\mathcal{S}$ with each world over a subtree of $\langle \mathcal{T}, \prec \rangle$, $\mathcal{A}$ and $\mathcal{B}$ are subsets of $\mathcal{W} \times \mathcal{T} \times \mathcal{W} \times \mathcal{T}$ defined only for tuples (w, t, w', t') for which t (t') is a time point in w (w') and w_t and $w'_{t'}$ share a common history (defined formally below), and $\mathcal{I}$ is a function $\mathcal{W} \times \mathcal{T} \to \mathcal{W}$ mapping each time point t in a world w to a subworld of w containing t.*

Definition 2. *A subworld of a world w over a time tree $\langle \mathcal{T}, \prec \rangle$ based on a set of states $\mathcal{S}$ is the world w restricted to a subtree of $\langle \mathcal{T}, \prec \rangle$ whose root is the root of w.*

As mentioned above, the agent needs to keep track of two senses of epistemic alternative: alternative actualities and alternative epistemic states with respect to one actual world. The relation $\mathcal{A}$ is for alternative actual worlds, while the relation $\mathcal{B}$ captures ignorance of an agent with respect to one actual world. More formally, the beliefs of the agent in some situation w_t (at a time point t in a world w) are precisely those propositions holding at all epistemic alternatives w' of w at t', i.e. in those situations $w'_{t'}$ such that $\mathcal{B}(w, t, w', t')$. The relation $\mathcal{A}$ is used as part of the definition of intentions; no matter how the world is actually, the agent believes it will eventually perform the intended action on all possible futures. Both relations $\mathcal{A}$ and $\mathcal{B}$ on situations are assumed to be serial, transitive and Euclidean, and in addition $\mathcal{A}$ is assumed to be reflexive. Also as noted above, w_t and $w'_{t'}$ are required to share a common history (defined formally below, but intuitively the sequence of prior states and the agent's beliefs at those states must be identical). As consequences, (i) the agent always "knows the time" in that the epistemic alternatives of a situation are always at corresponding time points in the execution structures, and (ii) w_t may have as an alternative another situation in w (though only one at a corresponding time point – the time at a situation can be counted as the number of situations in its history). Finally, the relations $\mathcal{B}$ and $\mathcal{I}$ are assumed to satisfy the condition that $\mathcal{B}(w, t, w', t')$ iff $\mathcal{B}(\mathcal{I}(w, t), t, \mathcal{I}(w', t'), t')$, i.e. the epistemic alternatives of $\mathcal{I}(w, t)$ at t are the intended subworlds of the epistemic alternatives of w at t.

Definition 3. *Let $\langle \mathcal{T}, \prec, \mathcal{S}, \mathcal{W}, \mathcal{A}, \mathcal{B}, \mathcal{I} \rangle$ be a BDI interpretation. Then a world $w \in \mathcal{W}$ satisfies a BDI-CTL formula at a time point t in w as follows.*

$$w \models_t \mathsf{B}\alpha \quad \text{if } w' \models_{t'} \alpha \text{ whenever } \mathcal{B}(w, t, w', t')$$
$$w \models_t \mathsf{I}\pi \quad \text{if } \mathcal{I}(w', t') \models_{t'} \mathsf{A}\Diamond do(\pi) \text{ whenever } \mathcal{A}(w, t, w', t')$$
$$w \models_t \mathsf{G}\gamma \quad \text{if } w \models_t \mathsf{I}(achieve\ \gamma)$$

We impose two additional constraints: (i) $w \models_t do(attempt\ \pi)$ iff $\mathcal{I}(w, t) \models_t do(\pi)$, and (ii) if $\mathcal{B}(w, t, w', t')$ then when $w \models_t do(attempt\ \pi)$, for any path p containing t, $\mathcal{B}(w, s_p(t), w', s_{p'}(t'))$ for any path p' containing a successor t' of t for which $(w'_{t'}, w'_{s_{p'}(t')}) \in R_{observe\ \alpha}$, and $\mathcal{B}(w, s_p(t), w, s_{p'}(t'))$ for any path p' containing a successor t' of t in w which satisfies α, for some α. The first constraint means that the agent's intended futures are exactly those where the actions attempted by the agent are successfully performed, and that the agent's attempts are based solely on its mental state, not on the state of the world. The second constraint means that the epistemic alternatives of the agent after performing an action are a partition of those derived from the set of prior epistemic alternatives using the semantics of action execution and belief update, as observations vary. The part of the definition relating to epistemic alternatives in the actual world is used to capture ignorance arising from a failure to distinguish the outcomes of a nondeterministic action.

We can now present the definition of Agent Dynamic Logic (ADL). Analogous to PDL, the language of ADL includes modal operators $[\pi]$ and $\langle \pi \rangle$ corresponding to each program π, and the semantics is based on computation trees, as in the approach of Harel [5]. The programs are assumed to consist of a set of atomic programs that can be combined with a unary operator $*$ (iteration) and binary operators ; (sequencing) and $\cup$ (alternation), and corresponding to any formula α of the base language $\mathcal{L}$ is a test statement α? – note, however, that the test is on whether α is a belief of the agent, not whether α holds in the environment. The language of programs also includes special actions *achieve* γ, *attempt* π and *observe* α (where γ and α are formulae of the base language $\mathcal{L}$ with α a conjunction of literals, and π is a program), an "empty" program Λ and a dummy action *env* that models the changes in the environment that occur over cycles in which the agent tests its beliefs.

The semantics of ADL is based on what we call *PRS interpretations*. Each program is modelled as a set of reduced BDI interpretations that arises by varying the actual world and belief accessibility relation $\mathcal{B}$; these are reduced BDI interpretations in that the relations $\mathcal{I}$ and $\mathcal{A}$ play no role and are therefore omitted from the definitions (note that the $\mathcal{B}$ relation is used to define the meaning of the test statements and the semantics of belief update, so cannot be omitted). In any reduced BDI interpretation b modelling a program π, one distinguished world b^* models the execution paths of π in the actual world and may have *non-final* situations, situations at leaf nodes in a computation tree where execution can continue (other worlds in b represent the agent's belief states, and final situations in b^* represent paths where program execution cannot continue). Each primitive action π (except for the special action *achieve* γ – see below) is modelled as in PDL as a binary relation on states (independent of the agent's beliefs), denoted R_π. In ADL, composite actions are modelled as sets of reduced BDI interpretations whose worlds derive from these state relations, one for each state in which the action is executable and each possible observation.

Definition 4. *A PRS interpretation is a pair $\langle \mathcal{S}, \mathcal{R} \rangle$, where $\mathcal{S}$ is a set of states and $\mathcal{R}$ is a family of sets of reduced BDI interpretations $\mathcal{R}_\pi$ based on $\mathcal{S}$, one such set for each program π, for which (i) for each atomic program π except those of the form achieve γ, $\mathcal{R}_\pi \subseteq \mathcal{R}_{attempt\ \pi}$, and (ii) in any reduced BDI interpretation $b \in \mathcal{R}_\pi$, transitions in b^* are state transitions from R_π while state transitions in other worlds in b are from $R_{observe\ \alpha}$ where α is some conjunction of literals β for which the postcondition of π logically implies either β or $\neg\beta$.*

Definition 5. *The binary state relation $R_{observe\ \alpha}$ is defined (for α a conjunction of literals) as follows.*

$$(s,t) \in R_{observe\ \alpha} \text{ iff } s \models \alpha \text{ and } t = \{s - \bar{\alpha} \cup \alpha^+\}$$

where if α is $\alpha_1 \wedge \cdots \wedge \alpha_n$, α^+ is the set of α_i and $\bar{\alpha}$ is the set of literals complementary to the α_i.

It is obvious that if s is a state (corresponding to a consistent complete theory over the base propositional language $\mathcal{L}$) and $(s,t) \in R_{observe\ \alpha}$, then t is also a state (i.e. is also a consistent and complete theory over $\mathcal{L}$), so the binary state relation is well defined. It is also clear that if K is a belief set of the agent (a consistent, but not necessarily complete, theory over $\mathcal{L}$) and K^*_α is the revised belief set as defined in PRS-like systems (extending the definition above to any consistent theory), then if $K = \cap \{s : s \in \mathcal{S}\}$, $K_\alpha^* = \cap\{t : s \in \mathcal{S}, K \subseteq s \text{ and } (s,t) \in R_{observe\ \alpha}\}$. This ensures that the state transitions based on an observation action taken from a set of epistemic alternatives correctly capture the update of the agent's belief set.

Definition 6. *The relations $\mathcal{R}_{achieve\ \gamma}$ corresponding to an achievement subgoal γ are defined as follows.*

$$\mathcal{R}_{achieve\ \gamma} = \biguplus \{\mathcal{R}_\pi \cap \Gamma : \pi \in L, post(\pi) \vdash \gamma\}$$

Here Γ is the set of reduced BDI interpretations b where the final situations of b^* satisfy γ, and $post(\pi)$ is the postcondition of a plan π in the plan library L.

Definition 7. *Let $\langle \mathcal{S}, \mathcal{R} \rangle$ be a PRS interpretation and $\langle T, \prec, \mathcal{S}, \mathcal{W}, \mathcal{B} \rangle$ be a reduced BDI interpretation. For a world $w \in \mathcal{W}$ over $\langle T, \prec \rangle$ containing a point t, let w^t be the subworld of w over $\langle T_t, \prec_t \rangle$, the subtree of $\langle T, \prec \rangle$ generated from t. Then w satisfies $do(\pi)$ and $[\pi]\alpha$ at a time point t in w as follows.*

- $w \models_t do(\pi)$ *if there is a reduced BDI interpretation b in $\mathcal{R}_\pi$ such that b^* is isomorphic to a prefix of w^t*
- $w \models_t [\pi]\alpha$ *if for every reduced BDI interpretation b in $\mathcal{R}_\pi$ such that b^* is isomorphic to a prefix of w^t, $w \models_u \alpha$ for every point u in w corresponding to a leaf node of b^**

Definition 8. *A world w is a prefix of a world w' if for each end node n of w, there is a world w_n such that replacing each n in w by w_n results in w'.*

Definition 9. *A world w^1 in a reduced BDI interpretation $\langle T_1, \prec_1, \mathcal{S}, \mathcal{W}_1, \mathcal{B}_1 \rangle$ is isomorphic to a world w^2 in a reduced BDI interpretation $\langle T_2, \prec_2, \mathcal{S}, \mathcal{W}_2, \mathcal{B}_2 \rangle$ if there is a one-one correspondence f between T_1 and T_2 such that for all $t, u \in T_1$, $t \prec_1 u$ iff $f(t) \prec_2 f(u)$, and for all $t \in T_1$, w_t^1 is equivalent to $w_{f(t)}^2$.*

Definition 10. *A situation $w_{t_1}^1$ in a reduced BDI interpretation $\langle T_1, \prec_1, \mathcal{S}, \mathcal{W}_1, \mathcal{B}_1 \rangle$ is equivalent to a situation $w_{t_2}^2$ in a reduced BDI interpretation $\langle T_2, \prec_2, \mathcal{S}, \mathcal{W}_2, \mathcal{B}_2 \rangle$ if $w_{t_1}^1 = w_{t_2}^2$ (i.e. they are equal as states) and $\{u_{t_1'} : \mathcal{B}_1(w^1, t_1, u, t_1')\} = \{v_{t_2'} : \mathcal{B}_2(w^2, t', v, t_2')\}$ (i.e. they satisfy the same basic beliefs).*

Definition 11. *Two situations $w_{t^1}^1$ and $w_{t^2}^2$ in reduced BDI interpretations b^1 and b^2 share a common history if all corresponding pairs of situations $w_{t_i}^1$ and $w_{t_i}^2$ in the sequences of situations $[w_{t_0}^1, \ldots, w_{t_n}^1]$ prior to $w_{t^1}^1$ in b^1 and $[w_{t_0}^2, \ldots, w_{t_n}^2]$ prior to $w_{t^2}^2$ in b^2 are equivalent (allowing here the possibility that both sequences are empty).*

We can now state the constraints on the sets of BDI interpretations $\mathcal{R}_\pi$ that ensure that the program construction operators respect their operational definitions.

$\mathcal{R}_{\pi;\chi} = \mathcal{R}_\pi \oplus \mathcal{R}_\chi$
$\mathcal{R}_{\pi \cup \chi} = \mathcal{R}_\pi \uplus \mathcal{R}_\chi$
$\mathcal{R}_{\pi^*} = \mathcal{R}_\pi^*$ (the reflexive transitive closure of $\mathcal{R}_\pi$ under $\oplus$)
$\mathcal{R}_{\alpha?} = \{b : b \in B_1, b^* \models \mathsf{B}\alpha \text{ and } b^* \text{ is isomorphic to a world in } \mathcal{R}_{env}\}$
$\mathcal{R}_{\neg\alpha?} = \{b : b \in B_1, b^* \not\models \mathsf{B}\alpha \text{ and } b^* \text{ is isomorphic to a world in } \mathcal{R}_{env}\}$

Here B_1 is the set of reduced BDI interpretations all of whose worlds are of depth 1. Note that test actions in the PRS-like architecture consume one cycle during which the environment may change. Hence the test $\alpha?$ ($\neg\alpha?$) succeeds only when the agent believes (does not believe) α, but the execution context, as captured in the non-final situations in the model, are those resulting from the changes in the environment, as reflected in $\mathcal{R}_{env}$.

The relations $\mathcal{R}_\pi$ for attempts are also subject to the following constraints.

$$\mathcal{R}_{attempt\ \Lambda} = \mathcal{R}_\Lambda,\ \mathcal{R}_{attempt\ \alpha?} = \mathcal{R}_{\alpha?},\ \mathcal{R}_{attempt\ \neg\alpha?} = \mathcal{R}_{\neg\alpha?}$$
$$\mathcal{R}_{attempt\ \pi;\chi} = \mathcal{R}_{attempt\ \pi;attempt\ \chi}$$
$$\mathcal{R}_{attempt\ \pi\cup\chi} = \mathcal{R}_{attempt\ \pi\cup attempt\ \chi}$$
$$\mathcal{R}_{attempt\ \pi^*} = \mathcal{R}_{(attempt\ \pi)^*}$$
$$\mathcal{R}_{attempt\ achieve\ \gamma} = \biguplus\{\mathcal{R}_\pi : \pi \in L, post(\pi) \vdash \gamma\}$$

As above, $post(\pi)$ is the postcondition of a plan π in the plan library L. The last constraint formally captures the intuition that execution of a plan in the plan library counts as an attempt to achieve its postcondition.

The program construction operators, sequencing, alternation and iteration, are modelled as operations on sets of BDI interpretations. The operation for sequencing is a kind of "concatenation" of worlds, denoted $\oplus$, analogous to concatenation of computation sequences. For alternation, we utilize an operation, denoted $\uplus$, that merges two worlds if they have equivalent initial situations.

Definition 12. *Let w^1 and w^2 be worlds (in reduced BDI interpretations) over time trees $\langle T_1, \prec_1 \rangle$ and $\langle T_2, \prec_2 \rangle$. Let S be the set of end points of T_1, and let S' be the subset of elements s of S for which w_s^1 is a non-final situation and equivalent to w_r^2, where r is the root of T_2. For each element s of S', let $w^2(s)$ be a world isomorphic to W_2 over a time tree $\langle T_2^s, \prec_2^s \rangle$, whose accessibility relations are the same as w^2 on corresponding elements. Then the* concatenation *of w^1 and w^2, denoted $w^1 \oplus w^2$ is defined over a tree consisting of $T_1 - S'$ and all the sets T_2^s with a precedence ordering $\prec$ extending $\prec_1$ and all the $\prec_2^s$ by also defining $t_1 \prec t_2$ if $t_1 \in T_1 - S'$, $t_1 \prec_1 s$ and $t_2 \in T_2^s$. The non-final situations of $w^1 \oplus w^2$ are defined to be those of all the $w^2(s)$ (there are no non-final situations if S' is empty).*

Definition 13. *Let w^1 and w^2 be worlds (in reduced BDI interpretations) over time trees $\langle T_1, \prec_1 \rangle$ and $\langle T_2, \prec_2 \rangle$ with roots r_1 and r_2, such that $w_{r_1}^1$ and $w_{r_2}^2$ are equivalent. Let the tree T be defined as the set of time points $T_1 \cup T_2$ in which r_1 and r_2 are identified, and with $\prec$ defined as $\prec_1 \cup \prec_2$ (so that the identified r_1 and r_2 is the root of T, and the children of this node are the children of r_1 from T_1 and of r_2 from T_2). Then the* merger *of w^1 and w^2, denoted $w^1 \uplus w^2$, is the world defined over the tree $\langle T, \prec \rangle$ that is inherited from w^1 and w^2, i.e. $(w^1 \uplus w^2)(t)$ is $w^1(t)$ if $t \in T_1$ and is $w^2(t)$ if $t \in T_2$. The non-final situations of $w^1 \uplus w^2$ are defined to be those of w^1 and w^2.*

4 Logical Properties of Attempts and Belief Update

We now describe some logical properties of action attempts and the logic of belief update implied by the above semantics for ADL. The logic by no means provides a complete axiomatization of these properties.

The first set of properties derive directly from the semantics for attempts.

(A1) $[attempt\ \pi]\alpha \Rightarrow [\pi]\alpha$
(A2) $[attempt\ \beta?]\alpha \Leftrightarrow [\beta?]\alpha$
(A3) $[attempt\ \pi;\chi]\alpha \Leftrightarrow [attempt\ \pi; attempt\ \chi]\alpha$
(A4) $[attempt\ \pi \cup \chi]\alpha \Leftrightarrow [attempt\ \pi \cup attempt\ \chi]\alpha$
(A5) $[attempt\ \pi^*]\alpha \Leftrightarrow [(attempt\ \pi)^*]\alpha$

Most of these are straightforward once it is noted that actions within square brackets are understood to be performed successfully. (A1) follows from the constraint that the models of π are all submodels of those of *attempt* π. (A2) says that all attempts to test the agents own beliefs are successful (the agent has accurate introspection abilities). (A3)–(A5) decompose complex attempts into constituent components.

A second pair of properties relate to attempts and achievement goals.

(B1) $[achieve\ \gamma]\gamma$
(B2) $[attempt\ achieve\ \gamma]\alpha \Leftrightarrow [\pi_1 \cup \cdots \cup \pi_n]\alpha$ where the π_i are the plans whose postcondition logically implies γ

(B1) is a definitive property of achievement goals which should hold in any theory: it basically states that successful executions of *achieve* γ actually achieve γ. However, the point of (B2) is that not all attempts to achieve γ are guaranteed to achieve γ, even those arising from successful executions of a plan whose postcondition implies γ, i.e. (B2) with *achieve* γ instead of *attempt achieve* γ is incorrect. So without a notion of attempts the correct axiom cannot be expressed.

A third set of properties capture simple properties of belief update.

(C1) $B A \bigcirc \alpha \Leftrightarrow A \bigcirc B \alpha$
(C2) $[observe\ \alpha]B\alpha$
(C3) $[observe\ (\beta_1 \wedge \beta_2)]\alpha \Leftrightarrow ([observe\ \beta_1]\alpha \wedge [observe\ \beta_2]\alpha)$
(C4) $[attempt\ achieve\ \gamma](B\gamma \vee B\neg\gamma)$

(C1) is a definitive property required for modelling belief update using the semantics of action, stating that the set of situations forming the epistemic alternatives of the agent after performing some action are exactly those resulting situations derived from executing the appropriate actions (the action itself or the observe actions) starting from each element of the set of initial epistemic alternatives. (C2) is valid only because we have assumed the agent's observations are veridical and because of a technicality of ADL that an observation of α can succeed only if α is true. (C3) is a simple belief revision property that holds because β_1 and β_2 are restricted to conjunctions of literals, making belief update on complete theories deterministic. (C4) captures the idea that the agent observes the postcondition of an action after attempted execution.

5 Conclusion

In this paper, we extended earlier work on modelling the mental states of PRS-like agents by considering the dynamics of belief. This has required addressing a series of related questions, including the correct modelling of action attempts (in turn both handling different types of success and failure and accommodating the present-directed and future-directed aspects of intention), and capturing the distinctions between two types of "possible" world, those that represent the ignorance of the agent about which world is the actual world, and those that reflect the agent's ignorance of the state of the world given that it is in some actual world. The resulting theory enables the dynamics of belief to be modelled using the semantics of action, and allows properties of belief update, attempts and observations to be represented in Agent Dynamic Logic.

Acknowledgements

This work is funded by an Australian Research Council Discovery Project Grant. Discussions with Krystian Ji have helped greatly in clarifying the main issues addressed in this paper. Thanks also to the Decision Systems Laboratory at the University of Wollongong for hosting a seminar on an earlier version of this work.

References

1. Bratman, M.E. (1987) *Intention, Plans and Practical Reason.* Harvard University Press, Cambridge, MA.
2. Cohen, P.R. & Levesque, H.J. (1990) 'Intention is Choice with Commitment.' *Artificial Intelligence,* **42**, 213–261.
3. Emerson, E.A. & Clarke, E.M. (1982) 'Using Branching Time Temporal Logic to Synthesize Synchronization Skeletons.' *Science of Computer Programming,* **2**, 241–266.
4. Georgeff, M.P. & Lansky, A.L. (1987) 'Reactive Reasoning and Planning.' *Proceedings of the Sixth National Conference on Artificial Intelligence (AAAI-87),* 677–682.
5. Harel, D. (1979) *First-Order Dynamic Logic.* Springer-Verlag, Berlin.
6. Pratt, V.R. (1976) 'Semantical Considerations on Floyd-Hoare Logic.' *Proceedings of the Seventeenth IEEE Symposium on Foundations of Computer Science,* 109–121.
7. Rao, A.S. & Georgeff, M.P. (1991) 'Modeling Rational Agents within a BDI-Architecture.' *Proceedings of the Second International Conference on Principles of Knowledge Representation and Reasoning (KR'91),* 473–484.
8. van der Hoek, W., van Linder, B. & Meyer, J.-J.Ch. (1999) 'An Integrated Modal Approach to Rational Agents.' in Wooldridge, M. & Rao, A. (Eds) *Foundations of Rational Agency.* Kluwer, Dordrecht.
9. Wobcke, W.R. (2002) 'Modelling PRS-like Agents' Mental States.' in Ishizuka, M. & Sattar, A. (Eds) *PRICAI 2002: Trends in Artificial Intelligence.* Springer-Verlag, Berlin.
10. Wooldridge, M.J. (2000) *Reasoning About Rational Agents.* MIT Press, Cambridge, MA.

Towards Belief Revision Logic Based Adaptive and Persuasive Negotiation Agents

Raymond Y.K. Lau and Siu Y. Chan

Centre for Information Technology Innovation
Faculty of Information Technology
Queensland University of Technology
GPO Box 2434, Brisbane, Qld 4001, Australia
{r.lau,s.chan}@qut.edu.au

Abstract. Human negotiators can persuade the opponents to revise their beliefs in order to maximise the chance of reaching an agreement. Existing negotiation models are weak in supporting persuasive negotiations. This paper illustrates an adaptive and persuasive negotiation agent model, which is underpinned by a belief revision logic. These belief-based negotiation agents are able to learn from the changing negotiation contexts and persuade their opponents to change their positions. Our preliminary experiments show that the belief-based adaptive negotiation agents outperform a classical negotiation model under time pressure.

1 Introduction

Negotiation refers to the process by which group of agents (human or software) communicate with one another in order to reach a mutually acceptable agreement on resource allocation (distribution) [1]. Many real-world negotiation problems are characterised by combinatorially complex negotiation spaces which involve many issues. In addition, a negotiation context is volatile rather than static because of the changing preferences of the negotiation parties. These problems are compounded with the challenge that negotiators are often bounded by limited resources, negotiation time, and information about the negotiation context. Classical negotiation models based on operational research methods or game-theoretic approach [2] have limited use in solving real-world negotiation problems because these models assume that complete information about a static negotiation space is available and the computational time for an agent to deliberate a solution is negligible. Argumentative logics have been proposed to formalise negotiation processes in which agents can use arguments to persuade the opponents to change their beliefs, desires, and intentions [3, 4]. Nevertheless, a full implementation of the proposed argumentative logics is yet to be conducted, not to say the empirical evaluation of the argumentative negotiation framework. As indicated by the advocates of the argumentative negotiation models [3, 4], the existing framework needs to be extended to support adaptive negotiations where the preferences of the agents may change over time.

2 Preliminary of Automated Negotiation

The basic negotiation model illustrated in this section is based on multi-attribute utility theory (MAUT) and is discussed in [5]. It is assumed that only a finite set of agents P participates in the negotiation processes. An *offer* is a tuple of attribute values $o = <I_{a1}, I_{a2}, \ldots, I_{an}>$ describing the buyers' (sellers') requirements of acquiring (allocating) resources. An attribute value (interval) I_{ai} is drawn from the domain D_{ai} of an attribute $a_i \in A$, where A is the set of attributes representing the relevant negotiation issues. Qualitatively, an agent p's preference is represented by a preference relation $\preceq_p$ over a finite set of permissible offers O_p. The set O_p is defined according to an agent p's *hard constraints* HC_p. The *valuations* of individual attributes and attribute values (intervals) are defined by the valuation functions $U_p^A : A \mapsto [0,1]$ and $U_p^{D_a} : D_a \mapsto [0,1]$ respectively, whereas U_p^A is an agent p's *valuation* for the attributes (issues) A, and $U_p^{D_a}$ is an agent's valuation for the attribute values of a domain D_a. By aggregating these *valuations* such as $u_p(o) = \sum_{a \in A} U_p^A(a) \times U_p^{D_a}(I_a)$, the utility $u_p(o)$ of an offer o can be defined [5].

For any $p \in P$, acceptance of an offer o proposed by other parties is defined by: (1) If $\forall_{o_x \in O_p} o_x \preceq_p o$, the agent p should accept o to maximize its own payoff; (2) If $o \in O'_p$ is true, the agent p should accept o because o is one of the elements from the set of previously proposed offers O'_p. If the offer o is neither p's most preferred offer nor one of its previous proposals, the agent p should reject the offer and propose a *counter-offer* according to its preference $(\preceq_p, O_p)$. In particular, a counter offer $o_{counter}$ with concession based on the least amount of utility decrement is defined by: $\exists_{o_{counter} \in \{O_p - O'_p\}} \forall_{o_x \in \{O_p - O'_p\}}$: $[o_x \preceq_p o_{counter}]$. It has been proved that the above model can guarantee *Pareto optimal* if it exists in a negotiation space [5]. A negotiation solution is at Pareto optimal if it is impossible to find an alternative such that at least one agent is better off while no other agent is worse off.

3 The AGM Belief Revision Framework

The AGM belief revision framework is one of the most influential works in the theory of belief revision [6]. In this framework, belief revision processes are taken as the transitions among belief states. A belief state (set) K is represented by a theory of a classical language $\mathcal{L}$. A belief is represented by a sentence of $\mathcal{L}$ supplemented with an entrenchment degree indicating the degree of firmness of such a belief. Three principle types of belief state transitions are identified and modelled by the corresponding belief functions: *expansion* (K_α^+), *contraction* (K_α^-), and *revision* (K_α^*). The AGM framework comprises sets of postulates to characterise these functions for *consistent* and *minimal* belief revision. In addition, the AGM framework also specifies the constructions of the belief functions based on various mechanisms. One of them is *epistemic entrenchment* ($\leqslant$) [7]. It captures the notions of *significance*, *firmness*, or *defeasibility* of beliefs. If inconsistency arises after applying changes to a belief set, the least significant beliefs are given up in order to restore consistency.

For a computer-based implementation of epistemic entrenchment and hence the AGM belief functions, Williams developed finite partial entrenchment rankings to represent epistemic entrenchment orderings [8]. The notion of finite partial entrenchment rankings is developed according to Spohn's ordinal conditional functions [9].

Definition 1. *A finite partial entrenchment ranking is a function $\mathbf{B}$ that maps a finite subset of sentences in $\mathcal{L}$ into the interval $[0,1]$ such that the following conditions are satisfied for all $\alpha \in dom(\mathbf{B})$:*

(PER1) $\{\beta \in dom(\mathbf{B}) : \mathbf{B}(\alpha) < \mathbf{B}(\beta)\} \not\vdash \alpha$;
(PER2) *If* $\vdash \neg\alpha$ *then* $\mathbf{B}(\alpha) = 0$;
(PER3) $\mathbf{B}(\alpha) = 1$ *if and only if* $\vdash \alpha$.

(PER1) states that the set of sentences ranked strictly higher than a sentence α cannot entail α. This property corresponds to the *Dominance* property of epistemic entrenchment [7]. $\mathbf{B}(\alpha)$ is referred to as the *degree of entrenchment* of an explicit belief α. The set of explicit beliefs of $\mathbf{B}$ is $\{\alpha \in dom(\mathbf{B}) : \mathbf{B}(\alpha) > 0\}$, and is denoted $exp(\mathbf{B})$. The set of implicit beliefs $Cn(exp(\mathbf{B}))$ is denoted $content(\mathbf{B})$, where Cn is the classical consequence operator.

For example, $\mathbf{B}$(shipment-fast) $= 0.6$ represents the entrenchment degree (i.e., firmness of a belief) of the belief "shipment-fast". The set of beliefs $\mathbf{B} = \{$(shipment-fast, 0.6), (shipment-fast $\rightarrow$ pay-more, 0.5), (pay-more, 0.5) $\}$ satisfies the property of a finite partial entrenchment ranking $\mathbf{B}$. However, the set $\mathbf{B} = \{$(shipment-fast, 0.6), (shipment-fast $\rightarrow$ pay-more, 0.5), (pay-more, 0.4) $\}$ does not satisfy the properties of $\mathbf{B}$ since beliefs with higher entrenchment degree in this set entail ($\vdash$) a belief with lower entrenchment degree (i.e., violating PER1). In particular, the belief "pay-more" does not have the same firmness as the set of beliefs which logically entail it. This is not a rational behaviour. If an agent always accepts a belief β whenever it is prepared to accept a belief α (i.e., $\alpha \vdash \beta$), the agent should believe β (e.g., "pay-more") at least as firmly as α (e.g., "shipment-fast", and "shipment-fast implying pay-more") [7].

In order to describe the epistemic entrenchment ordering ($\leqslant_\mathbf{B}$) generated from a finite partial entrenchment ranking $\mathbf{B}$, it is necessary to rank implicit beliefs.

Definition 2. *Let $\alpha \in \mathcal{L}$ be a contingent sentence. Let $\mathbf{B}$ be a finite partial entrenchment ranking and $\beta \in exp(\mathbf{B})$. The degree of entrenchment of an implicit belief α is defined by:*

$$degree(\mathbf{B},\alpha) = \begin{cases} sup(\{\mathbf{B}(\beta) \in ran(\mathbf{B}) : cut_\leqslant(\beta) \vdash \alpha\}) \\ \quad if\ \alpha \in content(\mathbf{B}) \\ 0 \quad otherwise \end{cases}$$

where the *sup* function returns the supremum from a set of ordinals. The $cut_\leqslant(\beta)$ operation extracts a set of explicit beliefs which is at least as entrenched as β according to a particular epistemic entrenchment ordering $\leqslant$ approximated by $\mathbf{B}$. $\vdash$ is the classical inference relation. Precisely, a *cut* operation is defined by: $cut_\leqslant(\beta) = \{\gamma \in dom(\mathbf{B}) : \mathbf{B}(\beta) \leqslant \mathbf{B}(\gamma)\}$.

In a belief revision based multiagent negotiation system, a negotiation context (i.e., an agent's preferences and constraints, and its beliefs about the opponents' preferences) is represented by a set of beliefs. When an agent's negotiation preferences change, the entrenchment degrees of the corresponding beliefs are raised or lowered in the agent's knowledge base. Raising or lowering the entrenchment degree of a belief is conducted via a belief revision operation $\mathbf{B}^\star(\alpha, i)$ where α is a sentence of $\mathcal{L}$ and i is the new entrenchment degree. A Maxi-adjustment operation [8] with $i > 0$ is an AGM belief revision operation (i.e., $content(\mathbf{B}^\star(\alpha, i)) = (content(\mathbf{B}))^\star_\alpha$). Based on the Maxi-adjustment method, a more efficient transmutation method called Rapid Anytime Maxi-adjustment (RAM) is developed and the details can be found in [10].

4 Belief Revision for Persuasive Negotiation

4.1 Representing Offers and Preferences

An offer comprises a set of propositions corresponding to the attribute values pertaining to that offer. The examples and experiments discussed in this paper are based on the classical propositional Horn language $\mathcal{L}_{Horn}$. As an example, a candidate offer o^{buyer} can be represented by: o^{buyer} = {buyer-pay-little, buyer-qty-small, buyer-get-fast} When an incoming offer is received by an agent, the corresponding labels are identified by an agent based on the overlapping attribute values.

Conceptually, agents' preferences are represented by epistemic entrenchment orderings of beliefs. For each negotiation agent, finite partial entrenchment rankings $\mathbf{B}$ are used to represent a *hierarchy of preferences* (e.g., a ranking of attributes, and from within each attribute a ranking of attribute values). For instance, the buyer agent's preferences are represented by an entrenchment ranking of attributes $\mathbf{B}_{attribute}$, rankings for price values $\mathbf{B}_{price}$, quantities $\mathbf{B}_{qty}$, and shipments $\mathbf{B}_{ship}$ respectively. The current negotiation context of the buyer agent is represented by the finite partial entrenchment ranking $\mathbf{B}_{Bcontext}$. If a user wants to specify conditional preferences (constraints) such as "buyer may accept above the average price if the items are shipped quickly", a rule window can be invoked. Initially, all the most entrenched beliefs from the respective entrenchment rankings of attribute values are selected to form an initial negotiation context. The entrenchment degree of a proposition is approximated by $U_p^A(a) \times U_p^{D_a}(I_a)$. The following theory base $\mathbf{B}^1_{Bcontext}$ reflects the buyer's view of the negotiation context at the beginning of the negotiation process. The conditional constraint states that the agent is willing to pay a bit more if the items are shipped quickly. The uncertainty about this conditional constraint is captured by the associated entrenchment degree of 0.9.

$\mathbf{B}^1_{Bcontext}$ = {(buyer-get-fast → buyer-pay-normal, 0.9),
(buyer-qty-small, 0.49),
(buyer-get-fast, 0.14),
(buyer-pay-little, 0.08)}

Table 1. Computing concessions based on entrenchment rankings.

Rankings	Beliefs		
$\mathbf{B}_{attr}$	quantity 0.7	shipment 0.2	price 0.1
$\mathbf{B}_{qty}$	qty-small 0.49	qty-standard 0.28	qty-large 0.07
$\mathbf{B}_{ship}$	get-fast 0.14	get-normal 0.08	get-slow 0.04
$\mathbf{B}_{price}$	pay-little 0.08	pay-normal 0.05	pay-much 0.01

4.2 Evaluating Incoming Offers

An agent determines if an incoming offer o should be accepted or not based on its beliefs about the current negotiation context (i.e., the agent's knowledge base $K = content(\mathbf{B}_{context})$). If the agent's current negotiation context nonmonotonically entails the logical representation ϕ of an incoming offer o, the agent may accept such a proposal otherwise the offer is rejected. So, the agents' decision making processes are underpinned by nonmonotonic reasoning, in particular, the *expectation inference* relation [11]. To enrich the operational characteristics of our belief-based negotiation agents, an *entrenchment-based* decision function $Accept_{\leqslant}(Context, o)$ is defined:

$$Accept_{\leqslant}(Context, o) = degree(\mathbf{B}_{context}, \phi) \qquad (1)$$

$\mathbf{B}_{context}$ represents the agent's current negotiation context and ϕ is the logical representation of the offer o. An optional negotiation threshold θ can be used by the negotiation agents to constraint the solutions (offers) in a more preferable region so that only the offers with acceptance scores (i.e., derived by Eq.(1)) higher than the acceptance threshold will be accepted. Concession computation adheres to the AGM principle of minimal change. For example, the buyer agent will use $\mathbf{B}_{attribute}$ to determine the least preferred attribute and then expand its current context based on the less preferred attribute values in subsequent rounds. The reason is that significant preferences should be kept intact to adhere to the principle of minimal change. According to empirical evaluation, maintaining stringent goals (preferences) can help maximise an agent's payoff [12]. A concession pointer is implicitly maintained for each entrenchment ranking to remember which attributes or attribute values have been used to revise an agent's current negotiation context $\mathbf{B}_{Bcontext}$ for concession generation. Therefore, at the first round, the concession pointers (underlined) as depicted in Table 1 are maintained. The prefix *buyer* is omitted for each label in Table 1.

4.3 Learning Changing Negotiation Contexts

A belief-based adaptive negotiation agent needs to: (1) revise its own preferential changes; (2) learn the opponents' preferential changes via their counter-offers; (3) consider the persuasions received from its opponents. Negotiation agents become more responsive to their negotiation contexts by continuously learning and revising all this information into their knowledge bases over time. The extent of incorporating the opponents' preferences into an agent's knowledge base depends on the credibility of the sources. The credibility $CR(p)$ for an agent p is derived by: $CR(p) = \frac{N_{success}}{N_{negotiation}}$; it is the fraction of $N_{success}$, the number of agreements made, over the total number $N_{negotiation}$ of negotiations recorded in the negotiation history file. A system wide default credibility $CR(default)$ will be applied if the negotiation partner p is new to the system.

In addition, the *time pressure* $TP(t)$ as well as an agent's attitude (i.e., eagerness factor e_p) towards a negotiation deadline also determines the degree of acceptance of others' preferences. A time pressure function for an agent p can be defined by: $TP(t) = (\frac{\min(t,t_p^d)}{t_p^d})^{\frac{1}{e_p}}$, where t_p^d is the agent p's deadline and t is the elapsed time. In our system, time can be expressed as absolute time or in terms of number of negotiation rounds. An agent p is *Boulware* (i.e., holding its own beliefs firmly and reluctant to change its preferences) if $0 < e_p < 1$ is set; for a conceder agent (i.e., easy to change its position in order to reach an agreement), $e_p > 1$ is true. If $e_p = 1$ is established, the agent holds *Linear* attitude towards a deadline. Three pre-defined eagerness modes $e_p = 0.1$ (Boulware agent), $e_p = 10$ (Concededr agent), and $e_p = 1$ (Neutral agent) are available in our system. Alternatively, a user can also set the eagerness factor directly via the client interface.

On the other hand, the time pressure function is also used to dynamically adjust (e.g., $\theta = (1 - TP(t)) \times \theta$) an agent's negotiation threshold θ if it is set via the client interface. Through the system's client interface, the user can specify the deadline of a negotiation session (in terms of number of rounds or absolute time). With reference to the Rapid Maxi-adjustment operator $\mathbf{B}^\star(\alpha, i)$ that executes the AGM belief revision functions, the new entrenchment degree i of a changing belief α is determined by:

$$i = \begin{cases} \text{if } \mathbf{B}_{p'}(\alpha) > \mathbf{B}_p(\alpha) \\ \mathbf{B}_p(\alpha) + (|\mathbf{B}_{p'}(\alpha) - \mathbf{B}_p(\alpha)|) \times CR(p') \times TP_p(t) \\ \text{if } \mathbf{B}_{p'}(\alpha) < \mathbf{B}_p(\alpha) \\ \mathbf{B}_p(\alpha) - (|\mathbf{B}_{p'}(\alpha) - \mathbf{B}_p(\alpha)|) \times CR(p') \times TP_p(t) \end{cases} \quad (2)$$

where $\mathbf{B}_p(\alpha)$ is the entrenchment degree of α for agent p, and $\mathbf{B}_{p'}(\alpha)$ is the degree of the same belief for agent p'. The time pressure function TP takes the elapsed time (rounds) t as input to generate an adjustment value in the unit interval $[0, 1]$. In *persuasive* mode of negotiation, an agent p' can selectively disclose its preferences by attaching the entrenchment degrees of attribute values to an outgoing offer.

For any propositions (i.e., attribute values) with entrenchment degrees disclosed, the negotiation agent p will use Eq.(2) to determine the adjustment values i. A user is allowed to manually override the system generated acceptance value by Eq.(2) via the client interface. Revising an agent's own preferences is more straightforward since an agent always trusts itself and accept 100% of the new beliefs. New beliefs or modified entrenchment degrees are revised into an agent's own knowledge base via the operator $\mathbf{B}^\star(\alpha, i)$ as well. As an example, the seller agent's first counter offer to the buyer agent is $o^{counter} = \{$ (seller-earn-much 0.9), (seller-ship-slow 0.8), seller-qty-large $\}$. In this case, the seller only discloses its preferences for the first two attribute values (i.e., the entrenchment degrees of the corresponding propositions). Assuming that the seller's credibility is $CR(seller) = 1.0$ and the buyer's current time pressure is $TP_{buyer}(t) = 0.5$, the buyer agent will execute the following adjustment algorithm to revise its negotiation context $\mathbf{B}_{Bcontext}$ before computing concession for the second round:

```
DO CASE
CASE (B(α) > B(β)) ∧ (i < B(β))
    B⁻_context(α, 0)
CASE (B(α) = B(β))
    IF (i < B(β))
        B⁻_context(α, 0)
    ENDIF
CASE (B(α) < B(β)) ∧ (i < B(β))
    SKIP
OTHERWISE
    B★_context(α, i)
END CASE
```

$\mathbf{B}(\beta)$ represents the entrenchment degree of a belief β pointed to by the implicit concession pointer. $\mathbf{B}(\alpha)$ is the degree of the changing belief α pertaining to an agent p, and $\mathbf{B}^-_{context}(\alpha, 0)$ is a belief contraction operation against agent p's current negotiation context. $\mathbf{B}^\star_{context}(\alpha, i)$ is a belief revision operation which could raise or lower the entrenchment degree of α in agent p's current negotiation context. The degree of adjustment i is computed based on Eq.(2) or directly entered from the client interface if an agent modifies its own preferences. The operation "SKIP" simply means no belief revision applied to agent p's negotiation context $\mathbf{B}_{context}$. The first CASE statement deals with the situation that the new entrenchment degree of the agent's changing belief α is lower than that of the belief β currently pointed to by the concession pointer. Since the entrenchment degree of α is originally higher than that of the belief β (i.e., it was added to the negotiation context before), the belief α should be contracted from the current negotiation context by $\mathbf{B}^-_{context}(\alpha, 0)$.

For each change related to an attribute value, the corresponding entrenchment ranking such as $\mathbf{B}_{ship}, \mathbf{B}_{qty}$, or $\mathbf{B}_{price}$ is always revised. For instance, the belief *seller-earn-much* is interpreted as *buyer-pay-much* by the buyer agent, and its new degree $i = 0.46 = 0.01 + (0.9 - 0.01) \times 0.5$ is computed according to Eq.(2). Accordingly, $\mathbf{B}^\star_{price}$(buyer-pay-much, 0.46) is invoked to revise $\mathbf{B}_{price}$. These changes are highlighted in Table 2. Moreover, the buyer agent's current negotiation context $\mathbf{B}_{Bcontext}$ is also revised by $\mathbf{B}^\star_{Bcontext}$(buyer-pay-much, 0.46) according to the above *context revision* algorithm. Similarly, the belief *seller-ship-slow* is converted to the belief *buyer-get-slow* by the buyer agent. The new entrenchment degree is computed according to Eq.(2): $i = 0.42 = 0.04 + (0.8 -$

Table 2. Entrenchment rankings after incorporating the seller's beliefs.

Rankings	Beliefs		
$\mathbf{B}_{attr}$	quantity 0.7	shipment 0.2	price 0.1
$\mathbf{B}_{qty}$	qty-small 0.49	qty-standard 0.28	qty-large 0.07
$\mathbf{B}_{ship}$	**get-slow 0.42**	get-fast 0.14	get-normal 0.08
$\mathbf{B}_{price}$	**pay-much 0.46**	pay-little 0.08	pay-normal 0.05

$0.04) \times 0.5$. After executing the belief revision operations, the buyer agent's negotiation context becomes: $\mathbf{B}^2_{Bcontext} = \{$(buyer-get-fast $\rightarrow$ buyer-pay-normal, 0.9), (buyer-qty-small, 0.49), (buyer-pay-much, 0.46), (buyer-get-slow, 0.42), (buyer-get-fast, 0.14), (buyer-pay-little, 0.08), (buyer-pay-normal, 0.05)$\}$. The agent's entrenchment rankings of attribute values are depicted in Table 2.

The last belief *buyer-pay-normal* is added to the current context because of concession generation at the beginning of round 2. Since the price attribute is less important for the buyer, the attribute value such as *buyer-pay-normal* is first added to the negotiation context to generate concession. The impact of the above learning process is that an offer such as $o^{seller} = \{$ seller-earn-much, seller-qty-small, seller-ship-slow $\}$ rejected in round 1 will be accepted in round 2 after persuasive negotiation initiated by the seller. The negotiation threshold θ is assumed zero in our example.

$$\phi = \text{buyer-pay-much} \wedge \text{buyer-qty-small}$$
$$\wedge \text{buyer-get-slow}$$

Round 1 Buyer rejects offer ϕ
$$\because content(\mathbf{B}^1_{Bcontext}) \not\models_E \phi$$
$$Accept_{\leqslant}(Context^1_{Buyer}, o) \not> \theta$$

Round 2 Buyer accepts offer ϕ
$$\because content(\mathbf{B}^2_{Bcontext}) \models_E \phi$$
$$Accept_{\leqslant}(Context^2_{Buyer}, o) > \theta$$

5 The Experiments

The negotiation spaces of our experiments were characterized by bilateral negotiations between a buyer agent p_B and a seller agent p_S. Each negotiation profile consists of 5 attributes with each attribute domain containing 5 discrete values represented by the natural numbers $D_a = \{1, 2, \ldots, 5\}$. The valuation of an attribute or a discrete attribute value was in the interval of $(0, 1]$. For each negotiation case, an agreement zone always exists since the difference between a buyer and a seller only lies on their valuations against the same set of negotiation issues (e.g., attributes and attribute values). For each agent, the size of the candidate offer set O_p is 3,125. 5 negotiation groups with each group containing 10 cases were constructed. For the first simulation group, each negotiation case contained identical buyer/seller preferences (i.e., the same weights for the attributes and the same valuations against the same set of attribute values). This

Table 3. Comparative negotiation performance Belief vs. Basic.

Group	Preferential Difference	$\Delta_{utility}$	Δ_{rate}
1	0%	0.0%	0.0%
2	20%	10.1%	12.5%
3	40%	16.1%	25.0%
4	60%	32.7%	42.9%
5	80%	39.2%	50.0%
	Average	19.6%	26.1%

Table 4. Impact of Persuasion on Negotiation Performance.

Persuasive Parties	Average Fairness	Average Joint-Utility
B S	0.97	1.33
B -	0.48	1.01
S -	1.41	0.97
- -	0.96	0.66

group was used as a control group and the other groups were the experimental groups. Each case in the succeeding group was injected a 20% increment of preferential difference.

In the first experiment, negotiation deadline was set to 500 rounds. If no agreement was made on or before the deadline, the utility achieved by each agent would be zero. In each negotiation round, 2 randomly selected attribute intervals and their entrenchment degrees pertaining to an agent (i.e., persuasion) were sent to the opponent. The credibility factor was set to 0.6 for each agent. Table 3 summarizes the average $\Delta_{utility} = \frac{JP_{Belief} - JP_{baseline}}{JP_{Baseline}} \times 100\%$ and $\Delta_{rate} = \frac{SR_{Belief} - SR_{baseline}}{SR_{Baseline}} \times 100\%$ for each negotiation group. $\Delta_{utility}$ and Δ_{rate} represent the comparative joint-payoff (JP) and success rate (SR) between the two negotiation systems respectively. An overall results of $\Delta_{utility} = 19.6\%$ and $\Delta_{rate} = 26.1\%$ were obtained. The reason is that the belief-based negotiation agents could learn and adapt to the changing context (e.g., persuasion sent by the opponent) and hence they were able to reach an agreement under a tough deadline in most of the cases. On the other hand, the basic negotiation system could not adapt to the changing negotiation context. Therefore, under a tough deadline, the system could not produce solutions in some cases even though the model should lead to optimal results theoretically.

The second experiment evaluated the persuasive negotiation of the belief-based negotiation agents. Both the joint-payoff and fairness ratio were used to measure the performance of the negotiation agents under various conditions such as both agents making persuasion (B, S), only the buyer persuading the seller (B, -), or no persuasion at all (-, -). Table 4 summarised the experimental results for various persuasion scenarios. The best result was achieved when each agent persuaded its opponent because each agent could take into account the other side's preference and reach an agreement quicker (e.g., before the deadline). On the other hand, if none of the agent tried to persuade the others, the performance was the poorest because an agreement could not be reached before the deadline.

6 Conclusions

Because of the belief revision based persuasive negotiation mechanisms, negotiation agents can take into account the opponents' changing negotiation preferences and become more responsive to the negotiation contexts. Our initial experiments show that under realistic negotiation conditions (e.g., time pressure), the effectiveness and the efficiency of the belief-based adaptive negotiation agents are better than that of the basic negotiation model which guarantees Pareto optimal. More quantitative evaluation against the belief-based adaptive negotiation agents will be conducted in the future.

References

1. Lomuscio, A.R., Jennings, N.R.: A classification scheme for negotiation in electronic commerce. Journal of Group Decision and Negotiation **12** (2003) 31–56
2. von Neumann, J., Morgenstern, O.: The Theory of Games and Economic Behaviour. Princeton University Press (1994)
3. Parsons, S., Sierra, C., Jennings, N.: Agents that reason and negotiate by arguing. Journal of Logic and Computation **8** (1998) 261–292
4. Kraus, S., Sycara, K., Evenchik, A.: Reaching agreements through argumentation: A logical model and implementation. Artificial Intelligence **104** (1998) 1–69
5. Barbuceanu, M., Lo, W.K.: Multi-attribute utility theoretic negotiation for electronic commerce. Agent-Mediated Electronic Commerce III. LNAI 2003, Springer-Verlag: Heidelberg, Germany (2001) 15–30
6. Alchourrón, C., Gärdenfors, P., Makinson, D.: On the logic of theory change: partial meet contraction and revision functions. Journal of Symbolic Logic **50** (1985) 510–530
7. Gärdenfors, P., Makinson, D.: Revisions of knowledge systems using epistemic entrenchment. In Vardi, M.Y., ed.: Proceedings of the Second Conference on Theoretical Aspects of Reasoning About Knowledge, Pacific Grove, California, Morgan Kaufmann (1988) 83–95
8. Williams, M.A.: Anytime belief revision. In Pollack, M.E., ed.: Proceedings of the Fifteenth International Joint Conference on Artificial Intelligence, Nagoya, Japan, Morgan Kaufmann Publishers (1997) 74–79
9. Spohn, W.: Ordinal conditional functions: A dynamic theory of epistemic states. In Harper, W., Skyrms, B., eds.: Causation in Decision, Belief Change and Statistics. Volume 2. D. Reidel, Dordrecht, Netherlands (1987) 105–134
10. Lau, R.: Context-Sensitive Text Mining and Belief Revision for Intelligent Information Retrieval on the Web. Web Intelligence and Agent Systems An International Journal **1** (2003) 1–22
11. Gärdenfors, P., Makinson, D.: Nonmonotonic inference based on expectations. Artificial Intelligence **65** (1994) 197–245
12. Krovi, R., Graesser, A., Pracht, W.: Agent behaviors in virtual negotiation environments. IEEE Transactions on Systems, Man, and Cybernetics **29** (1999) 15–25

Agents and Web Services Supported Business Exception Management*

Minhong Wang and Huaiqing Wang

Department of Information Systems, City University of Hong Kong,
83 Tat Chee Avenue, Hong Kong
{iswmh,iswang}@cityu.edu.hk

Abstract. The unpredictability of business processes requires that business applications support exception management with the ability to dynamically adapt to the changing environment. Exception management is a kind of complex process, in which multiple organizations and mixture of human activities and automated tasks may be involved. For a competitive solution to exception management, a web services and agents supported approach is elaborated in this paper. Agent technology is applied to deal with the dynamic, complex, and distributed processes in exception management; web services techniques are proposed for more scalability and interoperability in network-based business environment. By integrating knowledge-based agents with web services to make use of the advantages from both, this approach leads to more intelligence, flexibility and collaboration in business exception management. A case of exception management in securities trading is developed to demonstrate the validity and benefits of this approach.

1 Introduction

An exception is anything that prevents the successful completion of normal business processes [10]. In order for business management systems to support such unpredictability, they must support exception handling with the ability to adapt to today's dynamic, uncertain and error-prone environment [9]. Most efforts to handle exceptions have utilized workflow technology, which offers limited support for flexibility and collaboration in process management [10, 8]. An agents and web services supported approach is proposed in this paper. By analyzing, designing, and implementing complex processes as a collection of interacting and autonomous components, agent-oriented techniques are well appropriate for complex exception management. The agent-based approach proposed in this paper is characterized by the ability to continuously perceive the business environment and make real-time decisions on tasks based on underlying business logic. Business knowledge referring process routing, operational constraint, exception handling, and business strategy are essential for

---

* This research is supported by a UGC Research Grant ((No. CityU 1234/03E) from the Hong Kong Government.

agents to reason appropriate actions in current situations. Furthermore, as business environments are rapidly changing from centralized and closed to distributed and open in Internet computing, web services are adopted as promising technology to support open and distributed decision making for exception management. In our research, we try to integrate agent technology with web services to make use of the advantages from both. Compared with other techniques, the main benefits include flexible task management in complex environment, knowledge-based exception solving capabilities, and support for scalable and interoperable business environment.

2 Background

2.1 Exception Management

Exception management is a kind of complex and dynamic process. Exceptions may result from such sources as inconsistent data, divergence of tasks, unexpected contingencies, and un-modeled changes in the environment. Since business exceptions are more related to business activities or business processes, most efforts to handle exceptions have utilized workflow technology to include conditional branches in workflow model or redesign business systems to deal with anticipated exceptions. However, such approaches offer limited support for flexibility and collaboration during process management [10, 8], and may cost a lot on business redesign or reconstruction. If the system has to cope with undefined errors or failures, or there is a need for real-time collaboration, more flexible and robust approaches are needed.

2.2 Intelligent Agents

The term agent is used to denote a software-based computer system that enjoys the properties of autonomy, social ability, reactivity, and pro-activity [17, 18]. By modularizing a complex problem in terms of multiple autonomous components that can act and interact in flexible ways, agent-oriented techniques are well appropriate for complex, dynamic, and distributed software systems [8]. The benefits may include loosely coupled distributed system architecture, reactivity to changing environment, semantic interaction within organizations, etc. Given the limitations of conventional workflow systems, a number of researchers have considered using multi-agent systems for various aspects of processes management [8, 11, 19, 20]. Since exception management is a kind of complex process, agent technology has been employed as an alternative for more flexible and robust approaches [14, 2, 13].

2.3 Web Services

Web services are currently one of the trends in network-based business services, which offer a new paradigm for distributed computing. Web services are self-contained and modular business process applications based on open standards; they enable integration models for facilitating program-to-program interactions. While business environments are rapidly changing from centralized and closed to distributed and open mainly by virtue of the proliferation of WWW, scalability and interoperability features are getting more crucial to systems development. Among current web technologies, web services are promising for open web-based business applications and hence adopted in this paper.

3 Agents and Web Services Supported Exception Management

Typical agent architectures have many same features as web services, and extend web services in several ways [6]. Web services, unlike agents, are not designed to use and reconcile ontologies. A web service knows only about itself, while agents often have awareness of other agents and their capabilities as interactions among the agents occur. Agents are inherently communicative, whereas web services are passive until invoked. Agents are cooperative, and by forming teams and coalitions can provide high-level and more comprehensive service, while current standards for web services do not provide for composing functionalities. By integrating agent technology with web services, we seek to take advantages of both.

3.1 Multi-agent Framework

An exception-management system is one that can track the predictable events of business processes, and can identify errors and subsequently resolved errors. We can reengineer current business applications to support exception management functions, or develop an independent exception management system to link with legacy applications through which a business process would pass during its lifecycle. In this research, we try to fundamentally use internal resources to build software capabilities to interact with legacy systems. Relevant data are extracted from existing applications into the exception management system to perform monitoring activities on business transactions, and resolutions for identified exceptions will be sent back to legacy systems to repair such exceptions.

In a dynamic and complex business environment, exception management is more like real time dynamic decision making tasks. Based on this concern, agents are proposed to manage complex activities based on continuous awareness of situation and real-time decisions on activities. As described in Figure 1, agents orchestrates business activities dynamically at runtime and continues the evaluation of environment throughout execution, during which business changes occur and business rules are dynamically bound to decision of tasks. The evolution of business processes is driven by changes from environment and runtime decision of tasks in current situation. The changes from environment may activate some tasks, and the activated tasks may produce new changes into the environment and subsequently start the next round of decision making of tasks.

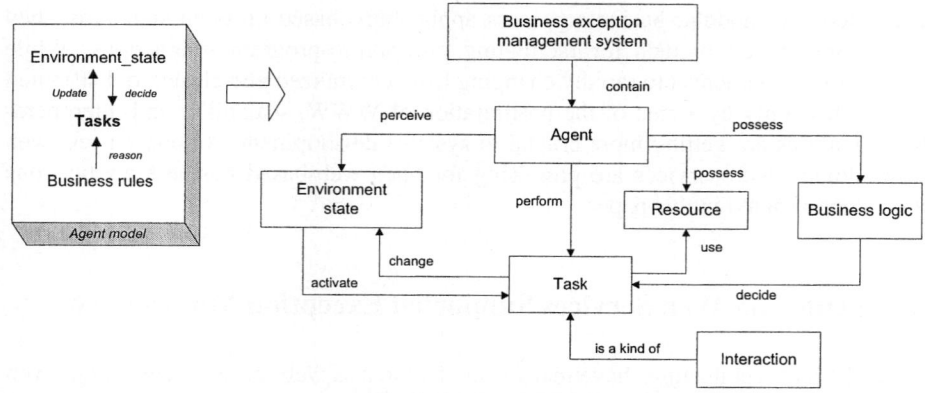

Fig. 1. Agent model

3.2 Knowledge-Based Agents

In a multi-agent system, software agents are proposed to perform tasks autonomously on user's behalf, which means that they can act independently of humans. Autonomous agents rely on the perception or awareness of its environment and the knowledge for problem solving. Various kinds of intelligence are supported by this kind of knowledge. Though there have been a few agent-oriented development methods based on knowledge engineering technology [4, 7], they are aiming at a general framework for agent-oriented computing and software engineering, not quite appropriate for the complex process management domain.

For the purpose for a flexible and robust approach to complex process management, we propose to construct the knowledge framework of agents in three layers, termed as situation knowledge, process control knowledge, and problem solving. 1) The **situation knowledge** of an agent is its beliefs about its environment, which may include information of resources, events, tasks, other agent, etc. This type of knowledge can be described in form of a collection of patterns modeling different classes of events, resources, etc. 2) The **process control knowledge** is used for an agent to control over its own internal states and over its activities. Such kind of knowledge usually concerns business rules, which are the user's expression of preference of policies followed by the agent to manage its task [1]. The separation of the process control knowledge from the problem solving knowledge enables the run-time system to assist users in coordinating and scheduling the tasks for problem solving, and contributes to simplify and speed up application development. 3) **Problem solving knowledge** of an agent describes its problem solving capability in form of methods and strategies. In business exception management, the knowledge for performing the tasks of exception capturing, analysis and resolution is required.

3.3 Web Services Support

Interaction among agents, an important aspect on research of multi-agent system, is set up on lower-level data communication as well as control information with semantic and knowledge. The most popular language for agent communication is Knowledge Query and Manipulation Language (KQML) [3]. Recently, there are researches focusing on the use of XML (Extensible Markup Language) in agent communication. In this research, web services are adopted as a promising web technology for open web-based exception management. Web services use the popular Internet standard technologies, such as XML, Simple Object Access Protocol (SOAP) and HTTP, to increase compatibility of the system. SOAP is the most common network communication protocol between software services. SOAP messages are represented by using XML, and can be sent over a transport layer, such as HTTP and SMTP. By integrating agent technology with web services, the agents deployed for exception management are wrapped as web services, and communicate with each other as well as interact with legacy business systems for necessary data exchange.

4 A Case: Exception Management in Securities Trading

Based on the above approach supported by agents and web services, a case of exception management in securities trading is elaborated in the following sections. More relevant information about this case can be found in [15, 16].

4.1 Case Description

With rising trading volumes and increasing risks in securities transactions, the securities industry is making an effort to shorten the trade lifecycle and minimize transaction risks. While attempting to achieve this, exception management is critical to pass trade information within the trade lifecycle in a timely and accurate fashion [12, 5]. Generally speaking, the process of exception management starts with the respective monitoring of trade details and trade agreement status. Any exception detected will result in the diagnosing activity, and subsequently, a diagnostic report with resolution advice will be produced. Once the advice is validated by the manager, resolution action will be carried out to resolve the exception. Concerning the distributed environment and complex processes, the agent-oriented approach is employed through delegating complex exception management tasks to a collection of agents. Furthermore, web services techniques are applied for more scalability and interoperability in network-based business environment in securities trading.

4.2 System Architecture

Based on the analysis in section 4.1, the agent hierarchy for exception management is described as follows. The Interaction agents, such as **trading interaction agent** and

settlement interaction agent, work as a bridge between our exception management system and the existing securities transaction systems. They convert legacy trade data into web service messages and convert web service messages into legacy messages when feeding back. Task agents are deployed to perform data monitoring and exception repair activities. **Trade details monitoring agent** is to detect any error contained within the details of each trade, e.g. an unusual component in a trade record. **Trade status monitoring agent** is applied to keep watch on the status of securities transactions. Those un-agreed confirmations, outstanding confirmations, and denied confirmations will be transmitted to the diagnostic agent for further investigation. When receiving the output from monitoring agents, **Diagnostic agent** will start its diagnosing process to investigate the nature of problems, and **Resolution agent** may take some initiatives to resolve the problem. **Repository agent** contains and manages several kinds of information about securities transactions and exceptions. Such shared information may form an important base for agents' collaboration in exception management. The architecture of our web-service and agents based exception management system is outlined in Fig.2, in which a society of agents are wrapped as web services to provide a set of services for exception management in securities trading. Following the model in Fig.1, each agent is built as an autonomous and cognitive entity that can perceive its environment by capturing events that occurred and monitoring states of tasks or resources, and perform appropriate tasks.

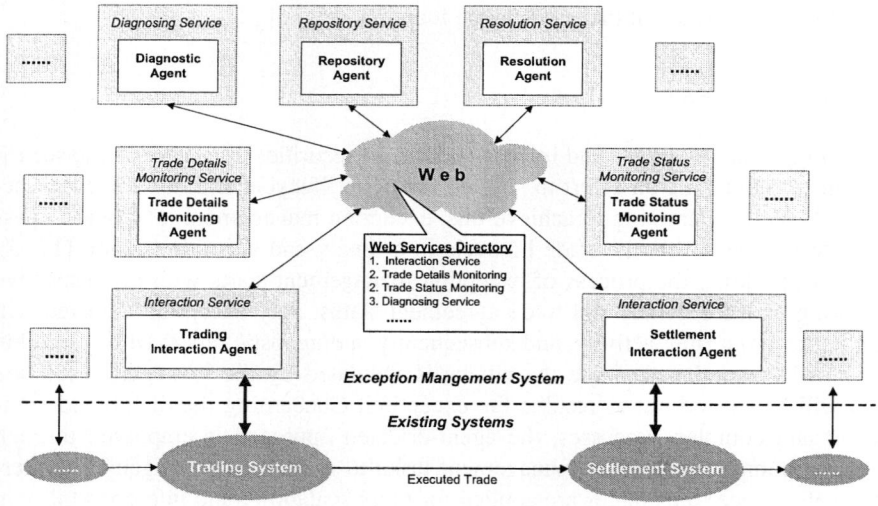

Fig. 2. System architecture

4.3 Knowledge-Based Agents

As suggested in section 3.2, the knowledge of agents in complex process management is constructed in three layers, i.e. situation knowledge, process control knowledge, and problem solving knowledge. Due to the limited space of this paper, only the Diagnostic Agent is described as an example for illustrating the knowledge engineering of agents in our system.

Situation Knowledge. The Diagnostic Agent may perceive the information of its environment, such as the information of error reports, diagnostic activities, data request, etc. Followed is an example that describes the information of an error report event. This error is numbered 102 and related to Trade No.12362.

```
(event (e-type error_report) (err-no 102) (trd-no 12362))
```

Process Control Knowledge. The knowledge for control usually concerns business rules followed by the agent to manage its tasks. The rule below specifies the check on exception resolutions to those trades of large value, since resolutions suggested the Diagnostic Agent to such trades are required to be confirmed by the diagnostic expert.

```
(defrule(defrule rule-7 "confirm resolution advice"
   (event (e-type resolution-advice) (trd-no ?t_no))
   (large-trade (trd-no ?t_no))
      =>    (assert   (task    (t-type  confirm_resolution)   (err-no
               ?e_no) (start-time (time))))))
```

Problem Solving Knowledge. Problem solving knowledge of an agent describes its capability to perform various tasks or solve problems on behalf of humans. When a trade is detected in pending status, i.e. a trade that has not been agreed by trade parties in a specified time, Diagnostic Agent will check if the trade agreement has been replied by the counterparty. This knowledge is specified in the rule below.

```
(defrule(defrule rule-7 "check agreement_reply"
   (error-report (err-no ?e_no) (trd-no ?t_no) (err-type pending)
   (transmission-record (trd-no ?t_no) (send-status ?s_status)
      (reply-status ?r_status))
      =>  (if (and (eq ?s_status successful)(eq ?r_status nil))
           then
              (assert (diag-report (err-no ?e_no) (trd-no ?t_no)
                    (diag-detail unreplied_agreement)))))
```

4.4 Implementation

The intelligent agents in our system are wrapped as web-services that provide exception management services on the Internet. The web service based agents have been developed using Java Web Services Development Package (JWSDP) (Java.sun.com). JWSDP brings together a set of Java APIs for XML-based Java applications by supporting key XML standards such as SOAP, WSDL and UDDI. These APIs and their reference implements are bundled together with a set of runtime tools to form a JWSDP. As we described before, the communication among agents are through

SOAP, which is done by Java API for XML Messaging (JAXM). Such JAXM messages follow SOAP standards, which prescribe the format for messages and specify the things that are required, optional, or not allowed. Furthermore, JESS (Java Expert system Shell and Scripting language) is adopted as the business rule engine. Jess is a rule engine and scripting environment written entirely in Java language (http://herzberg.ca.sandia.gov/jess). In our system, each agent contains a JESS rule set for reasoning. The reasoning results are asserted JESS facts. An agent can send such facts to other agents, by wrapping them to XML and SOAP messages. After our web-service agents have been set up, they can be published on the Web. The Web Services Description Language (WSDL) specification is used to describe and publish web-service agents in a standard way.

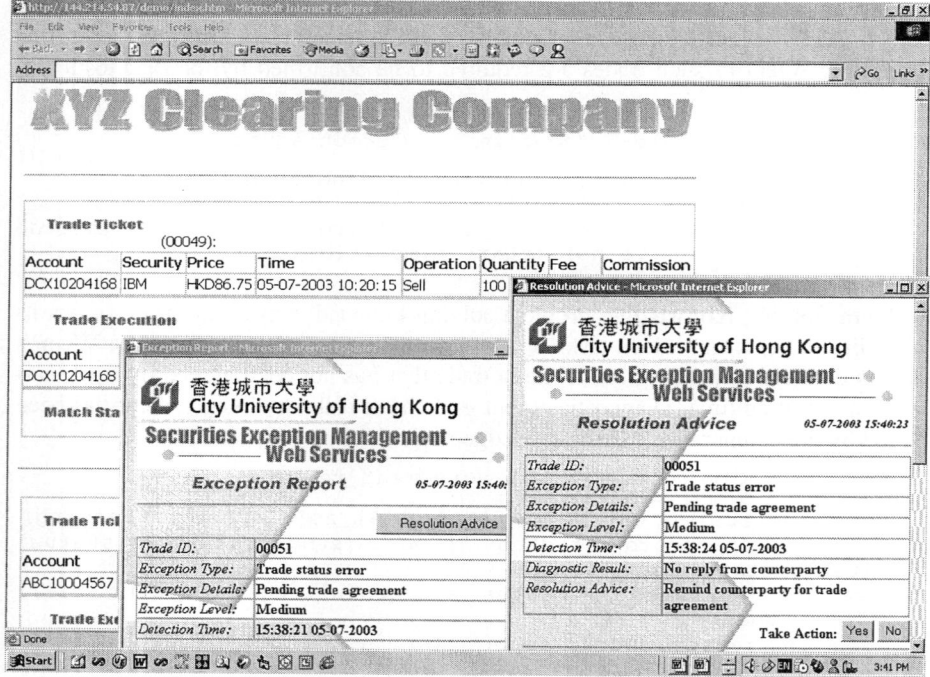

Fig. 3. Prototype

Fig.3 shows an interface screen of the prototype. The background window is a clearing company's regular interface window. We did not put any additional artifact into such existing interfaces. When an exception is detected, an additional window (the small one at the left hand side) will pop up to display the exception report. The user can read the resolution advice by clicking the "Resolution Advice" button in the exception report window. A "Resolution Advice" window will pop up, shown in the right hand. As to resolution advice, the user may accept it and take automatic repair action by clicking "Yes", or ignore it and take action through other ways.

5 Conclusion

This paper has explores the approach supported by agent-based techniques with web services technology for business exception management. Compared with traditional workflow approaches to exception handling, our approach provides more support for flexibility and collaboration by delegating complex exception management tasks to a collection of interacting and autonomous web-service-agents. Equipped with process control knowledge, agents may offer more flexibility of task management in dynamic business environment. Problem solving knowledge of agents, on the other hand, facilitates more capabilities in exception detection, diagnosis and resolution. Furthermore, by wrapping intelligent agents into web services, our approach provides more scalability and interoperability in network-based business environment.

Acknowledgement

The authors want to thank Kwok Kit Wan from City University of Hong Kong for his support on the system development.

References

1. Caglayan, A., and Harrison, C., Agent sourcebook: a complete guide to desktop, internet, and intranet agent, John Wiley & Sons, New York, 1997.
2. Chiu, D., Li, Q., and Karlapalem, K., Cooperative Exception Handling in ADOME Workflow Management System, Information Systems: an International Journal (special issue on Web Information Systems Engineering), 26(2), 2001, pp.93-120.
3. Finin, T., Fritzson, R., McKay, D., and McEntire, R., KQML as an agent communication language, Proceedings of the third international conference on Information and knowledge management, ACM Press, Nov.1994.
4. Glaser, N., The CoMoMAS Approach: From Conceptual Models to Executable Code, http://citeseer.nj.nec.com, 1997
5. Guerra A., Exception Management: The Safety Net You've Been Looking For? Wall Street & Technology Online, Sep 4, 2002, URL: http://www.wallstreetandtech.com
6. Huhns, M.N., Agents as Web services. IEEE Internet computing, 6 (4), 2002, 93-95.
7. Iglesias, C., Garijo, M., Gonzalez, J., and Velasco, J., A methodological proposal for multi-agent systems development extending CommonKADS, Proceedings of the tenth knowledge acquisition for knowledge-based systems workshop, 1996.
8. Jennings, N.R., Faratin, P., Norman, T. J., O'Brien, P. and Odgers. B., Autonomous Agents for Business Process Management, International Journal of Applied Artificial Intelligence, 14 (2), pp.145-189.
9. Kammer, P.J., Bolcer, G.A., Taylor, R.N., Hitomi, A.S., and Bergman, M., Techniques for Supporting Dynamic and Adaptive Workflow, Computer Supported Cooperative Work (CSCW), Vol. 9, November 2000, pp.269-292.
10. Klein, M., Dellarocas, C., A Knowledge-based Approach to Handling Exceptions in Workflow Systems, Computer Supported Cooperative Work (CSCW), Vol.9, November 2000, pp.399-412.

11. O'Brien, P.D., and Wiegand, W.E., Agent based process management: applying intelligent agents to workflow, The Knowledge Engineering Review, Vol. 13(2), 1998, pp.1-14.
12. U.S. Securities and Exchange Commission, Settling securities trades in one day, T+1, http://www.sec.gov, Oct. 2001.
13. Wang, H., and Wang, C., Intelligent Agents in the Nuclear Industry, IEEE Computer, 30(11), November 1997, pp. 28-34.
14. Wang, H., Mylopoulos, J., and Liao, S., Intelligent Agents and Financial Risk Monitoring Systems, Communications of the ACM, 45(3), 2002, pp. 83-88.
15. Wang, M., Wang, H., Wan, K.K., and Xu, D., The design of Intelligent Agents for Exception Management in Securities Trading, Proceeding of Americas Conference on Information Systems (AMCIS 2003), Tampa, US, August 2003.
16. Wang, M., Wang, H., Wan, K.K., and Xu, D., Knowledge-based Exception Handling in Securities Transactions, forthcoming in Proceeding of Hawaii International Conference on System Science (HICSS-37), Hawaii, US, January 2004.
17. Wooldridge, M., and Jennings, N., Intelligent agents: theory and practice, The Knowledge Engineering Review, 10(2), 1995, pp. 115-152.
18. Wooldridge, M., An introduction to multiagent systems, J. Wiley, Chichester, England, 2002.
19. Zhao, J.L., Nunamaker, J.F., and Briggs, R.O., Intelligent Workflow Techniques for Distributed Group Facilitation, Proceedings of the 35th Hawaii International Conference on System Sciences, January 7-10, 2002.
20. Zhuge, H., Workflow- and agent-based cognitive flow management for distributed team cooperation, Information & Management, 2003, Vol.40, pp.419-429.

Multi-agent Interaction Technology for Peer-to-Peer Computing in Electronic Trading Environments

Martin Purvis, Mariusz Nowostawski, Stephen Cranefield, and Marcos Oliveira

Information Science Department, University of Otago, Dunedin, New Zealand
Tel: +64-3-479-8318
{mpurvis,mnowostawski,scranefield,moliveira}
@infoscience.otago.ac.nz

Abstract. Open trading environments involve a type of peer-to-peer computing characterised by well-defined interaction protocols that are used by the traders and sometimes updated dynamically. New traders can arrive at any time and acquire the protocols that are current. Multi-agent system technology is appropriate for these circumstances, and in this paper we present an approach that can be used to support multiple trader agents on multiple computing platforms. The approach involves the use of FIPA-compliant trader agents which (a) incorporate micro-agents for specific local tasks and (b) use coloured Petri nets in order to keep track of the local context of agent conversations. In order to enhance efficiency and employ standard transport services, the trader agents interact with peers on other platforms by means of JXTA technology. We illustrate the working of our approach by examining the operation of an example multi-agent system in commodities trading scenario.

Keywords: electronic trading, agent interaction, JXTA, P2P

Content areas: multi-agent systems, E-commerce and AI, Agents

1 Introduction

Peer-to-peer computing applications in open economic trading spheres must be able to interoperate effectively in distributed, heterogeneous, and sometimes unreliable environments. Multi-agent system technology, wherein agents communicate by exchanging declarative statements, has the potential to provide a robust and scalable infrastructure to support such systems [1]. With agent architectures, individual agent participants can be replaced or supplemented by improved agents, which can enable the overall system to introduce improvements, adapt to changing conditions, and extend the scope of operations to new domains.

In the international e-business climate, autonomous agents or groups of such agents from distinct organizations may come together in a competitive environment and exchange information and services. In order for multi-agent systems to operate effectively under these circumstances, they must be able to coordinate their activities with other agents in a satisfactory manner, and this coordination is accomplished by having suitable interaction protocols between agents. In addition, the deployed agents must be able to respond rapidly in competitive trading environments, and so should be developed to employ standard infrastructural P2P services wherever possible. In this paper we describe our approach to the representation and use of agent interaction protocols and discuss our implementation that combines the use of standard agent [2] and P2P [3] technology. The implementation of our approach is demonstrated in the context of a commodities trading scenario. This represents a new approach to agent-based systems based on combining standard, FIPA-based protocols and P2P technology.

2 Multi-agent Systems

Agents must share an understanding of the possible message types and the terms that are used in their communication. A common approach that has been used to deal with the potential complexity of these messages is to have messages represented in a declarative format, with the basic message types limited to a few standard types and the individual terms used in the message content represented by an ontology that has been developed for the application domain of interest [4].

2.1 FIPA Agents

The Foundation for Intelligent Physical Agents Agent Communication Language (FIPA ACL) has a relatively small set of message types (the Communicative Act Library [2]) based on speech acts [5]. Examples of FIPA communicative acts are quite general, such as *inform, request, propose,* etc., and that to which the general communicative acts refer, *e.g.* what is being 'requested' or 'proposed', are contained in the bodies of the messages. The task of understanding the message body containing terms that refer to an ontology can require a considerable amount of reasoning, but this task can be assisted by employing conversation policies, or interaction protocols [6], which can reduce the number of options that need to be considered for appropriate response to an incoming message. An interaction protocol specifies a limited range of responses that are appropriate to specific message types when a particular protocol is in operation, and this is a way of situating a sequence of exchanged messages in a context. FIPA has produced a short list of specifications [7] for several standard interaction protocols, but these are somewhat limited and may not offer sufficient assistance for many of the potential interactions in which agents are likely to engage.

Interaction protocols represented in the FIPA specifications focus on the explicit exchange of information that takes place between the two agents, but there is no concern or representation to assist in the understanding of what is contained in the body of the message. That kind of task is left to the agent's own devices and is not treated by the FIPA interaction protocols. Instead of leaving all of the rest of what transpires in connection with the interaction outside of the specification and up to the individual agents, however, we consider it to be advantageous to consider within the protocol what the other agent is doing with the information.

2.2 Interaction Protocols

Although FIPA uses AUML [8] to represent its standard interaction protocols, we use coloured Petri nets (CPNs) [9,10], because their formal properties facilitate the modelling of concurrent conversations in an integrated fashion. The availability of net analysis tools [11] means that it is possible to check the designed protocols and role interactions for undesired loops and deadlock conditions, and this can then help eliminate human errors introduced in the design process.

Figures 1 and 2 show our representation of the FIPA *request* interaction protocol. Each interaction protocol is modelled in terms of the individual agent roles in the interaction: for each individual role there is a separate Petri net. The collection of individual Petri nets associated with all the relevant roles represents the entire interaction protocol. For every conversation, there are always at least two roles: that of the initiator of the conversation and the roles of the other participants in the conversation.

Figure 1 depicts the initiator of the FIPA *request* interaction, and Figure 2 shows the Participant interaction. For diagrammatic simplicity, we omit the inscriptions from the diagram, but we will describe some of them below. The *In* place (in this and the following Petri net diagrams) will have tokens placed there when the agent receives messages from other agents. The *In* place is a *fusion node* (a place common to two or more nets): the very same *In* place may exist on other Petri nets that also represent conversations in which the agent may be engaged. When the agent receives a message from another agent, a token with information associated with the message is placed in the *In* place, which may be shared by several Petri nets. The transitions connected to the *In* place have guards on them such that the transitions are only enabled by a token on the *In* place with the appropriate qualification. The Initiator of the request interaction will have a token placed in the *Start* place, and this will trigger the *Send request* transition to place a token in the *Out* place. We assume that the communication transport machinery causes tokens to disappear from a Petri net's *Out* place and (usually) a corresponding token to appear on the *In* place of another agent. The transfer may not be instantaneous, or even guaranteed to occur; it is possible for a token to disappear from one role's *Out* place without a corresponding token appearing at another agent's *In* place.

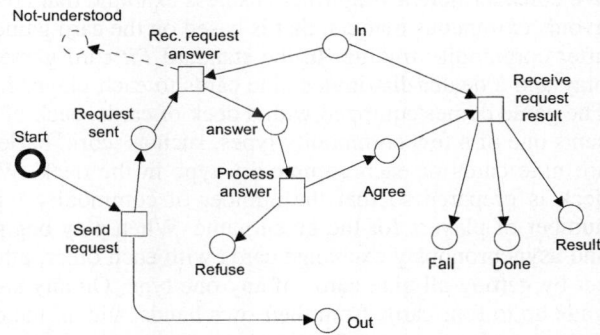

Fig. 1. Request interaction for the Initiator role.

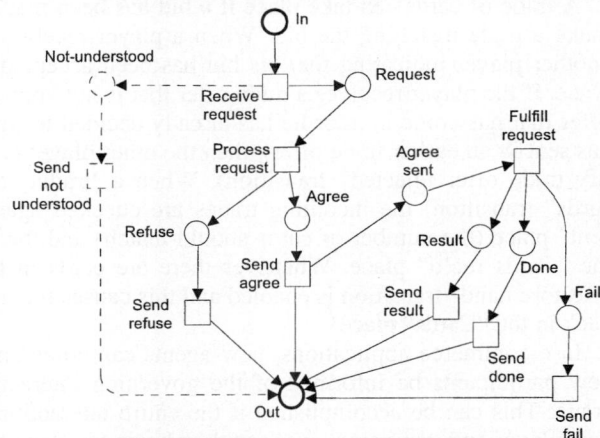

Fig. 2. Request interaction: the Participant role.

Note that the Initiator could be involved in several concurrent request interaction conversations, and the placement of specific tokens in the *Agree* place enables this agent to keep track of which responses correspond to which conversations. This shows how the coloured Petri net representation facilitates the management of concurrent interactions involving the same protocol.

3 Electronic Trading Scenario

We consider here a simplified business example that covers some essential issues but avoids extraneous matters, that is based on the card game, *Pit* [12], which is modelled after commodity trading. In the standard *Pit* card game, three to seven players may play and a dealer distributes nine cards to each player from a shuffled deck of cards. The game comes equipped with a deck of cards, each of which has a 'suit' that represents one of a few commodity types, such as corn, barley, wheat, rice, etc., and there are nine cards or each commodity type in the deck. When the game is played, the deck is prepared so that the number of commodity types in the deck matches the number of players for the given game. When play begins, the players independently and asynchronously exchange cards with each other, attempting to "corner" the market by getting all nine cards of any one type. On any single exchange, they can only trade up to four cards from their own hands, and all the cards traded must belong to a single commodity type. Trading is carried out by a player (the "bidder") announcing, for example, that he has some cards to trade. Whenever a player manages to get a 'corner', he announces that fact to the dealer, and the given "hand" is finished (the protocol shown here is for a single hand). Players who get a corner in 'wheat' (by getting all nine 'wheat' cards) get 100 points, a corner in 'corn' gets 75 points, in 'oats' gets 60 points, etc.

In course of play, a player (role shown in Figure 3) always checks to see if he has a corner, and if so, announces this to the Dealer, who, in turn, announces it to the rest of the players, signaling the end of the hand. Whenever an external bid is received, the player could choose to accept the bid. If the player accepts the bid, a message is sent to the bidding player (not the Dealer) and a token stored in the "cards offered" place.

A trade of cards can take place if a bid has been made and a player has offered to make a trade matching the bid. When a player receives a trade offer message from another player indicating that his bid has been accepted, it is stored in the "Accpt." place. If the player receives a trade offer that is not applicable (such as a second trade offer that has come in after he has already decided to trade cards with someone who has sent in an earlier trade offer), then the other player is sent a rejection notice ("Notify trade offer rejected" transition). When a 'trader' receives cards ("Rec. traded cards" transition) the incoming trades are checked against the token in the "Cards sent" place (the number of cards should match) and the received cards are placed in the "Cards rec'd" place. Whenever there are cards in the "Cards rec'd" place, the "Restore hand" transition is enabled and this causes the received cards to be deposited back in the "Cards" place.

In e-commerce applications, new agents can come and go, so it is necessary that new participants be informed of the governing interaction protocols in the trading arena. This can be accomplished if the entire interaction protocol can be sent to the new player and that new player can then begin to interact according to that prescribed

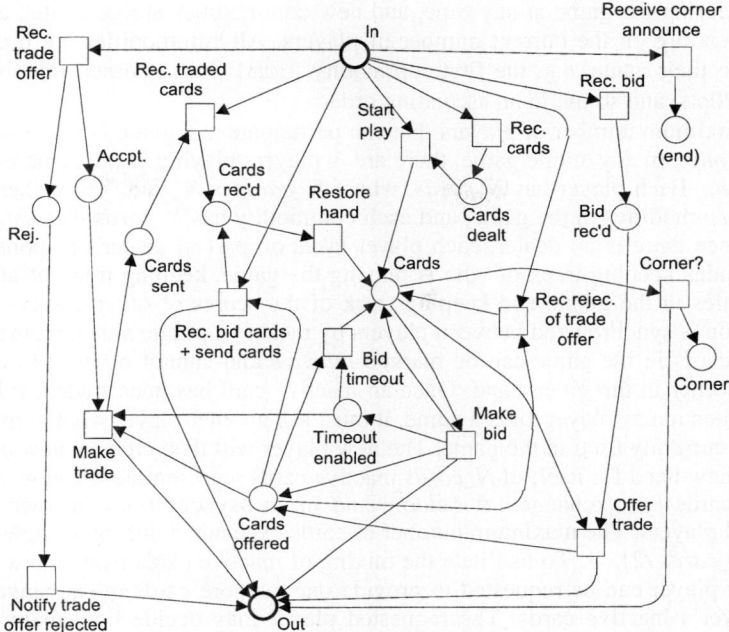

Fig. 3. The Pit game interaction protocol for the Player role.

protocol. In the next section we discuss our implementation of the interaction protocol scheme and how the dynamic situation of new agent participants is handled.

4 Peer-to-Peer Implementation for Electronic Trading

For our multi-agent implementation, we use Opal [13], a platform for agent-based development in Java that provides support for the FIPA agent specifications. Packed with Opal is JFern [14], a Java-based tool for the enactment and simulation of coloured Petri nets. When new agents appear and are to be incorporated into the network of available agents, they are sent a FIPA *Propose* message by the group manager with a message content containing an action proposal to interact according to an enclosed protocol specified by an XML serialization of a Petri net. The interaction protocol comprises a coloured Petri net and the associated ontology, represented in UML, for the terms used in the interaction protocol. Both the Petri net and the UML-encoded ontology information are encoded in XML and sent to the newcomer agent when it joins a group.

4.1 The P2P Pit Game

We have adapted the Pit game to make it more characteristic of a peer-to-peer environment of autonomous components. The modified game has the same goal as in the standard game: each player is playing for itself, and is trying to corner a single commodity. However, there is now no centralized dealer. In addition, players can leave and join during the game at any time, and new commodities are generated automatically depending on the current number of players. All commodities are ordered according to their value, e.g. the first commodity, `com1`, has a corner value of 10pts, `com2` = 20pts, and so on, in an ascending order.

The maximum number of players that can participate in a game is set to some high value, N_max. In any single game, there are N players playing at the same time, with $N < N\_max$. Each player has N_cards, where $N\_cards > N\_max$. Thus, there are always N commodities in the game, and each commodity has N_cards that are in circulation. Since there is no dealer, each player takes on part of dealer's responsibilities. That includes keeping track of who is playing the game, keeping track of all current commodities in the game, and keeping track of the scores of other players. All that information is synchronized between players by means of public announcements.

Some cards in the game can be marked *inactive* and cannot be used to count towards a corner in the given hand. Once an inactive card has been traded, it becomes *active*. When a new player joins a game, it must ask another player what commodities are being currently used in the game. The new player will then create a new commodity and a new hand for itself of N_cards inactive cards representing the new commodity. The cards are exchanged at random and in an asynchronous manner between individual players. The maximum number of cards exchanged during a single transaction is $(N\_cards /2) - 1$. To facilitate the mixing of inactive cards from a new player's hand, any player can be requested to provide one or more cards in exchange for another player's inactive cards. The requested player may decide how many cards it wants to exchange, but it cannot refuse the inactive card demand.

A new game starts when a single player creates a group, advertises it, and creates for itself N_cards cards of the lowest priced commodity. All the cards in his hand are marked inactive. This player sets the group players count, N, to 1, and records the value of the current highest commodity and lowest commodity. When a second player joins the group, it is informed of the current number of players in the group and what is the next commodity price (the second lowest). The newly joined player creates a hand of this commodity, and marks all its cards inactive. When a third player joins in, again, the player counter is incremented and a new commodity set is created. All players are aware of the number of players in the group, and all know what is the current highest priced commodity. This is kept in synchronisation by making public announcements within the group. After the third player joins the group, cards may be traded, and players can make bids and announcements.

New players can join a playing group at any time during the play. They simply join the group, ask about the number of players and the highest priced commodity, create a hand of inactive cards of a new commodity, and start exchanging cards with others.

There are two types of announcements: public announcements, and individual agent-to-agent messages. The former are done through the underlying network infrastructure to all the agents in the game. The latter are done between only two interested parties. This is discussed further in Section 5.

5 Implementation Infrastructure

The implementation using the Opal FIPA Platform also includes the KEA microagent framework [15]. The interaction architecture is shown in Figure 4. The use of

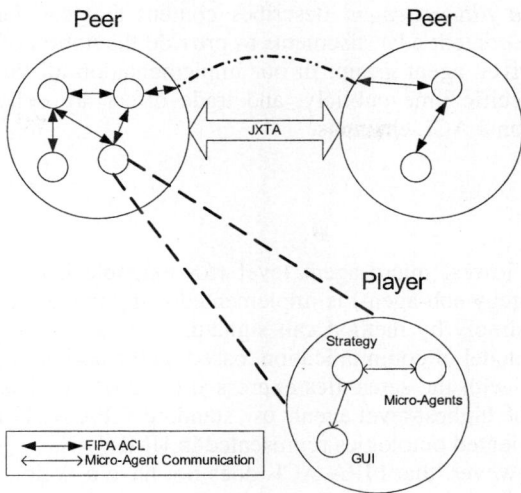

Fig. 4. Agent, micro-agent, and JXTA interaction.

micro-agents allows us to maintain agent-oriented software modelling and implementation on all levels of abstraction. GUI components and internal processing units, such as the *Strategy* mico-agent are represented and implemented as agents and/or roles. At a higher level all players are treated as individual FIPA agents, which communicate between each other using FIPA ACL messages. The player agents delegate particular tasks to appropriate micro-agents. This approach offers the advantage of reusing components, together with late dynamic binding between particular roles.

5.1 Use of JXTA

To facilitate the dynamic discovery of peers on the network and peer-to-peer messaging, we have used the JXTA infrastructure [3], which is a set of open protocols that allow any connected device on the network to communicate and collaborate in a P2P manner. In this paper we show how JXTA peers and JXTA announcements can co-exist with the notion of agent-to-agent messaging and FIPA ACL.

The fundamental notion in JXTA is a peer, which represents any networked device that implements one or more of the JXTA protocols. To send messages to one another, JXTA peers use pipes, which represent an asynchronous and unidirectional message transfer mechanism used for service communication. Another important JXTA mode of communication is *advertisements*, which are language-neutral metadata structures represented as XML documents and are used to describe and publish the existence of a peer resources. Peers discover resources by searching for their corresponding advertisements and may cache any discovered advertisements locally. Each advertisement is published along with a *lifetime* that specifies the time availability of its associated resource. Lifetimes enable the deletion of obsolete resources without requiring any centralized control (an advertisement can be republished before the original advertisement expires in order to extend the lifetime of a resource). In particular, *Content Advertisement* describes content that can be shared in a peer group, and we use content advertisements to provide the notion of "public announcements" within a given agent group. In our implementation all Pit game bids are announced for a specific time publicly, and trade offers are delivered to individual agents over traditional ACL channels.

5.2 Messaging

Messaging at the lowest micro-agent level (for example between the micro-agent Player and its Strategy sub-agent) is implemented using method calls, and its semantics is expressed simply by method call signatures. At a higher level, micro-agents employ a limited model of communication, based on the notion of goals, declarations, and commitments, with the semantics expressed by UML models of goals and their relationships. At the highest level agents use standard FIPA ACL augmented with the notion of object-oriented ontologies represented in UML [16].

We observe, however, that FIPA ACL does not have a notion of an agent group, and there is no notion of a public announcement to a group. FIPA messages are addressed to a set of recipients. If the set is empty, this corresponds to "broadcasting of messages such as in ad-hoc wireless networks" (FIPA Abstract Architecture [2]). If the set of recipients has more than one entry, this "corresponds to the situation where the message is multicast" (FIPA ACL Message Structure Specification [2]). However, the standard FIPA message transport protocols (MTPs), IIOP and HTTP, being based on TCP/IP, do not support multicasting. Therefore, most FIPA agent platforms must simulate multicasting by sending separate messages to each individually named recipient. This is where JXTA plays an important role. We have introduced a special "wrapper" agent, called a *Peer* agent. Currently, there is a single Peer Agent for each JXTA peer (*i.e.* a single Peer Agent per machine). All the communication between individual Players and a Peer is done by standard FIPA ACL; but the communication between Peer agents, themselves, is performed by means of JXTA announcements and pipes (*i.e.* outside normal FIPA ACL messaging). All public announcements are done via JXTA announcements, and all peer-to-peer communication, *i.e.* all the individual agent conversations, are performed using standard FIPA messaging mechanisms transmitted via the JXTA Pipe infrastructure. Thus in the P2P Pit game each agent sends bids over FIPA ACL to the Peer, which in turn performs multicast messaging on behalf of the agents (for public announcements like bids). All the public announcements are done in an asynchronous (and unreliable) manner over the standard JXTA Content Advertisements. Since the Peer also has a standard pipe for FIPA text-based ACL messaging, all communication can be considered to be performed over JXTA.

5.3 Integrating FIPA and Peer-to-Peer Messaging

In the previous section we discussed the use of peer agents to provide a bridge between FIPA-style and JXTA messaging. We are currently extending Opal's FIPA messaging system so that messages to groups are supported in a transparent manner, without the need for introducing extra peer agents. We believe this can be a useful extension to the FIPA model of messaging in its own right.

In some agent societies it may be important for agents to be able to send messages that are intentionally publicly observable. For example, in the original physical version of the card game Pit, all player communications and the exchanges of cards (but not the commodities of the cards being exchanged) are public. An electronic version of public announcements can be seen as a mechanism that reduces the possibility of cheating in that medium, thus ensuring a smoothly running agent society. Therefore, the use of JXTA-style multicast messages to groups may play a useful role in the design of agent institutions. A further extension of this idea would be to allow FIPA messages to be sent from one agent to another, but also 'carbon copied' to a group. An example of this type of message in human society is the public exchange of wedding vows between bride and groom in the presence of witnesses.

5.4 Wireless Implementation

Because we anticipate future applications involving wireless technology, we also implemented the Opal+JXTA system in J2ME Personal Profile in order to support mobile applications. The Pit game application has then been ported and demonstrated on the Sharp Zaurus c700 Personal Digital Assistant [17].

6 Discussion

In the current P2P implementation we have introduced an extra transport layer between the FIPA agent and the (FIPA-compliant) Transport System. This layer is provided by the specialist Peer Agent, which intercepts all Pit Game-related messages from individual Player agents, and propagates them appropriately for the P2P environment.

For messages addressed to a single individual agent registered on the local peer, the Peer Agent simply forwards the message directly to the recipient. If the receiver is registered on a remote peer, the local Peer Agent passes the message to that recipient's Peer Agent, which in turn passes the message down to the individual recipient. If, however, the original message is a public announcement (such as a bid), then the local Peer agent passes the announcement to all locally registered agents and also passes it to all other Peer Agents, which in turn pass it down to all their local players. In the current implementation, the Peer Agent is implemented on a level below the FIPA ACL level, so all its communications are not based on the FIPA ACL itself, but rather on a proprietary protocol implemented on our OPAL-specific platform.

Opal has been built to conform to the latest specification of the FIPA Abstract Architecture (FIPA AA). The standard set of transport protocols in OPAL (IIOP and HTTP) has been extended to include JXTA. At the present time the Transport Service, as specified in FIPA AA, is used solely to provide a communication protocol for ACL messages between two end-points. But the Transport Service does not cover some aspects of agent communication, such as discovery, multicasts or broadcasts. Since these were needed for our application, we implemented them using our own proprietary interfaces and protocols. From this work, we have come to believe that there would be advantages in extending the basic FIPA AA infrastructure to cover discovery and broadcasts. Dynamic discovery of other, FIPA-compliant, Transport Services would enable dynamic discovery of other agent platforms that appear in a networked environment. This in turn would provide a bootstrapping infrastructure for Agent Directory data exchange and dynamic caching of remote Agent Directory Services. With such an addition, all Pit game public announcements would be simpler at the agent level, without the necessity of using proprietary Peer Agents or JXTA Wrappers. We believe such an addition to the FIPA AA would facilitate agent usage in P2P applications.

References

1. Jennings, N. R., "Agent-oriented software engineering", *Proceedings of the 12th International Conference on Industrial and Engineering Applications of AI*, (1999).
2. FIPA. Foundation For Intelligent Physical Agents (FIPA). FIPA 2001 specifications, http://www.fipa.org/specifications/ (2003).
3. Project JXTA. http://www.jxta.org.
4. Ontology.org, http://www.ontology.org (2003).
5. Searle, J., *Speech Acts : An Essay in the Philosophy of Language,* Cambridge U. Press, Cambridge (1970).
6. Greaves, M, and Bradshaw, J. (eds.), *Specifying and Implementing Conversation Policies*, Autonomous Agents '99 Workshop, Seattle, WA, (May 1999).
7. FIPA Interaction Protocols, http://www.fipa.org/repository/ips.php3 (2003).
8. Odell, J, Parunak, H. V. D., Bauer, B., "Extending UML for agents", *Proceedings of the Agent-Oriented Information Systems Workshop at the 17th National conference on Artificial Intelligence*, pp. 3-17 (2000).
9. Cost, S., Chen, Y., Finin, T., Labrou, Y., and Peng, Y., "Using colored Petri nets for conversation modeling, *Issues in Agent Communication,* Lecture Notes in AI, Springer-Verlag, Berlin (2000).
10. Jensen, K., *Coloured Petri Nets – Basic Concepts, Analysis Methods and Practical Use,* Springer-Verlag, Berlin (1992).
11. See, for example, http://www.daimi.au.dk/PetriNets/tools/db.html (2003).
12. Pit Game, Parker Bros., Inc., Salem, MA (1904)
    see http://www.centralconnector.com/GAMES/pit.html.
13. Purvis, M., Cranefield, S., Nowostawski, M., and Carter, D., "Opal: A Multi-Level Infrastructure for Agent-Oriented Software Development", *Information Science Discussion Paper Series*, No. 2002/01, ISSN 1172-6024, University of Otago, Dunedin, New Zealand.
14. Nowostawski, M., *JFern,* version 1.2.1, http://sourceforge.net/project/showfiles.php?group_id=16338 (2002).
15. Nowostawski, M., Purvis, M., and Cranefield, S., "KEA - Multi-level Agent Infrastructure,Published", *Proceedings of the 2nd International Workshop of Central and Eastern Europe on Multi-Agent Systems (CEEMAS 2001)* University of Mining and Metallurgy, Krakow, Poland pp.355-362 (2001), http://www.sf.net/projects/javaprs
16. Cranefield, S. and Purvis, M., "A UML Profile and Mapping for the Generation of Ontology-specific Content Languages", Knowledge Engineering Review, Special Issue on Ontologies in Agent Systems, 17:21-39 (2002).
17. Sharp Corporation, Zaurus SL-C700, http://www.mobile-review.com/pda/review/sharp-zaurus-c700-en.shtml (2003).

$\mathcal{K}_2$: Animated Agents that Understand Speech Commands and Perform Actions

Takenobu Tokugana, Kotaro Funakoshi, and Hozumi Tanaka

Department of Computer Science, Tokyo Institute of Technology
Tokyo Meguro Ôokayama 2-12-1, Japan
{take,koh,tanaka}@cl.cs.titech.ac.jp

Abstract. This paper presents a prototype dialogue system, $\mathcal{K}_2$, in which a user can instruct agents through speech input to manipulate various objects in a 3-D virtual world. The agents' action is presented to the user as an animation. To build such a system, we have to deal with some of the deeper issues of natural language processing such as ellipsis and anaphora resolution, handling vagueness, and so on. In this paper, we focus on three distinctive features of the $\mathcal{K}_2$ system: handling ill-formed speech input, plan-based anaphora resolution and handling vagueness in spatial expressions. After an overview of the system architecture, each of these features is described. We also look at the future research agenda of this system.

1 Introduction

From a historical point of view, Winograd's SHRDLU [1] can be considered as the most important natural language understanding system. SHRDLU was a kind of software agent working in a block world. Although SHRDLU was not "embodied", having had only a small stick, it certainly had several features that a conversational agent is supposed to have. It could understand English through keyboard inputs and carry out some simple tasks such as "Pick up a red block on the table" by building a plan to achieve it. Furthermore, it could solve some of the anaphoric ambiguities in input sentences. In short, SHRDLU was clearly ahead of its time. It had a great potential, and it was very promising for future research on natural language understanding.

Recently better technologies have become available in speech recognition and natural language processing. Major breakthroughs in the area of computer graphics have enabled us to generate complex, yet realistic 3-D animated agents or embodied life-like agents in a virtual environment. Researchers are now in a good position to go beyond SHRDLU by combining these technologies [2].

According to Cassell et al. [3], conversational skills consist not only in the ability to understand and produce language, but also in the ability to perform the corresponding body movements (facial expressions, the use of hands, etc.), intonations and tonal expressions. All of them have regulatory functions for the process of conversation. Cassell and her collaborators have developed REA, an embodied conversational agent endowed with social, linguistic, and psychological knowledge. While REA stresses the importance of non-verbal functions in conversations, this paper presents a conversational animated agent system, $\mathcal{K}_2$, which emphasizes the importance of natural language understanding in spoken language. Although linguistic expressions handled by $\mathcal{K}_2$ are limited, a number of issues remain to be addressed.

Since all the actions carried out by an agent of the $\mathcal{K}_2$ system are visible, we can evaluate the performance of the system by observing its animation. Visualizing the agents' actions yields many interesting issues from a cognitive science point of view; more complex processes are involved than those found in most conventional natural language understanding systems. In this paper, we particularly focus on handling ill-formed speech input, resolving anaphora in the virtual world, handling vagueness in spatial expressions, and describe how the $\mathcal{K}_2$ system approaches these issues.

After sketching out the overview of the $\mathcal{K}_2$ system in Sect. 2, the above three issues are discussed in Sect. 3, 4, and 5. Finally, Sect. 6 concludes the paper and looks at future research agenda.

2 System Overview

A screen shot of $\mathcal{K}_2$ is shown in Fig. 1. There are two agents and several objects (colored balls and desks) in a virtual world. Through speech input, a user can command the agents to manipulate the objects. The current system accepts simple Japanese utterances with anaphoric and elliptical expressions, such as "Walk to the desk." and "Further". The size of the lexicon is about 100 words. The agent's behavior and the subsequent changes in the virtual world are presented to the user in terms of a three-dimensional animation.

Fig. 1. A screenshot of $\mathcal{K}_2$

The architecture of the $\mathcal{K}_2$ is illustrates in Fig. 2. system. The speech recognition module receives the user's speech input and generates a sequence of words. The syntactic/semantic analysis module analyzes the word sequence to extract a case frame. This module accepts ill-formed speech input including postposition omission, inversion, and self-correction. Handling ill-formedness is described in Sect. 3. At this stage, not all case slots are necessarily filled, because of ellipses in the utterance. Even in cases where there is no ellipsis, instances of objects are not identified at this stage.

Resolving ellipses and anaphora, and identifying instances in the world are performed by the discourse analysis module. Anaphora resolution and instance identification are achieved by using plan-knowledge, which will be described in Sect. 4.

The discourse analysis module extracts the user's goal as well and hands it over to the planning modules, which build a plan to generate the appropriate animation. In other words, the planning modules translate the user's goal into animation data. However, the properties of these two ends are very different and straightforward translation is rather difficult. The user's goal is represented in terms of symbols, while the animation data is a sequence of numeric values. To bridge this gap, we take a two-stage approach – macro- and micro-planning.

During the macro-planning, the planner needs to know the physical properties of objects, such as their size, location and so on. For example, to pick up a ball, the agent first needs to move to the location at which he can reach the ball. In this planning process, the distance between the ball and the agent needs to be calculated. This sort of information is represented in terms of coordinate values of the virtual space and handled by the micro-planner.

To interface the macro- and micro-planning, we introduced the SPACE object to represent a location in the virtual space by its symbolic and numeric character. The SPACE object is described in Sect. 5.

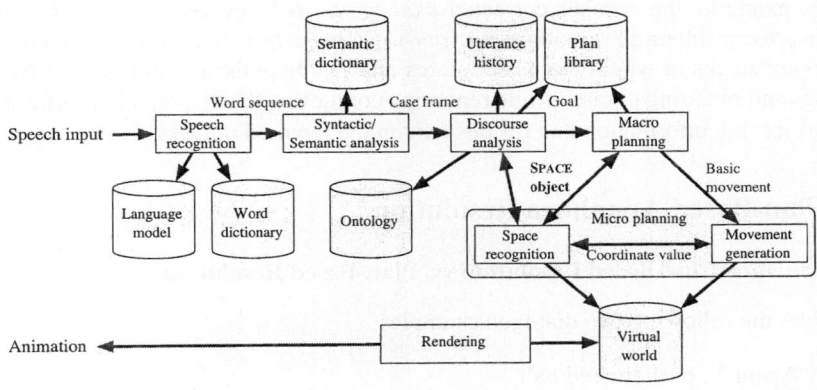

Fig. 2. The system architecture of $\mathcal{K}_2$

3 Handling Ill-Formed Speech Input

The syntactic/semantic analysis module in Fig. 2 adopts a phrase-based dependency parser in order to deal with spontaneous speech robustly. It handles the four types of ill-formed Japanese speech: postposition omission, inversion, self-correction, and hesitation. Here, we briefly describe the first three of them and how the parser deals with them. A more detailed description is found in [4].

Postposition Omission. In Japanese, the grammatical role of a noun phrase is marked by a postposition, and the order of postpositional phrases is relatively free. However, speakers often omit postpositions, and this causes difficulties in syntactic and semantic analysis. In addition, when we use automatic speech recognizers (ASRs) in dialogue systems, we have to cope with the misrecognition of postpositions. Because their acoustic energy tends to be weak, postpositions tend to be misrecognized (often deleted) more than content words by ASRs. The parser estimates omitted or deleted postpositions from semantic constraints.

Inversion. Since Japanese is a head-final language, sentences usually end with a predicate. In speech dialogue, however, speakers sometimes add several phrases after the predicate. We consider such cases to be inversion, and assume that these post-predicate phrases depend on the predicate. The parser only allows phrases that come after a main predicate to depend on the preceding predicate.

Self-correction. Self-correction is also known as speech repair, or simply repair. In Japanese, self-correction can be combined with postposition omission and inversion:

    akai tama-(wo)   mae-(ni)   osite migi-no   yatu-wo
    red ball-(ACC) front-(GOAL) push right-GEN one-ACC
          (Push the right red ball forward)

In this example, the speaker corrected *akai tama-(wo)* (*wo* was omitted) by adding the inverted pronoun phrase, *migi-no yatu-wo*. The parser detects self-corrections by observing stacks in which the parser stores analysis hypotheses, and merges repaired phrases and repairing phrases while removing conflicting (that is, repaired) information and preserving information that resides only in the repaired phrases.

4 Plan-Based Anaphora Resolution

4.1 Surface-Clue-Based Resolution vs. Plan-Based Resolution

Consider the following two dialogue examples.

(1-1) "Agent X, push the red ball."
(1-2) "Move to the front of the blue ball."
(1-3) "Push *it*."

(2-1) "Agent X, pick up the red ball."
(2-2) "Move to the front of the blue ball."
(2-3) "Put *it* down."

    The second dialogue is different from the first one only in terms of the verbs in the first and third utterances. The syntactic structure of each sentence in the second dialogue (2-1)–(2-3) is the same as the corresponding sentence in the first dialogue (1-1)–(1-3). However, pronoun "it" in (1-3) refers to "the blue ball" in (1-2), and pronoun "it" in (2-3) refers to "the red ball" in (2-1). The difference between these two examples is not explained by the theories based on surface clues such as the centering theory [5–7].
    In the setting of SHRDLU-like systems, the user has a certain goal of arranging objects in the world, and constructs a plan to achieve it through interaction with the system. As Cohen pointed out, users tend to break up the referring and predicating functions in speech dialogue [8]. Thus, each user's utterance suggests a part of plan rather than a whole plan that the user tries to perform. To avoid redundancy, users need to use anaphora. From these observations, we found that considering a user's plan is

indispensable in resolving anaphora in this type of dialogue system and developed an anaphora resolution algorithm using th relation between utterances in terms of partial plans (plan operators) corresponding to them.

The basic idea is to identify a chain of plan operators based on their effects and preconditions. Our method explained in the rest of this section finds preceding utterances sharing the same goal as the current utterance with respect to their corresponding plan operators as well as surface linguistic clues.

4.2 Resolution Algorithm

As described in Sect. 2, speech input is recognized by the ASR and the recognized word sequence is syntactically and semantically analyzed, then transformed into a case frame. At this stage, anaphora is not resolved. Based on this case frame, a plan operator is retrieved in the plan library. This process is generally called "plan recognition." Currently the mapping from an utterance to a plan operator is done based on the verb in the utterance. When a verb is missing in the utterance, the system recovers the missing verb by using clue words and referring to the history database and the plan library.

A plan operator used in our system is similar to that of STRIPS [9], which consists of precondition, effect and action description. There are cases in which the missing verb can be recovered by referring to constraints on variables in the plan operator.

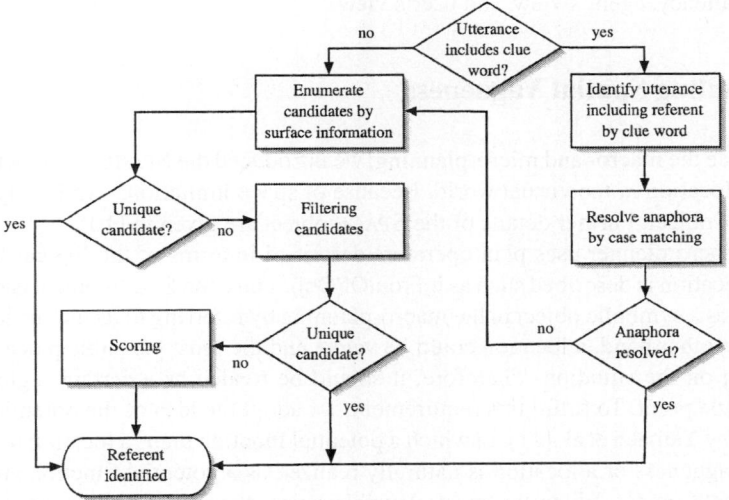

Fig. 3. Anaphora resolution algorithm

Variables in the retrieved plan operator are filled with case fillers in the utterance. There might be missing case fillers when anaphora (zero pronoun) is used in the utterance. The system tries to resolve these missing elements in the plan operator. To resolve the missing elements, the system again uses clue words and the plan library. An overview of the anaphora resolution algorithm is shown in Figure 3.

When the utterance includes clue words, the system uses them to search the history database for the preceding utterance that shares the same goal as the current utterance. Then, it identifies the referent on the basis of case matching.

There are cases in which the proper preceding utterance cannot be identified even with the clue words. These cases are sent to the left branch in Fig. 3 where the plan library is used to resolve anaphora.

When there is no clue word or the clue word does not help to resolve the anaphora, the process goes through the left branch in Fig. 3. First, the system enumerates the candidates of referents using the surface information, then filters them out with linguistic clues and the plan library. For example, demonstratives such as "this", "that" are usually used for objects that are in the user's view. Therefore, the referent of anaphora with demonstratives is restricted to the objects in the current user's view.

If the effect of a plan operator satisfies the precondition of another plan operator, and the utterances corresponding to these plan operators are uttered in discourse, they can be considered to intend the same goal. Thus, identifying a chain of effect-precondition relations gives important information for grouping utterances sharing the same goal. We can assume an anaphor and its referent appear within the same utterance group.

Once the utterance group is identified, the system finds the referent based on matching variables between plan operators.

After filtering out the candidates, there still might be more than one candidate left. In such a case, each candidate is assigned a score that is calculated based on the following factors: saliency, agent's view, and user's view.

5 Handling Spatial Vagueness

To interface the macro- and micro-planning, we introduced the SPACE object which represents a location in the virtual world. Because of space limitations, we briefly explain the SPACE object. Further details of the SPACE object are given in [10].

The macro planner uses plan operators described in terms of the logical forms, in which a location is described such as InFrontOf(Obj). Thus, the SPACE object is designed to behave as a symbolic object in the macro-planning by referring to its unique identifier.

On the other hand, a location could be vague and the most plausible place changes depending on the situation. Therefore, it should be treated as a certain region rather than a single point. To fulfill this requirement, we adopt the idea of the potential model proposed by Yamada et al. [11], in which a potential function maps a location to its plausibility. Vagueness of a location is naturally realized as a potential function embedded in the SPACE object. When the most plausible point is required by the micro-planner for generating the animation, the point is calculated by using the potential function with the Steepest Descent Method.

Consider the following short conversation between a human (H) and a virtual agent (A).

H: Do you see a ball in front of the desk?
A: Yes.
H: Put it on the desk.

When an utterance "Do you see a ball in front of the desk?" is given in the situation shown in Fig. 1, the discourse analysis module identifies an instance of "a ball" in the following steps.

(A) space#1 := new inFrontOf(desk#1, viewpoint#1, MIRROR)
(B) list#1 := space#1.findObjects()
(C) ball#1 := list#1.getFirstMatch(kindOf(BALL))

In step (A), an instance of SPACE is created as an instance of the class inFrontOf. The constructor of inFrontOf takes three arguments: the reference object, the viewpoint, and the axis order[1]. Although it is necessary to identify the reference frame that the speaker used to interpret the speaker's utterance correctly, we focus on the calculation of potential functions given a reference frame.

Suppose the parameters of inFrontOf have been resolved in the preceding steps, and the discourse analysis module chooses the axis mirror order and the orientation of the axis based on the viewpoint of the light-colored arrows in Fig. 4. The closest arrow to the viewpoint-based "front" axis ((1) in Fig. 4) is chosen as the "front" of the desk. Then, the parameters of potential function corresponding to "front" are set.

In step (B), the method matchObjects() returns a list of objects located in the potential field of space#1 shown in Fig. 5. The objects in the list are sorted in descending order of the potential value of their location.

In step (C), the most plausible object satisfying the type constraint (BALL) is selected by the method getFirstMatch().

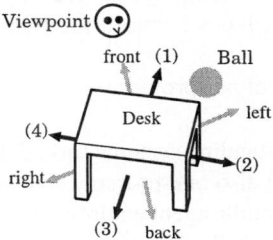
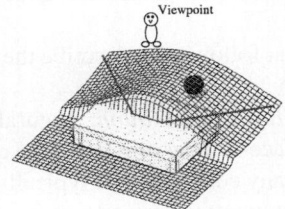

Fig. 4. Adjustment of axis   **Fig. 5.** Potential field of space#1

When receiving the next utterance, "Put it on the desk.", the discourse analysis module resolves the referent of the pronoun "it" and extracts the user's goal. The macro planner constructs a plan to satisfy the goal as follows:

1. walk(inFrontOf(ball#1, viewpoint#1, MIRROR) AND
   reachableByHand(ball#1) AND NOT(occupied(ball#1)))
2. grasp(ball#1)
3. put(ball#1,on(desk#1, viewpoint#1, MIRROR))

---

[1] We follow Herskovits' formulation [12] of spatial reference. There are two types of axis order: basic and mirror.

Walk, grasp, and put are defined as basic movements. They are handed over to the micro planner one by one.

The movement walk takes a SPACE object representing its destination as an argument. In this example, the conjunction of three SPACE objects is given as the argument. The potential function of the resultant SPACE is calculated by multiplying the values of the corresponding three potential functions at each point.

After moving to the specified location, the movement grasp is performed to grab ball#1. When putting the ball on the desk, the micro planner looks for a space on the desk that no other object occupies by composing the potential functions in a manner similar to the walk step.

As this example illustrates, the SPACE object effectively plays a role as a mediator between the macro and micro planning.

6 Concluding Remarks and Future Work

We have introduced our prototype system $\mathcal{K}_2$. $\mathcal{K}_2$ has several distinctive features, three of which are described in this paper: handling ill-formed Japanese speech input, plan-based anaphora resolution, and handling spatial vagueness by bridging between macro- and micro-planning.

The system achieved robustness by introducing ill-formed input handling. Plan-based anaphora resolution enables $\mathcal{K}_2$ to interpret the user's intention more precisely than the previous, surface-cue-based resolution algorithms. The SPACE object is designed to bridge the gap between the symbolic system (language processing) and the continuous system (animation generation), and it mediates between the two types of planners.

In what follows, we describe the research agenda of our project.

One-to-Many Conversation. Natural language understanding systems should deal with not only face-to-face or one-to-one conversations, but also one-to-many conversations. One-to-many conversations typically take place in a multi-agent environment [13, 14]. In a one-to-one conversation, it is easy to decide who is the intended listener. In contrast, in a one-to-many conversation, there are many potential listeners, hence it should be decided at the beginning who is the intended listener. The intended listener is often mentioned explicitly in the early utterance of the dialogue, but this is not always the case. Without identifying the agent appointed as an actor of the action, a proper animation will not be generated. The situation gets worse when a speaker is concerned with only performing an action without caring who does it. In such cases, agents have to request clarifications or negotiate among themselves.

Parallel Actions. Most intelligent agent systems perform only one action at a time. Yet, if we want to make systems become more flexible, we must enable them to handle more than one action at a time. Hence, they must speak while walking, wave while nodding, and so on.

Currently, the macro planner performs only a single action at a time, handing the micro planner the elements of each action one by one. To build a more versatile system, we have to develop a system able to carry out multiple actions at a time, simultaneously or sequentially, and we have to build an interface able to communicate between the macro- planner and the micro-planner.

Multimodality. In natural language understanding systems, multimodal information (gestures and gazing) is an important factor for interpreting a user's utterance. For example, pointing to a certain object could be an easy task if a pointing gesture is used together with an utterance. Obviously, this is what we are striving for: animated, natural looking agents.

Acknowledgment

This work is partially supported by a Grant-in-Aid for Creative Scientific Research 13NP0301, the Ministry of Education, Culture, Sports, Science and Technology of Japan. The URL of the project is http://www.cl.cs.titech.ac.jp/sinpro/en/index.html.

References

1. Winograd, T.: Understanding Natural Language. Academic Press (1972)
2. Tanaka, H., Tokunaga, T., Shinyama, Y.: Animated agents capable of understanding natural language and performing actions. In: Life-Like Characters. Springer (2004) 429–444
3. Cassell, J., Bickmore, T., Billinghurst, L., Campbell, L., Chang, K., Vilhjalmsson, H., Yan, H.: Embodiment in conversational interfaces: REA. In: Proceedings of CHI'99 Conference. (1999) 520–527
4. Funakoshi, K., Tokunaga, T., Tanaka, H.: Processing Japanese self-correction in speech dialog systems. In: Proceedings of the 19th International Conference on Computational Linguistics (COLING). (2002) 287–293
5. Grosz, B.J., Joshi, A.K.J., Weinstein, S.: Providing a unified account of definite noun phrases in discourse. In: Proceedings of ACL'83. (1983) 44–49
6. Grosz, B.J., Joshi, A.K., Weinstein, P.: Centering: A framework for modeling the local coherence of discourse. Computational Linguistics **21** (1995) 203–226
7. Walker, M.A., Joshi, A.K., Prince, E.F., eds.: Centering Theory in Discourse. Clarendon Press Oxford (1998)
8. Cohen, P.R.: The pragmatics of referring and the modality of communication. Computational Linguistics **10** (1984) 97–146
9. Fikes, R.E.: STRIPS: A new approach to the application of theorem problem solving. Artificial Intelligence **2** (1971) 189–208
10. Tokunaga, T., Koyama, T., Saito, S., Okumura, M.: Bridgin the gap between language and action. In: the 4th International Workshop on Intelligent Virual Agents. (2003) 127–135
11. Yamada, A., Nishida, T., Doshita, S.: Figuring out most plausible interpretation from spatial description. In: the 12th International Conference on Computational Linguistics (COLING). (1988) 764–769
12. Herskovits, A.: Language and Spatial Cognition. An Interdisciplinary Study of the Prepositions in English. Cambridge University Press (1986)
13. Ferber, J.: Multi-Agent Systems - An Introduction to Distributed Artificial Intelligence. Addison-Wesley Longman (1999)
14. Weiss, G., ed.: Multiagent Systems. The MIT Press (1999)

InCA: A Mobile Conversational Agent

Mohammed Waleed Kadous and Claude Sammut

University of New South Wales, Sydney, Australia
fwaleed,claudeg@cse.unsw.edu.au

Abstract. InCA is a distributed personal assistant conversational agent. The front-end runs on a handheld PDA and uses facial animation and natural speech input/output to interact with the user to provide services such as appointments, e-mail and weather reports. Existing conversational character research focuses on desktop platforms, but there are obvious differences when the platform is a mobile device, the two most obvious being the limited computational power and the restrictions on input modalities. This paper discusses the architecture and implementation of InCA, which addresses these two challenges.

Keywords: Conversational agents, speech interaction, mobile applications of artificial intelligence.

1 Introduction

Most conversational agents are designed to run on desktop computers. The user is assumed to have several modes of input, such as keyboard, mouse and voice.

However, recent years have seen an explosion of mobile devices, such as personal digital assistants, in-car computers and high-powered mobile phones. Techniques for conversational agents on such devices are under-explored. There are two particular challenges:

– Limited computational power. In particular, these devices do not have hardware acceleration of 3D graphics, and are not likely to in the near future.
– Limited I/O options. These devices may be small, have low resolution, lack keyboards etc.

A further problem, shared with desktop agents, is making these agents seem intelligent. Due to the limited computational power, this is even harder on a mobile platform.

While it is true that the computing power of mobile devices is continually increasing, mobile devices typically have one quarter of to one eighth the computing power and storage of their desktop equivalents. Therefore, using the network to provide additional computing power to mobile devices will allow, in certain circumstances, a circumvention of their limited computing power.

InCA (Internet-based Conversational Agent) is a mobile conversational agent that runs on a PDA, but uses network infrastructure to overcome some of the above limitations. It is part of the program of research being undertaken by the

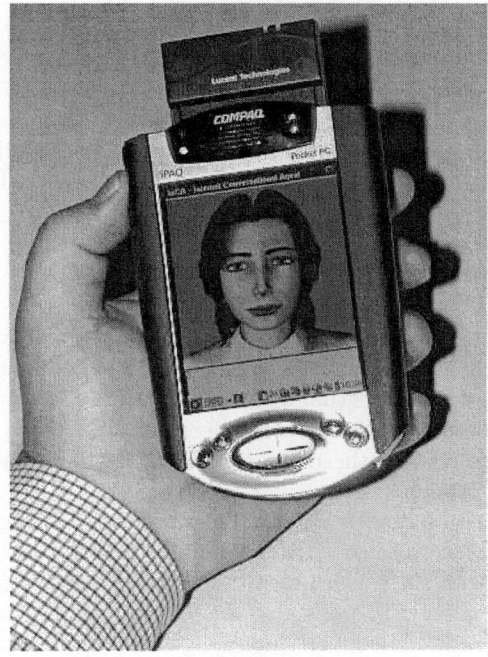

Fig. 1. InCA running on a PDA

Smart Internet Technology Cooperative Research Centre. A photograph of InCA running on a mobile device is shown in Figure 1. The current implementation of InCA has the following features:

- Provides the following personal assistant-type services: news headlines, emailreading, making and listing appointments (synchronised with the desktop), retrieving weather and exchange rates, and translations from English to several European language (albeit badly pronounced in English).
- Spoken (but speaker-dependent) natural language input. Users can say things like "Can you get me the weather for today, please?" Or "Yo InCA! What's the exchange rate for US dollars, man?" or "I want the local news, InCA." Our system does not force them to adhere to a constrained grammar.
- Speech output with facial animation, but currently without emotional expression.

The rest of this paper will discuss the architecture used by InCA to provide these capabilities; in particular, it will focus on the two most interesting problems: dialog management and facial animations. It will then discuss some recent refinements, before presenting plans for future work.

Table 1. Speech vs recognised words

What was said	Speech recognition
ok what about my appointments	that care about my point man
what's the weather going to be like	what the weather down to be light
uh francs please	a Frank's place
ok can you translate i'm tired to german	a cake can you translate I'm tied to German
no goodbye	know the by.

1.1 Related Work

Our work draws on the established study of embodied conversational agents. This includes the work of Cassell et al [2] on REA, and also Cyberella [3]. Both of these systems try to develop virtual agents that interact via speech and gesture.

The InCA project is also related to the work on TRIPS [1] and the CU Communicator system [8]. Both of these projects focus on the process of collaborative interaction through speech.

The underlying technologies for mobile conversational agents are also currently developing; for example, work on facial animation for mobile platforms [6]. There has also been some work on speech-based interaction with mobile devices of a limited form [11]. There is also the SmartKom Project at DFKI, which also aims to develop mobile conversational agents [12]; however, at the time of publication, details are unavailable. To our knowledge, this is the first published work on functional mobile conversational agents.

2 InCA Architecture

To provide the above features, InCA employs the architecture shown in Figure 2. It operates within three domains: the client, which runs on a PDA, the server that coordinates the speech recognition, speech synthesis and dialog management, and finally a coordinator that is responsible for real-time retrieval of data such as weather, appointments, and so on from the Internet.

2.1 Client

The InCA client currently runs on a Compaq iPaq H3870[1]. This device has the following specifications.

- StrongARM 206MHz processor.
- 32MB Flash ROM, 64MB RAM.
- 320x240 65,000 colour screen.
- Internal Microphone/Speaker.
- Linux operating system with Qt/Embedded GUI.
- 802.11b Wireless ethernet (WiFi).

---

[1] It also works with other StrongARM-based Linux devices, e.g. the Sharp Zaurus SL-5500.

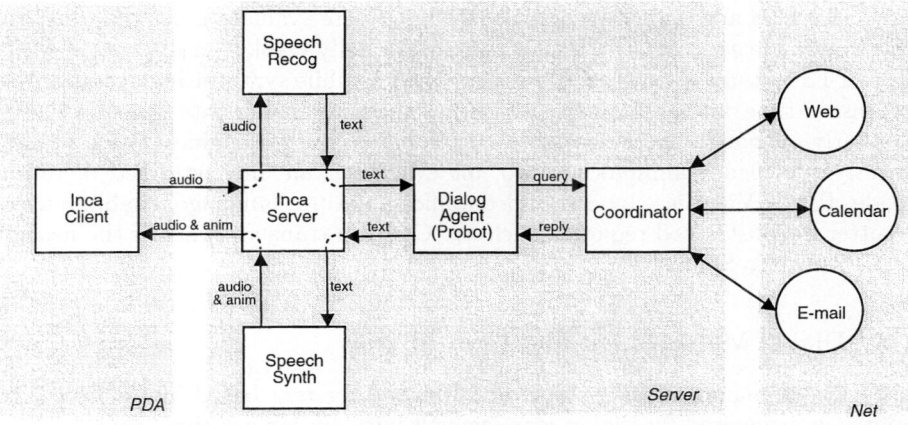

Fig. 2. InCA architecture

The StrongARM processor is designed for low-power consumption, and not computing power – it consumes no more than 400 milliwatts – two orders of magnitude less than a desktop processor. It does not have a oating-point unit. Obviously, its 3D capabilities are extremely limited.

The software that runs on the client is very "thin"; it streams audio (hopefully the speaker's voice) to the server and plays back audio and facial animation scripts once they have been downloaded to the client. To simplify detecting silence, a button on the side of the device – usually used as the "voice record" button – is used to signal when the user is speaking to InCA. It communicates to the server over WiFi. Audio is currently transferred uncompressed (22kHz 16-bit PCM), since this occupies less than 5 per cent of the maximum available bandwidth.

2.2 Server

The server coordinates several different components. It currently runs on a Linux workstation (Pentium III 800MHz, 256MB RAM). Firstly, it takes the audio coming from the client and reassembles it into a continuous audio stream (since the audio is streamed to the server, but it only goes to the speech recognition engine, delays in communication can be easily handled). It sends this data to the speech recognition engine. Currently, we are using IBM ViaVoice to provide speech recognition. It takes the the speech recognition engine's guess of the utterance and passes this to the dialog manager, which generates a reply. The InCA server then takes the reply and passes it to the Text-to-Speech (TTS) engine to generate both the audio and facial animation instructions. Currently, we are using IBM ViaVoice TTS for this, however we are evaluating other alternatives, such as Rhetorical's rVoice, and ScanSoft's RealSpeak. This information is conveyed back to the InCA client, and once the data is downloaded, the InCA client is told to begin playing the response.

Local TTS and speech recognition systems were evaluated, but did not have the required features, nor were they computationally viable. For instance, CMU's Flite TTS system [4] takes up 90 per cent of CPU while synthesising; leaving little processor time for animation; and with somewhat inadequate speech quality. Similarly, although there are mobile speech recognition engines, these require strictly specified grammars and do not even offer an unconstrained dictation mode. IBM's ViaVoice, by comparison, allows natural language, enabling users to utter unconstrained requests, such as "Can you translate where's the nearest restaurant into Spanish?"

2.3 Dialog Management and Coordinator

Most dialog management systems are designed for text-based interaction. The approaches required for dialog management with speech are significantly different, mainly because of the unreliability of speech recognition. Table 1 shows user utterances and the speech recognition engine's best guess of that utterance.

For this reason, we employed Probot [10] for dialog management. Probot has a number of features that make it well-suited to this problem. Probot is implemented as a rule-based system embedded in a Prolog interpreter. The rules consist of patterns and responses, where each pattern is matched against the user's utterance and the response is an output sentence. Both patterns and responses may have attached Prolog expressions that act as constraints in the patterns and can invoke some action when used in the response.

The pattern-response rules are grouped into contexts, which represents the current topic of conversation. A typical script consists of several contexts. Changing contexts is managed by making a Prolog call. To add further exibility and conversational agility, Probot also employs two other lists of pattern-response rules: filters and backups.

Filters are used to to detect utterances that require an instantaneous change of context. Utterances are first checked against filter patterns before being checked against patterns in the current context. Backups are used to handle utterances that did not cause any filter or context rules to fire.

This makes InCA very agile in conversation, while still allowing it to use context to constrain the recognition problem.

```
InCA: Hello. How can I help you?
User: I want the local news.
InCA: Headlines are: [...]
User: can you help me a bit?
InCA: I can tell you local, international
      or computer news.
User: well can you list my emails then?
InCA: You have 3 messages. [...]
User: help me.
InCA: To read a message, just tell me the message
      number. Or you can ask me to list your messages.
```

In the above conversation, InCA is able to offer context-specific help, while still being able to change context from news to e-mail in a single statement – no explicit indicators such as "can we do e-mail now?" are required.

One particular set of Prolog commands that is extensively used in our scripts is to retrieve information from dynamic information sources, such as the web, email and calendaring systems. This is accomplished through the Coordinator; a program which accepts instructions from the Probot and retrives the information from the network.

The current implementation of the Coordinator is a Perl script. It uses RSS (Rich Site Summary) to retrieve headlines; SOAP (Simple Object Access Protocol) to make the remote procedure calls to retrieve exchange rates and translations (through Babelfish) and POP3 to retreive e-mail.

These queries can form part of InCA's replies, as demonstrated below. An example of a rule employed by our system is:

```
c_language :: { french | german | spanish | italian };

* translat~ * {into | to } <c_language> ==>
  [
    ^coord_query([translate, ^4, ^2])
  ]
```

The above rule would fire on an utterance such as "could you please translate where is the nearest hotel into italian". The response generates a coordinator query asking to translate the second expression matched (in this case, "where is the nearest hotel") into the fourth expression matched ("italian").

2.4 Facial Animation

Clearly, for current generation mobile platforms, three-dimensional texture-mapped heads are out of the question, at least if any other processing is to be done. One possible approach would be to use a 2D polygonal face, as Perlin [9] does; however, for many mobile devices, even this small number of calculations may be excessive.

For the current version of InCA, we have used a very simple, "cartoon" approach. A face was generated using the commercial character animation package Poser. In addition to the face, we also manipulated the face to generate the mouth postions described in Nitchie [5] as conveyed in Parke et al [7]. In total, 18 mouth positions are generated. Each phoneme produced can be mapped to one of these mouth positions. Rather than the whole image being retained, only a rectangle including the mouth is kept.

When the TTS generates the audio for InCA, it also generates the phonemes and the corresponding timing information. This can be used to construct a "playlist" of which mouth position should be shown and for how long. The playlist and the audio are both transmitted to the client. Once both are received by the client, synchronised playback begins.

When playback begins, the whole face is drawn. When it is time to change the mouth position, the mouth area is "overwritten" by the mouth image corresponding to the phoneme.

A similar idea is used to implement random blinking.

3 Refinements

In addition to the basic plan above, we have applied several refinements.

3.1 Alternatives for Speech

We evaluated the accuracy of our system by having several conversations, and recording correct, confused and wrong responses. A "confused" response occurs when none of the Probot rules fire; and consequently InCA asks the user to repeat his last statement. A "wrong" response occurs when an incorrect rule fires, e.g, the user says: "List my e-mails", and InCA replies with "One Australian dollar is 0.55 US dollars", which obviously did not meet the user's request.

We found that with a sample of 99 utterances, from a user who had trained the speech recognition system, InCA was wrong only 2 per cent of the time, and confused 31 per cent of the time.

IBM ViaVoice, however, has a capability of producing alternative "interpretations" of an utterance – typically as many as 16 alternatives are generated. If there are no patterns in the current context that match an utterance, the InCA server requests an alternative from the speech recognition engine, and tests that to see if any patterns were matched this time. This is repeated until all alternatives are exhausted, at which point the user is asked to repeat his or her utterance. For example, consider the third example from Table 1: "uh francs please". The first guess, "a Frank's place" doesn't match any patterns, so a second alternative is requested. The second alternative is "francs Place", which – while not totally correct – is still recognised because the context is currently exchange rates, and one of the patterns picked up "francs" as a currency. Using this technique the confusion rate was reduced to 22 per cent – a 29 per cent reduction in the number of times the user was asked to repeat themselves.

3.2 Multiple Characters

It is relatively easy to generate new characters to be used with InCA – another set of 22 or so images must be generated, and the speech synthesis must be modified to generate a different voice.We have generated several interchangeable characters; in particular we have a male character as well. These characters are interchangeable with minimal effort.

3.3 Facial Gestures as State Indicators

Some of the InCA queries can take a few seconds to perform; since retrieval of information over the Internet is sometimes slow. The conventional way to convey this to the user might be to get InCA to say "Please wait". However, we have a facial expression that involves raising the eyebrows and looking up in a manner that is associated with thinking or contemplating. This facial expression is maintained until just before InCA is ready to speak. At this point, normal eye contact is restored. Similarly, when InCA is listening to the user, it raises its eyebrows. Exploring such use of facial expressions to express states such as thinking, confusion and so on is something we plan to explore.

3.4 Multimodal Interaction

A limited capability for multimodal interaction has been added to examine how extensible InCA was. Users can also now ask for a map of the University of New South Wales campus. A map of the University is brought up and the user is shown a map. Simple queries such as "what is this building" or "show me the library" are possible. The user can then ask InCA to show her face again.

To accomplish this, the user's multimodal interactions would be converted into a string; for example if the user clicked on a particular location (say 100,100) then the message sent back to the Probot would be:

+CLICK X 100 Y 100+ What is this place?

In the above, the '+' sign indicates something not said by the user, but containing additional information, in this case a click at 100,100. Similarly, the Probot script after analysing the location might respond with the following:

+CIRCLE 90 100 40+ That's the library, as shown by the red circle.

This would then be interpreted by the client on the PDA as an instruction to draw a circle on top of the campus map. Although simple, this approach does not scale well. For example, it is hard to write matching rules in Probot for more complex queries, such as "how would I get from here to here?" It is something we hope to address in future work.

4 Further Work

Obviously, InCA is in her infancy, and the avenues of research are many. Our plans for further work include:

- Evaluating how important the face is; would the device be equally useful without the face?
- Evaluating the "3D cartoon" face against a real-time 2D face similar to Perlin's [9].
- Adding a phone interface to InCA, so that instead of interacting via a PDA, the interaction could occur using a standard phone line.
- Learning user's preferences.

– Integrating more tightly between the speech recognition engine and the dialogue management system. In particular, the current model of taking alternatives from the speech recognition engine after recognition has been done is simplistic. We are looking at techniques for extracting probable words in the current context and using them to inform the search performed by the speech recognition engine.

5 Conclusion

InCA is a mobile conversational agent that uses speech I/O and addresses some of the unique challenges of the mobile environment. Simple facial animation techniques may be adequate; we are hoping to test this statistically. Further, the network can be used as a means to obtain additional computing power to effectively add features such as speech recognition and synthesis.

6 Web Page

Movies, photographs, conversation transcripts, etc are available from:
http://www.cse.unsw.edu.au/~inca/

Acknowledgements

The authors would like to acknowledge the support of the Smart Internet Technology CRC. They would also like to acknowledge the good work done by the crew at www.handhelds.org and the developers of Familiar.

References

1. James Allen, Donna Byron, Myroslava Dzikovska, George Ferguson, Lucian Galescu, and Amanda Stent. Towards conversational human-computer interaction. *AI Magazine*, 22(4):27–37, 2001.
2. J. Cassell, T. Bickmore, M. Billinghurst, L. Campbell, K. Chang, H. Vilhjalmsson, and H. Yan. Embodiment in conversational interfaces: Rea. In *Proceedings of the CHI'99 Conference*, pages pp. 520–527, 1999.
3. P. Gebhard. Enhancing embodied intelligent agents with affective user modelling. In *UM2001: Proceedings of the Eighth International Conference*, Berlin, 2001. Springer.
4. Kevin A. Lenzo and Alan W. Black, 2002. http://www.speech.cs.cmu.edu/ite/.
5. E. B. Nitchie. *How to Read Lips for Fun and Profit*. Hawthorne Books, New York, 1979.
6. Igor S. Pandzic. Facial animation framework for the web and mobile platforms. In *Web3D 2002*, pages pp. 27–34. ACM Press, 2002.
7. Frederic I. Parke and Keith Waters. *Computer Facial Animation*. A K Peters, 1996.
8. B. Pellom, W. Ward, and S. Pradhan. The CU Communicator: An architecture for dialogue systems. In *International Conference on Spoken Language Processing*, Beijing China, 2000.

9. Ken Perlin. Layered compositing of facial expressions. In *SIGGRAPH 1997 Technical Sketch*, 1997.
10. Claude Sammut. Managing context in a conversation agent. *Electronic Transactions on Artificial Intelligence*, 6(27), 2001. http://www.ep.liu.se/ea/cis/2001/027/.
11. Speereo. Speereo web site, 2002. http://www.speereo.com/.
12. WolfgangWahlster. Multimodal interfaces to mobile webservices. In *ICT Congress, Den Haag*, http://smartkom.dfki.de/, 2002.

Determination of Usenet News Groups by Fuzzy Inference and Kohonen Network

Jong-Wan Kim[1], Hee-Jae Kim[1], Sin-Jae Kang[1], and Byeong Man Kim[2]

[1] School of Computer and Information Technology, Daegu University
Gyeonsan. Gyeongbuk. 712-714 South Korea
{jwkim,kimhj,sjkang}@daegu.ac.kr
[2] School of Computer Engineering. Kumoh National Institute of Technology
Gumi, Gyungbuk, South Korea
bmkim@se.kumoh.ac.kr

Abstract. In this work, we present a service determining user's preferred news groups among various ones. For this end, candidate terms from example documents of each news group are extracted and a number of representative keywords among them are chosen through fuzzy inference. They are then presented to Kohonen network for learning representative keywords of each news group. From the observation of training patterns, we could find the sparseness problem that lots of keywords in training patterns are empty. Thus, a method to train neural network through reduction of unnecessary dimensions by the statistical coefficient of determination is used in this paper. Experimental results show that the method is superior to the method using every input dimension in terms of cluster overlap defined by using within-cluster distance and between-clusters distance.

1 Introduction

It is important to retrieve exact information coinciding with user's need from lots of Usenet news and filter desired information quickly. In Usenet news system, differently from email system, we must previously register our interesting news groups if we want to get the news information. However, it is not easy for a novice to decide which news group is relevant to his or her interests. This problem will be mitigated if it is possible to use profiles - key words representing user's interests – instead of news group. Thus, in this paper, we present a method to automatically determine news groups from user's profile and conduct performance evaluation of the method.

To determine news groups coinciding with user's profile, we must extract representative terms from each news group and select highly relevant news groups by comparing representative terms and user profile. To extract representative terms of a news group, firstly we have to connect news servers over the Internet and collect Usenet news documents. We then extract a number of terms called representative keywords (RKs) from them through fuzzy inference. Performance of our approach is heavily influenced by the effectiveness of selection method of RKs so that we choose fuzzy inference because it is more effective in handling the uncertainty inherent in selecting RKs within documents [1]. There are cosine similarity measure, neural network approach, and other learning methods to decide the similarity between user profiles and RKs of each news group in information retrieval field [2]. Naturally the performance of information retrieval system depends on the use of which method among three methods aforementioned. However, since we are focusing on the usability of the proposed method rather than the performance improvement, we choose the neural network approach that is familiar with us and is easy to deal with.

Kohonen network, one of unsupervised learning algorithms that do not request user's feedback continuously [3], can classify news groups with only RKs. So we adopted Kohonen network as a classification algorithm in this work. However, by observing input patterns used as training vectors of neural network, we found the sparseness problem that specific keywords chosen in many news groups were empty. To fix this sparseness problem, we first select input variables (= chosen RKs) relevant to the target variable (= similar news group) presented by the user and then train only these selected input variables. From experimental results, we can conclude that it is more useful than training all of input variables. Resulting from that, we will introduce statistical coefficient of determination that is a method to determine input variables highly relevant to the target variable.

In the next section, the related works on Internet filtering, extraction of RKs, and effects of dimensionality reduction are reviewed. Section 3 presents a method to determine news groups automatically. The experimental results to test the proposed method are shown in Section 4. Finally conclusion is followed.

2 Related Works

In our knowledge, there is no research work such as automatic determination of Usenet news groups from user profiles like this work. Of course, Usenet news filtering in the field of information filtering [4, 5, 6] is more or less related to this research topic. However it is not easy to directly compare these works and the proposed method, because the proposed method is not a filtering method but a new type of user interface to read electronic news. In also, the proposed method can be applied to the conventional news filtering techniques for reducing news documents to be compared. That is, since we don't need to process every news articles but only process articles included in the news group related to the profile, the proposed method has an advantage in terms of the processing speed.

It is very important to select RKs representing news groups well from example or training documents. To extract RKs and assign them weights are the same problem that the existing linear classifiers such as Rocchio and Widrow-Hoff algorithms [7] find centroid vector of a training document collection. Both of these algorithms use TF (Term Frequency) and IDF (Inverse Document Frequency) for re-weighting terms but they do not consider term co-occurrence relationship within feedbacked documents. Though the term showing the similar occurrence pattern with initial query terms should be treated more importantly than the term that not, currently high weight value is assigned to a term having only high TF value. To resolve this problem, we have to calculate term co-occurrences between these RKs and candidate terms within each example document. Since Kim et al. [1] showed satisfactory performance in the experiments conducted with a few positive example documents, we chose the method to extract RKs.

Determining which attributes are relevant to the learning task is a principal problem in machine learning. However, in the absence of such background knowledge, automatic techniques are required to identify such attributes. Nearest neighbor algorithms are presented to calculate an average similarity measure across all of the attributes. However, to reduce the contribution of irrelevant attributes within nearest neighbor algorithms, kinds of PCA (Principal Component Analysis) approach, are presented [8]. PCA involves a mathematical procedure that transforms a number of correlated variables into a smaller number of uncorrelated variables called principal components. Though PCA utilizes these transformed principal components for pattern classification, we could not know which of input attributes contribute to classify patterns. However, it is important to determine specific attributes that are contributed to pattern classification in this work. We are going to use statistical coefficient of determination useful to determine the degree of contribution for pattern classification.

3 The Method to Automatically Determine News Groups

The material described in this section is the core of a news reading system to read news articles easily by using user profile instead of news group identifier, which is to automatically determine news groups relevant to user profiles. A new type of newsreader is composed of two steps – training phase and testing phase. First, in training phase, if a user specifies specific Usenet news server, that is NNTP server, then the NNTP sever connects lots of news servers over the Internet and downloads news documents. These documents are transferred to the newsreader. Then the newsreader extracts RKs through fuzzy inference and reduces input dimensions by the use of coefficient of determination, and finally classifies news groups with the help of Kohonen network. In testing phase, the newsreader reads his or her keyword profile and presents it to Kohonen network, and then Kohonen network notifies the user a news group list very close to the user's desire. Finally the newsreader downloads news articles according to the conventional news protocol.

3.1 Representative Keyword Selection

It is important to select representative keywords or terms representing each news group well from example documents of news groups. To achieve this goal, we calculate weights of candidate terms by using the method of [1] that showed superior performance to the existing RK extraction methods and then select representative ones from them based on their contribution to the news group. Details are as follows.

Example documents are transformed to the set of candidate terms by eliminating stop words and stemming using Porter's algorithm. The TF (Term Frequency), DF (Document Frequency), and IDF (Inverse Document Frequency) of each term are calculated from this set. They are normalized and used as input variables for fuzzy inference. Normalization is performed as follows:

NTF (normalized TF) is calculated by dividing TF_i (= the frequency of term t_i in the example documents) by DF_i (= the number of documents having term t_i in the example documents). DF represents the frequency of documents having a specific term within the example documents and has been normalized as TF. NDF (normalized DF) is defined as the ratio of DF_i over the maximum DF value. IDF represents the inverse document frequency of a specific term within the example documents and the normalization of the IDF is performed by the same way of DF.

Figure 1 shows the membership functions of the fuzzy input and output variables used for fuzzy inference. Since the NTF, NDF, and NIDF values calculated for each term should have been fuzzified to the form suitable for fuzzy inference, we used normal triangular membership function. As you can see in Figure 1(a), NTF variable has {S (Small), L (Large)}, NDF and NIDF variables have {S (Small), M (Middle), L (Large)} as linguistic labels or terms. The fuzzy output variable, TW (Term Weight) which represents the importance of each term, has six linguistic labels as shown in Figure 1(b).

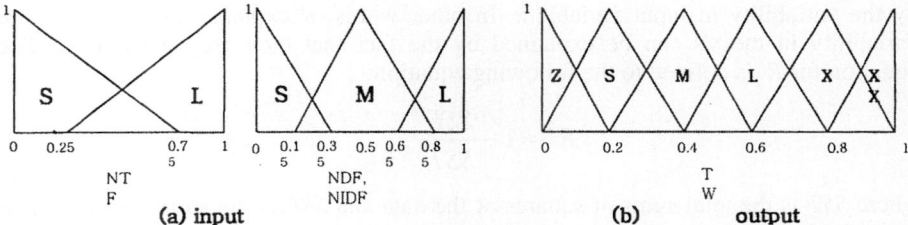

Fig. 1. Fuzzy input and out variables (Z: Zero, S: Small, M: Middle, L: Large, X: Xlarge, XX: XXlarge in TW)

Table 1 gives 18 fuzzy rules to inference the term weight TW, where NTF is considered as primary factor, NDF and NIDF as secondary ones. As shown in Table 1, we assign Z label which means almost none relevant to TW if all NTF, NDF, and NIDF values are S, because we think the term is never an important term. In another case when NTF is S, NDF is L which means the document frequency is large, and NIDF is S, S label is assigned to TW. Because both of NTF and NIDF values have Small labels, though we overestimate TW of the term due to high frequency of the term within most example documents. The other rules were set by the similar way.

Table 1. Fuzzy inference rules

NDF \ NIDF	S	M	L	NDF \ NIDF	S	M	L
S	Z	Z	S	S	Z	S	M
M	Z	M	L	M	S	L	X
L	S	L	X	L	M	X	XX
NTF = S				NTF = L			

We can get the term weight TW in the form of fuzzy set as output of inference. Thus, the output has to be converted to the crisp value by the following basic steps: firstly, we apply the NTF, NDF, and NIDF fuzzy values to the antecedent portions of

18 fuzzy rules and find the minimum value among the membership degrees of three fuzzy input values. Then all of 18 membership degrees are classified into 6 groups according to the fuzzy output variable TW and the maximum output value for each group is calculated. Finally these 6 values are defuzzified into a crisp value through the center of gravity defuzzification process [9] that is used most often.

3.2 Dimensionality Reduction by the Use of the Coefficient of Determination

A statistic that is widely used to determine how well a regression model fits to a given problem is the coefficient of determination (or multiple correlation coefficient), R^2 [10]. R^2 represents the fraction of variability in target variable y that can be explained by the variability in input variable x. In other words, R^2 explains how much of the variability in the y's can be explained by the fact that they are related to x. The equation for R^2 is defined to the following equation:

$$R^2 = 1 - \frac{SSE}{SST} \qquad (1)$$

where SST is the total sums of squares of the data and SSE is the sum of squares due to residual errors.

As shown in the equation (1), the bigger the coefficient of determination is, the stronger the usability of the regression model is. Thus, it is needed to reduce some variables having low R^2; the terms less contribute to the classification task should be eliminated from RKs. The task is to classify news groups of the target variable. By doing that, we can improve pattern classification ratio.

We can find the input variables affecting the target variable by using mentioned regression analysis. Instead of the complete model utilizing all of input variables including unnecessary variables, the reduced model to utilize necessary variables can be a more desirable regression model [10]. To construct this kind of reduced model, we calculate the coefficient of determination to select input variables identifying news group with every candidate input variable – terms derived through fuzzy inference.

To classify news group documents using the coefficient of determination, a target variable is needed. Thus class labels of news groups based on news group domains are assigned to a target variable in this work. For example, we classified 126 news groups in news.kornet.net of NNTP server based on domain names manually. We classified news groups by considering upper four domain names of a specific news group. Namely han.answers.all has class label 1, han.arts.architecture.all has class label 2, and the rest of news groups have their corresponding class labels. However some news groups are classified into the same one; for example, han.comp.os.linux.apps.all and han.comp.os.linux.misc.all have the same class label 33 because the upper four domain names of these two news groups are equal as "han.comp.os.linux". Finally 114 class labels are assigned to all the experimental data.

After we assigned these 114 class labels as values of a target variable temporarily and candidate terms relevant to the target variable as input variables, we calculate the coefficient of determination between every candidate term and the target variable. Backward elimination scheme is chosen to filter input variables in this paper. In the backward elimination scheme, the variable with the lowest coefficient under the predefined threshold value among previously calculated coefficients of determination is eliminated one by one. We can finally get necessary input variables by iterating the backward elimination scheme till all of remaining coefficients of determination are over the predefined threshold value.

4 Experiments and Analysis

4.1 Experimental Data and Training Method

In this paper, we have implemented a news reading system in Java. First we connected the news.kornet.net, one of Usenet news servers to collect training data, selected news groups through NNTP protocol, and downloaded news documents from each news group. At this time, news groups having less than 10 documents were excluded.

Experiments were performed for 126 news groups. Ten documents or twenty documents for each news group are randomly selected to extract RKs by fuzzy inference. The reason why we perform by the two ways is to confirm how much is dimensional reduction affected by the number of RKs extracted. The size of Kohonen map was fixed to 5×5 and training was performed for 1000 times. Training data were extracted from each news group by fuzzy inference, the remaining terms are stored into an internal database after excluding some low relevant attributes by the coefficient of determination. These stored terms were analyzed for training documents of each news group. In this experiment, 25 and 28 terms were finally extracted according to the number of documents used per news group, 10 or 20, respectively.

Since the term frequency of the news group having lots of documents is greater than the news group having small documents in general, we have to consider the number of documents in each news group. For example, 1448 documents are stored in the "han.comp.os.linux.networking" news group, but only 24 documents are stored in the database of the "han.answers" news group. In order to reduce this deviation, normalization is performed in this paper.

4.2 Induction Analysis of the Coefficient of Determination

To evaluate training performance, Kohonen network is used to cluster news groups reflecting user's intention. Test vectors were generated with keywords given by user. In order to calculate the distance between the keywords given by user and the keywords already stored in database, the values of keywords which user did not specify were set "0" and therefore the dimensions of two keyword vectors were same. The weight values of keywords given by user are averaged by dividing the weights of keywords already stored in database used during training phase by the frequency which the keyword are occurred in the news groups. Figure 2 shows a sample keyword profile given by some users.

If a test input vector is chosen among keyword profiles, it is presented to Kohonen network and then the output neuron with the minimum distance is determined. Finally the news groups being included in this output neuron are presented to the user. Figure 3 shows the very closest news groups determined with keywords given by a user and the previously trained information. As shown in Figure 3, not only similar news groups but also a non-relevant news group are classified into the output neuron (4,1) as a representative cluster. Surely, this results partially from the performance of classifier itself. But it mainly depends on the fact that representative terms used during training phase get mixed. In other words, the process to extract RKs should be more improved.

userId	password	keywords
kc	mpeg	html, http, 서버, 시스템
glide	prince	java, linux, office, xml
cybe	ecrm	information, mail, spam

Fig. 2. Users' keyword profile. The "서버" and "시스템" are Korean words and correspondent to "server" and "system", respectively

```
NumPatterns : 126    SizeVector : 25
Please type your user id : kc
Winner : 4, 1
Search Group : han.comp.os.windows.setup.all
Search Group : han.comp.security.all
Search Group : han.comp.www.misc.all
Search Group : han.politics.all
```

Fig. 3. Recommended news group for User (kc)

To analyze induction effect of the coefficient of determination for the case using reduced input dimension and the other case using every input dimension, the within-cluster distance (Dw) and the between-clusters distance (D_b) are defined as follows:

$$Dw_j = \frac{1}{|C_j|} \sum_{i \in C_j} \sqrt{[X_i - W_j]^2} \qquad (2)$$

where Xi is the i-th input pattern included in the j-th cluster, Wj is the weight vector of the j-th output neuron; the centroid vector of the j-th cluster, Cj is the set of patterns included in the j-th cluster, and $|Cj|$ is the number of patterns included in the j-th cluster. Therefore Dw_j means the distance between the centroid vector of the j-th cluster and the input patterns included in the j-th cluster. The equation (3) represents the average within-cluster distance (Dw) of all clusters.

$$Dw = \frac{1}{k} \sum_{j=1}^{k} Dw_j \qquad (3)$$

where k is the number of output neurons – the number of clusters.

$$Db_j = \sum_{m=1, \neq j}^{k} \sqrt{[W_j - W_m]^2} \qquad (4)$$

where *Wj* and *Wm* in the equation (4) are the weight vectors of the *j*-th output neuron and the *m*-th output neuron, respectively. So, the distance between *Wj* and *Wm* means the distance between clusters. The following equation defined by averaging the sum of distances between all output neurons represents the average between-clusters distance (D_b) of all clusters:

$$D_b = \frac{1}{k}\sum_{j=1}^{k} Db_j \qquad (5)$$

Since a good pattern classifier reduces intra-cluster distance and increases inter-clusters distance in general [11], the two measures are used to evaluate the effect of the proposed dimensionality reduction method. Table 2 shows the experimental results conducted with 10 documents per news group. We have used 0.01 and 0.02 as the threshold values of the coefficient of determination in the experiments. Twenty-five terms are used to evaluate the performance of the base method as shown in Table 2. However, in the case of the threshold value as 0.01, 20 terms are used to evaluate the performance; 20% of terms are reduced by the proposed method. At the threshold value as 0.02, only 16 terms are used to evaluate the performance and therefore 36% of terms are reduced too.

From experimental results, since not only the within-cluster distance but also the between-clusters distance decrease together as the threshold value of the coefficient of determination increases, the usefulness of the proposed method seems poor. However, the cluster overlap is defined in the Figure 4 by considering the within-cluster distance (Dw) and the between-clusters distance (D_b) together. As you can see in Figure 4, if the double within-cluster distance is less than the between-clusters distance, then two clusters are disjoint and we can say that the two clusters are separated. Similarly, if the double Dw is greater than or equal to D_b, then two clusters are overlapped. As shown in Table 2, all three methods are correspondent to the case 1 in Figure 4 because 2×Dw is less than D_b regardless of a cluster representing a circle or a square. That means, since the clusters of the proposed method are non-overlapped, the between-clusters distance does not affect the performance evaluation. As a result, Dw of the proposed method is less than the one of the base method and therefore the clustering result of the proposed method is much more compact than that of the base method.

Table 2. Experiments with 10 documents per news group (Th: threshold of the coefficient of determination)

Terms used	Base method	Proposed Th=0.01	Impv. (%)	Proposed Th=0.02	Impv. (%)
Dw	0.10	0.08	20.0	0.07	30.0
Db	0.49	0.36	-26.5	0.35	-28.6
Overlap	0	0	0	0	0

In the experimental results conducted with 20 documents per news group as shown in Table 3, the number of terms is increased to 28 as we expected. We can reduce 32% and 43% of the number of terms with the threshold values of the coefficient of determination as 0.01 and 0.02, respectively. Differently from Table 2, the experimental results on Table 3 show the overlap between clusters exists, because every method is correspondent to the case 2 in Figure 4 that D_b is less than $2 \times Dw$. In this work, we model a cluster as a square instead of a circle. The reason why we model a cluster as a square is that it is easier for us to calculate the degree of overlap from a square than from a circle. In this paper, we define the cluster overlap between clusters as the following equation (6):

$$overlap = (2D_w - D_b) \times D_w \qquad (6)$$

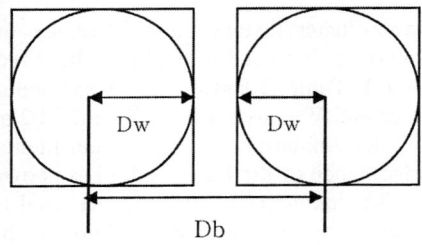 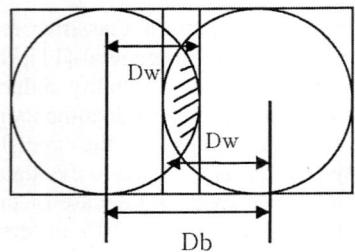

case1: disjoint clusters (Db>2Dw)   case2: overlapped clusters (Db≤2Dw)

Fig. 4. Cluster Overlap

Table 3. Experiments with 20 documents per news group (Th: threshold of the coefficient of determination)

Terms used	Base method	Proposed Th=0.01	Impv. (%)	Proposed Th=0.02	Impv. (%)
Dw	0.40	0.35	12.5	0.36	10.0
Db	0.61	0.62	1.6	0.63	3.3
Overlap	0.076	0.028	63.2	0.0324	57.4

As shown in the equation (6), we used half of the overlapped rectangle in order to make the overlap between clusters be similar to the case of a circle if possible. We found that the performance of the proposed method was improved over 50% in terms of the cluster overlap from the values in Table 3.

From these experimental results, we find that it is always not good to excessively reduce terms and it is very important to select terms to be reduced too. These results imply that the proposed method is especially effective to the problem having much more input dimensions. We also have experienced that the training time of Kohonen network is reduced. It may be caused by the reduction of unnecessary input.

5 Conclusions

In this paper, the core part of a user profile-based newsreader, a mapping method between a profile and news groups was proposed and its performance was evaluated.

The features of this work can be described as follows. First, the proposed method improved precision by extracting RKs from news documents with the help of fuzzy inference. Second, pattern classification was improved by using the coefficient of determination in statistics to exclude unnecessary redundant attributes for learning. Third, the within-cluster distance and the between-clusters distance were chosen to evaluate the proposed method in terms of pattern classification. We especially have defined the cluster overlap measure to integrate the two cluster distance measures and showed the proposed method was superior to the conventional method using every input dimension in terms of this cluster overlap. Finally the proposed method brought out an additional effect to reduce training time of neural network due to reduction of unnecessary input attributes.

In the future, we should find any other criteria to evaluate the effectiveness of the proposed method. In also, the effects of the proposed dimensionality reduction method using the coefficient of determination are to be verified by applying to the more complex problems with hundreds or thousands of input attributes.

References

1. Kim, B. M., Li, Q., and Kim, J. W.: Extraction of User Preferences from a Few Positive Documents, Proceedings of The Sixth International Workshop on Information Retrieval with Asian Languages (2003) 124-131
2. Salton, G. and McGill, M.: Introduction to Modern Information Retrieval, McGraw Hill, New York (1983)
3. Kohonen, T.: Self-Organizing Maps, Springer-Verlag, New York (1995)
4. Yan, T. W. and Garcia-Molina, H.: "Distributed selective dissemination of information," Proceedings of the Third International Conference on Parallel and Distributed Information Systems (1994) 89-98
5. Stevens, C.: "Automating the creation of information filters," Communications of the ACM, 35(12) (1992) 48
6. Resnick, P., Iacovou, N., etc.: "GroupLens: An open architecture for collaborative filtering of netnews, " Proceedings of the Conference on Computer Supported Cooperative Work, ACM (1994) 175-186
7. Lewis, D. D., Schapire, R. E., Callan, J. P., and Papka, R.: "Training algorithms for linear text classifiler", Proc. of SIGIR-96, 19th ACM International Conference on Research and Development in Information Retrieval (1996)
8. Payne, T. R. and Edwards, P.: "Dimensionality Reduction through Sub-Space Mapping for Nearest Neighbor Algorithms," European Conference on Machine Learning (2000) 331-343
9. Lee, C. C.: "Fuzzy logic in control systems: Fuzzy logic controller-part I," IEEE Trans. Syst. Man, Cybern., 20(2) (1990) 408-418
10. Ott, R. L.: An introduction to statistical methods and data analysis, Duxbury Press, Belmont, California (1993)
11. Duda, R. O. and Hart, P. E.: Pattern Classification and Scene Analysis, John Wiley and Sons (1973)

Using Context to Solve the Correspondence Problem in Simultaneous Localisation and Mapping

Margaret E. Jefferies, Wenrong Weng, Jesse T. Baker, and Michael Mayo

Department of Computer Science
University of Waikato, New Zealand
{mjeff,ww19,jtb5,mcc2,mmayo}@cs.waikato.ac.nz

Abstract. We present a method for solving the correspondence problem in Simultaneous Localisation and Mapping (SLAM) in a topological map. The nodes in the topological map are a representation for each local space the robot visits. The approach is feature based - a neural network algorithm is used to learn a signature from a set of features extracted from each local space representation. Newly encountered local spaces are classified by the neural network as to how well they match the signatures of the nodes in the topological network. Of equal importance as the correspondence problem is its dual, that of perceptual aliasing which occurs when parts of the environment which appear the same are in fact different. It manifests itself as false positive matches from the neural network classification. Our approach to solving this aspect of the problem is to use the context provide by nodes in the neighbourhood of the (mis)matched node. When neural network classification indicates a correspondence then subsequent local spaces the robot visits should also match nodes in the topological map where appropriate.

1 Introduction

In this paper we describe one of the approaches we are using to solve the corresponding problem in Simultaneous Mapping and Localisation (SLAM). This is regarded as one of the hard problems in SLAM. It is often termed cycle or loop closing because the problem presents itself when the robot traverses a cycle in its environment. The challenge is how to recognise that the cycle has been closed - that parts of the environment observed from different vantage points *correspond* to the same physical space.

The problem is encountered in both topological and absolute metric maps. For absolute metric maps current localisation methods provide consistent enough local maps but residual error accumulates over large distances. By the time a large cycle is encountered the map will contain significant inconsistencies. Current approaches use some form of probability evaluation to estimate the most likely pose of the robot given its current observations and the current state of its map [1-4]. Detecting the cycle allows the map to be aligned correctly but means the error has to be corrected backwards through the map.

Most topological approaches to robot spatial mapping partition the environment in some way and link these partitions as they are experienced to form a topological map [5-8]. The advantage of this approach is that global consistency is not an issue because the error cannot grow unbounded as in absolute metric maps. Consistency is not a problem within the partitions as they are usually around the size of a local environment. State of the art localisation methods are good enough for local environments. In closing cycles in a topological map the problem is to match two nodes in the topological map if they represent the same physical space (the correspondence problem) and to distinguish two nodes that look the same if they represent different parts of the environment (the perceptual aliasing problem).

Recently hybrid topological/metric approaches have emerged [6, 7, 9]. Hybrid approaches are popular in the cognitive mapping community [5, 8, 10] however the metric and topological maps do not have equal status. The topological map is the dominant representation in their models. Cognitive maps are often regarded as being like a "map in the head" that an agent (human, animal or robot) has for its experience of its spatial environment. In absolute metric maps the need to match the local map associated with a particular pose and the need to propagate error corrections backwards through the map has seen the introduction of topologically linked local metric maps for sequences of poses [1-3]. However these are a means to an end which is more consistent absolute metric maps.

Our mapping system is based on our previous work where a computational theory of cognitive mapping has been derived from empirical evidence of how humans and animals solve similar problems [8, 11]. An agent could be human animal or robot. Cognitive mapping researchers have been interested in the correspondence problem for some time but it was not clear from their computer simulations that their algorithms would handle all the uncertainties that a robot faces in the real world [8, 12]. Recently cognitive mapping researchers have begun to adapt their theories and algorithms for the real world problem robots encounter [13, 14].

Our approach to mapping the robot's environment extends the hybrid model of [8] and adheres to the dominant cognitive mapping tenet, that the prime representation is the topological map (see [5, 8] for a discussion on why this is so). Yeap and Jefferies' [8] topological map of metric local space descriptions has been implemented on a mobile robot with minor adaptations to handle input from a laser range sensor.

In this paper we demonstrate how topological matching can be used to solve the correspondence problem and at the same time reduce the false positives which are due to perceptual aliasing. The nodes in the topological map are the individual local spaces the robot visits connected as they are experienced. We detect correspondences in the topological map using feature matching. However we can not match every feature in a local space because when it is approached from different view points different parts of the local space may be occluded. Therefore a backprop neural network is used to learn a signature for each local space which is composed of the subset of features that are viewable from wherever the ASR is approached. New local spaces are classified according to these signatures. If the classification process indicates a match then the neural network is retrained to account for the different views the robot will have of the same space when it is approached from different routes. The key to solving the perceptual aliasing problem is to recognise that the nodes in the topological map do not exist on their own. They are organised according to their topological connections and the neighbourhoods which result provide a certain context for any node within the map. When neural network classification indicates a correspondence then subsequent local spaces the robot visits should also match nodes in the topological map where appropriate.

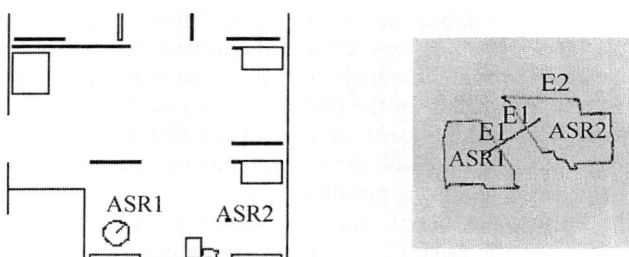

Fig. 1. (a) A section of the robot's environment. (b) The ASRs constructed correspond to thelabelled sections of the environment in (a). E1 and E2 are exits, E1 links ASR1 and ASR2.

2 The Basic Mapping Approach

The topological map comprises a representation for each local space visited with connections to others which have been experienced as neighbours. The local space is defined as the space which "appears" to enclose the robot. The local space representation is referred to as an Absolute Space Representation (ASR) a term which emphasises the separateness and independence of each individual local space. Each ASR in the topological map has its own local coordinate frame. Note that these are *local* absolute spaces in contrast to the *global* absolute metric representations referred to in section 1.

The basic algorithm described in [8] was modified to handle input from a laser range sensor and accumulating odometric and sensor errors. However the fundamentals of the algorithm remain. Yeap and Jefferies [8] argued that the exits should be constructed first because they are the gaps in the boundary which tell the robot how it can leave the current space. An exit will occur where there is an occlusion and is formed by creating the shortest edge which covers the occlusion. Once the exits are formed it is a straightforward process to connect the surfaces which lie between them to form the boundary of the ASR. At the same time surfaces which are viewed through the exits, and are thus outside the ASR, are eliminated. Fig.1 (b) shows a sequence of two ASRs so computed. See [8] for an in-depth description of the basic algorithm and [14, 15] for the details of how it is implemented on an autonomous mobile robot using laser range sensing. Rofer's [16] histogram correlation localisation method is used to provide consistency within ASRs. New ASRs are computed whenever the robot crosses an exit into an unexplored region and ASRs are linked, as they are experienced, via the exits which connect them to their neighbours in the topological map. The ASRs are the nodes of the topological map and the exits are its edges. Fig.1(b) shows an example of a topological map constructed in this way.

3 Using Feature Matching to Detect Correspondences

In this section we present a feature based matching approach to closing cycles in a topological map. As the robot enters a local space and constructs an ASR for it, the set of features for the ASR are classified by the neural network. The neural network returns its prediction, a score for each ASR in the topological map, which indicates its degree of similarity with the ASR the robot currently occupies. If all the values are below a chosen threshold then it is treated as a new ASR. The neural network is then trained on the new ASR's feature set to find a signature that will be used to recognise it when it is revisited. If a match is indicated from the classification process the neural network is retrained. Because the matching ASRs are computed from different view points not all the features in one ASR will be common to the other. Thus this process refines the signature so that better predictions are possible for future classifications.

3.1 Feature Selection

The feature set needs to accommodate sensing errors and be able to handle partial matches resulting from occlusions. We divide the ASR into segments, where each segment is a region of the ASR boundary which has a consistent gradient. The segments are divided into minor (short) segments and major (long) segments. Minor segments often result from spurious effects therefore they are not included in the feature set. The remaining segments are used to form the initial set of features given to the neural network. In addition to the segment, a feature comprises the angles corresponding to the change in gradient between adjacent segments, traversing the ASR in a clockwise direction. (see 2). Table 1 shows the segments extracted for the ASR depicted. There are 7 major segments labelled 1-7, and 3 minor segments. Segment 1 denotes an exit. Segment 3 represents a gap in the boundary but is turned into a surface because it is too small for the robot to pass through. The features extracted are listed in Table 1.

3.2 Signature Learning and ASR Classification

The requirements of the learning algorithm were as follows. The learning algorithm needed to be incremental and be able to add new classes (ASR signatures) online as new ASRs are encountered. There could be no restriction on either the number of boundary segments or the number of distinct ASRs in the environment. The algorithm needed to be able to decrement the effect of features common to many ASRs while strengthening the effect of those that distinguish ASRs. While the learning process could run in the background a fast prediction process was essential if it was to run in real time. Therefore, a back-propagation neural network was chosen to learn the ASR signatures and predict matches of newly computed ASRs with previously visited ASRs. Nguyen-Widrow Initialisation, Momentum and Batch updating of weights are used along with a bipolar sigmoid activation function.

The ranges of the input values (10m for length, and 360° for angles) are discretised into intervals. This is a practical requirement for a neural network but also accommodates sensor error. In the current implementation, a length interval of 200mm and angle interval of 45° are used. Each input neuron represents a particular length, angle, angle combination. When classifying an ASR, the output neuron associated with each ASR, outputs a value between 0 and 1 indicating the similarity of the new ASR with the visited ASR.

An example of a cycle is shown in Fig.2. The robot has traversed the environment depicted in Fig.2 (a) constructing the ASRs in the topological map (Fig.2 (b)) in the order they are numbered. The robot re-enters ASR2 via ASR7. The newly computed

668   Margaret E. Jefferies et al.

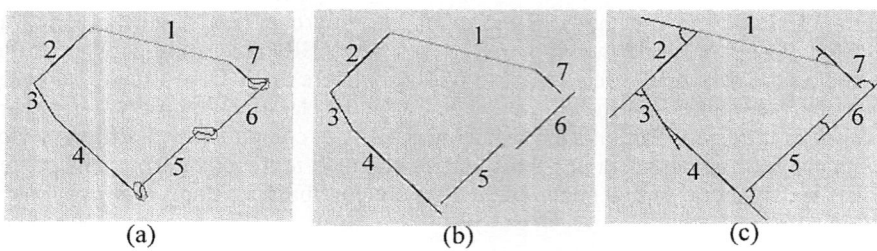

Fig. 2. The Features extracted from an ASR. (a) The ASR with minor segments encircled and major segments labelled 1-7. (b) Minor segments are removed. (c) The segments and angles which comprise the initial feature set.

Table 1. The initial features extracted for the ASR in Fig. 2.

Segment No	Length (mm)	Angle 1 (degrees)	Angle 2 (degrees)
1	1800	32.86	58.81
2	1008.9	58.81	-281.17
3	522.3	-281.17	10.6
4	1506.9	10.6	90.38
5	1014.9	90.38	0.07
6	991.3	0.03	88.44
7	392.8	88.44	32.86

Table 2. The similarity values for ASR 2* in Fig. 2.

ASR	1	2	3	4	5	6	7	8	9	10	11
pred	.78	.94	.89	.71	-.11	.72	.18	.51	.34	.36	.04

ASR2* is shown in 3 (c). The similarity predictions for ASRs 1 - 11 are shown in Table 2. Five values stand out, .78, .94, .89, .71, and .72 for ASRs 1, 2, 3, 4, and 6 respectively. If the threshold value were set at 0.7, say, then these would all be candidate matches. One cannot simply choose the best match because in many environments the ASRs for different local spaces will look similar (the perceptual aliasing problem). More evidence is needed to choose between them if indeed any of them should be chosen. In this case it is appropriate to choose the largest value. However this is not always so as can good threshold value, currently we take a conservative approach and reject similarity values below 0.9.i.

In the example in Fig.4 the robot re-enters ASR3 via ASR10. The similarity values for ASRs 1-10 are shown in Table 3. Four values stand out, .97, .91, .88, and .77 for ASRs 2, 3, 8, and 10 respectively. With a threshold value of 0.9 we need to choose

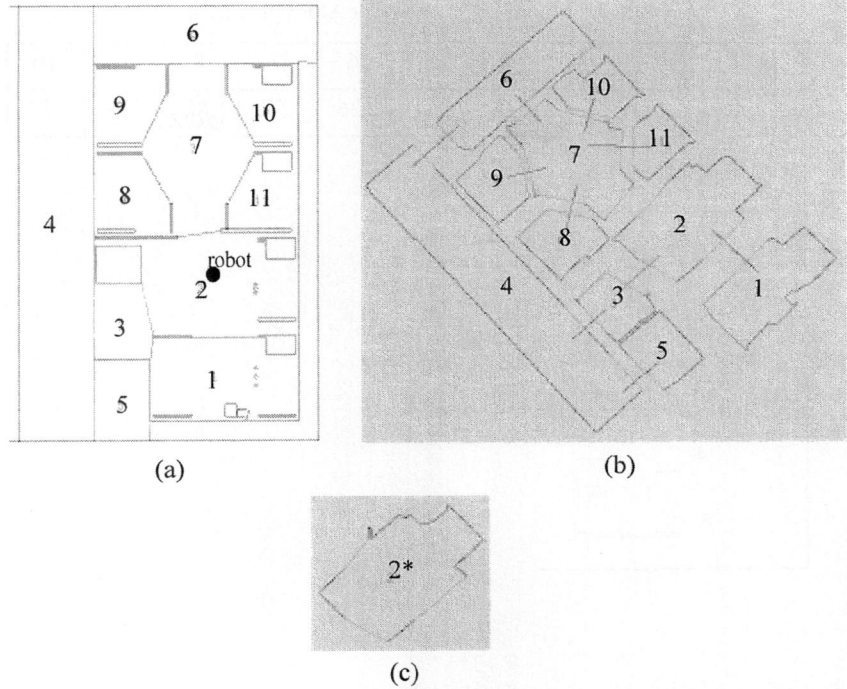

Fig. 3. A positive match. (a) The environment. (b) the topological map constructed in the order the ASRs are numbered. (c) The robot has re-entered ASR2 via ASR7. ASR2* depicts the newly computed ASR to be matched.

between 0.97 for ASR2 and 0.91 for ASR3. The highest value, for ASR2, is an example of a false positive.

Clearly in this case, the new ASR, ASR3* overlaps both ASR3 and ASR2, the ASRs with the highest predictions. If the new ASR does match a previously visited ASR then one would expect that its neighbours would match neighbours of the matched ASR. We currently gather evidence in this way for sequences of three ASRs, combining their predictions (see Section 4.3). However ASR3* in Fig.4 is not a good example to demonstrate this. None of its exits matches an exit in ASR3. The exit it would match is in ASR2.

There is evidence to suggest that the new ASR is a combination of both ASR3 and ASR2. This evidence comes in the form of the high predictions for ASR2 and ASR3 which are linked in the topological map and the overlap which occurs in the global metric map. However we need to do further testing to determine if there is any gain in matching under these circumstances. It may be that taking the conservative approach of rejecting the match would be less problematic. Note that missing a match in topological mapping is not catastrophic - an opportunity for a shortcut is missed but reliable (not necessarily optimal) navigation is still possible.

Table 3. The similarity values for ASR3* in Fig. 4.

ASR	1	2	3	4	5	6	7	8	9	10
pred	.46	.97	.91	.48	.64	.26	.57	.88	.15	.77

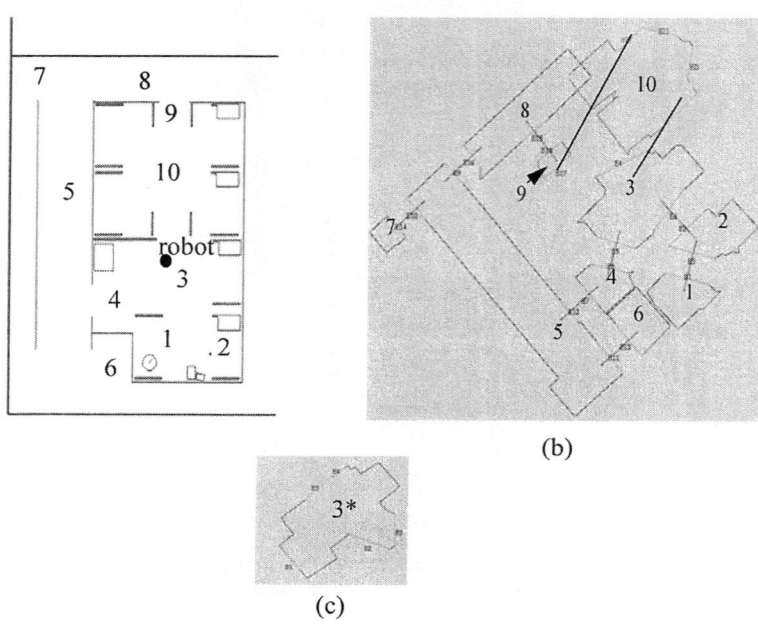

(b)

(c)

Fig. 4. An example of a false positive prediction (a) the environment (b) the topological map (c) the robot re-enters ASR3 and computes the ASR as depicted. It covers both ASR3 and ASR4 and extends into ASR2. The highest similarity value is for ASR2.

3.3 Topological Matching

The idea behind topological matching is to delay committing to a match in the topological map until it can be verified that a sequence of ASRs in the topological map containing the new ASR matches a sequence containing the previously computed ASR. We have found that sequences of order 3 give good results in the environments our robot navigates. A simple environment is used in Fig.5 to demonstrate the process. The robot traverses the environment computing ASRs which are numbered in the order they are encountered. In Fig.5 (b) the robot has re-entered ASR1 via ASR5. A new ASR is constructed and labelled ASR6. The ASR similarities for ASR6 are listed in Table 4. The robot continues to explore, obtaining the sequence of order 3, ASRs 6, 7 and 8 in Fig.5 (c). The sequence ASR 1-3 is the only sequence of order 3 containing ASR1. Classifying ASRs 7 and 8 give the predictions 0.92 and 0.93 respectively, that they match ASRs 3 and 2. All three predictions are above the 0.9 threshold indicating a positive match of ASR1 and ASR6 and the topological map can be adjusted to reflect this.

Table 4. The similarity values for ASR6 in.

ASR	1	2	3	4	5
pred	.9	.73	.74	.58	.55

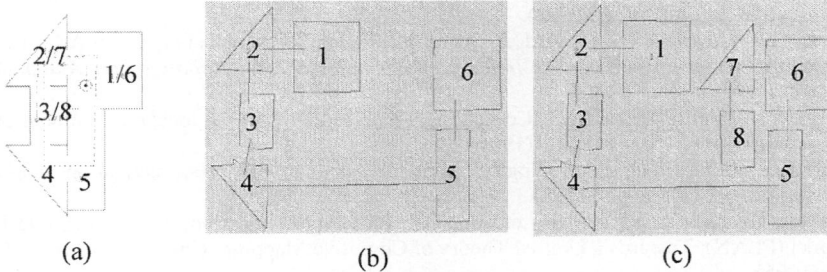

(a)   (b)   (c)

Fig. 5. Topological matching. (a) A simple environment (b) The topological map after the robot has re-entered ASR 1 via ASR5. A new ASR5 for the same space, ASR5 is linked to ASR5. (c) The sequence ASR6, ASR7, ASR8 match the sequence ASR1, ASR2, ASR3 confirming the match of ASRs 1 and 6.

In this example there was only one prediction to be validated. In more complex environments multiple hypotheses would be carried. We are currently investigating how best to converge to a winning hypothesis particularly in environments with a high similarity. Sequences of higher order may be needed in these environments.

4 Conclusion

In this paper we have shown how topological matching can be used to solve the correspondence problem and at the same time reduce the effect of false positives which are due to perceptual aliasing. ASRs in a topological map can be recognised from a characteristic subset of their features. Context plays an important role in eliminating false positive matches. The context of a matched node (its neighbourhood) is used to verify that it is in fact a true positive match. We are currently investigating how the robot can bale out of a committed match at some later time when it discovers a mismatch. It should be able to return to an alternative high prediction and test its validity against the accumulated data. This is for future work.

References

1. Hahnel, D., Burgard, W., Fox, D., and Thrun, S. A efficient fastSLAM algorithm for generating maps of large-scale cyclic environments from raw laser range measurements. in *Intelligent Robots and Systems*, (2003).
2. Thrun, S., Hahnel, D., Ferguson, D., Montemerlo, M., Triebel, R., Burgard, W., Baker, C., Omohundro, Z., Thayer, S., and Whittaker, W. A system for volumetric robotic mapping of abandoned mines. in *International Conference on Robotics and Automation*, (in press) (2003).

3. Hahnel, D., Thrun, S., Wegbreit, b., and Burgard, W. Towards lazy data association in SLAM. in *10th International Symposium of Robotics Research*, (2003).
4. Gutmann, J.-S. and Konolige, K. Incremental mapping of large cyclic environments. in *International Symposium on Computational Intelligence in Robotics and Automation*, (1999).
5. Kuipers, B., The spatial semantic hierarchy. *Artificial Intelligence*, 119: 191-233 (2000).
6. Tomatis, N., Nourbakhsh, I., and Siegwart, R. Hybrid simultaneous localization and map building: Closing the loop with multi-hypotheses tracking. in *International Conference on Robotics and Automation*, (2002).
7. Bosse, M., Newman, P., Leonard, J., Soika, M., Feiten, W., and Teller, S. An Atlas framework for scalable mapping. in *International Conference on Robotics and Automation*, (2003).
8. Yeap, W.K. and Jefferies, M.E., Computing a representation of the local environment. *Artificial Intelligence*, 107: 265-301 (1999).
9. Thrun, S., Learning metric-topological maps for indoor mobile robot navigation. *Artificial Intelligence*, 99(1): 21-71 (1998).
10. Chown, E., Kaplan, S., and Kortenkamp, D., Prototypes, Location, and Associative Networks (PLAN): Towards a Unified Theory of Cognitive Mapping. *Cognitive Science*, 19: 1-51 (1995).
11. Jefferies, M.E. and Yeap, W.K. Representing the local space qualitatively in a cognitive map. in *Twentieth annual conference of the Cognitive Society*, 525-530 (1998).
12. Kuipers, B.J. and Byun, Y.-T. A Robust, Qualitative method for Robot Spatial learning. in *Proceedings of the National Conference on Artificial Intelligence (AAAI-88)*, 774-779 (1988).
13. Kuipers, B. and Beeson, P. Bootstrap learning for place recognition. in *18th International Conference on Artificial Intelligence*, (2002).
14. Jefferies, M.E., Baker, J., and Weng, W. Robot cognitive mapping: A role for a global metric map in a cognitive mapping process. in *Workshop on Robot and Cognitive Approaches to Spatial Mapping*, (2003).
15. Jefferies, M.E., Yeap, W.K. and Baker, J.T. Robot mapping with a topological map of local space representations. *In Mastorakis, N.E., Kluev, V.V. and Djuro, K. (eds) Advances on Simulation, Systems Theory and Systems Engineering. WSEAS Press, 287-294 (2002)*.
16. Rofer, T. Using histogram correlation to create consistent laser scan maps. *In IEEE Conference on Robotics and Automation*, 625-630, (2002).

Knowledge-Based Interactive Robot: System Architecture and Dialogue Manager

Pattara Kiatisevi, Vuthichai Ampornaramveth, and Haruki Ueno

National Institute of Informatics (NII)
Graduate University for Advanced Studies (Sokendai)
2-1-2 Hitotsubashi, Chiyoda-ku
Tokyo, Japan 101-8430
pattara@grad.nii.ac.jp, {vuthi,ueno}@nii.ac.jp

Abstract. Development of robots that interact with people intelligently in the human-friendly manner is still a challenging research topic. Consider welfare and friend robots that will live with us in the long term, their interactions with human are different from those of traditional dialogue systems. They are usually multi-modal, and multi-topic. Robots should be also able to learn through the conversations in order to be capable of new things.

We aim to integrate robotics and knowledge technology to achieve such robot. This paper presents its system architecture and dialogue manager. The architecture is distributed. The robot is decomposed into multiple components called *primitive agents*. The special agent dialogue manager acts as the brain of the system. It perceives changes in the environment and makes actions by inferencing based on the knowledge base. Frame-based knowledge technique is used to represent the world of interest. It is extended to support time-based layer and frames actions priority. The current system can perform state-based and frame-based types of dialogue, and learn simple facts and rules given explicitly by human. The prototype system is developed on a humanoid robot and an example of multi-modal human-robot interaction is shown.

1 Introduction

Research in humanoid robots has made impressive progress in the past decades with significant improvement in the mechanical and electrical aspects. But most developed robots still cannot interact with human and the environment intelligently and autonomously. A lot of research has been conducted in the field of dialogue technology, but they are mostly focused on systems that act as front-end to certain computing resources, e.g., search and reservation system, and interact with human in a relatively short period of time [1,2].

Consider systems like friend or welfare robots that will stay with human in the longer term, the nature of the interaction becomes different. The dialogues are not limited to one specific subject but usually span over several topics. More importantly, as the robot interacts with human again and again, it must be able

to learn from the conversation so that human needs not to tell what to do all
the time, or to give the same information when having conversation in another
topic or at another time.

Learning can be done in various modes, for example, learning through explicit
human instruction, i.e., the human gives directly the new knowledge or new rule,
e.g., when the human says *"Alex is a student"*, the robot should learn that there
is an *is-a* relationship between *Alex* and the *Student* concept; learning through
implicit human instruction; and learning from demonstration. In this phase of
development, we are concerned only with the explicit case.

Moreover, the robot should support multi-modal input/output, to make the
interaction more human-friendly. For that it has to manage several sensors and
actuators efficiently. It should be as well easy to add new devices into the system.

This paper presents our development of an interactive robot that learns, as a
part of the *Symbiotic Information Systems (SIS)* research program [3]. In order
to enable efficient collaboration among hardware and software components that
compose the robot, a distributed system architecture is proposed [4]. To support
intelligent dialogue conversations, the knowledge technique is employed. We have
developed a general purpose software platform called SPAK [5] and used it to
manage the interaction.

In the next three sections we discuss the overall system architecture, SPAK
and the dialogue manager. In Section 5 we describe the demonstration prototype
and show an example of human robot interaction scenario.

2 System Architecture

Robots (in the context of service and friend robots) are typically composed
of various kinds of software and hardware components, e.g., robot arms, video
camera, microphone, face detection software, speech recognition software. These
components have different usages and programming interfaces depending on their
types, programming languages, and manufacturers. Some runs only on a specific
platform. Since all these components are to be combined into an integrated
system (i.e. the robot), a mechanism to allow efficient cooperations among them
and fast development process in order to cope with rapid change of technology,
is needed.

We design the system so that the robot is divided into small networked components called *primitive agents*[1]. Each primitive agent is either responsible for
a certain specific task, for example, speech recognition, face detection; or representing a certain robotics device it is connected to, e.g., video camera or speaker.
A primitive agent can be accessed from other primitive agents on the TCP/IP
network using the remote-procedure-call *XML-RPC* (http://www.xmlrpc.org).
An agent makes available the list of functions it offers in its *programming interface*.

---

[1] The term *agent* in this paper is referred to an individual computing element that
performs a specific task using the resource it controls. It can be autonomous or
non-autonomous, intelligent or non-intelligent.

A primitive agent is technically a piece of software performing a certain specific task wrapped by an XML-RPC server. This server waits for requests from other agents. When a request arrives, it is accepted and forwarded to the appropriate part of code that performs the real processing. Adding a new component to the system can be done by simply wrapping it with the XML-RPC server and making it accessible for other agents on the network. Figure 1 illustrates an example robot with its 6 primitive agents.

Example programming interface of a face detector primitive agent is as follow (in pseudo code):

- *string getStatus()*: check agent's status (common for all agents)
- *string ping()*: check agent's reachability (common for all agents)
- *void setImage(base64_encoded_data imagecontents)*: set the input image contents
- *string getFaceLocations()*: does the face detection, and return face location(s)

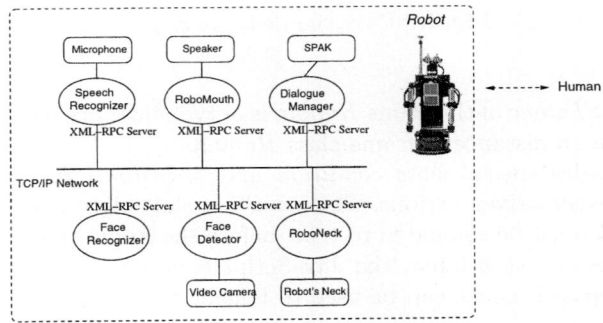

Fig. 1. Robot as a network of primitive agents

3 SPAK

SPAK (Software Platform for Agents and Knowledge Management) is a software platform for knowledge processing and coordination of tasks among several software modules [6]. SPAK features frame-based knowledge management [7]. It has a GUI knowledge editor for manual manipulation of the knowledge contents. It has a network interface allowing the interaction with other agents on the network. The knowledge content is stored in the XML format, hence easy to be exported to and manipulated by other programs. The current version of SPAK is implemented in Java in order to be multi-platform.

As shown in Figure 2, SPAK maintains its knowledge contents in hierarchy of *frames*. Each frame includes a set of *slots*. SPAK frame slots can be of scalar types: *string*, *integer*, *real* (real number); *list* (array); *instance* (as link to other frame instance); and procedural script. For the procedural script, SPAK supports JavaScript language and has a built-in JavaScript interpreter.

In each slot a condition can be attached. For example, the slot *Age* of the frame *Human* is of type integer and has a condition that *Age must be greater*

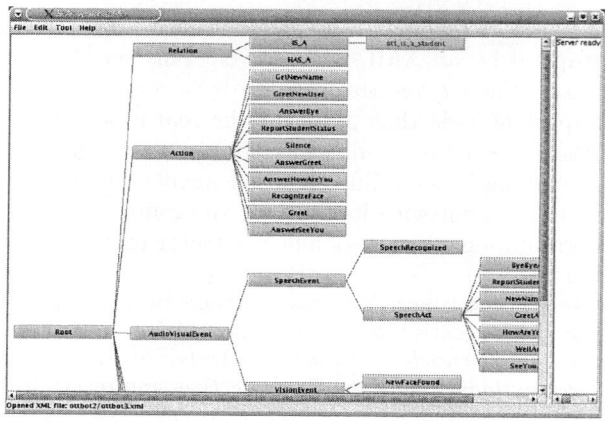

Fig. 2. SPAK knowledge manager

than 0. The slot *Father* of the frame *Human* is of type instance with the condition that it must be an instance of frame class *Human*.

SPAK provides special slots *condition* and *onInstantiate* to facilitate the realization of event-driven actions. The *condition* slot might contain JavaScript expression that must be evaluated to true, before the frame can be instantiated. Once the frame is instantiated, the JavaScript code specified in *onInstantiate* slot will be executed, hence can be used to trigger actions.

SPAK in Action: There are several ways to use SPAK to control robot behaviors. Here we show the method we used in our human-robot dialogue applications.

First the knowledge about the world of interest is created. Objects and concepts are mapped into frames, e.g., *Human, Student, Professor, Event, Behavior*. The event-action behavior is achieved by using the *Event* and *Behavior* frames. Event frames are designed for describing changes in the environment, e.g., *AudioVisualEvent – SpeechRecognized, SpeechAct, FaceDetected, KnownFaceRecognized; SensorEvent – HeadSensor, BellySensor* events. Behavior frames are designed with proper conditions in order to match those events and cause some actions.

When a primitive agent perceives a change in the environment, it passes that information to SPAK Knowledge Manager (through the SPAK network interface) in the form of event frames, which might consequently result in creation of a new behavior frame and trigger an action.

In the big picture, the SPAK Knowledge Manager acts as decision making module. It receives input events from other primitive agents, incorporates changes into its knowledge contents, and causes output actions.

An example from a human-robot experiment: when an unknown face is observed by the face recognizer primitive agent, an event frame, say *UnknownFaceFound*, is sent to the Knowledge Manager. Upon receiving this frame, the condition of a behavior frame *Greet,* which requires an existence of an unknown person in front of the robot (i.e. an *UnknownFaceFound* frame) is fulfilled. Therefore a new instance of *Greet* frame is created and some actions, e.g., say a greeting word, are triggered according to the contents of its *onInstantiate* slot.

By using SPAK in our robotics environment, we encountered two major problems. First, the conventional frame-based technique is found not able to handle the temporal information well. Second, it is ambiguous which frame action is to be processed first in case that there are many possible candidates. Therefore we propose two new extensions namely time-based layer and frame actions priority supports to solve the problems.

Time-Based Layer: In typical use of the frame-based knowledge representation, objects in the world of interest are represented by frames in the hierarchical structure. Properties of an object are encoded in the slots of the frame representing that object itself or the upper class frames. Frame hierarchies reflect the structural view of the world and the current instance frames correspond to existing objects in the world at the current time.

In our system, a change in the environment triggers the SPAK Knowledge Manager to perform actions, or make appropriate changes to its knowledge contents, e.g., instantiating a new frame, updating the slot value of a certain frame, deleting a frame. The knowledge is therefore up-to-date according to the current situation.

Knowledge about the world at the current point in time can be easily inferred or added into the system. However, it is difficult to deal with temporal information. For example, consider a knowledge hierarchy containing a *Human* frame and its sub-class frames: *Professor, Associate Professor, Lecturer.* The robot met a human of name *John,* learned that he was a lecturer, and saved into its knowledge. Some years later John changed his position from lecturer to associate professor and finally to professor. At the current time, with proper updates to its knowledge contents every time John changed his position, the robot can answer the question like *What is the position of John right now?* but it will have hard time answering the question like *When did John get promoted from lecturer to associate professor?* Tracking of temporal information changed is crucial in order to achieve such knowledge.

One can argue that we can simply create a special slot *PreviousPosition* in the *Human* frame to keep the old status information and probably another slot for keeping the time when the status changes, or even treat John's human frames with different positions as different frames . However, with these settings, we end up with either having an overwhelming number of slots for every information changes we would like to keep track of, or having extremely large amount of frame instances in the system.

Consider the situation of a service robot which stays with human for years, its knowledge content changes as time goes by (and actually the knowledge structure too, e.g. new hierarchy of frames, new slot in a frame, when the robot learns the new things, but we have yet to investigate this issue). This changes information which is recording of frames' activities, e.g. a frame is instantiated, a frame is deleted, a certain slot value of a frame is changed, grows larger as the robot lives its life. At the end it is possible that it becomes much larger than the current knowledge. Without proper handling of this high amount of information, it is hard to make use of it.

We propose that this temporal information should be recorded and made search-able by keeping track of all the changes to the knowledge contents and providing methods to access this data. The whole knowledge become layers of the knowledge contents at each point in time, stacking onto each other with the top most one, the one that we can see from the knowledge editor, as the current one.

With this time-based layer, the SPAK behavior varies depending on time (i.e. the history). The notation to specify timing information of slots is as follow. The current value of slot *age* of frame *s* is $s.age$[2]. That value at 10 seconds before is $s.age\{-10\}$.

It is now simple to specify frame's condition based on time. For example, if we want the robot to "*Do Action A if the face has not moved for 5 seconds*". Assume $A.myFace$ is an instance of a *Face* frame, and x,y are the slots of *Face* frames indicating the (x,y) position of the face. The condition slot of the action frame A can be set as follow:

$s.myFace.x == s.myFace.x\{-5\}$ && $s.myFace.y == s.myFace.y\{-5\}$

Priority Support for Frame Actions: Our use of SPAK for human-robot interaction is in event-action manner, i.e., an incoming event triggers SPAK to instantiate frame(s) and cause some actions. However, in many cases, there are many candidate frames to be instantiated at the same time, all caused by the same input event. Now which frame is to be instantiated first? The order is important since instantiation of a frame can cause changes to the environment and even to the knowledge contents itself. It might also invalidate the evaluation condition of another frame which was about to be instantiated at the same time.

We propose that it should be possible to assign priority value to each frame to indicate which one would win in the case that many frames are simultaneously qualified for frame actions, i.e., instantiation, changing of slot value, deletion. This can be manually-assigned, or as a general policy, e.g., the frame that has largest number of conditions always win (which might have to rely on the manual priority anyway in case there are more than one of such frames).

For example, imagine a robot is configured with a *ByeBye* action. It would normally say "*Bye bye, have a nice evening*" to the human when he is leaving the laboratory. But in case it knows that it is going to rain this evening and notices that he forgot to take his umbrella with him, another action to warn him "*It is going to rain this evening, would you like to take your umbrella?*" should be triggered first. It this case, both actions can actually be triggered by the same *Bye* event but the warning one should have higher priority so that it will be executed first.

---

[2] As a a notation used in SPAK, the symbol *s* means the current frame.

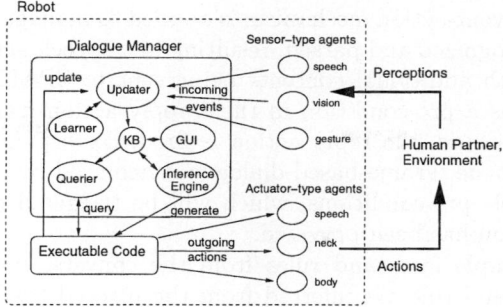

Fig. 3. Knowledge manager and interaction with other components

A new slot *priority* of type real is added in SPAK to indicate this priority. At the moment only manual priority specification is supported.

4 Dialogue Manager

Dialogue management is handled by the knowledge manager which is a part of SPAK. The knowledge manager and its interaction with other components are shown in Figure 3. Changes in the environment (e.g. new object detected, spoken text recognized) are noticed by sensor-type primitive agents (e.g, face detector, speech recognizer). They then submit corresponding information to the *Updater* component of the Knowledge Manager. The Updater incorporates changes into the knowledge data base (DB), which might trigger instantiation of new frames or manipulation of existing frames by *Inference Engine*. Instantiation of a new frame causes execution of program code according to the content of *onInstantiate* slot. This can generate requests to actuator-type agents in order to do some physical actions. The program code and the Inference Engine can optionally query more information about the world or history from the *Querier*.

Supported Dialogue Conversation Types: To handle state-based and frame-based types of dialogue, we use the event-action mechanism through *Event* and *Behavior* frames. Event frames are designed for describing changes in the environment, e.g., *SpeechRecognized*, *FaceDetected* events. Behavior frames are designed with proper conditions in order to match those events and cause some actions.

An example is as follow: when an unknown face is observed by the face recognizer agent, an event frame *UnknownFaceFound* will be sent to the Knowledge Manager. Upon receiving this frame, the condition of the behavior frame *Greet*, which requires an existence of an unknown person in front of the robot (i.e. an *UnknownFaceFound* frame), is fulfilled. Therefore a new instance of *Greet* frame is created and the actions specified in the *onInstantiate* slot, e.g., say a greeting word, are executed.

Similarly, the event-action mechanism is applied to manage the dialogue. The input speech is recognized and parsed, resulting in a speech act event containing a performative with additional contents being sent to SPAK. This speech act event can be set as a pre-condition in the a reply action frame. When such a speech act event occurs, the reply action is fired, corresponding to the state-based type of dialogue. Frame-based dialogue is achieved by creating an action frame with multiple pre-conditions, which will be triggered only when all the required information has been provided.

Learning of simple facts and rules from the conversation can be done as follows. New fact and rule are inferred from the uttered text and transformed into speech act. For example, assume the knowledge base contains a frame of type *Man*, the sentence "*Alex is a Man*" is parsed and results in the speech act as follow (in the frame-slot value representation):

Inform-type="is_a"; Inform-target1="Alex"; Inform-target2="Man"

Upon receiving this information, the Updater updates the knowledge database, causing the Inference Engine to create a new instance of the frame *Man*, with the slot *Name* filled with value *Alex*. In the future, a question like "*Who is Alex?*" can be answered by asking the Querier if there is any instance of *Human* frame (parent frame of Man and Woman) with the name *Alex*.

Learning of new rules can be done similarly. For example, telling of a new action to be done at a certain time results in a new *Action* frame with the value of slot *starttime* filled. The action will be fired by the Inference Engine at the specified time.

5 Demonstration Prototype

A multi-modal human-robot experiment with the Robovie humanoid robot (developed by ATR, Japan) was conducted. Robovie has human-like upper torso on top of an ActivMedia wheel robot. It has two eye-cameras and a speaker at its mouth. Robovie can interact with users by moving its arms and head, or using voice.

Overview diagram of the current system is illustrated in Figure 4(a). Robovie works with a number of primitive agents running on 4 different workstations to distribute the workload. Some important primitive agents are:

- *SpeechRecognizer:* uses the IBM ViaVoice speech recognition software as back-end.
- *RobovieMouth:* accepts strings of input text and output the speech sound to the Robovie's speakers using the Festival Text-to-Speech software.
- *FaceDetector:* finds face locations in the image using the software from Carnegie-Mellon University (http://www-2.cs.cmu.edu/~har/faces.html).
- *FaceRecognizer:* performs face recognition using MIT's Eigenface software.
- *TextParser*: parses the input text (from the SpeechRecognizer agent) and sends the result speech acts to SPAK.
- *RoboviePose:* offers low level functions to control the movement of Robovie's mechanical parts.

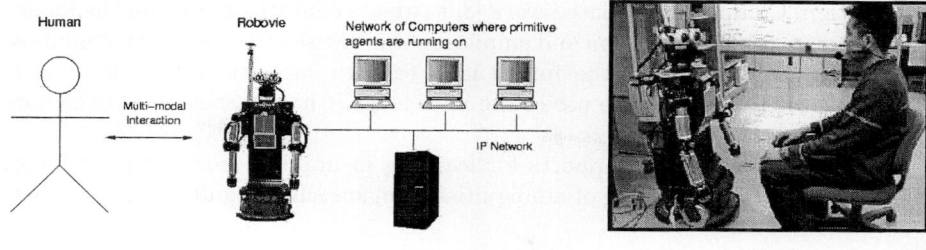

(a) Overview Diagram   (b) Experiment

Fig. 4. Prototype system

The developed system can handle multi-modal interaction in state-based, frame-based type of dialogues, and explicit learning as described in Section 4. To demonstrate a more realistic use, an example human-robot interaction scenario is designed as follows:

A welfare robot named *Robota* lives in the house with its master Alex. It is 8 o'clock in the morning. The robot detects a human face at far distance, then closer, and closer. It starts the face recognition process. Based on the this sequence of events, the Greet dialogue is triggered.

Robot: *Good morning, Alex* [also waves its hand]
Human: *Hi, Robot.*
R: *How are you today?*
H: *Not very well.*
Robot records the status of human. This value of *not very well* triggers more questions.
R: *That is not good. Did you sleep well last night?*
H: *No.*
R: *Sleep is very important for your health. How is your condition?*
H: *I have a headache.*
With the status of not very well, and having headache, the action to contact welfare center is fired.
R: *I see, I should report to the welfare service center to get some advice for you.*
[simulated] The robot contacts the welfare service center.
R: *A physical consultant advice you to visit the center. Should I reserve a visit for you?*
H: *Yes.*
To reserve a visit at the center, it needs to know the time.
R: *Do you want to visit just now or in the afternoon?*
H: *Afternoon is better.*
[simulated] The robot queries the welfare center, and found the afternoon time is OK. In order to visit the center, a transportation means is required. It then queries travel agent for the bus information.
R: *OK. A shuttle bus is available at 3. Do you reserve it?*
H: *Yes.*
Reserve action completed, the robot adds a reminding action to be done when the bus arrives, and reports the task.
R: *I have reserved a visit at 3:30 and the bus at 3:00. I will tell you when the bus arrives.*
H: *Thank you very much.*

Figure 4(b) displays the experiment environment. Robovie made a successful conversation with a human subject according to the scenario.

6 Conclusion and Future Work

The system architecture and dialogue manager of our multi-modal interactive robot are presented. The knowledge technique is employed to manage dialogue interaction. Compared to related work [8,9], we are concerned more on the longer term human-robot interaction and emphasize on the use of knowledge techniques, with which we believe in the future it is easy to support more complicated learning processes and make use of the knowledge it has learned than behavior-based approach.

Future work includes supports for learning in implicit mode and reinforcement learning, and handling of ambiguities from speech recognition and parsing.

References

1. McTear, M.F.: Spoken dialogue technology: enabling the conversational user interface. ACM Computing Surveys, vol. 34, pp. 90 - 169 (2002)
2. B. Pellom, W. Ward, J. Hansen, K. Hacioglu, J. Zhang, X. Yu, S. Pradhan: University of colorado dialog systems for travel and navigation. In: Proceedings of the Human Language Technology Conference (HLT-2001). (2001)
3. Ueno, H.: Symbiotic Information Systems: Towards an Ideal Relationship of Human-Beings and Information Systems. Technical Report of IEICE, KBSE2001-15:27-34 (August 2001)
4. P. Kiatisevi, V. Ampornaramveth, H. Ueno: A distributed architecture for knowledge-based interactive robots. In: Proceedings of the 2nd International Conference on Information Technology for Application (ICITA 2004), Harbin, China. (2004)
5. V. Ampornaramveth, P. Kiatisevi, H. Ueno: Toward a software platform for knowledge management in human-robot environment. Technical Report of IEICE, Vol. 103 No. 83, pg. 15-20 (2003)
6. V. Ampornaramveth, P. Kiatisevi, H. Ueno: SPAK: Software Platform for Agents and Knowledge Management in Symbiotic Robots. IEICE Trans. Information and Systems, Vol.E87-D No.4 (2004) 886–895
7. Minsky, M.: A framework for representing knowledge. MIT-AI Laboratory Memo 306 (1974)
8. L. Seabra Lopes, A. Teixeira: Human-robot interaction through spoken language dialogue. In: Proceedings of the IEEE/RSJ International Conference on Intelligent Robots and Systems, (IROS-2000). (2000)
9. John Fry, Hideki Asoh, Toshihiro Matsui: Natural dialogue with the jijo-2 office robot. In: Proceedings of the IEEE/RSJ International Conference on Intelligent Robots and Systems (IROS-98). (1998)

Complete Coverage by Mobile Robots Using Slice Decomposition Based on Natural Landmarks

Sylvia C. Wong and Bruce A. MacDonald

Department of Electrical and Computer Engineering
University of Auckland, New Zealand
{s.wong,b.macdonald}@auckland.ac.nz

Abstract. In applications such as vacuum cleaning, painting, demining and foraging, a mobile robot must cover an unknown surface. The efficiency and completeness of coverage is improved by the construction of a map while the robot covers the surface. Existing methods generally use grid maps, which are susceptible to odometry error and may require considerable memory and computation. We propose a new "slice decomposition" ideally suited to coverage by a simple zigzag path. Cell boundaries are large, easily detectable natural landmarks. Therefore, the decomposition is robust against uncertainty in sensors. It can also handle a wider variety of environments. The proposed method has been evaluated using simulation and real robot experiments.

1 Introduction

In a coverage application, a mobile robot must visit all the reachable surface in its environment. While coverage is similar to exploration, an exploring robot moves and sweeps its long range sensors, so as to *sense* all of its environment. During a coverage application, the robot or a tool must *pass over* all floor surface.

If the environment is unknown, the robot must use a strategy that ensures it covers all the space. It must use sensors to gather information about obstacles as it moves, and it must formulate and remember some form of map, so that it may return to areas it has seen but not yet covered.

The algorithmic strategy of "divide and conquer" is a powerful technique used to solve many problems, and many mapping procedures carry out a process of space decomposition, where a complex space is repeatedly divided until simple subregions of a particular type are created. The problem at hand is then solved by applying a simpler algorithm to the simpler subregions. Exact cell decompositions [1] and occupancy grids [2] are examples of such maps. Coverage algorithms commonly use some form of space decomposition as a map, because covered areas can be stored easily by marking individual subregions.

Occupancy grids are a widely used map representation for coverage algorithms; it is straightforward to mark covered areas. Zelinsky used the distance transform of a grid map [3]. A coverage path is formed by selecting the unvisited neighbouring cell with the highest distance transform. Unlike other coverage algorithms, a goal location must be selected. Gabriely and Rimon incrementally subdivide the environment into disjoint grid cells, while following a spanning tree of the partial grid map [4]. A disadvantage of grid maps is the requirement for accurate localisation to create and maintain a coherent map [5]. Grid maps also suffer from exponential growth of memory usage because the resolution does not depend on the complexity of the environment [6]. Also, they do not permit efficient planning through the use of standard graph searches [6].

Exact cell decomposition divides a complex structure S into a disjoint component cells, whose union is exactly S. The boundary of a cell corresponds to a criticality of some sort. Exact cell decomposition methods are commonly used in path planning for point to point tasks. The most common example is trapezoidal decomposition [1]. It is formed by sweeping a line L across the environment, and creating a cell boundary whenever a vertex is encountered. Obstacles are limited to polygons. Therefore, each cell of a trapezoidal decomposition is either a trapezoid or a triangle. For path planning, the decomposition is first reduced to a connectivity graph representing the adjacency relation among cells [1]. The associated connectivity graph is searched to find paths between any two cells.

However, trapezoidal decomposition creates convex cells that are unnecessarily small, and therefore inefficient, for coverage purposes. Some non-convex shapes can also be covered by simple coverage patterns. For example, the two cells on each side of the obstacle in Fig. 1(a) can be merged and the simple zigzag pattern shown can still cover the combined cells. Based on merging multiple cells in trapezoidal decomposition, Choset and Pignon proposed the first exact cell decomposition specifically designed for coverage [7]; the boustrophedon decomposition, shown in Fig. 1(b), signifying the relationship between the decomposition and the zigzag. Like trapezoidal decomposition, boustrophedon decomposition is limited to environments with only polygonal objects.

Butler proposed an exact cell decomposition for rectilinear environments, for his coverage algorithm CC_R [8]. Cell boundaries are formed when an obstacle boundary parallel to the sweep line is encountered. While trapezoidal and boustrophedon decompositions cannot handle obstacle surfaces parallel to the

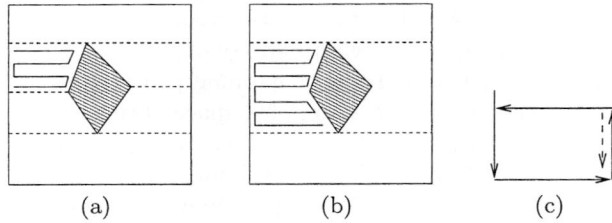

Fig. 1. (a) Trapezoidal decomposition creates cells that are unnecessarily small for coverage tasks. (b) Boustrophedon decomposition reduces the number of cells by combining multiple cells that can be covered by a zigzag. (c) The rectangular coverage pattern used in CC_R and Morse decomposition.

sweep line, the criticality in CC_R is specially defined for rectilinear environments. Another difference is that CC_R is calculated online by contact sensing robots, simultaneously with the coverage process. In other words, an associated coverage algorithm is devised to use a partial cell decomposition for coverage path planning, at the same time updating the map when new information becomes available. Instead of a zigzag, CC_R uses a rectangular coverage pattern that includes retracing, shown in Fig. 1(c). The retracing is added to ensure wall following on both side boundaries, because a contact sensing robot cannot detect obstacles except when wall following. If an opening in the side boundary occurs between consecutive strips of the zigzag, the robot will miss it.

Acar et al. introduced Morse decomposition [9] which can handle a larger set of environments than boustrophedon decomposition and CC_R. Cell boundaries in Morse decomposition are critical points of Morse functions. Put simply, a cell boundary occurs when the sweep line encounters an obstacle whose surface normal is perpendicular to the sweep line. Morse decomposition generalises boustrophedon decomposition to include non-polygonal obstacles. However, it cannot handle surfaces parallel to the sweep line. This excludes rectilinear environments. Similarly to CC_R, Morse decomposition also has an online decomposition algorithm. However, Morse decomposition cannot use a zigzag to cover individual cells. It uses the rectangular pattern in Fig. 1(c). The wall following offered by the pattern is needed because critical points occurring on the side boundary cannot be detected even with unlimited range sensors, except when wall following [10]. This is due to the difficulty in detecting critical points of Morse functions.

This paper introduces a new exact cell decomposition for complete coverage path planning, where the decomposed regions are precisely suited to a zigzag coverage pattern, with no retracing. The length of the coverage path is greatly reduced. Cell boundaries are large scale features that have physical extension over time, and can be detected even by noisy and inaccurate sensors. Also, our algorithm works on a larger variety of environments, including both rectilinear and non-rectilinear ones. Obstacles can be polygonal, or curved. Lastly, the cell decomposition can be constructed online, in an unknown environment, while the robot covers the space [11].

Section 2.1 explains the slices and segments created by a sweep line. Section 2.2 defines the criticality for cell boundaries. Section 2.3 presents the slice decomposition algorithm. Section 2.4 discusses the effects of step size and sweep direction. Section 3 presents results and section 4 discusses the work.

2 Slice Decomposition

2.1 Slice and Segments

A slice decomposition is created by sweeping a line from the top of an environment to the bottom. There are two types of region — obstacle and free space. At any time, the sweep line intersects a number of free space and obstacle regions determined by the topology of the environment and position of the sweep line.

We call the arrangement of regions intersected by the sweep line a *slice* and the regions within *segments*.

Fig. 2(a) shows an obstacle with the sweep line at two different positions. The slices created are shown on the right; at position 1 the slice contains one free space segment, an obstacle segment, and then another free space segment. The slice at position 2 has three free space segments and two obstacle segments.

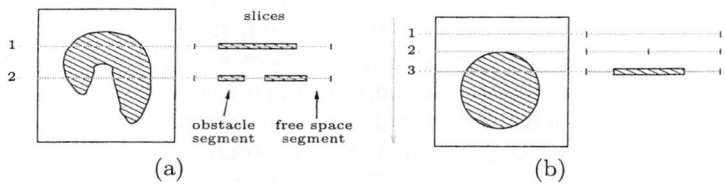

Fig. 2. (a) The arrangement of segments in slices made by the sweep line changes as it sweeps through the environment. (b) The number of segments present in a slice changes as the sweep line enters an obstacle.

In Fig. 2(b), at position 1, the slice contains only one free space segment. Obstacle segments begin to emerge at position 2, where the sweep line first intersects with the object.

The sweep line can be viewed as a ray passing through the segments on a slice. The ray intersection test [12] shows that every time an intersection is made, the line is in a different type of region. This guarantees that each segment is bounded by two intersection points, and also implies that the sweep line always has an even number of intersections on the slices, since the ray always starts and ends in the obstacle region outside the boundary.

2.2 Criticality

Two slices S_a and S_b are consecutive if they are from sweep line positions one time step apart. If the sweep line moves by a distance δx for each time step, and the slices S_a and S_b are from positions x_a and x_b respectively, then slice S_a and slice S_b are consecutive slices if and only if $\mid x_a - x_b \mid = \delta x$.

Cell boundaries occur when there is an abrupt change in the topology between segments in consecutive slices. There are two situations where this can happen:

1. A segment in the previous slice is split by the emergence of a new segment.
   - An obstacle segment emerges within a free space segment, as in Fig. 3(a).
   - A free space segment emerges within an obstacle segment, as in Fig. 3(b).
2. A segment from the previous slice disappears in the current slice.
   - An obstacle segment disappears, as in Fig. 3(c).
   - A free space segment disappears, as in Fig. 3(d).

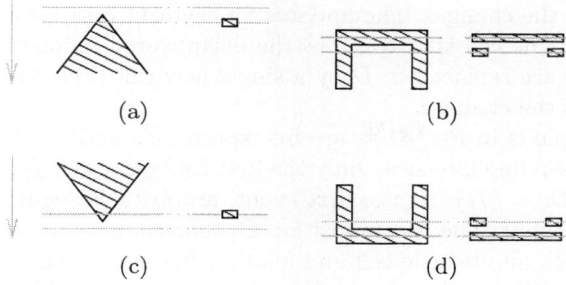

Fig. 3. (a), (b) One segment splits into multiple segments. (c), (d) Multiple segments merge into a single segment.

2.3 Decomposition Algorithm

The slice decomposition is formed by maintaining a list D of active obstacle and free space cells with segments present on the slices created by the sweep line as it sweeps through the environment, summarised in Algorithm 1. The history of list D, ie all the cells that have appeared in D, forms the decomposition. The sweep stops to process and update list D whenever a criticality occurs.

Algorithm 1 Offline Slice Decomposition.

1: $c \in \{\text{free space cell, obstacle cell}\}$
2: **for all** time t **do**
3:    Move sweep line downwards by δx
4:    $D_{t-1} = (\ldots, c_{i-2}, c_{i-1}, c_i, c_{i+1}, c_{i+2}, \ldots)$
5:    **for all** segments in D_{t-1} **do**
6:       **if** emergence inside c_i **then**
7:          $(c_i) \leftarrow (c_{e-1}, c_e, c_{e+1})$
8:          $D_t = (\ldots, c_{i-2}, c_{i-1}, c_{e-1}, c_e, c_{e+1}, c_{i+1}, c_{i+2}, \ldots)$
9:       **if** c_i disappears **then**
10:         $(c_{i-1}, c_i, c_{i+1}) \leftarrow (c_d)$
11:         $D_t = (\ldots, c_{i-2}, c_d, c_{i+2}, \ldots)$

The algorithm has two loops, one for moving the sweep line from top to bottom (line 2), the other for inspecting segments in the previous and the current slice for topology changes (line 5). At line 1 are specified all cells that are either free space cells or obstacle cells. Within the first loop, line 3 shows that the sweep line is moved by δx for each time step. Line 4 gives the format of the list D at the previous time step D_{t-1}. Lines 6 and 9 within the inner loop correspond to the two cases of criticality. For segment emergence (line 6), the segment that is split into two halves is replaced by three separate segments (line 7). The three segments belong to new cells and are therefore given new cell IDs, c_{e-1}, c_e, c_{e+1}. These new cell IDs identifying this slice contain a cell boundary. Line 8 shows the list D_t after the changes. The updates for segment disappearance are shown in lines 9 to 11. The cell that contains the disappeared segment, along with its two neighbours, are replaced in D by a single new cell (line 10). Line 11 shows the list D_t after the changes.

In the example is in Fig. 4, f_n are free space cells and o_n are obstacle cells. Initially, the sweep line intersects only the first free space cell f_1, giving just that one space cell, $D_t = (f_1)$. At the first event, an obstacle segment emerges and the first cell f_1 is split. The decomposition D_t then changes to contain three cells – a free space cell, an obstacle cell and another free space cell, $D_t = (f_2, o_1, f_3)$. Then obstacle cell o_1 is split when a free space cell emerges. The decomposition D_t changes to contain five cells, $(f_2, o_2, f_4, o_3, f_3)$. Next D_t changes to three cells, (f_5, o_3, f_3), as the left side bulge is passed. Finally the decomposition D_t contains only one free space cell f_6 when the sweep line exits the obstacle.

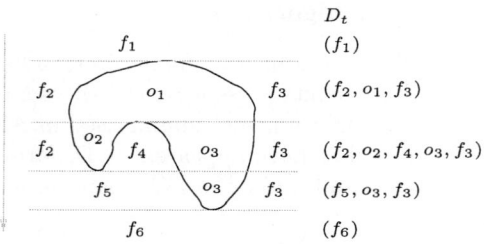

Fig. 4. An example of slice decomposition.

The algorithm tracks both free space and obstacle cells, although only the free space cells are of interest, since mobile robots cannot move inside obstacles.

2.4 Effect of Step Size and Sweep Direction

Since slice decomposition uses a discrete line sweep process, the step size between consecutive slices therefore affects the decomposition yield for a given environment. In practice the step size is determined by the width of the robot, to ensure no space is left uncovered in consecutive sweeps. If the step size is reduced to be infinitesimally small, $\delta x \to 0$, then the sweeping process becomes a continuous sweep, like other exact cell decompositions. However, slice decomposition also works for step sizes larger than infinitesimal.

To capture all cells in a particular environment, the maximum step size has to be smaller than the height of the smallest cell

$$\delta x \leq \min h(c_i) \qquad (1)$$

δx is the step size of the line sweep and $h(c_i)$ is the height of the i-th cell. Equation 1 guarantees that all cells will be present in at least one slice.

Fig. 5 illustrates the effect of varying the step size, on the decomposition created. When the steps are small, all cells in the environment are captured.

For example, in Fig. 5(a), the step size is small enough to guarantee a sweep line to pass through the small cell between the two lobes at the top of the obstacle. When the step size is increased to the height of the smallest cell, ie $\delta x = \min h(c_i)$, the second sweep position in Fig. 5(a) just barely touches the cell. If the step size is further increased, the smallest cell may be missed entirely, as is the case in Fig. 5(c).

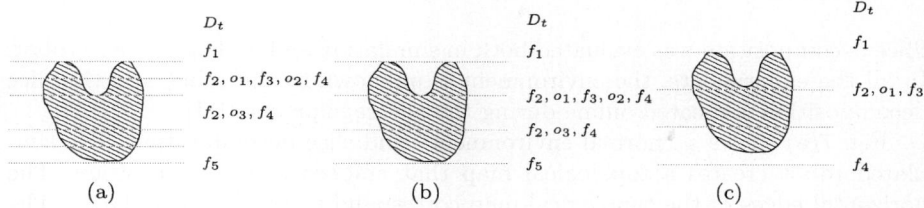

Fig. 5. Effect of step size on decomposition produced. All sweep lines are assumed to be slightly above the obstacle surface they are touching. The list of cells on the right shows where changes (criticalities) occur. (a) $\delta x = \frac{1}{2} \times \min h(c_i)$, (b) $\delta x = \min h(c_i)$, (c) $\delta x > \min h(c_i)$.

When equation 1 is satisfied, the decompositions created are independent of differences in the step size. Compare the slice decomposition in Fig. 5(a) and 5(b). Although the cells are discovered at different positions, the overall transitions of the list D are the same.

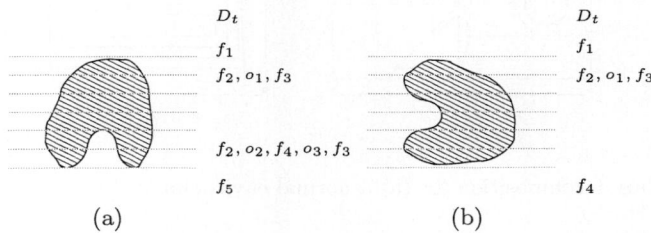

Fig. 6. (a) Forward and reverse sweep yield the same slice decomposition. (b) Rotation changes slice decomposition.

The decomposition created is the same whether the sweeping is in the forward (top to bottom) or the reverse (bottom to top) direction. The decomposition is dependent only on the position of the sweep lines, as illustrated in Fig. 6(a). It shows the same sweep line positions as Fig. 5(a), but the obstacle is upside down. The topology changes in the list D_t are essentially the same in both figures. The only change is to the numbering of cells.

However, if the environment is rotated, the decomposition will be different. Equation 1 guarantees the same decomposition being created only for a particular sweep angle. Fig. 6(b) shows the same obstacle as in Fig. 5, but rotated 90°. It can be seen that the decomposition will be different from that given in Fig. 5 no matter how small the step size is. This is not a shortcoming of a discrete sweep algorithm because continuous sweep based exact cell decomposition, such as trapezoidal decomposition, is also affected by rotational transforms.

3 Results

Slice decomposition was evaluated both in simulation and with a Khepera robot. In all the experiments, the environment is unknown to the robot and the slice decomposition is created online during the coverage process [11].

Fig. 7(a) shows a "normal environment" and slice decomposition. The simulated robot creates a topological map that embeds the decomposition. The horizontal edges of the topological map correspond to the cell boundaries. The environment is divided into 12 free space cells. Some vertical edges cross over the obstacles, because they are simply drawn as straight lines linking their nodes.

Fig. 7(b) shows a more unusual arrangement of obstacles. The free space in the spiral is divided into 9 free space cells.

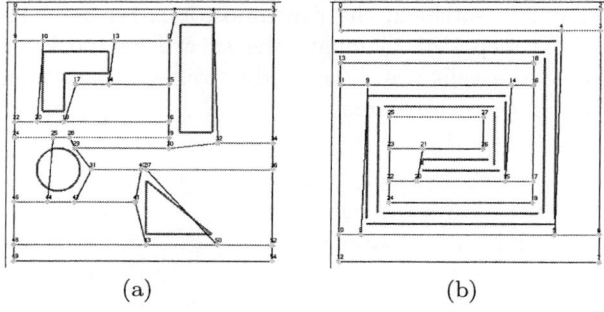

Fig. 7. Slice decomposition for (a) a normal environment, (b) a spiral environment.

Slice decomposition was also implemented and tested on the 53mm diameter Khepera robot [11]. It has 8 infra-red sensors which can detect objects up to 30 to 40mm away, and optical wheel encoders for dead reckoning. Fig. 8(a) shows the area covered and Fig. 8(b) the path the robot took in one of the experiments. The cell boundaries of the slice decomposition are shown in Fig. 8(c).

The step size Δx is set to the diameter of the robot, since we want to cover all the surface between consecutive strips of the zigzag. Since the robot is smaller than the free space cells, the step size Δx is always smaller than the height of the smallest cell; equation (1) is satisfied and all features in the environment are captured. If the robot is larger than some of the cells, then it cannot enter and cover these cells. The slice decomposition created by such a robot will therefore not have a representation of these cells.

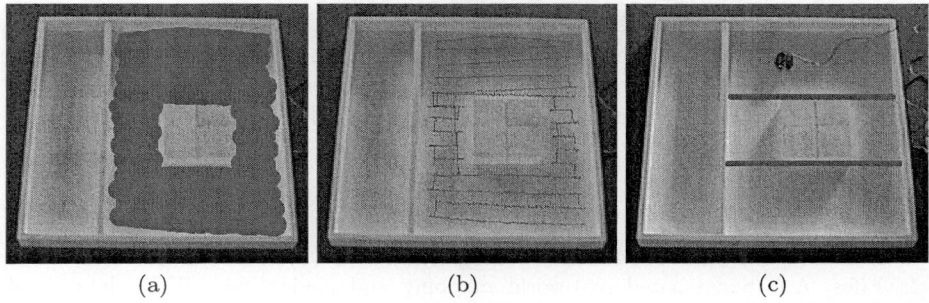

Fig. 8. Khepera robot: (a) area covered (b) path taken (c) slice decomposition created.

4 Discussion

Criticalities in exact cell decompositions are usually defined as small features, such as vertices in trapezoidal decomposition [13] and critical points in Morse decomposition [9]. In comparison, criticality in slice decomposition is defined using large features, segments. For example, obstacle segments are detected as proximity to obstacles along the sweep line [11]. These large features have physical attributes that are detectable over time. Spurious sensor errors are filtered out through averaging. As a result, the detection becomes robust against noisy and inaccurate sensing [14].

Trapezoidal decomposition forms regions more frequently than slice decomposition, by dividing the space as the sweep line crosses every vertex. While the larger regions formed by slice decomposition may not be convex, the regions are still covered by a simple zigzag algorithm, since the non–convex sides of the space are perpendicular to the zigs and zags.

The concept of non-zero step sizes is incorporated in slice decomposition. If the robot moves in a zigzag path to cover individual cells in the decomposition, then the long strips in the zigzag are the sweep lines. The distance between strips in the zigzag path becomes the step size in the slice decomposition.

Since mobile robots cannot move inside obstacles, some free space cells must be swept in the reverse direction, for example in the L-shaped obstacle of Fig. 7(a).

Slice decomposition can handle a larger variety of environments. Boustrophedon decomposition can only handle polygonal obstacles. CC_R can only handle rectilinear environments. Morse decomposition is more general and can handle obstacles with smooth surfaces, but is only defined for non-rectilinear environments because boundaries parallel to the sweep line are degenerate cases for Morse functions. In comparison, slice decomposition is defined on changes in the topology of slices. It can handle any environment with polygonal and smooth-surfaced objects, including rectilinear ones, for example that shown in Fig. 7(b).

5 Conclusion

This paper presents a new exact cell decomposition for coverage. Slice decomposition uses changes in topology to decompose an environment, where each cell intersects with the sweep line twice as it passes over. Cells formed can be covered by a zigzag. Our work uses large features for defining cell boundaries and can detect boundaries robustly. It also can cover a wider variety of environments. The decomposition is tested with simulation and real robot experiments.

References

1. Latombe, J.C.: Robot Motion Planning. Kluwer (1991)
2. Elfes, A.: Sonar-based real-world mapping and navigation. IEEE Journal of Robotics and Automation **RA-3** (1987) 249–265
3. Zelinsky, A.: A mobile robot exploration algorithm. IEEE Transactions on Robotics and Automation **8** (1992) 707–717
4. Gabriely, Y., Rimon, E.: Spiral-STC: An on-line coverage algorithm of grid environments by a mobile robot. In: Proceedings of the IEEE International Conference on Robotics and Automation, Washington, DC (2002) 954–960
5. Castellanos, J.A., Tardós, J.D., Schmidt, G.: Building a global map of the environment of a mobile robot: The importance of correlations. In: Proceedings IEEE International Conference on Robotics and Automation (ICRA). Volume 2. (1997) 1053–1059
6. Thrun, S.: Learning metric-topological maps for indoor mobile robot navigation. Artificial Intelligence **99** (1998) 21–71
7. Choset, H., Pignon, P.: Coverage path planning: The boustrophedon decomposition. In: Proceedings of the International Conference on Field and Service Robotics, Canberra, Australia (1997)
8. Butler, Z.J., Rizzi, A.A., Hollis, R.L.: Contact sensor-based coverage of rectilinear environments. In: Proceedings IEEE International Symposium on Intelligent Control/Intelligent Systems and Semiotics. (1999) 266–271
9. Acar, E.U., Choset, H., Rizzi, A.A., Atkar, P.N., Hull, D.: Morse decompositions for coverage tasks. International Journal of Robotics Research **21** (2002) 331–344
10. Acar, E.U., Choset, H.: Sensor-based coverage of unknown environments: Incremental construction of morse decompositions. International Journal of Robotics Research **21** (2002) 345–366
11. Wong, S.C., MacDonald, B.A.: A topological coverage algorithm for mobile robots. In: Proceedings IEEE/RSJ International Conference on Intelligent Robots and Systems (IROS). Volume 4., Las Vegas, Nevada (2003) 1685–1689
12. Foley, J.D., et al.: Computer graphics : principles and practice. Second edn. Addison-Wesley (1990)
13. Chazelle, B.: Approximation and decomposition of shapes. In Schwartz, J.T., Yap, C.K., eds.: Algorithmic and Geometric Aspects of Robotics. Lawrence Erlbaum Associates (1987) 145–185
14. Mataric, M.J.: Integration of representation into goal-driven behavior-based robots. IEEE Transactions on Robotics and Automation **8** (1992) 304–312

Shape Matching for Robot Mapping

Diedrich Wolter[1] and Longin J. Latecki[2]

[1] University of Bremen, FB 3 – Cognitive Systems, 28359 Bremen, Germany
[2] Temple University, CIS Department, PA 19122 Philadelphia, USA

Abstract. We present a novel geometric model for robot mapping based on shape. Shape similarity measure and matching techniques originating from computer vision are specially redesigned for matching range scans. The fundamental geometric representation is a structural one, polygonal lines are ordered according to the cyclic order of visibility. This approach is an improvement of the underlying geometric models of today's SLAM implementations, where shape matching allows us to disregard pose estimations. The object-centered approach allows for compact representations that are well-suited to bridge the gap from metric information needed in path planning to more abstract, i.e. topological or qualitative spatial knowledge desired in complex navigational tasks.

1 Motivation

The problems of self-localization, i.e. localizing the robot within its internal map, and robot mapping, i.e. constructing the internal map autonomously, are of high importance to the field of mobile robotics [16]. Coping with unknown or changing environments requires to carry out both tasks simultaneously, therefore this has been termed the SLAM problem: Simultaneous Localization and Mapping [4] – it has received considerable attention [4, 6, 16]. Successful stochastical approaches have been developed that tackle representation and handling of uncertain data which is one key point in SLAM. As todays stochastical models are powerful, even linking them to a very simple geometric representation already yields impressive results. Advances in stochastical means have improved the overall performance leaving the basic spatial representation untouched. As the internal geometric representation is a foundation for these sophisticated stochastical techniques, shortcomings on the level of geometric representation affect the overall performance.

We claim that an improved geometric representation enhances the overall performance dramatically. A compact, object oriented representation based on shape is an universal yet slender one. It can outperform often-used occupancy grids in storage as well as in computational resources, since smaller sets of data need to be processed. Object-centered representations have been judged necessary to represent dynamic environments [16]. Moreover, a more comprehensive spatial representation can allow to mediate between different aspects of spatial information that are desired or even necessary in applications. We propose a shape representation of the robot's surrounding that grants access to metric information as needed in robot motion or path planning alongside with more abstract, qualitative or topological knowledge which is desired in navigational tasks and a well-suited foundation for communication.

2 Related Work

Any approach to master the SLAM problem can be decomposed into two aspects: handling of map features (extraction from sensor data and matching against the (partially) existing map) and handling of uncertainty. To address uncertainty mainly statistical techniques are used. Particle filters or the extended Kalman filter are used in most current SLAM algorithms [15, 16, 6]. As this paper focusses exclusively on the map's geometric representation, we now review related aspects in detail.

Typically, map features extracted from sensor data (esp. range finder data) are either the positions of special landmarks [4], simple geometric features like lines [10, 11, 3], or range finder data is used uninterpreted [16]. Uninterpreted use results in constructing a bitmap-like representation of the environment termed occupancy grid [5]. The simplicity of this approach causes its strength, namely universality: It may be used in unstructured, unprepared environments. However, major drawbacks also exist. First, matching a scan against the map in order to localize the robot is formulated as a minimization [10, 16, 6]. Therefore, a good estimation of the robot's position is required to prevent minimization getting stuck in local minima. Second, occupancy grids grow with the environment's size, not its complexity. As grids need to fine, it ends up in handling large data sets. This is not only a problem of storage, but, far more important, it affects run-time of algorithms as huge amounts of data need to be processed. To keep path planning in a once constructed map feasible, a topological representation can be coupled with the metric one [14].

To maintain a map at manageable size from the beginning, representations based on features or landmarks provide excellent means. These so-called object maps represent only positions of landmarks and their distinctive features. Thus, these maps grow with the environment's complexity (i.e. the number of visible landmarks), allowing for efficient processing. Using natural landmarks is of special interest as environments do not need to be prepared, like, e.g., by installing beacons [4]. For example, mapping based on line segments has been shown to improve performance in office environments [11]. A key point in feature-based approaches is a matching of perceived features against the ones represented in the map. Wrong matching result in incorrect maps; complex features help to prevent such mixups. As features' presence is required, application is often limited to special environments only. Choosing simple, omnipresent features can easily inhibit a reliable matching of perceived features against the map. Unreliable feature extraction, e.g. extracting line segments from round objects causes problems, too, as additional noise gets introduced.

To overcome these problems, we propose a representation based on shape features. Shape information can be extracted in any environment, and already individual features provide distinctive information as shape respects a wide spatial context.

Matching of features is, thus, based on shape matching which has received much attention in the context of computer vision. The idea of applying shape matching in the context of robot mapping was suggested in the fundamental paper by Lu & Milios [10], scan matching has already been considered similar to model-based shape matching. Thrun considers this connection underexploited [16]. Recent advances in shape matching provide a good starting point to bring these fields together, which we propose in this paper.

In the domain of robot mapping two key aspects dictate the applicability of shape descriptors: partial shape retrieval and the ability to deal with simple shapes. Firstly, as only partial observations of the environment can be made, any approach to shape representation that cannot handle partial shapes renders itself unemployable. This includes, for example, encoding by feature vectors like Fourier or momentum spectra. Secondly, any robot's working environment must be representable in the framework of the chosen shape descriptor. Besides these confinements, another feature is required: Much shape information perceivable often is rather poor, like for instance straightaway walls with small protrusions only. Therefore, shape recognition processes must be very distinctive, even on rather featureless shapes.

Structural approaches represent shape as a colored graph representing metric data alongside configurational information. Amongst these so-called skeleton based techniques, especially shock graphs (cp. [13]) are worth consideration[1]. Though primarily structural approaches may very well bridge from metric to more abstract qualitative or topological information (cp. [14]), recognizing shapes lacking of a rich structure of configuration has not yet proven feasible. Moreover, robust computation and matching of a skeleton in the presence of noise and occlusion has not yet been solved. Thus, we propose a boundary based approach. Considering the discrete structure provided by sensors, using polygonal lines to represent the boundaries of obstacles may be achieved easily. Related matching techniques rely on a so-called similarity measure. Various measures, often metrics, have been developed. Arkin et al. ([1]) accumulate differences in turning angle in straightforward manner; their approach fails to account for noise adequately. Basically all improvements employ a matching of boundaries to establish a correspondence prior to summing up dissimilarities of corresponding parts. Basri et al. propose a physically motivated deformation energy ([2]). More recently, an alignment-based deformation measure has been proposed by Sebastian et al. which considers the process of transforming one outline into another ([12]). However, common to these approaches is that an equal sampling rate of the outlines is required to ensure good correspondences of sampling points. Considering shape information obtained by a range sensor, scanning the same object from different positions, however, would generate this effect.

---

[1] Skeleton based approaches relate closely to Voronoi based spatial representations used in the field of robotics (cp. [14, 13]).

An improved performance in similarity measures for closed contours has been achieved by Latecki & Lakämper who consider a matching on basis of an a-priori decomposition into maximal arcs (cp. [8]). We will formulate the presented approach on this basis. However, it is tailored to deal with any kind of open polyline and addresses the problem of noisy data in a direct manner. The representation is complemented by a structural representation of robust ordering information. Applicability of the elementary shape similarity measure has been shown in [9].

3 Structural Shape Representation

Shape information is derived from sensor readings by a range sensor, typically a laser range finder (LRF). Shape is represented as a structure of boundaries. Polygonal lines, called *polylines*, serve as the basic entity. They represent obstacles' boundaries. Much of the spatial information represented in the map can be captured by individual polylines which form visual parts (cp. [8]). The variety of perceivable shapes in a regular indoor scenario already yields a more reliable matching than other feature-based approaches. At the same time, we are able to construct a compact representation. However, we exploit even more context information than represented by a single polyline considering shape as a structure of polylines. This allows us to cope with environments displaying mostly simple shapes with almost no extra effort. The structure captured is ordering information. For any given viewpoint, perceivable objects can be ordered in a counter-clockwise manner. A first step in the presented approach is to extract shape information from LRF data.

3.1 Grouping and Simplification of Polylines

Let us assume that the range data is mapped to locations of reflection points in the Euclidean plane, using a local coordinate system. Now, these points are segmented into individual polylines. For this grouping a simple heuristic may be employed: An object transition is said to be present wherever two consecutive points measured by the LRF are further apart than a given distance threshold. We used a threshold of 20cm in our experiments, however, the precise choice is not crucial and possible differences are regarded (cp. section 4.2).

Polylines extracted this way still carry all the information (and noise) retrieved by the sensor. To make the representation more compact and to cancel out noise, we employ a technique called Discrete Curve Evolution (DCE) introduced by Latecki & Lakämper ([7]) to make the data more compact without loosing valuable shape information and to cancel out noise. DCE is a context-sensitive process that proceeds iteratively: *Irrelevant* vertices get removed until no irrelevant ones remain. Though the process is context-sensitive, it is based on a local relevance measure for a vertex v and its two neighbor vertices u, w [2]:

$$K(u,v,w) = |d(u,v) + d(v,w) - d(u,w)| \qquad (1)$$

---

[2] Context is respected as in the course of simplification the vertices' neighborhood changes.

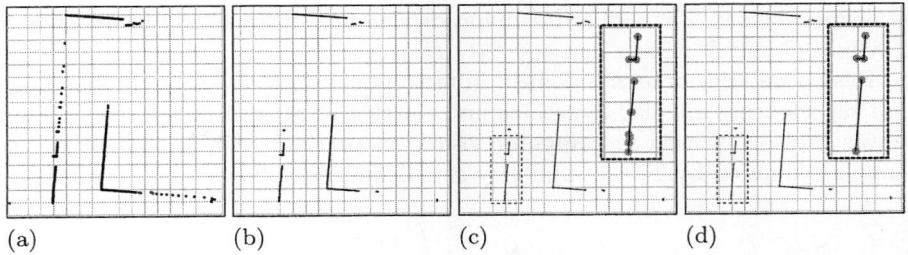

(a) (b) (c) (d)

Fig. 1. Extracting polylines from a scan. Raw scan points (a) are grouped to polylines (b), then simplified by means of DCE. The threshold used in figure (c) is 1 and 5 in (d). The two additional rectangles show magnifications of marked parts. The grid denotes 1 meter distance.

Hereby, d denotes the Euclidean distance. The process of DCE is very simple and proceeds in a straightforward manner. The least relevant vertex is removed until least relevance exceeds a given simplification threshold. Consequently, as no relevance measure is assigned to end-points, they remain fixed. The choice of a specific simplification threshold is not crucial; refer to Figure 1 for results. Proceeding this way we obtain a cyclic ordered vector of polylines.

4 Matching Shapes

To match two shapes means to match two ordered set of polylines against each other. Hence, we need to seek the *best* correspondence of individual polylines that preserves the structure, i.e. that does not violate the order. Shape similarity is the key point to quantify quality of a correspondence.

4.1 Similarity of Polylines

The similarity measure utilized in our approach is based on a measure introduced by Latecki & Lakämper; we will briefly summarize the approach and indicate changes necessary in this context – for details refer to [8]. To compute the basic similarity measure between two polygonal curves, we establish the best correspondence of maximal left- or right-arcuated arcs[3]. To achieve this, we first decompose the polygonal curves into maximal subarcs which are likewise bent. Refer to Figure 2 (c) for an illustration. Since a simple 1-to-1 comparison of maximal arcs of two polylines is of little use, due to the fact that the curves may consist of a different number of such arcs and even similar shapes may have different small features, we allow for 1-to-1, 1-to-many, and many-to-1 correspondences. The main idea here is that on at least one of the contours we have a maximal arc that corresponds to a part of the other contour that is composed of adjacent maximal arcs. The best correspondence can be computed using Dynamic Programming, where the similarity of the corresponding visual parts is

---

[3] The original work is based on convex and concave arcs, respectively. As we deal with open polylines here, the terms convex or concave would be meaningless.

as defined below. The similarity induced from the optimal correspondence of polylines C and D will be denoted $S(C,D)$.

Basic similarity of arcs is defined in tangent space, a multi-valued step function representing angular directions and relative lengths of line-segments only. It was previously used in computer vision, in particular, in [1]. Denoting the mapping function by T, the similarity gets defined as follows:

$$S_a(C,D) = (1 + (l(C) - l(D))^2) \cdot \int_0^1 (T_C(s) - T_D(s) + \Theta_{C,D})^2 ds \qquad (2)$$

where $l(C)$ denotes the arc length of C. The constant $\Theta_{C,D}$ is chosen to minimize the integral (cp. [8]) (it respects for different orientation) and is given by

$$\Theta_{C,D} = \int_0^1 T_C(s) - T_D(s) ds. \qquad (3)$$

More appropriately, this measure should be denoted a dissimilarity measure as identical curves yield 0, the lowest possible measure. This measure differs from the original work in that it is affected by an absolute change of size rather than by a relative one. It should be noted that this measure is based on shape information only, neither the arcs' position nor their orientation are considered. This is possible due to the wide context information of polylines.

When comparing polylines, the amount of noise and the size of shape features present are often challenging. Applying DCE to a degree that would certainly remove all noise would remove many valuable shape features as well. DCE makes vertex removal decisions in the context of a single object. A better noise identification can be made in the context of comparing corresponding polylines. We encapsulate the basic similarity measure S in another process that masks out noise in the context of corresponding polylines. It is similar to the initial curve evolution employed. When comparing two polylines C and D, we evolve each polyline by removing vertices if the similarity improves. Obviously, a counter weight is needed to prevent elimination of all differing shape features. This counter weight, a cost for removing a vertex from a polyline is defined on the basis of a noise model of the LRF. Vertices whose removal only results in a small contour shift can likely be caused by noise and may be removed with low cost, whereas bigger changes are inhibited by high costs. The cost function R for removing a set of vertices (respectively r for removing a single vertex v with neighbors u and w) from a polyline P is defined on the basis of area difference. It describes the summed up costs for iteratively removing a set of vertices $\{v_1, \ldots, v_n\}$ from polyline P.

$$R_P(\{v_1, \ldots, v_n\}) := \sum_{i=1}^{n} r_{P \setminus \{v_1, \ldots, v_{i-1}\}} v_i, \quad r_Q(v) := \left(\frac{h}{c}\right)^2$$

The similarity measure S^* is defined on the basis of the basic similarity S considering the optimal set of vertices to mask out.

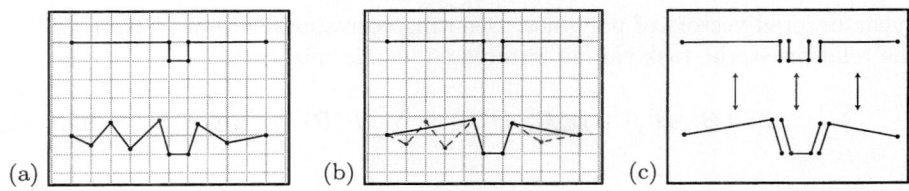

Fig. 2. (a) Two polylines from sensing an example scene with a simulated laser range finder. The upper polyline is free of noise, the lower one suffers from distortions of the magnitude of the shape features present. Using similarity measure $S^\star$, noise can be masked out when comparing the objects. Only the subsets shown in (b) are effective in the comparison; the determined similarity is enhanced by a factor of more than 10. Decomposition into maximal arcs and determined correspondence are shown in (c).

$$S^\star(C, D) := \min_{C^\star \subseteq C, D^\star \subseteq D} \{S(C \setminus C^\star, D \setminus D^\star) + R_C(C^\star) + R_D(D^\star)\} \quad (4)$$

Computation is formulated as a greedy algorithm[4]. A prerequisite here is to use a hughly distinctive basic similarity measure. An example is depicted in Figure 2. When comparing the two polylines shown in Figure 2 (a), vertices are removed if the removal cost is lower than the gain in shape similarity (i.e. the decrease of S). This results in removing small distortions from the lower polyline, while retaining the features of both (cp. Figure 2 (b)).

4.2 Matching Vectors of Polylines

The actual matching of two structural shape representations extracted from different scans is computed by finding the *best* correspondence of polylines which respects the cyclic order. Shape similarity is the key to measuring the quality of a matching. Additionally, we must take into account that (a) not all polylines may match as features' visibility changes and (b) that due to grouping differences (cp. section 3.1) not necessarily 1-to-1 correspondences exist. Noise or change of view point, for example, may lead to a different grouping. Moreover, since every correspondence of polylines induces an alignment that would align both scans involved, we demand all alignments induced to be very similar. This criterion is helpful to correctly match featureless shapes, e.g. short segments as obtained when scanning a chairs' legs. The clue in our approach is the exploitation of the correspondence of salient visual parts to correctly identify featureless parts even if no a-priori alignment is available. An estimation of the alignment is necessary to utilize an efficient matching algorithm. We will show (in Section 4.3) how to compute an estimate using shape similarity. Clearly, it can be derived from odometry if odometry data is available. Let us now assume that such an estimate exists. Further, let $B = (B_1, B_2, \ldots, B_b)$ and $B' = (B'_1, B'_2, \ldots, B'_{b'})$ be two

---

[4] Computing the true minimum may lead to combinatorial explosion, the greedy implementation avoids this problem and yields similar results.

cyclic ordered vectors of polylines. Denoting correspondence of B_i and B'_j [5] by the relation $\sim$, the task can be formulated as minimization.

$$\sum_{(B_i, B'_j) \in \sim} (S^\star(B_i, B'_j) + D(B_i, B'_j)) + \sum_{B \in \tilde{B}} P(B) + \sum_{B' \in \tilde{B}'} P(B') \stackrel{!}{=} \min \quad (5)$$

Hereby, $\tilde{B}$ (rsp. $\tilde{B}'$) denotes the set of unmatched polylines. P is a penalty function for not matching a polyline. This is necessary, as not establishing any correspondences would yield the lowest possible value 0 suggesting maximum similarity. The penalty function is chosen to linearly grow with the polyline's size modeling a higher likelihood for smaller polylines to appear or disappear[6]. D denotes the aforementioned alignment measure quantifying the deviation of the estimated alignment from the one induced by the correspondence $B_i \sim B'_j$. The best correspondence can so be computed by applying an extended Dynamic Programming scheme. The extension regards the ability to detect 1-to-many and many-to-1 correspondences and results in a linear extra effort such that the overall complexity is $O(n^3)$. The basic idea here is to consider in each step of the computation if it is advantageous to establish a grouping with the latest correspondence determined so far, if the summed up (dis-)similarity values and skipping penalties can be decreased.

4.3 Matching in the Absence of Odometry

The outlined matching is capable of tracking *complex* shapes even if no estimate of the induced alignment is available. We will detail now how to obtain an alignment estimate purely by shape similarity. If we had two corresponding polylines, hence, the induced alignment, we could use this as the estimation in the matching. Observing that many shapes can be matched only in consideration of shape similarity, the matching can be employed to obtain this correspondence. Thus, the matching can be computed in a two pass process. Within the first matching pass the consideration of induced alignments' similarity is ineffective. Then, the *most reliable* correspondence is selected. Finally, the actual matching is computed using the alignment induced by the selected matching. To quantify reliability, a measure based on shape similarity and shape complexity has been proposed [9]. A polyline's shape complexity may be expressed by summing up inner points' relevance measures (cp. equation 1). If a polyline has no inner points, complexity is given by half its length. Terming this complexity measure C, the reliability is defined as

$$Q(P, Q) = C(P) + C(Q) - S^\star(P, Q). \quad (6)$$

---

[5] To be more precise: correspondences of either B_i and $\{B'_j, B'_{j+1}, \ldots, B'_{j'}\}$ or $\{B_i, B'_{i+1}, \ldots, B'_{i'}\}$ and B'_j since we consider correspondences of types 1-to-many and many-to-1, too.

[6] When comparing polylines affected by similar noise, similarity values grow linearly with the polylines' size, too.

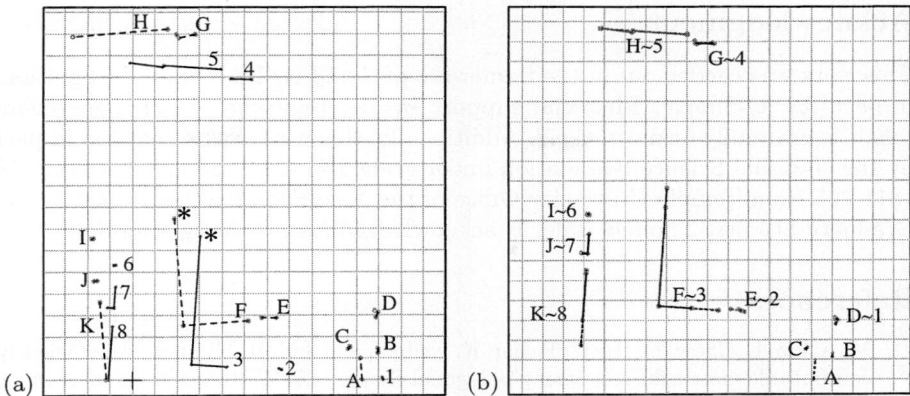

Fig. 3. The two scans depicted in (a) (numbered 1–8 and A–K) are matched only wrt. shape, the most reliable match (marked ⋆) is selected. The induced alignment helps to determine the final matching. The correspondences found and the two scans aligned according to the estimation are shown in (b). Observe that the scans' origins are farer apart than 1m (grid denotes 1m distance) and no odometry has been used.

The idea is to express reliability as high similarity of complex shapes (cp. [9] for details). An exemplary result is presented in Figure 3 where two scans are matched against each other only concerning shape (a). Based on the most reliable correspondence the estimated alignment is computed. Accordingly aligned scans and the matching is shown in (b). The presented technique can cope with differences in the scans' position of more than 1m without the help of any means of estimating the robot's current position. Observe, that this is a dramatical improvement compared to the precision required by standard scan matching approaches which typically rely on a hill climbing strategy [6].

5 Conclusion and Outlook

We have presented a comprehensive geometric model for robot mapping based on shape information. Shape matching has been tailored to the domain of scan matching. The matching is powerful enough to disregard pose information and cope with significantly differing scans. This improves performance of today's scan matching approaches dramatically. Based on the presented shape processing, we plan to propose a complete robot mapping architecture. This is the topic of a forthcoming paper. We believe mapping based on shape to be particularly promising. For example, shape matching can also be exploited to map alignment. Equation 3 already provides the rotational difference. We are aware that statistical methods are needed to guarantee robust performance, but did not include any as we concentrated on geometric models exclusively. So, future work comprises also the coupling with a state-of-the-art stochastical model besides attacking the problem of cycle detection.

Acknowledgment

This work was carried out in the framework of the SFB/TR 8 Spatial Cognition, project R3 [Q-Shape]. Financial support by the Deutsche Forschungsgemeinschaft is gratefully acknowledged. Additionally, this work was supported in part by the National Science Foundation under grant INT-0331786 and the grant 16 1811 705 from Temple University Office of the Vice President for Research and Graduate Studies. Thomas Röfer is acknowledged for providing scan data.

References

1. M. Arkin, L. Chew, D. Huttenlocher, K. Kedem, and J. S. B. Mitchell. An efficiently computable metric for comparing polygonal shapes. *IEEE Transactions on Pattern Analysis and Machine Intelligence*, 13, 1991.
2. R. Basri, L. Costa, D. Geiger, and D. Jacobs. Determining the similarity of deformable shapes. *Vision Research*, 38, 1998.
3. I. J. Cox. Blanche: Position estimation for an autonomous robot vehicle. In I. J. Cox and G. Wilfong, editors, *Autonomous Robot Vehicles*, pages 221–228. Springer-Verlag, 1990.
4. G. Dissanayake, P. Newman, S. Clark, H. Durrant-Whyte, and M. Csorba. A solution to the simultaneous localization and map building (SLAM) problem. *IEEE Transactions of Robotics and Automation*, 2001.
5. A. Elfes. *Occupancy Grids: A Probabilistic Framework for Robot Perception and Navigation*. PhD thesis, Department of Electrical and Computer Engineering, Carnegie Mellon University, 1989.
6. D. Hähnel, D. Schulz, and W. Burgard. Map building with mobile robots in populated environments. In *Proceedings of International Conference on Intelligent Robots and Systems (IROS'02)*, 2002.
7. L. J. Latecki and R. Lakämper. Convexity rule for shape decomposition based on discrete contour evolution. *Computer Vision and Image Understanding*, 73, 1999.
8. L. J. Latecki and R. Lakämper. Shape similarity measure based on correspondence of visual parts. *IEEE Trans. Pattern Analysis and Machine Intelligence*, 22(10), 2000.
9. L. J. Latecki, R. Lakämper, and D. Wolter. Shape similarity and visual parts. In *Proceedings of the 11th International Conference on Disrecte Geometry for Computer Imagery (DGCI)*, Naples, Italy, November 2003.
10. F. Lu and E. Milios. Robot pose estimation in unknown environments by matching 2D range scans. *Journal of Intelligent and Robotic Systems*, 1997.
11. T. Röfer. Using histogram correlation to create consistent laser scan maps. In *Proceedings of the IEEE International Conference on Robotics Systems (IROS-2002)*, 2002.
12. T. B. Sebastian, P. N. Klein, and B. B. Kimia. On aligning curves. *IEEE Transactions on Pattern Analysis and Machine Intelligence*, 25(1):116–125, 2003.
13. K. Siddiqi, A. Shokoufandeh, S. J. Dickinson, and S. W. Zucker. Shock graphs and shape matching. *International Journal of Computer Vision*, 35(1):13–32, 1999.
14. S. Thrun. Learning metric-topological maps for indoor mobile robot navigation. *Artificial Intelligence*, 99(1):21–71, 1998.
15. S. Thrun. Probabilistic algorithms in robotics. *AI Magazine*, 21(4):93–109, 2000.
16. S. Thrun. Robotic mapping: A survey. In G. Lakemeyer and B. Nebel, editors, *Exploring Artificial Intelligence in the New Millenium*. Morgan Kaufmann, 2002.

Covisibility-Based Map Learning Method for Mobile Robots

Takehisa Yairi

Research Center for Advanced Science and Technology, University of Tokyo
4-6-1 Komaba, Meguro-ku, Tokyo, Japan
yairi@space.rcast.u-tokyo.ac.jp

Abstract. In previous work, we proposed a unique landmark-based map learning method for mobile robots based on the "co-visibility" information i.e., very coarse qualitative information on "whether two objects are visible together or not". In this paper, we introduce two major enhancements to this method: (1) automatic optimization of distance estimation function, and (2) weighting of observation information based on reliability. Simulation results show that these enhancements improve the performance of this proposed method dramatically, not only in the qualitative accuracy measure, but also in the quantitative measure.

1 Introduction

Map building problem in unknown environments has long been a major research topic in the field of intelligent mobile robot, and a variety of methods have been developed so far. These map learning methods are often classified into two major categories – *metric*[8, 2] and *topological*[7, 10] methods, from the viewpoint of the way of map representation[1].

A noticeable trend in both the methodologies is the emergence of the framework called SLAM (simultaneous localization and mapping)[2] or CML (concurrent mapping and localization)[4, 13], in which accurate map building and self-localization are pursued simultaneously by integrating various quantitative information from proprioceptive and exteroceptive sensors.

Contrary to this trend, authors have proposed a *minimalist* approach to the map learning problem that requires neither quantitative sensor measurements nor the robot's own position, but instead exploits "co-visibility" information i.e., information about "what landmark objects are visible together"[14, 15]. This method utilizes a heuristics "if two objects are frequently observed together, then they are likely to be located near one another" in order to estimate spatial proximities among objects from the co-visibility information, and a well known multivariate analysis method called Multi-dimensional scaling (MDS) to obtain a 2-D configuration of all the landmark objects. In the previous work, it was shown that the method is able to build reasonably accurate maps in a qualitative measure using only such primitive and incomplete information and is robust

---
[1] There are several researches[12, 5] to integrate these two different paradigms.

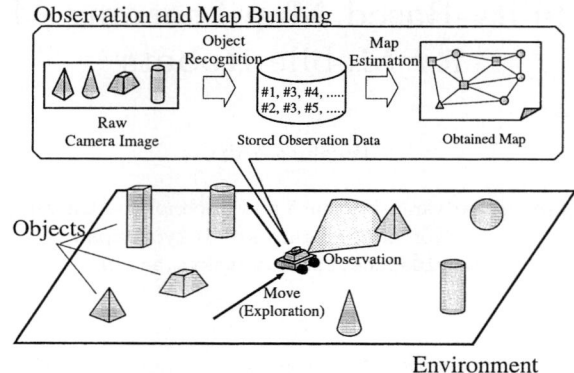

Fig. 1. Assumed map building task of a mobile robot (exploration, observation and map estimation)

against some classes of object recognition errors. Such qualitative maps can be used for various purposes such as qualitative navigation[6], communication with humans, and etc.

However, there were some restrictions in the previous version, which make the application in the real environment difficult. In this paper, we present two practical enhancements contributing to the improvement. One is the automatic optimization of parameters in the distance function which transforms the co-visibility frequencies into the spatial proximities, whereas in the previous versions these parameter values were manually determined. The other enhancement is the weighting of the distance matrix elements based on the reliability of related information, whereas in the old framework, all estimates are treated equally regardless of the difference in reliability of each estimate.

Due to these enhancements, the performance of the proposed map learning method is dramatically improved. Especially, it is remarkable that the enhanced version achieves high accuracy not only in the qualitative measure (evaluated by the triangle orientation error), but also in the quantitative measure (evaluated by the average positional error).

2 Covisibility-Based Map Learning and Extension

2.1 Assumption

We consider a map building task by a mobile robot, in which the robot estimates the positions of a set of objects in the environment by repeated explorations and observations (Figure 1).

At each observation site, the robot takes a 360° panoramic image and attempts to recognize all objects in it. Then, the list of objects which are recognized together is recorded and used for building a map later. It should be noted that neither quantitative measurements such as relative distance to the objects and directions nor the robot's own positions are utilized. As to the object recognition capability of the robot, we make an assumption that the recognition success rate generally decreases as the distance between the robot and object increases. Although the degree of validity of this assumption is dependent on the environment, objects, and recognition algorithm, we consider it to be roughly appropriate because the image size of an object becomes smaller and the chance of occlusion increases as the distance increases.

2.2 Co-visibility and Empirical Distance

The central idea of the covisibility-based map learning method is the use of an empirical rule that "a pair of objects observed simultaneously more frequently is likely to be located more closely together". More specifically, we define the *co-visibility frequency* $f_{i,j}$ between two objects as $f_{i,j} = \frac{n_{i,j}}{n_i+n_j-n_{i,j}}$, where n_i and $n_{i,j}$ denote the number of times each object is observed and the number of times each pair of objects is observed together respectively. It means the conditional probability that two objects are visible at the same time, given that at least one of them is visible. This definition of $f_{i,j}$ is also known as Jaccard's coefficient. With this definition, the empirical rule above can be interpreted as "distance between two landmark objects $d_{i,j}$ generally decreases as $f_{i,j}$ increases". We call the monotonic decreasing function ϕ which estimates $d_{i,j}^2$ from $f_{i,j}$ as *empirical distance function*, and defines *empirical distance* $\delta_{i,j}$ as the estimated distance from $f_{i,j}$ by ϕ. Say, $\delta_{i,j}^2 = \phi(f_{i,j})$.

Figure 2 (scattered points) illustrates the actual relationship between the real distance $d_{i,j}$ and co-visibility frequency $f_{i,j}$ in the simulation environment in section 5. We can see that this empirical rule is approximately appropriate.

2.3 Outline of Covisibility-Based Mapping

The outline of the map learning based on the co-visibility information is described below. Further details of the procedure are given in [14, 15].

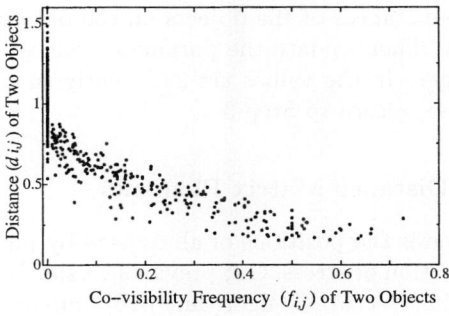

Fig. 2. Relationship between distance $d_{i,j}$ and co-visibility frequency $f_{i,j}$ of objects in the simulation environment

Step 1 The robot repeats the exploration and observation steps:
  (a) It moves to the next observation site, avoiding collisions with obstacles.
  (b) It obtains a list of visible objects L_o from the panoramic camera image captured at the current position, then updates n_i and $n_{i,j}$ as below:
  $n_i \leftarrow n_i + 1$ (for each object i in L_o)
  $n_{i,j} \leftarrow n_{i,j} + 1$ (for each pair of i, j in L_o)

Step 2 After a specified number of steps, the co-visibility frequency $f_{i,j}$ is computed for each pair of objects based on n_i, n_j, and $n_{i,j}$.

Step 3 Then the empirical distance $\delta_{i,j}$ of each pair is computed by the empirical distance function: $\delta_{i,j}^2 = \phi(f_{i,j})$.

Step 4 The robot obtains the estimated positions of all objects $\hat{X} = (\hat{x}_1, \cdots, \hat{x}_N)$ by applying Multi-Dimensional Scaling (MDS) to the empirical distance matrix Δ whose (i, j) element is $\delta_{i,j}$.

3 Enhancements

We make two enhancements in the Steps 3 and 4 of the above framework.

3.1 Automatic Optimization of Distance Function Parameters

A non-trivial issue in the original covisibility-based mapping method was how we should decide a suitable *empirical distance function* ϕ. In the previous implementation, we assumed that the function type and parameter values of ϕ are both determined manually beforehand. Although it would be possible to determine ϕ "optimally" if the statistical relationship between the co-visibility frequencies ($f_{i,j}$) and the real distances ($d_{i,j}$) were available, it is generally unrealistic.

In the enhanced method, a mechanism of on-line adaptation of the empirical distance function ϕ is developed. By this enhancement, parameter values in ϕ are automatically determined so that the loss function of MDS is locally minimized, though the function type is still needed to be decided manually. More specifically, *Step 5* is added to the basic algorithm.

Step 5 Compute the distances of the objects on the obtained configuration in the previous step. Then update the parameter values in ϕ by *least square fitting*. If the changes in the values are sufficiently small, return the result and exit. Otherwise, return to Step 3.

3.2 Weighting of Distance Matrix Elements

In Step 4, MDS estimates the positions of all objects by minimizing a criterion which is called loss function or stress. Our previous version based on the classical scaling (one of the simplest MDS algorithms)[16] employs the following loss function:

$$L_{old}(\hat{X}) = \sum_{i<j}(\delta_{i,j}^2 - d^2(\hat{x}_i, \hat{x}_j)) \qquad (1)$$

where, $d(\hat{x}_i, \hat{x}_j) \equiv d_{i,j}(\hat{X})$ denotes the distance between two objects computed on the configuration $\hat{X}$ obtained by MDS. This criterion can be regarded as "unweighted" in that the distances of all pairs of objects are treated with the same weight. In fact, however, object pairs with lower co-visibility frequencies have larger variances in the actual distances, as Figure 2 implies.

In this enhanced version, we employ a weighted loss function as below:

$$L_{new}(\hat{X}) = \sum_{i<j} w_{i,j} \cdot (\delta_{i,j} - d(\hat{x}_i, \hat{x}_j))^2 \qquad (2)$$

The weight $w_{i,j}$ for each object pair is determined based on the reliability of the empirical distance $\delta_{i,j}$. This kind of loss function is efficiently minimized by SMACOF algorithm[3, 1].

4 Qualitative and Quantitative Map Evaluation

In our previous work, we employed two different kinds of *qualitative* map evaluation criteria based on Delaunay triangulation[14] and triangle orientation[15]. Both of them are meant to measure how accurately the qualitative spatial relationships among the objects are preserved in the learned maps. On the other hand, we have not evaluated the method using *quantitative* measures so far, mainly because it seemed that high quantitative accuracy cannot be expected as long as neither quantitative measurements nor the robot's own positions are utilized.

In this paper, we employ a *quantitative* map evaluation criterion in addition to the qualitative one, in order to examine the performance of our method more exhaustively.

4.1 Qualitative Map Evaluation: Triangle Orientation Error

A widely used method to evaluate *qualitative* correctness of an obtained map is to count the number of triangles whose *orientations* (clockwise or anti-clockwise) are consistent between the real map and the obtained map[9, 11]. This is considered to be a reasonable criterion when we use an obtained map for *qualitative navigation*[6, 9], in which the order of visible landmark objects at each position is used as the major information source.

More specifically, *triangle orientation error* Err_{ori} is defined as the percentage of triangles with wrong orientations in the constructed map, i.e.,

$$Err_{ori} \equiv \frac{(\# \text{ of triangles with wrong orientation})}{{}_N C_3} \qquad (3)$$

Quantitative Map Evaluation: Position Error. The simplest way of evaluating the *quantitative* accuracy of an obtained map is to compute the average position error from the real position of an object x_i. However, such a simple comparison is inappropriate in this case because a map reconstructed by MDS generally has a different orientation and scaling from the real map.

Therefore, in this work, we assume that precise positions of a few objects are given beforehand, and the Affine transformation is applied to the original map obtained by MDS so that the differences between those object positions on the map and their real positions are minimized. We call these landmark objects whose exact positions are given beforehand *anchor objects*. Then we define *Landmark position error* Err_{pos} as the average error of each object position from the real one, i.e,

$$Err_{pos} \equiv \frac{1}{N} \sum_i^N \|x_i - \hat{x}'_i\| \qquad (4)$$

where, $\|\|\|$ stands for the ordinary Euclidean distance, and $\hat{x}'_i$ stands for the position of i-th landmark on the map after the Affine transformation.

5 Simulation

5.1 General Settings

We conducted a simulation study to examine how the performance is improved by the enhancements, using Cyberbotics' WEBOTS simulator (ver.2.0). The environment is a square field whose side length is 1.5[m] containing 30 landmark objects. Each landmark is a cylinder-shaped object (height: 160[mm], diameter: 48[mm]), and is given a unique ID number from 0 to 29. Figure 3(a) is an example of environment used in this simulation. We prepared 5 different configuration patterns.

We make a simplified assumption that the robot can recognize a landmark object if and only if its visual angle is larger than 6 degrees. At each observation position, the robot chooses its next moving direction randomly within the range of $\pm\theta_r = 45$[deg], and proceeds $l_r = 100$[mm] in the direction.

Those general settings are basically the same as those used in the previous study[15].

5.2 Results

Table 1 summarizes the condition of each case in this simulation study.

(A) Baseline Case. First, we re-examined the performance of the previous implementation[15] as a baseline case. In this, the empirical distance function ϕ is fixed to:

$$\phi(f_{i,j}) = max(min(0.3 \cdot \log f_{i,j}, 2.0), 0.1), \qquad (5)$$

and the classical scaling is employed. Dotted lines in Figure 4(a),(b) show how the qualitative and quantitative errors change, as the amount of observation data increases. Figure 3(b) illustrates a constructed map with this condition after 1500 steps in the environment of Figure 3(a).

Table 1. Conditions of Simulation Cases

Case	Empirical Distance Function		Weighting	MDS
	Type	Parameters		
(A)	log w. bounds	Fixed	No	classical scaling
(B-1)	log	Auto	No	SMACOF
(B-2)	exp	Auto	No	SMACOF
(B-3)	power	Auto	No	SMACOF
(C-1)	log	Auto	Yes (method 1)	SMACOF
(C-2)	log	Auto	Yes (method 2)	SMACOF

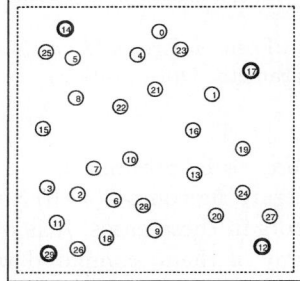
(a) Real configuration

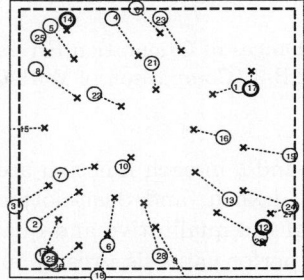
(b) Constructed Map in Case A

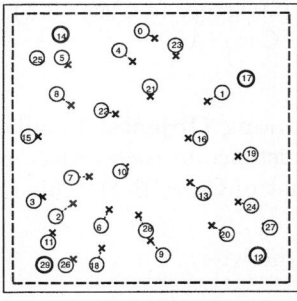
(c) Constructed Map in Case B-1

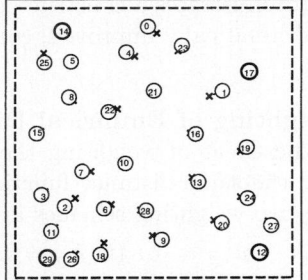
(d) Constructed Map in Case C-1

Fig. 3. A real configuration of landmarks (a) and obtained maps after 1500 steps by the proposed method(b-d). Four thick circles in each figure stand for the anchor objects. Dotted lines in (b-d) represent differences of object positions from their real positions. Side length of the field is 1.5[m]

(B) Automatic Optimization of Empirical Distance Functions. Next, we examined the performance of the method when the first enhancement (automatic optimization of empirical distance functions) is applied. This time we prepared 3 types of function classes below:

(B-1) : $\phi(f_{i,j}) = -a \cdot \log \frac{f_{i,j}+b}{1+b}$

(B-2) : $\phi(f_{i,j}) = a \cdot exp(b \cdot f_{i,j})$

(B-3) : $\phi(f_{i,j}) = a \cdot (1 - f_{i,j})^b$

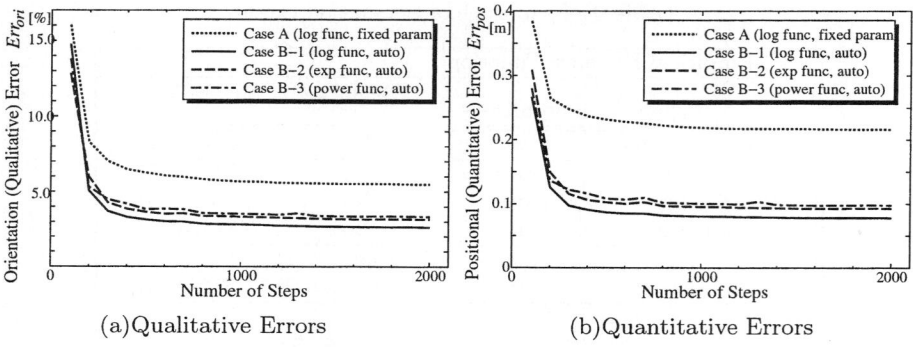

Fig. 4. Changes of Orientation Errors (Err_{ori}) and Position Errors (Err_{pos}) of Cases A,B-1,B-2,B-3 (Comparison of With / Without Parameter Optimization)

where, a and b in each function are the parameter to be optimized.

Solid, dashed, and dash-dotted lines in Figure fig:comp-1(a)(b) show the changes of the qualitative and quantitative errors in these cases. It is observed that the performance is greatly improved in any of them, compared with the baseline case. While Case (B-1) marked the best performance among the three cases, it is still difficult to conclude that this result is general in any environment. Figure 3(c) illustrates a constructed map after 1500 steps in Case (B-1). We can see it is dramatically improved, compared with Case (A).

(C) Weighting of Empirical Distances Among Objects. Finally, we examined the effect of weighting the empirical distance of each object pair. We employed the same distance function (ϕ) as that of Case (B-1). This time, the following two weighting schemes are tested:

(C-1) : $w_{i,j} = 0.1$ (if $f_{i,j} = 0.0$),   1.0 (otherwise)

(C-2) : $w_{i,j} = 1 - exp(-f_{i,j})$

Solid and dotted lines in Figure 5(a)(b) show the changes of the errors in these two cases. Note that the results in Cases (A) and (B-1) are also displayed in this figure for comparison. From this, we can see that the enhancement of distance weighting also leads to a large improvement in the performance, though there was no significant difference between the two weighting schemes.

Figure 3(d) illustrates a constructed map after 1500 steps in Case (C-1). The difference from the real configuration (Figure 3(a)) becomes smaller.

6   Conclusion

Covisibility-based mapping is a unique map building method that learns reasonably accurate maps using the information about "what landmark objects are seen together", without quantitative measurements or the robot's own position.

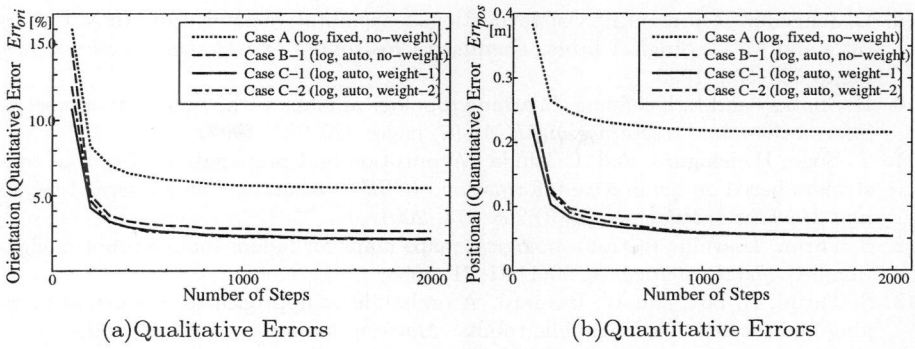

Fig. 5. Changes of Orientation Errors (Err_{ori}) and Position Errors (Err_{pos}) of Cases A,B-1,C-1,C-2 (Comparison of With / Without Distance Weighting)

In this paper, we presented two major extensions to this method: (1) automatic optimization of empirical distance function parameters, and (2) weighting of empirical distances based on reliability. It was shown that the constructed maps are greatly improved in both qualitative and quantitative measures by these extensions.

In future, we will investigate the effectiveness of this method in more realistic situations.

Acknowledgement

This work is partly supported by Tateishi Science and Technology Foundation.

References

1. I. Borg and P. Groenen. *Modern Multidimensional Scaling: Theory and Applications*. Springer, 1997.
2. J.A. Castellanos, J.M.M. Montiel, J. Neira, and J.D. Tardos. The SPmap: A probabilistic framework for simultaneous localization and map building. *IEEE Transactions on Robotics and Automation*, 15(5):948–953, 1999.
3. T. Cox and M. Cox. *Multidimensional Scaling*. Chapman & Hall/Crc, 2001.
4. H. Feder, J. Leonard, and C. Smith. Adaptive mobile robot navigation and mapping. *International Journal of Robotics Research*, 18(7):650–668, 1999.
5. B. Kuipers. The spatial semantic hierarchy. *Artificial Intelligence*, 119:191–233, 2000.
6. T. Levitt and D. Lawton. Qualitative navigation for mobile robots. *Artificial Intelligence*, 44(3):305, 361 1990.
7. M. Mataric. Integration of representation into goal-driven behavior-based robots. *IEEE Transactions on Robotics and Automation*, 8(3):304–312, 1992.
8. P. Moravec and A. Elfes. High resolution maps from wide angle sonar. In *Proc. IEEE Int. Conf. Robotics and Automation*, pages 116–121, 1985.

9. C. Schlieder. Representing visible locations for qualitative navigation. In N. P. Carret'e and M. G. Singh, editors, *Qualitative Reasoning and Decision Technologies*, pages 523–532. 1993.
10. H. Shatkay and L. Kaelbling. Learning topological maps with weak local odometric information. In *Proceedings of IJCAI-97*, pages 920–927, 1997.
11. T. Sogo, H. Ishiguro, and T. Ishida. Acquisition and propagation of spatial constraints based on qualitative information. *IEEE Transactions on Pattern Analysis and Machine Intelligence*, 23(3):268–278, 2001.
12. S. Thrun. Learning metric-topological maps maps for indoor mobile robot navigation. *Artificial Intelligence*, 99(1):21–71, 1998.
13. S. Thrun, D. Fox, and W. Burgard. A probabilistic approach to concurrent mapping and localization for mobile robots. *Machine Learning*, 31:29–53, 1998.
14. T. Yairi, K. Hirama, and K. Hori. Fast and simple topological map construction based on cooccurrence frequency of landmark observation. In *Proc. IEEE/RSJ Int. Conf. on Intelligent Robots and Systems (IROS'01)*, pages 1263–1268.
15. T. Yairi and K. Hori. Qualitative map learning based on co-visibility of objects. In *Proceedings of IJCAI-03*, pages 183–188, 2003.
16. G. Young and A. Householder. Discussion of a set of points in terms of their mutual distances. *Psychometrika*, 3:19–22, 1938.

Optimal Gene Selection for Cancer Classification with Partial Correlation and *k*-Nearest Neighbor Classifier*

Si-Ho Yoo and Sung-Bae Cho

Dept. of Computer Science, Yonsei University
134 Shinchon-dong, Sudaemoon-ku, Seoul 120-749, Korea
bonanza@sclab.yonsei.ac.kr, sbcho@cs.yonsei.ac.kr

Abstract. High density DNA microarrays are widely used in cancer research, monitoring thousands of genes at once. Due to small sample size and the large amount of genes in micrarray experiments, selection of significant genes via expression patterns is an important matter in cancer classification. Many gene selection methods have been investigated, but it is hard to find out the perfect one. In this paper we propose a new gene selection method based on partial correlation in regression analysis to find the informative genes to predict cancer. The genes selected by this method tend to have information about the cancer that is not overlapped by the genes selected previously. We have measured the sensitivity, specificity, and recognition rate of the selected genes with *k*-nearest neighbor classifier for colon cancer dataset. In most of the cases, the proposed method has produced better results than the gene selection methods based on correlation coefficients, showing high accuracy of 90.3% for colon cancer dataset.

1 Introduction

DNA microarrays provide the measurement of expression levels of thousands of genes simultaneously. These new techniques make it easy to monitor the expression patterns of thousands of genes simultaneously under particular experimental environments [1]. The use of microarrays has been shown in many cases to provide clear analysis of biomedical research. Many researchers have been studying on cancer prediction using microarray with gene expression profile data. To classify tumor samples using mircoarray data, it is necessary to decide which genes should be included in a predictor. Since some genes may have no function for cancer, it is very important to select few informative genes before classification. Also, reducing the dimensions of the data gives more accurate and fast prediction to classify the cancer.

There have been many papers about feature selection method for cancer prediction. Several feature selection methods for selecting informative genes to help classify the cancer were proposed [2]. However, the previous works based on the rank of genes did not consider the partial correlations between the selected genes. They only calculated the similarity between the target (cancer) and the gene itself one by one. Ignoring the

---
* This paper was supported in part by Biometrics Engineering Research Center, KOSEF, and Brain Science and Engineering Research Program sponsored by Korean Ministry of Science and Technology in Korea.

partial correlations of the genes selected, the subset of the chosen genes might have redundant information about cancer.

In this paper, we propose a new gene selection method based on partial correlation in regression analysis. In terms of selecting the genes not by their rank but by their partial correlation, this method is different from previous works. It takes care about the correlations between selected genes to minimize redundant information that could be in the subset of selected genes [3]. Reducing the redundant information about the cancer in the selected genes helps classifying the cancer. The selected genes go into a classifier as an input to conduct classification. The classifier is trained with this input to adjust for right result with the genes selected. Many classifiers have been used in cancer prediction, including support vector machine [4], self-organizing map [5], and k-nearest neighbor [6]. We have used k-nearest neighbor classifier to verify the proposed method with colon cancer dataset of gene expression profile. The results are compared with Pearson's and Spearman's correlation coefficients which are the representative feature selection methods based on correlation analysis. We have investigated the three measures (sensitivity, specificity and recognition rate) to evaluate the performance of the proposed method.

2 Backgrounds

2.1 DNA Microarray

DNA arrays consist of a large number of DNA molecules spotted in a systemic order on a solid substrate. Depending on the size of each DNA spot on the array, DNA arrays can be categorized as microarrays when the diameter of DNA spot is less than 250 microns, and macroarrays when the diameter is bigger than 300 microns. The arrays with the small solid substrate are also referred to as DNA chips.

There are two representative DNA microarray technologies: cDNA microarray technology and oligonucleotide microarray technology. cDNA microarrays are composed of thousands of individual DNA sequences printed in a high density array on a glass microscope slide using a robotic arrayer. High-density oligonucleotide microarrays [7] are made using spatially patterned, light-directed combinatorial chemical synthesis, and contain up to hundreds of thousands of different oligonucleotides on a small glass surface. For mRNA samples, the two samples are reverse-transcribed into cDNA, labeled using different fluorescent dyes mixed (red-fluorescent dye Cy5 and green-fluorescent dye Cy3). After the hybridization of these samples with the arrayed DNA probes, the slides are imaged using scanner that makes fluorescence measurements for each dye. The log ratio between the two intensities of each dye is used as the gene expression data.

$$gene\_expression = \log_2 \frac{\text{Int}(\text{Cy5})}{\text{Int}(\text{Cy3})} \tag{1}$$

where Int(Cy5) and Int(Cy3) are the intensities of red and green colors. Since at least hundreds of genes are put on the DNA microarray, we can investigate the genome-wide information in short time.

2.2 Related Works

It is essential to efficiently analyze DNA microarray data because the amount of DNA microarray data is usually very large. Among thousands of genes whose expression levels are measured, not all are needed for classification. Because microarray data consist of large number of genes in small samples, we need to select the informative genes for classification. This process is referred to as gene selection.

There have been various studies about gene selection methods for cancer classification. Pearson's and Spearman's correlation coefficients are based on statistical correlation analysis, Euclidean distance and cosine coefficient are used to calculate the similarity between genes, and information gain and mutual information are calculated for dependencies between genes [2]. GA/KNN method is used to identify discriminative genes between different classes of samples [6], and also Bayesian variable selection approach is adopted to select useful genes [8].

Some groups have reduced the dimensionality (number of features) by singular value decomposition (SVD), and principal component analysis (PCA) [9]. Other groups have published the results obtained using different feature subset selection procedures on microarray data. These methods evaluate each feature with respect to how well it distinguishes from different classes. Then they rank all genes according to the result and select the top k genes as the feature subset to be used. Some also employ a method to remove redundancy in the selected gene set; for example, some genes may provide the same information [10]. Bayesian approach to dimensionality reduction has been applied by West [9] where the singular-value decomposition is applied to the design matrix to reduce the dimension of the problem. Extracting the informative features for the classification using principal component analysis or genetic algorithm [11] is also studied.

Among them statistical correlation analysis such as Pearson's and Spearman's correlation coefficients are the most commonly used methods to select informative genes by calculating the similarity between the variables. These two correlation coefficients find correlation (linear relationship and the direction of relation) between two variables and also the degree of their correlation. The correlation coefficients have its value ranging from -1 to 1. Values close to 1 indicate strong positive correlation between two variables and -1 indicate strong negative correlation. This method selects a variable which is highly correlated with target variable in order by its rank.

Statistical correlation analysis is broadly used for feature selection, but has a pitfall of ignoring the inter-relations between the selected genes. The selected subset of genes may have redundant information to classify cancer.

3 Cancer Classification Using Partial Correlation

3.1 Regression Analysis

Regression analysis is a method of analyzing the partial correlations between the target variable and the variables that explain the target very well. Unlike the correlation analysis, regression analysis can predict or analyze the impact caused by one or more variables on the other variable [9]. This method sets one variable as a target, and finds out independent variables that affect the target variable. If there is only one independent variable that explains the model we call it a linear regression model and if there are more than one variable that explains the model we call it a multiple regression model.

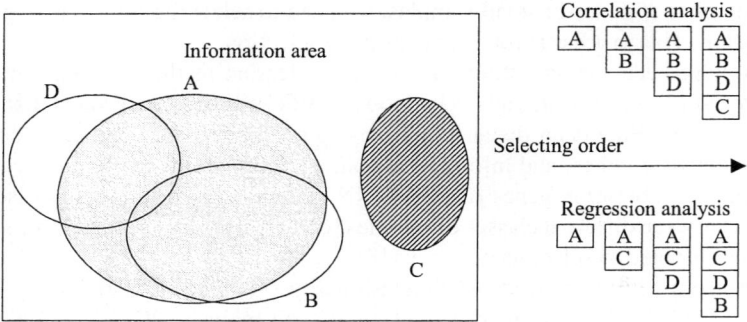

Fig. 1. Basic concept of correlation and regression analysis

The basic concept of regression analysis is shown in Fig 1. Although the amount of information represented by B is larger than that of C, regression model selects C first because it covers larger information area which is not covered by A. The order of selecting genes is quite different. The correlation analysis selects (A, B, D, C) in order by the size of the area they cover. However the regression analysis selects (A, C, D, B) in order by the size of exclusive area, excluding the area covered by the previously selected ones. The regression analysis considers the relations of selected genes to minimize the redundancy.

In the case of adapting gene expression profile data to regression analysis, we use a multiple regression model because there are multiple genes to explain the target variable which indicates the presence of cancer in the sample. Linear regression model with target variable y and the variable x which explains the target variable is constructed as (2) and multiple regression models with the same target variable y and the multiple x's that explain the target are constructed as (3).

$$y = \beta_0 + \beta_1 x_i + \varepsilon, \quad i = 1, 2, \ldots, n \qquad (2)$$
$$y = \beta_0 + \beta_1 x_{1i} + \beta_2 x_{2i} + \beta_3 x_{3i} + \varepsilon_i, \quad i = 1, 2, \ldots, n \qquad (3)$$

Here, β_0 and β_1 are the constants estimated by observed values of x and the target variable y. ε is estimated by normal distribution that has the mean of 0 with the variance of σ^2. In a regression model, selecting the variables which explain the target variable well depends on R^2 value of the variables.

$$R^2 = \frac{SSR}{SSTO} \qquad (4)$$

Here, *SSR* indicates the fluctuations made by regression model, while *SSTO* indicates the whole amount of change made by target variable y. The variable that can explain the target variable well will have large R^2 value because of large SSR. Regression models are verified by F-test. Each F-value of regression model is calculated and evaluated as the fitness of that model. Selecting the model depends on their fitness by F-value.

3.2 Gene Selection Algorithm

The label of the samples is set as a target variable of the model. If the sample is cancer the label is 1, and if it is normal the label is 0. The algorithm of the proposed gene selection method using partial correlation is shown as follows:

procedure
    var N: total number of genes
                G: set of selected genes
                x_G: genes in G
    function $Model(x)$: a regression model of gene x

begin
  for i=1 to N
    $Model(x_i)$
  find $Max\_R^2(x_i)$ and put x_j into G
  do
    for i=1 to N
      $Model(x_G, x_i)$, $x_G \ne x_i$
    find $Max\_R^2(x_G, x_i)$ and put x_i into G
  while $Max\_R^2(x_i) > 0$
end

G is a subset of selected genes and $Max(R^2)$ is the maximum value of R^2 in the developed regression models. At first, there are N genes and we make a regression model for each gene, thereby total numbers of N regression models are formed. Then we compute the R^2 value of each model and find out the maximum R^2 value. If the maximum value of R^2 is larger than 0 (which means that the model could explain the target), the gene of that model is added to G, which is a subset of the selected genes. If the maximum value of R^2 is equal to 0 (which means that the model is not good at explaining the target), the algorithm is terminated. After the first iteration, we make new gene sets ($gene_{selected} + gene_{new}$) by combining a new gene that is not included in the selected genes. After this combination, new regression models with the new gene sets are calculated and the model with the largest R^2 value is selected.

$$y = \beta_0 + \beta_1 gene_{selected} + \beta_2 gene_{new} + \varepsilon \tag{5}$$

Since this method selects the genes according to the relations with the selected genes, it decreases the redundant information about the cancer and constructs an optimal gene set to predict cancer.

3.3 k-Nearest Neighbor

We have used a k-nearest neighbor (KNN) classifier to classify the selected genes, because there are few samples available. Since the samples in microarray data are not many as other usual datasets, the classifiers with parameter tuning like neural network have difficulty in this domain. KNN is one of the most common methods for memory based induction. Given an input vector, KNN extracts k closest vectors in the reference set based on a similarity measure, and makes decision for the label of input vector using the labels of the k nearest neighbors. Pearson's correlation can be used as the similarity measure. When we have an input X and a reference set $D = \{d_1, d_2, \ldots, d_N\}$, the probability that X may belong to class c_j, $P(X, c_j)$, is defined as follows:

$$P(X, c_j) = \sum_{d_i \in KNN} \text{Sim}(X, d_i) P(d_i, c_j) - b_j \qquad (6)$$

where $\text{Sim}(X, d_i)$ is the similarity between X and d_i, and b_j is a bias term.

4 Experiments

4.1 Experimental Environments

The proposed method for discovering significant genes is applied to a colon cancer dataset that contains 62 samples. Each sample contains 2000 gene expression levels. 40 of 62 samples are colon cancer samples and the remaining are normal samples. Each sample was taken from tumors and normal healthy parts of the colons of the same patients and measured using high density oligonucleotide arrays. 31 out of 62 samples are used as training data and the remaining are used as test data in this paper. (Available at: http://www.sph.uth.tmc.edu:8052/hgc/default.asp) For evaluation, we have used sensitivity, specificity, and recognition rate. Sensitivity is the percentage of samples that are recognized as cancer which are really cancer. Specificity is the percentage of samples that are recognized as normal which are really normal.

4.2 Results

Table 1 shows the descriptions of the genes selected by the partial correlation method. We have selected 18 genes that have R^2 value which is larger than zero. The ID of the first gene selected is R8712 (MYOSIN HEAVY CHAIN, NONMUSCLE) and this gene shows higher specificity in Fig. 2 than sensitivity or recognition rate. This gene has useful information about normal samples, but not much information about tumor samples. The third selected gene U3662 (Human Y-chromosome RNA recognition m-otif protein gene) shows higher sensitivity than specificity in Fig. 2. This gene has useful information about tumor samples. Table 2 shows R^2 value, F-value and significant levels of F-value of the selected genes by the partial correlation method. Gene493 is the first selected gene among 2000 genes, with the greatest R^2 value in the regression models. This gene has 50.33 of F-value which is very high and significant level of F-value is less than 0.0001 which is very confident. In the case of the third gene selected, the gene has F-value of 9.74 which is lower than the other's, having low confidence. Except a few genes that have low F-value, most of the genes selected by the partial correlation method show quite high confidence level and prove to have important information about the cancer.

Table 1. Descriptions of the genes selected by the partial correlation method

Rank	Gene ID	Gene Annotation
1	R8712	MYOSIN HEAVY CHAIN, NONMUSCLE (Gallus gallus)
2	U0202	Human pre-B cell enhancing factor (PBEF) mRNA, complete cds.
3	U3662	Human Y-chromosome RNA recognition motif protein (YRRM) gene, exon 12, partial cds, subclone 7S2.
4	H6253	SPORE GERMINATION PROTEIN B2 (Bacillus subtilis)
5	T7102	Human (HUMAN);.
6	H5607	GTP CYCLOHYDROLASE I (Homo sapiens)
7	T9947	GLUCOSE-6-PHOSPHATASE (Homo sapiens)
8	J0014	Human dihydrofolate reductase pseudogene (psi-hd1).
9	M2821	Homo sapiens low density lipoprotein receptor (FH 10 mutant causing familial hypercholesterolemia) mRNA, 3' end.
10	H2475	FRUCTOSE-BISPHOSPHATE ALDOLASE A (HUMAN);.
11	R4985	COAGULATION FACTOR V PRECURSOR (Homo sapiens)
12	T9855	DNA-DIRECTED RNA POLYMERASES I AND III 16 KD POLYPEPTIDE (Saccharomyces cerevisiae)
13	T4964	MYRISTOYLATED ALANINE-RICH C-KINASE SUBSTRATE (Homo sapiens)
14	T6109	ENDOGLIN PRECURSOR (Homo sapiens)
15	M8473	Human autoantigen calreticulin mRNA, complete cds.
16	H6439	CALCINEURIN B SUBUNIT ISOFORM 1 (Homo sapiens)
17	T7258	GLUTAMATE RECEPTOR 5 PRECURSOR (Homo sapiens)
18	H1506	PROTEIN KINASE CLK (Mus musculus)

Table 2. R^2 value, F-value, and significance levels of the genes selected by the partial correlation method

Rank	Gene Number	Partial R-Square	F-Value	Pr>F
1	gene493	0.6344	50.33	<.0001
2	gene1147	0.1549	20.58	<.0001
3	gene1927	0.0559	9.74	0.0043
4	gene1587	0.057	15.15	0.0006
5	gene66	0.0322	12.29	0.0017
6	gene1427	0.0218	11.99	0.002
7	gene597	0.0157	12.94	0.0015
8	gene1919	0.0133	19.93	0.0002
9	gene1584	0.0053	11.94	0.0024
10	gene55	0.0031	9.74	0.0054
11	gene459	0.0028	14.74	0.0011
12	gene1340	0.0019	19.84	0.0003
13	gene2000	0.0007	13.09	0.0021
14	gene955	0.0004	10.26	0.0055
15	gene287	0.0002	8.78	0.0097
16	gene92	0.0002	11.68	0.0042
17	gene332	0.0001	14.83	0.002
18	gene858	0.0001	20.94	0.0006

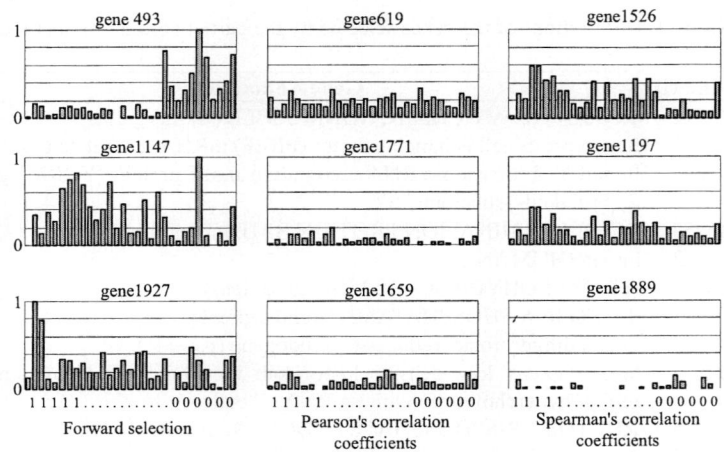

Fig. 2. Expression levels of the genes selected. Top three ranked gene's expression levels have been normalized 0 to 1 and the figure shows all 31 training sample's expression levels on top three ranked genes

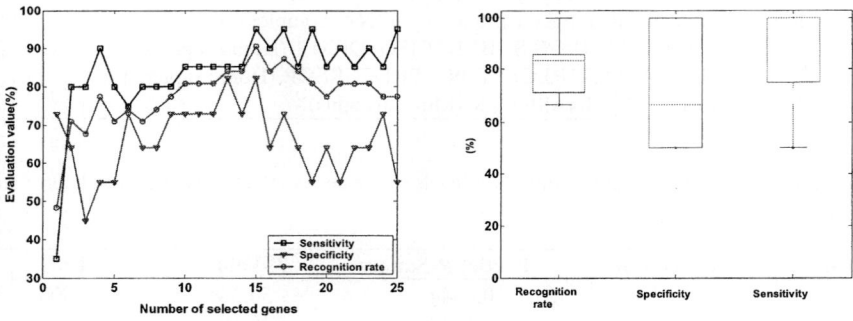

Fig. 3. Results of three evaluation criteria   **Fig. 4.** 10-fold cross validation results

In Fig. 2, the pattern of the genes that are selected by the partial correlation method is different and they have different expression levels on the same samples. They compensate each other and reduce the redundancy. However the genes that are selected by Pearson's correlation coefficients and Spearmans' correlation coefficient have similar pattern and similar expression levels. They are top 3 ranked genes which have high correlation coefficients individually, but not partially correlated to each other. Fig 3 shows the results by the partial correlation method. When only one gene has been selected, it has performed very poorly (sensitivity of 35.0%, specificity of 73.0%, and recognition rate of 48.4%). The highest of all the three criteria appears when the number of selected genes reaches around 15. Since the classifier's performance is heavily dependent on training dataset, we have applied 10-fold cross validation for more precise results. 10-fold cross validation results are shown in Fig 4. 62 samples are divided into 10 sets.

9 sets have been used as training set and 1 set has been used as a test set. The average values of the three measures after 10 runs are 82.37% (recognition rate), 73.34% (specificity), and 88% (sensitivity).

Table 3 shows the results of the best performance when the genes are selected by the partial correlation method. We have determined the optimal number of genes for each method from Fig. 2 (15 genes are used in all the cases). In Spearman's correlation coefficient, the sensitivity is perfect (100%) and even better than the partial correlation method (95%), but the specificity is very low. The proposed method has classified both of tumor and normal samples well and shows high performance in all the criteria. Table 4 shows a confusion matrix of the selected genes. The test sample predicted to be tumor is marked as 1 and that predicted as normal is marked as 0. The proposed method predicts 19 (19/20) samples as tumor, which are actually tumor and predicts 9 (9/11) samples as normal, which are actually normal. Compared with Pearson's and Spearman's correlation coefficients, the partial correlation method is superior in terms of sensitivity and specificity.

Table 3. Best results (%) of the evaluation measures by the three gene selection methods

	Sensitivity	Specificity	Recognition rate
Pearson	75.0	82.0	77.4
Spearman	100.0	9.0	67.7
Partial	95.0	82.0	90.3

Table 4. Confusion matrix of selected genes by three gene selection methods

	Pearson			Spearman			Partial		
		Predicted 0	Predicted 1		Predicted 0	Predicted 1		Predicted 0	Predicted 1
Actual	0	9	2	Actual 0	1	10	Actual 0	9	2
	1	5	15	1	0	20	1	1	19

5 Concluding Remarks

In this paper, we have proposed the partial correlation method for gene selection to classify cancer. The genes selected by the partial correlation method can minimize the redundant information about cancer. Previous works are based on one-to-one correlation. They do not consider the correlations between the selected genes. But the partial correlation method selects the genes that are partially correlated between the selected genes, reducing the redundancy in the subset of selected genes. In the experiments, we have used colon cancer datasets to show the usefulness of the proposed method. Actually, the genes selected by the partial correlation method have shown its power in predicting cancer.

Comparing with other classical methods to select genes would be needed in future work since we have compared only two kinds of methods and also comparing runtimes of the algorithm with other methods would be needed for better analysis in time complexity of the proposed method.

References

1. C. A. Harrington, C. Rosenow and J. Retief, Monitoring gene expression using DNA microarrays. *Curr. Opin. Microbiol*, 3 (2000) 285-291.
2. S.-B. Cho and J. Ryu, Classifying gene expression data of cancer using classifier ensemble with mutually exclusive features, *Proc. of the IEEE*, 90 (11) (2002) 1744-1753.
3. W. D. Shannon, M. A. Watson, A. Perry and K. Rich, Mantel statistics to correlate gene expression levels from microarrays with clinical covariates. *Genetic Epidemiology*, 23(1)(2002) 97-96.
4. T. S. Furey, N. Cristianini, N. Duffy, D. W. Bednarski, M. Schummer and D. Haussler, Support vector machine classification and validation of cancer tissue samples using microarray expression data. *Bioinformatics*, 16(10) (2000) 906-914.
5. P. Tamayo, Interpreting patterns of gene expression with self-organizing map: Methods and application to hematopoietic differentiation. *Proc. of the Natl. Acad. of Sci.* USA, 96 (1999) 2907-2912.
6. L. Li, C. R. Weinberg, T. A. Darden and L. G. Pedersen, Gene selection for sample classification based on gene expression data: study of sensitivity to choice of parameters of the GA/KNN method, *Bioinformatics*, 17 (12) (2001) 1131-1142.
7. R. J. Lipshutz, S. P. A. Fodor, T. R. Gingeras and D. J. Lockhart, High density synthetic oligonucleotide arrays, *Nature Genetics*, 21 (1999) 20-24.
8. K. E. Lee, N. Sha, E. R. Dougherty, M. Vannucci and B. K. Mallick, Gene selection: a Bayesian variable selection approach. *Bioinformatics*, 19(1) (2002) 90-97.
9. M. West, J. R. Nevins, J. R. Marks, R. Spang, C. Blanchette and H. Zuzan, DNA microarray data analysis and regression modeling for genetic expression profiling. *ISDS Discussion*, (2000) 00-15.
10. T. H. Bo and I. Jonassen, New feature subset selection procedures for classification of expression profiles. *Genome Biology*, 3(4) (2002) 0017.1-0017.11.
11. J. Liu and H. Iba, Selecting informative genes with parallel genetic algorithms in tissue classification. *Genome Informatics*, 12(2001) 14-23.

Prediction of the Risk Types of Human Papillomaviruses by Support Vector Machines

Je-Gun Joung[1,2], Sok June O[2,4], and Byoung-Tak Zhang[1,2,3]

[1] Biointelligence Laboratory, Graduate Program in Bioinformatics
[2] Center for Bioinformation Technology (CBIT)
[3] School of Computer Science and Engineering
Seoul National University, Seoul 151-742, Korea
[4] Department of Pharmacology, College of Medicine
Inje University, Busan 614-735, Korea
Phone: +82-2-880-5890, Fax: +82-2-883-9120
{jgjoung,juno,btzhang}@bi.snu.ac.kr

Abstract. Infection by high-risk human papillomaviruses (HPVs) is associated with the development of cervical cancers. Classification of risk types is important to understand the mechanisms in infection and to develop novel instruments for medical examination such as DNA microarrays. In this paper, we classify the risk type of HPVs by using the protein sequences. Our approach is based on the hidden Markov model and the Support Vector Machines. The former searches informative subsequence positions and the latter computes efficiently to classify protein sequences. In the experiments, the proposed classifier was compared with previous methods in accuracy and F-cost, also the prediction result of four unknown types is presented.

1 Introduction

Human papillomaviruses (HPVs) are small DNA viruses that infect epithelial tissues and relate to the diverse malignant tumors. Especially high-risk types could induce more than 95% of cervical cancer in woman. HPVs have a double-stranded DNA genome of approximately 8,000 bps that codes for 10 viral proteins, eight early gene products and two late gene products. More than 85 different HPV types have been described, with new types characterized because of significant differences in sequence homology compared with other defined HPV types [1]. Recently more than 120 have been partly reported [2]. The HPV types are often classified as low-risk or high-risk [3]. Low-risk viral types are associated with low-grade lesions such as condylomata and not cancers. On the other hand, high-risk viral types are associated with high-grade cervical lesions and cancers [4].

The most urgent and important thing for diagnosis and therapy is to discriminate which HPV genotypes are highly risky. Currently, the HPV risk types are classified manually by some experts. Furthermore, there is no method to test immediately if the new HPVs are detected from patients.

In this paper, we propose a novel method to classify HPV risk types, using protein sequence information. Our approach is based on the hidden Markov models (HMMs) and the support vector machines (SVMs). The former is suitable to search informative subsequence positions and the latter provides efficient computation to classify protein sequences. HMM is one of the most successful methods for biological sequence analysis. Especially, it has been quite successful in detecting conserved patterns in multiple sequences [5][6]. Whereas HMM is a generative model, the kernel-based classifier is a discriminant model. Ultimately, the proposed method uses the generative model to get easily distinguishable sequence source and the discriminant model to maximize classification ability.

The proposed SVM includes the string kernel that deals with protein sequences. The string kernel is an inner product in the feature space consisting of all subsequences of length k and maps to feature space from sequences. The string kernel-based approach is efficient to analyze the biological sequence data, because it can extract important features from biological sequences. Recently, several string kernel approaches have been studied in bioinformatics and these have been mostly applied to analyze the protein sequences. For example, the string kernel has been applied to the peptide cleavage site recognition and remote homology detection, outperforming other conventional algorithms [7][8][9][10]. In this paper, SVMs learn a linear decision boundary between the two classes (high-risk and low-risk viral types).

Our work addresses how to classify the viral protein through the kernel-based machine learning approach. It can provide a guide to determine the risk type, when someone finds a novel virus. The paper is organized as follows. In Section 2, the data set is summarized and data pre-processing using HMM is described. Then the kernel method for HPV sequence analysis is presented in Section 3. In Section 4, the experimental results are provided by the proposed method applied to HPV sequence data sets. Concluding remarks and directions on further research are given in Section 5.

2 Data Set

2.1 Data Resource

The data set was extracted from the HPV sequence database at Los Alamos National Laboratory (LANL). High-risk HPV types can be distinguished from other HPV types based on the structure and function of the E6 and E7 gene products. For this reason, we got sequences corresponding to the 72 types from E6. E6 is an early gene product and plays an important role in cellular transformation. E6 products from oncogenic types of HPV can bind to and inactivate the cellular tumor suppressor gene products. This process plays an important role in the development of cervical cancer. Fifteen HPV types were labeled as high-risk types [11]. The rest were labeled as low-risk types.

2.2 Data Pre-processing Using HMM

The training and test data sets consist of subsequences that are estimated as more informative segments in the whole E6 sequence. The procedure for data preprocessing is as follows. First, all known risk type sequences are aligned by the multiple alignment tool such as ClustalW [13]. Second, they are divided into positive and negative sequences, then an HMM is constructed from positive segments. Each segment is the subsequence that is a window with size w and is aligned over the same position by using the multiple alignment tool. Third, the log-likelihoods of positive and negative segments are calculated from the HMM model. Fourth, score is calculated by the difference between positive and negative log-likelihoods. The second and third steps are performed as the window shifts. Finally, the data set for classification is extracted from position that has the high score.

The biological sequence analysis has developed a reasonably successful solution using HMMs. HMMs are one of statistical sequence comparison techniques. They calculate the probability that a sequence was generated by a given model. In our approach, scoring is done by evaluating the probability that presents difference sequences by comparing the positive and negative segments.

3 Classifying by Support Vector Machines

3.1 Support Vector Machines

After the data-preprocessing, the string kernel-based SVM is trained on the HPV sequence data set and tested on the unknown sequences. Support vector machines were developed by Vapnik for classification of data based on a trained model [12]. Recently they have found several applications in biological data analysis. Given a kernel and a set of labelled training vectors (positive and negative input examples), SVMs learn a linear decision boundary in the feature space defined by the kernel in order to discriminate between the two classes. Any new unlabelled example is then predicted to be positive or negative depending on the position of its image in the feature space relatively to the linear boundary.

SVMs learn non-linear discriminant functions in an input space. This is achieved by learning linear discriminant function in a high-dimensional feature space. A feature mapping ϕ from the input space to the feature space maps the training data $S = \{\mathbf{x}_i, y_i\}_{i=1}^n$ into $\Phi(S) = \{\Phi(\mathbf{x}_i), y_i\}_{i=1}^n = \{\mathbf{z}_i, y_i\}_{i=1}^n$. In the feature space, SVMs learn $f(\mathbf{z}) = \langle \mathbf{w}, \mathbf{x} \rangle + b$ so that the hyperplane separates the positive examples from negative ones. Here if $f(\mathbf{z}) > 0$ ($f(\mathbf{z}) < 0$) then the example is classified as positive (negative). The decision boundary is the hyperplane $\langle \mathbf{w}, \mathbf{z} \rangle = 0$ and the margin of the hyperplane is $\frac{1}{\|\mathbf{w}\|}$. Among normalized hyperplanes, SVMs find the maximal margin hyperplane that has the maximal margin.

According to the optimization theory, SVM optimization problem is solved by the following dual problem:

$$\text{maximize} \quad \sum_{i=1}^n \alpha_i - \frac{1}{2} \sum_{i=1}^n \sum_{j=1}^n \alpha_i \alpha_j y_i y_j \langle \mathbf{z}_i, \mathbf{z}_j \rangle, \tag{1}$$

$$\text{subject to} \quad \alpha \geq 0 (1 \leq i \leq n), \sum_{i=1}^n \alpha_i y_i = 0, \tag{2}$$

where parameters α_i are called *Lagrange multipliers*. The parameters $(\mathbf{w}, b)$ are determined by the optimal α_i. For a solution $\alpha_1^*, \ldots, \alpha_n^*$, the maximal margin hyperplane $f^*(\mathbf{z}) = 0$ can be expressed in the dual representation in terms of these parameters:

$$f^*(\mathbf{z}) = \sum_{i=1}^{n} \alpha_i^* y_i \langle \mathbf{z}_i, \mathbf{z} \rangle + b. \quad (3)$$

The dual representation allows for using kernel techniques. In the dual representation, the feature mapping ϕ appears in the form of inner products $\langle \mathbf{z}_i, \mathbf{z}_j \rangle = \langle \Phi(\mathbf{x}_i), \Phi(\mathbf{x}_j) \rangle$.

3.2 Kernel Function

In this paper, the function of SVM is the mismatch-spectrum kernel. The mismatch-spectrum kernel is a new string kernel that was used to detect remote homology detection [8]. It is very simple and efficient to compute. In order to capture significant information from the sequence data, mismatch-spectrum kernels use the spectrum. The mismatch-spectrum kernel is the extended version of the spectrum kernel by adding the biologically important idea of mismatches. The k-spectrum kernel is based on a feature map from the space of all finite sequences to the vector space. Here the space of all finite sequences consists of an alphabet $\mathcal{A}$ of size $|\mathcal{A}| = l$ and the vector space is the l^k-dimensional vectors indexed by the set of k-length subsequences (k-mers) from $\mathcal{A}$.

For a simple feature map, the coordinate indexed by α of k-mer is the number of times α occurs in x. The k-spectrum feature map $\Phi_{(k)}(x)$ can be defined as:

$$\Phi_{(k)}(x) = (\phi_\alpha(x))_{\alpha \in \mathcal{A}^k}. \quad (4)$$

where $\phi_\alpha(x)$ is the number of occurrences of α in x and $\mathcal{A}^k$ is the alphabet of the amino acids constituting k-mers. Thus the k-spectrum kernel function $K(x, y)$ for two sequences x and y is obtained by taking the inner product in feature space:

$$K_{(k)}(x, y) = \langle \Phi_{(k)}(x), \Phi_{(k)}(y) \rangle. \quad (5)$$

The use of the kernel function makes it possible to map the data implicitly into a high-dimensional feature space and to find the maximal margin hyperplane in the feature space. More biologically realistic kernel is the model allowing mismatch in k-mer subsequences. A fixed k-mer subsequence of amino acids is defined as $\alpha = a_1 a_2 ... a_k$, with each a_i a character in $\mathcal{A}$. The (k, m)-neighborhood generated by α is the set of all k-length sequences β from $\mathcal{A}$ that differ from α by at most m mismatches. This set is denoted by $N_{(k,m)}(\alpha)$. The feature map $\Phi_{(k,m)}$ is defined as follows:

$$\Phi_{(k,m)}(\alpha) = (\phi_\beta(\alpha))_{\beta \in \mathcal{A}^k}, \quad (6)$$

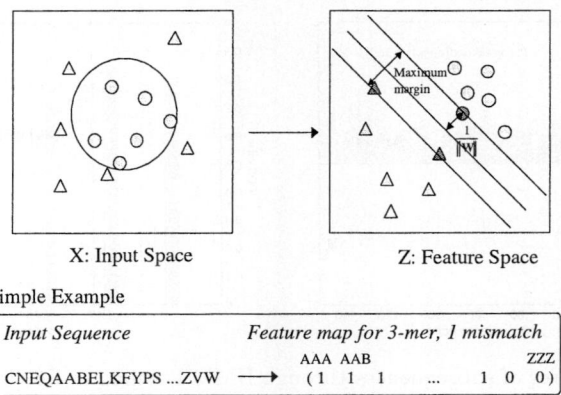

Input Sequence	Feature map for 3-mer, 1 mismatch
	AAA AAB ZZZ
CNEQAABELKFYPS ...ZVW →	(1 1 1 ... 1 0 0)

Simple Example

Fig. 1. The maximal margin classifier (or SVM) learns a linear discriminant function in high-dimensional feature so that the hyperplane optimally separates with maximum margin. For the mismatch-spectrum kernel, the feature map $\phi_\beta(\alpha)$ is given from input space into a high-dimensional feature space (vector space). The feature map is indexed by all possible k-mers.

where $\phi_\beta(\alpha) = 1$ if β belongs to $N_{(k,m)}(\alpha)$, $\phi_\beta(\alpha) = 0$ otherwise. Thus, a k-mer contributes weight to all the coordinates in its mismatch neighborhood.

The feature map on an input sequence x is defined as the sum of the feature vectors assigned to the k-mers in x:

$$\Phi_{(k,m)}(x) = \sum_{k-\text{mers } \alpha \text{ in } x} \Phi_{(k,m)}(\alpha) \tag{7}$$

Note that the β-coordinate for $\Phi_{(k,m)}(x)$ is just a count of all instances of the k-mer β occurring with up to m mismatches in x. The (k,m)-mismatch kernel $K_{(m,k)}$ is the inner product in feature space of feature vectors:

$$K_{(k,m)}(x,y) = \langle \Phi_{(k,m)}(x), \Phi_{(k,m)}(y) \rangle. \tag{8}$$

Mismatch kernels are used in combination with the SVM. Fig. 1 shows the classification task of discriminating the positive sequence class from the negative class. SVMs employing the mismatch-spectrum kernel perform the learning in a high-dimensional feature space.

For (k,m) mismatch kernel $K_{(k,m)}$, if Eq. (5) is applied, then the learned SVM classifier is represented as:

$$f(x) = \sum_{i=1}^{n} y_i \alpha_i \langle \Phi_{(k,m)}(x_i), \Phi_{(k,m)}(x) \rangle + b. \tag{9}$$

Here x_i are the training sequences, y_i are labels, and α_i are weights. It can be implemented by pre-computing and storing per k-mer scores so that the prediction can be calculated in linear time by look-up of k-mer scores [8].

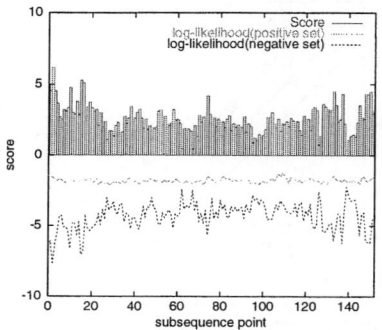 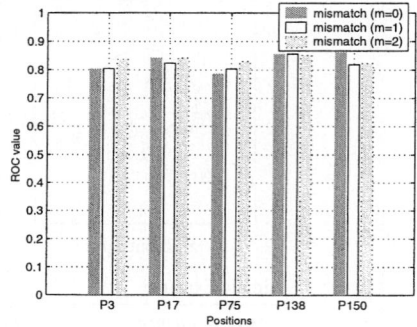

Fig. 2. High scores of subsequences through HMM learning in E6 (left). Point of High scores are 3, 17, 75, 138, and 150. These points are possible to play an important role in the tumor-related suppression or activation. The ROC scores of subsequences that present high scores by HMM (right). The point 138 indicates the highly conserved sequence position so that the highly conserved regions are associated with the classification performance.

4 Experiments

4.1 Searching Informative Subsequences

Left in Fig. 2 shows the scores that are computed through the HMM model to find more informative subsequence positions. Each score is the difference between the log-likelihood of the positive subsequences and one of negative subsequences. The positive data and negative data were selected from the believable types (the number of the positive data set: 15, the number of the negative data set: 11) The window size w is 12 and the number of shifted segments is 153.

In this figure, high scores by HMM are points 3, 17, 75, 138, and 150 that are positions of the starting residues of subsequences. These points are probably motifs that play an important role. The point 138 is zinc-binding region of E6 [16]. In E6, the zinc-binding region is necessary for *trans*-activation and transformation, and is involved in protein-protein interactions. E6 binds to p53 that is a cellular tumor suppressor protein [14]. E6 from high-risk HPV binds p53 with higher affinity than that from low-risk HPV, and mediates the degradation of p53 through the ubiquitin-dependent system.

4.2 Prediction Performance of Subsequences

Fig. 2 (right) shows the ROC (receiver-operating characteristic) values of subsequences that present high scores in Fig. 2 (left). An ROC represents the joint values of the true positive ratio (sensitivity) and false positive ratio (1−specificity). Each bar is an average value after 100 runs. The size of k-mers is 4. At this test, the point 138 has high accuracy for tree mismatches (m=0, 1, 2). Each ROC value is 86 (m=0), 86 (m=1) and 85 (m=2), respectively. The point 138 indicates the highly conserved sequence region as described in the above section. The result suggests that searching the highly conserved region improves the accuracy of the classifier.

Table 1. The performance comparison of sequence based classification (SVMs) and text based classification (AdaCost, AdaBost, navie Bayes).

	Sequence based classification	Text based classification		
Method	SVMs	AdaCost	AdaBoost	naive Bayes
Accuracy	93.15	93.05	90.55	81.94
F-score	85.71	86.49	80.08	63.64

Our approach was compared with textmining approaches in the classification performance. Table 1 shows the comparison of four learning methods. Three methods (AdaCost, AdaBoost, nave Bayes) had been reported in previous study that presented methods to classify the risk type from text data [15]. All results were values predicted by one-leave-out cross-validation. Here the F-score is usually used for Information Retrieval (IR) performance measures. The F-score is computed for given precision p and recall r as F-score $= (2pr)/(p+r)$. SVMs shows 93.15% of accuracy and 85.71% of F-score.

This result supports that sequence based classification can show higher classification performance than text-based classification or similar performance. When the documents of some types are available, text based approach can perform. However new types are detected from patients, text based approach is useless. Our approach can be used generally without additional information such as comments or descriptions.

4.3 Classification of Risk Types

Table 2 shows the comparison between the manually tagged answers and the string kernel based predictions. The manually tagged answers are based on the human papillomavirus compendium (1997 version) and Muñoz's [11] paper. Seventeen HPV types were classified as high-risk types (16, 18, 31, 33, 35, 39, 45, 51, 52, 56, 58, 59, 61, 66, 67, 68, and 72). If the type belongs to the skin-related or cutaneous HPV group reported at the human papillomavirus compendium, it is classified as a low-risk type. There was a good agreement between our epidemiologic classification and the classification based on phylogenetic grouping. In this table, symbol ? denotes the risk type that can not be determined, and there are three unknown types. The prediction is the result of one-leave-out cross-validation.

The most interesting is that the classifier predicted high-risks for HPV70. According to the previous study on HPV [17], the document contains that HPV70 also detected in genital intraepithelial neoplasia from one patient. This is very important result because the classifier in this paper provides the probability whether the unknown HPV types are high-risk or not.

The prediction of types 30, 32, 53, 66 and 68 has different answers for the manually tagged answer. HPV30 and HPV32 were associated specifically with a laryngeal carcinoma and Heck's disease, respectively. They were not classified as high-risk, but are probably associated with a high risk of carcinogenesis. In contrast to the two types, the prediction for HPV53, HPV66, and HPV68 is

Table 2. Comparison between the manually tagged answer (Man.) and the string kernel based prediction (Class.).

Type	Man.	Class.	Type	Man.	Class.	Type	Man.	Class.	Type	Man.	Class.
HPV1	Low	Low	HPV20	Low	Low	HPV38	Low	Low	HPV57	?	Low
HPV2	Low	Low	HPV21	Low	Low	HPV39	High	High	HPV58	High	High
HPV3	Low	Low	HPV22	Low	Low	HPV40	Low	Low	HPV59	High	High
HPV4	Low	Low	HPV23	Low	Low	HPV41	Low	Low	HPV60	Low	Low
HPV5	Low	Low	HPV24	Low	Low	HPV42	Low	Low	HPV61	High	High
HPV6	Low	Low	HPV25	Low	Low	HPV43	Low	Low	HPV63	Low	Low
HPV7	Low	Low	HPV26	?	Low	HPV44	Low	Low	HPV65	Low	Low
HPV8	Low	Low	HPV27	Low	Low	HPV45	High	High	HPV66	High	Low
HPV9	Low	Low	HPV28	Low	Low	HPV47	Low	Low	HPV67	High	High
HPV10	Low	Low	HPV29	Low	Low	HPV48	Low	Low	HPV68	High	Low
HPV11	Low	Low	HPV30	Low	High	HPV49	Low	Low	HPV70	?	High
HPV12	Low	Low	HPV31	High	High	HPV50	Low	Low	HPV72	High	High
HPV13	Low	Low	HPV32	Low	High	HPV51	High	High	HPV73	Low	Low
HPV15	Low	Low	HPV33	High	High	HPV52	High	High	HPV74	Low	Low
HPV16	High	High	HPV34	Low	Low	HPV53	Low	High	HPV75	Low	Low
HPV17	Low	Low	HPV35	High	High	HPV54	?	Low	HPV76	Low	Low
HPV18	High	High	HPV36	Low	Low	HPV55	Low	Low	HPV77	Low	Low
HPV19	Low	Low	HPV37	Low	Low	HPV56	High	High	HPV80	Low	Low

sure to make a mistake. HPV type 53 was detected in genital specimens of the 16 of the patients [18]. However, it is probably not associated with a high risk of carcinogenesis. To be exact in prediction, there is a need for the data set to contain sequences for E7 or L1 gene.

5 Conclusion

We proposed the use of a kernel based method to classify HPV risk types. The proposed kernel-based classifier includes the mismatch string kernel. The string kernels function as a mapping to feature space from sequences. These kernels compute sequence similarity based on shared occurrences of k-mer. The string kernel-based classifier is very powerful to analyze the biological sequence data, because it can extract important features from input sequences. When the classifier learns informative subsequences, the accuracy is better. The informative subsequences could indicate the highly conserved regions.

We predicted the risk type for all types via one-leave-out cross-validation. The most interesting question is 'what is the risk type of HPV70'. This paper provides the probability whether the unknown HPV types are high-risk or not. Our approach can provide a priori knowledge for probe selection in designing genotyping DNA-microarrays. In other words, it can catch specificity to classify high-risk and low-risk viral infection. For more accurate prediction, the input sequence data could be combined with information of the protein structure. Using the secondary structure is possible to have on effect HPV classification.

Acknowledgments

This research was supported in part by NRL, the Korean Ministry of Science and Technology (Korean Systems Biology Research Grant, M10309000002-03B5000-00110).

References

1. H. Pfister, J. Krubke, W. Dietrich, T. Iftner, P. G. Fuchs, Classification of the papilomavirues-mapping the genome, *Ciba Found. Symp.*, Vol. 120, pp. 3–22, 1986.
2. H. zur Hausen, Papillomaviruses causing cancer: evasion from host-cell control in early events in carcinogenesis, *Journal of National Cancer Inst.*, Vol. 92, pp. 690–698, 2000.
3. IARC Monographs on the Evaluation of the Carcinogenic Risks to Humans, Lyon, France: IARC Scientific Publications, 1995.
4. M. F. Janicek, H. E. Averette, Cervical cancer: prevention, diagnosis, and therapeutics, *A Cancer Journal for Clinicians*, Vol. 51, pp. 92–114, 2001.
5. P. Baldi, Y. Chauvin, et. al., Hidden Markov models of biological primary sequence information, *PNAS*, Vol. 91, pp. 1059–1063, 1994.
6. S. Eddy, Multiple alignment using hidden Markov models, *ISMB 95*, pp. 114–120, 1995.
7. C. Leslie, E. Eskin, W. Noble, The spectrum kernel: a string kernel for SVM protein classification, *Proceedings of the Pacific Symposium on Biocomputing 2002*, pp. 564-575, 2002.
8. C. Leslie, E. Eskin, J. Weston, W. Noble, Mismatch String Kernels for Discriminative Protein Classification, *Bioinformatics*, Vol. 20, pp. 467-476, 2004.
9. J.-P. Vert, Support vector machine prediction of signal peptide cleavage site using a new class of kernels for strings, *Proceedings of the Pacific Symposium on Biocomputing 2002*, pp. 649–660, 2002.
10. T. Jaakkola, M. Diekhans, D. Haussler, A discriminative framework for detecting remote protein homologies, *Journal of Computational Biology*, 2000.
11. N. Muñoz, F. X. Bosch, et. al., Epidemiologic classification of human papillomavirus types associated with cervical cancer, *N. Engl. J. Med.*, Vol. 348, pp. 518–527, 2003.
12. V. N. Vapnik, Statistical Learning Theory, Springer, 1998.
13. J. D. Thompson, D. G. Higgins, T. J. Gibson, CLUSTAL W: improving the sensitivity of progressive multiple sequence alignment through sequence weighting, position specific gap penalties and weight matrix choice, *Nucleic Acids Res.*, Vol. 22, pp. 4673–4680, 1994.
14. T. Ristriani, M. Masson, et al., HPV oncoprotein E6 is a structure-dependent DNA-binding protein that recognizes four-way junctions, *J. Mol. Biol.*, 10 (296), pp. 1189–1203, 2000.
15. S.-B. Park, S. Hwang, and B.-T. Zhang, Mining the Risk Types of Human Papillomavirus (HPV) by AdaCost, *Lecture Notes in Computer Science*, Vol. 2736, pp. 403-412, 2003.
16. C. G. Ullman, P. I. Haris, et al., Predicted -helix/ -sheet secondary structure for the zinc-binding motifs for human papillomavirus E7 and E6 proteins by consensus prediction averaging and spectroscopic studies of E7, *Biochem. J.*, Vol. 319, pp. 229–239, 1996.
17. M. Longuet, S. Beaudenon, G. Orth, Two novel genital human papillomavirus (HPV) types, HPV68 and HPV70, related to the potentially oncogenic HPV39, *J. Clin. Microbiol.*, 34 (3), pp. 738–744, 1996.
18. T. Meyer, R. Arndt, et al., Distribution of HPV 53, HPV 73 and CP8304 in genital epithelial lesions with different grades of dysplasia, *Int. J. Gynecol. Cancer.*, 11 (3), pp. 198–204, 2001.

Computational Methods for Identification of Human microRNA Precursors

Jin-Wu Nam, Wha-Jin Lee, and Byoung-Tak Zhang

Graduate Program in Bioinformatics
Center for Bioinformation Technology
Biointelligence Laboratory, School of Computer Science and Engineering
Seoul National University, Seoul 151-742, Korea
{jwnam,wjlee,btzhang}@bi.snu.ac.kr

Abstract. MicroRNA (miRNA), one of non-coding RNAs (ncRNAs), regulates gene expression directly by arresting the messenger RNA (mRNA) translation, which is important for identifying putative miRNAs. In this study, we suggest a searching procedure for human miRNA precursors using genetic programming that automatically learn common structures of miRNAs from a set of known miRNA precursors. Our method consists of three-steps. At first, for each miRNA precursor, we adopted genetic programming techniques to optimize the RNA Common-Structural Grammar (RCSG) of populations until certain fitness is achieved. In this step, the specificity and the sensitivity of a RCSG for the training data set were used as the fitness criteria. Next, for each optimized RCSG, we collected candidates of matching miRNA precursors with the corresponding grammar from genome databases. Finally, we selected miRNA precursors over a threshold (=365) of scoring model from the candidates. This step would reduce false positives in the candidates. To validate the effectiveness of our miRNA method, we evaluated the learned RCSG and the scoring model with test data. Here, we obtained satisfactory results, with high specificity (= 51/64) and proper sensitivity (= 51/82) using human miRNA precursors as a test data set.

1 Introduction

MicroRNAs (miRNAs) are a new class of ncRNA species, which are processed from long miRNA precursors by an enzyme Dicer [1]. The miRNAs participate in regulating gene expression directly by arresting the expression of specific mRNA, whereas other ncRNA participate in gene expression indirectly [2, 3, 4]. These miRNAs have been discovered by various experimental methods such as northern blot [5, 6], clone library [7], separation of microRNP, etc [8]. However, identifying miRNA by those experiments is considerably time-consuming and cost-expensive. Thus, we need a computational algorithm to efficiently predict miRNAs. The algorithms used for gene prediction are less efficient to predict miRNAs because miRNA sequences have a low similarity among sequences. Recently, some groups defined some statistical measures of miRNA precursors to predict miRNAs with respect to those of other species' miRNA precursors [6, 9]. However, these methods need the comparative analysis among miRNA precursors of evolutionarily similar species. If the miRNA precursors

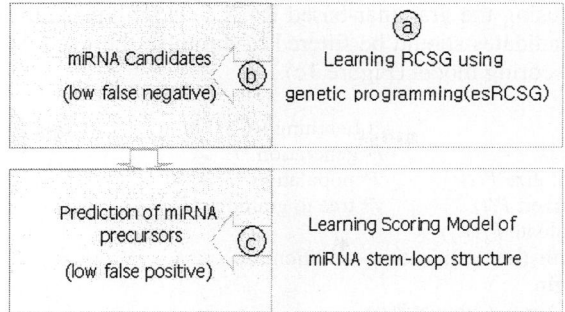

Fig. 1. The schematic overview of algorithm for predicting miRNAs. (a): Optimizing RCSG using genetic programming (b): Collecting miRNA candidates using the optimized RCSG (c): Selecting miRNA precursors from the candidates using the scoring scheme.

of one species have been not known, the method is impossible to predict putative miRNA precursors in the other similar species. Thus, it is essential to the general algorithm to identify putative miRNA only using the structure and sequence information of miRNA precursors. Also, the general algorithm is important to search the common structure and the conserved sequences. To do this, we applied genetic programming.

Genetic programming is an automated method to create working genetic programs, which are called individuals, from a high-level problem statement of a problem [10, 11]. These individuals are generally represented by tree structures. A genetic program consists of two elements, function symbol and terminal symbol. Function symbols appear as internal nodes. Terminal symbols are used to denote actions taken by the program. Genetic programming does this by genetically breeding a population of genetic programs using the principle of Darwinian natural selection and biologically inspired operations. Genetic programming uses crossover and mutation for transformation operators, which can endow variations to the genotype [10].

In this paper, we suggest a new method to detect putative miRNA precursors using a genetic programming and a scoring model of miRNA precursors. The method does not need the comparative analysis among similar species because it searches for the common-structure from miRNA precursors. To learn the common-structure, we define the RCSG (RNA Common-Structural Grammar), which is optimized by genetic programming.

2 Materials and Methods

2.1 Outline of Our Approach

In order to identify miRNA genes in genomes, we have developed an algorithm including a three-step (Figure 1). At first step, the genetic programming optimizes the RCSG according to a predefined fitness function (Figure 1a). The fitness function uses the specificity, the sensitivity and complexity of the structural grammars. At next step, with the optimized RCSG, we search for miRNA precursor candidates on genome sequences using the grammar-based RNA searching program [12] (Figure 1b). The precursor candidates should be filtered to diminish the false positive in the final results using the scoring model (Figure 1c).

```
begin                          /* Learning RCSG */
    t = 0                      /* generation */
    initialize P(t)            /* population */
    convert P(t)               /* tree to grammar*/
    evaluate P(t)
    while (not termination-condition) do
    begin
        S = S + above(P(t))
        t = t+1
        select P(t) from P(t-1)            /* selection */
        crossover-mutate P(t) except Best  /* genetic operators */
        convert P(t)
        evaluate P(t)                      /* fitness function */
        if (local search)
            while (not termination-condition) do
                j = j + 1
                P_j(t) = mutate P(t)
                if (evaluate P(t) < evaluate P_j(t) )
                    P(t) = P_j(t)
    end
end
```

Fig. 2. The pseudo-code of our genetic programming, which learns RCSG from a set of training data, known miRNA precursors.

2.2 Genetic Programming to Optimize RCSG

We have implemented a special genetic programming for the optimization of RCSG. The algorithm of the genetic programming can be illustrated by the pseudo-code as Figure 2. The procedures of the algorithm can be described as follows: (a) initialize the population with randomly generated trees; (b) convert all function trees into structural grammars; (c) calculate the fitness, specificity, sensitivity, and complexity for all grammars; (d) evaluate all structural grammars using the sensitivity, specificity and complexity against the positive and negative training set; (e) using ranking selection, select function trees that will generate offspring (next generation); (f) apply variations, such as mutation and crossover, with the selected function trees; (g) Iterate steps (b) through (f) for the user-defined number of generations.

2.2.1 Individual Representation

In order to convert structural grammars into function trees, we have defined the function f1, f2 and root as shown in Figure 3a. These functions can be formulated by some expression rules (Figure 3a). Therefore, using the expression rules, we can express the structural grammars (Figure 3c) as function trees (Figure 3b). We can use the function trees as individuals of genetic programming because one of the characteristics of genetic programming is that individuals are represented by tree structures.

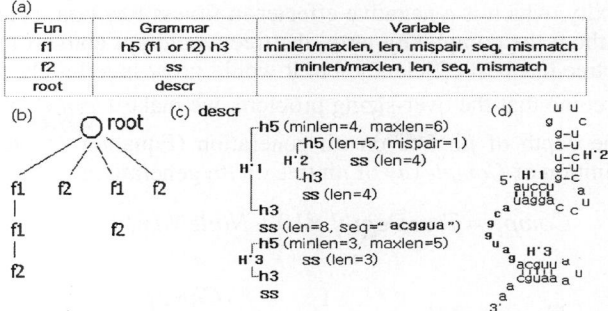

Fig. 3. (a): Function f1 generates recursively structural grammar, including one helix structure and either f1 or f2 as next deviation. Function f2 only represents ss (single strand), which means loop, bulge and single strand. Both f1 and f2 contain some variables, which measure structural information such as the length of helix (len), the number of pair (mispair) and mismatch, and sequence (seq). (b): A function tree to which can be converted into structural grammar (c): The child nodes of root in (b) conform to the first indentation of (c) and the nodes of second depth conform to the second indentation of (c). One helix that consists of the pair of h5-h3, h means helix, 5 and 3 mean 5' end and 3' end) (d): Secondary RNA structure is represented by structural grammar (c). H1, H2 and H3 in (c) and (d) are helix structures.

To avoid creation of invalid structural grammars, function trees have some constraints about the order of the function and the terminal node. First, f2 function should not appear consecutively in the same depth of the tree, contiguous f2 functions can be considered as only one. Second, f2 function can only appear as terminal node to terminate recursive generation of function tree. Finally, variables 'minlen' and 'maxlen' should always come in pair and should not coexist with variable 'len.'

2.2.2 Population Initialization

An initial population is randomly created with some constraints about function tree as described above. The initial population contains various function trees because there is no limitation in the number of nodes and the width of tree. That makes it possible to cover a wide range for searching start point. The broad coverage at start point is one of the major reasons the esRCSG is efficient for searching optimal solution.

2.2.3 Fitness Function

The fitness function (Equation 1) is defined by using specificity, sensitivity and the complexity that are defined at (Equation 4).

$$Fitness = spC * Specificity + stC * Sensitivity - Complexity \quad (1)$$

$$spC + stC = 1 \quad (2)$$

Two parameters, namely spC and stC were added as a way to regulate the effects of specificity and sensitivity. To normalize the fitness, the sum of spC and stC is always 1 (Equation 2). The parameters decide the trade-off between the specificity and the sensitivity on the fitness function.

The complexity, which is a negative effecter in fitness function, controls the growing of tree. Without the complexity term, the tree would not convert to the minimum size where the tree has best efficiency, but it would grow indefinitely during the evolution. To overcome that the over-sizing problem, we make $Comp_i^j$ include the node number and the depth of jth tree on ith generation (Equation 3). (Equation 4) describes the definition of *Complexity* of jth tree on ith generation.

$$Comp_i^j = TreeDepth_i^j \times 10 + NodeNum_i^j \quad (3)$$

$$Complexity_i^j = \frac{1}{(NS+PS)^2} \times \frac{Comp_i^j}{Comp_{i-1}^{best}} \quad (4)$$

where *Complexity* is normalized by square of the number of training data set (*NS + PS*). *NS* is the number of negative training data set and *PS* is the number of positive training data set. $Complexity_i^j$ depends on $Comp_{i-1}^{best}$, which is *Comp* of the best individual (tree) on (i-1)th generation. That dependency makes the trees have the minimum *Comp* as the progress of generation. Finally, the size of best tree on last generation is converged into minimum length as the principle of Occam's razor [13].

2.2.4 Variation

The variation operators are applied so that each descendent will have a different tree structure relative to the parents. The first operator to perturb the tree is the mutation. The mutation changes the value of the function variable by a random variable drawn from Poisson distribution. The crossover exchanges each sub-tree in two parent trees via single-point recombination to generate two new offspring trees. In the crossover, two parent function trees are selected at random from the population and then each single recombination point is selected at random from the each parent.

Table 1. Transition matrix.

	A	T	C	G
A	0.84			
T	-0.06	0.31		
C	-0.52	-0.24	1.40	
G	-0.47	-0.34	-0.93	1.28

2.3 Scoring Model to Predict miRNA Precursors

To construct the scoring scheme, we inspect the characteristics of the conserved sequences and structure over known miRNA precursors. Most miRNA precursors form long stem-loop structure of 70 ~100 nucleotides. Mature miRNAs are derived from the precursor transcript. Because the processing of the precursors is performed at specific region by Dicer enzyme, we believe that the conserved primary sequence or the conserved secondary structure exists in the stem-loop structure. Thus, we designed the scoring model with transition matrix, base paring score and IUPAC nucleotide ambiguity code (Equation 5).

$$Sm = \arg\max[\sum_{i=1}^{l}\sum_{j=1}^{n} \{S_{i,j} \cdot At\} + \sum_{i=1}^{l}\sum_{j=1}^{n} \{P_{i,j} \cdot Ap\}]$$ (5)

where are $S_{i,j}$ and $P_{i,j}$ a transition score and a pairing score respectively. At and Ap are constants that decide trade-off of transition score and paring score respectively. n is the number of all precursors and l is size of stem structure. The scoring model, Sm, is the paired sequences, which is represented with ambiguity codes and maximize the sum of the score.

We constructed the transition matrix through multiple structural alignments of miRNA precursors [14]. The transition matrix is described in Table 1.

3 Results

3.1 Dataset

For each step, training data set and test data set are described in Table 2. In order to extract extended stem-loop structures to be used as negative data set of scoring model in human genome, we predicted RNA secondary structures using RNAfold program (available at http://rna.tbi.univie.ac.at/ cgi-bin/RNAfold.cgi) for human chromosome 18 and 19. The stem-loop structures are selected under some criterions obtained through learning common structure of human miRNA precursors, which are sequence length (64 ~ 90 nucleotides), stem length (above 22 nucleotides), bulge size (under 15 nucleotides), loop size (3 ~ 20 nucleotides) and free energy (under -25 kcal).

Table 2. Data sets to train and test.

Steps	Class	Training number (Test number)	
Learning RCSG	Positive	50 (102)	http://www.sanger.ac.uk/software/
	Negative	200	Primary sequences, hairpins, RNA peudoknots, IRE, bulges and internal loops
Scoring model	Positive	85 (67)	http://www.sanger.ac.uk/software/
	Negative	1000	Stem-loop randomly extracted from Human chromosome 18 and 19

3.2 Learning RCSG of miRNA Precursor

The genetic programming succeeded in optimizing the RCSG of miRNA precursors (Figure 4a). The conditions and results of the experiment are described in Figure 4c. In this experiment, we tried a local search with the words of miRNA precursors. The optimal RCSG with the word 'gcaggga' allows one mismatch and has lower sensitivity than itself without the word. Figure 5 shows the plots of the fitness and the specificity of the best individual on each generation. Because using the elitism, the fitness readily increased or equaled according to growing generation.

(a)
descr (fitnss=0.93, specfty=0.96, sensty=0.71)
  h5(mispair=3)
    ss(minlen=5, maxlen=24)
    h5(len=5, mispair=1)
      h5(minlen=8, maxlen=14, seq='gcaggga', mismatch=1)
        ss(minlen=5, maxlen=27)
        h5(mispair=5)
          ss(minlen=5, maxlen=15)
        h3
      h3
    h3
  h3

(b)
descr (fitnss=0.74, specfty=0.84, sensty=0.84)
  h5(mispair=5)
    h5(mispair=1)
      ss(len=27, seq='gaguaaa', mismatch=0)
    h3
    ss(len=22)
  h3

(c)

Population size	30
Generation number	30
Iteration number for local search	30
spC	0.95
stC	0.05

Fig. 4. (a): The optimal RCSG of miRNA precursors. (c): The setting of parameters and the measures. (b): The RCSG is more general and more sensitive than the RCSG of (a) but less specific.

In order to evaluate the RCSGs for miRNA precursors, we performed the test with the test set consisting of 102 miRNA precursors (excluding training set) and 100 the negative data. In the results, we could measure sensitivity (= 0.71) with detecting 72 of 102 miRNA precursors and specificity (= 0.92) with 72 true positive of 78 positive candidates. The miRseeker of Lay group showed the validation results of the 75% (18/24) sensitivity and about 50% of specificity [1]. Our approach made a more specific identifier than miRseeker and could reduce the false positives. However, it seems that our strategy is less sensitivity than miRseeker [9]. If using alternative optimal RCSGs, such as Figure 4b, together, we think that it is enough to cover the low sensitivity.

3.3 Learning and Evaluation of Scoring Model

To reduce the false positives, we implemented the scoring model of stem-loop in miRNA precursor as described above. The scoring model was optimized with maximizing the Equation 5 (Figure 6).

Next, we tested the scoring model with a negative set and human miRNA precursors (Figure 7). Only thirteen of a thousand negative sets were bigger than the threshold (score = 365), the remaining was smaller. It means that our method shows high specificity. Also, 51 of 82 human miRNA genes were uncovered by our method and the sensitivity was 0.62, slightly higher than the sensitivity obtained by using miRseeker [9].

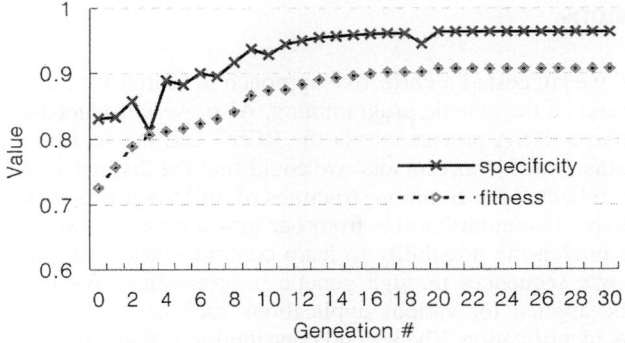

Fig. 5. The plot of the best RCSG for learning miRNA precursor.

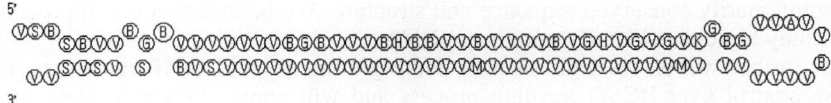

Fig. 6. The optimized scoring model of stem structure in miRNA precursor. This scoring model was learned in the direction of maximizing the score (Equation 5) for 69 training set (of human miRNA precursors).

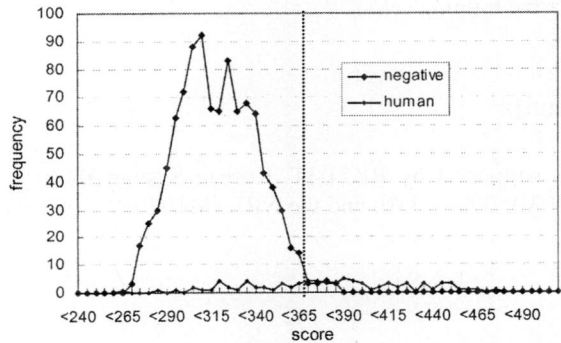

Fig. 7. The distribution of score of negative data and human as test data. The negative set was made of a thousand extended stem-loops extracted in human genome. The positive test sets consist of 82 sequences except training set. The dotted line is a score threshold.

Table 3. 5-fold Cross-validation of predicting miRNA precursor.

Accuracy (5-fold)	Average	Min	Max	S.D.
Sensitivity	0.63	0.56	0.70	0.06
Specificity	0.80	0.74	0.89	0.06

In general modeling situations, it is necessary to decide which models within a specific set are more compatible with all given data. Cross-validation is one established way for accomplishing this. We describe the result for 5-fold cross-validation [15] as shown in Table 3. The 152 miRNAs are randomly divided into 5 groups.

4 Discussions

In this paper, we suggested an effective approach to search for a RCSG with miRNA sequences based on the genetic programming. Also, we introduced a new approach to predict putative miRNA precursors via the RCSG and the scoring model. When applying the human miRNA precursors, we could find the distinctive RCSGs. The identified RCSGs reflected the common structures of miRNA precursors.

We can derive two contributions from our new approach. The first contribution is that we have proven the possibility to learn common-structural grammar from structurally unknown sequences through genetic programming. We believe that our approach can be applied for various applications such as RNA similarity search and putative RNA identification. The second contribution is that we have suggested a new approach to predict putative miRNA. Our approach is a sufficient method to minimize false positives because our method applies the common structure and the information of evolutionarily conserved sequence and structure. We believe that our approach can help many biologists identify putative miRNAs.

For further works, we will consider detail grammars, such as if statements, to increase control over RCSG learning process and will apply Hidden Markov models (HMM) instead of the scoring model to make stochastic learning model. Also, because the efficiency of the learning depends on how we constitute the negative training set, it is important to associate apt sequences having various secondary structures for the negative training sequence set. We are trying to develop a method to make more optimal negative training set.

Acknowledgments

This research was supported by BK21-IT, Korean System Biology Research Grant (M10309000002 -03B5000-00110) and the NRL (M10203000095-03J0000-04510).

References

1. Huttenhofer A., Brosius J. and Bachellerie JP. RNomics: identification and function of small, non-messenger RNAs. *Current Opinion in Chemical Biology*, 6:835-843, 2002.
2. Ambros V. Tiny regulators with great potential. *Cell*, 107:823-826, 2001.
3. Gottesman S. *Genes & Development*, 16:2829-2842, 2002.
4. Zamore P. D. Ancient Pathways programmed by small RNAs. *Science*, 296:1265-1269, 2002.
5. Lagos-Quintana M., Rauhut R., Lendeckel W. and Tuschl T. Identification of novel genes coding for small expressed RNAs. *Science*, 294:853-858, 2001.
6. Lim L. P., Glasner M. E., Yekta S., Burge C. B., and Bartel D. P. Vertebrate microRNA genes. *Science*, 299:1540, 2003.
7. Lagos-Quintana M., Rauhut R., Meyer J., Borkhardt A. and Tuschl T. New microRNAs form mouse and human. *RNA*, 9:175-179, 2003.
8. Dostie J., Mourelatos Z., Yang M., Sharma A., and Dreyfuss G. Numerous microRNPs in neuronal cell containing novel microRNA. *RNA*, 9:180-186, 2003.

9. Lai E.C., Tomancak P., Williams R.W. and Rubin G. M. Computational identification of Drosophila microRNA genes. *Genome Biology*, 4:R42. 2003.
10. Koza J. R. Genetic programming: On the programming of computers by means of natural selection. MIT Press. 1992.
11. Angeline P.J. and Kinnear K.E. Advances in Genetic Programming 2. Jr MIT Press. 1996.
12. Thomas J. Macke, David J. Ecker, Robin R. Gutell, Daniel Gautheret, David A. Case and Rangarajan Sampath. RNAmotif, an RNA secondary structure definition and search algorithms. *Nucleic Acids Research*, 29:4724-4735, 2001.
13. Zhang B.-T., Ohm P., and Mühlenbein H. Evolutionary neural trees for modeling and predicting complex systems. *Engineering Applications of Artificial Intelligence*, 10:473-483, 1997.
14. Siebert S. and Backofen R. MARNA: A Server for Multiple Alignment of RNAs. *In Proceedings of the German Conference on Bioinformatics*, 135-140, 2003.
15. Weiss S.M. and Kapouleas I. An empirical comparison of pattern recognition neural nets and machine learning classification methods. *In Proceedings of the 11th International Joint Conference on Artificial Intelligence*. Detroit, Mich: IJCA1 234–237, 1989.

Multi-objective Evolutionary Probe Design Based on Thermodynamic Criteria for HPV Detection

In-Hee Lee, Sun Kim, and Byoung-Tak Zhang

Biointelligence Laboratory
School of Computer Science and Engineering
Seoul National University, Seoul 151-742, Korea
{ihlee,skim,btzhang}@bi.snu.ac.kr

Abstract. DNA microarrays are widely used techniques in molecular biology and DNA computing area. It consists of the DNA sequences called probes, which are DNA complementaries to the genes of interest, on solid surfaces. And its reliability seriously depends on the quality of the probe sequences. Therefore, one must carefully choose the probe sets in target sequences. In this paper, the probe design for DNA microarrays is formulated as the multi-objective optimization problem. We propose a multi-objective evolutionary approach, which is known to be suitable for this kind of optimization problem. Since a multi-objective evolutionary algorithm can find multiple solutions at a time, we used thermodynamic criteria to choose the most suitable one. For the experiments, the probe set generated by the proposed method is compared to the sequences used in commercial microarrays, which detects a set of Human Papillomavirus (HPV). The comparison result supports that our approach can be useful to optimize probe sequences.

Contents Area: Bioinformatics and AI, Evolutionary computing

1 Introduction

DNA microarray is a small plate on which various kinds of oligonucleotide probes are attached. It is widely used to study cell cycle, gene expression profiling and other DNA-related phenomena in a cell. When the contents of a cell is hybridized to the microarray, if there exists a complementary molecule to one of the probes, it would hybridize to the probe so that a user can detect it. In this way, it can provide the information on whether a gene is expressed or not for hundreds of genes at a time. From this, a biologist can get an overview of gene expression level at a certain time point.

There are two kinds of DNA microarray, cDNA microarray and oligonucleotide microarray. In contrast to cDNA microarrays, one can choose or change the probe sequences on oligonucleotide microarrays. Therefore, the reliability of the information that a oligonucleotide microarray provides depends on the quality of probe sets that used. If a probe hybridizes to not only its target gene but also other genes, the microarray may produce misleading data. Thus, one needs to design the probe set carefully to get precise data.

In literature, lots of probe design methods are suggested reflecting its importance. In [4], the frequency matrix based method was suggested. And an information theoretical method based on Shannon entropy as a quality criterion was used in [5]. Li *et al.* suggested a method based on sequence information and hybridization free energy in [7]. The optimum probes are picked based on having free energy for the correct target, and maximizing the difference in free energy to other mismatched target sequences. And Bourneman *et al.* proposed two heuristics for minimizing the number of oligonucleotide probes needed for analyzing populations of ribosomal RNA gene clones on DNA microarrays [1]. One was a simulated annealing based method which was used to find the probe sets maximizing the number of distinguished pairs of clones for the given number of probes, and the other heuristic, the Lagrangian relexation, was applied to find a minimum number of probes that distinguish all given clones. Recently, a method based on machine learning algorithms such as naïve Bayes, decision trees, and neural networks has been also proposed for aiding probe selection [9]. It tests the probe sets which has high possibility for the hybridization experiments by the learning on the microarray data from *E. coli* and *B. subtilis*. But in spite of the variety of probe design methods, there exists no evolutionary computation-based approach.

We formulated the problem of selecting optimal set of probes as multi-objective optimization problem and applied multi-objective evolutionary algorithm. A multi-objective optimization problem usually has a set of Pareto optimal solutions instead of only one optimal solution. The multi-objective evolutionary algorithm has the advantage that one can get the Pareto optimal solutions at a time. But in the real-world application, one must choose one solution rather than the set of Pareto optimal solutions. As a final decision maker, we choose the thermodynamic criteria for it can provide a realistic evaluation of the set of probes.

In the following sections, we explain the suggested probe design method in detail. In section 2, we briefly introduce the multi-objective optimization problem and formulates the probe design problem as multi-objective optimization problem. Section 3 and 4 describe our probe design method and provide the experimental results. Conclusions are drawn in section 5.

2   Multi-objective Formulation of Probe Design

2.1   Multi-objective Optimization Problem

As the name suggests, a multi-objective optimization problem (MOP) has a number of objectives which are to be optimized [3]. And the problem usually has a number of constraints. The general form of multi-objective optimization problem is like the following:

$$\text{Optimize} \quad f_i(\mathbf{X}), \quad i = 1, \cdots, M;$$
$$\text{subject to} \quad g_j(\mathbf{X}) = 0, j = 1, \cdots, N.$$

Here, M denotes the number of objectives and N the number of constraints. And a solution can be represented as a vector in the objective space, denoted by $f(\mathbf{X}) = (f_1(\mathbf{X}), f_2(\mathbf{X}), \ldots, f_M(\mathbf{X}))$.

We suppose conflicting objectives and no priority between objectives in the further explanation. For non-conflicting objectives, the optimization of one objective implies the optimization of the other and both objectives can be treated as one objective. And if there exists priority between objectives, one can optimize objectives according to the priority by optimizing single objective which is the weighted sum of objectives. Therefore, for both cases, the given problem becomes a single objective optimization problem and we exclude such cases hereafter.

Given an optimization problem, one's goal is to find optimal solution(s). For a single objective case, the optimality of a solution is determined by simply comparing its objective function value to others. In multi-objective case, the optimality of a solution is determined by domination relation between solutions. A solution X is said to *dominate* other solution Y when the following two conditions are satisfied and denoted by $X \preceq Y$:

1. X is no worse than Y in all objectives.
2. X is strictly better than Y in at least one objective.

Therefore, the optimal solutions for a MOP are those that are not dominated by any other solutions. Thus, one's goal in MOP is to find such a *non-dominated set* of solutions.

There exist several methods to find such non-dominated set of solutions for an MOP. Among them, evolutionary method is most popular and currently most actively studied method. Because it is a population-based method, it has the advantage that it can provide a set of non-dominated solutions by one run.

2.2 Probe Design as an MOP

There exist several criteria to evaluate the set of probes. We list the generally used conditions for good probes as follows:

1. The probe sequence for each gene should not appear other genes except its target gene.
2. The non-specific interaction between probe and target should be minimized.
3. The probe sequence for each gene should be different from each other as much as possible.
4. The probe sequence for each gene should not have secondary structure such as hairpin.
5. The melting temperatures of the probes should be uniform.

The first three conditions concern with the specificity of the probes. And the secondary structure of a probe can disturb the hybridization with its target gene. Therefore, well-designed probes should have minimal secondary structure. Lastly, the probes on a oligonucleotide chip is exposed to the same experimental condition. If the melting temperatures of the probes are not uniform, some probes can not hybridize with its target. So, the probes must have the uniform melting temperatures.

Before going on the formulation of the problem, let us introduce some notations. We denote a set of n probes by $X = \{x_1, x_2, \ldots, x_n\}$, where $x_i = \{A, C, G, T\}^l$ for $i = 1, 2, \ldots, n$, l is the length of each probe. And we denote the set of target genes by $T = \{t_1, t_2, \ldots, t_n\}$.

The first condition is the basic requirement for a valid set of probes. Therefore it can be treated as a constraint as follows:

$$g(X) = \sum_{i \neq j} subsequence(x_i, t_j),$$

where $subsequence(x_i, t_j)$ is one if x_i occurs in t_j at least once and zero otherwise. From its definition, this constraint must be zero.

Other 4 conditions can be formulated as minimization objectives. These are formulated as follows:

$$f_1(X) = \sum_{i \neq j} hybridize(x_i, t_j),$$

$$f_2(X) = \sum_{i \neq j} similarity(x_i, x_j),$$

$$f_3(X) = \sum_{i} hairpin(x_i),$$

$$f_4(X) = \sigma_{Tm(X)}.$$

Here, $hybridize(x_i, t_j)$ has non-zero value in proportion to the hybridization likelihood between x_i and t_j. And $similarity(x_i, x_j)$ means the hamming distance between x_i, x_j including shifted comparison. For condition 4, we considered hairpin as the only possible secondary structure, because other structures are hard to compute or hardly occur in microarray probes. $hairpin(x_i)$ has non-zero value in accordance with the probability that x_i can form a hairpin. Condition 5 can be formulated as minimizing the standard deviation of melting temperatures of each probes $(Tm(X))$.

From above, the probe design problem is formulated as an MOP with 4 minimization objectives and 1 equality constraints.

$$\text{Minimize} \quad f_i(\mathbf{X}), \quad i = 1, \cdots, 4;$$
$$\text{subject to} \quad g(\mathbf{X}) = 0\ .$$

3 Evolutionary Oligonucleotide Probe Design

To design probe set that satisfies above condition, we propose an evolutionary computation-based approach. In this approach, we try to find various optimal solutions simultaneously using multi-objective evolutionary algorithm and then choose appropriate probe set according to thermodynamic criteria.

3.1 The Multi-objective Evolutionary Approach

We try to find optimal probe sets using multi-objective evolutionary algorithm. For the multi-objective evolutionary algorithm produces multiple solutions, we choose the most appropriate solution using thermodynamic criteria.

When we optimize probe sets, we applied multi-objective evolutionary algorithm for the following reasons. First, the probe design can be viewed as a kind of multi-objective optimization problem, and evolutionary algorithm showed good performance in optimization including multi-objective optimization. Second, evolutionary approach can provide a population of solutions rather than one solution. The probe design is a multi-objective optimization between conflicting objectives. For example, if we extremely maximize the difference between the probe sequences, the specificity of the probes may drop. Therefore, each set of probes is a trade-off between these conflicting objectives. Evolutionary multi-objective algorithm can find multiple trade-off solutions of various degree. Users can find the most suitable trade-off solution among the population according to appropriate criteria. In this paper, we choose the thermodynamic criteria.

We used the multi-objective evolutionary algorithm called NSGA-II [2]. It is based on the constrained domination concept. The constrained domination concept determines which solution is better than the other in multi-objective problem. Let x and y be two solutions. If both of them is infeasible, the one that violates less constraints dominates the other. If only one of them is feasible and the other is infeasible, the feasible one dominates the other. If both of them is feasible, the objective values are compared. If x is not worse than y in every objective and is strictly better than y in at least one objective, x dominates y. Applying above process to every pair of solutions in the population, each solution in the population can be ranked by the number of solutions it dominates. The objective of NSGA-II is to drive every solution towards the first rank through evolutionary process.

The NSGA-II algorithm is composed of the following steps:

1. Combine parents and offsprings in the previous generation.
2. Perform constrained non-dominated sorting within the combined population. This step produces several layers of populations with different ranking.
3. Generate the parent population for the next generation by selecting solutions from each layers in the previous step. The higher the rank of the layer, the more solutions are selected from that layer. When selecting solution in each layer, we used tournament selection.
4. Generate the offspring population for the next generation from the parent population in the previous step using genetic operations such as crossover and mutation.
5. Repeat 1 ~ 4 for fixed number of generations.

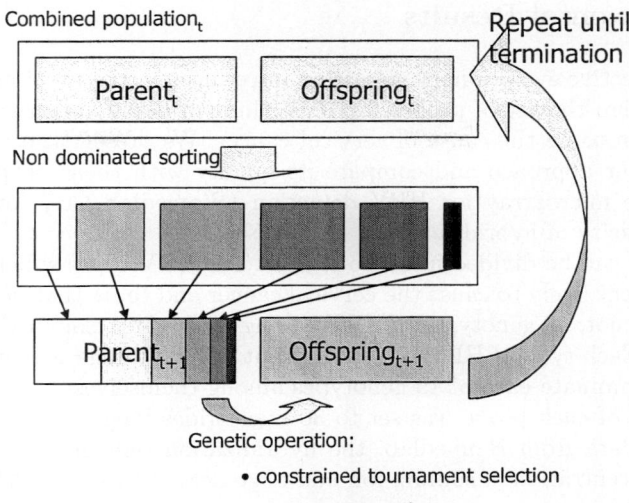

Fig. 1. The flow of NSGA-II.

The above procedure is shown in Fig. 1. While repeating above steps, the solution that has the lowest rank is removed from the population and the whole population moves towards trade-off surface. In the mean time, various trade-off solutions are evolved in the population. As a result, we can get a population of non-dominated trade-off solutions.

Among the previously mentioned conditions for good probes, we used the first condition as a constraint and the others as objectives in NSGA-II.

After the final generation, NSGA-II produces many non-dominated solutions. Among these the fittest one is chosen by using thermodynamic criteria.

3.2 The Thermodynamic Criteria

We used the thermodynamic criteria to determine if a probe hybridize to the wrong target gene. The thermodynamic criteria is based on the nearest neighbor model of DNA [8]. A probe candidate can hybridize to various site of a gene. Using the nearest neighbor model, we can calculate the free energy it takes to hybridize at each site and determine the corresponding melting temperature. If the melting temperature at a wrong hybridization site is higher than the actual hybridization temperature, misleading hybridization may occur. Using this way, we can determine if a candidate probe hybridizes to the wrong target gene or not.

Using this criteria, we chose the set of probes which have the least mis-hybridizing probes from the Pareto optimal solutions generated by multi-objective evolutionary algorithm.

4 Experimental Results

The multi-objective evolutionary algorithm introduced in the previous section is applied to design the set of probes for HPV (human papillomavirus) detection which is known to be the cause of cervical cancer. We present the result set of probes from our approach and compare its quality with those on pre-existing oligonucleotide microarray for HPV detection (Biomedlab Co., Korea) [6] in terms of specificity of hybridization.

HPV types can be divided into two classes. The HPV types which belong to one class are very likely to cause the cervical cancer and those that belong to the other class are not. 19 genotypes of HPV belong to the first class are selected as target genes. Each type of HPV has similar but different gene sequence. So our goal is to discriminate each of 19 genotypes among themselves.

The length of each probe was set to 30 nucleotides long. And based on the experimental data from Biomedlab, the hybridization temperature was set to 40°C. The concentration of sodium ion and oligomers were set to $1M$ and $1nM$ respectively.

The size of population was set as 1000 and the maximum generation number as 200. The generation number is chosen to be big enough for the population to converge to Pareto front. The crossover and mutation probabilities are set as 0.9 and 0.01 respectively.

To compare the quality of probes, we checked the specificity of hybridization for each probes. To do so, we used the following procedure. First, we compute the melting temperature of most stable configuration for every pair of probes and genes. Then, the average of the difference between these values and the melting temperature of probes is calculated. This procedure can be formulated as follows:

$$\frac{\sum_i (Tm(x_i) - \max_{j, i \neq j}(Tm(x_i, t_j)))}{|T|}$$

where, $Tm(x)$ denotes the melting temperature of probe x and $Tm(x,y)$ the melting temperature of most stable configuration of probe x and gene y. If a probe is not hybridized to its target gene specifically and is highly likely to cross-hybridize to other target genes, its melting temperature of most stable configuration with that gene would be high. Then, the difference between its own melting temperature and the cross-hybridization temperature would be small. By averaging these values for all probes, we can check specificity of hybridization of a probe set. The larger the average value is, the more specific the hybridization reactions between probes and its target genes are.

The probe set produced by the suggested algorithm has the value of 61.21 and that from Biomedlab Co. has 56.38 (see Table 1). As can be seen from the table, the suggested method could produce a more reliable probe set. The resulting probe set generated by the proposed approach is shown in Table 2.

Table 1. The comparison result between probes in commercial chip and produced sets of probes.

The Multi-objective Approach	Biomedlab. Probes
61.21	56.38

Table 2. The resulting sets of probes.

HPV Type	Probe Sequence
HPV6	GCATCCGTAACTACATCTTCCACATACACC
HPV11	GACACTATGTGCATCTGTGTCTAAATCTGC
HPV16	ACTAACTTTAAGGAGTACCTACGACATGGG
HPV18	ATGATGCTACCAAATTTAAGCAGTATAGCA
HPV31	TTGTGCTGCAATTGCAAACAGTGATACTAC
HPV33	AACTAGTGACAGTACATATAAAAATGAAAA
HPV34	GCACAAACTTTTCAGTTTGTGTAGGTACAC
HPV35	GTCTGTGTGTTCTGCTGTGTCTTCTAGTGA
HPV39	CCGTAGTACCAACTTTACATTATCTACCTC
HPV40	AGTAATTTCAAGGAATATTTGCGTCATGGG
HPV42	CAACATCTGGTGATACATATACAGCTGCTA
HPV44	CACAGTCCCCTCCGTCTACATATACTAGTG
HPV45	CCTCTACACAAAATCCTGTGCCAAGTACAT
HPV51	GGTTTCCCCAACATTTACTCCAAGTAACTT
HPV52	AGGTTAAAAAGGAAAGCACATATAAAAATG
HPV56	ACTATTAGTACTGCTACAGAACAGTTAAGT
HPV58	GCACTAATATGACATTATGCACTGAAGTAA
HPV59	ATTCCTAATGTATACACACCTACCAGTTTT
HPV66	ATTAATGCAGCTAAAAGCACATTAACTAAA

5 Conclusions

We formulated the probe design problem as a constrained multi-objective optimization problem and presented a multi-objective evolutionary method for the problem. Because our method is based on multi-objective evolutionary algorithm, it has the advantage to provide multiple choices to users. And to make it easy to choose among candidates, we suggested the thermodynamic criteria as an assistant to the decision maker. It is shown that the proposed method can be useful to design good probes by applying it to real-world problem and comparing them to currently used probes.

But in the proposed approach, several time consuming stages are contained such as the non-dominated sorting procedure. Thus, it is necessary to optimize such procedures. And our conditions for good probes are simplified and it needs more consideration on more appropriate conditions.

Acknowledgements

This research was supported in part by the Ministry of Education & Human Resources Development under the BK21-IT Program, the Ministry of Commerce,

Industry and Energy through MEC project, and the NRL Program from Korean Ministry of Science and Technology. The RIACT at Seoul National University provides research facilities for this study. The target gene and probe sequences are supplied by Biomedlab Co., Korea.

References

1. Bourneman, J. Chrobak, M., Vedova, G. D., Figueroa, A., and Jiang, T., Probe Selection Algorithms with Applications in the Analysis of Microbial Communities, *Bioinformatics*, **17**(Suppl.1):39–48, 2001.
2. Deb, K. and Goel, T., Controlled Elitist Non-dominated Sorting Genetic Algorithms for Better Convergence, *Proceedings of the First International Conference on Evolutionary Multi-Criterion Optimization (EMO-2001) LNCS 1993*, 67–81, 2001.
3. Deb, K., *Multi-Objective Optimization using Evolutionary Algorithms*, John Wiley & Sons, Ltd., England, 2001.
4. Drmanac, S., Stravropoulos, N. A., Labat, I., Vonau, J., Hauser, B., Soares, M.B., and Drmanac, R., Gene Representing cDNA Clusters Defined by Hybridization of 57,419 Clones from Infant Brain Libraries with Short Oligonucleotide Probes, *Genomics*, **37**:29–40, 1996.
5. Herwig, R., Schmitt, A. O., Steinfath, M., O'Brien, J., Seidel, H., Meier-Ewert, S., Lehrach, H., and Radelof, U., Information Theoretical Probe Selection for Hybridisation Experiments, *Bioinformatics*, **16**(10):890–898, 2000.
6. Hwang, T. S., Jeong, J. K., Park, M., Han, H. S., Choi, H. K., and Park, T. S., Detection and Typing of HPV Genotypes in Various Cervical Lesions by HPV Oligonucleotide Microarray, *Gynecol Oncol.*, **90**(1):51-56, 2003
7. Li, F. and Stormo, G.D., Selection of Optimal DNA Oligos for Gene Expression Arrays, *Bioinformatics*, **17**:1067–1076, 2001.
8. SantaLucia, John, Jr., A Unified View of Polymer, Dumbbell, and Oligonucleotide DNA Nearest-neighbor Thermodynamics, *Proceedings of National Academy of Science*, **95**:1460–1465, 1998.
9. Tobler, J. B., Molla, M. N., Nuwaysir, E. F., Green, R. D., and Shavlik, J. W., Evaluating Machine Learning Approaches for Aiding Probe Selection for Gene-expression Arrays, *Bioinformatics*, **18**(Suppl.1):164–171, 2002.

Synergism in Color Image Segmentation

Yuzhong Wang, Jie Yang, and Peng Ningsong

Institute of Image Processing and Pattern Recognition
Shanghai Jiaotong University, Shanghai 200030, P.R. China
{oliverwang,jieyang,pengningsong}@sjtu.edu.cn

Abstract. An improved approach for JSEG is presented for unsupervised color image segmentation. Instead of color quantization algorithm, an automatic classification method based on adaptive mean shift (AMS) based clustering is used for nonparametric clustering of image data set. The clustering results are used to construct Gaussian mixture modelling of image data set for the calculation of soft J value. The region growing algorithm used in JSEG is then applied in segmenting the image based on the multiscale soft J-images. Experiments show that the synergism of JSEG and the soft classification based on GMM overcomes the limitations of JSEG successfully and is more robust.

1 Introduction

Color image segmentation is useful in many applications. From the segmentation results, it is possible to identify regions of interest and objects in the scene. A variety of techniques have been proposed, for example: stochastic model based approaches [1,4,9], morphological watershed based region growing [11], energy diffusion [10], and graph partitioning [7]. However, due to the difficult nature of the problem, there are few automatic algorithms that can work well on a large variety of data.

The problem of segmentation is difficult because of image texture. In the reality, natural scenes are rich in color and texture. It is difficult to identify image regions containing color-texture patterns. Yining Deng [2] proposed a new approach called JSEG which can be used to segment images into homogeneous color-texture regions.

However, JSEG has two limitations which will affect the segmentation results. One is caused by color quantization parameter which determines the minimum distance between two quantized colors, and the quantization results directly influences the segmentation results. A good parameter value yields the minimum number of colors necessary to separate two regions. However, it's very difficult to select a good parameter. Facing a strange image, the user will have difficulty to select a suitable quantization parameter. In addition, it's inappropriate to process different kinds of images using the same parameter. Therefore, the existence of this parameter degrades the flexibility of JSEG. Another is caused by the varying shades due to the illumination. The problem is difficult to handle because, in many cases, not only the illuminant component, but also the color components of a pixel, change their values due to the spatially varying illumination [2] and this problem usually cause oversegmentation.

In this paper, a new approach is presented to improve JSEG. First, we use (AMS) based clustering to finish color classification instead of using original color quantization algorithm. By this classification method, image data can be divided into appropriate clusters automatically, so the adaptability of JSEG without quantization parameter is improved. Second, enlightened from segmentations based on fuzzy theories, we make an assumption that colors distributions in the image obey Gaussian mixture modeling (GMM), and calculate soft J values to construct soft J- image using GMM. This can effectively restrain the oversegmentation in those regions with color smooth transition. Experiments show that the synergism of JSEG and the soft classification based on GMM is successful.

2 Background

The basic idea of the JSEG method is to separate the segmentation process into two stages, color quantization and spatial segmentation. In the first stage, colors in the image are quantized to several representative classes that can be used to differentiate regions in the image. This quantization is performed in the color space without considering the spatial distributions of the colors. Then, the image pixel values are replaced by their corresponding color class labels, thus forming a class-map of the image. The class-map can be viewed as a special kind of texture composition. In the second stage, spatial segmentation is performed directly on this class-map without considering the corresponding pixel color similarity.

A criterion for "good" segmentation using spatial data points in class-map is proposed. Let Z be the set of all N data points in a class-map. Let $z = (x, y), z \in Z$, and m be the mean,

$$m = \frac{1}{N} \sum_{z \in Z} z \qquad (1)$$

suppose Z is classified into C classes, $Z_i, i = 1, ..., C$. Let m_i be the mean of the N_i data points of class Z_i,

$$m_i = \frac{1}{N_i} \sum_{z \in Z_i} z \qquad (2)$$

Let

$$S_T = \sum_{z \in Z} \|z - m\|^2 \qquad (3)$$

and

$$S_W = \sum_{i=1}^{C} S_i = \sum_{i=1}^{C} \sum_{z \in Z_i} \|z - m_i\|^2 \qquad (4)$$

S_W is the total variance of points belonging to the same class. Define

$$J = (S_T - S_W)/S_W \qquad (5)$$

In the case of image which consists of several homogeneous color regions, the color classes are more separated from each other and the value of J is large. However, if all color classes are uniformly distributed over the entire image, the value of J tends to be small. We can construct J-image whose pixel values correspond to these local J values calculated over small windows centered at the pixels. The higher the local J value is, the more likely that the corresponding pixel is near a region boundary. Contrarily, a small local J value indicates corresponding pixel be in a region interior. The size of the local window determines the size of image regions that can be detected. Windows of small size are useful in localizing color edges, while large windows are useful for detecting texture boundaries. Often, multiple scales are needed to segment an image.

The characteristics of the J-image allow us to use a region-growing method to segment the image. Consider the original image as one initial region. The algorithm starts the segmentation of the image at a coarse initial scale. Then, it repeats the same process on the newly segmented regions at the next finer scale.

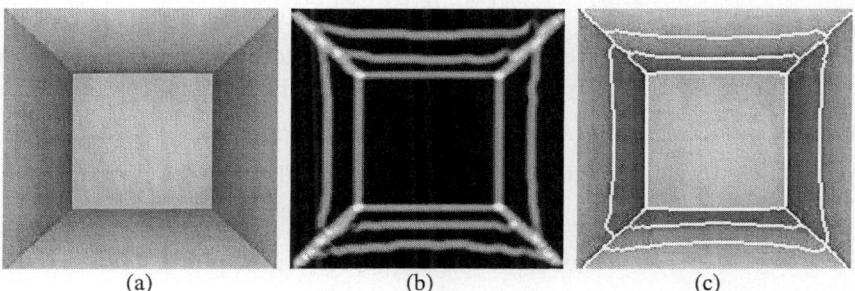

(a) (b) (c)

Fig. 1. (a) A synthetic image. (b) J-image at scale 2. (c) Result after segmentation at scale 2.

In fact, an accurate construction of class-map can result in an outstanding segmentation; furthermore, an exact quantization parameter can result in an accurate class-map. Therefore, the existence of quantization parameter, as mentioned above, degrades the flexibility of JSEG. In addition, the second limitation is caused by hard classification for colors. Because hard classification often divides colors with smooth transition into several classes, therefore makes several obvious visually different regions in class-map which originally belong to the same region.

A synthetic image, its J-image at scale 2 and segmentation result are shown in Fig.1 (quantization parameter is 200, scale threshold is 2 and region merge threshold is 0.4). In the synthetic image, there is phenomenon of colors smooth transition in yellow and blue regions. Therefore, it's impossible to avoid oversegmentation no matter what quantization parameter is selected. This simple example well shows the limitations of JSEG.

3 The Improved Method Based on GMM

To overcome the first limitation of JSEG, a nonparametric clustering based on AMS is used for colors quantization. While to overcome the second limitation, GMM of the image data set, instead of the hard classification, is constructed by using the results of AMS clustering for labeling every pixel.

3.1 Adaptive Mean Shift-Based Clustering

Here we only review some of the results described in [3] which should be consulted for the details.

Assume that each data point $x_i \in R^d, i = 1,...,n$ is associated with a bandwidth value $h_i > 0$. The sample point estimator

$$\hat{f}_K(x) = \frac{1}{n} \sum_{i=1}^{n} \frac{1}{h_i^d} k\left(\left\|\frac{x - x_i}{h_i}\right\|^2\right) \tag{6}$$

based on a spherically symmetric kernel K with bounded support satisfying

$$K(x) = c_{k,d} k\left(\|x\|^2\right) > 0 \quad \|x\| \leq 1 \tag{7}$$

is an adaptive nonparametric estimator of the density at location x in the feature space. The function $k(x), 0 \leq x \leq 1$ is called the profile of the kernel, and the normalization constant $c_{k,d}$ assures that $K(x)$ integrates to one. The function $g(x) = k'(x)$ can always be defined when the derivative of the kernel profile $k(x)$ exists. Using $g(x)$ as the profile, the kernel $G(x)$ is defined as $G(x) = c_{g,d} g\left(\|x\|^2\right)$.

By taking the gradient of (6) the following property can be proven

$$m_G(x) = C \frac{\hat{\nabla} f_K(x)}{\hat{f}_G(x)} \tag{8}$$

Where C is a positive constant and

$$m_G(x) = \frac{\sum_{i=1}^{n} \frac{1}{h_i^{d+2}} x_i g\left(\left\|\frac{x - x_i}{h_i}\right\|^2\right)}{\sum_{i=1}^{n} \frac{1}{h_i^{d+2}} g\left(\left\|\frac{x - x_i}{h_i}\right\|^2\right)} \tag{9}$$

is called the mean shift vector. The expression (8) shows that at location x the weighted mean of the data points selected with kernel G is proportional to the normalized density gradient estimate obtained with kernel K. The mean shift vector thus points toward the direction of maximum increase in the density. The implication of the mean shift property is that the iterative procedure

$$y_{j+1} = \frac{\sum_{i=1}^{n} \frac{1}{h_i^{d+2}} x_i g\left(\left\|\frac{y_j - x_i}{h_i}\right\|^2\right)}{\sum_{i=1}^{n} \frac{1}{h_i^{d+2}} g\left(\left\|\frac{y_j - x_i}{h_i}\right\|^2\right)} \quad j = 1, 2, ... \tag{10}$$

is a hill climbing technique to the nearest stationary point of the density, i.e., a point in which the density gradient vanishes. The initial position of the kernel, the starting point of the procedure y_1 can be chosen as one of the data points x_i. Most often the

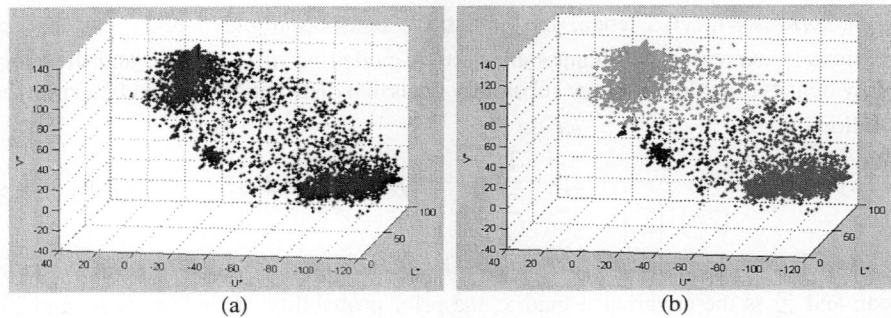

Fig. 2. (a) Colors distribution of the synthetic image in $L*U*V*$ color space. (b) Corresponding clustering result using FAMS clustering procedure.

points of convergence of the iterative procedure are the modes (local maxima) of the density.

There are numerous methods described in the statistical literature to define h_i, the bandwidth values associated with the data points, most of which use a pilot density estimate. For computational reasons, the simplest way to obtain the pilot density estimate is by nearest neighbors [8]. Let $x_{i,k}$ be the k-nearest neighbor of the point x_i. Then, we take $h_i = \|x_i - x_{i,k}\|_1$. In [5], an approximation technique, locality-sensitive hashing (LSH), was employed to reduce the computational complexity of AMS and we can call this fast algorithm as Fast Adaptive Mean Shift (FAMS) procedure, and the selection of k was proved flexible.

AMS clustering is employed to classify color image data. Images are usually stored and displayed in the RGB space. However, to ensure the isotropy of the feature space, a uniform color space with the perceived color differences measured by Euclidean distances should be used. We have chosen the $L*U*V*$ space, whose coordinates are related to RGB values by nonlinear transformations – thus allowing the use of spherical windows [6]. We assume image data obey GMM in $L*U*V*$ space, so we employ the multivariate normal kernel

$$K(x) = (2\pi)^{-d/2} \exp\left(-\frac{1}{2}\|x\|^2\right) \qquad (11)$$

in AMS procedure. In practical applications, we select k equal 500 and employ FAMS procedure. Convergence is declared when the magnitude of the shift becomes less than 0.1.

Fig.2 shows the colors distribution of synthetic image shown in Fig.1 in $L*U*V*$ color space and its colors classification result using FAMS clustering procedure. Visually the synthetic image should be classified into three color classes and it does be decomposed into three clusters with FAMS clustering procedure.

3.2 Soft J Value with GMM

Suppose $\{I_k\}, k = 1,...,N$ is the set of all pixels of the color image $I(x, y)$, and I_k obey Gaussian mixture distribution of C classifications. Mark sub-Gaussian distribution as $\omega_i, i=1,...,C$. Then, the statistical distribution $p(I_k)$ of I_k can be approximately expressed with Gaussian mixture modelling of C classes, and the probability density function of every subsidiary Gaussian distribution ω_i can be expressed as following

$$p(I_k | \omega_i, \theta_i) = \frac{1}{(2\pi)^{\frac{3}{2}}|\Sigma_i|^{\frac{1}{2}}} \exp\left\{-\frac{1}{2}(I_k - \mu_i)^T \Sigma_i^{-1}(I_k - \mu_i)\right\} \quad i=1,...,C \quad (12)$$

$\theta_i = (\mu_i, \Sigma_i)$ denotes the parameters of Gaussian mixture modelling, and μ_i is the mean and Σ_i is the covariance matrix; the prior probability of is $P(\omega_i)$. μ_i and Σ_i can be calculated with the data belonged to the ith class and $P(\omega_i)$ is the ratio of the number of pixels of the ith class to total number of pixels.

Then we can calculate every pixel's membership ($\mu_{I_k, j}(k=1,...,N, i=1,...,C)$) of every class with Bayesian equation

$$\mu_{I_k, i} = \frac{P(\omega_i) p(I_k | \omega_i, \theta_i)}{\sum_{j=1}^{C} P(\omega_j) p(I_k | \omega_j, \theta_j)} \quad k=1,...,N; i=1,...,C \quad (13)$$

After finishing calculation of pixel's membership, we redefine the calculation of J value, letting Z be the set of all N data points in a class-map and $z=(x, y), z \in Z$,. Suppose image data set is classified into C classes. Equations (1) □(3) and (5) needn't to be changed. Modify equation (2) as following

$$m_i = \frac{\sum_{z \in Z} z \cdot \mu_{z,i}}{\sum_{z \in Z} \mu_{z,i}} \quad i=1,...,C \quad (14)$$

and modify equation (4) as following

$$S_W = \sum_{i=1}^{C} S_i = \sum_{i=1}^{C} \sum_{z \in Z} \left(\mu_{z,i} \cdot \|z - m_i\|^2\right) \quad (15)$$

Then, the J value calculated with new rules is called soft J value, and the new J-image constructed by soft J values is called soft J-image. The second limitation can be overcome by using region growing in soft J-image.

Soft J-image of the synthetic image and corresponding segmentation result are shown in Fig.3. The experimental results prove that the improved method overcomes the limitations of JSEG successfully.

4 Experimental Results

The improved algorithm is tested on a variety of images. Generally speaking, the new method looks more robust than JSEG.

Fig.4 shows three examples. The parameters used in JSEG are the same as those used in the simple example shown in Fig.1 and the scale threshold and the region merging threshold used in our method also adopt the same values. The results of Fig.4

Fig. 3. (a) Soft J-image at scale 2 of the synthetic image. (b) Corresponding segmentation result.

(a) and (d) obtained from our method are obviously better than those obtained from JSEG. However, the result of Fig.4 (g) obtained from JSEG is similar to the result from our method. This can be explained as that the set of parameters is right suitable for Fig.4 (g); in another word, it indicates that our method has outstanding adaptability.

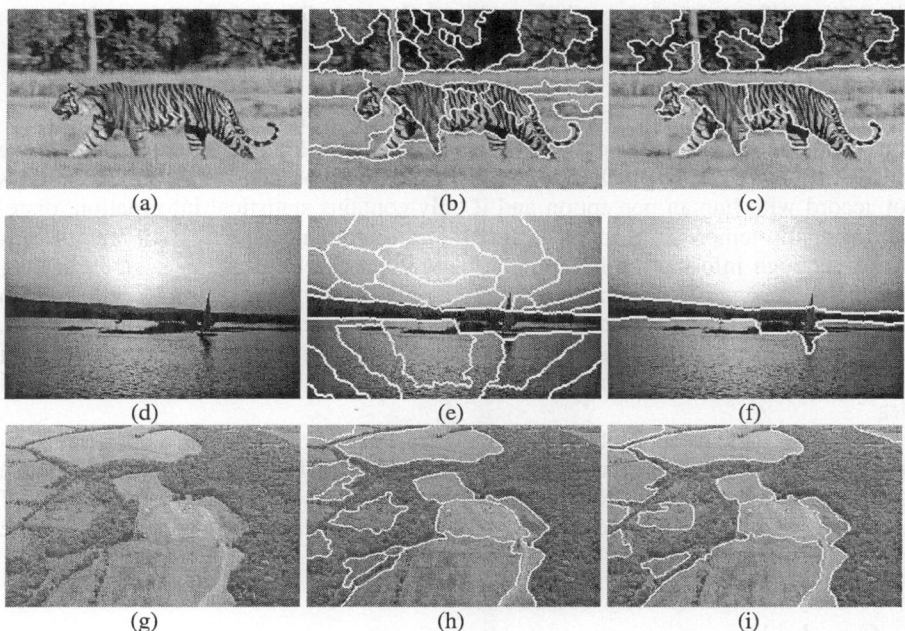

Fig. 4. The original images are shown in the left column while the results from JSEG in the middle column, and the results from our method in the right column.

5 Application

The improved algorithm is successfully applied in our tongue characterization system and is mainly used to segment homogenous regions of substance and coat for colors

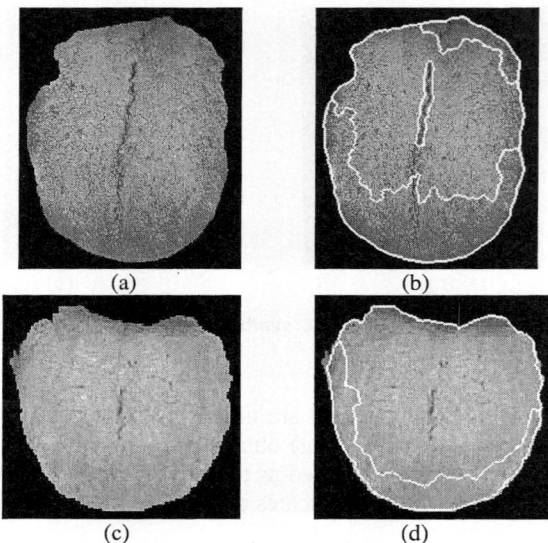

Fig. 5. (a), (c) Two original tongue images. (b), (d) Corresponding regions segmentation results of substance and coat.

identification. In [12] a tongue characterization system is introduced and segmentation of homogenous regions of substance and coat as well as colors identification are finished by recognizing pixels through the standard color samples. However, it does not accord with human perception and it only contains statistical information, disregarding spatio-temporal information that is very important to doctors. In fact, there is already enough information in a single tongue that can be used for segmenting homogenous regions of substance and coat. To obtain results that accord with human perception, we should employ a fine-to-coarse then coarse-to-fine method, that is, substance and coat should be segmented into different homogenous regions at first and then every pixel in different regions is recognized by using standard color samples.

Therefore, there is no doubt that it is a correct choice to segment homogenous regions in tongue by using our improved algorithm of JSEG through which we have achieved excellent results. Fig.5 shows two examples of regions segmentation of substances and coats. These results are quite according with human perception and are appreciated by experts on traditional Chinese medicine.

6 Conclusions

In this work, an improved approach for JSEG is presented for the fully unsupervised segmentation color-texture regions in color images. An automatic classification method based on FAMS clustering is used for nonparametric clustering of image data set. GMM of image data constructed with classifications achieved by FAMS clustering procedure is applied in the calculation of soft J value.

If we want to get good results by JSEG, the parameters used in JSEG must be adjusted repeatedly. Fortunately, the influence of scale threshold and region merging threshold are much less than quantization threshold. Therefore, the selection of quantization threshold degrades efficiency in practical application to a great extent. Repeated selecting quantization threshold will exhaust users and is forbidden in automatic systems. In the traditional clustering techniques, we know, the feature space is usually modeled as a mixture of multivariate normal distributions, which can introduce severe artifacts due to the elliptical shape imposed over the clusters or due to an error in determining their number. However, the AMS based nonparametric feature space analysis eliminates these artifacts. Therefore, GMM constructed from the results obtained by AMS based clustering method is consequentially more exact.

Experiments show the new method overcomes the limitations of JSEG successfully and is more robust. Excellent adaptability and flexibility of the improved method make it more applicable in practical systems.

References

1. Belongie, S. et. al.: Color- and texture-based image segmentation using EM and its application to content-based image retrieval. Proc. of ICCV. (1998) 675-682
2. Deng, Y., Manjunath, B.S.: Unsupervised Segmentation of Color-texture Regions In Images and Video. IEEE Trans. PAMI. 8 (2001) 800-810
3. Comaniciu, D.: An Algorithm for Data-Driven Bandwidth Selection. IEEE Trans. PAMI. 2 (2003) 281-288
4. Delignon, Y., et. al.: Estimation of generalized mixtures and its application in image segmentation. IEEE Trans. Image Processing. 6 (1997) 1364-1376
5. Georgescu, B., Shimshoni, I., Meer, P.: Mean Shift Based Clustering in High Dimensions: A Texture Classification example. Proc ninth Int'l Conf. Computer Vision. (2003) 456-463
6. D. Comaniciu, P. Meer: Robust Analysis of Feature Spaces: Color Image Segmentation. IEEE Proc. CVPR. (1997) 750-755
7. Shi, J. Malik, J.: Normalized cuts and image segmentation. Proc. of CVPR. (1997) 731-737
8. Duda, R.O., Hart, P.E., Stork, D.G.: Pattern Classification. Wiley (2001)
9. Wang, J.-P.: Stochastic relaxation on partitions with connected components and its application to image segmentation. IEEE Trans. PAMI. 6 (1998) 619-636
10. Ma, W.Y., Manjunath, B.S: Edge flow: a framework of boundary detection and image segmentation. Proc. of CVPR. (1997) 744-749
11. Shafarenko, L., Petrou, M., Kittler, J.: Automatic watershed segmentation of randomly textured color images. IEEE Trans. Image Processing. 11 (1997) 1530-1544
12. Shen, L.S., Wang, A.M., Wei, B.G.: Image Analysis for Tongue Characterization. ACTA ELECTRONICA SINICA. 12 (2001) 1762-1765

Face Recognition Using Direct-Weighted LDA

Dake Zhou and Xin Yang

Institute of Image Processing & Pattern Recognition, Shanghai Jiaotong University
Shanghai 200030, P.R. China
{normanzhou,yangxin}@sjtu.edu.cn

Abstract. This paper introduces a direct-weighted LDA (DW-LDA) approach to face recognition, which can effectively deal with the two problems encountered in LDA-based face recognition approaches: 1) Fisher criterion is nonoptimal with respect to classification rate, and 2) the "small sample size" problem. In particular, the DW-LDA approach can also improve the classification rate of one or several appointed classes by using a suitable weighted scheme. The proposed approach first lower the dimensionality of the original input space by discarding the null space of the between-class scatter matrix containing no significant discriminatory information. After reconstructing the between- and within-class scatter matrices in the dimension reduced subspace by using weighted schemes, a modified Fisher criterion is obtained by replacing the within-class scatter matrix in the traditional Fisher criterion with the total-class scatter matrix. LDA using the modified criterion is then implemented to find lower-dimensional features with significant discrimination power. Experiments on ORL and Yale face databases show that the proposed approach is an efficient approach to face recognition.

1 Introduction

Face recognition (FR) techniques could be roughly categorized into two main classes: feature-based approaches and holistic-based approaches [1]. Motivated by the need of surveillance and security, telecommunication and human-computer intelligent interaction, many FR techniques have been developed in the past two decades. Among various FR techniques, the most promising approaches seem to be those holistic-based approaches, since they can avoid difficulties of facial shape or features detection encountered in the feature-based approaches. For holistic-based approaches, feature extraction techniques are crucial to their performance. Linear discriminant analysis (LDA) and principle component analysis (PCA) are the two most used tools for feature extraction in holistic-based approaches, e.g., the famous Fisherfaces [2] and Eigenfaces [3] are based on the two techniques, respectively.

LDA, based on Fisher criterion to seek the projection which maximizes the ratio of the between- and within- class scatters, is a well-known classical statistical technique for dimension reduction and feature extraction [4]. Therefore, it is generally believed that, for the FR problem, LDA-based algorithms outperform PCA-based ones, since the former exploits the class information to build the most discriminatory features space for classification while the latter achieves simply object reconstruction in the sense of mean-square error. Belhumeur et al. first suggested a LDA-based approach to face recognition, which is also referred to as Fisherfaces [2]. Inspired of the success of Fisherfaces approach, at present there are many LDA extension approaches that try to find more effective features subspace for FR, such as direct-LDA (D-LDA) [5][6], Enhanced Fisher linear discriminant Model (EFM) [7], etc.

Although LDA has been successfully used for FR tasks in many cases, there are two problems in LDA-based FR approaches [2][6][8][9]. One is the so-called "small sample size" (SSS) problem, which widely exists in FR tasks because the number of training samples (typically less than 10 per person) is smaller than the dimensionality of the samples (typically larger than 10^4). A solution to the SSS problem is the "regularity techniques" that add some small perturbation to the with-in class scatter matrix and then increase the sample size [8]. Another option is the one that use PCA as a preprocessing step to discard the null space of the within-class scatter matrix for dimension reduction [2]. However, the discarded subspace may contain significant discriminatory information. Recently, direct-LDA (D-LDA) methods for face recognition are presented, in which the null space of the between-class scatter matrix or the complement space of the null space of the within-class scatter matrix, containing no significant discriminatory information, is discarded [5][6]. Another problem encountered in LDA-based approaches is that the traditional Fisher separability criterion is nonoptimal with respect to classification rate in multiclass case. Loog et al. proposed a weighted-LDA (W-LDA) method using an "approximation weighted pairwise Fisher criteria" to relieve this problem [9]. But this method cannot be directly applied in high-dimensional patterns, such as face images, because of its computational complexity and the existence of the SSS problem.

This paper introduces a direct-weighted LDA (DW-LDA) approach for face recognition, which relieves the above two problems to a great extent. In particular, the DW-LDA approach can also improve the classification rate of one or several appointed classes by using an appropriate weighted scheme. The basic idea of the DW-LDA comes from D-LDA and W-LDA. The proposed approach first lower the dimensionality of the original input space by discarding the null space of the between-class scatter matrix containing no significant discriminatory information. After introducing weighted schemes into the reconstruction of the between- and within-class scatter matrix in the dimension reduced subspace, a modified Fisher criterion is obtained by replacing the within-class scatter matrix in the traditional Fisher separability criterion with the total-class scatter matrix. LDA using the modified criterion is then implemented to find lower-dimensional features with significant discrimination power. Finally, the nearest neighbor (to the mean) rule and Euclidean distance measure are used for classification. Experimental results on ORL and Yale face databases show that the proposed approach is an effective method for face recognition.

2 Review of LDA

The problem of feature extraction in FR can be stated as follows: Given a set of N training face image $\{x_i\}_{i=1}^{N}$, each of which is represented as an n-dimensional vector. Let $c_1, c_2, ..., c_K$ denote the classes. The objective is to find a transformation T, based on optimization of certain separability criterion, to produce a low-dimensional feature vector y_i with significant discriminatory power, such that: $y_i = T(x_i)$.

LDA is one of the widely used linear feature extraction techniques in the FR community, which is also referred to as Fisher linear Discriminant Analysis (FLD). Let S_w and S_b denote the within-class scatter matrix and the between-class scatter matrix in the input space, respectively. The goal of LDA is to find a set of basis vectors, denoted as W that maximizes the Fisher criterion function $J(W)$ defined as:

$$J(W) = \frac{|W^t S_b W|}{|W^t S_w W|} \qquad (1)$$

Suppose matrix S_w is nonsingular, the criterion function $J(W)$ can be maximized when W consists of the eigenvectors of the matrix $S_w^{-1} S_b$. Unfortunately, the matrix S_w is often singular in FR tasks because of the existence of the SSS problem. As a result, LDA overfits to the training data and thus generalizes poorly to new testing data. Additionally, the traditional Fisher criterion defined by Eq. (1) is not directly related to classification rate in multiclass case.

3 Direct-Weighted LDA (DW-LDA)

The proposed DW-LDA approach, which uses the D-LDA techniques for dimensionality reduction while at the same time utilizes weighted schemes to obtain a modified Fisher criterion that it is more closely related to classification error, can effectively deal with the above two problems encountered in traditional LDA-based approaches. In particular, the DW-LDA can also improve the classification rate of one or several appointed classes by using a suitable weighted scheme. Fig.1 gives a conceptual overview of this algorithm.

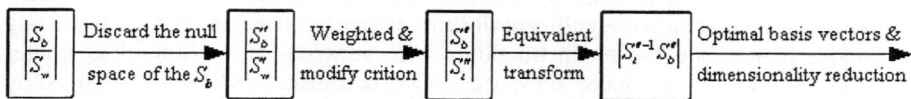

Fig. 1. Flow chart of the DW-LDA algorithm.

3.1 Dimensionality Reduction

Since those significant discriminatory information are in the null space of S_w or the complement space of the null space of S_b [5][6], one can safely discard the null space of S_b without losing useful information. To remove null space of S_b, we first diagonalize S_b:

$$E^t S_b E = \Lambda_b \qquad (2)$$

Where t denotes the transpose operator, $E = (e_1, e_2, ..., e_n) \in R^{n \times n}$ is the eigenvector matrix of S_b, and $\Lambda_b = diag(\lambda_1, \lambda_2, ..., \lambda_n) \in R^{n \times n}$ is the diagonal eigenvalue matrix of S_b with diagonal elements in decreasing order. We can then obtain matrices

$E' = (e_1, e_2, ..., e_m) \in R^{n \times m}$ and $\Lambda'_b = diag(\lambda_1, \lambda_2, ..., \lambda_m) \in R^{m \times m}$ ($m = rank(S_b) < K$), such that: $E''S_b E' = \Lambda'_b$. Now, project the training samples from the origin input space into the dimensionality reduced subspace spanned by vectors $e_1, e_2, ..., e_m$:

$$x'_i = E''x_i \qquad (3)$$

It should be noted that the direct eigen-decomposition of S_b is very difficult or impossible since its dimensionality is very high (typically larger than 10^4). Fortunately, S_b can be rewrited as: $S_b = \sum_{i=1}^{K} P_i(M_i - M)(M_i - M)^t = \Phi\Phi^t$, where $\Phi = (\sqrt{P_1}(M_1 - M), ..., \sqrt{P_K}(M_K - M))$, $M_1, M_2, ..., M_K$ and M are the means of the classes and the grand mean of the training samples, and P_i is the priori probability of the i-th class. According to the singular-value-decomposition (SVD) principle, the first m eigenvectors of S_b, which correspond to nonzero eigenvalues, can be indirectly computed by using an eigenanalysis on the matrix $\Phi^t\Phi$. As $\Phi^t\Phi$ is a $K \times K$ matrix, its eigenanalysis is affordable.

3.2 Weighted Schemes and Modified Criterion

Loog et al. has shown that the traditional Fisher criterion defined by Eq. (1) is not directly related to classification error in multiclass case [9]. They also demonstrated that the classes with larger distance to each other in output space are more emphasized while the Fisher criterion is optimized, which leads that the resulting projection preserves the distance of already well-separated classes, causing a large overlap of neighboring classes. To obtain a modified criterion that it is more closely related to classification error, weighted schemes should be introduced into the traditional Fisher criterion to penalize the classes that are close and then lead to potential misclassifications in the output space. However, we would like to keep the general form of Eq. (1) because then the optimization can be carried out by solving a generalized eigenvalue problem without having to resort to complex iterative optimization schemes. Therefore, in this paper, simple weighted schemes are introduced into the reconstruction of the between-class scatter matrix in the dimensionality reduced subspace, which is different to the one used in [9]. The weighted between-class scatter matrix S''_b is defined as follows:

$$S''_b = \sum_{i=1}^{K-1} \sum_{j=i+1}^{K} P_i P_j w(d_{ij})(M'_i - M'_j)(M'_i - M'_j)^t \qquad (4)$$

where M'_i is the mean of the i-th class and d_{ij} is the Mahanalobis distance between the i-th class and j-th class in the dimensionality reduced subspace. The weighted function $w(d_{ij})$ is a monotonically decreasing function of the distance d_{ij}, with the constraint that it should drop faster the square of d_{ij}:

$$w(d_{ij}) = \eta_{bij} d_{ij}^{-4} / \sum \eta_{bij} d_{ij}^{-4} \tag{5}$$

Additionally, correct coefficients η_{wi} are introduced into the weighted within-class scatter matrix S_w'' defined as:

$$S_w'' = \sum_{i=1}^{K} P_i \eta_{wi} E\{(x_i' - M_i')(x' - M_i')^t \mid x_i' \in c_i\} \tag{6}$$

where $E(\cdot)$ denotes the expectation operator, η_{bij} and η_{wi} are the correct coefficients designed to describe the "importance" of the *i-th* class, and $\eta_{bij} = \eta_{bji}$ ($i,j=1,...,K, i \neq j$). In general case, $\eta_{bij} = \eta_{wi} = 1$ ($i,j=1,...,K, i \neq j$). But in special case, in which we have special interest in the *i-th* class and want to improve its classification rate, we can achieve this by increasing its corresponding correct coefficients to force the resulting projection preferring to the class. Note that the improvement of the classification rate of one or several special classes will in turn increase the whole classification error and we will demonstrate this in our experiments.

As the within-class scatter matrix may be singular in the dimensionality reduced subspace, we further replace the within-class scatter matrix in traditional Fisher criterion with the total-class scatter matrix. Finally, the Fisher criterion is modified as:

$$J(W') = \frac{|W'^t S_b'' W'|}{|W'^t S_t'' W'|} \tag{7}$$

where the total-class scatter matrix $S_t'' = S_w'' + S_b'' > 0$, because of the fact that $S_w'' \geq 0$ and $S_b'' > 0$. It is easy to prove that the projection W' that maximizes the modified criterion defined by Eq. (7) can always maximize $\left|(W^t S_b'' W)/(W^t S_w'' W)\right|$ [8].

3.3 Overall Optimal Transformation Matrix

When the projection W' consists of the eigenvectors of the matrix $S_t''^{-1} S_b''$, the criterion defined by Eq. (7) is maximized:

$$S_t''^{-1} S_b'' W' = W' \Delta \tag{8}$$

where Δ is the corresponding diagonal eigenvalue matrix of $S_t''^{-1} S_b''$, with diagonal elements in decreasing order. To further reduce the dimensionality to l, W' only consists of the first l eigenvectors, which correspond to the first l largest eigenvalues ($l \leq m$). Therefore, the overall optimal transformation matrix T is:

$$T = E'W' \tag{9}$$

4 Experiment Results

We use the publicly available ORL and Yale face databases to test the DW-LDA approach, with the considerations that the first database is used as a baseline study while the second one is used to evaluate face recognition methods under varying lighting conditions. The ORL database contains 400 face images of 40 distinct subjects. Ten images are taken for each subject, and there are variations in facial expression (open or closed eyes, smiling or non-smiling), facial details (glasses or no glasses), and pose (tilting and rotation of up to about 20^0), but there are few illumination variations. The images are 256 grayscale levels with a resolution of 112×92. The Yale database consists of 165 face images of 15 subjects. There are variations in facial expression (open or closed eyes, smiling or non-smiling), facial details (glasses or no glasses), and illumination, but there are few pose variations. The original images are 256 grayscale levels with a resolution of 160×121. Note that for the images in Yale database, before they are used in our experiment, they are normalized to the size of 100×100 by using the geometrical normalization technique suggested by Brunelli et al. [10] and the histogram equalization technique. Fig. 2 illustrates some example images used in our experiment.

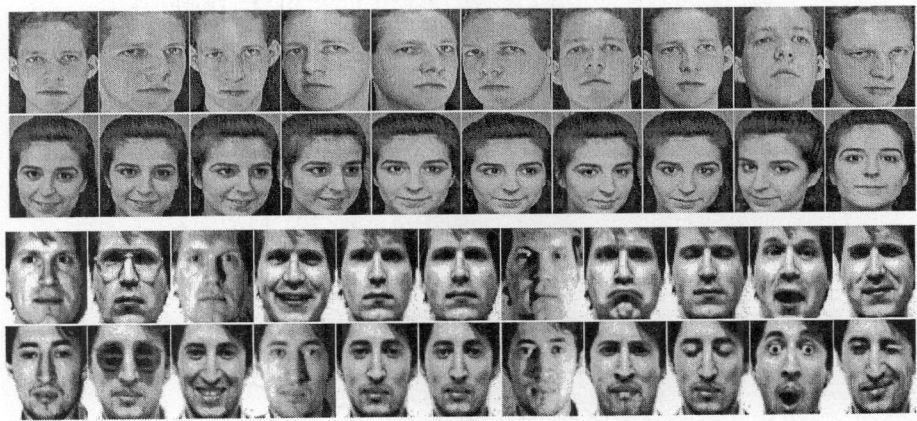

Fig. 2. Some example face images in ORL (Top) and Yale (Bottom) databases.

We compared the performance of five holistic-based face recognition methods, including the proposed DW-LDA method, the D-LDA method, the EFM method, the famous Eigenfaces and Fisherfaces. Note that since in this paper we focus only on feature extraction techniques for FR, a simple classifier, i.e., the nearest neighbor (to the mean) classifier with Euclidian similarity (distance) measure is used for classification. Our first series of experiments is implemented on ORL database. Fig.3 shows the classification rate curves of the five methods with respect to the dimensionality of features while 5 face images per person are selected randomly for training. The proposed method outperforms than the other four methods. In particular, our method achieves 94.8% recognition accuracy while only 27 features are used. The classification rate curves of the five methods are also shown in Fig.4 as functions of the number of training samples per person. One can see from this figure that our proposed method also performs the best among the five methods. The Eigenfaces outperforms the remaining three methods when there are only 2 training samples per person, because of the existence of the SSS problem.

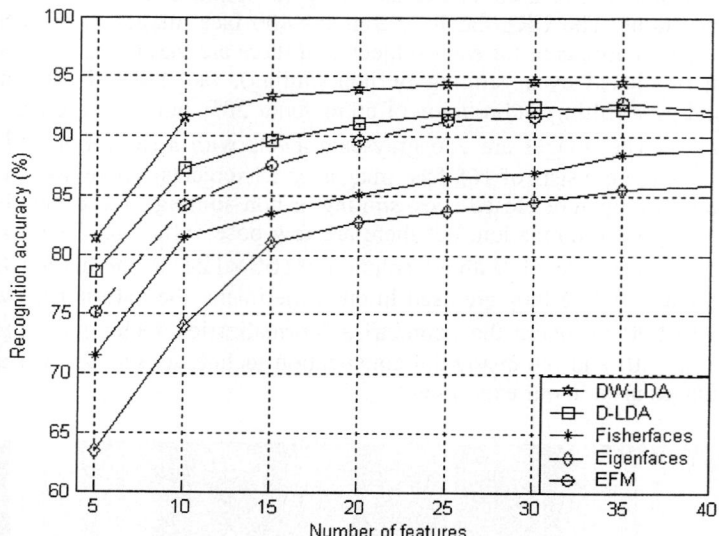

Fig. 3. Classification rate vs. feature dimensionality.

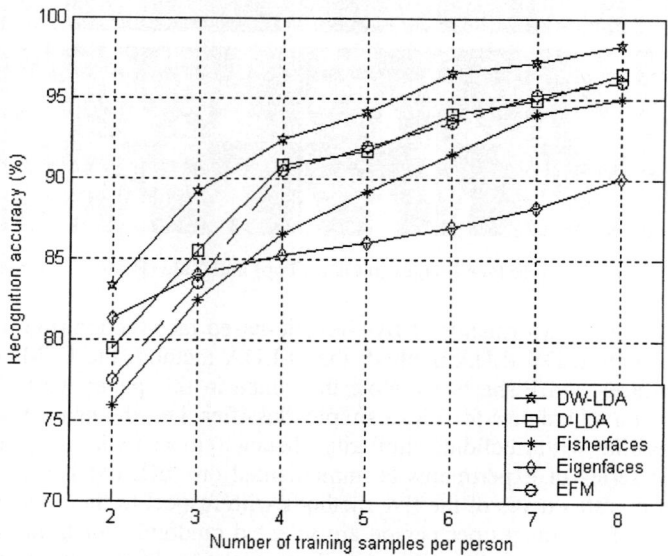

Fig. 4. Classification rate vs. number of training samples per person.

The next series of experiments on ORL database verify the fact that the proposed method can improve the classification rate of one or several appointed classes. In normal case (5 training samples per person, 39 features, $\eta_{bij} = \eta_{wi} = 1$, $i,j=1,...,40, i \neq j$), the classification accuracy of the *40-th* subject in ORL database is 44%, while the overall classification accuracy is 93.9%. If the correct coefficients η_{b40j} ($j=1,...,39$) are set as 4 and η_{w40} are set as 5, the classification accuracy of the *40-th* subject is 76%, while the overall classification accuracy is 84.6%. That is, the improvement of classification rate of one or several appointed classes is at cost of the degeneration of classification rate of the remaining classes.

To evaluate the recognition performance under varying lighting conditions, we performed last series of experiments on Yale database with 5 training samples per person. The proposed DW-LDA method also outperforms than the other methods as shown in Tab.1.

Table 1. Comparative face recognition performance of several methods.

Results\Methods	DW-LDA	D-LDA	EFM	Fisherfaces	Eigenfaces
Accuracy	95.6%	93.4%	93.9%	92.1%	87.8%
Feature dimensionality	14	14	14	14	15

5 Conclusions

Feature extraction is a key step for holistic-based face recognition approaches. In this paper, a LDA extension technique called direct-weighted LDA (DW-LDA), is proposed for face recognition. The proposed method, which combines the strengths of the D-LDA and W-LDA approaches while at the same time overcomes their disadvantages and limitations, can effectively find the significant discriminatory features for face recognition. In particular, the DW-LDA approach can also improve the classification rate of one or several appointed classes. Experiments on ORL and Yale face databases show that the proposed approach is an effective method for face recognition. Additionally, the DW-LDA can also be used as an alternative of LDA, for the high-dimensional complex data consisting of many classes.

Acknowledgements

This work was partially supported by National Natural Science Foundation of China (No. 30170264), National High-tech Program of China (No. 2003CB716104).

References

1. Chellappa, R., Wilson, C.L., Sirohey, S.: Human and machine recognition of faces: a survey. Proc. IEEE, Vol. 83 (1995) 705–740
2. Belhumeur, P., Hespanha, J., Kriegman, D.: Eigenfaces vs. fisherfaces: recognition using class specific linear projection. IEEE Trans. Patt. Anal. Mach. Intell., Vol. 19 (1997) 711-720

3. Turk, M., Pentland, A.: Eigenfaces for recognition. J. Cognitive Neurosci., Vol. 3 (1991) 71-86
4. Jain, A.K., Duin, R., Mao, J.: Statistical pattern recognition: a review. IEEE Trans. Patt. Anal. Mach. Intell., Vol. 22 (2000) 4-37
5. Chen, L. F., Mark Liao, H. Y., Ko, M.T., Lin, J.C., Yu, G.J.: A new LDA-based face recognition system which can solve the small sample size problem. Pattern Recognition, Vol. 33 (2000) 1713-1726
6. Yu, H., Yang, J.: A direct LDA algorithm for high-dimensional data with application to face recognition. Pattern Recognition, Vol. 34 (2001) 2067-2070
7. Liu, C., Wechsler, H.: Gabor feature based classification using the enhanced fisher linear discriminant model for face recognition. IEEE Trans. Image Processing, Vol. 11 (2002) 467-476
8. Liu, K., Cheng, Y. Q., Yang, J. Y., Liu, X.: An efficient algorithm for Foley–Sammon optimal set of discriminant vectors by algebraic method. Int. J. Pattern Recog. Artificial Intell., Vol. 6 (1992) 817-829
9. Loog, M., Duin, R.P.W., Haeb-Umbach, R.: Multiclass linear dimension reduction by weighted pairwise Fisher criteria. IEEE Trans. Pattern Anal. Machine Intell., Vol. 23 (2001) 762-766
10. Brunelli, R., Poggio, T.: Face recognition: Features versus templates, IEEE Trans. on Patt. Anal. Mach. Intell., Vol. 15 (1993) 1042-1052

Face Recognition Using Enhanced Fisher Linear Discriminant Model with Facial Combined Feature

Dake Zhou and Xin Yang

Institute of Image Processing & Pattern Recognition, Shanghai Jiaotong University
Shanghai 200030, P.R. China
{normanzhou,yangxin}@sjtu.edu.cn

Abstract. Achieving higher classification rate under various conditions is a challenging problem in face recognition community. This paper presents a combined feature Fisher classifier (CF^2C) approach for face recognition, which is robust to moderate changes of illumination, pose and facial expression. The success of this method lies in that it uses both facial global and local information for robust face representation while at the same time employs an enhanced Fisher linear discriminant model (EFM) for good generalization. Experiments on ORL and Yale face databases show that the proposed approach is superior to traditional methods, such as eigenfaces and fisherfaces.

1 Introduction

Face recognition (FR) techniques could be generally categorized into two main classes [1]: 1) feature-based methods, which rely on the detection and characterization of individual facial features (i.e., eyes, nose, and mouth etc.) and their geometrical relationships; 2) holistic-based methods, which are the template matching approaches based on the whole facial information. Motivated by the need of surveillance and security, telecommunication and human-computer intelligent interaction, FR techniques have got a great development in the past two decades, but there are still some problems [2]. The significant one is that most FR approaches perform poorly or even cannot work under various conditions, such as changing illumination, pose, and facial expression. A solution to this problem may be to use facial holistic as well as local information for face recognition, which is inspired by the fact that both holistic and local information are necessary for human recognition of faces [2][3]. In Ref. [4][5], eigenfaces plus eigenfeatures (eigeneyes and eigennose) is used to identify face, which leads to an expected improvement in recognition performance. This approach, however, has two main limitations: 1) it does not use class information, as it is only based on principal component analysis (PCA) technique; 2) it needs accurate facial features (eyes and nose) detection, which is very difficult in practice.

The main objective of this research is to improve the accuracy of face recognition subjected to varying facial expression, illumination and pose. In this paper, a combined feature fisher classifier (CF^2C) approach is proposed for face recognition, which is robust to moderate changes of illumination, pose and facial expression. In the CF^2C framework, face image is first divided into smaller sub-images and then the discrete cosine transform (DCT) technique is applied to the whole face image and some sub-images to extract facial holistic and local features. After concatenating these DCT based facial holistic and local features to a facial combined feature vector, the enhanced Fisher linear discriminant model (EFM) is employed to obtain a low-dimensional facial feature vector with enhanced discrimination power. Finally, the nearest neighbor (to the mean) rule with Euclidian distance measure is used for classification. Experimental results on ORL and Yale face databases show that the proposed approach is more robust than traditional FR approaches, such as Eigenface and Fisherfaces.

The rest of this paper is organized as following: In Section 2, we will introduce the DCT based facial combined feature extraction. In Section 3, our CF^2C algorithm is described. Experimental results are presented in Section 4 and our conclusions are drawn in Section 5.

2 The DCT Based Face Representation

Among various deterministic discrete transforms, the DCT best approaches to Karhunen-Loeve Transform (KLT), which is widely used for feature extraction in FR community. Additionally, the DCT can be computed more efficiently than the KLT because it can be implemented by using fast Fourier transform algorithm [6]. Therefore, we employ DCT for face representation, i.e., a low-to-mid frequency subset of the 2-dimensional (2-D) DCT coefficients of a face image is extracted as the facial global feature, which is similar to that used in Ref. [7]. In this paper, a square subset is used for the feature vector. The size of this subset is chosen such that it can sufficiently represent a face, but it can in fact be quite small, as will be shown in section 4.

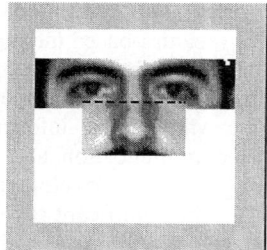

Fig. 1. A face image (Left) and its local regions of eyes and nose (Right).

The similar technique is used to extract facial local information. We first divide the whole face image roughly into several small-overlapping sub-images, such as the forehead, eyes and nose sub-images etc (First detect the centers of eyes, then the nose tip; By considering these location information and the size of face image, segmentation is done). Obviously, the regions of eyes, nose and mouth are the most salient regions for face recognition [1]. However, since the mouth shape is very sensitive to changes of facial expression, the mouth region is discarded and only the eyes and nose regions are used in this paper. DCT is then used to the two sub-images to extract local information. Fig. 1 shows a face image and its local regions of eyes and nose. Let X_h, X_{le}, X_{ln} denote the facial holistic feature vector, the eyes and nose regions feature vectors, respectively. Thus, X_h, X_{le}, X_{ln} can be defined as follows:

$$X_h = \mathrm{Re}\,shape(\Phi(f), n_h) \tag{1}$$

$$X_{le} = \mathrm{Re}\,shape(\Phi(f_{le}), n_{le}) \tag{2}$$

$$X_{\ln} = \mathrm{Re}\,shape(\Phi(f_{\ln}), n_{\ln}) \tag{3}$$

where $\Phi(\cdot)$ denotes the 2-D DCT, f, f_{le} and f_{ln} denote the face image, eyes and nose sub-images, respectively, *Reshape(A, n)* is a function that extracts the top-left $n \times n$ square matrix from matrix A and then transforms this square matrix into a n^2-dimensional column vector.

A new feature vector $\tilde{Y}$ is then defined as the concatenation of X_h, X_{le}, X_{ln}: $\tilde{Y} = \left(X_h^t, X_{le}^t, X_{\ln}^t \right)^t$. Therefore, the corresponding facial combined feature vector Y can be derived from $\tilde{Y}$ by:

$$Y = (\tilde{Y} - u)/\sigma \tag{4}$$

where $u = \dfrac{1}{n}\sum_{i=1}^{n}\tilde{Y}_i$ is the mean vector of training vectors, n is the number of training samples, σ consists of σ_j *(j=1,...,k)*, σ_j is the *j-th* component of the standard deviation of training vectors and k is the dimensionality of vector Y.

3 Combined Feature Fisher Classifier

In the process of the DCT based facial combined feature extraction, however, the class information is not used. To improve its classification performance, one needs to process further this combined feature with some discrimination criterion.

3.1 Fisher Linear Discriminant Analysis

Fisher linear Discriminant Analysis (FLD), which is also referred to as Linear Discriminant Analysis (LDA), is one of the widely used discrimination criterion in face recognition [8][9]. The basic idea of the FLD is to seek a projection that maximizes the ratio of the between-class scatter and the within-class scatter. Let S_w and S_b denote the within- and between- class scatter matrices, respectively. The goal of FLD is to find a projection matrix W that maximizes the Fisher criterion function $J(W)$ defined as:

$$J(W) = \left| (W'S_b W)/(W'S_w W) \right| \tag{5}$$

The criterion function $J(W)$ is maximized when W consists of the eigenvectors of the matrix $S_w^{-1} S_b$.

One main drawback of FLD is that it requires large training sample size for good generalization. When such requirement is not met, FLD overfits to the training data and thus generalizes poorly to the new testing data. For the face recognition problem, however, usually there are a large number of faces (classes), but only a few training samples per face. One possible remedy for this drawback is to artificially generate additional data and then increase the sample size [8]. Another remedy is to balance the need for adequate signal representation and subsequent classification performance by using sensitivity analysis on the spectral range of the within-class eigenvalues, which is also referred to as enhanced Fisher linear discriminant model (EFM) [10].

3.2 Enhanced Fisher Linear Discriminant Model

The enhanced Fisher linear discriminant model (EFM) improves the generalization capability of FLD by decomposing the FLD procedure into a simultaneous diagonalization of the within- and between- class scatter matrices. The simultaneous diagonalization is stepwisely equivalent to two operations: whitening the within-class scatter matrix and applying PCA on the between-class scatter matrix by using the transformed data [10]. The EFM first whitens the within-class scatter matrix:

$$S_w \tilde{\Xi} = \tilde{\Xi}\tilde{\Gamma}, \quad \tilde{\Gamma}^{-\frac{1}{2}}\tilde{\Xi}'S_w\tilde{\Xi}\tilde{\Gamma}^{-\frac{1}{2}} = I \qquad (6)$$

where $\tilde{\Xi} = (e_1, e_2, ..., e_k) \in R^{k \times k}$ is the eigenvector matrix of S_w, I is the unitary matrix and $\tilde{\Gamma} = diag(\lambda_1, \lambda_2, ..., \lambda_k) \in R^{k \times k}$ is the diagonal eigenvalue matrix of S_w with diagonal elements in decreasing order.

During the whitening step, the small eigenvalues corresponding to the within-class scatter matrix are sensitive to noise, which causes the whitening step to fit for misleading variations. So, the generalization performance of the EFM will degenerate rapidly when it is applied to new data. To achieve enhanced performance, the EFM keeps a good tradeoff between the need of adequate signal representation and generalization performance by selecting suitable principal components. The criterion of choosing eigenvalues is that the spectral energy requirement (which implies that the selected eigenvalues should account for most of the spectral energy) and the magnitude requirement (which implies that the selected eigenvalues should not be too small, i.e., better generalization) should be considered simultaneously. Suppose eigenvalues set $\{\lambda_i\}_{i=1}^m$ ($m<k$) are selected, which is based on this selecting criterion, thus m can be determined as the largest integer that satisfies the following equation:

$$(\sum_{j=1}^m \lambda_j / \sum_{i=1}^k \lambda_i) \geq \alpha \quad \text{and} \quad \lambda_m \geq \varepsilon \qquad (7)$$

where α and ε are the preset thresholds.

We can then obtain matrices $\Xi = (e_1, ..., e_m) \in R^{k \times m}$ and $\Gamma = diag(\lambda_1, ..., \lambda_m) \in R^{m \times m}$. The new between-class scatter matrix can be defined as follows:

$$\tilde{S}_b = \Gamma^{-\frac{1}{2}}\Xi'S_b\Xi\Gamma^{-\frac{1}{2}} \qquad (8)$$

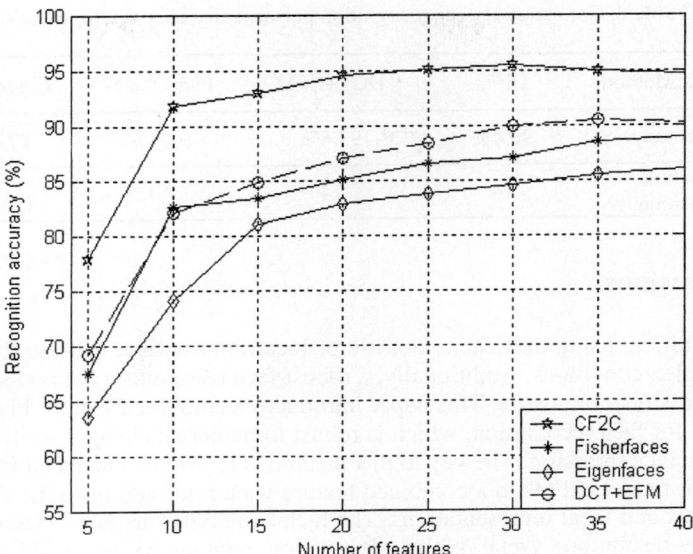

Fig. 3. Classification rate vs. Feature dimensionality.

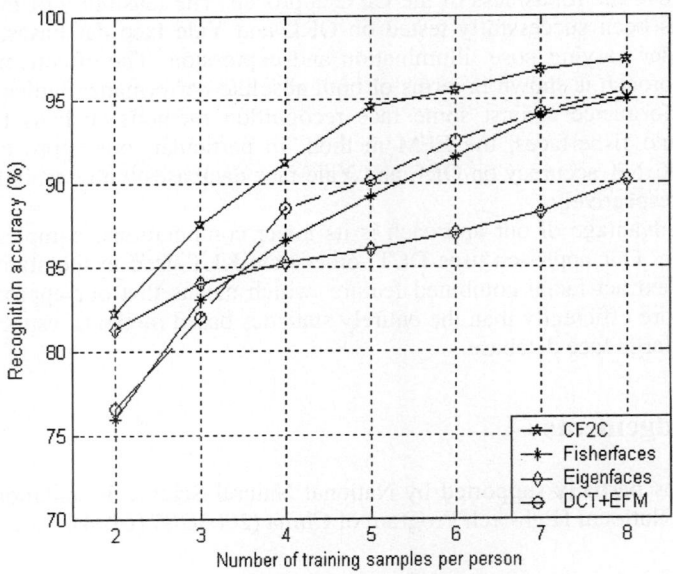

Fig. 4. Classification rate vs. Number of training samples per person.

To evaluate the recognition performance under varying lighting conditions, we performed last series of experiments on Yale database with 5 training samples per person. The proposed method also outperforms than the other three methods as shown in Tab.2.

Table 2. Comparative face recognition performance of several methods.

Results\Method	CF^{2}C	DCT+EFM	Fisherfaces	Eigenfaces
Accuracy	96.4%	93.6%	92.1%	87.8%
Feature dimensionality	14	14	14	15

5 Conclusions

Face recognition, using only facial holistic or local information, may not be accurate under complex conditions. Additionally, a robust face recognition method should also consider classification aspect. This paper introduces a combined feature Fisher classifier (CF^{2}C) for face recognition, which is robust to moderate changes of illumination, pose and facial expression. The key to this method is to use the enhanced fisher linear discriminant model (EFM) to a combined feature vector derived from the DCT based facial holistic and local representations. The facial combined feature, encompassing a coarse (low-resolution) facial global description augmented by additional (high-resolution) local details, can represent face more robustly. Using the EFM, developed from the traditional fisher classifier with improved generalization capability, can further improve the robustness of the CF^{2}C approach. The feasibility of the proposed approach has been successfully tested on ORL and Yale face databases, which are acquired under varying pose, illumination and expression. The effectiveness of the proposed approach is shown in terms of both absolute performance indices and comparative performance against some face recognition methods such as the popular eigenfaces and fisherfaces, the EFM method. In particular, our approach achieves 94.6% and 96.4 % accuracy on ORL and Yale face databases with 5 training samples per people, respectively.

Another advantage of our approach is its lower computational complexity during training stage. Our approach uses DCT, other than KLT used in the statistics based methods, to extract facial combined feature, which means that our approach can be computed more efficiently than the entirely statistics based methods, especially while running in a large face database.

Acknowledgements

The work was partially supported by National Natural Science Foundation of China (30170264), National High-tech Program of China (2003CB716104).

References

1. Chellappa, R., Wilson, C.L., Sirohey, S.: Human and machine recognition of faces: a survey. Proc. IEEE, Vol. 83 (1995) 705–740
2. Zhao, W., Chellappa, R., Rosenfeld, A., Phillips, P.J.: Face recognition: a literature survey. (2000) http://citeseer.nj.nec.com/374297.html

3. Sukthankar, G.: Face recognition: a critical look at biologically-inspired approaches. (2000) Technical Report: CMURI- TR-00-04, Carnegie Mellon University, Pittsburgh, PA.
4. Moghaddam, B., Pentland, A.: Probabilistic visual learning for object representation. IEEE Trans. Patt. Anal. Mach. Intel. Vol. 19 (1997) 696-710.
5. Pentland, A., Moghaddam, B., Starner, T.: View-based and modular eigenspaces for face recognition. Proceedings of the IEEE International Conference on Computer Vision and Pattern Recognition, Seattle, WA, (1994) 84-91.
6. Rao, K. and Yip, P.: Discrete Cosine Transform-Algorithms, Advantages, Applications. (1990) Academic: New York, NY
7. Hafed, Z.M. and Levine, M.D.: Face Recognition Using the Discrete Cosine Transform. International Journal of Computer Vision, Vol. 43 (2001) 167–188
8. Etemad, K. and Chellappa, R.: Discriminant analysis for recognition of human face images. Journal of the Optical Society of America A: Optics Image Science and Vision, Vol. 14 (1997) 1724-1733
9. Jain, A.K., Duin, R., Mao, J.: Statistical pattern recognition: a review. IEEE Trans. Patt. Anal. Mach. Intell., Vol. 22 (2000) 4-37.
10. Liu, C., Wechsler, H.: Gabor feature based classification using the enhanced fisher linear discriminant model for face recognition. IEEE Trans. Image Processing, Vol. 11 (2002) 467-476
11. Brunelli, R., Poggio, T.: Face recognition: Features versus templates. IEEE Trans. Patt. Anal. Mach. Intell., Vol. 15 (1993) 1042-1052.

Gradient Vector Flow Snake with Embedded Edge Confidence

Yuzhong Wang and Jie Yang

Institute of Image Processing and Pattern Recognition,
Shanghai Jiaotong University, Shanghai 200030, P.R. China
{oliverwang,jieyang}@sjtu.edu.cn

Abstract. Snakes, or active contours, are used extensively in computer vision and image processing applications, particularly in locating object boundaries. Problems associated with initialization and poor convergence to boundary concavities have limited their utility. Gradient vector flow (GVF) snake solved both problems successfully. However, boundaries in noisy images are often blurred even destroyed with smoothing and false results usually occur when such images are processed even with GVF snake model. We have incorporated embedded edge confidence (EEC) into GVF snake model. The improved method can solve this problem when noisy images were processed.

1 Introduction

Snake [1], or active contours model, is defined as an energy-minimizing spline – the snake's energy depends on its shape and location within the image. Local minima of this energy then correspond to desired image properties such as object boundary. Snakes may be understood as a special case of a more general technique of matching a deformable model to an image by means of energy minimization. Snakes are widely used in many applications, including edge detection, shape modeling, segmentation, and motion tracking.

There are two general types of active contour models in the literature today: parametric active contours [1] and geometric active contours [3,4]. The content of this paper focuses on the former. Parametric active contours synthesize parametric curves within an image domain and allow them to move toward desired features, usually edges.

There are two key difficulties with parametric active contour algorithms. The first one is that the initial contour must, in general, be close to the true boundary or otherwise, it will likely converge to the wrong result. The second one is that active contours have difficulties progressing into boundary concavities. Several methods have been proposed to address these problems including multiresolution methods [5], pressure forces [6], and distance potentials [7], control points [8], domain-adaptivity [9]. However, most of the methods proposed to address these problems solve only one problem while creating new difficulties [10]. A new class of external force for active contour models that addresses both problems listed above was presented in [10]. The new external force called gradient vector flow (GVF) is computed as a diffusion of the gradient vectors of the images. The active contour that uses the GVF as its external force is called GVF snake. Particular advantages of the GVF snake over a traditional snake are its insensitivity to initialization and its ability to move into boundary concavities.

There is also a common problem with all kinds of snake models that they have no antinoise capability. It's known that the external forces of snake models derive directly or indirectly from the gradient vectors of the images; furthermore, the gradient vectors derive directly from edges information within the images. Before processing, the noisy images must be smoothed which will make the object boundaries blurred even destroyed at the same time, thus, snake model with gradient vectors obtained from wrong edges information would doubtless produce wrong result. However, EEC [11] can indicate the reliability of edges. Therefore, EEC can be incorporated into the computation of gradient vectors to solve this problem.

In this paper, we construct new gradient vectors using EEC as weighting coefficient of original gradient vectors. Then, gradient vector flow is computed with new gradient vectors and experimental results show that GVF snake with EEC is more efficient and robust.

2 Gradient Vector Flow Snake

2.1 Traditional Snake Model

A traditional snake is a curve $X(s) = [x(s), y(s)]$ for $s \in [0,1]$, that moves through the spatial domain of a image $I(x, y)$ to minimize the energy function defined in [1] as

$$E_{energy} = \int_0^1 E_{energy}(X(s)) ds \qquad (1)$$

$$E_{energy} = \int_0^1 E_{in}(X(s)) + E_{ext}(X(s)) ds \qquad (2)$$

Where E_{in} is the internal energy that provides smoothness to the contour and E_{ext} is the external energy calculated from an image data which determines the relationship between snake and the image.

The internal energy E_{in} of snake which is found to be the sum of the two terms such as elasticity and bending, is defined as

$$E_{in} = \frac{1}{2} \left[\alpha \left| \frac{dX(s)}{ds} \right|^2 + \beta \left| \frac{dX(s)^2}{ds^2} \right|^2 \right] \qquad (3)$$

Where α and β are the weighted parameters to control snake's tension and rigidity respectively. By controlling them we can control the limitation up to which snake is allowed to stretch and bend. These parameters are to be fixed for detecting the boundary of interested object in the image. The term $\alpha\left|\dfrac{dX(s)}{ds}\right|^2$ is a first-order derivative of the position of the snake and controls the tension in snake. Hence, it is called the elasticity energy $E_{elastic}$ of snake. Again the term $\beta\left|\dfrac{dX(s)^2}{ds^2}\right|^2$ is second-order derivative of snake's position and controls the rigidity of snake. Therefore, it is called the bending energy $E_{bending}$ of snake.

Using Eq.(3) in Eq.(2) we get

$$E_{energy} = \int_0^1 \frac{1}{2}\left[\alpha|X'(s)|^2 + \beta|X''(s)|^2\right] + E_{ext}(X(s))ds \qquad (4)$$

Again from [1], the external energies which lead the active contour towards step edge are found as

$$E^1_{ext} = -|\nabla I(x,y)|^2 \quad \text{or} \qquad (5)$$
$$E^2_{ext} = -|\nabla(G_\sigma(x,y)*I(x,y))|^2$$

Where $G_\sigma(x,y)$ is a two-dimensional Gaussian function with standard deviation σ and ∇ as the gradient operator. In fact, $G_\sigma(x,y)*I(x,y)$ is the operation of image smoothing with Gaussian filter.

A snake that minimizes E_{energy} must satisfy the Euler equation

$$\alpha X''(s) - \beta X''''(s) - \nabla E_{ext} = 0 \qquad (6)$$

Note $F_{in} = \alpha X''(s) - \beta X''''(s)$ is the internal force that tries to stop the stretching and bending and $F^P_{ext} = -\nabla E_{ext}$ is the external potential that tries to pull the snake towards the desired image edge. Then the force balance equation becomes $F_{in} + F^P_{ext} = 0$. To solve Eq.(6), the snake is made dynamic i.e. X as function of time t and s then Eq.(6) becomes

$$X_t(s,t) = \alpha X''(s,t) - \beta X''''(s,t) - \nabla E_{ext} \qquad (7)$$

This gives the solution of Eq.(6) which is the traditional snake and its limitations which we have mentioned above. See [10] for a more detailed discussion of traditional snake's limitations.

2.2 Gradient Vector Flow Snake Model

GVF snake [10] is a modified form of the active contour. GVF snake keeps the strong and useful part of the traditional snake: the internal force. But, instead of image gradient, it creates its own force field called the GVF force field [10] which was the dense vector filed derived from image by minimizing energy function in a variational framework. The minimization is achieved by solving a pair of decoupled linear partial differential equations which defuses the gradient vectors of a gray level edge map computed from the image.

The new static external force field $F^p{}_{ext} = V(x,y)$ defined in [10], comes from the premise of mathematics of Helmholtz theorem. It states that most general static field can be decomposed into two components: irrotational i.e. curl-free component and solenoidal i.e. divergence-free component. Now (7) becomes

$$X_t(s,t) = \alpha X''(s,t) - \beta X''''(s,t) + V \qquad (8)$$

Where V is the external force filed and which is independent of t. The solution of the above equation gives a GVF snake. If we look at the traditional external force filed of snake, the only useful forces are the ones near the edges. The rest of the image normally has very little variation in gradient and hence it is ignored by snake deformation. Therefore, if we can find an algorithm to further extend the gradient force near the edges into the rest of the image, we could increase snake's capture range and have a better deformation at concaved edges. The algorithm in [10] goes through a computational diffusion process. The concept is to create a new vector field called gradient vector field from an image data. This force is located in a homogeneous region. Due to a diffusion process a force is assigned which points towards the edges of the objects. Now, the edge map $f(x,y)$ derived from the image $I(x,y)$ has the property that it is closest to the image boundaries. So for $i = 1$ and 2, $f(x,y) = -E^i{}_{ext}(x,y)$. The gradient vector force field has been defined in [10] as $V(x,y) = [u(x,y), v(x,y)]$, which minimizes the energy function

$$\varepsilon = \iint \mu \left(u_x^2 + u_y^2 + v_x^2 + v_y^2 \right) + |\nabla f|^2 |V - \nabla f|^2 \, dxdy \qquad (9)$$

The parameter μ is a regularization parameter governing the tradeoff between the first term and the second term in the integrand. This parameter should be set according to the amount of noise present in the image (more noise, increase μ). In fact, if there is a lot of noise in the image, a large μ can not restrain noise effectively, on the contrary, it would often lead to slow and wrong snake deformation. Hence, noise must still be removed by smoothing.

Computing the GVF field using variations of calculus in [2], we get the following Euler equations:

$$\mu \nabla^2 u - (u - f_x)(f_x^2 + f_y^2) = 0 \qquad (10)$$
$$\mu \nabla^2 v - (v - f_y)(f_x^2 + f_y^2) = 0$$

Where ∇^2 is the laplacian operator. GVF is then generalized to three dimensions with u and v as functions of time and GVF deformable surface is implemented.

$$u_t(x,y,t) = \mu\nabla^2 u(x,y,t) - (u(x,y,t) - f_x(x,y)) \cdot (f_x(x,y)^2 + f_y(x,y)^2) \quad (11)$$
$$v_t(x,y,t) = \mu\nabla^2 v(x,y,t) - (v(x,y,t) - f_y(x,y)) \cdot (f_x(x,y)^2 + f_y(x,y)^2)$$

The steady-state solution of the linear parabolic equations is the solution of equation (10). These equations are decoupled and hence can be solved as the separate scalar partial differential equations in u and v. The above equations are known as generalized diffusion equations and are from the description of desirable properties of external fields for active contours.

Before computing GVF, the edge map function must be first calculated. $f(x,y) = |\nabla(G_\sigma(x,y) * I(x,y))|^2$ can be used in case of noisy images. Any noise removal algorithm like median filtering morphological filtering and anisotropic diffusion can be used. However, if desired edges are weak in the noisy image, edges are usually destroyed after running noise removal algorithm. Then, we can not get an accurate result with snake even GVF snake.

3 Multiscale Gradient Map with Embedded Edge Confidence

The idea from [11] is illustrated in Fig.1. Assume that the two differentiation masks employed by the gradient operator are defined in a $n \times n$ window. These masks, together with the data in the window, can be represented as three vectors in R^{n^2}. The two vectors corresponding to the masks define the gradient subspace (a hyperplane), while the data is an arbitrary vector in R^{n^2}.

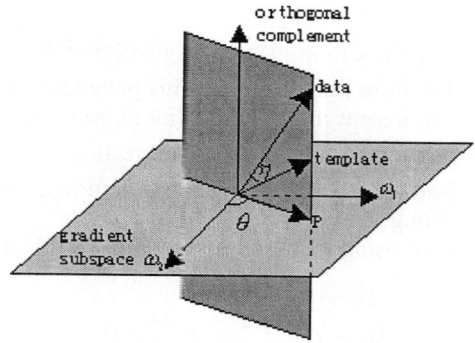

Fig. 1. The principle gradient and embedded edge confidence generation

Computation of the gradient vector is equivalent to projecting the data into the subspace with its orientation θ being the angle between the projected data and one of the mask vectors. Note that only the part of the data in the gradient subspace is employed in computing the gradient vector.

The parameter θ can be used to generate an ideal edge prototype, i.e., a unit step-edge passing through the center of the $n \times n$ window and oriented at θ. The value of a pixel of the prototype is obtained by integrating across its crosssection. The edge prototype is also a vector in R^{n^2} and in general will not be located in the gradient subspace, though, by definition must be in the plane of the projection and the data. The prototype is the template of the normalized pattern which would be present in the optimal case. Thus, EEC η, the cosine of the angle between the data and the template, measures the confidence in the presence of an edge obeying the assumed model. The critical observation is that η is computed in R^{n^2}, thus includes new information from the $(n^2 - 2)$-dimensional orthogonal complement of the gradient subspace. Therefore, η is a measure independent of the gradient magnitude.

Assume the employed $n \times n$ gradient operator are W^T (x-axis direction) and W (y-axis direction) and corresponding $n \times n$ sampling data in the image is A, we can obtain three vectors $\omega 1 = \text{vec}[W]$, $\omega 2 = \text{vec}[W^T]$ and $a = \text{vec}[A]$ by stacking up the columns of the corresponding matrices. We normalize the vector a to a unit vector a_{norm}. Therefore, the gradient magnitude g of point at center of A and the corresponding θ are:

$$g = \left[(a^T \cdot \omega 1)^2 + (a^T \cdot \omega 2)^2 \right]^{\frac{1}{2}} \quad (12)$$

$$\theta = \tan^{-1}\left(\frac{a^T \cdot \omega 1}{a^T \cdot \omega 2} \right)$$

The employed edge model A_{ref} ($n \times n$ matrix) is the traditional ideal step-edge passing through the center of the neighborhood and oriented at $-180^0 \leq \theta_e < 180^0$. And $\theta_e = \theta - 90^0$. The value of a pixel is computed by integrating across its unit area cross-section and, thus, the shape of the transition region depends on θ_e. The model $t = \text{vec}[A_{ref}]$ is normalized having zero-mean and Frobenius norm one. For computational reason, we can use a look-up table for the templates. Then, EEC η can be expressed as

$$\eta = \left| a_{norm}^T \cdot t \right| \quad (13)$$

The mask W obtained from the outer product of two one-dimensional sequences $s(i), d(j), (i, j = -\frac{n-1}{2}, \ldots 0, \ldots, \frac{n-1}{2})$ can be written as

$$W = s \cdot d^T \quad (14)$$

and is rank-one matrices since all the columns are scaled versions of the same vector s. See [12] for a more detailed discussion of the definition of s and d.

Then, we can get new gradient map G_c with EEC at different scales by using confidence η as weighting coefficient of corresponding original gradient magnitude. The new gradient magnitude g_c is

$$g_c = \eta \cdot g \tag{15}$$

New gradient map can preserve gradient magnitudes of real edges and relatively decrease gradient magnitudes from noise.

4 The Synergism of the Both Methods

From the definition of G_c, we can reach a conclusion that if the edge map is constructed with G_c as initialization of GVF field, the edges information will be well preserved with noise being restrained effectively and an excellent result will be achieved. The edge map $f(x, y)$ can be calculated as

$$f(x, y) = |G_c|^2 \tag{16}$$

The size of the masks employed by the gradient operator can decided depending on the quality of image. Generally speaking, the size of the masks should increase with the increase of noise.

5 Experimental Results and Discussions

A series of artificial and medical images have been used for the experiments. GVF snake using traditional edge map was compared with GVF snake with EEC. Two examples are respectively showed in Fig.2 and Fig.3. We used $\alpha=0.5$, $\beta=0$ and $\mu=0.2$ for the both methods and $s(i) = h_K(i;0,0), d(j) = h_K(i;1,1)$ (see [12]).

A sequence of GVF snakes (plotted in a shade of gray) and the GVF snake result (plotted in white) are respectively showed in (b) and (c) of Fig.2 and Fig.3. Edge map $|\nabla(G_\sigma * I)|^2$ has been used for GVF snake, however we could not obtain good result no matter what value σ was, because with little σ, noise couldn't be removed and the boundaries would become blurry even destroyed with the increase of σ. However, GVF snake with EEC can get ideal results for edge map with EEC can effectively preserve edge information and simultaneously get rid of noise. Therefore, the results from GVF snake with EEC are better than those from GVF snake with edge map $|\nabla(G_\sigma * I)|^2$. In addition, it's doubtless that the capture range of GVF snake with EEC is larger than that of traditional GVF snake when noisy images are processed.

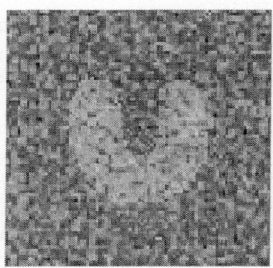 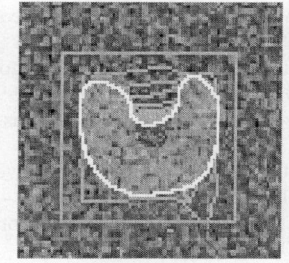 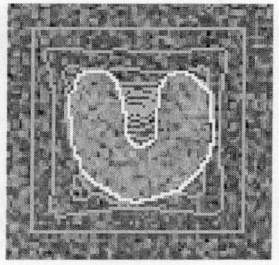

Fig. 2. (a) A noisy synthetic 88×88 -pixel image of a U-shaped object; (b) Convergence of the GVF snake with edge map $|\nabla(G_\sigma * I)|^2$ (σ=2.5); (c) Convergence of the GVF snake with EEC (template window size is 9×9)

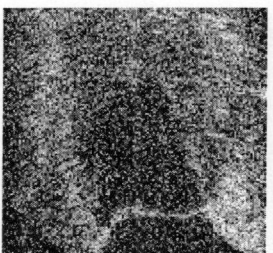 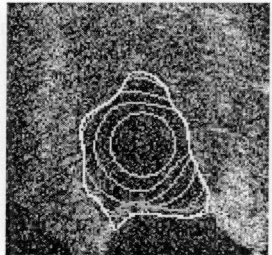 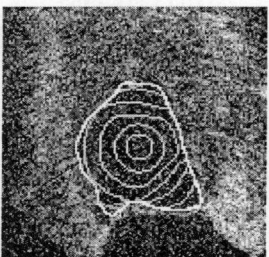

Fig. 3. (a) A noisy 130×130 -pixel ultrasonic image of the left ventricle of a human heart; (b) Convergence of the GVF snake with edge map $|\nabla(G_\sigma * I)|^2$ (σ=2.5); (c) Convergence of the GVF snake with EEC (template window size is 11×11)

In summary, ideal results can be obtained with both GVF snake and GVF snake with EEC when the images of high quality are processed. However, as edge map constructed with EEC can effectively preserve edges information and even weak ones, as well as decrease the influence of noise without smoothing, GVF snake with EEC is more robust when noisy images are being processed. There is still a limitation that we can't obtain accurate result when the shape of edges are zigzag in noisy images, because the more noise there is, the larger template window we will need for computation of EEC, however, in this complicated case, an enlarged template window which is originally a simple and idealized edge prototype will lose edge information. Of course, this limitation exists likewise in GVF snake.

References

1. Kass, M., Witkin, A., Terzopoulos, D.: Snakes: Active contour models. Int. J. Comput. Vis.1(1987) 321–331
2. Courant, R., Hilbert, D.: Methods of Mathematical Physics. New York: Interscience. 1 (1953)
3. Malladi, R., Sethian, J. A., Vemuri, B. C.: Shape modeling with front propagation: A level set approach. IEEE Trans. PAMI. 17 (1995) 158–175

4. Caselles, V., Kimmel, R., Sapiro, G.: Geodesic active contours. Proc. 5th Int. Conf. Computer Vision. (1995) 694–699
5. Leroy, B., Herlin, I., Cohen, L. D.: Multi-resolution algorithms for active contour models. 12th Int. Conf. Analysis and Optimization of System. (1996) 58–65
6. Cohen, L. D.: On active contour models and balloons. CVGIP: Image Understand. 53 (1991) 211–218
7. Cohen, L.D., Cohen, I.: Finite-element methods for active contour models and balloons for 2-D and 3-D images. IEEE Trans. PAMI. 15(1993) 1131–1147
8. Davatzikos, C., Prince, J. L.: An active contour model for mapping the cortex. IEEE Trans. Med. Imag. 14 (1995) 65–80
9. Davatzikos, C., Prince, J. L.: Convexity analysis of active contour models. Proc. Conf. Information Science and Systems. (1994) 581–587
10. Xu, C., Prince, J.L.: Snakes, Shapes and gradient vector flow. IEEE Trans. Image Processing. 7 (1998) 359-369
11. Meer, P., Georgescu, B.: Edge detection with embedded confidence. IEEE Trans. PAMI. 23 (2001) 1351-1365
12. Meer, P., Weiss, I.: Smoothed differentiation filters for images. J. Visual Comm. and Image Representation. (1992) 58-72

Object Boundary Edge Selection for Human Body Tracking Using Level-of-Detail Canny Edges

Tae-Yong Kim[1], Jihun Park[2], and Seong-Whan Lee[1]

[1] Department of Computer Science and Engineering
Korea University, Seoul, Korea
{tykim,swlee}@image.korea.ac.kr
[2] Department of Computer Engineering
Hongik University, Seoul, Korea
jhpark@hongik.ac.kr

Abstract. We propose a method for an accurate subject tracking by selecting only tracked subject boundary edges in a video stream with changing background and a moving camera. Our boundary edge selection is done in two steps; 1) remove background edges using an edge motion, 2) from the output of the previous step, select boundary edges using a normal direction derivative of the tracked contour. Our accurate tracking is based on reducing affects from irrelevant edges by selecting boundary edge pixels only. In order to remove background edges using the edge motion, we compute tracked subject motion and edge motions. The edges with different motion direction than the subject motion are removed. In selecting boundary edges using the contour normal direction, we compute image gradient values on every edge pixels, and select edge pixels with large gradient values. We use multi-level Canny edge maps to get proper details of a scene. Multi-level edge maps allow us robust tracking even though the tracked object boundary is not clear, because we can adjust the detail level of an edge map for the scene. The computed contour is improved by checking against a *strong (simple)* Canny edge map and hiring *strong* Canny edge pixels around the computed contour using Dijkstra's minimum cost routing. Our experimental results show that our tracking approach is robust enough to handle a complex-textured scene.

1   Introduction and Related Works

Tracking moving objects (subjects) is a hot issue because of a wide variety of applications in computer vision such as video coding, video surveillance, augmented reality, and robotics. This paper addresses the problem of selecting boundary edges for robust contour tracking in a single video stream.

We can classify the methods of representing an object contour into two categories depending on the method used; parameterized contour or nonparameterized contour. In tracking a parameterized contour, an object contour representing the tracked subject is represented by using parameters. These methods use

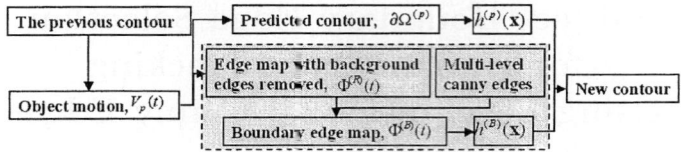

Fig. 1. Overview of our tracking method.

Snake models[1] in general; Kalman Snake[2] and Adaptive Motion Snake[3] are popular Snake models. In the method of tracking a nonparameterized contour, an object contour as an object border is represented. The contour created by these algorithms is represented as a set of pixels. Paragios's algorithm[4] and Nguyen's algorithm[5] are popular in these approaches.

In Nguyen's algorithm[5], a watershed line that was determined by using the watershed segmentation[6] and the watershed line smoothing energy[7,5] becomes the new contour of a tracked object. Nguyen's approach removed background edges by using object motion. But Nguyen's approach left many irrelevant edges that prohibit accurate contour tracking. To overcome this problem, this paper proposes the method of selecting only the edges in the boundary of the tracked object. In order to increase object contour tracking accuracy, we remove background edges using edge motions. The background edges whose motion directions are different from that of the tracked subject are removed. This is applied to a highly textured scene. After background edge removal, we compute average intensity gradient in the normal direction of the previous frame contour, and consider only the edges with high gradient values as the boundary edges of the tracked object. We use multi-level Canny edges to get a proper detail of a scene. Thus, we can obtain robust contour tracking results even though an object boundary is not clear.

The computed contour of a watershed line is checked against a *strong* Canny edges around the contour. We mean strong that the generated Canny edge map is simple and does not include highly textured edges. This edge map can be generated by adjusting control parameters of a Canny edge generator. We run a final routing using the computed contour pixels and *strong* Canny edge pixels. The resulting minimum cost contour becomes the final contour of the current image frame.

2 Efficient Contour Tracking

Nguyen[5] proposed a method for tracking a nonparameterized object contour in a single video stream. In this algorithm, a new tracked contour was determined by a watershed algorithm[6] with a watershed line smoothing energy[7,5] added in the energy minimization function. The contour is the border between a tracked object and background areas.

In the step of new contour detection, Nguyen used two edge indicator functions, $h^{(p)}(\mathbf{x})$ and $h^{(I)}(\mathbf{x})$, for deciding a new contour. $h^{(p)}(\mathbf{x})$ is an edge indicator function from the predicted contour, $\partial \Omega^{(p)}$, and $h^{(I)}(\mathbf{x})$ is an edge indicator function computed from the edge map resulting after background edges are removed by object motion vector. We create a boundary edge map, $\Phi^{(B)}(t)$, from $\Phi^{(R)}(t)$ and create $h^{(B)}(\mathbf{x})$ from $\Phi^{(B)}(t)$. We use two edge indicator functions, $h^{(p)}(\mathbf{x})$ and $h^{(B)}(\mathbf{x})$, for deciding a new contour. Figure 1 shows an overview of our tracking method.

3 Boundary Edge Selection

This section explains the method of selecting only boundary edges, $\Theta^{(B)}(t)$, for improving the accuracy of object contour tracking. We obtain $\Phi^{(B)}(t)$ from the edge map, $\Phi^{(R)}(t)$, resulting after background edges are removed by edge motion.

3.1 Background Edge Removal

Background Edge Removal Using Object Motion. Nguyen[5] removed background edges by using object motion vector, $V_p(t)$. But, Nguyen's approach left many irrelevant edges in the following cases: 1) an edge segment that has the same direction as $V_p(t)$ and its length exceeding the magnitude of $V_p(t)$, 2) a highly textured background, and 3) inner edges of a tracked object. These irrelevant edges prohibit accurate contour tracking.

Background Edge Removal Using Edge Motion. We remove background edges using an edge motion. We compute a tracked subject motion and background edge motions. The background edges whose motion directions are different from that of the tracked subject are removed. Edge motion is computed using optical flow[8]. We use Canny edge generator for edge generation, and compute optical flow from the edge map. The tracked subject motion vector is computed to be $V_p(t)$, and each edge pixel motion vector computed is tested against $V_p(t)$. If the difference between two vectors are bigger than a specified constant T_e, we consider it to be a background edge pixel. Let $\Phi^{(I)}(t)$ be the edge map detected at the current frame. Vector O_{Edge} is the computed optical flow of an edge pixel in $\Phi^{(I)}(t)$. The dominant translation vector $V_p(t)$ is estimated by

$$V_{(p)}(t) = \arg\min_{V \in \Psi} \sum_{p \in \Omega(t-1)} [I(p, t-1) - I(p+V, t)]^2 \quad (1)$$

where Ψ is the velocity space and $\Omega(t-1)$ is pixels that belong to an object area in frame (t-1).

$$\Phi_{background}(t) = \{Edge \in \Phi^{(I)}(t) \mid \|V_p(t) - O_{Edge}\| > T_e\} \quad (2)$$

$\Phi^{(R)}(t)$ is an edge of $\Phi^{(I)}(t)$ subtracted by $\Phi_{background}(t)$, where $\Phi_{background}(t)$ is a background edge map. The background edge removal method using edge motion removes edges with different motion than the tracked subject, and this method is independent of the degree of complexity in the edge map, while accurately removing all background edge pixels with different motion. The edge map without background edges is used in computing the boundary edge selection.

3.2 Calculating an Image Gradient in a Contour Normal Direction

In this paper, we present a novel method of removing noisy edges by computing an image gradient using the previous frame contour. We compute an image intensity gradient in the normal direction of the contour.

Suppose a contour is parametrically represented as $r(s) = \begin{pmatrix} x(s) \\ y(s) \end{pmatrix}$. The tangent direction of $r(s)$ is $r'(s)$ as presented in Figure 2(a). The orthogonal direction of $r'(s)$ is $r'_\perp(s)$. We consider only the image gradients in the direction of $r'_\perp(s)$. $I(m,n)$ is an image intensity function.

$$D(r(s)) = \frac{1}{\sqrt{\left(\frac{dx(s)}{ds}\right)^2 + \left(\frac{dy(s)}{ds}\right)^2}} \left(\frac{\partial I}{\partial n}\frac{dx(s)}{ds} - \frac{\partial I}{\partial m}\frac{dy(s)}{ds}\right) \qquad (3)$$

By extending equation (3), we compute an average color gradient, $\widehat{D}(r(s_i))$, along the normal direction at a pixel point $r(s_i)$ on the contour. $r(s_i)$ is one of a pixel point of $r(s)$. The computational process of $\widehat{D}(r(s_i))$ is as follows: (i) Make an ellipse with two major axes of $r'_\perp(s)$ and $r'(s)$ directions. Its size is adjusted properly. (ii) Separate the pixels inside the ellipse into two parts using a line along the $r'(s)$ direction in Figure 2(a). (iii) Calculate the mean intensity values of the pixels in two separate areas that were separated by $r(s)$ in Figure 2(a). The result of the computation is $\widehat{D}(r(s_i))$.

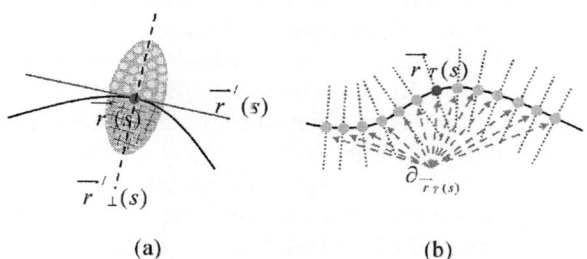

Fig. 2. (a) A normal direction of the parametric contour $r(s)$, and an ellipse with two inside areas separated by a contour for calculating $\widehat{D}$. (b) $\partial_{r_T(s_i)}$ and the contour normal directions at the pixels that belong to $\partial_{r_T(s_i)}$ for calculating $\widehat{TD}_i(r_T(s_i))$.

3.3 Advantages of Using a Normal Direction of a Contour

Our gradient values are not affected by intensity changes different from the normal direction of the contour because we compute the gradient only in the normal direction of the contour. This enables us to get high gradient values around the tracked object boundary even in a complex scene.

Figure 3 shows that we can get large gradient values at a real object boundary if we compute a gradient in the normal direction of the boundary. Then we add the concept of considering a textured area divided by the boundary contour. The concept of using average intensity values of an image area is blurring small changes or edges because of noises or small texture patterns.

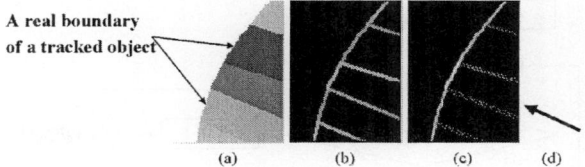

Fig. 3. (a) An example of image intensity change around a tracked subject. (b) An image gradient computed without considering any special direction. (c) An image gradient computed in the normal direction to the actual boundary of a tracked object. (d) The direction considered as the normal direction.

Fig. 4. Results of Canny edge detections in three different levels.

3.4 Boundary Edge Pixel Selection

Boundary edge pixels are selected after background edge removal by using edge motion. As explained in Section 3.1, $\Phi^{(R)}(t)$ is the edge map resulting after background edges are removed by edge motion. $r(s)$ is a parametric representation of a predicted contour, $\partial\Omega^{(p)}$, and the total number of pixels on $\partial\Omega^{(p)}$ is N. $r(s_i)$ is i-th pixel of $\partial\Omega^{(p)}$. Boundary edge pixel selection process is done along $\partial\Omega^{(p)}$. We process the selection on every pixel point, $r(s_i)$, where i=1,...,N, on $\partial\Omega^{(p)}$. We consider $\Phi_i^{(R)}(t)$, which is a part of the edge map, $\Phi^{(R)}(t)$, along $\partial\Omega^{(p)}$. $\Phi_i^{(R)}(t)$ has edges in a circular area centered at $r(s_i)$ with radius c_Φ, a specified constant. $r_T(s_i)$ is one of edge pixels in $\Phi_i^{(R)}(t)$. $r_T(s_i)$ can be considered to be one of a pixel point of $r_T(s)$, a parametric curve translated from $r(s)$ by $(r_T(s_i) - r(s_i))$. $\partial\Omega_T^{(p)}$ is a contour translated from $\partial\Omega^{(p)}$ by $(r_T(s_i) - r(s_i))$. The left side of Figure 6 shows $\partial\Omega^{(p)}$ and noisy edge pixels, $\Phi^{(R)}(t)$. The right side of Figure 6 shows a close up of a circular area of radius c_Φ centered at $r(s_i)$. This circular edge map is denoted as $\Phi_i^{(R)}(t)$. We compute a gradient of a normal direction of $\partial\Omega_T^{(p)}$ at $r_T(s_i)$ of pixel point of every edge on $\Phi_i^{(R)}(t)$. To detect k possible pixels for boundary edges, we compute a gradient of a normal direction of $\partial\Omega_T^{(p)}$ at every edge pixel point of $\Phi_i^{(R)}(t)$, where k is a specified constant. $\partial_{r_T(s_i)}$ is a set of the pixels of $r_T(s_i)$ on $\partial\Omega_T^{(p)}$ in the circular area of radius c_∂ centered at $r_T(s_i)$. $\widehat{TD}_i(r_T(s_i))$ is the sum of $\widehat{D}$s computed along the pixels of $\partial_{r_T(s_i)}$ with reference at $r_T(s_i)$. Figure 2 (b) shows $\partial_{r_T(s_i)}$ and the contour normal directions at the pixels that belong to $\partial_{r_T(s_i)}$ for calculating $\widehat{TD}_i(r_T(s_i))$.

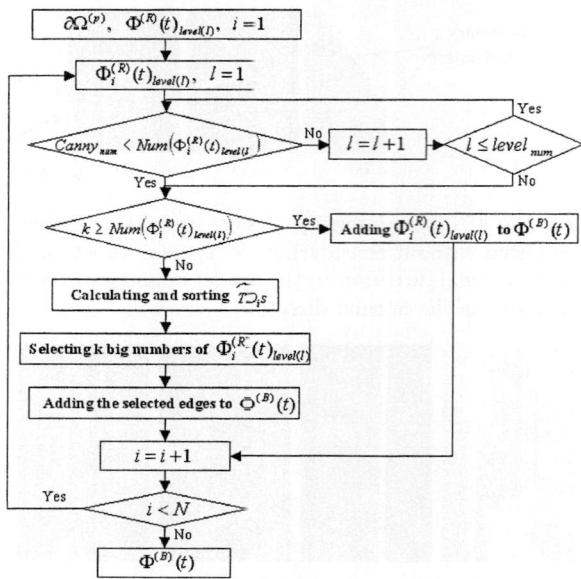

Fig. 5. The process of boundary edge selection.

We use the biggest $\widehat{TD}_i$s with large values in selecting boundary edges.

$$\widehat{TD}_i(r_T(s_i)) = \sum_{\partial r_T(s_i)} (\widehat{D}_i(r_T(s_i))) \qquad (4)$$

Figure 5 shows the process of selecting pixels for boundary edges. For Canny edge maps generated with lower image intensity gradient values, we compute Canny edge map and $\Phi_i^{(R)}(t)$ in each level. Multi-level Canny edges are results of Canny edge detection depending on the given thresholds. Figure 4 shows results of Canny edge detections in three different levels given a single image. We control the level of detail of a scene using multi-level Canny edge maps. Detailed Canny edge map of a scene confuses our tracking, and very simple edge map misses tracking information. $\Phi_i^{(R)}(t)_{level(l)}$ is $\Phi_i^{(R)}(t)$ calculated in level l. $\Phi_i^{(R)}(t)_{level(l)}$ has edges in a circular area centered at $r(s_i)$ with radius c_Φ in level l. At the i-th computation loop, if the number of $Num(\Phi_i^{(R)}(t))_{level(l)}$ is smaller than $Canny_{num}$, we use $\Phi_i^{(R)}(t)_{level(l)}$ in one step lower level, where $Canny_{num}$ is a specified constant. In other words, we use detailed Canny edge result if object boundary is not clear. Therefore we can obtain robust tracking results although object boundary is not clear. $Num(\Phi_i^{(R)}(t)_{level(l)})$ is the number of edge pixels in $\Phi_i^{(R)}(t)_{level(l)}$. At the i-th computation loop, we select k edge pixels with large $\widehat{TD}_i$ values. $level_{num}$ is the number of level of Canny edges computed.

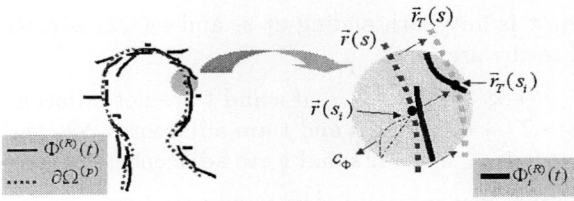

Fig. 6. A predicted contour and image operations along the contour. The operation is done on every edge pixel in a circular area.

4 Contour Tracking with Selected Boundary Edges

An overview of our tracking process is shown in Figure 1. User inputs an initial contour of a tracked object at the first frame.

In the steps of contour detection, using the concept of topographical distance, the watershed segmentation is done by a minimization[7, 5]. For this algorithm, we use two edge indicator functions, $h^{(B)}(\mathbf{x})$ and $h^{(p)}(\mathbf{x})$. Two edge indicator functions, $h^{(B)}(\mathbf{x})$ and $h^{(p)}(\mathbf{x})$, are derived from $\Theta_i^{(B)}(t)$ and $\partial \Omega^{(p)}$, respectively. An algorithm for edge indicator function is given in Nguyen's paper[5]. The boundary edge map, $\Theta_i^{(B)}(t)$, is obtained by an algorithm proposed in this paper. $\partial \Omega^{(p)}$ is obtained by translating $\partial \Omega(t-1)$ by $V_p(t)$[5]. A watershed line extracted using two edge indicator functions, $h^{(B)}(\mathbf{x})$ and $h^{(p)}(\mathbf{x})$, becomes a new contour at the current frame.

5 Final Routing with Strong Canny Edges

A *strong* Canny edge map has relatively small number of pixels in the edge map. The edge map is made using only large gradient value of the intensity changes in a scene. We do a final routing on strong Canny edges as well as the computed contour of watershed line. An union of edge map and the computed contour, denoted as I, is a pair (Γ, Υ) consisting of finite set Γ of pixels, and a mapping Υ that assigns to each pixel t in Γ a value $\Upsilon(t)$, value one or value two. Value one is for strong Canny edge pixels, and value two is for the computed contour pixels. An adjacency relation A is an irreflexive binary relation between pixels of Γ. I can be interpreted as a directed graph whose nodes are the pixels and whose arcs are the pixel pairs in A. sAt depends only on the four-connected neighbor of the pixels in I, and $(s,t) \in \Gamma \times \Upsilon$. A path is a sequence of pixels $\pi = <t_1, t_2, \cdots, t_k>$, where $(t_i, t_{i+1}) \in A$ for $1 \leq i \leq k-1$. t_1 is the origin, and t_k is the destination of the path. We assume given a function f that assigns to each path π a path cost $f(\pi)$, in some totally ordered set of cost values. The set of cost values contain a maximum element denoted by $+\infty$. The additive cost function satisfies

$$f_{sum}(\pi \cdot <s,t>) = f_{sum}(\pi) + w(s,t)$$

where $(s,t) \in A$, π is any path ending at s, and $w(s,t)$ is a fixed nonnegative weight assigned to the arc (s,t).

$$w(s,t) = \begin{cases} +\infty & \text{if s and t are not adjacent pixels} \\ \Upsilon(s) * \Upsilon(t) * \Upsilon(t) & \text{if s and t are adjacent pixels and } \Upsilon(s) \neq \Upsilon(t) \\ 1 & \text{if s and t are adjacent pixels and } \Upsilon(s) = \Upsilon(t) \end{cases}$$

This weight function guarantees to take stronger Canny edges in the optimum path routing. The routing is done using Dijkstra's minimum cost routing algorithm. The result of the routing becomes our final contour of a tracked image. Figure 7(a) is the computed contour of a watershed line, and this is used as an input to the final routing. The resulting final contour is shown in Figure 7(b).

(a) Computation result of a watershed line (b) Fixed contour using strong Canny edges

Fig. 7. Final contour fixed using strong Canny edges.

6 Experimental Results

We have experimented with easily available video sequences generated with a home camcorder, Sony DCR-PC3. Figure 8 shows the background edges removed by Nguyen's approach[5], and boundary edges selected by our approach. Figure 9 shows contour tracking results of a movie clip. We selected the boundary edges with k=2. We use $Canny_{num}=10$, $level_{num}=3$, $c_\partial=20$ and $c_\Phi=12$ in Figure 8 and Figure 9.

Figure 9 shows a man walking a subway hall. The hall tiles as well as the man's cross stripe shirt generate many complicated Canny edges. The contour shape changes as the man with a cross stripe shirt rotates from facing the front to the back. The size of the tracked subject changes as the man comes closer to a camera and then moves away from it. There are many edge pixels in the background and the subject has many edges inside the tracked contour. There are other people moving in different directions in the background. Even under this complex circumstance, our boundary edge-based tracking was successful. Walking people crossing our subject did not affect our tracking performance.

7 Conclusion

In this paper, we proposed a novel method of improving accuracy in tracking a highly textured object. We select only the edges around the tracked object boundary to overcome the noisy edge problem because of a complex scene.

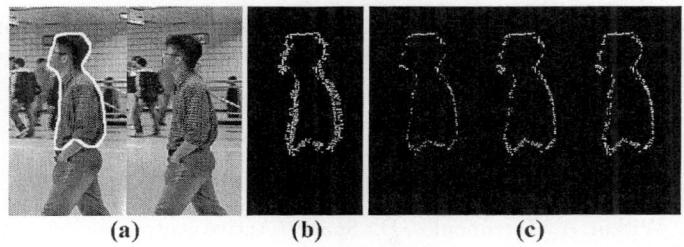

Fig. 8. (a) Two consecutive frames and a contour determined at the previous frame(marked by a white outline). (b) An output of background edge removal by Nguyen's approach (c) Outputs of boundary edge selections with k = 1, 3, 5.

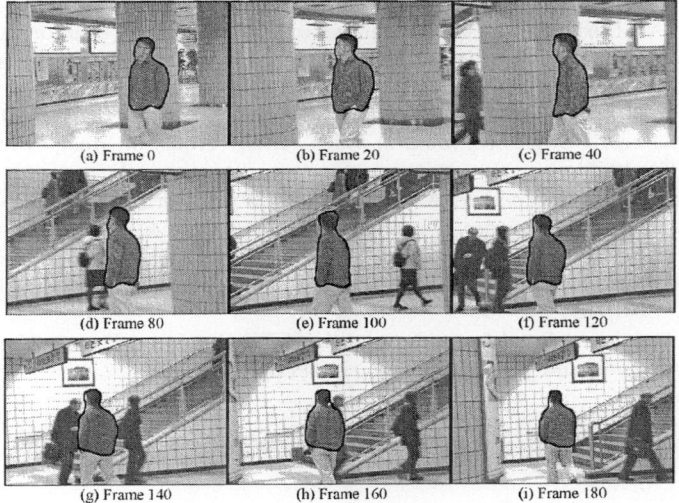

Fig. 9. Tracking results(marked by a black outline).

In order to remove background edges using the edge motion, we compute tracked subject motion and edge motions. The edges with different motion direction than the subject motion are removed. Then, we compute image intensity gradient in the normal direction of the previous frame contour to remove redundant edges from the edge map resulting after background edges are removed by edge motion. We can obtain robust tracking results, even though object boundary is not clear, by using multi-level Canny edges. By considering only the normal direction of a contour, we ignore edges with different slope than that of the subject boundary. The gradient computation in average intensity change involves a concept of considering change of a textured area divided by a contour. By using these methods, our computation is not bothered by noisy edges or small cross stripe textures, resulting in a robust tracking. By using our strong Canny edge based final routing, we can hire the edge pixels with large intensity changes as the tracked subject boundary. Our experimental results show that our tracking approach is reliable enough to handle a sudden change of the tracked subject shape in a complex scene[1].

References

1. Kass, M., Witkin, A., Terzopoulos, D.: Snakes: Active contour models. International Journal of Computer Vision **1** (1987) 321–331
2. Peterfreund, N.: Robust tracking of position and velocity with kalman snakes. IEEE Trans. on Pattern Analysis and Machine Intelligence **21** (1999) 564–569
3. Fu, Y., Erdem, A.T., Tekalp, A.M : Tracking visible boundary of objects using occlusion adaptive motion snake. IEEE Trans. on Image Processing **9** (2000) 2051–2060
4. Paragios, N., Deriche, R.: Geodesic active contours and level sets for the detection and tracking of moving objects. IEEE Trans. on Pattern Analysis and Machine Intelligence **22** (2000) 266–280
5. Nguyen, H.T., Worring, M., van den Boomgaard, R., Smeulders, A.W.M.: Tracking nonparameterized object contours in video. IEEE Trans. on Image Processing **11** (2002) 1081–1091
6. Roerdink, J.B.T.M., Meijster, A.: The watershed transform: Definition, algorithms and parallelization strategies. Fundamenta Informaticae **41** (2000) 187–228
7. Nguyen, H.T., Worring, M., van den Boomgaard, R.: Watersnakes: energy-driven watershed segmentation. IEEE Trans. on Pattern Analysis and Machine Intelligence **25** (2003) 330–342
8. Shi, J., Tomasi, C.: Good features to track. IEEE Computer Society Conference on Computer Vision and Pattern Recognition (1994) 593–600

---

[1] This work was partially supported by 2004 Hongik University Research Fund.

Unsupervised Multiscale Image Segmentation Using Wavelet Domain Hidden Markov Tree

Xu Qing, Yang Jie, and Ding Siyi

Inst. of Image Processing & Pattern Recognition, Shanghai Jiao tong Univ. Shanghai
Box251, 1954 Huashan Road, Shanghai, P.R.China
qingxu8@hotmail.com

Abstract. In this paper, we have improved the supervised multi-scale texture segmentation (HMTseg), where wavelet domain hidden Markov model is applied to capture the texture feature and a contextual model is employed to fuse multi-scale segmentation. In order to extend supervised HMTseg to an unsupervised one, we perform a hierarchical clustering in the blocks on the starting scale. The dissimilarity between sub-mages is measured by the Kullback-Leibler distance (KLD) between corresponding WD HMT models. Experiments show that the performance of our proposed method is promising and needs less prior information on textures present in the given images.

Keywords: multiscale texture segmentation, wavelet domain hidden Markov model, hierarchical clustering.

Content Areas: Bayesian network; Image processing

1 Introduction

Segmentation of texture images is a difficult low level vision problem with important applications in vision-guided autonomous robotics, product quality inspection, medical diagnosis, content-based image retrieval and in the analysis of remotely sensed images. The goal of texture segmentation is to identify homogenous regions, where distinct texture exists. The key step in texture segmentation can be done by testing the homogeneousness in term of the texture feature. So texture characterization plays an important role in the segmentation process. In fact, many approaches in extracting texture features have been proposed. For example, features based on statistical image models [8, 9], Markov random field models [10, 11] and wavelet transform [12] have been suggested for texture segmentation. In this paper, wavelet-domain (WD) hidden Markov model (HMM), in particular, the hidden Markov tree (HMT) model has been adopted to characterize the feature of textures in our proposed segmentation algorithm.

Recently, M.S.Crouse (1998) [1] has proposed wavelet domain hidden Markov tree (WD HMT). It provides an efficient way to model the texture [2, 3], because it effectively characterizes the joint statistics of the wavelet transforms by capturing the inter-scale dependences of the wavelet coefficients. Embedded in a multi-scale Bayesian segmentation framework, wavelet domain hidden Markov tree (WD HMT) has been applied to texture segmentation [4], called HMTseg This approach performed texture classification at a range of different scales using WD HMT and its fast training and likelihood computation algorithm. Then a Bayesian graph contextual model [5] is adopted to fuse these multi-scale classifications to gain a final segmentation. By concisely modeling and fusing the statistical behavior of textures at multiple scales, the HMTseg algorithm produces a robust and accurate segmentation of texture images. However, HMTseg is still a supervised method, since it needs homogenous training images for each texture in the image. It is inefficient to expect the training images to be manually provided in some practical application areas, in particular in content based image retrieval, where the segmentation is to be performed on several thousand images. On the other hand, there are already a large number of unsupervised algorithms in literature [6]. Most of them are a two step procedure: (1) a set of features are extracted from each texture; (2) then an unsupervised clustering algorithm is performed on the multi-dimensional feature space. However, none of them utilize the effective WD HMT model to extract feature of the texture. By combining this clustering-based segmentation and HMTseg, we proposed an unsupervised multi-scale segmentation using WD HMT, which assumes that types of textures present in the image are unknown in advance.

In this paper, our proposed algorithm first divides the given image into some sub-images, which are large enough to gain robust estimation of their models (WD HMT). Then WD HMT parameters are estimated from each sub-blocks using Expectation Maximum (EM) algorithm [1] and the dissimilarity between WD HMT models is measured by Kullback-Leibler distance [7]. After we have obtained the disparity between every pair of sub-images, hierarchical cluster analysis can be directly employed in the data set to group the sub-images to several homogenous regions. Thus, we gain a coarse segmentation and the WD HMT parameters are estimated again on each homogenous region. Finally, updated models are used to perform supervised segmentation, such as HMTseg.

This paper is organized as follows. First, we will review some previous work related to WD HMT in section2. Then, we propose our unsupervised algorithm in section 3, where HMTseg is used and hierarchical clustering is used to identify the training samples for unknown textures based on the Kullback-Leibler distance of WD HMT, so that the unsupervised segmentation problems can be converted into the supervised one. The simulation results and discussions are presented in section 4. Finally, conclusions are drawn in Section 5.

2 Related Works

2.1 Wavelet Domain Hidden Markov Tree Model

Crouse *et al.* [1] proposed a new framework for statistical signal processing based on wavelet domain hidden Markov models (WD-HMM). It provides an effective approach to model both the non-Gaussian statistics and the persistence property across scale of wavelet coefficients. The concept of WD HMM is briefly reviewed in this section.

First, due to Non-Gaussianity of the wavelet transform, a Gaussian mixture model (GMM) is employed to model the wavelet coefficients distribution density. In a 2D

HMT model (see Fig. 1.), denote $w^B_{j,i,k}$ to be the wavelet coefficient. In this presentation, B represents sub-band detail image ($B \in \{HH, HL, LH\}$). j indexes scale (1<j<J) –smaller j corresponds to higher resolution analysis. (i, k) is the spatial location of analysis. The wavelet coefficient $w^B_{j,i,k}$ is associated with a hidden state $S^B_{j,i,k}$, whose probability mass function can be expressed as, $P(S^B_{j,i,k} = m) = p^B_{j,i,k}(m)$ (m=0....M-1). Conditioning on its state $S^B_{j,i,k} = m$, $w^B_{j,i,k}$ follows a Gaussian distribution with zero mean and variance $S^B_{j,i,k}$. By increasing M and allowing nonzero means, we can approximate the real distributions arbitrarily close [1]. Furthermore, to obtain a robust estimation, the wavelet coefficients in the same scale are assumed to share the same statistics, which is called "tying" [1]. Therefore, we can parameterize the GMM of w^B_j by $\pi = \{p_s(m), \mu_m, \sigma_m^2 \mid m = 0......M-1\}$ and the overall probability density function of w^B_j is expressed as:

$$f_w(w) = \sum_{m=0}^{M-1} P_S(m) f_{W|S}(w \mid s = m), \qquad (1)$$

Where

$$f_{W|S}(w \mid s = m) = \frac{1}{\sqrt{2\pi\sigma_m^2}} \exp(-\frac{(w-\mu_m)^2}{2\sigma_m^2}) = g(w, \mu_m, \sigma_m^2), \qquad (2)$$

Second, to capture the persistence property of the wavelet transform, a wavelet-domain hidden Markov tree model (HMT) is developed in [1]. By connecting state variables vertically across scales, we obtain a graph with tree-structured dependencies between variable states. A state transition matrix for each link statistically quantifies the degree of persistence of small/large wavelet coefficients. Thus, the 2-D HMT (M=2) is parameterized by

$$\theta_{HMT} = \{P^B_J(m), \varepsilon^B_{j,j-1}(m,n), \sigma^2_{B,j,m} \mid B \in B; j = 1,......J; m = 0,1\}$$

Where $\varepsilon^B_{j,j-1}(m,n)$ is the transition probability of the Markov chain from scale j to scale (j-1) in sub-band B. Given W, θ_{HMT} can be estimated by the tree-structured EM training algorithm proposed in [1] which can maximize the HMT model likelihood $f(W \mid \theta_{HMT})$, and $f(W \mid \theta_{HMT})$ is defined as

$$f(W \mid \theta_{HMT}) = \sum_{B \in B} \sum_{k,j=0}^{N_J-1} \log(\sum_{m=0}^{1} f_m(T^B_{J,i,k} \mid \theta_{HMT}, m)) \qquad (3)$$

Where $T^B_{J,i,k}$ denotes the wavelet sub-tree rooted at $w^B_{J,i,k}$ and the three sub-bands are assumed to be independent. The $f(W \mid \theta_{HMT})$ can be computed using an Upward-Downward Algorithm.

The WD HMT has been successfully applied to texture classification [3]. Given the trained model parameter θ_{HMT} and the image data W, we can compute the model likelihood $f(W | \theta_{HMT})$ using equation (3). The $f(W | \theta_{HMT})$ measures how well the model fits the image data. Thus, the optimal classification becomes the maximum likelihood (ML) rule, which is to choose the class making the observed data most likely, i.e.

$$C_{ML} = \arg \max_{c \in \{1,......,N_c\}} f(W | \theta^c)$$

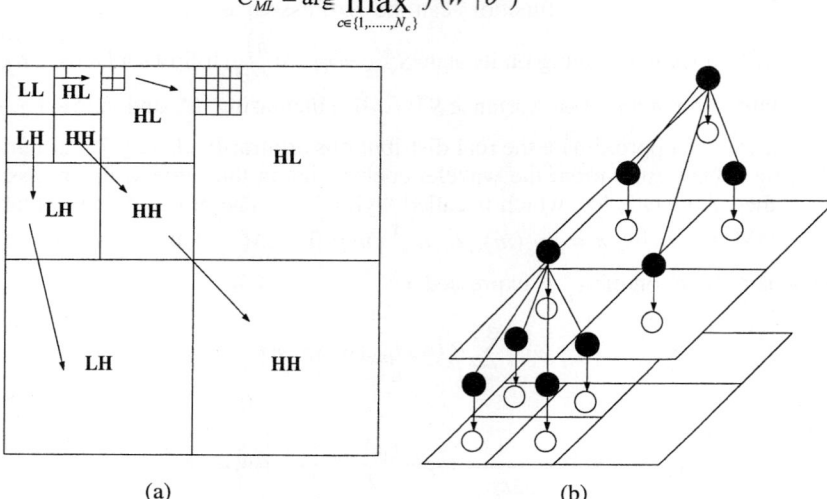

Fig. 1. (a) Spatial and frequency structure of 3-scale DWT (b) 2-D Hidden Markov Tree structure, where black node represents the hidden state and white node represents the wavelet coefficient decided by the hidden state and the line between black nodes capture the dependences across scales.

2.2 Multi-scale Segmentation Using Wavelet Domain Hidden Markov Tree

Bayesian approach provides a way to integrate both texture feature and prior knowledge about contextual properties of texture [4] [5], where maximum a posteriori (MAP) is usually involved. However, a drawback of these methods is that the high classification accuracy often requires high computation complexity [4]. Multi-scale image segmentation solves this problem by segmenting both large homogenous regions and detail boundary regions. It can improve the classification accuracy while retaining relatively low computation complexity. The two key ingredients of all multi-scale Bayesian segmentation algorithms are (1) the contextual model to capture dependencies of different scale features or classification labels and (2) the way to characterize the texture in each scale. In particular, a Bayesian segmentation algorithm, called HMTseg, was proposed in [4], which applies wavelet-based HMT to characterize texture multiscalely and uses a context vector to capture the dependencies of multi-scale class label.

Multi-scale segmentation framework obtains dyadic squares in different scales by recursively dividing the given image into four equal sub-images HMTseg captures the feature of each dyadic square by wavelet domain hidden Markov Tree model. Meanwhile, contextual information is described by a vector v^j, which is derived from a set of neighboring (3x3) dyadic squares. We denote a dyadic square and its class label respectively by $d_{i,k}^j$ and $c_{i,k}^j$. j indexes the scale. Each context vector $v_{i,k}^j$ contains two entries: the class label of the parent node and the dominant class label of the parent square and its eight neighbors. And given $v_{i,k}^j$, $d_{i,k}^j$ is independent with all other class label.

The HMTseg segmentation algorithm consists of three steps, including HMT training, multi-scale likelihood computation, and inter-scale fusion.

Step 1: wavelet domain HMT models are trained to characterize each different texture in the segmented image using homogenous training images.

Step 2: use the likelihood computation algorithm [1] to compute the likelihood of each dyadic image square at each different scale. This gives the conditional likelihoods $f(d_{i,k}^j \mid c_{i,k}^j)$ for each dyadic square.

Step 3: perform inter-scale fusion using the class label tree. First, choose a starting scale (j+1) such that we can gain a reliable raw segmentation c^{j+1} in that scale, which is performed by classifying each dyadic square using the conditional likelihood, computed in the step 2. Then, v^j is computed from the class labels of (j+1)th scale c^{j+1}. Moreover, EM algorithm is applied to estimate $p(c_{i,k}^j \mid v_{i,k}^j)$ by maximizing the likelihood of the image given the v^j. In this iterating process, each iteration updates the contextual posterior distribution $p(c_{i,k} \mid d_{i,k}, v_{i,k})$. When the iteration process converges, we determine the $c_{i,k}$, which maximizes the $p(c_{i,k} \mid d_{i,k}, v_{i,k})$. Then repeat this inter-scale fusion in (j-1)th scale based on v^{j-1}, which is computed from c^j. We continue this multi-scale fusion till the finest scale.

Note that we must provide training textures for the HMT training step, which makes HMTseg a supervised segmentation. That means we must have the prior texture type information for each texture present in given image before HMTseg is employed.

3 Unsupervised Multi-scale Texture Segmentation Using Wavelet Domain Hidden Markov Tree

An unsupervised segmentation suggests that there are no training textures available for identifying homogenous regions. Therefore, HMTseg can not be employed directly to obtain an unsupervised segmentation, since HMTseg needs the training data set to estimate the WD HMT parameters. In order to convert HMTseg to a self-supervised segmentation, a hierarchical clustering is performed on a starting scale with appropriate dissimilarity definition. The result clusters serve as the initial training data for HMTseg.

Assume that we know the number of different textures in given images; our proposed segmentation algorithm consists of 5 steps:

Step 1: Choose $j_0 (1 < j < J)$ for the starting scale. Then divide the given images into no-overlapping sub blocks (each one contains $2^{j_0} \times 2^{j_0}$ pixels) and perform j_0 scale Haar wavelet transform on each block. Next, EM algorithm is conducted on each block separately to estimate a set of WD HMT model parameters $\theta_{i,j}$ for every wavelet coefficient block (denote (i, j) to be the position of blocks in the j_0 scale). Here, tying [1] should be adopted to obtain a reliable estimation of model parameters.

Step 2: In this step, the statistical dissimilarity between each model is measured by Kullback-Leibler distance .we adopt the fast algorithm developed in [2], which employs an upward procedure to compute the upper bound of the KLD between each pair of WD HMT models.

Step 3: Link together pairs of models that are in close proximity using the dissimilarity information generated in step 2. As WD HMT models are paired into binary clusters, the newly formed clusters are grouped into larger clusters until a hierarchical tree is formed. Then, the hierarchical tree is cut off at an appropriate point to satisfy the assumed number of distinct textures.

Step 4: Use the clusters generated in step 3 as reliable training set for each type of textures. In order to obtain a reliable training set, the blocks on the boundary are discarded. Then, EM algorithm is conducted in these clusters again to estimate their corresponding WD HMT model. This step is just the training step of HMTseg.

Step 5: The supervised HMTseg reviewed in section 2 can be implemented completely to obtain a final segmentation.

The starting scale j_0 should be selected so large that each sub-block can contain enough statistical information to obtain a reliable estimation. Moreover, its size also should be small to result in a fine initial segmentation. So a trade-off should be made in the choice of starting scale. Haar wavelet transform is more appropriate for solving segmentation problem [4].Using the 2-D Haar wavelet transform, we can find a corresponding wavelet coefficient $w_{i,k}^j$ for each dyadic square $d_{i,k}^j$ .The wavelet coefficient $w_{i,k}^j$ can be computed from and only from the pixels in $d_{i,k}^j$. Thus Haar wavelet transform can more efficiently represent edge. In the clustering step, an effective proximity should be measured before any clustering is performed. The framework introduced in section 2 suggests that the Kullback-Leibler distance (KLD) should be used to compute the disparity between two WD HMMs [2]. The Monte-Carlo method can approximate the KLD simply. However, with this method, the accurate approximation demands a large number of randomly generated data set. This can be prohibitively expensive in practical situations. Moreover, due to the "random" nature of the Monte-Carlo method, the approximations of the distance could vary in different computations. These two drawbacks make the Monte-Carlo method inappropriate for our segmentation algorithm. M. Vetterli (2002) derived a fast algorithm to compute the KLD between WD HMMs [2]. Because of its low computational complexity, we adopt this algorithm in our segmentation. There are two ways to create clusters from the hierarchical tree using the hierarchical clustering algorithm. One is to set the number of classes to group data to several clusters. The other is to set an inconsistency threshold to cut off the hierarchical tree. If we want to segment a given image to different regions, the first way should be adopted. If we want to extract a texture object we are interested, we can employ the second way. The hierarchical clustering offers more flexibility for the applications.

4 Experiment Results and Discussions

We applied our texture segmentation algorithm to several images of composite textures with size 640×640 pixels and 256 grey levels. Textures from the Brodatz album [13] are used to make up the composite texture images. None of the textures used in our experiment can be discriminated by grey level values alone. We start our clustering in the 6th scale and set the cluster number to be 4. That is to say, we fist divide the given image into 10x10 sub blocks, whose size are 64 by 64. Then, their corresponding WD HMT models are estimated using EM algorithm, and the KLD between every pair of blocks is computed. Here, we cut off each depth-6 tree to 8x8 depth-3 trees and perform EM estimation with inner-scale and inter-scale tying [1] to avoid overfitting.

Figure 2 shows the segmentation results obtained for 2 composite texture images (640x640), which both consist of 4 distinct textures selected from Brodatz album.

Table 1 shows the numerical evaluation for the 2 experiments. We use the percentage of correct classification (PCC) as the evaluation criteria. A return of over 90% correctly classified pixels is very promising.

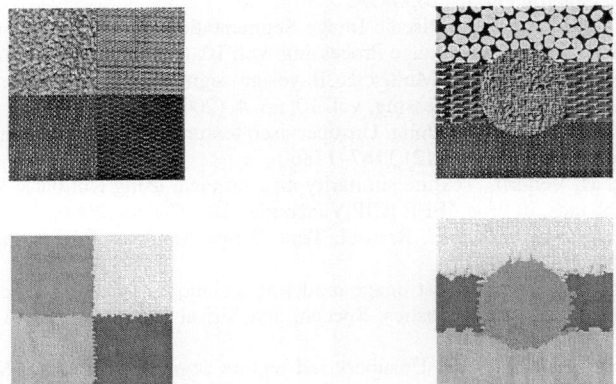

Fig. 2. Two composite texture images and their segmentation results. The first row shows the original image and the second row shows the segmentation results.

Table 1. Segmentation performance evaluation.

	Segmentation performance (PCC)
Composite texture 1	97.42%
Composite texture 2	93.71%

5 Conclusion

In this paper, we have improved the supervised multi-scale texture segmentation (HMTseg), where wavelet domain hidden Markov model is applied to capture the texture feature and a contextual model is employed to fuse multi-scale segmentation. In order to extend supervised HMTseg to an unsupervised one, we perform a hierarchical clustering in the sub-images on the starting scale. The dissimilarity between blocks is measured by the Kullback-Leibler distance (KLD) between corresponding WD HMT models. Experiments show that the performance of our proposed method is promising and needs less prior information on texture present in the given images. Currently, we are trying to employ this algorithm to solve color texture image segmentation problem.

Reference

1. M. S. Crouse, R. D. Nowak, R. G. Baraniuk, Wavelet-based statistical signal processing using hidden Markov model, IEEE Trans. Signal Proc. 46(4), (1998) pp. 886-902.
2. M. N. Do and M. Vetterli, Rotation Invariant Texture Classification and Retrieval using Steerable Wavelet-domain Hidden Markov models, IEEE Transactions on Multimedia, Vol. 4, No. 4 (2002).
3. G. Fan and X. G. Xia, Maximum Likelihood Texture Analysis and Classification Using Wavelet-Domain Hidden Markov Models, in Proc. 34th Asilomar Conf. Signals, Systems, and Computers Pacific Grove.(2000)CA.
4. H. Choi and R. Baraniuk, Multiscale Image Segmentation Using Wavelet-domain Hidden Markov Models, IEEE Trans. Image Processing, vol. 10, (2001) pp. 1309-1321.
5. H. Cheng and C. A. Bouman, Multiscale Bayesian segmentation using a trainable context model, IEEE Trans. Image Processing, vol. 10, no. 4, (2001) pp. 511-525.
6. Anil K. Jain and Farshid Farrokhnia, Unsupervised texture segmentation using gabor filters. Pattern Recognition, (1991) 24(12):1167–1186.
7. M. N. Do and M. Vetterli,, Texture similarity measurement using Kullback–Leibler distance onwavelet subbands, in Proc. IEEE ICIP,Vancouver, BC, Canada(2000)
8. G.E.P. Box, G.M. Jenkins, G.C. Reinsel, Time Series Analysis: Forecasting and Control, 3rd ed., Prentice Hall (1994).
9. R.L. Kashyap, K.B. Eom, Robust image modeling techniques with an image restoration application, IEEE Trans. on Acoustics, Speech, and Signal Processing 36 (6) (1988) 1313–1325
10. B.S. Manjunath, R. Chellappa, Unsupervised texture segmentation using Markov random fields models, IEEE Trans. on Pattern Analysis and Machine Intelligence 13 (5) (1991) 478–482.
11. H. Derin, H. Elliott, Modeling and segmentation of noisy and textured images using Gibbs random fields, IEEE Trans. on Pattern Analysis and Machine Intelligence 9 (1) (1987) 39–55.
12. A. Laine, J. Fan, Texture classification by wavelet packet signatures, IEEE Trans. on Pattern Analysis and Machine Intelligence 15 (11) (1993) 1186–1191.
13. P. Brodatz. Textures: A Photographic Album for Artists & Designers. Dover Publications, Inc., New York, 1966.

Adaptive Model for Foreground Extraction in Adverse Lighting Conditions

Stewart Greenhill, Svetha Venkatesh, and Geoff West

Department of Computing, Curtin University of Technology
GPO Box U1987, Perth 6845, Western Australia
{stewartg,svetha,geoff}@cs.curtin.edu.au

Abstract. Background elimination models are widely used in motion tracking systems. Our aim is to develop a system that performs reliably under adverse lighting conditions. In particular, this includes indoor scenes lit partly or entirely by diffuse natural light. We present a modified "median value" model in which the detection threshold adapts to global changes in illumination. The responses of several models are compared, demonstrating the effectiveness of the new model.

1 Introduction

The focus of this paper is on developing a robust foreground extraction module to be used in conjunction with tracking systems for tracking people in their home. These indoor environments do not have the controlled indoor conditions of office spaces or laboratories. By making long term recordings within a home we note that consideration must be given to the following factors:

- Illumination is spatially variable. A significant amount of the lighting is natural light, diffusing into the space via windows, doors, and skylights. The light sources are often very bright (ie. sunlight), although the overall level of illumination may be low. There is thus a large dynamic range in intensity which can lead to saturation in the images.
- Light sources may not be overhead. Most windows are close to ground level meaning that many objects are lit from the side. Objects (eg. people) may obscure light sources, casting broad shadows that are disconnected from the obscuring object.
- Illumination is temporally variable. Over the course of a day lighting is influenced by changes in external conditions due to clouds, shadows, and reflections. It is influenced by internal events such as the opening and closing of doors, windows and curtains, and the switching on and off of internal lighting.

A first step in motion analysis is to model the normal variation of the background of a scene. Two current approaches are to use a mixture of Gaussian distributions [1] or the median value over a short time window [2]. Both approaches have problems in situations where illumination changes rapidly. Adaptation in the mixture of Gaussians model is determined by a learning rate. To perform well under varying illumination, the number of distributions K and the learning rate α must be adapted to match the time scale of the input, which is not known *a priori*. The median value approach uses a single global threshold for foreground extraction. This is insufficient to deal with relatively long-term trends in the illumination level. An efficient alternative the Gaussian mixture model is to use clusters with varying weights [3] but these are subject to the same considerations with respect to learning rate.

This paper seeks to address the issues with these existing background elimination models. We use a median value model with an adaptive threshold to improve the quality of extracted foreground images. As part of this investigation a motion tracking system was implemented, and the performance of different background models was compared. This paper presents some results from this process, and describes an improved background elimination algorithm.

2 Background Elimination

The Gaussian mixture (GM) model [1] maintains a number of Gaussian distributions K for each pixel. These are characterised by a mean μ, variance σ and weight ω which are adjusted over time as new data becomes available. The rate at which the models adapt is determined by α, the *learning rate*. Small values of α make the model adapt slowly, favouring historical evidence over new evidence. Large values of α cause rapid adaptation, but can also introduce additional problems. If the learning rate is too high, the Gaussian models become too specific (ie. σ becomes small) too quickly and the background model becomes unstable as models are continually invalidated by new evidence. In practice it is necessary to balance α and K to cover the expected variation in the background.

The median value (MV) model [2] maintains a set S of N samples for each pixel. The background model is the value of the pixel that minimises the distance to all other pixels according to the *L-inf distance* in the RGB colour space:

$$Distance(a, b) = max(|a.c - b.c|) \quad c = R, G, B$$

A threshold T_L is used to identify which image pixels are different from the background value, according to the same distance measure. This defines the image foreground. As stated, this technique has a relatively short term memory. Within roughly $N/2$ samples, any previous evidence is replaced by new evidence. That is, in response to a step change in the input, the median value will have shifted to the new state. Cyclic changes are handled if their period is less than N. Typically, N is chosen to be a small number (eg. 8). The complexity of updating the background model is $O(N^2)$, but once this is done, frames can be classified in constant time. Therefore, it is usual to subsample the original input (eg. to one in 10 frames). In contrast, the cost of updating a GM model is $O(K)$ but the proportionality constant is higher due to the more complex calculation. It is uncommon to use more than 4 or 5 distributions in real-time applications.

The SAKBOT system [2] improves the stability of the MV background model by incorporating *adaptivity* and *object-level reasoning*. A background model B_t is maintained separate to the statistical background model B_t^s. Foreground regions are classified as moving object, shadow, ghost, or ghost-shadow. The background model is assigned the statistical background value B_t^s for background, ghost, and ghost-shadow

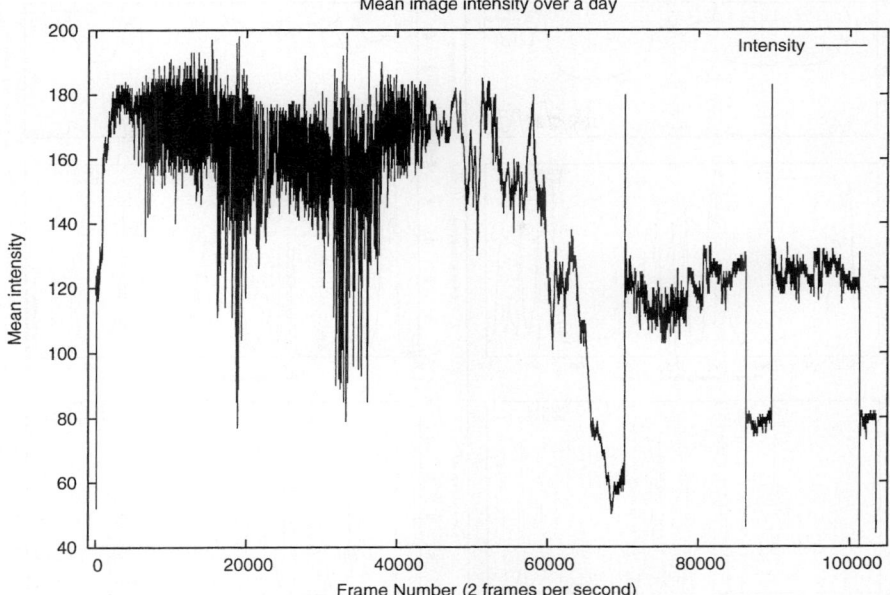

Fig. 1. Mean illumination for an indoor scene over approximately 14.5 hours.

regions, and the previous background value B_{t-1} for moving objects and their shadows. In this way, objects moving through the scene do not disrupt the background model. An adaptivity factor is included, adding B_t to the set S but weighting the distances used for the median function by a factor ω_b.

3 Response of Models to Illumination Changes

Both GM and MV models perform well in conditions of near constant lighting. However, rapid illumination changes produce a large disparity between the current pixel values and the background model. As a result, large areas of the image become classified as foreground. This interferes with object segmentation and tracking.

The problem arises from two sources. Firstly, under natural lighting external changes (due to shadows, clouds) cause significant changes in indoor illumination. The magnitude of the change is generally greater in the corresponding outdoor scene. Secondly, most cameras have an internal gain or aperture level that is adjusted to normalise the overall brightness of the image. The presence of a temporary bright object can cause the camera to suddenly change gain level.

Figure 1 shows the mean illumination for an indoor scene over approximately 14.5 hours. Mean illumination $\overline{I}$ is defined as the average over all image pixels of:

$$\sqrt{r^2 + b^2 + g^2}/\sqrt{3}$$

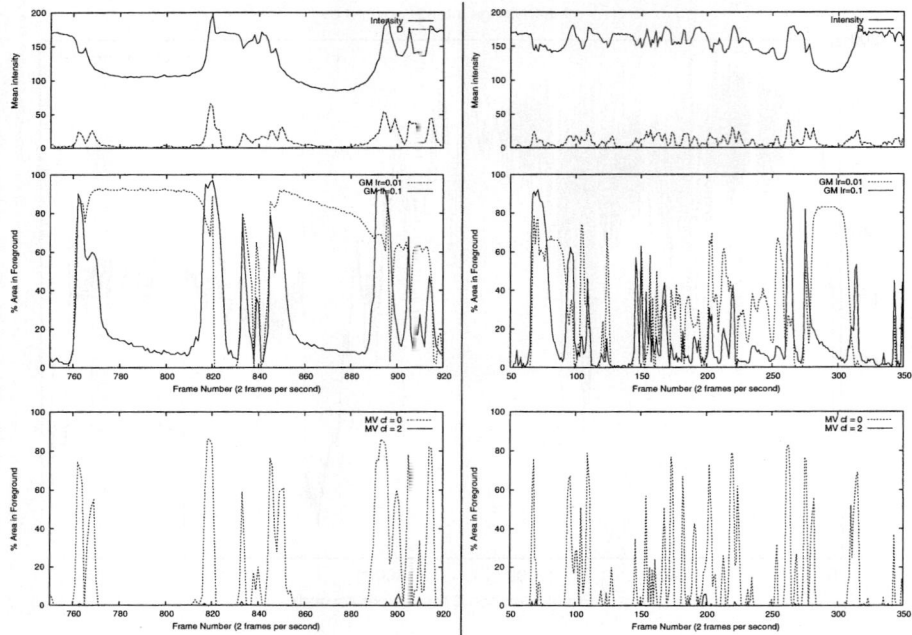

Fig. 2. Background elimination under natural illumination changes. Columns show two different time periods. Rows show intensity $\bar{I}$ and correction D (top), GM performance (centre) and MV performance (bottom). Scene has no moving objects. Foreground is all non-background pixels.

where r, g, and b are the values of the red, green and blue image channels. Most objects in the scene are small compared to the image size, so object motion generally has a small effect on mean illumination.

Over the course of a day $\bar{I}$ is influenced by changes in external conditions due to clouds, shadows, and reflections. It is influenced by internal events such as the opening and closing of doors, windows and curtains, and the switching on and off of internal lighting. In addition, since lighting is not always overhead people can temporarily obscure light sources (eg. by walking in front of windows).

Both GM and MV models eventually adapt to changed lighting conditions. The GM model generally has a slower response time, but maintains multiple models of background state so can be more stable under repetitive changes. The MV model responds relatively quickly (roughly $N/2$ frames), but both models produce disrupted images while adaptation takes place. As shown in the figure the fluctuation in illumination may be 20 to 50% of the mean value. The time scale of the fluctuations varies from a few seconds to a few minutes.

4 Adaptive Median Value Model

To improve image quality of the MV model during adaptation, we employed a correction to the detection threshold T_L that adapts in response to global illumination changes. The system works as follows:

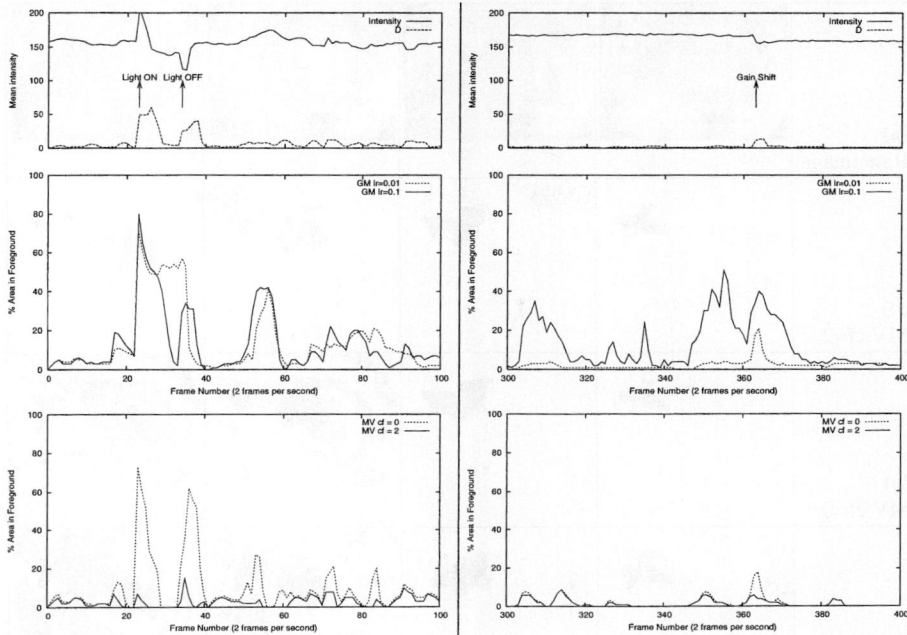

Fig. 3. Background elimination under imposed illumination changes. Left column includes lighting change. Right column shows response to camera gain shift (frame 363). Rows show intensity $\overline{I}$ and correction D (top), GM performance (centre) and MV performance (bottom). Scene includes moving objects. Foreground areas exclude "shadow" pixels. See Figure 4 for classified images.

The mean illumination $\overline{I}$ is computed for each image. The original model [2] maintains a history S of N images. In addition, we maintain a history H of $\overline{I}$ for the previous $M = N/2$ images. The difference D between the largest and smallest value in H approximates the worst-case disparity between the current and historical median value of $\overline{I}$. This value D is scaled by a correction factor cf and added to T_L to correct for differences due to shifts in mean illumination. This causes the detection threshold T_L to increase during periods of rapid change by an amount that is proportional to the difference in mean illumination.

Figure 2 shows the performance of various background models in response to natural changes in illumination. In this scene, no objects are moving, so any foreground pixels are due to artifacts of the background model. A measure of the disruption to the image is the proportion of the total image area detected as foreground. Ideally, this should be small. The figure shows values obtained by four background models working on the same image sequence. The best performance is obtained by the MV model with $cf = 2$. This peaks at only 6% (around frame 200 and 900), whereas all other models peak at between 85 and 90%. The "fast" GM model ($\alpha = 0.1$) adapts well to rapid changes, and is significantly better than the "slow" GM model ($\alpha = 0.01$) over long disturbances. Having less "inertia", the MV models respond better to long disturbances.

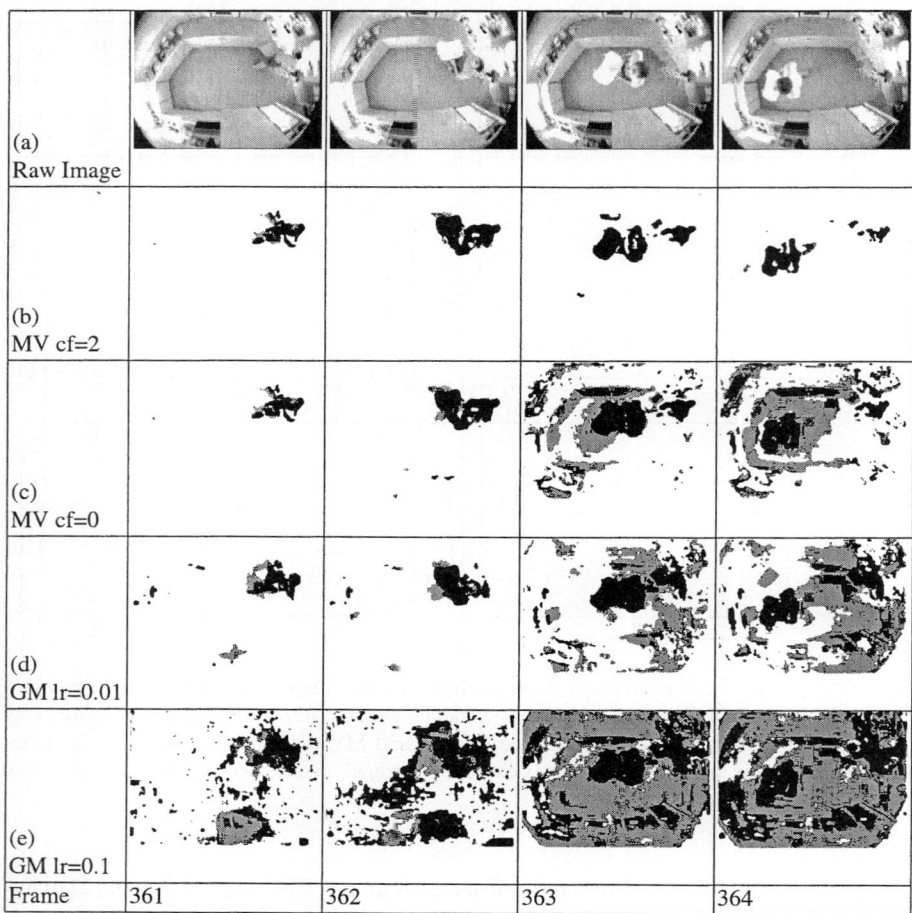

Fig. 4. Foreground (black) and shadow (grey) regions resulting from a camera gain shift. Note that a significant proportion of foreground pixels are removed by shadow reduction.

Figure 3 shows the response to sudden illumination changes. In this experiment an overhead light is turned on and off and a bright object (a white tray) is carried across the room, inducing a step change in the camera gain of about 5%. There is also some variation in natural lighting. Foreground pixels are classified as object or shadow. Shadow pixels are not included in the foreground area, so the overall performance of all models is better than the unclassified foreground values. Again, the adaptive MV model ($cf = 2$) shows least disruption to the image. This time the "slow" GM model outperforms the "fast" GM model, illustrating that the performance of the GM model depends on the match between model parameters and the input. In this scene there are moving objects which is an additional source of perturbations of the background model.

Figure 4 shows the effect of a rapid change in illumination (here, a shift in camera gain) on the background model. This occurs at frame 363 in the sequence shown in Figure 3. Since the scene becomes rapidly darker, there is a large disparity between the current frame and the background model. The background regions are shown in white in the bottom 4 image rows. Foreground regions are classified as shadow (grey) or object (black). An object moves from right to left, leaving a "ghost" in its initial location. Importantly, changing the MV foreground threshold T_L does not adversely affect the ability of the system to track objects moving in the scene. Again, the corrected MV model shows the least disruption to image quality. In this case, a decrease in illumination levels can be handled by normal shadow reduction techniques [4]. For an increase in illumination, the shadow regions shown here would not be distinguishable from foreground objects.

5 Conclusion and Future Work

This paper describes the response of various background elimination models to adverse, real-world lighting effects. Models are compared according to their ability to reject false foreground objects under rapid illumination changes. An adaptive median value model (MV) is described, which consistently performs better than for the uncorrected MV model, and Gaussian mixture (GM) models.

The MV model is attractive because it is computationally less intensive than GM models. MV has a global foreground threshold (T_L) which is easily adapted to lighting changes, as we have presented here. It may be possible to similarly improve GM models by perturbing the distribution means, although it is less clear over what time scales this might be possible. The full SAKBOT model [2] augments the MV statistical model with feedback. As such, it becomes vulnerable to rapid changes, and we have not yet studied the extent of this problem.

The adaptive MV model tends to suffer when rapid illumination changes are spatially non-uniform. One possible solution to this problem is to compute separate corrections for sub-regions of the original image. This is an area for future work.

References

1. Stauffer, C., Grimson, W.E.L.: Learning patterns of activity using real-time tracking. IEEE Transactions on Pattern Analysis and Machine Intelligence **22** (2000) 747–757
2. Cucchiara, R., Grana, C., Piccardi, M., Prati, A.: Detecting moving object, ghosts and shadows in video streams. IEEE Transactions on Pattern Analysis and Machine Intelligence **25** (2003) 76–81
3. Butler, D., Sridharan, S., V. Michael Bove, J.: Real-time adaptive background segmentation. In: Proceedings International Conference on Acoustics, Speech and Signal Processing (ICASSP 2003). (2003)
4. Prati, A., Mikic, I., Cucchiara, R., Trivedi, M.M.: Analysis and detection of shadows in video streams: A comparative evaluation. In: IEEE Computer Vision and Pattern Recognition Conference, Hawaii (2001)

Improvement of Binarization Method Using a Water Flow Model for Document Images with Complex Backgrounds

Hyun-Hwa Oh and Sung-Il Chien

School of Electrical Engineering and Computer Science
Kyungpook National University, Daegu 702-701, Korea
ohh@palgong.knu.ac.kr, sichien@ee.knu.ac.kr

Abstract. Binarization algorithm using a water flow model has been presented [6], in which a document image is efficiently separated into two regions, characters and backgrounds, due to the property of locally adaptive thresholding. However, this method has not decided when to stop the iterative process and required long processing time. Moreover, characters on poor contrast backgrounds often fail to be separated successfully. In the current paper, an improved approach is proposed to overcome above shortcomings of the existing method, by introducing a hierarchical thresholding technique as well as extracting the regions of interest (ROIs) for speed-up and an automatic stopping criterion.

1 Introduction

Binarization is a very important preprocessing step for document image analysis and character recognition, as the quality of the binarization is critical for subsequent phases [1, 2]. There are basically two groups of binarization techniques - global and local. Global methods binarize the entire image using a single threshold [3, 4]. For real document images with various background patterns or noises, and multiple styles of typesetting, a global thresholding results in severe deterioration in the quality of a binarized document image. To overcome such difficulties, many local methods have been proposed, in which the threshold value is determined based on local properties of an image, e.g. pixel-by-pixel or region-by-region [2] [5–7].

Recently, Kim et al. proposed a locally adaptive thresholding algorithm for a document image binarization using a water flow model [6]. In their study, an image is regarded as a three-dimensional (3-D) terrain that is composed of plateaus or mountains, corresponding to backgrounds, and valleys, corresponding to characters. If water falls onto the terrain, it travels down on the terrain and fills valleys. Since the amount of filled water represents the local characteristics of an original terrain, their method yields good segmentation results for document images, even with somewhat complex backgrounds. However, since Kim et al.'s method pours water onto the entire image surface iteratively, it requires longer processing time when the size of an image becomes bigger. Plus, their method contains a tedious task to determine the number of rainfall iteration manually for obtaining the best binarization result. Kim et al. obtained the final binary image by applying a global thresholding technique to the amount of filled water. Thus, characters over quite poor contrast background are most likely to be removed because the corresponding valleys are just filled with a little water.

The current paper proposes a modified version of Kim et al.'s method, overcoming the above drawbacks. The proposed method restricts rainfall onto the terrain surface to certain region with large gradient magnitudes, instead of the entire image surface. The iterative rainfall process is terminated automatically by introducing the stopping criterion. When thresholding the amount of filled water, this paper analyzes its histogram by introducing a separability factor, which is a measure to discriminate two classes, and then determines the adaptive threshold values to obtain the final binary image.

This paper is organized as follows. In Section 2, the proposed method for speeding up and overcoming the limitations of the Kim et al.'s method is described in detail. In Section 3, experimental results on real document images are shown, followed by conclusions in Section 4.

2 Proposed Binarization Algorithm for Document Image

This paper proposes an improved approach that can overcome the main shortcomings of Kim et al.'s binarization method based on a water flow model. An overall flow chart of the proposed method is depicted in Fig. 1.

2.1 Extraction of ROI and Automatic Stopping of Rainfall Process

In a gray-level document image $I(x,y)$, the gradient magnitude is usually large at the boundary between characters and backgrounds, yet relatively small for flat background regions. In this paper, the regions with large gradient magnitude are defined as ROIs, whereas the regions with a small gradient magnitude are regarded as desert regions where rain rarely falls. The threshold $Th_{gr} = 10\ln\left(\|\nabla I(x,y)\|_{avg}\right)$ is used for separating ROIs from desert regions, where $\|\nabla I(x,y)\|_{avg}$ is the average gradient magnitude of the image. Figure 2 presents an example of the search process to find the position with the locally lowest height in the 3-D terrain surface of an image. The slash-marked region represents the desert region, while the other region represents the ROI. A drop of water falls at (x_i, y_i) only within the ROI. The height of the terrain $I(x_i, y_i)$ is then compared with those of neighboring positions within the 7×7 search mask, and the position with the lowest height is determined as the position to where the water will flow next. This search process is executed repeatedly until the center position of the mask has the lowest height. Here, restricting the rainfall to ROIs reduces both the target region to be processed and the length of the flow route, thereby speeding up the binarization method based on a water flow model.

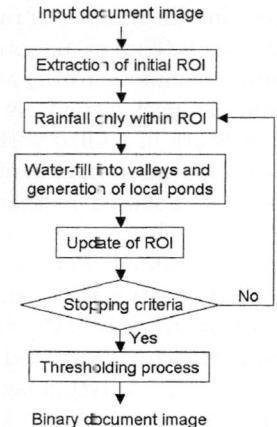

Fig. 1. Overall flow chart of proposed method.

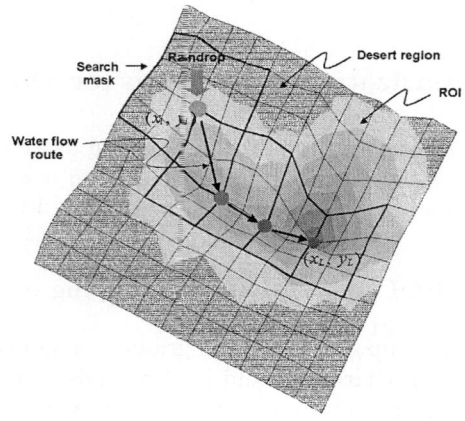

Fig. 2. ROI, desert region, and example of search procedure for locally lowest position using search mask.

When the water fallen at (x_i, y_i) reaches the lowest position (x_L, y_L) through above search process, the heights of the lowest position and its 3×3 neighboring positions are increased as follows:

$$I'(x_{L+j}, y_{L+k}) = I(x_{L+j}, y_{L+k}) + \alpha G(j+1, k+1), \quad -1 \leq j, k \leq 1. \quad (1)$$

Here, $I'(x, y)$ represents the water-filled terrain and $G(j, k)$ denotes the 3×3 Gaussian mask with variance of one. The parameter α controls the amount of water to be filled into a local valley. Above rainfall procedure is applied to all pixels of the ROI by sequential scanning, iteratively. In this way, if α is too small, the valley is filled with a little water at each iteration. Thus, to fill the valley with enough water, the number of iteration should be increased. Whereas, if α is too large, the valley water overflows into the neighboring region corresponding to background and noise excessively. In our experiments, α is set at two.

In consequence of rainfall process, a lot of ponds are generated at water-filled valleys. As the rainfall is iterated, depths of ponds become deeper and their sizes grow. Some adjacent ponds are merged into a single pond. Moreover, some positions within the ROI are flooded with water and become the bottom of a pond. Hence, if a drop of water falls at such a position in the next rainfall process, the water does not flow down to the neighboring position anymore. Therefore, this paper excludes such positions from the ROI at each iteration, thereby decreasing the area of the ROI. Here, let the area of the initial ROI be $A_{ROI(0)}$ and the area of the ROI after t-th iterations be $A_{ROI(t)}$. Then the iterative rainfall process is stopped when the following condition is satisfied:

$$A_{ROI(t)} < c A_{ROI(0)}, \qquad (2)$$

where the thresholding parameter c is set at 0.6 in the our experiments. After termination of the rainfall process, each pond connected with water-filled pixels is labeled and its average water level is calculated. Thereafter, the water level of each pond is assigned an average water level. Consequently, we obtain a water-filled terrain of the input document image, in which the character regions of the low gray-level are raised, while the background regions of the high gray-level are kept their original gray-levels.

2.2 Adaptively Hierarchical Thresholding

We now analyze the amount of water on the water-filled terrain and obtain the final binary document image. To do this, the gray-levels of the original image are subtracted from those of the water-filled image. Then water-filled ponds are extracted, in which their depths correspond to the amount of filled water. The pond depth varies widely according to the gray-level difference between characters and their neighboring backgrounds. If a global thresholding technique is used to threshold the pond depth, as in Kim et al.'s method, the shallow ponds corresponding to characters on poor contrast backgrounds are either partially or completely eliminated. To solve this problem, the threshold value need to be determined adaptively by analyzing the distribution of the pond depth.

Otsu's method [3] selects the optimal threshold k^* to discriminate two classes C_1 and C_2 (e.g., objects and background) in an image, by maximizing the following discriminant criterion measure

$$\eta = \frac{\sigma_B^2}{\sigma_T^2}, \qquad (3)$$

where σ_B^2 is the between-class variance and σ_T^2 is the total variance. This method also affords supplementary means to analyze further aspects other than the selection of the optimal threshold for a given image. As stated in [3], the maximum value $\eta(k^*)$, denoted simply by η^*, can be used as a measure to evaluate the separability of classes in the original image or the bimodality of the histogram. It is uniquely determined within the range $0 \leq \eta^* \leq 1$. The lower bound (zero)

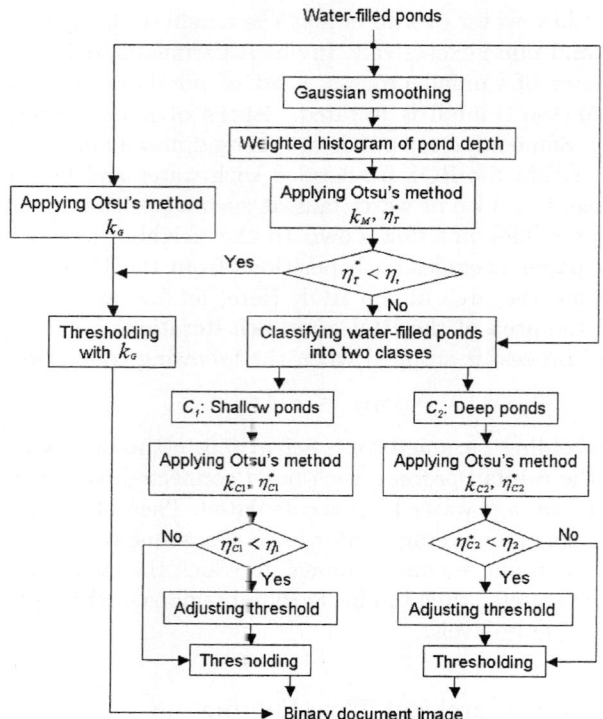

Fig. 3. Schematic diagram of proposed hierarchical thresholding method.

is attainable by, and only by, pictures having a single constant gray level, and the upper bound (unity) is attainable by, and only by, two-valued pictures. This property is an important criterion that we will use in our hierarchical thresholding to the pond depth.

For thresholding the water-filled ponds efficiently, this paper selectively categorizes them into two classes, which are a shallow pond class and a deep pond class. Here, the separability factor of Eq.(3) is used. Figure 3 represents the schematic diagram of the proposed thresholding method. First, the water-filled ponds are smoothed by 3×3 Gaussian filter, resulting in suppression of impulse noise on each pond. Normally, an extremely shallow pond is most likely to be noise. Therefore, if the maximum depth of a pond is quite small, then such a pond is removed. Usually, depths on every position of an isolated pond are not equal to one another due to the uneven topography of the pond's bottom. This paper regards the maximum depth of each isolated pond as its main depth. Then we compute a weighted histogram of main depths of ponds temporarily, in which the area of each pond is given to it as a weight. By applying Otsu's method to this histogram, the separability factor η_T^* and the threshold k_M are obtained. If η_T^* is less than predetermined η_t, this means the existing ponds are likely to be the same class. In other words, most of ponds correspond to characters with similar gray-level. Hence the water-filled ponds are thresholded by Otsu's threshold value k_G and then the final binary document image is obtained.

However, if η_T^* is greater than η_t, then the water-filled ponds are assumed to be modeled with two classes. Here, the threshold k_M is used to discriminate two classes; if the main depth of the pond is greater than k_M, then this pond is classified as the deep pond. Otherwise, the pond is categorized as the shallow pond. Now, two pond classes are analyzed by the separability factors η_{C1}^* and η_{C2}^*, which are computed from their pond depth histogram, respectively. In case of the shallow pond class, if $\eta_{C1}^* < \eta_1$, which assumes most of ponds correspond to noise, the threshold value is adjusted as $k'_{C1} = k_M$ to remove noise. Otherwise, this means characters coexist with noise and k_{C1} is used for thresholding the shallow pond class. Similarly, in case of the deep pond class, if $\eta_{C2}^* < \eta_2$, which indicates most of ponds correspond to the character, the threshold value is readjusted downwards as $k'_{C2} = \beta\, k_{C2} \times \eta_{C2}^*$, resulting in the better quality of the segmented character. Otherwise, this case means the deep pond class includes both characters and noise and k_{C2} is used for discriminating them. Here, η_1 and η_2 are empirically determined and parameter β is set at one. In consequence, the final binary document image is obtained by applying two adaptive threshold values to each class.

3 Experimental Results

For a performance evaluation, various document images obtained by a scanner with 200dpi were used in experiments. The test document images are 256 × 256 pixels with 8-bit gray-levels and contain various characters with different gray-levels and complicated backgrounds with poor contrasts. Figure 4 shows examples of the real document images.

For an objective evaluation of the binarization results, the performance of the proposed method was compared with those of three conventional methods, which are Otsu's method, Liu and Srihari's method, and Kim et al.'s method. For fair comparisons, the parameters of each method tested were carefully selected to obtain the best possible results. Especially, in case of Kim et al.'s method, we selected the number of rainfall iteration that appeared to yield the best binary image after repeatedly applying their method to the test image.

A visual inspection is made of the qualities of the binary document images obtained when using the different methods. Figure 5 shows the binarization results for the test image 1 that involves various gray-level characters on inhomogeneous backgrounds. Figure 5(a) represents the result of Otsu's method, in which the characters located in the upper right part are not separated. Figure 5(b) shows the result of Liu and Srihari's method, in which a lot of characters are partially or completely eliminated. In case of Kim et al.'s method, an improved result is obtained compared with the above two results, yet false objects are observed on the upper right part and some characters in bottom area are partially broken and eliminated completely, as in Fig. 5(c). Figure 5(d) shows the result of the proposed method, which produces the best binarization.

Fig. 4. Real document images for binarization: (a) test image 1 (T_1), in which vertical white line (237th line) is superimposed for later discussion, (b) test image 2 (T_2), and (c) test image 3 (T_3).

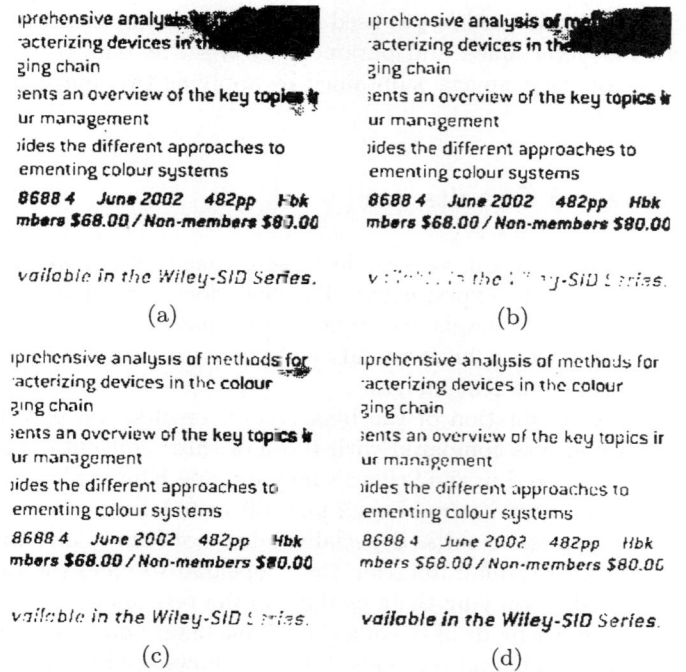

Fig. 5. Binarization results for test image 1: (a) Otsu's method, (b) Liu and Srihari's method, (c) Kim et al.'s method, and (d) proposed method.

Figures 6(a) and 6(b) show the binarization results when applying Otsu's method and Liu and Srihari's method to the test image 2, respectively. In those cases, small characters located in the upper region are not segmented from the background due to a severely poor contrast. As in Fig. 6(c), Kim et al.'s method still results in lots of missing characters on the upper region. In contrast, the proposed method yields a good performance as shown in Fig. 6(d).

(a) (b) (c) (d)

Fig. 6. Binarization results for test image 2: (a) Otsu's method, (b) Liu and Srihari's method, (c) Kim et al.'s method, and (d) proposed method.

Figures 7(a) and 7(b) show the results of Otsu's method and Liu and Srihari's method to the test image 3, in which many false objects are obtained. Figure 7(c) shows the result of the Kim et al's method, where the characters are successfully extracted from the backgrounds and the binarization quality is good. Figure 7(d) shows the result of the proposed method, which produced a satisfactory performance similar to that in Fig. 7(c).

Figure 8(a) shows the profiles of the original terrain and water-filled terrain along the 237th vertical white line superimposed in Fig. 4(a) when using the proposed method. After automatic stopping of the rainfall iteration, the local valleys were adequately filled with water, whereas most background regions remained as dry plains. Since the test image 1 contained diverse characters with different gray-levels in an inhomogeneous background, the depths of the ponds were very different from each other as in Fig. 8(b). Thus, a single threshold value, as determined by Otsu's method, could not effectively threshold the water-filled ponds, whereas the adaptive thresholds determined by the proposed method achieved a good segmentation performance.

The speed of the proposed method was measured, as implemented on a Pentium IV 1.6GHz PC and Windows 2000 OS. As for Otsu's method and Liu and Srihari's method, the average time taken to binarize the test images was under 0.01sec. In case of the proposed method, the average processing time was ap-

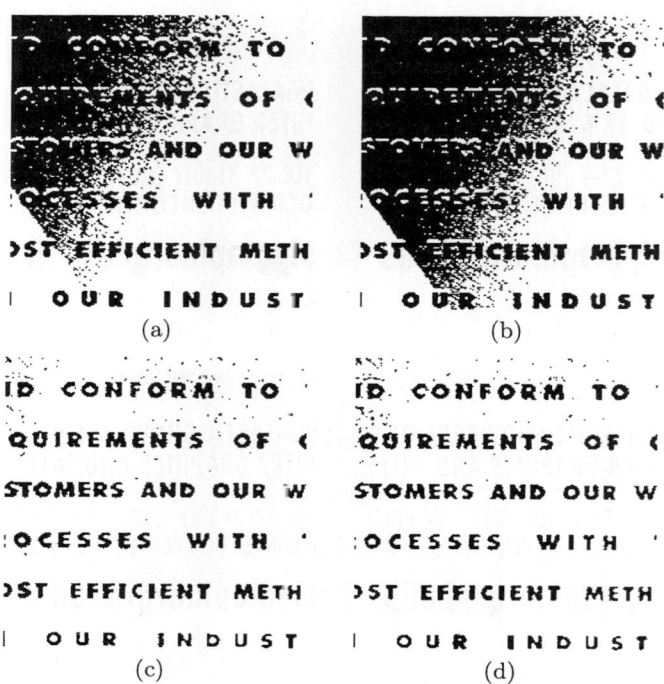

Fig. 7. Binarization results for test image 3: (a) Otsu's method, (b) Liu and Srihari's method, (c) Kim et al.'s method, and (d) proposed method.

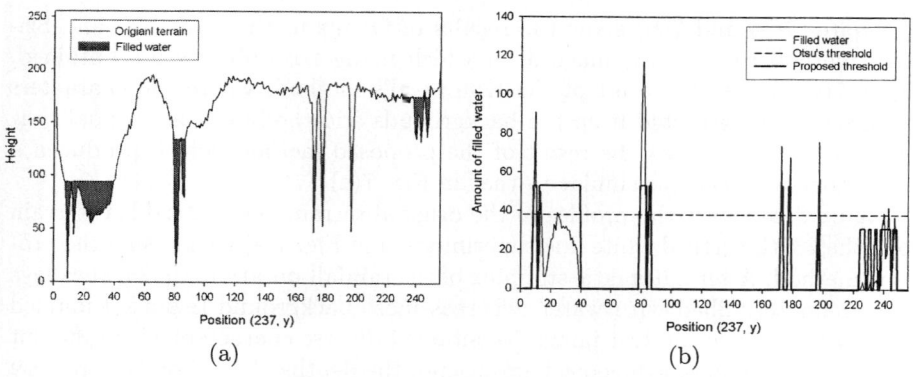

Fig. 8. Amount of filled water and threshold values: (a) profile of original terrain and water-filled terrain for 237th vertical line in test image 1 when using proposed method, and (b) amount of filled water in (a), Otsu's threshold, and proposed threshold.

proximately 0.65sec. Although this was longer than that for above two methods, it was drastically shorter than that for Kim et al.'s method, where the average processing time was about 4.23sec. Table 1 presents the number of rainfall iter-

Table 1. Number of rainfall iteration and processing time (sec) comparison between proposed method and Kim et al.'s method with respect to ten test images.

Test image		T_1	T_2	T_3	T_4	T_5	T_6	T_7	T_8	T_9	T_{10}
Kim et al.'	No. iter.	15	12	10	10	15	20	10	7	10	15
method	Proc. time	5.33	3.92	4.68	3.11	3.91	9.66	3.03	1.78	3.17	4.10
Proposed	No. iter.	4	3	3	3	2	3	2	4	3	5
method	Proc. time	0.66	0.42	1.20	0.48	0.66	0.72	0.45	0.44	0.84	0.66

ation and a processing time comparison between Kim et al.'s method and the proposed method with respect to the ten test images. The number of iteration, which is determined automatically by the proposed method, is smaller than that determined manually by Kim et al.'s method. Moreover, as seen in Table 1, the processing time for the proposed method was about 4 to 13 times shorter than that for Kim et al.'s method.

4 Conclusions

This paper suggested the improved approach of the document image binarization using a water flow model, which can produce a good binary image with high quality. The document image was divided into the iterative ROIs and the desert regions. Rainfall process occurred only within the ROIs, thereby speeding up the binarization process. Iterative rainfall process was automatically terminated by the proposed stopping criterion. Furthermore, the amount of filled water was adaptively thresholded by selectively dividing water-filled ponds into shallow and deep ponds and adjusting their thresholds based on histogram analysis, respectively. Experimental results showed that the proposed method achieved satisfactory binarized results to various document images with poor contrast backgrounds and also speeded up considerably the existing method based on a water flow model.

Acknowledgement

This work was supported by the Brain Korea 21 Project in 2003.

References

1. Cheng, H., Fan, Z.: Background Identification Based Segmentation and Multilayer Three Representation of Document Images. Proceedings of International Conference on Image Processing **3** (2002) 1005–1008
2. Sauvola, J., Pietikainen, M.:Adaptive Document Image Binarization. Pattern Recognition **33** (2000) 225–236
3. Otsu, N.: A Threshold Selection Method from Gray-Scale Histogram. IEEE Trans. Syst., Man, Cybern. **SMC-8** (1978) 62–66

4. Kitter, J., Illingworth, J.:On Threshold Selection Using Clustering Criteria. IEEE Trans. Syst., Man, Cybern. **SMC-15** (1985) 652–655
5. O'Gorman, L.: Binarization and Multithresholding of Document Image Using Connectivity. Graphical Models Image Process. **56(6)** (1994) 494–506
6. Kim, I.-K., Jung, D.-W., Park, R.-H.: Document Image Binarization Based on Topographic Analysis Using a Water Flow Model. Pattern Recognition **35** (2002) 265–277
7. Liu, Y., Srihari, S.N.: Document Image Binarization Based on Texture Features. IEEE Trans. Pattern Anal. Mach. Intell. **19(5)** (1997) 540–544

Learning and Integrating Semantics for Image Indexing

Joo-Hwee Lim[1] and Jesse S. Jin[2]

[1] Institute for Infocomm Research, 21 Heng Mui Keng Terrace, Singapore 119613
[2] University of New South Wales, Sydney 2052, Australia

Abstract. In this paper, we propose learning and integration frameworks that extract and combine local and global semantics for image indexing and retrieval. In the supervised learning version, support vector detectors are trained on semantic support regions without image segmentation. The reconciled and aggregated detection-based indexes then serve as an input for support vector learning of image classifiers to generate class-relative image indexes. In the unsupervised learning approach, image classifiers are first trained on local image blocks from a small number of labeled images. Then local semantic patterns are discovered from clustering the image blocks with high classification output. Training samples are induced from cluster memberships for support vector learning to form local semantic pattern detectors. During retrieval, similarities based on both local and global indexes are combined to rank images. Query-by-example experiments on 2400 unconstrained consumer photos with 16 semantic queries show that the proposed approaches outperformed the fusion of color and texture features significantly in average precisions by 55% and 37% respectively.

1 Introduction

Started more than a decade ago, content-based image retrieval research has yet to bridge the "semantic gap" between the information that one can extract from the visual data and the interpretation that the same data have for a user in a given situation [6]. In particular, broad domain such as unconstrained consumer photos pose great challenge for content-based image retrieval research as the amount of content variations is usually very high due to the spontaneous and casual nature during image capturing. The objects in the photos are ill-posed, occluded, and cluttered with poor lighting, focus, and exposure.

In this paper, we present learning and integration frameworks that extract and combine local and global semantics for image indexing and retrieval. In the supervised learning version, support vector detectors are trained on semantic support regions without image segmentation. The reconciled and aggregated detection-based indexes then serve as an input for support vector learning of image classifiers to generate class-relative image indexes. During retrieval, similarities based on both indexes are combined to rank images.

Town and Sinclair [7] described a semantic labeling approach to image retrieval. An image is segmented into non-overlapping regions and each subject to classification into 11 visual categories suited to outdoor scenes by neural networks. Similarity between a query and an image is the sum over all grids of the Euclidean distance between classification vectors, or their cosine of correlation. The evaluation was carried out on over 1000 Corel Photo Library images and about 500 home photos, with better results obtained for the Corel images. However, a major drawback of the supervised learning approach is the human effort required to provide labeled training image regions.

In the field of computer vision, researchers have developed object recognition systems from unlabeled and unsegmented images (e.g. [2]). Sophiscated generative and probabilistic model has been proposed to represent, learn, and detect object parts, locations, scales, and appearances from fairly cluttered scenes with promising results [2]. Motivated from a machine translation perspective, object recognition is posed as a lexicon learning problem to translate image regions to corresponding words. More generally, the joint distribution of meaningful text descriptions and entire or local image contents are learned from images or categories of images labeled with a few words [1,4]. While the results for the annotation problem on entire images look promising [4], the correspondence problem of associating words with segmented image regions remains very challenging [1].

We address the issue of minimal supervision differently. We do not assume availability of text descriptions for image or image classes as in [1,4]. Neither do we know the object classes to be recognized as in [2]. We wish to discover and associate local unsegmented regions with semantics and generate their samples to construct models for content-based image retrieval, all with minimal manual intervention. This is realized as a novel three-stage hybrid framework that interleave supervised and unsupervised learnings. Image classifiers are first trained on local image blocks from a small number of labeled images. Then local semantic patterns are discovered from clustering the image blocks with high classification output. Training samples are induced from cluster memberships for support vector learning to form local semantic pattern detectors. During retrieval, similarities based on local class pattern indexes and discovered pattern indexes are combined to rank images.

Query-by-example experiments on 2400 unconstrained consumer photos with 16 semantic queries show that the combined matching aproaches are better than matching with single indexes. Both the semantics design and the semantics discovery approaches also outperformed the linear fusion of color and texture features significantly in average precisions by 55% and 37% respectively.

2 Semantics Design Approach

From a semantics design perspective, we propose a cascading framework to combine local and global semantics that are learned and extracted from images. At the region level, local support vector detectors are trained on semantic support regions without image segmentation. The detection results are reconciled across multiple resolutions and aggregated spatially as image indexes. They also serve as input patterns for support vector image classifiers to learn and generate class-relative image indexes. During retrieval, similarities based on both types of indexes are combined to rank images.

2.1 Detection-Based Indexing

Semantic support regions (SSRs) are salient image patches that exhibit semantic meanings to us. A cropped face region, a typical grass patch, and a patch of swimming pool water etc can all be treated as their instances. In this paper, we train local support vector detectors [3] on multi-scale block-based image regions without a region segmentation step. Given a local image patch with feature vector z, a support vector classifier $\mathcal{S}_i$ is a detector for SSR i on z. The classification vector T for region z can be computed via the softmax function as

$$T_i(z) = \frac{\exp^{\mathcal{S}_i(z)}}{\sum_j \exp^{\mathcal{S}_j(z)}}. \tag{1}$$

As we are dealing with heterogeneous consumer photos, we adopt color and texture features to characterize SSRs. A feature vector z has two parts, namely, a color feature vector z^c and a texture feature vector z^t. For the color feature, we compute the mean and standard deviation of each color channel (i.e. z^c has 6 dimensions). We use the YIQ color space over other color spaces as it performed better in our experiments. For the texture feature, we adopted the Gabor coefficients [5]. Similarly, the mean and standard deviation of the Gabor coefficients (5 scales and 6 orientations) in an image block are computed as z^t (60 dimensions). Zero-mean normalization was applied to both the color and texture features. In this paper, we used polynomial kernels with a modified dot product similarity measure between feature vectors y and z,

$$y \cdot z = \frac{1}{2}\left(\frac{y^c \cdot z^c}{|y^c||z^c|} + \frac{y^t \cdot z^t}{|y^t||z^t|}\right) \tag{2}$$

To detect SSRs with translation and scale invariance, the image is scanned with windows of different scales, progressively from 20×20 to 60×60 at a step of 10 pixels, on a 240×360 size-normalized image. That is, after this detection step, we have 5 maps of detection. To reconcile the detection maps across different resolutions onto a common basis, we adopt the following principle: If the most confident classification of a region at resolution r is less than that of a larger region (at resolution $r + 1$) that subsumes the region, then the classification output of the region should be replaced by those of the larger region at resolution $r + 1$. Using this principle, we start the reconciliation from detection map based on largest scan window (60×60) to detection map based on next-to-smallest scan window (30×30). After 4 cycles of reconciliation, the detection map that is based on the 20×20 window would have consolidated the detection decisions obtained at other resolutions.

Suppose a region Z comprises of n small equal regions with feature vectors $z_1, z_2, \cdots, z_n$. To account for the size of detected SSRs in the spatial area Z, the SSR detection vectors of the reconciled detection map is aggregated as

$$T_i(Z) = \frac{1}{n}\sum_k T_i(z_k). \tag{3}$$

For the data set and experiments reported in this paper, we designed 26 classes of SSRs (i.e. $S_i, i = 1, 2, \cdots, 26$ in Eq. (1)), organized into 8 superclasses as illustrated in Fig. 1. We cropped 554 image regions from 138 images and used 375 of them (from 105 images) as training data and the remaining one-third for validation. Among all the kernels evaluated, those with better generalization result on the validation set are used for the indexing and retrieval tasks. A polynomial kernel with degree 2 and constant 1 ($C = 100$ [3]) produced the best result on precision and recall. Hence it was adopted in our experiments.

Fig. 1. Examples of semantic support regions (top-down, left-to-right): people (face, figure, crowd, skin), sky (clear, cloudy, blue), ground (floor, sand, grass), water (pool, pond, river), foliage (green, floral, branch), mountain (far, rocky), building (old, city, far), interior (wall, wooden, china, fabric, light)

For query by examples, the content-based similarity λ between a query q and an image x can be computed in terms of the similarities between their corresponding local regions. For example, the similarity based on L_1 distance measure (city block distance) between query q with m local regions Y_j and image x with m local regions Z_j is defined as

$$\lambda(q, x) = 1 - \frac{1}{2m} \sum_j \sum_i |T_i(Y_j) - T_i(Z_j)| \quad (4)$$

2.2 Class-Relative Indexing

Research on image categorization has received more attention lately. In general, the classifications were made based on low-level features such as color, edge directions etc (e.g. [8]). Instead of image classification, we wish to estimate the relevant class of images of a query. We define prior semantic image categories as prototypical instances of the relevance class and use categorical memberships in a similarity measure. As our test images are consumer photos, we designed a taxonomy for consumer photos as shown in Fig. 2. This hierarchy of categories is more comprehensive than that addressed in [8]. We trained support vector classifiers on the 7 disjoint categories represented by the leaf nodes (except the miscellaneous category) in Fig. 2. A support vector classifier $C_k, k = 1, \cdots, 7$ is trained to differentiate each category from others. Using the softmax function, the output of classification C_k for a given image x is computed as,

$$R_k(x) = \frac{\exp^{C_k(x)}}{\sum_j \exp^{C_j(x)}}. \quad (5)$$

For each class, a human subject was asked to define the list of ground truth images from a collection of 2400 images and 20% of the lists was used for training. To ensure unbiased training samples, we generated 10 different sets of positive training samples from the ground truth list for each class based on uniform random distribution. The negative training (test) examples for a class are the union of positive training (test) examples of the other 6 classes and the `miscellaneous` class. The classifier training for each class was carried out 10 times on these different training sets and the support vector classifier of the best run was retained.

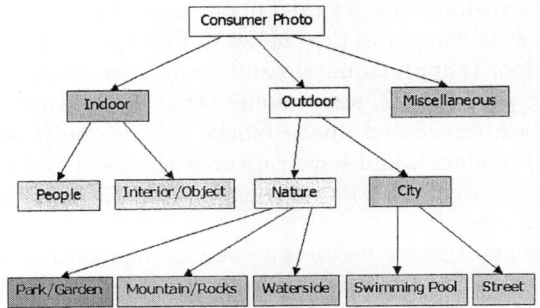

Fig. 2. Taxonomy for consumer photos

The feature vector for classification is the detection-based image index as described above. To be consistent with the SSR training, we adopted the polynomial kernels with degree 2 and constant 1 ($C = 100$ [3]) and the following modified dot product similarity measure between image indexes $u = T_i(Y_j)$ and $v = T_i(Z_j)$ is computed as

$$u \cdot v = \frac{1}{m} \sum_j \frac{\sum_i T_i(Y_j) T_i(Z_j)}{\sqrt{\sum_k T_k(Y_j)^2} \sqrt{\sum_k T_k(Z_j)^2}} \qquad (6)$$

The category-based similarity μ between a query q and an image x is defined as

$$\mu(q, x) = 1 - \frac{1}{2} \sum_k |R_k(q) - R_k(x)| \qquad (7)$$

3 Semantics Discovery Approach

First support vector machines (SVM) are trained on local image blocks from a small number of images labeled as several semantic categories. Then *typical* image blocks that produce high SVM outputs are grouped into Discovered Semantic Regions (DSRs) using fuzzy c-means clustering. The training samples for these DSRs are automatically induced from cluster memberships and subject to local support vector machine learning to form local semantic detectors for DSRs. An image is indexed as a tessellation of DSR histograms (similar to the

SSR indexing) and matched using histogram intersection. At the same time, the support vector image classifiers trained on local image blocks (i.e. Local Support Classes (LSC)) are also used to form detection-based image indexes in terms of local class patterns. During retrieval, similarities based on DSR and LSC indexes are combined to rank images.

3.1 Local Semantics Discovery

Given an application domain, some typical classes C_k with their image samples are identified. For consumer images used in our experiments, we trained 7 binary SVMs on the following categories (leaf nodes of Fig. 2): interior or objects indoor (inob), people indoor (inpp), mountain and rocky area (mtrk), parks or gardens (park), swimming pool (pool), street scene (strt), and waterside (wtsd). The training samples are tessellated image blocks z from the class samples. After learning, the class models would have captured the local class semantics and a high SVM output (i.e. $C_k(z) \gg 0$) would suggest that the local region z is typical to the semantics of class k.

The same color and texture features as well as the modified dot product similarity measure used in the supervised learning framework (Eq. (2)) are adopted for the support vector classifier training with polynomial kernels. With the help of the learned class models C_k, we can generate sets of local image regions that characterize the class semantics $\mathcal{X}_k$ as

$$\mathcal{X}_k = \{z | C_k(z) > \rho\} \quad (\rho \geq 0) \tag{8}$$

However, the local semantics hidden in each $\mathcal{X}_k$ is opaque and possibly multi-mode. We would like to discover the multiple groupings in each class by unsupervised learning such as Gaussian mixture modeling and fuzzy c-means clustering. The result of the clustering is a collection of partitions m_{kj}, $j = 1, 2, \cdots, N_k$ in the space of local semantics for each class, where m_{kj} are usually represented as cluster centers and N_k are the numbers of partitions for each class.

Once we have obtained the typical semantic partitions for each class, we can learn the models of Discovered Semantic Regions (DSRs) S_i $i = 1, 2, \cdots, N$ where $N = \sum_k N_k$ (i.e. we linearize the ordering of m_{kj} as m_i). We label a local image block ($x \in \cup_k \mathcal{X}_k$) as positive example for S_i if it is closest to m_i and as negative example for S_j $j \neq i$,

$$X_i^+ = \{x | i = \arg\min_t |x - m_t|\} \tag{9}$$

$$X_i^- = \{x | i \neq \arg\min_t |x - m_t|\} \tag{10}$$

where $|.|$ is some distance measure. Now we can perform supervised learning again on X_i^+ and X_i^- using say support vector machines $\mathcal{S}_i(x)$ as DSR models. To visualize a DSR S_i, we can display the image block s_i that is most typical among those assigned to cluster m_i that belonged to class k,

$$C_k(s_i) = \max_{x \in X_i^+} C_k(x) \tag{11}$$

In our experiments, we trained 7 SVMs with polynomial kernels (degree 2, constant 1, $C = 100$ [3]) for the leaf-node categories (except `miscellaneous`) on color and texture features (Eq. (2)) of 60×60 image blocks (tessellated with 20 pixels in both directions) from 105 sample images. Hence each SVM was trained on 16,800 image blocks. After training, the samples from each class k is fed into classifier C_k to test their typicalities. Those samples with SVM output $C_k(z) > 2$ (Eq. (8)) are subject to fuzzy c-means clustering. The number of clusters assigned to each class is roughly proportional to the number of training images in each class. We have 26 DSRs in total. To build the DSR models, we trained 26 binary SVM with polynomial kernels (degree 2, constant 1, $C = 100$ [3]), each on 7467 positive and negative examples (Eq. (9) and (10)). To visualize the 26 DSRs that have been learned, we compute the most typical image block for each cluster (Eq. (11)) and concatenate their appearances in Fig. 3.

Fig. 3. Most typical image blocks of the DSRs learned (left to right): china utensils and cupboard top (first four) for the `inob` class; faces with different background and body close-up (next five) for the `inpp` class; rocky textures (next two) for the `mtrk` class; green foliage and flowers (next four) for the `park` class; pool side and water (next two) for the `pool` class; roof top, building structures, and roadside (next five) for the `strt` class; and beach, river, pond, far mountain (next four) for the `wtsd` class

As mentioned, detection-based image indexing is carried out based on the steps similar to the semantics design approach. For query by examples, the local similarity λ between a query q and an image x can be computed in terms of the similarities between their corresponding local regions as given in Eq. (4).

3.2 Local Class Patterns

The classifiers C_k trained on local image blocks in order to derive DSRs can also be used to form image indexes based on local class patterns. That is, detection-based image indexing is carried out similar to SSR indexing with $S_i(z)$ replaced by $C_k(z)$ in Eq. (1). The global similarity μ between a query q and an image x is computed as given in Eq. (7).

4 Integrated Similarity Matching

We believe that both the local content-based similarity and global context-based similarity are important and complementary. They can be combined into a single similarity for ranking images relevant to a query example. A simple linear combination ($\omega \in [0,1]$) is

$$\rho(q, x) = \omega \cdot \lambda(q, x) + (1 - \omega) \cdot \mu(q, x) \qquad (12)$$

When a query has multiple examples, $q = \{q_1, q_2, \cdots, q_K\}$, the similarity $\rho(q, x)$ for any image in a database is computed as

$$\rho(q, x) = max_i \rho(q_i, x) \qquad (13)$$

5 Empirical Evaluation

In this paper, we evaluate our proposed approach on 2400 genuine consumer photos with indoor and outdoor settings as well as portrait and landscape layouts. After removing possibly noisy marginal pixels, the images are of size 240 × 360. The indexing process automatically detects the layout and applies the corresponding tessellation template. Photos of bad quality, e.g. faded, over-exposed, blurred, dark, etc. are retained in order to reflect the complexity of the original data. We defined 16 semantic queries and their ground truths (in brackets) among the 2400 photos (Table 1). Fig. 4 shows, in top-down left-to-right order, 2 relevant images for queries Q01 to Q16, respectively. As these unconstrained consumer images have highly varied and complex contents, we represent each query with 3 relevant photos as query examples in our experiments. The precisions and recalls were computed without the query images themselves in the lists of retrieved images.

Table 1. Semantic queries used in QBE experiments

Q01 (994)	indoor	Q02 (1218)	outdoor
Q03 (277)	people close-up	Q04 (840)	people indoor
Q05 (134)	interior or object	Q06 (697)	city scene
Q07 (521)	nature scene	Q08 (52)	at a swimming pool
Q09 (645)	street or roadside	Q10 (150)	along waterside
Q11 (304)	in a park or garden	Q12 (67)	at mountain area
Q13 (239)	buildings close-up	Q14 (73)	close up, indoor
Q15 (491)	small group, indoor	Q16 (45)	large group, indoor

We compare our proposed approaches ("Dsgn" for the semantics design framework and "Dscv" for the semantics discovery framework) with the feature-based approach that combines color and texture in a linearly optimal way (denoted as "CTO"). We have not compared with region-based approach as we believe that current image segmentation algorithms will not be robust enough for unconstrained consumer images such as those used in our experiments. All indexing are carried out with a 4 × 4 grid on the images.

For the color-based signature, local color histograms of b^3 ($b = 4$ to 17) number of bins in the RGB color space were computed and compared using histogram intersection. For the texture-based signature, we adopted the mean and standard deviation of Gabor coeffients and the associated distance measure as reported in [5]. The Gabor coefficients were computed with 5 scales and

Fig. 4. Sample consumer photos from the 2400 collection. They also represent 2 relevant images (top-down, left-right) for each of the 16 queries used in our experiments

Table 2. Average precisions at top retrieved images

Avg.Prec.	CTO	SSR	SSC	Dsgn	DSR	LSC	Dscv
At 20	0.64	0.76	0.71	0.84	0.71	0.70	0.80
At 30	0.59	0.70	0.68	0.78	0.68	0.69	0.76
At 50	0.52	0.62	0.64	0.72	0.63	0.63	0.70
At 100	0.46	0.54	0.58	0.65	0.57	0.58	0.62
Overall	0.38	0.45	0.53	0.59	0.48	0.48	0.52

6 orientations. Convolution windows of 20×20 to 60×60 were attempted. The distance measures between a query and an image for the color and texture methods were normalized within $[0, 1]$ and combined linearly similar to Eq. (12). Among the relative weights attempted at 0.1 intervals, the best overall average precision of 0.38 was obtained with a dominant influence of 0.9 from the color feature (2197 bins) and 0.1 influence from the texture feature (20×20 windows).

Table 2 shows the average precisions among the top $20, 30, 50$ and 100 retrieved images as well as the overall average precisions for the methods compared. In a nutshell, our proposed approaches Dsgn and Dscv achieved high average precisions of 0.59 and 0.52 respectively, which are significant improvements of 55% and 37% over that of the CTO method (last row of Table 2). The integrated matching (Eq. (12)) has also shown to be effective in combining the complementary indexes (i.e. Dsgn from SSR and SSC, Dscv from DSR and LSC) to produce better average precisions (Table 2). Retrieval is very efficient as similarity matching involves simple arithmetic operations only. Learning and indexing require more computation but they are carried out off-line and the algorithms are inherently parallel, hence concurrent and parallel implementation are straight forward.

6 Conclusion

In this paper, we have presented frameworks to combine local and global semantics from both semantics design and discovery perspectives. While the supervised framework provides a structured design methodology to build semantic image indexing and retrieval systems, the unsupervised framework provides an automatic approach to discover local semantics bootstrapped from semantic image classes. The proposed local and global image indexes are based on segmentation-free detection of SSRs and DSRs as well as class memberships of SSCs and LSCs that are all derived from statistical learning in a modular manner. An empirical evaluation has been carried out using 16 semantic queries on 2400 real unconstrained consumer images to verify the usefulness of the proposed framework against a typical feature-fusion approach.

References

1. K. Barnard et al. Matching words and pictures. *J. Machine Learning Research*, 3: 1107-1135, 2003.
2. R. Fergus, P. Perona, and A. Zisserman. Object class recognition by unsupervised scale-invariant learning. In *Proc. of IEEE CVPR*, 2003.
3. T. Joachims. Making large-scale SVM learning practical. *Advances in Kernel Methods - Support Vector Learning.* B. Scholkopf, C. Burges, and A. Smola (ed.). MIT-Press, 1999.
4. J. Li and J.Z. Wang. Automatic linguistic indexing of pictures by a statistical modeling approach. *IEEE Trans. on PAMI*, 25(10): 1-14, 2003.
5. B.S. Manjunath and W.Y. Ma. Texture features for browsing and retrieval of image data. *IEEE Trans. on PAMI*, 18(8): 837-842, 1996.
6. A.W.M. Smeulders et al. Content-based image retrieval at the end of the early years. *IEEE Trans. on PAMI*, 22(12): 1349-1380. 2000.
7. C. Town and D. Sinclair. Content-based image retrieval using semantic visual categories. *Technical Report 2000.14.* AT&T Research Cambridge. 2000.
8. A. Vailaya et al. Bayesian framework for hierarchical semantic classification of vacation images. *IEEE Trans. on Image Processing*, 10(1): 117-130, 2001.

PDA-Based Text Localization System Using Client/Server Architecture

Anjin Park and Keechul Jung

School of Media, College of Information Science, Soongsil University, Seoul, South Korea
kcjung@ssu.ac.kr
http://hci.ssu.ac.kr/

Abstract. Recently, several research results of image processing are proposed on the mobile vision systems. Many CPUs for Personal Digital Assistant(PDA) are integer CPUs, which have no floating-computation component. It results in slow computation of the algorithms constructed by using neural networks, which have much floating-computation. In this paper, in order to resolve this weakness, we propose an effective text localization system with the Client(PDA)/Server(PC) architecture which is connected to each other with a wireless LAN. The Client(PDA) compresses tentative text localization results in JPEG format for minimizing the transmission time to the Server(PC). The Server(PC) uses both the Multi-Layer Perceptron(MLP)-based texture classifier and Connected Components(CCs)-based filtering for a precise text localization based on the Client(PDA)'s tentative extracting results. The proposed method leads to not only faster running time but also efficient text localization.

1 Introduction

In the ubiquitous computing age which uses the high quantity network, anytime, anywhere, anydevice, handheld devices such as Personal Digital Assistant(PDA) with a small camera and a wireless communication module will be widely used in near future.

Based on the fact that texts within images captured by a camera attached to a PDA are very useful for describing the contents of the image and can be easily extracted comparing with other semantic contents, researchers have recently attempted text-based image indexing using various image processing techniques[1-11].

We encounter two major troubles when we try text localization and recognition on a PDA platform compared with a desktop PC[6].

First, limited computational resource. Almost all CPUs for a PDA are integer CPUs, which have no floating-computation component. And it results in slow computation because a compiler uses a float emulation library to implement floating-computation. For example, when we implement a text localization system on the PDA with a Multi-Layer Perceptron(MLP)-based texture classifier which is used in this paper, it takes about 4 minutes to process an 240×320 size image. It is 120 times slower than the desktop PC which is used in our implementation.

Second, limited memory. For example, a Pocket PC 2002-based system which is used in this paper has 16~64MB memory and a general Palm OS-based system has 8~16MB memory. The memory is used for both storage and program. This is not suitable for the text localization and the optical character recognition(OCR).

In order to resolve this weakness, Zhang et al.[6] substituted the floating-computation with a normalized integer computation to speed up it, which will surely bring the loss of the precision. Haritaoglu[7] used a Client/Server architecture, and he implemented a precise text localization system with many floating-computations on the Server(PC). However, a user had to manually select the tentative text regions in the PDA, and also the system requires much transmission time in the wireless LAN.

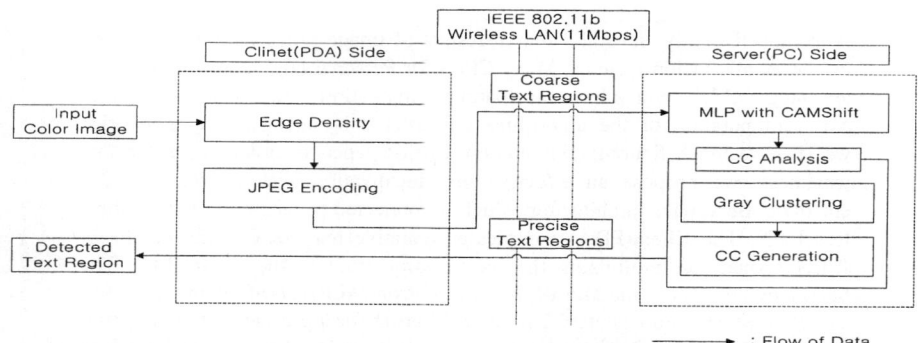

Fig. 1. Overview of the proposed text localization system.

Fig. 1 gives an overall structure of the proposed method. In order to resolve problems such as a limited computational resource and memory, we use the Client(PDA)/Server(PC) architecture, and in order to resolve a transmission time between Client(PDA) and Server(PC), an extracted tentative text regions in the PDA is compressed in JPEG format and send it to Server(PC). A Server(PC) implements a precise text localization based on Client(PDA)'s results. We use both a MLP-based texture classifier with high recall rates in the low resolution and a connected components(CCs)-based filtering with high precision rates. And then, the time-consuming texture analysis for less relevant pixels is avoided by using CAMShift.

The rest of the paper is organized as follows. We describe the Client(PDA) side and the Server(PC) side in Section 2 and 3, respectively. The experimental results are presented in Section 4. Finally, Section 5 summarizes the paper.

2 Client(PDA) Side

A Client(PDA) extracts tentative text regions using edge density and compresses the result images in JPEG format to minimize the transmission time.

The edge density is the number of edge points in each N×N window. If the edge density has a larger value than the given threshold value, then we assume the N×N window is a tentative text region. The edge density is appropriate for a PDA because of a simple computation in the texture classifier, and it results in the efficient running time in the overall structure.

We use the JPEG algorithm as the image compression method. Impressive compression ratios can be achieved by JPEG. Ratios of up to twenty to one can be achieved without noticeable difference from the original image[12].

In our implementation, edge point is computed by applying laplacian operators, the threshold for the edge density had been experimentally determined to be 50, and window size has used 20×20 window.

Because a Server(PC) implements text localization with the only gray image, we change the result images obtained by the edge density with gray images.

As shown in Fig. 2, we use the edge density for tentative text extraction, we can get sufficient extraction results with a low computation cost and low false dismissals. Figs. 2(a) are edge density images, and Figs. 2(b) are result images obtained by the edge density.

(a)   (b)

Fig. 2. Examples of result images obtained by the edge density.

3 Server(PC) Side

A Sever(PC) implements a precise text localization based on the Client(PDA)'s results, and it uses both a MLPs-based texture classifier and a CCs-based filtering.

The images captured by a camera attached to PDA are a low resolution, and it can include various backgrounds. When we use the MLP-based texture classifier, it seems the high recall rate with such images, and we use the CCs-based filtering to enhance the precision rate together.

3.1 MLP-Based Texture Classifier

We use a MLP to make a texture classifier that discriminates between text pixels and non-text ones. A received image data is scanned by the MLP, which receives the gray values of a given pixel and its neighbors within a small window. The MLP's outputs are combined into a text probability image (TPI), where each pixel's value is in the range [0,1] and represents the probability that the corresponding input pixel is a part of text. If a pixel has a larger value than the given threshold value, it is considered as a text pixel.

Fig. 3 describes the architecture of the MLP-based texture classifier. Adjacent layers are fully connected. Unlike other neural network-based text detection methods, we can simplify a laborious feature design task and can make a compact system as we use the raw image pixels as an input feature. Therefore no explicit feature extraction stage is used as opposed to the other text detection approaches with wavelet, FFT, gabor-based feature extraction stages, etc.[5]. Moreover, instead of using all pixels in the input window, a configuration for autoregressive feature (gray squares in Fig. 3) is used. This input configuration is well known for better performance and generalization power for texture analysis[5].

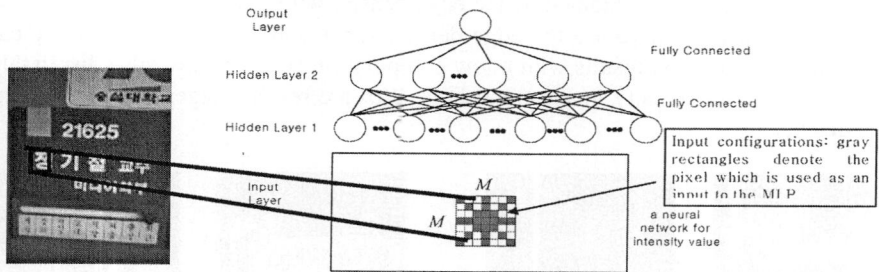

Fig. 3. A three-layer feed-forward neural network.

To handle practically infinite non-text images in the training stage of MLPs, we use the bootstrap method recommended by Sung and Poggio[8]. This bootstrap method is used to get non-text training samples more efficiently and to force the MLPs to learn a precise boundary between text and non-text classes. 4(a) and (b) are examples of text and non-text images, respectively, used as initial training samples. Fig. 4(c) shows a training image used in bootstrap. Fig. 4(d) depicts the pixels (marked as black) misclassified as texts. This bootstrap method is used to get non-text training samples more efficiently and to force the MLP to learn a precise boundary between text and non-text classes.

Fig. 4. Examples of training samples and misclassified results: (a) text samples, (b) non-text samples, (c) an image for bootstrap, and (d) classification results of (c).

3.2 CAMShift Algorithm

We use a CAMShift algorithm on the TPI for text detection, which is a modified version of the CAMShift algorithm[9]. To avoid the full scanning of an input image with MLP, which we mentioned as a drawback of the texture-based methods in Section 1, CAMShift algorithms are invoked at several seed positions on the TPI. This leads to great computational savings when text regions do not dominate the image. Fig. 5 is the CAMShift algorithm for text detection.

- Set up the initial locations ($mean_x(i)_0$, $mean_y(i)_0$) and sizes ($\lambda_x(i)_0$, $\lambda_y(i)_0$) of search windows Ws
- Do
  For each search window $W(i)$
  - Generate the TPI within $W(i)$ using MLP.
  - Based on the mean shift vector, derive the new position and size of a text region.
  - Modify $W(i)$ according to the derived values.
  Merge overlapping windows.
  Increment the iteration number t.
  While($\| mean_X(i)_t - mean_X(i)_{t+1} \| > \varepsilon_x$ or $\| mean_Y(i)_t - mean_Y(i)_{t+1} \| > \varepsilon_y$)
- Filter localized text regions using area and aspect ratio of the region-bounding rectangles

---

Fig. 5. CAMShift algorithm for text detection.

At the initial stage of the CAMShift algorithm on each search window, we decide whether the search window contain texts or not. During consecutive iterations, we estimate the size, position, skew angle of the text region using 2D moments[9], change the parameters of a search window depending on the estimated values, and then perform a window-merge operation to eliminate overlapping search windows. If the mean shift is larger than either of the threshold values ε_x (along x-axis) and ε_y (along y-axis), the iteration continues.

We convolve every pixel (x,y) in a search window. If a pixel (x,y) has been convolved by MLP in previous iterations, re-use $TPI(x,y)$. Otherwise we perform and convolution using MLP at pixel (x,y). The size, position, and skew angle of text regions are estimated by 2 dimensional moment calculations[9]. At each iteration, we have to merge some overlapping search windows to save processing time of the MultiCAMShift algorithm. When overlapping windows exist, we examine whether they are originally a single text or separate texts. This is done by checking the degree of overlap between two regions as follows. Let D_α and D_β be the areas covered by two text regions α and β. Then the degree of overlap between α and β is defined as

$$\Lambda(\alpha,\beta) = \max(size(D_\alpha \cap D_\beta)/size(D_\alpha),\ size(D_\alpha \cap D_\beta)/size(D_\beta)), \quad (1)$$

Where $size(\lambda)$ counts the number of pixels within λ. Regions α and β are determined to be a single text if $T_O \leq \Lambda(\alpha,\beta)$ where T_O is a threshold set to be 0.8. Otherwise they are separate texts.

Fig. 6. Examples of text localization using MLPs with CAMShift: (a) input images overlaid with tracks of mean locations, (b) final localized results.

Fig. 6 shows text localization results with a simple image. In Figs. 6(a), the white cross symbols show the transitions of mean locations in successive iterations. Figs. 6(b) show the extracted text regions.

3.3 Connected Component-Based Filtering

Although we use the bootstrap method to make the texture classification MLP learn the precise boundary between a text class and non-text one, the detection result from the MLPs includes many alarms because we want the MLPs to detect texts as many as possible. As shown in Fig. 7, texture-based text detection algorithms tend to give false alarms for high-contrast or high-frequency regions and the regions which have similar textural properties with characters. In Figs. 7(a), detected text regions are marked with black-and-white boundaries. In Figs. 7(b), the black pixels denote texts. In order to tackle the false alarm problem of the texture-based method, we use the CCs-based filtering.

Fig. 7. Text detection examples using MLPs with CAMShift: (a) a scene text image with marked text regions and (b) its corresponding filtered images (TPI).

CCs are not appropriate for low-resolution images because they depend on the effectiveness of the segmentation method. Therefore, we made assumptions; 1) Text regions appear sufficiently large in the scene. 2) The text is designed with high contrast to background. 3) Each character is composed of one or several connected components.

We use the single-link clustering algorithm for making connected component[11]. The single-link clustering algorithm combines the two nearest clusters of similar intensity. Input images(output of the MLPs) in our experiment generate 4 clusters.

Each pixel in the text regions of the input image is then replaced by the representative intensity of the group it belongs to. CCs are identified from this image. The morphological closing operation is applied to the CCs before we compute the attributes of the components, such as size and area. We have then the two stages filtering on the CCs:

Stage 1: Heuristics using features of CCs such as area, fill factor, and horizontal and vertical extents; The width of the text region must be larger than the predefined minimum width(Min_width), the aspect ratio of the text region must be smaller than Max_aspect, the area of the component should be larger than Min_area and smaller than Max_area, and the fill_factor should be larger than Min_fillfactor.

Stage 2: Geometric alignment of text components; We check the number of adjacent text components which have the same color in an identical text line. Texts have to be aligned in more than three consecutive components.

Fig. 8 shows the example images before and after CC analysis.

Fig. 8. CC analysis: (a) before CC-based filtering and (b) after CC-based filtering.

4 Experimental Results

In our implementation, we use the Client(PDA)/Server(PC) architecture. The Client(PDA) component consists of a HP iPAQ h5450 model, a everCAM LMC2001B camera, and a wireless communication module. The HP iPAQ h5450 model is the Pocket PC 2002-based system and has 64MB SDRAM/48MB Flash ROM and 400MHz Intel Xscale PXA 250 processor. The everCAM LMC2001B camera has 320k pixels. The Server(PC) component consists of a Pentium IV 2.66 GHz system and a internet connectivity.

The input image from the camera is used as a gray image with 240×320 pixel resolution. Fig. 9 shows result images per each step on the Server(PC).

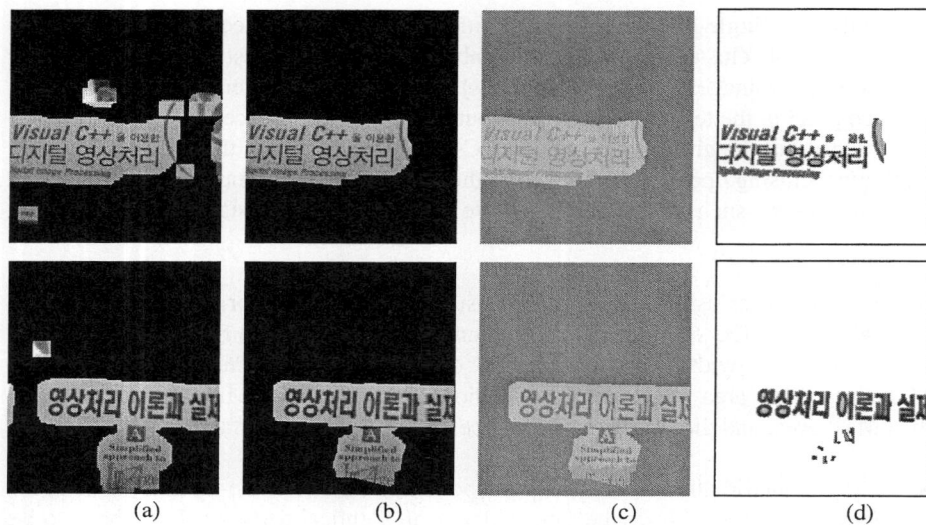

Fig. 9. Examples of result image per each step on the Server(PC): (a) images which is transmitted from the PDA, (b) text detection results using MLP, (c) single-link clustering, (d) text detection results(after CCs analysis).

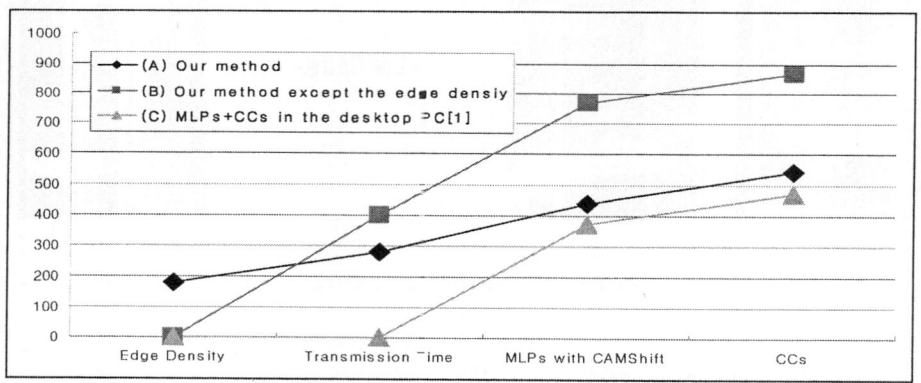

Fig. 10. the cumulative running time per each step: (A) the proposed method, (B) the proposed method except the edge density, (C) in the desktop PC.

Fig. 10 shows the comparison result with the running time. Fig. 10(A) is the proposed method, Fig. 10(B) is the method except the edge density, and Fig. 10(C) is the running time of the MLPs+CCs in the desktop PC[1]. As shown in Fig. 10, Fig. 10(A) takes the faster running time than Fig. 10(B) and is little difference comparison to Fig. 10(C), and the edge density has efficient running time in the overall structure.

We evaluate the localization rates on pixel level and use two metrics (precision and recall rates)[10]. Table 1 shows the pixel level precision and recall rate per each step. As shown in Table 1, the propose method takes higher precision rate than MLP-only method.

Table 1. Pixel level precision and recall rate per each step.

	Edge Density	MLPs	CCs
Precision rate	48%	73.48%	91.12%
Recall rate	100%	92.5%	84.34%

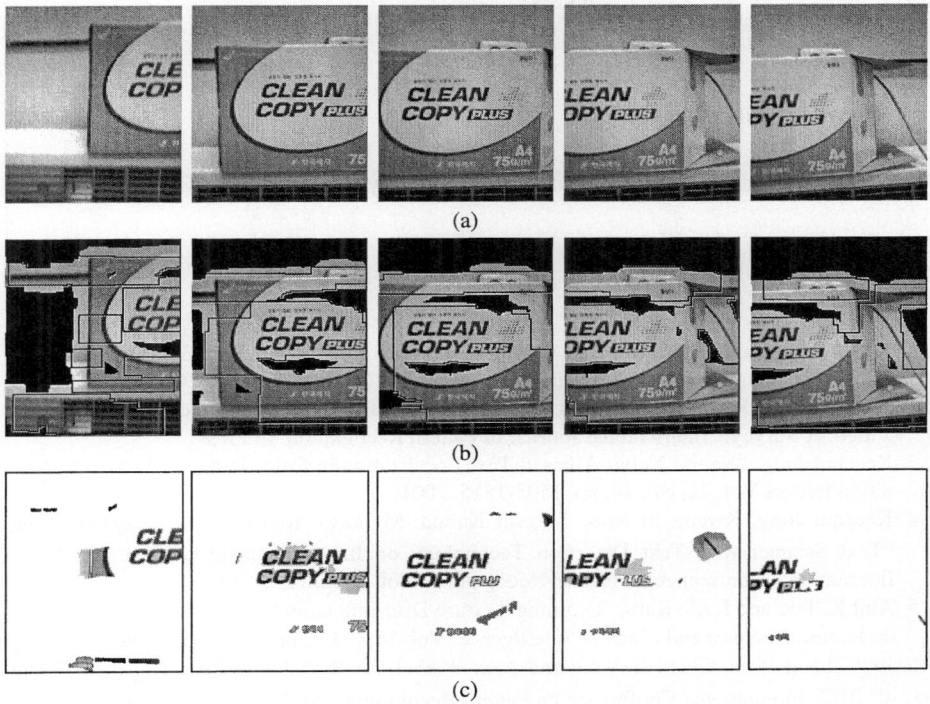

Fig. 11. The text localization examples.

Fig. 11 shows text localization examples. Fig. 11(a) shows the input images from the camera attached by PDA, Fig. 11(b) shows the result image in the PDA(Client), and Fig. 11(c) shows the result image in the Server(PC).

5 Conclusions

A floating-computation had much running time because almost all CPUs for PDA are integer CPUs. The text localization which is used in this paper was effective method in the desktop PC. However, it resulted in slow computation because of much floating-computation. In order to resolve this problem, we used the Client(PDA)/Server(PC) architecture. The purposed method leads to not only faster running time but also efficient text localization.

However, texts within the images from the PDA occasionally have following properties: 1) the text is designed with low contrast to background, 2) several characters are linked to one connected component after quantization because of low resolution. In this case, our system does not work well. However, the text information what we are aiming to is not include in these case. As a result, our system is suitable for the PDA.

Acknowledgement

This work was supported by the Soongsil University Research Fund.

Referrences

1. Keechul Jung and JungHyun Han, "Hybrid Approach to Efficient Text Extraction in Complex Color Images," Pattern Recognition Letters, Vol. 25, Issue 6, pp. 679-699, Apr. 2004.
2. Keechul Jung, Kwang In Kim, and Anil K. Jain, "Text Information Extraction in Image and Video: A Survey," International Journal of Pattern Recognition, In Press.
3. Keechul Jung, "Neural Network-based Text Localization in Color Images," Pattern Recognition Letters Vol. 22, No. 14, pp. 1503-1515, 2001.
4. Keechul Jung, Kwang In Kim, Takeshi Kurata, Maskastu Kourogi and JungHyun Han, "Text Scanner with Text Detection Technology on Image Sequences," The 16th IEEE International Conference on Pattern Recognition, Vol. 3, pp. 11-15, Aug. 2002.
5. Anil K. Jain and Kalle Karu, "Learning Texture Discrimination Masks," IEEE Transactions on Pattern Analysis and Machine Intelligence, Vol. 18, No. 2, pp. 195-205, 1996.
6. Jing Zhang, Xilin Chen, JieYang and Alex Waibel, "A PDA-based Sign Translator," The 4th IEEE International Conference on Pattern Recognition, pp. 216-219, Oct. 2002.
7. Ismail Haritaoglu, "Scene Text Extraction and Translation for Handheld Devices," IEEE Conference on Computer Vision and Pattern Recognition, pp. 408-413, 2001.
8. K. K. Sung and T. Poggio, "Example-based Learning for View-based Human Face Detection," IEEE Transactions on Pattern Analysis and Machine Intelligence, Vol. 20, No. 1, pp. 39-51, 1998.
9. Gary R. Bradski and Vadim Pisarevsky. "Intel's Computer Vision Library: Application in Calibration, Strereo, Segmentation, Tracking, Gesture, Face and Object Recognition," IEEE Conference of Computer Vision and Pattern Recognition, Vol. 2, pp. 796-797, 2000.
10. Huiping Li, David Doerman and Omid Kia, "Automatic Text Detection and Tracking in Digital Video," IEEE Transactions on Image Processing, Vol. 9, No. 1, Jan., pp. 147-156, 2000.
11. Anil. K Jain and Bin Yu, "Automatic Text Location in Images and Video Frames," Pattern Recognition, Vol. 31, No. 12, pp.2055-2076, 1998.
12. Randy Crane, "A Simplified Approach to Image Processing," Prentice Hall PTR, 1997.

Vision Technique for the Recognition of Billet Characters in the Steel Plant

Jong-hak Lee[1], Sang-gug Park[2], and Soo-joong Kim[3]

[1] Technical Research Institute of POSCO
790-785, 1 Goedong-dong, Nam-gu, Pohang, Kyungpook, Korea
jhak@posco.co.kr
http://www.springer.de/comp/lncs/index.html
[2] Department of Computer Engineering, Uiduk University
780-713, #50 Yu-gum, Kang-gong, Kyung-ju, Kyungpook, Korea
skpark@uiduk.ac.kr
[3] Dept. of Electronics and Electric Engineering, Kyungpook National University
702-701, Sin-am, Dong-gu, Taegu, Korea
sjkim@ee.knu.ac.kr

Abstract. This paper describes vision technique about the real time billet characters recognition system in the steel production line. Normally, the billets are mixed at yard so that their identifications are very difficult and very important processing. The character recognition algorithm used in this paper is base on the subspace method by K-L transformation. With this method, we need no special feature extraction steps, which are usually error prone. So the gray character images are directly used as input vectors of the classifier. To train the classifier, we have extracted eigen vectors of each character, which was included in the billet images. We have constructed vision system for the recognition of billet characters using this algorithm and tested this system in the steel production line. The recognition rate of our system in the field test has turned out to be 98.6 % if the corrupted characters are excluded. In the results, we have confirmed that our recognition system has a good performance in the poor environments and ill-conditioned marking system such as steel production plant.

1 Introduction

Nowadays, humans are being replaced by automated systems in many fields of applications, such as robotics [1], control system, system manufacturing, machine diagnosis and maintenances analysis, aircraft autopilot, and autopilot enhancement. The automated systems can save time, reduce cost, increase efficiency, performance, and reliability. This improvement has been reached in many systems, but it is far from being reached in other fields. One of the challenging fields that are still an open area of research is pattern recognition. So far, many approaches had been used and still a lot of research is needed to automate this problem. The character recognition technique is a part of the pattern recognition. In the field application, such as steel and iron plant, circumference environments have a serious effect in the character recognition. In the steel production line, the molten metal of a furnace is transformed into continuous casting slab or bloom via continuous casting processes and then move to the heating furnace of the hot rolling mill. A billet is extracted from bloom through the hot rolling processing. For the classification of the quality and uses of these slab or billet, material management numbers are marked in their front area. A small error in their classification causes serious results. Therefore, it is very important to recognize exactly this management numbers This paper describes about the real time billet number recognition system in the steel production line. Normally, the billets are mixed at yard so that their identifications are hardly tractable. The character recognition algorithm used in this paper is base on the subspace method by KLT(Karhunen-Loeve Transformation) [2]. With this method, we need no special feature extraction steps, which are usually error prone. So the gray images are directly used as input vectors of the classifier. To train the classifier, we have extracted eigen vectors of each character, which was included in the billet images. These characters are consists of 10 Arabia numbers and 26 alphabet characters, which are gathered from billet images of the production line. We have developed billet characters recognition system using this algorithm and tested this system in the steel production line during the 8-days. The recognition rate of the classifier in the field test has turned out to be 94.1 % and could be more improved to 98.6 % if the corrupted characters are excluded. By through the field test, we have confirmed that our recognition system has a good performance in the poor environments and ill-conditioned marking system. In some cases, wrong qualities of billets are injected into heating furnace, which result in bad quality products. To prevent miss injection, the billets are monitored by CCTV, which is installed in front of heating furnace. To build billet tracking control, the automatic billet identification is necessary condition.

2 Karhunen-Loeve Transformation

The Karhunen-Loeve(K-L) decomposition [3],[4], named after Karhunen [5] and Loeve [6], is used in many different applications that deal with large data sets. In the literature, K-L decomposition is known by several different names. It is known as K-L transformation, empirical orthogonal functions, quasiharmoic modes, singular value decomposition, Hotteling transform, proper orthogonal decomposition and principal component analysis. In these approaches, K-L decomposition was used as either a compression tool or as a feature identifier. In the last few years, K-L decomposition has been used extensively by Smaoui et al., in fluid flow in porous media, in the analysis of sand stones, and in the study of flames. In face recognition, K-L decomposition was used by Smaoui and Matar [7]. In this paper, recognition method by K-L transformation is use secondary variance of input data. If we define that input pattern $x = [x_1, x_2, ..., x_N]^T$ is random vector in the vector space of N-th order and c_x, m_x are covariance matrix, mean vector, respectively. Then we can denote as follows,

$$m_x = E[x] . \tag{1}$$

$$c_x = E[(x-m_x)(x-m_x)^T] . \tag{2}$$

Because c_x has a real number value and symmetry matrix form. There are exist eigen value, which has a positive value of N numbers, and eigen vector of each eigen values. Eigen vectors of each different eigen values are mutually orthonormal. Let assume that λ_i, φ_i are the eigen value, eigen vector of c_x, respectively and λ_i is arranged in order of $\lambda_i \geq \lambda_{i+1}$ ($i = 1, 2, ..., N-1$). Then, eigen vector matrix, Φ is represented as following Eq.(3).

$$\Phi = [\varphi_1 \; \varphi_2 \; \cdots \; \varphi_N] . \tag{3}$$

First column of matrix Φ has a eigen vector, which has a maximum eigen value and last column of matrix Φ has a eigen vector, which has a minimum eigen value. If we define Φ^T as a transform matrix, which has transform x into y. Then, we obtain following Eq.(4).

$$y = \Phi^T (x - m_x) . \tag{4}$$

In Eq. (4), we designate y as a Karhunen-Loeve transformation and Φ^T as a Karhunen-Loeve transformation matrix. In this case, transformed new random vector has following properties.

$$m_y = E[y] = \Phi^T(E[x] - m_x) = 0 . \tag{5}$$

$$\begin{aligned} c_y &= E[(y - m_y)(y - m_y)^T] \\ &= E^T c_x E \\ &= [a_{ij}] . \end{aligned} \tag{6}$$

here, $\qquad i, j = 1, 2, ..., N$

$$a_{ij} = \begin{pmatrix} \lambda_i & for & i = j \\ 0 & otherwise & \end{pmatrix}$$

Therefore, each components of vector y, which was transformed by KLT, is mutually uncorrelated. In generally, the size of eigen vector of K-L transformed vector, y is N when the size of input vector is N. In that case, most of transformed energy is concentrated in the M-dimensional space ($M \leq N$).

3 Vision Systems

3.1 Image Acquisition System

For the acquisition of the billet images, which is marked management numbers, we designed area image acquisition system using CCD camera and image processing devices. CCD camera has located at the input side of heating furnace of the hot rolling mill. Therefore, billet images are acquired before it is transferred to the heating furnace. Fig. 1 represents system layout for the image acquisition of billet. Trigger sensor sends a trigger signal to the camera controller whenever the billet is arriving at the target zone.

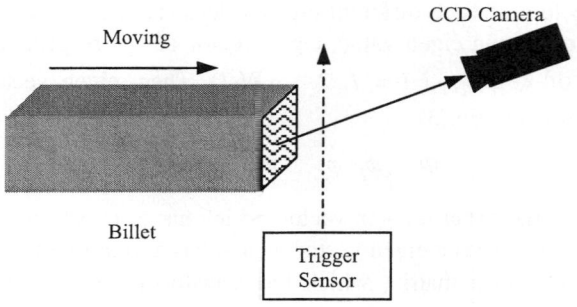

Fig. 1. System layout for the image acquisition

Fig. 2. Captured image of a billet

The CCD camera captures the image of a cross section, which was marked the management characters of billet. Frame grabber, Matrox Meteorl-II of PC is connected with CCD camera. The model number of a CCD camera is Pulinx 9701, which has supporting 768 × 484 image size and 256 gray level. Fig. 2 represents the captured image of billet. For the stability of gray image in the billet processing line, we shined a halogen lamp on the cross section of a billet.

3.2 Character Recognition

For the recognition of management characters from the billet image, we used several steps. Fig. 3 represents flowchart for the character recognition. In the steel processing line, billets can be rotated to the any directions, which are 0°, 90°, 180° and 270°.

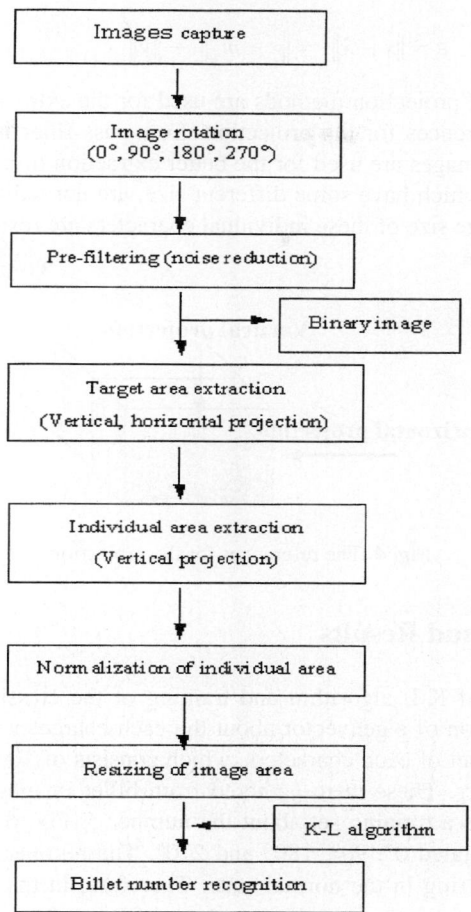

Fig. 3. Flowchart of the our algorithm

We should consider this rotation at the first step. In the case of rotation, 90°, 270°, it can be more easily distinguished than the rotation, 0°, 180° by the comparison of a format of character string and numbers of individual characters within a character string. In the case of rotation, 0°, 180°, we have distinguished their rotation angle using the voting methods, which are based on recognition rate. For this recognition, we compare their reconstruction error in the domain of KLT and inverse KLT between input character and candidate characters. Candidate characters, which are predefined, are alphabets 26 and Arabia numbers 10. The character classification is needed to find a final character, which has a minimum reconstruction error between input character and candidate character. The reconstruction error is calculated as Eq.(7). Here, the parameters of equation are as follows, x : input vector, $\hat{x}$: inverse transformed vector of x, m_x : mean of x, $\hat{y}$:K-L transform about the subspace area.

$$\varepsilon = \|x - \hat{x}\|^2 = \|x - m_x\|^2 - \|\hat{y}\|^2. \tag{7}$$

Horizontal or vertical projection methods are used for the extraction of a border. Fig. 4 represents the references for the projection. Low pass filter is applied in the prefiltering and binary images are used for the better extraction of a border. The individual character areas, which have some different size, are normalized to the same size, 40×40 and then, image size of these individual characters are resized for the reduction of the computing time.

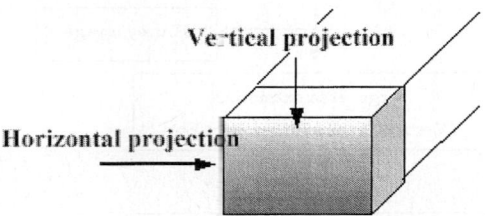

Fig. 4. The references for the projection

4 Experiments and Results

For the application of K-L algorithm and training of the classifier in the character recognition, calculation of eigenvector about the each character is need. For this, we constructed training set of each characters, which consists of 10 Arabia numbers and 26 alphabet characters. These were gathered from billet images of steel production line. Fig. 5 represents a training set about the number 5. Fig. 6 represents character images, which are rotated 0°, 90°, 180° and 270°. The numbers of character image have two character string in the normal state. Therefore, in the case of rotated 90°, and 270°, two strings from the topside are selected for the character recognition. Fig. 7 represents individual characters of extracted character string when the character image was rotated 0°, 90°. Fig. 8 represents individually extracted characters from the single character string. In this paper, we use original gray image instead of binary image. Therefore, our methods don't need binarization about the captured image. The profile of upper side represents mountain and valley. The mountain represents location of characters and the valley represents location of border between each characters. For the field test, we applied our system to the billets. Our system has located at the input side of heating furnace in the wire rod mill line. Test time was 8-days and 2503 billets were used for the test. The recognition rate of the system in the field test has turned out to be 94.1 %. The cause of the recognition fail is classified into three types. Two types are cannot recognize by human eyes as well as commuter system.

These cases include 113 billets (4.5 %). Only one type among the failed three cases could not recognized by our system despite of the normal state. This case includes 34 billets (1.4 %). Therefore, the maximum recognition rate of our system can be increased to the 98.6 % if the corrupted characters are excluded.

Vision Technique for the Recognition of Billet Characters in the Steel Plant 849

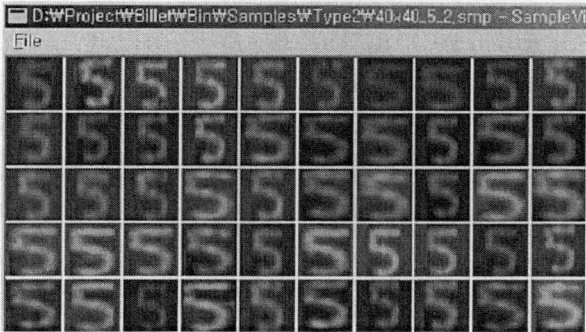

Fig. 5. Training set of number 5

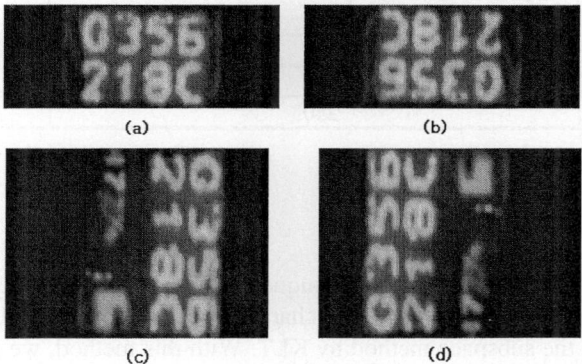

Fig. 6. Character images, which are rotated ((a) 0°, (b) 180°, (c) 90°, (d) 270°)

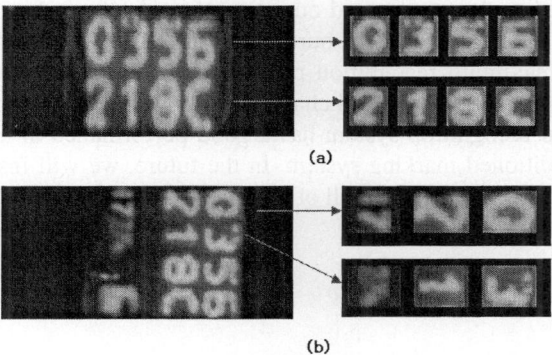

Fig. 7. Extracted character string when the image was rotated ((a) 0°, (b) 90°)

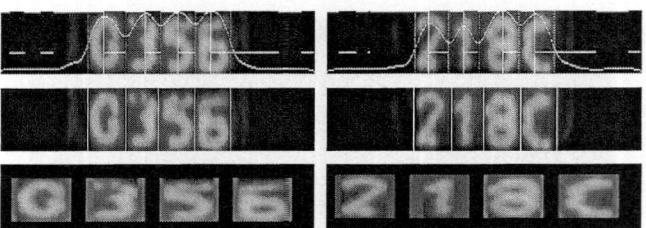

Fig. 8. Extracted individual characters

Table 1. Test results

Test results	State of billet	Numbers of test billets	Recognition rate
Successes	Normal	2356	2356 (94.1 %)
Failed	Different marking style	16	147 (5.9 %)
	Character damage	97	
	Normal	34	
Total		2503	2503(100 %)

5 Conclusions

In this paper, we described vision technique for the character recognition of billet image in the steel production line. The character recognition algorithm used in this paper is base on the subspace method by KLT. With this method, we need no special feature extraction steps, which are usually error prone. So the gray character images are directly used as input vectors of the classifier. To train the classifier, we have gathered the billet images from the their production line. We have developed billet number recognition system and tested our system during the 8-days in the steel production line. The recognition rate of our system has turned out to be 94.1 % in the worst case. The maximum recognition rate of our recognition system could be increased to the 98.6 % if the corrupted characters are excluded. In the results, we have confirmed that our recognition system has a good performance in the poor environments and ill-conditioned marking system. In the future, we will install our recognition system to the on-line wire rod mill of the steel production line.

References

1. G. Schweitzer: Mechatronics for the design of human oriented machines, IEEE/ASME Trans. on Mechatronics, Vol. 1 (1996) 120–126
2. Jeong-Hoe Ku: Design of freight train ID number recognition system based on Karhunen-Loeve transform, thesis of master degree of Pohang university of science and technology (1994)

3. K. Fukunaga, Warren L.G. Koontz: Application of the Karhunen-Loeve expansion to feature selection and ordering, IEEE trans. on computers, Vol. C-19, No. 4 (1970) 311–318
4. S. Watanabe: Karhunen-Loeve expansion and factor analysis theoretical remarks and applications, Proc. 4th Prague Conf. Inform. Theory (1965)
5. Karhunen K: Uber lineare methoden in der Wahrsccheillichkeitsrechung, annales academiae scientiarum fennicae, seried AI: mathematica-physica (1947) 3–79
6. Loeve, M, "probability theory," Van Nostrand, New York (1963)
7. N. Smaoui and M. Ibrahim, "Classification oh human faces using Karhunen-Loeve decomposition and radial basis function neural networks," Intern. J. Computer Math., Vol. 80(3) (2003) 325–345

Tagging Medical Documents with High Accuracy

Udo Hahn and Joachim Wermter

Text Knowledge Engineering Lab
Friedrich-Schiller-Universität Jena
Fürstengraben 30, D-07743 Jena, Germany
hahn@coling.uni-freiburg.de

Abstract. We ran both Brill's rule-based tagger and TNT, a statistical tagger, with a default German newspaper-language model on a medical text corpus. Supplied with limited lexicon resources, TNT outperforms the Brill tagger with state-of-the-art performance figures (close to 97% accuracy). We then trained TNT on a large annotated medical text corpus, with a slightly extended tagset that captures certain medical language particularities, and achieved 98% tagging accuracy. Hence, statistical off-the-shelf POS taggers cannot only be immediately reused for medical NLP, but they also achieve – when trained on medical corpora – a higher performance level than for the newspaper genre.

1 Introduction

The applicability of human language technology in the field of medicine, so-called medical language processing (MLP), is gaining rapid recognition [1].

For written language material, however, the development of training and test resources has almost exclusively focused on newswire or newspaper genres. This is most prominently evidenced by the PENN TREEBANK [2]. Its value as one of the most widely used language resources mainly derives from two features. First, it supplies everyday, non-specialist document sources, such as the *Wall Street Journal*, and, second, it contains value-added, *viz.* annotated, linguistic data. Since the understanding of newspaper material does not impose particular requirements on its reader, other than the mastery of general English and common-sense knowledge, it is easy for almost everybody to deal with. This is essential for the accomplishment of the second task, *viz.* the annotation and reuse of part-of-speech (POS) tags and parse trees, as the result of linguistic analysis. With the help of such resources, whole generations of state-of-the-art taggers, chunkers, grammar and lexicon learners have evolved.

The medical field poses new challenges. First, medical documents exhibit a large variety of structural features not encountered in newspaper documents (the genre problem), and, second, the understanding of medical language requires an enormous amount of a priori medical expertise (the domain problem). Hence, the question arises, how portable results are from the newspaper domain to the medical domain.

We will deal with these issues, focusing on the portability of taggers, from two perspectives. We first pick up off-the-shelf technology, in our case the rule-based Brill tagger [3] and the statistically-based TNT tagger [4], both trained on newspaper data, and run it on medical text data. One may wonder how the taggers trained on newspaper language perform with medical language. Furthermore, one may ask whether it is necessary (and, if so, costly) to retrain these taggers on a medical corpus, if one were at hand. These questions seem to be of particular importance, because the use of off-the-shelf language technology for MLP applications has recently been questioned [5]. Answers will be given in Section 2.

Once a large annotated medical corpus becomes available, additional questions can be tackled. Will taggers improve their performance substantially when trained on medical data, or is this more or less irrelevant? Also, if medical sublanguage particularities can already be identified on the level of POS co-occurrences, would it be a good idea to enhance newspaper-oriented, general-purpose tagsets with dedicated medical tags? Finally, does this extension have a bearing on the performance of tagging medical documents and, if so, to what extent? We will elaborate on these questions in Section 4.

2 Medical Tagging with Off-the-Shelf Technology

For the first series of experiments, we chose two representatives of the currently prevailing data-driven tagging approaches, Brill's rule-based tagger [3] and TNT, a statistical tagger [4]. As we are primarily concerned with German language input, for Brill's tagger, originally developed on English data, its German rule extension package was used. TNT, on the other hand, is based on a statistical model and therefore is basically language-independent. It implements the Viterbi algorithm for second-order Markov models [4], in which states of the model represent tags and the output represents words. The best POS tag for a given word is determined by the highest probability that it occurs with n previous tags. Tags for unknown words are assigned by a probabilistic suffix analysis; smoothing is done by linear interpolation.

2.1 Experiment 1: Medical Tagging with Standard Tagset Trained on NEGRA

The German default version of TNT was trained on NEGRA, the largest publicly available manually annotated German newspaper corpus (composed of 355,095 tokens and POS-tagged with the general-purpose STTS tagset [6]). The Brill tagger comes with an English default version also trained on general-purpose language corpora like the PENN TREEBANK [2]. In order to compare the performance of both taggers on German data, the Brill tagger was retrained on the German NEGRA newspaper corpus, with parameters recommended in the training manual.

In a second round, we set aside a subset of a newly developed German-language medical corpus (21,000 tokens, with 1800 sentences). We here refer to this text corpus as FRAMED$_{Stts}$ and describe its superset, FRAMED, in more depth in Section 4.1.

Three human taggers, trained on the STTS tagset and on guidelines used for tagging the NEGRA corpus, annotated FRAMED$_{Stts}$ according to NEGRA standards. The interrater reliability for this part of the manual annotation was 96.7% (standard deviation: 0.6%), based on a random sample of 2000 tokens (10% of the evaluation corpus). This score is still within acceptable bounds. The performance of both taggers, TNT and Brill, with their NEGRA newspaper-trained parameterization was then measured on the FRAMED$_{Stts}$ corpus. In addition, since both TNT and Brill allow the inclusion of an external backup lexicon, their performance was also measured by plugging in two such medical backups.

2.2 Results from Medical Tagging with Standard Tagset Trained on NEGRA

We measured *tagging accuracy* by the ratio of the number of correct POS assignments to text tokens (as defined by the gold standard, *viz.* the manually annotated corpus) and the number of all POS assignments to text tokens from the test set. Table 1 reveals that the n-gram-based TNT tagger outperforms the rule-based Brill tagger on the FRAMED$_{Stts}$ medical corpus, both being trained on the NEGRA newspaper corpus. The inclusion of a small medical backup lexicon (composed of 171 entries which account for the most frequently falsely tagged tokens such as measure units, Latinate medical terms, abbreviations) boosted TNT's performance to 96.7%, which is on a par with the state-of-the-art performance of taggers on newspaper texts. A much larger medical backup lexicon, which contained the first one plus the *German Specialist Lexicon*, a repository of domain-specific medical terms (totalling 95,969 entries), much to our surprise had almost no effect on improving the tagging results.

Table 1. Tagging Accuracy (Training on NEGRA Newspaper Corpus; Evaluation on FRAMED$_{Stts}$ Medical Corpus)

	TNT	BRILL
Default	95.2%	91.9%
+ Back-up Lexicon 1	96.7%	93.4%
+ Back-up Lexicon 2	96.8%	93.5%

The results for the German version of Brill's tagger, both its default version (91.9%) and the lexicon add-on (93.4%), are still considerably better than those of its default version reported by Campbell et al. [5] for English medical input (89.0%).

3 An Inquiry into Corpus Similarity

The fact that an n-gram-based statistical POS tagger like TNT, trained on newspaper and tested on medical language data, falls 1.5% short of state-of-the-art performance figures may at first come as a surprise. It has been observed by [5] and [1], however, that medical language shows *less* variation and complexity than general, newspaper-style language. Our second series of experiments, quantifying the grammatical differences/similarities between newspaper and medical language on the TNT-relevant POS n-gram level, may shed some explanatory light on the tagger's performance.

3.1 Experiment 2: Measuring Corpus Similarity

We collected a large medical document collection, referred to as BIGMED (it is composed of 2480K tokens), of mostly clinical texts (i.e., pathology, histology and surgery reports, discharge summaries). Next, we randomly split BIGMED into six subsamples of NEGRA size (355K tokens). This was meant to ensure a statistically sound comparability and to break up the medical subgenres. The same procedure was repeated for a collection of German newspaper and newswire texts collected from the Web. All twelve

Table 2. POS n-gram and χ^2 Comparsions between NEGRA-MED and NEGRA-NEWS (deviation of means of six MED and six NEWS samples in parentheses)

	NEGRA	MED	NEGRA	NEWS
POS trigram types	13,045	9,232.9 (217.5)	13,045	13,709.2 (86.8)
common POS trigram types: ratio (in %)	7,130.3 (144.2)		9,992.0 (33.6)	
	54.7 (1.1)	77.2 (0.4)	76.6 (0.3)	72.9 (0.3)
χ^2 significant common POS trigram types	2,793.8 (34.4) ratio: 41.7% (1.3)		1,202.0 (29.6) ratio: 12.1% (0.3)	
POS bigram types	1,441	1,169.0 (20.7)	1,441	1,441.8 (14.8)
common POS bigram types: ratio (in %)	1,076.5 (14.3)		1,270.8 (9.3)	
	76.4 (1.0)	92.0 (0.5)	88.2 (0.6)	88.1 (0.4)
χ^2 significant common POS bigram types	689.9 (5.5) ratio: 64.2% (0.9)		386.5 (12.2) ratio: 30.4% (0.9)	
POS unigram types	55	52.7 (0.5)	55	55.0 (0.5)
common POS unigram types	51.3 (0.5)		53.7 (0.5)	
χ^2 significant common POS unigram types	44.7 (0.8) ratio: 87.0% (1.5)		36.5 (2.4) ratio: 68.1% (4.9)	

samples (six medical ones, henceforth called MED, and six newspaper ones, henceforth called NEWS, also composed of 2480K tokens to ease partitioning) were then automatically tagged by TNT based on its newspaper-trained parameterization.

Since NEGRA is the newspaper corpus on which the default version of TNT was trained, its statistical comparison with MED should elucidate the tagger's performance on medical texts without changing the training environment. Moreover, a parallel comparison with other newspaper texts (NEWS) may help in further balancing these results. Because TNT is a Markovian tagger based on tri-, bi- and unigram POS sequences, the statistics were based on the POS n-gram sequences in the different corpora. For this purpose, we extracted all POS trigram, bigram and unigram type sequences from NEGRA, MED, and NEWS. Their numbers are reported in Table 2 (see rows 1, 4 and 7). We then generated a distribution of these types based on three ranges of occurrence frequencies. The results are reported in Table 3.

We then determined how many POS n-gram types were common between NEGRA and MED and common between NEGRA and NEWS (see Table 2, rows 2, 5 and 8). Each of these common POS n-gram types was subjected to a χ^2 test in order to measure whether their common occurrence in both corpora was just random (null hypothesis) or whether that particular n-gram was indicative of the similarity between the two corpora (i.e., between NEGRA and MED, on the one hand, and between NEGRA and NEWS, on the other hand). This interpretation of χ^2 statistics has already been evaluated against other corpus similarity measures and was shown to perform best [7], assuming a non-normal distribution (cf. also Table 3).

The χ^2 metric sums the differences between observed and expected values in all squares of the table and scales them by the magnitude of the expected values. The

Table 3. Three-part Distribution of POS n-gram Types in NEGRA, MED and NEWS

		POS n-gram types appearing		
		< 10 times	10-1000 times	≥ 1000 times
tri-grams	NEGRA	9402	3610	33
	MED	6571.2 (153)	2610.5 (66.5)	51.2 (0.8)
	NEWS	9972.5 (69)	3698.7 (31.6)	38 (0.6)
bi-grams	NEGRA	618	744	79
	MED	503.5 (18.2)	590.5 (16.3)	75 (1.9)
	NEWS	598.8 (14.)	762.2 (5.3)	80.8 (.6)
uni-grams	NEGRA	4	18	33
	MED	4.3 (0.8)	21.3 (0.8)	27 (0.6)
	NEWS	2.8 (1.0)	17.5 (0.8)	34.7 (0.5)

number of all common significant POS n-grams (i.e., those whose critical values are greater than 3.841 for a probability level of $\alpha = 0.05$) is indicative of the magnitude of corpus similarity. These results are reported in Table 2 (see rows 3, 6 and 9).

3.2 Results from Measuring Corpus Similarity

As shown in Table 2 (rows 1, 4 and 7), the number of unique POS n-gram types was considerably lower in MED. Compared with NEGRA, MED had 29% less trigram types, 19% less bigram types and 4% less unigram types (i.e., POS tags), whereas NEWS even had slightly more types at all n-gram levels. This much lower number of MED POS trigram and bigram types is also reflected in the three-part distribution in Table 3: The number of POS trigrams occurring less than ten times is almost one third less in MED than in NEGRA or in NEWS; similarly, but less pronounced, this can be observed for POS bigrams. On the other hand, the number of trigram types occurring more than 1000 times is even higher for MED, and the number of bigram and unigram types is about the same when scaled against the total number of types. This indicates a rather high POS trigram and bigram type dispersion in newspaper corpora, whereas medical narratives appear to be more homogeneous.

Table 2 (rows 2, 5 and 7) indicates that the number of POS trigram and bigram types common to both corpora was much smaller for the NEGRA-MED comparison than it was for NEGRA-NEWS. In other words, more of the NEGRA POS n-gram types appeared in the NEWS corpus as well, whereas far less showed up in the MED corpus. At this level of comparison, sublanguage differences clearly show up. If, however, compared with the total number of POS n-gram types in each corpus, the common ones cover much more of the MED corpus than of the NEGRA corpus. The coverage for NEGRA and NEWS is about the same.

The number of common POS n-gram types that are χ^2 significant (Table 2: rows 3, 6, and 9) shows the magnitude of corpus similarity. For the common trigram types, it was almost four times higher in the NEGRA-MED comparison than for NEGRA-NEWS; for the common bigram types it was more than twice as high, and for the unigram types 20% higher.

Finally, the top-ranked POS trigrams, bigrams and unigrams common to NEGRA and MED exhibit a strikingly different χ^2 magnitude compared to those common to NEGRA and NEWS. This means that, in regard to their top POS n-grams, NEGRA and MED are highly similar, whereas NEGRA and NEWS are less so. Interestingly, for each n-gram the top 5 ranks remain unchanged across all six NEGRA-MED comparisons, whereas they have a different ranking in almost each of the six NEGRA-NEWS comparisons. It seems as though the most characteristic similarities between medical sublanguage and newspaper language are highly consistent and predictable, whereas the intra-newspaper comparison shows weak and inconsistent similarities.

4 Medical Tagging with Medical Resources

4.1 FRAMED, an Annotated Medical Text Corpus

The FRAMED corpus [8] combines a variety of relevant medical text genres, with focus on clinical reports. The clinical text genres cover discharge summaries, pathology, histology and surgery reports. The non-clinical ones consist of medical expert texts (from a medical textbook) and health care consumer texts taken from the Web. Medical language, as used in these clinical documents, has some unique properties not found in newspaper genres. Among these features are the use of Latin and Greek terminology (sometimes also mixed with the host language, here German), various *ad hoc* forms for abbreviations and acronyms, a variety of (sometimes idiosyncratically used) measure units, enumerations, and some others. These may not be marginal sublanguage properties and thus may have an impact on the quality of tagging procedures. In order to test this assumption, we enhanced the NEGRA-rooted STTS tagset with three dedicated tags which capture ubiquitous lexical properties of medical texts not covered by this general-purpose tagset, thus yielding the STTS-MED tagset. The three tags are 'ENUM' (all sorts of enumerations), 'LATIN' (Latin forms in medical terms), and 'FDSREF' (reference patterns related to formal document structure).

Under the supervision of the second author, our three student annotators then annotated the FRAMED medical corpus with the extended STTS-MED tagset. The mean of the inter-annotator consistency of this annotation effort was 98.4% (with a standard deviation of 0.6). A look at the frequency ranking of the dedicated medical tags shows that they bear some relevance in annotating medical corpora. Out of the 54 tag types occurring in the FRAMED corpus, ENUM is ranked 14, LATIN is ranked 19, and FDSREF is ranked 33. In terms of absolute frequencies, all three additional tags account for 1613 (out of 100,141) tag tokens (ENUM: 866, LATIN: 560, FDSREF: 187). To test the overall impact of these three additional tags, we ran the default NEGRA-newspaper-based TNT on our FRAMED medical corpus and compared the resulting STTS tag assignments with those from the extended STTS-MED tagset. The additional tags accounted for only 24% of the differences between the two assignments (1613/6685). Hence, their introduction, by no means, fully explains any improved tagging results (compared with the reduced newspaper tagset). The other sublanguage properties mentioned above (e.g., abbreviations, acronyms, measure units etc.) are already covered by the original tagset.

4.2 Experiment 3: Re-training TNT on FRAMED

In a third experiment, we compared TNT's performance with respect to the general newspaper language and the medical sublanguage. For this purpose, the tagger was newly trained and tested on a random sample (100,198 tokens) of the NEGRA newspaper corpus with the standard STTS tagset, and, in parallel, re-trained and tested on the FRAMED medical corpus using STTS-MED, the extended medical tagset.

For this evaluation, we used learning curve values (see Table 4) that indicate the tagging performance when using training corpora of different sizes. Our experiments started with 5,000 tokens and ranged to the size of the entire corpus (minus the test set). At each size increment point, the overall accuracy, as well as the accuracies for known and unknown words were measured, while also considering the percentage of unknown words. The tests were performed on random partitions of the corpora that use up to 90% as training set (depending on the training size) and 10% as test set. In this way, the test data was guaranteed to be unseen during training. This process was repeated ten times, each time using a different 10% as the test set, and the single outcomes were then averaged.

Table 4. Averaged Learning Curve Values for Different Training Sizes (standard deviation in parentheses)

Training Size	NEGRA	FRAMED	NEGRA	FRAMED	NEGRA	FRAMED	NEGRA	FRAMED
	% unknown words		Accuracy unknown words only		Accuracy known words only		Overall Accuracy	
5,000	40.3 (1.4)	40.8 (3.3)	74.9 (2.5)	81.1 (2.5)	96.3 (0.4)	97.8 (0.7)	87.7 (1.2)	91.0 (1.5)
10,000	33.9 (0.6)	33.5 (3.2)	79.3 (1.2)	85.9 (2.0)	96.8 (0.3)	97.8 (0.4)	90.9 (0.5)	93.7 (1.1)
20,000	28.6 (1.0)	26.1 (2.2)	82.9 (1.1)	88.9 (1.6)	97.1 (0.3)	98.2 (0.2)	93.0 (0.3)	95.9 (0.6)
30,000	25.2 (1.0)	21.1 (1.6)	84.4 (1.1)	90.2 (1.2)	97.3 (0.4)	98.3 (0.2)	94.0 (0.3)	96.6 (0.4)
40,000	23.1 (0.9)	18.3 (1.6)	85.1 (1.1)	91.7 (1.7)	97.3 (0.2)	98.6 (0.3)	94.6 (0.4)	97.3 (0.5)
50,000	21.6 (1.0)	16.7 (1.8)	85.8 (1.2)	92.0 (1.8)	97.4 (0.2)	98.7 (0.3)	94.9 (0.4)	97.6 (0.5)
60,000	20.2 (0.9)	15.3 (1.8)	86.1 (1.3)	92.4 (1.7)	97.5 (0.2)	98.7 (0.2)	95.2 (0.4)	97.7 (0.5)
70,000	19.2 (1.0)	14.5 (1.9)	86.4 (1.7)	92.4 (2.0)	97.5 (0.3)	98.6 (0.4)	95.4 (0.4)	97.7 (0.7)
80,000	18.5 (0.9)	13.6 (1.6)	86.9 (1.4)	93.2 (2.1)	97.5 (0.2)	98.8 (0.3)	95.6 (0.4)	98.0 (0.5)
90,000	17.9 (1.3)	12.5 (1.7)	86.9 (1.3)	93.0 (1.9)	97.6 (0.3)	98.7 (0.3)	**95.7 (0.3)**	**98.0 (0.4)**

4.3 Results from Medical Tagging with Medical Resources

Table 4 (columns 4-9) reveals that the FRAMED-trained TNT tagger outperforms the NEGRA-trained one at all training points and across all types of accuracies we measured. Trained with the largest possible training size (*viz.* 90,000 tokens), the tagger's overall accuracy for its FRAMED parametrization scores 98.0%, compared to 95.7% for NEGRA. The performance differences between FRAMED and NEGRA range between 2.3 (at training points 90,000 and 70,000) and 3.3 percentage points (at training point 5,000). The tagging accuracy for known tokens is higher for both FRAMED and NEGRA (with 98.7% and 97.6%, respectively, at training point 90,000). The differences here are less pronounced, ranging from 1.0 to 1.3 percentage points.

By far the largest performance difference can be observed with respect to the tagging accuracy for unknown words (cf. Table 4 (columns 4 and 5)), ranging from 5.8 (at training point 30,000) to 6.6 percentage points (at training points 10,000 and 40,000). The FRAMED-trained tagger scores above 90% in seven out of ten points and never falls below 80%. The NEGRA-based tagger remains below 90% at all points, and even falls below 80% at the first two training points. This performance difference is clearly one factor which contributes to the FRAMED tagger's superior results. The difference in the average percentage of unknown words is the other dimension where both environments diverge (cf. Table 4, columns 2 and 3). Whereas the percentage of unknown words starts out to be equally high for low training sizes (5,000 and 10,000), this rate drops much faster for the FRAMED-trained tagger. At the highest possible training point, only 12.5% of the words are unknown, compared to still almost 18% unknown to the NEGRA-trained tagger, resulting in a 5.4 percentage point difference. Thus, both the high tagging accuracy for unknown words and their lower rate, in the first place, seem to be key for the superior performance of the FRAMED-trained TNT tagger.

5 Discussion and Conclusions

Campbell and Johnson [5] have argued that general-purpose off-the-shelf NLP tools are not readily portable and extensible to the analysis of medical texts. By evaluating the English version of Brill's rule-based tagger [3], they conclude that taggers trained on general-purpose language resources, such as newspaper corpora, are not suited to medical narratives but rather need timely and costly retraining on manually tagged medical corpora. Interestingly though, it has also been observed [1, 5] that medical language shows less variation and complexity than general, newspaper-style language, thus exhibiting typical properties of a sublanguage. Setting aside the difference in vocabulary between medical and non-medical domains, the degradation in performance of general-language off-the-shelf NLP tools for MLP applications then seems counter-intuitive. Our first and second series of experiments were meant to explain this puzzle.

The results of these experiments shed a different light on the portability and extensibility of off-the-shelf NLP tools for the analysis of medical narratives as was hypothesized by [5]. A statistical POS tagger like TNT, which is trained on general-purpose language by default, only falls 1.5% short of the state-of-the-art performance in a medical environment. An easy-to-set-up medical backup lexicon eliminates this difference entirely. It appears that it is the underlying language model which determines whether a POS tagger is more or less suited to be portable to the medical domain, not the surface characteristics of medical sublanguage. Moreover, lexical backup facilities show up as a significant asset to MLP. Much to our surprise, a full-scale, carefully maintained lexicon did not substantially improve the tagger's performance in comparison with a heuristically assembled brief list of the most common mistakes.

A reason for the statistical tagger's outperformance may be derived from our comparative corpus statistics, which was the focus of our second series of experiments. Concerning POS n-grams, the data points to a less varied and less complex grammar of medical sublanguage(s). Not only is the number of POS n-gram types much lower for medical narratives than for general-language newspaper texts, but the distribution also favors high-occurring (more than 1000 times) types in MED. Another indicator of a simpler POS n-gram grammar in medical narratives is the fact that the absolute number of POS n-gram types common to NEGRA and MED is much lower than for NEGRA and NEWS. Scaled against the total number of types in MED, however, the common ones cover a bigger part of the medical narratives, whereas they cover less of NEGRA. For POS trigrams, half of NEGRA is congruent with three quarters of MED; for POS bigrams three quarters of NEGRA is congruent with nine tenths of MED.

Common POS n-grams that are χ^2 significant indicate that two corpora are similar with respect to them. Their number was significantly higher for the NEGRA-MED comparison than for NEGRA-NEWS. Hence the congruency of a high proportion of POS n-gram types between NEGRA and MED is not accidental. At the POS n-gram type level, this shows a higher degree of similarity between NEGRA and medical narratives than between NEGRA and other newspaper texts.

Furthermore, the high χ^2 numbers for the top ranked POS n-grams indicate that they are especially characteristic of the NEGRA-MED similarity. Eight of the top-ranked trigrams and bigrams can be identified as parts of a noun phrase. All of them contain a prenominal adjective, six a common noun. The prenominal adjective is by far the most characteristic POS unigram for medical-newspaper inter-language similarity. None of these observations hold for newspaper intra-language similarity.

Our third series of experiments showed that Markovian taggers like TNT improve their performance substantially when trained on medical data. Indeed, we were able to achieve a performance boost which goes beyond current state-of-the-art numbers. This seems to be even more notable inasmuch as the tagger's retraining was done on a comparatively small-sized corpus (90,000 tokens).

These experiments suggest two explanations. First, annotating medical texts with a medically enhanced tagset accounts for sublanguage properties not covered by general-purpose tagsets. Second, several tagging experiments on newspaper language, whether statistical [9, 4] or rule-based [3], report that the tagging accuracy for unknown words is much lower than the overall accuracy[1]. Thus, the lower percentage of unknown words in medical texts seems to be a sublanguage feature beneficial to POS taggers, whereas the higher proportion of unknown words in newspaper language seems to be a prominent source of tagging errors. This is witnessed by the tagging accuracy for unknown words, which is much higher for the FRAMED-trained tagger than for the newspaper-trained one. For the medical tagger, there is only a 5 percentage point difference between overall and unknown word accuracy at training point 90,000, whereas, for the newspaper tagger, this difference amounts to 8.8 percentage points. This may be interrelated with yet another sublanguage property, *viz.* the lower number of word types: At each training point, the lexicon of the FRAMED tagger is 20 percentage points smaller than that of the newspaper tagger. TNT's handling of unknown words relies on the probability distribution for a particular suffix of some fixed length [4]. Guessing an unknown word's category is easier on a small-sized tagger lexicon, because there may be less choices for the POS category of a word with a particular suffix.

---

[1] These authors report on differences of overall and unknown word accuracy which range between 7.7 and 11.5 percentage points.

Only recently has the accuracy of data-driven POS taggers moved beyond the '97% barrier' as derived from newspaper corpora [10, 11]. This was partly achieved by computationally more expensive models than TNT's efficient unidirectional Markovian one. These figures must also be distinguished from those attributed to linguistically backuped taggers which come with 'heavy' parsing machinery [12]. Although reaching the 98% accuracy level constitutes a breakthrough, it is conditioned by the medical sublanguage we are working with. Still, it might be useful for the application of language technologies in sublanguage domains like medicine, genomics and biology.

Acknowledgements

We want to thank our students, Inka Benthin, Lucas Champollion and Caspar Hasenclever, for their excellent work as human taggers. This work was partly supported by Deutsche Forschungsgemeinschaft (DFG), grant KL 640/5-1.

References

1. Friedman, C., Hripcsak, G.: Natural language processing and its future in medicine. Academic Medicine **74** (1999) 890–895
2. Marcus, M.P., Santorini, B., Marcinkiewicz, M.A.: Building a large annotated corpus of English: The PENN TREEBANK. Computational Linguistics **19** (1993) 313–330
3. Brill, E.: Transformation-based error-driven learning and natural language processing: A case study in part-of-speech tagging. Computational Linguistics **21** (1995) 543–565
4. Brants, T.: TNT: A statistical part-of-speech tagger. In: Proceedings of the 6th Conference on Applied NLP, Seattle, WA (2000) 224–231
5. Campbell, D.A., Johnson, S.B.: Comparing syntactic complexity in medical and non-medical corpora. In: Proceedings of the Annual Symposium of the American Medical Informatics Association – AMIA 2001, Washington, D.C. (2001) 90–94
6. Skut, W., Krenn, B., Brants, T., Uszkoreit, H.: An annotation scheme for free word order languages. In: Proc. 5th Conference on Applied NLP, Washington, D.C. (1997) 88–95
7. Kilgarriff, A.: Comparing corpora. Intl. Journal of Corpus Linguistics **6** (2001) 97–133
8. Wermter, J., Hahn, U.: An annotated German-language medical text corpus as language resource. In: Proceedings 4th International LREC Conference, Lisbon, Portugal (2004)
9. Ratnaparkhi, A.: A maximum entropy model for part-of-speech tagging. In: Proceedings of the Conference on Empirical Methods in NLP, Philadelphia, PA (1996) 133–142
10. Giménez, J., Màrquez, L.: Fast and accurate part-of-speech tagging: The SVM approach revisited. In: Proceedings of the International Conference on 'Recent Advances in Natural Language Processing' – RANLP 2003, Borovets, Bulgaria (2003)
11. Toutanova, K., Klein, D., Manning, C.D., Singer, Y.: Feature-rich part-of-speech tagging with a cyclic dependency network. In: Proceedings of the HLT and the 3rd Conference of the North American Chapter of the ACL, Edmonton, Canada (2003) 252–259
12. Samuelsson, C., Voutilainen, A.: Comparing a linguistic and a stochastic tagger. In: Proceedings of the 35th Annual Meeting of the ACL & 8th Conference of the European Chapter of the ACL, Madrid, Spain (1997) 246–253

Pronominal Anaphora Resolution Using a Shallow Meaning Representation of Sentences

Hilda Ho, Kyongho Min, and Wai Kiang Yeap

Language Research Group, Institute for IT Research
Auckland University of Technology
Auckland, 1020 New Zealand
{hho,kyongho.min,wai.yeap}@aut.ac.nz

Abstract. This paper describes a knowledge-poor anaphora resolution approach based on a shallow meaning representation of sentences. The structure afforded in such a representation provides immediate identification of local domains which are required for resolving pronominal anaphora. Other kinds of information used include syntactic information, structure parallelism and salience weights. We collected 111 singular 3rd person pronouns from open domain resources such as children's novel and examples from several anaphora resolution papers. There are 111 third-person singular pronouns in the experiment data set and 94 of them demonstrate pronominal anaphora in domain of test data. The system successfully resolves 78.4% of anaphoric examples.

1 Introduction

Due to the variety of anaphors that could occur in text and the different knowledge sources needed to resolve anaphors, anaphoric resolution is an interesting and a difficult problem in language research. Some examples of the different types of anaphora are shown below:

1. intra-sentential (e.g. "Jack tried to start his car") versus inter-sentential (e.g. "Mary has a sister. Her name is Jane"),
2. according to a co-reference direction, anaphora (e.g. "Jack started his car") versus cataphora (e.g. "On his way to school, Tom met his friend"),
3. according to a syntactic category, definite noun phrase (e.g. "An intruder has stolen a vase. The intruder stole the vase from a cupboard"), pronominal (e.g. "Jack started his car"), reflexive (e.g. "John told us about himself"), and reciprocal (e.g. "Tom and Mary like each other"),
4. shared common knowledge between a speaker and a hearer within a context (extra-textual (e.g. "the sun")),
5. use of real world knowledge (associative (e.g. "John bought a new computer yesterday and he found that the keyboard was broken")),
6. pronoun "it" can mean one of a personal pronoun (e.g. "baby"), a non-personal pronoun (e.g. "company" or "cat"), a pleonastic pronoun (e.g. "it is raining"), or a referring event.
7. others include: anaphoric dependencies in ellipsis [5], associative anaphors [1], [7], quantifier [13], and anaphors in captions of pictures [3].

Methods developed in the past for anaphoric resolution include the use of syntactic information [6], syntactic information with constraints and preferences based on structural binding dependency between anaphors and antecedents [12], [15], a machine learning approach with limited semantic information (e.g. ISA hierarchy) from WordNet [14], and knowledge-poor approach (e.g. MARS system [4]) using results of a POS tagger rather than syntactic parses [8], [9].

Lappin and Lease [6] used syntactic information and an attentional state of antecedent candidate to resolve inter-/intra-sentential anaphoric expressions restricted to third person pronouns and lexical anaphors (reflexives and reciprocals). The syntactic salience was measured by using syntactic structure produced by McCord's Slot Grammar Parser. They tested 360 pronoun occurrences in computer manual texts. However, the structural salience measurement affected their algorithm's performance of inter-sentential anaphoric cases.

Soon et al. [14] studied coreference resolution of general noun phrases (e.g. definite/demonstrative noun phrases, proper names, and appositive) in terms of a machine learning approach. They used 12 features to resolve coreference problems including semantic class features such as a simple ISA hierarchy from WordNet. Among the 12 features, they found 3 features (ALIAS, APPOSITIVE, and STRING_MATCHING) were more highly informative than other features. Modjeska et al. [11] employed lexico-syntactic pattern and semantic knowledge extracted from the WWW to resolve other-anaphora in a machine learning framework. They employed a Naïve Bayes approach with 9 different features and tested the system with/without web information.

Palomar et al. [12] studied anaphora resolution in Spanish texts and their system was based on slot unification parser and constraints and preferences extracted from lexical, morphological, syntactic, and statistical knowledge. The preferential knowledge was retrieved from a training corpus to give more priority to resolve anaphoric coreference. Their system showed good performance to process a reflexive pronoun and a demonstrative pronoun in a prepositional phrase.

Stuckardt [15] studied anaphora resolution based on restrictions and preferences extracted from syntactic tree structures resulted from FDG (Functional Dependency Grammar of English). The system used binding constraints to extract rule patterns based on syntactic relations between anaphors and antecedents. In addition, a text-genre specific choice of preferred antecedent was applied. Among various preference factors, sentence recency was the most valuable factor in his system. Walker [16] studied anaphora resolution based on a centering model of discourse structure with a cache method. The centre in a hierarchical/linear discourse structure was stored in a cache for anaphoric resolution.

This paper describes a knowledge-poor anaphora resolution approach based on shallow meanings extracted from each sentence. The anaphoric resolution in this paper focuses on both intra- and inter-sentential anaphoric expressions of singular 3rd person pronouns. The system employed some syntactic (e.g. syntactic roles such as subject, object, indirect object, local domain, recency (position of antecedents)) and semantic features (e.g. gender, number) rather than syntactic dependency rules (e.g. c-command rule).

Section 2 briefly describes the input to the system and section 3, the basic algorithm developed. Section 4 presents some preliminary experimental results and section 5, the conclusion and future works.

2 Input

The anaphoric resolution system is developed as part of a text analysis system known as SmartINFO (Smart INFOrmation). SmartINFO processes paragraphs of text and generates a shallow meaning representation for each sentence. Such a representation captures the relationship between words in each sentence in a form that the system knows how to interpret. Some examples are shown below:

> (interpret '(The man who ordered the book foolishly paid the money))

[PAID (:ACTOR (PERSON (:SEX (MALE)) (:NUMBER (SINGULAR))
              (:MODIFIER (THE))
              (:WHO (ORDERED
                      (:WHAT (BOOK (:MODIFIER (THE))))))
              (:MANNER (FOOLISHLY))))
       (:WHAT (MONEY (:MODIFIER (THE))))]

> (interpret '(He got himself very dirty in the park))

[GOT (:ACTOR (HE (:SEX (MALE))))
      (:WHAT (HIMSELF))
      (:MODIFIER (VERY) (DIRTY))
      (:IN (PARK (:MODIFIER (THE))))]

From the above input, all nouns and pronouns that appear in them are extracted and each is given a unique identification and a reference to the sentences in which they belong. As the focus of this paper is not on the output of SmartINFO, we will not give a formal definition of the above representation schema here.

3 The Anaphora Resolution Algorithm

The anaphora resolution algorithm works as follows:

1. Input – a paragraph of text which will be processed by SmartINFO and turned into a list of shallow meanings representations.
2. For each of these representations, extract all the nouns and (third-person) pronouns that appear in them. When a pronoun appears in sentence, say, 5, then the candidate list of nouns for this pronoun contains all nouns (only those with the correct gender and number agreement) appearing in the first 5 sentences.
3. Using the candidate list, the pronouns are resolved in the following manner: first we use local domain and syntactic constraints, next we apply structure parallelism between sentences, and finally we apply salience weightings.

3.1 Local Domain and Syntactic Constraints

Many existing systems use Chomsky's Binding Theory [2] to define syntactic constraints for filtering invalid candidates with respects to c-command and local domain. The traditional definition of a local domain of a constituent C is defined as the set of constituents contained in the closest S or NP that contains C.

C-command is defined as follows ([10], pp 58): A node X c-commands a node Y if and only if:

(i) X does not dominate Y.
(ii) Y does not dominate X.
(iii) The first branching node dominating X also dominates Y.

Three syntactic rules using the notions of c-command and local domain were defined [10] as follows:

(i) A reflexive pronoun must co-refer with a NP that c-commands it and is in the same local domain.
(ii) A non-reflexive pronoun cannot co-refer to a c-commanding NP within the same local domain.
(iii) A non-pronominal NP cannot co-refer with a NP that c-commands it.

Many existing anaphora resolution systems have applied these syntactic rules to their algorithms. Our approach differs in the way in which the local domain is defined. The shallow meaning representation of each sentence has already restructured the sentence in such a way that words in the same list share the same local(/global) domain. (see Fig. 1).

Example1: Mary gave a book to Jane for her$_1$ to do the work for her$_2$.
[gave (:actor (person (:name (mary))))
       (:what (book (:modifier (a)))
              (:to (jane (:person (:name (jane)))
              (:for (her (:sex (female)))
                    (:to (do (:what (work (:modifier (the)))
                             (:for (her (:sex (female))))
                        ))))))))]

Example2: Mary told her$_1$ that she loves the picture of her$_2$.
[that (:ms2 (loves (:actor (she (:sex (female))))
                    (:what (picture (:modifier (the)) (:of (her (:sex (female))))))
                    (:number (singular))))
      (:ms1 (told   (:actor (person (:name (mary))))
                    (:what (her (:sex (female))))))]

Fig. 1. Identifying local domains: In example 1, her$_2$ is embedded inside the local domain of her$_1$ whereas this is not the case in example 2

It is interesting to compare the output for example 1 in Fig. 1 with the syntactic parse tree generated by link grammar[1]:

(S (NP Mary)
   (VP gave (NP a book)
             (PP to (NP Jane))
             (PP for (NP her))
             (S2 (VP to (VP do (NP the work)
                               (PP for (NP her)))))))

The above output shows that the local domain for her$_2$ is S2 but the local domain of her$_1$ is the top S. Thus, according to c-command rules, her$_1$ does not c-command her$_2$ and they're in different local domains, implying that they could co-refer.

---

[1] http://www.link.cs.cmu.edu/link/

Once the local domain of the pronoun is identified, several syntactic constraints are applied to filter out invalid antecedent candidates. Two sets of rules are defined: one for reflexive pronouns and the other for non-reflexive pronouns. Note that these rules are continually being refined as more examples are encountered.

The syntactic constraints for reflexive pronouns state that:

- If the local domain of the pronoun is an action word itself or a NP that is composed of possessive noun/possessive form of noun (e.g. "John's picture of himself"), the reflexive anaphor can only co-refer to the candidates that are located in the same local domain.
- If the local domain of the pronoun is an embedded action, such as an infinitive phrase, the reflexive anaphor cannot co-refer to any candidates that are located in the same local domain. For example, "Mary asks Jane to tell her about herself", the pronouns "her" and "herself" are both located in the local domain of the embedded action "to tell" and the two pronouns are not referring to the same person ("her" is referring to "Mary" and "herself" is referring to "Jane").
- If the local domain of the pronoun is an embedded action with a preposition phrase, such as the one in example 1 of Fig.1 above, then the semantic of the preposition is analysed. For example, "Mary is desperate for Jane to depend on herself", the preposition "for" indicates that "Jane" performs the embedded action "to depend". In this case, the reflexive pronoun co-refers to candidates that are located in the same local domain. In case of "Mary took the book from Jane to read it herself", the preposition "from" indicates that the embedded action is unlikely to be performed by "Jane" and the reflexive pronoun therefore does not co-refer to candidates that are located in the same local domain.

The syntactic constraints for non-reflexive pronouns state that:

- The pronoun cannot co-refer to any candidates that are located in the same local domain, except when the anaphor is a possessive pronoun such as "Peter loves *his* car".

SmartINFO's anaphora resolution system can also filter out invalid pronoun candidates as well as the NP candidates. To illustrate, consider the following example:

Peter met John and he$_1$ told him he$_2$ would leave early.

and the output generated by SmartINFO:

[and (:ms2 (told (:actor (he$_1$ (:sex (male))))
(:recipient (him (:sex (male))))
(:what (would (:actor (he$_2$ (:sex (male))))
(:what (leave (:what ?r)))
(:manner (early))))))
(:ms1 (met (:actor (person (:name (peter))))
(:what (john (:person (:name (john)))))))]

Although this sentence is very ambiguous, one can still be sure that the pronoun "he$_1$" does not co-refer to the pronoun "him". When SmartINFO is trying to resolve the pronoun "him", it searches for any pronoun within its same local domain (i.e. the pronoun "he$_1$") and filter it out as invalid antecedent candidate. Furthermore, the algorithm also filters the antecedent of that invalid pronoun from the candidate list of the current anaphor. In the example above, the pronoun "he_1" is resolved to co-refer to "Peter", then "Peter" is filter out from the candidate list of the pronoun "him", leaving only "John" as a valid antecedent candidate.

Once the invalid candidates are filtered out, structure parallelism is applied to resolve the anaphor. For this parallelism application, the anaphor and the antecedent candidate must share the same action word (i.e. verb) in the same/consecutive sentence(s) and they must have the same syntactic role (subject/object/indirect-object) (e.g. "Mary *gave* Jane a cat. She also *gave* her a book.") If these conditions are met, the anaphor is resolved; otherwise, salience weights are applied.

3.2 Salience Weights

Six salience factors are applied to select the most preferred antecedent from the set of competing candidates. The salience depends solely on simple syntactic and statistic information that are provided by SmartINFO. Additional information such as word class or syntactic tags (e.g. head nouns) is not used as salience in this system. As the SmartINFO system aims to be applied to an open domain, all of the salience factors are genre-free. However, two of them are specific to the local domain of embedded action. The antecedent candidates obtain a score between -2 to 2 for each salience factor. It should be noted that these salience factors are still under development at the point this paper is produced. Further refinements and modifications on these factors are expected in future.

Embedded Action - Infinitive Phrase

If a local domain of a current pronoun (anaphor) is an embedded action in the form of infinitive phrase and the pronoun has a prepositional phrase (PP) as its parent (e.g. "Mary asks Jane [to do it for *her*.]"), then the object of a sentence is not preferred. A candidate with its syntactic role as object is given a score of -2. If a pronoun is not within a prepositional phrase (e.g. Mary asks Jane [to tell *her* about Peter.]"), the subject of a sentence is more preferred as antecedent. A candidate with its syntactic role as subject is given a score of 2.

Embedded Action - Preposition Phrase

If a local domain of a current pronoun (anaphor) is an embedded action with a preposition phrase (e.g. "Mary is desperate [for Jane to depend on *her*.]" – the prepositional phrase for the action 'to depend' is 'for Jane'), and the pronoun does not have this prepositional phrase as its parent, then a candidate with its syntactic role as subject is more preferred and a score of 1 is assigned. If a pronoun has this prepositional phrase as its parent, which defines the pronoun's local domain (e.g. "Mary gave a book to Jane [for *her* to do the homework.]"), then a candidate with its syntactic role as indirect object is more preferred (scores 1).

Syntactic Roles

This salience factor simply says that subject is more preferred than object, which is more preferred than indirect object. A candidate with its syntactic role as subject is given a weight of 2, object scores 1, and indirect object scores 0.5.

Role Parallelism

> This role parallelism mechanism is different from the structure parallelism performed earlier in the AR process, which states that an anaphor and its antecedent are dominated by the same ACTION (i.e. verb) in the shallow meaning representations (see section 3.1). In this phase, only syntactic roles of an anaphor and its antecedent candidate are compared and if they match each other (e.g. both are subjects; "*Mary* loves Jane. *She* gave her a dog."), a score of 1 is assigned to the candidate.

Frequency of Occurrence in the paragraph

> Preference is given to candidates that appear more frequently in a paragraph in which an anaphor is located. Candidates that appear more then five times in the paragraph are given a score of 2. Candidates that appear between three to five times in the paragraph score 1 and those that appear twice in the paragraph are given a weight of 0.5.

Recency

> The most recent candidate is given a score of 0.5.

When all preferences are taken into account, each candidate has an accumulated salience weight. Candidates that have a negative score are removed from the candidate list. The most highly scored candidate is then selected as the antecedent. In case of a tie, the most recent candidate will be selected.

4 Preliminary Experimental Results

The SmartINFO's anaphora resolution system is tested against a set of experiment data, which is collected from open domain resources such as children's novel and examples form several anaphora resolution papers. The data is slightly modified to be parsed by SmartINFO (plural pronouns and words with apostrophes were manually modified). There are 111 singular third-person pronouns in the experiment data set and 17 (15%) of them do not have any antecedents within the scope of the test data. The application of salience factors to resolve anaphoric expression in the system is able to filter out 90% of invalid candidates and resolve 78.4% of anaphoric examples used to test the AR system. By using local domain information and syntactic constraints solely, the AR system is considered very successful in filtering invalid antecedent candidates.

Table 1 illustrates the evaluation of pronominal anaphors in this experiment. The pronominal anaphors that are examined in this experiment are the 3rd person singular pronouns such as she, her, he, his, him, and it. The success rate of masculine pronouns is much higher than that of feminine pronouns because the syntactic structure of sentences containing the masculine pronouns is simpler than those with feminine pronouns. In the case of pronoun "it", if real world text were tested, then its success rate would be worse.

Table 1. Evaluation of Pronominal Anaphors in Experiment

Type of Pronominal Anaphor	Total number of occurrences in data set	Number of correctly resolved anaphors	Correctly resolved anaphors (%)
She	34	28	82.3%
Her (objective)	39	31	79.5%
Her (possessive)	5	0	0%
He	12	12	100%
His	5	0	0%
Him	12	12	100%
It	5	4	80%
TOTAL	**111**	**87**	**78.4%**

Table 2. Evaluation of Intra-sentential & Inter-sentential Anaphors in Experiment

Type of Anaphor	Total number of occurrences in data set	Number of correctly resolved anaphors	Correctly resolved anaphors (%)
Intra-sentential	43	33	76.7%
Inter-sentential	68	54	79.4%
TOTAL	**111**	**87**	**78.4%**

Table 2 shows the evaluation of intra-sentential and inter-sentential anaphors tested. Of the 111 pronouns, 68 of them illustrate inter-sentential anaphors. SmartINFO correctly resolves 80% of inter-sentential anaphors and 77% of intra-sentential anaphors. As mentioned before, 15% of the pronouns in the experiment data do not have any antecedent in the test domain (e.g. "Peter asks Jane to tell Mary about *her*." – the pronoun does not co-refer to any of the NPs in the sentence.). By using the specially defined local domain and syntactic constrains, SmartINFO's anaphora resolution system can successfully identify 82% of these pronouns. Overall, SmartINFO is able to resolve 78% of the anaphors successfully.

In the test data 20.7% of the third-person pronouns are incorrectly resolved by the SmartINFO's anaphora resolution system. The causes of errors are shown in Table 3. The top two reasons of failure are parsing errors by SmartINFO (30%) and possessive pronouns (30%) that is not implemented in this system. As the SmartINFO system is still being developed, it has not reached maturity and some errors are produced during parsing. Such parsing errors therefore affect the performance of anaphora resolution. As mentioned in section 2, the SmartINFO extracts all the nouns and pronouns from the shallow meaning representation of sentences. However, it is currently unable to extract any possessive pronoun concepts. Hence, all of the possessive pronouns in the testing data are not resolved.

Salient weights results in 17% of the errors. A salient factor based on syntactic roles states that a candidate as a subject role is preferred, and the salient factor based on structure parallelism states that a candidate having the same syntactic role as an anaphor is preferred. These two salient factors work well with sentences/paragraph in which the theme is consistent. However, if the theme changes suddenly, these two salient factors will incorrectly assign more weight to an inappropriate candidate. For example, consider the paragraph:

"Mary lives in Auckland. She is ten years old. She loves singing. Mary has a sister. *She* is Jane."

SmartINFO's anaphora resolution system incorrectly resolved the last pronoun 'she' as Mary, which has been the focus of the paragraph in the previous four sentences.

Table 3. Major Error Types in SmartINFO's Anaphora Resolution System

Error Type	Number of Errors	%
Parsing Errors	7	30.4%
Possessive Pronouns	7	30.4%
Salience Weights	4	17.4%
Anaphor co-reference to pronoun	4	17.4%
Pleonastic It	1	4.2%
TOTAL	24	100%

Although the current system is able to filter out invalid pronoun candidates as well as their antecedents when solving an anaphor, it is currently unable to resolve any anaphors that co-refer to another pronouns. Such cases have caused 17% of the errors. The remaining 4% of errors are caused by pleonastic 'it' as it has not been implemented yet.

5 Future Works

Further research is needed to improve the accuracy of SmartINFO's anaphora resolution system. The current system can only handle singular third-person pronouns such as he, him, she, her, and it. Once the system is improved to extract possessive pronouns (e.g. 'Peter loves his photos.'), new syntactic constraints with respects to local domains can be added to the anaphora resolution algorithm for resolving possessive pronouns. Apart from this, more studies on the distribution of salience weights and discovery of new salience factors can enhance the chance for selecting the correct antecedent from the set of competing candidates. A pronoun-pronoun co-reference algorithm will also be investigated in future for resolving any anaphors that have another pronoun as their antecedents (e.g. "Mary gave a book to Jane. *She* told her that *she* love the story very much.") In addition, when the anaphora resolution system for singular third-person pronouns is mature enough, the system can be improved to handle plural pronominal anaphors and pleonastic 'it'.

Reference

1. Bunescu, R.: Associative Anaphora Resolution: A Web-based Approach. Proceedings of the EACL-2003 Workshop on the Computational Treatment of Anaphora. Budapest Hungary (2003) 47-52
2. Chomsky, N.: Lectures on government and binding. Foris, Dodrecht (1981)
3. Denber, M.: Automatic Resolution of Anaphora in English. Imaging Science Division, Eastman Kodak Co. (1998)
4. Evans R.: Mitkov's Anaphora Resolution System (MARS Demo). University of Wolverhampton. Available: http://clg.wlv.ac.uk/MARS/

5. Kehler, A., Shieber, S.: Anaphoric Dependencies in Ellipsis. Computational Linguistics. 23(3) (1997) 457-466
6. Lappin, S., Leass, H.: An Algorithm for Pronominal Anaphora Resolution. Computational Linguistics. 20(4) (1994) 535-561
7. Meyer, J., Dale, R.: Using the WordNet Hierarchy for Associative Anaphora Resolution. Proceedings of Building and Using Semantic Networks. Taipei Taiwan (2002)
8. Mitkov R.: Robust pronoun resolution with limited knowledge. Proceedings of COLING'98/ACL'98. Montreal Canada (1998) 869-875
9. Mitkov R.: 1999. "Anaphora resolution: The state of The Art". *Working paper (Based on the COLING'98/ACL'98 tutorial on anaphora resolution)*. University of Wolverhampton UK (1999)
10. Mitkov R: Anaphora Resolution. Pearson Education Limited. Longman. Great Britain. (2002)
11. Modjeska, N., Markert, K., Nissim, M.: Using the Web in Machine Learning for Other-Anaphora Resolution. Proceedings of EMNLP-2003. Sapporo Japan (2003) 176-183
12. Palomar, M., Ferrandez, A., Moreno, L., Martinez-Barco, P., Peral, J., Siz-Noeda, M. Munoz, R.: Am Algorithm for anaphora Resolution in Spanish Texts. Computational Linguistics. 27(4) (2001) 544-567
13. Polany, L., van den Berg, M.: Logical Structure and Discourse Anaphora Resolution. Proceedings of ACL99 Workshop on the Relation of Discourse/Dialogue Structure and Reference. College Park USA (1999) 110-117
14. Soon, W. Ng, H., Lim, D.: A Machine Learning Approach to Coreference Resolution of Noun Phrases. Computational Linguistics. 27(4) (2001) 521-544
15. Stuckardt, R.: Design and Enhanced Evaluation of a Robust Anaphora Resolution Algorithm. Computational Linguistics. 27(4) (2001) 481-50514.
16. Walker, M.: Centering, Anaphora Resolution, and Discourse Structure. In: Walker, M., Joshi, K. Prince, E. (eds.): Centering Theory in Discourse. Oxford University Press, UK (1998)

Multi-agent Human-Machine Dialogue: Issues in Dialogue Management and Referring Expression Semantics

Alistair Knott, Ian Bayard, and Peter Vlugter

Dept of Computer Science, University of Otago

1 Introduction

Human-machine dialogue systems typically support dialogue between two agents: the human user is one agent and the system plays the part of the other. In this scenario, the user and the system take turns at being the speaker, and when one of them is the speaker, the other is the addressee (the agent being spoken to).

However, in real life dialogue, there are frequently more than two participants. Automated dialogue systems can be configured in various ways to operate in a multi-speaker scenario. Firstly, a system can simulate each dialogue participant as a separate autonomous agent (e.g. Padilha and Carletta [1]). Secondly, a system can play the part of a single agent in a context where there are several human speakers (Wang, [2]). Finally, the system could support a dialogue between a single human user and several agents, all of which are played by the system. Here the agents can either be genuinely autonomous, or they can act in the service of a shared plan, delivering lines given to them by a central controller.

To extend a dialogue system to deal with multi-speaker interactions, whichever of the above scenarios is envisaged, a number of things must be supplied. At the dialogue level, we need a theory of turn-taking, to decide when to make an utterance, and who the addressees of other speakers' utterances are. At the level of sentence syntax and semantics, we need to pay special attention to constructions which are used to refer to dialogue participants (especially personal pronouns) and which are used to control turn-taking (especially terms of address).

We have already built a two-speaker dialogue system, which incorporates full sentence parsing and generation using a declarative grammar, and a range of standard dialogue management techniques (de Jager et al [3]; Bayard et al, [4]). This paper describes how we are extending this system to a multi-speaker environment, focussing on the additional syntactic constructions and dialogue management principles which are required, and on the interactions between these.

2 Te Kaitito: An English-Māori Dialogue System

Our dialogue system, called Te Kaitito[1], supports bilingual human-machine dialogues in English and Māori. The user and the system alternate in generating

---
[1] Online demos of Te Kaitito can be found at
http://tutoko.otago.ac.nz:8080/teKaitito/

contributions to a dialogue. When it is the user's turn to contribute, (s)he enters a sentence in English or Māori. The sentence is first parsed, using the LKB system (Copestake et al. [5]), and a set of syntactic analyses is computed. Each analysis is associated with a semantic interpretation. One interpretation is then selected, using various principles (Knott and Vlugter, [6]). The dialogue manager then decides what kind of dialogue act is being performed by the utterance, and responds accordingly. If it encounters a problem interpreting the utterance, it responds with a suitable clarification question.

2.1 Presuppositional DRT

When an incoming utterance is parsed, its semantic representation is derived. The grammar associates sentences with representations in the Minimal Recursion Semantics (MRS) formalism (Copestake et al, [7]). As a postprocessing stage, we convert these representations to a format called Discourse Representation Structures (DRSs; Kamp and Reyle [8]), with some additional annotations to deal with presuppositions and dialogue issues.

A DRS is a structure with two fields, one for representing **discourse referents**, and one for representing **conditions** or predications over these referents. DRSs are typically drawn as split boxes, where referents appear at the top, and conditions below. The discourse context is also represented by a DRS structure. This DRS represents the **common ground** of the conversation, in other words, the material which the speakers consider to be common knowledge between them.

A sentence's **presuppositions** are elements of its content which the speaker assumes are already part of the common ground. They are constraints on the kinds of context in which the sentence can be uttered. Here are two examples.

(1) The dog chased a cat.
(2) John's cat slept.

Sentence 1 presupposes that there is a dog in the discourse context (or more precisely, that there is exactly one *salient* dog in the context). Sentence 2 presupposes that there is someone called John, and also that this person has a cat. The DRSs for Examples 1 and 2 are shown in Figure 1. Notice that the presupposition DRSs are distinguished by dashed lines.

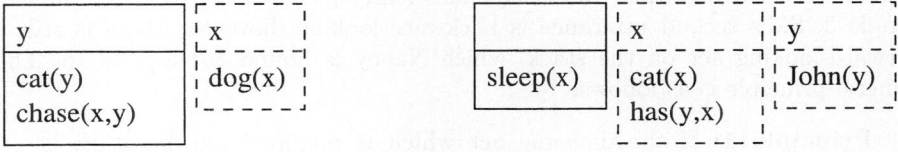

Fig. 1. *The dog chased a cat; John's cat slept*

2.2 Dialogue Management Concepts

Our dialogue system works with a number of different **dialogue acts**: assertions, questions, answers, acknowledgements and so on. We distinguish, as is traditional, between **forward-looking** and **backward-looking** dialogue acts. A forward-looking act is basically a new initiative taken by a speaker; for example a new assertion made apropos of nothing, or a question about some new topic. A backward-looking act is one which is taken in response to an earlier dialogue act; for example the answer to a question, or the acknowledgement of an assertion. We will refer to a pairing of a forward-looking dialogue act and a backward-looking act as a **subdialogue**.

Another well-known idea in dialogue theory is that subdialogues can be nested inside one another. Here is an example of a subdialogue involving a clarification question.

(3)   Sid: can you pass the syringe?
      Nancy: Which syringe?
      Sid: The one on the left.
      Nancy: Here you are.

The dialogue context can be thought of as containing a number of forward-looking acts which need to be responded to. These acts are sometimes referred to as the **dialogue stack**, or as a set of **questions under discussion**, unordered except for one **maximal** question, which is what a backward-looking act is assumed to respond to. In Example 3, after Sid's first utterance, there is one forward-looking act in the dialogue context, and after Nancy's first utterance, there are two, Nancy's being maximal. Sid's second utterance is therefore understood as responding to Nancy's question. In our system, we model the dialogue stack as a set of DRSs which are kept separate from the common ground.

3 Dialogue Management in Multi-agent Dialogue

3.1 Deciding on the Next Speaker

Who the next speaker is allowed to be depends on what the previous dialogue act was. A simple rule is that if the previous utterance was a forward-looking dialogue act, the next speaker must be the addressee of that act. However, in nested subdialogues, this rule is not sufficiently general. For instance, in Example 3, Sid's second utterance is backward-looking; however, there is still a forward-looking act on the stack, which Nancy is bound to respond to. The general principle is as follows:

> **Principle 1:** If the dialogue act which is maximal on the stack is forward-looking, the next speaker must be the addressee of that act.

When there is no forward-looking act on the stack – in other words, when the stack is empty – we assume anyone can talk next. Much has been written about how 'the floor is claimed' in such cases. In our system, we simply hand initiative to the user. The user can cede the floor, simply by pressing 'return' without entering a sentence. If this happens, the system currently selects one of the characters it plays at random to make a new initiative (either asking a new question, or making a new assertion).

3.2 Deciding on the Addressee

The next issue is to determine the addressee of an utterance. If the speaker is played by the system, this issue is one of content selection, which relates to what the system wants to achieve. In our case, we keep things very simple, by always talking to the user.

> Principle 2: If the system must make an utterance, the addressee is always the user.

If the speaker is the user, then determining the addresee is an interpretation issue. The remainder of this section sets out some principles which govern how this works.

Structurally-Defined Addressees. In cases where there is a forward-looking dialogue act on the stack, we can use an analogue of Principle 1 to determine the addressee.

> **Principle 1a:** If a speaker utters a backward-looking dialogue act, the addressee of this utterance is the speaker of the forward-looking dialogue act which is maximal on the stack.

In such a case, the addressee can be identified structurally, without being mentioned explicitly.

Explicit Identifications of the Addressee. Other methods of indicating the addressee are more explicit. Firstly there are methods which are entirely nonverbal. For instance, when saying an utterance, the speaker can look at a particular person, or can even indicate one or more addressees by actually pointing at them. However, our system does not have the multimodal capabilities to simulate these nonverbal methods. Alternatively, the speaker can be even more explicit, and identify the addressee or addressees linguistically, using what we will call an **addressee term.**

Addressee terms can be used in two dialogue contexts. Firstly, if the addressee is already specified structurally, an addressee term can be given which is consistent with this.

(4) Josephine [to Bert]: Shall we watch a video?
     Bert: Not tonight, Josephine[2]. I have a headache.

---

[2] We believe that an explicit addressee term in such cases carries connotations of intimacy or of a heightened emotional connection. This seems a good example.

If an addressee term is used which is inconsistent with the structurally specified addressee, we suggest the result is an incoherent dialogue.

(5) Josephine [to Bert]: Shall we watch a video?
     Bert: # Not tonight, Frank. I have a headache[3].

The second context in which addressee terms can be used is at a point when the speaker is making a forward-looking dialogue act; in other words, where s/he is taking some new initiative.

> **Principle 3:** If the speaker is making a forward-looking dialogue act, (s)he is free to choose any addressee or group of addressees.

For instance, in Example 6, Bob's first utterance is backward-looking, and has to be understood as being addressed to Sue even though there is no addressee term. But Bob's second utterance is forward-looking; he is thus free to address it to anyone, provided he makes this explicit with an addressee term.

(6) Sue: Shall we go to the cinema tonight, Bob?
     Bob: Good idea.
     Bob: Do you want to come, Svetlana?

Note that Principle 3 as stated above should apply to forward-looking acts inside nested subdialogues; we expect that nested forward-looking acts should be addressable to any person. Indeed, nested forward-lookig acts do seem to have this property, as the following example shows.

(7) Sue: Shall we go to the cinema tonight, Bob?
     Bob: Svetlana, do you want to come?
     Svetlana: Good idea.
     Bob: Okay.

Note that Svetlana's utterance closes her subdialogue with Bob, and thus that Bob's second utterance (a backward-looking act) has to be understood as being addressed to Sue, by Principle 1a.

Default Addressees. One final way of specifying an addressee is by default.

> **Principle 4:** If a forward-looking act F is made without an explicit addressee term, then the addressee is taken to be the set of speakers involved in the previous subdialogue, minus the speaker of F.

Here is an example of Principle 4 in action:

(8) Sue [addressing Bob and Mary]: Shall we go to the cinema tonight?
     Bob: Good idea.
     Mary: Good idea.
     Bob: What film do you want to see?

---

[3] At best, Bert's reply can be understood on the premise that Josephine was asking on Frank's behalf. We do not consider this kind of proxy dialogue move; however, see Section 4 for a related construction we do cover.

Sue's first statement, together with Bob and Mary's responses to it, consitute a subdialogue. Bob's second utterance (*What film do you want to see?*) is a forward-looking act. Since there is no explicit addressee term, we assume by Principle 4 that it is addressed to Sue and Mary. Note that the principle also covers the case where the speaker was not involved in the preceding subdialogue. Here is an example of this:

(9)   Sue [addressing Bob]: Shall we go to the cinema tonight?
      Bob: Good idea.
      Mary: Hi there, what's up?

Mary in this case is interpreted as entering a dialogue whose participants are Sue and Bob. In this context, her utterance should be interpreted as addressed to both participants, unless she includes an explicit addressee modifier indicating otherwise.

4   Personal Pronouns

In a multi-speaker context, there are some syntactic constructions which we need to pay special attention to, namely personal pronouns and addressee terms. We consider personal pronouns in this section, and addressee terms in Section 5.

Personal pronouns are devices which allow a speaker to refer anaphorically to him/herself, to the addressee, and to third parties. In each case, there is provision for the object of reference to be a single person, or a plural entity. The English personal pronoun system is quite simple, comprising first, second and third person pronouns, each of which can be singular or plural.

In other languages, the pronoun system encodes a a richer set of possibilities. For instance, in Māori, the language we are particularly interested in, there is a distinction between singular, dual and plural which is orthogonal to that between first and second person. Moreover, for first person plural, there is a further distinction between 'inclusive' and 'exclusive' pronouns, depending on whether the addressee is included in the set of people including the speaker.

Semantically, all pronouns introduce presuppositions about entities which are already in the discourse context. In the case of singular pronouns, the story is quite simple: first-person pronouns presuppose an object who is the speaker, and second-person pronouns presuppose an object who is the addressee. Consider the following dialogue:

(10) Bob: I love you.
      Sue: I love you too.

Both of these sentences can be represented as the DRS in Figure 2 (left). Clearly, in order to interpret such a DRS, the context needs to contain appropriate objects of which **addressee** and **speaker** are predicated. These predicates are unusual in two respects. Firstly, they need to change at each change of either speaker or addressee. For instance, when Bob's utterance in Example 10 is interpreted, the

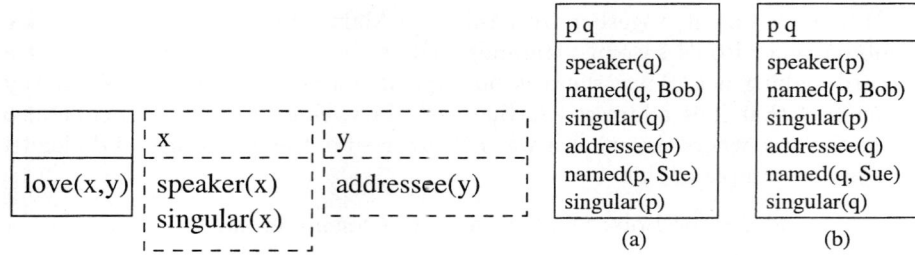

Fig. 2. DRS for *I love you*, with two possible contexts

context DRS should be as in Figure 2(a), while when Sue's utterance is processed, it should be as in Figure 2(b). Secondly, there can only be one `speaker` and one `addressee` predicate at any time; we assume there is only one conversation going on.

Plural Personal Pronouns. To represent plural objects in general, we assume each plural object is associated with a discourse referent, whose members can be identified with a series of `member` predicates, and about which other special predicates such as `plural-object` and `cardinality` can be asserted. Plural personal pronouns denote – or more accurately presuppose – groups which include the addressee. For instance, *we* presupposes a group which includes the speaker, and plural *you* presupposes a group which includes the addressee. The group referred to by a plural pronoun must be made salient linguistically, for instance, by using a conjunction of noun phrases, as in Example 11:

(11) Dean: Pearl and I went to the cinema yesterday.
      Hank: What did y'all watch?
      Dean: We watched 'Casablanca'.

The first utterance here introduces a group entity composed of Pearl and Dean. In Hank's responding utterance, *y'all* presupposes a salient plural entity one of whose members is the addressee (Dean); the group of Pearl and Dean satisfies this presupposition. In Dean's second utterance, *we* presupposes this same entity.

This general definition of personal pronouns subsumes an interesting case where the speaker or the addressee are *themselves* group entities. Consider this case:

(12) Bob: Sue and Mary, are you ready to go?

The group of people denoted by *you* in this example are not just being referred to, but being addressed; unlike the group denoted by *y'all* in Example 11, *you* in this example actually denotes the group of people who have to respond to the utterance. Note that the second person pronoun can still be defined as presupposing a salient group of people which includes the addressee, provided that (a) we are not talking about strict inclusion, and (b) we assume (reasonably) that the addressee of an utterance is always a salient entity in the discourse context.

According to our dialogue-managment principles, a forward-looking utterance with a group addressee must be responded to by that group. Is it possible for an utterance to have a group speaker? Genuine 'joint utterances' are of course virtually nonexistent (outside the theatre). Our approach is to allow the possibility of group speakers, with a very simple additional dialogue management principle:

Principle 5: utterances made by a group speaker are actually made by an individual member of the group, on behalf of the whole group.

This approach is in fact in keeping with a general assumption in our system that all communication is public, and that there are no disagreements between participants. But in a more realistic situation, clearly much more needs to be said about how members of a group negotiate a response in such cases.

5 Addressee Terms

Addressee terms function syntactically as sentence modifiers in English and Māori. In English, they can appear wherever a sentential adverb can appear; we believe they have the same distribution as conjunctive expressions like *however* or *therefore*. They are typically proper names (e.g. *Hello, John*) or bare nouns (e.g. *Hello, baby*). In Māori, they typically occur at the front of sentences:

(13)   William, kei te auau ngā kurī. (William, the dogs are barking.)

One important exception: greetings are best modified postsententially:

(14)   Kia ora William. (Hello William.)

What does an addressee term contribute semantically to a sentence? Our suggestion is that it contributes something very like a presupposition about the addressee, just as second-person pronouns do. For an addressee term, the presupposition has additional content as well, namely, all the properties which it mentions. For instance, here is an extract from Example 10 with heightened passion:

(15)   Bob: I love you, Sue.

The DRS for this example is given in Figure 3. There are two addressee presuppositions here, one contributed by *you*, and one by *Sue*. Note that the latter

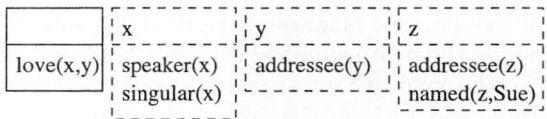

Fig. 3. DRS for *I love you, Sue*

presupposition does not bind to anything in the assertion DRS, but that because there is only ever one addressee entity in the context, the two addressee presuppositions are constrained to corefer in this case.

There are nonetheless some important differences between the semantics of an addressee term and that of a second-person pronoun. Firstly, a plural addressee term squarely presupposes the addressee entity, not simply an entity including the addressee. Secondly, as emphasised in Section 3.2, addressee terms can function to *change* the default addressee, not simply to refer. This process needs to be described in some detail.

Assume we are dealing with a new incoming utterance from the user. Before processing this utterance, the system the system deletes all the existing **speaker** and **addressee** predicates from the context, sets the new **speaker** to be the user, and sets the **addressee** predicate according to the defaults given in Section 3. For instance, consider Example 16:

(16) User: I like movies, Bob.
      Bob (played by the system): That's interesting.
      User: Do you like movies, Sue?

After Bob's utterance, the system will set **speaker** to User, and **addressee** to Bob, by Principle 4. The user's second utterance presupposes that Sue is the addressee. The only way of allowing this is by accommodation of an **addressee** predicate which holds of the object named Sue. Since there can only ever be one **addressee** predicate, this also means deleting the existing **addressee** predicate holding of Bob. Accommodation of presuppositions due to addressee terms is thus non-monotonic. One problem this raises is in how to handle the presupposition due to the pronoun *you* in the utterance. If it was processed before that of the addressee term, it ends up being bound to an object which is no longer the addressee! These complications make it important to handle presuppositions due to addressee terms before any other presuppoitions. We therefore augment the DRS language we use to represent utterances, to include a special sub-DRS for addressee terms.

6 An Example Dialogue for Practicing Pronouns in Conversational Māori

The main application we have in mind for our dialogue system is a computer-aided language learning system for Māori which uses dialogue as its paradigm. To teach the Māori pronoun system, it is useful to support more than two speakers. We have implemented all of the syntax and semantics of pronouns and addressee terms, and many of the dialogue management principles, but we still have some work to do in combining these into a unified framework. In the meantime, we give an example below of the kind of multi-speaker dialogue we have in mind. The student is Jason; Hone and Piri are characters whose utterances are generated by the dialogue system.

1	Hone/Piri	Kia ora, Jason!	Hello, Jason!
2	Jason	Tēna kōrua.	Hello (you two).
3	Hone	Kei te hiakai ahau.	I'm hungry.
4	Piri	Kāore ahau i te hiakai.	I'm not hungry.
5	Piri	Kei te hiakai koe, Jason?	Are you hungry, Jason?
6	Jason	Kāore.	No.
7	Hone	Jason, kei te hiakai kōrua ko Piri?	Jason, are you (dual) and Piri hungry?
8	Jason	Kāore māua i te hiakai.	No, we (dual, exclusive) aren't hungry.

In Utterance 1, Hone and Piri are the speakers. They address Jason explicitly to start with. When Jason responds, Hone and Piri are by default the addressees, and Jason's greeting uses the appropriate dual pronoun. In 3 and 4, Hone and Piri provide some information about themselves. In 5, Piri asks a question of Jason. Since Hone is the default addressee of this utterance, Piri has to identify Jason explicitly with an addressee term. In 6, Jason answers Piri. In 7, Hone jumps in; by default, his utterance therefore has Jason and Piri as its addressees. However, Hone's utterance has an explicit addressee term (*Jason*) which overrides this. Finally, in 8, Jason replies, using an appropriate dual and exclusive first-person pronoun to refer to himself and Piri. The utterance is assumed to be addressed to Hone by default.

Implementing a dialogue system which supports this kind of interaction will allow a student great flexibility in practicing Māori questions, answers, assertions, all in a context where distinctions between the alternative personal pronouns are clearly motivated.

References

1. Padilha, E., Carletta, J.: A simulation of small group discussion. In: Proceedings of the 6th workshop on the semantics and pragmatics of dialogue (EDILOG 2002), Edinburgh (2002) 117–124
2. Wang, H.C., Huang, C.Y., Yang, C.H., Wang, J.F.: Multi-speaker dialogue for mobile information retrieval. In: Proceedings of the international symposium on Chinese spoken language processing (ISCSLP), National Cheng-Kung University, Tainan, Taiwan (2002)
3. de Jager, S., Knott, A., Bayard, I.: A DRT-based framework for presuppositions in dialogue management. In: Proceedings of the 6th workshop on the semantics and pragmatics of dialogue (EDILOG 2002), Edinburgh (2002)
4. Bayard, I., Knott, A., de Jager, S.: A uni cation-based grammar for a fragment of Māori and English. In: Proceedings of the 2nd Australasian Natural Language Processing Workshop (ANLP 2002). (2002)
5. Copestake, A.: The (new) LKB system. CSLI, Stanford University (2000)
6. Knott, A., Vlugter, P.: Syntactic disambiguation using presupposition resolution. In: Proceedings of the 4th Australasian Language Technology Workshop (ALTW2003), Melbourne (2003)
7. Copestake, A., Flickinger, D., Sag, I., Pollard, C.: Minimal Recursion Semantics: An introduction. Manuscript, CSLI, Stanford University (1999)
8. Kamp, H., Reyle, U.: From discourse to logic. Kluwer Academic Publishers, Dordrecht (1993)

Coherent Arrangement of Sentences Extracted from Multiple Newspaper Articles

Naoaki Okazaki[1], Yutaka Matsuo[2], and Mitsuru Ishizuka[1]

[1] Graduate School of Information Science and Technology, The University of Tokyo
7-3-1 Hongo, Bunkyo-ku, Tokyo 113-8656, Japan
okazaki@miv.t.u-tokyo.ac.jp
[2] Cyber Assist Research Center, AIST Tokyo Waterfront
2-41-6 Aomi, Koto-ku, Tokyo 135-0064, Japan

Abstract. Multi-document summarization is a challenge to information overload problem to provide a condensed text for a number of documents. Most multi-document summarization systems make use of extraction techniques (e.g., important sentence extraction) and compile a summary from the selected information. However, sentences gathered from multiple sources are not organized as a comprehensible text. Therefore, it is important to consider sentence ordering of extracted sentences in order to reconstruct discourse structure in a summary. We propose a novel method to plan a coherent arrangement of sentences extracted from multiple newspaper articles. Results of our experiment show that sentence reordering has a discernible effect on summary readability. The results also shows significant improvement on sentence arrangement compared to former methods.

1 Introduction

There is a great deal of computerized documents accessible on-line. With the help of search engines, we can obtain a set of relevant documents that fits to our interest. Even though we narrow the range of documents to be read through the search phase, we often get disgusted with the quantity of retrieved documents. Automatic text summarization is a challenge to the information overload problem to provide a condensed text for a given document. Multi-document summarization (MDS), which is an extension of summarization to related documents (e.g., a collection of documents or web pages retrieved from a search engine, collected papers on a certain research field, etc.), has attracted much attention in recent years.

Figure 1 illustrates an example of typical MDS system. Given a number of documents, a MDS system yields a summary by gathering information from original documents. Important sentence or paragraph extraction, which finds significant textual segments to be included into a summary, plays a major role in most summarization system. There has been a great deal of research to improve sentence/paragraph extraction because the quality of extraction has much effect on overall performance in a MDS system.

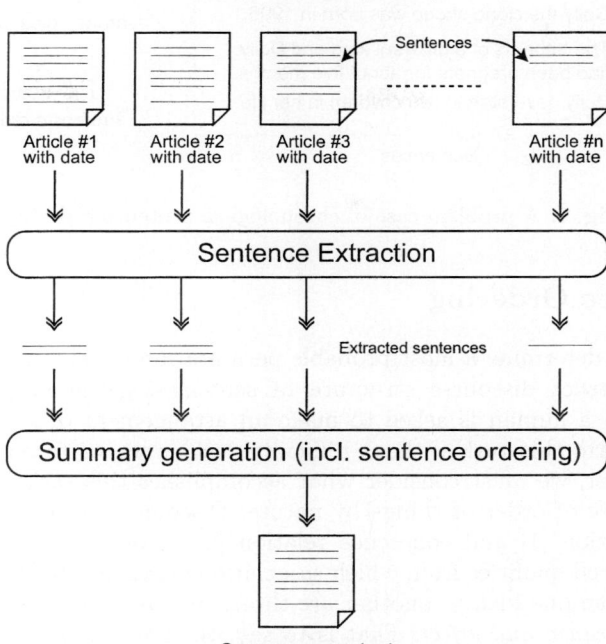

Fig. 1. A simplified summarization system with sentence extraction.

However, post-processing of extraction is also important to secure summary readability. We should eliminate unnecessary parts within extracted sentences to gain a higher compression ratio or insert necessary expressions to complement missing information. We should also break a long sentence into several sentences or combine several sentences into one sentence. Although there are numerous directions to improve summary readability as a post-processing phase of extraction, we consider a method to arrange extracted sentences coherently and inquire the necessity of a sequential ordering of summary sentences.

In this paper we propose our approach for coherent arrangement of sentences extracted from multiple newspaper articles. The rest of this paper is organized as follows. We present an outline of sentence ordering problem and related research including chronological sentence ordering, which is widely used in conventional MDS systems. We point an issue of chronological ordering and explain our approach to improve chronological ordering by complementing on presupposed information of each sentence. The subsequent section (Section 3) addresses evaluation metrics to validate the effectiveness of our algorithm in MDS and show experimental results. In Section 4 we discuss future work and conclusion of this paper.

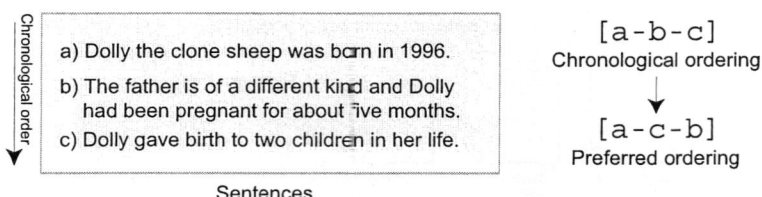

Fig. 2. A problem case of chronological sentence ordering.

2 Sentence Ordering

Our goal is to determine a most probable permutation of sentences or, in other words, reconstruct discourse structure of sentences gathered from multiple sources. When a human is asked to make an arrangement of sentences, he or she may perform this task without difficulty just as we write out thoughts in a text. However, we must consider what accomplishes this task since computers are unaware of order of things by nature. Discourse coherence, typified by rhetorical relation [1] and coherence relation [2], is of help to this question. Hume [3] claimed qualities from which association arises and by which the mind is conveyed from one idea to another are three: *resemblance*; *contiguity in time or place*; and *cause and effect*. That is to say we should organize a text from fragmented information on the basis of topical relevancy, chronological sequence, and cause-effect relation. It is especially true in sentence ordering of newspaper articles because we must arrange a large number of time-series events concerning several topics.

Barzilay et. al. [4] address the problem of sentence ordering in the context of multi-document summarization and the impact of sentence ordering on readability of a summary. They proposed two naive sentence-ordering techniques such as majority ordering (examines most frequent orders in the original documents) and chronological ordering (orders sentence by the publication date). Showing that using naive ordering algorithms does not produce satisfactory orderings, Barzilay et. al. also investigate through experiments with humans in order to identify patterns of orderings that can improve the algorithm. Based on the experiments, they propose another algorithm that utilizes topical segment and chronological ordering. Lapata [5] proposed another approach to information ordering based on a probabilistic model that assumes the probability of any given sentence is determined by its adjacent sentence and learns constraints on sentence order from a corpus of domain specific texts. Lapata estimates transitional probability between sentence by some attributes such as verbs (precedence relationships of verbs in the corpus), nouns (entity-based coherence by keeping track of the nouns) and dependencies (structure of sentences).

Against the background of these studies, we propose the use of antecedent sentences to arrange sentences coherently. Let us consider an example shown in Figure 2. There are three sentence a, b, and c from which we get an order [a-b-c] by chronological ordering. When we read these sentences in this order,

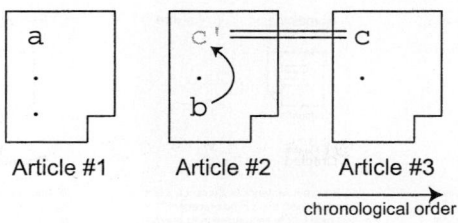

Fig. 3. Background idea of ordering refinement by precedence relation.

we find sentence b to be incorrectly positioned. This is because sentence b is written on the presupposition that the reader may know Dolly had a child. In other words, it is more fitting to assume sentence b to be an elaboration of sentence c. As you may easily be able to imagine, there are some precedent sentences prior to sentence b in the original document. Lack of presupposition obscures what a sentence is saying and confuses the readers. Hence, we should refine the chronological order and revise the order to [a-c-b], putting sentence c before sentence b.

2.1 Chronological Ordering

It is difficult for computers to find a resemblance or cause-effect relation between two phenomena: there is a great deal of possible relations classified in detail; and we do not have conclusive evidence whether a pair of sentences that we arbitrarily gather from multiple documents has some relation. A newspaper usually deals with novel events that have occurred since the last publication. Hence, publication date (time) of each article turns out to be a good estimator of resemblance relation (i.e., we observe a trend or series of relevant events in a time period), contiguity in time, and cause-effect relation (i.e., an event occurs as a result of previous events). Although resolving temporal expressions in sentences (e.g., *yesterday, the next year, etc.*) [7, 8] may give a more precise estimation of these relations, it is not an easy task. For this reason we first order sentences by the chronological order, assigning a time stamp for each sentence by its publication date (i.e., the date when the article was written).

When there are sentences having the same time stamp, we elaborate the order on the basis of sentence position and sentence connectivity. We restore an original ordering if two sentences have the same time stamp and belong to the same article. If sentences have the same time stamp and are not from the same article, we put a sentence which is more similar to previously ordered sentences to assure sentence connectivity.

2.2 Improving Chronological Ordering

After we obtain a chronological order of sentences, we make an effort to improve the ordering with the help of antecedent sentences. Figure 3 shows the

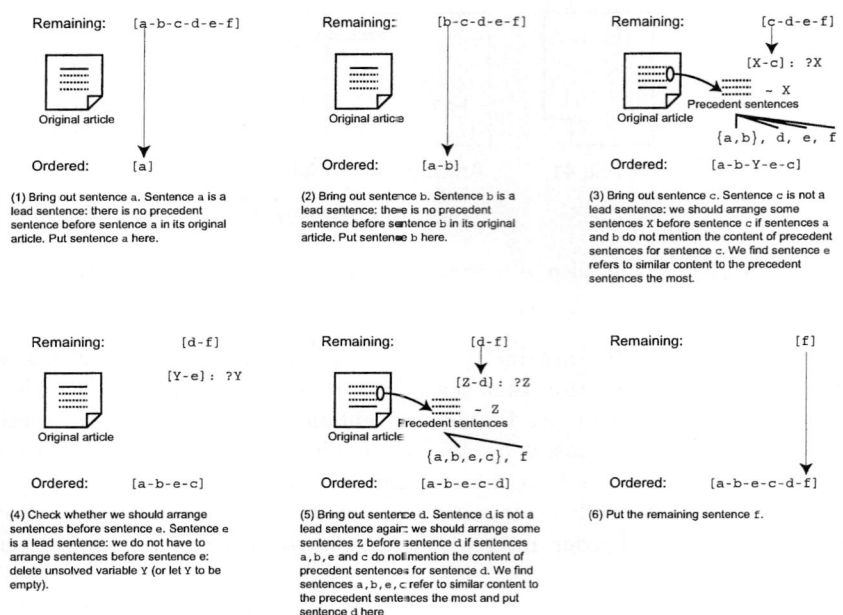

Fig. 4. Improving chronological ordering with the help of antecedent sentences.

background idea of ordering refinement by precedence relation. Just as the example in Figure 2, we have three sentences a, b, and c in chronological order. At first we get sentence a out of the sentences and check its antecedent sentences. Seeing that there are no sentences prior to sentence a in article #1, we take it acceptable to put sentence a here. Then we get sentence b out of remaining sentences and check its antecedent sentences. We find several sentences before sentence b in article #2 this time. Grasping what the antecedent sentences are saying, we confirm first of all whether if their saying is mentioned by previously arranged sentences (i.e., sentence a). If it is mentioned, we put sentence b here and extend the ordering to [a-b]. Otherwise, we search a substitution for what the precedence sentences are saying from the remaining sentences (i.e., sentence c in this example). In Figure 3 example, we find out sentence a is not referring to what sentence c' is saying but sentence c is approximately referring to that. Putting sentence c before b, we finally get the refined ordering [a-c-b].

Figure 4 illustrates how our algorithm refines a given chronological ordering [a-b-c-d-e-f]. In Figure 4 example we leave position of sentences a and b because they do not have precedent sentences in their original article (i.e., they are lead sentences[1]). On the other hand, sentence c has some preceding sentences in its original document. This presents two choices to us: we should check if it is safe to put sentence c just after sentences a and b; or we should arrange

---

[1] *Lead sentences* are sentences which appear at the beginning in an article.

some sentences before sentence c as a substitute of the precedent sentences. Preparing a term vector of the precedent sentences, we search a sentence or a set of sentences which is the most similar to the precedent content in sentences {a,b}, d, e, and f. In other words, we assume sentence ordering to be [a-b-X-c] and find appropriate sentence(s) X if any. Supposing that sentence e in Figure 4 describes similar content as the precedent sentences for sentence c, we substitute X with Y-e. We check whether we should put some sentences before sentence e or not. Given that sentence e is a lead sentence, we leave Y as empty and fix the resultant ordering to [a-b-e-c].

Then we consider sentence d, which is not a lead sentence again. Preparing a term vector of the precedent sentences of sentence d, we search a sentence or a set of sentences which is the most similar to the precedent content in sentences {a,b,e,c}, f. Supposing that either sentence a, b, e or c refers to the precedent content closer than sentence f, we make a decision to put sentence d here. In this way we get the final ordering, [a-b-e-c-d-f].

2.3 Compatibility with Multi-document Summarization

We describe briefly how our ordering algorithm goes together with MDS. Let us think the example shown in Figure 3 again. In this example, sentence extraction does not choose sentence c' while sentence c is very similar to sentence c'. You may think this is rare case for explanation, but it could happen as we optimize a sentence-extraction method for MDS. A method for MDS (e.g., [9]) makes effort to acquire information coverage under a condition that there is a number of sentences as summary candidates. This is to say that an extraction method should be able to refuse redundant information.

When we collect articles which describe a series of an event, we may find that lead sentences convey similar information over the articles since the major task of lead sentences is to give a subject. Therefore, it is quite natural that: lead sentences c and c' refer to similar content; an extraction method for MDS does not choose both sentence c' and c in terms of redundancy; and the method also prefers either sentence c or c' in terms of information coverage.

3 Evaluation

3.1 Experiment and Evaluation Metrics

We conducted an experiment of sentence ordering through multi-document summarization to test the effectiveness of the proposed method. We utilized the TSC-3 [10] test collection, which consists of 30 sets of multi-document summarization task. Performing an important sentence extraction for MDS [11] up to the specified number of sentences (approximately 10% of summarization rate), we made a material for a summary (i.e., extracted sentences) for each task. We order the sentences by six methods: *human-made ordering (HO)* as the highest anchor; *random ordering (RO)* as the lowest anchor; *chronological ordering (CO)* as a

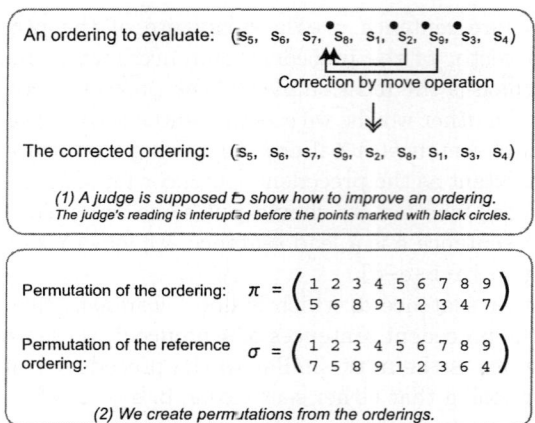

Fig. 5. Correction of an ordering.

conventional method; *chronological ordering with topical segmentation (COT)* (similar to Barzilay's method [4]); *proposed method without topical segmentation (PO)*; and *proposed method with topical segmentation (POT))*. Topical segmentation is a task to recognize topics in source documents to separate sentences referring to a topic from one another[2]. We asked three human judges to evaluate sentence ordering of 28 summaries out of TSC-3 test collection[3].

The first evaluation task is a subjective grading where a human judge marks an ordering of summary sentences on a scale of 4: 4 (*perfect*: we cannot improve any further), 3 (*acceptable*: makes sense even though there is some room for improvement), 2 (*poor*: requires minor amendment to bring it up to the acceptable level), and 1 (*unacceptable*: requires overall restructuring rather than partial revision).

In addition to the rating, it is useful that we examine how close an ordering is to an acceptable one when the ordering is regarded as *poor*. Considering several sentence-ordering patterns to be acceptable for a given summary, we think it is valuable to measure the degree of correction because this metric virtually requires a human corrector to prepare a correct answer for each ordering in his or her mind. Therefore, a human judge is supposed to illustrate how to improve an ordering of a summary when he or she marks the summary with *poor* in the rating task. We restrict applicable operations of correction to move operation to keep minimum correction of the ordering. We define a move operation here as removing a sentence and inserting the sentence into an appropriate place (see Figure 5-(1)).

---

[2] We classify articles by nearest neighbor method [6] to merge a pair of clusters when their minimum distance is lower than a given parameter $\alpha = 0.3$ (determined empirically). We calculate the distance by cosine distance of document vectors.

[3] We exclude two summaries because they are so long (approximately 30 sentences) that it is hard for judges to evaluate and revise them.

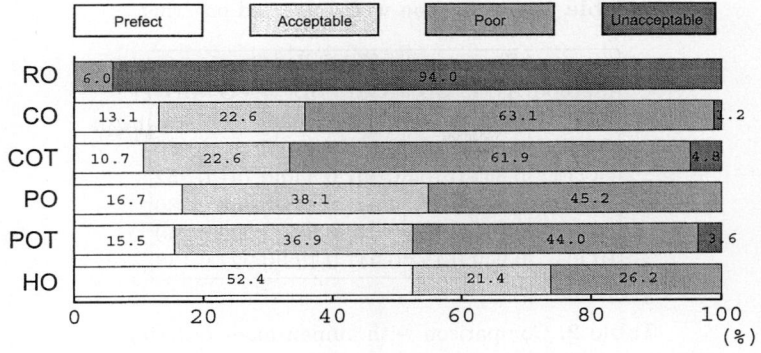

Fig. 6. Distribution of rating score of orderings in percentage.

Supposing a sentence ordering to be a rank, we can calculate rank correlation coefficient of a permutation of an ordering π and a permutation of the reference ordering σ. Spearman's rank correlation $\tau_s(\pi, \sigma)$ and Kendall's rank correlation $\tau_k(\pi, \sigma)$ are known as famous rank correlation metrics and were used in Lapata's evaluation [5]. These metrics range from -1 (an inverse rank) to 1 (an identical rank) via 0 (a non-correlated rank). In the example shown in Figure 5-(2) we obtain $\tau_s(\pi, \sigma) = 0.85$ and $\tau_k(\pi, \sigma) = 0.72$.

We propose another metric to assess the degree of sentence continuity in reading, $\tau_c(\pi, \sigma)$:

$$\tau_c(\pi, \sigma) = \frac{1}{n} \sum_{i=1}^{n} \text{equals}\left(\pi\sigma^{-1}(i), \pi\sigma^{-1}(i-1)+1\right), \tag{1}$$

where: $\pi(0) = \sigma(0) = 0$; $\text{equals}(x, y) = 1$ when x equals y and 0 otherwise. This metric ranges from 0 (no continuity) to 1 (identical). The summary in Figure 5-(1) may interrupt judge's reading after sentence S_7, S_1, S_2 and S_9 as he or she searches a next sentence to read. Hence, we observe four discontinuities in the ordering and calculate sentence continuity $\tau_c(\pi, \sigma) = (9-4)/9 = 0.56$.

3.2 Result

Figure 6 shows distribution of rating score of each method in percentage of 84 (28×3) summaries. Judges marked about 75% of human-made ordering (HO) as either perfect or acceptable while they rejected as many as 95% of random ordering (RO). Chronological ordering (CO) did not yield satisfactory result losing a thread of 63% summaries although CO performed much better than RO. Topical segmentation could not contribute to ordering improvement of CO as well: COT is slightly worse than CO After taking an in-depth look at the failure orderings, we found the topical clustering did not perform well during this test. We suppose that the topical clustering could not prove the merits with this test collection because the collection consists of relevant articles retrieved by

Table 1. Comparison with corrected ordering.

Method	Spearman AVG SD	Kendall AVG SD	Continuity AVG SD
RO	0.041 0.170	0.035 0.152	0.018 0.091
CO	0.838 0.185	0.870 0.270	0.775 0.210
COT	0.847 0.164	0.791 0.440	0.741 0.252
PO	0.843 0.180	0.921 0.144	0.856 0.180
POT	0.851 0.158	0.842 0.387	0.820 0.240
HO	0.949 0.157	0.947 0.138	0.922 0.138

Table 2. Comparison with human-made ordering.

Method	Spearman AVG SD	Kendall AVG SD	Continuity AVG SD
RO	-0.117 0.265	-0.073 0.202	0.054 0.064
CO	0.838 0.185	0.778 0.198	0.578 0.218
COT	0.847 0.164	0.782 0.186	0.571 0.229
PO	0.843 0.180	0.792 0.184	0.606 0.225
POT	0.851 0.158	0.797 0.171	0.599 0.237
HO	1.000 0.000	1.000 0.000	1.000 0.000

some query and polished well by a human and thus exclude unrelated articles to a topic. On the other hand, the proposed method (PO) improved chronological ordering much better than topical segmentation: sum of perfect and acceptable ratio jumped up from 36% (CO) to 55% (PO). This shows ordering refinement by precedence relation improves chronological ordering by pushing poor ordering to an acceptable level.

Table 1 reports closeness of orderings to the corrected ones with average scores (AVG) and the standard deviations (SD) of the three metrics τ_s, τ_k and τ_c. It appears that average figures shows similar tendency to the rating task with three measures: HO is the best; PO is better than CO; and RO is definitely the worst. We applied one-way analysis of variance (ANOVA) to test the effect of four different methods (RO, CO, PO and HO). ANOVA proved the effect of the different methods ($p < 0.01$) for three metrics. We also applied Tukey test to compare the difference between these methods. Tukey test revealed that RO was definitely the worst with all metrics. However, Spearman's rank correlation τ_S and Kendall's rank correlation τ_k failed to prove the significant difference between CO, PO and HO. Only sentence continuity τ_c proved PO is better than CO; and HO is better than CO ($\alpha = 0.05$). The Tukey test proved that sentence continuity has better conformity to the rating results and higher discrimination to make a comparison.

Table 2 shows closeness of orderings to ones made by human. Although we found RO is clearly the worst as well as other results, we cannot find the significant difference between CO, PO, and HO. This result revealed the difficulty of automatic evaluation by preparing a correct ordering.

4 Conclusion

In this paper we described our approach to coherent sentence arrangement for multiple newspaper articles. The results of our experiment revealed that our algorithm for sentence ordering did contribute to summary readability in MDS and improve chronological sentence ordering significantly. We plan to do further study on the sentence ordering problem in future work, explore how to apply our algorithm to documents other than newspaper and integrate ordering problem with extraction problem to benefit each other and overall quality of MDS.

Acknowledgment

We made use of Mainichi Newspaper and Yomiuri Newspaper articles and summarization test collection of TSC-3. We wish to thank reviewers for valuable comments on our paper.

References

1. Mann, W., Thompson, S.: Rhetorical structure theory: Toward a functional theory of text organization. *Text* **8** (1988) 243–281
2. Hobbs, J.: *Literature and Cognition*. CSLI Lecture Notes 21. CSLI (1990)
3. Hume, D.: *Philosophical Essays concerning Human Understanding*. (1748)
4. Barzilay, R., Elhadad, E., McKeown, K.: Inferring strategies for sentence ordering in multidocument summarization, *JAIR* **17** (2002) 35–55
5. Lapata, M.: Probabilistic text structuring: experiments with sentence ordering. In *Proceedings of the 41st ACL* (2003) 545–552
6. Cover, T. M., Hart, P. E.: Nearest neighbor pattern classification. Journal of *IEEE Transactions on Information Theory* **IT-13** (1967) 21–27
7. Mani, I. and Wilson, G.: Robust temporal processing of news. In *Proceedings of the 38th Annual Meeting of ACL'2000* (2000) 69–76
8. Mani, I., Schiffman, B., Zhang, J.: Inferring temporal ordering of events in news. In *Proceedings of HLT-NAACL'03* (2003)
9. Carbonell, J., Goldstein, J.: The use of MMR, diversity-based reranking for re-ordering documents and producing summaries. In *Proceedings of the 21st Annual International ACM-SIGIR Conference on Research and Development in Information Retrieval* (1998) 335–336
10. Hirao, T., Okumura, M., Fukushima, T., Nanba, H.: Text Summarization Challenge 3: Text summarization evaluation at NTCIR Workshop 4. In *Working note of the 4th NTCIR Workshop Meeting* (to appear in June 2004)
11. Okazaki, N., Matsuo, Y., Ishizuka, M.: TISS: An integrated summarization system for TSC-3. In *Working note of the 4th NTCIR Workshop Meeting* (to appear in June 2004)

Improvement of Language Models Using Dual-Source Backoff

Sehyeong Cho

MyongJi University, Department of Computer Science
San 38-2 Yong In, KyungGi, Korea
shcho@mju.ac.kr

Abstract. Language models are essential in predicting the next word in a spoken sentence, thereby enhancing the speech recognition accuracy, among other things. However, spoken language domains are too numerous, and therefore developers suffer from the lack of corpora with sufficient sizes. This paper proposes a method of combining two n-gram language models, one constructed from a very small corpus of the right domain of interest, the other constructed from a large but less adequate corpus, resulting in a significantly enhanced language model. This method is based on the observation that a small corpus from the right domain has high quality n-grams but has serious sparseness problem, while a large corpus from a different domain has more n-gram statistics but incorrectly biased. With our approach, two n-gram statistics are combined by extending the idea of Katz's backoff and therefore is called a dual-source backoff. We ran experiments with 3-gram language models constructed from newspaper corpora of several million to tens of million words together with models from smaller broadcast news corpora. The target domain was broadcast news. We obtained significant improvement (30%) by incorporating a small corpus around one thirtieth size of the newspaper corpus.

Area: Natural Language Processing

1 Introduction

Languages have redundancy and therefore have regularity, due partly to languages themselves and partly to regularity or predictability in the reality that is described by the language. Once you heard "in terms" you are more likely to hear "of" than "off". This is an example of linguistic regularity. Once you heard "U.S. open" you are more likely to hear "Tiger Woods" than "Pablo Picasso." This is due to regularity in reality.

Language modeling is an attempt to capture the regularities and make predictions. One use of language modeling has been automatic speech recognition. Optical character recognition and spelling correction also make use of language modeling.

Recent attempts in language modeling are mostly based on statistical approaches. This is because statistics has a solid theoretical foundation for dealing with uncertainty. It is easier to integrate information from various sources to reach a conclusion. If we see a linguistic process as a stochastic process, speech recognition can be modeled statistically by using Bayes's law as in equation 1.

$$\arg\max_s P(s \mid a) = \arg\max_s P(a \mid s)P(s) \tag{1}$$

In equation 1, a represents acoustic signal and s represents a sentence. Unless extra-sentential information is used, a statistical language model sees $P(s)$ as $\prod_{i=1..n} P(w_i \mid w_1 w_2 ... w_{i-1})$, where s is a sequence of words $w_1...w_n$. Further, if dependency is assumed to be local to previous $n-1$ words, that is, $\prod_i P(w_i \mid w_1 w_2 ... w_{i-1}) = \prod_i P(w_i \mid w_{i-n+1} ... w_{i-2} w_{i-1})$, then we call it an n-gram language model. We restrict our attention only to n-gram based models, approximating the probability of a sentence as $\prod_i P(w_i \mid w_{i-n+1} ... w_{i-2} w_{i-1})$. In this paper, we use 3-gram language model for practical reasons.

In order to use an n-gram language model, it is necessary to somehow estimate the probability of the form $P(w_i \mid w_{i-n+1} w_{i-n+2} ... w_{i-1})$. This is usually obtained by maximum likelihood estimation, which is simply a relative number of occurrences in a large text, or corpus. The process of collecting the occurrences (hence probabilities) is called training.

The biggest obstacle for training by a limited text is sparseness. For instance, if we had ten million words in a corpus and 10,000 words in the vocabulary. The average number of occurrences of a 3-gram is a mere 0.00001, since there are 10^{12} possible 3-gram types. This means that by simple MLE, most n-grams will have zero probabilities, which is certainly not correct. Therefore we need a means of estimating probabilities for zero-occurrence n-grams.

Smoothing, or discounting is a way of giving non-zero probabilities to n-grams that have zero MLE probabilities. Good-Turing[1] and Witten-Bell[2] are two examples of smoothing. They are also called *discounting* because part of the probabilities of existing n-grams are taken away and given to non-existent 3-grams, or *zerotons*.

The discounted probability mass can either be distributed uniformly or based on some linguistic information. With Katz's backoff method [3], we distribute the residual probability mass proportional to the n-1-gram probabilities. [4] has a good summary on more recent approaches to discounting.

Perplexity[5] is used as a measure to judge the quality of statistical language models. Perplexity is 2 to power of cross-entropy, where cross entropy is defined as equation 2.

$$H(L,M) = -\lim_{n \to \infty} \frac{1}{n} \sum_{x_{1..n}} P_L(x_{1..n}) \log P_M(x_{1..n}) \tag{2}$$

L represents the language and M represents the model. Perplexity is preferred to cross-entropy, because it is more intuitive. Cross entropy (and hence perplexity) will be minimized if the estimated probabilities were equal to actual probabilities of occurrences.

2 Motivation: The Lack of Right Corpus

What motivated this research is simply the lack of right corpus. By "right corpus," we mean sentences from the same domain. Further, the corpus should be big enough. For instance, to construct a reasonable 3-gram model, several million words are generally considered barely useable, though a billion words is considered to be a saturation point[6]. Some one hundred words will probably be considered to be unacceptable.

Table 1. Perplexity of models from various corpora. Test text from broadcast news.

Training corpus Size in 100,000 words	1	2	4	8	16	32
Broadcast corpus	582	567	485	420	331	248
Newspaper corpus	1170	1150	1051	926	793	631

As we see in Table 1, the perplexity of a language model constructed from a newspaper corpus is consistently greater than that of the language model constructed from the broadcast news corpus of the same size. This means newspaper language and broadcast news language are different. Therefore, no matter how large the corpus is, you cannot break the barrier of inherent perplexity. Unfortunately, it is extremely difficult to have corpora of sufficient size for each domain, like broadcast news, travel domain, dictation, and so on and so forth.

This granted, what we need then is a way of making use of existing information to help lower the perplexity of the language model. However, simply merging two corpora will not help much, as we shall see later in the next section.

3 Related Work

Linear combination is probably the simplest way of combining two language models as shown in equation 3.

$$P_{combined}(w \mid h) = \sum_{k=1..n} \lambda_k P_k(w \mid h) \qquad (3)$$

In this equation, h represents history, w represents a word, and n is the number of individual language models. The sum $\sum_{k=1..n} \lambda_k$ should be equal to unity, for the sake of consistency. Further, if there are only two information sources, equation 3 is simplified as equation 4.

$$P_{combined}(w \mid h) = \lambda_1 P_1(w \mid h) + \lambda_2 P_2(w \mid h) \qquad (4)$$

Rosenfeld[7] points out that the optimal coefficients can be found by Expectation-Maximization algorithm. If the information sources are only two, determining the practical optimum is much easier: just trial and error will do practically.

Linear interpolation has the advantage of extreme simplicity. It is easy to implement, easy to compute. Linear combination is consistent as far as n-gram models are concerned.

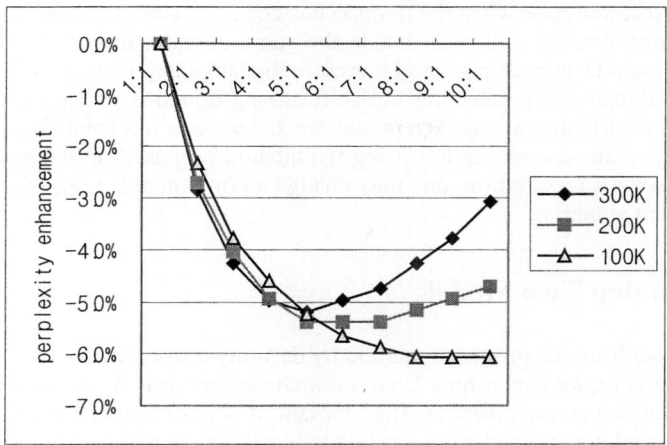

Fig. 1. Reduction in perplexity by linear interpolation. X axis is the ratio of $\lambda_1 : \lambda_2$ from 1:1 to 10. Improvements are depicted relative to 1:1 cases.

Maximum entropy method[7] is another option. Maximum entropy method gives a consistent solution even when the event spaces are not the same. For instance, suppose we had an n-gram model probability and a trigger pair model probability: $P(bank \mid in, the)$ and $P(bank \mid loan \in history)$. When the two conditions are both satisfied, that is, the history contained the word 'loan' and previous two words were "in the", then maximum entropy method can find a solution without sacrificing the consistency, by imposing that the constraints are satisfied *on the average*. On the other hand, linearly combining the two will give out inconsistent probabilities.

However, if we had the same event space, then Maximum entropy method will result in trouble.

1. With maximum entropy method, the expectation,

$$\mathop{E}_{h \text{ ends in 'in the'}} [P_{combined}(bank \mid h)] = P_1(bank \mid in, the).$$

2. Also, by the same token,

$$\mathop{E}_{h \text{ ends in 'in the'}} [P_{combined}(bank \mid h)] = P_2(bank \mid in, the)$$

Except by rare coincidence, $P_1(bank \mid in, the) \neq P_2(bank \mid in, the)$, which obviously is a contradiction. Therefore maximum entropy method is good only when we have different event spaces, but cannot be consistently used in our problem.

Akiba [8] proposed using selective backoff. Their approach is similar to ours in that they use backoff with two different models. One of the models is probabilistic model and the other is a grammar network. The aim of their combination is to delete probabilities of all unnecessary n-grams, that is, those that are not possible word sequences according to the simpler grammar-based transition network.

Adaptation([9], for example) is a dynamic switching of language models based on the present situation. Adaptation can further be divided into cross-domain adaptation and intra-domain adaptation. Cross-domain adaptation means switching the language model to a different one when the domain has changed. Intra-domain adaptation deals with the same domain, but even inside the same domain, topics or sub-topics may change, or speaker may change, and therefore the languages change. While adaptation focuses on dynamically detecting the shift among domains or topics, our problems deals with constructing a language model *per se* by using information from two models. We can create several models using the method proposed in this paper and in the process of speech recognition, one may change among models (i.e., adapt) depending on the current situation.

4 Combining Two Models

We start describing the proposed method by defining a few terms.

A *primary corpus* is a corpus from a domain of interest. A *secondary corpus* is a (relatively larger) corpus, from another domain. A *primary language model*, then, is a language model constructed from a primary corpus. A *secondary language model* is a language model constructed from a secondary corpus. C_1 is the primary corpus, and C_2 is the secondary corpus. P_1 denotes the probability obtained by maximum likelihood estimation from the primary corpus. $\overline{P}_1$ denotes a discounted primary probability. P_2 and $\overline{P}_2$ are likewise defined.

We prepared 3-gram models from corpora of various sizes. One set used broadcast news script, the other newspaper articles. The test data is from a separate text from broadcast news. It is not difficult to figure out, given the same size, the broadcast news corpora (primary corpus, hence primary language model) performed better (i.e., lower perplexity). What is interesting in the result is that given the same (or roughly the same) perplexity, the 3-gram hit ratio of the primary model is significantly lower. Conversely, with similar 3-gram hit ratios, the secondary model has significantly higher perplexity.

The reason for lower 3-gram hit ratio is simple: the model is constructed from smaller corpus. Nevertheless, it performs better because of the quality of n-gram probability distribution.

Conversely, once again, the secondary model had higher 3-gram hit ratio because it was constructed from a bigger corpus, but poorer because the difference in the language made the probability estimate inadequately biased. Then what if we combined the two merits: quality n-gram statistics and higher hit ratio. That is the basic idea behind our approach.

From the observations, it follows that by using a 3-gram probability obtained from the corpus of the same domain we can obtain lower perplexity. Then what about a 2-gram primary model and a 3-gram secondary model? We observed that if the primary model and the secondary model used the same size, then the 2-gram primary model performed far better than the 3-gram secondary model.(Table 3) However, this does not mean that 3-gram probabilities in the secondary model is useless, since usually secondary model is constructed from a far bigger corpus. For instance, a secondary 2-gram model constructed from a 10,000K size corpus outperformed a primary 3-gram model from a 800K size corpus.

Table 2. Perplexity and 3-gram his ratio(using Cambridge-CMU toolkit v.2, w/ Good-Turing discounting, range 1-7-7).

Test and training corpus from same domain (broadcast news)			Test corpus: broadcast news Training corpus: newspaper articles		
size	3-gram hit ratio	perplexity	size	3-gram hit ratio	perplexity
100K	14.2	582	100K	7.09	1170.47
200K	17.8	567.16	200K	10.06	1150.5
400K	22.67	485.1	400K	13.38	1051.69
800K	27.89	420.11	800K	17.44	926.91
1600K	34.53	331.07	1600K	23.19	793.34
3200K	42.15	248.19	3200K	29.15	631
5000K	47.47	200.96	5000K	33.48	543.27

Table 3. Perplexity measures of 2.3-gram models, primary and secondary.

	Primary model		Secondary model	
	2-gram model	3-gram model	2-gram model	3-gram model
100 K	587.75	582	1175.66	1170.47
200 K	585.09	567.16	1171.96	1150.5
400 K	514.78	485.1	1083.05	1051.69
800 K	459.53	420.11	970.69	926.91
1600 K	386.03	331.07	838.08	793.34
3200 K	313.25	248.19	694.9	631
10,000K			526.42	433.58
20,000K			457.79	348.24

Therefore given appropriate sizes, we may be able to take advantage of n-gram probabilities in both models. We assumed that the secondary corpus is at least one order of magnitude larger than the primary corpus, based on the observation in Table 2 and Table 3. Then we may conclude that the relative qualities of n-grams are:

3-gram(primary) $\succ$ 3-gram(secondary) $\succ$ 2-gram(primary)
$\succ$ 2-gram(secondary) $\succ$ 1-gram(primary) $\succ$ 1-gram (secondary),

where the $\succ$ stands for the (informal) relation "more important."

However, a straightforward solution will lead to inconsistency. In other words, the conditional probabilities do not sum up to unity (i.e.,

$$\sum_{xyz \in C_1} P_1(z \mid x, y) + \sum_{\substack{xyz \notin C_1 \\ xyz \in C_2}} P_1(z \mid x, y) \neq 1).$$

This is where Katz's idea comes into play. First, we note that the n-gram probabilities in the primary model is generally either overestimated (when the count is greater than zero) or underestimated (when the count is zero). Therefore we first discount the MLE probabilities of the non-zerotons. Let $\beta = 1 - \sum_{xyz \in C_1} \overline{P_1}(z \mid x, y)$. Then we redistribute the mass to zeroton 3-grams (i.e., the 3-gram xyz's, such that $xyz \notin C_1$). The redistribution is not uniform, but proportional to either secondary 3-gram probability or primary 2-gram. Assuming that the secondary corpus is larger by at least one order of magnitude,

$$\overline{P}(z\mid xy) = \begin{cases} \overline{P_1}(z\mid xy) & \text{if } xyz \in C_1 \\ \alpha_{xy}\overline{P_2}(z\mid xy)\gamma_1 & \text{if } xyz \notin C_1, xyz \in C_2 \\ \alpha_{xy}\overline{P}(z\mid y)\gamma_2 & \text{otherwise} \end{cases} \quad (4)$$

γ_1 and γ_2 are coefficients that reflect the relative importance of secondary 3-gram and primary 2-gram. However, we experienced these values other than 1:1 yielded no significant improvement, and equation 4' will be used instead.

$$\overline{P}(z\mid xy) = \begin{cases} \overline{P_1}(z\mid xy) & \text{if } xyz \in C_1 \\ \alpha_{xy}\overline{P_2}(z\mid xy) & \text{if } xyz \notin C_1, xyz \in C_2 \\ \alpha_{xy}\overline{P}(z\mid y) & \text{otherwise} \end{cases} \quad (4')$$

In the above formula, α_{xy} is a normalizing constant such that $\sum_{xyz}\overline{P}(z\mid xy)=1$.

Therefore

$$\alpha_{xy} = \frac{\beta}{\sum_{\substack{xyz \notin C_1 \\ xyz \in C_2}} \overline{P_2}(z\mid xy) + \sum_{\substack{xyz \notin C_1 \\ xyz \notin C_2}} \overline{P}(z\mid y)}. \quad (5)$$

Unlike Katz's coefficients, there is no simple computation procedure for α_{xy}, and thus repeated summation is required, which took hours in a machine with two Xeon 2GHz processors. Fortunately, the calculation needs to be done only once and it need not be calculated in real-time.

The 2-gram probability $\overline{P}(z\mid y)$ is recursively defined in a similar manner.

$$\overline{P}(z\mid y) = \begin{cases} \overline{P_1}(z\mid y) & \text{if } yz \in C_1 \\ \alpha_y\overline{P_2}(z\mid y)\delta_1 & \text{if } yz \notin C_1, yz \in C_2 \\ \alpha_y\overline{P}(z)\delta_2 & \text{otherwise} \end{cases} \quad (6)$$

or by the same reason equation 4' replaced 4, we use equation 6.

$$\overline{P}(z\mid y) = \begin{cases} \overline{P_1}(z\mid y) & \text{if } yz \in C_1 \\ \alpha_y\overline{P_2}(z\mid y) & \text{if } yz \notin C_1, yz \in C_2 \\ \alpha_y\overline{P}(z) & \text{otherwise} \end{cases} \quad (6')$$

Finally, 1-gram probability can also be defined in a similar fashion.

$$\overline{P}(z) = \begin{cases} \overline{P}_1(z) & \text{if } z \in C_1 \\ \alpha_0 \overline{P}_2(z) & \text{if } z \notin C_1, z \in C_2 \\ \alpha'_0 & \text{otherwise} \end{cases} \quad (7)$$

For practical purposes, equation 7 may be simplified to either 8 or 9.

$$\overline{P}(z) = \begin{cases} \lambda_1 \overline{P}_1(z) + \lambda_2 \overline{P}_2(z) \\ \alpha'_0 \quad \text{otherwise} \end{cases} \quad (8)$$

$$\overline{P}(z) = \begin{cases} \overline{P}_1(z) \\ \alpha'_0 \quad \text{otherwise} \end{cases} \quad (9)$$

5 Results

We used CMU-Cambridge toolkit to construct secondary models in ARPA-format from a newspaper corpus (Dong A Ilbo news) from 4 million to 8 million words. We also constructed 4 primary models from SBS broadcast news (100K to 400K words). Test corpus was a separate SBS broadcast news text of 10K size.

By simply mixing up primary and secondary models, we obtained 10 to 17 percent decrease in perplexity. With optimal mixing ratio by linear interpolation, additional 5 to 6 % decrease is seen (see Fig.1). The result of the dual-source experiment showed around 30% decrease in perplexity. Considering that 20% decrease in perplexity shows notable increase in the accuracy of the speech recognizer, this can be regarded a meaningful result.

6 Conclusion and Future Work

The experiment clearly showed that there is improvement. However, it is not certain if this is indeed the optimal. As we discussed earlier the relative quality of the primary and the secondary n-grams depend on the corpora sizes. For instance, if the size of the primary corpus is very small compared to the secondary model, the secondary 2-gram probability may prove to be more reliable than the primary 3-gram.

Table 5 shows how 3-gram log probabilities average in each case. Row and column headings represent case numbers, top heading for dual-source backoff and side heading for Katz's style original backoff. For instance, case 1 means the 3-gram exists in the primary corpus. Case 2 means the 3-gram does not appear in primary corpus but appears in secondary corpus, and so on. Therefore –27.5 in row 2 column 3 means the average log probabilities of next words (where Katz's method used 2-gram and the proposed method used 3-gram from secondary corpus) was enhanced by –27.5. Negative numbers indicate average log probability decreased and positive numbers indicate the reverse. Even though as a whole the average decreased, in some cases it turned out to the opposite. This may indicate there are possibilities for more enhancement.

Table 4. Resulting Perplexity of interpolated model and dual-source backoff model.

Mixture of primary and secondary	Linear Interpolation (1:1)	dual-source backoff
100K/4M	377	242
200K/5M	359	244
300K/6M	333	230
400K/8M	300	206

Table 5. Enhancement in average log probabilities.

	Case 1	Case 2	Case 3	Case 4	Case 5	Etc.
Case 1	0	0	0	0	0	...
Case 2	0	0	-27.5	0	-118	...
Case 3	0	0	**18.5**	0	0	...
Case 4	0	0	0	0	-78.7	...
Case 5	0	0	0	0	**17.59**	...
Etc.	...	...	...	...	...	...

Lastly, the algorithm needs to be generalized to n-gram models of arbitrary n values. Theoretically, it seems possible. However, the real problem is in determining the order of applications. This is not merely a theoretical a problem, but a practical one, since it may well depend on the sizes of the corpora – relative or absolute – and also on the similarity among primary, secondary, and the test corpora.

Acknowledgement

This work was supported by grant R05-2003-000-11830-0 from the Basic Research Program of the Korea Science and Engineering Foundation.

References

1. Good, I.J. "The Population frequencies of species and the Estimation of Population parameters," Biometrica, vol.40, parts 3,4 pp.237-264
2. Witten, I.H. and Bell, T.C. "The zero-frequency problem: Estimating the probabilities of novel events in adaptive text compression," in IEEE Transactions on Information Theory, vol. 37-4, pp.1085-1094. 1991
3. Katz, S.M. "Estimation of Probabilities from Sparse Data for the Language Model Component of a Speech Recognizer," IEEE Transactions on Acoustics, Speech and signal Processing, vol. ASSP-35, pp 400-401, March 1987
4. Goodman, J.T. "A Bit of Progress in Language Modeling," Computer Speech and Language vol. 15, pp.403-434, 2001
5. Jelinek, F. et al, "Perplexity – A Measure of the difficulty of speech recognition tasks," Journal of the Acoustics Society of America, 62, S63. Supplement 1, 1977
6. Jurafsky, D. and Martin, J.H., *Speech and Language Processing*, Prentice-Hall, 2000
7. Rosenfeld, R. Adaptive Statistical Language Modeling: A Maximum Entropy Approach, Ph.D. dissertation, April 1994, Carnegie-Mellon University
8. Akiba, T., Itou, K., Fujii, A. and Ishikawa, T. "Selective Backoff smoothing for incorporating grammatical constraints into the n-gram language model," in Proc. International Conference on Spoken Language Processing, pp. 881-884, Sept. 2002
9. Chen, S. F. et al, "Topic Adaptation for Language Modeling Using Unnormalized Exponential Models," in Proc. ICASSP'98, Vol. 2, pp. 681-684, May 12-15, 1998

Speaker Identification Based on Log Area Ratio and Gaussian Mixture Models in Narrow-Band Speech

Speech Understanding / Interaction

David Chow and Waleed H. Abdulla

Electrical and Electronic Engineering Department, The University of Auckland
Auckland, New Zealand
ccho071@ec.auckland.ac.nz, w.adbulla@auckland.ac.nz
http://www.ele.auckland.ac.nz/~wabd002

Abstract. Log area ratio coefficients (LAR) derived from linear prediction coefficients (LPC) is a well known feature extraction technique used in speech applications. This paper presents a novel way to use the LAR feature in a speaker identification system. Here, instead of using the mel frequency cepstral coefficients (MFCC), the LAR feature is used in a Gaussian mixture model (GMM) based speaker identification system. An F-ratio feature analysis was conducted on both the LAR and MFCC feature vectors which showed the lower order LAR coefficients are superior to MFCC counterpart. The text-independent, closed-set speaker identification rate, as tested on the down-sampled version of TIMIT database, was improved from 96.73%, using the MFCC feature, to 98.81%, using the LAR features.

1 Introduction

Feature extraction is the key to the front-end process in speaker identification systems. The performance of a speaker identification system is highly dependent on the quality of the selected speech features. Most of the current proposed speaker identification systems use mel frequency cepstral coefficients (MFCC) and linear predictive cepstral coefficients (LPCC) as feature vectors [1]. Currently, researches are focusing on improving these two cepstral features. Orman had developed a new filter-bank to replace the mel frequency filter banks used in MFCC calculation [2]. On the other hand, there are many new features proposed to be used along with MFCC and LPCC [3, 4, 5]. Although MFCC and LPCC were proved to be two very good features in speech recognition, they are not necessarily being as good in speaker identification. In 1976, Sambur proposed to use orthogonal linear prediction coefficients as features in speaker identification [6]. In his work, he pointed out that for a speech feature to be effective, it should reflect the unique properties of the speaker's vocal apparatus and contains little or no information about the linguistic content of the speech [6]. As a result, he had tried to use linear prediction coefficients (LPC), parcor and log area ratio coefficients (LAR) as the speech features and then using orthogonal technique to reduce the linguistic content in those features. According to his work, log area ratio feature and parcor feature gave better results than LPC feature [6]. In this paper, LAR feature are chosen instead of parcor feature because it has a linear spectral sensitivity and is more robust to quantization noise [7]. In 1995, Reynolds demonstrated a Gaussian mixture model (GMM) based classifier work well in text-independent speaker identification even with speech feature that contains rich linguistic information like MFCC [3, 8]. With the above results, the authors believe that using LAR based features as feature vectors in the GMM-based speaker identification system will yield a very good identification result.

In this paper, LAR feature is investigated thoroughly by using the F-ratio analysis. A series of experiments about the performance of LAR feature on a speaker identification system had been conducted. This paper is organized as follows; section 2 gives a description of the LAR feature. Section 3 analyses LAR computational complexity. Section 4 explains the GMM-based speaker identification system used in this paper. Section 5 compares the performance of LAR feature with the MFCC feature. Section 6 derives conclusions out of this work.

2 Log Area Ratio Coefficients

The log area ratio (LAR) coefficients are derived from the linear prediction coefficients (LPC). Linear prediction coefficients are a highly effective representation of the speech signal. In this analysis, each speech sample is represented by a weighted sum of p past speech samples plus an appropriate excitation. The corresponding formula for the LPC model is:

$$s_n = \sum_{k=1}^{p} a_k s_{n-k} + Gu_n \tag{1}$$

where p is the order of the LPC filter, s_n is n^{th} speech sample and a_k is the kth coefficients of the LPC vector. These coefficients are found by Durbin algorithm which minimizes the mean square prediction error of the model [7, 9].

The LPC model characterizes the vocal tract of a person. It can be transformed into other coefficients called Log area ratio coefficients (LAR). In LAR analysis, the vocal tract of a person is modelled as a non-uniform acoustic tube formed by cascading p uniform equal length cylindrical tubes with different cross-section areas [9]. The glottis connected to the first tube is assumed to have zero area while the lips connected to the last tube is assumed to have infinite area. Figure 2.1 illustrates the acoustic tubes speech production model.

In this model, the length of each cylindrical tube is closely related to the sampling period and the number of coefficients in the LPC model. Therefore, in calculating the LAR coefficients, the vocal tract length is not needed to be specified.

The LAR coefficients are formed by the log area ratio between the cross-section areas of every two connected tubes. The number of cylindrical tubes in the model is equal to the number of LAR coefficients plus one. The relationship between the LAR coefficients and the LPC is:

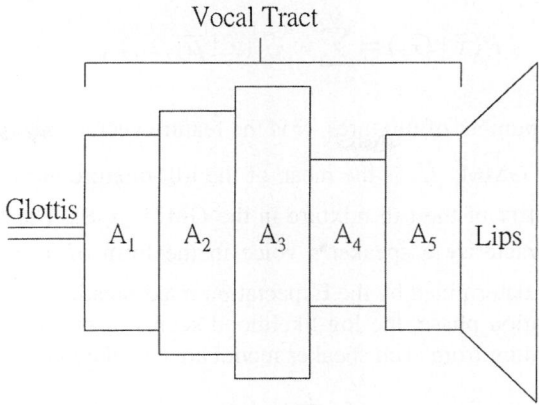

Fig. 2.1. Acoustic tubes speech production model.

$$LAR_i = \log\left(\frac{A_i}{A_{i+1}}\right) = \log\left(\frac{1+\alpha_i}{1-\alpha_i}\right), A_{p+1} = 1 \qquad (2)$$

where α_i is the ith parcor coefficients which can be found by:

$$\alpha = a_i^{(i)}, 1 \leq i \leq p \qquad (3)$$

where $a_i^{(i)}$ is the ith LPC calculated by the ith order LPC model [9].

3 Computation Complexity Analysis

According to Karpov, the time to compute MFCC feature is about 1.2 times slower than computing LPCC feature [10]. The computation of LAR feature is very similar to LPCC feature. Both the LAR and LPCC algorithms required to compute the autocorrelation matrix and both require the Durbin algorithm to solve the system of equations formed by the autocorrelation matrix. However, the last step to compute LAR feature is different to LPCC feature. The computation complexity of the last step of LAR feature is 4p operations while the LPCC counterpart is p(p+1) operations [10] where p is the order of the analysis. In conclusion, the computation complexity of LAR feature is slightly less than LPCC for $p > 3$ and accordingly less than MFCC.

4 Gaussian Mixture Model Based Speaker Identification System

In this speaker identification system, each speaker enrolled in the system is represented by a Gaussian mixture model (GMM). The idea of GMM is to use a series of Gaussian functions to represent the probability density of the feature vectors produced by a speaker. The mathematical representation is:

$$P(\vec{x} \mid G_s) = \sum_{i=1}^{M} w_i G_i(\vec{x} \mid \overline{\mu}_i, \Sigma_i) \quad (4)$$

where M is the number of mixtures, $\vec{x}$ is the feature vector, w_i is the weight of the i-th mixture in the GMM, $\overline{\mu}_i$ is the mean of the i-th mixture in the GMM and Σ_i is the covariance matrix of the i-th mixture in the GMM [3, 8]. The Model parameters $(w_i, \overline{\mu}_i, \Sigma_i)$ characterize a speaker's voice in the form of a probabilistic density function. They are determined by the Expectation maximization (EM) algorithm [11].

In the identification phase, the log-likelihood scores of the incoming sequence of feature vectors coming from each speaker model are calculated by:

$$L(X, G_s) = \sum_{t=1}^{F} P(\vec{x}_t \mid G_s) \quad (5)$$

where $X = \{\vec{x}_1, \vec{x}_2, \cdots, \vec{x}_F\}$ is the sequence of speaker feature vectors and F is the total number of feature vectors [3, 8]. The speaker whose speaker model generates the highest score is identified as the producer of the incoming speech signal. This decision method is called maximum likelihood (ML).

5 Experimental Method and Results

The speech data used in our speaker identification experiments consist of 112 males and 56 females selected from the testing set of the TIMIT database. TIMIT is a noise free speech database recorded using a high quality microphone sampled at 16 kHz. In this paper, the speech signal used was down sampled from 16 kHz to 8 kHz in order to test the identification accuracy under narrow-band (0–4000Hz) speech. Each speaker produces 10 sentences, the first 8 sentences were used for training and the last 2 sentences were used for testing. The average length of each sentence is 3 seconds. In other word, there was about 24 seconds of speech for training and 6 seconds for 2 tests with 3 seconds for each test.

The speech signal was extracted by using an energy based algorithm [12]. No pre-emphasis filter was applied to the signal. The analysis of speech signal was conducted over the speech frames of 20ms duration with 10ms overlapping. The windowing function used was Hamming window. The length of the window is chosen so that there are enough speech samples in each frame to estimate the speech spectrum and make it insensitive to window placement with respect to pitch periods. The classification engine used in this experiment was a 32 mixtures GMM classifier initialized by vector quantization (VQ) [13].

5.1 F-Ratio Analysis

F-ratio is a figure of merit to evaluate the effectiveness of feature coefficients. The formula of the F-ratio is:

$$F-ratio = \frac{\text{speaker variance among classes}}{\text{speaker variance within classes}} \qquad (6)$$

Figure 5.1 shows the F-ratio of the MFCC feature and LAR feature. It can be clearly seen that the lower order coefficients of LAR feature has higher F-ratio score than the MFCC counterpart. For the application of text-independent speaker identification, the F-ratio scores provide a good indication on the quality of the features but it is not perfect. That is because the three assumptions required by the F-Ratio are not fully achieved. These three assumptions are: [14]

The feature vectors within each class must have Gaussian distribution.
The features should be statistically uncorrelated.
The variances within each class must be equal.

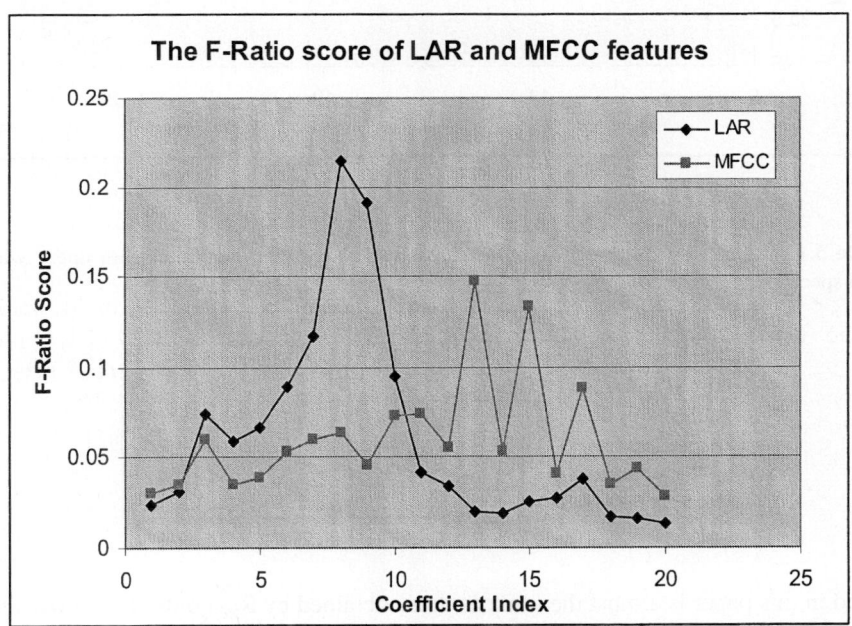

Fig. 5.1. The F-ratio score of the LAR and MFCC features.

5.2 Identification Results

The identification tests were conducted by 168 speakers according to the experimental setup described at the beginning of section 5. In each test, each speaker conducted 2 trials on the system.

Table 5.1 compares the wide-band speech (0 – 8000Hz) identification accuracies obtained by three different experiments with a similar setup and using similar speaker identification system. As can be seen from the table, the identification accuracy ob-

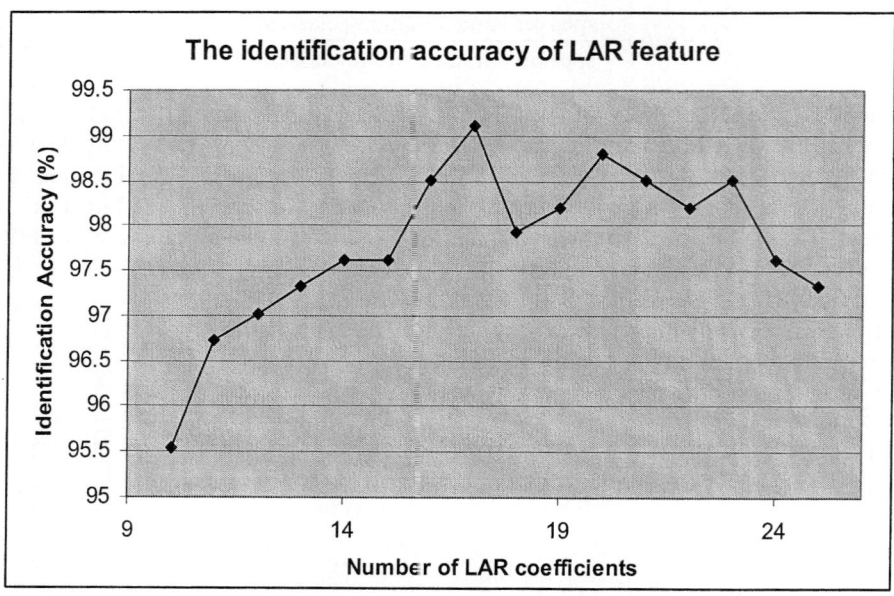

Fig. 5.2. The identification rate of the LAR feature.

Table 5.1. The identification rate of MFCC based speaker identification system under wideband speech.

	Identification rate
This paper (168 speakers from TIMIT)	99.4%
Reynolds's result in [8] (630 speakers from TIMIT)	99.5%
Reynolds's result [15] (168 speakers from TIMIT)	99.1%

tained in this paper is almost the same as those obtained by Reynolds. This proves the correct implementation of MFCC and GMM based speaker identification system used in this paper.

Figure 5.2 shows that the identification rate based on 17 LAR coefficients produces the best result where the identification rate of 99.11% was achieved. Table 5.2 compares the identification rate using 20 MFCC and 20 LAR coefficients. It also shows the identification rate obtained by replicating Reynolds work. The reason of using 20 LAR coefficients instead of 17 LAR coefficients is because in Reynolds's study, 20 MFCC coefficients were used. Therefore, 20 LAR coefficients were used in this study to give fair comparison. From the table, the identification rate of MFCC is 96.73% as compared to 98.81% obtained by LAR. A 2.08% improvement is achieved. The identification results obtained in this paper is higher than that obtained by Reynolds. One reason that explains the slightly worst result obtained by Reynold is the MFCC feature used by him only covered the telephone pass-band (300Hz – 3400Hz) where the MFCC feature used in this paper covered the whole 0 – 4000Hz bandwidth.

Table 5.2. The identification rate of LAR and MFCC features

	Identification rate
20 LAR coefficients	98.81%
20 MFCC coefficients	96.73%
Reynolds's result [15]	95.2%

6 Conclusions

This paper presents a novel way of utilising the LAR feature in a GMM-based speaker identification system. The new speaker identification system using 20 LAR coefficients achieved an identification rate of 98.81% as opposed to 96.73% obtained by the MFCC-based speaker identification system.

The F-ratio analysis showed that the LAR feature is more efficient than the MFCC feature in capturing the speaker's related information.

The computation of LAR feature has less computation complexity than the MFCC counterpart. Also, LAR feature is robust to quantization. These advantages make LAR feature extraction method easy to be implemented in embedded systems.

Acknowledgement

This work is supported by The University of Auckland Vice Chancellor Development Fund, project 23109 and The University of Auckland Research Fund, project 3602239/9273.

References

1. Premakanthan P. and Mikhad W. B. (2001) Speaker Verification/Recognition and the Importance of Selective Feature Extraction: Review. *MWSCAS*. **Vol 1,** 57-61.
2. Orman O. D. (2000) Frequency Analysis of Speaker Identification Performance. Master thesis, Bo aziçi University.
3. Sanderson S. (2002) Automatic Person Verification Using Speech and Face Information. PhD thesis. Griffith University.
4. Petry A. and Barone D. A. C. (2001) Fractal Dimension Applied to Speaker Identification. *ICASSP (Salt Lake City).* May 7-11. 405-408.
5. Liu C. H., Chen O. T. C. (2002) A Text-Independent Speaker Identification System Using PARCOR and AR Model. *MWSCAS*. **Vol 3,** 332-335.

6. Marvin R. S. (1976) Speaker Recognition Using Orthogonal Linear Prediction. *IEEE Transactions on Acoustic, Speech and Signal Processing.* **Vol 24,** 283-289.
7. Makhoul J. (1975) Linear Prediction: A Tutorial Review. *Proceedings of the IEEE.* **Vol 63,** 561-579.
8. Reynolds D. A. (1995) Speaker identification and verification using Gaussian mixture speaker models. *Speech Communication.* **Vol 17,** 91 – 108.
9. Campell J.P. and Jr. (1997) Speaker recognition: a tutorial. *Proceeding of the IEEE.* **Vol 85,** 1437-1462.
10. Karpov E. (2003) Real-Time Speaker Identification. Master thesis, University of Joensuu.
11. Bilmes J. A. (1998) A Gentle Tutorial of the EM Algorithm and its Application to Parameter Estimation for Gaussian Mixture and Hidden Markov Models. Technical Report, University of Berkeley.
12. Rabiner L. and Sambur B. (1975) An Algorithm for Determining the Endpoints of Isolated Utterances. *The Bell System Technical Journal.* **54,** pp 297 – 315.
13. Linde Y., Buzo A., Gray, R. (1980) An Algorithm for Vector Quantizer Design. *IEEE Transactions on Communications.* **Vol. 28(1),** 84-95.
14. Paliwal K. K. (1992) Dimensionality Reduction of the Enhanced Feature Set for the HMM-Based Speech Recognizer. Digital Signal Processing. **Vol. 2.** 157-173.
15. Reynolds D. A., Zissman M. A., Quatieri T. F., O'Leary G. C., Carlson B. A. (1995) The Effects of Telephone Transmission Degradations on Speaker Recognition Performance. *ICASSP (Detroit).* May 9-12. 329-331.

Automatic Sound-Imitation Word Recognition from Environmental Sounds Focusing on Ambiguity Problem in Determining Phonemes

Kazushi Ishihara[1], Tomohiro Nakatani[2],
Tetsuya Ogata[1], and Hiroshi G. Okuno[1]

[1] Graduate School of Informatics, Kyoto University, Kyoto, Japan
[2] NTT Communication Science Laboratories

Abstract. Sound-imitation words (SIWs), or onomatopoeia, are important for computer human interactions and the automatic tagging of sound archives. The main problem in automatic SIW recognition is ambiguity in the determining phonemes, since different listener hears the same environmental sound as a different SIW even under the same situation. To solve this problem, we designed a set of new phonemes, called the *basic phoneme-group* set, to represent environmental sounds in addition to a set of the articulation-based phoneme-groups. Automatic SIW recognition based on Hidden Markov Model (HMM) with the basic phoneme-groups is allowed to generate plural SIWs in order to absorb ambiguities caused by listener- and situation-dependency. Listening experiments with seven subjects proved that automatic SIW recognition based on the basic phoneme-groups outperformed that based on the articulation-based phoneme-groups and that based on Japanese phonemes. The proposed system proved more adequate to use computer interactions.

1 Introduction

The recent development of interface technology has enhanced human-computer interactions and enabled us to talk with robots as we would humans. Current systems, however, can deal only with speech, although non-speech sounds also have much information [1–5]. Automatic speech recognition (ASR) systems fail to recognize non-speech sounds, in particular environmental sounds such as friction, impact and electronic sounds. To communicate such environmental sounds, Japanese speaking people often use sound-imitation words called "*giongo* onomatopoeia". This means the naming of a thing by vocal imitations of the sound associated with it. For example, a sound-imitation word "r-i-N r-i-N" in Japanese, and "ting-a-ling" in English, stand for the sound of bell. Sound-imitation words are very effective for situational communication as well as for environmental sounds. Tanaka proposed the use of sound-imitation words to detect machine errors [6]. Sound-imitation words are also a means of symbolic grounding, as they transform sounds into symbolic representations. In digital archives, sound-imitation words may be used for annotations, such as in MPEG-

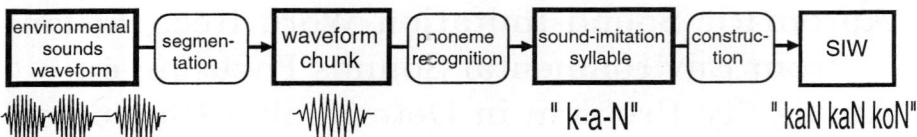

Fig. 1. Sound-imitation word recognition processing

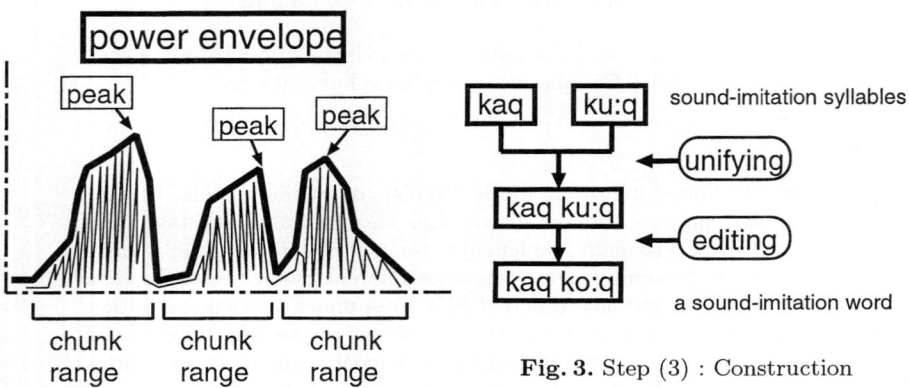

Fig. 2. Step (1) : Waveform segmentation

Fig. 3. Step (3) : Construction

7 for sound signals. Wake constructed a retrieval system using sound-imitation words as the retrieval key [7].

Our aim is to automatically transform environmental sounds into Japanese sound-imitation words. The critical issue in this transformation is how to resolve the ambiguity problem in literal representations. In this paper, we propose *phoneme-group expressions* to solve this problem.

In section 2, we describe the processing of sound-imitation word recognition. In section 3, we present the details of the ambiguity problem and an approach using phoneme-group expressions. In section 4, we evaluate our new approach. In section 5, we present our conclusions.

2 Sound-Imitation Word Recognition

Based on the relationship between a waveform chunk and one syllable of a word, we developed an approach to transform sounds into sound-imitation words (SIWs) in three stages [8]:

(1) The whole waveform is divided into waveform chunks.   (segmentation)
(2) Each segment is transformed into a sound-imitation syllable by phoneme recognition.   (phoneme recognition)
(3) A sound-imitation word is constructed from sound-imitation syllables according to Japanese grammar and culture.   (Construction)

This process is shown in Fig. 1. This paper primarily focuses on step (2).

Table 1. Conditions of phoneme recognition

system	HMM-based system (16-mixture monophone model)
sound stimuli	6011 short environmental sounds (from RWCP Sound Scene Database[S1])
label file	written by one person using three kinds of phoneme sets (section 3)
features	MFCC(16) + power(1) + ΔMFCC(16) + Δpower(1) frame size: 50 ms, frame shift: 10 ms
decoder	HVite in HTK[9]

2.1 Step (1): Segmentation

In the first step, the waveforms are divided into waveform chunks. A waveform chunk equals a short sound, called *tanpatsu-on* in Japanese [10]. The *tanpatsu-on* is used as a unit of the environmental sounds. Based on the sonority theory [11] and perceptual experiments, we know that the number of syllables is equal to the number of peaks in a power envelope. From this theory, we developed a segmentation method that involves calculating the ratio of the local minima between two peaks in a power envelope to the lesser of the two peaks, and then segmenting at the index of the local minima, if the ratio is less than a threshold (Figure 2). The details of this segmentation method and perceptual experiments are introduced in our paper [8].

Additionally, we think that a repeat recognition method for environmental sounds [12] can be applied to this process. The method recognizes what sound was repeated, and how many times the sound was repeated, based on the degree of similarity between each segment. To use this method, the recognition system can express an environmental sound repeated using a brief expression. For instance, when the system hears "k-a-N k-a-N k-a-N k-a-N k-a-N k-a-N k-a-N k-a-N k-a-N", the system represents the sound as "k-a-N k-a-N k-a-N" or "nine times [k-a-N]". Such brief expressions sound very natural and human.

2.2 Step (2): Phoneme Recognition

In the second step, each segment is transformed into a sound-imitation syllable by means of Japanese phoneme. This process is referred to as phoneme recognition in this paper. For recognition systems, we used HMM-based systems, trained on 6,011 environmental sound stimuli and their associated transcriptions. The sound stimuli are obtained from RWCP Sound Scene Database [S1]. The acoustic features consist of 16 MFCCs plus energy, together with their delta coefficients, resulting in 34 parameters per frame. The frame size was 50 ms, with a frame shift of 10 ms. This system is a 16-mixture monophone model. These conditions are shown in Table 1.

We believe that the MFCCs are effective for environmental sound recognition as well as speech recognition [13], because the Mel frequency and filterbank analysis were designed to imitate the human hearing system. In our preliminary

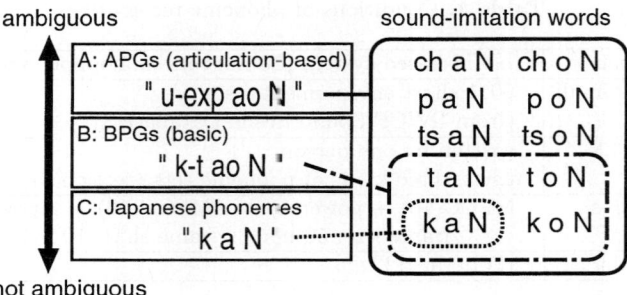

Fig. 4. Expressions using each phoneme set

experiments, we confirmed that the HMM-based system was more effective than the decision-tree based one and that the MFCCs were more effective than the LPCs and FBANKs [9]. The parameters shown above were determined based on the results of these experiments.

However, the ambiguity problem of sound-imitation words prevents the recognizer from appropriately training and determining the phoneme. This critical issue is described in sections 3 and 4

2.3 Step (3): Construction

In the final step, a sound-imitation word is constructed from all of sound-imitation syllables, and the word is edited to determine the most appropriate one, according to the requirements of the Japanese language. For example, the system would express a cry of a cuckoo as "ka-q ko:-q" while the system heard as "ka-q ku:-q". This is because "ka-q ko:-q" is a well known symbolic expression in Japanese. The influence of language and culture is dealt with in this step. How to design editing strategies will be studied in the future.

3 Ambiguity of Determining Phonemes

The critical issue, in sound-imitation word recognition, is the ambiguity in determining the phonemes. The literal representation of sound-imitation words is not unique, but there are a lot of variations that depend on the listeners. For instance, a certain impact sound may be heard as "b-a:-N", "d-a:-N", or "d-o:-N". It is very difficult for the system to train and output the proper sound-imitation words because expressions written in Japanese phonemes cannot appropriately represent environmental sounds. To solve this problem, we designed and compared three sets of phonemes:

- $\mathcal{A}$: *articulation-based phoneme-group* [APG] set   (Section 3.1)
- $\mathcal{B}$: *basic phoneme-group* [BPG] set   (Section 3.2)
- $\mathcal{C}$: *Japanese phoneme* set   (Section 3.3)

The first and second sets are ones of phoneme-groups, consisting of some Japanese phonemes, that can also represent ambiguous words. For example,

Table 2. Consonants of articulation-based phoneme-groups [$\mathcal{A}$]

phoneme-group	Japanese phoneme	associated articulation
/nasal/	m n	nasal
/fric/	j s sh z	fricative
/hf/	f h	fricative
/semiv/	w y	semi-vowel
/v-exp/	b d g	voiced plosive
/u-exp/	ch k p t ts	unvoiced plosive

Table 3. Other phonemes of articulation-based phoneme-groups (APGs) [$\mathcal{A}$]

APG	phoneme	APG	phoneme	APG	phoneme	APG	phoneme	APG	phoneme
/ao/	a o	/ao:/	a: o:	/i/	i	/i:/	i:	/u/	u
/u:/	u:	/e/	e	/e:/	e:	/q/	q	/N/	N

if a phoneme-group /α/ consists of /b/ and /d/, and another phoneme-group /β/ consists of /a:/ and /o:/, the expression "α-β-N" generates four sound-imitation words, "b-a:-N", "d-a:-N", "b-o:-N" and "d-o:-N" (Fig. 4). In this section, we describe how to design the two sets of phoneme-groups, and how to train Japanese phoneme transcriptions for ambiguous words. We prepared a set of Japanese phonemes in order to evaluate the effectiveness of $\mathcal{A}$ and $\mathcal{B}$.

3.1 Phonemes $\mathcal{A}$: Articulation-Based Phoneme-Groups

In this subsection, we describe how to design a set of the "articulation-based phoneme-groups (APGs)." An APG is a Japanese vowel or a new phoneme consisting of several Japanese consonants articulated in the same manner (Tables 2 and 3). There are six consonants, — /nasal/, /fric/, /semiv/, /hf/, /v-exp/, and /u-exp/ —, eight new vowels — /ao/, /i/, /u/, /e/, /ao:/, /i:/, /u:/ as well as /e:/ —, moraic silence /q/ and moraic nasal /N/. /ao/ represents a sound that can be heard not only as /a/, but also as /o/. We designed these phoneme-groups based on a hypothesis that phonemes articulated in the same manner tend to exhibit similar properties to environmental sounds. The hypothesis is confirmed by an analysis of perceptual experiments and the sound-symbolism theory, which is the study of the relationships between the sound of an utterance and the meaning [14]. The study claims that the phoneme itself suggests a meaning. For example, /m/ and /n/ (nasal consonants) tend to be used in soft expressions.

Expressions made from the APGs generate more sound-imitation words than expressions from the Japanese phonemes and basic phoneme-groups. Thus, the recall ratio is high, and the precision ratio is low. Therefore, a set of APGs can be used for the automatic tagging of sound archives, while inappropriate words are often generated when transformed into sound-imitation words.

3.2 Phonemes $\mathcal{B}$: Basic Phoneme-Groups

In this subsection, we describe how to design a set of the "basic phoneme-groups (BPGs)." The BPG set includes all kinds of combinations of Japanese conso-

Table 4. Phonemes of basic phoneme-groups [$\mathcal{B}$]

/t/, /k-t/, /b/, /p/, /t-ch/, /f-p/, /t-p/, /z-j/, /k/, /g/, /r/, /k-p/, /k-t-ch/, /b-d/, /j/, /t-ts/, /ts-ch/, /s-sh/, /d-g/, /b-d-g/, /w/, /sh-j/, /k-t-r/, /k-g/, /t-d/, /ch/, /sh/, /ao/, /a/, /i/, /u/, /e/, /o/, /ao:/, /a:/, /i:/, /u:/, /e:/, /o:/, /N/, /q/, /q-N/

Table 5. Japanese phonemes [$\mathcal{C}$]

/w/, /y/, /p/, /t/, /k/, /b/, /d/, /g/, /ts/, /ch/, /m/, /n/, /h/, /f/, /s/, /sh/, /z/, /j/, /r/, /q/, /N/

nants. Table 4 shows a list of the BPGs that appears in the listening data. For example, /k-t/ is a BPG representing a sound that can be heard not only as /k/, but also as /t/, and that cannot be heard as other Japanese phonemes. The difference between the APG and the BOG is determined by whether Japanese phonemes are allowed to be an element in two or more groups.

It is difficult to train the HMMs of all BPGs adequately, because the numbers of groups in the set is huge. So, when the number of samples from a certain phoneme-group is insufficient to build adequate HMMs, we use the transcriptions of Japanese phonemes for training instead of those made from the BPGs. For instance, HMMs train transcriptions without using /p-w/, but using /p/ and /w/, since there are very few samples of /p-w/.

3.3 Phonemes $\mathcal{C}$: Japanese Phoneme

In this subsection, we describe how to train "Japanese phoneme" expressions. A set of Japanese phonemes is shown in Table 5. We used *OSPT training*[1] to solve the ambiguity problem in training. OSPT training is a technique for training a sound stimulus with two or more transcriptions. When there is a sound stimulus that has two transcriptions, we use both transcriptions, one by one. Although OSPT training is effective for training with respect to the literal ambiguity of environmental sounds, the output from this method is listener-dependent, since each Japanese phonemic expression generates only one sound-imitation word.

4 Experiments

To evaluate the three kinds of phoneme sets, we conducted listening experiments. We used seven subjects ranging in age from 22 to 24. For testing data,

---

[1] OSPT is an abbreviation for "one sound with plural transcriptions".

Table 6. Comparison of three phoneme sets

phoneme	example 1	example 2	ambiguity
$\mathcal{A}$: APGs	u-exp ao N	fric u: Q	much (it generates a lot of SIWs)
$\mathcal{B}$: BPGs	k-t ao N	s-sh u: Q	a little (it generates some SIWs)
$\mathcal{C}$: Japanese phonemes	k a N	sh u: Q	no (it generates only one SIW)

Table 7. Results of listening experiment

phoneme	recall ratio	precision ratio	score
$\mathcal{A}$: APGs	81/140 (57.9%)	27/104 (26.0%)	—
$\mathcal{B}$: BPGs	79/140 (56.4%)	26/36 (72.2%)	3.89
$\mathcal{C}$: Japanese phonemes	56/140 (40.0%)	17/22 (77.3%)	3.66

we prepared 20 environmental sound stimuli, which were sounds recorded in a real environment or obtained from different CDs than the sounds used in training [S2,S3]. They were mainly impact and friction sounds. The process of this experiment is as follows:

1. Subjects listened to environmental sound stimuli.
2. Subjects transcribed them, using their own sound-imitation words [*answer SIWs*]. They could write down two or more sound-imitation words for each sample.
3. All SIWs generated from the systems were shown to the subjects [*result SIWs*].
4. According to the level of appropriateness, the subjects evaluated all of the *result SIWs*, using five kinds of scoring, — 1 for inappropriate SIWs and 5 for appropriate SIWs.

We defined the *answer SIWs* as correct transcriptions, and three phoneme sets were evaluated on the recall and precision ratio of the *result SIWs*, generated by their expressions. Additionally, we used scores of appropriateness to evaluate them.

The results are shown in Table 7. Expressions using "$\mathcal{B}$: basic phoneme-groups" obtained a high precision ratio, and could output more than half of the answer SIW though they are very various. Moreover, the average score in this phoneme set was the highest of all. $\mathcal{A}$-expressions aren't evaluated by scores, because they often generate too many SIWs for the subjects to be able to evaluate all the words. We predict that scores will be less than 3.00 if the evaluation is performed, based on the recall and precision ratio. Expressions using $\mathcal{A}$: articulation-based phoneme-groups have a low precision ratio, even though the recall ratio was the highest of the three. As a result, we confirmed that $\mathcal{A}$-expressions are more ambiguous and varied than human answers. In contrast, expressions using "$\mathcal{C}$: Japanese phonemes" have a low recall ratio, even though the precision ratio is the highest. The $\mathcal{C}$-expression evaluations are too dependent on the listeners, because one $\mathcal{C}$-expression generates only one SIW.

Table 8. Result SIWs and Answer SIWs

No.	Result SIWs of $\mathcal{A}$	Result SIWs $\mathcal{B}$	Result SIWs $\mathcal{C}$
		Answer SIWs	
02	u-exp i N (—)	t-ch i N (3.45)	ch i N (3.22)
	t i N [3], k i N [3], ch i N [3], k a N [1], t u w i: N [1]		
04	u-exp ao q (—)	k-t ao q (2.97)	t o q(2.00)
	k a q [4], t a q [4], ch a q [1], t a N [1], ch i q [1], t e q [1], ts a q [1]		
05	u-exp i N (—)	k-t-ch i N (4.33)	ch i N (4.67)
	k i N [4], t i N [3], ch i N [3], ch i q [2], t i q [2], t u q [1], p i q [1]		
06	u-exp i: N (—)	t-ch i: N (4.45)	ch i N (3.67)
	ch i: N [4], ch i N [3], t i: N[3], k i: N [3], k i N [2], p i N [1]		
07	fric u: q (—)	s-sh u: q (3.50)	s u: q (2.89)
	sh u: q [5], sh i: q [5], sh a: q [1], j i: q [1]		
08	u-exp o q (—)	ch u: q (1.44)	ch o q (3.22)
	ch a q [4], ch i q [3], ch i: q [1], ch a: N [1], t o: N [1], t o q [1], ts u q [1]		
09	u-exp o q (—)	p ao q (3.45)	p o q (3.33)
	p a q [6], p o q [4], t a q [1], k a q [1], p o w a q [1], k u q [1], t u q [1], ts u q [1]		
10	u-exp ao q (—)	t ao q (3.06)	t o q (2.56)
	p a q [3], t a q [3], t o q [2], k a q [2], p u q [1], ts u q [1], k a N [1], k o N [1], p i q [1]		
11	u-exp i: N (—)	r i N (2.22)	r i: N (4.44)
	r i: N [5], ch i: N [3], t i: N [3], p i: N [3], k i: N[2]		
12	fric u: q (—)	sh u: q (2.11)	sh o q (2.44)
	sh a q [4], ch a q [2], ch i i q [1], ch i i r i [1], sh a: q [1], sh u q [1]		
13	u-exp o: N (—)	p o: N (4.33)	p o: N (4.33)
	p o: N [7], k o: N [2], b e: N [1], p a: N [1], k w a: N [1], k w o: N [1]		
14	u-exp e: N (—)	p e: N (3.78)	p e: N (3.78)
	p o: N [3], p a: N [2], p e: N [2], p i: N [2], p w o: N [1], b i: N [1], t o: N [1], p e: q [1]		
15	u-exp i: q (—)	f-p i: q (3.78)	f i: q (3.00)
	p i: q [5], p i: q [2], ky u i: q [1], k i: q [1], py u i: q [1], ch i: q [1], f i: q [1]		
16	u-exp i q (—)	p i q (4.44)	p i q (4.44)
	p i q [7], b i q [2], py u i q [1]		
17	v-exp u: q (—)	b u: q (4.56)	b u: q (4.56)
	b u: q [5], b u: q [4], b u a: q [1], d u: q [1], p a: q [1], b a: q [1], b o: q [1]		
18	v-exp u: q (—)	g u: q (2.67)	g u: q (2.67)
	j i: q [3], g i: q [2], w i: q [1], j i w a j i w a [1], j i i: q [1], b i: q [1], d i d i d i [1]		

Table 8. (Continued)

No.	Result SIWs of $\mathcal{A}$	Result SIWs $\mathcal{B}$	Result SIWs $\mathcal{C}$
	Answer SIWs		
19	u-exp i: N (—)	t-ch u: q (1.56)	t i: N (4.00)
	ch i N [4], t i: N [3], k i N [2], t i N [2], k i i N [1], k i i: N [1], ch i i: N [1]		
20	v-exp u: N (—)	b u: N (4.56)	g u: N (3.44)
	b u: q [4], b u: N [2], g u: N [2], b i: q [1], d u: N [1], b a: N [1], b o: N [1], b u w a: q [1]		

From the listening experiment, we confirmed that expressions using the BPGs are very suitable for expressing the literal ambiguity of the Japanese speaking people. The *answer* and *result SIWs* are shown on Table 8. In this table, the value in parentheses shows the average score of the targets, and the value in square brackets shows the number of listeners who answer the SIW. Original sounds are illustrated at "http://winnie.kyoto-u.ac.jp/members/ishihara/onomatopoeia_e.html".

5 Conclusion

In this paper, we proposed three-stage procedure to transform environmental sounds into sound-imitation words. In particular, we discussed the literal ambiguity problem of sound-imitation words. To solve this problem, three kinds of phoneme sets were designed. The APGs represent very ambiguous expressions, the BPGs represent less ambiguous expressions, and the Japanese phonemes represent no ambiguity. Based on the listening experiment, we confirmed that expressions using the BPGs are very suitable for expressing the literal ambiguity of Japanese speaking people. An important future project is to design a strategy that can choose the most suitable sound-imitation word for the user from a selection of SIWs.

This study was conducted using the non-speech sound dry sources of the RWCP Sound Scene Database in Real Acoustic Environment.

Acknowledgements

This research was partially supported by the Ministry of Education, Science, Sports and Culture, Grant-in-Aid for Scientific Research (A), 15200015, 2003, and the JPSP 21st Century COE Program. It was partially conducted as joint researches with NTT Communication Science Laboratories.

We would like to express our thanks to Dr. Yasuhiro Minami (NTT Communication Science Lab.), Dr. Atsushi Nakamura (NTT Communication Science Lab.), Mr. Yasushi Tsubota (Kyoto Univ.), and Mr. Tetsuro Kitahara (Kyoto Univ.), for their guidance and numerous helpful suggestions.

References

1. G. Jahns et al.: Sound Analysis to Recognize Individuals and Animal Conditions, *XIII CIGR Congress on Agricultural*, 1998.
2. K. Nagahata: A study of how visually impaired persons identify a place using environmental sounds, *Journal of the Acoustic Society of Japan*, Vol.56, No.6, pp406-417, 2000.
3. T. Zhang and C.C. Jay Kuo: Audio-guided audiovisual data segmentation, indexing, and retrieval, *Proc. of the SPIE The International Society for Optical Engineering*, 3656, pp316-327, 1998.
4. Darvishi A., World Wide Web access for blind people: problems, available solutions and an approach for using environmental sounds, *Proc. of the 5th International conference on Computers helping people with special needs*. vol.1, pp369-373, 1996.
5. T. Ashiya et al.: IOSES: An Indoor Observation System Based on Environmental Sounds Recognition Using a Neural Network, *Trans. of the Institute of Electrical Engineers of Japan*, Vol.116-C, No 3, pp341-349, 1996.
6. K. Tanaka: Study of Onomatopoeia Expressing Strange Sounds (Case if Impulse Sounds and Beat Sounds) (in Japanese), *Trans. of the Japan Society of Mechanical Engineers* Series C, Vol.61, No.592, 1995.
7. S. Wake and T. Asahi: Sound Retrieval with Intuitive Verbal Descriptions, IEICE 2001, *Trans. on Information and Systems* Vol.E84-D No.11, pp.1568-1576, 2001.
8. K. Ishihara, Y. Tsubota, and H.G. Okuno: Automatic Transformation of Environmental Sounds into Sound-Imitation Words Based on Japanese Syllable Structure, Proc. of EUROSPEECH-2003, pp.3185-3188, 2003.
9. HTK3.0: http://htk.eng.cam.ac.uk/
10. K. Hiyane: Study of Spectrum Structure of Short-time Sounds and its Onomatopoeia Expression (in Japanese), *IEICE Technical Report*, SP97-125, 1998.
11. P. Ladefoged: *A Course In Phonetics*, Harcourt Brace College Publishers, 1993.
12. Y. Hattori et al.: Repeat recognition of Continuous Environmental Sound (in Japanese), *Information Processing Society of Japan*, 2003.
13. Michael Cowling and Renate Sitte: Comparison of techniques for environmental sound recognition, *Pattern Recognition Letters* 24, pp.2895-2907, 2003.
14. I. Tamori, L. Schourup: "*Onomatopoeia - ke-i-ta-i to i-mi -*" (in Japanese), Kuroshio Publisher, 1999.

[S1] RWCP Sound Scene Database in Real Acoustical Environments, http://tosa.mri.co.jp/sounddb/indexe.htm
[S2] *SHI-N KO-KA-O-N DA-I-ZE-N-SHU* (in Japanese), KING RECORD.
[S3] *KO-KA-O-N DA-I-ZE-N-SHU* (in Japanese), KING RECORD.

Statistical Pitch Conversion Approaches Based on Korean Accentual Phrases

Ki Young Lee[1], Jong Kuk Kim[2], and Myung Jin Bae[2]

[1] Department of Information Communication Engineering, Kwandong University
7 San Imcheon-ri, Yangyang-eup, Yangyang-gun, Gangwon-do, Korea
kylee@mail.kwandong.ac.kr
[2] Department of Information & Telecommunication Engineering, Soongsil University
Sangdo 5-dong, Dongjak-gu, Seoul, Korea
kokjk@hanmail.net, mjbae@ssu.ac.kr

Abstract. In performing speech conversion from a source speaker to a target speaker, it is important that the pitch contour of the source speakers utterance be converted into that of the target speaker, because pitch contour of a speech utterance plays an important role in expressing speaker's individuality and meaning of the of the utterance. This paper describes statistical algorithms of pitch contour conversion for Korean language. Pitch contour conversions are investigated at two levels of prosodic phrases: intonational phrase and accentual phrase. The basic algorithm is a Gaussian normalization in intonational phrase. The first presented algorithm is combined with a declination-line of pitch contour in an intonational phrase. The second one is Gaussian normalization within accentual phrases to compensate for local pitch variations. Experimental results show that the algorithm of Gaussian normalization within accentual phrases is significantly more accurate than the other two algorithms in intonational phrase.

1 Introduction

Voice conversion requires transformation of all perceptually important aspect of the human voice: pitch, loudness, timbre and timing(tempo and rhythm). Tempo has more to do with the overall speed while rhythm is more about the local variations in speed. Timbre deals with how the voice itself sounds, while the other aspects reflect how a person speaks. There are many researchers to investigate how to convert the pitch and timing. Practically through varying pitch contours, a speaker who converses or reads can present not only state of emotion but also meaning of sentence. A conversion of prosody features including pitch contour therefore plays an important role to express desired characteristics of a speaker and meaning of an utterance Through varying pitch contours, a speaker who converses or reads can present not only state of emotion but also meaning of sentence. A conversion of prosody features including pitch contour therefore plays an important role to express desired characteristics of a speaker and meaning of an utterance. Psychoacoustic experiments support the theory that pitch contours contain speaker individuality [1, 2]. Pitch contour has been used to make high quality synthetic speech through TTS (text-to-speech) systems that are capable of expressing speaker individuality, and intonation as expressed by pitch contours is generated in accordance with the unit of sentence or other structures defined by such systems [3,4]. In TTS systems, prosodic phrases have been shown beneficial to naturalness of synthetic speech [5]. Currently there are two approaches to pitch contour conversion. One is a statistical approach such as Gaussian normalization, the other is a dynamic programming method using non-linear time warping based on pitch contours from a training sentence database [6,7]. The statistical method of a Gaussian normalization is easy to process because the average pitch value of a given speaker can be mapped to that of a target speaker. However this method is insufficient to capture local pitch variations as perceived in the utterance of the target speaker. The dynamic programming method requires a large training database of utterances spoken by at least two speakers.

The purpose of this study is to present two algorithms based on prosodic phrases for converting the pitch contour of a sentence for the sake of imparting perceptually important characteristics of a desired speaker, where the statistical method of Gaussian normalization is improved to compensate for local pitch variations. The basic algorithm is a Gaussian normalization that is performed on pitch contour using the average pitch and the standard deviation of pitch statistics. In the first presented algorithm, the pitch contour of an intonation phrase is first fitted by a declination line and the resulting pitch residues are then converted by Gaussian normalization. The second one performs Gaussian normalization on pitch contour of every accentual phrase for each sentence to compensate for local pitch variation. Experiments are carried out for several declarative sentences uttered by a source and a target speaker, and pitch contour error within every accentual phrase of modified speech relative to that of the target speaker is measured to evaluate their converting abilities because the scale of pitch contour modification are not large enough to be clearly perceived in listening tests. The result shows that the second method is able to accurately convert pitch contour of a source speaker to pitch contour of a target speaker that is rich of local variation structure.

2 Prosodic Phrases of Korean

Nespor and Vogel [8] proposed that human languages have a universal hierarchical structure that consists of seven prosodic units, including syllables, feet, phonological words, clitic group, phonological phrases, intonational phrases and phonological utterance. These units are closely related to the prosodic and phonological rules appropriate to each language. Sun-Ah Jun [9] proposed that not all seven prosodic units of Nespor and Vogel are necessary for each language, but to each language there are a few units that are linguistically significant. The intonational phrases(IP) of Sun-Ah Jun is a prosodic unit which corresponds to the intonational phrase of Nespor and Vogel, and is characterized by an intonationl contour made up of two tonal levels H(igh) and L(ow). The intonational contour of the IP is derived from two constituents: the pitch accent and the phrase tone. The pitch accent is a pitch event phonologically linked to a particular stressed syllable in an utterance. The phrase tone is an autosegment which exists independently of lexical entries, and consists of phrase accents and a boundary tone. The phrase accent occur after the rightmost pitch accent, and a boundary tone occurs at the right edge and optionally at the left edge of the IP. Thus, the phrase accent marks the boundary of intermediate phrase which are smaller units than the IP. The smaller units than the IP are accentual phrase(AP) which are submit of the IP. In sum, the natural utterance is composed of the hierarchical structure which has APs and IPs as its constituents.

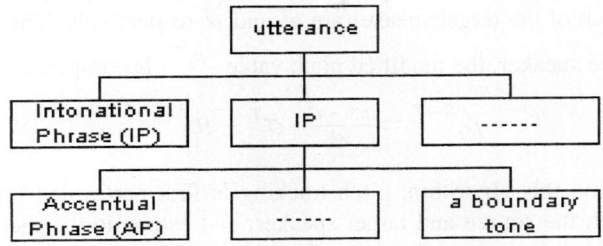

Fig. 1. Korean prosodic phrases

For Korean, accentual phrases(APs) and intonational phrases(IPs) are linguistically significant. Experimental results support her suggestion to be valid in reading sentences [10]. This paper develops the statistical algorithms of pitch contour conversion based on prosodic phrases of Korean.

3 Statistical Algorithms of Pitch Contour Conversion

The presented methods of converting the pitch contours of a given speaker to those of a target speaker are summarized in Table 1. The first two algorithms perform pitch contour conversion in the prosodic unit of IP. The Gaussian normalization is a basic algorithm, and the other one is a combination of declination line fitting followed by Gaussian normalization, referred to as declined Gaussian. The last algorithm performs pitch contour conversion according to every AP by Gaussian normalization, referred to as accentual Gaussian. The PSOLA [11] technique is used for synthesizing speech waveform after the described pitch contour conversion.

Table 1. Pitch contour conversion algorithms

Prosodic phrase	Algorithm	Approach	Assumption	Main Idea
Intonational Phrase	Gaussian	statistics	Gaussian distributuion	Gaussian normalzaion
	Declined Gaussian	declination line, statistics	pitch declination base line	effective distribution
Accentual Phrase	Accentual Gaussian	accentual phrase, statistics	accentual phrase	effective distribution, prosody phrase

3.1 Pitch Contour Conversion in IP

3.1.1 Gaussian Normalization Algorithm

The method of Gaussian normalization involves matching the average pitch and the standard deviation of pitch of a given source speaker to those of target speaker for each IP. Assume that pitch measurement values are i.i.d. Gaussian random variables, where the average pitch and standard deviation of pitch of the source speaker before pitch conversion are μ^S and δ^S respectively, and the average pitch and the standard deviation of pitch of the target speaker are u^T and δ^T respectively. Then given a pitch value of a source speaker, the modified pitch value $p_t^{S \to T}$ is computed as

$$p_t^{S \to T} = \frac{p_t^S - \mu^S}{\delta^S} \cdot \sigma^T + \mu^T \tag{1}$$

In implementation this algorithm, pitch tracking is first performed on training sentences from both the source and target speaker, and estimation is then made on the mean and standard deviation of pitch values of each IP for each speaker. It is not complicated to show that the converted pitch values $p_t^{S \to T}$ by equation (1) has the mean and standard deviation matched to those of the target speaker in IP.

3.1.2 Declined Gaussian Algorithm

$$D_t = p_{t_0} + (t - t_0) \cdot \frac{p_{t_N} - p_{t_0}}{t_N - t_0} \tag{2}$$

where p_{t_0} and p_{t_N} are the pitch values at a starting time, t_0 and an ending time, t_N, respectively. Then the pitch residues Δp_t of each speaker are calculated as $\Delta p_t = p_t - D_t$. The residues Δp_t^S and Δp_t^T of the source and the target speaker are modeled as two i.i.d. Gaussian random variables and Gaussian normalization is applied to obtain the converted residue $p_t^{S \to T}$ by equation (1). Finally the modified pitch value is computed as

$$p_t^{S \to T} = \Delta p_t^{S \to T} + \left\{ p_{t_0}^T + (t - t_0) \cdot \frac{p_{t_N}^T - p_{t_0}^T}{t_N - t_0} \right\} \tag{3}$$

3.2 Accentual Gaussian Algorithm in AP

Accentual phrases are constituents of IP. In Korean, syntactic phrases are divided in orthography by a space, and are in general in accordance with APs. There is a strong correlation between syntactic and prosodic phrases in Korean language. Within an IP, an AP that is characterized by a pitch contour pattern LH (low-high) includes three syllables at maximum, and another AP that is characterized by a pitch contour pattern LHLH includes four syllables at least. The last AP is a boundary tone that is different from the LH pattern [9, 10]. The accentual Gaussian algorithm makes use of the local pitch patterns of the APs and carry out pitch contour conversion according to every AP by Gaussian normalization at a time. Then given a pitch value $p_t^{S_i}$ in the i-th AP of a source speaker, the modified pitch value $p_t^{S_i \to T_i}$ is computed as

$$p_t^{S_i \to T_i} = \frac{p^{S_i}_t - \mu^{S_i}}{\delta^{S_i}} \cdot \sigma^{T_i} + \mu^{T_i} \qquad (4)$$

where, μ^{S_i}, σ^{S_i} and σ^{T_i}, μ^{T_i} are the average pitch and the standard deviation of pitch of the source speaker and target speaker according to the i-th AP, respectively.

4 Experimental Results and Evaluation

Speech data were obtained at 10 kHz sampling rate. Script used for data collection was composed of 16 sentences with all declarative sentences. Two male speakers of standard Korean read the script in their natural style without any guideline. Prosodic phrase boundaries were hand marked at the levels of IPs and APs.

4.1 Conversion Results

Figure 2 shows the conversion results performed by the three algorithms of Table 1. Speech waveform is shown in figure (a), and figure (b) is the pitch contour of a source speaker, A, and (c) and (d) are the speech waveform and pitch contour of a target speaker, B. The vertical lines in (b), (d), (f), (h) and (j) are hand-marked boundaries of prosodic phrases such as IP and APs, where the boundaries of IP are the same of one spoken sentence and the smaller units than the IP are APs. The speech waveform and pitch contour after Gaussian normalization are shown in figure (e) and (f).

The speech after Gaussian normalization has the same average pitch and standard deviation of pitch as those of the target speaker in each IP. Figure (g) and (h) are speech waveform and pitch contour modified by using the declined Gaussian algorithm. The result shows that only the starting and ending pitch values of the modified speech are identical to those of the target speakers. However, in the view of the AP unit, the resulting pitch contours are different from the target ones. The results from using accentual Gaussian algorithm are shown in Figure 2 (i) and (j). It is observed that this algorithm is able to accurately modify pitch contours even for large local pitch variations.

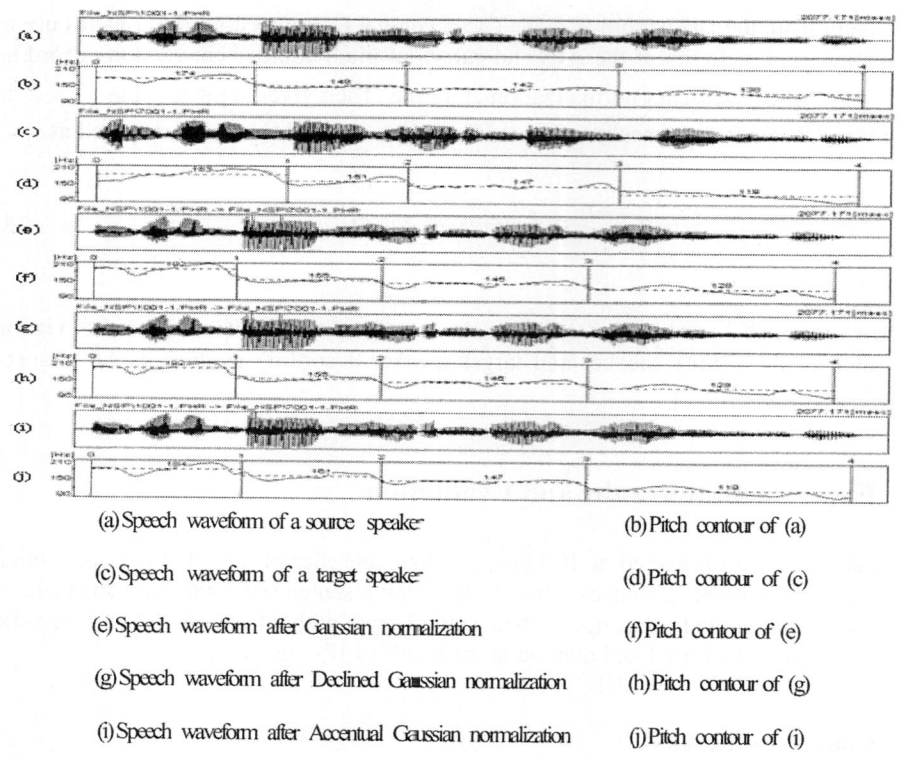

(a) Speech waveform of a source speaker
(b) Pitch contour of (a)
(c) Speech waveform of a target speaker
(d) Pitch contour of (c)
(e) Speech waveform after Gaussian normalization
(f) Pitch contour of (e)
(g) Speech waveform after Declined Gaussian normalization
(h) Pitch contour of (g)
(i) Speech waveform after Accentual Gaussian normalization
(j) Pitch contour of (i)

Fig. 2. Results of pitch contour conversion

4.2 Evaluation

Both subjective and objective measures may be used to evaluate the results of pitch contour conversion. In subjective evaluation, human subjects would listen to pitch-modified speech data and their opinions are collected for scoring each method. In objective evaluation, pitch contour error in the modified speech data relative to that of the target speaker is directly measured.

4.2.1 Objective Evaluation

Since in certain cases the scale of pitch contour modification are not large enough to be clearly perceived in listening tests, the objective measure is used to quantify the error of pitch conversion. Define the pitch error in the i-th accentual phrase as

$$e_u^i = \frac{1}{M} \sum_{m=0}^{M} \left(u_m^{T_i} - u_m^{S_i \to T_i} \right) \tag{5}$$

$$e_\delta^i = \frac{1}{M}\sum_{m=0}^{M}\left(\left|\delta_m^{T_i} - \delta_m^{S_i \to T_i}\right|\right) \qquad (6)$$

where $u_m^{S_i \to T_i}$ and $\delta_m^{S_i \to T_i}$ represents the average pitch and the standard deviation of pitch for i-th accentual phrase of the modified speech from a source speaker to a target speaker, respectively, with $1 \leq m \leq M$ and M is the number of the spoken texts. Figure 3 shows comparisons of pitch error values computed by equation (5) and (6) performed by three algorithms. In figure 4, the comparison of three algorithms is presented by their average of pitch error values for all APs.

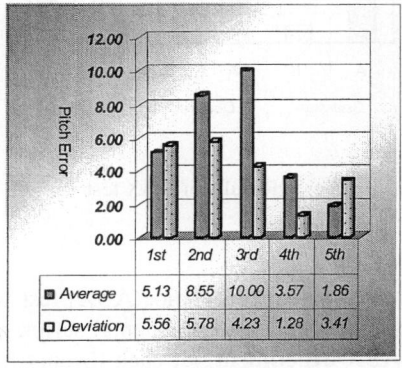

(a) Gaussian Normalization

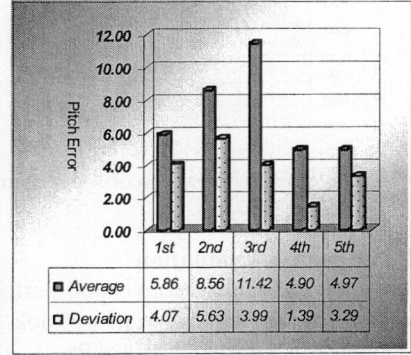

(b) Declined Gaussian algorithm

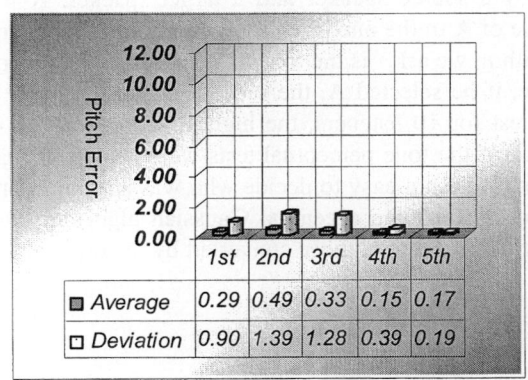

(c) Accentual Gaussian algorithm

Fig. 3. Pitch error comparisons of each algorithm

In the case of Gaussian normalization, the average of pitch error for all accentual phrases is about 5.82 and the deviation error is about 4.05. In the declined Gaussian algorithm, the average of pitch error is about 7.14 and the deviation is about 3.67. In the accentual Gaussian algorithm, the errors are converged near to 0, because this algorithm uses a conversion unit as an AP smaller than an IP. Since within each AP the ranges of pitch variation is much less than the range of pitch variation in the IP, this proposed algorithm using APs can modify pitch contours more accurately than others using IPs.

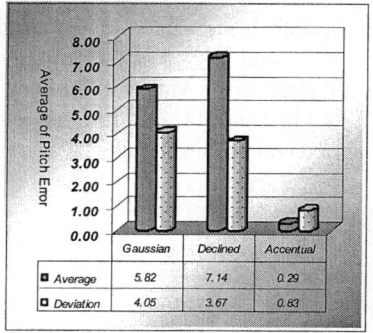
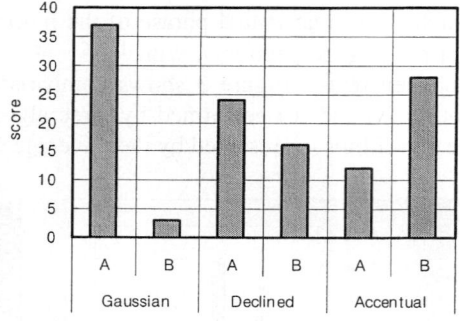

Fig. 4. Average error comparison of 3 algorithms   **Fig. 5.** Results of ABX test

4.2.2 Subjective Evaluation

To subjectively evaluate conversion performance, one forced-choice(ABX) test was carried out. In this test material, we took 4 sentences in the experimental script, and each sentence is consisted of 4 APs. In the ABX experiment, let each listener hear several speeches of source, target and converted speech, and A and B were speech utterances spoken by a source speaker and a target spaeker. X was the converted speech from the tone of A to the one of B by each algorithm. When listener listen to three Xs by 3 algorithm, we ask, "is the tone of X closer to the one of A or to the one of B?" For example, if he selected A, the score is increased by 1. Since we used 4 sentences to ABX test for 10 listeners, the highest score is 40 (= 4 sentences * 10 listeners). The result of the tone perceptual tests were shown in figure 5. In this experiment, 10 listeners were not easy to decide who was speaking, but they could recognise that the tone of X by the accentual Gaussian algorithm would be different from A and more simillar to B than those converted by the other algorithms.

5 Conclusion

The same sentence spoken by two speakers in general has different prosodic characteristics including duration, intensity and tone. In the current work, statistical algorithms of pitch contour conversion are proposed to modify the pitch contours of prosodic phrases from a source speaker to those of a target speaker. In the level of IP, the results of the basic algorithm of Gaussian normalization and the other algorithm using a declination line of pitch contour show that it is not good to modify pitch contour to a target speaker, since the IP unit is too long to compensate pitch variation in one sentence including several APs that have multiple patterns of tonal levels. Experimental results show that the proposed algorithm of Gaussian normalization at the level of APs is capable of modifying pitch contours more accurately than the algorithms for IPs, since within each AP the ranges of pitch variation is much less than the range of pitch variation in the IP.

Acknowledgement

This work was supported by the Korean Science and Engineering Foundation, grant no. R01-2002-000-00278-0.

References

1. M. Akagi, T. Ienaga,"Speaker Individualities in Fundamental Frequency Contours and Its Control", Proc. EuroSpeech'95, pp. 439-442, Sep. 1995.
2. H. Kuwabara, Y. Sagisaka,"Acoustic Characteristics of Speaker Individuality : Control and Conversion", Speech Communication, Vol. 16, pp.165-173, 1995.
3. A. Kain, M.W. Macon,"Spectral Voice Conversion for Text-To-Speech Synthesis", Proc. ICASSP'98, Vol. 1, pp. 285-288, 1998.
4. J. P. H. van Santen,"Prosodic Modeling in Text-to- Speech Synthesis", Proc. EuroSpeech'97, KN 19-KN 28, 1997.
5. Y. J. Kim, H. J. Byeon, Y. H. Oh,"Prosodic Phrasing in Korean; Determine Governor, and then Split or Not", Proc. EuroSpeech'99, pp.539-542, 1999.
6. L. M. Arslan, D. Talkin,"Speaker Transformation using Sentence HMM based Alignments and Detailed Prosody Modification", Proc. ICASSP'98, Vol. 1, pp. 289-292, 1998.
7. D. T. Chappel, J. H. L. Hansen,"Speaker-Specific Pitch Contour Modeling and Modification", Proc. ICASSP'98, Vol. 1, pp. 885-888, 1998.
8. M. Nespor, I. Vogel, Prosodic Phonology, Dordrecht : Foris Publication
9. Jun, Sun-Ah, The Phonetics and Phonology of Korean Prosody, Ph. D. Dissertation, The Ohio State University, 1993.
10. K. Y. Lee, M. S. Song, "Automatic Detection of Korean Accentual Phrase Boundaries", The Journal of Acoustic Society of Korea, Vol. 18, No.1E, pp.27-31, 1999.
11. E. Moulines, F. Charpentier,"Pitch-Synchronous Waveform Processing Techniques for Text-to-Speech Synthesis Using Diphones", Speech Communication 9(5,6) pp.453-467, 1990.

On the Stability of a Dynamic Stochastic Capacity Pricing Scheme for Resource Allocation in a Multi-agent Environment

Alain Gaetan Njimolu Anyouzoa and Theo D'Hondt

Programming Technologies Labs. Vrije Universiteit Brussel Pleinlaan 2
1050 Brussels, Belgium
anyouzoa_njimolu@ieee.org, tjdhondt@vub.ac.be

Abstract. Following the view point of Evolutionary Dynamics, we have built a multi-agent system to study resource allocation in a heterogeneous network of resources. Resources are modeled as strategies, and agents distribute processing requirements onto them using imperfect information and local decision making. Agents are endowed with bounded rationality in an imperfect information structure environment. Our intent is to achieve cooperative equilibrium using competitive dynamics by controlling congestion through capacity pricing. A distributed differentiated pricing scheme is proposed to improve loose coupling between agents and resources through a loosely coupled interaction model. However, the benefits of greater decentralization and increased local decision-making come at the expense of greater stochastic dynamics which can have unpredictable effects on the stability of the system. We had to come up with an appropriate approach for its stability analysis. This poster outlines the system built and some aspects of our stability analysis approach.

Keywords: Muli-Agent systems, Evolutionary Game Theory, Nash Equilibrium, Evolutionary Stable Strategy, Multi-Level Selection

1 Goal of the Poster

① Show how distributed load balancing can be achieved through a co-evolutionary approach using evolutionary game theory mixed with transaction cost economics.
② Introduce a new stability analysis approach based on a physics approach (Statistical mechanics and Quantum mechanics).
③ Show how stability analysis of adjustment model with persistent randomness can be dealt with.

2 Previous Publication or Use of This Material

① Spontaneous emergence and extinction of resources in distributed systems - Resources Allocation as Evolving Strategy revisited - A. G. Njimolu Anyouzoa, B. Manderick - *In the Proc. 4th Argentine Symposium on Artificial Intelligence Sept. 9-13 2002 Santa Fe Argentina.*

② Dynamic Stochastic Capacity Pricing for Resource Allocation Alain G. N. Anyouzoa, Prof. Dr. T. D'Hondt, M. Ba, D. Akoa - *In the proceeding of IEEE/WIC IAT-Oct. 2003, Halifax, Canada.*
③ On the Stability of a Dynamic Stochastic Capacity Pricing Scheme for Resource Allocation in a Multi-Agent environment - Alain G. N. Anyouzoa, Theo D'Hondt - *To appear in WIAS (Web Intelligence and Agent Systems).*

3 Poster Layout

① Resources use rational heuristics to set unit prices using pricing functions. The two graphics in the upper level of the figure are example of pricing functions used.
② Lower level-Left: Different level of details of our stability analysis methods.
③ Lower Level-Right: Details of the three different energy levels in "B" on the left side.

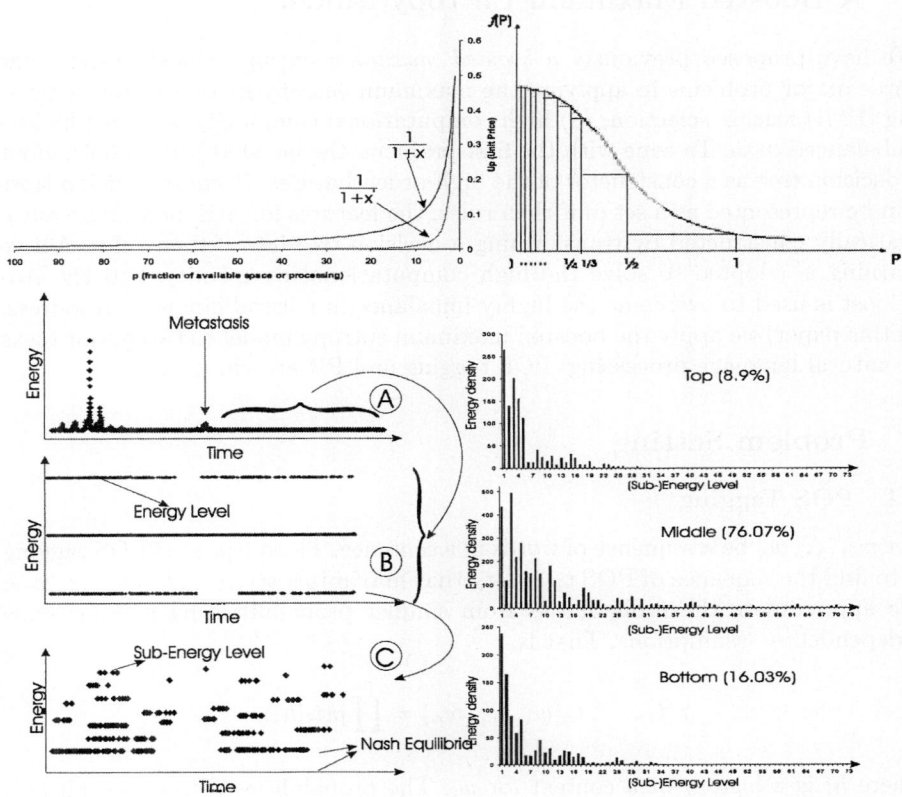

Fig. 1. Example of pricing functions and stability analysis

Part-of-Speech Tagging and PP Attachment Disambiguation Using a Boosted Maximum Entropy Model

Seong-Bae Park[1], Jangmin O[2], and Sang-Jo Lee[1]

[1] Department of Computer Engineering
Kyungpook National University, 702-701 Daegu, Korea
{seongbae,sjlee}@knu.ac.kr
[2] School of Computer Science and Engineering
Seoul National University, 151-744 Seoul, Korea
jmoh@bi.snu.ac.kr

1 A Boosted Maximum Entropy Model

We have proposed previously *a boosted maximum entropy model* to overcome three major problems in applying the maximum entropy models to text chunking [1]: (i) feature selection, (ii) high computational complexity, and (iii) highly-imbalanced data. To cope with the first problem, the boosted ME models adopt a decision tree as a constructor of the high-order features. Because decision trees can be represented as a set of if-then rules, the features for ME models are automatically constructed by transforming a decision tree into if-then rules. Active learning is adopted to solve the high computational complexity, and the AdaBoost is used to overcome the highly imbalance in natural language resources. In this paper, we apply the boosted maximum entropy model to two major tasks in natural language processing: POS tagging and PP attachment.

2 Problem Setting

2.1 POS Tagging

Let $w_1, \ldots, w_n$ be a sequence of words in a sentence. The purpose of POS tagging is to find the sequence of POS $t_1, \ldots, t_n$ that maximizes $p(t_1, \ldots, t_n | w_1, \ldots, w_n)$. We approximate the probabilities from simpler probabilities by making some independence assumptions. That is,

$$p(t_1, \ldots, t_n | w_1, \ldots, w_n) = \prod_{i=1}^{n} p(t_i | h_i),$$

where h_i is a history or a context for w_i. The probabilities $p(t_i | h_i)$ for all w_i's are computed by the ME model. Two words on the left context and the right context respectively are used as the first-order features. That is, h_i is

$$h_i = \{w_{i-2}, w_{i-1}, w_i, w_{i+1}, w_{i+2}, t_{i-2}, t_{i-1}\}.$$

Table 1. Accuracy of the proposed method in POS tagging and PP attachment.

Method	POS Tagging	PP Attachment
Normal ME model	96.89%	77.7%
Boosted ME model	96.78%	85.3%

2.2 PP Attachment

The goal of PP attachment is to determine the correct attachment $y \in \{N, V\}$ about 4-tuples of the form (v, n_1, p, n_2), where v is a head verb, n_1 is a head noun which is an object of v, p is a preposition, and n_2 a head noun of the prepositional phrase. Formally, the task can be formulated to comparing the probabilities of each attachment:

$$f(v, n_1, p, n_2) = \arg\max_{y \in \{N, V\}} p(y|v, n_1, p, n_2),$$

where $p(y|v, n_1, p, n_2)$ is estimated by a ME model with the first-order features of $v, n_1, p,$ and n_2.

3 Experimental Results and Conclusions

The dataset for the experiments is derived from Wall Street Journal corpus. Table 1 shows the performance of the proposed method. The performance of the proposed method in POS tagging is slightly worse than that of normal ME model with the features by human experts [2][1], but it is not statistically insignificant at 0.05 level of significance. In PP attachment, the proposed method achieved 85.3% of accuracy, while the normal ME yielded only 77.7%.

In both tasks, human labor is confined to choose the simple first-order features. Therefore, the cost of modeling the tasks is minimized. Though the cost is minimized, the proposed method gives the performance as high as the state-of-the-art method. In other words, it shows that we can develop a good system without so much knowledge on specific domain.

Acknowledgements

This research was supported by Kyungpook National University Research Fund, 2004.

References

1. S.-B. Park and B.-T. Zhang, "A Boosted Maximum Entropy Model for Learning Text Chunking," In *Proceedings of ICML-02*, pp. 482-489, 2002.
2. A. Ratnaparkhi, "A Maximum Entropy Model for Part-of-speech Tagging," In *Proceedings of EMNLP-96*, pp. 133–142, 1996.

---

[1] This is the state-of-the-art in POS tagging.

Solving Pickup and Delivery Problems with Refined Construction and Repair Heuristics

Vincent Tam and M.C. Kwan

Department of E.E.E., The University of Hong Kong
Pokfulam, Hong Kong
Phone: +852-2859-2697
vtam@eee.hku.hk

Abstract. Pickup and delivery problems with time windows (PDP-TW) involve assigning all paired pickup-and-delivery requests to various vehicles to satisfy relevant time-window requirements while minimizing certain objective measures including the total number of vehicles used. In some previous work, the conventional push forward insertion heuristic (PFIH) was successfully adapted to work with a new swap operator for repairs so as to effectively solve PDP-TWs. Here, we firstly adapted the PFIH to efficiently construct a better initial solution which will then be iteratively improved by another refined swapping scheme which systematically revises its neighborhood size for opportunistic improvements. The prototype using our refined heuristics gained impressive results against those of a tabu-embedded metaheuristic search on a set of modified Solomon's test cases. More importantly, the refined heuristics prompts for future investigation and improvement to effectively solve related scheduling problems.

1 A Summary of Our Search Proposal

In Artificial Intelligence [2] or Operations Research [1], a wealth of published results has been established for the challenging and well-known delivery problems with time windows (DP-TWs). Basically, solving a DP-TW is to schedule a fleet of vehicles in order to satisfy a number of customers' requests with user-specified service time windows, that is to restrict each delivery to occur within a limited period. The pickup and delivery problems with time windows (PDP-TWs) [1, 2] are extended from DP-TWs with additional coupling constraints to demand every pair of pickup and delivery requests to be serviced by the same delivery vehicle. PDP-TWs represent a more challenging and general class of delivery problems occurring widely in the modern logistics industry for land, sea or air transport. Examples of PDP-TWs include the dial-a-ride application [2] and bus scheduling [1].

In this paper, we mainly proposed the following two heuristics to construct and iteratively repair the currently best solution so as to effectively solve PDP-TWs.

- **The Refined Insertion Heuristic:** The original push forward insertion heuristic (PFIH) was a route construction heuristic proposed by Solomon to handle DP-TW. Basically, PFIH carefully considers the lowest possible cost of inserting a new customer into the current route whenever possible against that of inserting into a new route before actually creating any new route. one obvious shortcoming of the originally adapted PFIH is that it does not even guarantee to return a locally optimal solution with respect to all the available routes during the search. Accordingly, we decided to improve the adapted PFIH to aggressively look for the best-fit positions among all the existing routes for each customer pair for insertion.
- **The Adaptive Swap Operator:** the original Swap operator [2] will randomly remove a "few" pairs of customers, put them temporarily into a relocation pool, and later re-insert those removed pairs of customers into any new/old vehicle based on any possible improvement on the objective measure. In case there is no possible position to re-insert the customer pair(s) in the relocation pool, a new vehicle will be created. In fact, the Swap operator can be efficiently run several times per iteration with a flexibly adjusted relocation pool size to opportunistically look for a better solution. A direct result is the refined Adaptive Swap (AD-Swap) operator.

Using the above heuristics, our proposed optimizer will find a locally, and possibly the globally, optimal solution to the concerned PDP-TW after a fixed number of iterations. For detail, refer to [2]. Table 1 compares the overall results, in terms of the total number of vehicles used (TV), the total distance traveled (TD) and their product as $TV * TD$, of our heuristic search proposals against Li & Lim's metaheuristic approach [1] over 56 modified test cases. The smallest figure in each column was boldfaced for ease of comparison. Clearly, the BPFIH+ID-Swap optimizer overwhelmingly bettered the original PFIH+Swap optimizer on both TV and TD.

Table 1. Overall results of different optimizers on all 56 modified benchmarks

Optimizers	Overall Results		
	TV	TD	$TV * TD$
PFIH+Swap	417	58,410	481,426
BPFIH+ID-Swap	410	57,766	467,197
Li & Lim's approach	405	58,185	462,873

References

1. Li, H., Lim, A.: A Metaheuristic for the Pickup and Delivery Problem with Time Windows. in *Proceedings* of the 13th IEEE International Conference on Tools with Artificial Intelligence, Nov 7-9, 2001.
2. Tam, V., Tseng, L.: Effective Heuristics to Solve Pickup and Delivery Problems with Time Windows. in *Proceedings* of the 15th IEEE International Conference on Tools with Artificial Intelligence, Nov 3-5, 2003.

Mining Multi-dimensional Data with Visualization Techniques

Danyu Liu and Alan P. Sprague

Department of Computer & Information Science
University of Alabama at Birmingham
153 Campbell Hall, 1300 Univ. Blvd
Birmingham AL 35294-1170
{liudy,sprague}@cis.uab.edu

Abstract. This paper describes a method to generate classification rules by using an interactive multidimensional data visualization and classification tool, called PolyCluster. PolyCluster is a system that adopts state-of-the-art algorithms for data visualization and integrates human domain knowledge into the construction process of classification rules. In addition, PolyCluster proposes a pair of novel and robust measurements, called the Average External Connecting Distance and the Average Internal Connecting Distance to evaluate the quality of the induced clusters. Experimental evaluation shows that PolyCluster is a visual-based approach that offers numerous improvements over previous visual-based techniques.

1 Introduction

In this paper, an interactive classification rules construction and exploration system is introduced, called PolyCluster. The motivation for PolyCluster is taken from several existing popular visual-based visualization systems [1, 2, 5, 4]. PolyCluster offers several unique features as novel contributions:

- PolyCluster uses classification rules as its classification mechanism. Classification rules are similar to decision trees and are a viable alternative.
- PolyCluster introduces a new classification construction mechanism that can help users build a classification model interactively, as well as visualize records in multi-dimensional spaces.
- For evaluating the quality of induced clusters, PolyCluster also proposes two new measurements, Average External Connecting Distance (AECD) and Average Internal Connecting Distance (AICD). These are extension to the ECD and ICD measurements [3].

These features enable PolyCluster to be an effective and efficient data mining solution. PolyCluster applies classification rules to finding structure, identifying patterns, and pinpointing relationships via multidimensional data visualization techniques. This framework is a major contribution of PolyCluster.

2 Experimental Results and Conclusions

Experimental results show that PolyCluster performs quite well compared with state-of-the-art classifiers. Because the classification rules are built by users manually rather than automatically built by underlying algorithms, the precision of the PolyCluster is quite dependent on the pattern-perception capabilities of humans. In particular, it seems that PolyCluster can obtain the same accuracy as that of the famous visual classifier PBC.

The paper introduces PolyCluster, an interactive multidimensional data visualization and classification tool. Experimental results have shown that PolyCluster is an effective and efficient approach to find structures, features, patterns, and relationships in underlying datasets. In addition, PolyCluster integrates a pair of novel and robust measurements, called AECD and AICD which users can adopt as a criterion to choose a best clustering combination from several available options. With further improvement such as the integration of automatic algorithms to build classifiers and the capabilities to handle categorical attributes, PolyCluster can become an even more powerful visual-based classification system.

References

1. M. Ankerst, C. Elsen, M. Ester and H.-P. Kriegel, Visual Classification: An Interactive Approach to Decision Tree Construction, Proceedings of the 5th ACM SIGKDD International Conference on Knowledge Discovery and Data mining, 1999, pp. 392-396.
2. M. Ankerst, M. Ester and H.-P. Kriegel, Towards an Effective Cooperation of the User and the Computer for Classification, Proceedings of the 6th ACM SIGKDD International Conference on Knowledge Discovery and Data mining, Boston, MA, 2000.
3. Y. Song and A. Zhang, Cluster and Compactness, Technical Report, Department of Computer Science and Engineering, State University of New York at Buffalo, 2001.
4. S. T. Teoh and K.-L. Ma, PaintingClass: Interactive Construction, Visualization and Exploration of Decision Trees, Proceedings of the 9th ACM SIGKDD International Conference on Knowledge Discovery and Data mining, 2003.
5. S. T. Teoh and K.-L. Ma, StarClass: Interactive Visual Classification Using Star Coordinates, Proceedings of the 3rd SIAM International Conference on Data Mining, 2003.

Believability Based Iterated Belief Revision*

Pei Yang, Yang Gao, Zhaoqian Chen, and Shifu Chen

State Key Laboratory for Novel Software Technology
Nanjing University, Nanjing 210093, China
yangpei@ai.nju.edu.cn

Abstract. Classical iterated belief revision methods rarely take into account the impact of the uncertain information. In this paper, an approach of believability based iterated belief revision(BIBR) is presented. BIBR relates the belief revision in the multi-agent system to the believability of information, which plays an important role in the revision process. Based on the Dempster-Shafer theory of evidence and believability function formalism, the believability of information can be obtained. The revised belief set by BIBR is dependent on the history of revision, namely, on the information received prior to the current belief set. It is proved that the BIBR operation meets the AGM postulates for belief revision and the Darwiche and Pearl postulates for iterated belief revision.

The classical account of belief change proposed by Alchourrón, Gärdenfors, and Makinson[1], commonly known as the AGM account of belief revision, is geared to dealing with *one-shot* belief change. The AGM framework gives a number of postulates that describe how the beliefs of an agent should change upon receiving the new information. Darwiche and Pearl proposed four further postulates on the AGM revision operation[2], to address the problem of iterated revision, i.e, of how an epistemic agent should act in the face of the continuous stream of new information. Although many researchers have contributed to the study of iterated belief revision, they mainly focus on the consistency of belief change, with little concern of the uncertainty of it in the multi-agent system, in which the information comes from a variety of human or artificial sources with different degrees of reliability, and thus the believability of information in the belief revision in the multi-agent system should be taken into consideration.

According to the Dempster-Shafer theory of evidence[3], each agent provides evidence for the frame of discernment and generates the basic probability assignment(BPA). All these BPAs will then be combined by the Dempster's rule of combination. On the basis of the believability function formalism[4], the believability of the information can be estimated.

In classical AGM framework, Alchourrón et al. proposed an approach of maximal consistent subset revision[1]. In general, there is more than one maximal

---

* This work is supported by the National Natural Science Foundation of China (No.60103012), the National Grand Fundamental Research 973 Program of China (No.2002CB312002) and the Natural Science Foundation of Jiangsu Province, China (No.BK2003409).

consistent subset of the belief set K. The maximal consistent subset revision is to arbitrarily select a maximal consistent subset K_M, and then use the selected K_M and the incoming information to make up the revised belief set. Although the information in each K_M is consistent with the incoming information, the believability of the information in different K_Ms is not equal. In other words, the K_Ms are not equally trustworthy. Hence, it is unreasonable to choose the *best* maximal consistent subset at random. In our work, we improve the Alchourrón's maximal consistent subset revision, i.e., give an ordering on the K_Ms of the belief set. Thus, we can choose the best maximal consistent subset K_B. We use an *average method*, which ranks the K_Ms according to the average believability of the statements in them. The BIBR operation ⊕ is defined as follows:

Definition 1. $K \oplus a = Cn(K_B \cup \{a\})$

Cn and a denote the consequence operation and the new information.

The procedure of BIBR is such that after every receipt of the new information a, the agent selects the best maximal consistent subset K_B from its belief set K. According to our average method, K_B is the maximal consistent subset with the biggest average believability of the statements. Then the agent expands K_B with a to generate a new belief set.

In the AGM framework, it is a general assumption that given any belief set K and information a, a revision operation ∗ determines a unique belief set $K' = K * a$. Consequently, whenever the agent has the belief set K and accepts the information a, it will end up in the same revised belief set K'. We would argue that, by the proposed BIBR, the revised belief set also depends on the history of revision, namely, the previously received information (excluding the statements in the belief set K). Thus, the agents having logically equivalent belief set and receiving the same information do not necessarily obtain the same revised belief set, since they may have different histories of revision.

References

1. Alchourrón, C.E., Makinson, D.: On the logic of theory change: Contraction functions and their associated revision functions. Theoria. 48 (1982) 14-37
2. Darwiche, A., Pearl, J.: On the logic of iterated belief revision. Proceedings of the Fifth Conference on the Theoretical Aspects of Reasoning about Knowledge. (1994) 5-23
3. Shafer, G.: A mathematical theory of evidence. Princeton University Press, Princeton (1976)
4. Shafer, G., Srivastava, S.: The bayesian and belief-function formalisms: A general perspective for auditing. Auditing: A Journal of Practice and Theory. Supplement (1990) 110-148

On Designing a Reduced-Order Fuzzy Observer

Behzad Moshiri, Farhad Besharati,
Abdrreza Dehghani Tafti, and Ali Akhavan Bitaghsir

Control and Intelligent Processing Center of Excellence
Department of Electrical and Computer Engineering University of Tehran
P.O. Box 14395/515, Tehran, Iran
Islamic Azad University, Science & Research Branch, Tehran, Iran

Abstract. In this paper, a method for designing reduced-order fuzzy observers for systems expressed in Takagi-Sugeno fuzzy model is proposed.

1 Introduction

In this paper, the fuzzy model is Takagi-Sugeno in which the dynamics of the system is expressed by linear state space equations in different regions of the work space; also, the system is controlled by using the state feedback for each of the local dynamics and thus the significance of designing the observer will become apparent [2], [3].

2 The Design of Reduced-Order Fuzzy Observer

The T-S fuzzy continuous-time dynamics model is expressed by **IF-THEN** rules.

$$\dot{X}(t) = \sum_{i=1}^{r} \mu_i.A_i.X(t) + \sum_{i=1}^{r} \mu_i.B_i.u(t) \tag{1}$$

The T-S fuzzy system's output will be defined as in the next equation.

$$y(t) = \frac{\sum_{i=1}^{r} w_i(z(t)).C.X(t)}{\sum_{i=1}^{r} w_i(z(t))} = \sum_{i=1}^{r} \mu_i(z(t)).C.X(t) \tag{2}$$

By considering the same fuzzy system's definitions, the final fuzzy controller's output will be:

$$u(t) = -\sum_{i=1}^{r} \mu_i.K_i.X(t) \tag{3}$$

By substituting equation 5 in equation 2, and also having $\sum_{j=1}^{r} \mu_j = 1$, we conclude that:

$$\dot{X} = \sum_{i=1}^{r}\sum_{j=1}^{r} \mu_i\mu_j(A_i - B_i.K_j)X(t)$$

The stability condition for the above system depends on the existence of a positive matrix P for which [1]:

$$(A_i - B_i.K_i)^T p + p(A_i - B_i.K_i) < 0, 1 \leq \forall i \leq r$$

and

$$\left(\frac{A_i - B_i.K_j + A_j - B_j.K_i}{2}\right)^T .p + p.\left(\frac{A_i - B_i.K_j + A_j - B_j.K_i}{2}\right) < 0,$$
$$for \ i < j \leq r \tag{4}$$

Several methods has been proposed for designing full-order observers [1], [4]. Each rule in the Takagi-Sugeno fuzzy model can be written like this:

If $z_1(t)$ is F_{i1} and ... and $z_g(t)$ is F_{ig} Then
$\dot{\bar{X}} = P.A_i.P^{-1}.X + P.B_i.u$
$\bar{Y} = C.P^{-1}.\bar{X} = C.Q.\bar{X} = [\,I_{q,q}\ 0\,]\,\bar{X}$

---

in which R is selected so that P will become nonsingular(regular).

Consider the inverted pendulum system. It can be seen that that the estimation error for state x_2 will become zero very soon in the specified time interval, which indicates the high precision of the observer.

3 Conclusion

In this paper, we've proposed a designing method for a reduced-order fuzzy observer in a T-S fuzzy system; also, the stability condition for the observer was studied. By considering the stability condition of the whole system, we observe that if the Takagi-Sugeno dynamics model is a correct estimation for the non-linear system, the proposed method for designing the observer and the controller can be an effective approach in controlling complex non-linear processes.

References

1. X. Jun, Z.Q. Sun, Analysis and design of fuzzy controller and fuzzy observer, IEEE Trans.on Fuzzy Systems voL.6,no.1,pp 41-51,(Feb. 1998)
2. R. Palm, Sliding mode observer for a T-S fuzzy system, IEEE Trans.on Fuzzy Systems. pp. 665-670, 2000
3. A. Fayaz, On the Sugeno- type fuzzy observers, IEEE conference, pp. 4828-4833, 1999.
4. R. Palm, P. Bergesten, Thau-Lunenberger observer for a T-S fuzzy system, IEEE Trans.on Fuzzy Systems, pp. 671-676, 2000.

Using Factorization Algorithm for 3D Reconstruction over Long Un-calibrated Sequences

Yoon-Yong Jeong, Yong-Ho Hwang, and Hyun-Ki Hong

Dept. of Image Eng., Graduate School of Advanced Imaging Science, Multimedia and Film
Chung-Ang Univ., 221 Huksuk-dong, Dongjak-ku, Seoul, 156-756, Korea
{kburngae,hwangyongho}@hotmail.com, honghk@cau.ac.kr

3D reconstruction over long sequences has been to the main problem of computer vision. For 3D reconstruction in Euclidean space, projective reconstruction, which is classified into the merging method and the factorization, is needed as a preceding step. The factorization methods suffer less from drift and error accumulation than the merging. However, they assume that most of corresponding points must remain in all frames. This paper presents a new projective reconstruction method for recovery of 3D structure over image sequences. For application of the factorization method over long sequences, we derive a new quantitative measure to break the full sequence into sub-sequences. Good grouping frames from a video sequence can produce a more appropriate input to geometry recovery and thereby improve the final result. The goal of our measure is to determine frame groups that are suitable for multi-view pose and geometry estimation based on the factorization. Correspondences between the first frame and the successive frames gradually diminish as the frame number grows over video sequence. The number of corresponding points on both the first and the second frame in the sequence, N_f, is used for frame grouping. At the first, we examine how many corresponding points on the first pair remain on the successive frames as $N_r = (1 - N_m / N_f)$, where N_m is the number of corresponding points on both the present frame and the previous. In general, the motion between frames has to be fairly small so that a precise correspondence can be established by using automatic matching, while significant parallax and large baseline is desirable for 3D analysis. The homography error (H_{err}) represents how much a camera moves between frames, and is used to evaluate the baseline length between two views. In addition, it means how many feature points are distributed on a planar surface. To estimate the fundamental matrix precisely, corresponding points should not be concentrated on a planar surface or a line segment. If corresponding points are distributed on many surfaces, it is difficult to establish one-to-one correspondences due to self-occlusion, so the homography error increases. If corresponding points are evenly distributed on the image, we can obtain a more precise fundamental matrix. Since the fundamental matrix contains all available information of the camera motion, the use of evenly distributed points improves motion and camera estimation results. To evaluate the degree of the point distribution in the image, we divide the entire image uniformly into sub-regions based on the number of corresponding points, and then calculate the point density of sub-region and that of the image. Standard deviation of the point density to represent the distribution of correspondences: $\sigma_p = \sqrt{N^{-1}\sum_{i=1}^{N}\left(N_{S_i}/A_s - N/A\right)^2}$, where N and N_{Si} are the total number of corresponding points, and that in the ith region. A and A_s are the area of the image and that of each sub-region, respectively. We define a new quantitative measure based on the above considerations: $S = \omega_1 N_r + \omega_2(1/H_{err}) + \omega_3 \sigma_p$, where S and ω_n are the score for grouping frames and the relative weights for each term, respectively. If S is above the threshold value, a new sub-sequence is generated. The full sequence is divided into several sub-sequences, and then we register the projective matrix of each sub-sequence. In order to proceed from projective matrix by three views to a complete description of the scene, it is necessary register all projective relations into the same coordinate frame. We iterate LmedS (Least median of square) based sampling and compute residuals, then find ADQ (Absolute dual quadric) with minimum median residual for rejection of the key-frames causing ADQ estimation to fail. ADQ is re-estimated from the selected camera matrix set, and we recover camera matrices of the rejected frames by using the camera resection, and then reconstruct finally the scene structure. For experiments, the proposed algorithm is compared with the merging method on the real images. The number of frames and the image size are 20 and 800×600. Our method divides the sequence into two groups and registers projective relations directly. The comparison of accumulation errors of camera parameters shows that the proposed method can estimate more precisely camera parameters, and thence reconstruct more robust 3D model as the frame number increases. The merging method estimates projective matrices from all of the views in order, while the proposed algorithm achieves projective reconstruction at a time on each group. Our reconstruction times are less than 20 seconds, and those of the previous 43 seconds. Therefore, our method has more computational efficiency than the merging method.

Acknowledgment

This research was supported by the Ministry of Education, Korea, and under the BK21 project, and the Ministry of Science and Technology, Korea, under the NRL(2000-N-NL-01-C-285) project.

A Hybrid Algorithm for Combining Forecasting Based on AFTER-PSO[*]

Xiaoyue Feng[1], Yanchun Liang[1,2,**], Yanfeng Sun[1], Heow Pueh Lee[2], Chunguang Zhou[1], and Yan Wang[1]

[1] College of Computer Science and Technology, Jilin University, Key Laboratory of Symbol Computation and Knowledge Engineering of the Ministry of Education Changchun 130012, China
[2] Institute of High Performance Computing, Singapore 117528, Singapore
liangyc@ihpc.a-star.edu.sg

Abstract. A novel hybrid algorithm based on the AFTER (Aggregated forecast through exponential re-weighting) and the modified particle swarm optimization (PSO) is proposed. The combining weights in the hybrid algorithm are trained by the modified PSO. The linear constraints are added in the PSO to ensure that the sum of the combining weights is equal to one. Simulated results on the prediction of the stocks data show the effectiveness of the hybrid algorithm.

1 Introduction

Combining forecasting was first proposed by Bates in 1969 [1]. A better performance can be achieved by combining different forecasting methods. In this paper, the combining weights are trained by the particle swarm optimization (PSO) [2]. To avoid the difficulty in employing the conventional PSO directly, a modified PSO is proposed. Using the high stability of AFTER [3] algorithm and the high searching ability of PSO, a hybrid algorithm is proposed and is abbreviated as AFTER-PSO.

2 Hybrid Algorithm Based on AFTER-PSO

Particle swarm optimization (PSO) is an evolutionary computational model which is based on swarm intelligence. The sum of the weights of combining forecasting must be equal to 1 which cannot be satisfied by the standard PSO. So a modified particle swarm optimization is proposed by adding linear constraints in the PSO based on the following theorem.

THEOREM The attributes of particles with added linear constraints
In the stage of initialization, if $Present_i(0)$, $pBest_i(0)$, $gBest_i(0)$ and $v_i(0)$ satisfy the following constraints

---

[*] This work is supported by the science-technology development project of Jilin Province of China (Grant No. 20030520) and the key science-technology project of the National Education Ministry of China (Grant No. 02090).
[**] Corresponding author.

$$\sum_i \Pr esent_i(0) = 1, \sum_i pBest_i(0) = 1, \sum_i gBest_i(0) = 1, \sum_i v_i(0) = 0. \quad (1)$$

then the parameters of particles will satisfy the constraints in each iteration. That is

$$\sum_i \Pr esent_i(t) = 1, \sum_i pBest_i(t) = 1, \sum_i gBest_i(t) = 1, \sum_i v_i(t) = 0. \quad (2)$$

The procedure of assigning weights based on AFTER and PSO is summarized as follows:

1) Getting a series of weights based on the AFTER;
2) Using these weights to initialize a particle of PSO and then produce several particles around this particle;
3) Employing the modified PSO to train the swarm and obtain the result of the AFTER-PSO.

3 Simulation Results

In order to examine the effectiveness of the proposed algorithm, we apply it to the stock price forecasting. Compared with the AFTER, the AFTER-PSO is more superior to the AFTER. The MSE of the AFTER-PSO is about 33% of that of the AFTER-PSO for both training data (0.00011 and 0.00035 respectively) and testing data (0.00008 and 0.00024 respectively). The accuracy of the prediction is improved significantly by the proposed algorithm.

4 Conclusions

A novel hybrid algorithm is presented based on the AFTER and the PSO, in which the combining weights are assigned by using the advantages of the AFTER and the PSO. Constraints are added into the PSO which can reduce the normalization time. Simulations show that the proposed hybrid algorithm has a relatively fast operational speed and good performance in the forecasting for many different kinds of data.

References

1. Bates JN and Granger CWJ. The combination of forecasts. Operations Research Quarterly. 1969, 20: 319-325
2. Kennedy J and Eberhart RC. Particle swarm optimization. Proceedings of the IEEE International Conference on Neural Networks. 1995, Vol. IV: 1942-1948
3. Yang Y. Combining time series models for forecasting. International Journal of Forecasting. 2004, 20 (1): 69-84

A Multi-strategy Approach for Catalog Integration

Ryutaro Ichise[1,2], Masahiro Hamasaki[2], and Hideaki Takeda[1,2]

[1] National Institute of Informatics, Tokyo 101-8430, Japan
[2] The Graduate University for Advanced Studies, Tokyo 101-8430, Japan
{ichise,takeda}@nii.ac.jp, hamasaki@grad.nii.ac.jp

Abstract. When we have a large amount of information, we usually use categories with a hierarchy, in which all information is assigned. This paper proposes a new method of integrating two catalogs with hierarchical categories. The proposed method uses not only the contents of information but also the structures of both hierarchical categories. We conducted experiments using two actual Internet directories, and the results show improved performance compared with the previous approach.

In this paper, we introduce a novel approach for catalog integration problem. The problem addressed in this paper is finding an appropriate category C_t in the target catalog T_C for each information instance I_{si} in the source catalog S_C. What we need to do is determine an appropriate category in T_C for an information instance. In order to solve the problem, we proposed the Similarity-based integration (SBI) [3]. SBI has a higher performance compared with the Naive Bayes (NB) approach, even with the extension proposed by [1]. In this paper, we propose a method which combines the SBI approach and the NB approach. In order to combine handling the meaning of information, we propose using NB after SBI.

A problem of SBI is that it is hard to learn a mapping rule when the destination category is in a lower category in the target concept hierarchy. In other words, the learned rules are likely to assign relatively general categories in the target catalog. In order to avoid this type of rules, we propose to combine a contents-based classification method after we apply the SBI algorithm. Since NB is very popular and easy to use, we adopt NB as the contents-based classification method. In order to apply the NB algorithm for hierarchical classification, we utilize the simple method of the *Pachinko Machine* NB. The Pachinko Machine classifies instances at internal nodes of the tree, and greedily selects sub-branches until it reaches a leaf [4]. This method is applied after the rule induced by SBI decides the starting category for the Pachinko Machine NB.

In order to evaluate the proposed algorithm, we conducted experiments using real Internet directories collected from Yahoo! [5] and Google [2]. The data was collected during the period from December 2003 to January 2004. The locations in Yahoo! and Google are Photography. We conducted ten-fold cross validations for the links appeared in both directories. The shared links were divided into

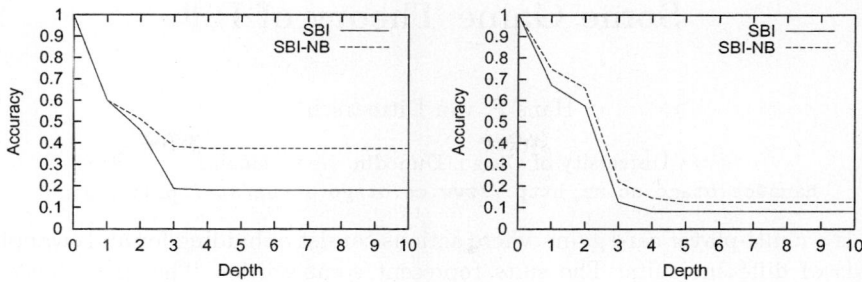

Fig. 1. Experimental Results

ten data sets; nine of which were used to construct rules, and the remaining set was used for testing. Ten experiments were conducted for each data set, and the average accuracy is shown in Figure 1. The accuracy is measured for each depth of the Internet directories. The vertical axes in Figure 1 show the accuracy and horizontal axes show the depth of the concept hierarchies. The left side of Figure 1 shows the results obtained using Google as the source catalog and Yahoo! as the target catalog, and the right side of Figure 1 shows the results obtained using Yahoo! as the source catalog and Google as the target catalog. For comparison, these graphs also include the results of SBI. SBI-NB denotes the results of the method proposed in this paper. The proposed algorithm performs much better in accuracy than the original SBI. One reason for this is that the NB works well. In other words, the contents-based classification is suited for this domain. According to [3], the NB method does not achieve the performance of SBI in the Photography domain. However, our proposed algorithm effectively combines the contents-based method with the category similarity-based method.

In this paper, a new technique was proposed for integrating multiple catalogs. The proposed method uses not only the similarity of the categorization of catalogs but also the contents of information instances. The performance of the proposed method was tested using actual Internet directories, and the results of these tests show that the performance of the proposed method is more accurate for the experiments.

References

1. R. Agrawal and R. Srikant. On integrating catalogs. In *Proc. of the 10th Int. World Wide Web Conf.*, 603–612, 2001.
2. Google. http://directory.google.com/, 2003.
3. R. Ichise, H. Takeda and S. Honiden. Integrating Multiple Internet Directories by Instance-based Learning. In *Proc. of the 18th Int. Joint Conf. on AI*, 22–28, 2003.
4. A. K. McCallum, et al. Improving text classification by shrinkage in a hierarchy of classes. In *Proc. of the 15th Int. Conf. on Machine Learning*, 359–367, 1998.
5. Yahoo! http://www.yahoo.com/, 2003.

Some Game Theory of Pit

Hans P. van Ditmarsch*

University of Otago, Dunedin, New Zealand
hans@cs.otago.ac.nz, http://www.cs.otago.ac.nz/staffpriv/hans/

Pit is a multi-player card game where actions consist of bidding for and swapping cards of different suits. The suits represent commodities. The first player to declare that he holds a full suit, wins the game. That player is said to corner the market in that commodity. From different points of view the Pit game has been investigated in [1, 2]. The former uses Pit to illustrate the supply and demand cycle in the general economics classroom. The latter may be seen as a study in requirements engineering for electronic market simulations. The logical dynamics of the game is spelled out in full detail in [3], using the language of [4]. This epistemic analysis is necessary to define Pit as a game. This poster is an exploration into the game theory of Pit.

A simplification of the real game is a Pit game for three players Anne, Bill, and Cath (a, b, and c) that each hold two cards from a pack consisting of two Wheat, two Flax, and two Rye cards (w, x, and y). For the card deal where Anne holds a Wheat and a Flax card Bill a Wheat and a Rye card, and Cath a Flax and a Rye card, we write $wx.wy\ xy$, etc. We call this the SixPit game. One of the deals that does not immediately end in a corner is $wx.wy.xy$. In such a deal, all players are 'equally well' informed.

All players now offer one card for trade. Suppose that given the card deal $wx.wy.xy$ at the outset of the game, Anne and Bill are chosen to trade. The four possible outcomes of their trade are $wx.wy.xy$, $xy.ww.xy$, $ww.xy.xy$ and $wy.wx.xy$. In the third case Anne will declare a corner in Wheat and wins, and in the second case Bill declares a corner in Wheat and wins. In the other cases a further move has to be made, possibly ad infinitum. In the first case, when the deal is again $wx.wy.xy$, the game state therefore *appears* to be the same as when the cards had just been dealt, but this is not true: a simple argument shows that Anne and Bill, but not Cath, now happen to know what the card deal is. Anne can therefore distinguish between 'the card in her hand that she shares with Bill, with whom she just traded', namely her Wheat card, and 'the card in her hand that she shares with Cath, with whom she did not just trade', namely her Flax card. Other card game states for SixPit also reveal only these options. In general:

– $shared_n$
  "if player n traded in the previous round, then he offers the card for trade that he knows to share with the player whom he traded with, and otherwise he chooses his card randomly."

---

* I acknowledge contributions from Stephen Cranefield, Johan Lövdahl, Martin Purvis, and Miklos Szilagyi. For the Pit game rules, see www.hasbro.com/common/-instruct/pit.pdf. For a simulation, see http://www.ida.liu.se/~jolov/pit/.

- $distinct_n$
 "if player n traded in the previous round, then he offers the card for trade that he knows to share with the player whom he did not trade with, and otherwise he chooses his card randomly."

We have computed the equilibria for the one-round game where Anne and Bill know the card deal. We may assume that this game is zero-sum, where a win means 2 points for the winner (who corners the market) and a loss -1 for both losers (that fail to corner the market). For example, Anne now plays $shared_a$ and thus offers w, Bill plays $distinct_b$ and thus offers y, and Cath plays $distinct_c$ and thus randomly chooses a card, and this is x. If Anne and Cath are now randomly chosen to trade, then the resulting deal is $xx.wy.wy$ and thus the payoff $(2, -1, -1)$. If no corner results, the payoff is $(0, 0, 0)$. As Cath's choice is blind in this one-round game, we can restrict ourselves to the game matrix for Anne and Bill. This contains the *expected* payoffs for a and b given random selection of two players for trading.

$a \backslash b$	$distinct_b$	$shared_b$
$distinct_a$	$(-\frac{1}{3}, -\frac{1}{3})$	$(\frac{1}{3}, -\frac{1}{6})$
$shared_a$	$(-\frac{1}{6}, \frac{1}{3})$	$(\frac{1}{6}, \frac{1}{6})$

This game has two pure equilibria, $(distinct_a, shared_b)$, and $(shared_a, distinct_b)$, and a mixed equilibrium where a plays $\frac{1}{2} \cdot distinct_a + \frac{1}{2} \cdot shared_a$ and b plays $\frac{1}{2} \cdot distinct_b + \frac{1}{2} \cdot shared_b$, with associated payoff $(0, 0)$. That equilibrium has the peculiar property, that when a plays a random card, b cannot affect his own expected payoff but only a's expected payoff, and vice versa. In other words: when a doesn't think at all, b cannot take advantage of that.

The game matrix is of the so-called 'chicken' type, where playing $shared_n$ may be seen as the cooperating strategy and playing $distinct_n$ as the defecting strategy, and $(shared_a, shared_b)$ is the unstable outcome where both players 'chickened out'. In terms of Pit: *if* Anne and Bill form a coalition, they can outwit Cath and each increase their expected gain from 0 to $\frac{1}{6}$. If instead one acts after all in his own interest, he can increase his expected gain to $\frac{1}{3}$, but, unfortunately, if they both do that, they both lose $\frac{1}{3}$ instead. Cath is then the laughing bystander who gains $\frac{2}{3}$.

References

1. Holt, C.: Trading in a pit market. Journal of Economic Perspectives **10(1)** (1996) 193–203
2. Purvis, M., Nowostawski, M., Cranefield, S., Oliveira, M.: Multi-agent interaction technology for peer-to-peer computing in electronic trading environments. In Moro, G., Sartori, C., Singh, M., eds.: Second International Workshop on Agents and Peer-to-Peer Computing, Melbourne (2003) 103–114
3. van Ditmarsch, H.: Logic and game theory of pit. Manuscript (2004)
4. van Ditmarsch, H.: Descriptions of game actions. Journal of Logic, Language and Information **11** (2002) 349–365

Dynamically Determining Affect During Scripted Dialogue

Tory Meyer

IIMS, Massey University, Auckland, New Zealand
T.A.Meyer@massey.ac.nz

Abstract. Autonomous synthetic actors performing in live stage performances must be capable of generating speech with characteristics appropriate to each moment in the performance. This paper describes a statistical technique used to classify lines of dialogue given a token set and prior knowledge base. The words in each line formed the basic tokens; results improved with each piece of additional information (punctuation, parts of speech, character name and previous lines) generated from the lines of the script, and also by normalisation of the basic tokens (normalisation of case, removal of punctuation, and word stemming). Results are two to three times improved over a simple random choice, allowing only the text of each line of dialogue as data.

Introduction

Synthetic actors in live stage performances must deliver dialogue with characteristics (e.g. pitch, volume, and rate of speech) appropriate to the specific interval in the performance during which the line is delivered. As part of a project investigating the use of synthetic actors in rehearsals for such performances, a speech system was given the task of identifying the delivery method most likely to satisfy the director of the rehearsal. Seven methods were available; five basic emotions (anger, sadness, disgust, gladness, fear), as well as surprised [1] and 'neutral' speech.

A strength, or score, of each method is also required. The actor is also expected to offer variations of its performance; one such technique is to generate dialogue using alternate methods – for example, the second most likely method, rather than the first, or a weighted combination of the first and second. For this task, the only data available to the actor are the scripted lines of dialogue (including the words and punctuation to be generated and the name of the character that delivers the line).

Implementation

Each line was converted into a set of tokens (specific tokenisation is outlined below). To classify, the probability of each token appearing in each type of delivery method was determined (based on the ratio of appearance to non-appearance in the training data). These probabilities were combined in a chi-squared distribution using Fisher's rule to give a final probability for each emotion that the message should be delivered via that method.

A variety of tokenisation methods were examined, each obtaining a different set of data from the lines of dialogue. In the most simplistic case, the line was split on any white space (i.e. into words with 'attached' punctuation). Case normalisation and stripping the 'attached' punctuation were also examined. More complex tokenisation included stemming the word tokens and generating tokens based on the parts of speech that the line included. Tokens were also generated for the name of the character delivering the line and based on the previous line.

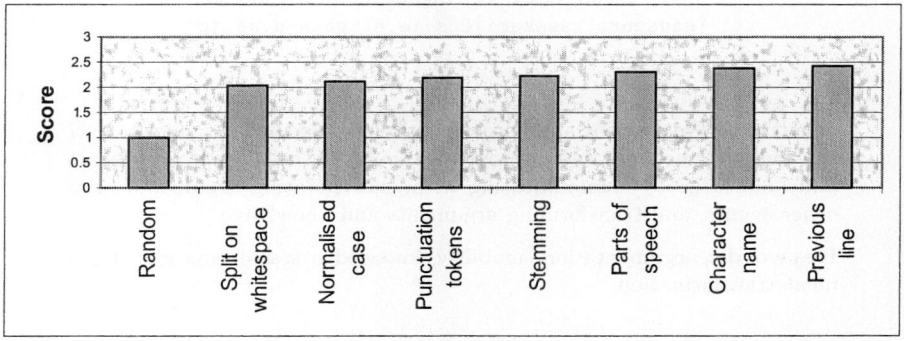

Fig. 1. Results Summary

Results

Randomly selecting a method to use results in around 14 percent accuracy; use of this system allows accuracy to increase to forty to fifty percent and of the remaining lines, the system is able to determine that it is unsure for ten to fifteen percent (of the total. Given the three attempts at each line allowed within the rehearsal context, 65 to 75 percent of lines are appropriately delivered, leaving less than fifteen percent incorrect and ten percent unsure.

References

1. J. E. Cahn, "The Generation of Affect in Synthesized Speech," *Journal of the American Voice I/O Society*, 1990.

Knowledge and Argument Transformation for Arguing Mobile Agents

Hajime Sawamura and Wataru Kawakami

Dept. of Information Engineering, Niigata University
8050, 2-cho, Ikarashi, Niigata, 950-2181 Japan
{sawamura,kawakami}@cs.ie.niigata-u.ac.jp

Abstract. We describe an approach to growing agents that migrate over the computer network and improve the quality of their logical arguments and knowledge by communicating with, incorporating arguments from other agents, and transforming arguments and knowledge.

Keywords: argumentation, mobility, knowledge transformation, argument transformation

1 Basic Components for Growing Agents

In this paper, we address ourselves to agents that grow over the computer network. The term "growing" has a meaning similar to recent concepts such as those appearing in learning, evolutionary computing, genetic computing, emergent computing and so on, whose purpose is to realize not behavior-fixed computing entities but environment-sensitive ones. We then think argumentation, mobility, and knowledge and argument transformation are the most basic components for growing agents. Argumentation is a way to seek truth by dialogue where truth is not a priori concept in the open and changing networked society. Mobility is a way to encounter with unexpected agents and their knowledge and ideas. Knowledge and argument transformation is a way to reorganize, improve and refine acquired knowledge from other agents through argumentation (dialogue) and mobility, and initial arguments to more convincing ones.

2 Argument and Knowledge Transformation

We introduce a variety of argument and knowledge transformations.

Argument Transformation Rules. These consist of (i) Rule replacement for information *refinement* and *diversification*, (ii) Fact replacement for information refinement and diversification, and (iii) Weak literal replacement for information *completion*. Rule replacement allows agents to employ more persuasive or preferable rules in their arguments. Fact replacement allows agents to introduce more evidences to arguments. Weak literal replacement allows agents to reduce incomplete knowledge (belief) included in arguments. These are subject to the following acceptability conditions under which an agent can accept the offered subarguments from other agents concerned: (1) The agent can neither undercut nor rebut any part of subarguments proposed by other agents. This acceptability condition is important since the agent should keep its knowledge base consistent, (2) The agent replaces subtrees in arguments if the number of facts as evidences can be increased after the replacement, and (3) let arg be a subargument to be replaced and arg' an argument offered. Then, arg' is acceptable if the number of weak literals in arg' is less than or equal to the number of weak literals in arg. In addition to the argument transformation introduced above, there are other useful and versatile directions. They include: (iv) Argument transformation based on the concept of similarity (for example, an argument on the issue $p(a)$ is changed into the argument on the issue $p(b)$, using a certain similarity relation $a \sim b$), (v) Argument transformation based on the concept of strengthening (or specificity) (for example, an argument on the issue p is changed into the argument on the issue q, where $p \to q$), and (vi) Argument transformation based on the concept of weakening (for example, an argument on the issue p is changed into the argument on the issue q, where $q \to p$). These three transformations are subject to such a condition that the transformed arguments are justified.

Knowledge Transformation Rules. We provide two rules: (vii) The reductant of rules and (viii) The rule abridgment. The reductant is a result obtained by reducing several rules with the same head to a single rule. The reductant is known to be a logical consequence from the several rules used. The rule abridgment, on the other hand, is its converse operation of the reductant. That is sort of a detachment and has a role of digesting complicated rules generated by the reductant. For example, $\{a \leftarrow b, c, d, e.\}$ is a reductant from $\{a \leftarrow b, c, .\}$ and $\{a \leftarrow d, e.\}$. Conversely, $\{a \leftarrow b, d.\}$ is an abridgment of the reductant, including b from the first rule and d from the second rule in their rule premises, where b and d are assumed to have most significant and relevant relationship with the conclusion a.

3 Argumentation Protocols for Growing Agents

We have constructed two kinds of agents that can grow through three fundamental capabilities: argumentation, mobility, and argument and knowledge transformation. One has the following scenario of agents' behavior on the network. Suppose an agent has an opinion in the form of argument on its issue. However, it is usual for such an argument to be made in terms of uncertain beliefs and knowledge. So, the agent would have a desire to make its argument more convincing one for its own self or its principal. Then the agent starts going out and visits (moves around) agents' places on the network with its own knowledge base and argument (inference) engine, where a number of other agents reside and act for their own goals with their own belief and knowledge. Through argumentative dialogue, it then tries to make its argument a better one by applying the subtree replacement transformations. For the other scenario of agents' behavior on the network, we assume such a virtual agents society that both antagonists and protagonists reside, as two major parties in our parliament. Then, the agent starts roaming around the network to resolve its baffling matter, expecting to meet those two kinds of agents over the network and argue about it. This style of meeting is important for agent growing since meeting only one of either antagonists or protagonists tends to lead to a biased formation of knowledge base.

In either case, our approach obviously differs from the usual information retrieval and finding by search engines on the internet in the sense that the issue is made clear from scratch in the form of arguments, and the agent's goal is to refine, complete its own arguments and find arguments based on varied grounds. In this model, agents continue to keep their first opinion on the issues without changing their minds while they are visiting and arguing with other agents.

References

1. H. Sawamura, W. Kawakami and Y. Umeda: *Argument Transformation for Growing Agents with Mobilit*, Proc. of the Second International Joint Conference on Autonomouse Agents and Multi Agent Systems (AAMAS2003), Melbourne, Australia, 14-18 July, 2003.

Improving Newsgroup Clustering by Filtering Author-Specific Words*

Yuval Marom and Ingrid Zukerman

School of Computer Science and Software Engineering
Monash University, Clayton, Victoria 3800, Australia
{yuvalm,ingrid}@csse.monash.edu.au

Introduction. This paper describes the first step in a project for topic identification in help-desk applications. In this step, we apply a clustering mechanism to identify the topics of newsgroup discussions. We have used newsgroup discussions as our testbed, as they provide a good approximation to our target application, while obviating the need for manual tagging of topics.

We have found that the postings of individuals who contribute repeatedly to a newsgroup may lead the clustering process astray, in the sense that discussions may be grouped according to their author, rather than according to their topic. To address this problem, we introduce a filtering mechanism, and evaluate it by comparing clustering performance with and without filtering.

The Filtering Mechanism. Our filtering mechanism operates in two stages. First, a 'profile' is built for each person posting to a newsgroup. This profile is a distribution of *word document frequencies*, where the document frequency of a word is the number of postings where the word is used. Next, word-usage proportions are calculated for each person. These are the word document frequencies divided by the person's total number of postings. We then filter out words that (1) have a high usage proportion, and (2) are posted by frequent contributors. For more details, see [1].

Clustering Newsgroups. We use the K-Means algorithm for clustering. This algorithm separates a dataset into k clusters based on the Euclidean distance between data points, where each data 'point' corresponds to one document (newsgroup thread). The output of the clustering process is evaluated by calculating the F-score for each cluster, and the combined F-score for all the clusters (the F-score measure reflects how many documents a cluster and a newsgroup have in common [2]). Our data representation consists of a bag-of-words with TF.IDF scoring [2]: a word-vector is made up from a chosen and fixed set of words; the vector components are determined based on how frequently each word appears in a document and how infrequently it occurs in other documents. For more details, see [1].

In order to determine the useful range of applicability of our filtering mechanism, we have evaluated clustering (and filtering) performance along the dimension of topical similarity between newsgroups. That is, we vary the level of relatedness between the newsgroups in our datasets. The least related newsgroups provide a benchmark for clustering performance, while the more related ones exemplify help-desk applications.

Results. Figure 1 shows the results obtained for three datasets with different values of k. The newsgroups in the first dataset were downloaded from the Internet. They

---

* This research was supported in part by Linkage Grant LP0347470 from the Australian Research Council and by an endowment from Hewlett Packard.

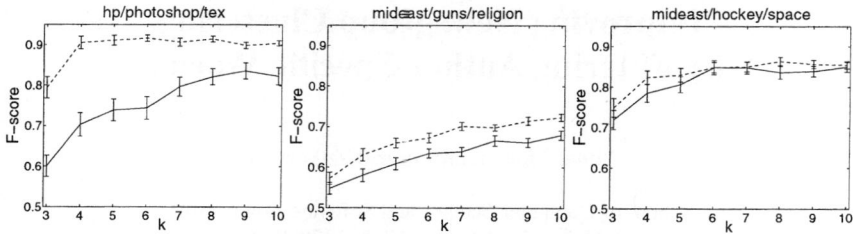

Fig. 1. Overall results for the three datasets.

are lp.hp (related to printing), comp.graphics.apps.photoshop (related to graphics), and comp.text.tex (related to text editing). These newsgroups are computing-related, but discuss fairly different topics. We see that for this dataset, performance is much poorer without filtering, particularly for low values of k. This suggests that author-specific words create undesirable overlaps between the clusters, which are resolved as the value of k increases because finer differences between the clusters are detected. In contrast, when filtering is used, the clustering procedure reaches its best performance with $k = 4$, where the performance is extremely good. The fact that it converges for such a low value of k suggests that there is little 'true' topical overlap between the newsgroups.

The second and third datasets were obtained from the "20-newsgroups" corpus (http://people.csail.mit.edu/people/jrennie/20Newsgroups). The second set consists of the newsgroups talk.politics.mideast, talk.politics.guns, and talk.religion.misc. These newsgroups discuss fairly similar topics, related to politics and religion. Because there is a large topical overlap between the newsgroups, clustering performance for this dataset is overall much poorer than for the first (and the third) dataset. As for the first dataset, the performance steadily improves as k increases, both with and without filtering. Notice also that filtering consistently improves clustering performance, which means that there are also undesirable overlaps created by author-specific words.

The third dataset is made up of the newsgroup talk.politics.mideast, which was also used in the second dataset, as well as rec.sport.hockey and sci.space. These newsgroups discuss very different topics, which explains why filtering has the least effect on this dataset: the documents are different enough for the clustering to perform similarly with and without filtering. That is, there are enough discriminating topical words to diminish the effect of author-specific words. Nonetheless, filtering has an effect for lower values of k, suggesting that some overlap is created by author-specific words – when enough clusters are used to account for this overlap ($k = 6$), the effect of the filtering mechanism disappears.

Conclusion. Newsgroup clustering generally benefits from a filtering mechanism that removes subjective influences of frequent contributors. The magnitude of this effect depends on the topical similarity between the newsgroups involved, and the level of granularity used in the clustering (*i.e.* the value of k).

References

1. Zukerman, I., Marom, Y.: Filtering speaker-specific words from electronic discussions. In: Proceedings of The 20th International Conference on Computational Linguistics. (2004)
2. Salton, G., McGill, M.: An Introduction to Modern Information Retrieval. McGraw Hill (1983)

Evolving Artificial Ant Systems to Improve Layouts of Graphical Objects

Vincent Tam[1], Simon Koo[1], and Kozo Sugiyama[2]

[1] Department of E.E.E., The University of Hong Kong
Pokfulam, Hong Kong
Phone: +852-2859-2697
vtam@eee.hku.hk

[2] School of Knowledge Science
The Japan Advanced Institute of Science and Technology, Japan
sugi@jaist.ac.jp

Abstract. Artificial ant systems (AAS) have been widely applied to solve many important industrial applications including network configuration or vehicle routing that involve constrained optimisation. In this paper, we explore the possible uses of AAS to handle layouts of graphical objects using constrained optimisation approach. In our evolving AAS, the stepwise movement of each individual ant naturally corresponds to the iterative adjustment of each graphical object in both x- and y-coordinates until a local minimum of a predefined objective function is reached. Up to our knowledge, this work represents the first attempt of applying AAS to improve layouts of graphical objects with simpler computation as compared to existing approaches, thus presenting new opportunities for further investigations.

1 Background and Motivation

Artificial ant systems (AAS) [1] or their extended ant colony optimisation (ACO) techniques have recently received due attention as a powerful optimisation approach to solve many hard constrained optimisation problems including the network configuration problems [1] and traveling salesman problems (TSPs) [1]. Also widely occurring in many industrial applications, *automatic adjustment* of graphical objects represents another class of challenging constrained optimisation problems for concise information visualization. Among the many possible alignment problems between the graphical objects in any planar graph, node overlappings are essentially local conflicts that can be effectively handled by local search methods such as a modified EGENET solver [2] proposed to successfully resolve both node and edge overlappings while minimising the predefined objective function on a set of 8 arbitrarily generated test graphs. In this paper, we proposed an interesting *AAS_Layout* search framework using each artificial ant as an autonomous agent to focus on avoiding local conflicts while optimising the objective functions through their indirect communication in the global pheromone matrix.

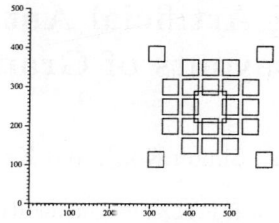

(a) The original symmetrical graph

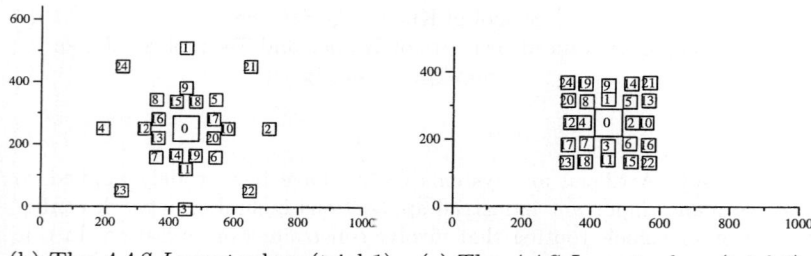

(b) The *AAS_Layout* solver (trial 1)   (c) The *AAS_Layout* solver (trial 2)

Fig. 1. A Symmetrical Graph.

2 An Empirical Evaluation

Figure 1(a) shows a symmetrical graph of 25 nodes involving some node overlappings. Figure 1(b) shows the result in which the ant system of our proposed *AAS_Layout* algorithm biases towards the diagonal symmetries whereas Figure 1(c) is the result in which our ant system biases toward the x- and y-symmetry, thus demonstrating the flexibility of our proposal.

Possible directions for further investigation may include: trying an alternative strategy to minimize the total number of moves at each iteration whenever appropriate so as to produce more compact layouts, experimenting with different parameters such as α and β to fine-tune the performance of our proposed *AAS_Layout*, and integrating our AAS-based search proposal with other local or heuristic search methods such as the modified EGENET solver [2].

References

1. Dorigo, M., Caro, G.D., Gambardella, L.M.: Ant Algorithms for Discrete Optimization. *Artificial Life*, **Vol. 5, No. 3**, pp. 137-172, 1999.
2. Tam, V.: Removing Node and Edge Overlapping in Graph Layouts by A Modified EGENET Solver. in *Proceedings* of the 11th IEEE International Conference on Tools with Artificial Intelligence, Chicago IL, Nov 9-11, 1999.

MASCONTROL: A MAS for System Identification and Process Control

Evelio J. González, Alberto Hamilton, Lorenzo Moreno,
Roberto L. Marichal, and Vanessa Muñoz

Departamento de Física Fundamental y Experimental, Electrónica y Sistemas
Av. Astrofísico Fco. Sánchez, S/N.Universidad de La Laguna.
38207. Tenerife, Spain
ejgonzal@ull.es

Abstract. In this paper, a MAS, called MASCONTROL for system identification and process control is presented, including an Ontology Agent. It implements a self-tuning regulator (STR) scheme. Defined classes, properties, axioms and individuals in the ontology are mainly related to control concepts. These definitions and other ones allow the system to make some interesting inferences from some axioms defined in the ontology.

1 MASCONTROL Agent Framework: Results

MASCONTROL framework is composed of 8 different types of agents, apart from FIPA ones.

ReaderCommandAgent (RCA) This agent samples the output of the system, calculates the command and sends it to the system.

IdentificationAgent (IA) Each IA tries to identify the system from the input-output vector. For this purpose, it uses Evenet2000 modules [1].

LinearIdentificationAgent (LIA) Similar to the IA, but it assumes a linear model.

CentralIdentificationAgent (CIA) This agent manages the IAs (linear or not). It asks for the results of the current optimizations selecting that optimization with the best results and informing the rest of the IAs with the same model.

OptimizerAgent (OpA) This agent optimizes the controller parameters.

CentralControlAgent (CCA) Manages the optimization of model parameters.

InputOutputAnalyzerAgent (IOAA) It analyzes process input and output data, testing, in an intuitive way, if the system input is rich enough.

Ontology Agent (OA)
Due to the transmission rate and optimization time, MASCONTROL should be used for controlling not-excessively fast processes. In this context the authors have tested the MAS controlling an interconnected tank system through three different control actions: P, PI and pole replacement and optimizing different system models through different optimization methods.

Process control is carried out in two phases. In the first phase, reference input value is continually modified, looking for a better identification. When it is considered that identification is good enough reference input is set to the desired value. OpAs optimization is carried with a variable reference. This way, model behaviour is supposed to be more independent from a given reference input.

Regarding to the PI control action, the closed-loop model has to be modified for including integral control action and the control action implemented by the RCA. These modifications are easy to carry due to MAS modularity.

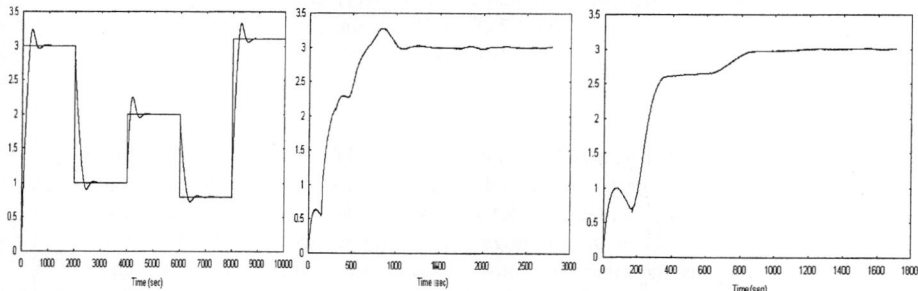

Fig. 1. MASCONTROL results: OpAs optimization (left), identification and control phases (center) and OA effect (right)

Figure 1 (left) shows an example of OpAs optimization. In this case system output reaches reference input in each section. Moreover, overshoot is low. This optimization is reflected in the system output: it reaches the desired reference input (3 V) and with a low overshoot. The training and desired reference input phases can be distinguished. (Figure 1, center)

This case instructs about the use of an OA in control system. Figure 1 (right) shows the output evolution initially controlled by a P control action. When IOAA realizes that the system output is stabilized and that it has not reached the reference input, RCA asks OA for the suitable control action for this situation. At this point, OA looks for this fact in the system ontology and inform RCA that the answer is a PI control action. Then, MASCONTROL makes the necessary modifications. As it was expected, process output reaches the desired reference input after these modifications.

Once the goodness of the agent architecture has been tested for system identification and P and PI control action, following work has focused on studying that goodness for a totally different control action, concretely, pole replacement. This control action critically depends on system identification.

References

1. Gonzalez E.J., Hamilton A., Moreno L., Aguilar R.M., Marichal R.L.. Neural networks teaching using Evenet-2000. Computer Applications in Engineering Education. Volume 11, Issue 1, 2003.1-5.

Vision Based Acquisition of Mouth Actions for Human-Computer Interaction

Gamhewage C. de Silva, Michael J. Lyons, and Nobuji Tetsutani

ATR Media Information Science Labs
2-2-2 Hikaridai, Keihanna Science City, Kyoto, 619-0288, Japan

Abstract. We describe a computer vision based system that allows use of movements of the mouth for human-computer interaction (HCI). The lower region of the face is tracked by locating and tracking the position of the nostrils. The location of the nostrils determines a sub-region of the image from which the cavity of the open mouth may be segmented. Shape features of the open mouth can then be used for continuous real-time data input, for human-computer interaction. Several applications of the head-tracking mouth controller are described.

1 System Description

Humans have fine motor control of the shape of the mouth, so it is reasonable that mouth action could be used in HCI. Our vision-based system takes the nostrils as anchor points for robustly tracking the lower face. Parameters of the mouth cavity region are extracted for interaction with applications.

Focusing on the lower region of the face makes efficient use of available pixels, devoting greater resolution to the mouth area. The system is initialized by positioning nostrils in a specific rectangular region of the image (Fig. 1a) and clicking a mouse button. Nostrils, appear darker relative to the surrounding face region under most lighting conditions. Vertical and horizontal projections of an image region containing the nostrils produces characteristic profiles, if the face is upright. The minima of these profiles can be used to estimate the x, y coordinates of the nostril centers, (N_1x, N_1y) and $N_2 = (N_2x, N_2y)$ (Fig. 1 b,c). The length, D_N, orientation angle, A_N, and mid-point, C_N of the segment joining the nostril center is calculated from these coordinates and used to determine a search window of the next tracking frame as well as a region for segmenting the mouth (Fig. 1 d). During tracking, the nostril and mouth search windows are rotated by angle $-A_N$ around C_N, and D_N and A_N are smoothed using a weighted sum of the previous and current values. Pixels corresponding to the shadow in the open mouth are segmented with intensity and colour thresholding and morphological processing on the segmented blob. The number of pixels in the blob is a measure of the **area**, A_m of the open mouth. The height H_m and width W_m of the open mouth are estimated with the standard deviations of blob pixel x and y coordinates. The **aspect ratio**, R_m of the open mouth is estimated by $R_m = H_m/W_m$. Use of statistical functions over all segmented pixels reduces noise in the shape parameter estimates.

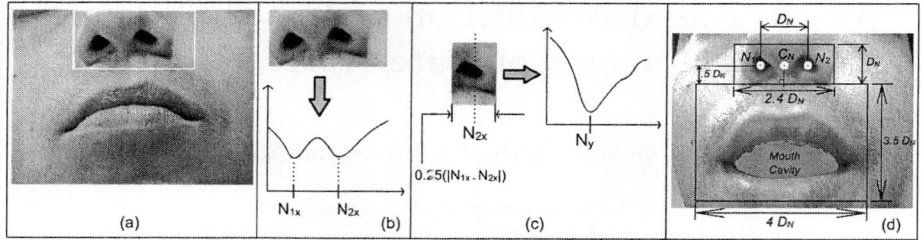

Fig. 1. Nostril detection and mouth region localization

2 Applications

Here we describe three applications for the mouth controller. With the *Mouthesizer* [1], mouth shape parameters are converted to MIDI control change signals to control musical effects. With a good mapping of action to audio effect, this is a compelling new way to play. The *Mouthbrush* system [2] allows the user to control brush qualities such as size, hardness, opacity, and color, with their mouth, while they are drawing using a graphics tablet and stylus. Artists who used the system reported an interesting and expressive experience. *MouthType*, is a prototype system for text entry by hand and mouth [3] on small keyboards, such as those on mobile phones. To enter Japanese text entry using MouthType, the vowel of syllable is chosen with mouth shape, while the consonant is simultaneously selected with a key press. This allows Japanese text entry with fewer keypresses and higher speed than existing methods.

Acknowledgments

We thank Chi-ho Chan for his input. This work was supported in part by the National Institute of Information and Communications Technology.

References

1. Michael J. Lyons, Michael Haehnel, Nobuji Tetsutani: Designing, Playing, and Performing with a Vision-Based Mouth Interface. Proceedings, 2003 Conference on New Interfaces for Musical Expression (NIME-03). (2003) 116–121
2. Chi-ho Chan, Michael J. Lyons, Nobuji Tetsutani: Mouthbrush: Drawing and Painting by Hand and Mouth. Proceedings, ACM ICMI-PUI. (2003) pp. 277–280
3. Michael J. Lyons, Chi-ho Chan, Nobuji Tetsutani: MouthType: Text Entry by Hand and Mouth. Proceedings, ACM CHI'04. (2004) pp. 1383-1386.

Unsupervised Image Segmentation with Fuzzy Connectedness

Yuanjie Zheng, Jie Yang, and Yue Zhou

Institute of Image Processing & Pattern Recognition
Shanghai Jiaotong University, Shanghai, 200030, China
yuanjiezheng@yahoo.com.cn, {jieyang,zhouyue}@sjtu.edu.cn

Abstract. In this paper, we report a method to do unsupervised image segmentations based on fuzzy connectedness with scale space theory. A new measure for doing segmented regions' mergence is also proposed. The method can be used in many applications like content based image retrieval and medical image analysis, etc.

1 Introduction

Image segmentation, also referred to recognize objects in an image in some cases, is a difficult problem. Unsupervised segmentation of image is even more like a nettlesome one. However, unsupervised segmentation often plays an important role in some applications like in content based image retrieval, etc.

In this paper, we report our method to do unsupervised segmentation, which unifies the two advantages of fuzzy connectedness [1] and scale space theory [2], i.e. addressing the graded composition of intensity values and hanging togetherness of image elements in object regions and accessing unsupervisedly the underlying structures of an image respectively.

2 Seeds Specification, Regions' Extraction and Their Mergence

We first utilize the approach in [2] to access the underlying structures of an image with Gaussian filtering and zero crossing. Pixels whose features vector locates near enough to the reference features of one cluster are labelled as the corresponding candidate seeds. All the connected components, in each of which elements are all seeds and have the same label, are, if their areas exceed a threshold, candidate seed regions. For a candidate seed region, we use the element which locates nearest to the centroid of the region area as the corresponding seed element.

Then each seed is considered as belonging to a different part of object. Segmented region of each seed is acquired by the iterative relative fuzzy objects extraction method in [1]. The number of segmented regions equalizes to the one of seeds. Then we construct a measure between any two segmented regions to determine the degree of their belonging to a same object, and some of the segmented regions are merged because they look more like belonging to a same object according to the measure values. The measure is defined as bellows.

Definition: For two seeds s_1 and s_2, $s_1 \neq s_2$ whose segmented regions are adjacent, for a given affinity k, if a,b are any two corresponding adjacent elements of the regions respectively, we define the *adherent strength* of s_1 and s_2 through a,b as $AS(s_1,s_2;a,b) = \min(\mu_{K_{s_1}}(a), \mu_{K_{s_2}}(b), \mu_{\kappa}(a,b))$, where $\mu_{K_{s_1}}$, $\mu_{K_{s_2}}$ refer to iterative relative fuzzy connectedness values. The measure *adherent strength* of s_1 and s_2 is defined as the maximum value of $AS(s_1,s_2;a,b)$ in all the corresponding adjacent elements, and denoted by $AS(s_1,s_2)$. If $s_1 = s_2$, we set $AS(s_1,s_2) = 1$, and there is no meaning for $AS(s_1,s_2;a,b)$.

Based on some of our theoretical conclusions (here we abbreviate them and their proofs for economy), the measure *adherent strength* is proven to be reasonable to do mergence.

3 Experiments Results

Figure 1 shows the segmented results on a slice of simulated MR brain image. Through experiments on a large amount of simulated and real MR images and color images, we find that our methods can provide more precise segmentation results compared with many of other methods.

This research is supported by China National Science Foundation, No: 30170274.

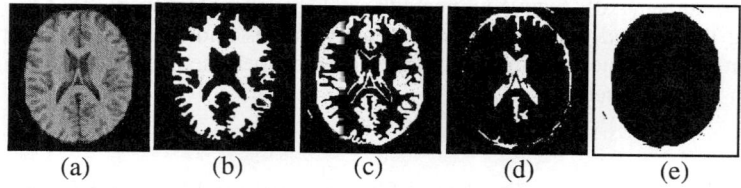

(a) (b) (c) (d) (e)

Fig. 1. (a) The original slice simulated brain image. (b)~(e) show the segmented results of white matter, gray matter, cerebrospinal fluid and background respectively

References

1. Saha, P.K., Udupa, J.K.: Iterative relative fuzzy connectedness and object definition: Theory, algorithms, and application in image segmentation. Proceedings of IEEE Workshop on Mathematical Methods in Biomedical Image Analysis. Hilton Head (2000) 28-35
2. Tang, M., Ma, S., General scheme of region competition based on scale space. IEEE Trans. PAMI. 23 (2001) 1366-1378.

Personalized Image Recommendation in the Mobile Internet

Yoon Ho Cho[1], Chan Young Kim[2], and Deok Hwan Kim[2,*]

[1] School of e-Business, Kookmin University
861-1 Jungnung, Sungbuk, Seoul, 136-702, Korea
www4u@kookmin.ac.kr
[2] School of Computer & information, Dongyang Technical College
62-160 Kochuk, Kuro, Seoul, 152-714, Korea
{cykim,dhkim}@dongyang.ac.kr

1 Image Recommender System

As mobile Internet technology becomes more increasingly applicable, the mobile contents market, especially character image downloading for mobile phones, has recorded remarkable growth. In spite of this rapid growth, however, most of the customers experience inconvenience, lengthy search processes and frustration in searching for the specific character images they want due to inefficient sequential search. This article describes a personalized image recommender system designed to reduce customers' search efforts in finding desired character images on the mobile Internet. The system combines two of the most popular information filtering techniques: Collaborative Filtering [1] and Content-Based Image Retrieval [2].

Two agents, CF and CBIR, collaborate and interact each other to support a customer in finding a desired image by generating personalized recommendations of character images. The CF agent generates a list of recommended images and provides an initial image to the CBIR agent. This agent creates the customer profile using purchase and preference information to identify neighbors and generate recommendations. When the CF-generated recommendation list is presented as shown in (a) of Fig. 1, a customer skims through the list to see if there are any images of interest. Then, the customer selects an entry to view the image, as shown in (b) of Fig. 1. After viewing, the customer may decide to purchase the image or decide whether to use the image as a query for CBIR-based search of similar images or to go back to the CF-generated recommendation list.

When the customer decides to use the viewed image as a starting query for further search, the viewed image is passed to the CBIR agent as an initial query, and the agent retrieves images based on similarity between the query and other images in the database. For all images in the database, this agent calculates the distances from the query and generates a list of k most similar images as recommendations. It then presents the retrieved k images to the customer one by one, as shown in (c) of Fig. 1, and interactively elicits the user's preference

---

* This work was supported by the Post-doctoral Fellowship Program of Korea Science & Engineering Foundation (KOSEF)

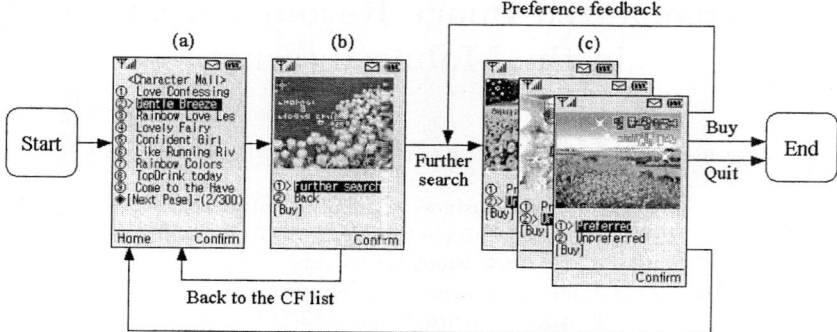

Fig. 1. System overview

judgment on the presented images. At any point in this presentation session, the customer may decide to buy an image or decide to quit. After all of k preference judgment are made, the CBIR agent updates the preference information and purchase databases with all the fed back preference and/or purchase information respectively for later use by the CF agent when the customer revisits the site. If all of k images are marked as unpreferred, the search session returns to the CF-generated recommendation list. Otherwise, this agent learns the customer's current preference using the preferred set, applies the result of learning in query refinement and distance function renewal, and uses the refined query and the updated distance function for the next iteration of retrieval.

2 Conclusion

The image recommender system described here offers the following benefits to both consumers and suppliers of mobile contents: (1) Customers can purchase contents with much less search effort and much lower connection time to the mobile Internet, because they can much more easily find desired mobile contents. (2) Mobile contents providers can improve the profitability of their business because lower customer frustration in finding desired contents increases revenue through an improved purchase conversion rate.

References

1. Y.H. Cho, J.K. Kim: Application of Web Usage Mining and Product Taxonomy to Collaborative Recommendations in E-Commerce. Expert Systems with Applications. **26** (2) 2004 233–246
2. D.H. Kim, C.W. Chung: Qcluster: Relevance Feedback Using Adaptive Clustering for Content-Based Image Retrieval. Proc. ACM SIGMOD International Conference. 2003 599–610

Clustering IP Addresses Using Longest Prefix Matching and Nearest Neighbor Algorithms

Asim Karim, Syed Imran Jami, Irfan Ahmad, Mansoor Sarwar, and Zartash Uzmi

Dept. of Computer Science
Lahore University of Management Sciences
Opposite Sector U, DHA, Lahore, 54792, Pakistan
akarim@lums.edu.pk

Abstract. This paper summarizes a new algorithm for clustering IP addresses. Unlike popular clustering algorithms such as k-means and DBSCAN, this algorithm is designed specifically for IP addresses. In particular, the algorithm employs the longest prefix match as a similarity metric and uses an adaptation of the nearest neighbor algorithm for search to yield meaningful clusters. The algorithm is automatic in that it does not require any input parameters. When applied to a large IP address dataset, the algorithm produced 90% correct clusters. Correct cluster analysis is essential for many network design and management tasks including design of web caches and server replications.

1 Background

Clustering is a key task in the discovery of useful patterns in large datasets. Clustering algorithms divide the data objects in the dataset into disjoint sets such that the objects within a set are more similar than to the objects in other sets. Over the years, many clustering algorithms have been developed employing various similarity metrics and search heuristics [1]. In general, these algorithms are general-purpose data clustering techniques that rely on domain-independent similarity metrics and search heuristics.

Internet protocol (IP) addresses are universally used for computer network communication today. The analysis of IP addresses contained within network traffic flows can yield useful patterns for traffic engineering such as the design of web caches and server replications. Clustering is an attractive technique for segmenting network traffic flows based on IP addresses. However, popular clustering algorithms such as k-means, k-medoids, and DBSCAN [1] do not produce meaningful clusters when applied to IP addresses [2].

2 Our Algorithm

We have developed a new algorithm for clustering large IP address datasets that uses the longest prefix match as the similarity metric and an adaptation of the nearest neighbor heuristic for clustering. This is a domain-specific algorithm that takes into consideration the unique characteristics of IP addresses. An IP address can be represented by a 32-bit-long string. The longest prefix match between two IP addresses is the largest number of prefix bits that are identical in the two addresses [3]. This concept is used to determine similarity between IP addresses; the larger the longest prefix match the greater the similarity and likelihood that the addresses belong to the same network domain [2].

The nearest neighbor clustering algorithm merges a data object into the existing cluster to which it is the most similar provided the similarity is greater than a pre-specified threshold value; otherwise, it is created as a new cluster [1]. Our algorithm adapts the nearest neighbor algorithm by using the longest prefix match as the similarity metric and eliminating the need for a threshold value to be pre-specified.

The new algorithm for clustering IP addresses is summarized next. First, the longest prefix match among the IP addresses in the dataset is calculated and stored in an adjacency matrix. Then, each IP address is considered in turn and its cluster is created with all IP addresses with which it has the largest longest prefix match. In other words, the nearest neighbor concept is applied. However, unlike in the original nearest neighbor algorithm, a new cluster is created for every IP address with the IP addresses with which it has the largest longest prefix match. As such, IP addresses may be relocated from one cluster to another whenever their longest prefix match is greater with another IP address. In this way, clusters are modified iteratively as each IP address is considered based on the longest prefix match, a natural measure of similarity for IP addresses. Notice that our algorithm does not require the input of a threshold value for the similarity, as required in the original nearest neighbor algorithm. This makes the algorithm automatic.

3 Results

The algorithm is tested on a dataset containing 10,525 distinct IP addresses. The clustering results are verified by using domain name lookup (nslookup) utilities [4]. It is found that about 90% of the clusters formed by the algorithm are valid clusters representing natural groups of IP addresses. In other words, the algorithm is able to find clusters of IP addresses belonging to the same network domain in almost all cases.

References

1. Maragaret H. Dunham, "Data Mining: Introductory and Advanced Topics", Pearson Education, 2003
2. Balachander Krishnamurthy, Jia Wang, "On Network-Aware Clustering of Web Clients", ACM SIGCOMM '00, Stockholm, Sweden, 2000
3. Marcel Waldvogel, "Fast Longest Prefix Matching: Algorithms, Analysis, and Applications", Swiss Federal Institute of Technology, Zurich,
  http://marcel.wanda.ch/Publications/waldvogel00fast.pdf
4. NS lookup Utility, http://ws.arin.net/cgi-bin/whois.pl

A Fuzzy Clustering Algorithm for Analysis of Gene Expression Profiles[*]

Han-Saem Park, Si-Ho Yoo, and Sung-Bae Cho

Dept. of Computer Science, Yonsei University
134 Shinchon-dong, Sudaemoon-ku, Seoul 120-749, Korea

Abstract. Advancement of DNA microarray technology has made it possible to get a great deal of biological information by a single experiment. Clustering algorithm is to group genes and reveal their functions or analyze unknown genes, which is categorized into hard and fuzzy clustering. For analyzing DNA microarray, fuzzy clustering can be better since genes can have several genetic information. In this paper, we present the GG (Gath-Geva) algorithm, which is one fuzzy clustering method, for clustering gene expression data. The GG algorithm is an improved version of the fuzzy c-means and GK (Gustafson-Kessel) algorithms and is appropriate for clustering gene expression data that have high dimension and ambiguous distribution. We have clustered serum and yeast data by the GG algorithm and compared it with the fuzzy c-means and GK algorithms. Through these experiments, we confirm that the GG algorithm is better for clustering gene expression data than other two algorithms.

1 Gath-Geva Fuzzy Clustering Method

Even though there are several fuzzy clustering algorithms and many researchers have applied them to gene expression data, most of them use the fuzzy c-means algorithm [1]. The fuzzy c-means algorithm is representative and the most frequently used fuzzy clustering algorithm, but it has limit that clusters are of spherical shapes with uniform density. The GK algorithm and the GG algorithm are proposed to remedy this restriction. Using the GK algorithm, instead of only spherical clusters, elliptical ones can also be recognized, and the GG algorithm, which is an extension of the GK algorithm, considers the size and density of the clusters as follows [2].

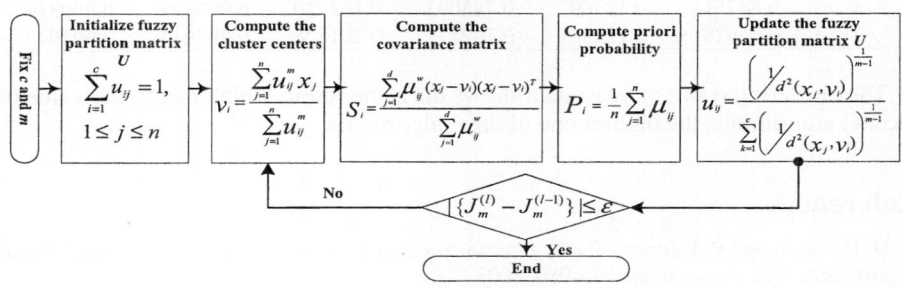

---

[*] This work was supported by the Korea Science and Engineering Foundation (KOSEF) through the Biometrics Engineering Research Center (BERC) at Yonsei University.

Here, μ_{ij} is the membership degree of x_j in the ith cluster, an element of the membership matrix $U = [\mu_{ij}]$, and m is the fuzziness parameter, which means the level of fuzziness of each datum's membership degree and should be bigger than 1.0. J_m is the objective function that is for terminal condition.

Because the GG algorithm considers many conditions, it is appropriate for clustering gene expression data. It also has the strength that is able to find the overlapped clusters and is less influenced by noisy data. For this reason, it is better to cluster the data with an ambiguous and complex distribution than the fuzzy c-means and GK algorithms. Besides, it can be a reason that the microarray chip, which is the source of gene expression data, has much noise that leads experiments wrong way although it is a useful device.

2 Experimental Results

We have used serum and yeast data for experiments. Serum data have 421 genes and 17 attributes, and yeast data have 517 genes and 19 attributes. After clustering serum and yeast data using the fuzzy c-means, GK, and GG algorithms, we compare them in terms of the *PC* and *CE* values that are cluster validity measures to evaluate the clustering result as compactness of clusters. In experiments, we have fixed fuzziness parameter value as 1.2 [1], and terminal condition value as 0.0000001.

Table 1 shows *PC* and *CE* values of the results of serum data when the number of clusters changes from 2 to 7. Cluster # means the number of clusters. The closer the *PC* value is to one (or the *CE* value to zero), the better clusters are formed. Here, it can be confirmed that the value of the GG algorithm is much higher than those of the fuzzy c-means and GG algorithms.

Table 1. Clustering results of serum data

	Fuzzy c-means		GK		GG	
Cluster #	PC	CE	PC	CE	PC	CE
2	0.941050	0.445610	0.957834	0.033238	0.999547	0.000345
3	0.922499	0.060756	0.847608	0.107245	0.999854	0.000097
4	0.872628	0.100212	0.798629	0.164987	0.999114	0.000793
5	0.833843	0.134836	0.779208	0.177488	0.989824	0.007438
6	0.847554	0.123697	0.782093	0.183229	0.999599	0.000319
7	0.846281	0.125561	0.762771	0.201828	0.997044	0.001043

The clustering result of yeast data shows the same result, which means the value of the GG algorithm is the highest one of three algorithms.

References

1. D. Dembele and P. Kastner, "Fuzzy c-means method for clustering microarray data," *Bioinformatics*, vol. 19, no. 8, pp. 973-980, 2003.
2. F. Hoppner, F. Klawonn, R. Kruse, and T. Runkler, *Fuzzy Cluster Analysis*, Wiley, pp. 43-39, 1999.

Evaluation of a Boosted Cascade of Haar-Like Features in the Presence of Partial Occlusions and Shadows for Real Time Face Detection

Andre L.C. Barczak

Massey University, Institute of Information and Mathematical Sciences
Albany Campus Private bag 102 904
North Shore Mail Centre, Auckland, New Zealand
a.l.barczak@massey.ac.nz
http://www.massey.ac.nz

Abstract. This paper presents further evaluation of the rapid object detection scheme developed by Viola and Jones and later extended by Lienhart et al. In this work the hypothesis that it is possible to train a classifier to find partially occluded objects was tested experimentally.

1 Introduction

Viola and Jones [1] developed an object detection method that calculates features very rapidly and uses Adaboost to train a cascade of classifiers. Their method was later extended by Lienhardt et al. [2].

This paper uses the same methods via the OpenCV [3] implementation to evaluate partially occluded object detection. The hypothesis was that it is possible to improve the classifier's hit rate in the presence of partial occlusions by training the classifier with random occluded examples.

experiment 1976 images of a person were acquired by a web camera and parts of the background were used to occlude the face. These images were used to train *Classifier 1*. The second experiment used 4767 FERET frontal faces with no occlusion to train *Classifier 2*. On the third experiment 1938 of the FERET frontal images were partially occluded with random pixels instead of background pixels. Each image was filled by either 12x12 or by 12x24 occlusion patches. The initial set of 1938 images composed a total of 13566 positive examples used to train *Classifier 3*. Figure 1 shows an example of an occluded face.

2 Experimental Results

The sample classifier provided with OpenCV library works very well for free frontal faces, but it is often unable to detect faces that present partial occlusion and strong shadows. Hit rates were measured for the image sequence *Akiyo*, detecting faces frame by frame. Other three sets were created using a web camera and acquiring images of a single person. Each sequence of frames had different percentages of partial occlusions. The results for each classifier are shown in table 1.

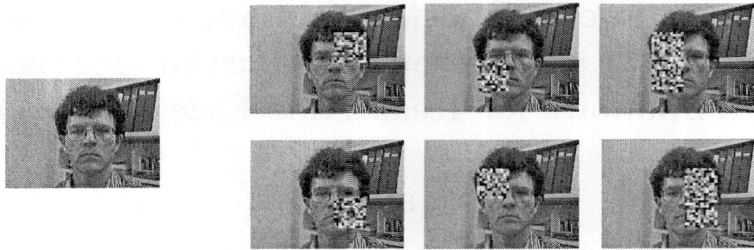

Fig. 1. The occlusion process creates 6 additional positive examples for each frontal face. This image does not belong to the FERET database.

Table 1. Hit ratios (%) for the sets of images using different classifiers.

	OpenCV Classifier	Class. 1	Class. 2	Class. 3
Akiyo (90 frames, 0% occl.)	100.0	0	46.6	97.7
Set 1 (92 frames, 73% occl.)	61.9	65.2	53.3	67.4
Set 2 (94 frames, 88% occl.)	59.6	47.8	42.6	78.7
Set 3 (91 frames, 91% occl.)	49.5	18.7	37.4	75.8

3 Conclusions, Future Work and Acknowledgements

The Viola and Jones classifier can be robust to partial occlusions and shadow effects. The problem of getting good training sets was minimized using randomly generated patches to cover parts of the positive examples.

A systematic study using objects other than faces would provide more substance to the claim that these methods are fairly generic for object detection.

Portions of the research in this paper used the *Color FERET* database of facial images collected under the *FERET* program. The author would like to thank Dr. Chris Messom and Dr. Martin Jonhson for their valuable suggestions.

References

1. Viola, P. and Jones, M., "Rapid Object Detection using a Boosted Cascade of Simple Features", *Proceedings IEEE Conf. on Comp. Vision and Patt. Recog.*, 2001.
2. Lienhart, R. and Maydt, J., "An Extended Set of Haar-like Features for Rapid Object Detection", *Proceedings of the ICIP2002*, 2002.
3. http://www.intel.com/research/mrl/research/opencv/
4. Phillips, P. J., Moon, H., Rizvi, S. A. and Rauss, P. J., "The FERET Evaluation Methodology for Face Recognition Algorithms", *IEEE Trans. Pat. Analys. and Mach. Intell.*, Vol. 22, pp. 1090-1104, October 2000.

Classifying Human Actions Using an Incomplete Real-Time Pose Skeleton

Patrick Peursum[1], Hung H. Bui[2], Svetha Venkatesh[1], and Geoff West[1]

[1] Dept of Computing, Curtin University of Technology, Perth, Western Australia
{peursump,svetha,geoff}@cs.curtin.edu.au
[2] Artificial Intelligence Center, SRI International, 333 Ravenswood Ave, Menlo Park, CA
bui@ai.sri.com

Abstract. Currently, most human action recognition systems are trained with feature sets that have no missing data. Unfortunately, the use of human pose estimation models to provide more descriptive features also entails an increased sensitivity to occlusions, meaning that incomplete feature information will be unavoidable for realistic scenarios. To address this, our approach is to shift the responsibility for dealing with occluded pose data away from the pose estimator and onto the action classifier. This allows the use of a simple, real-time pose estimation (stick-figure) that does not estimate the positions of limbs it cannot find quickly. The system tracks people via background subtraction and extracts the (possibly incomplete) pose skeleton from their silhouette. Hidden Markov Models modified to handle missing data are then used to successfully classify several human actions using the incomplete pose features.

1 Introduction

Human motion/action recognition has been an active field for many years, with various methods of obtaining features for the classifier to work on. Most action recognition research has so far concentrated on classification using simple, always-observed features such as trajectory, bounding boxes or flesh-coloured areas [1–3]. However, this paper argues that as more complex motions are modelled, incomplete information due to occlusions is an unavoidable fact in real-world situations – although self-occlusions can be handled by fully-articulated human body models, occlusions by scene objects cannot. To address the problem of occlusions, this paper proposes that the action classifier must handle the incomplete pose via missing data in the observation vector. The Hidden Markov Model (HMM) was chosen as the basis for an action recognition system since it has proven successful in modelling human motion and can also be modified to allow for missing data in both training and classification. This allows the use of a simple, fast pose estimation via the "star" skeletonisation (stick figure) proposed in [4] and extended to fuse multiple views into 3D. See [5] for a more detailed description of this research.

2 Methodology

The Expectation-Maximisation (EM) algorithm for HMMs was modified to allow for missing data in the observation vector [5]. Six different actions were then performed in an indoor laboratory monitored by four cameras (one in each corner). The six actions

Table 1. Confusion matrix for classification of actions from 5-fold cross-validation

	Drink	Read	Type	Walk	Sit Down	Stand Up
True Positives	90	55	40	50	50	50
False Positives	5	1	0	0	0	0
Recall	98.9%	91.7%	100%	100%	100%	100%
Precision	94.7%	98.2%	100%	100%	100%	100%

are walking, sitting into a chair, standing up from a chair, typing, reading and drinking. Pose estimation is produced via "star" skeletonisation [4] modified for this research to fuse multiple views into a 3D skeleton [5]. The skeleton does not attempt to estimate the position of limbs which it cannot directly detect, thus producing missing data for those undetected limbs that the recognition system must deal with in both training and testing. Features extracted are: horizontal speed, height, torso length, torso angle, leg lengths, angle between the legs, arm lengths and angles between the arms and the torso.

3 Results

Classification accuracy is quite high (see Table 1), with the only failures resulting from confusion between the drinking and reading actions. This is because *Drinking* and *Reading* differ only slightly – *Drinking* involves bringing an object (cup) to the actor's mouth whereas *Reading* involves bringing an object (book) to the actor's body. Analysis of the skeleton reveals that these results are produced from a skeleton that is missing approximately 25% of its pose data (on average) due to undetected arms (42% of the time) and legs (26% of the time). Other features are always observed. Although this seems to be a high tolerance of missing data, only a few movements are important in each action and these are often fairly prominent (eg: reaching out an arm).

4 Conclusions

It has been shown that incomplete pose information is no barrier to limb-level human action recognition. Even under conditions where a significant amount of pose information is missing (25%), the action recognition system is able to compensate and classify actions highly accurately. Thus using missing data to shift the responsibility of handling occlusions onto the action classifier is a natural and effective solution to the problem of occlusion in real-world situations.

References

1. Chowdhury, A.K.R., Chellappa, R.: A factorization approach for activity recognition. In: IEEE Computer Vision and Pattern Recognition. (2003)
2. Peursum, P., Venkatesh, S., West, G., Bui, H.H.: Object labelling from human action recognition. In: IEEE Intl Conf. on Pervasive Computing and Communications. (2003) 399–406
3. Moore, D.J., Essa, I.A., Hayes, M.H.: Exploiting human actions and object context for recognition tasks. In: IEEE Intl Conf. on Computer Vision. Volume 1. (1999) 80–86
4. Fujiyoshi, H., Lipton, A.: Real-time human motion analysis by image skeletonization. In: Workshop on Application of Computer Vision. (1999)
5. Peursum, P., Bui, H.H., Venkatesh, S., West, G.: Technical report 2004/01: Human action recognition with an incomplete real-time pose skeleton. Technical report, Curtin University of Technology, WA Australia (2004) http://impca.cs.curtin.edu.au/publications/techreports.html.

Multiclass Support Vector Machines Using Balanced Dichotomization

Boonserm Kijsirikul, Narong Boonsirisumpun, and Yachai Limpiyakorn

Department of Computer Engineering, Chulalongkorn University, Thailand
{Boonserm.K,Yachai.L}@chula.ac.th
Narong.Bo@student.chula.ac.th

The Support Vector Machine (SVM) has been introduced as a technique for solving a variety of learning and function estimation problems. The technique was originally designed for binary classification learning with its outstanding performance. However, many real world applications involve multiclass classification. Typical SVM solutions to N-class problems are to construct and combine several two-class classifiers into an N-class classifier such as the one-against-the-rest approach (1-v-r) and the one-against-one approach (1-v-1). The one-against-one methods solve $N(N-1)/2$ binary classifiers where each one is trained on data from two classes. There are different methods for the evaluation of the correct class after all $N(N-1)/2$ classifiers have been constructed. The Max Wins method takes the majority vote of a certain class as the final output [3]. A drawback of the 1-v-1 SVMs is their inefficiency of classifying data as the number of SVMs grows superlinearly with the number of classes. To improve the efficiency in classifying data, Platt et al. [5] proposed the Decision Directed Acyclic Graph (DDAG) with $N(N-1)/2$ internal nodes and N leaves. Only $N-1$ decision nodes will be evaluated in order to derive an answer, that is lower than $N(N-1)/2$ decisions required by Max Wins. To reduce the unnecessarily high number of node evaluations for the correct class, Kijsirikul, et al. [4] proposed the Adaptive Directed Acyclic Graph (ADAG) method, which is a modification of the DDAG. Like the DDAG, the ADAG requires $N-1$ decisions in order to derive an answer. However, using the reversed triangular structure reduces the number of evaluations the correct class is tested against other classes to $\lceil \log_2 N \rceil$ times or less, which is considerably lower than that of $N-1$ times required by the DDAG.

In this paper, we introduce a new method for constructing multiclass SVMs using binary classifiers, called *Balanced Dichotomization*. For an N-class problem, the system constructs $N(N-1)/2$ binary classifiers during its training phase like other one-against-one methods. Among those binary hyperplanes having been constructed, the system searches for the hyperplane at the most balanced position among all candidate classes, called *balanced dichotomization classifier* that separates the data classes into half-and-half on each side. Using a balanced dichotomization classifier can thus remove half of the candidate classes during each evaluation for the correct class, that is a higher number of elimination compared to other methods, such as the DDAG, the ADAG, which eliminate only one class using an ordinary binary classifier. As a result, the technique can optimally reduce the number of decisions in order to derive an answer to $\lceil \log_2 N \rceil$ times, rather than $N-1$ times in the DDAG and the ADAG.

The basic idea of the primary SVM classification is to find the optimal hyperplane separating the two classes of data as illustrated in Figure 2 (a). The hyperplane maximizes the margin between the data in class 1 and class 2. However, the hyperplane in Figure 2 (a) is not a balanced dichotomization classifier because when considering the positions of all candidate classes, it is not at the most balanced position as depicted in

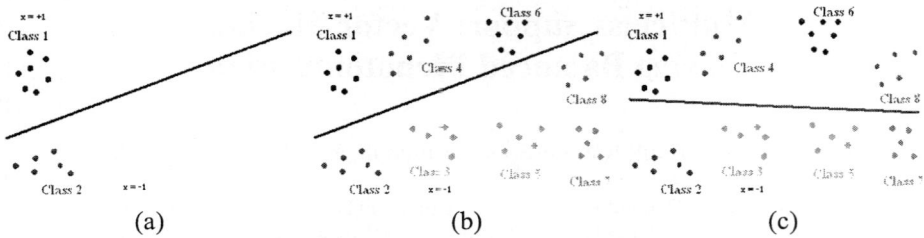

Fig. 2. (a) The optimal hyperplane for classes 1 and 2, (b) the hyperplane is not a balanced dichotomization classifier when considering other classes, and (c) an optimal balanced hyperplane.

Figure 2 (b). The hyperplane shown in Figure 2 (c) is an example of the balanced dichotomization hyperplane. It is posed at the optimal balanced position that separates candidate classes into half-and-half on each side.

Since Balanced Dichotomization requires considering positions of all candidate classes to arrive at a balanced hyperplane, there may be cases where a hyperplane in consideration is posed in between data of certain classes. To deal with these cases, two parameters are introduced in our approach, i.e. the optimal range of generalization error and the optimal pruning percentage. *Pruning percentage* is used as the threshold for the removal of data on either side of the hyperplane in consideration. The strategy of pruning is to achieve the balanced dichotomization that provides the minimum number of evaluations for the correct class while maintaining the accuracy within the range of generalization performance [1]. If the ratio between data of a class on one side and all data of the class is less than pruning percentage, the data on that side will be ignored. Moreover, using *the optimal range of generalization error*, only hyperplanes with the generalization error within the range will be considered.

We evaluate the performance of our method on several datasets from the UCI Repository of machine learning databases [2]: Glass, Satimage, Segment, Shuttle, Vowel, Soybean, Letter, and Isolet. The experimental results show that Balanced Dichotomization runs faster and maintains accuracy comparable to Max Wins and better than the ADAG and the DDAG methods.

References

1. Bartlett, P. L. and Shawe-Taylor, J. (1999) *Generalization performance of support vector machines and other pattern classifiers*, In B.Schölkopf, C. Burges, & A. Smola (Eds.), Advances in Kernel Methods – Support Vector Learning, pp. 43-54, MIT Press, USA.
2. Blake, C., Keogh, E., and Merz, C. (1998) *UCI Repository of Machine Learning Databases*, Department of Information and Computer Science, University of California, Irvine. http://www.ics.uci.edu/~mlearn/MLSummary.html
3. Friedman, J. H. (1996) *Another Approach to Polychotomous classification*, Technical report, Department of Statistics, Stanford University.
4. Kijsirikul, B., Ussivakul, N., and Meknavin, S. (2002) *Adaptive Directed Acyclic Graphs for Multiclass Classification*, The Seventh Pacific Rim International Conference on Artificial Intelligence.
5. Platt, J., Cristianini, N. and Shawe-Taylor, J. (2000) *Large Margin DAGs for Multiclass Classification*, Advances in Neural Information Processing Systems, MIT Press, 12, 547-553.

Time Series Pattern Discovery by Segmental Gaussian Models

Imahara Shuichiro, Sato Makoto, and Nakase Akihiko

Toshiba Corporation
1 Komukai Toshiba-Cho, Saiwai-Ku, Kawasaki, Kanagawa, Japan
Tel: +81-44-549-2235
{shoe16,satom,nakase}@isl.rdc.toshiba.co.jp

As a result of diversification of sensor data due to advances in sensing technology in recent years, large amounts of multidimensional sensor data are stored in various areas such as plants and social systems. It is difficult to take the first step in time series analysis to visualize such sensor data in its entirety. Reflecting the increasing need to analyze data whose features are not clearly understood, the time series analysis method using the features of an economic time series (e.g., ARMA) cannot necessarily be applied. Therefore, methods for analyzing time series data without assuming features of the data are of great interest. The method for extracting features of time series data without assuming features of the data is a time series pattern discovery method [3]. A time series pattern discovery method is used to find the waveforms automatically as time series patterns that arise frequently from time series data.

Since time series data rarely contains identical waveforms, it is necessary to make some allowances in the time and height directions in the matching waveforms. The use of Deformable Markov Models is one solution [1]. In this method, the time series patterns correspond to probability models on a one-to-one basis. This method spoils the detailed forms of the waveforms and is a pattern matching method, but not a pattern discovery method. In this paper, we propose probability models named Segmental Gaussian Models (SGMs) that are based on Deformable Markov Models and a time series pattern discovery method that uses these models as time series patterns.

In the algorithm of the time series pattern discovery method using SGMs, time series data are divided into segments (by a segmentation method as in [2]) and SGMs are first created from all of the L-successive segments. The likelihood function of SGMs to the L-successive segment $Q(S, Y)$ consists of scale $p_{s_i}(s_i)$ and form $p_{y_i}(y_i|s_i)$ probabilities. In the form probability, the waveform is normalized. Normalization eliminates the influence of scale from the form and equalizes the dimensions of the original waveform y_i and the average vector μ_{y_i}. Both of these vectors are compared in terms of Euclidean distance.

$$Q(S,Y) = \prod_{i=1}^{L} p_{s_i}(s_i) p_{y_i}(y_i|s_i)$$

$$p_{s_i}(s_i) = (2\pi)^{-\frac{d_s}{2}} |\Sigma_{s_i}|^{-\frac{1}{2}} \exp(-\frac{1}{2}(s_i - \mu_{s_i})^T \Sigma_{s_i}^{-1}(s_i - \mu_{s_i}))$$

$$p_{y_i}(y_i|s_i) = (2\pi\sigma_{y_i}^2)^{-\frac{d_y}{2}} \exp(-\frac{1}{2\sigma_{y_i}^2}(f(y_i,s_i) - \mu_{y_i})^T(f(y_i,s_i) - \mu_{y_i}))$$

In the second step of the algorithm, the likelihood between models is calculated and the model pair whose likelihood is the maximum of all pairs is merged. Since likelihood is calculated by assigning a value to a likelihood function, the likelihood between a model pair cannot be determined simply. It is therefore approximated by the average of likelihoods calculated by assigning the original waveforms making up model j to a likelihood function of model i. Since there are two types of pair likelihoods, let the smaller one serve as the representative value from the pair likelihood. The maximum likelihood pair is merged by the following update equation.

$$\alpha = \frac{n_1}{n_1 + n_2}, \quad \beta = \frac{n_2}{n_1 + n_2}, \quad \mu_s = \alpha \mu_{s_1} + \beta \mu_{s_2}, \quad \mu_y = \alpha \mu_{y_1} + \beta \mu_{y_2}$$
$$\Sigma_s = \alpha(\Sigma_{s_1} + (\mu_s - \mu_{s_1})(\mu_s - \mu_{s_1})^T) + \beta(\Sigma_{s_2} + (\mu_s - \mu_{s_2})(\mu_s - \mu_{s_2})^T)$$
$$\sigma_y^2 = \alpha(\sigma_{y_1}^2 + \frac{1}{d_y}(\mu_y - \mu_{y_1})^T(\mu_y - \mu_{y_1})) + \beta(\sigma_{y_2}^2 + \frac{1}{d_y}(\mu_y - \mu_{y_2})^T(\mu_y - \mu_{y_2}))$$

In the framework of bottom-up clustering, these calculations and merge steps are repeated. After several iterations, the obtained models are time series patterns. Since a large amount of time is needed for visualization when many patterns are obtained, only 10 high-order-frequency patterns may be output, for example.

The effectiveness of the proposed method has been confirmed using acceleration data from a wristwatch-type sensor. This method was compared with bottom-up clustering in which similarity is the Euclidean distance and the pattern length is fixed. Fig.1 shows that the time series patterns discovered by this method are obtained from waveforms with lower variance than in the method that uses the Euclidean distance. For this reason, the representation patterns of the comparative method (bold line) have slow forms.

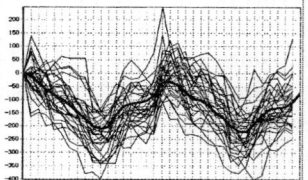
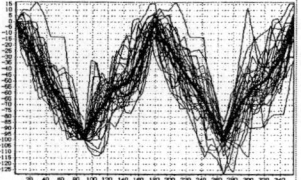

Fig. 1. left: Euclidean distance, right: proposed method.

References

1. X. Ge and P. Smyth: Deformable Markov model templates for time-series pattern matching. *Proc. KDD 2000*, pp.81-90, 2000.
2. E. Keogh and P. Smyth: A probabilistic approach to fast pattern matching in time series databases. *Proc. KDD'97*, pp 24-30, 1997.
3. G. Das, K. Lin, H. Mannila, G. Renganathan, and P. Smyth: Rule discovery from time series. *Proc. KDD'98*, pp.16-22, 1998.

A Model for Identifying the Underlying Logical Structure of Natural Language

Vasile Rus and Alex Fit-Florea

Indiana University, South Bend, IN 46634, USA
vasile@cs.iusb.edu
Southern Methodist University, Dallas, TX 75205, USA
alex@engr.smu.edu

Abstract. This paper introduces a model for identifying the underlying logical arguments, such as logical subject, of predicates, namely verbs, in sentences. The model's features are selected based on lexico-syntactic and shallow semantic principles. Reported results are promising.

To overcome the drawback of modern parsing technology to identify the underlying logical structure of English sentences, novel methods are necessary that offer accurate, robust and scalable solutions to the problem of finding syntactic functional information. In this work a model is introduced which is then used to induce automated tools able to detect functional information (logical) in English sentences. The tools are obtained using the C4.5 package for decision tree induction.

1 Related Work

Our approach is similar to approaches that address the problem of shallow semantic parsing - the process of annotating texts with semantic roles specified either using predicate specific labels (FrameNet project) or predicate independent labels (Propbank project). They address the problem of shallow semantic parsing as a classification problem using a diversified pool of formalisms to induce a classifier (Support Vector Machines, Decision Trees) and sets of features (the sets used by different approaches have many features in common). Our work is similar to those approaches in many ways: (1) we address the task of detecting logic roles (as opposed to semantic roles) as a classification problem (2) we use a set of features similar, at some extent, to those used by the mentioned studies (3) the induced classifier plays an important role in a natural language based knowledge representation [1],[2].

2 The Model

The basic approach is to address the argument identification task as a classification problem: given a verb in a sentence and a candidate phrasal head find the most appropriate syntactic role the head plays. The set of possible roles contains: subject, direct object, indirect object, prepositional object or norole (a value which indicates that the candidate head does not play any role for the given verb). To preview our results, we demonstrate that combining a set of indicators automatically extracted from large text corpora provide good performance.

The key to any automatic classification task is to determine a set of useful features for discriminating the items to be classified. Observing the patterns of logic syntactic roles for verbs we derived a set of features for our classification task including: head word of candidate phrase for a syntactic role, the verb, the type of sentence (S, SINV, etc.), the relative position of the two, and some others. Those features could be automatically extracted from large corpus, either manually annotated or automatically generated.

3 Experimental Setup

Previous work on verb meaning research, such as [1] reported experiments on a set of 14 target verbs that exhibit multiple argument patterns: {\it ask, begin, believe cause, expect, find, give, help, like, move, produce, provide, seem, swing}. We adopted those 14 verbs since we believed it would be a good starting point to have a small set, on one hand, with many argument ambiguities, on the other hand, thus balancing challenges with manageability of the experiments.

Next, we looked for a corpus. Treebank is a good candidate since it contains limited role annotations. We started by developing patterns for tgrep, a tree retrieval pattern-based tool, to identify sentences containing target verbs from Wall Street Journal (WSJ) corpus (the version with part-of-speech tags) and used the online form to retrieve the data. The training set is further processed: a stemmer is applied to obtain the stem of individual words and then the target verb is identified and the features extracted. One or more training examples (positive and negative) are generated from a sentence. As learning paradigm we opted for decision trees.

We did two major experiments: (1) using our set of features as a standard model and (2) use the dependency feature as a filter instead of being part of the model. The models presented yield high performance, especially the model with the extended feature. They can form reliable components in larger text understanding systems such as logic form idenfication, automated textual inference engines, text interpretation and question answering.

References

1. A. Korhonen and G. Gorrell and D. McCarthy, *Statistical filtering and subcategorization frame acquisition*, in Proceedings of the Joint SIGDAT Conference on Empirical Methods in Natural Language Processing and Very Large Corpora, Hong Kong
2. Rus, Vasile, *High Precision Logic Form Transformation*, Proceedings of the International Conference with Tools in Artificial Intelligence, 2001, Dallas, TX, November, IEEE Computer Society, IEEE Press

A Reputation-Based Trust Model for Agent Societies

Yuk-Hei Lam[1], Zili Zhang[1,2], and Kok-Leong Ong[1]

[1] School of Information Technology, Deakin University
Waurn Ponds, Victoria 3217, Australia
{yuk,zzhang,leong}@deakin.edu.au
[2] Faculty of Computer and Information Science
Southwest China Normal University
Chongqing 400715, China

1 Problem

Trust and security issues are prevalent in agent societies, where agents are autonomously owned and operated in a networked environment. Nowadays, trust and reputation management is a promising approach to manage them. However, many reputation models suffered from a major drawback – there is no mechanism to discourage agents from lying information when making a recommendation. Although some works do take into account of this issue, they usually do not penalize an agent for making poor referrals. Worse, some systems actually judge an agent's referral reputation based on its service reputation. In situations where this is unacceptable, we need to have a mechanism where agents are not only discouraged from making poor referrals, but are also penalized when doing so. Towards this, we propose a reputation-based trust model that considers an agent's referral reputation as a separate entity within the broader sense of an agent's reputation. Our objective is not to replace any existing reputation mechanisms, but rather to complement and extend them.

2 Solution

Within our model, the broad-sense reputation for an agent is defined by considering its performance as a **provider** (i.e., providing service to another agent), and an **advisor** (i.e., making referrals). Hence, an agent is able to evaluate another agent along three dimensions: its overall reputation, its reputation as a service provider, and its referral reputation. As a result, an agent can now judge another agent's credibility in a fair and accurate manner.

To gauge the reputation of an agent, we introduce a quantitative measure called the **total net trust value**. This measure overcomes the shortcomings of averaging past performances or referrals by taking into account the experience of an agent in the past transactions. In particular, we penalize agents who make poor referrals by downgrading its broad-sense reputation, and the total net trust value of its reputations as an advisor. Moreover, it also discourage agents from making poor referrals.

To allow an agent questions about the trustworthiness of another agent, our proposed model also incorporates another measure called **Trust Degree**, which qualifies the amount of trust an agent has on another agent. The broad-sense reputation rating and the total net trust value are the main elements for calculating the trust degree of the target agent. It is because when an agent decides to initiate a new transaction, it needs to reconcile its knowledge with the global score before passing a judgement. In our model, a positive trust degree of the target agent concludes that the decision making agent considers the target agent as a trustworthy agent.

Consider an agent that sends a service request message to a service agent. The service agent will decide whether to provide the requested service based on a number of factors, in which one of them is trust. The service agent can query about the trustworthiness of the target agent by evaluating the total net trust value and the broad-sense reputation of the target agent. A positive net trust value indicates an agent has performed good transactions more that bad ones in the past. Conversely, a negative net trust value indicates that an agent has performed poor transactions more that good ones in the past. Finally, the service agent applies those values to calculate the trust degree of the target agent. Since the broad-sense reputation rating will always be positive and the total net trust value can be either positive or negative, the sign of the trust degree will reveal the trustworthiness of the target agent.

3 Results

Experiments have been carried out in order to verify the effectiveness and benefits of our proposed model. One of the experiment results shows that an agent, who always provide good services but poor referrals, will always have a chance to provide good services but not for making recommendations. This contrast approaches where agents are removed altogether (if they provide bad services or recommendation), or assumed to be good in referrals by the fact that is has a good service reputation. Thus, the largest benefit of our model is that we do not exclude the agent altogether because it does have its value in providing a service. Yet, we also prevented the agent from being malicious in its referral. From our initial simulation results, we believe we have evidence to support the feasibility and suitability of our proposal. More details of the paper can be obtained from [1].

References

1. Lam, Y., Zhang, Z., Ong, K.: A Reputation-based Trust Model for Agents Societies. Technical Report TRC04/04, School of Information Technology, Deakin University, http://www.deakin.edu.au/~yuk/TechReports/trustmodel04.pdf (2004)

A Model of Rhetorical Structure Analysis of Japanese Texts and Its Application to Intelligent Text Processing: A Case for a Smart Help System

Noriko Ito[1], Toru Sugimoto[1], Shino Iwashita[1], Ichiro Kobayashi[1,2], and Michio Sugeno[1]

[1] RIKEN Brain Science Institute 2-1 Hirosawa, Wako, Saitama 351-0198 Japan
{itoh,sugimoto,iwas,koba,msgn}@brain.riken.jp
[2] Faculty of Science, Ochanomizu University
2-1-1 Otsuka, Bunkyo-ku, Tokyo 112-8610 Japan

The purpose of this paper is to propose an algorithm of rhetorical structure analysis of Japanese instructional texts with special reference to wordprocessor help texts and ways of utilizing the rhetorical structure of the help texts in the course of providing the response to the user so that we can bring the computer closer to the people and make effective use of the existing resources.

In rhetorical structure theory (RST), the structure of a text is interpreted as a tree structure consisting of text segments tied together by various types of rhetorical relations. Rhetorical relations are often indicated by discourse markers, such as conjunctions. We adopt this in describing the semantic relations among the clauses and sentences in the help texts. We assume that a rhetorical structure is a tree whose nodes are called rhetorical units, and define text segments consisting of clauses or sentences as rhetorical units. A unit consists of a rhetorical relation type that is seen among the child rhetorical units, i.e., *sequence* and *solutionhood*, and a role that this unit is considered to play for the parent unit, i.e., Nucleus and Satellite, following RST. Fig. 1 shows a sample help text and the rhetorical structure drawn from the sample.

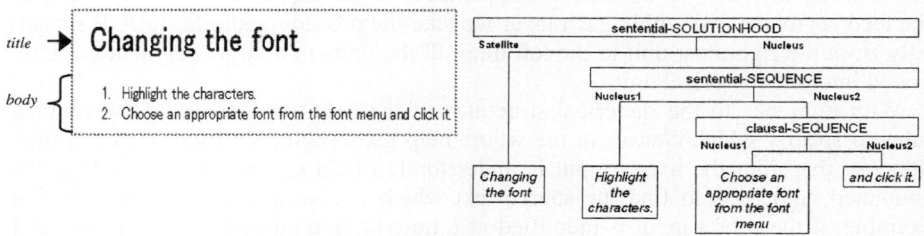

Fig. 1. Sample help text and its rhetorical structure

Fig. 2 shows the flow of the rhetorical structure analysis. Our model of the rhetorical structure analysis involves two tasks: (i) identification of the possible rhetorical relations between given adjacent rhetorical units and (ii) construction of the structure of these units. In the clausal rhetorical structure analysis, we construct a tree structure in which a leaf corresponds to a clause simplex and the root corresponds to a sentence.

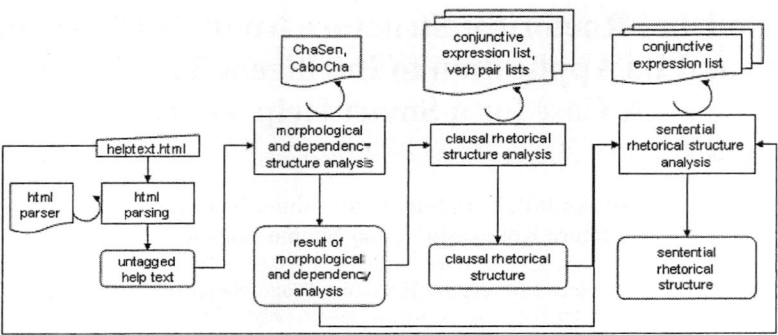

Fig. 2. Overview of the model of rhetorical structure analysis

Regarding identification of clausal rhetorical relations, we refer to information of the child units, e.g., conjunctive expressions and verbs.

As to construction of the structure of the clausal rhetorical units, we take the following procedure repeatedly from the rightmost clause to the left until all the clauses in a sentence are integrated into one rhetorical unit.

A. Construct a rhetorical unit whose right child is the rightmost clause or rhetorical unit, which is constructed just before, and left child is the clause or the rhetorical unit that is on the left to the rightmost one.
B. Identify the rhetorical relation of that unit by referring to the information of the child units mentioned above.

In the sentential rhetorical structure analysis, we construct a tree structure in which the leaf corresponds to a sentence and the root corresponds to the entire help text. By applying the method similar to the one for the clausal analysis, we can obtain the possible rhetorical relations between given adjacent rhetorical units.

As to construction of the structure of the sentential rhetorical units, we refer to the hierarchical structure of document that consists of help title/body, numbered lists, linefeed segments and within each layer we take the procedure similar to A-B repeatedly from the rightmost unit to the left until all the units in a target segment are integrated into one rhetorical unit.

With reference to the rhetorical structures of the help texts, we establish ranking rules to specify which clauses in the whole help texts should be tried to match first. Suppose that after the user's input is understood, a help system starts searching the annotated help texts to find the source text which is appropriate to the output. For example, if the user's input is identified as a how-to type question (e.g., "How can I center the characters?") as the result of the understanding process, the titles and the Satellite units of the *clausal-purpose* relation which represent (sub) goals will be processed first. If there is no match, the Nucleus units of the *clausal-means* which represent very specific (sub) goals will be processed.

The rhetorical structure can be used also to find unnecessary text segments and to decide the order of presentation to the user.

The model of the rhetorical structure analysis presented in this paper is applicable to 25 texts (118 sentences) extracted from "formatting text" section in the help texts accompanying Microsoft Word 2000.

Explicit State Duration HMM for Abnormality Detection in Sequences of Human Activity

Sebastian Lühr[1], Svetha Venkatesh[1], Geoff West[1], and Hung H. Bui[2]

[1] Department of Computing, Curtin University of Technology
GPO Box U1987, Perth, Western Australia
{luhrs,svetha,geoff}@cs.curtin.edu.au
[2] Artificial Intelligence Center, SRI International
333 Ravenswood Ave, Menlo Park, CA
bui@ai.sri.com

1 Introduction

Much of the current work in human behaviour modelling concentrates on activity recognition, recognising actions and events through pose, movement, and gesture analysis. Our work focuses on learning and detecting abnormality in higher level behavioural patterns. The hidden Markov model (HMM) is one approach for learning such behaviours given a vision tracker recording observations about a person's activity. Duration of human activity is an important consideration if we are to accurately model a person's behavioural patterns. We show how the implicit state duration in the HMM can create a situation in which highly abnormal deviation as either less than or more than the usually observed activity duration can fail to be detected and how the explicit state duration HMM (ESD-HMM) helps alleviate the problem.

2 Experimentation Methodology

We recorded 150 video sequences of normal behaviour in a kitchen scenario using a single camera, each recording belonging to one of five normal classes of activity sequences one might observe in a kitchen. Motion in the room was segmented using a robust tracker and a Kalman filter was employed to track moving objects between frames. A subject's proximity to one of six areas of interest was calculated, mapped to discrete observations and recorded approximately every 1.5 seconds.

The normal classes of behaviour were designed to highlight the importance of modelling duration given the limitations of the tracking system. That is, using an impoverished observation set, the classes would have the same sequence of observations but would differ in the duration spent in a location. The first two classes, preparing cereal and making toast for breakfast, are identical in the order that the areas of interest in the room are visited and hence it is only possible to distinguish between the two classes by considering the time spent at the kitchen bench, the act of making toast taking considerably longer than the preparation of a bowl of cereal. Similarly, the classes representing dinner preparation and reheating differed only in the duration spent standing by the stove. The fifth class differs to the other classes in both the activity duration and the order in which the activities are performed. A further 24 sequences of abnormal behaviour, differing to the norm only in terms of shorter or longer times spent at any of the six locations, were recorded.

Each normal class was modelled using a standard fully connected HMM, a left-right HMM, an explicit state duration HMM (ESD-HMM) and a left-right ESD-HMM. The optimal number of states were empirically found to be 12, 2, 3 and 2 respectively. The models were trained on a random sample of 60% of the normal activity sequences and tested on the remainder. A single Gaussian distribution was used to estimate the duration probabilities in the ESD-HMM case, the model otherwise requiring an unrealistic amount of training data to accurately estimate the state duration probabilities.

3 Results

The HMM was the weakest model for classification of the unseen normal sequences with 81% accuracy, its dynamic time warping property rendering it unsuitable for use as a classifier given the type of observation sequences used in this experiment. The left-right HMM was an improvement with 97% accuracy. Although the model performed well empirically, the limited number of parameters in a two state HMM is inadequate to properly encode the sequences and hence properly discriminate between classes. Confusion between the similar activity classes was the prime source of error in both cases. The ESD-HMM models performed equally well with 100% accuracy. Explicit duration allows the model to clearly differentiate between all classes.

We classified unseen observation sequences as either normal or abnormal by thresholding on the highest log likelihood, normalised by the total length of a sequence. ROC curves were used to investigate the suitability of each of the models as a detector of abnormality. Neither the HMM nor left-right HMM models are able to reliably differentiate between our normal and abnormal sequences using the thresholding approach. The ESD-HMM increased our ability to reliably detect duration abnormality, its main cause of error a result of the model treating the observations as a cyclic activity. The left-right ESD-HMM did not exhibit this behaviour and produced good results.

Long term abnormality was investigated by artificially varying the duration of a primary activity in a randomly selected test sequence. The normalised likelihood returned by the HMM and the left-right HMM increased in proportion to the duration of the activity. The HMM and left-right HMM are therefore not suitable for the detection of highly abnormal activity duration. The ESD-HMM exhibited a similar trend, the lack of transition constraints allowing the model to briefly enter a state with a sub-optimal emission probability in order to maximise the overall sequence likelihood. The left-right ESD-HMM behaved correctly, the sequence likelihood rapidly decreasing as the activity duration was increased.

4 Conclusion

This work has highlighted the importance of explicit duration modelling for classification of sequences of human activity and the reliable and timely detection of duration abnormality. The incorporation of duration in models of human behaviour is an important consideration for systems seeking to provide cognitive support and to detect deviation in the behavioural patterns of the elderly.

References

1. Lühr, S., Venkatesh, S., Bui, H.H.: Duration abnormality detection in sequences of human activity. Technical Report TR-2004/02, Department of Computing, Curtin University (2004)

An Augmentation Hybrid System for Document Classification and Rating

Richard Dazeley and Byeong-Ho Kang

School of Computing, University of Tasmania, Hobart, Tasmania 7001, Australia*
Smart Internet Technology Cooperative Research Centre, Bay 8, Suite 9/G12
Australian Technology Park Eveleigh NSW 1430*
{rdazeley,bhkang}@utas.edu.au

Abstract. This paper introduces an augmentation hybrid system, referred to as Rated MCRDR. It uses Multiple Classification Ripple Down Rules (MCRDR), a simple and effective knowledge acquisition technique, combined with a neural network.

Introduction

As we move from the Information Age to the Age of Information Overload, Information Filtering (IF) has gained significant attention in the research community. This paper briefly introduces a new method based on a variant to the Multiple Classification Ripple Down Rules (MCRDR) methodology, called Rated MCRDR (RM) [1]. Rated MCRDR is an augmentation hybrid intelligent system developed to provide both classifications and a relevance ranking of cases and can be applied in many domains [1]. One of the key areas that the algorithm was designed for was information filtering and in fact draws heavily on ideas found in the information filtering research. The main idea behind the system is to significantly reduce the feature space, so that it is of a size that a neural network is capable of handling, in such a way that we don't effectively loose any relevant information.

Rated MCRDR (RM)

To achieve this, RM adopted the basic premise that while the majority of features may be statistically relevant [2] it is safe to assume that an individual user is not interested in all the possible features. Therefore, RM attempts to identify keywords, groups of words, phrases or even compressed features, outputted from some other feature reduction method, by using simple user interrogation, by using the Multiple Classification Ripple Down Rules (MCRDR) [3]. This incremental Knowledge Acquisition (KA) methodology allows a user to perform both the KA process and the maintenance of a Knowledge Based System (KBS) over time [3]. The basic concept behind MCRDR is to use the user's knowledge within the context it is provided [1, 3] to produce multi-

---

* Collaborative research project between both institutions.

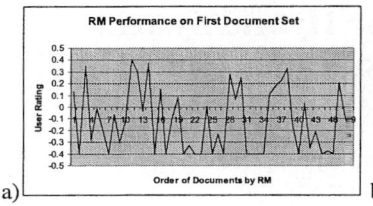 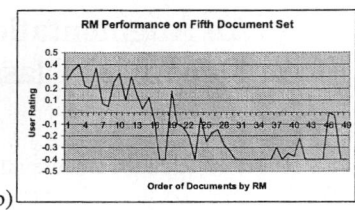

Fig. 1. Ability of RM to order cases according to the simulated-user's preference. a) Shows RM's performance prior to any training. b) Shows RM's performance after 5 document sets.

ple classifications for an individual document. Therefore, if the expert disagrees with one or more of the conclusions found by the system, knowledge can be easily added to improve future results.

It then learns further information, through observing user behaviour, about the relationships between groups of identified features to capture a deeper sociological meaning behind the selected features as well as to associate a set of relevance rankings. When a new feature or set of features are identified by the user, the specifically designed neural network steps to a rating that accurately identifies its relevance to the user immediately. After the initial learning step, any further documents receiving the same classification allow the network to learn more intricate non-linear relationships. Thus, RM has the ability to learn both classifications for documents if required, as well as being able to learn both linear and non-linear ratings effectively. The remainder of this paper will discuss RM in detail.

Results and Discussion

The system has undergone preliminary testing with a simulated expert using a randomly generated data set. Figure 1, illustrates how RM was able to place the documents with a higher relevance to the user first after only seeing 5 groups of 50 documents. These tests were done primarily to show that the system was able to learn quickly and to be used for parameter tuning purposes. Clearly a more rigorous testing regime needs to be used in order to fully justify the algorithm's ability to learn within the information domain.

References

1. R. Dazeley and B. H. Kang. Rated MCRDR: Finding non-Linear Relationships Between Classifications in MCRDR. in *3rd International Conference on Hybrid Intelligent Systems*. 2003. Melbourne, Australia: IOS Press
2. T. Joachims. Text Categorization with Support Vector Machines: Learning with Many Relevant Features. in *European Conference on Machine Learning (ECML)*. 1998: Springer
3. B. H. Kang, Validating Knowledge Acquisition: Multiple Classification Ripple Down Rules. 1996, University of New South Wales: Sydney.

Study and Comparison of 3D Face Generation

Mark Chan, Patrice Delmas, Georgy Gimel'farb,
Chia-Yen Chen, and Philippe Leclercq

Department of Computer Science, University of Auckland, New Zealand
patrice@cs.auckland.ac.nz

Abstract. Four techniques to generate 2.5 D face surfaces from a set of 2D images are compared using both rendering results and surface distance comparison for Orthogonal Views (OV), Photometric Stereo (PSM), Automatic and Interactive Binocular Stereo (ABS and IBS) using Dur database of 20 face surfaces. PSM obtains the best rendered surfaces.

1 Used Methods

- IBS computes depth information from a pair of images with calibrated cameras. A set of feature points is manually extracted, its 3D is obtained by triangulation and interpolated onto a generic model – CANDIDE3 (MPEG4) [1] was upgraded using the radial basis function [2].
- ABS matches pixels to compute the disparity map. In this experiment, as a first step, sum of absolute difference (SAD) [3] was used for its simplicity.
- PSM creates a 3D representation from intensity images [4]. It estimates the surface normals using apriori knowledge of the illumination geometry. Three images are acquired with a different light source direction. PSM generates a complete face dense map with approximately 40000 vertices.
- OV [5] one camera is placed in front of the test subject and a second one orthogonally. Feature point's 3D coordinates are manually extracted – x and y coordinates are obtained from the frontal image and z from the orthogonal image – and mapped onto a generic model.

2 Results

Reconstructed surfaces are compared with respect to their rendering quality. Figure 1 presents 3D faces generated by different methods. Results show that PSM has the best rendering, due to the large amount of vertices. Results from ABS could not be used for quantitative comparison due to low camera resolution – the quantization effect gives an insufficient disparity range: 16 pixels.

Because of the use of different methods, normalisation is needed: rotation, scaling and translation. Rotation adjusts all the surfaces to face the same direction. Feature points are manually extracted from PSM and used as reference. They were interpolated onto 3D face meshes for scaling purpose. Finally surfaces are translated to the minimum distance apart. Further details can be found in [6].

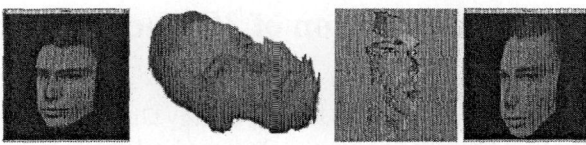

Fig. 1. Experimental results generated – from left to right – by: IBS, ABS, PSM and OV

In this experiment, results from 20 test subjects were used. Table 1 shows pixels absolute differences between 3D surfaces and table 2 gives additional statistics.

3D face surfaces generated from IBS have a smaller distance to the PSM – used as a reference – results than OV. OV and IBS are similar: ~ 74% of the vertices have pixel differences less than 5. In addition, their comparisons against PSM are nearly identical.

Table 1. Overall Comparison Result on different 3D surfaces

	≤ 5	≤ 10	≤ 15	≤ 20	≥ 20
PSM vs OV	49.3	26.1	13	4.69	6.8
PSM vs IBST	51.7	26.7	10.4	5.4	5.5
OV vs IBT	74	18	4.5	1.6	1.9

Table 2. Statistical Comparison Result on different 3D surfaces

	Max.	Mean	Variante	Std Dev.
PSM vs OV	80.88	9.17	163.5	12.78
PSM vs IBST	80.18	8.43	136.22	11.67
OV vs IBST	36.1	4.1	26.22	5.12

3 Conclusion

In this paper, 3D face surfaces are compared qualitatively and quantitatively. PSM generates 3D face surfaces with the best rendering. Surfaces generated from IBS and OV are very similar. Future work include a broader taxonomy of stereo vision algorithm as well as disparity map post processing introducing a ground truth of test subjects to use as benchmarks.

References

1. Ahlberg, J.: Candide3 – an updated pararneterized face. In: Report No.LiTH-ISY-R-2326, Department of Electrical Engineering, Linkoping University, Sweden (2001)
2. J. Noh, D.F., Neumann, U.: Animated deformations with radial basis function. In: ACM Virtual Reality and Software Technology (VRST), University of Southern California, California, United States (2000) 166–174
3. Leclercq, P., J.Morris: Robustness to noise of stereo matching. In: International Conference on Image Analysis and Processing, Mantova, Italy (2003) 606–611
4. Woodham, R.: Photometric method for determining surface orientation from multiple images. In: Optimal Engineering. Volume 19. (1980) 139–144
5. Ip, H., Yin, L.: Constructing a 3D individualized head model from two orthogonal views. In: The Visual Computer. Volume 12. (1995) 254–266
6. Chan, M.: 3D face analysis and synthesis. In: Masters Thesis, University of Auckland, Auckland, New Zealand (April, 2004)

Stable Solutions Dealing with Dynamics in Scheduling Based on Dynamic Constraint Satisfaction Problems

Hiromitsu Hattori, Toramatsu Shintani, Atsushi Isomura,
Takayuki Ito, and Tadachika Ozono

Graduate School of Engineering, Nagoya Institute of Technology
Gokiso-cho, Showa-ku, Nagoya, Aichi 466-8555, Japan
{hatto,tora,isomura,itota,ozono}@ics.nitech.ac.jp

Abstract. The real-life scheduling problems are often over-constrained, and there is often one intractable case where unexpected events are added and a sudden change is required. In this paper, we describe such problems as the Dynamic Valued Constraint Satisfaction Problem (DyVCSP). In DyVCSP, although the previous schedule would be modified when there is some change, the new schedule should be similar to the current one. We propose a method for achieving solution stability, which maintains portions of the current schedule using the provisional soft constraint. The provisional constraint ensures each variable keeps its value as much as possible. In this paper, we formalize the nurse scheduling problem as DyVCSP and use our method to achieve solution stability.

1 Nurse Scheduling as a Dynamic VCSP

In a DyVCSP, the nurse scheduling problem could be defined as a sequence of VCSPs, each of which represents the problem at each time step. Each VCSP is changed to the next VCSP by loss or gain of values, variables, or constraints. A VCSP at a time step i is defined by $\mathcal{VP}_i = (X_i, D_i, C_i, S, \varphi)$, where $X_i = \{x_{(1,1)}, x_{(1,2)}, ..., x_{(s,t)}, ...\}$. $x_{(s,t)}$ is the working shift of nurse s on day t. D_i is the set of domain. $d_{(s,t)}$ is the domain of $x_{(s,t)}$. On the nurse roster, $d_{(s,t)}$ is $\{free, morning, evening, night\}$. S is the valuation structure defined by $E = [0, 9]$, $\succ = >$, $\bot = 0$, $\top = 9$, $\otimes = +$, and the valuation function φ is simply summation of values. C_i is the set of constraints. The constraints are described in the following form:

$$constraint(lower\_lim, upper\_lim, assignment\_list, weight).$$

This constraint is satisfied if the number of elements in the current assignment corresponding to those in the *assignment_list* are more than the *lower_lim* and less than the *upper_lim*. This is an example of a personal constraint:

$$constraint(1, 3, \{x_{(s,1)} = morning, ..., x_{(s,t)} = morning, ...\}, 4)$$

This is satisfied if the number of corresponding elements between the current assignment and the *assignment_list* is 1 to 3. Then, a DyVCSP could be described as follows:

$$\mathcal{DP} = \{\mathcal{VP}_0, \mathcal{VP}_1, ..., \mathcal{VP}_i, ...\}$$

The problem with solution stability [1,2] in DyVCSP can be defined as the problem of sequentially computing a solution for each of the VCSPs $\{\mathcal{VP}_0, \mathcal{VP}_1, ..., \mathcal{VP}_i, ...\}$ given some existing static constraint satisfaction algorithms.

2 Re-scheduling with Dynamic VCSP

We focus on a case where a nurse suddenly needs to change his/her schedule and re-scheduling is needed. As mentioned above, we deal with the solution stability. In this paper, the solution stability is defined as follows:

Solution Stability: The results after re-scheduling should be similar to those of previously completed scheduling because users are confused if there are extensive changes.

In our method for solution stability, we introduce a provisional constraint. The provisional constraint is used to maintain the previous value of each variables as much as possible. For example, when $v_{(i,j)}$ is assigned to the variable $x_{(i,j)}$ in the previous problem, the provisional constraint which is used to keep the value $v_{(i,j)}$ is:

$$constraint(1, 1, \{x_{(i,j)=v_{(i,j)}}\}, w)$$

where, w is the weight of the provisional constraint. The value of w is predefined.

The process of re-scheduling for achieving solution stability is as follows:

Step 1: New constraints for sudden requests are generated and the constraints C_{new} are added to current problem $\mathcal{VP}_i$. The problem then changes $\mathcal{VP}_i$ to $\mathcal{VP}_{i+1}$. The new constraints C_{new} is the cause of re-scheduling.

Step 2: The provisional constraints C^i_{prov} to maintain the current solution are generated and added to the set of provisional constraints C_{prov}, which consists of all provisional constraints. C_{prov} is as follows:

$$C_{prov} = \bigcup_{j=0}^{i} C^j_{prov} \quad (\forall j\ c \in C^j_{prov}, c \notin C_{prov})$$

Step 3: C_{prov} is added to $\mathcal{VP}_{i+1}$. Then, $\mathcal{VP}_{i+1}$ is changed to $\mathcal{VP}'_{i+1}$. If the summation of the weight of newly added provisional constraints ($W_{C^i_{prov}}$) is higher than that of the weight of C_{new} in Step 1 ($W_{C_{new}}$), the re-scheduling process stops. This is because the schedule is not modified when $W_{C_{new}} \leq W_{C^i_{prov}}$.

Step 4: The problem $\mathcal{VP}'_{i+1}$ is solved based on basic stochastic hill climbing. Since the provisional constraints that keep the previous value of each variable are included in Step 3, a stable solution would be obtained.

Step 5: All provisional constraints included in C_{prov} are removed, and then the problem $\mathcal{VP}'_{i+1}$ is changed back into $\mathcal{VP}_{i+1}$. Here, all satisfied provisional constraints are removed from C_{prov} to avoid duplication of them in solving $\mathcal{VP}_{i+2}$.

References

1. Wallace, R.J., Freuder, E.C.: Stable solutions for dynamic constraint satisfaction problems. In: Proceedings of the 4th International Conference on Principles and Practice of Constraint Programming. (1998) 447–461
2. Verfaillie, G., Schiex, T.: Solution reuse in dynamic constraint satisfaction problems. In: Proceedings of the 12th National Conference on Artificial Intelligence(AAAI-94). (1994) 307–312

Analyzing Emotional Space in Sensitivity Communication Robot "Ifbot"

Masayoshi Kanoh*, Shohei Kato, and Hidenori Itoh

Dept. of Intelligence and Computer Science, Nagoya Institute of Technology
Gokiso-cho, Showa-ku, Nagoya 466-8555, Japan
{kanoh,shohey,itoh}@ics.nitech.ac.jp

The "Ifbot" robot communicates with people by considering its own "emotions" and theirs. Figure 1 has a front and side view of Ifbot. It has sensibility technology. This is able to detects the emotions of its interlocutor from the tone of his/her voice and the words used. Ifbot also has unique facial-expression mechanisms. Figure 2 outlines the mechanisms, which it has 10 motors and 104 LEDs. Ifbot expresses its emotions, moods and other feelings on its face by using these mechanisms in communication. We first attempt to extract characteristics of Ifbot's facial expressions by mapping these to its emotional space, and then analyze its emotional space psychologically.

Creating and Analyzing Ifbot's Emotional Space

We applied a five-layer perceptron [1] to extract the characteristics of Ifbot's facial expressions. We used output of the third layer of the perceptron to map Ifbot's emotional space and used the values of 15, 45, 3, 45 and 15 for the number of units in each layer to create the emotional space. We prepared some questionnaires to observe Ifbot's emotional space, in which we showed respondents the 29 facial sequences which were used to train the perceptron network, and they chose the best emotion corresponding each sequence. We provided seven options for classifying emotions: six basic emotions [2] and no classification. Table 1 lists that each 2 facial sequences of anger, happiness, sadness, and surprise that were the most popular in the questionnaires. Figure 3 plots Ifbot's emotional space

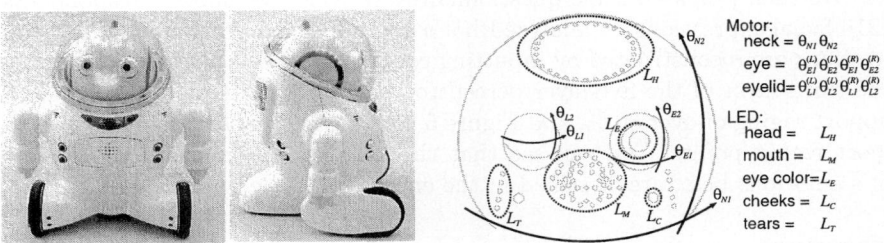

Fig. 1. Front and side views of Ifbot. **Fig. 2.** Ifbot's Facial-expression mechanisms.

---

* Presently with Chukyo University. Address: 101 Tokodachi, Kaizu-cho, Toyota 470-0393, Japan. E-mail: mkanoh@life.chukyo-u.ac.jp

Table 1. Results of questionnaires (%).

Face	Anger	Disgust	Fear	Happiness	Sadness	Surprise	No class.
exp 1	78	14	0	0	4	0	4
exp 2	84	4	4	2	0	2	4
exp 3	0	0	0	14	0	66	20
exp 4	0	0	2	22	0	72	4
exp 5	2	6	4	0	86	0	2
exp 6	0	0	8	2	90	0	0
exp 7	0	4	0	84	0	6	6
exp 8	0	0	0	96	0	4	0

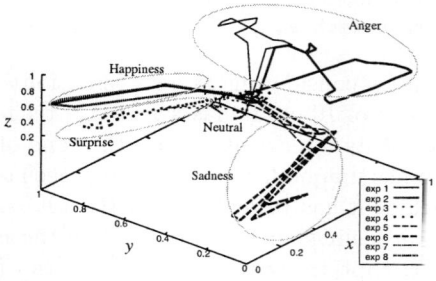

Fig. 3. Emotional space in Ifbot.

Fig. 4. High support rating points on Ifbot's emotional space (over 80 %).

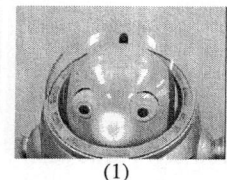 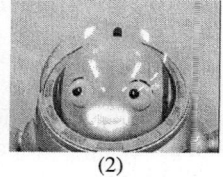 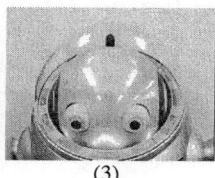 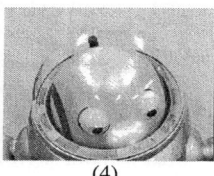

(1) (2) (3) (4)

Fig. 5. Facial expressions on high support rating points: (1) surprise, (2) happiness, (3) sadness, (4) anger.

constructed by training the network. The lines in the figure are the results of mapping Ifbot's facial sequences listed in Table 1. You can see that the facial sequences, which express Ifbot's emotions best, are classified in the emotional space. We then prepared some questionnaires, in which we showed respondents the 216 facial expressions, to analyze Ifbot's emotional space in detail. The facial expressions are reconstructed by inputting coordinate points at regular intervals to the third layer of the five-layer perceptron. Figure 4 plots points which earn a support raging of over 80 %, and Figure 5 shows the facial expressions on high support rating points. You can see that the facial expressions, which express Ifbot's emotions best, are classified in the emotional space approximately.

References

1. Bishop, C.M.: Neural Networks for Pattern Recognition. Oxford University Press (1995)
2. Ekman, P.: Unmasking the Face. Prentice-Hall (1975)

Human-Centric Approach for Human-Robot Interaction

Mariko Narumi[1] and Michita Imai[1,2]

[1] Keio University
3-14-1 Hiyoshi, Kohoku-ku Yokohama 223-0061 Japan
{narumi,michita}@ayu.ics.keio.ac.jp
[2] PRESTO, JST

1 Our Aim

Many intelligent robots have already been developed for entertaining people or providing useful information. Such robots need capability of human-robot interaction to be a communication partner of the human. Our aim is to achieve human-robot interaction which is as natural as human-human interaction.

2 Why Do People Feel Shy About Interaction with Robot?

a. The person feel shy to interact with the robot even if the robot behaves like humans.

b. The person reads the robot's feeling when the robot utters something include feeling.

Fig. 1. Breaing the Shyness on Human-Robot Interaction

When we exhibited our robots ROBOVIE in ROBODEX2003, many people could not interact properly with robots. They seemed to be shy and have no ideas how to reply to robots(Fig1a). If a customer feels shy about communicating wit ha service providing root, the robot may not be able to provide enough service because it cannot get enough information about the task from him/her.

People can interact with the robot without being shy when we concentrate on the interaction with it. However human-robot interaction studies did not take care of the problem that people can not concentrate on the interaction with the robot and they feel unnatural on the interaction itself. We assumed 2 reasons which cause "shyness": **"robot factors"** and **"human factors."** Robot factor is the lack of robot's capability of expressing and processing information that causes people to feel unnatural for the interaction. Recent robotics studies achieved the robots that perform almost "human-like" and can resolve robot factors and the unnaturalness felt for the person's performance on the interaction with the robot. But they can not put out shyness from his/her mind. Human factors are that people feel unnatural for the interaction itself and do not concentrate on the interaction with the robot.

3 Our Approach – Developing Common Quality of Sense

Why does the interaction with the robot make us feel unnatural, even if the robot performs like humans? In human-human interaction, we unconsciously concentrate on it since we can read the partners' mind and predict partners' intention. It is easy for us because we know that partners can "feel" the same sense as ourselves. When a person have the same sense(ex: the beauty of flower) with the partner(s), we call this situation that "they are sharing the common quality of sense." Can people concentrate and do not feel shy about the interaction with the robot when they predict robot's feeling(Fig1b)? We have developed an experimental system named "i-Director", which directs interaction to develop the common quality of sense between the person and the robot.

4 Experiment

We conducted a psychological experiment to confirm that people feel "shyness" on human-robot interaction and it could be broken by sharing common quality of sense between the person and the robot. 21 subjects were devided into 2 groups, Experimental Group(ExpG) and Control Group(CtlG). For ExpG subjects, i-Director generated utterances including feeling about the object in real world. For CtlG subjects, i-Director generated utterances including information of the object. In the experiment, all CtrG subjects agreed with robot's utterance including feeling(ex. "This flower smells good, isn't it?") so that common quality of sense had developed between the subjects and the robot. After some topics of the scenario the robot gave a sweet to the subject and told him/her to eat it. All of CtrG subjects ate it though a half of CtlG subjects did not eat. This result indicates that the CtlG subjects did not feel shy about interaction with robot. (Please see [Imai et al, 2003] for details of the experiment.)

References

Imai, M. and Narumi, M.: "Generating common quality of sense by directed interaction", 12th IEEE International Workshop on Robot and Human Intaractive Communication(RO-MAN 2003), pp.199–204, 2003.

Complexity of Coordinating Autonomous Planning Agents

Adriaan ter Mors, Jeroen Valk, and Cees Witteveen

Faculty of Electrical Engineering, Mathematics and Computer Science,
Delft University of Technology
P.O. Box 5031, 2600 GA Delft, The Netherlands
{a.w.termors,j.m.valk,c.witteveen}@ewi.tudelft.nl

We assume that a number of agents have to work together on some joint task T consisting of a number of elementary tasks t_j, partially ordered by a set of precedence constraints[1]. The elementary tasks are allocated to the agents using some given task allocation protocol (cf. [2]). We assume that *(i)* to perform its set of tasks, an agent needs to make a plan, and that *(ii)* each agent wishes to retain full *planning autonomy*, i.e., to retain the freedom to decide how to best perform its tasks.

The precedence constraints, however, induce dependencies between the agents: if a task t, allocated to agent A_j, is preceded by a task t' from a different agent A_i, then A_j is dependent on A_i. To manage these dependencies between agents, some form of *coordination* is required, as illustrated in the following example:

Consider a joint task of four tasks t_1, t_2, t_3, t_4, such that $t_1 \prec t_2$ and $t_3 \prec t_4$. There are two agents: A_1 is allocated t_1 and t_4, A_2 is allocated t_2 and t_3. Suppose A_1 decides to execute t_4 before t_1, and agent A_2 decides to perform t_2 prior to t_3. It is easily verified that joint execution of these plans fails, because now $t_1 \prec t_2 \prec t_3 \prec t_4 \prec t_1$.

In general, the plan coordination problem for multi-agent systems is not an entirely new topic. Most approaches in the coordination literature either take a *post-planning* approach (cf. [5]), where agents initially plan independently, but where combination of individual plans into a joint plan requires *replanning*, or coordination and planning are *intertwined* (cf. [1]). Especially in the latter case, coordination requires exchanging planning information to arrive at a feasible joint plan. If, however, there exist competitive relations between the agents, then agents may be reluctant to reveal details of their plans to other agents, rendering the aforementioned approaches inappropriate.

To guarantee planning autonomy, we therefore take a *pre-planning* approach to coordination: prior to planning, additional constraints may be imposed on the agents so that, subsequently, a feasible joint plan can be found simply by combining whatever plans the individual agents come up with. Pre-planning coordination is not a new concept either; *social laws* also enable agents to operate independently, e.g. by requiring all agents to drive on the right. Social laws are

---

[1] If a task t_1 precedes a task t_2, denoted by $t_1 \prec t_2$, then work on t_2 may not start until t_1 has been completed.

constructed off-line, however, and are therefore unable to deal with the dependencies arising from cooperating on a joint task.

As a result, we concentrate on the following *coordination problem*:

> *How to find a minimal set of additional dependencies, such that irrespective of the plans developed by the autonomous planning agents, these plans can always be combined into a feasible joint-agent plan without the need to revise any of them?*

This coordination problem can be decomposed into two subproblems: *verifying* that a given set of additional constraints allows agents to plan independently (the coordination verification problem), and finding out whether a coordination set is of minimal size (the minimal coordination problem). The coordination-verification problem alone turns out to be co-NP-complete; the coordination problem itself can be solved in non-deterministic polynomial time if we have an NP-oracle for the coordination verification problem. In fact, we can show that the coordination problem is Σ_2^p-complete[2].

Even rather simple cases of the coordination problem, e.g., where each agent has only to plan two elementary tasks, turn out to be intractable and we can prove that it is very unlikely that constant-ratio approximation algorithms for this problem exist even if each agent has only a trivial planning task to perform.

As it is unlikely that we will find constant-ratio approximations for the coordination problem, even in simple cases, we have focused our attention instead on developing distributed heuristics to solve the coordination problem. These *partitioning heuristics* can be used both *centrally* by broker agents (e.g. supply chain managers) or *distributively* by the collection of planning agents themselves. Elsewhere [4], we show that these distributed coordination protocols perform well on multi-modal logistic planning problems. Our results show that (*i*) a distributed, pre-planning coordination approach can outperform a centralized planning approach, and (*ii*) that we can (re-)use single-agent planning software to solve multi-agent planning problems, if we coordinate the agents prior to planning using our coordination algorithms.

References

1. Keith S. Decker and Victor R. Lesser. Designing a family of coordination algorithms. In *Proceedings of the Thirteenth International Workshop on Distributed Artificial Intelligence (DAI-94)*, pages 65–84, 1994.
2. Onn Shehory and Sarit Kraus. Methods for task allocation via agent coalition formation. *Artificial Intelligence*, 1998.
3. Adriaan ter Mors, Jeroen Valk, and Cees Witteveen. Complexity of coordinating autonomous planning agents: Technical report, 2004.
4. Jeroen Valk and Cees Witteveen. Multi-agent coordination in planning. In *Seventh Pacific Rim International Conference on Artificial Intelligence*, pages 335–344, Tokyo, Japan, august 2002. Springer.
5. Frank von Martial. *Coordinating Plans of Autonomous Agents*, volume 610 of *Lecture Notes on Artificial Intelligence*. Springer Verlag, Berlin, 1992.

---

[2] For a full account, we refer the reader to a technical report on this subject [3].

An Approach for Multirelational Ontology Modelling

Pedro J. Vivancos-Vicente, Rafael Valencia-García, Jesualdo T. Fernández-Breis,
Rodrigo Martínez-Béjar, and Fernando Martín-Rubio

Grupo de Tecnologías del Conocimiento y Modelado Cognitivo, Campus de Espinardo
Universidad de Murcia, CP 30071, Murcia, Spain
{pedroviv,valencia}@um.es,
{jfernand,rodrigo,fmartin}@dif.um.es
http://klt.dif.um.es

Abstract. This paper presents a work which is concerned with both the theoretical and practical foundations of ontology development. An ontological model that covers several types of relations between concepts is described. Also, an ontology editor for building ontologies according to this particular ontological model is presented in this paper and its benefits and drawbacks with respect to other available ontological engineering tools are discussed.

1 Introduction

The motivation for our research comes from the need of 'well-built' ontologies. In this paper, the prototype of a system for editing and visualizing domain ontologies built according to a new model is presented. The model allows domain experts to define ontologies in a friendly way, and the consistency of the knowledge defined by the human modeller is checked and guaranteed. Besides, the model allows for inferring new (ontological) knowledge from that modeled in the ontology. The ontological model has been implemented on top of a formal ontological schema defined and described in this paper.

2 The Ontology Editor

In this work, an ontology is viewed as a specification of a domain knowledge conceptualisation (Van Heijst et al, 1997), and represented a set of concepts related each other using a number of relationships. Although one user can define a relationship for its domain, there are predefined relationships. Each concept is structurally defined through a name (and, in some cases, a list of alternative names) and some attributes which can take a range of values, like integer, string, and so on. In this model, a number of different types of conceptual relations in real domains are covered. The system incorporates modules with different purposes:

1. Top-level modelling: The top-level ontology proposed by Sowa (Sowa, 2000) is used in this editor. So, each concept must be assigned one of the top-level categories contained in this top-level ontology.

2. 'Clean' Taxonomies: This module assists the user in the creation of well-defined taxonomies according to the principles introduced in (Guarino and Welty, 2004).
3. Consistency: This is a critical issue in the construction of ontologies. This implies that all the properties and axioms defined for concepts, attributes, and each type of relation are checked and they must be held by the ontologies.
4. XML: The ontologies are stored in XML format. We are currently extending the editor to deal with OWL ontologies.

3 Conclusions

This paper describes a methodology for designing the taxonomic subsystem so that each taxonomic node will correspond to one of the properties defined in "clean" taxonomies (Guarino and Welty, 2004). In our work, topological relations can also be inferred from the proper structure of the ontology rather than being explicitly specified. In order to evaluate the adequacy of the ontology editor to build ontologies, some properties of the edited ontologies were checked, namely, precision, breadth, consistency, completeness and utility. The ontologies that have been used for validating the system meet these properties. The ontologies, which are accessible at our web page and whose knowledge was directly acquired from experts, belong to biological and medical domains. This tool allows users to specify richer ontologies than the ones that can be defined by using other existing ontology editors, which are mainly constrained by the number of relations that can be defined and which do not include facilities for modelling good taxonomies and the top-level categories of concepts. Furthermore, the editor guarantees the consistency of the ontologies built.

Acknowledgements

We thank the Spanish Ministry for Science and Technology for its support for the development of the system through projects TIC2002-03879, FIT-110100-2003-73 and FIT-150500-2003-503, the Regional Government of Murcia (Spain) through project 2I03SIU0039; and Seneca Foundation through project PI-16/0085/FS/01. We also thank the European Commission for its support under project ALFA II0092FA.

References

Guarino, N., Welty, C. (2004) An overview of OntoClean. In S.Staab, R. Studer (eds), Handbook on Ontologies, Springer-Verlag.
Sowa, J.F. (2000). Knowledge Representation. Logical, Philosophical and Computational Foundations. Brooks-Cole.
Van Heijst, G., Schreiber, A.T. and Wielinga, B.J. (1997). Using explicit ontologies in KBS development, International Journal of Human-Computer Studies, 45, 183-292.

SNR-Invariant Normalization of the Covariance Measure for Template Matching[*]

Jong Dae Kim

Division of Information and Communication Engineering
Hallym University, 1 Okchon-dong, Chunchon, 200-702, Korea
kimjd@hallym.ac.kr

1 Theory

An unbiased estimator of signal variance is presented for normalizing the covariance that is widely selected as a similarity measure in vast template-matching applications. It is the variance estimator of the pure signal instead of the observed signal whose variance has been typically selected to normalize the covariance.

In order to estimate the pure signal variance, this paper employs two assumptions on the statistics of the intensity distribution in the template region. First, a local histogram in the template will be bi-modal showing two clusters: one is for the object area and the other is for the background. Under this assumption, the variance of each cluster will be the same as that of noise. Besides, the mean distance of the clusters will approximate to the variance of the pure signal. This assumption is reasonable because the imaged signal of the targeting object is usually homogeneous in most applications. Second, the clusters can be discriminated by the mean intensity of the whole template region. This assumption is brought from the idea that the total mean is often chosen as the initial estimate of the iterative selection methods for the threshold of two clusters. It must be the best choice for partitioning the clusters especially when the template is tested around the matched position. In which case, the intensities of the background and the object tend to be clearly separated. Furthermore this assumption is fairly desirable because the mean intensity is available from the calculation of the covariance. From the assumptions, this paper proposes that the pure signal variance can be estimated by the difference between the mean intensities of two clusters which are separated by the mean in the total template region.

The covariance normalized by the proposed estimator was compared with the classical normalized covariance for the stability of the response and the success rate under the white Gaussian noise. It was also tested for a set of real images where the target objects had disparate backgrounds. Both simulation and experiments proved the superiority of the normalization by the proposed estimator.

2 Results and Conclusion

One-dimensional simulation was performed to verify the performance of the proposed method. The left picture in Fig. 1 shows the magnitude variation over the noise stan-

---

[*] This work was supported by grant No. R05-2003-000-10603-0 from the Basic Research Program of the Korea Science & Engineering Foundation.

dard deviation. It shows that the proposed method delivers a stable response even when the signal is severely corrupted.

We selected the test images with more than two identical objects suffering different backgrounds. They were chosen because the matching measures might deliver different responses. Hence the covariance normalized by the classical estimator and by the proposed one might produce the different distributions of the match-responses. One of such examples was finding letters in an image with a text string on a picture background, such as posters or magazine covers. The uppermost image in the right picture of Fig. 1 shows one of the test images, where the template of 'O' is embedded in its right bottom corner. The middle and the bottommost graphs depicted the horizontal profiles along the matched positions of the template matching responses. The middle graph was for the covariance normalized by the classical estimator (labeled as 'NC') and the bottom one was for that by the proposed estimator (labeled as 'proposed'), respectively. The 'o' marked peaks in each profile represented the match-responses and the dashed lines indicated the maximum mismatch-responses. In the graphs, one of match-responses was smaller than the maximum mismatch-response with the classical normalization, while all of them were great enough with the proposed normalization. From this idea, we defined 'failed-case' as the case that there was at least one of the match-responses below the maximum mismatch-response. Table 1 summarizes the number of the failed-cases for 30 arbitrary chosen test images. While the proposed method failed for only 4 images, there were 8 failed-cases for the classical normalization. It was remarkable that the classical method did fail for all the failed-cases of the proposed method.

Both one-dimensional simulation and the experimental results on the real images proved that the proposed method gave more stable response on the SNR variation than the classical normalization.

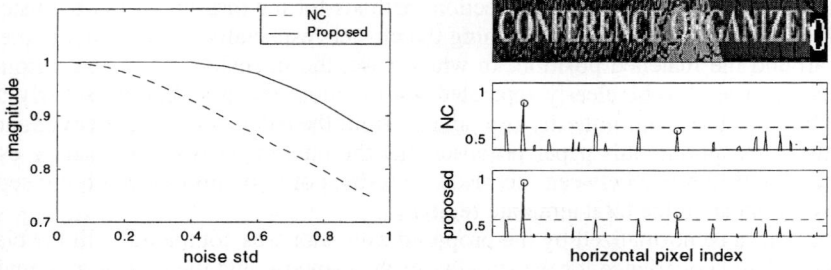

Fig. 1. One-dimensional simulation result (left) and the example result on a real image where the proposed method was superior to the classical normalization (right).

Table 1. The number of failed-cases for the 30 test images (the number of the test images for which at least one match-response was smaller than the maximum mismatch-response).

	NC	Proposed
Number of failed-cases for each method	8	4
Number of failed-cases for both methods		4

Brain Emotional Learning Based Intelligent Controller Applied to Gas Metal Arc Welding System

Mahdi Jalili-Kharaajoo

Young Researchers Club, Azad University, Tehran, Iran
mahdijalili@ece.ut.ac.ir

Abstract. Modeling emotions has attracted much attention in recent years, both in cognitive psychology and design of artificial systems. In this paper, we will apply Brain Emotional Learning Based Intelligent Controller (BELBIC) to Gas Metal Arc Welding System (GMAWS). Simulation results reveal the effectives of BELBIC.

1 Introduction

Biologically motivated intelligent computing has in recent years been successfully applied to solving complex problems [1]. Whether called emotional control or merely an analog version of reinforcement learning with critic, the method is increasingly being utilized by control engineers, robotic designers and decision support systems developers and yielding excellent results. To this end, BELBIC has been proposed that acts better than some classic controllers [2]. In this paper, we will make use of BELBIC to current and arc length control in GMAW systems [3].

2 Architecture of BELBIC

It has been adopted a network model developed by Moren and Balkenius [4], as a computational model that mimics amygdala, orbitofrontal cortex, thalamus, sensory input cortex and generally, those parts of the brain thought responsible for processing emotions, namely, BELBIC in [2]. There are two approaches to intelligent and cognitive control. In the indirect approach, the intelligent system is utilized for tuning the parameters of the controller. We have adopted the second, so called direct approach, where the intelligent system, in our case the computational model termed BELBIC, is used as the controller block (Fig. 1). BELBIC is essentially an action generation mechanism based on sensory inputs and emotional cues.

Since amygdala does not have the capability to unlearn any emotional response that it ever learned, inhibition of any inappropriate response is the duty of orbitofrontal cortex. Controllers based on emotional learning have shown very good robustness and uncertainty handling properties [2], while being simple and easily implementable. To utilize the version of the Moren-Balkenius model as a controller [4], we note that it essentially converts two sets of inputs into the decision signal as its output. We have implemented a closed loop configuration using this block (termed BELBIC) in the feed forward loop of the total system in an appropriate manner so that the input signals have the proper interpretations (Fig. 2).

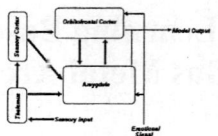

Fig. 1. The abstract structure of BELBIC

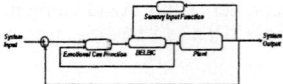

Fig. 2. Control system configuration using BELBIC

3 Simulation Results

To evaluate the performance of BELBIC, we apply it to current and arc length control in GMAW systems, which have been described in details in [3]. In order to investigate the effects of parameter uncertainty over the performance of the controller we perform the simulation with 30% random parameter variations. The performance of the controller in the case of parameter uncertainty is depicted in Fig. 3, which is better than that of obtained in [3].

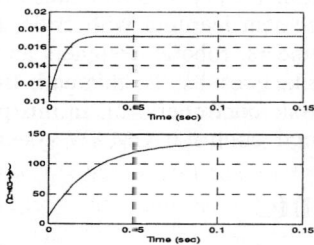

Fig. 3. Closed-loop system performance using BELBIC

4 Conclusion

In this paper, we applied BELBIC to current and arc length control in GMAW systems. The closed-loop system results were satisfactory in comparison with the results by [3].

References

1. S. Hofmeyr, S. Forrest, Architecture for an Artificial Immune System, Evolutionary. Comp. J., 2000.
2. Lucas, C., Shahmirzadi, D. and Zandesh, A., Introducing brain emotional learning based intelligent controller (BELBIC), Auto Soft Journal, 2004.
3. Abdel-Rahman, M. Feedback linearization control of current and arc length in GMAW systems, Proc. American Control Conference (AACC98), Philadelphia, 1757-1762, 1998.
4. J. Moren, C. Balkenius, A Computational Model of Emotional Learning in The Amygdala, From animals to animals 6: Proc. 6th Int. Conf. Simu. Adaptive behavior, Cambridge, MA, MIT Press, 2000.

Qualitative Spatial Arrangements and Natural Object Categories as a Link Between 3D-Perception and Speech

Reinhard Moratz, Michael Wünstel, and Robert Ross

Transregional Collaborative Research Center "Spatial Cognition"
Universität Bremen, FB 03
Postfach 330 440, D-28334 Bremen, Germany
{moratz,wuenstel,robertr}@informatik.uni-bremen.de

Overview

The visionary goal of an easy to use service robot implies intuitive styles of interaction between humans and robots. Such natural interaction can only be achieved if means are found to bridge the gap between the forms of object perception and spatial knowledge maintained by such robots, and the forms of language, used by humans, to communicate such knowledge. Part of bridging this gap, is allowing user and robot to establish joint reference on objects in the environment - without forcing the user to use unnatural means for object reference.

Our approach to establishing joint object reference makes use of natural object classification, and a computational model of basic intrinsic and relative reference systems. The system, utilizing $2\frac{1}{2}$ D laser range data, assigns natural category (e.g. "door", "chair", "table") to new objects based on their functional design. The recognizer - based on the concepts of affordances, form and function - identifies certain geometries that lead to certain functions, and therefore allow their identification [2]. With basic objects within the environment classified, we can then make use of a computational reference model, to process natural projective relations (e.g. "the briefcase to the left of the chair"), allowing users to reference objects which cannot be classified reliably by the recognition system alone.

In the current version, we mainly focus on the concept of the *supporting plane*. When the function of an object part is to support a potential other object, this part has to be parallel to the ground. A full three-dimensional segmentation based approach is not necessary when additional clues like object arrangement information is given by the user. In the future, we will augment the system with more refined 3D reconstruction abilities. The approach performs best for objects having strong functional constraints at the system's current perceptual granularity (e.g. desks, tables, chairs). However, smaller objects on the ground (e.g. waste paper baskets, briefcases etc.) can be detected but not classified reliably by our current system. These objects can however be referred to by a human and furthermore they can be referred to with reference to other objects in the environment (e.g. "the bin behind the table").

A projection of the recognized 3D objects onto the plane produces a 2D map, defined in terms of object location for directed and undirected objects, object categorization (if available), and camera position and angle. This map, is used as input for our reference processing module. Our model of projective relations (e.g. "left", "right", "in front of", "behind") uses a reference axis which is a directed line through the center of the object used as relatum (e.g. the robot itself, the group of objects, or other salient objects) [1]. If the robot itself is the relatum then the reference direction is given by it's view direction (which normally corresponds to the symmetry axis of the robot). Otherwise the directed line from robot to the center of the relatum serves as reference axis. The partitioning into sectors of equal size is a sensible model for the directions "left", "right", "front" and "back" relative to the relatum. However, this representation only applies if the robot serves as both relatum and origin. If a salient object or the group is employed as the relatum, front and back are exchanged, relative to the reference direction. The result is a qualitative distinction, as formally specified in [1].

As mentioned, this model was developed with a modest visual recognition system. However, since our new, 3D, object recognition system, is capable of detecting objects like chairs which have an intrinsic reference frame, we wish to account for intrinsic reference cases within our model. For example, "In front of the chair" is the direction into which a human would look if he sat on this chair. For such a case we can take the intrinsic reference model which we used for the robot itself. The difference is that a chair seen from a different point of view induces a "front" and a "back" acceptance area but typically no "left" or "right" area. However, we did not systematically test this intuition with human test subjects yet.

In our initial system demonstrator, users interact with the system by verbally issuing simple requests to the system. These requests - to identify items in the system's perceptual range - are detected with a Nuance Speech Recognizer[1], before being fed to a semantic analysis component. This analysis attempts to identify the category of object to be identified, the referent object, and the relationship used by the user to relate the referent object to the target object. The reference processing module then attempts to identify the target object in the 2D map using the projective relations defined. The most probable target object once computed, is then highlighted. For images of the perceived scenes and the corresponding results of the system see
http://www.sfbtr8.uni-bremen.de/A2

In future work, our vision system is to be augmented with a light camera to combine the two- and three-dimensional recognition methods, thus allowing for a wider range of objects which can be perceived. With this new resolution capability, we will also be expanding our qualitative reference model, examining - amongst other things - differences between spatial models appropriate for English, as well as German speakers.

References

1. R. Moratz, K. Fischer, and T. Tenbrink. Cognitive Modeling of Spatial Reference for Human-Robot Interaction. *International Journal on Artificial Intelligence Tools*, 10(4):589–611, 2001.
2. Michael Wünstel and Reinhard Moratz. Automatic object recognition within an office environment. In *Canadian Conference on Computer and Robot Vision (CRV2004)*, 2004.

---

[1] We gratefully thank Nuance Communications Inc. (www.nuance.com) for the use of their systems.

Integrating Feature Information for Improving Accuracy of Collaborative Filtering

Hyungil Kim[1], Juntae Kim[1], and Jonathan L. Herlocker[2]

[1] Department of Computer Engineering, Dongguk University, Seoul, Korea
{hikim,jkim}@dongguk.edu
[2] Department of Computer Science, Oregon State University, Corvallis, Oregon, USA
herlock@cs.orst.edu

Abstract. *Collaborative filtering (CF)* has been widely used and successfully applied to recommend items in practical applications. However, the collaborative filtering has two inherent problems: data sparseness and the cold-start problems. In this paper, we propose a method of integrating additional feature information of users and items into CF to overcome those difficulties and improve the accuracy of recommendation. We apply a two-pass method, first filling in unknown preference values, then generating the top-N recommendations.

1 Introduction

Recommendation systems analyze a user's preference and suggest items such as books, movies, music, web pages, etc. Collaborative filtering (CF) recommendation systems compare the rating information between users, discover similar users, and then predict a user's preference for certain item based on the similar users' preference for that item. CF has many advantages and has been applied successfully for various applications. However, when there are very few known preferences, it is difficult to find similar users, and therefore the accuracy is degraded. This weakness is more serious in the initial stage of the system.

One possibility to overcome the data sparseness is to use the additional feature information on users and items. There have been various attempts to combine content information into the collaborative filtering. In this paper, we propose a method of integrating feature information into CF by filling unknown preference values to overcome the difficulties caused by the sparseness and to improve the accuracy of recommendation. We call this method as *data blurring*.

2 Integrating Feature Information

In many practical applications, we have some information on user and item attributes in addition to the preference data itself, such as the user's gender, age, or the item's category. By using that information, we can alleviate the problems of data sparseness. In this section, we present our data blurring method.

Let P be a Boolean user-item preference matrix. $P_{ij} = 1$ if user U_i prefers item I_j, and $P_{ij} = 0$ if we have no information regarding U_i's preference for item I_j. Associated with each user U_i is a vector $X_i = <x_1, x_2, \ldots, x_n>$, where x_k is the value of k-th feature for users, and associated with each item I_j is a vector $Y_j = <y_1, y_2, \ldots, y_m>$, where y_k is the value of k-th feature for items. We use a two-pass method, first filling missing preference information, then using the complete preference data to generate top-N recommendations. For $P_{ij} = 0$, we can predict the value of P_{ij} either by using item feature information or by using user feature information, before apply the CF. We call the former as a *row-wise blurring* and the later as a *column-wise blurring*.

The probability that the user U_i has preference for item I_j is the probability that user U_i has preference for items with same feature vector as I_j, multiplied by the probability that item I_j is preferred among those items. Therefore, the row-wise blurring can be computed as in equation (1).

$$P(I_j | U_i) = P(I_j | y_1, \ldots, y_m) \cdot P(y_1, \ldots, y_m | U_i) \approx P(I_j | y_1, \ldots, y_m) \cdot \prod_{k=1}^{m} P(y_k | U_i) \quad (1)$$

The probabilities in equation (1) can be estimated by counting corresponding 1's in the preference matrix P. The user feature information can be used in a similar way to compute column-wise blurring, and these values are combined to predict the unknown preference values. After all the unknown preference values are predicted, the modified preference matrix is used to generate CF recommendation.

3 Experimental Results and Conclusion

The accuracy of the recommendation with the blurred data is compared to the accuracy of the recommendation with the original data. The dataset used for the experiment is selected from the EachMovie dataset. In this experiment, we randomly selected 1,000 users and 1,000 movies, and converted the rating values to Boolean values. The dataset is divided into 10 groups, and 10-fold cross validation is performed. The final accuracy is measured in terms of the hit ratio. The hit ratio is measured by 1) eliminating each known preference in turn, 2) generate CF top-N recommendations, and 3) check whether it is included in top-N recommendation. Vector similarity is used for finding similar users in CF. Table 1 shows the results.

Table 1. Accuracy (hit ratio) of CF recommendations

	Original data		Blurred data	
k	Top 10	Top 20	Top 10	Top 20
k=1	19.51%	24.06%	25.63%	37.05%
k=5	39.10%	47.52%	39.96%	50.13%
k=10	43.00%	53.33%	43.34%	54.15%
k=20	44.14%	55.94%	44.23%	55.08%
k=50	43.54%	56.13%	43.42%	55.30%

For most of cases, the blurred data produced a higher hit ratio, and the improvement is greater for smaller values of k. This is because the sparseness has greater effect for smaller values of k. Since the blurred data reflects the probability obtained from the feature information, it is possible to make recommendations even if the data is very sparse or there are no known preferences available.

An Ordered Preprocessing Scheme for Data Mining

Laura Cruz R., Joaquín Pérez, Vanesa Landero N., Elizabeth S. del Angel, Victor M. Álvarez, and Verónica Peréz

Instituto Tecnológico de Ciudad Madero, México
lcruzreyes@prodigy.net.mx,
{landerov,eliza_stgo}@hotmail.com

Abstract. Data preprocessing plays an important role in many processes of data mining. The practice widely adopted in this area is only to use a preprocessing method like discretization. In this paper we propose an ordered scheme to combine various important methods of data preprocessing. The aim is to increase the accuracy of the most used classification algorithms. The experimental results showed that our proposed scheme is better than the classical scheme.

1 Preprocessing Scheme for Classification

Data mining is the process of extracting useful knowledge from large datasets. Generally, the collected data are inconsistent, which can affect directly to the efficiency of mining process. For this reason, many preprocessing tasks must be carried out before the actual data analysis starts. These are: Handling missing values [1]; Balancing the classes which are not equally represented, the natural distribution in the data set is not often the best distribution for learning a classifier [2]; Features selection for identifying and removing much of the irrelevant and redundant information that can be ignored without degrading the results of learning [3]; and discretization, because the classification performance tends to be better when quantitative attributes are discretized [4].

There are several works using two preprocessing methods in an independent way [1–7], but the common practice is only to use one preprocessing method. In this paper, we propose an ordered scheme to combine various important methods of data preprocessing as follows: handling missing values, balancing datasets, selecting features and discretization. The aim is to increase the accuracy of the most used classification algorithms. We compare our proposal with the common scheme, in which the only used method is discretization.

We implemented the methods for handling missing values and balancing datasets. For feature selection and discretization tasks we used the methods implemented in the WEKA System [8]. Preliminary experiments were carried out to determine the best method for each corresponding preprocessing task: mean imputation, over-sampling by duplicating instances (we proposed improvements to SMOTE balanced method to use a wide variety of cases with more than two classes), CBS (Consistency Subset Evaluation), EMD (Entropy Minimization Discretization). These methods are well described in [1, 2, 6, 9].

2 Experimental Results and Conclusions

We collected 26 machine learning dataset, which includes a wide variety of domains from UCI repository. We applied our ordered scheme and the classical scheme for preprocessing the test cases. After that, we classified these preprocessed cases with C4.5, Naïve Bayes, LBR, SNNB, and AODE algorithms (we used classes of WEKA system, only SNNB was implemented). For evaluation purpose, we compare the average accuracy of all classification algorithms that were used with each preprocessing scheme. The average was calculated from 10 tenfold cross-validations (using a different tenfold partition of the data). The significance of the results was confirmed with the t-statistic test on a 1% confidence level.

The results of the final experiments were satisfactory. The averages were 87.68 % for our scheme, and 85.55 % for the classic scheme. We obtained an improvement of 2.13% with our proposed scheme. For future works, we are planning to experiment with different orders in the combined scheme, a promised alternative could be to consider feature selection like first step, followed by other preprocessing methods. For extending our results, we have plans to compare our proposal with the cases and classification algorithms that were used in [3]. Our goal is to find a general scheme that can be automatically configurable to each particular problem.

References

1. Farhangfar, Alireza: Experimental analysis of methods for imputation of missing values in databases. (2004)
2. Chawla, Nitesh V.: C4.5 and imbalanced data sets: Investigating the effect of sampling method, probabilistic estimate, and decision tree structure. Canada. (2002)
3. Raman, Baranidharan: Enhancing inductive learning with feature selection andexample selection. (2003)
4. Yang, Ying; Webb, Geoff I.: Discretization For Naive-Bayes Learning: Managing Discretization Bias And Variance. Australia. (2002)
5. Liu, Huiqing; Li, Jinyan; Wong, Limsoon: A Comparative Study on Feature Selection and Classification Methods Using Gene Expression Profiles and Proteomic Patterns. Singapore. (2002)
6. Yang, Ying; Webb, Geoff I.: A Comparative Study of Discretization Methods for Naive-Bayes Classifiers. (2002)
7. Kerdprasop, Nittaya; Kerdprasop, Kittisak; Saiveaw, Yawd and Pumrungreong, Preecha: A comparative study of techniques to handle missing values in the classification task of data mining. Thailand. (2003)
8. Ian H. Witten, Eibe Frank: Data Mining, Practical Machine Learning Tools and Techniques with Java Implementations. Morgan Kaufmann Publisher. (2000)
9. Gunnalan, Rajesh; Menzies, Tim; Appukutty, Kalaivani; Srinivasan, Amarnath: Feature Subset Selection with TAR2less. USA. (2003)

Spatial Function Representation and Retrieval

Yutaka Matsuo, Akira Takagi, Shigeyoshi Hiratsuka,
Koiti Hasida, and Hideyuki Nakashima

Cyber Assist Research Center
National Institute of Advanced Industrial Science and Technology
Aomi 2-41-6, Koto-ku, Tokyo 135-0064

Spatial information has been received much attention recently. A ubiquitous computing environment enables us to monitor a user behavior and potentially provide tailored information services depending on the user situations such as location. Navigation and city tours are some of the major applications of GIS (Geographic Information Service) using location information.

We consider that space has a meaning. For example, when one is in a lounge, that person may be able to drink something. She may be relaxing talking with someone else, or thinking alone while smoking. We understand the meaning of spaces unconsiously. This study is an attempt to capture the meaning of space by explicitly describing the meaning of space to utilize for for advanced location-based information services.

We consider space as an artifact. It is usually considerately designed by humans to have functionality. For example, a lounge has functions such as "enable one to drink," "provide something to drink," and "enable one to be seated." These functions are realized by the functions of objects that exist in that space: a coffee server offers the function of providing coffee. A chair enables one to be seated. And the function of space is sometimes more than the function of inner objects. According to Sasajima, a function is defined as a result of interpretation of a behavior under an intended goal [2]. We define a spatial function as a result of interpretation of a property that is realized by a structure of a space under an intended goal. Unlike divice functionality, spatial functionality involves human factors. For different types of users, a space offers different functions, e.g., a student and a teacher in a classroom, and a doctor and a patient in a hospital. Therefore, we claim that a spatial function should be conditional upon the type of user.

Moreover, there is a concrete distinction between what we call the *physical function* and the *social function* of a space. For example, if a room has chairs, a table, and an ash tray, smoking is physically possible. However, smoking might be socially prohibited in the room. On the other hand, smoking is physically and socially possible in a smoking room. In other words, there is a function to "enable smoking" (physically) and "permit smoking" (socially) in the room.

The importance of explicit conceptualization for reusability of knowledge has been widely recognized [1]. In this study, we discuss a meaning of a space from the functional point of view and propose a knowledge representation of a space with high applicability and reusability. Developing a spatial representation is an essential issue in revealing how humans understand a space.

```xml
<?xml version="1.0" standalone="yes'?>
<spaces>
 <place type="restaurant" label="Udon">
  <space>
   <function>
    <user><aattr name="position">guest</aattr></user>
    <permit id="func:permit:eat">eat</permit>
    <enable id="func:enable:eat">eat</enable>
    <service>restaurant
     <achievedby>
      <func ref="func:enable:eat"/>
      <func ref="func:permit:eat"/>
     </achievedby>
    </service>
   </function>
   <function>
    <user><aattr name="position">staff</aattr></user>
    <enable>cook</enable>
   </function>
  </space>
 </place>
</spaces>
```

Fig. 1. An example of spatial function representation.

Figure 1 is a (simplified version of) spatial functions description of a restaurant space. The merit of our representation is threefold: (i) it considers a space as an artifact; a space is described from its function, property and structure. (ii) a space has different meanings to different persons; thus our representation conditions a spatial function by user type. (iii) not only physical function but also social function is considered; a space has a social meaning, and our representation describes spatial meaning both physically and socially.

Through construction of a spatial representation that concurs with our common sense, we can produce a more intelligent spatial information system. We propose an example of such advanced information system called *spatial function retrieval* which searches spatial functions to satisfy a user's need. The system can respond to the input "I am hungry": It searches for a place to get something to eat and a place where we can take a seat and eat. Then it can suggest "How about buying sandwiches at the store and going to the park to eat it?" This is a combination of multiple spatial functions.

We can also apply user modeling based on our spatial function representation. A user's location history is changed into a history of functions that the user experiences.

References

1. Y. Kitamura and R. Mizoguchi. Functional ontology for functional understanding. In *Workshop Notes for QR-98*, pages 88–98, 1998.
2. M Sasajima, Y Kitamura, M Ikeda, and R Mizoguchi. FBRL: A function and behavior representation language. In *Proc IJCAI-95*, pages 1830–1836, 1995.
3. M. Weiser. The computer for the twenty-first century. *Scientific American*, 268(3):94–104, 1991.

Fuzzy Project Scheduling with Multiple Objectives

Hongqi Pan and Chung-Hsing Yeh

School of Business Systems, Monash University
Victoria 3800, Australia
{Hongqi.Pan,ChungHsing.Yeh}@infotech.monash.edu.au

Abstract. Due to two-page limitations for being accepted as a poster paper, the paper can only briefly describe a hybrid fuzzy goal programming approach for solving multiple objectives in fuzzy multi-mode project scheduling. To simplify such complex scheduling, a rule knowledge base for mode assignment combines into fuzzy goal programming, thus a multi-mode scheduling problem is decomposed into a simpler single mode scheduling problem.

1 Introduction

Fuzzy multi-mode resource-constrained project scheduling (MMRCPS) with multi-objectives optimization inherently exists in real-word applications. It represents generalized circumstances of project scheduling where activities can be performed in one of several executive modes under the fuzzy environment, and where multiple objectives are taken into consideration simultaneously, such as finance, time, and other industry-specific objectives. In the case of dredge breakdown repair, two objectives, timing and the cost are often required. However, the degree of priorities of these two objectives often varies depending on the current circumstances of budget status and workload of a dredging company. These objectives often conflict with each other. There is no single solution that is the best for these two objectives. A better schedule generated for the dredge repair should match the degree of requirements for these individual objectives.

2 Formulation of Scheduling Dredge Repair

The objective function of minimizing the project completion time is equal to the last activity finished at time $F\widetilde{T}_n$.

$$\text{Min } f_1 = F\widetilde{T}_n \qquad (1)$$

The objective function of minimizing the repair cost (project cost) can be given as

$$\text{Min } f_2 = \sum_{r=1}^{R}\sum_{j=1}^{J}\sum_{m=1}^{M_j}(k_{jmr}\times C_r + k^*_{jmr}\times C^*_r)\sum_{s=\tilde{t}}^{\tilde{t}+d_{jm}-1}x_{jms} + dp_j \times \tilde{l}_j \qquad (2)$$

where k_{jmr} and k^*_{jmr} are the amounts of resource consumed by activity j and the extra resource r respectively. C_r and C^*_r are the unit costs of the available and the extra resource r respectively. dp_j is the daily penalty rate after due days $\tilde{l}_j$ in activity j.

The start time $\widetilde{ST}_j$ and finish time $\widetilde{FT}_j$ of an activity j should be satisfied as

$$\widetilde{ST}_j + \tilde{d}_j = \widetilde{FT}_j \qquad j = 1,2,\ldots,J \tag{3}$$

The precedence between activities should have the following relationships

$$\widetilde{FT}_i \leq \widetilde{ST}_j; \quad \forall (i,j): i \ll j \tag{4}$$

Let rk_{jr} and rk^*_{jr} be respectively the percentages of the required amount from both the available and extra resource r consumed by activity j. They should be

$$rk_{jr} + rk^*_{jr} = 1 \tag{5}$$

Let u_{jmr} represent the amount of resource r consumed by activity j. The amounts consumed both from the available (k_{jmr}) and the extra (k^*_{jmr}) resources should be

$$u_{jmr} = k_{jmr} + k^*_{jmr} \tag{6}$$

Let $S_{\tilde{t}}$ denote the set of activities scheduled at the time $\tilde{t}$, and the amount of resource r, allocated to activities should be satisfied as the following condition

$$\sum_{j \in S_{\tilde{t}}} \sum_{m=1}^{M_j} x_{jm\tilde{t}} \times u_{jmr} \times rk_{jr} \leq K_r \quad \forall \tilde{t} \in \tilde{T} \tag{7}$$

The amount of resource r, consumed from the available resource by activity j is

$$k_{jmr} = u_{jmr} \times rk_{jr} \tag{8}$$

The amount of resource r, consumed from the extra resource by activity j is

$$k^*_{jmr} = u_{jmr} \times rk^*_{jr} \tag{9}$$

To reduce constraints in the model for improving its computational efficiency, five rules for mode assignment are constructed for supporting decisions on selecting activity modes. The mode will be decided by the rules before processing the model. Because of the limitation of the paper, these rules are not listed here.

3 Conclusion

This approach developed allows a loose aspiration level to suit practical requirements under a fuzzy environment. To reduce complex constraints in the fuzzy goal programming model, and to speed up computation, a rule-based knowledge has been constructed to decide which mode will be performed for an activity based on the current partial schedule status, the current resource availabilities, and the current critical paths, preset by the experienced decision maker. Such an interactive approach facilitates the implement of fuzzy goal programming in an efficient and effective way, and yields the best compromised solution among conflicting objectives. This model gives a significant scheduling control under frequently changeable conditions.

A New Approach for Applying Support Vector Machines in Multiclass Problems Using Class Groupings and Truth Tables

Mauricio Kugler, Hiroshi Matsuo, and Akira Iwata

Department of Computer Science and Engineering
Nagoya Institute of Technology
Gokiso-cho, Showa-ku, 466-8555, Nagoya, Japan
mauricio@kugler.com, {matsuo,iwata}@nitech.ac.jp

The Support Vector Machines (SVMs) had been showing a high capability of complex hyperplane representation and great generalization power. These characteristics lead to the development of more compact and less computational complex methods than the One-versus-Rest (OvR) and One-versus-One (OvO) [1] classical methods in the application of SVMs in multiclass problems. This paper proposes a new method for this task, named *Truth Table Fitting Multiclass SVM* (TTF-MCSVM), in which less SVMs are used than other classical methods. The main objective of this research is the development of an efficient method to be applied in problems with very large number of classes, like in the recognition of East Asian languages characters (e.g. Japanese and Chinese kanji).

The TTF-MCSVM is based on the combination of many simple binary SVMs, like the OvR and OvO. The N classes are divided in M combinations of two groups, where M is:

$$M = \lceil \log_2 N \rceil \tag{1}$$

The two groups obtained in each combination will correspond to two pseudo-classes, and these two pseudo-classes will form a grouping. As the M groupings are binary, they can be applied to M simple and independent binary SVMs. This approach can be also represented by the encoding scheme described in [2], in which large encodings were used to increase the classifiers performance. However, the focus in the present work is the opposite, i.e. to use the smallest possible encoding size, resulting in less SVMs than other classical methods. If the groupings are consistent (i.e. each class has a different associated pseudo-class combination), the M groupings are arranged in a Boolean truth table, where the inputs are the results of all SVMs and the output is the winner class, which is chosen by the overlap of the decision hyperplanes of the SVMs. During the training phase, each SVM is trained independently, and the margin is maximized to divide the two pseudo-classes of that SVM. On the test phase, the results of the M SVMs are applied on the truth table and, if the groupings are correct, it will be possible to choose the winner class.

A basic example is shown in Fig. 1. The same 9 class problem was solved using the TTF-MCSVM (Fig. 1(a), with the groupings drawn in the figure), OvR (Fig. 1(b)) and OvO (Fig. 1(c)) methods. All of them used gaussian kernel with

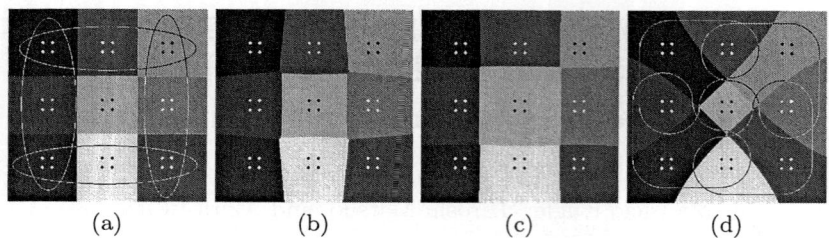

Fig. 1. Nine classes problem: (a) TTF-MCSVM (4 SVMs, 16 SV, Grouping Set A), (b) OvR (8 SVMs, 47 SV), (c) OvO (28 SVMs, 108 SV), (d) TTF-MCSVM (4 SVMs, 20 SV, Grouping Set B)

$\sigma=1.5$ and $C=100$. Using the TTF-MCSVM method, less classifiers were used, less support vectors (SV) were found and a better generalization was obtained when compared to the other methods. However, a different grouping set, such as the one shown in (Fig. 1(d)), can clearly result in a smaller margin.

Table 1 shows the comparison of three UCI benchmark problems, *iris*, *wine* and *glass*, solved by the TTF-MCSVM (with random groupings), OvR and OvO methods. The results shows the smaller number of support vectors for the best performance parameters combinations, calculated over the average of a 10-fold cross validation (p means d for polynomial kernel and σ for gaussian kernel).

Table 1. UCI benchmark experiments comparison

Problem	TTF-MCSVM				OvR				OvO			
(N, samples)	M	CR%	#SV	p,C	M	CR%	#SV	p,C	M	CR%	#SV	p,C
Polynomial Kernel												
iris (3, 150)	2	99.33	31	2, 1.0	3	99.33	52	2, 0.9	3	94.67	95	2, 0.03
wine (3, 178)	2	98.82	50	1, 0.2	3	98.82	106	2, 0.07	3	98.82	40	1, 0.2
glass (6, 214)	3	66.19	304	2, 0.2	6	69.52	844	3, 0.004	15	70.95	502	2, 0.02
Gaussian Kernel												
iris (3, 150)	2	98.67	19	4, 80	3	98.67	43	3, 60	3	96.00	76	1, 1
wine (3, 178)	2	98.82	49	20, 100	3	99.41	87	10, 9	3	99.41	86	10, 3
glass (6, 214)	3	75.71	363	0.9, 4	6	75.71	603	1, 6	15	76.19	560	1, 4

The TTF-MCSVM performance shows no statistically significant difference from the OvR and OvO methods, using a smaller number of classifiers and, in almost all cases, considerably less SV. In the case of the *glass* problem, optimized groupings sets could increase the performance. The small number of classifiers, specially when the kernel matrix is calculated in advance, leads to smaller training time. Future works include the study on the groupings optimization and experiments dealing with more complex real world problems.

References

1. Jason Weston and Chris Watkins. Support vector machines for multi-class pattern recognition. In *Proceedings of the 7th European Symposium On Artificial Neural Networks*, pages 219–224, Bruges, 4 1999.
2. Thomas G. Dietterich and Ghulum Bakiri. Solving multiclass learning problems via error-correcting output codes. *Journal of Artificial Intelligence Research*, 2:263–286, 1995.

Imitation of Bee Reproduction as a Crossover Operator in Genetic Algorithms

Ali Karcı

Fırat University, Faculty of Engineering, Department of Computer Engineering
23119, Elazığ / Turkey
akarci@firat.edu.tr

Abstract. There are lots of methods inpired by the natural observations (i.e. fuzzy logic, artificial neural networks, genetic algorithms, simulated annealing algorithms, etc.) This paper proposes a novel crossover operator type inspired by the sexual intercourses of honey bees. The method selects a specific chromosome in present population as queen bee. While the selected queen bee is one parent of crossover, all the remaining chromosomes have the chance to be next parent for crossover in each generation once. For this purposes, we defined three honey bee crossover methods: In the first method, the chromosome with the best fitness score is queen honey bee and it is a fixed parent for crossover in the current generation. The second method handles the chromosome with the worst fitness score. Finally, queen bee is changed sequentially in each generation.

1 Introduction

Sometimes, some effective ideas are inspired from nature. In fact, human beings have often simulated natural phenomena to create new technologies resulting in created technologies different from the natural simulated phenomena sometimes [1,2,3].

Similar to these methods, we introduced a new crossover type, which is called Bee Crossover (BC), in this study for improving the GA performance. We were inspired from the bee sexual intercourses, since we are at the aim of improving the performance of GAs. The bee queen has the sexual intercourses with other male bees, and similarly a specified chromosome can be considered as bee queen and it is a parent for crossover and the oether parent is one of the remaining chromosomes in the colony. Each remaining chromosome in the colony has sexual intercourses (being parent for crossover) at least once.

2 Bee Crossover

Bee is a four-winged insect with a sting, that lives in a colony and collects nectar and pollen from flowers to produce wax and honey. The bee queen has the sexual intercourses with all the male bees in the colony for the reproduction of bees. The sexual intercourses in the colony of bees can be considered as crossover type. There are three different crossover types can be defined.

First Type (BC1): The chromosome with the best fitness value is a fixed parent and all the remaining chromosomes are crossed over with this fixed parent at least once in each generation. The best chromosome can be changed from generation to generation. The fixed parent is the chromosome with the best fitness value, not the fixed parent in the previous generation.

Second Type (BC2): The chromosome with the worst fitness value is a fixed parent and all the remaining chromosomes are crossed over with this fixed parent at least once in each generation. The worst chromosome can be changed from generation to generation. The fixed parent is the chromosome with the worst fitness value, not the fixed parent in the previous generation.

Third Type (BC3): The fixed parent determination does not depend on the fitness values and it depends on the order of chromosome in the colony, while population is sorted with respect to the fitness values. The fixed parent in the first generation is the first chromosome. The fixed parent in the second generation is the second chromosome, and so on. The fixed parent in the ith generation is the $(i \bmod |P|)^{th}$ chromosome, where i is the current generation number and |P| is the size of population.

3 Conclusions

In this paper, we inspired by the sexual intercourses of honey bees. Some specific chromosomes in the population can be selected as queen bees.

The superiority of honey bee crossovers with respect to uniform crossover were verified in three ways. Number of iterations: In the most of time, honey bee crossovers obtained results in less number of iterations with respect to number of iterations of uniform crossover. The uniform crossover obtained the worst results with respect honey bee crossovers, and this point is significant. Finally, uniform crossover lost the diversity of population in a small range of time, however, honey bee crossovers lost the population diversity in the larger ranges of time.

The application of proposed crossover methods are as easy as the applications of single-point, two-point, n-point and uniform crossovers. The idea for partial mapped crossover, cyclic crossover, order crossover is also applicable in the proposed methods, since only difference is the selection of parents.

References

1. D. Goldberg, "Genetic Algorithm in Search, Optimization and Machine Learning", Massachusetts, Addison-Wesley Publishing Company Inc., 1989.
2. A. Karcı, A. Arslan, "Bidirectional evolutionary heuristic for the minimum vertex-cover problem" Journal of Computers and Electrical Engineerings, vol. 29, pp.111-120, 2003.
3. A. Karcı, A. Arslan, " Uniform Population in Genetic algorithms", İ.Ü. Journal of Electrical & Electronics, vol.2 (2), pp.495-504, 2002.

An Intelligent Robot Navigation System Based on Neuro-Fuzzy Control

Osama Fathy Hegazy[1], Aly Aly Fahmy[2], and Osama Mosaad El Refaie[3]

[1] Cairo Higher Institute for Computer, Information and Management, Cairo Academy
Golf Region, Cairo, Egypt
osamahegazy488@hotmail.com
[2] Faculty of Computer and Information, Cairo University, Cairo, Egypt
afahmy@frcu.eun.eg
[3] Faculty of Engineering -Tanat University, Tanta, Egypt
osamamosaad331@hotmail.com

Controlling mobile robot navigation system that operates in an unknown and uncertain environment is a difficult operation. Much of this difficulty is due to environmental inconsistencies and sensor inadequacies. We present a new neuro-fuzzy controller that controls the navigation system of a mobile robot to move safely in an unknown environment in presence of obstacles. Training data is accumulated from robot's sensors to generate a set of fuzzy rules that govern the robot navigation system on-line. The proposed controller based on the following two algorithms:
- obstacle avoidance algorithm based on combine goal seeking and open-area seeking schemes [1], and
- on-line learning algorithm that combines both backpropagation learning and a fuzzy similarity measure schemes [2].

The obstacle avoidance algorithm is based on the assumptions that the model of the robot kinematics and dynamic constraints are available, and the sensory system that needed to explore the unknown environment surrounding the robot is available and can be modeled to produce all needed input data. The sensory system consists of IR sensor to produce a set of angle-distance pair, GPS to know the current position, and a video camera for supervised feedback signal processing. The proposed algorithm is described as follows: Consider $P_s(x, y)$, $P_c(x, y)$, and $P_g(x, y)$ are the start, the current, and the goal position of the robot, respectively, then

Start from $P_s(x, y)$
1. Apply goal seeking algorithm
2. IF $P_s(x, y) = P_g(x, y)$ THEN stop
3. Apply on-line structure-parameter learning algorithm
4. IF an obstacle is found THEN
   - Apply open-area seeking algorithm
   - $P_s(x, y) = P_c(x, y)$
   - Apply on-line structure-parameter learning algorithm
5. IF the obstacle is not avoided THEN repeat Step-4
6. $P_s(x, y) = P_c(x, y)$, and go to Step-1

The model of the neuro-fuzzy controller is consists of three layers. Nodes in input layer transmit the input values to the next layer through the link weight that represented by fuzzy numbers. Nodes in the second layer represent the rule layer, hence, the integration function and the activation function perform two different fuzzy AND operation, Zadeh's and Lukasiewicz T-norm's [3]. Nodes in layer three act as a defuzzifier. The flow chart of the on-line structure-parameter learning algorithm is shown in Fig. 1.

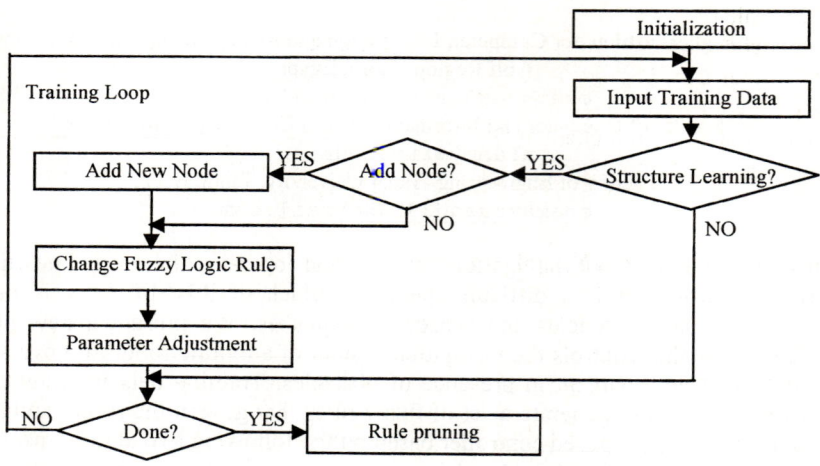

Fig. 1. Flow chart of the on-line structure-parameter learning algorithm

The results of simulated robot experiments are provided to demonstrate the effectiveness of the proposed approach to robot learning. The proposed on-line obstacle avoidance algorithm succeeded to extract dynamically fuzzy rules from training examples based on fuzzy similarity measure, which is used to control the behaviours of a non-holonomic vehicle through an unknown environment.

References

1. Ahmed M. Mahmoud and Asim Nabawi,. "mobile robot navigation system based on fuzzy logic controller", Egyptian Information Journal, Vol. 4, No. 2, pp. 1-9, December 2003.
2. Aly Aly Fahmy and Osama Fathy Hegazy, "Fuzzy Adaptive Learning Decision System with on-line neural learning", INFOS2004, 6-8 March, Cairo, Egypt, 2004.
3. Yager R.R., Connectives and quantifiers in fuzzy sets, Fuzzy Sets and Systems 40 (1991) 39-75.

Author Index

Abdulla, Waleed H.   901
Adilakshmi, T.   154
Ahmad, Irfan   965
Akihiko, Nakase   975
Álvarez, Victor M.   1007
Ampornaramveth, Vuthichai   673
Anbulagan   173
Andreae, Peter   585
Angel, Elizabeth S. del   1007
Anyouzoa, Alain Gaetan Njimolu   928
Axnick, Karl   322

Bae, Myung Jin   919
Bain, Stuart   144
Baker, Jesse T.   664
Baluja, Shumeet   3
Barczak, Andre L.C.   969
Bayard, Ian   872
Beaumont, Matthew   134
Bekmann, J.P.   361
Besharati, Farhad   938
Bitaghsir, Ali Akhavan   938
Boonsirisumpun, Narong   973
Bui, Hung H.   971, 983

Cao, Longbing   85
Cerezci, Osman   422
Chan, Mark   987
Chan, Siu Y.   605
Chen, Chia-Yen   987
Chen, Hung-Ming   262
Chen, Jian-Hung   262
Chen, Qingfeng   33
Chen, Shifu   936
Chen, Yiqiang   544
Chen, Zhaoqian   936
Chien, Sung-Il   812
Cho, Sehyeong   892
Cho, Sung-Bae   391, 713, 967
Cho, Yoon Ho   963
Choi, Ho-Jin   272
Choi, Jong Soo   464

Chow, David   901
Chu, Shu-Chuan   534
Collins, Richard   585
Cranefield, Stephen   625
Cruz R., Laura   1007

D'Hondt, Theo   928
Dai, Honghua   201, 352
Dazeley, Richard   985
Delmas, Patrice   987
Denzinger, Jörg   381
Ditmarsch, Hans P. van   946

Easwarakumar, K.S.   429

Fahmy, Aly Aly   1017
Feng, Jun   95
Feng, Xiaoyue   942
Fernández-Breis, Jesualdo T.   997
Fit-Florea, Alex   977
Fong, Alvis Cheuk Ming   485
Foo, Norman   13
Fu, Yan   544
Funakoshi, Kotaro   635

Gao, Wen   544
Gao, Xiaoying   585
Gao, Yang   936
George, Sarah   311
Gimel'farb, Georgy   987
González, Evelio J.   957
Greenhill, Stewart   805
Gunturkun, Rustu   422

Hahn, Udo   852
Hamasaki, Masahiro   944
Hamilton, Alberto   957
Hang, Xiaoshu   352
Hasegawa, Ryuzo   43
Hasegawa, Tomoharu   524
Hasida, Koiti   1009
Hassine, Ahlem Ben   124

Hattori, Hiromitsu 989
He, Simin 544
Hegazy, Osama Fathy 1017
Herlocker, Jonathan L. 1005
Hiratsuka, Shigeyoshi 1009
Ho, Hilda 862
Ho, Jack 164
Ho, Shinn-Ying 262
Hoffmann, Achim 361
Hong, Hyun-Ki 940
Hope, Lucas R. 322
Horsch, Michael C. 104
Hui, Siu Cheung 485
Hwang, Yong-Ho 940

Ichise, Ryutaro 944
Idrissi, Abdellah 124
Imai, Michita 993
Inoue, Masato 282
Ishihara, Kazushi 909
Ishizuka, Mitsuru 882
Isomura, Atsushi 989
Ito, Noriko 981
Ito, Takayuki 524, 989
Itoh, Hidenori 991
Iwashita, Shino 981
Iwata, Akira 1013

Jalili-Kharaajoo, Mahdi 1001
Jami, Syed Imran 965
Jauregui, Victor 13
Jefferies, Margaret E. 664
Jeon, Jun-Cheol 241
Jeong, Yoon-Yong 940
Jie, Yang 797
Jin, Jesse S. 823
Joung, Je-Gun 723
Jung, Keechul 411, 833

Kadous, Mohammed Waleed 644
Kang, Byeong-Ho 985
Kang, Sin Kuk 401
Kang, Sin-Jae 654
Kanoh, Masayoshi 991
Karcı, Ali 1015
Karim, Asim 965

Kasabov, Nikola 231
Katayama, Susumu 75
Kato, Shohei 991
Kavitha, V. 429
Kawakami, Wataru 950
Khan, M. Shamim 454
Khor, Sebastian W. 454
Kiatisevi, Pattara 673
Kijsirikul, Boonserm 973
Kim, Byeong Man 495, 654
Kim, Chan Young 963
Kim, Deok Hwan 963
Kim, Eun Yi 401, 411
Kim, Hang Joon 401
Kim, Hee-Jae 654
Kim, Hyun-jung 505
Kim, Hyungil 1005
Kim, Jinsoo 495
Kim, Jong Dae 999
Kim, Jong Kuk 919
Kim, Jong-Wan 495, 654
Kim, Juntae 1005
Kim, Myung Won 332
Kim, Soo-joong 843
Kim, Sun 742
Kim, Tae-Yong 787
Kim, TaeYong 464
Knott, Alistair 872
Kobayashi, Ichiro 981
Koo, Simon 955
Korb, Kevin B. 322
Küngas, Peep 23
Kugler, Mauricio 1013
Kurt, Tarkan 201
Kwan, Alvin 164
Kwan, M.C. 932
Kwon, Suhn-beom 505

Lam, Yuk-Hei 979
Landero N., Vanesa 1007
Latecki, Longin J. 693
Lathrop, Richard 1
Lau, Raymond Y.K. 605
Leclercq, Philippe 987
Lee, Heow Pueh 373, 942
Lee, In-Hee 742

Lee, Jong-hak 843
Lee, Ki Young 919
Lee, Sang-Jo 930
Lee, Seong-Whan 787
Lee, Tae-Seung 272
Lee, Wha-Jin 732
Legaspi, Roberto 114
Li, Dequan 544
Li, Gang 201
Li, Guo-Zheng 292
Li, Qing 495
Liang, Yanchun 373, 942
Ligozat, Gérard 53
Lim, Joo-Hwee 823
Limpiyakorn, Yachai 973
Ling, Charles X. 544
Liu, Danyu 934
Liu, Guo-Ping 292
Liu, Li 85, 474
Lu, Jingli 474
Lühr, Sebastian 983
Luo, Chao 85
Luo, Dan 85
Lyons, Michael J. 959

MacDonald, Bruce A. 683
Maher, Michael 134
Makoto, Sato 975
Marichal, Roberto L. 957
Marom, Yuval 953
Martín-Rubio, Fernando 997
Martínez-Béjar, Rodrigo 997
Matsumoto, Satoshi 211
Matsuo, Hiroshi 1013
Matsuo, Yutaka 882, 1009
Mayo, Michael 664
McCalla, Gordon 301
Meyer, Tony 948
Min, Hyeun-Jeong 391
Min, Kyongho 862
Mitra, Debasis 65
Mittal, Vibhu 3
Miyahara, Tetsuhiro 211
Moratz, Reinhard 1003
Moreno, Lorenzo 957
Mors, Adriaan ter 995

Moshiri, Behzad 938
Mould, David 104
Mukai, Naoto 95
Muñoz, Vanessa 957

Nakashima, Hideyuki 1009
Nakatani, Tomohiro 909
Nam, Jin-Wu 732
Narumi, Mariko 993
Nicholson, Ann E. 322
Niemann, Michael 311
Ningsong, Peng 751
Nowostawski, Mariusz 625
Numao, Masayuki 114

O, Jangmin 930
O, Sok June 723
Ogata, Tetsuya 909
Oh, Hyun-Hwa 812
Okada, Masato 282
Okazaki, Naoaki 882
Okuno, Hiroshi G. 909
Oliveira, Marcos 625
Ong, Kok-Leong 979
Ou, Yuming 474
Ozawa, Seiichi 231
Ozono, Tadachika 524, 989

Pagnucco, Maurice 13
Pan, Hongqi 1011
Pan, Jeng-Shyang 534
Pang, Shaoning 231
Park, Anjin 833
Park, Han-Saem 967
Park, Hyeyoung 282
Park, Jihun 787
Park, Sang-gug 843
Park, Seong-Bae 930
Park, Taejin 342
Pérez, Joaquín 1007
Peréz, Verónica 1007
Peursum, Patrick 971
Potts, Duncan 221
Pujari, Arun K. 154
Purvis, Martin 625

Qing, Xu 797

Ralescu, Anca   191
Refaie, Osama Mosaad El   1017
Renz, Jochen   53, 65
Roddick, John F.   534
Ross, Robert   1003
Rowley, Henry   3
Rus, Vasile   977
Ryu, Joung Woo   332
Ryu, Kwang Ryel   342

Sahami, Mehran   3
Sammut, Claude   644
Sarwar, Mansoor   965
Sattar, Abdul   134, 144
Sawamura, Hajime   950
Shi, Zhongzhi   563
Shin, Kyung-shik   505
Shintani, Toramatsu   524, 989
Shirai, Yasuyuki   43
Shoudai, Takayoshi   211
Shuichiro, Imahara   975
Sierra, Carles   2
Silva, Gamhewage C. de   959
Sison, Raymund   114
Siyi, Ding   797
Smart, Will   251
Snow, Paul   445
Sprague, Alan P.   934
Su, Che-Jen   534
Sugeno, Michio   981
Sugimoto, Toru   981
Sugiyama, Kozo   955
Sun, Ruixiang   544
Sun, Yanfeng   942
Suzuki, Yusuke   211

Tafti, Abdrreza Dehghani   938
Takagi, Akira   1009
Takeda, Hideaki   944
Tam, Vincent   164, 932, 955
Tan, Colin Keng-Yan   515
Tanaka, Hozumi   635
Tang, Tiffany   301
Temurtas, Fevzullah   422
Temurtas, Hasan   422
Tetsutani, Nobuji   959

Thornton, John   134, 144
Tokugana, Takenobu   635
Tu, Yiqing   201

Ueno, Haruki   673
Uzmi, Zartash   965

Valencia-García, Rafael   997
Valk, Jeroen   995
Vance, Dan   191
Venkatesh, Svetha   805, 971, 983
Vivancos-Vicente, Pedro J.   997
Vlugter, Peter   872

Wang, Haipeng   544
Wang, Huaiqing   615
Wang, Jingchun   183
Wang, Minhong   615
Wang, Ruili   436
Wang, Yan   942
Wang, Yuzhong   751, 778
Watanabe, Toyohide   95
Watson, Ian   554
Weng, Wenrong   664
Wermter, Joachim   852
West, Geoff   805, 971, 983
Williams, Tim   381
Wills, Anna   554
Witteveen, Cees   995
Wobcke, Wayne   595
Wolter, Diedrich   693
Wong, Sylvia C.   683
Wu, Chunguo   373
Wu, Zhaohui   575
Wünstel, Michael   1003

Xiang, Wei   373
Xue, Li   292

Yairi, Takehisa   703
Yang, Hui   563
Yang, Jie   292, 751, 778, 797, 961
Yang, Pei   936
Yang, Qiang   544
Yang, Xin   760, 769
Yeap, Wai Kiang   862
Yeh, Chung-Hsing   1011

Yoo, Kee-Young 241
Yoo, Si-Ho 713, 967
Yumusak, Nejat 422

Zeng, Rong 544
Zhang, Byoung-Tak 723, 732, 742
Zhang, Changshui 183
Zhang, Mengjie 251
Zhang, Minjie 563
Zhang, Shichao 33, 474
Zhang, Yongping 436

Zhang, Zili 979
Zheng, Yuanjie 961
Zhou, Baoyao 485
Zhou, Chunguang 373, 942
Zhou, Dake 760, 769
Zhou, Hu 544
Zhou, Xuezhong 575
Zhou, Yonglei 183
Zhou, Yue 961
Zukerman, Ingrid 311, 953